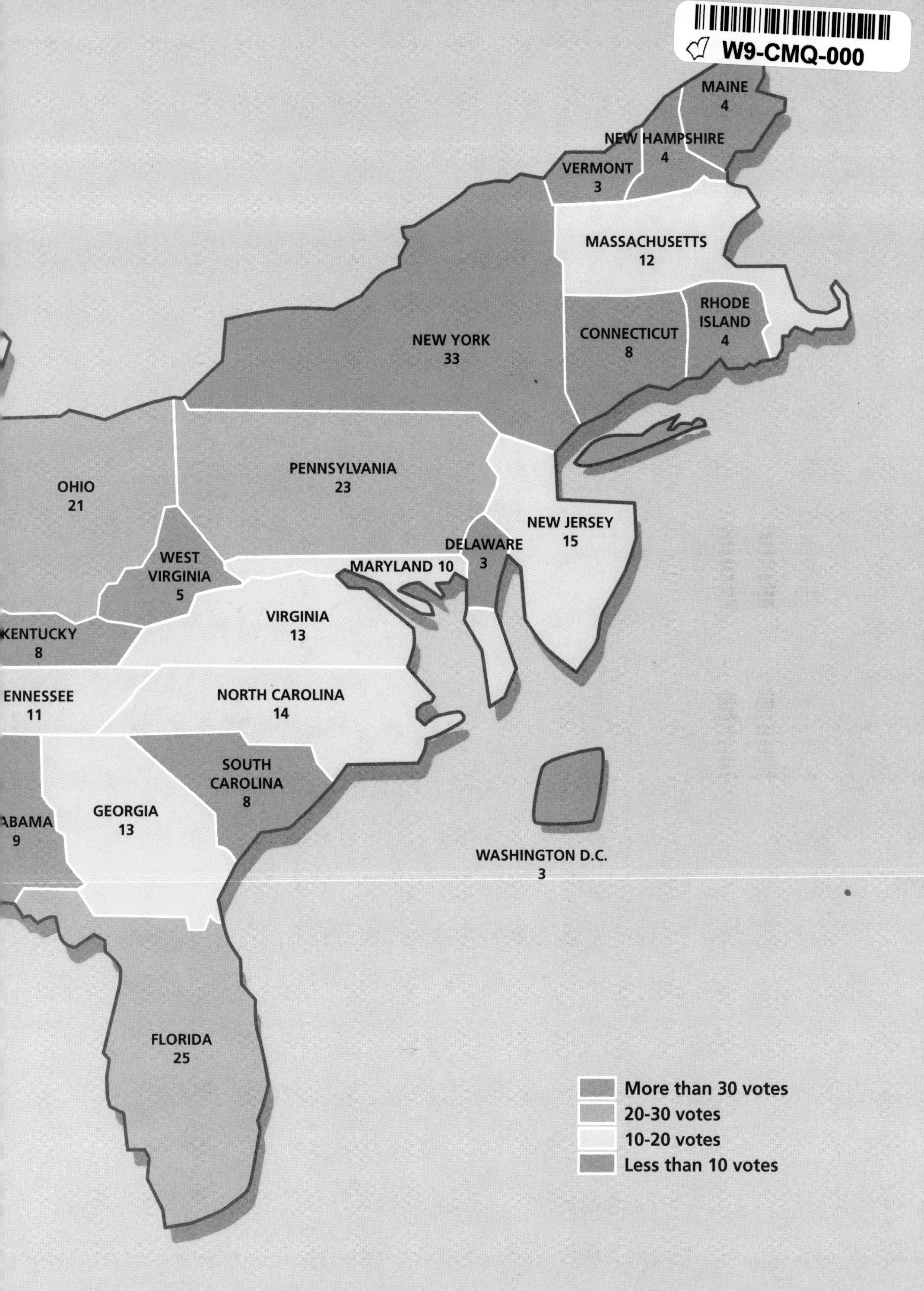

W9-CMQ-000
MAINE
4
NEW HAMPSHIRE
4
VERMONT
3
MASSACHUSETTS
12
RHODE
ISLAND
4
CONNECTICUT
8
NEW YORK
33
PENNSYLVANIA
23
OHIO
21
NEW JERSEY
15
DELAWARE
3
MARYLAND 10
WEST
VIRGINIA
5
VIRGINIA
13
KENTUCKY
8
ENNESSEE
11
NORTH CAROLINA
14
SOUTH
CAROLINA
8
GEORGIA
13
ABAMA
9
WASHINGTON D.C.
3
FLORIDA
25
More than 30 votes
20-30 votes
10-20 votes
Less than 10 votes

GOVERNMENT BY THE PEOPLE

National Version

Eighteenth Edition

James MacGregor Burns
University of Maryland, College Park and Williams College

J.W. Peltason
University of California

Thomas E. Cronin
Whitman College

David B. Magleby
Brigham Young University

Prentice Hall, Upper Saddle River, New Jersey 07458

Library of Congress Cataloging-in-Publication Data
Government by the people : national version / James MacGregor Burns ... [et al]. — 18th ed.
p. cm.
Includes bibliographical references and index.
ISBN 0-13-011656-4
1. Local government—United States. 2. United States—Politics and government. I. Burns, James MacGregor.
JK274.B855 2000
320.473—dc21 99-15982
CIP

Editorial Director: *Charlyce Jones Owen*
Editor in Chief: *Nancy Roberts*
Senior Acquisitions Editor: *Beth Gillett Mejia*
Associate Editor: *Nicole Conforti*
Editorial Assistant: *Brian Prybella*
Marketing Manager: *Christopher DeJohn*
Development Editor and Project Manager: *Serena Hoffman*
Development Consultant: *Jane Tufts*
Copy Editor: *Ann Hofstra Grogg*
AVP, Director of Production and Manufacturing: *Barbara Kittle*
Manufacturing Manager: *Nick Sklitsis*
Buyer: *Ben Smith*
Creative Design Director: *Leslie Osher*
Interior and Cover Designer: *Anne DeMarinis*
Line Art Coordinator: *Guy Ruggiero*
Director, Image Resource Center: *Melinda Reo*
Image Specialist: *Beth Boyd*
Manager, Rights and Permissions: *Kay Dellosa*
Photo Researcher: *Eloise Donnelley*
Supervisor of Production Services: *John Jordan*
Electronic Page Layout: *Joh Lisa and Scott Garrison*
Illustrations: *ElectraGraphics*
Cover Art: *Detail of large crowd, Ken Fisher/Tony Stone Images*
"Red & White Stripes," Friend & Johnson, Inc.

This book was set in 10/12.5 Minion
by Prentice Hall Production Services and was
printed and bound by RR Donnelley & Sons.
The cover was printed by Phoenix Color Corp.

Printed in the United States of America
10 9 8 7 6 5 4 3 2 1

ISBN 0-13-011656-4

Prentice-Hall International (UK) Limited, London
Prentice-Hall of Australia Pty. Limited, Sydney
Prentice-Hall Canada Inc., Toronto
Prentice-Hall Hispanoamericana, S.A., Mexico
Prentice-Hall of India Private Limited, New Delhi
Prentice-Hall of Japan, Inc., Tokyo
Pearson Education Asia Pte. Ltd., Singapore
Editora Prentice-Hall do Brasil, Ltda., Rio de Janeiro

BRIEF CONTENTS

PART ONE: CONSTITUTIONAL PRINCIPLES

PART TWO: RIGHTS AND LIBERTIES

PART THREE: THE POLITICAL PROCESS

PART FOUR: POLICY-MAKING INSTITUTIONS

PART FIVE: THE POLITICS OF NATIONAL POLICY

APPENDIX

CONTENTS

PART ONE: CONSTITUTIONAL PRINCIPLES

PART TWO: RIGHTS AND LIBERTIES

PART THREE: THE POLITICAL PROCESS

PART FOUR: POLICY-MAKING INSTITUTIONS

PART FIVE: THE POLITICS OF NATIONAL POLICY

APPENDIX

FEATURES

PEOPLE DEBATE

A CLOSER LOOK

WE THE PEOPLE

YOU DECIDE!

A MESSAGE FROM THE AUTHORS

As we enter the new millennium, the endurance and stability of American government are impressive. Many U.S. citizens take for granted civil liberties, civil rights, free and fair elections, the peaceful transfer of power, and economic freedom and prosperity. Yet many people in the world live in places where these freedoms are nonexistent. This is a time for testing for new democracies as well as old ones. Contempt for government and politics is expressed in the United States and abroad, yet politics and partisan competition are the life blood by which free societies can achieve the ideals of a government by the people.

Constitutional democracy—the kind we have in the United States—is exceedingly hard to win, equally hard to sustain, and often hard to understand without rigorous study. Our political history is an evolution toward an enlarged role for citizens and voters. Citizens have more rights and political opportunities in 2000 than they had in 1800 or 1900. The framers of our Constitution warned that we must be vigilant in safeguarding our rights, liberties, and political institutions. But to do this, we must first understand these institutions and the forces that have shaped them.

The world we live in remains highly volatile. Although our defense policy changed with the collapse of communism and the emergence of a less powerful Russia, the world has not suddenly become a safer place in which to live. Regional strife and terrorism continue to plague us. The United States has entered a period of reassessment of its role in the world, in the United Nations, in regional defense organizations like NATO, and in its economic relations with other countries.

Over the last half century, voters in this country have preferred divided government, with a president from one party and a Congress from the other. Both major parties are seeking to broaden their base to become the dominant party. Americans have never liked political parties, but our parties do work, and they do offer choices. Campaign financing and reform initiatives have become serious challenges. Also hotly debated are how to improve educational opportunity, lessen crime, combat racism, promote trade, and encourage better paying jobs.

Although we constantly turn to government and to our elected officials with problems and requests, we are critical of their shortcomings. A recurrent theme of this book is the absolute need for politics and politicians, despite the widespread tendency to criticize nearly everything political. The reality is that our political system should not be taken for granted, even as we seek ways it can be improved.

We want you to come away from reading this book with a richer understanding of American politics, government, and the job of politicans, and we hope you will participate actively in making this constitutional democracy more vital and responsive to the urgent problems of the twenty-first century.

REVIEWERS

The writing of this book has profited from the informed, professional, and often sharp, critical suggestions of our colleagues around the country. This and previous editions have been considerably improved as a result of reviews by the following individuals, for which we thank them all.

David Gray Adler, Idaho State University
James E. Anderson, Texas A&M University
David Barnum, De Paul University
Robert Bartlett, Purdue University
Robert C. Benedict, University of Utah
Thad Beyle, University of North Carolina
Robert R. Bland, University of North Texas
Robert P. Bradshaw, Brigham Young University
Gary Bryner, Brigham Young University
J. Ranson Clark, Muskingum College
Jeanne Clarke, University of Arizona
Leif Carter, University of Georgia
Morgan Chawawa, De Kalb College
Richard Chesteen, University of Tennessee
Ray Christensen, Brigham Young University
Peggy J. Connally, North Central Texas College
Gary Cornia, Brigham Young University
Elmer Cornwell, Brown University
Gary Covington, University of Iowa
Douglas Crane, De Kalb College
Richard Davis, Brigham Young University
James D. Decker, Macon College
Robert DiClerico, West Virginia University
Lois Lovelace Duke, Georgia Southern University
Pat Dunham, Duquesne University
Robert Elias, University of San Francisco
Larry Elowitz, Georgia State College
Lee Epstein, Washington University
Steven Finkel, University of Virginia
Amy Fried, Colgate University
Earl H. Fry, Brigham Young University
David B. Galbraith, Brigham Young University
Mark Gibney, Purdue University
L. Tucker Gibson, Trinity University
Eugene Goss, Long Beach City College
James A. Graves, Kentucky State University
Eugene R. Grosso, Long Beach City College
Gail Harrison, Georgia Southern University
Paul Herrnson, University of Maryland
Marjorie Hershey, Indiana University
Michael J. Horan, University of Wyoming
Ronald J. Hrebenar, University of Utah

Diane P. Jennings, De Kalb College
Loch K. Johnson, University of Georgia
Bill Kelly, Auburn University
Janet M. Kelly, Clemson University
J. Landrum Kelly, Georgia Southern University
Donald F. Kettl, University of Wisconsin
Dwight Kiel, Central Florida University
Ronald F. King, Tulane University
Michael E. Kraft, University of Wisconsin
Fred A. Kramer, University of Massachusetts
William Lammers, University of Southern California
Ned Lebow, Ohio State University
James P. Lester, Colorado State University
Paul Light, Brookings Institution
William Louthan, Ohio Weslyan University
Vincent N. Mancini, Delaware County Community College
Richard Matthews, Lehigh University
Robert McCalla, University of Wisconsin
Christopher B. Mobley, De Paul University
Theodore R. Mosch, University of Tennessee-Martin
Max Neiman, University of California
David Nice, Washington State University
Richard Pacelle, University of Missouri
Glen Parker, Florida State University
Kelly D. Patterson, Brigham Young University
William A. Pelz, Elgin Community College
B. Guy Peters, University of Pittsburgh
Richard Pious, Barnard College
George Pippin, Jones County College
John Portz, Northeastern University
Pamela Rodgers, University of Wisconsin
David Rosenbloom, American University
Alan Rosenthal, Rutgers University
Henry Shockely, Boston University
Steven Shull, University of New Orleans
Christine Marie Sierra, University of New Mexico
Christopher D. Skubby, Lakeland Community College
Robert W. Small, Massasoit Community College
Gregory W. Smith, Gettysburg College
Richard Smolka, American University
Neil Snortland, University of Arkansas at Little Rock
Michael W. Sonnleitner, Portland Community College
Jacqueline Vaughn Switzer, Northern Arizona University
Thaddeus J. Tocza, University of Colorado at Boulder
Roy Thoman, West Texas A&M University
John Tierney, Boston College
Richard Valelly, Massachusetts Institute of Technology
R. Lawson Veasey, University of Arkansas
Frank L. Wilson, Purdue University
Cheryl D. Young, Texas Technical University
Joseph F. Zimmerman, State University of New York at Albany

ACKNOWLEDGMENTS

Writing this book requires teamwork—first, among the authors, who read and rewrite each other's first drafts, then with our research assistants, who track down loose ends and give us the perspective of students, and with the editors and other professionals at Prentice Hall. Important to each revision are the detailed reviews by teachers and researchers, who provide concrete suggestions on how to improve the book. We are grateful to all who helped with this edition.

Research assistants for the eighteenth edition of *Government by the People* were: Brant Avondet, Jason Beal, Marianne Holt, Anna Nibley, Eric Smith, Kim Spears, Peter Stone, and Jon Tanner at Brigham Young University; Elizabeth Schiller at University of Californa, Irvine and Donna Jones and JoAnn Collins at Whitman College provided secretarial assistance.

Books for major college courses like this involve state of the art teaching tools and electronic ancillaries. We are grateful to Marla Danziger and Alison Pendergast for their work on the CD ROM, to Larry Elowitz for the Study Guide and Instructor's Manual, and to Gregg Scott for the Test Item File. Finally, in a real sense, this book is being constantly updated on our home page at **http://www.prenhall.com/burns**, thanks to the excellent work of David Garson and Brian Werner.

We are most indebted to our excellent production editor, Serena Hoffman. She is knowledgeable, thorough, and cares greatly about our book. Her orchestration of all parts of the project, including keeping us on schedule while facilitating our being able to maximize the currency of the book, is remarkable. We also thank Beth Gillett, who has joined Prentice Hall as Political Science Editor and has brought considerable energy and experience to the design and content of this new edition. Our thanks, too, to Nicole Conforti, who kept track of supplements production, and to editorial assistant Brian Prybella. Others at Prentice Hall we wish to thank for their continued support are Phil Miller, Charlyce Jones Owen, Nancy Roberts, and Christopher DeJohn.

Many skilled professionals were important to the publication of this book. They include Joh Lisa and Scott Garrison for page layouts, Eloise Donnelley for photo research, Guy Ruggiero for art coordination, Anne DeMarinus for interior and cover design, and Leslie Osher for design supervision.

We also want to thank you, the professors and students who use our book and who send us letters with suggestions for improving *Government by the People*. We welcome your notes, phone calls, and e-mail. Please write us care of the Political Science Editor at Prentice Hall, 1 Lake Street, Upper Saddle River, New Jersey 07458, or contact us directly:

James MacGregor Burns
Academy of Leadership
University of Maryland
College Park, MD 20742

J.W. Peltason
School of Social Sciences
University of California
Irvine, CA 92717-5700
jwpeltas@uci.edu

Thomas E. Cronin
Office of the President
Whitman College
Walla Walla, WA 99362
cronin@whitman.edu

David B. Magleby
Department of Political Science
Brigham Young University
Provo, UT 84602
david_magleby@byu.edu

A MESSAGE FROM THE PUBLISHER

For nearly 50 years, Burns, Peltason, Cronin, and Magleby's *Government by the People* has taught students the ins and outs of American Government. Now, as we enter a new millennium, no other book is better poised to take students from onlookers to participants in the fascinating processes of democratic government. The gratifying success the text has enjoyed over the years results from a distinguished authorship team who always treat each new edition as a fresh challenge—and, in many ways, a virtually new book.

New to This Edition

- NEW! *"The People Debate":* Most instructors agree that debate and critical thinking are main objectives of their courses. These two-page spreads throughout the book give students a chance to participate in a pro/con debate in the text, online, and through essays and links on the CD ROM and the web. Controversial topics such as Bilingual Education, the Role of the Independent Council, and Affirmative Action are argued by scholars, journalists, and politicians. In addition, through the popular "You Decide" and "Thinking It Through" feature, students can learn to think actively about the issues and events of the day.
- NEW! *CD ROM:* **Free** in every new book, an interactive CD ROM helps students read, review, and explore the text. The computer disk provides the text in its entirety, with introductions to each chapter by David Magleby, one of the authors. Also provided are video clips, illustrations, charts, and graphs from the text, review questions, further exploration for "The People Debate" feature through audio introductions, essay questions, web links, critical thinking questions, and much more.
- NEW! *Additional Learning Tools:* In order to accommodate the many learning styles of introductory students, *Government by the People* now offers a running glossary in the margin of the text pages to clarify key terms and concepts. A list of these terms at the end of each chapter helps with review, and a full glossary at the end of the book serves as a further reference.
- NEW! *Emphasis on Comparative Material:* Comparative material that puts information into a global context by comparing the United States with other nations is highlighted in the text and boxed features by a special icon.
- NEW! *Streamlined Policy Section:* The chapters on economic and regulatory policy have been combined in Chapter 18 for ease of instruction and for their logical connections.
- NEW! *Completely Redesigned:* To help increase readability, this edition has been totally redesigned to open up the space and reduce the number of items in the margins. Photos, tables, charts, and figures have all been recast to make them easier for students to read and digest the information.

Features of the Text

- COMPREHENSIVE AND BALANCED PRESENTATION: Known for its balanced coverage of constitutional principles, political processes, and political institutions, this latest edition offers the best of previous editions and exciting changes in content that include:
  - A thematic examination of constitutional democracy-its ideals, its conditions, and the American struggle to realize its possibilities and potential.
  - Much revised treatment of the presidency (Chapter 15), Congress (Chapter 14), and the bureaucracy (Chapter 17) to reflect current issues, including Bill Clinton's battles with Congress and the independent council.
  - A unique chapter, "Making Social Policy" (Chapter 20), covers past policy initiatives, such as the New Deal and the Great Society, as well as current debates over welfare reform, health care, crime control, and education policies.
  - "The American Political Landscape" (Chapter 8), examines social and economic diversity in American society and some of the political consequences of living in an increasingly multicultural nation.
  - Extensive interpretation of the 1998 election, including data from the National Election Study, will prepare students to follow and interpret the 2000 presidential race.
  - Substantially revised policy chapters reflect current policy initiatives and the priorities of the president and Congress.
  - Innovative treatment of political ideology and culture, political participation, voter turnout, voting behavior, and campaign financing.
  - Expanded coverage of state and local politics in the *National, State, and Local Version,* including full updates on 1998 election results.
- CURRENCY: Altlhough Introduction to American Government courses are not courses on current events, students are always interested in what is going on around them.

Throughout the text, we use examples that are at the forefront of the news. From the 2000 presidential race to Bill Clinton's battles with the independent council, students are enabled to put today's headlines into a meaningful context.

- YOU DECIDE/THINKING IT THROUGH: This participatory question-and-answer feature is designed to strengthen students' critical thinking skills as well as introduce interesting and challenging issues and ideas about American politics. A question is presented on the left page, and on the facing page a "Thinking It Through" discussion examines possible answers. This unique feature has long been a favorite of readers.
- A CLOSER LOOK: These journalistic-style boxes combine text, photographs, and art on relevant issues of high student appeal. Some of the topics include: Hate Speech on Campus, What Is Sexual Harrassment? Campaign Finance Reform, The Don't Ask, Don't Tell Controversy, and Violence in the Public Schools.
- WE THE PEOPLE: These unique boxes are designed to reflect the concerns and experiences of ethnic and minority groups in American politics. Some of the topics include: Coming to America, Distribution of Education in the United States, Portrait of the Electorate, Needed: Minority Law Clerks at the Court, and Women Governors.
- POLITICS ONLINE: End-of-chapter Internet exercises are designed to engage and educate students about the vast potential of the Internet. The exercises present information, pose questions, and provide web addresses to enable students to access the plentiful resources available online.

Technology Initiatives

With the development of new technologies, we have discovered effective new ways of helping students understand and retain information. In this edition, we have made every effort to give both instructors and students a large array of multi-media tools to help in the presentation and the learning of the material.

- **www.prenhall.com/burns**: Prentice Hall's exclusive *Companion Website*™ that accompanies *Government by the People* offers unique tools and support that make it easy for students and instructors to integrate this online study guide with the text. Containing a wealth of additional resources, this free website includes practice tests, the original text of more than 150 primary source documents mentioned in the text, an update section for the latest election news, an interactive survey, and additional web links.
- GOVERNMENT BY THE PEOPLE: INTERACTIVE EDITION: Free in every new book, this exciting electronic version of the text will help students read, review, and explore the text. See description of the CD ROM earlier in this preface.
- POLITICAL SCIENCE ON THE INTERNET: This timely supplement provides an introduction to the Internet and the numerous political sites on the World Wide Web. It describes e-mail, list servers, browsers, and how to document sources. It also includes web addresses for the most current and useful political websites. This 96-page supplementary book, shrink-wrapped to the text, is free to students.
- DISTANCE LEARNING SOLUTIONS: For instructors interested in distance learning, Prentice Hall and WebCT Educational Technologies offer a fully customizable, online course using the popular WebCT online course architecture. Using Prentice Hall's wealth of content, we have put together a package including online lectures, online testing, online quizzes, links, communication tools, as well as many course management features commonly available with WebCT. See your local Prentice Hall representative or visit our special Demonstration website at **www.prenhall.com/webct** for more information.

Supplements for the Instructor

In addition to the Faculty Resources material found on the companion website, *Government by the People* offers instructors a wide range of proven as well as new instructional aids. The supplements have been completely revised, not only to incorporate material new to this edition, but also to ensure the highest quality and accuracy possible.

- INSTRUCTOR'S RESOURCE MANUAL: This supplement provides the following resources for each chapter of the text: summary, review of major concepts, lecture suggestions and topic outlines, suggestions for classroom discussions, additional resource materials, and a detailed content outline for lecture planning.
- POWER POINT PRESENTATION SLIDES: The charts and graphs from the book, along with lecture outlines tied to each chapter, are all available on Power Point slides. To preview them, go to **www.prenhall.com/burns** and click on Faculty Resources.
- STRATEGIES FOR TEACHING AMERICAN GOVERNMENT: A GUIDE FOR THE NEW INSTRUCTOR: This unique guide offers a wealth of practical advice and information to help new instructors face the challenges of teaching courses in American Government. Available at **www.prenhall.com/burns** under Faculty Resources.
- TEST ITEM FILE: Completely reviewed and revised to ensure the highest level of quality and accuracy, this test item file contains over 2,000 questions in multiple choice, true/false, and essay format covering factual, conceptual, and applied material from the text.

- PRENTICE HALL TEST MANAGER: A computerized version of the test item file, this program allows full editing of questions and the addition of instructor-generated items. Other special features include random generation, scrambling question order, and test preview before printing. Available for IBM and Macintosh computers.
- AMERICAN GOVERNMENT TRANSPARENCIES, SERIES VI: This set of over 125 four-color transparency acetates reproduces illustrations, charts, and maps from the text as well as from additional sources. A brief guide provides descriptions, teaching suggestions, and discussion questions for each transparency.
- FILMS FOR THE HUMANITIES AND SCIENCES: With a qualifying order of textbooks from Prentice Hall, you may select from this high quality library of political science videos from Films for the Humanities and Sciences. Please contact your local representative for a complete listing.

Supplements for the Student

In addition to the Companion Website and the CD ROM, *Government by the People* offers a complete array of study and supplemental material for the student.

- THEMES OF THE TIMES SUPPLEMENT: Prentice Hall and *The New York Times* expand students' knowledge beyond the classroom and into the world we live in. Users of *Government by the People* can receive a complimentary newspaper supplement containing recent articles pertinent to American Government. These articles, featuring the best in reporting and journalistic integrity associated with *The New York Times*, update the text material and contribute real-world applications to the topics covered in the course.

- THE WRITE STUFF: WRITING AS A PERFORMING AND POLITICAL ART, SECOND EDITION: This brief booklet, written by Thomas E. Cronin, provides ideas and suggestions on writing style and methods in political science. Also available on the web at **www.prenhall.com/burns** under Student Resources.
- A GUIDE TO CIVIC LITERACY: This brief booklet provides suggestions for getting students involved in politics. It includes nine political activities for individuals or groups on agenda building, coalition building, registering and mobilizing voters, education, and increasing accountability. The guide was written by James Chesney and Otto Feinstein, both of Wayne State University.
- STUDY GUIDE: Each chapter includes outlines, study notes, a glossary, practice tests, Political Science Today study assignments, and data analysis worksheets that reinforce student learning. The guide was prepared by Larry Elowitz of Georgia College and State University.

ABOUT THE AUTHORS

JAMES MACGREGOR BURNS

James MacGregor Burns is a Senior Scholar at the Academy of Leadership, University of Maryland, College Park, and Woodrow Wilson Professor Emeritus of Government at Williams College. He has written numerous books, including *The Power to Lead* (1984), *The Vineyard of Liberty* (1982), *Leadership* (1979), *Roosevelt: The Soldier of Freedom* (1970), *The Deadlock of Democracy: Four-Party Politics in America* (1963), and *Roosevelt: The Lion and the Fox* (1956). His most recent book is *A People's Charter: The Pursuit of Rights in America* (1991), which he wrote with his son, Stewart Burns. Burns is a past president of the American Political Science Association and winner of numerous prizes, including the Pulitzer Prize in History.

J.W. PELTASON

J.W. Peltason is a leading scholar on the judicial process and public law. He is Professor Emeritus of Political Science at the University of California, Irvine. As past president of the American Council on Education, Peltason has represented higher education before Congress and state legislatures. His writings include *Federal Courts in the Political Process* (1955), *Fifty-Eight Lonely Men: Southern Federal Judges and School Desegration* (1961), and *Understanding the Constitution* (1997). Among his awards are the James Madison Medal from Princeton University and the American Political Science Association's Charles E. Merriam Award.

THOMAS E. CRONIN

Thomas E. Cronin is a leading student of the American presidency, leadership, and policy-making processes. He teaches at and serves as president of Whitman College. He was a White House Fellow and a White House aide and has served as president of the Western Political Science Association. His writings include *The State of the Presidency* (1980), *U.S. v. Crime in the Streets* (1981), *Direct Democracy: The Politics of Initiative, Referendum, and Recall* (1989), *Colorado Politics and Government* (1993), and *The Paradoxes of the American Presidency* (1998). Cronin is a past recipient of the American Political Science Association's Charles E. Merriam Award.

DAVID B. MAGLEBY

David B. Magleby is nationally recognized for his expertise on direct democracy, voting behavior, and campaign finance. He is Professor of Political Science at Brigham Young University and has taught at the University of California, Santa Cruz, and the University of Virginia. His writings include *Direct Legislation* (1984), *The Money Chase: Congressional Campaign Finance Reform* (1990), and *The Myth of the Independent Voter* (1992). He was president of Pi Sigma Alpha, the national political science honor society, and has received numerous teaching awards. In 1996 he was a Fulbright Scholar at Nuffield College, Oxford University.

COMPANION WEBSITE

www.prenhall.com/burns

Your Internet companion to the most exciting state of the art educational tools on the Web!

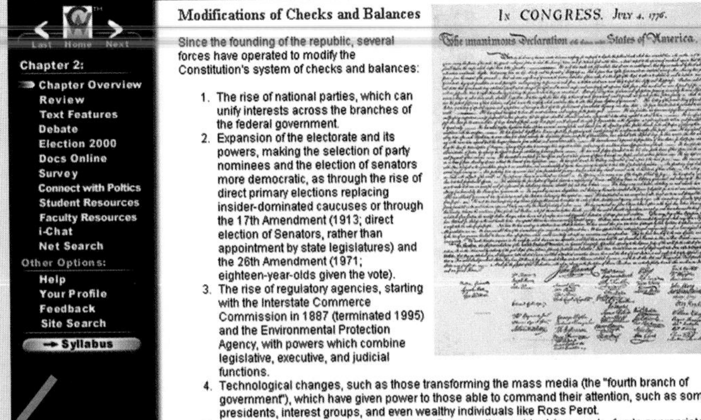

Gives students summary information of the chapter.

Connects features in the text such as "We the People" and "A Closer Look" to Internet sites for further information.

Follows the 2000 presidential race with updated information and links throughout the election.

Interactive survey questions show students how their opinions on political issues compare to those of other students around the country.

Writing help, career and internship information, and links to state web pages are found here.

Join the discussion of debate issues, current events, and other issues online.

Allows students to email instructors and provides a vehicle for feedback on the site.

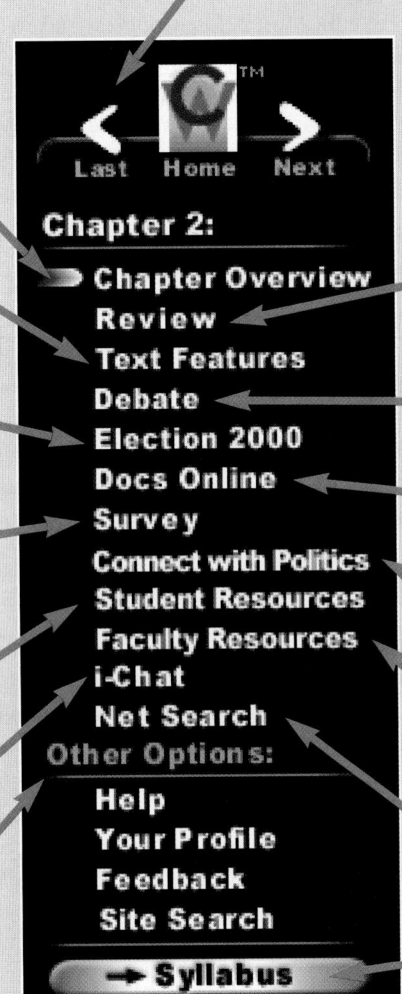

Students can test their knowledge of the chapter through a series of multiple choice, true/false, fill-in-the-blank, and essay questions.

Offers students the opportunity to further investigate "The People Debate" through Internet links and essay questions.

Links students to text of over 150 primary source documents mentioned in the book.

Links students directly with the most popular Internet sites for American Government.

Faculty can download Power Point slides and information about teaching the American Government course.

Searches the Net for key words.

Allows instructors to post their syllabus and lecture notes for their class.

GOVERNMENT BY THE PEOPLE INTERACTIVE CD-ROM

THIS EXCITING NEW ELECTRONIC VERSION OF THE TEXT ON CD-ROM features video tips from the author, interactive graphics, review questions, links to further research, debate destinations, video and audio clips, and the complete text of ***Government by the People***, 18th edition.

How to install:

WINDOWS: Insert CD. Wait for menu. Click the Install button. **MAC:** Insert CD. Double click on the Install icon.

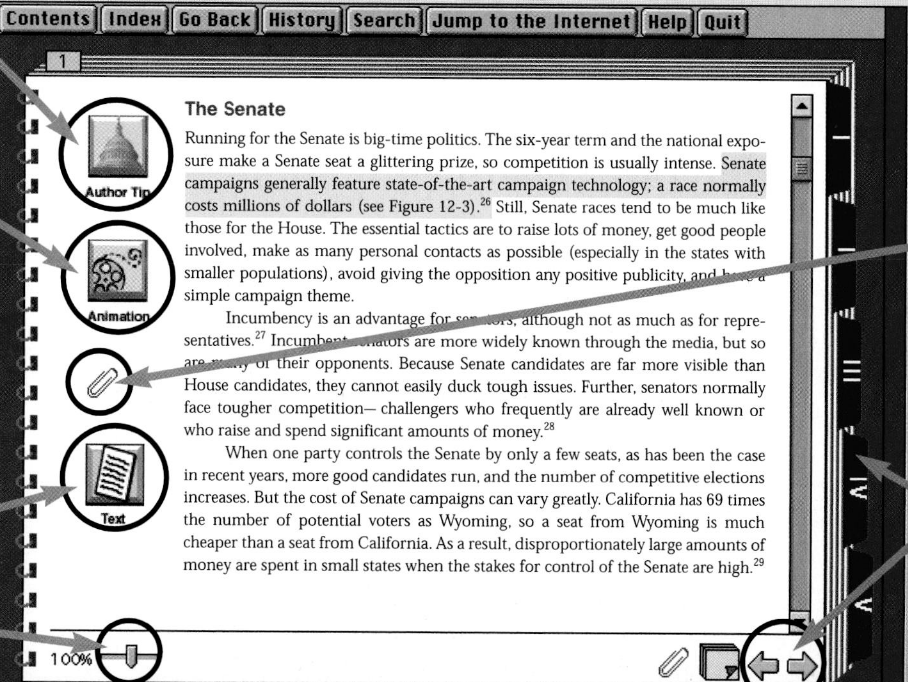

*Additional Features

How to Highlight text:

Just as you can use a highlighter marker to highlight text in traditional print books, you can also highlight text electronically in this CD-ROM. **To highlight text:**

1. Select the text you want to highlight.
2. From the Edit menu, choose *Highlight Selection*. Your selection is highlighted.
3. Unhighlight text using the same steps.

How to Annotate text:

You can add your own comments or "margin notes" to any paragraph in the CD-ROM. The program places a paper clip next to the paragraph you annotate. You can add one annotation per paragraph. **To annotate:**

1. Scroll until the text position you want to annotate is at the top of the main page.
2. From the Edit menu in the menu bar, select *Annotate*. The *Define Annotation* dialog appears.
3. In the *Text:* box, enter your notation. Click *Add*. To make corrections, the backspace key erases the last character typed.
4. A paper clip icon appears next to the paragraph you annotated.

OR

1. Drag the *Annotation icon* to a location.
2. Repeat steps 3 and 4.

How to Bookmark text:

You can set up your book to include bookmarks that you place in locations you want to revisit. When you select yourself as the user, your personal set of bookmarks appears.
To define and use bookmarks:

1. Activate the bookmark editor by clicking on the yellow "sticky note" pad icon at the bottom of the window. The *Define Bookmark* dialog appears.
2. Change the default bookmark name if desired.
3. Click the *Add* button. The program will place a yellow numbered bookmark at the top of the page you are reading.

To revisit a bookmarked page: Click the yellow bookmark at the top of the page. **To remove a bookmark,** click *Define*, then click *Delete* in the window that appears.

See back page for system requirements and license agreements.

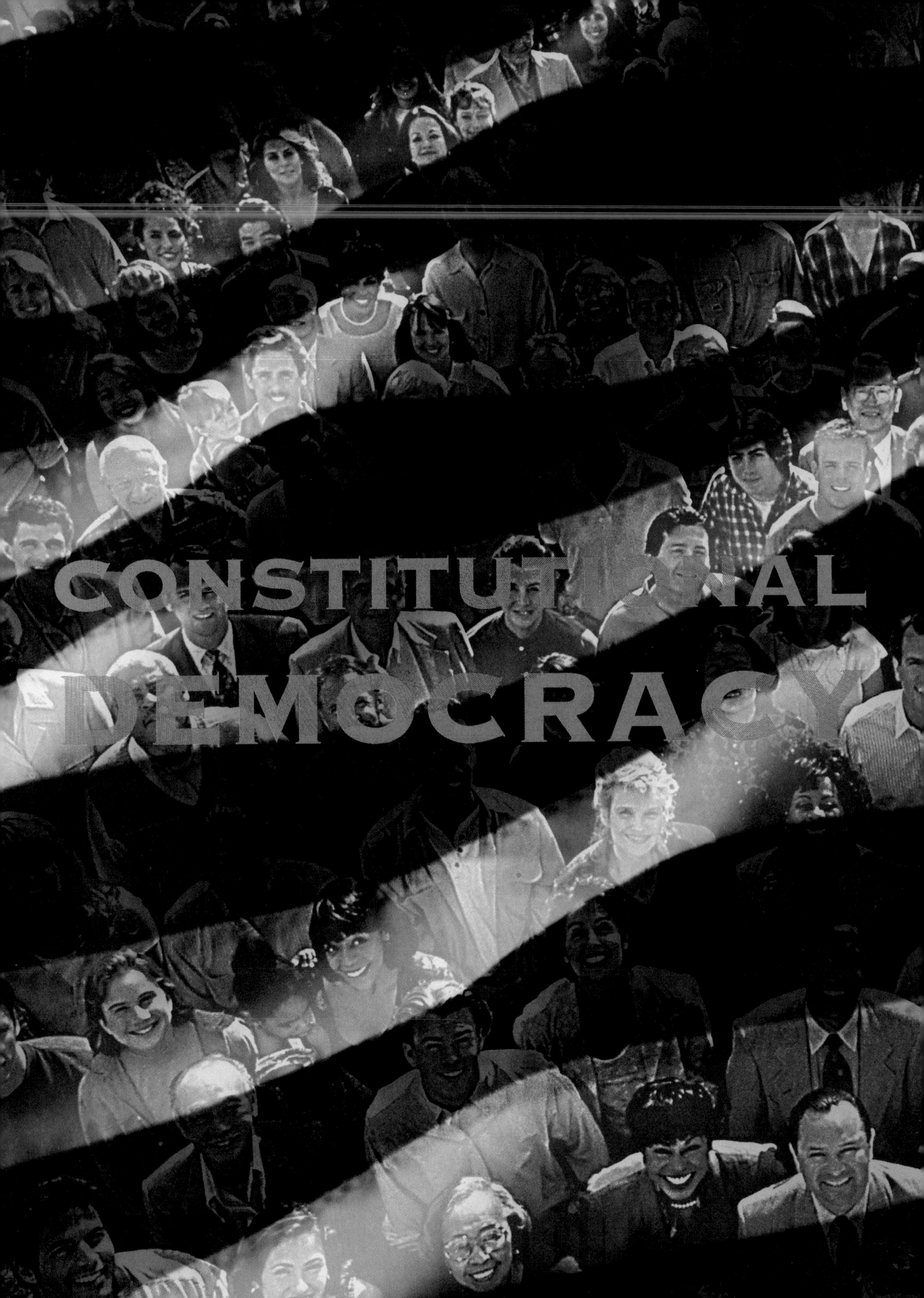
CONSTITUTIONAL
DEMOCRACY

1

CHAPTER OUTLINE

- Defining Democracy
- The Constitutional Roots of the American Experiment
- The Constitutional Convention, 1787
- To Adopt or Not to Adopt?

AS THIS NATION ENTERS THE TWENTY-FIRST CENTURY, THERE ARE SOME DISQUIETING SIGNS, SOME WIDESPREAD CONCERNS ABOUT THE VITALITY OF OUR DEMOCRATIC system. Politician bashing has always been part of our tradition, but now Americans tend to be especially cynical about politics and politicians—and with good reason. Revelations about President Bill Clinton's conduct with a White House intern and his attempts to conceal the nature of the relationship threw the country into an emotional examination of how to deal with elected officials who violate accepted standards of conduct.

For months Congress and the country debated whether Bill Clinton's actions were "high crimes and misdemeanors," or whether they were serious mistakes in judgment but not grounds for impeachment and removal from office. Public opinion and congressional votes on the matter reflected a deeply divided country and Congress. Ultimately the question of what is an impeachable offense is a political question, one that must be decided by a majority of the U.S. House of Representatives and two-thirds of the Senate. Removal of an elected president from office is so serious because it sets aside the wishes of the electorate that the Constitution requires removal from office only after trial and conviction on impeachment charges. Although the House majority passed two articles of impeachment for perjury and obstruction of justice against President Clinton, the Senate did not reach the two-thirds vote (67 senators) needed to convict and remove the president.

The debate over what to do about President Clinton's actions forced a reassessment of what we expect of elected officials. Defenders of President Clinton stressed the private nature of his behavior and also pointed to public opinion polls showing large majorities approving his job performance. Detractors of the president countered that it is never right to lie under oath or lie to the American people. In addition, it was argued, presidents are role models and should set a high standard in personal conduct.

The nature of the impeachment issue and the unrelenting media coverage of the Clinton/Lewinsky matter forced discussion of the topic in the homes of most Americans. Surveys of parents found that they were more likely to discuss politics with their children as a result of the scandal, and these discussions were often initiated by the children. Not surprisingly, the White House scandal resulted in large numbers of young people losing respect for politicians.[1] But children were not the only ones who lost trust and confidence in elected officials. Older Americans were also turned off. Some were alienated by Independent Counsel Kenneth Starr's relentless pursuit of the president and the content of his report to Congress, while others were disgusted by the actions of the president and the highly partisan tactics of Congress.

It will take some time to discover whether the Clinton-Lewinsky matter further discourages people from voting, entering government service, or running for office. But the popular perceptions that politics is corrupting, that politicians are dishonest, that elected officials are more concerned about their party than about the good of the country have all been reinforced by this scandal. These are all mistaken notions and misperceptions.

The truth is that most politicians are honorable women and men who care deeply for their country and are willing to sacrifice their privacy and earn less money when they seek office. They do not often agree on what is the best course of action, but neither do we as citizens. How they work out their differences in a large and complex country is fascinating and important to understand. It is why the study of government is important. Even with the deep divisions in the country over the Clinton impeachment, Congress met its constitutional obligations. The country was able to bring closure to the matter and move on.

As we enter the twenty-first century, our Republic will have survived for more than two hundred years. During that time we have held—even in the midst of a civil war, depressions, and world wars—54 presidential elections and the peaceful transfer of power from one party to another scores of times. Not many democracies have survived this long. We made it through the centuries for many reasons, but a major one has been that all Americans—women and men; Republicans and Democrats; business leaders and labor leaders; Protestants, Catholics, and Jews; Northerners and Southerners; New Yorkers and Peorians; Whites, African Americans, and Hispanics; rich and poor—all have shared a common commitment to our Constitution, to one another, and to the belief that our differences are best reconciled by debate, compromise, and voting, and that politicians who get the most votes in an election govern better than do generals who win wars, or businesspeople who produce wealth, or college professors who produce knowledge, or clergy who teach religion.

Government by the people is necessarily government by politicians. A central tenet of democracy is that those who hold power should do so only by winning an election. In our political system, the fragmentation of powers requires politicians to mediate among factions, build coalitions, and work out compromises among and within the branches of our government to produce policy and action.

We expect a lot from our politicians. We expect them to operate within the rules of democracy, be honest, humble, patriotic, compassionate, sensitive to the needs of others, well-informed, competent, fair-minded, self-confident, and inspiring. They must be candidates of the people, not of the money. They must not want power for itself, but lead because of their concern for the public good. And finally, they must be willing to do the job and get out when finished. Yet as we close out this century, Americans have generally negative views about politicians.

"The Athenians are here, Sire, with an offer to back us with ships, money, arms, and men—and, of course, their usual lectures about democracy."

Why the gap between expectations about the actual and the ideal politician? The gap exists in part because we have such unrealistic expectations. We want politicians to be perfect, to have all the answers, and to have all the correct (in our minds) values. We want politicians to solve our problems, yet we also want them to serve as scapegoats for the things we dislike about government: taxes, regulations, hard times, and limits on our freedom. It is impossible for anyone to live up to these ideals. Like all individuals, politicians live in a world in which perfection may be the goal, yet compromise, ambition, fund raising, and self-promotion are necessary. "Ideal" leaders are usually dead. Ideal politicians exist only in a community in which conflict does not exist—and probably where liberty and rights do not exist.

This book is about how our democracy works. When you finish reading it, we hope you will come to see that politicians are essential to making democracy work and recognize that to get rid of politics from public affairs would be to get rid of democracy.

Defining Democracy

The word "democracy" is nowhere to be found in the Declaration of Independence or in the U.S. Constitution, nor was it a term used by the founders of the Republic. It is both a very old term and a new one. It was used at the time of the founding of this nation to refer to various undesirable things: mobs, lack of standards, and a system that encouraged leaders who gained power by appealing to the emotions and prejudices of the rabble.

The distinguishing feature of democracy is that government derives its authority from its citizens. In fact, the word comes from two Greek words: *demos* (the people) and *kratos* (authority or power). Thus **democracy** means *government by the people*—not government by one person (a monarch, a dictator, a priest) or government by the few (an oligarchy or aristocracy).

Ancient Athens and a few other Greek cities had a **direct democracy** in which citizens came together to discuss and pass laws and select their rulers. These Greek city-states did not last. Most turned to mob rule and then resorted to dictators. Thus, when the word "democracy" came into English usage in the seventeenth century, it denoted this kind of direct democracy. It was a term of derision, a negative word, usually used to refer to mob rule.

James Madison, writing in *The Federalist*, No. 10, reflected the view of many of the framers of the U.S. Constitution when he wrote, "Such democracies [as the Greek and Roman] . . . have ever been found incompatible with personal security, or the rights of property; and have in general been as short in their lives, as they have been violent in their deaths" (*The Federalist*, No. 10 appears in the Appendix at the back of this book).

Today it is no longer possible, even if desirable, to assemble the citizens of any but the smallest towns to make their laws or to select their officials directly from among the citizenry. Rather, we have invented a system of representation. Democracy today means **representative democracy**, or, to use Plato's term, a *republic*, in which those who have governmental authority get and retain authority directly or indirectly as a result of winning free elections in which all adult citizens are allowed to participate. The framers preferred to use the term "republic" to avoid any confusion between direct democracy, which they disliked, and representative democracy, which they liked and thought secured all the advantages of a direct democracy while curing its weaknesses. Today, and in this book, *democracy* and *republic* are used interchangeably.

In defining democracy, several other terms need to be clarified. **Constitutional democracy** as used here refers to a government in which those who exercise substantial governmental powers do so as the result of winning free and relatively frequent elections. It is a government in which there are recognized, enforced limits on the powers of all governmental officials.

Constitutionalism is a label we apply to arrangements such as checks and balances, federalism, separation of powers, rule of law, due process, and the Bill of Rights that require our leaders to listen, think, bargain, and explain before they make laws. We then hold them politically and legally accountable for how they exercise their powers. Other constitutional democracies use some, but not necessarily all, of these devices as well as some that we do not use; for example, *ombudsmen*, officials who investigate wrongdoing by public officials.

Like most political concepts, democracy encompasses many ideas and has many meanings. Democracy is a way of life, a form of government, a way of governing, a type of nation, a state of mind, and a variety of processes. We can divide these

democracy
Government by the people, either directly or indirectly, with free and frequent elections.

direct democracy
Government in which citizens come together to discuss and pass laws and select rulers.

representative democracy
Government that derives its powers indirectly from the people, who elect those who will govern; also called a *republic*.

constitutional democracy
A government in which those who exercise governmental powers do so as a result of winning free and relatively frequent elections and are subject to recognized, enforced limits on the power of all government officials. It is the elections that make the government democratic; it is the recognized and enforced limits on power that make it constitutional.

constitutionalism
The set of arrangements such as checks and balances, federalism, separation of powers, rule of law, due process, and the Bill of Rights that requires our leaders to listen, think, bargain, and explain before they make laws. We then hold them politically and legally accountable for how they exercise their powers.

many meanings into three broad categories: democracy as a system of interacting values, a system of interrelated political processes, and a system of interdependent political structures.

Democracy as a System of Interacting Values

Today the democratic faith may be as near a universal faith as the world has. A belief in human dignity, freedom, liberty, individual rights, and other democratic values is widely shared in most corners of the world. The essence of democratic values is contained in the ideas of personal liberty, respect for the individual, popular consent, and equality of opportunity.

PERSONAL LIBERTY Liberty has been the single most powerful value in American history. It was for "life, liberty, and the pursuit of happiness" that independence was declared; it was to "secure the Blessings of Liberty" that the Constitution was drawn up and adopted. Even our patriotic songs extol the "sweet land of liberty." The essence of liberty is *self-determination*, meaning that all individuals must have the opportunity to realize their own goals. Liberty is not simply the absence of external restraint on a person (freedom *from*); it is the individual's freedom and capacity to act positively to reach his or her goals (freedom *to*). Moreover, both history and reason suggest that individual liberty is the key to social progress. The greater the people's freedom, the greater the chance of discovering better ways of life.

RESPECT FOR THE INDIVIDUAL Popular rule in a democracy flows from a belief that every individual has the potential for common sense, rationality, and fairness. Individuals have important rights; collectively, those rights are the source of all legitimate governmental authority and power. These concepts pervade all democratic thought. They are woven into the writings of Thomas Jefferson, especially in the Declaration of Independence: "All men . . . are endowed by their Creator with certain unalienable rights" (the Declaration of Independence appears in the Appendix). Constitutional democracies make the *person*—rich or poor, black or white, male or female—the central measure of value. The state, the union, and the corporation are measured in terms of their usefulness to individuals. Not all political systems, of course, put the individual first. Some promote **statism**, considering the state supreme. In a modern democracy, the nation, or even the community, is less important than are the individuals who compose it.

EQUALITY OF OPPORTUNITY The importance of the individual is enhanced by the democratic value of *equality*: "All men are created equal and from that equal creation they derive rights inherent and unalienable, among which are the preservation of liberty and the pursuit of happiness." So reads Jefferson's first draft of the Declaration of Independence, and the words indicate the primacy of the concept. Alexis de Tocqueville and other international visitors who have studied American democracy were all struck by the strength of egalitarian thought and practice in our political and social lives.

But what does equality mean? Equality for whom? For blacks as well as whites? For women as well as men? For Native Americans, descendants of the Pilgrims, and recent immigrants? And what kind of equality? Economic, political, legal, social, or some other kind of equality? *Equality of opportunity?* Does equality of opportunity simply mean that everyone should have the same place at the starting line? Or does it mean an effort should be made to equalize the factors that determine how well a person fares economically or socially?

POPULAR CONSENT The animating principle of the American Revolution, the Declaration of Independence, and the resulting new nation was **popular consent**, the

statism
The idea that the rights of the state (meaning nation) are supreme over the rights of the individual.

popular consent
The idea that a just government must derive its powers from the consent of the people it governs.

idea that a just government must derive its powers from the *consent of the people* it governs. A commitment to democracy thus entails a community's willingness to participate and make decisions in government. These principles sound unobjectionable intellectually, but in practice they mean that certain individuals or groups may not get their way. A commitment to popular consent must involve a willingness to lose when most people vote the other way.

DEMOCRATIC VALUES IN CONFLICT The basic values of democracy do not always coexist happily. Individualism may conflict with the collective welfare or the public good. Self-determination may conflict with equal opportunity. For example, the right of a home owner to add another floor to her home may conflict with the right of her neighbor to have an unobstructed view. Or the right of a person to smoke an after-dinner cigar in a restaurant may conflict with the right of others not to have to breathe tobacco smoke.

Much of our political combat revolves around how to strike a balance among democratic values—how to protect the Declaration of Independence's unalienable rights of life, liberty, and the pursuit of happiness while trying to "form," as the Constitution announces, "a more perfect Union, establish Justice, insure domestic Tranquility, provide for the common defence, promote the general Welfare, and secure the Blessings of Liberty to ourselves and our Posterity" (see the Preamble to the Constitution, which follows Chapter 2). Over the years the American political system has moved, despite occasional setbacks, toward greater freedom and more democracy.

A strong commitment to democracy is in many ways a twentieth-century idea. People throughout the world are more attracted to democracy today than ever before. Recent events in Indonesia, Germany, Poland, the Czech Republic, Slovakia, Russia, and South Africa are evidence that the dream of freedom and democratic government is universal.

Democracy as a System of Interrelated Political Processes

Far more people dream about democracy than ever experience it, and many new democracies fail. To be successful, democratic government requires a well-defined political process as well as a governmental structure. To become reality, democratic values must be incorporated into a political process, the essence of which is the tradition of free and fair elections, majority rule, freedom of expression, and the right to assemble and protest.

FREE AND FAIR ELECTIONS Democratic government is based on free and fair elections held at intervals frequent enough to make them relevant to policy choices. Elections are one of the most important devices for keeping officials and representatives accountable.

We previously described *representative democracy* as a government in which those who have the authority to make decisions with the force of law acquire and retain this authority either directly or indirectly as the result of winning free elections in which the great majority of adult citizens are allowed to participate. Crucial to modern-day definitions of democracy is the idea that opposition political parties can exist, can run candidates in elections, and can at least have a chance to replace those who are currently holding public office. Thus political competition and choice are crucial to the existence of democracy.

Although all citizens should have equal voting power, free and fair elections do not imply that everyone must or will have equal political influence. Some people, because of wealth, talent, or position, have more influence than others. How much extra influence key figures should be allowed to exercise in a democracy is an ongoing question. But at the polls, a president or a plumber, a corporate CEO or a ditch digger, each casts only one vote.

MAJORITY RULE **Majority** rule is a basic rule of democracy. It means that the candidate or the party that receives more than half the votes wins the election and takes charge of the government until the next election. In practice, however, majority rule is often **plurality** rule, in which the candidate or party with the most votes wins the election, even though it may not constitute a true majority of more than half the votes. For example, in the 1996 presidential election, Bill Clinton received 49 percent of the votes, Bob Dole 41 percent, and Ross Perot 8 percent. Clinton won a plurality of the votes, not a majority. Once elected, officials do not have a right to curtail the attempts of political minorities to use all peaceful means to become the new majority. Even as the winners take power, the losers are at work to try to get it back at the next election.[2]

Should the will of the majority prevail in all cases? Americans answer this question in a variety of ways. Some insist majority views should be enacted into laws and regulations. However, an effective representative democracy involves far more than simply ascertaining and applying the statistical will of most of the people. It is a more complicated and often untidy process in which the people and their agents debate, compromise, and arrive at a decision only after thoughtful deliberation.

The framers wanted to guard society against any one part acting unjustly toward any other part. The Constitution reflects their fear of tyranny by majorities, especially momentary majorities that spring from temporary passions. They insulated certain rights and institutions from popular choice. Effective representation of the people, the framers insisted, should not be based solely on parochial interests or shifting breezes of opinion.

FREEDOM OF EXPRESSION Free and fair elections depend on access to information relevant to voting choices. Voters must have access to facts, competing ideas, and the views of candidates. Free and fair elections require a climate in which competing, non-government-owned newspapers, radio stations, and television stations can flourish. If the government controls what is said and how it is said, there is no democracy. Without free speech there are no free and fair elections.

THE RIGHT TO ASSEMBLE AND PROTEST Citizens must be free to organize for political purposes. Obviously, individuals can be more effective if they join with others in a party, a pressure group, a protest movement, or a demonstration. The right to oppose the government, to form opposition parties, and to have a chance of defeating incumbents is not only vital; it is a defining characteristic of a democracy.

Democracy as a System of Interdependent Political Structures

Democracy is, of course, more than values and processes. It also entails a system of political structures that safeguard these values and processes. The Constitution and the Bill of Rights create an ingenious structure—one that both grants and checks government power. This constitutional structure is reinforced by a political system of parties, interest groups, media, and other institutions that mediate between the electorate and those who govern and thus help to maintain democratic stability.

The American constitutional system is remarkable for four elements: (1) *federalism*, the division of powers between the national and state governments; (2) *separation of powers* among the legislative, executive, and judicial branches; (3) a system of *checks and balances* in which each branch is given the constitutional means, the political independence, and the personal motives to check the powers of the other branches; and (4) a judicially enforceable, written, explicit *Bill of Rights* that provides a guarantee of individual liberties and due process before the law.

Conditions Conducive to Constitutional Democracy

How do we explain the relatively small number of long-lived, strong democracies? Although it is hard to specify the precise conditions that are essential for the establishment and maintenance of a democracy, here are a few things we have learned.

majority
A candidate or party wins more than half the votes cast to win an election.

plurality
A candidate or party wins the most votes cast, not necessarily more than half.

IT'S NOT EASY TO BE FREE

New democracies often fail. It is one thing to espouse democratic values, another to put them into practice. Some people believe in democracy until they lose power in an election. Or the citizens grow weary of the political wrangling that comes with democracy and long for a strong charismatic leader with simple solutions for complex problems. The struggle to convert to a market economy in Russia has produced this kind of turmoil. Leaders like Napoleon or Adolf Hitler promise to make a country work more smoothly, often by disbanding democratic institutions. Citizens may turn to such leaders when they face economic difficulties or are under threat from a foreign power. Sectional differences can also pull apart the fabric of democracy. Parts of a country that have a distinctive racial, religious, or ethnic composition often distrust the national majority and seek guarantees or special concessions—as have French-speaking residents in Quebec and ethnic Albanians in Kosovo.

Because democracies are so difficult to sustain, comparatively few have lasted long. More than half the world's constitutions have been written in the past four decades. On the entire continent of Asia, no democracy predates World War II, when a democratic constitution was imposed on Japan. In Africa, the oldest democracy is Botswana, which has had free elections and a multiparty system since 1966.

Arctic
Greenland (Den.)
Bering Sea
United States
Canada
Iceland
Norway
Sweden
Finland
Russia
United Kingdom
Den.
Neth.
Estonia
Latvia
Lithuania
Eire
Poland
Byelarus
Belgium
Germany
Aust.
Ukraine
Kazakhstan
Mongolia
France
Switz.
Hung.
Romania
Italy
Spain
Portugal
Bulg.
Greece
Georgia
Azerbaijan
Uzbekistan
Kyrgyzstan
Turkey
Armenia
Turkmen.
Tajikistan
N. Korea
S. Korea
Japan
United States of
Atlantic
Morocco
Lebanon
Syria
Israel
Iraq
Iran
Afghanistan
China
Jordan
Kuwait
Pakistan
Nepal
Bhutan
Mexico
Cuba
The Bahamas
Western
Algeria
Lybia
Egypt
Saudi
U.A.E.
India
Bangladesh
Taiwan
United States
Haiti
Dominican
Mauritania
Myanmar
Laos
Pacific Ocean
Beli
Jamaica
Puerto
Guatamala
El Salvador
Honduras
Nicaragua
Costa Rica
Panama
Colombia
Trinidad
Guyana
Suriname
French Guiana (France)
Venezuela
Ecuador
Senegal
Gambia
Guinea-Bissau
Guinea
Sierra
Liberia
Ivory Coast
Ghana
Mali
Niger
Burkina
Nigeria
Chad
Sudan
Central African Republic
Oman
Yemen
Ethiopia
Somalia
Thailand
Cambodia
Vietnam
Philippines
Brunei
Sri Lanka
Malaysia
Singapore
Palau (US)
Irian Java (INDO)
Papua New
Indonesia
Solomon Islands
Benin
Togo
Gabon
Congo
Cameroon
Rwanda
Uganda
Zaire
Burundi
Kenya
Tanzania
Malawi
Pacific Ocean
Brazil
Peru
Bolivia
Paraguay
Chile
Argentina
Uruguay
Angola
Zambia
Mozambique
Madagascar
Zimbabwe
Namibia
Botswana
Swaziland
Lesotho
South Atlantic
Indian Ocean
Australia
South Africa
New Zealand
Falkland Islands (U.K.)
S.Georgia Islands
Antarctica

Not Free | Partly Free | Free

Map of Freedom

SOURCE: *Freedom Review*, January/February 1998. © 1998 by Freedom House.

You Decide . . .

"Bowling Alone." Does this mean a decline in "social capital"?

Political scientist Robert D. Putnam has pointed to a decline in American political involvement and a decline in confidence in our political institutions. He notes that in recent decades fewer people engage in politics—voting, attending a political rally, working for a political party, or taking part in the political process in other ways. There has also been a decline in church membership and attendance, membership in labor unions, involvement in the PTA, membership in civic and fraternal organizations, volunteering for the Boy Scouts, the Red Cross, and other organizations, and membership in fraternal organizations such as Lions, Elks, Shriners, and Masons.

Putnam writes, "The most whimsical yet discomforting bit of evidence of social disengagement in contemporary America that I have discovered is this: More Americans are bowling today than ever before, but bowling in organization leagues has plummeted in the last decade or so." Noting that members of bowling leagues consume three times as much beer and pizza as do those who bowl alone, he theorizes that "The broader social significance. . . lies in the social interaction and even occasionally civic conversations over beer and pizza that solo bowlers forgo." Whether or not bowling beats balloting in the eyes of most Americans—more bowl than vote—"bowling teams illustrate yet another vanishing form of *social capital*."* Do you agree with him?

*Robert D. Putnam, "Bowling Alone: America's Declining Social Capital," *Journal of Democracy* 6, no. 1 (January 1995), p. 20.

social capital
Participation in associations that reinforce democratic habits of discussion, compromise, and respect for differences.

ideology
One's basic beliefs about power, political values, and the role of government—beliefs that arise out of educational, economic, and social conditions and experiences.

EDUCATIONAL CONDITIONS Clearly, the exercise of voting privileges takes some level of education on the part of the citizenry. But a word of caution: A high level of education does not cause or guarantee democratic government, as the example of Nazi Germany readily illustrates. And there are some democracies, such as India, where large numbers of people are illiterate. Still, voting makes little sense unless a considerable number of the voters can read and write and express their interests and opinions. The poorly educated and illiterate get left out in a democracy.

ECONOMIC CONDITIONS A relatively prosperous nation, with an equitable distribution of wealth, provides the best context for democracy. Starving people are more interested in food than in voting. Where economic power is concentrated, political power is likely to be concentrated. Well-to-do nations have a greater chance of sustaining democratic governments than do those with widespread poverty. The reality is that extremes of wealth and poverty undermine the possibilities for a healthy constitutional democracy. Thus the prospects for an enduring democracy are greater in Canada or France than in Rwanda or Russia.

Some measure of private ownership of property and a relatively favorable role for the market economy are also related to the creation and maintenance of democratic institutions. Democracies can range from heavily regulated economies with public ownership of many enterprises, such as Sweden, to those in which there is little government regulation of the marketplace. But there are no democracies with a command economy and little private ownership of property, although there are many nations with a market economy and no democracy. There are no truly democratic communist states, nor have there ever been any.

SOCIAL CONDITIONS Economic development generally makes democracy possible, yet proper social conditions are necessary to make it real.[3] In a society fragmented into warring groups that differ fiercely on fundamental issues, government by discussion and compromise is difficult, as we are discovering in Serbia. When ideologically separated groups consider the issues at stake to be vital, they may prefer to fight rather than accept the verdict of the ballot box. But in a society that consists of many overlapping associations and groupings, individuals are not as likely to identify completely with a single group and give their allegiance to it. For example, Joe Smith is a Baptist, an African American, a southerner, a Democrat, an electrician, a member of the National Rifle Association, and he makes $50,000 a year. On some issues Joe thinks as a Baptist, on others as a southerner, and on still others as an African American. Sue Jones is a Catholic, a white Republican, an auto dealer, and a member of the National Organization for Women; she comes from a Polish background, and she makes $150,000 a year. Sometimes she acts as a Republican, sometimes as an American of Polish descent, and sometimes as a member of NOW. Jones and Smith differ on some issues yet agree on others. In general, the differences between them are not likely to be greater than their common interest in maintaining a democracy.[4]

Democracy is more likely to survive in a nation where the people have acquired democratic habits, what is coming to be called **social capital.**[5] Democratic social capital is generated when there are a rich variety of associations and social institutions that bind people together. Participation in these social institutions helps build and reinforce democratic habits of discussion, compromise, and respect for differences.

IDEOLOGICAL CONDITIONS **Ideology** refers to basic beliefs about power, government, and political practices—beliefs that arise out of the educational, economic, and social conditions individuals experience. Out of these conditions must also develop a general acceptance of the ideals of democracy and a willingness of a substantial part of the people to agree to proceed democratically. This acceptance is sometimes called the *democratic consensus.*

The Constitutional Roots of the American Experiment

We Americans take democracy for granted. We somehow consider it inevitable. We take pride in our ability to make it work, yet we have essentially inherited a functioning system. Its establishment was the work of others, ten or more generations ago. The challenge for us is not just to keep it going but to improve it. To do so, however, we must first understand it, and this requires careful consideration of our democratic and constitutional roots.

The Colonial Beginnings

There were many reasons one might have expected our democratic experiment to fail. The thirteen states (formerly colonies) were independent and could have gone their separate ways. Sectional differences based on social and economic conditions and slavery were an obvious problem. Religious, ethnic, and racial diversity, which challenges so many governments around the world today, existed in substantial degree in the United States during its formative years.

Given these potential problems, how did democracy survive? How did this nation establish democratic principles for its government? How did it limit potential abuses? These questions are of importance not only to Americans but to all who value freedom and democracy everywhere.

The framers of the U.S. Constitution had experience to guide them. For almost two centuries, Europeans had been sailing to the New World in search of liberty—especially religious liberty—as well as land and work. While still aboard the *Mayflower*, the Pilgrims drew up a compact to protect their religious freedom and to make possible "just and equal laws." In the American colonies, editors found they could speak freely in their newspapers, dissenters could distribute leaflets, and agitators could protest in taverns or in the streets. But the picture of freedom in the colonies was a mixed one. The Puritans in Massachusetts soon established a **theocracy**, a system of government in which religious leaders claimed divine guidance and in which not all religious sects were granted religious liberty. Dissenters were occasionally chased out of town, and some printers had their shops closed or were even physically attacked.

In short, the colonists in those early centuries were struggling with the balance of unity and diversity, stability and dissent, order and liberty. Puritans continued to worry "about what would maintain order in a society lacking an established church, an attachment to place, and the uncontested leadership of men of merit."[6] Nine of the thirteen colonies eventually set up a state church. Throughout the 1700s Puritans in Massachusetts barred certain men from voting on the basis of church membership. To the Anglican establishment in Virginia, campaigns for toleration were in themselves subversive. Women and slaves could not vote at all.

Still, most colonial Americans enjoyed a wide array of liberties. When John Peter Zenger, a New York newspaper printer, was jailed in 1734 by royal authority on the charge of seditious libel, Zenger's attorney appealed to a jury and won a "not guilty" verdict. The case helped establish freedom of the press. Increasingly, questions arose about how people could secure their liberties, rather than leave them in the hands of mobs, sheriffs, or religious establishments. The answer was to bind liberties tightly into colonial laws and constitutions. The Maryland Act for the Liberties of the People legislated that "all the inhabitants of this Province being Christians [slaves excepted] should have such rights, liberties, immunities, privileges, and free customs" as any natural-born subject of England. The Massachusetts Body of Liberties of 1641, which served as a model for later New York and Pennsylvania charters, guaranteed freedom of speech and petition at public meetings, right of counsel, trial by jury, and "the same justice and law" for every person.[7]

theocracy
Government by religious leaders, who claim divine guidance.

Thinking it Through...

While more Americans may be bowling alone, what about the growth of new organizations such as the Sierra Club, the National Organization for Women, the American Association of Retired Persons, and so on? Doesn't that show a counter trend? Putnam found that the vast majority of the members of these associations only write a check or read a newsletter; few ever attend meetings or have any connection to other members. He acknowledges the growth of "support groups" as offsetting the erosion of conventional civic organizations.

Americans still rank high compared with other countries in social capital, but if there has been a deterioration in social capital, it could have consequences for the stability of our political system. What has caused this decline? Putnam discounts the movement of women into the labor force or the increasing mobility of our population as causes of this decline, but suggests that television—and, it may be assumed, the computer—have made our communities wider but shallower.

Putnam's work has its critics who believe that there has not been a serious decline in social involvement. Anyone living and working on an American college campus certainly finds active student participation in all kinds of organizations and associations. Others challenge his conclusion that television is largely responsible for this decline in political participation. The growth of radio talk shows, C-SPAN, CNN, Fox News, and Internet chat groups may be new ways to build social capital.

Do you think Putnam's arguments are convincing? How would you gather evidence to test his hypothesis? You might begin with a look at Sidney Verba, Kay Leman Scholzman, and Henry E. Brady, *Voice and Equality: Civic Volunteerism in American Politics* (Harvard University Press, 1995) and Pippa Norris, "Does Television Erode Social Capital? A Reply to Putnam," *P.S.: Political Science & Politics* 29 (September 1996), pp. 474–79.

The Declaration of Independence committee set down on paper the ideas and goals that would later be incorporated in the Constitution. Shown here are (left to right) Thomas Jefferson, Roger Sherman, Benjamin Franklin, Robert Livingston, and John Adams.

The Rise of Revolutionary Fervor

As resentment against British rule mounted during the 1770s and revolutionary fervor rose, Americans became determined to fight the British to win their rights and liberties. A year after the fighting broke out in Massachusetts, the Declaration of Independence proclaimed in ringing tones that all men are created equal, endowed by their Creator with certain unalienable rights; that among them are "life, liberty, and the pursuit of happiness"; that to secure those rights governments are instituted among men; and that whenever a government becomes destructive of those ends, it is the right of the people to alter or abolish it. (Read the full text of the Declaration of Independence in the Appendix.)

We all have heard these great ideals so often that we take them for granted. Revolutionary leaders did not. They were deadly serious about these rights and willing to fight and pledge their lives, fortunes, and sacred honor for them. Bills of rights in the new state constitutions guaranteed free speech, freedom of religion, and the natural rights to life, liberty, and property. All their constitutions spelled out the rights of persons accused of crime, such as knowing the nature of the accusation, being confronted by their accusers, and receiving a timely and public trial by jury.[8] Moreover, these guarantees were in *written* form, a sharp contrast to the unwritten British constitution.

Articles of Confederation
The first constitution of the American states, drafted in 1777, ratified in 1781, and replaced by the present Constitution in 1789.

Annapolis Convention
A convention held in September 1786 to consider problems of trade and navigation, attended by five states and important because it issued the call to Congress and the states for what became the Constitutional Convention.

Constitutional Convention
The convention in Philadelphia, May 25 to September 17, 1787, that framed the Constitution of the United States.

Toward Unity and Order

As the war against the British widened, the need arose for a stronger central government that could pull the colonies together and conduct a revolutionary war. For a time the Continental Congress, which had led the way toward revolution, tried to direct hostilities against the British, but it took a man of George Washington's iron resolve to unify and direct the war effort. Sensing the need for more unity, Congress established a new national government under a written document called the **Articles of Confederation**. At first hardly worthy of the term "government," the Articles were not approved by all the state legislatures until 1781, after Washington's troops had been fighting for six years.

This new Confederation was a move toward a stronger central government, but a limited and inadequate one. Having fought a war against a strong central government in London, Americans were understandably reluctant to create another one, so the Articles established a fragile league of friendship rather than a national government. From 1777 to 1788, Americans made progress under this Confederation, but with the end of the war in 1783, the sense of urgency that had produced unity began to fade. Conflict between creditors and debtors within the states grew intense. Foreign threats continued; territories ruled by England and Spain surrounded the new nation, which—internally divided and lacking a strong central government—made a tempting prize.

As pressures on the Confederation mounted, many leaders became convinced it would not be enough merely to revise the Articles of Confederation. To create a union strong enough to deal with internal diversity and factionalism as well as resist external threats, a stronger central government was needed.

Weaknesses of the Articles of Confederation

1. Congress had no direct authority over citizens but had to work through the states; it could not pass laws or levy taxes in order to carry out its responsibilities to defend the nation and promote its well-being.
2. Congress could not regulate trade between the states or with other nations. States taxed each others' goods and even negotiated their own trade agreements with other nations.
3. Congress could not forbid the states from issuing their own currencies, further complicating interstate trade and travel.
4. Congress had to handle all administrative duties because there was no executive branch.
5. The lack of a judiciary system meant that the national government had to rely on state courts to enforce national laws and settle disputes between the states. In practice, state courts could overturn national laws.

In September 1786, under the leadership of Alexander Hamilton, those who favored a truly national government took advantage of the **Annapolis Convention**, a meeting in Annapolis, Maryland, on problems of trade and navigation attended by delegates from five states, to issue a call for a convention that would have full authority to consider basic amendments to the Articles of Confederation. The delegates in Annapolis asked the legislatures of all the states to appoint commissioners to meet in Philadelphia on the second Monday of May 1787, "to devise such further provisions as shall appear to them necessary to render the Constitution of the Federal Government adequate to the exigencies of the Union." The convention they called for became the **Constitutional Convention**.

For a short time all was quiet. Then, late in 1786, messengers rode into George Washington's plantation at Mount Vernon with the kind of news he and other leaders had dreaded. Led by Daniel Shays, farmers in western Massachusetts, crushed by debts and taxes, were rebelling against foreclosures, forcing judges out of their courtrooms, and freeing debtors from jails. Washington was appalled. "What, gracious God, is man?" he exclaimed. Ten years before, he had been leading Americans in a patriotic war against the British, and now Americans were fighting Americans!

Clearly, liberty had been allowed to go too far. Indeed, such disorder was a threat to liberty itself. If government could not check such disorders, Washington wrote to his friend James Madison, "what security has a man for life, liberty or

American colonists, resentful of crushing taxes and the denial of their basic liberties by the British, flung boxes of tea into Boston harbor in what we now know as "The Boston Tea Party."

Under the leadership of Daniel Shays, a group of farmers took possession of the courthouse in Northampton, Massachusetts in 1786.

property?" Without a stronger central government, "thirteen Sovereignties pulling against each other, and all tugging at the federal head will soon bring ruin on the whole."

Not all Americans reacted as Washington did to what became known as **Shays' Rebellion**. When Abigail Adams, the politically knowledgeable wife of John Adams, sent news of the rebellion to Thomas Jefferson, the Virginian replied, "I like a little rebellion now and then," noting also that the "tree of liberty must be refreshed from time to time" with "the natural manure" of the blood of patriots and tyrants.

Shays' Rebellion petered out after the farmers attacked an arsenal and were cut down by cannon fire. Yet this "little rebellion" sent a stab of fear into the established leadership. It also acted as a catalyst. The message now was plain: Action must be taken to strengthen the machinery of government. Seven states appointed commissioners to attend a convention in Philadelphia to strengthen the Articles of Confederation. Congress finally issued a cautiously worded call to all the state legislatures to appoint delegates for the "sole and express purpose of revising the Articles of Confederation." The suspicious congressional legislators specified that no recommendation would be effective unless approved by Congress and confirmed by all the state legislatures, as provided by the Articles.

The Constitutional Convention, 1787

The delegates who assembled in Philadelphia that May had to establish a national government powerful enough to prevent the young nation from dissolving but not so powerful that it would crush individual liberty. What these men did continues to have a major impact on how we are governed. It also provides an outstanding lesson in political science for the world.

The Delegates

Seventy-four delegates were appointed by the various states, but only 55 arrived in Philadelphia. Of these, approximately 40 took a real part in the work of the convention. It was a distinguished gathering. Many of the most important men of the nation were there: successful merchants, planters, bankers, lawyers, and former and present governors and congressional representatives (39 of the delegates had served in Congress). Most had read the classics of political thought. Most had participated vigorously in the practical task of constructing local and state governments. Many had also worked hard to create and direct the national Confederation of the states. And 8 of the 56 signers of the Declaration of Independence were present at the Constitutional Convention.

The convention was as representative as most political gatherings at the time: the participants were all white male landowners. These well-read, well-fed, well-bred, and often well-wed delegates were mainly state or national leaders, for in the 1780s ordinary people were not likely to participate in politics. (Even today farm laborers, factory workers, and truck drivers are seldom found in Congress, although a haberdasher, a peanut farmer, and a movie actor have made their way to the White House.)

Several of the participants at the convention stand out as the prime movers. Alexander Hamilton had been the engineer of the Annapolis Convention, and as early as 1778 he had been urging that the national government be made stronger. Hamilton had come to the United States from the West Indies and while still a college student had won national attention for his brilliant pamphlets in defense of the Revolutionary cause. During the war he served as General Washington's aide, and his experiences confirmed his distaste for a Congress so weak it could not even supply the Revolution's troops with enough food or arms.

From Virginia came two of the leading delegates: George Washington and James Madison. Although active in the movement to revise the Articles of Confederation, Washington had been reluctant to attend the convention. He accepted only when per-

Shays' Rebellion
Rebellion by farmers in western Massachusetts in 1786–87, protesting mortgage foreclosures; led by Daniel Shays and important because it highlighted the need for a strong national government just as the call for a Constitutional Convention went out.

suaded that his prestige was needed for its success. He was selected unanimously to preside over the meetings. According to the records, he spoke only twice during the deliberations, yet his influence was felt in the informal gatherings as well as during the sessions. The assumption that Washington would become the first president under the new constitution inspired confidence in it. James Madison was only 36 years old at the time of the convention, yet he was one of its most learned members. He had helped frame Virginia's first constitution and had served both in the Virginia Assembly and in the Confederation's Congress. Madison was also a leader of those who favored the establishment of a stronger national government.[9]

The proceedings of the convention were kept secret. To encourage everyone to speak freely, delegates were forbidden to discuss the debates with outsiders. It was feared that if a delegate publicly took a firm stand on an issue, it would be harder for him to change his mind after debate and discussion. The delegates also knew that if word of the inevitable disagreements got out, it would provide ammunition for the many enemies of the convention. There were critics of this secrecy rule, but without it, agreement might not have been possible.

Consensus

The Constitutional Convention is usually discussed in terms of its three famous compromises: the compromise between large and small states over representation in Congress, the compromise between North and South over the regulation and taxation of foreign commerce, and the compromise between North and South over the counting of slaves for the purpose of taxation and representation. There were many other important compromises; yet on many significant issues, most of the delegates were in agreement.

Although a few delegates might have personally favored a limited monarchy, all supported a republican form of government. This was the only form seriously considered and the only form acceptable to the nation. Equally important, all the delegates opposed arbitrary and unrestrained government.

The common philosophy accepted by most of the delegates was that of

WE THE PEOPLE

The Framers: Hamilton and Madison

In the Constitution the framers offered perhaps the most brilliant example of collective intellectual genius—of combining both theory and practice—in the history of the Western world. How could a country 70 times smaller in population than it is today produce several dozen men of genius in Philadelphia, and probably another hundred or so equally talented political thinkers who did not attend? The lives of two prominent delegates, Alexander Hamilton and James Madison, help explain the origins of this collective genius.

Like most of the other framers, Hamilton and Madison were superbly educated. Both had extensive private tutoring—a one-to-one teacher-student ratio. Like scores of other thinkers of the day, both combined extensive practical experience with their schooling. Both were active in their political and religious groups; both took part in political contests and electoral struggles; both helped build political coalitions.

Both men were "moral philosophers" as well as political thinkers. They had strong views on the supreme value—liberty—as well as on current issues. Instead of simply sermonizing about liberty, they analyzed it; they debated what kind of liberty, how to protect it, how to expand it. They also thought hard about other values enshrined in the Declaration of Independence, such as the virtues and dangers of equality and what kind of "happiness" Americans should pursue.

James Madison

Alexander Hamilton

"Remember, gentlemen, we aren't here just to draft a constitution. We're here to draft the best damn constitution in the world."

balanced government. They wanted to construct a national government in which no single interest would dominate. Because most of the delegates represented citizens who were alarmed by the tendencies of desperate farmers to interfere with the property rights of others, they were primarily concerned with balancing the government in the direction of protection for property and business.

Benjamin Franklin, the 81-year-old delegate from Pennsylvania, favored extending the right to vote to all white males, but most of the delegates believed that owners of land were the best guardians of liberty. James Madison voiced the fear that those without property, if given the right to vote, would combine to deprive property owners of their rights. The delegates agreed in principle on limited voting rights, but differed over the kind and amount of property one must own in order to vote. Because the states were in the process of relaxing qualifications for the vote, the framers recognized they would jeopardize approval of the constitution if they made the qualifications to vote in federal elections more restricted than those of the states. As a result, each state was left to determine the qualifications for electing members of the House of Representatives, the only branch of the national government that was to be elected directly by the voters.

Within five days of its opening, the convention—with only Connecticut dissenting—voted that "a national government ought to be established consisting of a supreme legislative, executive, and judiciary." This decision to establish a supreme national government profoundly altered the nature of the union from a loose confederation of states to a truly national government.

Few dissented from proposals to give the new Congress all the powers of the old Congress plus all other powers necessary to ensure that the harmony of the United States would not be challenged by state legislation. The framers agreed that a strong executive, which had been lacking under the Articles of Confederation, was necessary to provide energy and direction. An independent judiciary was also accepted without much debate. Other issues, however, sparked considerable conflict.

Conflict and Compromise

There were serious differences among the various delegates, especially between those from the large and small states. One of the most contentious issues was how to distribute the land extending westward to the Mississippi, land that had been secured through the Revolution. Several large states asserted claims to these western lands, but the small states generally objected. The large states also favored a strong national government (which they expected they could dominate), while the delegates from the small states were anxious to avoid being dominated.

This tension surfaced in the first discussions of representation in Congress. Franklin favored a single-house national legislature, but most states had had two-chamber legislatures since colonial times, and the delegates were used to the system. **Bicameralism**—the principle of the two-house legislature—reflected the delegates' belief in the need for balanced government. The Senate, the smaller chamber, would represent the aristocracy and offset the larger, more democratic House of Representatives.

bicameralism
The principle of a two-house legislature.

Virginia Plan
Proposal at the Constitutional Convention made by the Virginia delegation for a strong central government with a bicameral legislature, the lower house to be elected by the voters and the upper chosen by the lower.

THE VIRGINIA PLAN The Virginia delegation took the initiative. They had met during the delay before the convention, and as soon as the convention was organized, they presented 15 resolutions. These resolutions, the **Virginia Plan**, called for a strong central government with a legislature composed of two chambers. The members of the more representative chamber were to be elected by the voters; those of the smaller and more aristocratic chamber were to be chosen by the larger chamber from nominees submitted by the state legislatures. Representation in both houses would be on the basis of either wealth or numbers, which would give the more populous and wealthier states—Massachusetts, Pennsylvania, and Virginia—a majority in the national legislature.

The Congress thus created was to be given all the legislative power of its predecessor under the Articles of Confederation, as well as the right "to legislate in all cases in which the separate States are incompetent." Further, it was to have the authority to veto state legislation that conflicted with the proposed constitution. The Virginia Plan also called for a national executive with extensive jurisdiction who would be chosen by the legislature. The national Supreme Court, along with the executive, was to have a qualified veto over acts of Congress.

New Jersey Plan
Proposal at the Constitutional Convention made by William Paterson of New Jersey for a central government with a single-house legislature in which each state would be represented equally.

THE NEW JERSEY PLAN The Virginia Plan dominated the discussion for the first few weeks. But by June 15 additional delegates from the small states arrived, and they began a counterattack. They rallied around William Paterson of New Jersey, who presented a series of resolutions known as the **New Jersey Plan.** Paterson did not question the need for a strengthened central government, but he was concerned about how this strength might be used. The New Jersey Plan would give Congress the right to tax and regulate commerce and to coerce states, yet it would retain the single-house legislature (as under the Articles of Confederation) in which each state, regardless of size, would have the same vote. The New Jersey Plan contained the germ of what eventually came to be a key provision of our Constitution: the *supremacy clause.* The national Supreme Court was to hear appeals from state judges, and the supremacy clause would require all judges—state and national—to treat laws of the national government and the treaties of the United States as superior to the constitutions and laws of each of the states. Table 1-1 outlines the key features of both plans.

Paterson maneuvered to force concessions from the larger states. He favored a strong central government, but not one the big states could control. Further, he raised the issue of practical politics. To adopt the Virginia Plan—which would create a powerful national government dominated by Massachusetts, Pennsylvania, and Virginia and eliminate the states as important units of government—would guarantee that the states would reject the new constitution. Still, the large states resisted, and for a time the convention was deadlocked. The small states believed all states should be represented equally in Congress, at least in the upper house. The large states insisted representation in both houses be based on population or wealth, and that

TABLE 1-1 Differences Between the Virginia and New Jersey Plans

Issue	Virginia Plan	New Jersey Plan
Source of Legislative Power	Derived from the people and based on popular representation	Derived from the states and based on equal votes for each state
Legislative Structure	Bicameral	Unicameral
Executive	Size undetermined, elected and removable by Congress	More than one person, removable by state majority
Judiciary	Life-tenured, able to veto state legislation in council of revision	No power over states
State Laws	Legislature can override	Government can compel obedience to national laws
Ratification	By the people	By the states

SOURCE: Larry Berman and Bruce Murphy, *Approaching Democracy*, 2nd ed. (Prentice Hall, 1999), p. 59.

Creating the Republic

April 1775 American Revolution begins at Lexington and Concord

June 1775 George Washington assumes command of Continental forces

July 1776 Declaration of Independence approved

November 1777 Articles of Confederation adopted by Continental Congress

March 1781 Articles of Confederation ratified by all the states

October 1781 British defeated at Yorktown

April 1784 Congress ratifies peace treaty with British

August 1786 to February 1787 Shays' Rebellion in western Massachusetts

May 1787 Constitutional Convention opens in Philadelphia

September 1787 Constitution of the United States adopted by Constitutional Convention

June 1788 Constitution ratified by nine states

January and February 1789 First national elections

March 1789 United States Congress meets for the first time in New York

April 1789 George Washington inaugurated as first president

September 1789 John Jay becomes first chief justice of the United States

September 1789 Congress proposes Bill of Rights

December 1791 Bill of Rights (first 10 amendments) ratified as part of the U.S. Constitution

Note: It took about 15 years to win independence, form an interim government that tried to govern, fashion a "more perfect union," and actually get a national government, with functioning legislative, executive, and judicial branches.

national legislators be elected by the voters rather than by state legislatures. Finally, a Committee of Eleven was elected to devise a compromise. On July 5 it presented its proposals.

THE CONNECTICUT COMPROMISE Because of the prominent role of the Connecticut delegation in constructing this plan, it has since been known as the **Connecticut Compromise**. It called for one house in which each state would have an equal vote and a second house in which representation would be based on population and in which all bills for raising or appropriating money would originate. This proposal was a setback for the large states, which agreed to it only when the smaller states made it clear this was their price for union. After equality of state representation in the Senate was accepted, most objections to a strong national government dissolved.

NORTH-SOUTH COMPROMISES Other issues split the delegates North and South. Southerners were afraid a northern majority in Congress might discriminate against southern trade. They had some basis for this concern. John Jay, secretary of foreign affairs for the Confederation, had proposed a treaty with Great Britain that would have given advantages to northern merchants at the expense of southern exporters. To protect themselves, the southern delegates insisted a two-thirds majority be required in the Senate before presidents could ratify treaties.

Differences between the North and South were also evident on the issue of representation in the House of Representatives. The question was whether to count slaves for purposes of apportioning seats in the House. The South wanted to count slaves, thereby enlarging its number of representatives; the North resisted. After heated debate, the delegates agreed on the **three-fifths compromise**. Each slave would be counted as three-fifths of a free person for the purposes of apportionment in the House and of direct taxation; this fraction was chosen because it maintained a balance of power between the North and South. The issue of "balance" would recur in the early history of our nation as territorial governments were established and territories applied for statehood.

Connecticut Compromise
Compromise agreement by states at the Constitutional Convention for a bicameral legislature with a lower house in which representation would be based on population, and upper house in which each state would have two senators.

three-fifths compromise
Compromise agreement between northern and southern states at the Constitutional Convention in which the slave population would be counted at three-fifths for determining direct taxation and representation in the House of Representatives.

OTHER ISSUES Delegates found other issues to argue about. Should the national government have lower courts, or would one federal Supreme Court be enough? This issue was resolved by postponing the decision. The Constitution states that there shall be one Supreme Court and that Congress may establish lower courts.

How should the president be selected? For a long time the convention accepted the idea that the president should be chosen by Congress. Yet the delegates feared Congress would dominate the president, or vice versa. Election by the state legislatures was rejected because the delegates distrusted the state legislatures. Finally, the Electoral College system was devised. This was perhaps the most novel and contrived contribution of the delegates, and has long been one of the most criticized provisions in the Constitution.[10] (Consult Article II, Section 1, of the Constitution.)

After three months the delegates stopped debating. On September 17, 1787, they assembled for the impressive ceremony of signing the document they were recommending to the nation. All but three of those still present signed; others who opposed the general drift of the convention had already left. Their work well done, delegates adjourned to the nearby City Tavern to relax and celebrate.

According to an old story, Benjamin Franklin was confronted by a woman as he left the last session of the Constitutional Convention in Philadelphia in September 1787.

"What kind of government have you given us, Dr. Franklin?" she asked. "A Republic or a Monarchy?"

"A Republic, Madam," he answered, "if you can keep it."

To Adopt or Not to Adopt?

The delegates had gone far. They had disregarded Congress's instruction to do no more than revise the Articles. They had ignored Article XIII of the Articles of Confederation, which declared the Union to be perpetual and prohibited any alteration of the Articles unless agreed to by Congress and by *every one of the state legislatures*, a provision that had made it impossible to amend the Articles. The convention delegates, however, boldly declared that their newly proposed Constitution should go into effect when ratified by popularly elected conventions in nine states.

They turned to this method of ratification for practical considerations as well as for reasons of principle. Not only were the delegates aware that there was little chance of securing approval of the new Constitution in all state legislatures; many also believed the Constitution should be ratified by an authority higher than a legislature. A constitution based on approval by the people would have higher legal and moral status. The Articles of Confederation had been a compact of state governments, but the Constitution was based on "We the People." Nevertheless, even this method of ratification would not be easy. The nation was not ready to adopt the Constitution without a thorough debate.

Federalists versus Antifederalists

Supporters of the new government, by cleverly appropriating the name **Federalists**, took some of the sting out of charges they were trying to destroy the states and establish an all-powerful central government. By calling their opponents **Antifederalists**, they pointed up the negative character of the arguments of those who opposed ratification.

The split was in part geographical. Seaboard and city regions tended to be Federalist strongholds; backcountry regions from Maine (then a part of Massachusetts) through Georgia, inhabited by farmers and other relatively poor people, were generally Antifederalist. But as in most political contests, no single factor completely accounted for the division between Federalists and Antifederalists. Thus in Virginia the leaders of both sides came from the same general social and economic class. New York City and Philadelphia strongly supported the Constitution, yet so did predominantly rural New Jersey.

The great debate was conducted through pamphlets, papers, letters to the editor, and speeches. The issues were important, but with few exceptions the argument about the merits of the Constitution was carried on in a quiet and calm manner. Out of the debate came a series of essays known as ***The Federalist***, written by Alexander Hamilton, James Madison, and John Jay to persuade the voters of New York to ratify the Constitution. *The Federalist* is still, said Charles Beard, "widely regarded as the most profound single treatise on the Constitution ever written and as among the few masterly works in political science produced in all the centuries of history."[11] (Three of the most important *Federalist* essays, Nos. 10, 51, and 78, are found in the Appendix of this book. We urge you to read them.) The great debate stands even today as an outstanding example of free people using public discussion to determine the nature of their fundamental laws.

Federalists
Supporters of ratification of the Constitution whose position promoting a strong central government was later voiced in the Federalist party.

Antifederalists
Opponents of ratification of the Constitution and of a strong central government generally.

The Federalist
Series of essays promoting ratification of the Constitution, written by Alexander Hamilton, John Jay, and James Madison in 1787 and 1788.

TABLE 1-2 Ratification of the U.S. Constitution

State	Date
Delaware	December 7, 1787
Pennsylvania	December 12, 1787
New Jersey	December 18, 1787
Georgia	January 2, 1788
Connecticut	January 9, 1788
Massachusetts	February 6, 1788
Maryland	April 28, 1788
South Carolina	May 23, 1788
New Hampshire	June 21, 1788
Virginia	June 25, 1788
New York	July 26, 1788
North Carolina	November 21, 1789
Rhode Island	May 29, 1790

The Antifederalists' most telling criticism of the proposed Constitution was its failure to include a bill of rights.[12] The Federalists believed a bill of rights was unnecessary because the proposed national government had *only* the specific powers delegated to it by the states and the people. Thus there was no need to specify that Congress could not, for example, abridge freedom of the press because the states and the people had not given it power to regulate the press. Moreover, the Federalists argued, to guarantee some rights might be dangerous, because it would then be thought that rights not listed could be denied. The Constitution already protected some important rights—trial by jury in federal criminal cases, for example. Hamilton and others also insisted that paper guarantees were weak supports on which to depend for protection against governmental tyranny.

The Antifederalists were unconvinced. If some rights were protected, what could be the objection to providing constitutional protection for others? Without a bill of rights, what was to prevent Congress from using one of its delegated powers to abridge free speech? If bills of rights were needed in state constitutions to limit state governments, why was a bill of rights not needed in the national constitution to limit the national government? This was a government farther from the people, they contended, with a greater tendency to subvert natural rights.

The Politics of Ratification

The absence of a bill of rights in the proposed constitution dominated the struggle over its adoption. In taverns and church gatherings and newspaper offices up and down the eastern seaboard, people were muttering, "No bill of rights—no constitution!" This feeling was so strong that some Antifederalists, who were far more concerned with states' rights than individual rights, joined forces with bill of rights advocates in an effort to defeat the proposed Constitution.

The Federalists were first to begin the debate over the Constitution that opened as soon as the delegates left Philadelphia in mid-September 1787. The Federalists' tactic was to secure ratification in as many states as possible before the opposition had time to organize. The Antifederalists were handicapped. Most newspapers were owned by supporters of ratification. Moreover, Antifederalist strength was concentrated in rural areas, which were underrepresented in some state legislatures and difficult to arouse to political action. The Antifederalists needed time to perfect their organization and collect their strength, while the Federalists, composed of a more closely knit group of leaders throughout the colonies, moved in a hurry.

In most of the small states, now satisfied by equal Senate representation, ratification was gained without difficulty. Delaware was the first state to ratify, and by early 1788, Pennsylvania, New Jersey, Georgia, and Connecticut had also ratified. Reports were coming in from Massachusetts, however, that opposition was broadening. The position of such key leaders as John Hancock and Samuel Adams was in doubt. The debate in the ratifying convention in Boston pitched some of the most polished Federalist speakers against an array of eloquent but plainspoken Antifederalists. The debate raged for most of January 1788 into February. At times it looked as though the Constitution would lose, as Antifederalists raised the cry of "Why no Bill of Rights?" and other objections. But in the end the Constitution was narrowly ratified in Massachusetts, by 187 to 168 (see Table 1-2).

The struggle over ratification continued through the spring of 1788. By June 21, Maryland, South Carolina, and New Hampshire had ratified, putting

Despite the many serious problems facing our country, a spirit of optimism is still evident in our hopes for the future, as this church bulletin testifies.

the Constitution over the top in the number (nine) required for ratification. But two big hurdles remained: Virginia and New York. Virginia was crucial. As the most populous state, the home of Washington, Jefferson, and Madison, it was a link between North and South. The Virginia ratifying convention rivaled the Constitutional Convention in the caliber of its delegates. Madison, who had only recently switched to favoring the bill of rights position after saying earlier it was unnecessary, captained the Federalist forces. The fiery Patrick Henry led the opposition. In an epic debate, Henry cried that liberty was the issue: "Liberty, the greatest of earthly possessions . . . that precious jewel!" But Madison quietly rebutted him and then played his trump card, a promise that a bill of rights embracing the freedoms of religion and speech and assembly would be added to the Constitution as the first order of business once the new government was established. At a critical moment, Washington himself tipped the balance with a letter urging ratification. News of the Virginia vote, 89 for the Constitution and 79 opposed, was rushed to New York.[13]

The great landowners along the Hudson, unlike their southern planter friends, were opposed to the Constitution. They feared federal taxation of their holdings, and they did not want to abolish the profitable tax New York had been levying on trade and commerce with other states. When the convention assembled, the Federalists were greatly outnumbered, but they were aided by Alexander Hamilton's strategy and skill and by word of Virginia's ratification. New York approved by a margin of three votes. Although North Carolina and Rhode Island still remained outside the Union (the former ratified in November 1789, and the latter six months later), the new nation was created. In New York, a few members of the old Congress assembled to issue the call for elections under the new Constitution. Then they adjourned without setting a date for reconvening.

Challenges for Our Constitutional Democracy

1. *"All men are created equal"*: What kinds of equality are—and should be—protected by the Constitution, and by what means?
2. *"Government by the people"*: Does the evolving constitutional system, including political parties and interest groups, strengthen fair and effective representation of the people?
3. *Federalism*: Does the Constitution provide an efficient and realistic balance between national and state power?
4. *Checks and balances*: Does the constitutional separation of powers between the president and Congress lead to gridlock and delay?
5. *Minority rights*: Does the Constitution adequately protect the rights of women, African Americans, Native Americans, Hispanic Americans, other ethnic groups, and recent immigrants?
6. *Suspects' rights*: Can representative government uphold the rights of the criminally accused and yet protect its citizens?
7. *Individual liberties*: Are individual liberties adequately protected in the Constitution? Do big government and big business diminish the freedom of the individual?
8. *The judicial branch*: Is it too powerful? Are the federal courts exceeding their proper powers as interpreters of the Constitution?
9. *War and peace*: What are the responsibilities of the United States as the only superpower?
10. *Constitutional responsibilities*: Are Americans participating adequately in our democratic system? Do citizens take civic responsibilities too lightly? Is our democracy in jeopardy?

Student anti-government protesters push against a line of riot police in Jakarta, Indonesia, demanding political and economic reform. Today, as in the past, the love of democracy inspires people all over the world.

POLITICS online

The Internet and American Government

The study of American government has been made more accessible through the Internet. Original documents, library catalogs, news reports, interviews, and research by public and private agencies are now at your fingertips, and some services are free of charge. We have prepared a brief section for each chapter that illustrates ways the Internet can facilitate your study of politics. We provide Internet addresses and invite you to access the *Government by the People* home page, which will provide helpful links to other home pages plus constantly updated addresses for useful sources of information.

A great first stop in your political surfing would be "Politics1," which provides comprehensive links to all presidential, gubernatorial, and congressional candidates, plus updated election results, coverage of all 50 states, and political issue debates:

http://www.politics1.com

"Politics on the Web" contains links to all branches of the federal government, political parties, and government agencies:

http://www.members.aol.com/govtdc/welcome.html

"Political Resources on the Net" contains links to government, parties, and policies for countries throughout the world:

http://www.agora.stm.it/politics/

If you are looking for information about the U.S. Constitution or other historical documents, try:

http://www.access.gpo.gov/congress/senate/constitution

http://www.law.emory.edu/FEDERAL

Other examples of resources relating to the U.S. Constitution can be found on the "Founding Fathers Page" maintained by the National Archives and Records Administration at:

http://dolley.nara.gov/exhall/charters/constitution/confath.html

More generally, the National Archives and Records Administration is a good place to check for documents on our national government:

http://www.nara.gov

For more Internet resources on the Constitution, see our home page:

http://www.prenhall.com/burns

SUMMARY

1. Americans have long been skeptical of politicians and politics. Yet politics is a necessary activity for a democracy. Indeed politics and politicians are indispensable to making our system of separated institutions and checks and balances work.
2. "Democracy" is an often misused term, and it has many different meanings. We use it here to refer to a system of interacting values, interrelated political processes, and interdependent political structures. The vital principle of democracy is that a just government must derive its powers from the consent of the people, and that this consent must be regularly renewed at free and fair elections.
3. Stable constitutional democracy is encouraged by various conditions, such as an educated citizenry, a healthy economy, and overlapping associations and groupings within a society in which major institutions interact to create a certain degree of consensus.
4. There has recently been some concern about a decline in *social capital*—the experiences people gain in working together in community groups. Lessons about compromise, accommodation, and participation are important building blocks for democracy.
5. Constitutionalism is a general label we apply to arrangements such as checks and balances, federalism, separation of powers, due process, and the Bill of Rights that force our leaders and representatives to listen, think, deliberate, bargain, and explain before they act and make laws. A constitutional government enforces recognized and regularly applied limits on the powers of those who govern.
6. Democracy developed gradually. A revolution had to be fought before a system of representative democracy in the United States could be tried and tested. It took several years before a national constitution could be written, and almost another year to be ratified. It took still another two years before a Bill of Rights could be adopted and ratified. It has taken more than two hundred years for democratic institutions to be refined and for systems of competition and choice to be hammered out. Democratic institutions in the United States are still evolving.

KEY TERMS

democracy 3
direct democracy 3
representative democracy 3
constitutional democracy 3
constitutionalism 3
statism 4
popular consent 4
majority 6
plurality 6
social capital 8
ideology 8
theocracy 9
Articles of Confederation 10
Annapolis Convention 10
Constitutional Convention 10
Shays' Rebellion 12
bicameralism 14
Virginia Plan 14
New Jersey Plan 15
Connecticut Compromise 16
three-fifths compromise 16
Federalists 17
Antifederalists 17
The Federalist 17

FURTHER READING

THORTON ANDERSON, *Creating the Constitution: The Convention of 1787 and the First Congress* (Pennsylvania State University Press, 1994).

BERNARD BAILYN, ED., *The Debate on the Constitution: Federalist and Antifederalist Speeches, Articles, and Letters During the Struggle over Ratification*, 2 vols. (Library of America, 1993).

LANCE BANNING, *The Sacred Fire of Liberty: James Madison and the Founding of the Federal Republic* (Cornell University Press, 1995).

M. E. BRADFORD, *Founding Fathers: Brief Lives of the Framers of the United States Constitution* (University Press of Kansas, 1994).

JAMES MACGREGOR BURNS, *The Vineyard of Liberty* (Knopf, 1982).

JAMES MACGREGOR BURNS AND STEWART BURNS, *The People's Charter* (Knopf, 1991).

THOMAS E. CRONIN, *Direct Democracy: The Politics of the Initiative, Referendum, and Recall* (Harvard University Press, 1989).

ROBERT A. DAHL, *Democracy and Its Critics* (Yale University Press, 1989).

ROBERT A. DAHL, *Toward Democracy: A Journey: Reflections, 1940–1997* (Institute of Governmental Studies, University of California, 1997).

AMY GUTMANN AND DENNIS THOMPSON, *Democracy and Disagreement* (Belknap, 1996).

ALEXANDER HAMILTON, JAMES MADISON, AND JOHN JAY, *The Federalist Papers*, ed. Clinton Rossiter (New American Library, 1961). Also in several other editions.

SAMUEL P. HUNTINGTON, *The Third Wave: Democratization in the Late Twentieth Century* (University of Oklahoma Press, 1991).

STEVEN H. JAFFE, *Who Were the Founding Fathers? Two Hundred Years of Reinventing American History* (Holt, 1996).

DREW R. MCCOY, *The Last of the Fathers: James Madison and the Republican Legacy* (Columbia University Press, 1989).

RICHARD B. MORRIS, *Witnesses at the Creation: Hamilton, Madison, and Jay and the Constitution* (Holt, Rinehart and Winston, 1985).

ROBERT D. PUTNAM, *Making Democracy Work: Civic Traditions in Modern Italy* (Princeton University Press, 1993).

JACK N. RAKOVE, *Original Meanings: Politics and Ideas in the Making of the Constitution* (Vintage Books, 1997).

ALEXIS DE TOCQUEVILLE, *Democracy in America*, 2 vols., 1835 (Vintage, 1955).

SIDNEY VERBA, KAY LEMAN SCHOLZMAN, AND HENRY E. BRADY, *Voice and Equality: Civic Volunteerism in American Politics* (Harvard University Press, 1995).

GORDON S. WOOD, *The Creation of the American Republic, 1776–1787* (University of North Carolina Press, 1969).

See also the *Journal of Democracy*, published quarterly for the National Endowment for Democracy by the Johns Hopkins University Press.

THE
LIVING
CONSTITUTION

2

CHAPTER OUTLINE

- Checking Power with Power
- Judicial Review and the "Guardians of the Constitution"
- The Constitution as an Instrument of Government
- Changing the Letter of the Constitution

THE ORIGINAL, UNAMENDED CONSTITUTION IN 1789 WAS A SKINNY DOCUMENT OF SOME 4,543 WORDS (YOU CAN CARRY IT AROUND IN YOUR COAT POCKET), YET IT packed a powerful punch. It was a document into which citizens of the early Republic, if optimistic, read their hopes, or, if pessimistic, their fears. Most of them would be surprised to learn that more than two hundred years later, we still have not written another constitution—let alone two or three!

As the Constitution won the support of Americans, it began to take on the aura of **natural law,** law that defines right from wrong, law that is higher than human law. "The Fathers grew ever larger in stature as they receded from view; the era in which they lived and fought became a Golden Age; in that age there had been a fresh dawn for the world, and its men were giants against the sky."[1] This early Constitution worship helped bring unity to the diverse new nation. Like the Crown in Great Britain, the Constitution became a symbol of national loyalty, evoking both emotional and intellectual support from all Americans, regardless of their differences. The framers' work became part of the American creed.[2] It stood for liberty, equality before the law, limited government—indeed, for just about whatever anyone wanted to read into it.

Even today, Americans love the Constitution, yet many do not know what is in it. A recent poll by the National Constitution Center found that nine out of ten Americans are proud of the Constitution and feel it is important to them. However, a third think the Constitution establishes English as the country's official language. One in six believes the Constitution establishes America as a Christian nation. Only one out of four could name a single First Amendment right. Although two out of three knew that the Constitution creates three branches of the national government, only one in three could name all three branches.[3]

The Constitution, however, is more than a symbol. It is a *supreme and binding law that both grants and limits powers.* "In framing a government which is to be administered by men over men," wrote James Madison in *The Federalist,* No. 51, "the great difficulty lies in this: you must first enable the government to control the governed; and in the next place oblige it to control itself" (see *The Federalist,* No. 51 in the Appendix of this book). The Constitution is both a positive instrument of government, which enables the governors to control the governed, and a restraint on government, which enables the ruled to check the rulers.

"And there are three branches of government, so that each branch has the other two to blame everything on."

In what ways does the Constitution limit the power of the government? In what ways does it create governmental power? How has it managed to serve as a great symbol of national unity and at the same time a somewhat adaptable and changing instrument of government? The secret is an ingenious separation of powers and a system of checks and balances that check power with power.

Checking Power with Power

It may seem strange to begin by stressing the ways in which the Constitution *limits* governmental power, but you must keep in mind the dilemma the framers faced. They wanted a stronger and more effective national government than they had under the Articles of Confederation; at the same time, they were keenly aware that the people would not accept too much central control. Efficiency and order were important concerns, but they were not as important as *liberty.* The framers wanted to ensure domestic tranquillity and prevent future rebellions, but they also wanted to forestall the emergence of a homegrown King George III. Accordingly, they allotted certain powers to the national government and reserved the rest for the states, thus establishing a system of *federalism* (whose nature and problems we take up in Chapter 3). Even this was not enough. They believed they needed additional means to limit the national government.

The most important way they devised to make public officials observe the constitutional limits on their powers was through *free and fair elections*; voters would be able to throw out of office those who abuse power. Yet the framers were not willing to depend solely on such political controls, because they did not fully trust the people's judgment. "Free government is founded on jealousy, and not in confidence," said Thomas Jefferson. "In questions of power, then, let no more be heard of confidence in man, but bind him down from mischief by the chains of the Constitution."[4]

Even more important, the framers feared that a majority might deprive minorities of their rights. "A dependence on the people is, no doubt, the primary control on the government," Madison admitted in *The Federalist,* No. 51, "but experience has taught mankind the necessity of auxiliary precautions." What were these "auxiliary precautions" against popular tyranny?

Separation of Powers

The first step was the **separation of powers**, that is, the allocation of constitutional authority to each of the three branches of the national government. In *The Federalist,* No. 47, Madison wrote, "No political truth is certainly of greater intrinsic value, or is stamped with the authority of more enlightened patrons of liberty, than that . . . the accumulation of all powers, legislative, executive, and judiciary, in the same hands . . . may justly be pronounced the very definition of tyranny." (Chief among the "enlightened patrons of liberty" to whose authority Madison was appealing were John Locke and Montesquieu, whose works were subscribed to by most educated Americans.)

The intrinsic value of the principle of dispersion of power does not by itself account for its inclusion in our Constitution. Such dispersion of power had been the general practice in the colonies for more than one hundred years. Only during the Revolutionary period did some of the states concentrate authority in the hands of the legislature, and that unhappy experience confirmed the framers' belief in the merits of separation of powers. Many attributed the evils of state government and the lack of energy in the central government to the fact that there was no strong executive both to check legislative abuses and to give energy and direction to administration.

natural law
God's or nature's law that defines right from wrong and is higher than human law.

separation of powers
Constitutional division of powers among the legislative, executive, and judicial branches, with the legislative branch making law, the executive applying and enforcing the law, and the judiciary interpreting the law.

Still, separating power was not enough. There was always the danger—from the framers' point of view—that different officials with different powers might pool their authority and act together. Separation of powers by itself might not prevent governmental branches and officials from responding to the same pressures—from the demand of an overwhelming majority of the voters to suppress an offensive book, for example, or to impose confiscatory taxes on rich people. If separating power was not enough, what else could be done?

checks and balances
Constitutional grant of powers that enables each of the three branches of government to check some acts of the others and therefore ensure than no branch can dominate.

Checks and Balances: Ambition to Counteract Ambition

The framers' answer was a system of **checks and balances.** "The great security against a gradual concentration of the several powers in the same department," wrote Madison in *The Federalist*, No. 51, "consists in giving to those who administer each department the necessary constitutional means and personal motives to resist encroachments of the others. . . . Ambition must be made to counteract ambition." Each branch therefore has a role in the actions of the others (see Figure 2-1). Congress enacts laws, yet the president can veto them. The Supreme Court can declare laws passed by Congress and signed by the

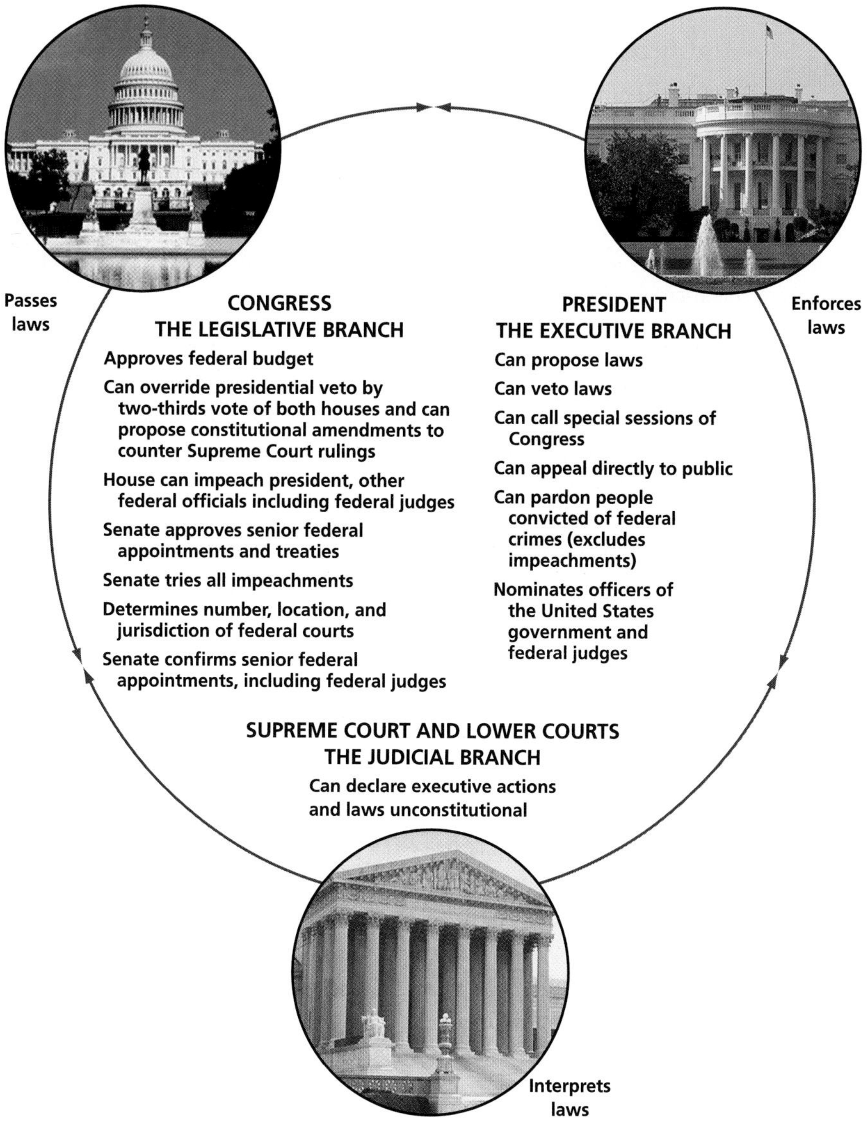

FIGURE 2-1 The Separation of Powers and Checks and Balances

The Exercise of Checks and Balances, 1789–1999

Vetoes

The president has vetoed more than 2,500 acts of Congress.
Congress has overridden presidential vetoes more than 100 times.

Judicial Review

The Supreme Court has ruled 150 congressional acts or parts thereof unconstitutional. Its 1983 decision on legislative vetoes (*INS v Chadha*) affects another 200 provisions.

Impeachment

The House of Representatives has impeached 17 federal officials, 2 presidents and 15 federal judges; of these, the Senate has convicted 7 judges but has not convicted a president.

Confirmation

The Senate has refused to confirm 9 cabinet nominations, and many other cabinet and subcabinet appointments were withdrawn because of likely Senate rejection.

president unconstitutional, but the president appoints the justices and all the other federal judges with the Senate's approval. The president administers the laws, but Congress provides the money. Moreover, the Senate and the House of Representatives have an absolute veto over each other in the enactment of a law, because bills must be approved by both houses.

Not only does each branch have some authority over the others, but each is politically independent of the others. The president is popularly elected, senators are chosen by the voters in each state, and members of the House are chosen by voters in their districts. And although federal judges are appointed by the president with the consent of the Senate, once in office they hold terms until they choose to retire.

The framers also ensured that a majority of the voters could win control over only part of the government at one time. Although in an off-year (nonpresidential) election a new majority might take control of the House of Representatives, the president, representing a previous majority, would still have at least two years to go, and senators stay on for six years. Finally, independent federal courts, which have developed their own powerful checks, were also provided.

Modifications of Checks and Balances

Distrustful of both the elites and the masses, the framers deliberately *built inefficiency into our political system.* They designed the decision-making process so that the national government can act decisively only when there is a consensus among most of the interest groups and after all sides have had a chance to have their say. Even though the fragmentation of political power written into the Constitution remains, several developments have modified the way the system of checks and balances works.

THE RISE OF NATIONAL POLITICAL PARTIES Political parties can serve as unifying factors—at times drawing together the president, senators, representatives, and sometimes even judges behind common programs. Yet the parties, in turn, can be splintered and weakened by having to work through a system of fragmented governmental power, so they never become strong or cohesive. Moreover, when one party controls the Congress and the other the White House, as has generally been the case since the end of World War II, parties may intensify checks and balances, rather than moderate them, to the point that action on some important issues may be difficult.[5]

Divided government may lead to so much competition between the two branches that we find "each institution protecting and promoting itself through a broad interpretation of its constitutional and political status, even usurping the other's power when the opportunity presents itself."[6] Thus we have had battles over presidential **impoundment** of funds appropriated by Congress, budget gridlock, and unseemly and angry confirmation hearings for the appointment of federal judges, especially for justices of the Supreme Court. Divided government also makes it difficult for the voters to hold anybody or any party accountable. "Presidents blame Congress . . . while members of Congress attack the president. . . . Citizens genuinely cannot tell who is to blame."[7]

divided government
Governance divided between the parties, especially when one holds the presidency and the other controls Congress.

impoundment
Presidential refusal to allow an agency to spend funds authorized and appropriated by Congress.

Yet when all the shouting dies down, political scientist David R. Mayhew concludes, there have been just as many congressional investigations and just as much important legislation passed when one party controls Congress and another controls the presidency as when the same party controls both branches.[8] And Charles Jones, a noted scholar of Congress and the presidency, adds that not only is divided government not that important in determining how our government responds to crises, but divided government is precisely what the voters appear to have wanted through much of our history.[9]

President Bill Clinton's first term confirmed Jones's thesis. There was more major legislation signed into law during his second two years (104th Congress, 1995–1996) when the Republicans controlled both houses, than during his first two years (103d Congress, 1993–1995), when President Clinton worked with a Democratic-controlled Congress. During his second term (1996–2000), however, there was continual partisan conflict between the Republican-controlled Congress and the Democratic White House. Congressional committees spent most of their time investigating allegations of misconduct on the part of the president and members of his cabinet. The Senate slowed down confirmation of President Clinton's judicial nominations, rejected his nominee for secretary of the Air Force, as well as many of his legislative recommendations, such as regulating the sale of tobacco to teenagers. Congress did, however, pass a major transportation bill authorizing billions of infrastructure improvements, and the Senate ratified the president's recommendation to amend the NATO treaty to include Poland, the Czech Republic, and Hungary.

EXPANSION OF THE ELECTORATE AND CHANGES IN ELECTORAL METHODS The framers wanted the president to be chosen by the Electoral College—wise, independent citizens free from popular passions and hero worship—rather than by ordinary citizens. Almost from the beginning, however, that is not the way the Electoral College worked. Rather, the voters actually select the president, since presidential electors chosen by the voters no longer have any discretion but are pledged in advance to cast their electoral votes for their party's candidates for president and vice president. And with the passage of the Seventeenth Amendment, senators are no longer elected by state legislatures but are chosen directly by the people.

The kind of "people" entitled to vote has expanded from white property-owning males to all citizens over 18 years of age. During the past century, American states have expanded the role of the electorate within the states by adopting **direct primaries** in which the voters select party nominees, by permitting the voters in about half the states to vote directly on laws (**initiative** and **referendum**), and even by removing elected state and local officials from office (**recall**). At the national level, the electorate has been given a major voice in choosing party nominees for the House and Senate and even for president.

direct primary
Election in which party members choose party nominees.

initiative
Procedure whereby a certain number of voters may, by petition, propose a law or constitutional amendment and have it submitted to the voters.

referendum
Procedure for submitting to popular vote measures passed by the legislature or proposed amendments to a state constitution.

recall
Procedure for submitting to popular vote the removal of officials from office before the end of their term.

ESTABLISHMENT OF AGENCIES DELIBERATELY DESIGNED TO EXERCISE LEGISLATIVE, EXECUTIVE, AND JUDICIAL FUNCTIONS When the national government began to regulate the economy, it issued detailed rules on such complex matters as railroad safety, bank and stock exchange practices, employment conditions, union negotiations, and automobile emissions. It was impossible to assign these regulatory responsibilities without providing the power to make and apply rules and to decide disputes. Beginning in 1887, Congress created *independent regulatory commissions* such as the Interstate Commerce Commission (which went out of business in 1995, although many of its functions were transferred to the Surface Transportation Board within the Department of Transportation) and the Federal Communications Commission. More recently it established *independent executive agencies* such as the Environmental Protection Agency.

CHANGES IN TECHNOLOGY The system of checks and balances operates differently today from the way it did in 1789. Back then there were no televised congressional committee hearings, no electronic communications, no *Larry King Live* or *Rush Limbaugh* talk shows, no *New York Times, Wall Street Journal, USA*

The European Union

Most European nations have signed the European Convention of Human Rights, which establishes a long list of civil liberties. In most cases, these countries have also accepted the jurisdiction of the European Court of Human Rights to resolve allegations of human rights abuses that cannot be settled at the national level and to enforce the Convention of Human Rights. This court has interpreted its powers broadly and has asserted its right to invalidate national laws that contravene obligations that the nations accepted in signing the convention.

Fifteen countries of the European Union have accepted the jurisdiction of the European Court of Justice (ECJ). The ECJ has the power to declare national laws invalid when they conflict with treaty obligations accepted as part of the European Union. In effect, the ECJ has established that treaty obligations take precedence over national laws and constitutions.

For the most part, the issues before the ECJ have been economic and commercial in nature. Courts in several nations, including the United Kingdom, are now vigorously reviewing governmental actions, if only to avoid the embarrassment of cases being decided by the ECJ.

Even with these trends toward more active judicial review, courts in the United States continue to exercise the power of judicial review more frequently and more broadly than do the newer constitutional and international courts.

Today, CNN, or C-SPAN, no nightly news programs with national audiences, no presidential press conferences, and no live coverage of wars and of Americans being held hostage in foreign lands. Nuclear bombs, television, computers, cellular telephones, fax machines, public opinion polls, the World Wide Web—these and other innovations create conditions very different from those of two centuries ago. We also live in a time of instant polls that tell us what people think about public issues.

In some ways these new technologies have added to the powers of presidents by permitting them to appeal directly to millions of people and giving them immediate access to public opinion. And these new technologies have also added leverage to organized interests by making it easy for them to target thousands of letters and calls at Congress, to organize letters to the editor, and to stage media events. New technologies have also given greater independence and influence to nongovernmental agencies such as the press. They have made it possible for rich people like Ross Perot and Steve Forbes and religious leaders like Pat Robertson, who have access to large resources, to bypass political parties and carry their message directly to the electorate.

THE EMERGENCE OF PRESIDENTIAL POWER Today problems anywhere in the world—China, Kosovo, North Korea, Iraq—often become crises for the United States. The need to deal with perpetual emergencies has concentrated power in the hands of the chief executive and the presidential staff. The president's role as the most significant player on the world stage and the coverage of summit conferences with foreign leaders enhance his status. Headline-producing events give the president a visibility no congressional leader can achieve. The office of the president has on occasion served to modify the system of checks and balances and provide some measure of national unity. Drawing on constitutional, political, and emergency powers, the president is sometimes able to overcome the restraints imposed by the Constitution on the exercise of governmental power—to the applause of some and the alarm of others.

Judicial Review and the "Guardians of the Constitution"

Judges have become so important in our system of checks and balances that they deserve special attention. Judges did not claim the power of **judicial review**—the power of a court to refuse to enforce a law or a government regulation that in the opinion of the judges conflicts with the Constitution—until some years after the Constitution was in operation. From the beginning, however, judges were expected to restrain legislative majorities. "The independence of judges," wrote Alexander Hamilton in *The Federalist*, No. 78 (which appears in the Appendix), "may be an essential safeguard against the effects of occasional ill humors in the society."

Judicial review is a contribution of the United States to the art of government, a contribution adapted by other nations. In Japan, Germany, France, Italy, and Spain, constitutional courts are responsible for reviewing laws referred to them to ensure constitutional compliance, including compliance with the charter of rights that is now part of these constitutions.[10] The Canadian Constitution allows either a provincial legislature or the national parliament to override certain sections of the Charter of Rights for a renewable period of six years.[11]

judicial review
The power of a court to refuse to enforce a law or a government regulation that in the opinion of the judges conflicts with the Constitution.

Origins of Judicial Review

Chief Justice John Marshall (1755–1835), our most influential Supreme Court justice. Appointed in 1801, Marshall served until 1835. Earlier he had been a staunch defender of the U.S. Constitution at the Virginia ratifying convention, a member of Congress, and a secretary of state. He is one of those rare people who served in all three branches of government.

The Constitution says nothing about who should have the final word in disputes that might arise over its meaning. Whether the delegates to the Constitutional Convention of 1787 intended to give the courts the power of judicial review is a question long debated. The framers clearly intended for the Supreme Court to have the power to declare state legislation unconstitutional, but whether they intended to give it the same power over congressional legislation is not clear. Edward S. Corwin, an outstanding authority on the American Constitution, concluded that unquestionably "the framers anticipated some sort of judicial review. . . . But it is equally without question that the ideas generally current in 1787 were far from presaging the present vast role of the court."[12] Why, then, didn't the framers not specifically provide for judicial review? Probably because they believed the power could be inferred from certain general provisions.

The Federalists—those who wrote the Constitution and controlled the national government until 1801—generally supported a strong role for federal courts and favored judicial review. Their opponents, the Jeffersonian Republicans (called Democrats after 1832), were less enthusiastic. In 1798 and 1799 Jefferson and Madison (who by this time had left the Federalist camp), with the Kentucky and Virginia Resolutions, came close to the position that state legislatures—and not the Supreme Court—had the ultimate power to interpret the Constitution. These resolutions seemed to question whether the Supreme Court even had the final authority to review state legislation, something about which there had been little doubt.

When the Jeffersonians defeated the Federalists in the election of 1800, it was still undecided whether the Supreme Court would actually exercise the power of judicial review. Logical reasons to support such a doctrine were at hand, and some precedents could even be cited; nevertheless judicial review was not an established power. Then in 1803 came *Marbury v Madison*, one of the most famous Supreme Court decisions of all time.[13]

Marbury versus Madison

The election of 1800 marked the rise to power of the Jeffersonian Republicans. President John Adams and fellow Federalists did not take their defeat easily. Indeed, they were greatly alarmed at what they considered to be the "enthronement of the rabble." Yet there was nothing much they could do about it before leaving office—or was there? The Constitution gives the president, with the consent of the Senate, the power to appoint federal judges to hold office during "good Behaviour." With the judiciary in the hands of good Federalists, thought Adams and his associates, they could stave off the worst consequences of Jefferson's victory.

The outgoing Federalist Congress then created dozens of new federal judicial posts. By March 3, 1801, Adams had appointed and the Senate had confirmed loyal Federalists to all these new positions. Adams signed the commissions and turned them over to John Marshall, his secretary of state, to be sealed and delivered. Marshall had just received his own commission as chief justice of the United States, but he was continuing to serve as secretary of state until Adams's term as president expired. Working right up until nine o'clock on the evening of March 3, Marshall sealed, but was unable to deliver, all the commissions. The only ones left were for the justices of the peace for the District of Columbia. The newly appointed chief justice left these commissions for his successor to deliver.

Jefferson, now inaugurated as president, was angered by this "packing" of the judiciary. When he discovered that some of the commissions were still lying on a

WHY THE INDEPENDENT COUNSEL LAW DESERVES TO LIVE

Samuel Dash

Samuel Dash, chief counsel for the Senate Watergate Committee and former ethics adviser to Kenneth Starr, maintains that if the current independent counsel legislation is killed, Congress would find it necessary to to reauthorize it in a few years. "Without it, there is no way to investigate possible crimes by the president or any of his top aides or cabinet officials. Is that what we really want?"

Dash points out that people are incorrect in complaining that the law "authorizes an uncontrollable prosecutor with unlimited resources and time who can abuse power and persecute citizens." He explains that the independent counsel is bound to follow Justice Department guidelines and is subject to the same rules of evidence, constitutional restrictions, and rules of professional conduct as any other federal prosecutor. If he abuses his authority, he can be removed by the attorney general.

If the public is offended by the behavior of independent counsels, the remedy is not to kill the independent counsel law, but to demand higher standards of fairness.

According to Dash, "If the public is offended by the behavior of independent counsels, the remedy is not to kill the independent counsel law, but to demand higher standards of fairness from federal prosecutors generally." Thus he would prohibit counselors from broadening the jurisdiction of an investigation unless the matter is directly related to the original mandate.

He also recommends that the independent counsel not be required to file a final report. "This requirement has caused some special prosecutors to continue to investigate longer than necessary and to expand their inquiries in order to justify their conduct and expenditures in their final report. Moreover, there is a tendency to justify an investigation by opining about the official's guilt in the report, even if the individual was not indicted. This runs contrary to federal prosecution practice, in which no such comments may be made."

Dash also criticizes the procedure of sending the investigation report to the House of Representatives. "This provision, originally intended to assure a flow of relevant information to the House, has been seen as giving the independent counsel the role of initiating the impeachment process—a role Congress never intended because it would be unconstitutional."★

SOURCE: Samuel Dash, "Why the Independent Counsel Law Deserves to Live," *The New York Times*, February 17, 1999, p. Al7.

AN OFFICE WITH AN INCENTIVE FOR ZEALOTRY

Cass R. Sunstein

Cass Sunstein, a law professor at the University of Chicago, urges that the Independent Counsel Act be allowed to die a peaceful death when it expires.

He maintains that the act has aggravated the tendency to turn political disagreements into criminal charges. "A president's opponents can use the appointment of an independent counsel to claim that the executive branch is rife with corruption, or they can just as easily exploit a decision not to appoint an independent counsel to generate public suspicion of the White House. No wonder that since the law was passed, every administration has been faced with at least one investigation."

Sunstein points out that the tendency of the press to focus on scandals, real or imagined, drowns out more important issues. The potential for personal destruction also makes qualified people reluctant to accept high-level government positions.

He counters the argument that only an independent counsel can prevent official lawlessness by crediting the Justice Department with the ability to do the job:

"Even during Watergate, no independent counsel law was necessary. Public opinion and ordinary professionalism prompted the Justice Department to give its two special prosecutors, Archibald Cox and Leon Jawarski, a degree of independence from presidential control."

According to Sunstein, ordinary prosecutors have a limited budget and a full caseload, so they are unlikely to concentrate on a partular person or pursue a case that may not lead to a jail sentence. "The Independent Counsel Act, however, creates an office with a single target and an unlimited budget, creating an incentive toward zealotry."

Even if the law were to be amended, Sunstein does not see it making the situation any better. "The office of the independent counsel, a case study in the law of unintended consequences, is a cure worse than the disease. The best approach would be to end it, not to mend it."★

SOURCE: Cass R. Sunstein, "An Office with an Incentive for Zealotry," *The New York Times*, February 17, 1999, p. A17.

The Independent Counsel Act creates an office with a single target and an unlimited budget, creating an incentive toward zealotry.

For further information about this debate, go to **http://www.prenhall.com/burns** *and click on the Debate Icon in Chapter 2.*

In 1857 the Supreme Court denied Dred Scott his freedom by ruling that slaves were property and protected as such by the Constitution. This decision declared an act of Congress—the Missouri Compromise—to be unconstitutional. This decision was later overruled by the Fourteenth Amendment, which made slaves citizens.

table in the Department of State, he instructed a clerk not to deliver them. Jefferson could see no reason why the District needed so many justices of the peace, especially Federalist justices.[14]

Among the commissions not delivered was one for William Marbury. After waiting in vain, Marbury decided to seek action from the courts. Searching through the statute books, he came across Section 13 of the Judiciary Act of 1789, which authorized the Supreme Court "to issue writs of *mandamus*, in cases warranted by the principles and usages of law, to . . . persons holding office under the authority of the United States." A **writ of *mandamus*** is a court order directing an official, such as the secretary of state, to perform a duty about which the official has no discretion, such as delivering a commission. So, thought Marbury, why not ask the Supreme Court to issue a writ of *mandamus* to force James Madison, the new secretary of state, to deliver the commission? Marbury and his companions went directly to the Supreme Court, and, citing Section 13, they made the request.

What could Marshall do? If the Court issued the writ, Madison and Jefferson would probably ignore it. The Court would be powerless, and its prestige, already low, might suffer a fatal blow. On the other hand, by refusing to issue the writ, the judges would appear to support the Jeffersonian Republicans' claim that the Court had no authority to interfere with the executive. Would Marshall issue the writ? Most people thought so; angry Republicans even threatened impeachment if he did so.

On February 24, 1803, the Supreme Court delivered its opinion. The first part was as expected. Marbury was entitled to his commission, said Marshall, and Madison should have delivered it to him. Moreover, a writ of *mandamus* could be issued by the proper court, even against so high an officer as the secretary of state.

Then came the surprise. Section 13 of the Judiciary Act seems to give the Supreme Court original jurisdiction in cases such as that in question. But Section 13, said Marshall, is contrary to Article III of the Constitution, which gives the Supreme Court original jurisdiction only when an ambassador or other foreign minister is affected or when a state is a party. Even though this is a case of original jurisdiction, Marbury is neither a state nor a foreign minister. If we follow Section 13, wrote Marshall, we have jurisdiction; if we follow the Constitution, we have no jurisdiction.

Marshall then posed the question in a more pointed way: Should the Supreme Court enforce an unconstitutional law? Of course not, he concluded. *The Constitution is the supreme and binding law*, and the courts cannot enforce any action of Congress that conflicts with it.

The real question remained unanswered. Congress and the president had also read the Constitution, and according to their interpretation, which was also reasonable, Section 13 was compatible with Article III. Where did the Supreme Court get the right to say Congress and the president were wrong? Why should the Supreme Court's interpretation of the Constitution be preferred to that of Congress and the president?

Paralleling Hamilton's argument in *The Federalist*, No. 78, Marshall reasoned: the Constitution is law; judges—not legislators or executives—interpret law; therefore, judges should interpret the Constitution. "If two laws conflict with each other, the courts must decide on the operation of each," he said. Case dismissed.

Marshall's decision, important as it was, did not by itself establish the Supreme Court's power to review and declare acts of Congress unconstitutional. Not until the *Dred Scott* case in 1857 did the Supreme Court declare another act of Congress unconstitutional,[15] and not until after the Civil War did the modern use of judicial review become established.

writ of *mandamus*
Court order directing an official to perform an official duty.

Marbury v Madison might have been interpreted by subsequent generations in a very limited way. It could have been interpreted to mean that the Supreme Court had the right to determine the scope of its own powers under Article III, but Congress and the president had the authority to interpret their own powers under Articles I and II. One scholar insists that is what Marshall intended, and that the more expansive interpretation of *Marbury v Madison* is part of a myth designed to perpetuate judicial dominance.[16] However, Marshall's decision has not been interpreted in this way. On the contrary, building on Marshall's precedent over the decades, the Court has taken the commanding position as the authoritative interpreter of the Constitution.

Several important consequences follow from the acceptance of Marshall's argument that judges are the official interpreters of the Constitution. The most important is that people can challenge laws enacted by Congress and approved by the president. Simply by bringing a lawsuit, those who lack the clout to get a bill through Congress can often secure a judicial hearing. And organized interest groups often find that goals unattainable by legislation can be achieved by litigation. Litigation thus supplements, and at times takes precedence over, legislation as a way to make public policy.[17]

The British and American Systems: A Study in Contrasts

It is possible for a government to be constitutional without our kind of checks and balances. The British system is a good example (see Figure 2-2). Under the British system, voters elect members of the House of Commons from districts throughout the nation, much as we elect members of the House of Representatives. The House of Commons, when it chooses to act, has almost complete constitutional power. Leaders of the majority party serve as executive ministers who collectively form the cabinet, with the prime minister as its head. The prime minister is chosen by the majority party. Like the other cabinet members, he or she represents a *constituency* (a district). When the ruling party loses the support of the majority in the Commons on a major issue, it must resign or call for new elections. Formerly, the House of Lords could check the Commons, but it is now almost powerless. There is no high court in Great Britain with the power to declare acts of Parliament unconstitutional. The prime minister cannot veto them, although he or she may ask the Crown to dissolve Parliament and call new elections for members of the House of Commons.

The British system is based on *majority* (50 percent plus one) or *plurality rule* (largest number); that is, a plurality of the voters elects a parliamentary majority. Like us, the British elect legislators from districts, and the party with the most votes in a district wins the seat, so that even with three or more parties, a plurality of the popular vote usually results in a majority of the parliamentary seats. So long as the parliamentary majority stays together, it can enact into law the majority party's program. British parties are cohesive and disciplined; party members vote together and support their parliamentary leaders. In Britain the party that wins an election has a very good chance of seeing its policy goals enacted.

Our system usually depends on the agreement of many elements of society. The party that wins a presidential or congressional election or even one that controls both these branches will still have a tough time carrying out its platform promises. The British system *concentrates* control and responsibility in the legislature; ours *diffuses* control and responsibility among several organs of government.

If a British or American citizen is thrown into prison without cause, each can appeal to the courts of their respective countries for protection. A British judge may free a person because he or she has been illegally detained contrary to the law, but a British judge, unlike an American one, may *not* declare a law duly enacted by

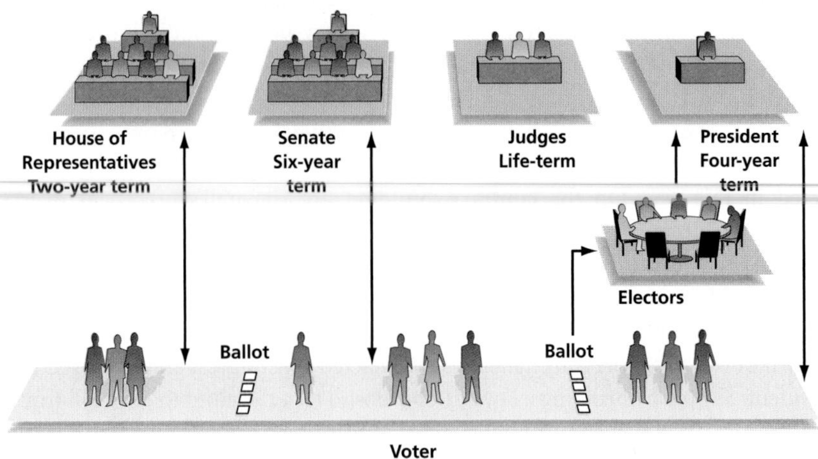

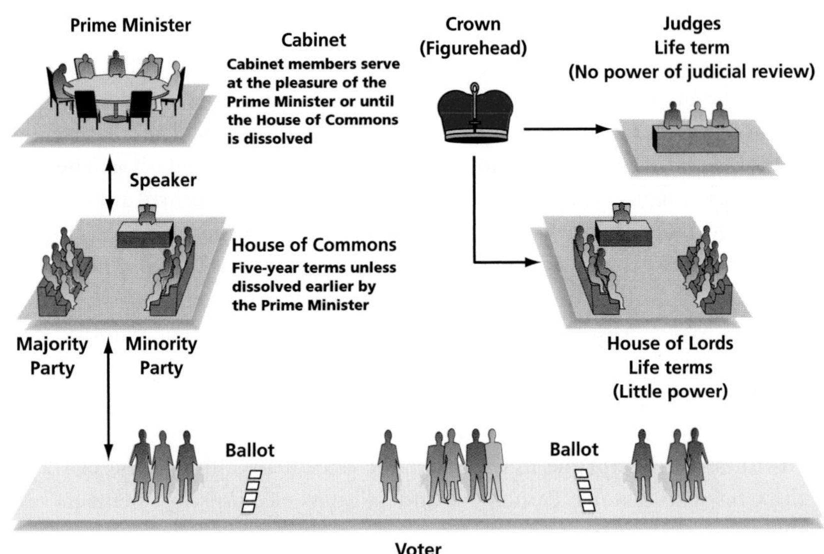

FIGURE 2-2 **A Comparison of the British and American Systems**

Parliament null and void because the judge believes it violates the British constitution. Parliament is the guardian of the British constitution. In the United States it is the courts, ultimately the Supreme Court, that are the keepers of the constitutional conscience—not Congress and not the president.

We have a written document called the Constitution; Britain has no such single document. Yet both systems are "constitutional" in the sense that the rulers are subject to defined restraints. The limits in our written Constitution and the conventions in the unwritten British constitution rest on underlying national values and attitudes.

The Constitution as an Instrument of Government

As careful as the Constitution's framers were to limit the powers they gave the national government, the main reason they had assembled in Philadelphia was to create a stronger national government. Having learned that a weak central government, incapable of governing, was a danger to liberty, they wished to establish a national government within the framework of a federal system with enough authority to meet the needs of all times. They made general grants of power, leaving it to succeeding generations to fill in the details and organize the structure of government in accordance with experience.

Hence our formal, written Constitution is only the skeleton of our system. It is filled out in numerous ways that must be considered part of our constitutional system in its larger sense. In fact, it is primarily through changes in the informal, unwritten Constitution that our system is kept up to date. These changes are found in certain basic statutes and historical practices of Congress, presidential practices, customs and usages of the nation, and decisions of the Supreme Court.

Impeachment charges against Andrew Johnson in 1868 failed to receive the necessary two-thirds vote in the Senate.

Congressional Elaboration

Because the framers gave Congress authority over many of the structural details of the national government, it is not necessary to amend the Constitution every time a change is needed. Rather, Congress can create legislation to meet the need. Examples of congressional elaboration appear in such legislation as the Judiciary Act of 1789, which laid the foundations of our national judicial system; in the laws establishing the organization and functions of all federal executive officials subordinate to the president; and in the rules of procedure, internal organization, and practices of Congress.

IMPEACHMENT AND REMOVAL POWER A dramatic example of congressional elaboration of our constitutional system is the use of the impeachment and removal power. An **impeachment** is a formal accusation against a public official and the first step in removal from office. Constitutional language about the impeachment process defining the grounds for impeachment is sparse. Look at your copy of the Constitution, and note that Article II (the Executive Article) calls for removal of the president, vice-president, and all civil officers of the United States on impeachment for, and conviction of, "Treason, Bribery, or other High Crimes and Misdemeanors." It is up to Congress to give meaning to that language.

President Richard Nixon avoided impeachment by resigning when it became clear that the House was prepared to vote in favor of articles of impeachment.

Article I (the Legislative Article) gives the House of Representatives the sole power to initiate impeachments and the Senate the sole power to try impeachments. When sitting for that purpose, senators "shall be on Oath or Affirmation." In the event the president is being tried, the chief justice of the United States presides. Article I also requires conviction on impeachment charges to have the agreement of two-thirds of the senators present. Judgments shall extend no further than removal from office and disqualification from holding any office under the United States, but a person convicted shall also be liable to indictment, trial, judgment, and punishment according to the law. Article I also exempts cases of impeachment from the president's pardoning power. Article III (the Judicial Article) exempts cases of impeachment from the jury trial requirement. That is all the relevant constitutional language. We must look to history to answer most questions about the proper exercise of these powers.[18]

Fortunately, past experience has triggered few acute constitutional disputes about the interpretation of impeachment procedures, so there is little history to go on. The House of Representatives has investigated 67 individuals for possible impeachment and has impeached 17—2 presidents and 15 federal judges.

The Senate convicted seven, all federal judges. The recent spate of impeachment proceedings involving federal judges—three since 1986—caused the Senate to decide, not without controversy, that the responsibility to hear evidence against impeached federal judges should be delegated to a Senate committee. The Supreme Court confirmed that the Senate may so delegate and, in fact, stated that the House and Senate possess the constitutional authority to decide what the precise impeachment process shall be, subject to little, if any, judicial review.[19] This precedent, however, about delegating to Senate committees the responsibility for hearing evidence against impeached judges does not apply to impeachment trials of presidents, which have to be held before the full Senate with, as the Constitution prescribes, the Chief Justice of the United States presiding.

impeachment
Formal accusation against a public official and the first step in removal from office.

President Clinton tried to shield his conversations with presidential adviser Bruce Lindsey under executive privilege during the independent counsel investigation concerning Monica Lewinsky, but the courts rejected such use of the privilege.

Only two presidents have been impeached—Andrew Johnson in 1868 and William Clinton in 1998. The Senate failed by one vote to muster the two-thirds necessary to support the charges against Johnson. In December of 1998 the House of Representatives adopted two articles of impeachment against President Clinton. The first article was adopted by a vote of 228 to 206, with all but five Republicans voting for it and all but five Democrats voting against it. It charged that President Clinton committed perjury—lying under oath about material matters before a federal grand jury. The alleged perjury was about the precise nature of his sexual relations with Monica Lewinsky. The second article of impeachment, adopted by a closer vote of 221 to 212, accused the president of obstructing justice by trying to withold evidence about, and to influence others to conceal, his affair with Monica Lewinsky.

Proponents of President Clinton's removal from office contended that lying under oath and obstruction of justice rise to the constitutional definition of "High Crimes and Misdemeanors" justifying the immediate removal of the president from office. Opponents argued that the facts did not justify either charge, and that although the president's actions deserved serious condemnation, concealment of a sexual affair is not an offense against the United States or an abuse of presidential power, and thus does not rise to the level of an impeachable offense. The Senate rejected the perjury charge 55 to 45 and the obstruction charge 50 to 50. Ten Republicans on the perjury charge and five on the obstruction charge joined all 45 Democratic senators in voting "not guilty."

What precisely constitutes impeachable offenses are political questions, that is, questions the Constitution directs to the House and Senate for resolution and not reviewable by the courts.[20] Most historical evidence about what constitutes an impeachable offense relates to charges against federal judges, who are not elected by the voters and who serve for "good behavior"—a standard different from that which applies to the president and vice-president, who are elected by the voters for fixed terms.

Congressional precedents have consistently rejected the broadest view that the Constitution authorizes removal of presidents or other United States officers or federal judges because of political objections to them, or dislike of the decisions they make, or because of their unpopularity (a view that night have moved us more in the direction of a parliamentary type of government). Congress has also rejected the narrowest construction that impeachable offenses are only those that involve violations of the criminal laws. Rather, the firmly established position, challenged by the House but reconfirmed by the Senate in the Clinton case, is that impeachment and conviction of a president are justified only if there have been serious violations of constitutional responsibilities by abuse of governmental powers and a clear dereliction of duty.[21]

Presidential Practices

Although the formal constitutional powers of the president have not changed, the office is dramatically more important and more central today than it was in 1789. Vigorous presidents—George Washington, Thomas Jefferson, Andrew Jackson, Abraham Lincoln, Theodore Roosevelt, Woodrow Wilson, Franklin Roosevelt, Harry Truman, Lyndon Johnson, Bill Clinton—have boldly exercised their political and constitutional powers, especially during times of national crisis. Their presidential practices have established important precedents, building the power and influence of the office.

Presidential practices include the claim of **executive privilege** (the right to confidentiality of executive communications, especially those that relate to national security), impoundment of funds previously appropriated by Congress, the right to send our armed forces into hostilities, and, most important, the right to propose legislation and work actively to secure its passage by Congress. President Clinton requested executive privilege to prevent testimony by two of his advisers before the grand jury investigating his relationship with Monica Lewinsky, but the request was denied.

executive privilege
The right to confidentiality of executive communications, especially those that relate to national security.

Foreign and economic crises as well as nuclear age realities expand to the president's role as the nation's "final arbiter." Political scientist Richard Neustadt says, "When it comes to action risking nuclear war, technology has modified the

Constitution: the President, perforce, becomes the only such man in the system capable of exercising judgment under the extraordinary limits now imposed by secrecy, complexity, and time."[22] The presidency has also become the pivotal office for regulating the economy and protecting the general welfare. Plainly, the president has also become our chief legislator as well as our chief executive.

Custom and Usage

Custom and usage round out our governmental system. The development of structures *outside* the formal Constitution—such as national political parties and the extension of the suffrage within the states—have democratized our Constitution. One example of custom and usage is televised presidential and vice-presidential debates under the sponsorship of the independent and nonprofit Commission on Presidential Debates. Through such developments, the president has become responsive to the people and has a political base different from that of Congress. Consequently, the constitutional relationship between the branches today is considerably different from that envisioned by the framers.

Judicial Interpretation

As discussed earlier, judicial interpretation of the Constitution, especially by the Supreme Court, has played an important part in keeping the constitutional system up to date. As social and economic conditions have changed and new national demands have developed, the Supreme Court has changed its interpretation of the Constitution accordingly. In the words of Woodrow Wilson, "The Supreme Court is a constitutional convention in continuous session." Because the Constitution adapts to changing times, it does not require frequent formal amendment. The advantages of this flexibility may be appreciated by comparing the national Constitution with the rigid and often overly specific state constitutions. Many state constitutions are so detailed that they tie the hands of the public officials and must be amended or replaced frequently.

Changing the Letter of the Constitution

The idea of a constantly changing system disturbs many people. How, they contend, can you have a constitutional government when the Constitution is constantly being twisted by interpretation and changed by informal methods? This view fails to distinguish between two aspects of the Constitution. As an expression of *basic and timeless personal liberties*, the Constitution does not, and should not, change. For example, a government cannot destroy free speech and still remain a constitutional government. In this sense the Constitution is unchanging. But when we consider the Constitution as an *instrument of government* and a positive grant of power, we realize that if it does not grow with the nation it serves, it will soon be ignored. The framers could never have conceived of the problems facing the government of a large, powerful, and wealthy nation of about 275 million people at the beginning of the twenty-first century. Although the general purposes of government remain the same—to establish liberty, promote justice, ensure domestic tranquillity, and provide for the common defense—the powers of government that were adequate to accomplish these purposes in 1787 are simply insufficient more than two hundred years later. Through its remarkable adaptability, our Constitution has survived democratic and industrial revolutions, the turmoil of civil war, the tensions of major depressions, and the dislocations of world wars.

The framers knew that future experiences would call for changes in the text of the Constitution and that some means for formal amendment was necessary. In Article V they gave responsibility for amending the Constitution to Congress and to the states. The president has no formal authority over constitutional amendments; presidential veto power does not extend to them, although presidential political influence is often crucial in getting amendments proposed and ratified. (President Abraham Lincoln won passage of the Thirteenth Amendment abolishing slavery, negating the efforts of

President James Buchanan prior to the Civil War to win passage of an amendment that would have guaranteed the maintenance of slavery.[23]) Nor may governors veto ratification of amendments by either state legislatures or state ratifying conventions.

Proposing Amendments

The first method for proposing amendments—and the only one used so far—is *by a two-thirds vote of both houses of Congress.* Dozens of resolutions proposing amendments are introduced in every session. Thousands have been introduced since 1789, but few make any headway. Throughout our history Congress has proposed only 31 amendments, including the Bill of Rights, of which 27 have been ratified—including the Twenty-seventh, which was originally part of the Bill of Rights but took more than two hundred years for ratification!

In recent decades there has been a flurry of congressional attempts at constitutional amendments.[24] None has been formally proposed by both chambers; many are currently under consideration. One given serious consideration is the Balanced Budget Amendment. Such an amendment has several times secured the two-thirds vote it needs in the House but failed to do so in the Senate. Republicans tend to favor it, Democrats to oppose it. The fact that, as a result of good economic times and some fiscal restraint, the budget actually started to generate a surplus for the first time in decades in fiscal year 1998 has somewhat reduced the pressure to pass a Balanced Budget Amendment. Nevertheless, in view of strong public support for it, the debate is likely to continue and be centered on the details. Recent versions call for a balanced budget starting in 2002, unless three-fifths of both houses of Congress vote to suspend the requirement. The proposed amendment also contains a clause limiting the role of the courts by specifying: "The judicial power of the United States shall not extend to any case or controversy arising under this article, unless Congress specifically authorizes such judicial intervention."

WE THE PEOPLE

Gregory Watson and the Twenty-seventh Amendment

In March 1982, Gregory Watson, a student at the University of Texas writing a paper on the Equal Rights Amendment, came across an amendment proposed in 1789 as part of the Bill of Rights that would prohibit a pay raise for members of Congress until the intervention of an election for members of the House. He found that only 6 of the original 13 states had ratified it, and that during the intervening years only 3 more states had done so.

Watson decided to start a ratification movement. He got some publicity for his efforts and, with the help of Texas Republican State Representative Don Mielke, persuaded 6 more state legislatures to ratify this long-forgotten proposed amendment. (By the way, Watson got only a C on his paper, although he is credited with influencing 26 state legislatures to ratify the Twenty-seventh Amendment.)*

After members of Congress tried unsuccessfully in 1989 to avoid public anger by delegating their decision to increase their own salaries to an independent commission, anti-Congress sentiment began to grow, and the ratification movement picked up steam. On May 7, 1992, the Michigan legislature became the thirty-eighth state to ratify the amendment.

The first reaction of some congressional leaders was to question this action because the Supreme Court had made it clear that amendments must be ratified within a "reasonable time." However, when members of Congress realized that the issue could be used against them in the next election, they declared the Twenty-seventh Amendment to be "valid as part of the Constitution of the United States." The vote was 99 to 0 in the Senate, 414 to 3 in the House.

*Ruth Ann Strickland, "The Twenty-seventh Amendment and Constitutional Change by Stealth," *PS: Political Science and Politics* (December 1993), p. 720.

Why has proposing amendments to the Constitution become such a popular pastime? In part because interest groups unhappy with Supreme Court decisions seek to overturn them. In part because groups frustrated by their inability to get things done in Congress hope to bypass Congress. And in part because scholars or interest groups (not necessarily mutually exclusive categories) seek to change the procedures and processes of government to make the system more responsive.[25]

The second method for proposing amendments—*a convention called by Congress* at the request of the legislatures in two-thirds of the states—has never been used. This method presents some difficult questions.[26] First, can state legislatures apply for a convention to propose specific amendments on one topic, or must they request a convention with full powers to revise the *entire* Constitution? How long do state petitions remain alive? How should delegates be chosen? How should a convention be run? Congress has considered bills to answer some of these questions but has not passed any, in part because most members do not wish to encourage a constitutional convention for fear that once in session it might propose amendments on any and all topics.

Under Article V of the Constitution, Congress could call for such a convention without the concurrence of the president. Under most proposals, each state would have as many delegates to the convention as it has representatives and senators in Congress. Finally—a crucial point—the convention would be limited to considering only the subject specified in the state legislative petitions and described in the congressional call for the convention. Scholars are divided, however, on whether Congress has the authority to limit what a constitutional convention might propose.[27]

Ratifying Amendments

After an amendment has been proposed, it must be ratified by the states. Again, two methods are provided by the Constitution: approval by the legislatures in three-fourths of the states, or approval by specially called ratifying conventions in three-fourths of the states. Congress determines which method is used. All amendments except one—the Twenty-first (to repeal the Eighteenth, the Prohibition Amendment)—have been submitted to the state legislatures for ratification (see Figure 2-3).

Seven state constitutions specify that their state legislatures must ratify a proposed amendment to the U.S. Constitution by majorities of three-fifths or two-thirds of each chamber. Although a state legislature may change its mind and ratify an amendment after it has voted against

The Japanese Constitution

The Japanese Constitution is easier to amend than is ours. A proposed amendment needs only to be passed by a two-thirds majority of both houses of Japan's parliament and then be ratified by a majority vote of the people in a national referendum. Despite the fact that after Japan's defeat in World War II its constitution was written by Americans, it has never been amended. In fact, no amendment has even been formally proposed.

What explains this reluctance of the Japanese to amend their constitution? Part of the explanation may be that the Japanese constitution goes well beyond our Bill of Rights to include a variety of economic and social rights, so that progressive Japanese vigorously object to any change in it. Another explanation is that the Japanese have learned to reinterpret controversial provisions of their constitution, as have Americans, in such a way as to make amending the document unnecessary. For example, although Article 9 of the Japanese Constitution forbids the maintenance of "land, sea, and air forces," and includes a renunciation of war, the Japanese have interpreted Article 9 to permit them to maintain "self defense forces," thus making it less urgent to change the constitution.

Japan has developed the sixth largest military force in the world as it takes upon itself a larger military role.

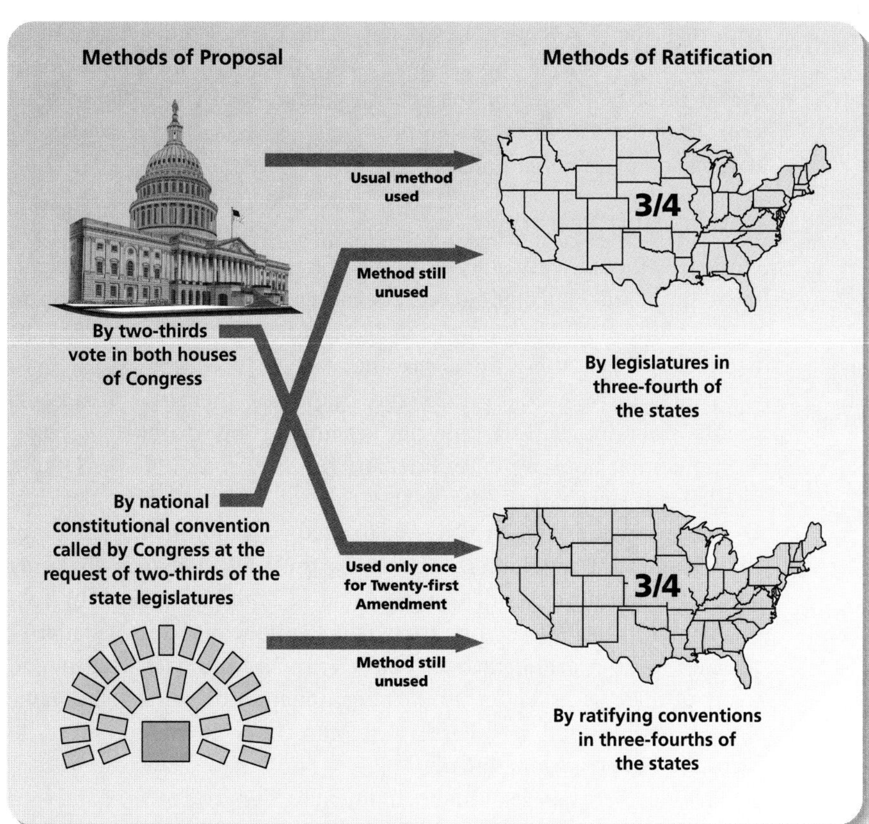

FIGURE 2-3 **Four Methods of Amending the Constitution**

How the Amending Power Has Been Used

To Add or Subtract National Government Power

The Eleventh took some jurisdiction away from the national courts.

The Thirteenth abolished slavery and authorized Congress to legislate against it.

The Sixteenth enabled Congress to levy an income tax.

The Eighteenth authorized Congress to prohibit the manufacture, sale, or transportation of liquor.

The Twenty-first repealed the Eighteenth and gave states the authority to regulate liquor sales.

The Twenty-seventh limited the power of Congress to set members' salaries.

To Expand the Electorate and Its Power

The Fifteenth extended the suffrage to all male African Americans.

The Seventeenth took the right to elect their United States senators away from state legislatures and gave it to the voters in each state.

The Nineteenth extended suffrage to women.

The Twenty-third gave voters of the District of Columbia the right to vote for president and vice-president.

The Twenty-fourth prohibited any state from taxing the right to vote (the poll tax).

The Twenty-sixth extended the suffrage to otherwise qualified persons 18 years of age or older.

To Reduce the Electorate's Power

The Twenty-second took away from the electorate the right to elect any person to the office of president for more than two full terms.

To Limit State Government Power

The Thirteenth abolished slavery.

The Fourteenth granted national citizenship and prohibited states from abridging privileges of national citizenship; from denying persons life, liberty, and property without due process; and from denying persons equal protection of the laws. This amendment has come to be interpreted as imposing restraints on state powers in every area of public life.

To Make Structural Changes in Government

The Twelfth corrected deficiencies in the operation of the Electoral College that were revealed by the development of a two-party national system.

The Twentieth altered the calendar for congressional sessions and shortened the time between the election of presidents and their assumption of office.

The Twenty-fifth provided procedures for filling vacancies in the vice-presidency and for determining whether presidents are unable to perform their duties.

ratification, the weight of opinion is that once a state has ratified an amendment, it cannot "unratify" it.[28]

Procedures can make a difference. The decision to submit the Twenty-first Amendment repealing Prohibition to ratifying conventions came about because the "wets" rightly believed that repeal had a better chance of success with conventions than with the rural-dominated state legislatures. Since no convention had ever been held before, scholars debated whether Congress or the state legislatures had the authority to set up conventions. State legislatures went ahead and did so. Since voters selected delegates on the basis of their pledge for or against ratification, the conventions were brief affairs (New Hampshire's lasted 17 minutes), so that this method amounted in essence to a direct referendum by the voters.[29] Also for tactical reasons, southern Democrats joined with eastern Republican conservatives in an unsuccessful effort to submit the Nineteenth Amendment to give women the vote, also called the Susan B. Anthony Amendment, to ratifying conventions.

The Supreme Court has said that ratification must take place within a "reasonable time" and has suggested that Congress should police this requirement (see Table 2-1). When Congress proclaims an amendment to be part of the Constitution, it must decide whether the amendment has been ratified within a reasonable time so that it is "sufficiently contemporaneous to reflect the will of the people."[30] However, Congress approved ratification of the Twenty-seventh Amendment, which had been before the nation for almost 203 years, so there seems to be no limit to what it will consider to be a "reasonable time." It is conceivable, but not likely, the Supreme Court could some day rule that the Twenty-seventh Amendment was not properly ratified.[31]

The question of reasonableness of time for ratification is not likely to become an issue for future amendments. Because of the experience with the Twenty-seventh Amendment, Congress will probably continue the current practice of stipulating in the text of a proposed amendment that it must be ratified by the necessary number of states *within seven years* from the date of submission by Congress. In fact, ratification ordinarily takes place rather quickly.[32]

Ratification Politics

Ordinarily the existence of a political coalition sufficient to get an amendment proposed by Congress reflects enough support in the nation to ensure ratification. The failure of the Equal Right Amendment to be ratified makes it clear this is not always the case.

First introduced in 1923 and frequently thereafter, the Equal Rights Amendment (ERA) did not get much support until the 1960s. An influential book by Betty Friedan, *The Feminine Mystique* (1963), challenged stereotypes about the role of women. The National Organization for Women (NOW), formed in 1966, made passage of ERA its central mission. By the 1970s the ERA had overwhelming support in both houses of Congress and in both national party platforms; not until 1980 did one party (the Republican) adopt a stance of neutrality. Every president from Harry Truman to Ronald Reagan, and many of their wives, endorsed the amendment. More than 450 organizations with a total membership of more than 50 million were on record in support of the ERA.[33]

Soon after passage of the amendment by Congress in 1972 and submission to the states, many legislatures ratified it quickly—sometimes

TABLE 2-1 The 27 Constitutional Amendments and Their Times for Ratification

	Amendment	Time to Ratify	Ratified		Amendment	Time to Ratify	Ratified
1–10.	Bill of Rights	2 years, 2½ months	1791	19.	Women's suffrage	1 year, 2½ months	1920
11.	Lawsuits against states	3 years, 10 months	1795	20.	Terms of office	11 months	1933
12.	Presidential elections	9½ months	1804	21.	Repeal of prohibition	9½ months	1933
13.	Abolition of slavery	10½ months	1865	22.	Limit on presidential terms	3 years, 11½ months	1951
14.	Civil rights laws	2 years, 11½ months	1868	23.	Washington, D.C., vote	9 months	1961
15.	Suffrage for all races	1 year, 1 month	1870	24.	Abolition of poll taxes	1 year, 5½ months	1964
16.	Income tax	3 years, 7½ months	1913	25.	Presidential succession	1 year, 7 months	1967
17.	Senatorial elections	1 year, ½ month	1913	26.	18-year-old suffrage	3½ months	1971
18.	Prohibition	1 year, 1½ months	1919	27.	Congressional salaries	202 years, 7½ months	1992

without hearings—and by overwhelming majorities. By the end of 1972, 22 states had ratified the amendment.[34] It appeared that the ERA would soon become part of the Constitution. Then the opposition organized under the articulate leadership of Phyllis Schlafly, a prominent spokesperson for conservative causes, and the ERA became controversial.

Opponents argued that "women would not only be subject to the military draft but also assigned to combat duty. Full-time housewives and mothers would be forced to join the labor force. Furthermore, women would no longer enjoy existing advantages under state domestic relations codes and under labor law."[35] The ERA also became embroiled in the controversy over abortion. Many opponents contended that its ratification would jeopardize the power of states and Congress to regulate abortion and would compel public funding of abortions.[36]

After the ERA became controversial, state legislatures held lengthy hearings, and floor debates became heated. Legislators hid behind parliamentary procedures and avoided making a decision for as long as possible. Opposition to ratification

Women came from every state in the country to march in support of the Equal Rights Amendment, demanding an extension of the deadline for final passage.

The Equal Rights Amendment (ERA)

Proposed March 22, 1972. Died June 30, 1982, three state legislatures shy of the thirty-eight needed for ratification.

Section 1. Equality of rights under the law shall not be denied or abridged by the United States or by any State on account of sex.

Section 2. The Congress shall have power to enforce, by appropriate legislation, the provisions of this article.

Section 3. This amendment shall take effect two years after the date of ratification.

arose chiefly in the same cluster of southern states that had opposed ratification of the Nineteenth Amendment, which gave women the vote. As the opposition grew more active, proponents redoubled their efforts. The National Organization for Women called for an economic boycott of cities in nonratifying states, and many organizations refused to hold their conventions in Chicago, Kansas City, Las Vegas, Miami, Atlanta, and New Orleans.

In the autumn of 1978 it appeared that the ERA would fall three short of the necessary number of ratifying states before the expiration of the seven-year limit—March 22, 1979. After an extended debate, and after voting down provisions that would have authorized state legislatures to change their minds and rescind prior ratification, Congress, by a simple majority vote, extended the time limit until June 30, 1982. It was argued that because the seven-year time limit was not in the body of the ERA amendment, it was subject to congressional modification by simple majority. Nonetheless, by the final deadline the amendment was still three state legislatures short. Its failure to be ratified made moot the pending court test of the extension's constitutionality.

The framers intended that amending the Constitution should be difficult. The ERA ratification battle demonstrated how well they planned.

POLITICS online

Using the Internet to Amend the Constitution

One of the strengths of our Constitution is that it can be amended. Today, various groups use the Internet to propose constitutional amendments and circulate petitions to be delivered to Congress. The agenda of Internet constitutional amendments reflects both conservative and liberal positions. Examples of proposed constitutional changes include eliminating federal taxes, prohibiting lawyers from holding public office, outlawing the death penalty, and setting term limits for public officials.

Your Web browser can find these petitions, but here is the address for two of them:

To abolish the death penalty:

http://www.unix.oit.umass.edu/~mellis/dp/npedp.html

To impose term limits on members of Congress:

http://www.senate.gov/~ashcroft/termlimits/

Two resources on the Web related to *The Federalist* essays are:

http://www.mcs.net/~knautzer/fed/fedpaper.html

http://www.auger.demon.co.uk/federalist-papers/index.htm

Links to the historical archives of the University of Illinois can be found at:

http://www.uis.edu/~lib-arch/

http://www.uiuc.edu/

For more Internet resources on the Constitution, see our home page:

http://www.prenhall.com/burns

SUMMARY

1. Our Constitution both grants and limits powers. The framers established a government by ordinary people. They did not anticipate Americans would be so virtuous and civic minded that they could be trusted to operate a government without checks and balances. The framers were suspicious of people, especially of those having political power, so they separated and distributed the powers of the newly created national government in a variety of ways.
2. The framers were also concerned to create a national government strong enough to solve national problems. Thus they gave the national government substantial grants of power, but these grants were made with such broad strokes that it has been possible for the constitutional system to remain flexible and adapt to changing conditions.
3. Although the American governmental system has its roots in British traditions, our separation of powers and checks and balances systems differ sharply from the British system of concentrated responsibility. It is also different because our courts have the power of judicial review.
4. The constitutional system has been modified over time, adapting to new conditions through congressional elaboration, presidential practices, customs and usages, and judicial interpretation.
5. Although adaptable, the Constitution itself needs to be altered from time to time, and the document provides a procedure for its own amendment. An amendment must be both proposed and ratified: proposed by either a two-thirds vote in each chamber of Congress or by a national convention called by Congress on petition of the legislatures in two-thirds of the states; ratified either by the legislatures in three-fourths of the states or by specially called ratifying conventions in three-fourths of the states. The Constitution has been formally amended 27 times. The usual method has been proposal by a two-thirds vote in both houses of Congress and ratification by the legislatures in three-fourths of the states.

KEY TERMS

natural law 24
separation of powers 24
checks and balances 25
divided government 26
impoundment 26
direct primary 27
initiative 27
referendum 27
recall 27
judicial review 28
writ of *mandamus* 32
impeachment 35
executive privilege 36

FURTHER READING

BRUCE A. ACKERMAN, *We the People* (Harvard University Press, Belknap Press, 1991).

LANCE BANNING, *The Sacred Fire of Liberty: James Madison and the Founding of the Federal Republic* (Cornell University Press, 1995).

RICHARD B. BERNSTEIN, *Amending America: If We Love the Constitution So Much Why Do We Keep Trying to Change It?* (Time, 1993).

JAMES BRYCE, *The American Commonwealth* (Macmillan, 1889), vols. 1 and 2.

JAMES MACGREGOR BURNS, *The Vineyard of Liberty* (Knopf, 1982).

RUSSELL L. CAPLAN, *Constitutional Brinkmanship: Amending the Constitution by National Convention* (Oxford University Press, 1988).

GERHARD CASPER, *Separation Powers: Essays on the Founding Period* (Harvard University Press, 1997).

ROBERT LOWRY CLINTON, *Marbury v. Madison and Judicial Review* (University Press of Kansas, 1989).

LOUIS FISHER, *Constitutional Conflicts Between Congress and the President*, 4th ed. (University Press of Kansas, 1997).

SCOTT DOUGLAS GERBER, *To Secure These Rights: The Declaration of Independence and Constitutional Interpretation* (New York University Press, 1995).

CHARLES HARDIN, *Constitutional Reform in America: Essays on the Separation of Powers* (Iowa State University Press, 1989).

BARBARA B. KNIGHT, *Separation of Powers in the American Political System* (George Mason University Press, 1989).

DAVID E. KYVIG, *Explicit and Authentic Acts: Amending the U.S. Constitution, 1776–1995* (University Press of Kansas, 1996).

LIBRARY OF CONGRESS, CONGRESSIONAL RESEARCH SERVICE, The Constitution of the United States of America: Analysis and Interpretation, Senate Document 100-9 (U.S. Government Printing Office, 1991).

FORREST MCDONALD, *Novus Ordo Seclorum: The Intellectual Origins of the Constitution* (University Press of Kansas, 1985).

J. W. PELTASON, *Understanding the Constitution*, 14th ed. (Harcourt Brace, 1997).

BARBARA A. PERRY, *Unfounded Fears: Myths and Realities of a Constitutional Convention* (Greenwood Press, 1989).

WILLIAM H. REHNQUIST, *Grand Inquests: The Historic Impeachments of Justice Samuel Chase and President Andrew Johnson* (Morrow, 1992).

JAMES L. SUNDQUIST, *Constitutional Reform and Effective Government* (Brookings Institution, 1986).

JOHN R. VILE, *The Constitutional Amending Process in American Political Thought* (Praeger, 1992).

JOHN R. VILE, *Encyclopedia of Constitutional Amendments, Proposed Amendments, and Amending Issues, 1789–1995* (ABC-CLIO, 1996).

On Reading the Constitution

More than two hundred years after its ratification, our Constitution remains the operating charter of our republic. It is neither self-explanatory nor a comprehensive description of our constitutional rules. Still, it remains the starting point. Many Americans who swear by the Constitution have never read it seriously, although copies can be found in the back of most American government and American history textbooks.

Justice Hugo Black, who served on the Supreme Court for 34 years, kept a copy of the Constitution with him at all times. He read it often. Reading the Constitution would be a good way for you to begin (and then reread again to end) your study of the government of the United States. Thus, we have included a copy of it at this point in the book. Please read it carefully.

The Constitution of the United States

The Preamble

We the People of the United States, in Order to form a more perfect Union, establish Justice, insure domestic Tranquility, provide for the common defense, promote the general Welfare, and secure the Blessings of Liberty to ourselves and our Posterity, do ordain and establish this Constitution for the United States of America.

Article I—The Legislative Article

Legislative Power

Section 1 All legislative Powers herein granted shall be vested in a Congress of the United States, which shall consist of a Senate and House of Representatives.

House of Representatives: Composition; Qualifications; Apportionment; Impeachment Power

Section 2 The House of Representatives shall be composed of Members chosen every second Year by the People of the several States, and the Electors in each State shall have the Qualifications requisite for Electors of the most numerous Branch of the State Legislature.

No Person shall be a Representative who shall not have attained to the Age of twenty five Years, and been seven Years a Citizen of the United States, and who shall not, when elected, be an Inhabitant of that State in which he shall be chosen.

Representatives and direct Taxes[1] shall be apportioned among the several States which may be included within this Union, according to their respective Numbers, *which shall be determined by adding to the whole Number of free Persons, including those bound to Service for a Term of Years, and excluding Indians not taxed, three fifths of all other Persons.*[2] The actual Enumeration shall be made within three Years after the first Meeting of the Congress of the United States, and within every subsequent Term of ten Years, in such Manner as they shall by Law direct. The Number of Representatives shall not exceed one for every thirty Thousand, but each State shall have at least one Representative; and until each enumeration shall be made, the State of New Hampshire shall be entitled to chuse three, Massachusetts eight, Rhode-Island and Providence Plantations one, Connecticut five, New-York six, New Jersey four, Pennsylvania eight, Delaware one, Maryland six, Virginia ten, North Carolina five, South Carolina five, and Georgia three.

When vacancies happen in the Representation from any State, the Executive Authority thereof shall issue Writs of Election to fill such Vacancies.

The House of Representatives shall chuse their Speaker and other Officers; and shall have the sole Power of Impeachment.

Senate Composition: Qualifications, Impeachment Trials

Section 3 The Senate of the United States shall be composed of two Senators from each State, *chosen by the Legislature thereof,*[3] for six Years; and each Senator shall have one Vote.

Immediately after they shall be assembled in Consequence of the first Election, they shall be divided as equally as may be into three Classes. The Seats of the Senators of the first Class shall be vacated at the Expiration of the second Year, of the second Class at the Expiration of the fourth Year, and of the third Class at the Expiration of the sixth Year, so that one third may be chosen every second Year; *and if Vacancies happen by Resignation, or otherwise, during the Recess of the Legislature of any State, the Executive thereof may make temporary Appointments until the next Meeting of the Legislature, which shall then fill such Vacancies.*[4]

No person shall be a Senator who shall not have attained to the Age of thirty Years, and been nine Years a Citizen of the United States, and who shall not, when elected, be an inhabitant of that State for which he shall be chosen.

The Vice President of the United States shall be President of the Senate, but shall have no Vote, unless they be equally divided.

The Senate shall chuse their other Officers, and also a President pro tempore, in the Absence of the Vice President, or when he shall exercise the Office of President of the United States.

The Senate shall have the sole Power to try all Impeachments. When sitting for that Purpose, they shall be on Oath or Affirmation. When the President of the United States is tried, the Chief Justice shall preside: And no Person shall be convicted without the Concurrence of two thirds of the Members present.

Judgment in Cases of Impeachment shall not extend further than to removal from Office, and disqualification to hold and enjoy any Office of honor, Trust or Profit under the United States; but the Party convicted shall nevertheless be liable and subject to Indictment, Trial, Judgment and Punishment, according to law.

Congressional Elections: Times, Places, Manner

Section 4 The Times, Places and Manner of holding Elections for Senators and Representatives, shall be prescribed in each State by the Legislature thereof; but the Congress may at any time by Law make or alter such Regulations, except as to the Places of chusing Senators.

The Congress shall assemble at least once in every Year, *and such Meeting shall be on the first Monday in December, unless they shall by Law appoint a different Day.*[5]

[1]Modified by the 16th Amendment
[2]Replaced by Section 2, 14th Amendment

[3]Repealed by the 17th Amendment
[4]Modified by the 17th Amendment
[5]Changed by the 20th Amendment

Powers and Duties of the Houses

Section 5 Each House shall be the Judge of the Elections, Returns and Qualifications of its own Members, and a Majority of each shall constitute a Quorum to do Business; but a smaller Number may adjourn from day to day, and may be authorized to compel the Attendance of absent Members, in such Manner, and under the Penalties as each House may provide.

Each House may determine the Rules of its Proceedings, punish its Members for disorderly Behaviour, and, with the Concurrence of two thirds, expel a Member.

Each House shall keep a Journal of its Proceedings, and from time to time publish the same, excepting such Parts as may in their Judgment require Secrecy; and the Yeas and Nays of the Members of either House on any question shall, at the Desire of one fifth of those Present, be entered on the Journal.

Neither House, during the Session of Congress, shall, without the Consent of the other, adjourn for more than three days, nor to any other place than that in which the two Houses shall be sitting.

Rights of Members

Section 6 The Senators and Representatives shall receive a Compensation for their Services, to be ascertained by Law, and paid out of the Treasury of the United States. They shall in all Cases, except Treason, Felony and Breach of the Peace, be privileged from Arrest during their Attendance at the Session of their respective Houses, and in going to and returning from the same; and for any Speech or Debate in either House, they shall not be questioned in any other Place.

No Senator or Representative, shall, during the time for which he was elected, be appointed to any civil Office under the Authority of the United States, which shall have been created, or the Emoluments whereof shall have been encreased during such time; and no Person holding any Office under the United States, shall be a Member of either House during his Continuance in Office.

Legislative Powers: Bills and Resolutions

Section 7 All Bills for raising Revenue shall originate in the House of Representatives; but the Senate may propose or concur with Amendments as on other Bills.

Every Bill which shall have passed the House of Representatives and the Senate, shall, before it becomes a Law, be presented to the President of the United States; if he approve he shall sign it, but if not he shall return it, with his Objections to that House in which it shall have originated, who shall enter the Objections at large on their Journal, and proceed to reconsider it. If after such Reconsideration two thirds of that House shall agree to pass the Bill, it shall be sent, together with the Objections, to the other House, by which it shall likewise be reconsidered, and if approved by two thirds of that House, it shall become a Law. But in all such Cases the Votes of both Houses shall be determined by yeas and Nays, and the Names of the Persons voting for and against the Bill shall be entered on the Journal of each House respectively. If any Bill shall not be returned by the President within ten Days (Sundays excepted) after it shall have been presented to him, the Same shall be a Law, in like Manner as if he had signed it, unless the Congress by their Adjournment prevent its Return, in which Case it shall not be a Law.

Every Order, Resolution, or Vote to which the Concurrence of the Senate and House of Representatives may be necessary (except on a question of Adjournment) shall be presented to the President of the United States; and before the Same shall take Effect, shall be approved by him, or being disapproved by him, shall be repassed by two thirds of the Senate and House of Representatives, according to the Rules and Limitations prescribed in the Case of a Bill.

Powers of Congress

Section 8 The Congress shall have Power To lay and collect Taxes, Duties, Imposts and Excises, to pay the Debts and provide for the common Defence and general Welfare of the United States; but all Duties, Imposts and Excises shall be uniform throughout the United States.

To borrow Money on the Credit of the United States;

To regulate Commerce with foreign Nations, and among the several States, and with the Indian Tribes;

To establish an uniform Rule of Naturalization, and uniform Laws on the subject of Bankruptcies throughout the United States;

To coin Money, regulate the Value thereof, and of foreign Coin, and fix the Standard of Weights and Measures;

To provide for the Punishment of counterfeiting the Securities and current Coin of the United States;

To establish Post Offices and post Roads;

To promote the Progress of Science and useful Arts, by securing for limited Times to Authors and Inventors the exclusive Right to their respective Writings and Discoveries;

To constitute Tribunals inferior to the supreme Court;

To define and punish Piracies and Felonies committed on the high Seas, and Offences against the Law of Nations;

To declare War, grant Letters of Marque and Reprisal, and make Rules concerning Captures on Land and Water;

To raise and support Armies, but no Appropriation of Money to that Use shall be for a longer Term than two Years;

To provide and maintain a Navy;

To make Rules for the Government and Regulation of the land and naval Forces;

To provide for calling for the Militia to execute the Laws of the Union, suppress Insurrections and repel Invasions;

To provide for organizing, arming, and disciplining, the Militia, and for governing such Part of them as may be employed in the Service of the United States, reserving to the States respectively, the Appointment of the Officers, and the Authority of training the Militia according to the discipline prescribed by Congress;

To exercise exclusive Legislation in all Cases whatsoever, over such District (not exceeding ten Miles square) as may, by Cession of particular States, and the Acceptance of Congress, become the Seat of the Government of the United States, and to exercise like Authority over all Places purchased by the Consent of the Legislature of the State in which the Same shall be, for the Erection of Forts, Magazines, Arsenals, dock-Yards, and other needful Buildings;—And

To make all Laws which shall be necessary and proper for carrying into Execution the foregoing Powers, and all other Powers vested by this Constitution in the Government of the United States, or in any Department or Officer thereof.

Powers Denied to Congress

Section 9 The Migration of Importation of such Persons as any of the States now existing shall think proper to admit, shall not be prohibited by the Congress prior to the Year one thousand eight hundred and eight, but a Tax or Duty may be imposed on such Importation, not exceeding ten dollars for each Person.

The privilege of the Writ of Habeas Corpus shall not be suspended, unless when in Cases of Rebellion or Invasion the public Safety may require it.

No Bill of Attainder or ex post facto Laws shall be passed.

No Capitation, or other direct, Tax shall be laid, unless in Proportion to the Census or Enumeration herein before directed to be taken.[6]

No Tax or Duty shall be laid on Articles exported from any State.

No Preference shall be given by any Regulation of Commerce or Revenue to the Ports of one State over those of another; nor shall Vessels bound to, or from, one State, be obliged to enter, clear, or pay Duties in another.

[6]Modified by the 16th Amendment

No Money shall be drawn from the Treasury, but in Consequence of Appropriations made by Law; and a regular Statement and Account of the Receipts and Expenditures of all public Money shall be published from time to time.

No Title of Nobility shall be granted by the United States; And no Person holding any Office of Profit or Trust under them, shall, without the Consent of Congress, accept of any present, Emolument, Office, or Title, of any kind whatever, from any King, Prince, or foreign State.

Powers Denied to the States

Section 10 No State shall enter into any Treaty, Alliance, or Confederation; grant Letters of Marque and Reprisal; coin Money; emit Bills of Credit; make any Thing but gold and silver Coin a Tender in Payment of Debts; pass any Bill of Attainder, ex post facto Law, or Law impairing the Obligation of Contracts, or grant any Title of Nobility.

No State shall, without the Consent of the Congress, lay any Imposts or Duties on Imports or Exports, except what may be absolutely necessary for executing its inspection Laws: and the net Produce of all Duties and Imposts, laid by any State on Imports or Exports, shall be for the Use of the Treasury of the United States; and all such Laws shall be subject to the Revision and Controul of the Congress.

No State shall, without the Consent of Congress, lay any Duty of Tonnage, keep Troops, or Ships of War in time of Peace, enter into any Agreement or Compact with another State, or with a foreign Power, or engage in War, unless actually invaded, or in such imminent Danger as will not admit of Delay.

ARTICLE II—THE EXECUTIVE ARTICLE

Nature and Scope of Presidential Power

Section 1 The executive Power shall be vested in a President of the United States of America. He shall hold his Office during the Term of four Years and, together with the Vice President, chosen for the same Term, be elected as follows:

Each State shall appoint, in such Manner as the Legislature thereof may direct, a Number of Electors, equal to the whole Number of Senators and Representatives to which the State may be entitled in the Congress: but no Senator or Representative, or Person holding an Office of Trust or Profit under the United States, shall be appointed an Elector.

The Electors shall meet in their respective States, and vote by Ballot for two Persons, of whom one at least shall not be an Inhabitant of the same State with themselves. And they shall make a List of all the Persons voted for, and of the Number of Votes for each; which List they shall sign and certify, and transmit sealed to the Seat of the Government of the United States, directed to the President of the Senate. The President of the Senate shall, in the Presence of the Senate and House of Representatives, open all the Certificates, and the Votes shall then be counted. The Person having the greatest Number of Votes shall be the President, if such Number be a Majority of the whole Number of Electors appointed; and if there be more than one who have such Majority and have an equal Number of Votes, then the House of Representatives shall immediately chuse by Ballot one of them for President; and if no person have a Majority, then from the five highest on the List the said House shall in like Manner chuse the President. But in chusing the President, the Votes shall be taken by States, the Representation from each State having one Vote; A quorum for this Purpose shall consist of a Member or Members from two thirds of the States, and a Majority of all the States shall be necessary to a Choice. In every Case, after the Choice of the President, the person having the greatest Number of Votes of the Electors shall be the Vice President. But if there should remain two or more who have equal Vote, the Senate shall chuse from them by Ballot the Vice President.[7]

The Congress may determine the Time of chusing the Electors, and the Day on which they shall give their Votes; which Day shall be the same throughout the United States.

No Person except a natural born Citizen, or a Citizen of the United States, at the time of the Adoption of this Constitution, shall be eligible to the Office of President; neither shall any Person be eligible to that Office who shall not have attained to the Age of thirty five Years, and been fourteen Years a Resident within the United States.

In Case of the Removal of the President from Office, or of his Death, Resignation, or Inability to discharge the Powers and Duties of the said Office, the same shall devolve on the Vice President, and the Congress may by Law provide for the Case of Removal, Death, Resignation, or Inability, both of the President and Vice President, declaring what Officer shall then act as President, and such Officer shall act accordingly, until the Disability be removed, or a President shall be elected.[8]

The President shall, at stated Times, receive for his Services, a Compensation, which shall neither be encreased nor diminished during the Period of which he shall have been elected, and he shall not receive within that Period any other Emolument from the United States, or any of them.

Before he enter on the Execution of his Office, he shall take the following Oath or Affirmation:—"I do solemnly swear (or affirm) that I will faithfully execute the Office of President of the United States, and will to the best of my Ability, preserve, protect and defend the Constitution of the United States."

Powers and Duties of the President

Section 2 The President shall be the Commander in Chief of the Army and Navy of the United States, and of the Militia of the several States, when called into the actual Service of the United States, he may require the Opinion, in writing, of the principal Officer in each of the executive Departments, upon any Subject relating to the Duties of their respective Offices, and he shall have the Power to grant Reprieves and Pardons for Offences against the United States, except in Cases of Impeachment.

He shall have Power, by and with the Advice and Consent of the Senate to make Treaties, provided two thirds of the Senators present concur; and he shall nominate, and by and with the Advice and Consent of the Senate, shall appoint Ambassadors, other public Ministers and Consuls, Judges of the supreme Court, and all other Officers of the United States, whose Appointments are not herein otherwise provided for, and which shall be established by Law: but the Congress may by Law vest the Appointment of such inferior Officers, as they think proper, in the President alone, in the Courts of Law, or in the Heads of Departments.

The President shall have Power to fill up all Vacancies that may happen during the Recess of the Senate, by granting Commissions which shall expire at the End of their next Session.

Section 3 He shall from time to time give to the Congress Information of the State of the Union, and recommend to their Consideration such Measures as he shall judge necessary and expedient; he may, on extraordinary Occasions, convene both Houses, or either of them, and in Case of Disagreement between them, with Respect to the Time of Adjournment, he may adjourn them to such Time as he shall think proper; he shall receive Ambassadors and other public Ministers; he shall take Care that the Laws be faithfully executed, and shall Commission all the Officers of the United States.

Section 4 The President, Vice President and all civil Officers of the United States, shall be removed from Office on Impeachment for, and Conviction of, Treason, Bribery, or other High Crimes and Misdemeanors.

ARTICLE III—THE JUDICIAL ARTICLE

Judicial Power, Courts, Judges

Section 1 The judicial Power of the United States, shall be vested in one supreme Court, and in such inferior Courts as the Congress may from time to time ordain and establish. The Judges, both the supreme and inferior Courts,

[7]Changed by the 12th and 20th Amendments

[8]Modified by the 25th Amendment

shall hold their Offices during good Behaviour, and shall, at stated Times, receive for their Services, a Compensation, which shall not be diminished during their Continuance in Office.

Jurisdiction

Section 2 The judicial Power shall extend to all Cases, in Law and Equity, arising under this Constitution, the Laws of the United States, and Treaties made, or which shall be made, under their Authority;—to all Cases affecting Ambassadors, other public Ministers and Consuls;—to all Cases of admiralty and maritime Jurisdiction;—to Controversies to which the United States shall be a Party;—to Controversies between two or more States; *between a State and Citizens of another State;*[9]—between Citizens of different States;—between Citizens of the same State claiming Lands under Grants of different States, and between a State, or the Citizens thereof, and foreign States, Citizens, or Subjects.

In all Cases affecting Ambassadors, other public Ministers and Consuls, and those in which a State shall be Party, the supreme Court shall have original Jurisdiction. In all the other Cases before mentioned, the supreme Court shall have appellate Jurisdiction, both as to Law and Fact, with such Exceptions, and under such Regulations as Congress shall make.

The Trial of all Crimes, except in Cases of Impeachment, shall be by Jury; and such Trial shall be held in the State where the said Crimes shall have been committed; but when not committed within any State, the Trial shall be at such Place or Places as the Congress may by Law have directed.

Treason

Section 3 Treason against the United States, shall consist only in levying War against them, or in adhering to their Enemies, giving them Aid and Comfort. No Persons shall be convicted of Treason unless on the Testimony of two Witnesses to the same overt Act, or on Confession in open Court.

The Congress shall have Power to declare the Punishment of Treason, but no Attainder of Treason shall work Corruption of Blood, or Forfeiture except during the Life of the Person attainted.

ARTICLE IV—INTERSTATE RELATIONS

Full Faith and Credit Clause

Section 1 Full Faith and Credit shall be given in each State to the public Acts, Records, and judicial Proceedings of every other State. And the Congress may by general Laws prescribe the Manner in which such Acts, Records and Proceedings shall be proved, and the Effect thereof.

Privileges and Immunities; Interstate Extradition

Section 2 The Citizens of each State shall be entitled to all Privileges and Immunities of Citizens in the several States.

A person charged in any State with Treason, Felony or other Crime, who shall flee from Justice, and be found in another State, shall on Demand of the executive Authority of the State from which he fled, be delivered up, to be removed to the State having jurisdiction of the Crime.

No person held to Service or Labour in one State, under the Laws thereof, escaping into another, shall, in Consequence of any Law or Regulation therein, be discharged from such Service or Labour, but shall be delivered up on Claim of the Party to whom such Service or Labour may be due.[10]

Admission of States

Section 3 New States may be admitted by the Congress into this Union; but no new State shall be formed or erected within the Jurisdiction of any other State; nor any State to be formed by the Junction of two or more States, or Parts of States, without the Consent of the Legislatures of the States concerned as well as of the Congress.

The Congress shall have Power to dispose of and make all needful Rules and Regulations respecting the Territory or other Property belonging to the United States; and nothing in this Constitution shall be so construed as to Prejudice any Claims of the United States, or of any particular State.

Republican Form of Government

Section 4 The United States shall guarantee to every State in this Union a Republican Form of Government, and shall protect each of them against Invasion; and on Application of the Legislature, or of the Executive (when the Legislature cannot be convened) against domestic Violence.

ARTICLE V—THE AMENDING POWER

The Congress, whenever two thirds of both Houses shall deem it necessary, shall propose Amendments to this Constitution, or, on the Application of the Legislatures of two thirds of several States, shall call a Convention for proposing Amendments, which, in either Case, shall be valid to all Intents and Purposes, as Part of this Constitution, when ratified by the Legislatures of three fourths of the several States, or by Conventions in three fourths thereof, as the one or the other Mode of Ratification may be proposed by the Congress; Provided that no Amendment which may be made prior to the Year One thousand eight hundred and eight shall in any Manner affect the first and fourth Clauses in the Ninth Section of the first Article; and that no State, without its Consent, shall be deprived of its equal Suffrage in the Senate.

ARTICLE VI—THE SUPREMACY ARTICLE

All Debts contracted and Engagements entered into, before the Adoption of this Constitution, shall be as valid against the United States under the Constitution, as under the Confederation.

This Constitution, and the Laws of the United States which shall be made in Pursuance thereof; and all Treaties made, or which shall be made, under the Authority of the United States, shall be the supreme Law of the Land; and the Judges in every State shall be bound thereby, any Thing in the Constitution or Laws of any State to the Contrary notwithstanding.

The Senators and Representatives before mentioned, and the Members of the several State Legislatures, and all executive and judicial Officers, both of the United States and of the several States, shall be bound by Oath or Affirmation, to support this Constitution; but no religious Test shall ever be required as a Qualification to any Office or public Trust under the United States.

ARTICLE VII—RATIFICATION

The Ratification of the Conventions of nine States, shall be sufficient for the Establishment of this Constitution between the States so ratifying the Same.

Done in Convention by the Unanimous Consent of the States present the Seventeenth Day of September in the Year of our Lord one thousand seven hundred and Eighty seven and of the Independence of the United States of America the Twelfth *In Witness whereof We have hereunto subscribed our Names.*

AMENDMENTS

The Bill of Rights

[The first ten amendments were ratified on December 15, 1791, and form what is known as the "Bill of Rights."]

AMENDMENT 1—RELIGION, SPEECH, ASSEMBLY, AND POLITICS

Congress shall make no law respecting an establishment of religion, or prohibiting the free exercise thereof; or abridging the freedom of speech, or of the press; or the right of the people peaceably to assemble, and to petition the government for a redress of grievances.

[9]Modified by the 11th Amendment
[10]Repealed by the 13th Amendment

Amendment 2—Militia and the Right to Bear Arms

A well regulated Militia, being necessary to the security of a free State, the right of the people to keep and bear Arms, shall not be infringed.

Amendment 3—Quartering of Soldiers

No Soldier shall, in time of peace be quartered in any house, without the consent of the Owner, nor in time of war, but in manner to be prescribed by law.

Amendment 4—Searches and Seizures

The right of the people to be secure in their persons, houses, papers, and effects, against unreasonable searches and seizures, shall not be violated, and no Warrants shall issue, but upon probable cause, supported by Oath or affirmation, and particularly describing the place to be searched, and the persons or things to be seized.

Amendment 5—Grand Juries, Self-Incrimination, Double Jeopardy, Due Process, and Eminent Domain

No person shall be held to answer for a capital, or otherwise infamous crime, unless on a presentment or indictment of a Grand jury, except in cases arising in the land or naval forces, or in the Militia, when in actual service in time of War or public danger; nor shall any person be subject for the same offence to be twice put in jeopardy of life or limb; nor shall be compelled in any criminal case to be a witness against himself, nor be deprived of life, liberty, or property, without due process of law; nor shall private property be taken for public use, without just compensation.

Amendment 6—Criminal Court Procedures

In all criminal prosecutions, the accused shall enjoy the right to a speedy and public trial, by an impartial jury of the State and district wherein the crime shall have been committed, which district shall have been previously ascertained by law, and to be informed of the nature and cause of the accusation; to be confronted with the witnesses against him; to have compulsory process for obtaining Witnesses in his favor, and to have the Assistance of Counsel for his defense.

Amendment 7—Trial by Jury in Common Law Cases

In Suits at common law, where the value in controversy shall exceed twenty dollars, the right of trial by jury shall be preserved, and no fact tried by a jury shall be otherwise re-examined in any Court of the United States, than according to the rules of the common law.

Amendment 8—Bail, Cruel and Unusual Punishment

Excessive bail shall not be required, nor excessive fines imposed, nor cruel and unusual punishments inflicted.

Amendment 9—Rights Retained by the People

The enumeration in the Constitution, of certain rights, shall not be construed to deny or disparage others retained by the people.

Amendment 10—Reserved Powers of the States

The powers not delegated to the United States by the Constitution, nor prohibited by it to the States, are reserved to the States respectively, or to the people.

Amendment 11—Suits Against the States [Ratified February 7, 1795]

The Judicial power of the United States shall not be construed to extend to any suit in law or equity, commenced or prosecuted against one of the United States by Citizens of another State, or by Citizens or Subjects of any Foreign State.

Amendment 12—Election of the President [Ratified June 15, 1804]

The Electors shall meet in their respective states, and vote by ballot for President and Vice-President, one of whom, at least, shall not be an inhabitant of the same state with themselves; they shall name in their ballots the person voted for as President, and in distinct ballots the person voted for as Vice-President, and they shall make distinct lists of all persons voted for as President, and of all persons voted for as Vice-President, and of the number of votes for each, which lists they shall sign and certify, and transmit sealed to the seat of the government of the United States, directed to the President of the Senate;—The President of the Senate shall, in presence of the Senate and House of Representatives, open all the certificates and the votes shall then be counted;—The person having the greatest number of votes for President, shall be the President, if such number be a majority of the whole number of Electors appointed; and if no person have such majority, then from the persons having the highest numbers not exceeding three on the list of those voted for as President, the House of Representatives shall choose immediately, by ballot, the President. But in choosing the President, the votes shall be taken by states, the representation from each state having one vote; a quorum for this purpose shall consist of a member or members from two-thirds of the states, and a majority of all states shall be necessary to a choice. And if the House of Representatives shall not choose a President whenever the right of choice shall devolve upon them, *before the fourth day of March next following*, then the Vice-President shall act as President, as in the case of the death or other constitutional disability of the President.[11] The person having the greatest number of votes as Vice-President, shall be the Vice-President, if such a number be a majority of the whole numbers of Electors appointed, and if no person have a majority, then from the two highest numbers on the list, the Senate shall choose the Vice-President; a quorum for the purpose shall consist of two-thirds of the whole number of Senators, and a majority of the whole number shall be necessary to a choice. But no person constitutionally ineligible to the office of President shall be eligible to that of Vice-President of the United States.

Amendment 13—Prohibition of Slavery [Ratified December 6, 1865]

Section 1 Neither slavery nor involuntary servitude, except as a punishment for crime whereof the party shall have been duly convicted, shall exist within the United States, or any place subject to their jurisdiction.

Section 2 Congress shall have power to enforce this article by appropriate legislation.

Amendment 14—Citizenship, Due Process, and Equal Protection of the Laws [Ratified July 9, 1868]

Section 1 All persons born or naturalized in the United States, and subject to the jurisdiction thereof, are citizens of the United States and of the State wherein they reside. No State shall make or enforce any law which shall abridge the privileges or immunities of citizens of the United States; nor shall

[11]Changed by the 20th Amendment

any State deprive any person of life, liberty, or property, without due process of law; nor deny to any person within its jurisdiction the equal protection of the laws.

Section 2 Representatives shall be apportioned among the several States according to their respective numbers, counting the whole number of persons in each State, excluding Indians not taxed. But when the right to vote at any election for the choice of electors for President and Vice President of the United States, Representatives in Congress, the Executive and Judicial officers of a State, or the members of the Legislature thereof, is denied to any of the male inhabitants of such State, being twenty-one[12] years of age, and citizens of the United States, or in any way abridged, except for participation in rebellion, or other crime, the basis of representation therein shall be reduced in the proportion which the number of such male citizens shall bear to the whole number of male citizens twenty-one years of age in such State.

Section 3 No person shall be a Senator or Representative in Congress, or elector of President and Vice President, or hold any office, civil or military, under the United States, or under any State, who, having previously taken an oath, as a member of Congress, or as an officer of the United States, or as a member of any State legislature, or as an executive or judicial officer of any State, to support the Constitution of the United States, shall have engaged in insurrection or rebellion against the same, or given aid or comfort to the enemies thereof. But Congress may by a vote of two-thirds of each House, remove such disability.

Section 4 The validity of the public debt of the United States, authorized by law, including debts incurred for payment of pensions and bounties for services in suppressing insurrection or rebellion, shall not be questioned. But neither the United States nor any State shall assume or pay any debt or obligation incurred in aid of insurrection or rebellion against the United States, or any claim for the loss or emancipation of any slave; but all such debts, obligations and claims shall be held illegal and void.

Section 5 The Congress shall have power to enforce, by appropriate legislation, the provisions of this article.

Amendment 15—The Right to Vote
[Ratified February 3, 1870]

Section 1 The right of citizens of the United States to vote shall not be denied or abridged by the United States or by any State on account of race, color, or previous condition of servitude.

Section 2 The Congress shall have power to enforce this article by appropriate legislation.

Amendment 16—Income Taxes
[Ratified February 3, 1913]

The Congress shall have power to lay and collect taxes on incomes, from whatever source derived, without apportionment among the several States, and without regard to any census or enumeration.

Amendment 17—Direct Election of Senators
[Ratified April 8, 1913]

The Senate of the United States shall be composed of two Senators from each State, elected by the people thereof, for six years; and each Senator shall have one vote. The electors in each State shall have the qualifications requisite for electors of the most numerous branch of the State legislatures.

When vacancies happen in the representation of any State in the Senate, the executive authority of such State shall issue writs of election to fill such vacancies: *Provided*, That the Legislature of any State may empower the executive thereof to make temporary appointment until the people fill the vacancies by election as the legislature may direct.

This amendment shall not be so construed as to affect the election or term of any Senator chosen before it becomes valid as part of the Constitution.

Amendment 18—Prohibition
[Ratified January 16, 1919. Repealed December 5, 1933 by Amendment 21]

Section 1 After one year from the ratification of this article the manufacture, sale, or transportation of intoxicating liquors within, the importation thereof into, or the exportation thereof from the United States and all territory subject to the jurisdiction thereof for beverage purposes is hereby prohibited.

Section 2 The Congress and the several states shall have concurrent power to enforce this article by appropriate legislation.

Section 3 This article shall be inoperative unless it shall have been ratified as an amendment to the Constitution by the legislatures of the several states, as provided in the Constitution, within seven years from the date of the submission hereof to the States by the Congress.[13]

Amendment 19—For Women's Suffrage
[Ratified August 18, 1920]

The right of the citizens of the United States to vote shall not be denied or abridged by the United States or by any State on account of sex.

Congress shall have power, by appropriate legislation, to enforce the provision of this article.

Amendment 20—The Lame Duck Amendment
[Ratified January 23, 1933]

Section 1 The terms of the President and Vice President shall end at noon on the 20th day of January, and the terms of the Senators and Representatives at noon on the 3rd day of January, of the years in which such terms would have ended if this article had not been ratified; and the terms of their successors shall then begin.

Section 2 The Congress shall assemble at least once in every year, and such meeting shall begin at noon on the 3rd day of January, unless they shall by law appoint a different day.

Section 3 If, at the time fixed for the beginning of the term of the President, the President elect shall have died, the Vice President elect shall become President. If a President shall not have been chosen before the time fixed for the beginning of his term, or if the President elect shall have failed to qualify, then the Vice President elect shall act as President until a President shall have qualified; and the Congress may by law provide for the case wherein neither a President elect nor a Vice President elect shall have qualified, declaring who shall then act as President, or the manner in which one who is to act shall be selected, and such person shall act accordingly until a President or Vice President shall have qualified.

Section 4 The Congress may by law provide for the case of the death of any of the persons from whom the House of Representatives may choose a President whenever the right of choice shall have developed upon them, and for the case of the death of any of the persons from whom the Senate may choose a Vice President whenever the right of choice shall have devolved upon them.

[12]Changed by the 26th Amendment

[13]Repealed by the 21st Amendment

Section 5 Sections 1 and 2 shall take effect on the 15th day of October following the ratification of this article.

Section 6 This article shall be inoperative unless it shall have been ratified as an amendment to the Constitution by the legislatures of three-fourths of the several States within seven years from the date of its submission.

Amendment 21—Repeal of Prohibition
[Ratified December 5, 1933]

Section 1 The eighteenth article of amendment to the Constitution of the United States is hereby repealed.

Section 2 The transportation or importation into any State, Territory, or Possession of the United States for delivery or use therein of intoxicating liquors, in violation of the laws thereof, is hereby prohibited.

Section 3 This article shall be inoperative unless it shall have been ratified as an amendment to the Constitution by conventions in the several States, as provided in the Constitution, within seven years from the date of the submission hereof to the States by the Congress.

Amendment 22—Number of Presidential Terms
[Ratified February 27, 1951]

Section 1 No person shall be elected to the office of the President more than twice, and no person who has held the office of President, or acted as President, for more than two years of a term to which some other person was elected President shall be elected to the Office of the President more than once. But this Article shall not apply to any person holding the office of President when this article was proposed by the Congress, and shall not prevent any person who may be holding the office of President, or acting as President, during the term within which this Article becomes operative from holding the office of President or acting as President during the remainder of such term.

Section 2 This Article shall be inoperative unless it shall have been ratified as an amendment to the Constitution by the legislatures of three-fourths of the several states within seven years from the date of its submission to the States by the Congress.

Amendment 23—Presidential Electors for the District of Columbia
[Ratified March 29, 1961]

Section 1 The District constituting the seat of Government of the United States shall appoint in such manner as the Congress may direct:

A number of electors of President and Vice President equal to the whole number of Senators and Representatives in Congress to which the District would be entitled if it were a State, but in no event more than the least populous State; they shall be in addition to those appointed by the States, but they shall be considered, for the purposes of the election of President and Vice President, to be electors appointed by a State; and they shall meet in the District and perform such duties as provided by the twelfth article of amendment.

Section 2 The Congress shall have power to enforce this article by appropriate legislation.

Amendment 24—The Anti-Poll Tax Amendment
[Ratified January 23, 1964]

Section 1 The right of citizens of the United States to vote in any primary or other election for President or Vice President, for electors for President or Vice President, or for Senator or Representative in Congress, shall not be denied or abridged by the United States or any State by reason of failure to pay any poll tax or other tax.

Section 2 The Congress shall have power to enforce this article by appropriate legislation.

Amendment 25—Presidential Disability, Vice Presidential Vacancies
[Ratified February 23, 1967]

Section 1 In case of the removal of the President from office or his death or resignation, the Vice President shall become President.

Section 2 Whenever there is a vacancy in the office of the Vice President, the President shall nominate a Vice President who shall take the office upon confirmation by a majority vote of both houses of Congress.

Section 3 Whenever the President transmits to the President pro tempore of the Senate and the Speaker of the House of Representatives his written declaration that he is unable to discharge the powers and duties of his office, and until he transmits to them a written declaration to the contrary, such powers and duties shall be discharged by the Vice President as Acting President.

Section 4 Whenever the Vice-President and a majority of either the principal officers of the executive departments, or of such other body as Congress may by law provide, transmit to the President pro tempore of the Senate and the Speaker of the House of Representatives their written declaration that the President is unable to discharge the powers and duties of his office, the Vice President shall immediately assume the powers and duties of the office as Acting President.

Thereafter, when the President transmits to the President pro tempore of the Senate and the Speaker of the House of Representatives his written declaration that no inability exists, he shall resume the powers and duties of his office unless the Vice President and a majority of either the principal officers of the executive departments, or of such other body as Congress may by law provide, transmit within four days to the President pro tempore of the Senate and the Speaker of the House of Representatives their written declaration that the President is unable to discharge the powers and duties of his office. Thereupon Congress shall decide the issue, assembling within forty-eight hours for that purpose if not in session. If the Congress, within twenty-one days after receipt of the latter written declaration, or, if Congress is not in session, within twenty-one days after Congress is required to assemble, determines by two-thirds vote of both houses that the President is unable to discharge the powers and duties of his office, the Vice President shall continue to discharge the same as Acting President; otherwise, the President shall resume the powers and duties of his office.

Amendment 26—Eighteen-Year-Old Vote
[Ratified July 1, 1971]

Section 1 The right of citizens of the United States, who are eighteen years of age, or older, to vote shall not be denied or abridged by the United States or by any State on account of age.

Section 2 The Congress shall have power to enforce this article by appropriate legislation.

Amendment 27—Congressional Salaries
[Ratified May 7, 1992]

No law, varying the compensation for the services of the Senators and Representatives, shall take effect, until an election of Representative shall be intervened.

AMERICAN
FEDERALISM

3

QUESTIONS ABOUT THE RELATIONS BETWEEN THE NATIONAL GOVERNMENT AND THE STATES HAVE ALWAYS BEEN A HOT ISSUE FOR AMERICANS,[1] AND THIS DEBATE has become a central theme of recent congressional and presidential elections, with Republicans leading the charge against the national government and urging a massive return of powers and responsibilities to the states. Antigovernment themes, most particularly those directed against entitlements, are part of today's campaign rhetoric from both political parties.

But it is not just in the United States that federalism issues have come to the top of the political agenda. In Canada the very nature of the federal system is at stake as the French-speaking province of Quebec demands special status and a considerable measure of autonomy.[2] The former Soviet Union—a highly centralized government that was federal in form but not in fact—broke apart into 15 independent nations, and now Russia (or more precisely, the Russian Federation) is going through a struggle to redefine its federal relationship to its 21 autonomous republics. Throughout Central Europe tensions erupt into violence as nations divide and subdivide, with the violence against ethnic Albanians in Kosovo as the most recent outbreak. And even in the United Kingdom, devolution is taking place in Scotland and Wales. In September 1997 the people of Scotland voted overwhelmingly for a local parliament in Edinburgh with considerable power, including the power to tax. It is scheduled to begin its work on January 1, 2000. In Wales the vote for devolution was approved by the narrowest of margins; the Welsh Assembly will have less authority than its Scottish counterpart, and because it will not have the power to tax, it will have to rely on funding from the central government.[3]

In the United States, from the days of the New Deal in the 1930s to today, there has been a steady drift of power and responsibility from the states to the national government. But although presidents from Nixon to Clinton put some brakes on the growth of the national government, it was not until the elections of 1994, when the Republicans took control of both houses of Congress, that a major, almost revolutionary, attempt to return many functions back to the states—the **devolution revolution**—occurred, at least at the level of the rhetoric.[4]

Although in 1995, to the surprise of most observers, some Supreme Court justices reopened *constitutional* questions about the powers of the national government,[5] debates today about federalism are not likely to be about constitutional issues. For despite the Court's recent cautioning Congress that there are some limits

CHAPTER OUTLINE

on the scope of its powers,[6] the national government's constitutional authority over an enormous range of subjects is clearly established, including civil rights, highway speed limits, or teenage smoking.

National and state governments are the arenas in which battles take place between consumers and producers, workers and employers, airlines and railroads, pro-choice and right-to-life advocates, pro-growth and anti-growth forces, and all the other contending groups that make up our political system. People who think they can get more of what they want from the national government are likely to advocate national action. Those who see state governments as more sympathetic are likely to argue for decentralization. Advocates of environmental protection, for instance, have generally found a more receptive audience in Washington than in their state capitals, especially in the West. They are likely to complain about "special interests" at the statehouse. Opponents of such regulation are likely to denounce the Washington bureaucrats.

In this chapter we begin by defining federalism and discussing its advantages. Next we look at the constitutional basis of our federal system. Then we see how court decisions and political developments have shaped, and continue to shape, our modern system of federalism.

Federalism was strained in Kosovo as ethnic Albanians fought to throw off the repressive regime of the Serbian national government and establish their own nation, or at least achieve greater local control.

Defining Federalism

Scholars have argued and wars have been fought about what federalism really means. One scholar counted 267 definitions.[7]

- *Dual federalism* interprets the Constitution as giving a limited list of powers—primarily foreign policy and national defense—to the national government, leaving most power to sovereign states. Each level of government is dominant within its own sphere. The Supreme Court serves as the umpire between the national government and the states in case of a dispute over which government is in charge of a particular activity. During our first hundred years, dual federalism was the favored interpretation most of the time by the Supreme Court.
- *Cooperative federalism* stresses federalism as a system to deliver governmental goods and services to the people and calls for cooperation among various levels of government.
- *Marble cake federalism*, a term coined by political scientist Morton Grodzins, conceives of federalism as a marble cake in which all levels of government are involved in a variety of issues and programs, rather than a layer cake with uniform divisions between layers or levels of government.[8]
- *Competitive federalism*, a term created by political scientist Thomas R. Dye, suggests that federalism provides us with a national government, 50 states, and thousands of other units, each competing with the others in the way in which they put together packages of services and taxes and vying with the others for the support of citizens. Applying the analogy of the marketplace, Dye emphasizes that at the state and local levels we have some choice about which state and city we want "to use," just as we have choices about which automobile we wish to drive.[9]
- *Permissive federalism* implies that although federalism provides "a sharing of power and authority between the national and state government, the states'

devolution revolution
Movement beginning with the 1994 congressional elections to transfer functions and responsibilities from the national government to the states; for example, for providing welfare.

share rests upon the permission and permissiveness of the national government."[10]

- *New federalism,* favored by Richard Nixon, Ronald Reagan, and George Bush, emphasizes their view that we should return fiscal resources and management responsibilities to the states in the form of large block grants and revenue sharing, and that we should sort out functions between national and state governments.

TABLE 3-1 Number of Governments

U.S. government	1
States	50
Counties	3,043
Municipalities	19,279
Townships or towns	16,656
School districts	14,422
Special districts	31,555
Total	85,006

SOURCE: U.S. Bureau of the Census, *Statistical Abstract of the United States, 1998.*

Federalism, as we define it, is a form of government in which a constitution distributes powers between a central government and subdivisional governments—usually called states, provinces, or republics—giving to both the national government and the regional governments substantial responsibilities and powers, including the power to collect taxes and to pass and enforce laws regulating the conduct of individuals.

The mere existence of both national and state governments does not make a system federal. What is important is that a *constitution divides governmental powers between the national government and the subdivisional governments,* giving clearly defined functions to each. Neither the central nor the subdivisional government receives its powers from the other; both derive them from a common source—a constitution. No ordinary act of legislation at either a national or a state level can change this constitutional distribution of powers. Both levels of government operate through their own agents and exercise power directly over individuals. Other countries with federal systems include Canada, Switzerland, Mexico, and Australia. "Nearly 40 percent of the people of the world now live in nations with a federal form of government. Another third live in countries that use some elements of federalism."[11]

Constitutionally, the federal system of the United States consists of only the national government and the 50 states. "Cities are not," the Supreme Court reminded us, "sovereign entities." But in a practical sense, we are a nation of about 85,000 governmental units—from the national government to the school board district (see Table 3-1). This does not make for a tidy, efficient, easy-to-understand system; yet, as we shall see, it does have its virtues.

Alternatives to Federalism

Among the alternatives to federalism are **unitary systems** of government, in which a constitution vests all governmental power in the central government. The central government, if it so chooses, may delegate authority to constituent units, but what it delegates it may take away. Britain, France, Israel, and the Philippines have unitary governments. In the United States, state constitutions usually create this kind of relationship between the state and its local governments.

At the other extreme are **confederations,** in which sovereign nations by a constitutional compact create a central government but carefully limit the power of the central government and do not give it the power to regulate the conduct of individuals directly. The central government makes regulations for the constituent governments, but it exists and operates only at their direction. The 13 states under the Articles of Confederation operated in this manner, as did the southern Confederacy during the Civil War (see Figure 3-1). The European Union is an example of a confederation from the modern era.[12]

Why Federalism?

In 1787, federalism was an obvious choice. Confederation had been tried and found wanting. A unitary system was out of the question because most people were too deeply attached to their state governments to permit subordination to central rule. Federalism was, and still is, thought to be ideally suited to the needs of a heterogeneous people spread over a large continent, suspicious of concentrated power, and

federalism
Constitutional arrangement whereby power is distributed between a central government and subdivisional governments, called states in the United States. The national and the subdivisional governments both exercise direct authority over individuals.

unitary system
A constitutional arrangement in which power is concentrated in a central government.

confederation
A constitutional arrangement in which sovereign nations or states, by compact, create a central government but carefully limit its power and do not give it direct authority over individuals.

desiring unity but not uniformity. Federalism offered, and still offers, many advantages for such a people.[13]

FEDERALISM CHECKS THE GROWTH OF TYRANNY Although in the rest of the world federal forms have not been notably successful in preventing tyranny, and many unitary governments are democratic, Americans tend to associate freedom with federalism.[14] As James Madison pointed out in *The Federalist*, No. 10: If "factious leaders . . . kindle a flame within their particular states," national leaders can check the spread of the "conflagration through the other states" (*The Federalist*, No. 10, appears in the Appendix of this book). Moreover, when one political party loses control of the national government, it is still likely to hold office in a number of states. It can then regroup, develop new policies and new leaders, and continue to challenge the party in power at the national level.

Such diffusion of power creates its own problems. It makes it difficult for a national majority to carry out a program of action, and it permits those who control a state government to frustrate the policies enacted by Congress and administered by national agencies. To our Constitution's framers, these obstacles were an advantage. They were fearful that a single-interest group might capture the national government

Government under the Articles of Confederation: 1781–1788

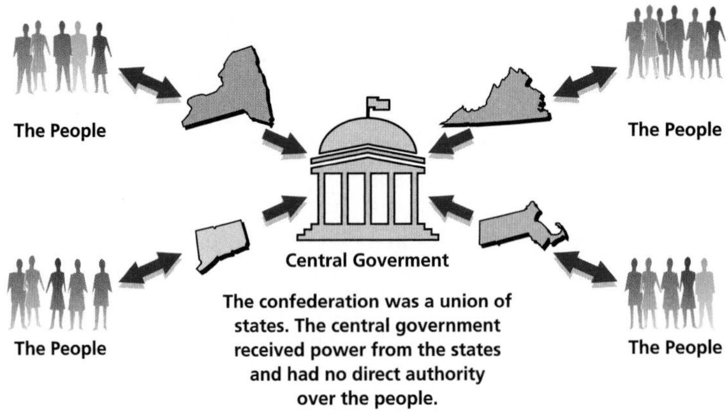

Government under U.S. Constitution (Federation): 1789–

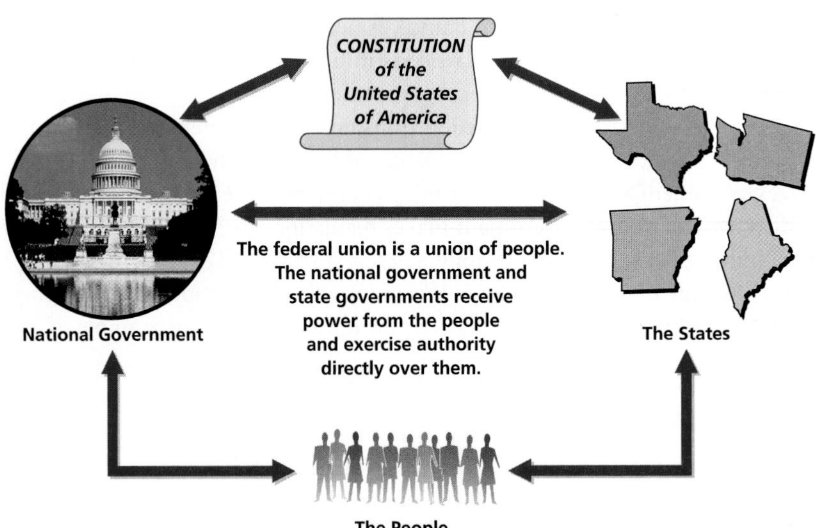

FIGURE 3-1 A Comparison of Federalism and Confederation

and attempt to suppress the interests of others. Of course the size of the nation and the many interests within it are the greatest obstacles to the formation of a single-interest majority—a point often overlooked today but emphasized by Madison in *The Federalist*, No. 10. If such a majority were to occur, having to work through a federal system would act to check its power.

FEDERALISM ALLOWS UNITY WITHOUT UNIFORMITY National politicians and parties do not have to iron out every difference on every issue that divides us, whether it be abortion, same-sex marriages, gun control, capital punishment, welfare financing, or assisted suicide. Instead, these issues are debated in state legislatures, county courthouses, and city halls. But this advantage of federalism is becoming less significant as many local issues become national and as events and outcomes in one state immediately affect policy debates at the national level.

FEDERALISM ENCOURAGES EXPERIMENTATION Supreme Court Justice Louis Brandeis pointed out that state governments provide great "laboratories" for public policy experimentation, with states serving as proving grounds. If they adopt programs that fail, the negative effects are limited; if programs succeed, they can be adopted by other states and by the national government. Georgia, for example, was the first state to permit 18-year-olds to vote; Oregon is holding elections by mail and is permitting physician-assisted suicide; New York has been vigorous in its assault on water pollution; California has pioneered air pollution control programs, especially automobile emission standards; Oregon and Hawaii are pioneers in creating new systems for the delivery of health care; Nevada is the only state, so far, to legalize statewide gambling, but aspects of legalized casino gambling are now found in more than half the states. Not all innovations, even those considered successful, are widely adopted. Nebraska is the only state to have a unicameral legislature, although in recent years such a change has been discussed, not too seriously, in both Minnesota and California.

Should Puerto Rico Become a State?

Puerto Rico has been a commonwealth since 1952. Its almost four million people are American citizens. As long as they live in Puerto Rico, they cannot vote in federal elections and they do not pay federal taxes. Spanish is the language used in schools and in government circles.

The U.S. House of Representatives in 1998 voted to authorize Puerto Rico to choose among statehood, independence, or continued commonwealth status. Puerto Rico held a nonbinding referdum in December 1998, just as it had in 1993. In 1993 almost 49 percent voted to maintain commonwealth status, 43 percent supported statehood, and 4 percent voted for independence. In 1998, 46.5 percent voted for statehood, followed by independence with 2.5 percent, "free association" with 0.3 percent, and commonwealth with 0.1 percent. However, 50.2 percent voted for the fifth choice, "none of the above," the choice backed by pro-commonwealth political parties. Although Governor Pedro Rossello, a champion of statehood, tried to interpret the vote as a victory for statehood, the vote seemed to stop the immediate likelihood of congressional action. President Clinton said he would work to help Puerto Ricans clarify their choices.*

If Puerto Rico were to be added to the Union, Congress would have to accommodate two more United States senators and six new members of the House of Representatives. With the House membership fixed by law at 435, unless the law is changed to increase the size of the House, there would have to be a reduction in the representation of the six least populous states.

*William Branigan, *The Washington Post*, December 10, 1998, p. A10.

FEDERALISM KEEPS GOVERNMENT CLOSER TO THE PEOPLE By providing numerous arenas for decision making, federalism involves many people and helps keep government closer to the people. Every day thousands of Americans are busy serving on city councils, school boards, neighborhood associations, and planning commissions. And since they are close to the issues and have firsthand knowledge of what needs to be done, they may be more responsive to the problem than the experts in Washington.

We should be cautious, however, about generalizing that state and local governments are necessarily "closer to the people" than is the national government. True, more people are involved in local and state politics than in national affairs, and confidence in state governments has gone up while respect for national agencies has diminished (see Figure 3-2). Yet national and international affairs are more often on people's minds than are state or local politics. Fewer voters participate in state and local elections than in congressional and presidential elections.

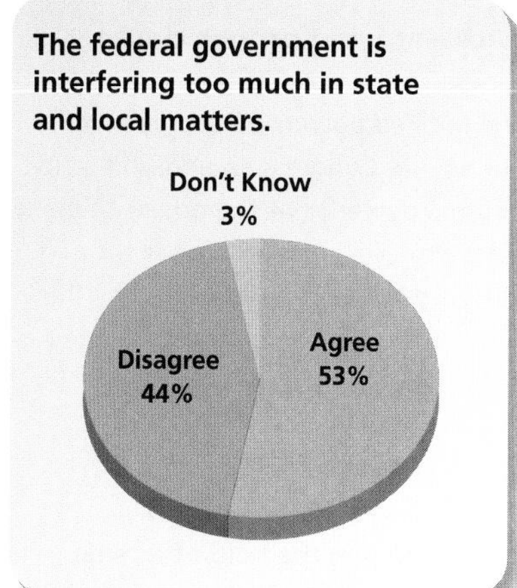

FIGURE 3-2 The Public's View on the Role of Government

SOURCE: The Pew Research Center for The People and The Press, October 1998.

The Constitutional Structure of American Federalism

Dividing powers and responsibilities between the national and state governments requires thousands of court decisions, hundreds of books, and endless speeches to explain—and even then the division lacks precise definition. Nonetheless it is helpful to get a basic understanding of how the Constitution divides these

An Expanding Nation

A great advantage of federalism—and part of the genius and flexibility of our constitutional system—has been the way in which we acquired territory and extended rights and guarantees by means of statehood, commonwealth, or territorial status, and thus grew from 13 to 50 states, plus territories.

Louisiana Purchase	1803
Florida	1819
Texas	1845
Oregon	1846
Mexican Cession	1848
Gadsden Purchase	1853
Alaska	1867
Hawaii	1898
Philippines	1898–1946
Puerto Rico	1899
Guam	1899
American Samoa	1900
Canal Zone	1904–2000
U.S. Virgin Islands	1917
Pacific Islands Trust Territory	1947

powers and responsibilities among the national and state governments and what obligations it imposes on each level of government in its relations to the other.

The formal constitutional framework of our federal system may be stated relatively simply:

1. The national government has only those powers delegated to it by the Constitution (with the important exception of the inherent power over foreign affairs).
2. Within the scope of its operations, the national government is supreme.
3. The state governments have the powers not delegated to the central government, except those denied to them by the Constitution and their state constitutions.
4. Some powers are specifically denied to both the national and state governments; others are specifically denied only to the states; still others are denied only to the national government.

Powers of the National Government

The Constitution, chiefly in the first three articles, delegates legislative, executive, and judicial powers to the national government. In addition to these **express powers**, such as the power to appropriate funds, the Constitution delegates to Congress **implied powers**, such as the power to create banks, which may be inferred from express powers. The constitutional basis for the implied powers of Congress is the **necessary and proper clause** (Article I, Section 8, Clause 18). This clause gives Congress the right "to make all Laws which shall be necessary and proper for carrying into Execution the foregoing Powers, and all other Powers vested . . . in the Government of the United States."

express powers
Powers specifically granted to one of the branches of the national government by the Constitution.

implied powers
Powers inferred from express powers that allow Congress to carry out its functions.

necessary and proper clause
Clause of the Constitution setting forth the implied powers of Congress. It states that Congress, in addition to its express powers, has the power to make all laws necessary and proper for carrying out all powers vested by the Constitution in the national government.

inherent powers
Those powers of the national government in the field of foreign affairs that the Supreme Court has declared do not depend upon constitutional grants but rather grow out of the very existence of the national government.

In the field of foreign affairs the Constitution gives the national government **inherent powers**, so that the national government has the same authority to deal with other nations as if it were the central government in a unitary system. These inherent powers do not depend on specific constitutional grants. For example, the government of the United States may acquire territory by purchase or by discovery and occupation, though no specific clause in the Constitution allows such acquisition. Even if the Constitution were silent about foreign affairs—which it is not—the national government would have the right to declare war, make treaties, and appoint and receive ambassadors.

Together, these express, implied, and inherent powers create a flexible system that has allowed the Supreme Court, Congress, the president, and the people to expand the central government's powers to meet the needs of a modern industrial nation operating in a global economy. This expansion of central government functions has rested on four constitutional pillars.

These four constitutional pillars—*the national supremacy article, the war power, the commerce clause,* and, most especially, *the power to tax and spend for the general welfare*—have permitted a tremendous expansion of the functions of the national government, so much so that the national government has in effect almost full power to enact any legislation that Congress thinks will promote the general welfare, so long as it does not conflict with those provisions of the Constitution designed to protect individual rights.

THE NATIONAL SUPREMACY ARTICLE One of the most important pillars is found in Article VI of the Constitution: "This Constitution, and the Laws of the United States which shall be made in Pursuance thereof; and all Treaties made . . . under the

Authority of the United States, shall be the supreme Law of the Land; and the Judges in every State shall be bound thereby; any Thing in the Constitution or Laws of any State to the Contrary notwithstanding." All officials, state as well as national, are bound by constitutional oath to support the Constitution of the United States. States may not override national policies; this restriction also applies to local units of government since they are agents of the states. National laws and regulations of federal agencies *preempt* the field, so that conflicting state and local rules and regulations are unenforceable.

The power to regulate interstate commerce allowed Congress to forbid discrimination like this in places of public accommodation in the 1964 Civil Rights Act.

THE WAR POWER The national government is responsible for protecting the nation from external aggression and, when necessary, for waging war. In today's world, military strength depends not only on troops in the field but also on the ability to mobilize the nation's industrial might and to apply scientific knowledge to the tasks of defense. The national government has the power to do whatever is necessary and proper to wage war successfully. Thus the national government has the power to do almost anything not in direct conflict with constitutional guarantees.

THE POWER TO REGULATE COMMERCE Congressional authority extends to all commerce that affects more than one state. Commerce includes the production, buying, selling, renting, and transporting of goods, services, and properties.[15] The **commerce clause** (Article 1, Section 8, Clause 3) packs a tremendous constitutional punch; it gives Congress the power "to regulate Commerce with foreign Nations, and among the several States, and with the Indian Tribes." In these few words the national government has been able to find constitutional justification for regulating a wide range of human activity, since few, if any, aspects of our economy today affect commerce in only one state and are thus outside the scope of the national government's constitutional authority.

The commerce clause can also be used to sustain legislation that goes beyond commercial matters. When the Supreme Court upheld the 1964 Civil Rights Act forbidding discrimination because of race, religion, or national origin in places of public accommodation, it said: "Congress's action in removing the disruptive effect which it found racial discrimination has on interstate travel is not invalidated because Congress was also legislating against what it considers to be moral wrongs." Discrimination restricts the flow of interstate commerce; therefore, Congress could legislate against discrimination. Moreover, the law could be applied even to local places of public accommodation because local incidents of discrimination have a substantial and harmful impact on interstate commerce. "If it is interstate commerce that feels the pinch, it does not matter how local the operation that applies the squeeze."[16]

THE POWER TO TAX AND SPEND Congress lacks constitutional authority to pass laws solely on the ground that they will promote the general welfare, but it may raise taxes and spend money for this purpose. Congress, for example, lacks constitutional power to regulate education or agriculture directly, yet it does have the power to appropriate money to support education or to pay farm subsidies. By attaching conditions to its grants of money, Congress may thus regulate what it cannot directly control by law.

When Congress puts up the money, it determines how the money will be spent. By withholding or threatening to withhold funds, the national government can influence or control state operations and regulate individual conduct. For example, Congress has stipulated that federal funds should be withdrawn from any program

commerce clause
The clause (Article I) in the Constitution that gives Congress the power to regulate commerce among the states, with other nations, and with the Indian tribes. This clause provides the constitutional basis for most national regulations of our economy, as well as for much civil rights legislation.

federal mandate
A requirement imposed by the federal government as a condition of receipt of federal funds.

concurrent powers
Powers the Constitution gives to both the national and state governments, such as the power to levy taxes.

in which any person is denied benefits because of race, color, or national origin; subsequently the categories of sex and physical handicap were added. Congress has also used its power of the purse to force states to raise the drinking age to 21 by tying such a condition to federal dollars for highways.

Congress frequently requires states to do certain things—for example, provide services to indigent mothers and take action to clean up the air and water. These requirements are called **federal mandates.** Often, Congress does not supply the funds required to carry out these mandates, and its failure to do so has become an important issue in states facing growing expenditures with limited resources.

Powers of the States

The Constitution *reserves for the states all powers not granted to the national government,* subject only to the limitations of the Constitution. Powers not given exclusively to the national government by provision of the Constitution or by judicial interpretation may be exercised concurrently by the states, as long as there is no conflict with national law. Such **concurrent powers** with the national government include the power to levy taxes and regulate commerce internal to each state (see Table 3-2).

In general, a state may levy a tax on the same item as the national government, but a state cannot, by a tax, "unduly burden" commerce among the states, interfere with a function of the national government, complicate the operation of a national law, or abridge the terms of a treaty of the United States. Where Congress has not preempted the field, states may regulate interstate businesses, provided these regulations do not cover matters requiring uniform national treatment or unduly burden interstate commerce.

Who decides what matters require uniform national treatment or what actions might place an undue burden on interstate commerce? Congress does, subject to final review by the Supreme Court. When Congress is silent or does not clearly state its intentions, the courts—ultimately the Supreme Court—decide if there is a conflict with the national Constitution or if there has been federal preemption by law or regulation.

Constitutional Limits and Obligations

To make federalism work, the Constitution imposes certain restraints on both the national and the state governments. States are prohibited from:

1. Making treaties with foreign governments
2. Authorizing private persons to prey on the shipping and commerce of other nations-what the Constitution refers to as "granting letters of marque and reprisal," a practice common during times of war in the eighteenth century

TABLE 3-2 The Federal Division of Powers

Types of Powers Delegated to the National Government	Some Powers Reserved for the States	Some Concurrent Powers Shared by the National and State Governments
■ Express powers stated in Constitution	■ To create a republican form of government	■ To tax citizens and businesses
■ Implied powers that may be inferred from express powers	■ To charter local governments	■ To borrow and spend money
■ Inherent powers that allow nation to present a united front to foreign powers	■ To conduct elections	■ To establish courts
	■ To exercise all powers not delegated to the national government or denied to the states by the Constitution	■ To pass and enforce laws
		■ To protect civil rights

3. Coining money, issuing bills of credit, or making anything but gold and silver coin a tender in payment of debts
4. Taxing imports or exports
5. Taxing foreign ships
6. Keeping troops or ships in time of peace (except the state militia, now called the National Guard)
7. Engaging in war, unless invaded or in such imminent danger as will not admit of delay

The national government, in turn, is required by the Constitution to refrain from exercising its powers, especially its powers to tax and to regulate interstate commerce, in such a way as to interfere substantially with the states' abilities to perform their responsibilities. Today, whatever protection states have comes primarily from the political process—in restraints that our system provides because individuals elected from the states participate in the decisions of Congress—rather than from judicially enforced limitations.

The Constitution also requires the national government to guarantee to each state a "Republican Form of Government." The framers used this term to distinguish a republic from a monarchy, on the one side, and from a pure, direct democracy, on the other. Congress, not the courts, enforces this guarantee and determines what is or is not a republican form of government. By permitting the congressional delegation of a state to take its seat in Congress, Congress acknowledges that the state has the republican form of government guaranteed by the Constitution.

In addition, the national government is obliged by the Constitution to protect states against *domestic insurrection.* Congress has delegated to the president the authority to dispatch troops to put down such insurrections when so requested by the proper state authorities. If there are contesting state authorities, the president decides which are the proper ones.[17] The president does not have to wait, however, for a request from state authorities to send federal troops into a state to enforce federal laws.

Secessionism Lives On

Secession—an effort by a local region to break away from the parent state—recurs periodically in American and world history. England fought an unsuccessful war to prevent the 13 colonies from forming an independent nation. The United States waged the Civil War to prevent secession by the southern states. The Soviet Union dissolved after failing to hold its member republics together. Yugoslavia has been violently torn apart by ethnic hatreds. And today the Kurds in Turkey and ethnic Albanians in Kosovo are fighting for their own independent homelands.

In 1992 the citizens of southwestern Kansas called for a constitutional convention to withdraw from Kansas and form the fifty-first state. The citizens of Staten Island recently voted to secede from New York City, but the New York legislature refused to approve. In past years, citizens in Alaska, northern Maine, the Eastern Shore of Maryland (proposal is to create a new state of Delmarva), Massachusetts, Virginia, Nebraska, Colorado, and California have also made unsuccessful attempts to secede from their states. Some people in that part of Minnesota called the Northwest Angle even got their member of Congress to propose a constitutional amendment to allow them to join Canada. A northern California legislator is pushing for a statewide referendum to break California into three separate states. Texas, when admitted into the Union, received congressional consent to break into five states if it ever should wish to do so.

Most of these efforts are likely to be futile since they would require approval of the legislatures, and most are only ways to publicize local grievances. Perhaps the only movement that has any chance is the effort by some citizens of San Fernando Valley to withdraw from Los Angeles.

SOURCE: Pam Belluck, "The Nation: Declarations of Independence; The New American Spirit: Divided We Stand," *The New York Times*, Week in Review, May 31, 1998. See also New York Times Web archives (http://archives.nytimes.com/archiv).

Interstate Relations

Three clauses in the Constitution, taken from the Articles of Confederation, require states to give full faith and credit to each other's public acts, records, and judicial proceedings; to extend to each other's citizens the privileges and immunities of their own citizens; and to return persons who are fleeing from justice.

FULL FAITH AND CREDIT The **full faith and credit clause** (Article IV, Section 1), one of the more technical provisions of the Constitution, requires state courts to enforce the civil judgments of the courts of other states and accept their public records and acts as valid. It does not require states to enforce the criminal laws of other states; in most cases, for one state to enforce the criminal laws of another would raise constitutional issues. The clause applies especially to enforcement of judicial settlements and court awards.

full faith and credit clause
Clause in the Constitution requiring each state to recognize the civil judgments rendered by the courts of the other states and to accept their public records and acts as valid documents.

INTERSTATE PRIVILEGES AND IMMUNITIES Under Article IV, Section 2, states must extend to citizens of other states the privileges and immunities granted to their own citizens, including the protection of the laws, the right to engage in peaceful occupations, access to the courts, and freedom from discriminatory taxes. Because of this clause, states may not impose unreasonable residency requirements,

A Closer Look

SAME-SEX MARRIAGES AND THE FULL FAITH AND CREDIT CLAUSE

The full faith and credit clause has become part of a national debate because of the possibility that a state could recognize same-sex marriages. The court in Hawaii had ruled that such marriages were legal. If Hawaii recognizes such marriages, would other states that do not allow them have to give full faith and credit to the marriage between bona fide Hawaiian residents who move into the state? Congress said no. In 1996 it passed and President Bill Clinton signed the Defense of Marriage Act, which relieves states of any obligation to recognize same-sex marriages and stipulates that the national government will recognize only heterosexual marriages for federal benefits such as Social Security and government pensions. This act is certain to be challenged in the courts as being beyond the power of Congress to provide states with an exemption from their constitutional obligation under the full faith and credit clause. Those supporting the act will point to the Constitution, which gives Congress the responsibility for prescribing the manner in which states are to comply with the clause. They may also point to the debates of the nineteenth century over polygamy.

In a ballot initiative in the November 1998 elections, voters in Hawaii gave their legislature authorization to overturn the court ruling and ban same-sex marriages. At the same time, Alaskans voted 2 to 1 in favor of a constitutional amendment that defines marriage as a union between one man and one woman.

The Supreme Court has yet to address this issue squarely, and past precedents provide no clear answer. It is the view of one authority that in light of recent Court rulings showing the present Court's tilt toward states' rights and "the fact that marriage has traditionally been an almost exclusive sphere of state authority, the Court would likely maintain the noncentralized and dual nature of American domestic relations that exist today, and allow the states to decide whether to recognize same-sex marriages."*

*John P. Feldmeier, "Federalism and Full Faith and Credit: Must States Recognize Out-of-State Same-Sex Marriages?" *Publius* 25, no. 4 (Fall 1995), p. 126. But for contrary view, see William Eskridge, "Credit Is Due," *The New Republic*, June 17, 1996, p. 11.

Gay couples renew their vows to each other in this ceremony in San Francisco's Metropolitan Community church.

that is, withhold rights to American citizens who have recently moved to the state and thereby have become citizens of that state. For example, a state may not set unreasonable time limits to withhold state-funded medical benefits from new citizens or to keep them from voting. How long a residency requirement may a state impose? A day seems about as long as the Court will tolerate to withhold welfare payments or medical care, 50 days or so for voting privileges, and one year for eligibility for in-state tuition for state-supported colleges and universities. Financially independent adults who move into a state just before enrolling in a state-supported university or college may be required to prove that they have become citizens of that state and intend to remain after finishing their schooling by supplying such evidence of citizenship as tax payments, a driver's license, car registration, voter registration, and a continuous, year-round off-campus residence. Students who are financially dependent on their parents remain citizens of the state of their parents.

EXTRADITION In Article IV, Section 2, the Constitution asserts that when individuals charged with crimes have fled from one state to another, the state to which they have fled is to deliver them to the proper officials upon the demand of the executive authority of the state from which they fled. This process is called **extradition.** "The obvious objective of the Extradition Clause," the courts have claimed, "is that no State should become a safe haven for the fugitives from a sister State's criminal justice system."[18] Congress has supplemented this constitutional provision by making the governor of the state to which fugitives have fled the agent responsible for returning them. Despite their constitutional obligation, governors of asylum states have on occasion refused to honor a request for extradition. So far in modern times no federal judge has had to try to enforce an extradition request.

INTERSTATE COMPACTS The Constitution also requires states to settle disputes with one another without the use of force. States may carry their legal disputes to the Supreme Court, or they may negotiate **interstate compacts**. Interstate compacts often establish interstate agencies to handle problems affecting the entire region. Before most interstate compacts become effective, congressional approval is required. After a compact has been signed and approved by Congress, it becomes binding on all signatory states, and its terms are enforceable by the Supreme Court. A typical state may belong to 20 compacts dealing with such subjects as environmental protection, crime control, water rights, and higher education exchanges.[19]

The Role of the Federal Courts: Umpires of Federalism

The political process ultimately decides how power will be divided between the national and the state governments. Still, the federal courts—and especially the Supreme Court—have often been called on to umpire the ongoing debate about which level of government should do what, for whom, and to whom. This role for the Courts was claimed in the celebrated case of *McCulloch v Maryland.*

McCulloch versus Maryland

In *McCulloch v Maryland* (1819), the Supreme Court had the first of many chances to define the division of power between the national and state governments.[20] Maryland had levied a tax against the Baltimore branch of the Bank of the United States, a semipublic agency established by Congress. James William McCulloch, the cashier of the bank, refused to pay on the grounds that a state could not tax an instrument of the national government.

Maryland was represented before the Court by some of the country's most distinguished lawyers, including Luther Martin, who had been a delegate to the Constitutional Convention. Martin said the power to incorporate a bank is not expressly delegated to the national government. He maintained that the necessary and proper clause gives Congress only the power to choose those means and to pass those laws absolutely essential to the execution of its expressly granted powers. Because a bank is not absolutely necessary to the exercise of any of its delegated powers, Congress had no authority to establish it. As for Maryland's right to tax the bank, the power to tax is one of the powers reserved to the states; they may use it as they see fit.

The national government was represented by equally distinguished counsel, chief among whom was Daniel Webster. Webster conceded the power to create a bank is not one of the express powers of the national government. However, the power to pass laws necessary and proper to carry out Congress's express powers is specifically delegated to Congress. Therefore, Congress may incorporate a bank as an

extradition
Legal process whereby an alleged criminal offender is surrendered by the officials of one state to officials of the state in which the crime is alleged to have been committed.

interstate compact
An agreement among two or more states. The Constitution requires that most such agreements be approved by Congress.

You Decide . . .

Do we need a stronger or a weaker government in Washington?

Should responsibility for former functions of national government, such as welfare and Medicare, be given back to the states? If the national government sets the standards, should it provide the funds but leave the details to the states? Do the facts, as you know them, support the need for federal standards? Or can state and local governments be trusted to handle most domestic problems in their own way?

appropriate, convenient, and useful means of exercising the granted powers of collecting taxes, borrowing money, and caring for the property of the United States. Although the power to tax is reserved to the states, Webster argued that states cannot interfere with the operations of the national government. The Constitution leaves no room for doubt; in cases of conflict between the national and state governments, the national government is supreme.

Speaking for a unanimous Court, Chief Justice John Marshall rejected every one of Maryland's contentions. He summarized his views on the powers of the national government in these now-famous words: "Let the end be legitimate, let it be within the scope of the Constitution, and all means which are appropriate, which are plainly adapted to that end, which are not prohibited, but consist with the letter and spirit of the constitution, are constitutional." Having thus established the doctrine of *implied national powers*, Marshall set forth the doctrine of **national supremacy**. No state, he said, can use its reserved taxing powers to tax a national instrument. "The power to tax involves the power to destroy. . . . If the right of the States to tax the means employed by the general government be conceded, the declaration that the Constitution, and the laws made in pursuance thereof, shall be the supreme law of the land, is empty and unmeaning declamation."

The long-range significance of *McCulloch v Maryland* in providing support for the developing forces of nationalism cannot be overstated. The arguments of the states' righters, if they had been accepted, would have strapped the national government in a constitutional straitjacket and denied it powers needed to handle the problems of an expanding nation.

Federal Courts and the Role of the States

The authority of federal judges to review the activities of state and local governments has expanded dramatically in recent decades because of modern judicial interpretations of the Fourteenth Amendment forbidding states to deprive any person of life, liberty, or property without due process of the law; nor can states deny to any person the equal protection of the laws and congressional legislation enacted to implement this amendment. Today almost every action by state and local officials is subject to challenge before a federal judge as a violation of the Constitution or of federal law.

In carrying out their judgments, federal judges have sometimes taken over the supervision of state prison systems, public hospitals, public schools, and other public facilities. Although a recent decision called the validity of some such takeovers in doubt, the Supreme Court has gone so far as to sustain a federal judge's right to order a local school board in Missouri to ignore the state's constitutional constraints and to raise taxes and sell bonds to fund the operation of a racially integrated magnet school.[21]

One of the major instruments for opening these issues for federal court review is the Supreme Court's revitalization—some would say rewriting—of an 1871 civil rights act originally written to combat the Ku Klux Klan. This act permits individuals to go into federal court to sue cities and counties for damages or seek injunctions against any person acting "under the color of law"—that is, in an official capacity—who they believe has deprived them of any right secured by the Constitution or by any one of the several thousands of federal laws.[22] Federal judges have also become agencies to enforce federal mandates. For example, doctors and hospitals may sue a state to force it to provide "reasonable" reimbursement as required by federal Medicare law, and parents may sue a state for allegedly failing to provide their disabled children with a "free appropriate public education" or otherwise reimburse such parents for tuition in a private school.[23]

Preemption occurs when a federal law or regulation takes over and precludes enforcement of a state or local law or regulation. State and local laws are preempted not only when they conflict directly with federal laws and regulations, but also if they

national supremacy
Constitutional doctrine that whenever conflict occurs between the constitutionally authorized actions of the national government and those of a state or local government, the actions of the federal government take priority.

preemption
The right of a federal law or regulation to preclude enforcement of a state or local law or regulation.

centralists
Those who favor national action over action at the state and local levels.

decentralists
Those who favor state or local action rather than national action.

touch a field in which the "federal interest is so dominant that the federal system will be assumed to preclude enforcement of state laws on the same subject."[24] Examples of federal preemption include the Coast Guard Authorization Act directing the secretary of transportation to develop standards for determining when people are considered intoxicated while operating a marine recreational vessel; laws regulating hazardous substances, water quality, and clean air standards; and many civil rights acts, most especially the Civil Rights Act of 1964 and the Voting Rights Act of 1965.

Over the years federal judges, under the leadership of the Supreme Court, have favored the powers of the federal government over the states. However, the Supreme Court has recently returned to the states several explosive political issues. Perhaps most notably in 1989 in *Webster v Reproductive Health Services* and in 1992 in *Planned Parenthood of Southeastern Pennsylvania v Casey*, the Court gave the states considerable latitude to regulate abortion, setting off intense clashes between pro-choice and right-to-life groups in the state legislatures.[25]

Despite the Supreme Court's bias in favor of national over state authority, few would deny the Supreme Court the power to review and set aside state actions. As Justice Oliver Wendell Holmes of the Supreme Court once remarked: "I do not think the United States would come to an end if we lost our power to declare an Act of Congress void. I do think the Union would be imperiled if we could not make that declaration as to the laws of the several States."[26]

The Great Debate—Centralists versus Decentralists

From the beginning of the Republic there has been an ongoing debate about the "proper" distribution of powers, functions, and responsibilities between the national government and the states. The constitutional arguments revolving around federalism grow out of specific political issues: Did the national government have the authority to outlaw slavery in the territories? Did the states have the authority to operate racially segregated schools? Could Congress regulate labor relations? Does Congress have the power to regulate the sale and use of firearms? Does Congress have the right to tell states how to regulate air and water pollution? The debates in the past and those today are frequently phrased in constitutional language, with appeals to the great principles of federalism. But they are also arguments over who gets what, where, and how.

During the Great Depression of the 1930s, the nation debated whether Congress had the constitutional authority to enact legislation on agriculture, labor, education, housing, and welfare. Only 40 years ago some legislators and public officials—as well as some scholars—questioned the constitutional authority of Congress to legislate against racial discrimination. The debate continues, although no longer couched primarily in constitutional terms, between **centralists**, those who favor national action, and **decentralists**, those who favor action at the state and local levels.

THE DECENTRALIST POSITION Among those favoring the decentralist or states' rights interpretation were Thomas Jefferson, John C. Calhoun, the Supreme Court from the 1920s to 1937, and more recently, Ronald Reagan, George Bush, the Republican leaders of Congress, Chief Justice William H. Rehnquist, and Justices Antonin Scalia, Clarence Thomas, and Sandra Day O'Connor. Most decentralists contend the Constitution is a treaty among sovereign states that created the central government and gave it carefully limited authority. As Justice Thomas, a modern-day ardent decentralist, wrote in a dissenting opinion supporting the argument that a state has the power to impose term limits on members of Congress, "The ultimate source of the Constitution's authority is the consent of the people of each individual State, not the consent of the undifferentiated people of the Nation as a whole."[27] Thus the national government is nothing more than an agent of the states, and every one of its powers should be narrowly defined. Any question about whether the states have

Thinking it Through...

The great debate about which level of government can best perform functions continues to rage. The Republican party started its history as the party of the National Union, while the Democrats were then the champion of states' rights, but for the past several decades there has been a switch. After winning majority status in Congress in 1994, Republicans led the charge on Washington, demanding the return of functions back to the states. Democrats tend to be reluctant about removing all federal standards, especially with respect to regulation of the environment and of the workplace, and they tend to be in favor of providing minimum standards for programs, especially welfare and health care.

Centralists' Arguments

1. State and local officials tend to be less competent than national officials.
2. State and local officials tend to be concerned only with the interests of their own areas.
3. State and local governments are unable or unwilling to raise taxes needed to carry out vital government functions.
4. State and local governments are more apt to reflect local racial and ethnic biases as well as the biases of dominant local industries.
5. State and local governments are afraid to regulate industries for fear the industries will move elsewhere.

Decentralists' Arguments

1. Increased urbanization has made states more responsive to the needs of city people.
2. In recent years state and local governments have shown greater willingness to raise taxes than the national government.
3. State and local governments have become as sensitive to the needs of the poor and minorities as is the national government.
4. State and local governments have reformed and modernized and thus become more effective governments.

given a particular function to the central government or have reserved it for themselves should be resolved in favor of the states.

Decentralists hold that the national government should not interfere with activities reserved for the states. The Tenth Amendment, they claim, makes this clear: "The powers not delegated to the United States by the Constitution, nor prohibited by it to the States, are reserved to the States respectively, or to the people." Decentralists insist state governments are closer to the people and reflect the people's wishes more accurately than does the national government. The national government, they add, is inherently heavy-handed and bureaucratic; to preserve our federal system and our liberties, central authority must be kept under control.

THE CENTRALIST POSITION The centralist position has been supported by Chief Justice John Marshall, Abraham Lincoln, Theodore Roosevelt, Franklin Roosevelt, and throughout most of our history by the Supreme Court. Centralists reject the whole idea of the Constitution as an interstate compact. Rather, they view the Constitution as a supreme law established by the people. The national government is an agent of the people, not of the states, because it was the people who drew up the Constitution and created the national government. They intended that the central government's powers should be liberally defined and that the central government should be denied authority only when the Constitution clearly prohibits it from acting.

Centralists argue that the national government is a government of all the people, whereas each state speaks only for some of the people. Although the Tenth Amendment clearly reserves powers for the states, it does not deny the national government the right to exercise to the fullest extent all the powers given to it by the Constitution. On the other hand, the supremacy of the national government, it is argued, restricts the states, because governments representing part of the people cannot be allowed to interfere with a government representing all of them.

Currently there are powerful political pressures and champions of a decentralist constitutional interpretation on the Supreme Court. Chief Justice Rehnquist, joined by Justices Scalia, Thomas, O'Connor, and frequently Justice Anthony M. Kennedy, have veered the court back to a more decentralist position. President Clinton's two appointees, Justices Ruth Bader Ginsburg and Stephen Breyer, joined by Justices David Souter and John Paul Stevens, are resisting this movement back to a states' rights interpretation of our federal system.

The Supreme Court and the Role of Congress

From 1937 until 1995 the Supreme Court essentially had removed federal courts from what had been their traditional role of protecting states from acts of Congress. The Supreme Court had broadly interpreted the commerce clause to allow Congress to do whatever Congress thought to be necessary and proper to promote the common good, even if the federal laws and regulations infringed on the activities of state and local governments. In 1985 the Supreme Court went so far as to tell the states that they should look to the political process to protect their interest, not to the federal courts.[28]

A decade later, however, the Supreme Court signaled that federal courts would no longer remain passive in resolving federalism issues. In the first of two important cases in the 1995 term, the Supreme Court declared the Gun-Free School Zones Act of 1980 unconstitutional.[29] In a second case, the Court declared that a state could not impose term limits on its members of Congress, but it did so by only a 5 to 4 vote. Justice John Paul Stevens, writing for the majority, built his argument on the concept of the federal union as espoused by the great Chief Justice John Marshall, as a compact among the people, with the national government serving as the people's agent. Justice Clarence Thomas, writing for the minority of four, espoused a view of federalism not heard from a justice of the Supreme Court since prior to the New Deal. He interpreted the Tenth Amendment as requiring the national government to justify its actions in terms of an enumerated power and granting to the states all other powers not granted to the national government.[30]

In the very next term, the Court declared that the clause in the Constitution empowering Congress to regulate commerce with the Indian tribes did not give Congress the power to authorize federal courts to hear suits against a state brought by Indian tribes.[31] The effect of this decision goes beyond Indian tribes. It means that, except to enforce rights stemming from the Fourteenth Amendment, which the Court explicitly acknowledged to be within Congress's power, Congress may no longer authorize individuals to bring legal actions against states in federal courts.

In the 1997 term the Supreme Court declared two acts of Congress unconstitutional because of interfering with powers of the states, once again asserting its role as the umpire of the federal system. It declared unconstitutional the Religious Freedom Restoration Act of 1993 (which is explained in some detail in Chapter 4) in large part because Congress tried to force judges to interpret the First and Fourteenth Amendments in a way that would interfere with the discretion of states in regulating the public welfare.[32] And then the Court ruled that the Brady Act, previously passed by Congress, could not require local law enforcement officers to do background checks on prospective gun buyers.[33]

These Supreme Court decisions—most of which split the Court 5 to 4 along ideological lines, with the conservative justices favoring states' rights—may presage a major shift in the Court's interpretation of the constitutional nature of our federal system. Federalism issues are likely to come up in future Senate judicial conformation hearings, and the appointment of new Supreme Court justices could well determine how these federalism issues are decided.

Regulatory Federalism, Federal Grants, and Federal Mandates

Congress authorizes programs, establishes general rules for how the programs will operate, and decides whether and how much room should be left for state or local discretion. Most important, Congress appropriates the funds for these programs and, until recently, has had deeper pockets than even the richest states. One of Congress's most potent tools for influencing policy at the state and local levels has been the federal grant.

Federal grants serve four purposes, the most important of which is the fourth:

1. To supply state and local governments with revenue.
2. To establish minimum national standards for such things as highways and clean air.
3. To equalize resources among the states by taking money from people with high incomes through federal taxes and spending it, through grants, in states where the poor live.
4. To attack national problems yet minimize the growth of federal agencies.

Types of Federal Grants

Three types of federal grants are currently being administered: categorical-formula grants, project grants, and block grants (or, as the Clinton administration calls them, flexible grants). From 1972 to 1982 there was also **revenue sharing**—federal grants to state and local governments to be used at their discretion and subject only to very general conditions. But when budget deficits soared in the second Reagan administration (1985–89) and there was no revenue to share, revenue sharing was terminated—to the states in 1986 and to local governments in 1987.

revenue sharing
Program from 1972 to 1987 whereby federal funds were provided to state and local governments to be spent largely at the discretion of the receiving governments, subject to very general conditions.

CATEGORICAL-FORMULA GRANTS Congress appropriates funds for specific purposes, such as school lunches or the building of airports and highways. These funds are allocated by formula and are subject to detailed federal conditions, often on a matching basis; that is, the local government receiving the federal funds must put up some of its own dollars. Categorical grants, in addition, provide federal supervision to ensure that the federal dollars are spent as Congress wants. There are hundreds of grant programs, but two dozen, including Medicaid, account for more than half of total spending for categoricals.

PROJECT GRANTS Congress appropriates a certain sum, which is allocated to state and local units and sometimes to nongovernmental agencies, based on applications from those who wish to participate. Examples are grants by the National Science Foundation to universities and research institutes to support the work of scientists or grants to states and localities to support training and employment programs.

BLOCK GRANTS These are broad grants to states for prescribed activities—welfare, child care, education, social services, preventive health care, and health services—with only a few strings attached. States have great flexibility in deciding how to spend block grant dollars, but when the federal funds for any fiscal year are gone, there are no more matching federal dollars.

The Politics of Federal Grants

Republicans "have consistently favored fewer strings, less federal supervision, and the delegation of spending discretion to the state and local governments."[34] Democrats have generally been less supportive of broad discretionary block grants, favoring instead more detailed, federally supervised spending. The Republican-controlled 104th Congress (1995–97) gave a high priority to the creation of block grants. However, Republicans ran into trouble when they tried to lump together welfare, school lunch and breakfast programs, prenatal nutrition programs, and child protection programs in one block grant.

With President Clinton's enthusiastic support, the Republicans were successful, however, in making one major change in federal-state relations—a devolution of responsibility for welfare from the national governments to the states. The Personal Responsibility and Work Opportunity Reconciliation Act of 1996 put an end to the 61-year-old program of Aid to Families with Dependent Children (AFDC), a federal guarantee of welfare checks for all eligible mothers and children. The 1996 act substituted for AFDC a welfare block grant to each state, with caps on the amount of federal dollars that the state will receive. It also put another big federal child care program into another block grant—Child Care and Development Block Grant (CCDBG).

These new welfare block grants give states considerable flexibility in how they provide for welfare, but there are federal strings. Most important, no federal funds can be used to cover recipients who do not go to work within two years, and no person can receive federally supported benefits for more than five years. And in order to slow down "the race to the bottom" in which states may try to make themselves "the least attractive state in which to be poor,"[35] Congress also stipulated that in order for states to receive their full share of federal dollars, they must continue to spend at least 75 percent of what they had been spending on welfare.[36]

The battle over the appropriate level of government to control the funds tends to be cyclical. A scholar of federalism explains, "Complaints about excessive federal control tend to be followed by proposals to shift more power to state and local governments. Then, when problems arise in state and local administration—and problems inevitably arise when any organization tries to administer anything—demands for closer federal supervision and tighter federal controls follow."[37]

Steve Greenberg. Courtesy Seattle Post-Intelligencer.

Federal Mandates

Fewer federal dollars do not necessarily mean fewer federal controls. On the contrary, the federal government has imposed mandates on states and local governments, often without providing federal funds. State and local officials complain that new federal regulatory devices are far more intrusive than the old-fashioned conditions they used to complain about.

Protests from state and local officials against unfunded federal mandates were effective. Congress, with President Clinton's support, passed the Unfunded Mandates Reform Act of 1995.[38] The act called on the Congressional Budget Office (CBO) and federal agencies to issue reports about the impact of unfunded mandates. The act also imposed some mild constraints on Congress itself. A congressional committee that approves any legislation containing a federal mandate must draw attention to the mandate in its report and describe its cost to state and local governments. If the committee intends any mandate to be partially unfunded, it must explain why it is appropriate for the cost to be borne by state and local government.

Whether the Unfunded Mandates Reform Act significantly slows downs federal mandates remains to be seen. So far it has had little effect. The Americans with Disabilities Act, for example, called on state and local governments to build ramps and alter curbs—renovations that are costing millions. Environmental Protection Agency regulations require states to build automobile pollution testing stations and take other actions to reduce pollution, but without corresponding federal dollars. Still, state officials praise the law for increasing congressional awareness of unfunded mandates. It has forced members of Congress to take into account how a bill would affect state and local governments, and to check with the Congressional Budget Office to avoid exposing a bill to a point of order that could slow down or even block its passage.

The Politics of Federalism

The formal structures of our federal system have not changed much since 1787, but the political realities, especially during the last half-century, have greatly altered how federalism works. To understand these changes, we need to look at some of the trends that continue to fuel the debate about the meaning of federalism.

The Growth of Big Government

Over the past 200 years there has been a drift of power to the national government. "No one planned the growth, but everyone played a part in it."[39] How did this shift come about? For a variety of reasons. One is that many of our problems have become national in scope. Much that was local in 1789, in 1860, or in 1930 is now national—even global. State governments could supervise the relations between small merchants and their few employees, but only the national government can supervise relations between a multinational corporation and its thousands of employees, many organized in national unions.

As industrialization proceeded, powerful interests made demands on the national government. Business groups called on the government for aid in the form of tariffs, a national banking system, subsidies to railroads and the merchant marine, and uniform rules relating to the environment. Farmers learned that the national government could give

New Techniques of Federal Control

- *Direct Orders* In a few instances, federal regulation takes the form of direct orders that must be complied with under threat of criminal or civil sanction. An example is the Equal Employment Opportunity Act of 1972, barring job discrimination by state and local governments because of race, color, religion, sex, and national origin.
- *Cross-cutting Requirements* The first and most famous of these requirements (so called because a condition on one federal grant is extended to all activities supported by federal funds, regardless of their source) is Title VI of the 1964 Civil Rights Act, which holds that no person may be discriminated against in the use of federal funds because of race, color, or national origin. Other laws extend these protections to persons because of gender or handicapped status. More than 60 cross-cutting requirements concern the environment, historic preservation, contract wage rates, access to governmental information, the care of experimental animals, the treatment of human subjects in research projects, and so on.
- *Cross-over Sanctions* These sanctions permit the use of federal dollars in one program to influence state and local policy in another. One example is a 1984 act that threatened to reduce federal highway aid by up to 15 percent for any state that failed to adopt a minimum drinking age of 21 by 1987.
- *Total Preemption* This kind of control rests not on the national government's power to spend but on its powers under the supremacy and commerce clauses to preempt conflicting state and local activities. Building on this constitutional authority, federal law in certain areas just preempts state and local governments from the field. "There are fourteen types of total preemption laws, ranging from ones removing all regulatory powers from the states to ones authorizing states to cooperate in enforcing a statute."*
- *Partial Preemption* In these instances, federal law establishes basic policies but requires states to administer them. Some programs give states an option not to participate, but if a state chooses not to do so, the national government then steps in and runs the programs. Even worse from the state's point of view is *mandatory partial preemption*, in which the national government requires the state to act on peril of losing other funds but provides no funds to support the state action. The Clean Air Act of 1990 is an example of mandatory partial preemption; the federal government set national air quality standards and required states to devise plans and pay for their implementation and enforcement.** Medicaid is another example of the national government providing some funds but mandating states to provide services that cost more than the federal funds cover.

*Joseph F. Zimmerman, "Congressional Regulation of Subnational Governments," *PS: Political Science and Politics* 26 (June 1993), p. 179.

**Mel Dubnick and Alan Gitelson, "Nationalizing State Policies," in *The Nationalization of State Government*, ed. Jerome J. Hanus (D.C. Heath, 1981), pp. 56–57.

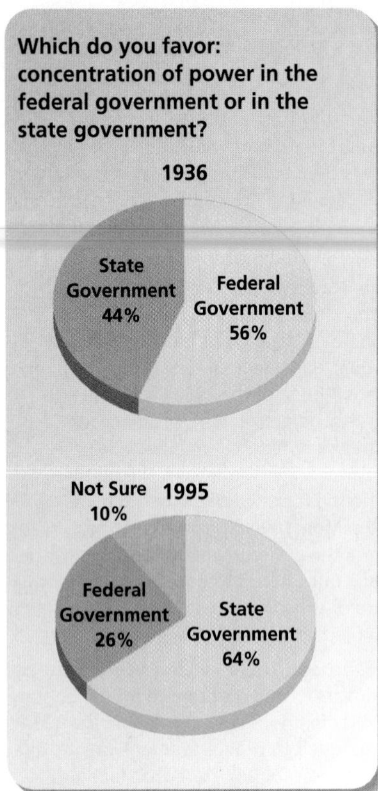

FIGURE 3-3 A Changing View of the Federal Government

SOURCE: *The Public Perspective*, a publication of the Roper Center for Public Opinion Research, University of Connecticut, Storrs. Reprinted by permission.

more aid than the states, and they too began to demand help. By the beginning of this century, urban groups in general and organized labor in particular pressed their claims. Big business, big agriculture, and big labor all added up to big government.

The growth of the national economy and the creation of national transportation and communications networks altered people's attitudes toward the national government (see Figure 3-3). Before the Civil War, the national government was viewed as a distant, even foreign, government. Today, in part because of television, most people identify as closely with Washington as with their state capitals. We are apt to know more about our president than about our governor, more about our national senators and representatives than about our state legislators or even about the local officials who run our cities and schools.

The Great Depression of the 1930s stimulated extensive national action on such issues as welfare, unemployment, and farm surpluses. World War II brought federal regulation of wages, prices, and employment, as well as national efforts to allocate resources, train personnel, and support engineering and inventions. After the war the national government helped veterans obtain college degrees and inaugurated a vast system of support for university research. The United States became the most powerful leader of the free world, maintaining substantial military forces even in times of peace. The Great Society programs of the 1960s poured out grants-in-aid to states and localities. City dwellers who had migrated from the rural South to northern cities began to seek federal funds for—at the very least—housing, education, and mass transportation.

Although economic and social conditions created many of the pressures for expansion of the national government, so did political claims. Until the overwhelming federal budget deficits of the 1980s and early 1990s, members of Congress, presidents, federal judges, and federal administrators actively promoted federal initiatives. With the return of the more balanced federal budgets in the late 1990s, it will be interesting to see if Congress returns to active promotion of federal programs. True, when there is widespread conflict about what to do—how to reduce the federal deficit, adopt a national energy policy, reform Social Security, provide health care for the indigent—Congress waits for a national consensus. But when an organized constituency wants something and there is no counterpressure, Congress "responds often to everyone, and with great vigor."[40] Once established, federal programs generate groups with vested interests in promoting, defending, and expanding them. Associations are formed, alliances are made. "In a word, the growth of government has created a constituency of, by, and for government."[41]

The politics of federalism are changing, however, and Congress is being pressured to reduce the size and scope of national programs. Tax laws no longer permit automatic increases to compensate for inflation, so Congress faces reduced federal revenues. Second, the cost of entitlement programs such as Social Security and Medicare are going up because there are more older people and they live longer. These programs have widespread public support, and to cut them is politically risky. "With all other options disappearing, it is politically tempting to finance tax cuts by turning over to the states many of the social programs . . . that have become the responsibility of the national government."[42]

The Devolution Revolution—A Revolution or Just Rhetoric?

The Republican sweep of the Congress in the 1994 elections carried with it a pledge to return many functions, most especially welfare, back to the states. President Clinton appeared to agree with the general tone of the Republicans. In his State of the Union Address before the 104th Congress in 1996, he proclaimed, "The era of big government is over." However, he tempered his comments by saying, "But we cannot go back to the time when our citizens were left to fend for themselves." Congress and the president came together for a major overhaul of welfare that turned responsibility over to the States. Congress also freed the states to set their own highway speed limits, changed the Safe Drinking Water Act to allow states to operate certain programs, and gave states a greater role over how federal rural development funds can be used.

Yet despite these dramatic shifts, recent Congresses, like their predecessors, have increased the authority of the national government in many areas. "Legislation cleared by the first Republican majority in four decades established national criteria for state-issued driver's licenses, ended state registration of mutual funds, created national food safety standards, nullified state laws that had restricted telecommunications competition, and extended federal criminal penalties to cover certain violent crimes."[43] Legislators made a whole host of crimes federal crimes, including carjacking and stalking, and federalized the crime of rape committed while carjacking. Appropriation bills pressured states to keep criminals behind bars by threatening to take grants away from states that failed to meet federal standards. And President Clinton, despite his pledge that the era of big government is over, pushed for an expanded federal role in many areas, calling for restrictions on guns, for changes in the 911 system, and for national educational test standards. One reporter concluded, "The 'Devolution' promised by Congressional Republicans . . . has mostly fizzled. Instead of handing over authority to state and local governments, they're taking it away."[44]

Republicans united behind Newt Gingrich and the Contract with America in 1994 in a "revolution" to turn back power to the states.

The Future of Federalism

In 1933, seeing state governments helpless during the Great Depression, one writer stated, "I do not predict that the states will go, but affirm that they have gone."[45] Those prophets of doom were wrong. States are stronger now than ever. During recent decades state governments have undergone a major transformation. Most have improved their governmental structures, taken on greater roles in funding education, launched programs to help distressed cities, and—despite new constitutional limitations—expanded their tax bases. Able men and women have been attracted to many governorships. "Today, states, in formal representational, policy making, and implementation terms at least, are more representative, more responsive, more activist, and more professional in their operations than they ever have been. They face their expanded roles better equipped to assume and fulfill them."[46]

Until the civil rights revolution of the 1960s, segregationists had feared that national officials—responding to different political majorities—would work for racial integration. Thus they praised local government, emphasized the dangers of overcentralization, and argued that the protection of civil rights was not a proper function of the national government. As one political scientist observed, "Federalism has a dark history to overcome. For nearly two hundred years, states' rights have been asserted to protect slavery, segregation, and discrimination."[47]

Today the politics of federalism, even with respect to civil rights, is more complicated than in the past.[48] The national government is not necessarily more favorable to the claims of minorities than are state or city governments. When the Supreme Court did not extend marital privacy rights to gays and lesbians, some state courts interpreted their state constitutions to provide more protection for these rights than does the U.S. Constitution. However, other states are passing legislation that would eliminate such protections.

As states more actively regulate the economy, and as state attorneys general prosecute many businesses for anticompetitive practices, business interests have been arguing that conflicting state regulations are unduly burdening interstate commerce. They are asking for preemptive federal regulation to save them not only from stringent state regulations, but from having to adjust to 50 different state laws.[49] "One national dumb rule is better than 50 inconsistent rules of any kind," says a lawyer who represents trade groups in the food industries and medical devices.[50]

The national government is not likely to retreat to a pre-1930 posture or even a pre-1960 one. The underlying economic and social conditions that generated the demand for federal action have not been altered substantially. On the contrary, in addition to such traditional issues as helping people find jobs and preventing inflation and depressions—which still require national action—countless new issues have been added to the national agenda by the growth of a global economy based on high technology, service, and information.

Most Americans have strong attachments to our federal system—in the abstract. They remain loyal to their states and show a growing and healthy skepticism about the national government. Some evidence suggests, however, that the anti-Washington sentiment "is 3,000 miles wide but only a few miles deep."[51] The fact is that Americans are pragmatists and are prepared to use whatever level of government—national, state, or local—that will get the job done.

POLITICS online

Using the Net to Track Welfare Reform

Welfare reforms enacted in 1996 will have important ramifications for federalism for years to come. Under the Personal Responsibility and Work Opportunity Act, states are experimenting with a variety of different programs. What are these programs? How are they working?

Because many of the alternatives being tried in the states are new and decentralized, the media may not pay much attention to them. But an alternative source of current information is the Internet, and one of the best places to go is the Health and Human Services website:

http://www.acf.dhhs.gov

Welfare reform is such an important issue for all levels of government that several think tanks are also following the issue. One of these think tanks, the Urban Institute, has prepared an in-depth report on current welfare issues:

http://www.urban.org

Additional information on welfare reform can be obtained in many states by clicking on the home page for the state or the governor of the state.

Other places to check include the Council of State Governments:

http://www.statesnews.org

and the Nelson A. Rockefeller Institute of Government:

http://rockinst.org

The Center for the Study of Federalism website is

http://www.temple.com\federalism

For more Internet resources on federalism, see our home page:

http://www.prenhall.com/burns

SUMMARY

1. A federal system checks the growth of tyranny, allows unity without uniformity, encourages experimentation, and keeps government closer to the people.
2. Alternatives to federal systems are unitary systems in which all constitutional power is vested in the central government, and loose compacts among sovereign states.
3. The national government has the constitutional authority, stemming primarily from the national supremacy article, from its powers to tax and spend and to regulate commerce among the states, and from its war powers, to do what Congress thinks is necessary and proper to promote the general welfare and to provide for the common defense. These constitutional pillars have permitted tremendous expansion of the functions of the federal government.
4. States must give full faith and credit to each other's public acts, records, and judicial proceedings; extend to each other's citizens the privileges and immunities it gives its own; and return fugitives from justice.
5. The federal courts umpire the division of power between the national and state governments.
6. Today debates about federalism are less often about its constitutional structure than over whether action should come from the national or state and local levels. Recent Supreme Court decisions favor a decentralist position and may presage a major shift in the Court's interpretation of the constitutional nature of our federal system.
7. The major instruments of federal intervention in state programs have been various kinds of financial grants-in-aid, of which the most prominent are categorical-formula grants, project grants, and block grants. The national government also imposes federal mandates and controls the activities of state and local governments by direct orders, cross-cutting requirements, cross-over sanctions in the use of federal funds, total preemption, and partial preemption.
8. Over the past 200 years there has been a drift of power to the national government, but recently Congress has been pressured to reduce the size and scope of national programs and to shift some existing programs back to the states. While responsibility for welfare has been turned over to the states, the authority of the national government has increased in many areas.

KEY TERMS

devolution revolution 54
federalism 55
unitary system 55
confederation 55
express powers 58
implied powers 58
necessary and proper clause 58
inherent powers 58
commerce clause 59
federal mandate 60
concurrent powers 60
full faith and credit clause 61
extradition 63
interstate compact 63
national supremacy 64
preemption 64
centralists 64
decentralists 64
revenue sharing 67

FURTHER READING

Samuel H. Beer, *To Make a Nation: The Rediscovery of American Federalism* (Harvard University Press, 1993).

Center for the Study of Federalism, *The Federalism Report* (published quarterly by Temple University; this publication, notes research, books and articles, and scholarly conferences).

Center for the Study of Federalism, *Publius: The Journal of Federalism* (published quarterly by Temple University; one issue each year is an "Annual Review of the State of American Federalism").

Thomas R. Dye, *American Federalism: Competition Among Governments* (Lexington Books, 1990).

Daniel J. Elazar, *The American Mosaic: The Impact of Space, Time, and Culture on American Politics* (Westview Press, 1994).

Michael Fix and Daphne A. Kenyon, *Coping with Mandates* (Urban Institute Press, 1990).

Al Gore, *From Red Tape to Results—Creating a Government That Works Better and Costs Less: Report of the National Performance Review* (U.S. Government Printing Office, 1993).

Christopher Hamilton and Donald T. Wells, *Federalism, Power and Political Economy* (Prentice Hall, 1990).

Ellis Katz and G. Alan Tarr, eds., *Federalism and Rights* (Roman & Littlefied, 1996).

John Kincaid, ed., "American Federalism: The Third Century," *Annals of the American Academy of Political and Social Science* 509 (May 1990).

Vincent Ostrom, *The Meaning of American Federalism* (ICS Press, 1991).

Paul E. Peterson, *The Price of Federalism* (Brookings Institution, 1995).

Martin Redish, *The Constitution as Political Structure* (Oxford University Press, 1995).

William H. Riker, *The Development of American Federalism* (Academic Publishers, 1987).

Harry N. Scheiber, *Federalism and the Judicial Mind: Essays on American Constitutional Law and Politics* (Institute of Governmental Studies, University of California at Berkeley, 1992).

Denise Scheberle, *Federalism and Environmental Policy: Trust and the Politics of Implementation* (Georgetown University Press, 1997).

Thomas R. Schwartz and John E. Peck, *The Changing Face of Fiscal Federalism* (M. E. Sharpe, 1990).

David B. Walker, *The Rebirth of Federalism: Slouching Toward Washington* (M. E. Sharpe, 1990).

Joseph F. Zimmerman, *Contemporary American Federalism: The Growth of National Power* (Praeger, 1992).

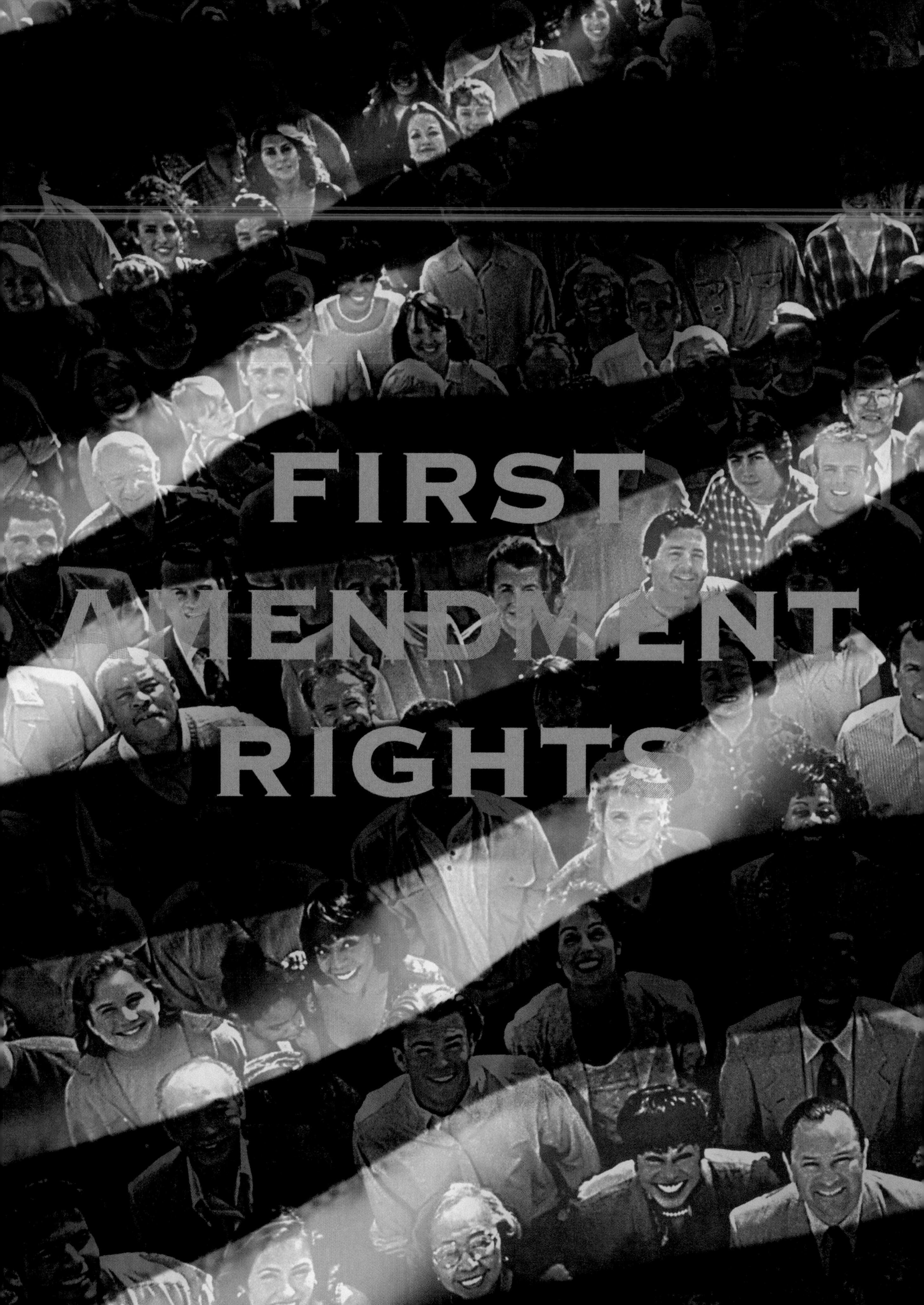
FIRST
AMENDMENT
RIGHTS

4

CHAPTER OUTLINE

- The Bill of Rights and the States
- Freedom of Religion
- Free Speech and Free People
- Freedom of the Press
- Other Media and Other Messages
- Nonprotected Speech
- Freedom of Assembly

"CONGRESS SHALL MAKE NO LAW," DECLARES THE FIRST AMENDMENT, "RESPECTING AN ESTABLISHMENT OF RELIGION, OR PROHIBITING THE FREE EXERCISE THEREOF, or abridging the freedom of speech, or of the press, or the right of the people peaceably to assemble, and to petition the Government for a redress of grievances. In this one sentence our Constitution lays down the fundamental principles of a free society: freedom of conscience and freedom of expression.

Although it was the framers who wrote the Constitution, in a sense it was the people who drafted our basic charter of rights. As we have seen, the Constitution drawn up in Philadelphia included guarantees of a few basic rights, but it lacked a specific bill of rights similar to that found in most state constitutions. This omission aroused widespread suspicion. To persuade delegates to the state ratification conventions to vote for the Constitution, the Federalists had to promise to correct this deficiency. In its first session, the new Congress made good on this promise by proposing twelve amendments, ten of which were ratified by the end of 1791 and became part of the Constitution. These ten amendments are known as the Bill of Rights.[1]

A judicially enforceable bill of rights is an American invention, although in recent decades more than 60 nations have added a bill of rights to their constitutions. In many instances these bills of rights have had no effect, since the legal resources to implement them were lacking. Even in the United States, the Bill of Rights was "nearly ignored by courts for a century and a half."[2]

In any discussion of rights and privileges, certain terms—liberties, rights, freedoms, privileges—are often used interchangeably. To clarify their meanings, we offer these definitions:

Civil liberties—rights of all persons that cannot be denied by governmental power: freedom of conscience, religion, or expression; generally, the freedoms secured by the First Amendment.

Civil rights—rights of all persons, not just citizens, to equal protection of the laws; the constitutional right not to be discriminated against by *governments* because of race, ethnic background, religion, or gender. Civil rights include the right not to be denied our lives, liberties, or property by government without due process of law. Civil rights can also be secured by laws of national and state governments not to be discriminated against by *persons* because of race, ethnic background, religion, or gender. These civil rights are protected by the due process and equal protection clauses of the Fifth and Fourteenth Amendments and by the civil rights laws of national and state governments.

Political rights—rights of citizens to participate in the process of governance flowing from the right to vote. These are the rights secured by the Fifteenth, Nineteenth, and Twenty-Third Amendments.

Rights of persons of accused of crimes—rights that protect all persons from abusive use by government of the power to prosecute and punish persons who violate the criminal laws. These are the rights secured by the Fourth, Fifth, Sixth, Eighth, and Fourteenth Amendments.

Legal privileges—privileges granted by governments to which we have no constitutional or legal right; for example, the right to welfare payments or a license to drive an automobile. However, once such legal privileges are granted, we have a legal right to them, and they cannot be denied except for "reasonable reasons" and by appropriate procedures.

Civil law—law that evolved from Roman law; in contrast to *common law,* which evolved from English tradition. Civil law is also used in contrast to *criminal law,* which refers to law that applies to disputes between individuals or between individuals and the government that carry no criminal sanctions.

THE BILL OF RIGHTS AND THE STATES

Note that the Bill of Rights literally applies *only to the national government,* not state governments.[3] Why not the states? The framers were confident that states could control their own state officials; also, most state constitutions already had bills of rights. But it was the new and distant central government they feared. As it turned out, those fears were largely misdirected. The national government, responsive to tens of millions of voters from a variety of races, creeds, religions, and economic interests, has shown less tendency to curtail civil liberties than have state and local governments.

When the Fourteenth Amendment, which does apply to the states, was adopted in 1868, supporters contended that its **due process clause**—which states that no person shall be deprived of life, liberty, or property without due process of law—limits states in precisely the same way the Bill of Rights limits the national government. At least, they argued, freedom of speech is protected by the Fourteenth Amendment. But for decades the Supreme Court refused to interpret the Fourteenth Amendment in this way. Then in 1925, in *Gitlow v New York,* the Court announced: "For present purposes we may and do assume that freedom of speech and of the press—which are protected by the First Amendment from abridgment by Congress—are among the fundamental personal rights and 'liberties' protected by the due process clause of the Fourteenth Amendment from impairment by the States."[4]

Gitlow v New York was a revolutionary decision. For the first time, the U.S. Constitution protected freedom of speech and of the press from abridgment by state and local governments. By the 1940s the other provisions of the First Amendment—religion, assembly, and petition—had been brought within the scope of the Fourteenth Amendment. Today the First Amendment's restraints are applied to all who exercise governmental authority at national, state, or local levels.

If the First Amendment applies to the states, why not the other parts of the Bill of Rights, most of which have to do with the rights of persons accused of crimes and with restraints on police procedures? Beginning in the 1930s and continuing at an accelerated pace during the 1960s, the Supreme Court **selectively incorporated** pro-

civil liberties
Rights of all persons that cannot be denied by governmental power: freedom of conscience, religion, or expression; generally, the freedoms secured by the First Amendment.

civil rights
Rights of all persons to equal protection of the laws; the constitutional right not to be discriminated against by government because of race, ethnic background, religion, or gender; guaranteed by the Fifth and Fourteenth Amendments.

political rights
Rights of citizens to participate in the process of governance flowing from the right to vote; secured by the Fifteenth, Nineteenth, and Twenty-third Amendments.

rights of persons accused of crimes
Rights that protect all persons from abusive use by government of the power to prosecute and punish persons who violate the criminal laws; secured by the Fourth, Fifth, Sixth, Eighth, and Fourteenth Amendments.

legal privileges
Privileges granted by government to which we have no constitutional or legal right; once granted, they cannot be denied except by appropriate procedures.

civil law
Law that evolved from Roman law; in contrast to *common law,* which has evolved from English tradition; also in contrast to *criminal law,* which refers to law that applies to disputes between individuals or between individuals and the government.

due process clause
Clause in the Fifth Amendment limiting the power of the national government; similar to clause in the Fifteenth Amendment prohibiting state governments from depriving any person of life, liberty, or property without due process of law.

vision after provision of the Bill of Rights into the due process clause. Today the Fourteenth Amendment imposes on the states all the provisions of the Bill of Rights except those of the Second, Third, Seventh, and Tenth Amendments and the grand jury requirements of the Fifth Amendment.

This *selective incorporation* of most provisions of the Bill of Rights into the Fourteenth Amendment is probably the most important constitutional development since the writing of the Constitution. It has profoundly altered the relationship between the national government and the states. It has made the federal courts, under the guidance of the Supreme Court of the United States, the most important protectors of our liberties.

After the Supreme Court incorporated most of the national Bill of Rights into the Fourteenth Amendment, little attention was paid by state judges—or anybody else—to the bills of rights in their respective state constitutions.[5] Recently, however, there has been a renewal of interest in state constitutions as independent sources of additional protection for civil liberties and civil rights.[6]

Advocates of what has come to be called **new judicial federalism** contend that the U.S. Constitution should set minimum but not maximum standards to protect our rights. There is nothing, they argue, to keep state courts from using similar provisions of the bill of rights in their own state constitutions to provide more protection for rights than is to be found in the U.S. Constitution. Moreover, state bills of rights sometimes encourage a more expansive protection of rights than does the national Bill of Rights. For example, a dozen states have an equal rights amendment in their constitutions, and 11 explicitly protect the right of privacy.[7] The Louisiana state constitution prohibits age discrimination; 35 state constitutions affirm the right of free speech; 36 state constitutions have clauses that could easily be construed as going beyond the Second Amendment in protecting the right to bear arms.[8]

However, if a state supreme court goes too far beyond public sentiment in its own state, its decisions run the risk of being overturned by amending the state constitution. In 1990, for example, victims' rights amendments were added to the California and Alaska constitutions to reverse the effect of decisions by state judges that extended the rights of criminal defendants beyond the protections provided by the U.S. Constitution. Since most state judges lack lifetime tenure and are subject to electoral contests, state judges "who stray too far from most of the people of their state's understanding of their state constitutions are likely to get chucked out of office,"[9] as happened in California in 1988 with the defeat of Chief Justice Rose Bird and two other liberal justices. Thus, despite the revival of interest in state bills of rights, the U.S. Supreme Court and the national Bill of Rights remain the dominant protectors of civil liberties and civil rights.

The separation of church and state was challenged by this county judge in Alabama, who refused to remove the plaque of the Ten Commandments from his courtroom despite a court ruling to do so.

selectively incorporated
Process by which provisions of the Bill of Rights are brought within the scope of the Fourteenth Amendment and so applied to state and local governments.

new judicial federalism
The practice of some state courts of using the bill of rights in their state constitutions to provide more protection for some rights than is provided by Supreme Court interpretation of the Bill of Rights in the Constitution.

establishment clause
Clause in the First Amendment that states that Congress shall make no law respecting an establishment of religion. It has been interpreted by the Supreme Court to forbid governmental support of any or all religions.

Freedom of Religion

The first words of the First Amendment are emphatic and brief: "Congress shall make no law respecting an *establishment* of religion, or prohibiting the *free exercise* thereof." Note there are two religion clauses: the establishment clause and the exercise clause. The Supreme Court has struggled to find a neutral course between the two religion clauses, both of which are cast in absolute terms, and either of which, if expanded to a logical extreme, would tend to clash with the other."[10]

The Establishment Clause

In writing what has come to be called the **establishment clause**, the framers were reacting to the English system, wherein the Crown was the head not only of the government but also of the established church—the Church of England—and public officials were required to take an oath of support for the established church as a condition of holding office. The establishment clause goes beyond merely forbidding the

You Decide...

Do Christmas trees or menorahs on public property violate the separation of church and state?

The Capital Square Review Board is responsible for regulating access to a ten-acre, state-owned plaza surrounding the state house in Columbus, Ohio. For more than a century the square has been used for public speeches, gatherings, and festivals advocating a variety of causes, both secular and religious. To use the square, a group has to fill out an official application form meeting several speech-neutral criteria.

In the 1993 Christmas season, the board authorized the state to put up its annual Christmas tree and granted a rabbi's application to erect a menorah next to it. The board also received an application from an officer of the Ohio Ku Klux Klan to place a cross on the square. To grant permission might violate the establishment clause. To deny permission might be a violation of the Klan's rights under the free speech and free exercise clauses. What should the board do?

establishment of a religion. It is designed to prevent three evils: government sponsorship of religion, government financial support of religion, and the active involvement of the government in religious matters.[11] On the other hand, the clause does not prevent governments from accommodating religious needs. To what extent and under which conditions governments may accommodate these needs is at the heart of much of the debate among the justices in interpreting the clause.

Establishment clause cases are not easy. They stir deep feelings, and the justices are often divided among themselves. The prevailing interpretation stems from a 1947 Supreme Court decision, *Everson v Board of Education*, that the establishment clause creates a *wall of separation* between church and state and prohibits any law or governmental action designed to benefit any religion, even if all religions are treated the same.[12]

This strict separation of church and state was further elaborated in *Lemon v Kurtzman* (1971). Under this three-part test: (1) a law must have a secular legislative purpose; (2) it must neither advance nor inhibit religion; and (3) it must avoid "excessive government entanglement with religion."[13]

Another test, championed by Justice Sandra Day O'Connor, is the *endorsement test*. Justice O'Connor believes that the clause forbids governmental practices that a reasonable observer would view as endorsing religion, even if there is no coercion.[14] The endorsement test has been honed in a series of decisions as the Court struggled with the question of whether governments may allow religious symbols to be displayed on, in, or near public properties and in public places. For example, the Court concluded that when a city displayed a nativity scene in a shopping district along with Santa's house and other secular and religious symbols of the Christmas season, there was little danger that a reasonable person would conclude that the city was endorsing religion.[15] But the Constitution does not permit a city government to display the nativity scene on the steps of the city hall, because, in this context, the city gives the impression that it is endorsing the display's religious message.[16]

The Court's three most conservative justices—Chief Justice William Rehnquist and Justices Antonin Scalia and Clarence Thomas—are edging toward a *nonpreferentialist test*.[17] They appear to believe that the Constitution prohibits favoritism toward a particular religion but does not prohibit government accommodation of religious activities or even nonpreferential support for religious organizations, so long as individuals are not legally coerced into participating in religious activities, and religious activities are not singled out for favorable treatment.

Applying these generalizations, we find that the establishment clause forbids states—including state universities, colleges, and school districts—to introduce devotional exercises into the public school curriculum, including school graduations.[18] However, the Supreme Court has not, as some people assume, prohibited prayer in public schools. It is not unconstitutional for students to pray in a school building. What is unconstitutional is sponsorship or encouragement of prayer *by public school authorities*.[19] Devotional reading of the Bible, recitation of the Lord's Prayer, and posting of the Ten Commandments on the walls of classrooms in public schools are also prohibited by the Constitution. A state may not forbid the teaching of evolution or require the teaching of "creation science"—the belief that human life did not evolve but rather was created by a single act of God.[20]

free exercise clause
Clause in the First Amendment that states that Congress shall make no law prohibiting the free exercise of religion.

Tax exemptions for church properties, similar to those granted other nonprofit institutions, are constitutional. State legislatures and Congress may hire chaplains to open each day's legislative session—a practice that has continued without interruption since the first session of Congress. But if done in a public school, this practice would be unconstitutional. Apparently, the difference is that legislators, as adults, are not "susceptible to religious indoctrination or peer pressure."[21] Also, as the joke goes, legislators need the prayer more.

Aid for Children Attending Parochial Schools

A troublesome area involves attempts by many states to provide financial assistance to students who attend parochial schools. The Supreme Court has tried to draw a line between permissible tax-provided aid to school children and impermissible aid to religion.

At the college level the problems are relatively simple. Tax funds may be used to construct buildings and operate educational programs at church-related schools, as long as the money is not spent directly on buildings used for religious purposes or on teaching religious subjects. Even if students choose to attend religious schools and become ministers, government aid to these students is permissible, because such aid has a secular purpose. Its effect on religion is the result of individual choice "and it does not confer any message of state endorsement of religion."[22]

At the elementary and secondary levels, however, the constitutional problems become more complicated.[23] Here the secular and religious parts of institutions and instruction are much more closely interwoven. Also, students are younger and more susceptible to indoctrination, so the chances are greater that aid to church-operated schools might become aid to religion.

Despite the constitutional obstacles, some states have provided tax credits or deductions for those who send their children to private, largely church-affiliated schools. Such deductions or credits available *only* to parents of children attending nonpublic schools are unconstitutional, but allowing tax-paying parents to deduct or take a credit from their state income taxes for what they paid for tuition and other costs to send their children to school—public or private—is constitutional, even if most of the benefit goes to those who send their children to private religious schools.[24]

The Supreme Court has also approved using tax funds to provide students who attend primary and secondary church-operated schools (except those that deny admission because of race or religion) with textbooks, standardized tests, lunches, transportation to and from school, and diagnostic services for speech and hearing problems.[25] Reversing an earlier decision, the Court has upheld programs that provide tax-supported teachers to teach remedial and enrichment classes to disadvantaged students in both public and parochial schools. Absent evidence showing that these teachers engaged in religious instruction, these programs pass the *Lemon* test.[26] The Court has also upheld the assignment of a sign-language interpreter, paid for by public funds, to accompany a deaf child to a parochial school on the grounds that this is aid to a student, not to a religion.[27]

Tax funds may *not* be used in religious schools to pay teachers' salaries, purchase equipment, produce teacher-prepared tests, repair facilities, or transport students on field trips. School authorities may not permit religious instructors to come into public school buildings during the school day to provide *religious* instruction, even on a voluntary basis.

The Free Exercise Clause

The right to hold any or no religious belief is one of our few absolute rights. The **free exercise clause** affirms that no government has authority to compel us to accept any creed or to deny us any right because of our beliefs or lack of them. Requiring religious oaths as a condition of public employment or as a prerequisite to running for public office is unconstitutional. In fact, the only time the Constitution mentions the word religion is to state: "No religious Test shall ever be required as a Qualification to any Office or public Trust under the United States" (Article VI).

The tension between the establishment and free exercise clauses became evident in 1995 when the University of Virginia denied a student group funds to pay for printing their religious newspaper. The university felt that because of the establishment clause, it could not allocate student-fee money to support a newspaper that

Children may pray in public schools, provided that the prayer is not authorized, organized, or endorsed by the school authorities.

Thinking it Through...

The board decided not to allow the Klan to put up the cross because to do so might be construed as state support for religion, which would be contrary to the establishment clause. But the courts, ultimately the U.S. Supreme Court, concluded that under these circumstances the board had violated the Klan's free speech rights. Justice Antonin Scalia, speaking for three other justices, wrote: "Religious expression cannot violate the Establishment Clause where (1) it is purely private and (2) occurs in a traditional or designated public forum, publicly announced and open to all on equal terms." Justice Sandra Day O'Connor concurred, creating a majority, because she concluded that in these circumstances there was no endorsement of religion.*

**Capitol Square Review Board v Pinette,* 515 US 753 (1995).

You Decide...

Should the Bill of Rights be amended to prohibit flag burning?

The American flag arouses patriotic emotions in Americans, many of whom fought or saw friends die under that banner. It is understandable that they would be angry to see that flag burned by protesters. Do you think the Constitution should be amended to give Congress the right to prohibit desecration of the American flag?

"primarily promotes a belief in or about a deity." The students alleged that the university had deprived them of their right to freedom of speech, including religious speech, and the Supreme Court agreed with the students.[28]

Although carefully protected, the right to practice a religion has had less protection than the right to hold particular beliefs. Prior to 1990 the Supreme Court carefully scrutinized laws alleged to infringe on religious practices and insisted that the government provide some *compelling public purpose* to justify actions that might infringe upon somebody's religion: "Only those interests of the highest order . . . can overbalance legitimate claims to the free exercise of religion."[29] In other words, the Constitution was thought to throw "a mantle of protection" around religious practices, and the burden was on the government to justify interfering with them.

Then, in *Employment Division v Smith* (1990), the Rehnquist Court significantly altered the interpretation of the free exercise clause by discarding the compelling interest test. As long as a law does not single out and ban religious practices because they are engaged in for religious reasons, the law may be applied to conduct even if it is religiously inspired.[30]

The Religious Freedom Restoration Act of 1993

The Supreme Court's decision in *Employment Division v Smith* prompted "an extraordinary congressional reaction."[31] Congress passed and President Bill Clinton signed the Religious Freedom Restoration Act of 1993 (RFRA), which was explicitly designed to reverse the *Smith* decision and restore the use of the compelling interest test. In signing the bill, President Clinton commented that reversing a decision of the Supreme Court "is a power that is rightly hesitantly and infrequently exercised by the United States Congress. But this is an issue in which that extraordinary measure was clearly called for."[32]

The Religious Freedom Restoration Act (RFRA) prohibited government—federal, state, or local—from limiting a person's exercise of religion unless the government could demonstrate a compelling governmental interest, and the law was the least restrictive means of furthering that interest. Congress asserted it had the power to pass RFRA because the Fourteenth Amendment gives it the authority to do whatever is necessary and proper to protect the rights secured by that amendment, including the right to free exercise of religion.

Reverend Anthony Cummins, pastor of St. Peter The Apostle Church, in front of his church in Boerne, Texas, after a battle with city officials who denied the church permission to build an addition to the historic structure.

When the Catholic archbishop of San Antonio was denied a building permit in 1997 to enlarge a church in Boerne, Texas, because the remodeling did not comply with the city's historical preservation plan, he claimed that the city's denial of a building permit interfered with religious freedom as protected by the Religious Freedom Restoration Act. The Supreme Court then ruled RFRA to be unconstitutional, charging that Congress had unconstitutionally intruded into the role of the courts and the states, and the act contradicted "vital principles necessary to maintain separation of powers and the federal balance."[33]

Supporters of RFRA—a rather strange combination of conservatives such as Republican Senator Orrin Hatch of Utah and liberals such as Democratic Senator Edward Kennedy of Massachusetts—countered the Supreme Court's decision with a proposal they called the Religious Liberty Protection Act. This act would build on congressional powers to regulate interstate commerce and spend for the general welfare. It stipulates that a government would lose federal funds for a program if it substantially burdens a person's religious exercise, unless the government can demonstrate a compelling interest, and it is the least restrictive means of furthering that compelling interest. If Congress should pass such a law, clearly there would be a challenge of its constitutionality before the Supreme Court.[34]

Police arrest Scott Tyler of Chicago after he set fire to an American flag on the steps of the Capitol building in Washington. The Supreme Court ruled that freedom of speech even covers "symbolic speech" like burning the U.S. flag.

FREE SPEECH AND FREE PEOPLE

Government by the people is based on every person's right to speak freely, to organize in groups, to question the decisions of the government, and to campaign openly against them. Only through free and uncensored expression of opinion can government be kept responsive to the electorate and political power be transferred peacefully. Elections, separation of powers, and constitutional guarantees are meaningless unless all persons have the right to speak frankly and to hear and judge for themselves the worth of what others have to say.

Despite the fundamental importance of free speech to a democracy, some people seem to believe speech should be free only for those who agree with them. Americans overwhelmingly support principles of tolerance when such principles are presented in general, abstract fashion—for example, "Do you believe in freedom of speech?" They are less tolerant, however, when the speech is directed at them or is critical of their race, religion, or ethnic origin.

Free speech is not simply the personal right of individuals to have their say; it is also the right of the rest of us to hear them. John Stuart Mill, whose *Essay on Liberty* (1859) is the classic defense of free speech, put it this way:

> The peculiar evil of silencing the expression of opinion, is that it is robbing the human race. . . . If the opinion is right, they are deprived of the opportunity of exchanging error for truth; if wrong, they lose what is almost as great a benefit, the clearer perception and livelier impression of truth, produced by its collision with error.[35]

As Justice Oliver Wendell Holmes, Jr., wrote:

> Persecution for the expression of opinions seems to me perfectly logical. If you have no doubt of your premises or your power and want a certain result with all your heart, you naturally express your wishes in law and sweep away all opposition. . . . But when men have realized that time has upset many fighting faiths, they may come to believe even more than they believe the very foundations of their own conduct that the ultimate good desired is better reached by free trade in ideas—that the best test of truth is the power of the thought to get itself accepted in the competition of the market, and that truth is the only ground upon which their wishes safely can be carried out. That at any rate is the theory of our Constitution. It is an experiment, as all life is an experiment.[36]

Yet some who say they believe in free speech draw the line at ideas they consider dangerous. What is a dangerous idea? Who decides? In the realm of political ideas, who can find an objective, eternally valid standard of right? Or as Chief Justice William H. Rehnquist put it for the Supreme Court, "The First Amendment recognizes no such thing as a 'false' idea."[37] The search for truth involves the possibility—even the inevitability—of error. The search cannot go on unless it proceeds freely in the minds and speech of all. This means, in the words of Justice Robert Jackson, "Freedom to differ is not limited to things that do not matter much. That would be a mere shadow of freedom. The test of its substance is the right to differ as to things that touch the heart of the existing order."[38]

Thinking it Through . . .

On June 21, 1989 the Supreme Court, in *Texas v Johnson*, decided by a 5 to 4 vote that the First Amendment protects the expressive act of burning the flag. President George Bush denounced the decision and called for a constitutional amendment that would nullify it. Congress responded by passing a federal law that would make it a crime to burn or to deface the flag—whatever one's purposes or intent. In June 1990 the Supreme Court declared that law unconstitutional in *United States v Eichman*.

A Flag Amendment to the Constitution would give Congress the power to prohibit flag desecration. Public opinion polls show strong support for it. Forty-nine state legislatures have already indicated they would ratify such an amendment, far more than the 36 needed. A Senate majority has several times voted in favor of such an amendment, but has fallen short of the two-thirds majority needed to pass a constitutional amendment.

Before you decide, you might want to read the opinions of the Supreme Court justices in *Texas v Johnson*, 491 U.S. 397 (1989) and *United States v Eichman*, 496 U.S. 310 (1990).

Even though the First Amendment explicitly denies Congress the power to pass any law abridging freedom of speech, the amendment has never been interpreted in absolute terms. Like almost all rights, the freedoms of speech and of the press are limited. In discussing the constitutional power of government to regulate speech, it is useful to distinguish among *belief, speech*, and *action*.

At one extreme is the right to *believe* as we wish. Despite occasional deviations in practice, the traditional American view is that beliefs are inviolable. No government has the right to punish a person for beliefs or to interfere in any way with freedom of conscience.

At the other extreme is *action*, which is usually subject to governmental restraint. As has been said, "The right to swing your arm ends where the other person's nose begins."

Speech stands somewhere between belief and action. It is not an absolute right, as is belief, but neither is it as exposed to governmental restraint, as is action. Some kinds of speech—obscenity, child pornography, libel, sedition, or fighting words—are not entitled in most circumstances to constitutional protection. Many problems arise in distinguishing between what does and does not fit into the categories of "nonprotected speech."

Historic Constitutional Tests

It is useful to start with the three constitutional tests developed in the first part of the twentieth century: the bad tendency doctrine, the clear and present danger doctrine, and the preferred position doctrine. Although they are no longer applied in these precise terms, they continue to reflect basic judicial and public attitudes toward governmental regulation of speech.

THE BAD TENDENCY DOCTRINE According to the **bad tendency doctrine**, the Constitution authorizes legislative bodies to forbid speech that has a tendency to cause people to engage in illegal action. Many legislators, city council members, and some state courts appear to hold this position.[39] It also seems to be the view of some college students who want to see their institution punish student colleagues or faculty who express "hateful" or "offensive" ideas.

Does the Constitution permit a city council or the trustees of a public university to punish people who publicly utter abusive racial remarks or insulting sexual taunts because they are so demeaning as to be the equivalent of a physical attack? Those who hold to the bad tendency test contend that such regulations are constitutional because abusive racial or insulting sexual remarks can in fact provoke violence, inflict injury on individuals, and create damaging racial divisions. These regulations, they contend, are a reasonable means to preserve public order and protect the rights of persons not to be abused because of their race or sex.

THE CLEAR AND PRESENT DANGER DOCTRINE Justice Oliver Wendell Holmes, Jr., is the author of this celebrated doctrine (*Schenck v United States*, 1919). "The question in every case is whether the words are used in circumstances and are of such a nature as to create a clear and present danger that they will bring about substantive evils that Congress has a right to prevent."[40] Justice Louis D. Brandeis further elaborated in a later case, "No danger flowing from speech can be deemed clear and present, and unless the incidence of the evil" that will result from a speech "is so imminent that it may befall before there is opportunity for full discussion."[41] Supporters of the **clear and present danger doctrine** concede speech is not an absolute right. Yet they believe free speech to be so fundamental to the operations of a constitutional democracy that no government should be allowed to restrict speech unless it can demonstrate a close connection between the speech and an illegal action. To shout "Fire!" *falsely* in a crowded theater is the most famous example. A government should not be allowed to interfere with speech unless it can prove, ultimately to a skeptical judiciary, that the particular speech in question presented an immediate danger of a

bad tendency doctrine
Interpretation of the First Amendment that would permit legislatures to forbid speech that has a tendency to cause people to engage in illegal action.

clear and present danger doctrine
Interpretation of the First Amendment that holds government cannot punish a person for speech unless the speech presents a clear and present danger that it will lead to illegal acts. To shout "Fire!" falsely in a crowded theater is Justice Oliver Wendell Holmes's famous example.

HATE SPEECH ON CAMPUS

A Closer Look

The Constitution limits how public universities and colleges may punish students for what they say, and cases challenging so-called "hate codes" are working their way through the courts. That speech may be insulting or racially offensive or sexist does not mean that it lacks constitutional protection. As the Supreme Court has said, "If there is a bedrock principle underlying the First Amendment, it is that the Government may not prohibit the expression of an idea simply because society finds the idea offensive or disagreeable."*

The speech of faculty and staff at universities and colleges, public or private, is also protected by the Constitution from government regulation. What of the power of the university or college itself to regulate the speech of its employees, including faculty, and its students? As state agencies, public universities and colleges are subject to the restrictions of the Constitution. Nonetheless, as an employer a public university has some leeway in regulating the speech of its employees, more leeway than it has in regulating the speech of its students—especially student speech outside of the classroom or away from residence halls. A university, for example, has some discretion—in fact, under federal laws, some obligation—to control racially or sexually harassing speech by faculty and staff. In its role of landlord for residence halls, universities and colleges have greater authority to impose reasonable time, place, and manner regulations against insulting racial, sexual, or religious slurs directed toward fellow residents.

Private universities and colleges are not subject to constitutional limitations on how they may regulate the speech of their students. However, state governments may protect the speech of students against undue regulation, and private universities that receive federal funds may find that their freedom to regulate the use of offensive speech by students is limited by federal laws and regulations. Federal and state laws regulating the responsibilities of employers to provide a workplace free from sexual harassment also apply to universities, private and public.

*United States v Eichman, 496 US 310 (1990), repeated and reemphasized in *Simon & Schuster v New York State Crime Victims Board,* 502 US 105 (1991).

Rutgers University students protest allegedly racist comments by their president, Francis Lawrence, outside a Board of Regents meeting.

major evil—for example, speech leading to a riot, destruction of property, corruption of an election, or direct interference with recruitment of soldiers.

Consider our earlier example of hate speech at a public university. Advocates of the clear and present danger doctrine would argue that, even though the public university had made such speech grounds for disciplining a student or faculty member, the regulation could not be applied constitutionally unless the university presented convincing evidence that the particular remarks would lead to a riot, or to injury to specific individuals, or be the direct cause of some other serious activity.

THE PREFERRED POSITION DOCTRINE Those who hold to the **preferred position doctrine** come close to the position that freedom of expression—that is, the use of words and pictures—should never be curtailed. This does not mean that

preferred position doctrine
Interpretation of the First Amendment that holds that freedom of expression is so essential to the operation of a democracy that judges should give it special protection and should almost never allow governments to punish persons for what they say, only for what they do.

You Decide . . .

Should the Constitution be amended to permit prayer in schools?

Congress has been considering an amendment that reads:

> "To secure the people's right to acknowledge God according to the dictates of conscience:
>
> Neither the United States nor any state shall establish any official religion, but the people's right to pray and to recognize their religious beliefs, heritage or traditions on public property, including schools, shall not be infringed.
>
> Neither the United States nor any state shall require any person to join in prayer or other religious activity, prescribe school prayers, discriminate against religion, or deny equal access to a benefit on account of religion."

The amendment is being pushed by the Christian Coalition, a national religious lobbying group. In 1998 it received the support of 224 members of the House of Representatives, a majority but not the 289 two-thirds majority the Constitution requires from each chamber in order to propose an amendment for possible ratification by three-fourths of the states.

Would you be in favor of such an amendment to the Constitution?

prior restraint

Restraint or censorship imposed before a speech is made or a newspaper published, usually presumed to be unconstitutional.

there is nothing left for judges to decide, for a line must still be drawn between speech and nonspeech.

This interpretation of the First Amendment gives these freedoms, especially freedom of speech and of conscience, a *preferred position* in our constitutional hierarchy. Judges have a special duty to protect these freedoms and should be most skeptical about laws trespassing on them. Legislative majorities are free to experiment with and to adopt various schemes regulating our lives in general, but when they tamper with freedom of speech, they interfere with the channels of the political process.

Current Constitutional Tests

The three historic doctrines continue to provide the background for debates on freedom of speech. Today, however, the Supreme Court is more apt to use the following doctrines to measure the limits of governmental power to regulate speech.

PRIOR RESTRAINT Of all the forms of governmental interference with expression, judges are most suspicious of those that impose **prior restraint**—censorship before publication. Prior restraints include governmental review and approval before a speech can be made, before a motion picture can be shown, or before a newspaper can be published. The Supreme Court has refused to declare all forms of prior censorship unconstitutional, but a "prior restraint on expression comes to this court with a 'heavy presumption' against its constitutionality."[42] Most examples of the Court's actual approval of prior restraints relate to military and security matters. Yet the Court has upheld the right of high school authorities to exercise control over the style and content of high school student newspapers.[43] It is likely that the Supreme Court would have a different view of the college press and would conclude that such publications are entitled to the same protections as other newspapers, especially college newspapers that have their own sources of funds and are operated by a corporation separate from the university.

VAGUENESS Laws touching First Amendment freedoms are required to pass rigid standards regarding vagueness. Laws must not allow those who administer them so much discretion that they could discriminate against those whose views they dislike. They must also not be so vague that people are afraid to exercise protected freedoms. The Supreme Court has struck down laws that condemn "sacrilegious" movies or publications of "criminal deeds of bloodshed or lust . . . so massed as to become vehicles for inciting violent and depraved crimes."[44]

LEAST DRASTIC MEANS Even for an important purpose, a legislature may not pass a law that impinges on First Amendment freedoms if there are other ways to handle the problem. To illustrate, a state may protect the public from unscrupulous lawyers, but it may not do so by forbidding attorneys from advertising their fees for simple services. The state could adopt other ways to protect the public from such lawyers that do not impinge on freedom of speech; it could, for example, provide for the disbarment of lawyers who mislead their clients.

CONTENT AND VIEWPOINT NEUTRALITY Laws concerning the time, place, or manner of speech that regulate some kinds of speech but not others, or that regulate speech expressing some views but not others, are much more likely to be struck down than those that are *content-neutral* or *viewpoint-neutral*; that is, laws that apply to *all* kinds of speech and to *all* views.[45] For example, the Constitution does not prohibit laws forbidding the posting of handbills on telephone poles. Yet laws prohibiting only religious handbills or handbills advocating racism or sexism would, in all probability, be declared unconstitutional because they would relate to the kind of handbills or what is being said, rather than applying to all handbills regardless of what they say.

The lack of viewpoint neutrality was the grounds for the Court striking down a St. Paul, Minnesota, ordinance that prohibited the display of a symbol that would arouse anger on the basis of race, color, creed, religion, or gender. The ordinance was not considered viewpoint neutral because it did not forbid displays that might arouse anger for other reasons, for example, because of political affiliation or sexual orientation.[46]

COMMERCIAL SPEECH Commercial speech is constitutionally protected but it is subject to more regulation than other kinds of speech. Advertising the sale of anything illegal—for example, narcotics—can be forbidden, as can false and misleading advertising. For example, television commercials for various medications must now list the various side effects that may result from taking the medication. However, a law forbidding false and misleading *political* speech or *political* advertising is clearly unconstitutional because government does not have the right to forbid anyone from expressing ideas because they are thought to be false or misleading.

The Act of Judging

Plainly, neither doctrines nor constitutional tests decide cases; judges do. Doctrines are judges' starting points. Each case requires a judge to weigh a variety of factors: What was said? Where was it said? How was it said? What was the intent of the person who said it? Which level of government is attempting to regulate the speech—a city council speaking for a few people, or the Congress speaking for many? (The Supreme Court is much more deferential to acts of Congress than to those of a city council or state legislature. Few acts of Congress have ever been struck down because of conflict with the First Amendment.) How is the government attempting to regulate the speech? By prior restraint or censorship? By punishment after the speech? Why is the government acting? To preserve the public peace? To prevent criticism of those in power? These and scores of other considerations are involved in the never-ending process of determining what the Constitution permits and what it forbids.

Freedom of the Press

Courts have carefully protected the press's right to publish information, no matter how the journalists get it. But reporters, editors, and others argue that this is not enough. They insist that the First Amendment gives them the right to ignore legal requests and to withold information. They also contend that the First Amendment gives them a *right of access*, a right to go wherever they need to go to get information.

Does the Press Have the Right to Withold Information?

Although most reporters have challenged the right of public officials to withold information, they claim the right to do so themselves, including the right to keep information from grand juries and legislative investigating committees. Without this right to withold information, reporters insist they cannot assure their sources of confidentiality, and they will not be able to get the information they need to keep the public informed.

The Supreme Court, however, has refused to acknowledge that reporters, and presumably scholars, have a constitutional right to ignore legal requests such as subpoenas and to withold information from governmental bodies.[47] If any privilege is to be given to newspeople, said the Court, it should be done by act of Congress and of the states. Congress has not yet responded to this suggestion, but many states have passed so-called *shield laws* that provide some protection for reporters from state court subpoenas.

Does the Press Have the Right to Know?

The press has argued that if reporters are excluded from places where public business is being conducted or denied access to information in government files, they are not able to perform their historic function of keeping the public informed. In similar fashion, some reporters argue that they may enter facilities such as food markets,

Thinking it Through...

Supporters—including its chief sponsor in the House of Representatives, Congressman Earnest J. Istook, a Republican from Oklahoma—argue that the Religious Freedom Amendment is necessary to reverse the impact of Supreme Court decisions since 1962, which he contends have undermined the original meaning of the First Amendment. Proponents of the amendment deny that it would interfere with religious freedom, but it would permit voluntary prayer in classrooms and at graduation exercises and allow expressions of faith in workplaces and public places, including the display of religious symbols.

Opponents contend that the amendment is both unnecessary and dangerous. It is unnecessary because the First Amendment already permits students and others to pray silently in school or in public places and to engage in other religious activities, such as wearing religious T-shirts and organizing prayer meetings and Bible clubs. The Religious Freedom Amendment, its opponents contend, is dangerous because it would undermine the establishment clause and allow religious majorities in every community to impose their beliefs on others, including putting government-sponsored religious symbols in public buildings.

SOURCE: Joan Lowy, "Republicans Pushing Prayer Amendment," *San Francisco Examiner*, March 1, 1998, p. A13; Jack Torry, "School Prayer Amendment Falls Short," *Washington Post-Gazette*, June 5, 1998. See also The Freedom Forum Online, "Religious Freedom Amendment (www.freedomforum.org/religion).

You Decide...

Should Congress require the National Endowment for the Arts (NEA) to consider "general standards of decency" when it judges the artistic merit of grant applications?

Such a requirement was adopted by Congress after the NEA made a grant for a Robert Mapplethorpe retrospective including homerotic photographs and another showing Adres Errano's photograph of a crucifix immersed in urine.

Does such a decency standard violate the First Amendment as interpreted by the Supreme Court to forbid any government from restricting expression because of objection to the viewpoint it presents? Does it violate the constitutional requirement that protects artists from arbitrary and discriminatory enforcement of vague standards?

child care centers, and homes for the mentally ill, even using false identities, to expose racial discrimination, employment discrimination, and financial frauds. The Supreme Court, however, has refused to acknowledge *a constitutional right of the press to know*, although it did concede that there is a First Amendment right for the press, along with the public, to be present at criminal trials.[48]

After a North Carolina jury awarded Food Lion, a supermarket chain, $5.5 million in punitive damages because ABC's *Primetime Live* reporters lied to get jobs at the supermarket to show bad food handling, ABC appealed, claiming reporters had a right to get inside the store by trespassing with hidden cameras to expose how unsafe and outdated food was relabeled and passed off to customers.[49]

Although they have no constitutional obligation to do so, many states have adopted *sunshine laws* requiring public agencies to open their meetings to the public and the press. Congress requires most federal executive agencies to open hearings and meetings of advisory groups to the public, and most congressional committee meetings are open to the public. Federal and state courtroom trials are also open, but judicial conferences, when the judges discuss how to decide the cases, are not.

Congress has authorized the president to establish a classification system to keep some public documents and governmental files secret, and it is a crime for any person to divulge such classified information. So far, however, although they have been threatened, no newspapers have been prosecuted for doing so.

The 1966 Freedom of Information Act

The Freedom of Information Act (FOIA) of 1966 as amended liberalized access to nonclassified government records. This act makes the records of federal executive agencies available subject to certain exceptions, such as private financial transactions, personnel records, criminal investigation files, interoffice memoranda, and letters used in internal decision making. If federal agencies fail to move promptly on requests for information, applicants are entitled to speedy judicial hearings. The burden is on an agency to explain its refusal to supply material, and if the judge decides the government has improperly withheld information, the government has to pay the legal fees. Since the inception of FOIA, more than 250,000 people have requested information, and more than 90 percent of these requests have been granted.

Some critics are concerned that FOIA has had an adverse effect on our ability to carry out confidential investigations and that its implementation costs too much. Others are concerned that FOIA may be used by businesses to obtain competitors' secrets. But most observers, especially newspaper reporters and scholars, believe that FOIA gives real meaning to the citizen's right to know.[50]

In 1995 President Clinton issued an executive order that called for automatic declassification of almost all government documents after 25 years. Any person who wants access to documents that are not declassified can appeal to an Interagency Security Classification Appeals panel, which has a record of ruling in favor of releasing documents. For example, it ordered release of papers from the Ford administration on nuclear weapons development in North Korea.

The Freedom of Information Act was supplemented by the Electronic Freedom of Information Act of 1996, calling on federal agencies to put their files online and to establish an index of all their records. Some agencies have moved to do so; others are still working to comply. NASA has done the most of the federal agencies. One of the most frequent requests to NASA's Electronic Reading Room is documents relating to unidentified flying objects (UFOs).

Argentine journalists have also used the FOIA, since it is open to any person, to get to American records about what happened during the time of military dictatorship in Argentina. The official archives in Argentina are in poor condition with many documents missing.

The worldwide importance of the Freedom of Information Act was shown by a recent tragic example from Japan, where there is no such act, although reform politicians have been advocating similar legislation for Japan.

When scientists discovered the AIDS virus and its transmission through the blood supply to hemophiliacs, pharmaceutical companies quickly developed heat-treated blood products that stopped the spread of the virus through the blood supply. When this development was announced, officials of Japan's Ministry of Health and Welfare met with officials of the dominant pharmaceutical companies in Japan and decided that there was no need to immediately require the use of heat-treated blood products in Japan. They delayed government regulations for two years.

This delay allowed these companies to develop their own versions of the blood products not to lose market share to their competitors. However, during the two-year delay hundreds of Japanese people contracted the AIDS virus unnecessarily through the blood supply. The victims later sued the Ministry of Health and Welfare and the pharmaceutical companies, but their lawsuit stalled because they had no evidence of how the ministry had made its decision. The ministry refused to acknowledge that such documents even existed. The logjam was broken only when reformist politician Naoto Kan became the minister of health and welfare and forced the ministry to release the relevant documents. When these documents became public, the lawsuit was quickly settled and the victims or their survivors received compensation. Mr. Kan is a strong proponent of a Freedom of Information Act for Japan.

Free Press Versus Fair Trials

When newspapers and television report in vivid detail the facts of a crime, interview prosecutors and police, question witnesses, and hold press conferences for defendants and their attorneys—as in the O. J. Simpson and Oklahoma City bombing cases—they may so inflame the public that finding a panel of impartial jurors and conducting a fair trial is difficult. In England, strict rules determine what the media may report, and judges do not hesitate to punish newspapers that comment on pending criminal proceedings. In the United States, in contrast, free comment is emphasized. Yet the Supreme Court has not been indifferent to protecting persons on trial from inflammatory publicity. Its remedies have been to order new trials or to instruct judges to impose sanctions on prosecutors and police, not on reporters.

Federal rules of criminal procedure forbid radio or photographic coverage of criminal cases in federal courts, but most states permit televising courtroom proceedings, and court TV programs have become very popular. People around the world followed the O. J. Simpson criminal case, one of the most publicized trials ever. Dissatisfaction with the results in high profile cases has led judges in some states to prohibit television coverage. Defendants always have the right to present evidence that television interfered with their trial, prevented fair hearings, and deprived them of due process.[51]

Thinking it Through...

The Supreme Court ruled that this "decency standard," even though vague, would not be declared unconstitutional on its face.* It explained that when the government makes grants, it is acting as a patron rather than as a sovereign, and thus the consequences of applying an imprecise standard are not constitutionally severe. More important, even conceding that the First Amendment does not allow Congress to forbid the display of art that may violate "general standards of decency," the Amendment does not require Congress to subsidize such art.

Justice David Souter, the lone dissenter, contended that when the government provides financial support for expressive works, it cannot apply a standard that discriminates because the views expressed are thought to be offensive or indecent.

*_National Endowment for Arts v Finley_, 141 L Ed 2d 500 (1998).

Other Media and Other Messages

When the Constitution was written, freedom of "the press" referred to leaflets, newspapers, and books. Today the Constitution protects other media as well—the mails, motion pictures, billboards, radio, television, cable, telephones, fax machines, and the new electronic media. Because each form of communication entails special problems, each needs a different degree of protection.

The Mails

Nearly 80 years ago, Justice Oliver Wendell Holmes, Jr., wrote in dissent: "The United States may give up the Post Office when it sees fit, but while it carries it on, the use of the mails is almost as much a part of free speech as is the right to use our

Former White House aide G. Gordon Liddy analyzes political events from a strongly conservative viewpoint on his daily radio show.

tongues."[52] In 1965 the Court adopted Holmes's view by striking down an act that had directed the postmaster general to detain foreign mailings of "communist political propaganda" and to deliver these materials only upon the addressee's request.[53] The Court has also set aside federal laws authorizing postal authorities to exclude from the mails materials they consider obscene.

Although government censorship of mail is unconstitutional, household censorship is not. The Court has sustained a law giving householders the right to ask the postmaster to order mailers to delete their names from all mailing lists and to refrain from sending any advertisements that they believe to be "erotically arousing or sexually provocative."[54] Moreover, Congress may forbid—and has forbidden—the use of mailboxes for any materials except those sent through the United States mails.

Motion Pictures and Plays

Films may be treated differently from books or newspapers, and prior censorship of films to prevent the showing of obscenity is not necessarily unconstitutional. However, laws calling for submission of films to a government review board are constitutional only if there is a prompt judicial hearing. The burden is on the government to prove to the court that the particular film in question is obscene. Prior censorship of films by review boards used to be rather common in some places. Live performances, such as plays and revues, are also entitled to constitutional protection.[55]

Handbills, Sound Trucks, and Billboards

Religious and political pamphlets, leaflets, and handbills have been historic weapons in the defense of liberty, and their distribution is constitutionally protected. So, too, is the use of their more contemporary counterparts—sound trucks and billboards. A state, for example, cannot restrain the distribution of leaflets merely to keep its streets clean.[56]

On the other side, the Supreme Court sustained a Tennessee statute prohibiting solicitation of votes and distribution of campaign literature within 100 feet of the entrance to a polling place. Even though this regulation applied to political speech in a public forum, the Court concluded that the 100-foot limit protected the integrity of the vote and the secrecy of the ballot.[57]

Radio and Television

Television today is the most important means of distributing news, as well as the primary forum for appealing for votes. Yet of all the mass media, broadcasting has received the least First Amendment protection. Congress has established a system of commercial broadcasting, supplemented by the Corporation for Public Broadcasting, which provides funds for public radio and television. The Federal Communications Commission (FCC) regulates the entire system by granting licenses and making regulations for their use.

The First Amendment would prevent censorship if the FCC tried to impose it. The First Amendment does not, however, prevent the FCC from imposing sanctions on stations that broadcast filthy words, even though such indecencies are not legally obscene. The FCC did precisely that in 1993 when it fined Infinity Broadcasting for indecent remarks by "shock jock" Howard Stern. Nor does the First Amendment prevent the FCC from refusing to renew a license if in its opinion a broadcaster has not served the public interest.

fairness doctrine
Doctrine interpreted by the Federal Communications Commission that imposed on radio and television licensees an obligation to ensure that differing viewpoints were presented on controversial issues or persons; repealed in 1987.

The First Amendment did not prevent the FCC from adopting what came to be known as the **fairness doctrine**, requiring broadcasters to cover issues of public significance and to reflect differing viewpoints. Thus, if licensees made editorial statements or endorsed candidates, they had to give people representing a different point of view an opportunity to respond. But in 1987 a Court of Appeals ordered the FCC to remove these constraints on the editorial freedom of broadcasters.[58]

Congress used to impose an *equal-time requirement* requiring licensees to give all candidates for public office equal air time. Congress later modified this requirement and then abolished it, to make possible televised presidential debates between candidates of only the two major parties.[59] Private television stations can now exclude from debates those who in their editorial judgment are not serious candidates. The Court has extended this same editorial freedom to public television stations, provided they exclude candidates not on the basis of their viewpoint but on objective standards, such as excluding candidates who have no chance to win.[60]

The Supreme Court has allowed more governmental regulation of broadcasters than of newspaper and magazine publishers because there were a limited number of airwaves. However, technological changes such as cable television, videotapes, and satellite broadcasting have opened up new ways to broadcast and have brought competition to the electronic media. Congress, acknowledging these changes, passed the Telecommunications Act of 1996, allowing telephone companies, broadcasters, and cable TV to compete with one another. In adopting the act, Congress did not abandon all government regulation of the airways. On the contrary, the act calls for many new regulations, for example requiring that all new television sets sold in the United States be equipped with V-chips that allow viewers to block programs containing violent and/or sexual material.

The Court has upheld a congressional requirement that cable television stations must carry signals of local broadcast television stations, a requirement that clearly could not be imposed on the print media or even on broadcast television.[61] The Court has also held that Congress may authorize cable operators to refuse access to leased channels for "patently offensive" programs. The Court, however, struck down congressional requirements that if a cable operator allows such offensive programming, it must be blocked and unscrambled through special devices.[62]

Telephones, Fax, E-Mail, and the World Wide Web

More than 30 million Americans log on to the Internet and are beginning to use it to buy books, clothing, jewelry, airplane tickets, stocks, and bonds. It is becoming a commercial marketplace and a major channel for communication. Congress is struggling with issues raised by cyberspace communication. Should the national government preempt state taxation? Should Congress make it a federal crime for pedophiles to stalk children over the Web? Do the existing laws against copyright piracy apply to the Web? Should there be national regulation of junk e-mail, or can state laws take care of the problem? Should Congress try to protect the privacy of those who use the Web?[63]

New technologies like the Internet have opened up the question of whether the government can constitutionally control or censor material aimed at children.

As Congress and the state legislatures begin to deal with these problems, legislators and the judges who will be reviewing subsequent lawsuits will have to apply traditional constitutional principles to new situations. For example, what about pornography and obscenity over telephones and e-mail? Congress, reflecting concern about "dial-a-porn" directed to persons under age 18, imposed a total ban on obscene and sexually oriented indecent interstate commercial telephone messages to any person, whatever their age. The Supreme Court found no constitutional obstacles to the law as it relates to "obscene" messages but declared unconstitutional the provision relating to sexually oriented messages that are not "obscene" as constitutionally defined, no matter how indecent. Justice Byron R. White wrote for the Court:

> It may well be that there is no fail-safe method of guaranteeing that never will a minor be able to access the dial-a-porn system . . . but from all we know . . . the FCC's technological approach to restricting dial-a-porn messages to adults who seek them would be extremely effective, and only a

few of the most enterprising and disobedient young people will manage to secure access to such messages.[64]

The Court has distinguished between a limited ban on indecent messages via radio and broadcast television and the ban on such messages over telephones. Radio and broadcast messages are readily available to children and can intrude into the privacy of the home without prior warning. Telephone messages, on the other hand, are available only to people who want to hear them. It may also be possible, as the Court suggested, to deny minors access to indecent telephone messages more readily than to indecent broadcasting, excepting, of course, "enterprising and disobedient young people."

What of the thousands of electronic bulletin boards, chat rooms, and the World Wide Web on which people from all over the world communicate with each other by computer? Should those who provide these services be held responsible for obscene and indecent messages? Do they have a right to exclude hate messages or racially or sexually offensive matter? And if government agencies are involved, to what extent do the First and Fourteenth Amendments limit the ability of the agencies to control the content of the messages?[65]

Nonprotected Speech

As we have noted, some kinds of speech are not entitled to constitutional protection. This does not mean that the constitutional issues relating to these kinds of speech are simple. How we prove *libel*, how we define *obscenity*, and how we determine which words are *fighting words* or *seditious speech* are hotly contested issues.

Libel

At one time newspaper publishers and editors had to take considerable care about what they wrote for fear they might be prosecuted for **libel**—written defamation—by the government or sued by individuals. Today, through a progressive raising of constitutional standards, it has become more difficult to win a libel suit against a newspaper or magazine.

In *The New York Times v Sullivan* (1964) and subsequent cases, the Supreme Court established guidelines for libel cases. The Constitution severely limits a state's power to award damages in a libel action brought by a public official against critics of official conduct. Neither public officials nor public figures can collect damages for any comments made about them, unless they can prove with "convincing clarity" the comments were made with "actual malice."[66] *Actual malice* means not merely that the defendant had bad motives but that the "statements were made with a reckless disregard for the truth," which in turn means that the defendant must have made the false publication with a high degree of awareness that the statement was not true.[67]

Public figures cannot collect damages even when subject to outrageous, clearly inaccurate, and false cartoons. Such was the case when *Hustler* magazine printed a cartoon of the Reverend Jerry Falwell; the Court held such cartoons cannot reasonably be understood as describing actual facts or actual events.[68] Nor does the mere fact that a public figure is quoted as saying something that he or she did *not* say amount to a libel. Unless the alteration in what the person said "results in material change," the mere fact that the words were deliberately altered does not equate with the constitutionally required knowledge of falsity.[69]

Constitutional standards for libel charges brought by private persons are not as rigid. State laws may permit private persons to collect damages without having to prove actual malice if they can prove the statements made about them are false and negligently published.

libel
Written defamation of another person. Especially in the case of public officials and public figures, the constitutional tests designed to restrict libel actions are very rigid.

Obscenity

Obscene publications are not entitled to constitutional protection, but members of the Supreme Court, like everybody else, have great difficulty in defining obscenity. Almost 100 separate opinions have been written on the matter.

In *Miller v California* (1973), the Court was finally able to assemble a majority opinion. Speaking for five members of the Court, Chief Justice Warren Burger tried to clarify the constitutional definition of **obscenity**. A work may be considered legally obscene provided: (1) the average person, applying contemporary standards of the particular community, would find that the work, taken as a whole, appeals to a prurient interest in sex (that is, patently offensive interests "over and beyond those that would be characterized as normal");[70] (2) the work depicts or describes in a patently offensive way sexual conduct specifically defined by the applicable law or authoritatively construed; and (3) the work, taken as a whole, lacks serious literary, artistic, political, or scientific value.[71]

Obscenity, then, is not entitled to constitutional protection. What about X-rated movies that fall short of the constitutional definition of obscenity? They are entitled to some constitutional protection, but less protection than political speech, and they are subject to greater government regulation. "The state may legitimately use the content of these materials as the basis for placing them in a different classification from other motion pictures."[72] Cities may, as New York City has done, also regulate where adult motion picture theaters may be located by zoning laws.

Sexually explicit materials either about minors or aimed at them are not protected by the First Amendment. Provided they act under narrowly drawn statutes, state and local governments can, for example, ban the knowing sale of "adult" magazines to minors, even if such materials would not be considered legally obscene if sold to adults.[73] And governments can make it a crime to depict sexual conduct by children, even if the depicted behavior would not be considered obscene if performed by adults. Nonetheless, although there is a recognized governmental interest in protecting children from harmful materials, the interest does not justify governments doing so in a manner that results in broad suppression of speech addressed to adults.[74]

Just as governments may protect minors, so apparently may they protect members of the armed forces. The Supreme Court left standing a ruling of a lower court upholding a 1996 act of Congress that forbids the sale or rental on military property of magazines or videos whose "dominant theme " is to portray nudity "in a lascivious way." The law was challenged unsuccessfully by the publishers of *Penthouse*.[75]

The Communications Decency Act of 1996

The Communications Decency Act of 1996, a part of the 1996 Telecommunications Act, made it a federal crime to use the Internet to knowingly transmit obscene or indecent and "patently offensive" words or pictures to minors. *Indecency* is defined as communication that depicts patently offensive materials about sexual or excretory activities, as measured by contemporary community standards.

In defending the act before the Supreme Court, the Justice Department contended: "The Internet threatens to give every child a free pass into the equivalent of every adult bookstore and every adult video store in the country." The American Civil Liberties Union countered, "The government cannot reduce the adult population to reading or viewing only what is appropriate for children."

The Supreme Court struck down the provisions against transmission of indecent communication and agreed with the district judge that the Internet "as the most participatory form of mass speech yet developed, deserves the highest protection from governmental intrusion." Cyberspace, the Supreme Court concluded, should be treated like books and magazines and thus subject to their broad constitutional protection.* The Internet, unlike broadcasting, is not a scarce commodity and should not be subject to the same kind of regulation as the broadcast industry. Moreover, the Internet is not as invasive as radio or television and should be given the same constitutional protection as the print media.

Congress followed with the Child Online Protection Act of 1998, which its supporters contend is narrower than the Communicators Decency Act. The new law makes it a crime for the operator of a commercial website to knowingly make available to those under age 17 sexually explicit material considered "harmful to minors." It has been immediately challenged and is now before the courts.**

This decision, *Reno v ACLU* (1997), merits your close attention. Appropriately, the decision and the oral argument can be found on the World Wide Web (www.findlaw.com). You can also learn more about this case and its implications by pulling up the home page of your favorite newspaper and searching for articles on the case, or find it and the comments about it on the Freedom Forum's home page (http://www.freedomforum).

*Benjamin Wittes, "Taming Cyberspace," *The Recorder*, December 29, 1995, p. 5. Mark Walsh, "Telecom Fight Just Beginning," *The Recorder*, February 9, 1996, p. 1.

**Pamela Mendels, "Online Smut Law Heads into Court," *The New York Times*, January 18, 1999, p. C3.

Pornography

Pornography used to be merely a synonym for *obscenity*. Pressure for regulating pornography came primarily from political conservatives and religious fundamentalists concerned that it undermines moral standards. More recently, some feminists have joined them, arguing "pornography is central in creating and maintaining sex as a basis for discrimination."[76] They contend that pornography promotes sexual abuse of individual women and perpetuates social subordination of women as a class. Some feminists define pornographic materials as sexually explicit pictures or words that depict women as sexual objects enjoying pain and humiliation or that

obscenity
Quality or state of a work that taken as a whole appeals to a prurient interest in sex by depicting sexual conduct in a patently offensive way and that lacks serious literary, artistic, political, or scientific value.

present abuse of women as a sexual stimulus for men. Some have argued that the line should be drawn to permit regulation of "depictions of sexuality that involve rape and violence against women."[77]

Advocates of regulation of pornography argue that just as sexually explicit materials about minors are not entitled to First Amendment protection, so should there be no such protection for pornographic materials. They propose that civil penalties be imposed on pornographers, and that women—and others who have had pornography forced upon them—be given the right to file complaints and sue for damages.

Not all feminists favor antipornography ordinances, yet those who do have been joined by social conservatives, and thus a new era in the battle over pornography has begun. For this new antipornography coalition to be successful, a substantial alteration in constitutional doctrine will be required.[78] The Canadian Supreme Court redefined obscenity to include materials that degrade women, and several cities in the United States have been considering the adoption of antipornography ordinances.[79] Indianapolis passed such a law, but it was declared unconstitutional.[80]

Women and men have usually differed significantly in their attitudes toward pornography. Men are less likely than women to think pornography damages adults who read it, and women are more likely to favor laws banning the sale of pornography, regardless of the age of the buyer, while men tend to favor restricting the sale of pornography to minors.

Fighting Words

Governments may punish certain well-defined and narrowly limited classes of speech that "by their very utterance inflict injury or tend to incite an immediate breach of peace."[81] These **fighting words** "have a direct tendency to cause acts of violence by the person to whom, individually, the remarks are addressed."[82] That the words are abusive, harsh, or insulting, or that they create anger, alarm, or resentment is not sufficient. Thus, a four-letter word worn on a sweatshirt was not judged to be a fighting word in the constitutional sense, especially when it was not directed to any specific person.[83] The "fighting words" category has taken on additional significance in recent years in view of the attempts by many state universities and colleges to regulate insulting racial, ethnic, and sexual slurs.

Seditious Speech

"If there is any fixed star in our constitutional constellation," Justice Robert Jackson said, "it is that no official, high or petty, can prescribe what shall be orthodox in politics, nationalism, religion, or other matters of opinion."[84] Any group can champion whatever position it wishes: vegetarianism, feminism, sexism, communism, fascism, black nationalism, white supremacy, Zionism, anti-Semitism, Americanism. It is one thing to punish persons for what they do; it is another to punish them for what they say. The story of the development of constitutional democracy is in large measure the story of making this distinction between seditious *action* and seditious *speech.*

fighting words
Words that by their very nature inflict injury upon those to whom they are addressed or cause acts of violence by them.

sedition
Attempting to overthrow the government by force or to interrupt its activities by violence.

THE SEDITION ACT OF 1798 The adoption of the Constitution and the Bill of Rights did not result in a quick, easy victory for those who wished to establish free speech in the United States.[85] In 1798, only seven years after the First Amendment had been ratified, Congress passed the first national law aimed against **sedition**—attempting to overthrow the government by force or to interrupt its activities by violence. Those were perilous times for the young Republic, for war with France seemed imminent. The Federalists, in control of both Congress and the presidency, persuaded themselves that national safety required some suppression of speech. Popular reaction to the Sedition Act helped defeat the Federalists in the elections of 1800.

They had failed to grasp the democratic idea that a person may criticize the government, oppose its policies, and work for its downfall, but still be loyal to the nation.

THE SMITH ACT OF 1940 Another attempt to limit criticism of the government was the Smith Act of 1940. The act forbids advocating overthrow of the government, distributing material teaching or advising the overthrow of government by violence, and organizing any group having such purposes. In 1950 the Supreme Court agreed that the Smith Act could be applied to the leaders of the Communist party who had been charged with conspiring to advocate the violent overthrow of the government.[86]

Since then, however, the Court has substantially modified constitutional doctrine. Now, neither Congress nor any government may outlaw mere advocacy of the abstract doctrine of violent overthrow: "The essential distinction is that those to whom the advocacy is addressed must be urged to do something now or in the future, rather than merely to believe in something."[87] Moreover, advocacy of the use of force may not be forbidden "except where such advocacy is directed to inciting or producing imminent lawless action and is likely to incite or produce such action."[88] Such narrow interpretation of the sedition laws means people are free to work for their political objectives as long as they abandon the use of force.

Freedom of Assembly

In the winter of 1977, Frank Collins, "a self-avowed Nazi," threatened to lead his small band, dressed in brown shirts and carrying swastikas, in a jack-booted march through the streets of Skokie, Illinois, a Chicago suburb with a large Jewish population.[89] Skokie's citizens included survivors of Hitler's extermination camps; many of them had relatives who lost their lives in the Holocaust. Many people, including the officials of Skokie and a local judge, argued that Collins and his followers should not be allowed to march. This would be like shouting "Fire!" in a crowded theater, they said, and to permit such a use of the streets presented a clear and present danger of inciting people to violence. Collins never actually marched in Skokie, but he did march in another part of Chicago.[90]

Another such incident occurred in the fall of 1998. Khallid Abdul Muhammad, a known racist and anti-Semite, organized a "Million Youth March" in New York City. Mayor Rudolph Giuliani denied a permit for the march on grounds that it would be a "hate march." A federal appeals court upheld a lower court ruling

New York City police in riot gear formed a human wall in front of the Million Youth March and charged the stage after Khallid Abdul Muhammad, organizer of the rally, urged the audience to riot and kill.

A street preacher addressing passersby in New York City's Times Square exercises the freedom of expression in a public forum.

that denial of the permit was unconstitutional. However, the three-judge panel placed restrictions on the event, limiting its duration to four hours and scaling it back to a six-block area. The march was surrounded by police in riot gear, who broke up the meeting after Muhammad delivered a vitriolic speech against police, Jews, and city officials.[91]

It took judicial authorities to defend the rights of these unpopular speakers and marchers. But it is not always the "bad guys" whose rights have to be protected by the courts. It also took judicial intervention in the 1960s to preserve for Martin Luther King, Jr., and for those who marched with him, the right to demonstrate in the streets of southern cities on behalf of civil rights for African Americans.

Such incidents present the classic free speech problem of the "heckler's veto," when the audience becomes so abusive that it is impossible for the speaker to be heard. It is almost always easier, and certainly politically more prudent, to maintain order by curbing public demonstrations of unpopular groups than by moving against those who are threatening them. On the other hand, if police did not have the right to order groups to disperse, public order would be at the mercy of those who resort to street demonstrations to create tensions and provoke street battles.

Public Forums and Time, Place, and Manner Regulations

The Constitution protects the right to speak, but it does not give people the right to communicate their views to everyone, every place, at every time they wish. No one has the right to block traffic or to hold parades or make speeches in public streets or on public sidewalks whenever he or she wishes. Governments may not specify what can or cannot be said, but they can make reasonable *time, place, and manner* regulations for protests or parades. The extent of government regulation varies with where the assembly takes place.

The Supreme Court has divided public property into three categories: public forums limited public forums, and nonpublic forums. The extent to which governments may limit access depends on the kind of forum involved. *Public forums* are public places historically associated with the free exercise of expressive activities, such as streets, sidewalks, and parks. Courts look closely at time, place, and manner regulations that apply to these traditional public forums to ensure that they are being applied evenhandedly, and that action is not taken because of what is being said rather than how and where or by whom it is being said.[92]

Other kinds of public property, such as designated rooms in a city hall or after-hour use of school buildings, may be designated as *limited public forums*, available for assembly and speech for limited purposes, a limited amount of time, and even for a limited class of speakers (such as only students, only teachers, or only employees), provided the distinctions between those allowed access and those not allowed access are viewpoint neutral.

Nonpublic forums include public facilities such as libraries, courthouses, schools, swimming pools, and government offices that are open to the public but are not public forums. As long as people use such facilities within the normal bounds of conduct, they may not be constitutionally restrained from doing so. However, people may be excluded from such places as a government office or a school if they engage in activities for which the facilities were not created. They have no right to interfere with programs or try to appropriate facilities—especially facilities such as a university president's office—in order to stage a political protest.

Does the right of peaceful assembly and petition include the right to violate a law nonviolently but deliberately? We have no precise answer, but in general, **civil disobedience**, even if peaceful, is not a protected right. When Dr. Martin Luther King, Jr., and his followers refused to comply with a state court's injunction forbidding them to parade in Birmingham without first securing a permit, the Supreme Court sustained their conviction, even though there was serious doubt about the constitutionality of the injunction and the ordinance on which it was based.[93]

civil disobedience
When people refuse to obey the law or refuse to comply with the orders of public officials as a means of expressing their opposition to the government or some of its laws.

The First Amendment right of anti-abortion protesters to picket in front of abortion clinics has come into conflict with a woman's right to go to an abortion clinic. Protesters have often massed in front of clinics shouting at employees and patrons and blocking entrances to the clinic. The Supreme Court has struck down provisions that prohibit protesters from peacefully, even if forcefully, expressing their views. But the Court has upheld injunctions that keep anti-abortion protesters outside of a reasonable buffer zone around abortion clinics, and also upheld injunctions that were issued because of prior unlawful conduct by the protesters. The proper constitutional test for such injunctions is "whether the challenged provisions . . . burden no more speech than necessary to serve a significant government interest," such as public safety or the right of women to go into such a clinic.[94]

Forms of Citation

In this and the next several chapters, we discuss constitutional rules at length, and to talk about the Constitution is to talk about Supreme Court decisions. Many of these decisions are cited in the notes at the back of the book so that you can look them up if you wish. Two forms of citation are used:

1. Official Supreme Court reports are cited as: *Gitlow v New York*, 268 US 652 (1925). This means that this case can be found in the 268th volume of the *United States Supreme Court Reports* on page 652, and it was decided in 1925. These reports are published by the U.S. Government Printing Office.
2. For more recent cases, see the advance sheets of *United States Supreme Court Reports*, published by the Lawyers' Cooperative Publishing Company of Rochester, New York. An example is a case involving First Amendment issues, *National Endowment for Arts v Finley*. It is cited 141 L Ed 2d 500 (1998). This means that it can be found in volume 141 of the Lawyers' Edition, second series, starting on page 500, and it was decided in 1998.

Assembly on Private Property

The right to assemble to petition the government for a redress of grievances does not include the right to trespass on private property. A state may protect property owners against those who attempt to convert property to their own uses, even if they are doing so to express ideas.

The profusion of large, privately owned shopping malls that cover many acres and are larger than some towns presents some difficult constitutional issues. The Supreme Court has set the following guidelines: privately owned shopping malls are neither public streets nor places of public assembly; no one has a constitutional right to use such a mall to hand out political leaflets, to picket for political purposes, or otherwise to exercise First Amendment freedoms. On the other hand, states and cities may legally obligate the owners of such centers to permit their use for peaceful political purposes, such as distributing handbills or getting people to sign petitions.[95]

In other words, although people have no constitutional right to engage in political action in a nonpublic shopping center, neither do the owners of such centers have a constitutional right to close them to political action in the face of reasonable state or local regulations providing for access that does not interfere with their primary commercial purposes.

online

First Amendment Issues on the Internet

For comprehensive coverage of all First Amendment issues, see the home page of the Freedom Forum:

http://www.freedomforum.org

Also see the home page of the Reporters Committee for Freedom of the Press:

http://www.rcfp.org/rcfp

For a liberal perspective on the First Amendment, check out the American Civil Liberties Union at:

http://www.aclu.org

For Supreme Court decisions and opinions:

http://www.findlaw.com/casecode/supreme.html

For a conservative perspective, check out the American Center for Law and Justice:

http://www.ACLj.org.

There is also a site for the Student Press Law Center:

http://www.splc.org

For more Internet resources on First Amendment Rights, see our home page at:

http://www.prenhall.com/burns

SUMMARY

1. First Amendment freedoms—freedom of religion, freedom from the establishment of religion, freedom of speech, freedom of the press, freedom of assembly and petition, and freedom of association—are at the heart of a healthy constitutional democracy.
2. Since World War I, the Supreme Court has become the primary branch of government for giving meaning to these constitutional restraints. And since 1925 these constitutional limits have been applied not only to Congress but to all governmental agencies—national, state, and local.
3. Clashes about First Amendment freedoms are not usefully thought of as battles between the "good guys" and the "bad guys" or as dramas in which judges rush to the rescue of liberty. Rather, these are arguments over conflicting notions of what is in the public interest.
4. Over the years, the Supreme Court has taken a practical approach to First Amendment freedoms. It has refused to make them absolute rights above any kind of governmental regulation, direct or indirect, or to say that they must be preserved at whatever price. But the justices have recognized that a constitutional democracy tampers with these freedoms at great peril. They have insisted upon compelling justification before permitting these rights to be limited. How compelling the justification is, in a free society, will always remain an open question.

KEY TERMS

civil liberties 76
civil rights 76
political rights 76
rights of persons accused of crimes 76
legal privileges 76
civil law 76
due process clause 76
selectively incorporated 77
new judicial federalism 77
establishment clause 77
free exercise clause 78
bad tendency doctrine 82
clear and present danger doctrine 82
preferred position doctrine 83
prior restraint 84
fairness doctrine 88
libel 90
obscenity 91
fighting words 92
sedition 92
civil disobedience 94

FURTHER READING

STEPHEN BATES, *Battleground* (Poseidon, 1993).

LEE C. BOLLINGER, *Images of a Free Press* (University of Chicago Press, 1991).

JAMES MACGREGOR BURNS AND STEWART BURNS, *A People's Charter: The Pursuit of Rights in America* (Knopf, 1991).

T. BARTON CARTER, *The First Amendment and the Fifth Estate: Regulation of Electronic Mass Media*, 4th ed. (Foundation Press, 1996).

T. BARTON CARTER, MARC A. FRANKLIN, AND JAY B. WRIGHT, *The First Amendment and the Fourth Estate*, 7th ed. (Foundation Press, 1997).

ZECHARIAH CHAFEE, JR., *Free Speech in the United States* (Harvard University Press, 1941).

JESSE CHOPER, *Securing Religious Liberty: Principles for Judicial Interpretation of Religion Clauses* (University of Chicago Press, 1995).

EDWARD J. CLEARY, *Beyond the Burning Cross: A Landmark Case of Race, Censorship, and the First Amendment* (Random House, 1995).

DONALD L. DRAKEMAN, *Church-State Constitutional Issues: Making Sense of the Establishment Clause* (Greenwood, 1991).

MIKE GODWIN, *Cyber Rights: Defending Free Speech in the Digital Age* (Times Books, 1998).

MARK A. GRABER, *Transforming Free Speech: The Ambiguous Legacy of Civil Libertarianism* (University of California Press, 1991).

KENT GREENAWALT, *Fighting Words: Individuals, Communities, and Liberties of Speech* (Princeton University Press, 1995).

MARJORIE HEINS, *Sex, Sin and Blasphemy: A Guide to America's Censorship Wars* (New Press, 1993).

NAT HENTOFF, *Living the Bill of Rights: How to Be an Authentic American* (HarperCollins, 1998).

EUGENE W. HICKOK, JR., ED., *The Bill of Rights: Original Meaning and Current Understanding* (University Press of Virginia, 1991).

PETER IRONS, ED., *May It Please the Court: The First Amendment—Live Recordings and Transcripts of the Oral Arguments Made Before the Supreme Court in Sixteen Key Decisions* (New Press, 1997).

JAMES E. LEAHY, *The First Amendment, 1791–1991: Two Hundred Years of Freedom* (McFarland, 1991).

LEONARD W. LEVY, *The Establishment Clause: Religion and the First Amendment* (Macmillan, 1986).

ANTHONY LEWIS, *Make No Law: The Sullivan Case and the First Amendment* (Random House, 1991).

CATHARINE A. MACKINNON, *Only Words* (Harvard University Press, 1993).

JOHN STUART MILL, *Essay on Liberty* (1859), in *The English Philosophers from Bacon to Mill*, ed. Arthur Burtt (Random House, 1939), pp. 949–1041.

MELVILLE B. NIMMER, *Nimmer on Freedom of Speech: A Treatise on the Theory of the First Amendment* (Mathew Binder, 1987).

JOHN T. NOONAN, JR., *The Lustre of Our Country: The American Experience of*

Religious Freedom (University of California Press, 1998).

J. W. PELTASON, *Understanding the Constitution*, 14th ed. (Harcourt Brace, 1997).

LUCAS A. POWE, JR., *The Fourth Estate and the Constitution: Freedom of the Press in America* (University of California Press, 1991).

DAVID M. RABBAN, *Free Speech in Its Forgotten Years* (Cambridge University Press, 1997).

JONATHAN RAUCH, *Kindly Inquisitors: The New Attacks on Free Thought* (University of Chicago Press, 1993).

ROBERT D. RICHARDS, *Freedom's Voice: The Perilous Present and Uncertain Future of the First Amendment* (Brassey's Inc., 1998).

GEOFFREY R. STONE, RICHARD A. EPSTEIN, AND CASS R. SUNSTEIN, EDS., *The Bill of Rights in the Modern State* (University of Chicago Press, 1992).

NADINE STROSSEN, *Defending Pornography: Free Speech, Sex, and the Fight for Women's Rights* (Scribner's, 1995).

CASS R. SUNSTEIN, *Democracy and the Problems of Free Speech* (Free Press, 1993).

ROBERT J. WAGMAN, *The First Amendment Book* (World Almanac, 1991).

EQUAL
RIGHTS
UNDER
THE
LAW

5

CHAPTER OUTLINE

- Equality and Equal Rights
- Equal Protection of the Laws: What Does It Mean?
- Voting Rights
- Education Rights
- Rights to Public Accommodations, Jobs, and Homes
- Affirmative Action: Is It Constitutional?
- Equal Rights Today

CONSIDER AGAIN THE RINGING WORDS OF THE DECLARATION OF INDEPENDENCE: "WE HOLD THESE TRUTHS TO BE SELF-EVIDENT, THAT ALL MEN ARE CREATED equal, that they are endowed by their Creator with certain unalienable Rights, that among these are Life, Liberty, and the pursuit of Happiness." In this one sentence the Declaration affirmed the precious rights of *equality* and *liberty* and appeared to rate equality at least on a par with liberty. The Declaration does not specify equality of white, Christian, or Anglo-Saxon men, but of *all* men (which at that time meant white, property-owning Anglo-Saxon men). It has taken more than two hundred years for that definition to be expanded to include all races, all religions, and all women. This creed of individual dignity and equality is older than our Declaration of Independence; its roots go back into the teachings of Judaism and Christianity.

What about the Constitution? What was the framers' attitude toward liberty and equality in that historic document? Although you will not find any reference to the idea of equality (not even the word itself appears in the Constitution or in the array of liberties that form the Bill of Rights), we know the framers believed that all men—at least all white men—were equally entitled to life, liberty, and the pursuit of happiness. But like the Declaration, the Constitution referred to "men" or "him," not to women, and none of its lofty sentiments applied to slaves, who enjoyed neither liberty nor equality.

The framers resolved their ambiguity about what kind of equality and for whom by creating a system of government designed to protect what they called *natural rights.* (Today we speak of *human rights*, but the idea is the same.) By **natural rights** the framers meant that every person has an equal right to protection against arbitrary treatment, an equal right to the liberties guaranteed by the Bill of Rights. These rights do not depend on citizenship; they are not granted by governments. They are the rights of *all* people.

The terms *civil liberties* and *civil rights* are often used interchangeably to refer to rights that are protected by the constitutional systems of constitutional democracies. *Civil liberties* is sometimes used more narrowly to refer to freedom of conscience, religion, and expression. *Civil rights* is used to refer to the right not to be discriminated against because of race, religion, gender, ethnic origin, or sexual orientation. Our Constitution provides two ways of protecting civil rights: first, it ensures that government officials *do not discriminate* against us; second, it grants national and state governments the power to *protect* these civil rights against interference by private individuals.

This chapter is concerned with both the protection of our rights from *abuse by government* and the protection through government of our right to be free from *abuse by our fellow citizens.* In this chapter we focus on the struggles of African Americans, women, Hispanics, Asian Americans, and Native Americans to secure the basic civil rights to the vote, to an education, to a job, and to a place to live on equal terms with their fellow citizens.

A person growing up in an affluent community faces a very different set of opportunities from a person growing up in a slum neighborhood.

EQUALITY AND EQUAL RIGHTS

Americans are committed to equality. *Equality,* however, is an elusive term. The concept for which there is the greatest consensus and is most clearly written into the Constitution is that everybody should have *equality of opportunity* regardless of race, ethnic origin, religion, and, in recent years, gender and sexual orientation. Ensuring this equality of opportunity has led to the historic struggle for civil rights in this country.

A variation of the concept of equal opportunity is *equality of starting conditions.* There is not much equal opportunity if one person is born into a well-to-do family, lives in a quiet suburb, is well fed, and receives a good education, while another is born into a poor, broken family, lives in an inner-city neighborhood, and attends inferior schools. Thus, it is argued, if we are to have equality of opportunity in a meaningful sense, we must compensate the disadvantaged through federal programs such as Head Start, which provides children from poor families with preschool experiences to prepare them for elementary school.

Compensating people so they will have equality of starting conditions can be accomplished by ensuring that individuals are not placed at a disadvantage because of prejudice or poverty. Traditional emphasis has been upon *individual* achievement, but such action sometimes shades into a concept of *equality between groups.* When large disparities in wealth and advantage exist between groups—as between blacks and whites or between women and men—equality becomes a highly divisive political issue. The disadvantaged tend to emphasize economic and social factors that exclude them from the mainstream. They champion programs like **affirmative action**, which are designed to provide special help to people based upon their group memberships. Whether such programs promote or deny equality is one of the most controversial current debates, as exemplified by the passage of Proposition 209 in California to end affirmative action programs.

Finally, equality can also mean *equality of results.* One perennial debate, especially among college students, is whether social justice and genuine equality can exist in a nation in which some people have so much and others have so little. Socialists and others call for a more equal distribution of wealth, yet such a view has had little support in the United States. There is considerable support for guaranteeing a minimum floor—a "safety net"—below which no one should be allowed to fall, but many people fear that insistence on equality of results would undermine equality of opportunity. The American view is not that everybody should have the same amount of material goods, but that, whatever a person's economic status for the moment, he or she should be able to expect that things will get better, and that hard work and risk-taking will be rewarded.

To put into perspective the court decisions, laws, and other governmental actions relating to civil rights for women and minorities, we review next the political and social contexts in which these constitutional issues were raised. Constitutional questions do not involve only court decisions, laws, and constitutional amendments; they encompass the entire social, economic, and political system. Although the struggles of all groups are interwoven, they are not identical, so we comment briefly and separately on each.

natural rights
Rights of all people to dignity and worth.

affirmative action
Remedial action designed to overcome the effects of past discrimination against minorities and women.

The Struggle for Racial Justice

Americans had a painful confrontation with the problem of race before, during, and after the Civil War. As a result of the northern victory, the Thirteenth, Fourteenth, and Fifteenth Amendments became part of the Constitution. During the Reconstruction period that followed, Congress passed a series of civil rights laws to implement these amendments and established programs to provide educational and social services for the freed slaves.

SEGREGATION AND WHITE SUPREMACY Before Reconstruction programs had any significant effect, however, the southern political leadership was restored to power, and by 1877, Reconstruction was ended. Northern political leaders abandoned African Americans to their fate at the hands of their former white masters, presidents no longer concerned themselves with the enforcement of civil rights laws, and Congress enacted no new ones. The Supreme Court either declared old laws unconstitutional or interpreted them so narrowly that they were ineffective. The Court also gave such a limited construction to the Thirteenth, Fourteenth, and Fifteenth Amendments that they failed to accomplish their intended purpose of protecting the rights of African Americans.

White supremacy was unchallenged in the South, where most African Americans lived. They were kept from voting; they were forced to accept menial jobs; and they were denied educational opportunities. African Americans were being lynched on an average of one every four days, and few whites raised a voice in protest.

During World War I, African Americans began to migrate to northern cities to seek jobs in war factories. This relocation was accelerated by the New Deal and World War II. As migration of African Americans out of the rural South into southern and northern cities shifted the racial composition of cities, the African American vote became important in national elections. Although discrimination continued, there were more jobs and more social gains. Above all, these changes created an African American middle class opposed to segregation as a symbol of servitude and a cause of inequality. By the middle of the twentieth century, urban African Americans in northern cities were active and politically powerful citizens. There was a growing demand for the abolition of color barriers.

THE NATIONAL GOVERNMENT RESPONDS In the 1930s, African Americans, who at that time lacked political power to make their demands effective, began resorting to lawsuits to challenge the doctrine of segregation. After World War II, this civil rights litigation began to have an impact. In the years that followed, the Supreme Court outlawed all forms of government-imposed segregation and struck down most of the devices that had been used by state and local authorities to keep African Americans from voting.

Presidents Truman and Eisenhower used their executive authority to fight segregation in the armed services and the federal bureaucracy, and directed the Department of Justice to enforce whatever civil rights laws were available. Still Congress held back. Then as the 1950s came to a close, the emerging national consensus in favor of governmental action to protect civil rights and the growing political voice of African Americans in the northern states began to have some influence on Congress. In 1957 Congress overrode a southern filibuster in the Senate and enacted the first federal civil rights laws since Reconstruction.

A TURNING POINT Decades after the Supreme Court had declared government-imposed racial segregation to be unconstitutional, most African Americans still were kept from voting. In the North many legal barriers in the path of equal rights had fallen, yet most African Americans still could not buy houses where they wanted, secure the jobs they needed, or find educational opportunities for their children. In

COLOR-BLINDED

Glenn C. Loury

Affirmative action is an application of positive discrimination, a principle essential for rectifying social and economic inequalities.

Glenn Loury, an economics professor at Boston University, defends affirmative action as an application of positive discrimination, a principle essential for rectifying social and economic inequalities. He begins by stating that the "nondiscrimination principle"—which "holds that personal characteristics like race, sex, or ethnicity should have no moral relevance"—sounds very good in theory. In this "color-blind" theory, everyone is judged on merit alone, and the better qualified person gets admitted to the elite college or gets the job regardless of his or her ethnicity. According to Loury, however, "For multiracial, multiethnic America, this [color-blindness] poses a permanent, intractable dilemma." Most simply, the dilemma is that the nondiscrimination principle sacrifices moral ends for the sake of legitimate means.

Loury frames his arguments in the terms of a timeless political debate: the distinction between substantive and procedural justice. Substantive justice is the idea that people get what they deserve. In its extreme formulation, it occurs when the guilty are convicted and the innocent acquitted, regardless of the fairness of the procedures that gain the conviction or acquittal. Procedural justice is the concept that justice is achieved when essential legal procedures, such as informing defendants of the charges against them and allowing them the assistance of counsel and the ability to call witnesses, are faithfully executed. In its purely theoretical sense, procedural justice means that justice is achieved if all essential procedures are followed, regardless of whether or not the guilty are convicted and the innocent go free.

Loury maintains that the nondiscrimination principle guarantees only procedural justice. He admits that procedural justice does provide limited fairness in selection procedures. He insists, however, that "fairness is neither a necessary nor a sufficient condition for the attainment of substantive justice in a racially divided democracy" because "public policy can be color-blind yet unfairly contrary to the interests of a racial minority—'benign neglect' being the most obvious example."★

Source: Glenn C. Loury, *New Republic* 219, August 24, 1988, p. 12.

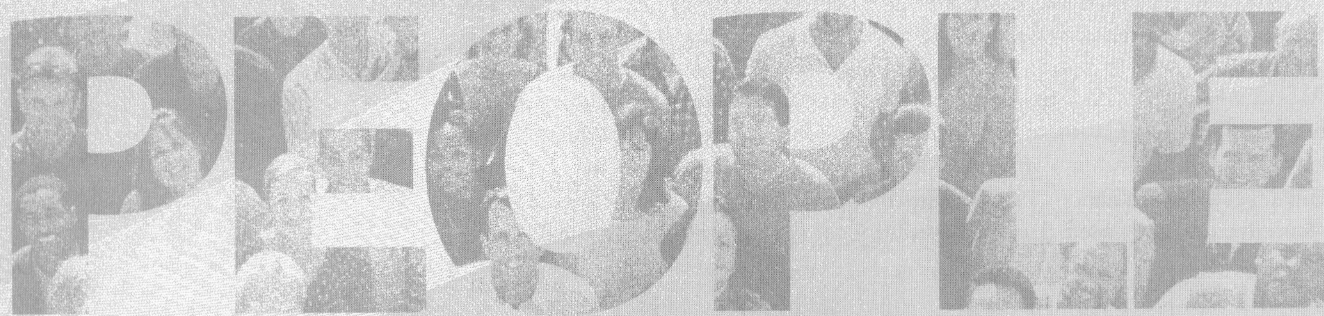

THE NEXT RECONSTRUCTION

Tamar Jacoby

Tamar Jacoby, a senior fellow at the Manhattan Institute, is also disappointed with racial inequality in America. She disagrees with Loury, however, on the role of positive discrimination in achieving equality. Even positive discrimination, Jacoby believes, highlights our distinguishing characteristics, such as skin color, and if genuine equality and harmony are to be achieved, we must come to realize that our similarities surpass our differences.

For Jacoby, the city of Atlanta, Georgia, illustrates America's profound racial problems. Atlantans appear to live in better racial harmony than people in other cities with large minority populations like Detroit. "Atlanta's public life, in restaurants, theaters, parks, and shopping malls, is encouragingly integrated, and both blacks and whites feel they have a stake in the booming future." Despite the appearance of harmony, however, poverty-stricken blacks are neglected in Atlanta just as elsewhere, and although Atlanta's workplaces are harmoniously integrated, neighborhoods, country clubs, and schools are usually exclusively white or black. "Almost everyone in the city has occasion to work with someone of the other race, but very few have made real friendships across the color line."

Jacoby objects to Atlanta's deep racial divisions: "[W]hat prevails in Atlanta isn't racial harmony. It's peaceful coexistence—a wary truce between two groups who believe they are fundamentally different and will always live separately." To Jacoby, separation perpetuates distrust and distinction. The problem with affirmative action and other forms of positive discrimination is that they institutionalize a focus on differences that perpetuates voluntary segregation. Proponents of affirmative action "have argued that it's worth reinstating preferences in order to preserve what little integration we have. But to settle for that would be to miss the opportunity to achieve much more."

Jacoby admits that she asks a lot. Overcoming racial separation means forsaking the peaceful coexistence for which blacks as well as whites have settled. "Peaceful coexistence is easier than forging new, more respectful and equitable ways to live together. Peaceful coexistence allows everyone to hold on to stereotypes: we never get close enough, after all, to disabuse ourselves." ★

If genuine equality and harmony are to be achieved, we must come to realize that our similarities surpass our differences.

SOURCE: Tamar Jacoby, "The Next Reconstruction," *New Republic* 218, June 22, 1998, pp. 19–21.

For further information about this debate, go to **http://www.prenhall.com/burns** *and click on the Debate Icon in Chapter 5.*

Fire fighters in Birmingham, Alabama, turn their hoses full blast on African American civil rights demonstrators in the 1960s. At times the water came with such force, even on children demonstrating, that it literally tore the bark off fully grown trees.

the South they could not eat in a restaurant or walk on the streets of so-called "white neighborhoods" without being insulted.

But times were changing. What had once been thought of as a "southern problem" was finally being recognized as a national challenge. A massive social, economic, and political movement began to supplement the struggles in the courtrooms. It began in Montgomery, Alabama, on December 1, 1955, when Rosa Parks refused to give up a seat in the front of a bus and was removed from the bus. The black community responded by boycotting city buses.

The boycott worked. It also produced a charismatic national civil rights leader, the Reverend Martin Luther King, Jr. Through his doctrine of nonviolent resistance, Dr. King gave a new dimension to the struggle. By the early 1960s, new organizational resources came into existence in almost every city to support and sponsor sit-ins, freedom rides, live-ins, and nonviolent demonstrations. These measures were often met with violence, and at times state and local governments failed to protect the victims or to prosecute those responsible for the violence.[1]

The forces of social discontent exploded in the summer of 1963. The explosion started with a demonstration in Birmingham, Alabama, which was countered with fire hoses, police dogs, and mass arrests. It ended in a march in Washington, D.C., where at least 250,000 people heard Dr. King and other civil rights leaders speak, and countless millions watched them on television. By the time the summer was over, there was hardly a city, North or South, that had not had demonstrations, protests, or sit-ins. Some also had violence.

This direct action had some effect. Many cities enacted civil rights ordinances, more schools were desegregated, and President John Kennedy urged Congress to enact a comprehensive civil rights bill. Late in 1963, the nation's grief over the assassination of President Kennedy, who had become identified with civil rights goals, added political fuel to the drive for decisive federal action to protect civil rights.[2] President Lyndon Johnson made civil rights legislation his highest priority, and on July 2, 1964, after months of debate, he signed into law the Civil Rights Act of 1964.[3]

women's suffrage
The right of women to vote.

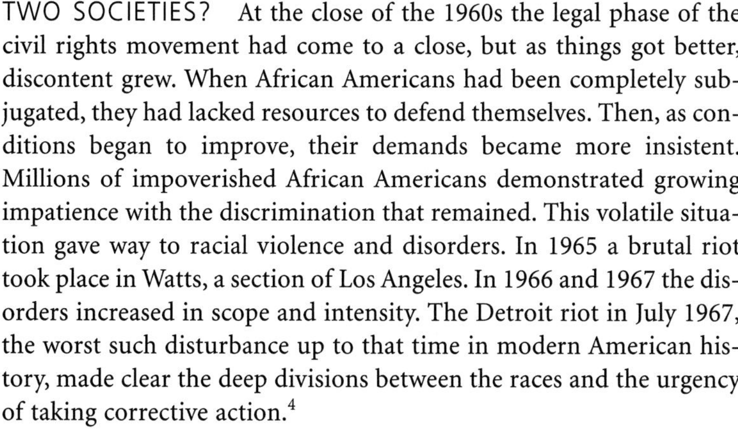

TWO SOCIETIES? At the close of the 1960s the legal phase of the civil rights movement had come to a close, but as things got better, discontent grew. When African Americans had been completely subjugated, they had lacked resources to defend themselves. Then, as conditions began to improve, their demands became more insistent. Millions of impoverished African Americans demonstrated growing impatience with the discrimination that remained. This volatile situation gave way to racial violence and disorders. In 1965 a brutal riot took place in Watts, a section of Los Angeles. In 1966 and 1967 the disorders increased in scope and intensity. The Detroit riot in July 1967, the worst such disturbance up to that time in modern American history, made clear the deep divisions between the races and the urgency of taking corrective action.[4]

THE KERNER COMMISSION After the racial disturbances in 1967, President Johnson appointed a special Advisory Commission on Civil Disorders to investigate the origins of the riots and to recommend measures to prevent or contain such disasters in the future. When the commission (called the Kerner Commission after its chair, Governor Otto Kerner of Illinois) issued its report, it said in stark, clear language: "What white Americans have never fully understood—but what the Negro can never forget—is that white society is deeply implicated in the ghetto. White institutions created it, white institutions maintain it, and white society condones it." The basic conclusion of the commission was that "our nation is moving toward two societies, one black, one white—separate and unequal" and that "only a commitment to national action on an unprecedented scale" could change this trend.[5]

The commission made sweeping recommendations on jobs, education, housing, and the welfare system. But other events diverted attention from these recommendations: the Vietnam War; Watergate; the election of Ronald Reagan and George Bush, who were reluctant to take governmental actions to enforce civil rights; and a growing skepticism about the effectiveness of governmental action generally.

The Clinton administration has been somewhat more sympathetic toward the use of governmental power to deal with issues of inequality than its immediate predecessors, but because of budgetary constraints, it has been unable or unwilling to promote any major initiatives directly aimed at the problems of the inner cities.

Women's Rights

The struggle for equal rights for women was intertwined with the battle to secure equal rights for African Americans. The Seneca Falls Women's Rights Convention (1848), which launched the women's movement, involved men and women who had been active in the campaign to abolish slavery. But as the Civil War approached, women were urged to abandon their cause and devote their energies to getting rid of slavery.[6] The Civil War brought the women's movement to a halt, and the Fourteenth and Fifteenth Amendments did not advance voting rights for women, even as they guaranteed that right to freed male slaves. The temperance movement to prohibit the sale of liquor diverted attention away from women's rights as well.

By the turn of the century, however, a vigorous campaign was under way for **women's suffrage**—the right to vote. The first victories came in western states, where Wyoming led the way. As a territory,

I Have a Dream . . .

"Five score years ago, a great American in whose symbolic shadow we stand signed the Emancipation Proclamation. This momentous decree came as a great beacon light of hope to millions of Negro slaves who had been seared in the flames of withering injustice. It came as a joyous daybreak to end the long night of captivity. But one hundred years later, we must face the tragic fact that the Negro is still not free. One hundred years later, the life of the Negro is still sadly crippled by the manacles of segregation and the chains of discrimination. One hundred years later, the Negro lives on a lonely island of poverty in the midst of a vast ocean of material prosperity. One hundred years later, the Negro is still languishing in the corners of American society and finds himself an exile in his own land. So we have come here today to dramatize an appalling condition. . . .

I have a dream that one day this nation will rise up and live out the true meaning of its creed: 'We hold these truths to be self-evident, that all men are created equal.'

I have a dream that one day on the red hills of Georgia the sons of former slaves and the sons of former slave owners will be able to sit down together at the table of brotherhood.

I have a dream that one day even the state of Mississippi, a desert state sweltering with the heat of injustice and oppression, will be transformed into an oasis of freedom and justice.

I have a dream that my four little children will one day live in a nation where they will not be judged by the color of their skin but by the content of their character."

SOURCE: Martin Luther King, Jr., address at the Lincoln Memorial, August 28, 1963.

WE THE PEOPLE

Women's History Is Half of History

1840 – 1880

Lucretia Mott, Elizabeth Cady Stanton barred from the World Antislavery Convention

Declaration of Sentiments, Seneca Falls

Women's Rights Convention

Harriet Beecher Stowe, *Uncle Tom's Cabin*

Sojourner Truth

Women's Loyal League

Clara Barton, Mother Bickerdyke, nurses

Equal Rights Association

Clara Barton, Red Cross

Radcliffe, Bryn Mawr founded

Woman's Christian Temperance Union

Mother Mary Jones, labor organizer

Emily Dickinson died 1886

1840 1860 1880

14th Amendment makes blacks citizens and adds the word "male" to the Constitution

15th Amendment provides for black male suffrage

Transcontinental railroad completed, 1869

Emancipation Proclamation

Texas admitted to the Union

Dred Scott decision

Lincoln elected

Lee surrenders to Grant

Reconstruction

Civil service reform

1900 – 1920

International Council of Women

National American Women Suffrage Association

Jane Addams, Hull House

Susan B. Anthony

Women's Trade Union League

Brandeis brief, protective legislation

National Woman's Party

Suffragists jailed for White House demonstration

Margaret Sanger birth control

Women get the vote

League of Women Voters formed

Alice Paul introduces Equal Rights Amendment (ERA)

Margaret Mead, *Coming of Age in Samoa*

Eleanor Roosevelt active first lady

Frances Perkins, secretary of labor

1900 1920

Populists

Battle of Wounded Knee

Progressive Era

Theodore Roosevelt

Woodrow Wilson

U.S. enters World War I

19th Amendment secures women's suffrage

Treaty of Versailles

Prohibition

Herbert Hoover

Depression

FDR, New Deal

1940 – 1980

Rosie the Riveter

800,000 women fired by aircraft companies

Women's Service Corps

Betty Friedan, *The Feminine Mystique*

Mary McCarthy, *The Group*

Title VII prohibits sex discrimination in employment

National Organization for Women (NOW)

ERA passed by Congress

The "Pill"

Supreme Court legalizes abortion in *Roe v Wade*

Title IX prohibits sex discrimination in education

International Women's Year

ERA ratification deadline extended

Women's Educational Equity Act passed

Sandra Day O'Connor, first woman Supreme Court justice appointed

ERA deadline passed without ratification

1940 1960 1980

Pearl Harbor

Atomic bomb

World War II ends

Korean War

Dwight D. Eisenhower

The New Frontier

Civil Rights Act

Kennedy assassinated

The Great Society

March on Washington, Martin Luther King Jr.

Vietnam

Student unrest

Peace movement

Executive order mandates affirmative action

Richard Nixon

Moon landing

Watergate

Cambodia

Jimmy Carter

Ronald Reagan

1990 – 2000

Geraldine Ferraro nominated as vice-presidential candidate of Democratic party

Supreme Court restricts *Roe v Wade*

Clarence Thomas Supreme Court confirmation hearings

54 women elected members of Congress in "The Year of the Woman"

Supreme Court reaffirms core holding of *Roe v Wade*

Ruth Bader Ginsburg appointed to the Supreme Court

Janet Reno named attorney general

Madeleine Albright named secretary of state

Increase of women executives in major corporations

1990 2000

Challenger explodes

George Bush

Bill Clinton

Wyoming had given women the right to vote. It is said when members of Congress in Washington grumbled about this "petticoat provision," the Wyoming legislators replied they would stay out of the Union one hundred years rather than come in without women's suffrage. Congress gave in and admitted Wyoming to the Union, women's suffrage and all. By the end of World War I, more than half the states had granted women the right to vote in some or all elections.

To many suffragists this state-by-state approach seemed slow and uncertain. They wanted a decisive victory—a constitutional amendment that would force *all* states to allow qualified women to vote. Finally, in 1919, Congress proposed the Nineteenth Amendment. Opposition to its adoption and ratification was intertwined with opposition to the voting rights of African Americans. Many southerners opposed the amendment. Not only would it extend the franchise to black women, but because it gave Congress enforcement power, it might also bring federal officials to investigate elections to ensure that the amendment was being obeyed, an interference that might call attention to how blacks were being kept from voting.

Susan B. Anthony and Elizabeth Cady Stanton were the two most influential leaders of the women's suffrage movement in the nineteenth century.

With the ratification of the Nineteenth Amendment in 1920, women won the right to vote, but they were still denied equal pay and equal rights, and they suffered numerous legal disabilities imposed by both national and state laws. The unsuccessful struggle to secure the adoption of the Equal Rights Amendment occupied much of the attention of the women's movement, but there are now other goals, and the political clout of women is being mobilized increasingly behind issues that range from pay, through pensions, to world peace, sexual harassment, abortion rights, and election to office.[7]

Hispanics

The struggle for civil rights has not been limited to women and African Americans. Each new wave of immigrants has been considered suspect by those who arrived earlier—all the more so if its members were not white or English speaking. Formal barriers of law and informal barriers of custom combined to deny equal rights. But as groups established themselves—first economically, then politically—most of these barriers were swept away, and constitutionally guaranteed rights were asserted.

Most Hispanics, many of whose ancestors have been Americans for generations, are bilingual, speaking English as well as Spanish. However, the fact that English is often not their first language has made it difficult for them to establish themselves educationally or to advance into the ranks of executives and professionals. Although not as visible a minority as African Americans, Hispanics have suffered the same kinds of discrimination in employment, education, and accommodations.

The largest group of Hispanics are the 18 million Mexican Americans—most of whom live in California, Texas, Arizona, and New Mexico. The second largest group consists of more than 3 million Puerto Ricans who reside on the mainland, often in the "barrios" of New York, Chicago, and other northern cities. They retain close ties with Puerto Rico and move back and forth from the island to the mainland. A third subgroup consists of more than a million refugees who fled from Castro's Cuba early in the 1960s, and a second wave, called the Mariel refugees, who fled in the 1980s. These Cubans, many of whom live in south Florida, include a substantial number of well-educated, successful businesspeople and professionals. A fourth group includes a rapidly growing number of refugees from Central and South America who presently number about 4 million.[8]

Hispanic political clout has been unrealized for a variety of reasons: internal political differences, and the fact that many Hispanics are young, many are not citizens, and many are not registered to vote. However, after California adopted Proposition 187 in 1994 denying medical, educational, and social services to illegal immigrants, and Congress amended the welfare laws to curtail benefits to noncitizens, many immigrants rushed to become naturalized. A million more Hispanics voted in 1996 than in 1992, with big increases in California and Texas.

A Closer Look

WHAT IS SEXUAL HARASSMENT?

The Supreme Court has interpreted Title VII of the Civil Rights Act of 1964 to impose on employers an obligation to provide a workplace environment that does not subject any employee to sexual harassment, including same-sex harassment. Sexual harassment comes in two forms: "quid pro quo," in which an employer makes it a condition of employment (hiring, promotion, etc.) that a person provide sexual favors; and discrimination because of being forced to work in a "hostile environment."

A hostile environment is defined as a workplace "permeated" with intimidation, ridicule, and insult that is severe or pervasive. Sexual harassment may be in the form of mere words; but the mere utterance of an epithet that is offensive does not by itself create a hostile environment. The psychological harm done to the victim is a relevant fact to be taken into account, but the plaintiff has the burden of proving that a reasonable person would consider the speech or conduct abusive.*

In the words of Justice Scalia, "We have never held that workplace harassment, even harassment between men and women, is automatically discrimination because of sex merely because the words used have sexual content or connotations." However, a majority of the Court recently ruled that an employer can be held liable for the conduct of supervisors who create a hostile work environment, even if the victim is not subjected to adverse tangible job consequences, and even if she did not notify her employer of her supervisor's conduct.** The Supreme Court has also ruled that Title IX of the Education Amendments of 1972 does not protect students from sexual harassment by a teacher unless the teacher's supervisor knew of the abuse and had failed to end it.†

Questions of sexual harassment have been brought to national attention by accusations made against Justice Clarence Thomas by Anita Hill at the time of his Senate confirmation, by the lawsuit brought by Paula Jones against President Clinton for allegedly seeking sexual favors when he was governor of Arkansas and she was an employee, and by Kathleen Willey, who contended that President Clinton had groped her.

In the Paula Jones case, the judge dismissed the charge on the grounds that, even if what Ms Jones said was true, there was no evidence that she had been deprived of her constitutional or legal rights, nor had she suffered any job discrimination. However, this was the case that would not die, and Ms Jones and her lawyers sought to appeal the decision. After prolonged negotiations over the amount of money, in November 1998 President Clinton agreed to pay $850,000 to settle the claim of sexual harassment, and Ms Jones dropped her demand that he apologize. On December 19, 1998 the second article of impeachment against Bill Clinton, which pertained to possible perjury in the Jones case, did not pass in the House of Representatives.

**Meritor Savings Bank, FSB v Vinson*, 477 US 57, 1986; *Harris v Forklift Systems, Inc.*, 510 US 17 (1993).

***Oncale v Sundowner Offshore Services*, 140 L Ed 2d 201 (1998); *Burlington Industries v Ellerth*, 141 L Ed 2d 633; *Faragher v City of Boca Raton*, 141 L Ed 2d 662 (1998).

†*Gebser v Lago Vista School Dist.*, 141 L Ed 2d 277 (1998).

Herblock. *The Washington Post*, July 6, 1998. Reprinted by permission.

Paula Jones and her attorney, Susan Carpenter McMillan, respond to reporters' questions regarding her harassment charges against Bill Clinton.

Asian Americans

The term "Asian American" describes approximately 10 million individuals from many different countries and many different ethnic backgrounds. Most do not think of themselves as "Asians" but as Americans of Chinese, Japanese, Vietnamese, Cambodian, Korean, or other specific ancestry. They live chiefly in the western states, but there has been a rapid increase in Asian Americans in New York and Texas.

Although Asian Americans are often considered a "model minority" because of their general success in education and business, the U.S. Civil Rights Commission found that "Asian-Americans do face widespread prejudice, discrimination and barriers to equal opportunity," and that racially motivated violence against them "occurs with disturbing frequency."[9]

CHINESE AMERICANS The Chinese were the first Asians to come to the United States. Beginning in 1847, when young male peasants came here to get away from poverty and to work in mines, on railroads, and on farms, the Chinese encountered economic and cultural fears of the white majority, who did not understand them or their culture. In response, the Chinese seldom tried to assimilate but instead gravitated to "Chinatowns." Discriminatory immigration and naturalization restrictions, imposed beginning in 1882, were strengthened in later years and were not removed until the end of World War II. Since that time, the Chinese have moved into the mainstream of American society, and they are beginning to run for and win local political offices. In 1996 Gary Locke, a Democrat and a graduate of Yale and Boston University, was elected governor of Washington, the first Chinese American to become governor of a continental state.

JAPANESE AMERICANS The Japanese first migrated to Hawaii in the 1860s and then to California in the 1880s. Most Japanese immigrants remained in the West Coast states. By the beginning of the twentieth century, they faced overt hostility. In 1905 labor leaders organized the Japanese and Korean Exclusion League, and in 1906 the San Francisco Board of Education excluded all Chinese, Japanese, and Korean children from neighborhood schools. Some western states passed laws denying the right to own land to aliens who were ineligible to become citizens—meaning, aliens of Asian ancestry.

During World War II, anti-Japanese hysteria provoked the internment of West Coast Japanese—most of whom were American citizens guilty of no crimes—in prison camps at Manzanar and Tule Lake, California. During this time Japanese property was often sold at confiscatory rates. Following the war, the exclusionary acts were repealed. In 1988 President Ronald Reagan signed a law providing $20,000 restitution to each of the approximately 60,000 surviving World War II internees.

OTHER ASIAN AMERICANS Koreans—more than 800,000 of them—are concentrated in southern California, Colorado, Honolulu, and New York City. Like other Asian Americans, they faced overt discrimination in jobs and housing, but a Korean middle class has been growing, with many becoming teachers, doctors, and lawyers. Many others operate small family businesses such as dry cleaners, florist shops, service stations, and small grocery stores, often in inner cities.[10] As prosperous small businesspeople, they are often the target of the anger of the poor people whose neighborhoods they serve. Many Korean stores were destroyed in the 1992 Los Angeles riots.

When Filipinos first came to the United States in the early part of this century, they were considered American nationals because the United States owned their native country. Nonetheless, they were denied their rights to full citizenship and faced discrimination and even violence, including anti-Filipino riots in the state of Washington in 1928 and later in California, where nearly one-third of the approximately 1.5 million Filipinos live.[11] Their economic status has improved, but their influence in politics remains as small as their numbers.

These Sioux Indians took part in a 220-mile March of Memory to mark the 100th anniversary of the Wounded Knee massacre.

The newest Asian arrivals consist of more than a million refugees from Vietnam, Laos, and Cambodia, who first came to the United States in 1975 and settled in California. Although this group included middle-class people who left during the fall of Saigon following the end of the Vietnam War, it also consisted of large numbers of "boat people" who came to our shores without any financial resources. In a relatively short time, most established themselves economically. Although they are starting to have political influence, they remain socially and economically segregated.

Native Americans

Almost half of the more than two million Native Americans live on or near a *reservation*—a tract of land given to the tribal nations by treaty—and are enrolled as members of one of the 550 federally recognized tribes, including 226 groups in Alaska.[12] Native Americans speak 200 languages.

Native Americans speak of their tribes as "nations," yet they are not possessed of the full attributes of sovereignty. Rather, they are a separate people with power to regulate their own internal affairs, subject to congressional supervision. States are precluded from regulating or taxing the tribes or extending the jurisdiction of their courts over the tribes unless authorized to do so by Congress.[13] In recent years Congress has stepped in to mediate growing tensions between Indian tribes who used their sovereignty over reservations to operate gambling casinos and the states in which these reservations are located.

By acts of Congress, Native Americans are citizens of the United States and of the states in which they live. They have the right to vote. Native Americans living off reservations and working in the general community pay taxes the same as everybody else; off reservations they have the same rights as any other Americans. If they are enrolled members of a recognized tribe, they are entitled to certain benefits created by law and by treaty. These benefits are administered by the Bureau of Indian Affairs of the Department of the Interior.

During the period of assimilation that began in 1887 and lasted until 1934, tribal governments were weak, some reservations were dissolved, and more than 100 tribes had their relationship with the federal government severed.[14] The civil rights movement of the 1960s created a more favorable climate for the concerns of Native Americans. Their goals were to reassert treaty rights and secure greater autonomy for the tribes. Under the leadership of the Native American Rights Fund (NARF), more Indian law cases were brought in the last several decades than at any time in our history.[15]

As a result of the militancy of Native American leaders and a greater national consciousness of the concerns of minorities, most Americans are now aware that many Native Americans live in poverty. Native Americans "are in far worse health than the rest of the population, dying earlier and suffering disproportionately from alcoholism, accidents, diabetes, and pneumonia."[16] Some reservations lack adequate health care facilities, educational opportunities, decent housing, and jobs. Congress has started to compensate Native Americans for past injustices and provide more opportunities for the development of tribal economic independence, and judges are showing greater vigilance in the enforcement of Indian treaty rights.

In 1986 Ben Nighthorse Campbell became the first Native American to be elected to Congress. He was elected as a Democrat from Colorado but changed to a Republican after being elected to the Senate in 1992.

Equal Protection of the Laws: What Does it Mean?

The **equal protection clause** of the Fourteenth Amendment declares no state (including any subdivision thereof) shall "deny to any person within its jurisdiction the equal protection of the laws." Although there is no parallel clause explicitly limiting the national government, the Fifth Amendment's **due process clause**, which states that no person shall "be deprived of life, liberty, or property, without due process of law," has been interpreted to impose the same restraints on the national government as the equal protection clause imposes on the states.

The Equal Protection Clause

Note the equal protection clause applies only to the *actions of governments*, not to those of private individuals. If a discriminatory action is performed by a private person, it does not violate the Constitution, although it may violate federal and state laws.

The equal protection clause does not, however, prevent governments from creating various classifications of people in its laws. What the Constitution forbids is *unreasonable* classifications. In general, a classification is unreasonable when there is no relation between the classes it creates and permissible governmental goals. A law prohibiting redheads from voting, for example, would be unreasonable. On the other hand, laws denying persons under 18 the right to vote, to marry without the permission of their parents, or to apply for a license to drive a car appear to be reasonable (at least to most persons over 18).

One of the most troublesome constitutional questions is how to distinguish between constitutional and unconstitutional classifications. The Supreme Court uses three tests for this purpose: (1) the traditional *rational basis* test for most laws; (2) the *heightened scrutiny* test, a middle-tier test; and (3) the most stringent test of all, a *strict scrutiny* test for laws dealing with suspect classes and fundamental rights.

Gambling on the Reservations

In 28 states Native American tribes sponsor gambling casinos on their reservations. In 1988 Congress, exercising its powers under the Indian Commerce Clause, passed the Indian Gaming Regulatory Act, which allows a tribe to conduct the gaming activities that would be legal in the surrounding state. This federal law also requires states to negotiate compacts with the tribes that give them the right to provide kinds of gambling not permitted elsewhere in the state. The act made the state's obligation to negotiate in good faith judicially enforceable, but the Supreme Court held that the Eleventh Amendment precludes Congress from allowing an Indian tribe to force a state into a federal court.*

A conflict developed in California between some Native American casinos and the state government over the use of slot machines like those used in Nevada casinos but forbidden in California. Governor Pete Wilson refused to amend the compact to allow the slot machines, and the tribes opened a public relations campaign contending that if they were not allowed to use the slot machines, it would lead to the loss of revenue and jobs needed for Indian education.

In 1998 Proposition 5 was presented to California voters to allow casino gaming in all its present forms on the reservations. There would be no limit on the number of video gambling machines, and the minimum gambling age would be 18. The casinos would be regulated primarily by the tribes themselves, with little state oversight or restrictions, but in accordance with federal laws established by the Indian Gaming Regulatory Act of 1988. In a battle that became the most expensive fight ever waged over a state initiative, the voters ignored the advertising campaign by Nevada casinos and broadly backed the expansion of casino gambling on tribal lands in California.

**Seminole Tribe of Florida v Florida*, 517 US 44 (1996).

THE RATIONAL BASIS TEST The traditional test to determine whether a law complies with the equal protection requirement places the burden of proof on those attacking the law. They must show that the law has no legitimate governmental goals. For example, the Supreme Court has held that a state might deny unemployment benefits to those who attend day school but make them available to those who attend night school. This classification of schools meets the rational basis test since it is reasonable to assume that those who go to school during the day are less likely to be available for employment than are those who go to school after work.[17]

SUSPECT CLASSIFICATIONS AND STRICT SCRUTINY When a law is subject to strict scrutiny, it is not sufficient that the law be a reasonable means to handle a particular problem. Rather, the courts must be persuaded that there is both a "compelling public interest" to justify such a classification and no less restrictive way to accomplish this compelling purpose.

A *suspect class* is a class of people deliberately subjected to unequal treatment in the past, or relegated by society to a position of such political powerlessness as to require extraordinary judicial protection.[18] Classifications based on race or national origin are always suspect. It does not make any difference if the laws are designed for so-called benign purposes—that is, to help persons of a particular race or national origin. For example, the Supreme Court has held that laws that give preference for public employment based on race are subject to strict scrutiny. The judges must be

equal protection clause
Clause in the Constitution that forbids any state to deny to any person within its jurisdiction the equal protection of the laws. By interpretation, the Fifth Amendment imposes the same limitation on the national government. This clause is the major constitutional restraint on the power of governments to discriminate against persons because of race, national origin, or sex.

due process clause
Clauses in the Fifth and Fourteenth Amendments stating that the national (Fifth) and state (Fourteenth) governments shall not deprive any person of life, liberty, or property without due process of law.

persuaded that such laws meet a "compelling public interest," and that there is no other way to serve this public interest.

QUASI-SUSPECT CLASSIFICATIONS AND HEIGHTENED SCRUTINY The heightened scrutiny test applies to what the court has called "quasi-suspect" classes. To sustain a law under this test, the burden is on the government to show that its classification serves "important governmental objectives" and is substantially related to these objectives.

Classifications based on gender are subject to heightened scrutiny. Not until 1971 was any classification based on gender declared unconstitutional. Before that time, many laws that purported to provide special protection for women—such as a Michigan law forbidding any woman other than the wife or daughter of a tavern owner to serve as barmaid—were upheld. As Justice William J. Brennan, Jr., wrote for the Court in 1973: "There can be no doubt that our nation has had a long and unfortunate history of sex discrimination. Traditionally such discrimination was rationalized by an attitude of 'romantic paternalism' which in practical effect put women, not on a pedestal, but in a cage."[19]

Today the Court's view is that gender classifications, although not as suspect as those based on race, are subject to the heightened scrutiny test. Treating women differently from men (or vice versa) is forbidden when supported by no more substantial justification than "archaic and overbroad generalizations," "old notions," and "the role-typing society has long imposed upon women."[20] If the government's objective is "to protect members of one sex because they are presumed to suffer from an inherent handicap or to be innately inferior," that objective is illegitimate.[21] The Supreme Court has struck down most, but not all, laws brought before it that were alleged to discriminate against women. The Court has refused to strike down the males-only draft and veterans' preference in civil service jobs.[22]

POVERTY AND AGE Just as racial minorities and women are entitled to special constitutional protection, it is argued, so should the poor and the elderly be. The Supreme Court, however, "has never held that financial need alone identifies a suspect class for purposes of equal protection analysis."[23] Thus, so far as the Constitution is concerned, a state may rely on property taxes for funds for schools, even if this means that schools in "rich" districts spend more per pupil than those in "poor" districts.

Age is neither a suspect nor a quasi-suspect class. Many laws commonly make distinctions based on age: to obtain a driver's license, to marry without parental consent, to attend schools, to buy alcohol, and so on. Many governmental institutions have age-specific programs: for senior citizens, for adult students, for midcareer persons. Although the Supreme Court has refused to make age a suspect classification requiring extra judicial protection, Congress, responding to "gray power," frequently treats age as a protected category. Congress has made it illegal for most employers to discriminate on the basis of old age, and except for a few exempt occupations, Congress prohibits employers from imposing mandatory retirement requirements.

FUNDAMENTAL RIGHTS AND STRICT SCRUTINY The Court also strictly scrutinizes laws impinging on *fundamental rights.* What makes a right fundamental in the constitutional sense? It is not the importance or the significance of the right that makes it fundamental, but whether it is explicitly or implicitly *guaranteed by the Constitution.* Under this test, the rights to travel and to vote have been held to be fundamental, as well as such First Amendment rights as the right to associate for the advancement of political beliefs. Rights to an education, to housing, or to welfare benefits have been held not fundamental. Important as these rights may be, there are no constitutional provisions specifically protecting them from governmental regulation.

Proving Discrimination

Does the fact that a law or a regulation has a differential effect—what has come to be known as *disparate impact*—on persons of a different race or sex by itself establish that the law is unconstitutional? In one of its most important decisions, *Washington v Davis* (1976), the Supreme Court said no.[24] "An unwavering line of cases" from the Supreme Court "hold that a violation of the Equal Protection Clause requires state action motivated by discriminatory intent; the disproportionate effects of state action are not sufficient to establish such a violation."[25] Or, as the Court said in another case: "The Fourteenth Amendment guarantees equal laws, not equal results."[26]

What do these rulings on disparate impact mean in practical terms? They mean, for example, that even when city ordinances permit only single-family residences and thus make low-cost housing projects impossible, they are not unconstitutional—even if their effect is to keep minorities from moving into the city—unless it can be shown that they were adopted with the *intent to discriminate* against minorities. Another example: preference for veterans in public employment does not violate the equal protection clause, even though its effect is to keep many women from getting jobs; the distinction between veterans and nonveterans was not adopted deliberately to create a sex barrier.

What is constitutional can nonetheless be made illegal. Things that are unconstitutional are always illegal, but what is illegal may not be unconstitutional. For example, state laws creating legislative districts with no intent to discriminate against African Americans, but which in effect dilute their voting power, are unconstitutional. But in the Voting Rights Act of 1965, Congress made voting requirements that do in fact dilute the voting power of African Americans illegal, even if they were adopted with no such intention. The Voting Rights Act of 1965 tests the legality of state voting laws and practices by their *effects* rather than by the *intentions* of those who passed them.

VOTING RIGHTS

Under our Constitution, it is the states, not the federal government, that regulate elections and voting qualifications. However, Article I, Section 4, gives Congress the power to supersede state regulations as to the "Times, Places and Manner" of elections for representatives, senators, and presidential electors. Congress has used this authority to set age qualifications and residency requirements to vote in national elections, to establish a uniform day for all states to hold elections for members of Congress and presidential electors, and to give American citizens who reside outside the United States the right to vote for members of Congress and presidential electors in the states in which they previously lived.

Limitations on the states' power to set voting qualifications are contained in the Fourteenth Amendment (forbidding qualifications that have no reasonable relation to the ability to vote), the Fifteenth Amendment (forbidding qualifications based on race), the Nineteenth Amendment (forbidding qualifications based on sex), and the Twenty-sixth Amendment (forbidding states to deny citizens 18 years of age or older the right to vote on account of age). These amendments also empower Congress to enact the laws necessary to enforce their provisions.

Getting Around the Fourteenth and Fifteenth Amendments

Fierce opposition followed ratification of the Fourteenth and Fifteenth Amendments. African American men were allowed to participate in the political life of southern states only when the federal government insisted upon it. As soon as federal troops were withdrawn from the South in 1877, southern Democrats regained control of state governments and set out to keep African Americans from voting. They used social pressure and violence. Organized secret societies like the Ku Klux Klan engaged in terrorist activities such as midnight shootings, burnings, whippings, and lynchings.

In the 1940s the Supreme Court began to strike down one after another of the devices that had been used to keep African Americans from voting. In 1944 (*Smith v Allwright*) the Court declared the **white primary** (a primary operated by the Democratic party which, in the then one-party South, was where public officials were actually chosen) unconstitutional.[27] In 1960 it held that **racial gerrymandering**—the drawing of election districts to ensure that African Americans would be a minority in all districts—was contrary to the Fifteenth Amendment.[28] In 1964 the Twenty-fourth Amendment eliminated the **poll tax**—payment required as a condition for voting—in presidential and congressional elections. In 1966 the Court held that the Fourteenth Amendment forbade the poll tax as a condition in any election.[29]

In many southern areas, **literacy tests** were used to discriminate against African Americans. Some states required applicants to demonstrate that they understood the national and state constitutions and, furthermore, that they were persons of good character. Although poor whites often avoided registration out of fear of embarrassment from failing a literacy test, the tests were more often used to discriminate against African Americans.[30] Whites were often asked simple questions; blacks were asked questions that would baffle a Supreme Court justice. "In the 1960s southern registrars were observed testing black applicants on such matters as the number of bubbles in a soap bar, the news contained in a copy of the *Peking Daily*, the meaning of obscure passages in state constitutions, and the definition of terms such as *habeas corpus*."[31] In Louisiana, 49,603 illiterate white voters were able to persuade election officials they could understand the Constitution, but only two illiterate black voters were able to do so.

Those wishing to deny African Americans the right to vote were forced to rely on registration requirements. On the surface such requirements appeared to be perfectly proper, but it was the way they were administered that had kept African Americans from the polls. White election officers confronted African Americans trying to register while white police stood guard; white judges heard appeals of decisions made by registration officials. Officials often seized on the smallest error in an application form as an excuse to disqualify a black voter. In one parish in Louisiana, after four white voters challenged the registration of some black voters on the grounds that those voters had made an "error in spilling" (*sic*) in their applications, registration officials struck 1,300 out of approximately 1,500 black voters from the rolls.[32]

white primary
Primary operated by the Democratic party in southern states that, before Republicans gained strength in the "one-party South," essentially constituted an election; ruled unconstitutional in *Smith v Allwright* (1944).

racial gerrymandering
The drawing of election districts so as to ensure that members of a certain race are always a minority in the district; ruled unconstitutional in *Gomillion v Lightfoot* (1960).

poll tax
Payment required as a condition for voting; prohibited for national elections by the Twenty-fourth Amendment (1964) and ruled unconstitutional for all elections in *Harper v Virginia Board of Election* (1966).

literacy test
Literacy requirement imposed by some states as a condition of voting, generally used to disqualify blacks from voting in the South; now illegal.

The Voting Rights Act of 1965

For two decades after World War II, under the leadership of the Supreme Court, federal judges carefully scrutinized voting laws and procedures in cases brought before them, but this approach still did not open the voting booth to African Americans. Finally Congress began to act. The Civil Rights Act of 1964 set aside, for elections for members of Congress and the president, literacy tests for persons who had completed the equivalent of the sixth grade and prohibited denial of the right to vote because of minor errors on application forms.

The Civil Rights Act of 1964 had hardly been enacted when events in Selma, Alabama, dramatized the inadequacy of depending on the courts to prevent racial barriers in polling places. A voter registration drive in Selma, led by Martin Luther King, Jr., produced arrests, marches on the state capital, and the murder of two civil rights workers. Still there was no dent in the color bar at the polls. Responding to events in Selma, President Lyndon Johnson made a dramatic address to Congress and the nation calling for federal action to ensure that no person would be deprived of the right to vote in any election for any office because of color or race. Congress responded with the Voting Rights Act of 1965.

Section 2 of the Voting Rights Act prohibits voting qualifications or standards that result in a denial of the right of any citizen to vote on account of race and color. Section 5 requires that states that had a history of denying African Americans or Hispanic citizens the right to vote must clear with the Department of Justice changes in voting practice or laws that might dilute the voting power of these groups.[33]

What precisely constitutes "dilution" and how it is to be measured is the subject of much litigation. Examples include changes in the location of polling places; changes in candidacy requirements and qualifications; changes in filing deadlines; changes from ward to at-large elections; changes in boundary lines of voting districts; and changes that affect the creation or abolition of an elective office and imposition by state political parties of fees to become delegates to nominating conventions.[34]

Following the 1990 census, the Department of Justice refused to certify redistricting plans of southern state legislatures that failed to draw as many districts as possible in which minorities would constitute a majority of the electorate. Most of these districts tended to be Democratic, leaving the other congressional districts in these states heavily white and Republican. The lower federal courts sustained the Department of Justice's interpretation. As a result, there was a considerable increase in the number of congressional districts represented by minorities and Republicans.[35]

The Supreme Court, however, in a series of cases beginning with *Shaw v Reno*, announced that although it was a legitimate goal for state legislatures to take race into account when they drew electoral districts in order to increase the voting strength of minorities, they may not make race the *sole* or predominant reason for drawing district lines. The Department of Justice, said the Supreme Court, was wrong in forcing states to create as many **majority-minority districts** as possible. A test case involved the North Carolina legislature's creation of a majority-minority district 160 miles long and in some places only an interstate highway wide. "If you drove down the interstate," said one legislator about this district, "with both car doors open, you'd kill most of the people in the district." North Carolina's reapportionment scheme, the Supreme Court declared, was so "irrational on its face that it can be understood only as an effort to segregate voters into separate voting districts because of their race." To comply with the Voting Rights Act, the Supreme Court explained, states must provide for districts roughly proportional to the minority voters' respective shares in the voting-age population.[36]

Major Civil Rights Laws

- Civil Rights Act, 1957: Makes it a federal crime to prevent persons from voting in federal elections.
- Civil Rights Act, 1964: Bars discrimination in employment or in public accommodations on the basis of race, color, religion, sex, or national origin; created the Equal Employment Opportunity Commission.
- Voting Rights Act, 1965: Authorizes the appointment of federal examiners to register voters in areas that have been discriminating.
- Age Discrimination in Employment Act, 1967: Prohibits job discrimination against workers or job applicants ages 40 through 65 and prohibits mandatory retirement.
- Fair Housing Act, 1968: Prohibits discrimination on the basis of race, color, religion, or national origin in the sale or rental of most housing.
- Title IX. Education Amendment of 1972: Prohibits discrimination on the basis of sex in any education program receiving federal financial assistance.
- Rehabilitation Act, 1973: Requires that recipients of federal grants greater than $2,500 hire and promote qualified handicapped individuals.
- Fair Housing Act Amendments, 1988: Gives the Department of Housing and Urban Development authority to prohibit housing bias against the handicapped and families with children.
- Americans with Disabilities Act, 1991: Prohibits discrimination based on disability and requires that facilities be made accessible to those with disabilities.
- The Civil Rights Act of 1991: Places the burden on employers to justify practices that negatively affect women and minorities by requiring employers to justify such practices as being job-related or showing that there are no alternative practices that would have a less negative impact. Also establishes a commission to examine the "glass ceiling" that seems to keep women from becoming executives and to make recommendations on how to increase promotion of women and minorities to management positions.

Since then the Court has expanded *Shaw* by clarifying that it was not meant to suggest that a "district must be bizarre on its face before there is a constitutional violation." Legislatures may be aware of racial considerations when they draw district lines, but when race becomes the overriding motive, the state violates the equal protection clause.[37] As a result, many southern states had to redraw legislative districts. However, when African-American incumbents ran in newly drawn districts with majority Euro-American electors in subsequent elections, they were all reelected.[38]

majority-minority district
A congressional district created to include a majority of minority voters; ruled constitutional so long as race is not the only factor.

Education Rights

Until the Supreme Court struck down such laws in the 1950s, southern states made it illegal for whites and blacks to ride in the same train cars, attend the same theaters, go to the same schools, be born in the same hospitals, or be buried in the same cemeteries. **Jim Crow laws**, as they came to be called, blanketed southern

Jim Crow laws
State laws formerly pervasive throughout the South requiring public facilities and accommodations to be segregated by race; ruled unconstitutional.

life. How could these laws stand in the face of the equal protection clause? This was the question raised in 1896 in *Plessy v Ferguson.*

In the *Plessy* decision, the Supreme Court endorsed the view that governmentally imposed racial segregation in public transportation, and presumably in public education, did not necessarily constitute discrimination if "equal" accommodations were provided for the members of both races.[39] The *Plessy* decision required equality as the price for compulsory segregation but, the "equal" part of the formula was meaningless. States segregated African Americans into unequal facilities, and they lacked the political power to protest effectively. The passage of time did not lessen the inequalities. Beginning in the late 1930s, African Americans started to file lawsuits challenging the doctrine. They cited facts to show that in practice, separate but equal always resulted in discrimination against African Americans.

Thurgood Marshall (center), George E. C. Hayes (left), and James Nabrit, Jr., (right) argued and won Brown v Board of Education of Topeka *before the Supreme Court in 1954.*

The End of Separate But Equal: Brown v Board of Education

At first the Supreme Court was not willing to upset the separate but equal doctrine, but in the spring of 1954, in *Brown v Board of Education of Topeka,* the Court finally reversed the *Plessy* doctrine as it applied to public schools by holding that "separate but equal" is a contradiction in terms. Segregation is itself discrimination.[40] A year later the Court ordered school boards to proceed with "all deliberate speed to desegregate public schools at the earliest practical date."[41]

In the years following the *Brown* decisions, federal judges struck down a whole battery of schemes designed to evade the Supreme Court's ruling. In 1969 the Court reversed its decision that had granted school districts time to prepare for desegregation. It declared: "Continued operation of racially segregated schools under the standard of 'all deliberate speed' is no longer constitutionally permissible. School districts must immediately terminate dual school systems based on race and operate only unitary school systems."[42]

In the 1960s Congress and the president joined even more directly in the battle against school segregation. Title VI of the Civil Rights Act of 1964, as subsequently amended, stipulates that federal dollars under any grant program or project must be withdrawn from an entire school or institution of higher education that discriminates "on the ground of race, color, or national origin" gender, age, or disability in "any program or activity receiving federal financial assistance."

From Segregation to Desegregation—But Not Yet to Integration

School districts that had operated two kinds of schools, one for whites and one for African Americans, now had an obligation to develop plans and programs to move from segregation to integration. For such school districts, desegregation would not be enough; they would have a duty to bring about integration. If they failed to do so on their own initiative, federal judges would supervise the school districts to ensure that they were doing what was necessary and proper to overcome the evils of segregation.

But since most whites and most African Americans live in separate neighborhoods, merely removing legal barriers to school integration does not by itself integrate the schools. To overcome this residential clustering by race, some federal courts mandated busing across neighborhoods, moving white students to once predominantly black schools and vice versa. Busing students was not popular and fostered widespread protest in many cities.

de jure segregation
Laws that made it a crime for black or white people to go to school together, or to be served together in public places, or to sit together in public transportation.

de facto segregation
Segregation that comes about because of economic or social conditions or results from individual choices.

The Supreme Court sustained busing only if it was to remedy the consequences of *officially* sanctioned, that is, ***de jure* segregation**. The Court refused to permit federal judges to order busing to overcome the effects of ***de facto* segregation**, segregation that arises as a result of social practices.

Since *Brown v Board of Education,* the federal government has intervened in more than 500 southern school desegregation cases. However, there has been no such judicial action for northern schools that have de facto segregation. As a result, many southern cities now have more integrated schools than do large northern cities. Yet even in the South, many school districts in central cities are predominantly African American or Hispanic. This segregated pattern of schools is partly the result of "white flight" to the suburbs and private schools to escape court-ordered busing. In more recent years it is also due to higher birth rates and immigration among African Americans and Hispanics.[43]

After a period of vigorous federal court supervision of school desegregation programs, the Supreme Court has started to restrict the role of federal judges.[44] Moreover, it has instructed them to restore control of a school system to the state and local authorities and to release districts from any busing obligations once the judge concludes that the authorities "have done everything practicable to overcome the past consequences of segregation."[45]

Political support for busing and for other efforts to integrate the schools is fading.[46] School districts are beginning to eliminate mandatory busing, with the result, according to one expert, that we may get "to a level of segregation we haven't seen since before the civil rights movement."[47] Some African American leaders, while still supporting desegregation efforts, are paying more attention to improving the quality of inner-city schools than to desegregating them.

Rights to Public Accommodations, Jobs, and Homes

As we have noted, the Fifth and Fourteenth Amendments apply only to governmental action, not to private discriminatory conduct. As Justice William Douglas said, our Constitution creates "a zone of privacy which precludes government from interfering with private clubs or groups. The associational rights which our system honors permit all-white, all-black, all-brown, and all-yellow clubs to be established. They also permit all-Catholic, all-Jewish, or all-agnostic clubs. . . . Government may not tell a man or a woman who his or her associates must be. The individual may be as selective as he desires."[48]

Families, churches, or private groups organized for political, religious, cultural, social, or expressive purposes are constitutionally different from large associations organized along other lines. The Supreme Court, for example, has upheld the application of laws forbidding sex or racial discrimination by organizations such as the Jaycees, the Rotary Club, and large (in this case more than 400 members) private eating clubs. Such associations and clubs are not small intimate groups. Nor were they able to demonstrate that allowing women or minorities to become members would change the content or impact of their purposes.[49]

In 1883 the Supreme Court had declared unconstitutional an act of Congress that made it a federal offense for any operator of a public conveyance, hotel, or theater to deny accommodations to any person because of race or color on the grounds that the Fourteenth Amendment does not give Congress such authority.[50] Since the 1960s, however, the constitutional authority of Congress to legislate against discrimination by private individuals is no longer an issue. The Court has broadly construed the **commerce clause**—which gives Congress the power to regulate interstate and foreign commerce—to justify almost any action that Congress might want to take against discriminatory conduct by individuals. Congress has also used its power to tax and spend to prevent not only racial discrimination but also discrimination based on ethnic origin, sex, disability, and age.

commerce clause
The clause (Article I) in the Constitution that gives Congress the power to regulate commerce among the states, with other nations, and with the Indian tribes. This clause provides the constitutional basis for most national regulations of our economy, as well as for much civil rights legislation.

The Civil Rights Act of 1964

With this law, for the first time since Reconstruction, Congress authorized the massive use of federal authority to combat *privately* imposed racial discrimination.

TITLE II: PLACES OF PUBLIC ACCOMMODATION Title II makes it a federal offense to discriminate against any customer or patron in a place of public accommodation because of race, color, religion, or national origin. It applies to any inn, hotel, motel, or lodging establishment (except establishments with fewer than five rooms and occupied by the proprietor—in other words, small boardinghouses); to any restaurant or gasoline station that serves interstate travelers or serves food or products, a substantial portion of which have moved in interstate commerce; and to any movie house, theater, concert hall, sports arena, or other place of entertainment that customarily presents films, performances, athletic teams, or other sources of entertainment that are moved in interstate commerce. Within a few months after its adoption, the Supreme Court sustained the constitutionality of Title II.[51] As a result, public establishments, including those in the South, opened their doors to all customers.

TITLE VII: EMPLOYMENT Title VII of the Civil Rights Act made it illegal for any employer or trade union in any industry affecting interstate commerce and employing 15 or more people (and, since 1972, any state or local agency such as a school or university) to discriminate in employment practices against any person because of race, color, national origin, religion, or sex. Employers have an obligation to create workplaces that avoid abusive environments. Related legislation makes it illegal to engage in discriminatory activities that affect those with physical handicaps, veterans, or persons over 40.

There are a few exceptions. Religious institutions such as parochial schools may use religious standards. Age, sex, or handicap may be considered where occupational qualifications are absolutely necessary to the normal operation of a particular business or enterprise—for example hiring only women to work in women's locker rooms. In 1991, Congress amended Title VII to set aside several Supreme Court decisions and to make it easier to challenge employment practices that, whatever the intent, have a disparate adverse impact on women and minorities. Title VII was passed to protect minorities and women; nonetheless, employers who discriminate against white males also violate its provisions.

Title VII has several special features. Not only do aggrieved persons have a right of private action to sue for damages for themselves, but also they can do so for other persons similarly situated in a **class action suit**. In addition, Congress created the Equal Employment Opportunity Commission (EEOC) to enforce its provisions. The commission, which consists of five members appointed by the president with the consent of the Senate, works together with state authorities to try to bring about compliance with the act and may seek judicial enforcement of complaints against private employers. The attorney general prosecutes Title VII violations by public agencies. The vigor with which the EEOC and the attorney general have acted has varied over the years, depending on the commitment of the president in office and the willingness of Congress to provide an adequate budget for the EEOC.[52]

Title VII is supplemented by a 1965 presidential executive order requiring all contractors of the federal government, including universities, to adopt and implement affirmative action programs to correct "underutilization" of women and minorities. Such programs may not establish racial or ethnic quotas for minorities or women, but they do call on contractors to establish timetables and goals; to follow open recruitment procedures; to keep records of applicants by race, sex, and national origin; and to explain why their labor force does not reflect the same proportion of persons within the appropriate labor market pools. Failure of contractors to file and implement an approved affirmative action plan may lead to loss of federal contracts or grants.

The Fair Housing Act and Amendments, 1968 and 1988

Housing is the last frontier of the civil rights crusade, the area in which progress is slowest and genuine change most remote.

> Segregated housing contributes mightily to a vicious circle that also includes educational and employment discrimination. . . . Because of poor schools for

class action suit
Lawsuit brought by an individual or a group of people on behalf of all those similarly situated.

many minorities, they cannot find well-paying jobs. Without such jobs they often cannot afford to live in nicer neighborhoods with decent housing. And because of their location in less desirable communities, good educational systems are less likely to be available."[53]

For half a century the Supreme Court has made **racial or religious restrictive covenants** (a provision in a deed to real property restricting its sale) legally unenforceable.[54] The 1968 Fair Housing Act forbids discrimination in housing, excluding from its protection so-called "Mrs. Murphy boarding houses," housing owned by private individuals who own no more than three houses, dwellings that have no more than four separate living units in which the owner maintains a residence; and religious organizations and private clubs housing their own members on a noncommercial basis. For all other housing, the act forbids owners to refuse to sell or rent to any person because of race, color, religion, national origin, sex, or physical handicap or because a person has children. Housing for older persons is exempted from this family provision. No discriminatory advertising is permitted.

The Department of Justice has filed hundreds of cases, especially those involving large apartment complexes, yet African Americans and Hispanics continue to be discriminated against when they attempt to rent apartments or buy houses. Realtors continue to steer African Americans and Hispanics toward neighborhoods that are not predominantly white, to require larger rental deposits from minorities than from whites, and even to refuse outright to sell or rent to minorities.[55]

Less than 1 percent of these discriminatory actions are complained about because they are often so subtle that victims are often unaware that they are being discriminated against. The number of discrimination complaints received by the Department of Housing and Urban Development and local and state agencies has been increasing as the result of more aggressive enforcement. Complaints about discrimination in housing also cover lending discrimination where the discrimination may often be subtle, but the results are to deny loans to minorities.

Voluntary segregation obviously exists. "It's a fact of life that blacks like to live in black neighborhoods and whites like to live in white neighborhoods. . . . And real estate agents generally like to bring customers to places they will like and where the agent can make a sale."[56] Whatever the reasons, housing segregation persists.

Affirmative Action: Is It Constitutional?

Prior to 1954, when white majorities were using governmental power to segregate African Americans and to discriminate against them, civil rights advocates cited with approval the famous words of Justice John Marshall Harlan: "Our Constitution is color-blind and neither knows nor tolerates class among citizens."[57] It was not until 1954 that Justice Harlan's views triumphed in *Brown v Board of Education.* The Court emphasized that the rights protected belong to each and every individual, not to the group to which he or she may belong.

But by the 1960s there was a new set of constitutional and national policy debates. Many people began to assert that government neutrality is not enough. If governments and universities and employers stopped discriminating yet changed nothing else, those previously discriminated against would still be kept from equal participation in American life. Because they had been so disadvantaged by past discrimination, they suffered disabilities not shared by white males in the competition for openings in medical schools, for skilled jobs, or for their share of government grants and contracts.

Remedies to overcome the consequences of past discrimination against African Americans, Hispanics, Native Americans, and women may be known as *affirmative action* by those who support them, but they are regarded as *reverse discrimination* by those who oppose them. The Supreme Court's first major statement on the

racial or religious restrictive covenants
A provision in a deed to real property excluding its sale to persons of a particular race or religion. Judicial enforcement of such deeds is unconstitutional.

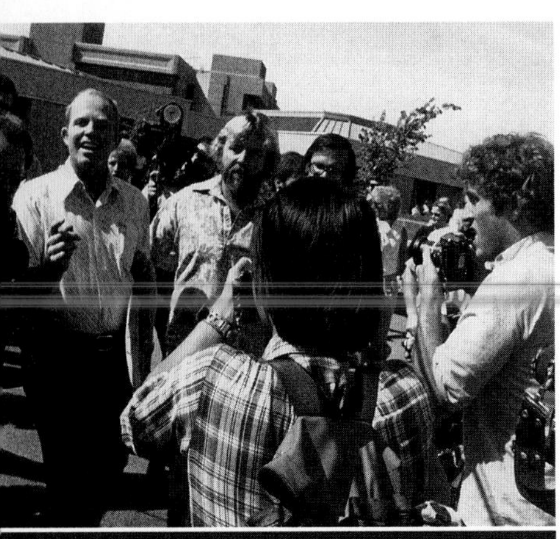

Alan Bakke, who won a historic affirmative action suit, is surrounded by reporters as he leaves class after his first day at the University of California medical school.

constitutionality of affirmative action programs came in a celebrated case relating to university admissions. Allan Bakke—a white male and a top student at Minnesota and Stanford Universities, as well as a Vietnam War veteran—applied both in 1973 and 1974 to the medical school of the University of California at Davis. In each of those years the school admitted 100 new students, 84 in a general admissions program and 16 in a special admissions program created for African Americans, Chicanos, Asian Americans, and Native Americans—groups who had been underrepresented until a special admissions program was established. Bakke's application was rejected each year while students with lower grade-point averages, test scores, and interview ratings were admitted under the special admissions program. After his second rejection, Bakke brought suit in federal court claiming he had been excluded because of his race, contrary to requirements of the Constitution and Title VI of the Civil Rights Act of 1964.

In *University of California Regents v Bakke* (1978), the Supreme Court ruled the Davis plan unconstitutional.[58] But in an opinion for the Court by Justice Lewis Powell, which no other member of the Court completely shared, the Court also declared that affirmative action programs are not necessarily unconstitutional. In order to achieve a diversified student body, a state university may properly take race and ethnic background into account as one of several factors in choosing students. However, the university's goal may not be to redress past misconduct by society or to ensure that more minority members become doctors. The problem with the California plan was it created a category of admissions from which whites were excluded solely because of their race.

After Bakke: Refinements and Uncertainty

Following *Bakke*, the Court dealt with a variety of affirmative action programs, sustaining most but not all of them. Yet, as Justice Byron White said, "Agreement upon a means for applying the Equal Protection Clause to an affirmative-action program has eluded this Court every time the issue has come before us."[59]

In *Richmond v Croson* in 1989, a Court majority struck down a regulation of the city of Richmond requiring nonminority city contractors to subcontract at least 30 percent of the dollar amount of their contracts to one or more minority business enterprises. Said Justice Sandra Day O'Connor for the Court, in language that called into question the validity of most government affirmative action plans, "Race-sensitive remedial measures are to be justified only after a strong basis in evidence has established that remedial action is necessary to overcome the consequences of past discriminatory action."

Justice Thurgood Marshall in dissent contended that there is "a profound difference separating governmental actions that themselves are racist, and governmental actions seeking to remedy the effects of prior racism." The proper test, he wrote, for race-conscious classifications designed to further remedial goals is merely that they have to be justified as serving important governmental objectives and must be substantially related to the achievement of those objectives. The majority, he said, "sounds a full-scale retreat from the effort to deliver on the century-old promise of equality and scuttled the efforts of a city to surmount its discriminatory past."[60]

After a brief period in which the Court majority upheld the right of the national government to make benign racial classifications with respect to radio and television licenses, the Court has returned to its more stringent review of affirmative action.[61] The Court has rejected the view that racial classifications, whether benign or hostile, should ever be subject to less than strict scrutiny by either the national or state and local governments and could be justified only if such a classification serves a compelling governmental interest. And as we have noted, the Court is similarly opposed to the use of race as the sole criteria in cases relating to the drawing of electoral district lines, where the injury to nonprotected groups is much less a concern.[62]

In the spring of 1996, the Court of Appeals for the Fifth Circuit, in *Hopwood v Texas*, set aside the University of Texas law school's affirmative action plan for admission of students.[63] It appeared to these judges that the decision in the *Bakke* case no longer had the support of the Supreme Court, and that the use of race as one factor in the admission process violated the equal protection clause. Texas University then modified its plan and petitioned the Supreme Court to review the court of appeals decision. On the last day of the 1995–96 term, the Supreme Court announced that it would not do so.

Justices Ruth Bader Ginsburg and David Souter took the unusual step of explaining that the Supreme Court's refusal to review the *Hopwood* decision should not be construed as indicating that the Court agreed with the Court of Appeals. Rather, the issue of constitutionality was no longer before the courts, since the law school had modified its plan. Justice Ginsburg noted, "Whether it is constitutional for a public college or graduate school to use race or national origin as a factor in its admission processes is an issue of great national importance." But, she concluded, "this Court reviews judgments, not opinions."[64]

As a result of the Supreme Court's skepticism about affirmative action, civil rights groups made an out-of-court settlement of a case in 1997 that challenged the right of a New Jersey school district to reduce its work force by dismissing a white teacher while keeping its only African American teacher with the same seniority. Civil rights groups were fearful that the Court might use this case to rule that diversity is not a legitimate reason for a racial preference, and thus call into question other affirmative action programs.[65]

Thus, until matters are clarified by the Supreme Court, as far as the United States Constitution is concerned, race—and presumably gender—may no longer be considered as a factor for admission to public universities and colleges in the Fifth Circuit (Texas, Louisiana, and Mississippi), but may be considered in the rest of the nation. It is clear, however, that the Supreme Court is closely scrutinizing programs that provide a preference based on race or ethnic origin or gender.

California's Proposition 209

In July 1995, at the urging of Governor Pete Wilson, the Regents of the University of California voted to eliminate race or gender as factors in employment, purchasing, contracting, or admissions at the University of California. Then in November 1996, Californians voted overwhelmingly for Proposition 209 to amend the state constitution to forbid state agencies—including schools, colleges, and universities—to discriminate against or grant preferential treatment to any individual or group on the basis of race, sex, color, ethnicity, or national origin in public employment, public education, or public contracting, except where necessary to comply with a federal requirement.

A variety of constitutional issues flow from California's Proposition 209. For example, although Proposition 209 clearly forbids universities and other state agencies from taking race and gender into account, does it also make unconstitutional state-supported outreach programs designed to recruit and encourage more women and minorities to become scientists and engineers? Does it prevent state universities from continuing outreach programs aimed at schools with large minority enrollments?

Opponents of affirmative action hoped that the adoption of Proposition 209 in California would start a national movement to restrict or eliminate affirmative action programs. President Clinton restricted some federal programs designed to give women and minority owned businesses greater access to federal contracts. And universities, under pressure from the Office of Civil Rights, have stopped offering scholarships based solely on race or ethnicity.[66] Congress has not as yet moved to limit other federal affirmative action programs.

The issue is very much alive. Public support for affirmative action as measured in public opinion polls varies by race, social class, education, and life experience, but close inspection suggests that "whites and blacks are not separated by unbridgeable gaps on affirmative action issues, at least not insofar as college admissions decisions are concerned."[67] The responses seem to depend to a significant degree on how the question is put. If the question asked is something like, "Are you in favor of abolishing preferences in hiring or college admissions based on race or gender?" most people say yes. But if the question is something like, "Do you favor affirmative action programs to increase the number of minorities in colleges or in jobs?" there is general support for such programs.

In Houston, Texas, the voters opposed, by 55 percent to 45 percent, an initiative that asked, "Shall the Charter of the City of Houston be amended to end the use of affirmative action for women and minorities?"[68] (A judge subsequently set aside the referendum because public officials had made a change from the original wording).[69] In the state of Washington, Initiative 200, almost identical in language with California's Proposition 209, called for abolishing preferential treatment in hiring or contracts. It garnered 58 percent of the popular vote, despite the fact that Governor Gary Locke and most of the leading businesses outspent their opponents three to one. Heartened by this victory, opponents of affirmative action are considering putting the question before the voters in other states, including Nebraska, Michigan, and Florida.[70]

Clearly the debate over the merits and constitutionality of affirmative action is not over. There are more decisions to come as the courts—and the nation—debate whether affirmative action is a vital tool to overcome decades of discrimination that needs to be "amended not ended." Or, as the proponents of Proposition 209 contend, has affirmative action served its purpose, so that government-mandated preference for any person based on race or gender is always unfair and unjust to those not given the preference and demeaning to those to whom it is offered?

Equal Rights Today

Today legal barriers have been lowered, if not removed, by civil rights legislation, executive orders, and judicial decisions. Important as these victories are, "They were victories largely for the middle class—those who could travel, entertain in restaurants, and stay in hotels. Those victories did not change life conditions for the mass of blacks who are still poor."[71]

More than a generation after the Kerner Commission issued its report, life for inner-city minorities is worse. As middle-class African Americans have moved out of the inner city, the remaining *underclass*, as they are coming to be called, has become even more isolated from the rest of the nation.[72] Children are growing up on streets where drug abuse and crime are everyday events. These Americans live in "separate and deteriorating societies, with separate economies, diverging family structures and basic institutions, and even growing linguistic separation within the core ghettos. The scale of their isolation by race, class, and economic situation is much greater than it was in the 1960s, impoverishment, joblessness, educational inequality, and housing insufficiency even more severe."[73]

Despite the lack of improvement in social conditions, the push for integration has lessened.

> In fact, power on both sides of the color line is based to some extent on acceptance of segregation. On the black side of the color line, it is advantageous to keep African Americans within black electoral areas and keep black-controlled resources within black institutions; integrationist policies are often viewed as posing larger threats than they actually do. On the white side of the line . . . some residents in outlying suburbs see critical advantages in their almost all-white and all middle-class status.[74]

Some contend attention should be paid to the plight of the underclass, and that instead of focusing on issues of race, what is needed is a policy of increasing jobs and improving education.[75] Others say there has to be a revival of the civil rights crusade, a restoration of vigorous civil rights enforcement, job training, and, above all, an attack on residential segregation.[76]

One of the difficulties is that, as conditions have become better for many African Americans and Hispanics, they are experienced by them as getting worse because conditions for the rest of Americans are getting better much faster. At the same time, most Americans see conditions for minorities to be improving. "Both perceptions will be correct. And the fact that both are correct in arriving at opposite perceptions of what is going on will itself lead to further misunderstanding."[77]

To help overcome these misunderstandings, President Clinton inaugurated the President's Initiative on Race in 1997 and appointed a seven-member Advisory Board chaired by a distinguished historian, John Hope Franklin. The president charged the Board to start a continuing national conversation about race throughout the United States.[78] The Board issued its final report in the fall of 1998. Its recommendations were: a substantial increase in the funds to enforce civil rights laws because, despite progress, discrimination on the basis of race, color, and ethnicity continues to be a factor of life; a national program to improve early childhood learning; expansion of programs to help small business; and a continuing national dialogue about race. To this end, the board recommended that the president appoint a permanent Council for One America.[79] Little action followed from these recommendations.

At the same time as the report on the Initiative on Race was issued, the Council of Economic Advisors released a fact book of essential indicators about the well-being of minorities. The Council's report made it clear that race and ethnicity continue to be predictors of well-being. Non-Hispanic whites and Asian Americans continue to be better off in terms of health, education, and economic status than African Americans, Hispanics, or Native Americans. As a result of civil rights laws, African Americans made substantial educational, social, and economic progress, but this progress slowed down after the mid-1970s. Hispanics have seen their relative economic status decline over the past 25 years, in considerable part because of immigration by those with lower levels of education and income than second and third generation Hispanics.[80]

What is clear, as we enter the twenty-first century, is that the issue of race and the treatment of ethnic minorities are still dominant domestic problems.

The President's Iniative on Race is a campaign to educate the nation about race issues. Advisory board members include (left to right) former New Jersey Governor Thomas Kean, board chairman John Hope Franklin, and Los Angeles attorney Angela Oh.

online

POLITICS

Using the Internet to Reduce Sexual Harassment

Sexual harassment and other workplace abuses have become major issues. While not a problem exclusively for women, most victims are female. The National Organization for Women (NOW) uses its home page to advocate a "Women-Friendly Workplace Campaign." This campaign encourages employers to pledge to observe standards such as providing a discrimination-free workplace and refusing to tolerate sexual or racial harassment. NOW also advocates getting consumers to sign a pledge that they will support businesses that are women-friendly. The document also goes on to encourage local NOW chapters to set up a "Speak-Out-Line" on which women can call in and report harassment and discrimination. These calls can then be counted and used to identify examples of problems in the community. The document also provides a sample press release, camera-ready copies of the consumer and employer pledges, and a list of suggested Women-Friendly Workplace actions, such as asking consumers and politicians to sign the pledge, targeting businesses that refuse to sign, holding a forum on workplace issues, and planning a "Women-Friendly Workplace" May Day rally.

It is hard to predict how much impact this particular NOW campaign will have, but it is clear that the Internet provides an effective means of getting extensive organizational information out to a lot of people quickly. One of the problems with the Internet for disseminating such information is that it is public. Critics of NOW and the media have the same access to the document as local NOW leaders have. For campaigns where mobilization strategy needs to be less public, the Internet poses problems.

If you want to read about this particular issue, go to:

http://www.now.org/issues/wfw/wfwlet.html

Several civil rights organizations maintain active home pages. See, for instance, the NAACP at:

http://www.naacp.org

or the United States Commission on Civil Rights at:

http://www.usccr.gov

or the National Organization for Women (NOW):

http://www.now.org

For more Internet resources on Equal Rights, see our home page at:

http://www.prenhall.com/burns

SUMMARY

1. Americans are committed to equality, an elusive term, with most support for equality of opportunity, some for equality of starting conditions, and some for equality of results.

2. Progress in securing civil rights for African Americans was a long time in coming. After the Civil War the national government briefly tried to secure some measure of protection for the freed slaves and to enforce the Thirteenth, Fourteenth, and Fifteenth Amendments and the civil rights laws passed to implement them. But when federal troops withdrew from the South in 1877, the national government withdrew from the field and blacks were left to their own resources. Not for nearly a century did the national government take action to prevent racial segregation and discrimination against blacks.

3. The crusade for women's rights was born partly out of the struggle to abolish slavery. Similarly, the modern women's movement learned and gained power from the civil rights movements of the 1950s and early 1960s. The fate of these two social movements has long been intertwined. Women secured the right to vote in the Nineteenth Amendment.

4. Concern for equal rights under the law continues today for African Americans and women and has been expanded to include the rights of Hispanics, Asian Americans, and Native Americans.

5. The Supreme Court uses a three-tiered approach to evaluate the constitutionality of laws challenged as violating the equal protection clause. Laws touching economic concerns are sustained if they are rationally related to the accomplishment of a legitimate government goal. Laws that classify people because of sex or illegitimacy are subject by the courts to heightened scrutiny and are sustained only if they serve important governmental objectives. Strict scrutiny is used to review laws that touch fundamental

rights or classify people because of race or ethnic origin. Such laws will be sustained only if the government can show a compelling public purpose.

6. A series of constitutional amendments, Supreme Court decisions, and laws passed by Congress have now secured the right to vote to all Americans, age 18 and over. Following the Voting Rights Act of 1965, the Justice Department can oversee practices in locales with a history of discrimination. Recent Supreme Court decisions have refined the lengths to which legislatures can go, or are obliged to go, in creating minority-majority districts.

7. *Brown v Board of Education of Topeka* (1954) struck down the "separate but equal" doctrine that had justified segregated schools in the South, but school districts responded slowly. In 1969 the Supreme Court demanded immediate compliance, and some federal courts mandated busing children across neighborhoods to comply. Still, full integration has proved elusive, as "White Flight" has made many inner cities, and their schools, predominantly black or Hispanic.

8. Discrimination in public accommodations was outlawed by the Civil Rights Act of 1964. This act also provided for equal employment opportunity. The Fair Housing Act of 1968 and its 1988 amendments forbid discrimination in housing.

9. The desirability and constitutionality of affirmative action programs that provide special benefits to those who have been subjected to past discrimination divide the nation and the Supreme Court. Remedial programs tailored to overcome specific instances of past discrimination are likely to pass the Supreme Court's suspicion of race, national origin, and sex classifications. However, the courts must still clarify constitutional issues concerning preferential treatment in school admissions and hiring practices.

KEY TERMS

natural rights 100
affirmative action 100
women's suffrage 104
equal protection clause 111
due process clause 111
white primary 114
racial gerrymandering 114
poll tax 114
literacy test 114
majority-minority district 115
Jim Crow laws 115
***de jure* segregation 116**
***de facto* segregation 116**
commerce clause 117
class action suit 118
racial or religious restrictive covenants 119

FURTHER READING

Barbara R. Bergman, *In Defense of Affirmative Action* (Basic Books, 1996).

Janet K. Boles, ed., "American Feminism: New Issues for a Mature Movement." *Annals of the American Academy of Political and Social Science* (May 1991).

William G. Bowen and Derek Bok, *The Shape of the River: Long-Term Consequences of Considering Race in College and University Admissions* (Princeton University Press, 1998).

Taylor Branch, *Parting the Waters: America in the King Years, 1954–1963* (Simon & Schuster, 1988).

Taylor Branch, *Pillar of Fire: America in the King Years, 1963–65* (Simon & Schuster, 1998).

Stephen L. Carter, *Reflections of an Affirmative Action Baby* (Basic Books, 1991).

Linda Chavez, *The Color Bind: California's Battle to End Affirmative Action* (University of California Press, 1998).

Chandler Davidson and Bernard Grofman, eds., *Quiet Revolution in the South* (Princeton University Press, 1994).

Janet Dewart, ed., *The State of Black America* (National Urban League, published annually).

Ronald J. Fiscus, *The Constitutional Logic of Affirmative Action* (Duke University Press, 1992).

Bernard Grofman and Chandler Davidson, eds., *Controversies in Minority Voting: The Votings Rights Act in Perspective* (Brookings Institution, 1992).

Bernard Grofman, Lisa Handley, and Richard G. Niemi, *Minority Representation and the Quest for Voting Equality* (Cambridge University Press, 1992).

Andrew Hacker, *Two Nations: Black and White, Separate, Hostile, Unequal* (Charles Scribner's Sons, 1992).

Randall Kennedy, *Race, Crime, and the Law* (Pantheon, 1997).

Richard Kluger, *Simple Justice* (Knopf, 1976).

Oren Lyons et al., *Exiled in the Land of the Free: Democracy, Indian Nations, and the U.S. Constitution* (Clear Light Publishers, 1992).

Susan Gluck Mezey, *In Pursuit of Equality: Women, Public Policy, and the Federal Courts* (St. Martin's Press, 1992).

Gary Orfield, Susan E. Eaton, and the Harvard Project on School Desegregation, *Dismantling Desegregation: The Quiet Reversal of Brown v Board of Education* (New Press, 1996).

Orlando Patterson, *The Ordeal of Integration: Progress and Resentment in America's Racial Crisis* (Civitas/Counterpoint, 1997).

J. W. Peltason, *Fifty-eight Lonely Men: Southern Federal Judges and School Desegregation* (University of Illinois Press, 1971).

David K. Shipler, *A Country of Strangers* (Vintage Books, 1998).

Peter Skerry, *Mexican Americans: The Ambivalent Minority* (Free Press, 1993).

Shelby Steele, *The Content of Our Character: A New Vision of Race in America* (St. Martin's Press, 1990).

Roberto Suro, *Strangers Among Us: How Latino Immigration Is Transforming America* (Alfred A. Knopf, 1998).

Stephen Thernstrom and Abigail Thernstrom, *America in Black and White* (Simon & Schuster, 1997).

RIGHTS
TO
LIFE
LIBERTY
AND
PROPERTY

6

CHAPTER OUTLINE

- Rights in the Original Constitution
- Citizenship Rights
- Property Rights
- Privacy Rights
- Rights of Persons Accused of Crimes
- The Short and Not Too Happy Life of John Crook
- How Just is Our System of Justice?
- The Supreme Court and Civil Liberties

THROUGHOUT MUCH OF THE WORLD MEN AND WOMEN ARE REBELLING AGAINST THE POLICE STATES UNDER WHICH THEY LIVE, AGAINST GOVERNMENTS IN WHICH the police are unrestrained in how they go about finding, capturing, and punishing so-called enemies of the people. When we in the United States get impatient about the time-consuming steps that must be followed before criminals are taken off the streets, or about the endless rounds of appeals and reviews available to those charged with crimes, we need to remember how fortunate we are to live in a society that values **due process**—established rules and regulations that restrain those in government who exercise power. Such procedures are not available to citizens in Serbia, China, Rwanda, Liberia, Kosovo, and many other parts of the world.

Public officials in the United States do have great power. Under certain conditions they can seize our property, throw us into jail, and—in extreme circumstances—even take our lives. The framers of our Constitution recognized that it is necessary to give power to those who govern. But it is also dangerous. It is so dangerous that to keep our officials from becoming tyrants, we do not depend on the ballot box alone. Because political power can threaten our liberty, we parcel it out in small chunks and surround it with restraints. No single official can decide to take our lives, liberty, or property. Officials must act according to the rules. If they act outside the scope of their authority or contrary to the law, they can be restrained, dismissed, or punished. These rights to due process are the precious rights of all who live under the American flag—rich or poor, young or old, black or white, man or woman, alien or citizen. In this chapter, we look at the safeguards that protect our rights to life, liberty, and property.

Rights in the Original Constitution

Even though most of the framers did not think a Bill of Rights was necessary, they considered certain rights important enough to be included in the original Constitution. These include the right of a writ of *habeas corpus* and protection against *ex post facto* laws and bills of attainder.

The Writ of Habeas Corpus

Foremost among constitutional rights is the **writ of *habeas corpus*.** Literally meaning "produce the body," this writ is a court order directing any official having a person in custody to produce the prisoner in court and explain to the judge why the prisoner is

Rights in the Original Constitution

1. Writ of *habeas corpus*
2. No bills of attainder
3. No *ex post facto* laws
4. No titles of nobility
5. Trial by jury in national courts
6. Protection for citizens as they move from one state to another, including the right to travel
7. Protection against using crime of treason to restrict other activities; limitation on punishment for treason
8. Guarantee that each state has a republican form of government
9. No religious test oaths as a condition for holding a federal office.

being held. As originally used, the writ was merely a judicial inquiry to determine whether a person in custody was being held as the result of the action of a court with proper jurisdiction. But over the years it has developed into a remedy "available to effect discharge from any confinement contrary to the Constitution or fundamental law."[1] Persons being held apply to a judge, usually through an attorney, stating why they believe they are being held unlawfully and requesting release. The judge then orders the jailer to show cause why the writ should not be issued. If a judge finds a petitioner is being detained unlawfully, the judge may order the prisoner's immediate release. Although state judges lack jurisdiction to issue writs of *habeas corpus* to find out why federal authorities are holding persons, federal district judges may do so to find out if state and local officials are holding people in violation of the Constitution or laws or treaties of the United States.

In recent years a challenge has been put forward by those who believe the writ has been abused by state prisoners to touch off an endless and unessential round of reviews, which sometimes lead to convictions being set aside by a federal judge after the matter has been carefully reviewed by at least two state courts. As evidence, critics point to the many prisoners on death row who have successfully used *habeas corpus* to raise objection after objection, delaying the execution of their sentence for years.

Partly because of this criticism, partly from concern for maintaining the principles of federalism, and partly in response to a growing overload on federal courts, the Supreme Court and Congress have severely restricted the *habeas corpus* discretion of federal judges.[2] Congress, in the 1996 Antiterrorism and Effective Death Penalty Act, restricted the number of times persons could be granted a *habeas corpus* review, stopped appeals for most *habeas* petitions at the level of the U.S. courts of appeals, and called for deference by federal judges to the decisions of state judges on matters of fact and law unless those decisions are clearly "unreasonable."[3]

Ex Post Facto Laws and Bills of Attainder

The Constitution forbids both the national and the state governments from passing *ex post facto* laws and enacting bills of attainder (Article I, Sections 9 and 10). An ***ex post facto* law** is a retroactive criminal law making a particular act a crime that was not a crime when the act was committed, or increasing punishment for a crime after the crime was committed, or lessening proof necessary to convict for a crime after it was committed. The prohibition does not prevent the retroactive application of laws that work to the benefit of an accused person—a law decreasing punishment, for example. Nor does the prohibition prevent the retroactive application of civil laws; an increase in income tax rates applied to income already earned, for example.

A **bill of attainder** is a legislative act inflicting punishment, including deprivation of property, without trial on named individuals or members of a specified group. For example, Congress enacted a bill of attainder when it accused three federal employees of being disloyal in an appropriations bill and fired them.

due process
Established rules and regulations that restrain those in government who exercise power.

writ of *habeas corpus*
Court order directing any official having a person in custody to produce the prisoner in court and explain to the judge why the prisoner is being held.

***ex post facto* law**
Retroactive criminal law that works to the disadvantage of an individual; forbidden in the Constitution.

bill of attainder
Legislative act inflicting punishment, including deprivation of property, without trial on named individuals or members of a specified group.

Citizenship Rights

Every nation has rules that determine nationality and define who is a member of, owes allegiance to, and is a subject of the nation. But in a democracy, citizenship is more than nationality, more than merely being a subject.[4] Citizenship is an *office*, and, like other offices, it carries with it certain powers and responsibilities. How citizenship is acquired and retained is therefore a matter of considerable importance.

How Citizenship Is Acquired and Lost

The basic right of citizenship was not given constitutional protection until 1868, when the Fourteenth Amendment was adopted. The Fourteenth Amendment states: "All persons born or naturalized in the United States, and subject to the jurisdiction thereof, are citizens of the United States and of the State wherein they reside." This means that all persons born in the United States, except children born to foreign ambassadors and ministers, are citizens of this country regardless of the citizenship of their parents. (Congress has defined the United States for this purpose to include Puerto Rico, Guam, the Northern Marianas, and the Virgin Islands.) A child born to an American citizen living abroad is an American citizen if the American parent has lived in the United States for ten years, including two years after age 14. Although the Fourteenth Amendment does not make Native Americans citizens of the United States and of the states in which they live, Congress did so in 1924.

The Fourteenth Amendment confers citizenship according to the principle of *jus soli*—by place of birth. In addition, Congress has granted, under certain conditions, citizenship at birth according to the principle of *jus sanguinis*—by blood.

NATURALIZATION Citizenship may also be acquired by either collective or individual **naturalization**, a legal action conferring citizenship upon an alien. The granting of citizenship to the people of the Northern Marianas in 1977 by an act of Congress is an example of collective naturalization.

Congress determines individual naturalization requirements. Today, with minor exceptions, nonenemy aliens over age 18 who have been lawfully admitted for permanent residence and who have resided in the United States for at least five years and in the state for at least six months are eligible for naturalization. Any state or federal court of record in the United States or the Immigration and Naturalization Service (INS) can grant citizenship. The INS, with the help of the Federal Bureau of Investigation (FBI), makes the necessary investigations.

Any person denied citizenship after a hearing before an immigration officer may appeal to a federal district judge. Citizenship is granted if the judge is satisfied that the applicant has met all the requirements after reviewing the FBI check that no disqualifying felony conviction has been found. The applicant renounces allegiance to his or her former country, swears to support and defend the Constitution and laws of the United States against all enemies, and promises to bear arms on behalf of the United States when required to do so by law. Those whose religious beliefs prevent them from bearing arms are allowed to take an oath swearing that, if called to duty, they will serve in the armed forces as noncombatants or will perform work of national importance under civilian direction. The court or INS then grants a certificate of naturalization.

Naturalized citizenship may be revoked by court order if the government can prove citizenship was secured by deception. In addition, citizenship, however acquired, may be renounced voluntarily. But citizenship cannot be taken from people because of what they have done—for example, for committing certain crimes, voting in foreign elections, or serving in foreign armies. Some actions, however, such as taking out citizenship in another country or swearing allegiance to another nation, may be taken into account as "highly persuasive evidence of a purpose to abandon citizenship." Even so, the government must prove that the citizen "not only voluntarily committed the expatriating act prescribed in the statute, but also intended to relinquish his citizenship."[5]

DUAL CITIZENSHIP Because each nation has complete authority to decide for itself the definition of nationality, it is possible for a person to be considered a citizen by two or more nations. **Dual citizenship** is not unusual, especially for persons from nations that do not recognize the right of individuals to renounce their citizenship, called the **right of expatriation**. (One of the issues of the War of 1812 was

naturalization
A legal action conferring citizenship upon an alien.

dual citizenship
Citizenship in two or more nations.

right of expatriation
Right of individuals to renounce their citizenship.

WE THE PEOPLE

Coming to America

Although natural-born Americans tend to take citizenship for granted, most naturalized citizens cherish it, for it represents hard work and a sincere commitment on their part. Would natural-born Americans appreciate citizenship more if they had to meet the same standards as foreign-born applicants?

Naturalization Requirements

An applicant for naturalization must:

1. Be over age 18.
2. Be lawfully admitted to the United States for permanent residence and have resided in the United States for at least five years and in the state for at least six months.
3. File a petition of naturalization with a clerk of a court of record (federal or state) verified by two witnesses.
4. Be able to read, write, and speak English.
5. Possess a good moral character.
6. Understand and demonstrate an attachment to the history, principles, and form of government of the United States.
7. Demonstrate that he or she is well disposed toward the good order and happiness of the country.
8. Demonstrate that he or she does not now believe in, nor within the last ten years has ever believed in, advocated, or belonged to an organization that supports opposition to organized government, overthrow of government by violence, or the doctrines of world communism or any other form of totalitarianism.

Category	Number
Total legal permanent immigrants	720,461*
Family- sponsored immigrants	238,122
Immediate relatives (spouses, children, and parents of U.S. citizens)	220,360
Employment- based immigrants	85,336
Refugees and asylees	114,669
Other immigrants	61,979
Undocumented (illegal) immigrants	300,000

SOURCES: U.S. Bureau of the Census, *Statistical Abstract of the United States, 1997* (Government Printing Office, 1997); The Federation for American Immigration Reform (http://www.fairus.org/04118604.htm).

*Includes persons allowed to enter under amnesty and refugee provisions in addition to the 675,000 other aliens allowed to come in each year.

Immigrants arriving at Ellis Island in 1900 came with high hopes but few material possessions.

that England did not recognize sailors born in England as having abandoned their English citizenship on becoming naturalized American citizens.) Children born abroad to American citizens may also be citizens of the nation in which they were born. Children born in the United States of parents from a foreign nation may also be citizens of their parents' country.

Among the nations that allow dual citizenship are Canada, Mexico, France, and the United Kingdom. One expert estimates that, based on the number of American children born to foreign-born parents, the number of Americans eligible to hold citizenship in another country grows by at least 500,000 a year.[6] Moreover, with more than 7 million Mexican-born immigrants in the United States and their American-born children now becoming eligible to apply for Mexican citizenship, the number of dual citizens in the United States is on the rise. Dual citizenship carries negative as well as positive consequences; for example, a person with dual citizenship may be subject to national service obligations and taxes in both countries.

Rights of American Citizens

An American becomes a citizen of one of our states merely by residing in that state. *Residence* as understood in the Fourteenth Amendment means the place one calls home. The legal status of residence should not be confused with the fact of physical presence. A person may be living in Washington, D.C., but be a citizen of California—that is, consider California home and vote in that state.

Most of our most important rights flow from *state* citizenship rather than from United States citizenship. In the Slaughter-House Cases (1873), the Supreme Court carefully distinguished between the privileges of United States citizens and those of state citizens. It held that the only privileges attaching to national citizenship are those that "owe their existence to the Federal Government, its National Character, its Constitution, or its laws."[7] These privileges have never been completely specified, but they include the right to use the navigable waters of the United States, to assemble peacefully, to petition the national government for redress of grievances, to be protected by the national government on the high seas, to vote if qualified to do so under state laws, to have one's vote counted properly, and to travel throughout the United States.

THE RIGHT TO LIVE IN THE UNITED STATES This right, which is not subject to any congressional limitation, is perhaps the most precious aspect of American citizenship. Aliens have no such right. They may be stopped on the high seas or at the borders and turned away if they fail to meet the terms and conditions stipulated by the Congress for admission to the United States. Today millions of people around the world yearn to come and live in the United States, but only American citizens have a constitutionally guaranteed right to do so.

THE RIGHT TO TRAVEL ABROAD The right to international travel can be regulated within the bounds of due process. Under current law it is unlawful for citizens to leave or enter the United States without a valid passport (except as otherwise provided by the president, as has been done for travel to Mexico, Canada, and parts of the Caribbean). The president, acting through the secretary of state, may refuse to grant or may revoke a passport if the government concludes that a holder's activities in foreign countries are causing, or are likely to cause, serious damage to our national security or foreign policy.

Rights of Aliens

We are in a period of growing hostility toward aliens, so the protections of citizenship become even more precious, especially the right to live here. True, the Constitution protects many rights of all *persons,* not just of American citizens; for example, neither Congress nor the states can deny to aliens the right of freedom of religion or the right of freedom of speech. Nor can any government deprive any person, alien or citizen, the due process of the law or equal protection under the laws.

However, Congress can deny welfare and many other kinds of benefits to aliens, as it did in 1996. In response to a political reaction, many of these benefits were later restored for aliens in the United States legally.

Congress, however, has denied most federally assisted benefits to *illegal* immigrants and has permitted states to deny them most other benefits, making an exception only for emergency medical care, disaster relief, and some nutrition programs. Congress debated a proposal allowing states to prohibit illegal immigrant children from attending public schools, but backed down under threat of a presidential veto. This legislation would have challenged the Supreme Court's 1982 decision that states cannot constitutionally exclude children of undocumented aliens from the public schools or charge their parents tuition.[8]

Admission to the United States

President Franklin Roosevelt, reminding us of our heritage as a haven for people fleeing religious and political persecution, opened his address to a convention of the Daughters of the American Revolution with the salutation, "Fellow immigrants and revolutionaries." Some Americans, however, are concerned that admitting so many people from abroad will dilute American traditions and values. Throughout our history debates have flared among those wishing to open our borders and those wishing to close them.

Aliens do not have a constitutional right to enter the United States. Congress has wide discretion in setting the numbers, terms, and conditions under which aliens can enter and stay in the United States. By 1882 Congress began to restrict the entry of persons alleged to be "undesirable," such as prostitutes and revolutionaries. During World War I, Congress, for the first time, set limits on the number of aliens who could be admitted each year. The Immigration Act of 1924 created a system that discriminated against immigrants from southern Europe and southeast Asia on the basis of national origin.

The Immigration Act of 1965 as amended in 1990 and 1996 sets an annual ceiling of 675,000 for nonamnesty, nonrefugee aliens allowed to come here as permanent residents, but when refugees and other exempt categories are added, more than 800,000 people enter the United States each year. The law also sets an annual limit on immigrants from any single country. Preference is given for family reunification. Second preference is provided to people who have special job skills or who are needed to fill jobs for which U.S. workers are not available. Included in this category are professionals holding advanced degrees, persons of exceptional ability, and skilled workers. Another provision allows for the admission of "millionaire immigrants" who are willing and able to invest a substantial sum in the United States to create or support a business that will provide jobs for Americans. There have been few takers for admission under this provision. There is also a "diversity" category to provide visas for 55,000 immigrants from 34 countries, chiefly but not exclusively European, whether or not they have relatives living in the United States. These visas are drawn annually by lottery from a pool of qualified applicants.

In addition to regularly admitted aliens, in recent years more than 100,000 political refugees have been admitted. *Political refugees* are defined by law as persons who have well-founded fears of persecution in their own countries based on their race, religion, nationality, social class, or political opinion. Persons who are admitted as political refugees can apply to become permanent residents after one year.

The attorney general, acting through the U.S. Immigration and Naturalization Service, may also grant *asylum,* if the attorney general agrees with the applicants that they, like political refugees, have well-founded fears of persecution in the country to which they would otherwise be returned, based on their race, religion, nationality, membership in a particular social group, or political opinion. It is not enough, however, that applicants face the same terrible conditions that all other citizens of their country face, or that they wish to escape from bad economic or political conditions. They must show specific danger of persecution. Where political conditions are extremely fluid, the Department of Justice can grant an individual "temporary protected status" while it tries to determine the peril the applicant actually faces at home.

The Immigration and Naturalization Service may turn back at the border persons seeking asylum when it considers their requests insubstantial, or it may even hold them in detention camps.[9] The president may order the Coast Guard—as both George Bush and Bill Clinton did with respect to Haitian and Cuban refugees—to stop persons on the high seas before they enter the territorial waters of the United States and return them to the country from which they have fled without determining whether they qualify as refugees.[10] Nonetheless, many people are still willing to risk great danger to get here and suffer detention once they arrive, just for the chance of being granted asylum.

The love of freedom is so strong that these Cuban "balseros" (boat people) were willing to risk death to get to the United States in this flimsy raft.

Once in the United States, aliens are subject to the full range of obligations, including the payment of taxes.[11] Aliens are counted in the census for the purpose of apportioning seats in the U.S. House of Representatives. Legally admitted aliens may be deported for a variety of reasons—for example, conviction of crimes involving moral turpitude, incitement of terrorist activity, illegal voting in elections, and conviction of domestic violence.[12]

Undocumented Aliens

How should the United States government deal with the estimated 2.3 to 2.4 million undocumented aliens—mostly from Mexico and other nations in Central and South America and a few from Canada and Poland—who illegally cross our borders not because they fear political persecution but because they see greater economic opportunity in the United States?[13] It should be noted, however, that most undocumented immigrants from Mexico return to Mexico after only two years. "By 10 years, almost 70 percent of those who came to the United States have returned."[14]

Inability to keep illegal aliens out of the country is not a question of constitutional power, for "over no conceivable subject is the legislative power of Congress more complete than it is over the admission of aliens."[15] Rather, the problems are political and practical. Although Congress in 1996 authorized an increase in the number of border patrol guards by 1,000 each year, for a total by 2001 of 10,000, and funded additional fencing of the California-Mexican border, there are thousands of miles of borders. Moreover, it is difficult to track down undocumented aliens inside the United States, round them up, and expel them in a fashion consistent with the practices and policies of a free society.

Once here, undocumented aliens do not find it hard to become invisible and find jobs, especially in our larger cities. Some employers prefer to hire them because they work for less money than those who are here lawfully, and they are unprotected. One of the sponsors of the Immigration Reform and Control Act of 1986 described the vulnerability of this "subculture of human beings who are afraid to go to the cops, afraid to go to a hospital, afraid to go to their employer who says, 'One peep out of you, buster, and you are down the road.' "[16]

Congress has been faced with conflicting pressures: from Hispanic groups concerned that making it illegal to hire undocumented workers will make employers hesitate to hire any Hispanics; from employers who do not want to keep costly records and investigate the legal status of everybody they hire; from employers of farm workers who want to be sure they will have enough laborers to pick seasonal crops; from American workers who do not want undocumented workers being used to keep wages low; and from city and local governmental officials who have to find the funds to provide social services for undocumented aliens.

The United States government tends to consider immigration policy a purely internal matter, yet it clearly affects our relations with other nations, most especially with Mexico, as the lengthy negotiations over the North American Free Trade Agreement (NAFTA) demonstrated. Whereas officials of the United States view immigration policy as a matter of sovereignty, Mexicans see it as a matter that directly affects them and a matter that should involve discussions between the two nations.[17]

Property Rights

Constitutional Protection of Property

Property does not have rights. People do. **Property rights** are the rights of an individual to own, use, rent, invest in, buy, and sell property. Historically, the close connection between liberty and ownership of property, between property and power, has been emphasized in American political thinking and American political institutions. A major purpose of the framers of the Constitution was to establish a government strong enough to protect people's rights to use and enjoy their property. At the same time, the framers wanted to limit government so it could not endanger that right. As a result, the framers included in the Constitution a variety of clauses protecting property rights.

property rights
The rights of an individual to own, use, rent, invest in, buy, and sell property.

contract clause
Clause of the Constitution that was originally intended to forbid state governments to modify contracts made between individuals; for a while interpreted to forbid state governments from adversely affecting property rights; no longer interpreted so broadly and no longer constrains state governments from exercising their police powers.

police powers
Inherent powers of state governments to pass laws to protect the public health, safety, and welfare; national government has no directly granted police powers, but through other delegated powers accomplishes the same goals.

eminent domain
Power of a government to take private property for public use; the U.S. Constitution gives national and state governments this power and requires them to provide just compensation for property so taken.

THE LEGAL TENDER AND CONTRACT CLAUSES Of special concern to the framers were the efforts of some state legislatures to protect debtors at the expense of their creditors by issuing paper currency and setting aside private contracts. To prevent these practices, the Constitution forbids states from making anything except gold or silver *legal tender* for the payment of debts and from passing any "Law impairing the Obligation of Contracts."

The **contract clause**, Article I, Section 10, was designed to prevent states from extending the period during which debtors could meet their payments or otherwise get out of contractual obligations. The framers had in mind an ordinary contract between private persons. However, beginning with Chief Justice John Marshall, the Supreme Court expanded the coverage of the clause to prevent states from altering privileges previously conferred on corporations. In effect, the contract clause was used to protect property and to maintain the status quo at the expense of the power of the states to guard the public welfare.

In the 1880s, however, the Supreme Court gradually began to restrict the coverage of the contract clause and to subject contracts to what in constitutional law is known as **police powers**—the power to protect the public health, safety, welfare, and morals. By 1934 the Supreme Court actually held that even contracts between individuals—the very ones the contract clause was intended to protect—could be modified by state law in order to avert social and economic catastrophe.[18] Although the contract clause is still invoked occasionally to challenge state regulation of property, it is no longer a significant limitation on governmental power.

What Happens When the Government Takes Our Property?

Both the national and state governments have the power of **eminent domain**—the power to take private property for public use—but the owner must be fairly compensated. This limitation, contained in the Fifth Amendment, was the first provision of the Bill of Rights to be enforced as a limitation on state governments as well as on the national government.[19]

What constitutes a "taking" for purposes of eminent domain?[20] The clause does not require compensation merely because governmental action may result in property loss. For example, if a zoning regulation restricts an area to single-family residential use and thus lowers the value of a particular property, no compensation is due. Ordinarily, but not always, the taking must be direct, and a person must lose title and control over the property. Sometimes, especially in recent years, the courts have found that a governmental regulation has gone "too far" and must be deemed a "taking" for which the government must pay compensation to its owners, even when title is left in the hands of the owners.[21] These are called **regulatory takings**. Thus, if a government creates landing and takeoff paths for airplanes over property adjacent to an airport, making the land no longer suitable for its prior use (say, raising chickens), compensation is warranted.

"Just compensation" is not always easy to define. In case of a dispute, the courts make the final resolution. By and large, "the owner is entitled to receive what a willing buyer would pay in cash to a willing seller at the time of the taking."[22] An owner is not entitled to compensation for the personal value of an old, broken-down house that is loved dearly. The compensation will only be for an old, broken-down house.

The *taking clause* has received renewed judicial attention in the last several years as many state and local units strive to protect the environment and quality of life by regulating the terms and conditions under which land may be developed. The Supreme Court has begun using the taking clause to review these governmental regulations. For example, the Supreme Court held that if a government has prevented a property owner from developing property by regulations that turned out to be unconstitutional, the owner is entitled to just compensation for the temporary taking, even if the government finally withdraws the regulation.[23] The Court also ruled that a government has engaged in a taking if it imposes an unrelated condition before issuing a building permit—requiring, for example, that the owner of a beach-front home allow the public to walk across the property to the beach as a condition for receiving a permit to enlarge the house.[24]

Due Process: Old and New

Perhaps the most difficult parts of the Constitution to understand are the clauses in the Fifth and Fourteenth Amendments that forbid national and state governments to deny any person life, liberty, or property without due process of law. Cases involving these clauses have resulted in hundreds of Supreme Court decisions. Even so, it is impossible to explain *due process* precisely. In fact, the Supreme Court has refused to give due process a precise definition and has emphasized that "due process, unlike some legal rules, is not a technical conception with a fixed content unrelated to time, place and circumstances."[25]

PROCEDURAL DUE PROCESS There are two kinds of due process: procedural and substantive. **Procedural due process** generally refers to the *methods* by which a law is enforced. But a law may violate the procedural due process requirement if it is too vague or if it creates an improper presumption of guilt. A vague statute fails to provide adequate warning and does not contain sufficient guidelines for law enforcement officials, juries, and courts.

A statute that creates an improper presumption of guilt denies due process by shifting the burden of proof from the government to the accused person. Laws presuming, for example, that all marijuana or cocaine in a person's possession must have been obtained illegally have been declared unconstitutional. But the Court did uphold a presumption with respect to heroin; as virtually all heroin is illegally imported, it is therefore not unreasonable to presume that a person who possesses heroin obtained it illegally.[26]

regulatory taking
Government regulation of property so extensive that government is deemed to have taken the property by the power of eminent domain, for which it must compensate the property owners.

procedural due process
Constitutional requirement that governments proceed by proper methods; places limits on how governmental power may be exercised.

You Decide...

Is a college education a constitutional right?

Scott E. Ewing was dismissed by the University of Michigan from a medical educational program after failing an examination required to qualify for the final two years. His request to retake the examination was denied. He brought an action in a federal district court alleging that all other medical students who had failed the examination had routinely been given at least a second chance to take the test. He contended his dismissal was arbitrary and capricious and was thus in violation of his substantive due process rights guaranteed by the Fourteenth Amendment. The university said he had been dismissed for legitimate academic reasons, that no one has a constitutional right to a second examination, and that what it had done was perfectly reasonable.

Did Ewing have a due process right to continued enrollment free from arbitrary state action? Did the state of Michigan violate Ewing's substantive property right to a college education?

Traditionally, however, procedural due process refers not to the law itself but to the *way in which a law is applied.* To paraphrase Daniel Webster's famous definition, it requires a procedure that hears before it condemns, proceeds upon inquiry, and renders judgment only after a trial or some kind of hearing. Originally, procedural due process was limited to criminal prosecutions, but it now applies to most kinds of governmental proceedings. It is required, for instance, in juvenile hearings, disbarment proceedings, proceedings to determine eligibility for welfare payments, revocation of drivers' licenses, and disciplinary proceedings in state universities and public schools.

The liberty that is protected by due process is more than freedom from being thrown into jail, and the property that is secured goes beyond the mere ownership of real estate, things, or money. Rather, liberty includes "the right of the individual to contract, to engage in any of the common occupations of life, to acquire useful knowledge, to marry, to establish a home and bring up children, to worship God according to the dictates of his own conscience, and generally to enjoy those common law privileges long recognized as essential to the orderly pursuit of happiness by free men."[27] The property protected by due process includes a variety of rights that may be conferred by state law, such as certain kinds of licenses, protection from being fired from some jobs except for just cause (for example, incompetence) and according to certain procedures, protection from deprivation of certain pension rights, and so on.

"Once it is determined that due process applies, the question remains what process is due."[28] What is due varies with the kind of interest involved, the reliability of the procedures used, and the governmental purposes to be served. In a federal courtroom, due process requires the careful observance of the provision of the Bill of Rights. In a state courtroom, due process requires the careful observance of all provisions of the Bill of Rights except indictment by grand jury and jury trials in civil cases. What is due in other kinds of proceedings is what must be done to ensure fundamental fairness. It is hard to generalize because many kinds of proceedings are involved, but at a minimum the person involved must have adequate notice and an opportunity to be heard.

SUBSTANTIVE DUE PROCESS Procedural due process places limits on *how* governmental power may be exercised; **substantive due process** places limits on *what* a government may do. Procedural due process pertains to the procedures of the law, substantive due process to the content of the law. Procedural due process mainly limits the executive and judicial branches; substantive due process mainly limits the legislative branch. Substantive due process means that an "unreasonable" law, even if properly passed and properly applied, is unconstitutional. It means that there are certain things governments *should not be allowed to do,* no matter how they do it.

Before 1937, substantive due process was used primarily to protect liberty of contract—that is, the right of employers to make contracts with employees freely, without government interference. Indeed, the adoption of the doctrine of substantive due process and the simultaneous expansion of the meaning of liberty and property made the Supreme Court, for a time, the final judge of our economic and industrial life. During this period the Supreme Court was dominated by conservative jurists who considered almost all social welfare legislation unreasonable. They used the due process clause to strike down laws setting maximum hours of labor, establishing minimum wages, regulating prices, and forbidding employers to fire workers because they joined a union.

substantive due process
Constitutional requirement that governments act reasonably and that the substance of the laws themselves be fair and reasonable; places limits on what a government may do.

The trouble with the substantive interpretation of due process is that what a person, including a judge, thinks is a "reasonable" law depends on economic, social, and political views rather than on legal doctrine. In democracies, elected officials are supposed to accommodate opposing notions of reasonableness and to decide what regulations of liberty and property are needed. When the Supreme Court substitutes its own ideas of reasonableness for those of Congress or state legislatures, it acts like a superlegislature.

In response to this criticism, the Supreme Court since 1937 has largely refused to apply the doctrine of substantive due process in reviewing laws regulating business enterprises. The Court now believes that deciding what constitutes reasonable regulations of business and commercial life is a legislative, not a judicial, responsibility. As long as the justices find a conceivable connection between a law regulating business and the promotion of the public welfare, the Supreme Court will not interfere. This does not mean, however, that the Court has abandoned substantive due process. On the contrary, substantive due process has taken on new life as a protector of civil liberties, most especially the right of privacy.

Substantive due process, resting on the notion that laws must be reasonable, has deep roots in concepts of natural law and a long history in the American constitutional tradition. For most Americans most of the time, it is not enough merely to say that a law reflects the wishes of the popular or legislative majority. We also want our laws to be just, and we continue to rely heavily on judges to decide what is just.

Privacy Rights

The most important extension of substantive due process in recent decades has been its expansion to protect the right of privacy, especially marital privacy. Although there is no mention of the right of privacy in the Constitution, the Supreme Court has put together some elements from the First, Fourth, Fifth, Ninth, and Fourteenth Amendments to recognize that personal privacy is one of the rights protected by the Constitution.

There are three aspects of this right: (1) the right to be free from governmental surveillance and intrusion, especially in marital matters; (2) the right not to have private affairs made public by the government; and (3) the right to be free in thought and belief from governmental compulsion.[29]

Abortion Rights

The most controversial aspect of constitutional protection for privacy relates to the extent of state power to regulate abortions. In *Roe v Wade*, decided in 1973, the Supreme Court ruled: (1) during the first trimester of a woman's pregnancy, it is an unreasonable and therefore unconstitutional interference with her liberty and privacy rights for a state to set any limits on her choice to have an abortion or on her doctor's medical judgments about how to carry it out; (2) during the second trimester, the state's interest in protecting the health of women becomes compelling, and a state may make a reasonable regulation about how, where, and when abortions may be performed; and (3) during the third trimester, when the life of the fetus outside the womb becomes viable, the state's interest in protecting the unborn child is so important that the state can prohibit abortions altogether, except when necessary to preserve the life or health of the mother.[30]

The *Roe* decision led to decades of heated public debate and attempts by Presidents Ronald Reagan and George Bush to select Supreme Court justices who could be expected to vote to reverse it. Nonetheless, in 1992 *Roe v Wade* was reaffirmed. A bitterly divided Rehnquist Court, by a five-person majority (O'Connor, Kennedy, Souter, Blackmun, and Stevens), upheld the view that the due process clauses of the Constitution protect a woman's liberty to choose an abortion prior to viability. The Court, however, held that the right to have an abortion prior to viability is subject to state regulation that does not "unduly burden" it. In other words, states may make reasonable regulations on how a woman exercises her right to an abortion so long as "the State does not prohibit any woman from making the ultimate decision to terminate her pregnancy before viability."[31]

Thinking it Through . . .

Eight members of the U.S. Supreme Court said that even if it is assumed that Ewing had such a right, the responsibility for determining academic matters belongs to the faculty, and judges should interfere only if there is "a substantial departure from accepted academic norms as to demonstrate that the faculty did not exercise professional judgment and acted clearly in an arbitrary and capricious manner."

Justice Lewis F. Powell, Jr., concurred, but would not even concede that Ewing might, for purposes of the decision, have a substantive due process property right not to be dismissed by a state university in an arbitrary manner.

You might want to read this short opinion. You can find it in many libraries. Give this citation to the librarian: *Regents of the University of Michigan v Ewing*, 474 US 214 (1985).

Applying the "undue burden" test, the Court has held, for instance, that states can prohibit the use of state funds and facilities for performing abortions, that a state may make a minor's right to an abortion conditional on her first notifying at least one parent or a judge, that a state may condition an abortion on a 24-hour waiting period during which a doctor must inform the woman about alternatives in a state-prescribed talk. On the other hand, a state may not condition a woman's right to an abortion on her first notifying her husband.[32]

Sexual Orientation Rights

Although there is general agreement on how much constitutional protection is provided for marital privacy, in 1986 the Supreme Court refused to extend such protection to relations between homosexuals. By a 5 to 4 vote, the Court refused to declare unconstitutional a Georgia law that made consensual sodomy as practiced by homosexuals a crime. That homosexual conduct occurs in the privacy of the home, said the majority, does not affect the result. But in 1998 the Georgia Supreme Court struck down this very same Georgia law in a case involving two consenting heterosexual adults as a violation of the right of privacy under the Georgia constitution. This is part of a trend of a number of state courts to find greater privacy protection in their state constitutions than the U.S. Supreme Court has found in the U.S. Constitution.[33]

Without mentioning its 1986 decision, a decade later the U.S. Supreme Court struck down a provision of the Colorado Constitution enacted by the voters through the initiative process, which prohibited all legislative, executive, or judicial action designed to protect homosexuals at any level of state or local government. This provision, declared the Court, violates the equal protection clause because it identifies persons by a single trait and then denies them across the board protection. Justice Antonin Scalia in dissent accused the Court of taking sides in "the cultural wars through an act not of judicial judgment but of political will."[34]

Because of the strong emotions on both sides of this issue, the right of privacy as an element of substantive due process is one of the developing edges of constitutional law, one about which people both on and off the Court have strong feelings. How the Supreme Court handles privacy issues has become front-page news.

Rights of Persons Accused of Crimes

According to the Fourth Amendment, "The right of the people to be secure in their persons, houses, papers, and effects, against unreasonable searches and seizures, shall not be violated, and no Warrants shall issue, but upon probable cause, supported by Oath or affirmation, and particularly describing the place to be searched, and the persons or things to be seized." Despite what we sometimes see in television police dramas and read in the press, law enforcement officers have no general right to break down doors and invade homes. They are not supposed to search people except under certain conditions, and they have no right to arrest them except under certain circumstances.[35]

Freedom from Unreasonable Searches and Seizures

Seizures, or what we now call police detentions and arrests, are in fact given less protection than searches of property. Police may arrest people without warrants in public places, provided there is *probable cause*—a fair probability that the persons in question have committed or are about to commit crimes. No later than two days after making an arrest, the police must take the arrested person to a magistrate so that the magistrate—not just the police—can decide whether probable cause existed to justify the warrantless arrest.[36] Probable cause, however, does not, except in extreme emergencies, justify a warrantless arrest of people in their own homes.

Under the common law, police officers apprehending a fleeing suspected felon could use weapons that might result in the felon's serious injury, even death. But the Fourth Amendment places substantial limits on the use of what is called *deadly force.* It is unconstitutional to shoot at an apparently unarmed, fleeing, suspected felon unless the officer has probable cause to believe that the suspect poses a significant threat of death or serious injury to the officer or others. Also, when feasible, the officer must first warn the suspect: "Halt or I'll shoot."

Police may detain and search cars and their passengers if they have probable cause to believe that the cars are involved in criminal activity, including even minor traffic offenses.

Not every time the police stop a person to ask questions or to seek that person's consent to a search is there a seizure or detention requiring probable cause or a warrant. If the police just ask questions or even seek consent to search that individual's person or possessions in a noncoercive atmosphere, there is no detention. "So long as a reasonable person would feel free 'to disregard the police and go about his business,' the encounter is consensual and no reasonable suspicion is required. The encounter will not trigger Fourth Amendment scrutiny unless it loses its consensual nature." But if the person refuses to answer questions or consent to a search, and the police, by either physical force or a show of authority, restrain the movement of the person, even though there is no arrest, the Fourth Amendment comes into play.[37] For example, if police approach people in airports and request identification, this act by itself does not constitute a detention. The same is true if police ask bus passengers for consent to search their luggage for drugs. But if the police do more, especially after consent is refused, then their actions require them to have some objective justification for the search beyond mere suspicion.

Various administrative searches by nonpolice government agents, such as teachers and health officials, do not require search warrants. Rules governing the conduct of such administrative searches are more lenient than are those for searches by police investigating crimes. Administrative searches conducted without grounds for suspicion of particular individuals have been upheld in certain limited circumstances.[38]

One troublesome area relates to compulsory drug testing. The Court has upheld the constitutionality of blood and urine tests of rail employees involved in train accidents; of customs officials who are directly involved in drug interdiction or who are required to carry a firearm; and of random drug testing for high school students engaged in interscholastic athletic competitions. But it struck down a Georgia law requiring candidates for designated state offices to certify that they had taken a drug test and that the test result was negative, because Georgia failed to show why this invasion of personal privacy was necessary.[39]

Some of the exceptions to the general rule against warrantless searches and seizures of what is found by police and customs officials are as follows:

1. *The Automobile Exception*: If officers have probable cause to believe that an automobile is being used to commit a crime, even a traffic offense, or that it contains persons who have committed crimes, or that it contains evidence of crimes or contraband, they may stop the automobile, detain the persons found therein, and search them and any containers or packages found inside the car.[40] Once an automobile has been lawfully detained, the police officers may order the driver and passengers to get out of the car without violating the Fourth Amendment.[41]
2. *The Terry Exception*: First discussed in *Terry v Ohio*, these searches were originally justified only when officers had reason to believe they were dealing with armed and dangerous persons, but they have subsequently been expanded to cover stops when the police have reason to believe that a person has committed or is about to commit a criminal offense. The intrusion permitted under a *Terry* search is limited to a quick pat-down to check

The Crime Control and Safe Streets Act of 1968

1. Makes it a crime for any unauthorized person to tap telephone wires or to use or sell, in interstate commerce, electronic bugging devices.
2. Empowers the United States attorney general to secure a warrant from a federal judge authorizing federal agents to engage in bugging in order to track down persons suspected of certain federal crimes. ("About 12,000 court-ordered criminal wiretaps are conducted every year by federal, state, and local authorities' and the number has been rising steadily in recent years, largely as a result of their frequent use in drug-trafficking cases.")*
3. Permits wiretaps without prior court approval for 48 hours in emergency situations involving certain crimes, such as child pornography, illegal currency transactions, offenses against witnesses of crimes, or immediate danger of death or serious injury.
4. Authorizes the principal prosecuting attorney of any state or political subdivision to apply to a state judge for a warrant approving wiretapping or other intercepts for felonies. (Most state and local jurisdictions allow such intercepts.)
5. Permits judges to issue warrants only if they decide probable cause exists that a crime is being, has been, or is about to be committed, and that information relating to that crime may be obtained only by wiretapping.

*Robert Suro and Elizabeth Corcoran, "Crossed Wires on Digital-Age Wiretapping," *The Washington Post National Weekly Edition*, April 6, 1998, p. 30.

for weapons that might be used to assault the arresting officer, to check for contraband, to determine identity, or to maintain briefly the status quo while obtaining more information.[42] If an officer stops and frisks a suspect to look for weapons and finds criminal evidence that might justify an arrest, then the officer can make a full search.[43]

3. *Searches Subsequent to Valid Arrest*: When making a lawful arrest, either with an arrest warrant or because of probable cause, police may make a warrantless search of persons involved, the areas under their immediate control, and all the possessions they take with them to the place of detention. And police may make a protective sweep of the immediate area to be sure it does not harbor other dangerous persons.[44]
4. *Searches for Evidence*: When there is probable cause to make an arrest, even if one is not made, limited searches are permitted if necessary to preserve easily disposed of evidence, such as scrapings under fingernails.[45]
5. *Consent*: Searches based on voluntary consent are allowed, even if the persons who give the consent are not told they are free to go and have a right to refuse to grant permission.[46]
6. *Border Searches*: Searches of persons and the goods they bring with them are permissible at border crossings.[47] The border search exception also permits officials to open mail entering the country if they have "reasonable cause" to suspect it contains merchandise imported contrary to the law.[48]
7. *Plain-View Exception*: The plain-view exception permits officers to seize evidence without a warrant if: (1) they are lawfully in a position from which the evidence can be viewed; (2) it is immediately apparent to them that the items they observe are evidence of a crime or are contraband; and (3) they have probable cause to believe—a reasonable suspicion will not do—that the evidence uncovered is contraband or evidence of a crime.[49]
8. *Exigent Circumstances*: Searches are permissible under *exigent circumstances*, that is, when officers do not have time to secure a warrant before evidence is destroyed, or a criminal escapes capture, or when there is need "to protect or preserve life or avoid serious injury." An example of exigent circumstances is that fire fighters and police may enter a burning building without a warrant and may remain there for a reasonable time to investigate the cause of the blaze after the fire has been extinguished. However, after the fire has been put out, the emergency is not to be used as an excuse to make an exhaustive, warrantless search for evidence not in plain sight.[50]
9. *Foreign Agents*: Although never directly sustained by the Supreme Court, Congress has endorsed a presidential claim that the president can authorize warrantless wiretaps and physical searches of agents of foreign countries. Congress has created a special Foreign Intelligence Surveillance Court to approve such requests. This court, consisting of seven federal district judges, meets in secret.[51]

search warrant
A warrant issued by a magistrate that authorizes the police to search a particular place or person, specifying the place to be searched and the objects to be seized.

Outside of these exceptions, a police search without consent is constitutionally unreasonable unless it has been authorized by a valid **search warrant**, issued by a magistrate after the police indicate under oath that they have probable cause to justify its issuance. Magistrates must perform this function in a neutral and detached manner and not serve merely as rubber stamps for the police.

The Constitution not only ordinarily requires a search warrant, but it also requires a specific one because *general search warrants*—warrants that authorize police to search a particular place or person without limitation—are unconstitutional. When a magistrate issues a warrant, the warrant must describe: (1) what places are to be searched, and (2) what things are to be seized. And a warrant is needed to search a person in any place he or she has an "expectation of privacy that society is prepared to recognize as reasonable," for example, in a hotel room, in a rented home, in a friend's apartment.[52] In short, the Fourth Amendment protects people, not places, from unreasonable governmental intrusions.

"The court finds itself on the horns of a dilemma. On the one hand, wiretap evidence is inadmissable, and on the other hand, I'm dying to hear it."

THE EXCLUSIONARY RULE In *Mapp v Ohio* (1961), the Supreme Court adopted a rule excluding from a criminal trial evidence that the police obtained unconstitutionally or illegally.[53] This **exclusionary rule** was adopted to prevent police misconduct. Critics of the exclusionary rule, including Chief Justice William H. Rehnquist, question why criminals should go free just because of police misconduct or ineptness,[54] but so far the Supreme Court has refused to abandon the rule. It has started making some exceptions to it, however, such as cases in which police relied in good faith on a search warrant that subsequently turned out to be granted improperly.[55]

The Right to Remain Silent

During the seventeenth century, certain special courts in England forced confessions from religious dissenters. The British privilege against self-incrimination developed in response to these practices. Because they were familiar with this history, the framers of our Bill of Rights included in the Fifth Amendment the provision that persons shall not be compelled to testify against themselves in criminal prosecutions. This protection against self-incrimination is designed to strengthen the fundamental principle that no person has an obligation to prove innocence. Rather, the burden is on the government to prove guilt.

The privilege against self-incrimination applies literally only in criminal prosecutions, but it has always been interpreted to protect any person subject to questioning by any agency of government, such as a congressional committee. It is not enough, however, to contend that answers might be embarrassing or might lead to loss of a job or even to civil suits; persons must have a reasonable fear that their answers might support a criminal prosecution against them or "furnish a link in the chain of evidence needed to prosecute" a crime they may have committed.[56]

Sometimes authorities would rather have information from witnesses than prosecute them. Congress has established procedures so that prosecutors and congressional committees may secure a grant of **immunity** for such a witness. There are two types of immunity: the narrowest type, *use immunity*, means that prosecutors cannot use the testimony to prosecute; *transactional immunity* means that a person who responds truthfully cannot be prosecuted for any crime related in the compelled testimony. After either kind of immunity has been granted, a witness no longer has a constitutional right to refuse to testify. A person granted use immunity can still be prosecuted for crimes subject to such investigations, but the government cannot use the information derived directly from the compelled testimony in any subsequent prosecution.

This grant of use immunity can be a formidable bar to successful prosecution, as was indicated by the government's inability to prosecute Oliver North and others involved in the Iran-Contra affair. Transactional immunity is seldom granted, but Independent Prosecutor Kenneth Starr granted such sweeping immunity to Monica Lewinsky and her mother in exchange for their agreement to tell all about the young intern's sexual affair with President Bill Clinton.[57]

exclusionary rule
Requirement that evidence unconstitutionally or illegally obtained be excluded from a criminal trial.

immunity
Protection granted by prosecutors to witnesses in exchange for giving up their constitutional right not to testify against themselves. There are various kinds of immunity; the most extensive is *transactional*, which means witnesses cannot be prosecuted for any offenses uncovered by their testimony; *use immunity* only protects witnesses from having their testimony used in subsequent criminal trials.

The Miranda warning is read to a suspect by a police officer before questioning him to inform him of his rights, such as the right to remain silent and the right to have an attorney present.

The Miranda Warning

Police questioning of suspects is a key procedure in solving crimes. Roughly 90 percent of all criminal convictions result from guilty pleas and never reach a full trial. Police questioning, however, can easily be abused. Police officers sometimes forget or ignore the constitutional rights of suspects, especially those who are frightened and ignorant. Unauthorized detention and lengthy interrogation to wring confessions from suspects, common practice in police states, were not unknown in the United States.

What good is the presumption of innocence if, long before the accused are brought before the court, they are detained and forced to prove their innocence to the police? Judges have done much to stamp out such police brutality. The Supreme Court has ruled that admission into evidence of a coerced confession violates the self-incrimination clause, deprives a person of the assistance of counsel guaranteed by the Sixth and Fourteenth Amendments, deprives a person of due process, and undermines the entire proceeding.[58]

Federal and state laws require police officers to take those whom they have arrested before magistrates promptly so that the magistrates may inform them of their constitutional rights and allow them to get in touch with friends and seek legal advice. Despite these requirements, in the past police were often tempted to quiz suspects first, trying to get them to confess before a magistrate informed them of their constitutional right to remain silent.

To put an end to such practices, the Supreme Court, in *Miranda v Arizona* (1966), announced that no conviction—federal or state—could stand if evidence introduced at the trial had been obtained by the police during "custodial interrogation" unless suspects have been: (1) notified that they are free to remain silent; (2) warned that what they say may be used against them in court; (3) told that they have a right to have attorneys present during questioning; (4) informed that if they cannot afford to hire their own lawyers, attorneys will be provided for them; and (5) permitted to terminate any stage of the police interrogation. If suspects answer questions in the absence of an attorney, the burden is on the prosecution to demonstrate that suspects knowingly and intelligently gave up their rights to remain silent and to have their own lawyers present. Failure to comply with these requirements leads to reversal of a conviction, even if other evidence is sufficient to establish guilt.[59]

Critics of the *Miranda* decision believe the Court has severely limited the ability of the police to bring criminals to justice, but the Supreme Court has refused to abandon the *Miranda* doctrine. It has modified the original ruling in order to deter perjury (lying under oath) by allowing evidence obtained contrary to the *Miranda* guidelines to be used to attack the credibility of defendants who offer testimony at their trials that conflicts with their statements to the police.

Crime and Punishment

The ban against cruel and unusual punishment limits government in three ways:

1. It limits the kinds and methods of punishment that may be imposed, prohibiting, for example, torture, intentional denial of medical care, inhumane conditions, unnecessary or wanton inflicting of pain, and deliberate indifference to medical and other needs of prisoners.[60]
2. It prohibits punishments grossly disproportionate to the severity of the crime. However, the Court has been reluctant to review legislative prescriptions of terms of punishment, and successful challenges to the severity of punishments have been extremely rare.[61]
3. It limits the power of the government to decide what can be made a criminal offense. For example, the mere act of being a chronic alcoholic may not be made a crime because alcoholism is an illness. However, being drunk in public may be a criminal offense.

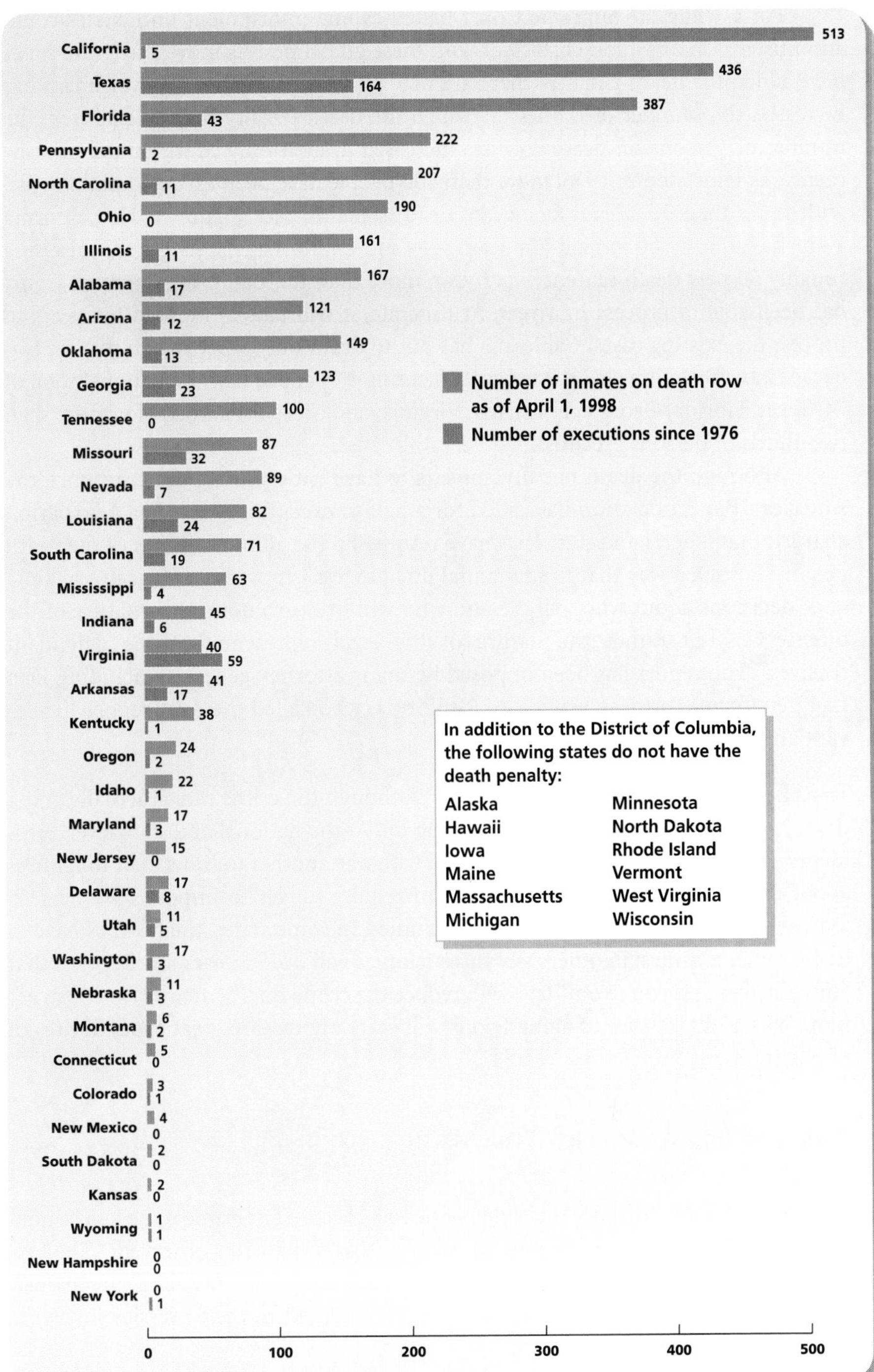

FIGURE 6-1 Under Sentence of Death

SOURCE: Death Penalty Information Center, NAACP Legal Defense Fund, as reported in *Los Angeles Times,* December 19, 1998, p. A10.

THE DEATH PENALTY After much soul searching, the Supreme Court has ruled that the death penalty is not necessarily cruel and unusual punishment if it is imposed for conviction of crimes that have resulted in a victim's death, if the procedures used by the courts "ensure that death sentences are not meted out wantonly or freakishly," and if these processes "confer on the sentencer sufficient discretion to take account of the character and record of the individual offender and the circumstances of the particular offense to ensure that death is the appropriate punishment in a specific case."[62]

For a while the Supreme Court halted capital punishment until states could administer it in a fashion consistent with these guidelines. As more and more states have added the death penalty (there are now 38), and the national government has increased the number of crimes for which the death penalty may be imposed, the number of persons on death row has increased dramatically. Since capital punishment was reinstated in 1976, more than 500 people have been executed nationwide, with more than 3,300 still facing the death sentence (see Figure 6-1). California alone has almost 500 inmates on death row, and California trial judges are imposing roughly 50 new death sentences per year, more than the California Supreme Court has been able to process in a year. At this rate, it will take more than ten years to process the existing cases. California has put to death only 5 persons in the last two decades. In 1997 Texas led the nation, executing 37 people, half the national total of 74. Texas, Florida, Georgia, Louisiana, Virginia, and Missouri account for more than two-thirds of persons executed.[63]

Although the death penalty appears to have widespread public support, the American Bar Association has called for a halt to executions. The Bar Association charged that federal and state laws have resulted in the administration of the death penalty in such a way that fundamental due process is now systematically lacking, and "decisions about who will die and who will live turn not on the nature of the offense ... but rather the nature of the legal representation the defendant receives." The report has been opposed by many attorney generals, including Dan Lungren, former attorny general of California, who called the ABA report "irrelevant and outrageous."[64]

THREE STRIKES AND YOU'RE OUT Although the crime rate is actually going down, public concern about crime is going up. At the national and state level, presidents, governors, and legislators are vying with one another to show their toughness about crime. Laws have been proposed to require judges to impose lifetime sentences upon persons convicted of three felonies. In some states, the felonies have to be for violent crimes; in others any three felonies will do. Scholars are skeptical that "three strikes and you're out" laws will reduce the crime rate. Moreover, to construct more jails and take care of aging felons will certainly require great expenditures of public funds.

The Short and Not Too Happy Life of John Crook

Many people consider the rights of persons accused of crime to be less important than other rights. But, as Justice Felix Frankfurter observed, "The history of liberty has largely been the history of observance of procedural safeguards." Further, these safeguards have frequently "been forged in controversies involving not very nice people."[65]

The rights of persons accused of crime by the national government can be found in the Constitution and in the Fourth, Fifth, Sixth, and Eighth Amendments. To gain some idea of how these constitutional safeguards are applied, let us follow the fortunes and misfortunes of a fictitious character, John Crook, as he is prosecuted for a federal crime.

John Crook sent circulars through the mail selling shares in a nonexistent gold mine—an action contrary to dozens of federal laws. When postal officials uncovered these activities, they went to the district court and secured from a United States magistrate a warrant to arrest Crook and another warrant to search his home for copies of the circulars. They found Crook at home and read the *Miranda* warning to him, emphasizing especially his right to remain silent and to have the assistance of counsel. They showed him the warrant, arrested him for using the mails to defraud, and found and seized some of the circulars mentioned in the search warrant.

The Preliminary Hearing and Right to Counsel

Crook was promptly brought before a federal magistrate, who again emphasized that Crook had a constitutional *right to assistance of counsel.* Unless the record clearly shows that the accused were fully aware of what they were doing and gave up the right to counsel, or intelligently exercised the right to represent themselves, the absence of counsel will render criminal proceedings unconstitutional. The right extends to all hearings for all offenses for which an accused could be deprived of liberty, whether or not a jury trial is required. Trials in which fines are the only penalty are exempt from the assistance-of-counsel requirement. This assistance is required at every stage of a criminal proceeding after the initiation of formal charges—preliminary hearings, bail hearings, trial, sentence, and first appeal. When Crook told the judge he could not afford to hire his own attorney, the judge appointed one paid by the federal government to represent him.

At this point Crook had not been convicted of anything. In fact, he had not even been formally charged with any crime, and he was entitled to be free without having to pay excessive *bail.* (Note that the Eighth Amendment does not require that bail be set, but forbids excessive bail.) Suspects are entitled to a hearing within five days, and, when bail is imposed, judges or magistrates must explain in writing why they believe there is clear and convincing evidence that release of the suspect might endanger the safety of other persons and the community.[66] The judge set Crook's bail at $5,000, and Crook was held over until the convening of the next federal grand jury. After hiring a professional *bondsman,* who posted the bail and collected a 10 percent fee, Crook was free as long as he remained within the judicial district.

The Indictment

Except for members of the armed forces, the national government cannot require anyone to stand trial for a serious crime except on a *grand jury indictment.* Grand jurors are concerned not with a person's guilt or innocence but merely with whether there is enough evidence to warrant a trial. The **grand jury** has wide-ranging investigatory powers and "is to inquire into all information that might bear on its investigations until it is satisfied that it has identified an offense or satisfied itself that none has occurred."[67] The strict rules that govern jury proceedings do not apply. The grand jury may admit hearsay evidence, and the exclusionary rule to enforce the Fourth Amendment does not apply. If a majority of the grand jurors agree that a trial is justified, they return what is known as a *true bill,* or **indictment**.

When the next grand jury was convened, the United States district attorney brought evidence before the 23 jurors to indicate that Crook had committed a federal crime. In Crook's case the grand jury was in agreement with the United States district attorney and returned a true bill against Crook.

After a copy of the indictment was served on Crook, he was again ordered to appear before a federal district judge. The Constitution guarantees the accused *the right to be informed of the nature and cause of the accusation* so that he or she can prepare a defense. Consequently, the federal prosecutor took care that the indictment clearly stated the nature of the offense, and she saw to it that copies were properly served on Crook and his lawyer.

Actually, prior to his hearing, Crook's attorney discussed with the United States attorney's office the possibility of Crook's pleading guilty to a lesser offense, in return for which he would not have to stand trial for the more serious charge of using the mails to defraud. Prosecutors, faced with more cases than they can handle, like this kind of **plea bargain**. Likewise, defendants are often willing to "cop a plea" for a lesser offense to avoid the risk of more serious punishment.

When defendants plead guilty, they are usually forever prevented from raising objections to their convictions. That is why, before accepting guilty pleas, a judge questions defendants to be sure their attorneys have explained the alternatives and

grand jury
A jury of 12 to 23 persons who, in private, hear evidence presented by the government to determine whether persons shall be required to stand trial. If the jury believes there is sufficient evidence that a crime was committed, it issues an indictment.

indictment
A formal charge issued by a grand jury against an individual for a specified crime; also called a *true bill.*

plea bargain
Negotiations between prosecutor and defendant aimed at getting the defendant to plead guilty in return for the prosecutor's agreeing to reduce the seriousness of the crime for which the defendant will be charged.

they know what they are doing. It never came to this in Crook's case, however. After discussing the matter with his attorney, Crook elected to stand trial on the charge and entered a plea of not guilty.

The Trial

After indictment, Crook's bail was raised to $50,000. Now the federal government was obligated to give him a *speedy and public trial.* Do not, however, take the word "speedy" too literally. Crook had to be given time to prepare his defense. Defendants, in fact, often ask for delays, because delay often works to their advantage. If, in contrast, the government denies the accused a speedy trial in a constitutional sense, the remedy is drastic. Not only is the conviction reversed, but also the case must be dismissed outright.

Crook's lawyer pointed out that under the Sixth Amendment, Crook had a *right to trial* before a **petit jury** selected from the state and district in which the alleged crime was committed because he was being tried for a serious crime, that is, one punishable by more than six months in prison or a $500 fine.[68] Although federal law requires juries of 12 members, the Constitution requires only that juries consist of at least six persons. Conviction in federal courts must be by unanimous vote. (The Constitution permits state courts to render guilty verdicts by nonunanimous juries, provided such juries consist of six or more persons.)

An *impartial* jury, one that meets the requirements of due process and equal protection, consists of persons who represent a fair cross-section of the community. Although defendants are not entitled to juries on which there are necessarily members of their own race, sex, religion, or national origin, they are entitled to be tried by juries from which jurors have not been *excluded* because of these categories. Government prosecutors cannot strike persons from juries because of race or gender, and neither can defense attorneys use what are called *peremptory challenges* to keep people off juries because of race, ethnic origin, or sex.[69]

Crook told his lawyer he had had dinner with George Witness on the night on which he was charged with sending the damaging circulars. The attorney took advantage of Crook's constitutional *right to obtain witnesses in his favor* and had the judge subpoena Witness to appear at the trial and testify. Although Witness could have refused to testify on the grounds that his testimony would tend to incriminate him, he agreed to appear. Crook himself, however, chose to use his constitutional right not to be a witness against himself and refused to take the stand. He knew that if he did so, the prosecution would have a right to *cross-examine* him, and he was fearful of what might be uncovered. To protect Crook's right against self-incrimination, the judge conducting the trial was required to caution the jury against drawing any conclusions from Crook's decision not to testify. All prosecution witnesses appeared in court and were available for defense cross-examination; the Constitution also insists that accused persons have the *right to be confronted with the witnesses against them.*

The Sentencing

At the conclusion of the trial, the jury brought in a verdict of guilty. The judge then raised Crook's bail to $75,000 and announced that she would hand down a sentence on the following Monday. The Eighth Amendment forbids the levying of *excessive fines and the inflicting of cruel and unusual punishments.*

The judge, following the guidelines set down by the United States Sentencing Commission, gave Crook the maximum punishment of a $50,000 fine and three years in the penitentiary. Such a sentence could not be considered cruel and unusual. Crook could have appealed both his conviction and the length of his sentence to the court of appeals, but he chose not to do so.

petit jury
A jury of 6 to 12 persons that determines guilt or innocence in a civil or criminal action.

A Closer Look

JURIES ON TRIAL

Public cynicism about the role of juries has increased in recent years as people learned the intimate details of some notorious trials because of around-the-clock television coverage and front-page newspaper attention. Resentment and bewilderment followed when juries failed to convict persons for what appeared to be obvious crimes. Examples included the 1992 acquittal of Los Angeles police officers whose extended beating of Rodney King had been videotaped and then witnessed by the entire nation (two officers were subsequently convicted of federal crimes); and the 1995 acquittal of O. J. Simpson after the criminal "trial of the century." Televised details of the Simpson trial dominated the news not only in the United States but throughout much of the world. A year later, in a civil trial that was also closely covered by the media, Simpson was held responsible for the wrongful deaths of his ex-wife and her friend and subject to total damages of $33 million.

A majority of whites believed that the jury in the first Simpson trial—nine African Americans, two Hispanics, and one white—had ignored the evidence and had voted to acquit Simpson because of their resentment of the unfair treatment of African Americans at the hands of the Los Angeles Police Department. Most African Americans believed that the jury had done its duty. Opinions about fairness of the jury system again divided along racial lines and added to demands to revise the rules for jury trials.[*]

In a trial that was front page news in England and the United States, Louise Woodward, a teenage British nanny, was accused of first degree murder for shaking to death Matthew Eappens, the eight-month-old baby she was caring for. Her defense attorneys claimed that her shaking did not cause the baby's death, which they argued was caused by a prior incident. Many people in England as well as in the United States championed her cause and contended that she should not be sent to prison.

The jury brought in a conviction of second degree murder and set the sentence as life in prison. The trial judge, to the surprise of most observers, set aside the jury's verdict in favor of involuntary manslaughter with a sentence of 279 days in jail, time she had already served. Woodward was set free but required to live in the United States pending appeal. The Massachusetts Supreme Court sustained the judge's decision, and Woodward returned home.[**]

[*]Abigail Goldman and Mary Curtius, "For Many, It's as Simple as Black and White," *Los Angeles Times*, February 5, 1997, p. A16.

[**]Court TV, "*Massachusetts v Woodward*: The Nanny Murder Trial" (www.courtv.com/trials/woodward).

O.J. Simpson

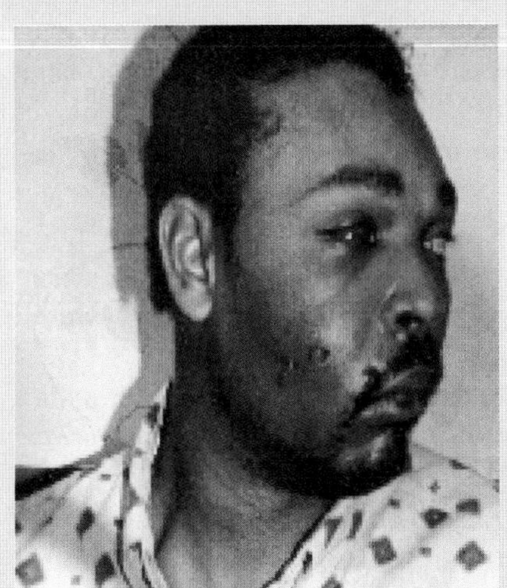

Rodney King

Louise Woodward

Double Jeopardy

While he was in the federal penitentiary, federal authorities took Crook before the state courts to answer charges that when he solicited shares in his nonexistent gold mine, he also violated several state laws. Through his state-appointed attorney, Crook protested that the federal government had already tried him, and he pointed to the Fifth Amendment provision that no person shall be "subject for the same offense to be twice put in jeopardy of life or limb."[70] The judge answered: "The Supreme Court has said that *double jeopardy* prevents two criminal trials by the *same* government for the *same* criminal offense." **Double jeopardy** does not prevent punishment by the national and the state governments for the same offense or for successive prosecutions for the same crime by two states. Nor does the double jeopardy clause forbid civil prosecutions, even after acquittal in a criminal trial for the same conduct, as most readers remember from watching the *civil* suit against O. J. Simpson for the wrongful death and battery of his ex-wife and for causing the wrongful death of her friend *after he had been acquitted in a criminal* trial for their murder.[71]

What constitutional rights can Crook claim in the state courts? He can claim both the rights secured by this state constitution and those provided by the U.S. Constitution. Every state constitution contains a bill of rights listing practically the same guarantees found in the national Bill of Rights. And, as we have noted, the Fourteenth Amendment does apply to the states. The Supreme Court has interpreted the due process clause of that amendment to impose all the provisions of the national Bill of Rights that protect persons accused of crime except for the grand jury requirements of the Fifth Amendment.

HOW JUST IS OUR SYSTEM OF JUSTICE?

What are the major criticisms of the American system of justice? How have they been answered? How accurate are TV shows and movies that highlight criminals going free and innocent people being imprisoned? Do they accurately reflect how our system of justice works?

Too Many Loopholes?

Some observers argue that by overprotecting the criminals and placing too much of a burden on the government not to make any mistakes, we delay justice, encourage disrespect for the law, and allow guilty persons to go unpunished. Justice should be swift and certain without being arbitrary. But under our procedures, criminals may go unpunished because: (1) the police decide not to arrest them; (2) the judge decides not to hold them for a trial; (3) the prosecutor decides not to prosecute them; (4) the grand jury decides not to indict them; (5) the jury decides not to convict them; (6) the judge decides not to sentence them; (7) an appeals court decides to reverse the conviction; (8) a judge decides to release them on a *habeas corpus* writ; or (9) the president or governor decides to pardon, reprieve, or parole them if convicted. As a result, the public never knows whom to hold responsible when laws are not enforced. The police can blame the prosecutor, the prosecutor can blame the police, and they can all blame the juries and judges.

Others take a different view and point out that there is more to justice than simply securing convictions. All the steps in the administration of criminal laws have been developed over centuries of trial and error, and each step has been constructed to protect ordinary persons against particular abuses by those in power. History warns against entrusting the instruments of criminal law enforcement to a single officer. For this reason, responsibility is vested in many officials.

double jeopardy
Trial or punishment for the same crime by the same government; forbidden by the Constitution.

Too Unreliable?

Critics who say that our system of justice is unreliable often point to trial by jury as the chief source of trouble. No other country relies as heavily on trial by jury as does the United States. Jury trials are also time consuming and costly. Trial by jury, critics argue, leads to a theatrical combat between lawyers who base their appeals on the prejudices and sentiments of the jurors. "Mr. Prejudice and Miss Sympathy are the names of witnesses whose testimony is never recorded, but must nevertheless be reckoned with in trials by jury."[72]

The jury system allows for what has come to be called *jury nullification*, in which jurors ignore their instructions to consider only the evidence presented in court, and, by voting for acquittal, express their displeasure with the law or the actions of prosecutors or police. Jury nullification has a long history. In colonial times juries refused to convict colonists of political crimes against the king as a way to protest British rule. Prior to the Civil War, northern juries refused to convict persons for helping runaway slaves. Before the 1970s, white southern juries sometimes refused to convict police for actions of brutality against blacks. And there were many who accused the jury in the O. J. Simpson criminal trial of voting to acquit him in order to express their displeasure with the Los Angeles Police Department and their belief that African Americans were routinely subject to police harassment.

Responding to growing public disenchantment with juries after a raft of unpopular verdicts, "State legislatures and court systems across the nation are starting to rewrite the rules of the jury system."[73] These changes include making it more difficult for people to be excused from jury service, allowing for nonunanimous decisions, limiting how long jurors can be sequestered, and exerting more control by judges over lawyer's statements to jurors in order to prevent appeals to jurors' emotions.

Defenders of the jury system reply that trial by jury provides a check by nonprofessionals on the actions of judges and prosecutors.[74] There is no evidence that juries are unreliable; on the contrary, decisions of juries do not systematically differ from those of judges.[75] Moreover, the jury system helps to educate citizens and enables them to participate in the application of their country's laws.

The grand jury has also come under attack. Critics charge that the grand jury has become a tool of the prosecutor. Said Justice William O. Douglas, "It is, indeed, common knowledge that the grand jury, having been conceived as a bulwark between the citizen and the Government, is now a tool of the Executive."[76]

During the 1960s critics on the left of the political spectrum charged that grand juries had become instruments to intimidate radicals, blacks, and antiwar militants. However, by the 1970s grand juries were being used to investigate the executive branch. In the Watergate investigation of the Nixon administration, it was through the use of the grand jury that the special prosecutor was able to argue that the president had no constitutional right to withhold information about wrongdoing, and Independent Counsel Kenneth Starr used the grand jury to force President Clinton to testify about his affair with White House intern Monica Lewinsky.

Too Discriminatory?

During the last several decades, the Supreme Court has worked particularly hard to enforce the ideal of equal justice under the law. Persons accused of a crime who cannot afford attorneys must be furnished them at government expense. If transcripts are required for appeals, such transcripts must be made available to those who cannot afford to purchase them. If appeals are permitted, the government must provide attorneys for at least one appeal of the decision of the trial court.

Poor people cannot be imprisoned because of inability to pay a fine. Nor, once sentenced, can poor persons be kept in jail beyond the term of the sentence because they cannot afford to pay a fine. Even for civil proceedings—divorce proceedings, for example—fees cannot be imposed that deny poor persons their fundamental rights, such as the right to obtain a divorce. If a state provides for civil appeals, it cannot deny a mother or father an appeal from a decree terminating parental rights because they cannot pay the fees for such an appeal. A state has no obligation, however, to waive fees for those seeking to be declared bankrupt. The Court apparently believes that people have a great right to be absolved of the ties that bind but not of their debts.[77]

Unfair to Minorities?

One of the more acute problems of our society is the tension between the police and the African American and Hispanic communities congregated in the ghettos and barrios of our large cities. Such tensions were evident in the Rodney King beating and the 1992 Los Angeles riots that followed. Many members of minorities do not believe they have equal protection under the law. The revelations of detective Mark Furhman's racist remarks during the O. J. Simpson trial confirmed the view of many—especially African Americans—that the police are instruments of white intolerance. "Even before the Simpson trial 83 percent of blacks said in a poll . . . that they didn't trust the criminal justice system."[78] "Whether the stated belief is well founded or not is at least partly beside the point. The existence of the belief is damaging enough."[79]

Blacks consider the police to be enforcers of white law. Studies proving prejudice on the part of some white police officers and examples of rough, if not brutal, police treatment of blacks are ample evidence to support this viewpoint. One study in California found that "the rate of unfounded arrest was four times higher for African Americans than Anglos. Latino rates were double those of Anglos."[80]

Police brutality was an issue in New York City in August 1997 when four white police officers were charged with brutally beating a black Haitian immigrant, Abner Louima, in the police car and the station house. Louima was hospi-

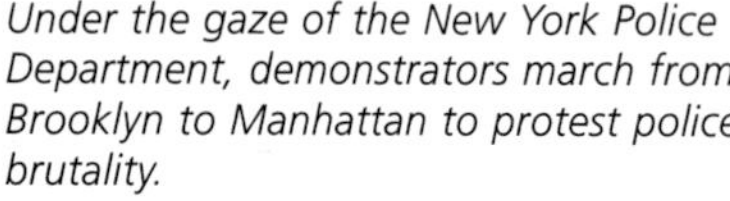

Under the gaze of the New York Police Department, demonstrators march from Brooklyn to Manhattan to protest police brutality.

talized for serious internal injuries, and the incident received wide coverage in the newspapers and on TV. A federal grand jury indicted the four officers on charges of violating Mr. Louima's civil rights and indicted a sergeant of attempting to cover up the incident.

In recent decades action has been taken to recruit more African Americans, Hispanics, and women as police officers, including appointment to command posts. In larger cities there are now oversight boards including civilians to which complaints about police misconduct can be brought. **Community policing** is being substituted for the traditional police procedures. Police departments work with churches and other local community groups and take police out of patrol cars to walk the beat and work in neighborhoods. Community policing, when combined with working with community organizations to sponsor crime-prevention programs, appears not only to reduce crime but to improve minorities' confidence in the police.[81]

community policing
Recent programs to move police from patrol cars into neighborhoods, where they walk the beat and work with churches and other community groups to reduce crime and improve relations with minorities.

The Supreme Court and Civil Liberties

Clearly, judges—especially those on the Supreme Court—play a major role in enforcing constitutional guarantees. This combination of judicial enforcement and written guarantees of liberty is one of the basic features of the American system of government. As Supreme Court Justice Robert H. Jackson wrote:

> The very purpose of a Bill of Rights was to withdraw certain subjects from the vicissitudes of political controversy, to place them beyond the reach of majorities and officials and to establish them as legal principles to be applied by the courts. One's right to life, liberty, and property, to free speech, a free press, freedom of worship and assembly, and other fundamental rights may not be submitted to vote: they depend on the outcome of no elections.[82]

This emphasis on constitutional limitations and judicial enforcement is an example of the "auxiliary precautions" James Madison believed were necessary to prevent arbitrary governmental action. In other free nations citizens rely more on elections and political checks to protect their rights; in the United States we appeal to judges when we fear our freedoms are in danger.

Such reliance on judicial protection of our civil liberties focuses attention on the Supreme Court. Yet only a small number of controversies are actually carried to the Supreme Court, and a Supreme Court decision is not the end of the judicial process. Lower-court judges as well as police, superintendents of schools, local prosecutors, school boards, state legislatures, and thousands of others clarify the Court's doctrines.

The Supreme Court can do little unless its decisions over time reflect a national consensus. Judges by themselves cannot guarantee anything; neither can the First Amendment. As Supreme Court Justice Robert H. Jackson (on the Court 1941–54) asked:

> Must we first maintain a system of free political government to assure a free judiciary to guarantee free government? It is my belief that the attitude of a society and of its organized political forces, rather than its legal machinery, is the controlling force in the character of free institutions. Any court that undertakes by its legal processes to enforce civil liberties needs the support of an enlightened and vigorous public opinion.[83]

Thus, the Bill of Rights—and the other procedural and substantive liberties of our Constitution—cannot rest on a foundation merely of tradition. The preservation of these rights depends on wide, continuing, and knowledgeable public support.

POLITICS online

Are Your E-Mail Messages Private?

In an experiment designed to prove to Fortune 500 companies that none of their computer systems are invulnerable to break-ins, *Fortune* magazine commissioned a Texas security firm to break into a major corporation's presumably secure computer system. Over a long Christmas weekend, the hackers were able to gain "root access" (access available only to the corporation's computer system administrators) to five computers at corporate headquarters, including the one used to do taxes. They also invaded the "electronic heart" of the corporation, the computer used exclusively by the corporation's Technology Department.

Once hackers gain access to a computer, they can "steal trade secrets, destroy data, sabotage operations, even subvert a particular deal or career." One study found that 40 percent of companies and institutions reported recent break-ins, and break-ins have not been limited to the private sector. In one publicized case, a 16-year-old British youth and his associate broke into the Rome Laboratory, the U.S. Air Force top research and development facility, and used its computer to gain access to the South Korea Atomic Research Institute.[84]

What about the privacy of your e-mail? If you are sending or receiving e-mail at work or school, you may not have much privacy. Even messages that you have deleted may be backed up on the company's main-frame computer. One alternative is to send personal messages on your own account.

For information on criminal justice, consult an annotated bibliography maintained by the Emery University Law School:

http://www.law.emory.edu/CRIMPRO/scholarlit/bibindex.html

The home page for the U.S. Department of Justice provides information on federal law enforcement:

http://www.usdoj.gov

For the perspective of trial lawyers on our criminal justice system:

http://www.nacdl.org

For more Internet resources on Rights to Life, Liberty, and Property, see our home page at:

http://www.prenhall.com/burns

SUMMARY

1. One of the basic distinctions between a free society and a police state is that in a free society there are effective restraints on the way public officials, especially law enforcement officials, perform their duties. In the United States the courts enforce these constitutional restraints.

2. The Constitution protects our right to seek a writ of *habeas corpus* and forbids *ex post facto* laws and bills of attainder.

3. The Constitution protects the acquisition and retention of citizenship. It protects the basic liberties of citizens as well as aliens.

4. The Constitution protects our property from arbitrary governmental interference, although debates about which interferences are reasonable and which are arbitrary are not easily settled.

5. The Constitution imposes limits not only on the procedures government must follow but also on the ends it may pursue. Some actions are out of bounds no matter what procedures are followed. Legislatures have the primary role in determining what is reasonable and what is unreasonable. However, the Supreme Court continues to exercise its own independent and final review of legislative determinations of reasonableness, especially on matters affecting civil liberties and civil rights.

6. The Supreme Court has put together elements from the First, Fourth, Fifth, Ninth, and Fourteenth Amendments to recognize a constitutionally protected right to personal privacy, especially with regard to marital privacy, including the right of a woman to choose an abortion.

7. The framers knew from their own experiences that in their zeal to maintain power and to enforce the laws, public officials are often tempted to infringe on the rights of those accused of crimes. To prevent such abuse, the Bill of Rights requires federal officials to follow detailed procedures in making searches and arrests and in bringing people to trial.

8. The Supreme Court interprets the Constitution, especially the Fourteenth Amendment, to impose on state and local governments almost the same restraints in the administration of justice as it imposes on the national government.

9. The Supreme Court continues to play a prominent role in developing public policy to protect the rights of the accused, to ensure that the innocent are not punished, and to guarantee that the public is protected against those who break the laws. The Court's decisions influence what the public believes and how police officers and others involved in the administration of justice behave. But the Court alone cannot guarantee fairness in the administration of justice.

KEY TERMS

due process 128
writ of *habeas corpus* 128
***ex post facto* law 128**
bill of attainder 128
naturalization 129
dual citizenship 129
right of expatriation 129
property rights 134
contract clause 134
police powers 134
eminent domain 134
regulatory taking 135
procedural due process 135
substantive due process 136
search warrant 140
exclusionary rule 141
immunity 141
grand jury 145
indictment 145
plea bargain 145
petit jury 146
double jeopardy 148
community policing 151

FURTHER READING

LAURENCE A. CANTER AND MARTHA S. SIEGEL, *U.S. Immigration Made Easy*, 6th ed. (Nolo Press, 1998).

GEORGE F. COLE, *Criminal Justice: Law and Politics*, 6th ed. (Wadsworth, 1993).

RICHARD EPSTEIN, *Bargaining with the State* (Princeton University Press, 1993).

MACKLIN FLEMING, *The Price of Perfect Justice* (Basic Books, 1974).

LAURENCE H. GELLER AND PETER HEMENWAY, *Last Chance for Justice: The Juror's Lonely Quest* (NCDS Press, 1997).

NATHAN GLAZER, ED., *Clamor at the Gates: The New American Immigration* (ICS Press, 1985).

JOHN GUINTHER, *The Jury in America* (Facts-on-File Publications, 1988).

WAYNE R. LAFAVE, *Search and Seizure: A Treatise on the Fourth Amendment*, 2d ed. (West Publishing Co., 1987).

LEONARD W. LEVY, KENNETH L. KARST, AND DENNIS J. MAHONE, *Criminal Justice and the Supreme Court* (Macmillan, 1990).

ROBERT E. LITAN, ED., *Verdict: Assessing the Civil Jury System* (Brookings Institution, 1993).

J. W. PELTASON, *Corwin and Peltason's Understanding the Constitution*, 14th ed. (Harcourt Brace, 1997).

JUDITH N. SHKLAR, *American Citizenship: The Quest for Inclusion* (Harvard University Press, 1991).

SPECIAL COMMISSION ON CRIMINAL JUSTICE IN A FREE SOCIETY, *Criminal Justice in Crisis* (American Bar Association, 1988).

U.S. COMMISSION ON IMMIGRATION REFORM, *Report to Congress: Executive Summary: Becoming an American, Immigration and Immigrant Policy* (U.S. Commission on Immigration Reform, 1997).

ROBERT V. WOLF AND AUSTIN SARAT (EDITORS), *The Jury System* (Chelsea House, 1998).

POLITICAL CULTURE AND IDEOLOGY

CHAPTER OUTLINE

CRUCIAL TO A DEMOCRATIC POLITICAL CULTURE IS PEOPLE COMING TOGETHER, LISTENING TO EACH OTHER, EXCHANGING IDEAS, LEARNING TO APPRECIATE EACH OTHER'S differences, and coordinating their responses to social or political problems. This kind of interaction can happen in political gatherings, yet it also happens in other social settings—the PTA, labor unions, veterans groups, or even bowling leagues. Political scientist Robert Putnam believes there has been a loss of the skills and learned behaviors people develop in such settings—what he calls *social capital.* He defines civic or social capital as "features of social organization such as networks, norms, and social trust that facilitate coordination and cooperation for mutual benefit."[1]

Putnam uses as one example the decline in the number of bowling leagues. He has documented that people bowl now more than ever, but they do it alone; between 1980 and 1993 the number of bowlers increased by 10 percent while bowling leagues diminished by 40 percent.[2] Putnam contends that this decline can be attributed to: more women in the workplace, thus reducing the amount of time women have for these involvements; greater mobility, which disrupts the development of roots in a community; changing family structure; and greater reliance on impersonal leisure activities like watching television and using computers.

Putnam's argument has political relevance because it helps explain declining levels of trust and confidence in political institutions that can result in a weaker democracy. Putnam, however, has his critics. He has been criticized on at least three fronts: (1) government and institutions establish more trust than Putnam recognizes;[3] (2) participation is not necessarily good for society—take, for example, joining the Ku Klux Klan;[4] and (3) Putnam's concern with civic trust misses the more important goal of "civic skepticism," a questioning of those in power, their motives and agenda.[5]

Some critics contend that the desire for more civic or social capital is a form of nostalgia—a longing for "the good old days." Political scientist Jean Bethke Elshtain responds that concerns about civil society arise not from nostalgia, but because the good things of democracy cannot exist without responsibility and accountability on our part—involvement in schools, churches, and other associations that enable us to work and live together.[6] Observers agree that the dramatic social changes of recent decades fostered discontent with government and dislocations in communities, but optimists argue that previous generations of Americans were able to deal with change. They point to the inventiveness of Teddy Roosevelt's Progressives or the creation of Social Security, Medicare, and Medicaid. Social reconstruction, they contend, is not only possible but essential.

Values We Share

Americans distrust government: 57 percent think "government regulation of business usually does more harm than good," and 64 percent think that "when something is run by the government, it is usually inefficient and wasteful."

Americans are more distrustful of the federal government than of local government: 75 percent think "the federal government should run only those things that cannot be run at the local level."

Americans are patriotic and share a sense of civic responsibility: 90 percent say they are "very patriotic," 89 percent feel it is their "duty to always vote," and 67 percent think that voting gives them some say in how the government runs things.

Most Americans believe in providing equal opportunity: 91 percent of Americans believe that "our society should do what is necessary to make sure that everyone has an equal opportunity to succeed."

Americans believe that government should help those in need: 61 percent of Americans believe that "it is the responsibility of government to take care of people who can't take care of themselves," and 62 percent think "the government should guarantee every citizen enough to eat and a place to sleep."

Americans are religious: 88 percent of Americans believe in the existence of God, and 78 percent see prayer as an important part of their daily life.

Americans see family and marriage as important: 85 percent of Americans say they have "old-fashioned values about family and marriage," and 74 percent think "too many children are being raised in day-care centers these days."

Americans distrust large corporations: 73 percent of Americans think "too much power is concentrated in the hands of a few big companies," and 58 percent think "business corporations make too much profit."

Americans are optimistic: 71 percent think that the United States "can always find a way to solve our problems and get what we want."

SOURCE: The Pew Research Center for the People and the Press, *Pew Values Update: American Social Beliefs, 1997–98*, April 1998 (http://www.people-press.org/valuetop.htm).

This chapter explores American political culture and the values that underlie it. The "bowling alone" debate has rekindled an interest in the nature and viability of the American political culture and an examination of how it is changing. Americans have conflicting ideas and beliefs about the proper role of government and where and how political power should be exercised. These beliefs and ideas are called *ideology*. In this chapter, we look at the political culture that unites us as well as the ideologies that sometimes divide us.

THE AMERICAN POLITICAL CULTURE

Political scientists use the term **political culture** to refer to the widely shared beliefs, values, and norms concerning the relationship of citizens to government and to one another. American democratic values include liberty, equality, individualism, democracy, justice, the rule of law, and nationalism, optimism, and idealism. There is no definitive list of American political values, however, for as we noted in Chapter 1, these widely shared democratic values overlap and sometimes conflict.

Shared Values

Before the American and French Revolutions, concern with individual liberty, freedom, equality, private property, limited government, and popular consent was not widespread. Europe had been dominated by aristocracies, had experienced centuries of political and social inequality, and had been ruled by governments that were often arbitrary in the exercise of power. Liberal political philosophers rebelled against these traditions and instead postulated the principles of classical liberalism. They claimed individuals have certain **natural rights**—the rights of all people to dignity and worth—and that the state (or government), as a primary threat to these rights, must be limited and controlled. During this same period, the economic system was changing to a free market system. People began to think they could improve their lot in life and own property. Radical new ideas like these influenced the thinking of the founders of our nation.

LIBERTY Americans have always been united by a commitment to liberty or freedom. No value in the American political culture is more revered. "We have always been a nation obsessed with liberty. Liberty over authority, freedom over responsibility, rights over duties—these are our historic preferences," wrote the late Clinton Rossiter, a noted political scientist. "Not the good man, but the free man has been the measure of all things in this sweet 'land of liberty'; not national glory but individual liberty has been the object of political authority and the test of its worth."[7]

EQUALITY Jefferson's famous words in the Declaration of Independence express the primacy of our views of equality: "We hold these truths to be self-evident, that all men are created equal, that they are endowed by their Creator with certain unalienable rights, that among these are life, liberty, and the pursuit of happiness." Americans have always believed in social equality. In contrast to the Europeans, our nation shunned aristocracy, and the Constitution explicitly banned titles of nobility.

Equality also refers to *political equality*, the idea that every individual has a right to equal protection under the law and equal voting power. While political equality has always been a goal, it has not always been a reality. African Americans, Native Americans, and women have been denied political equality in the past.

Equality encompasses the idea of equality of opportunity, especially with regard to improving economic status. Americans believe that social background

political culture
The widely shared beliefs, values, and norms concerning the relationship of citizens to government and to one another.

natural rights
The rights of all people to dignity and worth; also called *human rights*.

should not limit our opportunity to achieve to the best of our ability, nor should race, gender, or religion. The nation's commitment to public education—programs like Head Start for underprivileged preschool children, state support for public colleges and universities, and federal financial aid for higher education—reflects our belief in equality.

INDIVIDUALISM The United States is characterized by a persistent commitment to the individual. Under our system of government, individuals have both rights and responsibilities. Concern for preserving individual freedom of choice and what limits, if any, to place on individual choice generate intense political conflict. The debate over legalized abortion is often framed in these terms. While Americans agree with individual rights and freedoms, they also understand that rights conflict with other rights or with the government's need to maintain order.

Americans have faith in the common sense of the ordinary person. We prefer action to reflection. We are often anti-expert and sometimes anti-intellectual. The emphasis on practicality and common sense has become part of our image. Poets like Walt Whitman and Carl Sandburg and storytellers like Mark Twain, Will Rogers, Eudora Welty, and Garrison Keillor have helped shape this tradition. This reverence for the common person helps explain our ambivalence toward power, politics, and government authority. In the United States, government is often viewed as a necessary evil.

DEMOCRACY, GOVERNMENT, AND THE CONSTITUTION The American political culture includes attitudes and beliefs about principles of government, procedures, documents, and institutions. A *democratic consensus*—a fairly widespread agreement on fundamental principles of governance and the values that undergird them—is essential to the maintenance of democracy. Americans have strong opinions about who has power to do what, how people acquire power, and how they are removed from power. These are fundamental "rules of the game" in which widespread consensus is important.

We believe in **majority rule**—governance according to the expressed preferences of the majority. Yet we also believe that people in the minority should be free to try to win majority support for their opinions. We also strongly favor a two-party system and regular elections. Our institutions are based on the principle of representation and consent of the governed. We believe in **popular sovereignty**—that ultimate power resides in the people. Government, from this perspective, exists to serve the people rather than the other way around. The means by which the government learns the will of the people is through *elections*, perhaps the most important expression of popular consent. But there are instances when popular sovereignty and majority rule must be limited by other fundamental rights, as in the case of referenda limiting civil rights.[8] Examples include California's 1964 vote to permit people to discriminate in the sale of residential housing and 1996 vote to overturn affirmative action.

Many of the limits on government are specified in the Constitution and the Bill of Rights. The Constitution is revered as a national symbol, yet we often differ over the precise meaning of the framers' original intentions. We honor many of these rights more in the abstract than in the particular. Almost half of us, for instance, think that books with dangerous ideas should be banned from public school libraries (see Table 7-1). Intolerance of dissenting or offensive views is amply demonstrated in many public opinion polls and is observed on college and university campuses. Still, Americans can ordinarily be characterized as affirming support for democratic and constitutional values.

majority rule
Governance according to the expressed preferences of the majority.

popular sovereignty
A belief that ultimate power resides in the people.

JUSTICE AND THE RULE OF LAW Inscribed over the entrance to the U.S. Supreme Court are the words "Equal Justice Under Law." The rule of law means that government is based on a body of law applied equally and by just procedures, as opposed to rule by an elite in which the whims of those in power decide policy or resolve disputes. Chief Justice John Marshall succinctly summarized this principle: "The government of the United States has been emphatically termed a government of laws, not of men."[9] Americans believe strongly in the principle of fairness: all individuals are entitled to the same legal rights and protections.

For government to adhere to the rule of law, its policies and laws should follow these five rules:

- *Generality*: Laws should be stated generally, not singling out any group or individual.
- *Prospectivity*: Laws apply to the future, not punish something someone did in the past.
- *Publicity*: Laws cannot be kept secret and then enforced.
- *Authority*: Valid laws are made by those with legitimate power, and the people legitimate that power through some form of popular consent.
- *Due Process*: Laws must be enforced impartially with fair processes.

NATIONALISM, OPTIMISM, AND IDEALISM Americans are highly nationalistic. We are proud of our past and tend to forget our nation's intolerance, diplomatic and military setbacks, the shame of slavery, and the denial of suffrage to women for more than a century. We are optimistic—though more about people than about government. We believe in opportunity, choice, individualism, and most of all, in freedom to improve ourselves and to achieve success with as little interference as possible from others or from government. As Table 7-2 indicates, U.S. citizens are more satisfied with their democratic government than are citizens of other countries.

We Americans know our system is not perfect. We often grumble that elected officials have lost touch with us, we are disgusted by scandals, and we are impatient

TABLE 7-1 It Depends on What You Mean by Rights and Freedoms

	Agree	Disagree	Don't Know
I have old-fashioned values about family and marriage.	85%	14%	1%
Welfare benefits should be denied to unwed teenagers.	36	56	8
Books that contain dangerous ideas should be banned from public school libraries.	50	46	4
Affirmative action programs to help blacks, women, and other minorities get better jobs and education should be continued.	58	36	6
The police should be allowed to search the houses of known drug dealers without a court order.	49	49	2
School boards ought to have the right to fire teachers who are known homosexuals.	33	63	4

Which is more important to you: that the government be able to censor news stories it feels threaten national security OR that the news media be able to report stories they feel are in the national interest?

Government be able to censor	58%
News media able to report	32
Both equal (volunteered)	5
Don't know	5

SOURCE: The Pew Research Center for the People and the Press, *Values Update Survey,* November 5–9 and 13–17, 1997, Question 21; and The Pew Research Center for the People and the Press, *Republicans: A Demographic and Attitudinal Profile*, August 7, 1996, p. 16.

with the slowness of the system to solve problems like health care, crime, drug abuse, and campaign finance. Yet we have an abiding faith in government by the people. Despite the dissatisfactions, a remarkable belief persists that the nation is better, stronger, and more virtuous than other nations. Like every country, the United States has interests and motives that are selfish as well as generous, cynical as well as idealistic. Still, our support of human needs and rights throughout the world is evidence of an abiding idealism.

TABLE 7-2 Satisfaction with the Way Democracy Works

	Satisfied	Dissatisfied
Canada	62%	24%
United States	64	27
Iceland	54	23
Germany	55	27
Costa Rica	52	25
Thailand	54	27
Chile	43	31
France	43	32
Taiwan	25	18
Japan	35	32
Dominican Republic	40	38
Spain	31	30
United Kingdom	40	43
India	32	43
Venezuela	28	59
Hungary	17	50
Mexico	17	67
China	na	na

SOURCE: "People Throughout the World Largely Satisfied with Personal Lives," *The Gallup Poll Monthly,* June 1995, p.6.

The American Dream

Many of our political values come together in the **American Dream**, a complex set of ideas about the economy and its relation to individuals holding that the United States is a land of opportunity, and individual initiative and hard work can bring economic success. Whether realized or not, this American Dream speaks to our most deeply held hopes and goals. The essence of the American Dream can be found in our enthusiasm for **capitalism**, an economic system characterized by private property, competitive markets, economic incentives, and limited government involvement in the production and pricing of goods and services.

The concept of private property enjoys extraordinary popularity in our political culture. In many European democracies, the state owns and operates transportation systems, the media, and other businesses that are privately owned and operated in the United States, although there is increasing privatization of state-owned communications systems like telephone companies and broadcast media. Americans cherish the dream of acquiring property. Moreover, most Americans believe that those who own property have the right to decide how to use it.

The right to private property is just one of the economic incentives that cement our support for capitalism and fuel the American Dream. This is the land of opportunity for the enterprising. Here the competitive, practical go-getter can make a fortune and build a dream home. We assume that people who have more ability or work extremely hard will get ahead, earn more, and enjoy economic rewards. We also believe that people should be able to pass most of what they have accumulated along to their children and relatives. Even the poorest Americans oppose high inheritance taxes or limits on how much someone can earn.

Americans believe the mixed free enterprise system gives almost everyone a fair chance, that capitalism is necessary, and that freedom depends on it. We reject communism and socialism—a rejection fortified in the past decade as most communist nations shifted toward capitalism. In the United States, individuals and corporations have acquired wealth and, at the same time, exercised political clout. Their power has, in turn, bred some resentment.

The conflict in values between a *competitive economy*, in which individuals reap large rewards for their initiative and hard work, and an *egalitarian society*, in which everyone earns a decent living, carries over into politics. How the public resolves this tension changes over time. For instance, social programs that sought to extend equality of opportunity enjoyed broad support in the 1960s. During the 1980s they were attacked and partially dismantled as President Ronald Reagan sought to implement a more conservative, procapitalist policy. In the 1990s President Bill Clinton and Congress modified existing welfare programs by requiring persons on welfare to actively seek employment.

As important as the American Dream is to the national consciousness, Americans know it remains unfulfilled. Many millions in this country are still denied equality of opportunity because of race, ethnic background, or gender. An underclass persists in the form of impoverished families, ill-nourished and ill-educated

American Dream
The widespread belief that individual initiative and hard work can bring economic success, and that the United States is a land of opportunity.

capitalism
An economic system characterized by private property, competitive markets, economic incentives, and limited government involvement in the production and pricing of goods and services.

children, and people living on the streets.[10] Many cities are actually two cities, where some live in luxury while others live in squalor. The gap between rich and poor has grown in recent years.[11] And a sharp difference between white and black income persists tenaciously. Far more than people want to admit, chances for success still depend on the family you were born in, the neighborhood you grew up in, or the college you attended.

The use of child labor in factories is one aspect of the industrial transformation that still exists in parts of the world today.

Political and Economic Change

Political values are clearly affected by historical developments and by economic and technological growth. The Declaration of Independence and the Constitution identified such important political values as individual liberty, property rights, and limited government.[12] Early in our history we emphasized separation of powers, checks and balances, states' rights, and the Bill of Rights. It took an additional generation or two before we also began to take seriously the expansion of suffrage and competitive nominations and elections. Notions of political equality and effective participation emerged during the presidency of Andrew Jackson and matured in the course of the nineteenth century. By the end of the nineteenth century, populists and suffragists turned ideals into action and formed large-scale movements to achieve more democratic forms of participation and more responsive forms of governance.

THE INDUSTRIAL TRANSFORMATION By 1900, the agrarian society the framers knew had been largely replaced by industrial capitalism and the growth of large corporations. With these changes, ideology was irreversibly transformed. Large privately owned corporations changed the economic order, including changes in the role of government and how people viewed each other. No one captures the implications of this shift better than political scientist Robert A. Dahl:

> One of the consequences of the new order has been a high degree of inequality in the distribution of wealth and income—a far greater inequality than had ever been thought likely or desirable under an agrarian order by Democratic Republicans like Jefferson and Madison, or had ever been thought consistent with democratic or republican government in the historic writings on the subject from Aristotle to Locke, Montesquieu, and Rousseau. Previous theorists and advocates had, like many of the framers of our own Constitution, insisted that a republic could exist only if the citizen body continued neither rich nor poor. Citizens, it was argued, must enjoy a rough equality of conditions.[13]

The success of the American industrial economy led to the accumulation of great wealth in the hands of a few—the robber barons or tycoons. Many had taken great risks and earned their fortunes through inventions and efficient production practices. But as disparities of income grew, so did disparities in political resources. Economic resources can be converted into political resources, like time to spend on politics and money to contribute to parties and candidates.[14]

At the turn of the century, the rise of the large corporation and the concentration of individual wealth in the United States created divisions and resentment. Muckraking journalists charged that the huge corporations had become **monopolies**, using their dominance of their industry to exploit workers and limit competition. Unsafe work conditions led to regulation of the workplace by the states, but only the national government, it seemed, had the power to ensure fair treatment in the marketplace. This sentiment not only gave rise to the nation's first **antitrust legislation**—federal laws that try to prevent monopolies from dominating an industry and restraining trade—but also sowed the idea that government could—and should—as the Constitution asserts, "promote the general welfare" by regulating working conditions, product safety, and labor-management disputes.

monopolies
Large corporations or firms that dominate their industries and are able to artificially fix prices and discourage competition.

antitrust legislation
Federal laws (starting with the Sherman Act of 1890) that try to prevent monopolies from dominating an industry and restraining trade.

Breadlines like this provided handouts of food to thousands of unemployed and destitute people during the Great Depression.

THE GREAT DEPRESSION AND THE NEW DEAL Much of our thinking about the role of government in a capitalistic system is shaped by the Great Depression and the near collapse of the capitalistic system. Unrestrained capitalism and the unregulated market were faulted as a cause of the Depression. The collapse of the stock market, massive unemployment, and a failed banking system brought the nation to the brink of disaster. There was no unemployment compensation, no guarantee on bank savings, no federal regulation of the securities exchanges, no Social Security. Americans turned to government to improve the lot of millions of jobless and homeless citizens. Beginning with Franklin D. Roosevelt's New Deal, the idea gradually gained widespread acceptance that government should use its powers and resources to ensure some measure of equal opportunity and social justice.

Today, free enterprise is no longer unbridled. Government regulations, antitrust laws, job safety regulations, environmental standards, and minimum wage rates all balance the freedom of enterprise against the rights of individuals. Most people today support a semiregulated or mixed free enterprise system that checks the worst tendencies of capitalism, but they reject excessive government intervention (see Table 7-3). Much of American politics centers on how to achieve this balance.

TABLE 7-3 Attitudes on Business and Welfare, 1997

	Agree	Disagree	Don't Know
There is too much power concentrated in the hands of a few big companies.	73%	25%	2%
Business corporations make too much profit.	58	38	4
It is the responsibility of the government to take care of people who can't take care of themselves.	61	37	2
The government should help more needy people even if it means going deeper into debt.	44	53	3
The government should guarantee every citizen enough to eat and a place to sleep.	62	36	2

SOURCE: The Pew Research Center for the People and the Press, *Values Update Survey,* November 5–9 and 13–17, 1997, Questions 9,15.

President Franklin Roosevelt's State of the Union Address in 1944 articulated a "Second Bill of Rights" for all citizens. Roosevelt declared that this nation must make a firm commitment to "economic security and independence." Included in his Second Bill of Rights were:

- The right to a useful and remunerative job in the industries, shops, farms, or mines of the nation
- The right to earn enough to provide adequate food and clothing and recreation
- The right of every farmer to raise and sell his products at a return that would give him and his family a decent living
- The right of every businessman, large and small, to trade in an atmosphere of freedom from unfair competition and domination by monopolies at home or abroad
- The right of every family to a decent home
- The right to adequate medical care and the opportunity to achieve and enjoy good health
- The right to adequate protection from the economic fears of old age, sickness, accident, and unemployment
- The right to a good education.[15]

Roosevelt's policies and later efforts by John F. Kennedy and Lyndon Johnson in the 1960s to pass civil and voting rights legislation and launch a War on Poverty defined the ideological and political fights of the last half of the twentieth century. Modern-day liberalism and conservatism turn, in large measure, on how much one believes in Roosevelt's Second Bill of Rights and how much government assistance one thinks is owed to minorities, women, and others who have suffered discrimination or have been left behind by the industrial or technological revolutions of the twentieth century.

Today's political divisions are still based in large part on differing perspectives on the role of government in pursuit of social and economic policies. Passage of Johnson's Great Society programs of the 1960s gave renewed emphasis to an expanded view of rights and a larger federal role. President Bill Clinton's efforts to provide health care to all Americans can be seen as an application of expanded rights. In calling for health care reform, Clinton referred to Roosevelt's Second Bill of Rights, asserting that "health care is a basic right all should have."[16]

Ideology and Attitudes about the Role of Government

Ideology refers to a person's ideas or beliefs about political values and the role of government. It includes the views people have about how government should work and how it actually works. Ideology links our basic values to the day-to-day operations or policies of government.

Two major, yet rather broad, schools of political thinking dominate American politics today: *liberalism* and *conservatism*. Two lesser, but more defined, schools of thought, *socialism* and *libertarianism*, also help define the spectrum of ideology in the United States.

Liberalism

In the seventeenth and eighteenth centuries, classical liberals fought to minimize the role of government. They stressed individual rights and perceived government as the primary threat to rights and liberties. Classical liberals favored *limited government* and sought ample protections from governmental harassment. Over time, the emphasis on individualism remained constant, but the perception of the need for

ideology
One's basic beliefs about political values and the role of government.

WHERE WE LEARN THE AMERICAN POLITICAL CULTURE

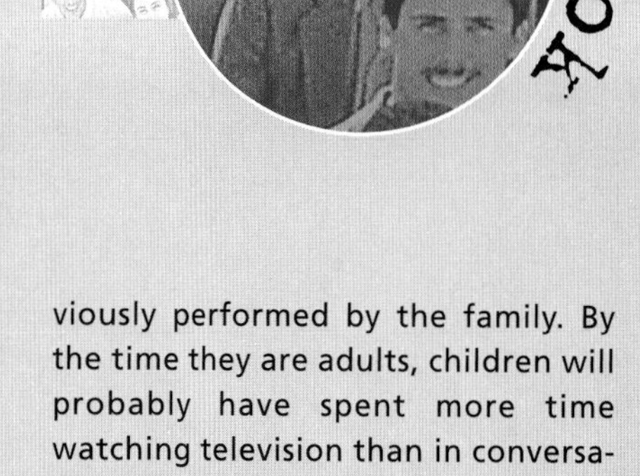

The Family

One of the important sources of political culture in the United States and in other nations as well is the family. Children are taught from an early age what it means to be an American. They are curious about why people vote, what the president does, and whether Grandpa fought in World War II. The questions may vary somewhat from family to family, but the themes of authority, freedom, equality, liberty, and partisanship are common. Families are the most important reference groups, and compared to families in other cultures, American families are much more egalitarian.

The Schools

Public schools are another source of the American political culture. Children and teachers often begin the school day by saluting the flag, reciting the Pledge of Allegiance, or singing the national anthem. Teaching American political and economic values is part of the curriculum. Not only are values taught in American history classes, but they are put into practice in school elections and newspapers and in encouraging students to participate in small-scale economic ventures.

Colleges and universities also play a role in fostering the American political culture. Students who attend college are often more confident than other persons in dealing with bureaucracy and politics generally, more likely to participate in politics and vote, and more knowledgeable about government. States require students at state colleges and universities to take courses in American government or state government, in part to instill a sense of civic duty while imparting knowledge about state and national governments.

Religious and Civic Organizations

Religious freedom and diversity have played a part in the formation and maintenance of the American political culture. American churches, synagogues, and mosques have long fostered a common understanding of right and wrong. Freedom, including freedom of religion, individualism, pluralism, and civic duty, have all been fostered by churches. As churches do not all take the same positions on political issues, their impact is sometimes mitigated, but they have been important to such major social and political movements as abolition of slavery, expansion of civil rights, and opposition to war. Civic organizations like the Boy Scouts, 4-H, League of Women Voters, Rotary Club, and Chamber of Commerce encourage citizen participation and pride in community and nation.

The Mass Media

In modern times the mass media have taken over some functions previously performed by the family. By the time they are adults, children will probably have spent more time watching television than in conversation with their parents. They may have had more political instruction from MTV than from their parents or their schools.

Political Activities

Finally, Americans educate each other about political values in the workplace, at the PTA meeting, or in more expressly political activities.

SOURCES: Charles W. Dunn, ed., *Religion in American Politics* (Congressional Quarterly Press, 1989); and Kenneth D. Wald, *Religion and Politics in the United States* (Congressional Quarterly Press, 1992).

government changed. Today liberals view government as protecting individuals from being abused by a variety of governmental and nongovernmental forces such as market vagaries, business decisions, and discriminatory practices.

"He's trustworthy, loyal, obedient, cheerful, and all that, but he leans to the left."

CONTEMPORARY LIBERALS In its modern American usage, **liberalism** refers to a belief in the positive uses of government to bring about justice and equality of opportunity. Modern-day liberals wish to preserve the rights of the individual and the right to own private property, yet they are willing to have the government intervene in the economy to remedy the defects of capitalism. Liberals seek protection against inadequate or deficient medical assistance, housing, and education. They generally believe in affirmative action programs, workers' health and safety protections, tax rates that rise with income, and unions' right to organize and strike.

On a more philosophical level, liberals generally believe in the possibility of progress. They believe that the future will be better, that obstacles can be overcome. This positive set of beliefs may explain their willingness to trust government programs. Liberals contend that the character of modern technology and the side effects of industrialization cry out for government programs to offset the loss of liberties suffered by the less well-to-do and the weak. Liberals such as Edward Kennedy, Hillary Rodham Clinton, and Jesse Jackson frequently stress the need for a compassionate and affirmative government.

Liberals charge that conservatives usually act in self-interest and follow the maxim, "Let the government take care of the rich, and the rich in turn will take care of the poor." Liberals, on the other hand, prefer that government take care of the weak, for the strong can always take care of themselves. "We have rejected the discredited theory that the fortunes of the nation should be in the hands of a privileged few," said President Harry Truman. "Instead, we believe that our economic system should rest on a democratic foundation and that wealth should be created for the benefit of all. . . . Every segment of our population and every individual has a right to expect from his government a fair deal."[17]

The liberal view holds all people equal. Equality of opportunity is essential, and toward that end, discriminatory practices must be eliminated. Some liberals favor the reduction of great inequalities of wealth that make equality of opportunity impossible. Most favor a certain minimum level of income. Rather than placing a cap on wealth, they want a floor placed beneath the poor. In short, liberals seek to lessen the impact of great inequalities of wealth and work to extend opportunities to all, regardless of their economic standing.

Liberals come in many varieties. Those who emphasize economic issues and call for government regulation to remedy the defects of capitalism may be called *New Deal liberals*; those who call for government assistance for the homeless or handicapped may be called *social liberals*; and *peace liberals* seek nonmilitary solutions to international tensions. Some liberals have lost faith in welfare programs and are skeptical about the efficiency and responsiveness of large bureaucracies but still favor government solutions to social and economic problems; they have named themselves *neoliberals.*[18]

CRITICISMS OF LIBERALISM Not everyone is convinced that liberals, in whatever form, have the answers for the policy challenges of the twenty-first century. Critics of liberalism, old and new, say liberals place too much reliance on governmental solutions, higher taxes, and bureaucracy. Opponents of liberalism argue that somewhere along the line liberals forgot that government, to serve our best interests, has to be limited. Power tends to corrupt, and too much dependence on government can corrupt the spirit, undermine self-reliance, and make people forget those cherished personal freedoms and property rights our Republic was founded to secure and protect. Too many governmental regulations and too much taxation tend to undermine the self-help ethic that "made America great." In short, critics of liberalism con-

liberalism
A belief in the positive uses of government to bring about justice and equality of opportunity.

tend that the welfare and regulatory state pushed by liberals will ultimately destroy individual initiative, entrepreneurial spirit, and the very engine of economic growth that might lead to true equality of economic opportunities.

In recent elections, Republicans made liberalism a villain and positioned their own candidates more in the mainstream. George Bush consistently referred to Michael Dukakis as from the "Liberal Democratic Party." Bill Clinton fought back and was careful not to label his program as liberal, focusing on the need for economic growth, jobs, and a lower budget deficit. He insisted he was a "New Democrat" to avoid the liberal stereotype. The battle over ideological definition persisted throughout the Clinton presidency, with Republicans pointing to his health care proposals as evidence of his tax-and-spend liberalism, and with Clinton countering that his leadership had significantly reduced the size of the federal budget deficit and had secured welfare reform.

Some liberals or progressives suggested a new agenda for the Democrats in response to the events of the 1990s and the success of conservative thinkers. E. J. Dionne, Jr.'s book on how progressives can regain power is aptly titled *They Only Look Dead*, referring to the conventional wisdom that liberal or progressive ideas are in decline. Dionne contends that "the current political upheaval can thus be defined less as a revolt against *big* government than as a rebellion against *bad* government—government that has proven ineffectual in grappling with the political, economic, and moral crises that have shaken the country."[19] Dionne challenges the claims of Clinton and Gingrich that big government is bad or even over. Pointing to past progressive or liberal successes, Dionne contends Americans want a government that eases economic transitions, helps "preserve a broad middle class," and "expands the choices available to individuals."[20]

As the agenda of American politics changes, so does the popularity of liberal or conservative positions. We have shifted from a preoccupation with budget deficits in the late 1980s and early 1990s to budget surpluses in the late 1990s. With the demise of communism, many Americans are now less concerned about defense spending and generally want less government. At the same time, we live in a global economy in which our jobs and economic progress are linked to our neighbors and to other countries around the world. The net effect of these changes is that our national government, while focusing on domestic issues like health care, crime, and welfare, does so in a context much more aware of budget constraints and the demand for lower taxes.

Conservatism

American **conservatism** has its roots in the political thinking of John Adams, Alexander Hamilton, and many of their contemporaries, who believed in limited government and encouraged individual excellence and personal achievement. Private property rights and belief in free enterprise are cardinal attributes of contemporary conservatism. In contrast to liberals, conservatives want to keep government small, except in the area of national defense. However, because conservatives take a more pessimistic view of human nature than liberals do, they maintain that people need strong leadership institutions, firm laws, and strict moral codes to keep their appetites under control. Government, they think, needs to ensure order. Conservatives also believe that those who fail in life are in some way the architects of their own misfortune and must bear the main responsibility for solving their own problems. Conservatives have a preference for the status quo and desire change only in moderation.

conservatism
A belief that limited government ensures order, competitive markets, and personal opportunity.

TRADITIONAL CONSERVATIVES Most conservatives opposed the New Deal programs of the 1930s, the War on Poverty in the 1960s, and the aggressive civil rights and affirmative action programs of the last three decades. Human needs, they say, can and should be cared for by families and charities. Conservatives place their faith in the private sector and consider social justice to be essentially an economic question. They dislike the tendency to turn to government, especially the national government, for solutions to societal problems. Government social activism, they say, has been expensive for taxpayers and counterproductive. They prefer private giving and individual voluntary efforts targeted at social and economic problems rather than government programs.

"With the end of the Cold War, the case for a strong central government has been dramatically weakened," according to Newt Gingrich. "The time has come for a reversion to first principles. In America, one of those first principles is that power resides first and foremost with the individual citizen. In America, individual citizens earn their bread, and the government had better have an overwhelming reason for taking it away from them."[21]

Traditional conservatives are emphatically pro-business. They oppose higher taxes and resist all but the most necessary antitrust, trade, and environmental regulations on corporations. The functions of government should be to encourage family values, protect the nation from foreign enemies, preserve law and order, enforce private contracts, foster competitive markets, and encourage free and fair trade.

Traditional conservatives favor dispersing power broadly throughout the political and social systems to avoid concentration of power at the national level. They favor having the market, rather than the government, provide services. Yet some conservatives, like 1996 vice-presidential candidate Jack Kemp, advocate a role for government in helping the worst-off climb out of poverty. Kemp believes government should create "enterprise zones" in impoverished urban areas by giving the private sector incentives to invest in poverty-stricken inner-city neighborhoods and create jobs for the urban poor.

WE THE PEOPLE

Differences in Political Ideology

	Conservative	Moderate	Liberal
Sex			
Male	41%	34%	24%
Female	37	39	24
Race			
White	40	37	23
Black	32	40	28
Age			
18–34	37	34	29
35–45	39	40	21
46–55	41	35	24
56–64	42	38	20
65+	41	41	18
Religion			
Protestant	47	39	14
Catholic	41	36	23
Jewish	15	25	60
Education			
Less than high school	33	45	21
High school diploma	38	45	17
Some college	36	39	25
Bachelor's degree	50	24	26
Advanced degree	40	22	37
Party			
Democrat	22	40	38
Independent	24	62	14
Republican	65	27	8

SOURCE: Center for Political Studies, University of Michigan, *American National Election Study*, 1998.

Note: We have combined with the moderates persons who do not know their ideology or had not thought much about it. For party identification, we have combined Independent leaners with their respective parties. Rows may not add up to 100 percent due to rounding.

THE NEW RIGHT Another brand of conservatism—sometimes called the New Right, ultraconservatism, or even the Radical Right—emerged in the 1980s. The New Right shares the love of freedom of traditional conservatives and backs an aggressive effort to combat international communism. It favors the return of organized prayer in the public schools, supports strict limits on abortion, and opposes policies like job quotas, busing, and tolerance of pornography and homosexuality. In sum, a defining characteristic of the New Right is a strong desire to impose various social controls.

A very active New Right or Religious Right group that supports social conservatism is the Christian Coalition, founded by Pat Robertson, a minister who sponsors a nightly cable television program. The coalition has become a major political force. Although ostensibly working in a bipartisan fashion, it is more at home in the Republican party. The coalition lobbies for and funds candidates who are pro-family, anti-abortion, anti-gay. It favors a constitutional amendment that would guarantee the rights to prayer in public schools and religious symbols in public places. It works at all levels of government and especially targets candidates who have voted for abortion rights legislation.

Some conservatives question the moralistic tone of the Christian Coalition. For example, Barry Goldwater, the late senator and 1964 Republican presidential candidate, worried that too much prominence and influence have been granted to the New Right, especially those he called the "checkbook clergy." Our Constitution, Goldwater said, seeks to allow freedom for everyone, not merely those professing certain moral or religious views. Goldwater pointed to the bloody divisions in Northern Ireland, the holy wars in Lebanon, and the pernicious religious righteousness in Iran as examples of the politicalization of churches. "The Moral Majority has no more right to dictate its moral and political beliefs to the country than does any other group, political or religious," said Goldwater. "The same is true of pro-choice, abortion, or other groups. They are free to persuade us because this land is blessed with liberty, but not to assign religious or political absolutes—complete right or wrong."[22] Goldwater feared that the great danger of the Christian Coalition was that it would tear his beloved Republican party apart.

CRITICISMS OF CONSERVATISM Not everyone agreed with Ronald Reagan's statement that "government is the problem."[23] Indeed, critics of conservatism before and during the Reagan-Bush era saw hostility to government as counterproductive and inconsistent. Conservatives, they argued, have a selective opposition to government. They want more government when it serves their needs—regulating pornography and abortion, for example—but are opposed to it when it serves somebody else's. Critics point out that government spending, especially for defense, grew during the 1980s when the conservatives were in control.

A growing political force in recent years is the Religious Right. They are active in local school boards and town councils as well as on the national scene.

CONSERVATIVE MANIFESTO

Pete DuPont

Former governor of Delaware and Republican presidential candidate Pete DuPont is a strong advocate for what he calls "contemporary conservatism." According to DuPont, conservatives are troubled by the inability of many individuals to accept the responsibility that living independently and morally in a free society entails.

Conservatives are troubled by the inability of many individuals to accept the responsibility that living independently and morally in a free society entails.

Pointing to the Declaration of Independence, which states that "that all men are created equal, that they are endowed by their creator with certain unalienable rights," DuPont asserts that people receive their rights from God rather than from government. The problem is that today's government has unnecessarily restricted rights and freedoms by regulating the economy and replacing private initiative with publicly financed social programs. These actions have encouraged many individuals to abandon responsibility for their own welfare in favor of dependence upon government programs. DuPont asserts that, "Even in America, amidst the greatest success of political and economic freedom in the history of the world, generations of central social and economic planning have finally fostered a new culture—a culture of dependency, rampant crime, single parenthood, broken families, tribal-like group competition, and a turn away from personal responsibility."

Human beings, in the conservative view, are competitive and individualistic. Like many conservatives, DuPont applauds the open marketplace in which people can establish their own businesses and compete freely to build enterprises that contribute to the general welfare of society. Conservatives enjoy the exhilaration of risk and competition. They find personal dignity in facing adversity with courage and overcoming obstacles with determination. They find personal irresponsibility and immorality to be the two most negative features of human nature. Irresponsible people rely on government or private handouts or resort to crime to meet their needs; immoral people have extramarital affairs and desert their families in their pursuit of pleasure.

What, then, is the conservative vision of the good society? DuPont repeatedly emphasizes strength as he identifies explicit principles for creating a prosperous and just society. Conservatives would: (1) strengthen our national defense by increasing the military forces and improving technology; (2) strengthen law enforcement by building more prisons, reinvigorating drug enforcement programs, and reaffirming the public's right to own firearms; (3) strengthen our economy by reducing taxes, minimizing government regulation of business, abolishing affirmative action programs, and paring down social programs such as health and welfare subsidies; (4) strengthen families by making divorce and abortion more difficult and allowing families to select the schools their children will attend.★

SOURCE: "Conservative Manifesto," *National Review* 46, March 21, 1994, pp. 32–38.

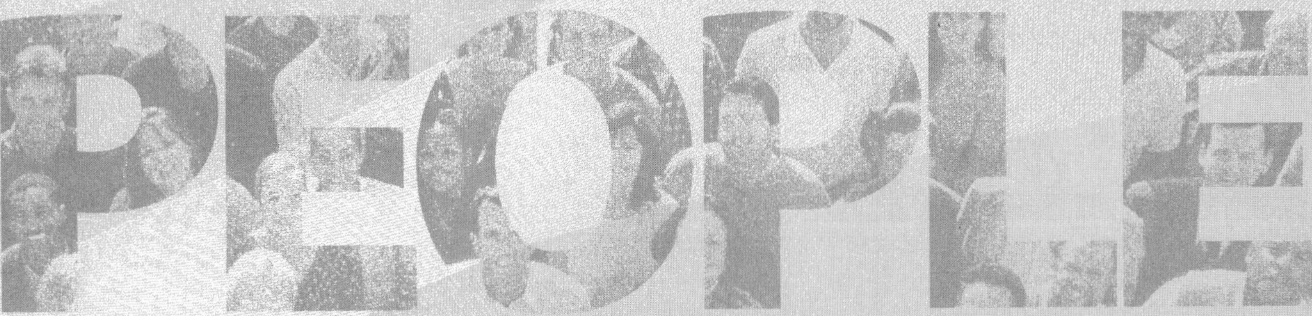

WHY I'M STILL LEFT

Mitchell Cohen

Mitchell Cohen, an editor of *Dissent* magazine, offers a different vision: one of American liberalism (or "social democracy," as he calls it). He explains that he uses the word "left" in order to identify with three "entwined" ideas: "liberty, equality, and solidarity." Conservatives, he says, have distorted what it means to be "liberal" or "left" and have tried to give these words negative connotations. Cohen maintains that at the heart of leftist values are democracy and social justice. This does not mean creating a utopia in which all people are forced to be equal. It does, however, include "siding with working people and the dispossessed, especially against private economic power." He hopes to convince people that "democracy ought to pervade socioeconomic in addition to political domains of life so that. . .the conditions for the freedom of one would be the conditions for the freedom of all."

Cohen insists that when conservatives claim that all people are equally free to pursue opportunity in our society, this is a myth. Citizens don't begin life at the same starting place. Our "free market" economy is in fact highly undemocratic because of the power of corporations and the advantages enjoyed by the upper social strata. People are not actually born with equal resources. We are born into a world in which some possess considerable advantages and many others are at a disadvantage. Cohen writes (following philosopher John Rawls) that "Our parents are a matter of chance, not choice. Unless you can be said to have rated your progenitors, why should advantages or disabilities that attend accidents of birth be translated into social privileges?" He points to national income data that indicates that the top 20 percent of the population has *nine times* as much wealth as the bottom 20 percent. This imbalance, he believes, is inherently unjust.

Cohen also thinks that conservatives are too one-sided when they say that people are competitive, "rugged individualists" by nature. Cohen argues that we are "social individuals" who want freedom, but who also feel solidarity with other human beings. So while Cohen believes markets are an important part of economic life, he also contends that they need to be regulated on behalf of broader human values. Cohen advocates an "equality-friendly society" and "social citizenship." He wants to ensure equal access to education and health care and to restrain the power of large corporations. According to Cohen, a healthy political democracy requires economic democracy.★

We are "social individuals" who want freedom, but who also feel solidarity with other human beings.

SOURCE: Mitchell Cohen, "Why I'm Still Left," *Dissent* 44 (Spring 1997).

For further information about this debate, go to **http://www.prenhall.com/burns** *and click on the Debate Icon in Chapter 7.*

Bernard Sanders, former mayor of Burlington, Vermont, and a self-described Socialist, was elected to the House of Representatives by Vermont voters as an Independent.

Conservatives place great faith in the market economy—critics would say too much faith. This posture often puts conservatives at odds with labor unions and consumer activists and in close alliance with businesspeople, particularly large corporations. Hostility to regulation and a belief in competition leads them to push for deregulation. This approach has not always had the intended positive effects, as the collapse of many savings and loans revealed.[24] Conservatives counter that relying on market solutions and encouraging the free market are still the best course of action in most policy areas.

The policy of the Reagan years of lowering taxes was consistent with the conservative hostility to government. Many conservatives embraced the idea that if we lower taxes on the rich, their economic activity will "trickle down" to the poor. This view was criticized by many Democrats, who pointed out that the growth in income and wealth in the 1980s was largely concentrated among the well-to-do.[25]

Conservatives are also criticized for their failure to acknowledge and endorse policies that deal with racism and sexism in the United States. Their opposition to the civil rights laws in the 1960s and to affirmative action in the 1990s are examples of this perspective. Not only have conservatives opposed new laws in these areas; they have hampered the activity of the executive branch when in power and have sought to limit the activity of the courts in these matters as well.

Socialism

socialism
An economic and governmental system based on public ownership of the means of production and exchange.

Socialism is an economic and governmental system based on public ownership of the means of production and exchange. Karl Marx once described socialism as a transitional stage of society between capitalism and communism. In a capitalist system, the means of production and most of the property are privately owned; in a communist system, property is "owned" by the state in common for all the people. In the ultimate communist country, justice is achieved by having participants determine their own needs and take what is appropriate from the common product of society. Marx's dictum was, "From each according to his ability, to each according to his needs."[26] Socialism can be combined with democracy as in Sweden, while communist countries like Cuba are ruled by one party, the Communist party.

In one of the most dramatic transformations in recent times, Russia, its sister republics, and its former European satellites abandoned communism and are now attempting to establish free markets. These countries had previously rejected capitalism, opting for state ownership and centralized government planning of the economy. But by the 1990s the disparities in economic well-being between capitalist and communist nations produced a tide of political and economic reform that left communism intact in only a few countries, such as Cuba and China.

American socialists—of whom there are very few prominent examples—favor a greatly expanded role for the government. They would nationalize certain industries, institute a public jobs program so that all who want work would be put to work, place a much steeper tax burden on the wealthy, and drastically cut defense spending as well.[27] Most of the democracies of Western Europe are more influenced by socialist ideas than we are in the United States, but they remain, like the United States, largely market economies. Governments generally appear to be turning more and more to market solutions to problems once assumed to be the responsibility of government. Some of the most important debates of the next century are going to be about what is the proper role of government and what the market can do better.[28]

Libertarianism

libertarianism
An ideology that cherishes individual liberty and insists on a sharply limited government, promoting a free-market economy, a noninterventionist foreign policy, and an absence of regulation in the moral and social spheres.

Libertarianism is an ideology that cherishes individual liberty and insists on a sharply limited government. It carries some overtones of anarchism, of the classical English liberalism of the past, and of a 1930s-style conservatism. The Libertarian party has gained a modest following among people who believe that both liberals and conservatives lack consistency in their attitude toward the power of the national government.

Libertarians preach opposition to just about all government programs. They favor massive cuts in government spending and an end to the Federal Bureau of Investigation, the Central Intelligence Agency, and most regulatory commissions; they favor a defense establishment that would defend the United States only if directly attacked. They oppose *all* government regulation, including, for example, mandatory seat-belt and helmet laws. Unlike conservatives, libertarians would repeal laws that regulate personal morality, including abortion, pornography, prostitution, and recreational drugs.

A Libertarian party candidate for president has been on the ballot in all 50 states in recent presidential elections, although never obtaining more than 1 percent of the vote. The Libertarian candidate for president in 1996, Harry Browne, ran on a platform that emphasized freedom from government. The 1996 Libertarian platform was committed to a smaller government, limited by the Constitution's specifications, and proposed immediate and complete removal of the federal government from education, energy, regulation, crime control, welfare, housing, transportation, health care, and agriculture; repeal of the income tax and all other direct taxes; decriminalization of drugs and pardons for prisoners convicted of nonviolent drug offenses; and withdrawal of overseas military forces. Libertarian positions are rarely timid; at the very least, they prompt intriguing political debates.[29]

Harry Browne, Libertarian candidate for president in 1996, was on the ballot in all 50 states but got only 1 percent of the total vote.

A Word of Caution

Political labels have different meanings across national boundaries as well as over time. To be a liberal in certain European nations is to be on the right; to be a liberal in the 1990s in the United States is to be on the left. In recent elections, "liberal," which back in Franklin Roosevelt's day had been popular, became "the L-word," a label most politicians sought to avoid. During his first presidential election, Bill Clinton defined himself as a "New Democrat," someone more in the country's political mainstream than past Democratic candidates had been. Republicans repeatedly accused Clinton of masquerading as a moderate, espousing Republican concerns like ending welfare. The varying ideological interpretations of Bill Clinton teach us that labels are rarely static and that politicians seek to define the opposing party as extremists and their own party as moderates.

On big questions—such as the role of government in the economy, in promoting equality of opportunity, in regulating the behavior of individuals or businesses, and on such issues as abortion—real differences separate conservative and liberal groups. This does not mean that persons who are conservative in one area are necessarily conservative in another.

It is important to appreciate that ideology both causes events and is affected by them. Just as the Great Depression resulted in a tidal wave of ideological change, so did our involvement in World War II, Korea, and Vietnam, each in its own way. World War II, with its positive example of how government can work to defend freedom, strengthened positive views about the role of the national government. The Vietnam War probably had the opposite effect, producing disillusionment with government. The antigovernment sentiment in recent presidential elections is undoubtedly related to Vietnam, the Watergate scandal, and allegations of sexual misconduct.

Debates about communist expansionism are increasingly dated and irrelevant in American politics. There is little fear today that the United States will become communist, and the communist threat around the world is greatly diminished. But people of varying ideologies do indeed worry about whether the United States is becoming too soft and losing ground in the global economy. Today we are more likely to debate what will make us beat, or at least compete with, a unified European economy.

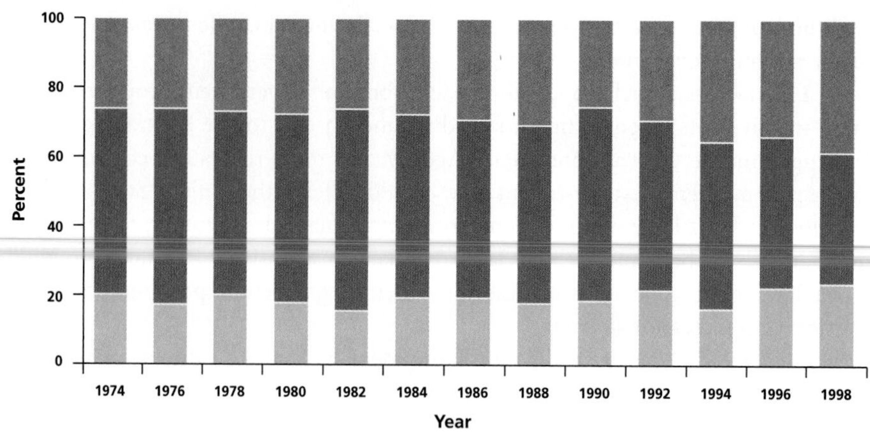

FIGURE 7-1 Ideology over Time

SOURCE: Center for Political Studies, University of Michigan, National Election Study Cumulative Data File, 1952–1992, *1994 National Election Study* and *1998 National Election Study.*

IDEOLOGY AND THE AMERICAN PEOPLE

Ideological controversy today centers on how we can improve schools, encourage a stronger work ethic, and stop the flow of drugs into the country; whether to permit openly gay people into the military or sanction gay marriages; and the best ways to instill religious values, build character, and encourage cohesive and lasting families.

Despite the twists and turns of American politics, the distribution of ideology in the nation has been remarkably consistent (see Figure 7-1). Conservatives outnumber liberals, but the proportion of conservatives did not increase substantially with the decisive Republican presidential victories of the 1980s.

Another important fact about ideology in the United States is that few people see themselves as extremists. In 1998 only 3 percent of the population saw themselves as extreme conservatives, and the same percent saw themselves as extreme liberals (see Figure 7-2). These percentages have changed very little over time. The tendency towards muted ideology is also demonstrated by the fact that there are more people who consider themselves slightly liberal rather than liberal. Despite claims by ideological factions in both parties to move to the right or move to the left, there are simply more votes in the middle.[30] (We analyze party identification in Chapter 10, but it is important to note here that there are liberal and conservative wings in both parties.)

For those who have a liberal or conservative preference, ideology provides a lens through which to view politics. It helps simplify the complexities of politics, policies, personalities, and programs. An ideology may be an accurate or an inaccurate description of reality, yet it is still the way a person thinks about people, power, and society. However, most Americans do not organize their attitudes systematically. A voter may want increased spending for defense but vote for the party that is for reducing defense spending because he or she has always voted for that party or prefers its stand on the environment. Or a person may favor tax cuts and balancing the budget while not cutting spending substantially.

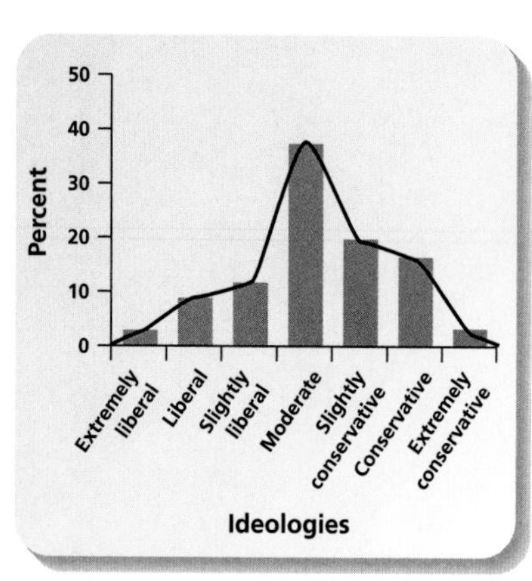

FIGURE 7-2 Ideology Curve

SOURCE: Center for Political Studies, University of Michigan, *1998 National Election Study.*

Consistency among various attitudes and opinions is often relatively low. Much of the time people view political issues as isolated matters and do not apply a general standard of performance in evaluating parties or candidates. Indeed, many citizens find it difficult to relate what happens in one policy situation to what happens in another. This problem becomes worse as government gets into more and more policy areas. Hence, many people, not surprisingly, have difficulty finding candidates who reflect their ideological preferences across a range of issues.

The absence of widespread and solidified liberal and conservative positions in the United States makes for politics and policy-making processes that are markedly different from those in many European and other nations. Policy making here is characterized more by coalitions of the moment than by fixed alignments that pit one set of ideologies against another. Our politics is marked more by moderation, pragmatism, and accommodation than by a prolonged battle between two, three, or more competing philosophies of government. Elsewhere, especially in countries where a strong Socialist or Christian Democratic party exists, things are different.

This does not, however, mean that policies or ideas are not elements in American politics. There has been, for instance, a shift to more partisan and ideological voting in the House of Representatives. Part of the explanation for the increasing importance of ideology in Congress is Republican gains in the South, with remaining southern Democrats becoming more liberal; in other parts of the country where moderate Republicans were once successful, liberal Democrats now hold many of the seats.

IDEOLOGY AND TOLERANCE

Is there a connection between support for civil liberties and tolerance for racial minorities and the ideologies of liberalism and conservatism? Some political scientists assert that conservatives are generally less tolerant than liberals. This view is stoutly contested by conservatives, who have charged liberals with trying to impose a "politically correct" position on universities and the media. Liberals are usually more tolerant of dissent and the expression of unorthodox opinions. However, liberals, too, can be intolerant—of anti-abortion forces, for example, or the National Rifle Association, or the views of Rush Limbaugh.

Most liberals are strongly opposed to crime and lawbreaking, yet they are as concerned about the roots or causes of crime as they are about the punishment of criminals. Perhaps for this reason, liberals exhibit somewhat greater concern than conservatives for the rights of the accused and are more willing to expand the rights of due process. Conservatives usually take a harder line and, in recent years, have won widespread popular support for their greater concern for the victims of crime than for the rights of the accused.

Such differences are most evident in the responses of liberals and conservatives to questions of civil rights and civil liberties. In the area of free speech, conservatives are usually seen as less willing to permit speech that is out of the political or cultural mainstream. Perhaps conservatives are less tolerant because those who claim to be exercising the right of free speech often attack established values. Liberals also favor limiting speech in areas like cigarette advertising or campaign spending.[31]

Conservatives believe that the United States has become too permissive. Many conservatives, especially in the New or Religious Right, are highly critical of homosexuals, drug users, prostitutes, unwed mothers, and pornographers. They worry about what they claim has been a decline in moral standards and, interestingly, call on government to help reverse these trends. Liberals, on the other hand, generally accept nonconformity in conduct and opinion as an inescapable by-product of freedom.[32] In this regard, liberals are like libertarians.

Ideologies have consequences. It is these sharp cleavages in political thinking that stir opposing interest groups into action. Groups such as the Christian Coalition, the American Civil Liberties Union, Amnesty International, Mothers Against Drunk Driving, Queer Nation, and countless others promote their views of what is politically desirable. It is also these differences in ideological perspectives that reinforce party loyalties and divide us at election time. Policy fights in Congress, between Congress and the White House, and during judicial confirmation hearings also have their roots in our uneasily coexisting ideological values.

Although Americans share many ideas in common, we as a people also hold many contradictory ideas. Our hard-earned rights and liberties are never entirely safeguarded; they are fragile and are shaped by the political, economic, and social climate of the day. In the next chapters we examine the interest groups and political parties that are battling to advance their values and compete in the American political culture. But before turning to those topics, we will examine the social and economic diversity of the American political landscape in Chapter 8 and see why agreement on shared democratic values is all the more remarkable.

POLITICS online

Electronic Communities

In this chapter we discussed the idea that Americans are increasingly detached from each other—the "bowling alone" idea. If people use the Internet as a mode of entertainment through which to look for information, shop, or pass their recreational time, this new technology will do little to reverse the trend of social disengagement. The stereotypical Internet "surfer" is antisocial, more interested in technology than people. Computer games, played in isolation from other people, seem to reinforce this sense that Web users are isolated from one another.

But the Internet is also used by people to talk to each other through chat rooms that provide important organizing information, bring people together, and help mobilize voters.

Examples of such "electronic communities" include:

http://www.talkspot.com/chan_news.html

http://www.4-lane.com/politicalchat

Even with these "electronic communities," the question remains whether people learn the essential political skills of listening, compromise, accommodation, and mobilization through such a process. Face-to-face interactions may develop different interpersonal skills than chat lines do. To explore this idea, listen to or participate in one of these electronic conversations yourself.

For more Internet resources on Political Culture and Ideology, see our home page:

http://www.prenhall.com/burns

SUMMARY

1. The United States, like every other nation or society, has a distinctive political culture. It consists of a widely held set of fundamental political values and accepted processes and institutions that help us manage conflict and resolve problems. In the United States, there is, at least in the abstract, respect for the Constitution, the Bill of Rights, a two-party system, and the right to elect officials on the basis of majority rule. Our belief in social equality has fostered acceptance of the notion that government should guarantee equality of opportunity through programs like education and job training.
2. Americans share a widespread commitment to classical liberalism, which embraces the importance of individual liberty, freedom, equality, private property, limited government, and popular consent. They also believe that the American Dream should be something we can all pursue.
3. American political values have been affected by the industrial transformation, the development of large corporations and other large institutions, the Great Depression, and a global economy.
4. The sources of the American political culture include the family, schools, religious and civic organizations, the mass media, and political activities.
5. Two broad schools of thought are important in American politics today: liberalism, a belief in the positive uses of government to bring about justice and equality of opportunity, and conservatism, a belief that limited government

ensures order, competitive markets, and personal opportunity. Socialism and libertarianism also attract a following in America. Few Americans are extremists.

6. Although many Americans are nonideological and are guided primarily by moderate pragmatism, a significant segment of Americans are either conservatives or liberals.
7. Ideological orientation has a bearing on how tolerant we are of the views and conduct of others. Liberals tend to be more permissive, whereas conservatives generally favor tradition, stability, and greater levels of "law and order." These differences have consequences for electoral contests, judicial interpretation, and policy development in our political system.

KEY TERMS

political culture 156
natural rights 156
majority rule 157
popular sovereignty 157
American Dream 159
capitalism 159
monopolies 160
antitrust legislation 160
ideology 162
liberalism 164
conservatism 165
socialism 170
libertarianism 170

FURTHER READING

LEON P. BARADAT, *Political Ideologies: Their Origins and Impact*, 6th ed. (Prentice Hall, 1996).

WILLIAM J. BENNETT, *Death of Outrage: Bill Clinton and the Assault on American Ideals* (Free Press, 1998).

WILLIAM F. BUCKLEY AND CHARLES R. KESLER, *Keeping the Tablets: Modern American Conservative Thought* (Harper & Row, 1988).

JAMES MACGREGOR BURNS, *Uncommon Sense* (Harper & Row, 1972).

JAMES CARVILLE, *We're Right, They're Wrong: A Handbook for Spirited Progressives* (Random House, 1996).

JAMES W. CEASER, *Reconstructing America: The Symbol of America in Modern Thought* (Yale University Press, 1997).

ALEXIS DETOCQUEVILLE, *Democracy in America* (Knopf reprint, 1994).

E.J. DOINNE, JR., *They Only Look Dead: Why Progressives Will Dominate the Next Political Era* (Simon & Schuster, 1996).

JOHN EHRMAN, *The Rise of Neoconservatism: Intellectuals and Foreign Affairs, 1945–1994* (Yale University Press, 1995).

JEAN BETHKE ELSHTAIN, *Democracy on Trial* (Basic Books, 1995).

DAVID FRUM, *What's Right* (HarperCollins, 1996).

NEWT GINGRICH, *To Renew America* (HarperCollins, 1995).

AMY GUTMANN AND DENNIS THOMPSON, *Democracy and Disagreement: Why Moral Conflict Cannot Be Avoided in Politics, and What Should Be Done About It* (Harvard University Press, 1996).

LOUIS HARTZ, *The Liberal Tradition in America* (Harcourt Brace, 1955).

JENNIFER HOCHSCHILD, *What's Fair: American Beliefs About Distributive Justice* (Harvard University Press, 1981).

IRVING KRISTOL, *Neoconservatism: The Autobiography of an Idea* (Free Press, 1995).

MICHAEL LERNER, *Politics of Meaning* (Viking Press, 1998).

WILLIAM MARTIN, *With God on Our Side: The Rise of the Religious Right in America* (Broadway Books, 1996).

HERBERT MCCLOSKY AND JOHN ZALLER, *The American Ethos: Public Attitudes Toward Capitalism and Democracy* (Harvard University Press, 1984).

CHARLES MURRAY, *What It Means to Be a Libertarian: A Personal Interpretation* (Broadway Books, 1997).

THEODORE SORENSEN, *Why I Am a Democrat* (Henry Holt, 1996).

DANIEL YERGIN AND JOSEPH STAINSLAW, *The Commanding Heights: The Battle Between Government and the Marketplace That Is Remaking the Modern World* (Simon & Schuster, 1998).

THE
AMERICAN
POLITICAL
LANDSCAPE

8

CHAPTER OUTLINE

- A Land of Diversity
- Who We Are
- Family Structure
- Unity in a Land of Diversity

WHEN THE IMMIGRANT PARENTS OF 90 CHILDREN DECIDED THEY DID NOT WANT THEIR CHILDREN TO CONTINUE WITH BILINGUAL EDUCATION IN THE NINTH Street School in Los Angeles, they did not know that their boycott would spark intense media attention and launch a statewide initiative to end bilingual education. One parent, Juana Jacobo, summarized the view of the parents when she said, "Home is for speaking Spanish, sure, but school is for learning English, and so we did the boycott." But to many Latino leaders in California, bilingual education represented the Anglo majority showing respect to the large Hispanic minority.

Bilingual education began in the mid-1970s. It was designed to help students learn English while not falling behind in other subjects that were taught in their native language. Roughly one-quarter of California's schoolchildren speak little or no English. Their native language is typically Spanish, although children entering school speak more than 100 different languages and some speak more than one non-English language, like the large group of students in Massachusetts from Cape Verde (Africa). Their native language is an ancient dialect called Kriolu, but they would have been taught to speak and write only in Portuguese in Cape Verde schools. In Massachusetts they are taught in Kriolu.[1] One California school district reported that over two-thirds of its students have "limited English proficiency"—the technical term used to define this population of students needing bilingual education. The California state education agency estimates a shortage of 20,000 teachers qualified to teach in two languages, despite bonuses of up to $5,000 for those who can.[2] The problem is not limited to California, as more than 3 million children nationwide lack basic skills in English, and more than one in four students in Houston and El Paso, Texas, school districts qualify for bilingual education.[3]

Ron Unz—a multimillionaire from California's Silicon Valley and an unsuccessful Republican gubernatorial candidate—had long been opposed to bilingual education and saw in the Ninth Street School boycott a chance to galvanize opposition to the practice and enact his "English for the Children" ballot initiative, Proposition 227. Also supporting the proposition was a famous Los Angeles math teacher, Jaime Escalante, whose story inspired the movie *Stand and Deliver.*

Proposition 227 requires immigrant students to enroll in one year of structured English immersion and then moves them into regular classes. Parents have the option to waive the English immersion and move the child immediately into an English class or a bilingual class taught in their native language. The initiative reflects Unz's view that "a young child can learn English in months. A year max. And to deny them that is the worst kind of paternalism."[4] The issue assumed greater symbolic importance to opponents of the initiative, who saw it as a successor to California's votes against illegal immigration in 1994 and affirmative action in 1996. Congressman Xavier Becerra (D.–Calif.) described Proposition 227 as "immigrant bashing."[5] California voters enacted the proposition by a margin of more than one million votes, setting the stage for similar measures in other states.

This controversy is part of the continuing debate in the United States over language, culture, and politics. In recent decades, voters in Arizona, Colorado, California, and Florida have voted overwhelmingly to make English—or as some insist, "American"—the official language. Nearly three out of four Californians and more than eight out of ten Floridians voted for English as the official language, and other states have considered similar measures.

What can you learn from these debates over language? Whatever side you choose in this debate, you have to be careful not to generalize from your own experiences. Most of us do not stop to consider how people from other backgrounds see things differently. This **ethnocentrism**—selective perception based on individual background, attitudes, and biases—is not uncommon, even among college students, who often assume that others share their economic opportunities, social attitudes, sense of civic responsibility, and self-confidence.

Albert Einstein once said few people are capable of expressing opinions that differ much from the prejudices of their social upbringing.[6] In this chapter we consider to what extent our social environment explains, or at least shapes, our opinions and prejudices. We also look at our diversity as Americans and the implications of geographic, social, and economic divisions for politics and government. Specifically, this chapter explores the effects of regional or state identity on political perspectives; the implications of differences in race, ethnicity, gender, family structure, religion, wealth and income, occupation, and social class for opinions and voting choices; and the relationship between age and education and political participation.

A Land of Diversity

Most nations consist of groups of people who have lived together for hundreds of years and who speak the same language, hold the same concept of deity, and share a common history. Although Japan, for example, has some people from other nations, most of its citizens are Japanese in the fullest sense of the word, and it is the same in Germany, Sweden, Saudi Arabia, China, and France. The United States is different. We are largely a land of immigrants. We have attracted the poor and oppressed, the adventurous and the talented, from all over the world, and we have been more open to accepting these people than have other nations.

One reason so many people want to come to the United States is that it holds a promise of religious, political, and economic freedom. It is also a place of opportunity for the enterprising. Our economic system has provided widespread (but not universal) opportunity for individuals to improve their economic standing. The American Dream—that everyone can "make it"—is widely shared.

Some elements of our diversity have become traditions that have political significance. Sectional differences persist between the South and the rest of the country, in part because of tradition. Third- or fourth-generation Americans may retain an identity with the native land of their ancestors, even though their spouses and neighbors do not share that identity.

Holding onto such differences is often the result of socialization in families, churches, and other closely knit groups. **Political socialization** is the process by which parents and others teach children about political values, beliefs, and attitudes. This teaching occurs during interactions in the home, on the playground, in school,

ethnocentrism
Selective perception based on individual background, attitudes, and biases that leads one to believe in the superiority of one's nation or ethnic group.

political socialization
The process by which we develop our political attitudes, values, and beliefs.

and in the neighborhood. In addition to fostering group identities, political socialization strongly influences how individuals see politics and which political party they prefer.

Because where we live and who we are in terms of our age, education, religion, and occupation affects how we vote, many who study voting and make predictions about it do so in terms of these and other factors, referred to as **demographics**. A **political predisposition** is a characteristic of individuals that is predictive of political behavior. Although demographics can be important, there are large individual differences within socioeconomic and demographic categories.

When social and economic differences coincide, they reinforce each other and make the differences between groups more important. Social scientists call these differences **reinforcing cleavages**; where they occur, political conflict becomes more intense and there is greater polarization in society. In Italy, for example, the regional divide between North and South is reinforced by the tendency of the North to be Socialist or Communist and the South to be Christian Democratic and Catholic in orientation. Nations can also have **cross-cutting cleavages**, instances where differences do not reinforce each other. To illustrate, let's look at religion and income. If all the rich individuals in a society are of one religion and the poor another, we would have reinforcing cleavages, and political conflict would be intensified. But if there are both rich and poor in all religions, and if people sometimes vote on the basis of their religion and sometimes on the basis of their wealth, then we would say the divisions are cross-cutting. American diversity has generally been more of the cross-cutting type than the cleavage type, lessening political conflict because individuals have multiple allegiances.

In some societies, politics centers largely upon passions over economic and religious differences. In Northern Ireland, for instance, the religious differences between Catholics and Protestants have produced centuries of violent division that may finally be resolved. Although socioeconomic differences are important to understanding American government and politics, they are not as central to the form and structure of politics as religion is in Bosnia or tribal identity in Rwanda.

Despite the fact that America, in the past as well as today, has been more hospitable to people from different religions, classes, or races than almost any other nation in the world, some Americans have not been tolerant. We often associate only with people "like us" and are suspicious of people "like them." From hostility toward different religions in the early colonies, to the anti-immigration movements of the late 1800s and early 1900s, to the various anti-immigration and anti-civil rights ballot initiatives of the 1990s, some Americans have exhibited ethnocentrism. For much of our history, minorities have been excluded from full participation in American political and economic life. Recently, many Americans have begun to take greater pride in their differing racial, ethnic, and religious traditions and cultures, and language is increasingly seen as part of a group's identity—an identity that minorities want to protect legally. Whether groups should assimilate or maintain a strong group identity is much debated within such groups and in the society at large.

Geography and National Identity

The United States is a geographically large and historically isolated country. Alexis de Tocqueville observed in 1835 that the country had no major political or economic powers on its borders "and consequently no great wars, financial crises, invasions, or conquests to fear."[7] Geographic isolation from the major powers of the world during our government's formative period helps explain American politics. The Atlantic Ocean served as a barrier to foreign meddling, giving us time to establish our political tradition and develop our economy. It also reinforced our sense of isolation from Europe and foreign alliances. This reluctance to become involved in foreign wars and controversies still arises in debates over foreign policy.

demographics
The study of the characteristics of populations.

political predisposition
A characteristic of individuals that is predictive of political behavior.

reinforcing cleavages
Divisions within society that reinforce one another, making groups more homogeneous or similar.

cross-cutting cleavages
Divisions within society that make groups more heterogeneous or different.

manifest destiny
A notion held by nineteenth-century Americans that the United States was destined to rule the continent, from the Atlantic to the Pacific Oceans.

In our entire history we have fought only one foreign enemy on our own soil—England in the War of 1812. (The war against Mexico of 1846–48 was fought almost entirely on Mexican land, some of which later became American land as a result of the war. The only other war fought on our soil was, of course, the Civil War.) In contrast, during the same period, Poland was invaded repeatedly and eventually partitioned by Austria, Prussia, and Russia. The difference is explained largely by location: Poland was surrounded by Europe's great powers. Had the United States been closer to Europe, it might have been overrun like Poland, and our Constitution and institutions repeatedly changed or eliminated to suit the victorious invaders. Having powerful and aggressive neighbors makes it difficult for relatively weak nations to nurture democracy.

The United States is a large country. Its land mass exceeds that of all but three nations in the world. In contrast, India has a population more than three times larger than the United States on a land mass one-third the size. Geographic space gave the expanding population of the United States room to spread out. This meant that some of the political conflicts arising from religion, social class, and national origin were diffused because groups could isolate themselves from one another. (See James Madison, *The Federalist*, No. 10, in the Appendix, for a development of the large republic idea.) Moreover, the large and accessible land mass helped foster the perspective that the United States had a **manifest destiny** to be a continental nation reaching from the Atlantic to the Pacific oceans. This notion that the United States was "destined" to expand across the continent was used to justify taking land occupied by Native Americans and Mexicans, especially the land acquired following victory in the Mexican-American War.

The United States is also a land of abundant natural resources. We have rich farmland, which not only feeds our population but makes us one of the three major exporters of food in the world. We are rich in such natural resources as coal, iron, uranium, and precious metals. All these resources enhance economic growth, provide jobs, and stabilize government. "The physical causes, unconnected with laws, which can lead to prosperity are more numerous in America than in any other country at any other time in history," observed Alexis de Tocqueville. "In the United States not legislation alone is democratic, for Nature herself seems to work for the people."[8]

Geography also helps explain our diversity. Parts of the United States are wonderfully suited to agriculture, others to mining or ranching, and still others to shipping. These differences produce different regional economic concerns, which in turn influence politics. For instance, a person from the agricultural heartland may

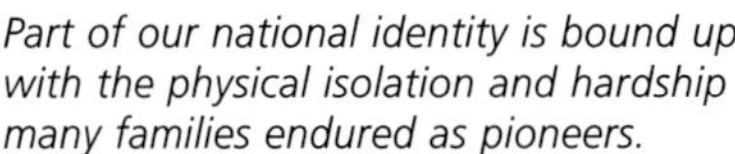

Part of our national identity is bound up with the physical isolation and hardship many families endured as pioneers.

have a different perception of foreign trade than an automobile worker in Detroit. But if that automobile worker is African American, this fact may be more important to her politics than what she does or where she lives. To understand American politics, we must appreciate these differences and their relative importance.

Unlike many other countries, geography in the United States does *not* define an ethnic or religious division. All the Serbs in the United States do not live in one place, all French-speaking Catholics in another, and all German immigrants in another. Sectional differences in the United States are primarily geographic, not ethnic or religious.

Sectional Differences

The most distinct section of the United States remains the South, although the South's differences are diminishing. From the beginning of the Republic, the agricultural South differed from the North, where manufacturing was more significant. But the most important difference between the regions was the institution of slavery. Northern opposition to slavery, which grew increasingly intense by the middle of the nineteenth century, reinforced the sectional economic interests that divided the nation. The eleven Confederate states, by virtue of their decision to secede from the Union, reinforced a common political identity, and after the Civil War sectional differences were strengthened by the policy of Reconstruction and the problems of race relations.

Things have changed in the last few decades, and as a result the South is becoming less distinct from the rest of the United States. A large in-migration has diminished the sense of regional identity, and the South has undergone tremendous change. The civil rights revolution gave African Americans the right to vote, opened up new educational opportunities, and helped to integrate the South into the national economy. African Americans still lag behind whites in voter registration, but the gap is now no wider in the South than elsewhere and is explained more by differences in education than by race.[9] In economic terms, the South still falls below the rest of the country in per capita income and education, but much less so than 50 years ago. The religious and moral conservatism of the South remains notable.

Until recently, political observers spoke of the "solid South"—a region that voted for Democrats at all levels. The reason for the connection between the South and Democrats is simple: "The Civil War made the Democratic party the party of the South, and the Republican party, the party of the North."[10] The Democratic "solid South" was to remain a fixture of American politics for more than a century. Since 1968 that has changed dramatically, first at the presidential level and increasingly at the state and local levels. As two respected observers of the region comment, "The fall of the South as an assured stronghold of the Democratic party in presidential elections is one of the most significant developments in modern American politics."[11] The political alignment has shifted as African Americans have been enfranchised and become overwhelmingly Democrats, and many whites have shifted to the Republicans. By 1992 and 1996, even with two southerners (Bill Clinton and Al Gore) on the ticket, Democrats won only four of the eleven former Confederate states.

What explains this dramatic reversal? Part of the explanation is that the Democrats' advocacy of aggressive action on civil rights in the 1960s alienated some southern whites. In addition, the debate within the Democratic party over Vietnam policy in the late 1960s and 1970s was "perceived by many southern voters as unpatriotic."[12] Republican presidential candidates have more recently exploited family values and law-and-order issues that appeal to conservative southern voters.

Republican success at the presidential level was slow to reach contests for Congress and state legislatures. Yet in 1994 and 1996, Republicans had more than

TABLE 8-1 Voting Patterns in the Eleven Former Confederate States

Republican Vote for President

1980	50%
1984	62
1988	59
1992	43
1996	46

Republican Vote for U.S. Representatives

1980	40%
1982	39
1984	42
1986	41
1988	42
1990	43
1992	48
1994	58
1996	53*
1998	58

Republican Share of State Legislators

	House	Senate
1980	18%	17%
1982	22	14
1984	23	17
1986	24	20
1988	27	24
1990	28	26
1992	31	31
1994	37	37
1996	44	44
1998	**42**	40

SOURCES: U.S. Bureau of the Census, *Statistical Abstract of the United States, 1995* (Government Printing Office, 1995), pp. 273, 275; *Statistical Abstract of the United States, 1993* (Government Printing Office, 1993), p. 279; *Statistical Abstract of the United States, 1989* (Government Printing Office, 1989), p. 254; *Statistical Abstract of the United States, 1987* (Government Printing Office, 1987), p. 239; *Congressional Quarterly Report*, November 9, 1996, pp. 3250–57; "Election Results," *Congressional Quarterly*, November 7, 1998, pp. 3027–3035.

*The 1996 Texas runoff elections are not included.

half of southern votes for the U.S. House of Representatives (see Table 8-1), and by 1995 they had seven of the eleven governorships in the former Confederate states. In the state legislatures of several southern states, remnants of the old "solid South" remain, but Republicans have made major inroads, and politics in the region is now much more competitive.

Another common sectional division is the *sun belt*—the eleven former Confederate states plus Oklahoma, New Mexico, Arizona, and the southern half of California. Sun belt states have been growing in population much more rapidly than the rest of the country, and as a result of population shifts after the last census, these states gained 17 seats in the U.S. Congress. Early projections call for states like Arizona, Colorado, Florida, Georgia, Montana, and Texas to gain seats following the 2000 census.[13] However, population growth in the South and West is occurring in different age groups. In the South, population growth is largest among those over 65; in the West, it is younger persons who provide the growth. Sun belt states have also experienced greater economic growth as industries headed south and southwest, where land is cheaper and more abundant, and where labor is cheaper as well (see Figure 8-1).

State and Local Identity

Americans identify with the politics of the state in which they live. Mention Wyoming, Mississippi, Oregon, New York, or Kansas, and it brings to mind a certain type of politics. The same is true for many other states. Like most stereotypes, these images are often misleading, but they reflect the fact that there is a sense of identity to states as political units that goes beyond demographic characteristics and is supported by recent empirical evidence. States have distinctive political cultures that affect public opinion and policy outcomes.[14] These state identities are reinforced by our electoral rules and other laws.

In American politics today, one state—California—stands out. More than one out of eight Americans is a Californian.[15] In terms of economic and political importance, California is in a league by itself; its 52 members of the House of Representatives exceed the total number of representatives from the smallest 20 states. No presidential candidate can afford to lose California's 54 electoral votes.[16]

The Kinds of Places in Which We Live

Most Americans, 80 percent of them, now live in central cities and their suburbs—what the Census Bureau calls *metropolitan areas.* During the early twentieth century, the movement of population was from rural areas to central cities, but the movement since the 1950s has been from the central cities to their suburbs. Today the most urban state is California (92.6 percent of its population lives in cities or suburbs). Vermont is the least urban, with only 32 percent living in cities or suburbs. Regionally, the West and Northeast are the most urban, the South and Midwest the most rural. The four-fifths of the population that now lives in cities and suburbs occupies only 2.5 percent of the nation's land.[17]

People move from cities to the suburbs for many reasons—better housing, new transportation systems that make it easier to get to work, the desire for cleaner air and safer streets. Another reason is *white flight*, the movement of whites away from the central cities so that children can avoid being bused for racial integration and attend generally better schools. White, middle-class migration to the suburbs means that American cities have become increasingly poor, increasingly African American, and increasingly Democratic. More than half of all African Americans now live in central cities, as opposed to only about one-quarter of whites, and the poverty level among blacks living in central cities is 50 percent higher than whites living in the same cities.[18] The proportions are very nearly reversed for suburbs, where more than half of all white Americans reside. Almost one-third of American suburbanites are now African American, up from one-fifth in 1980.[19]

In large cities such as Washington, D.C., Detroit, Baltimore, Atlanta, and New Orleans, the city population is now more than 50 percent African American (see Table 8-2). Hispanics constitute nearly two-thirds of the population of El Paso, Texas, and Santa Ana, California, and more than half of the population of Miami and San Antonio.[20] As population shifts occur, the tax base of cities declines because the richer people have gone to the suburbs, where they now pay local sales and property taxes. At the same time, service needs in the cities increase as the remaining less affluent population must pay for education, police protection, and health care.

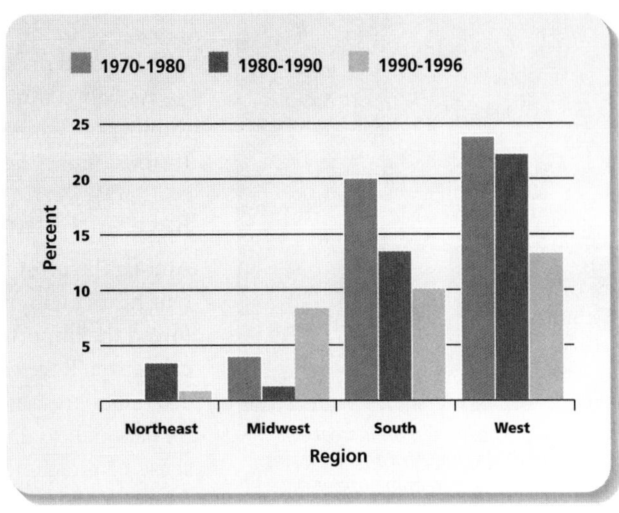

FIGURE 8-1 Population Gains by Region, 1970–1996

SOURCE: U.S. Bureau of the Census, *Statistical Abstract of the United States, 1998* (Government Printing Office, 1998), p. 131.

Suburbs vary in relative affluence. Many older ones now face the same problems as the inner cities, but their populations typically have higher per capita income, fewer minorities, and more Republicans. Companies employing professionals or engaging in high-tech or service activities frequently relocate to the suburbs to avoid city congestion and to be closer to the bedroom communities of their workers. Political boundaries, which define local governments and delineate responsibility for services, create understandable tensions among cities, suburbs, and rural areas. Tax revenues, legislative representation, zoning laws, and governmental priorities are hotly contested issues on the local level.

TABLE 8-2 Cities with Populations of 100,000 or More That Are at Least 50 Percent African American, 1998

	Population	Percent African American
Atlanta, Ga.	394,000	67%
Baltimore, Md.	736,000	59
Birmingham, Ala.	265,000	63
Detroit, Mich.	1,028,000	76
Gary, Ind.	117,000	81
Inglewood, Calif.	110,000	52
Jackson, Miss.	197,000	56
Macon, Ga.	107,000	52
Memphis, Tenn.	619,000	55
Newark, N.J.	275,000	59
New Orleans, La.	497,000	62
Richmond, Va.	203,000	55
Savannah, Ga.	138,000	51
Washington, D.C.	607,000	66

SOURCE: U.S. Bureau of the Census, *Statistical Abstract of the United States, 1998* (Government Printing Office, 1998), p. 47.

Recent years have seen an increase in wealth among some African Americans that enables them to enjoy upper-class comforts and opportunities.

Who We Are

Sectional distinctions are less prominent today than they were a century or even a half century ago. Today Americans are more likely to define themselves by a number of characteristics, each of which may influence how they vote or think about various candidates, issues, or policies.

Race and Ethnicity

Among the most important distinctions in American politics are race and ethnicity. Our history as a nation of immigrants and our struggle with race relations have reinforced the importance of these differences, and they have become part of our political debate. **Race** can be defined as a grouping of human beings with common characteristics presumed to be transmitted genetically. **Ethnicity** is a social division based on national origin, religion, and language, often within the same race, and includes a sense of attachment to that group. In the United States, race and ethnicity issues focus on African Americans, Asians, and Hispanics.

Four out of five Americans are white. African Americans are the largest nonwhite racial group. There are more than 33 million African Americans in the United States, roughly 13 percent of the population. Asian Americans constitute just under 4 percent of the population, and Native Americans just under 1 percent. Most American Hispanics are classified as white by the Census Bureau, although Hispanics can be of any race. The Census Bureau estimates that there are 28 million American Hispanics, constituting over 10 percent of the population.[21] Because of differences in immigration and birth rates, whites in America will have declined to just under three-quarters of the population by the year 2050. Hispanics are the fastest growing ethnic group.

AFRICAN AMERICANS Most people came to this country of their free choice in search of freedom and opportunity. African Americans came as slaves. Although they were freed as a result of the Civil War, racial divisions continue as one of the enduring issues of American politics,[22] as seen in the recent battles over affirmative action in California and Washington.

Until 1900, more than 90 percent of all African Americans lived in the South.[23] By 1995 the figure was 52 percent.[24] Many African Americans left the South after the turn of the century, hoping to improve their lives by settling in the large cities of the Northeast, Midwest, and West. The reality for many was urban poverty. More recently, some African Americans have been returning to the South, especially to its urban areas.

In economic terms, African Americans are much worse off than whites in the United States. African American median family income in 1996 was $25,970, compared to $42,646 for whites. Incomes of about one-third of African Americans are below the poverty level, compared to 11 percent of whites.[25] Another way to measure economic well-being is in terms of assets including property and possessions, or wealth. *Wealth* encompasses the things of economic value (savings, stocks, property) you possess; *income* is how much money you make from your job or investments. African Americans' net wealth is only one-tenth that of whites, and Hispanics have only slightly more wealth than African Americans (see Figure 8-2). As a result, African Americans and Hispanics have fewer resources to fall back on in hard times, and they are less likely to have the savings to help a child pay for college.[26] Some African Americans have become relatively prosperous; 17 percent of African American households had earnings in 1995 of over $50,000, a proportion still only half that for whites.[27] Some African Americans, like Michael Jordan and Oprah Winfrey, have risen to the top in earnings in their fields of endeavor.

Middle-class African Americans provide role models for the young and leadership for the civil rights movement, yet their comparatively small number serves as a reminder that most African Americans remain behind whites in an economy that

race
A grouping of human beings with common characteristics presumed to be transmitted genetically.

ethnicity
A social division based on national origin, religion, language, and often race.

relies more and more on education and job skills. About 24 percent of whites graduate from college, whereas only about 14 percent of African Americans do.[28] Among 18-to-21-year-old high school graduates, 45 percent of whites go on to college, but only 33 percent of African Americans.[29]

Finally, the African American population is much younger than the white population; the 1996 median age for whites was 35.7, compared to 29.5 for African Americans.[30] The combination of a younger African American population, a lower level of education, and concentration in economically hard-pressed urban areas has resulted in a much higher unemployment rate for young African Americans. Unemployment, in turn, can lead to social problems like crime, drug and alcohol abuse, and family dissolution.

What's My Name?

The terms "Latino" and "Chicano" are preferred to "Hispanic" by some persons of Spanish-speaking descent to disassociate themselves from Spain, a colonial power against which their ancestors fought wars of independence. "Hispanic" is the term most widely used by government agencies and the media, while "Latino" appears more popular among leaders of the group. "Chicano" is often associated with the politically active Mexican American movement of the 1960s and 1970s. Most Mexican Americans, Puerto Rican Americans, and Cuban Americans prefer to be called American rather than Latino or Hispanic.

SOURCE: Richard Santillan and Carlos Munoz, Jr., "Latinos and the Democratic Party," in *The Democrats Must Lead*, ed. James MacGregor Burns, William Crotty, Lois Lovelace Duke, and Lawrence D. Longley (Westview Press, 1992), pp. 182–83; Rodolfo O. de la Garza, Louis DeSipio, F. Chris Garcia, John Garcia, and Angelo Falcon, *Latino Voices: Mexican, Puerto Rican, and Cuban Perspectives on American Politics* (Westview Press, 1992), p. 13.

African Americans have had limited rights and little political power for most of the period since emancipation. Owing their freedom to the "party of Lincoln," most African Americans initially identified with the Republicans, but this loyalty started to change with Franklin Roosevelt, who insisted on equal treatment for African Americans in his New Deal programs.[31] In the period after World War II, African Americans came to see the Democrats as the party of civil rights. The 1964 Republican platform position on civil rights espoused states' rights—then the creed of southern segregationists—in what appeared to be an effort to win the support of southern white voters. Virtually all African Americans voted for Lyndon Johnson in 1964, and in presidential elections between 1964 and 1996, their Democratic vote has averaged 85 percent.[32]

Recently, African Americans have become much more important politically because of their increased voter participation and their concentrated population. African Americans constitute only .3 percent of Montana and .4 percent of South Dakota, but 36 percent of Mississippi, 33 percent of Louisiana, and 30 percent of South Carolina.[33] Southern senators and representatives cannot afford to ignore the African American vote.[34] Evidence of growing African American political power is the dramatic increase in the number of African American state legislators, which rose from 168 in 1970 to 575 in 1996.[35]

HISPANICS/LATINOS Latinos are not a monolithic group, and while they share a common linguistic heritage, they often differ from one another, depending on which country they emigrated from. Cuban Americans, for instance, tend to be Republicans, while Mexican Americans and Puerto Ricans are disproportionately Democrats.[36] Socioeconomically, Cuban Americans approximate the higher end of the population, while Puerto Rican Americans and Mexican Americans are generally at the lower end of the scale.[37] A recent study found differences among Latinos of Mexican, Puerto Rican, and Cuban descent in partisanship, ideology, and rates of participation but widespread support for a liberal domestic agenda, including increased spending on health care, crime and drug control, education, the environment, child services, and bilingual education.[38]

Given the overall growth of the Latino population, it is not surprising that both major parties have aggressively sought to cultivate Latino candidates. Two Latinos have won elections to the U.S. Senate, both from New Mexico, and President Clinton has had several Hispanics in his cabinet.

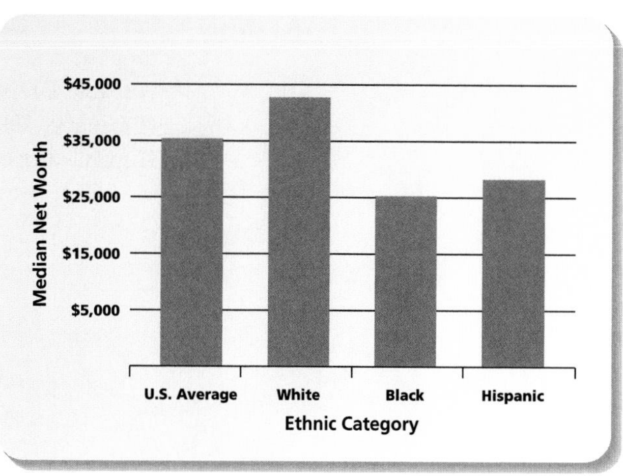

FIGURE 8-2 Wealth Distribution in the United States by Race

SOURCE: U.S. Bureau of the Census Home Page (http://www.census.gov/ftp/pub/hhes/wealth/wlth93f.html).

WHY EVEN LATINO PARENTS ARE REJECTING A PROGRAM DESIGNED FOR THEIR CHILDREN'S BENEFIT

Rosalie Pedalino Porter

The accumulated research of the past thirty years reveals almost no justification for teaching children in their native languages to help them learn either English or other subjects.

"Bilingual education is a classic example of an experiment that was begun with the best of humanitarian intentions but has turned out to be terribly wrongheaded," concludes Rosalie Pedalino Porter. Porter notes that following World War II, influential educators believed that children who did not speak English needed a three-year transition period in which they would learn English while receiving instruction in their original language. This belief resulted in "an education industry" in which "many bilingual programs became more concerned with teaching in the native language and maintaining the ethnic culture of the family than with teaching children English in three years."

Porter insists that these programs have not had the intended beneficial results. "The accumulated research of the past thirty years reveals almost no justification for teaching children in their native languages to help them learn either English or other subjects. . . ." She notes that although bilingual classes were expected to raise student self-esteem and relieve stress, there is no evidence that these objectives have been achieved. Nor has the original goal—reducing the dropout rate—been accomplished. The Hispanic Dropout Project's final report (February 1998) indicates that the Hispanic dropout rate is still between 30 and 35 percent, more than double the rate for African Americans and more than three times the dropout rate for non-Hispanic whites.

Why is bilingual education such a failure? First, according to Porter, national polls have shown that most Hispanics value learning English much more highly than they value speaking Spanish in order to retain their native culture. Second, Hispanic parents are unhappy that in some cases children stay in bilingual programs for up to six years, delaying their complete integration into English language classrooms.

Porter cites several situations around the country in which Spanish-speaking parents have protested bilingual education programs because they believed the programs were not helping their children succeed in an English-speaking America. She concludes that "bilingual education has had a sufficient trial period to be pronounced a failure. It is time finally to welcome immigrant children into our society by adding to the language they already know a full degree of competency in the common language of their new country—to give these children the very best educational opportunity for inclusion."★

SOURCE: Rosalie Pedalino Porter, "Why Even Latino Parents Are Rejecting a Program Designed for Their Children's Benefit," *Atlantic Monthly* 281, May 1998, pp. 28–39.

SHOULD ENGLISH BE THE LAW?

Robert D. King

Robert D. King, a professor at the University of Texas, takes direct aim at the English-only movement. "The question that lies at the root of most of the uneasiness is this: Is America threatened by the preservation of languages other than English? Will America, if it continues on its traditional path of benign linguistic neglect, go the way of Belgium, Canada, and Sri Lanka—three countries among many whose unity is gravely imperiled by language and ethnic conflicts?" The problem, says King, is that language is key to cultural identity. "Scratch most nationalist movements and you find a linguistic grievance. The demands for independence of the Baltic states (Latvia, Lithuania, and Estonia) were intimately bound up with fears for the loss of their respective languages and cultures in a sea of Russianness."

Still, some countries like Finland and Switzerland have a long and successful multilingual heritage. Why? Because they have a strong national identity that transcends language boundaries. Although the Swiss speak German, Italian, and French, they see themselves not as French, German, or Italian, but share what King calls "unique otherness."

According to King, language conflicts pose no lasting problem to the United States because "America has that unique otherness . . . In spite of all our racial divisions and economic unfairness, we have the frontier tradition, respect for the individual, and opportunity; we have our love affair with the automobile; we have in our history a civil war that freed the slaves and was fought with valor; and we have sports, hot dogs, hamburgers, and milk shakes—things big and small, noble and petty, important and trifling. 'We are Americans; we are different.'" ★

The problem is that language is key to cultural identity.

Source: Robert D. King, "Should English Be the Law?" *Atlantic Monthly*, April 1997, pp. 55–64.

For more information about this debate, go to **http://www.prenhall. com/burns** *and click on the Debate Icon in Chapter 8.*

The divisions among Latinos are politically important because of the tendency of the groups to settle in different areas. Nearly two-thirds of Cuban immigrants live in Florida, especially greater Miami; Puerto Rican immigrants are concentrated in or around New York City; and Mexican American immigrants in the southwest and California. The Census Bureau estimates that more than 10.6 million Hispanics live in California alone.[39]

WE THE PEOPLE

Percentage of the Population by Race and Origin

	1990	2000	2025	2050
White	83.9%	82.1%	78.3%	74.8%
African American	12.3	12.9	14.2	15.4
American Indian, Inuit, Aleut	0.8	0.9	1.0	1.1
Asian and Pacific Islander	3.0	4.1	6.6	8.7
Hispanic	9.0	11.4	17.6	24.5

SOURCE: U.S. Bureau of the Census, *Statistical Abstract of the United States, 1996* (Government Printing Office, 1997), p. 14.

Percentages do not equal 100 percent because Hispanics can be of any race. Figures for 2000, 2025, and 2050 are projections.

The issue of illegal aliens became the focus of a much publicized ballot initiative in California in 1994—Proposition 187. California voters, by a margin of 59 percent to 41 percent, adopted a measure that would deny most state spending on illegal immigrants. The constitutionality of the initiative was immediately challenged in court.

ASIAN AMERICANS Asian Americans are a heterogeneous group of persons classified together by the census for statistical purposes but with significant differences in culture, language, and political experience in the United States. The group includes persons of Chinese, Japanese, Korean, Vietnamese, Filipino, and Thai origin, as well as persons from the Pacific Islands. Asian Americans as a group are the most successful economically and educationally. More than three out of every five Asian Americans have graduated from college, compared to one out of every four white Americans and one in seven African Americans.[40]

In 1996, the United States was home to nearly 10 million Asian Americans and Pacific Islanders, residing primarily in the western states, especially Hawaii, California, and Washington.[41] The numbers of Asian Americans grew during the 1970s and 1980s, largely as a result of Southeast Asian immigration. In the 1990 census, persons from Asia had climbed to one of four of all foreign-born persons living in the United States, and the Philippines was surpassed only by Mexico as the country of birth for foreign-born persons living in this country. In states with heavy concentrations of Asian immigrants, these groups are now becoming more politically important and visible in politics. In 1996, Washington elected the first Chinese American governor of a state in the continental United States—Gary Locke.

THE TIES OF ETHNICITY Except for Native Americans, all Americans are immigrants or are descended from immigrants. The country's early settlers were generally English-speaking Protestants; even today, people of English, Scottish, and Welsh background make up the largest ethnic group in the United States. Irish immigrants, largely Catholics, started coming before the potato famine in the 1840s and came in larger numbers after it. Upon their arrival, they experienced economic exploitation and religious bigotry. The Irish American response was often to retreat among themselves, forming a strong ethnic group consciousness. Other ethnic groups that followed—Italians, Greeks, Chinese—each experienced a similar cycle: flight from their homeland and happy arrival here; then discrimination, exploitation, residential clustering, and the formation of a strong group identity.

The largest number of immigrants came between 1900 and 1924, when 17.3 million people relocated to the United States—by far the largest immigration to one country in any quarter-century in human history. From 1991 to 1995, there were more than 5.2 million immigrants,[42] primarily from the Caribbean and Mexico, and from Asian

gender gap
The difference between the political opinions or political behavior of men and women.

countries such as the Philippines, Vietnam, and China. The foreign-born proportion of the U.S. population has increased in recent years, rising from 14 million in 1980 to nearly 26 million in 1997, the largest number of foreign-born in U.S. history.[43] Recently the proportion of Asian and Mexican immigrants has pulled even with or surpassed the number of Europeans.

Having large numbers of immigrants can pose challenges to any political and social system. The immigrants are often the source of social conflict as they compete with more established groups for jobs, rights, political power, and influence.

EMILY's List and Wish List

One of the groups that has most aggressively promoted female candidates is EMILY's List, a group that funds pro-choice Democrats. EMILY is an acronym for "Early Money Is Like Yeast," meaning that campaign contributions given to candidates early in their campaigns can help raise more money, just as yeast helps dough to rise. EMILY's List supporters are proud of the fact that there are more women in the U.S. House than ever before in history. EMILY's list has also helped fund racial and ethnic female candidates, with roughly one-third of the candidates supported being African American or Latina. Republicans have duplicated EMILY's List with their own political action committee, Wish List, which gives to Republican female candidates who are pro-choice.

Gender

For most of U.S. history, politics and government were men's business. As discussed in Chapter 5, women gained the right to vote primarily in the western territories, beginning with Wyoming in 1869 and Utah in 1870, and then in Colorado and Idaho before the turn of the century.[44] The right was not extended nationally until 1920 with passage of the Nineteenth Amendment. The fears of some opponents of women's suffrage—that women would form their own party and vote largely for women or fundamentally alter our political system—have not been realized. During Susan B. Anthony's suffrage campaign, Jonas H. Upton, editor of the *Democratic Salem Monitor* in Salem, Oregon, contended that women, if given the right to vote, would combine to vote for war because they were exempt from the draft.[45] Others said women would unite to vote for prohibition.[46]

For most of the period after gaining the right to vote, American women voted at a lower rate than women in other Western democracies, but this trend appears to be changing.[47] For the past 20 years, women have voted at nearly the same rate as men, with the result that in recent elections, because females in the population outnumber males, the female vote has outnumbered the male vote.

WOMEN IN POLITICS The numbers of women elected to public office have been low; since 1917, less than 6 percent of representatives in the U.S. House have been women, but the number of women elected to the House of Representatives and U.S. Senate reached new highs in the 1990s. Following the 1998 elections there were 3 female governors, 9 women serving in the Senate, and 58 in the U.S. House of Representatives. The rising number of women holding office now is due to more women running for office, especially in contests with no incumbent running.[48]

Instead of voting as a bloc, women have typically divided their vote between the two major political parties. However, in 1992 and 1996 women were more likely than men to vote for Clinton and less likely to vote for Ross Perot (see Figure 8-3). Women have chosen to work within the existing political parties and do not overwhelmingly support female candidates, especially if they must cross parties to do so.

The women's movement in American politics encompasses a comprehensive agenda, including voting and political rights as well as extending the basic liberties of the Bill of Rights and Fourteenth Amendment. In addition to rights and liberties, women seek equal opportunity, education, jobs, skills, and respect in what has been a male-dominated system.[49]

There is a **gender gap**—significant differences between men and women—in public opinion and voting. Women are more likely to oppose violence in any form—death penalty, new weapons systems, or the possession of handguns. Evidence suggests that women as a group are more compassionate than men and so are more likely to favor government that provides health insurance and family services. Women are more concerned than men about women's rights—enforcement of child support, punishment for sexual abuse and rape, and unequal treatment in the legal system. These so-called "gender issues" are becoming increasingly important.

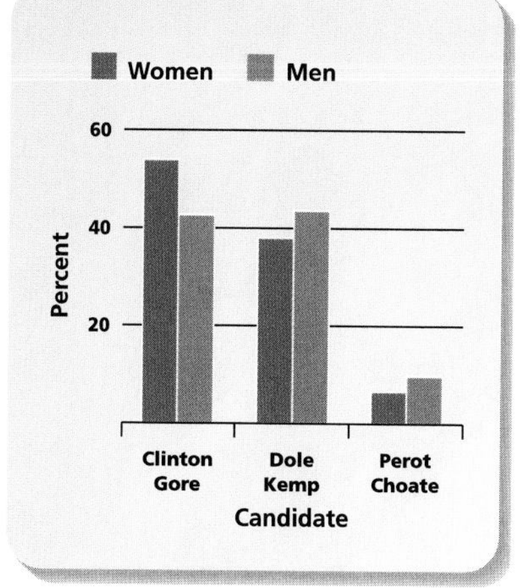

FIGURE 8-3 Gender and the Vote for President, 1996

SOURCE: "Voter News Service Exit Poll," *The New York Times*, November 10, 1996, p. 16.

Charles Brett, Copley News Service.

American women identify work and family issues such as day-care, prenatal and postnatal leave, and equal treatment in the workplace as important.[50] Other gender issues, some of them focal points in recent elections, include reproductive rights, restrictions on pornography, and sexual harassment.[51]

There are serious inequalities between men and women in income. About 79 percent more women than men work at or below the minimum wage.[52] In 1993, 45 percent of women earned less than $10,000, compared to only 25 percent of men.[53] While women now earn on average only about 72 cents for every dollar earned by men, this figure has improved from the 60 cents for every dollar in 1980.[54] Because an increasing number of women today are the sole breadwinners for their families, the implications of this low income level are even more significant. The problem of lower pay for women is not restricted to working mothers. Among college graduates ages 25 to 34, women earn an average of 80 cents for every dollar earned by men of the same age and education. As age increases, the earnings gap widens, so that 55- to 64-year-old college educated women earn only 60 cents for every dollar earned by men of the same age and education.[55] Increasing women's income is an important issue to the women's movement.

Family Structure

The changing nature of the family is one of the most important demographic facts as we enter the new century. Over the past half-century the family has been transformed from a "traditional family" (mother and father married with children in the home) to a range of living arrangements and varying family structures. Part of the changing nature of families is due to liberalization of attitudes toward sexuality. Today, Americans are much more likely to approve of premarital sex than in the early 1970s. And at some point in their lives, over half of Americans will *cohabit* (live with someone of the opposite sex to whom they are not married). Cohabitation raises policy questions as well, such as whether the live-in partner is eligible for employment benefits and welfare payments. Contraception is widely used and accepted, and yet one-third of all births are now illegitimate. These children will often be in need of social services and financial assistance.

People now marry later in life, with men marrying at average age 26.5 and women at 24.5. Yet marrying later has not improved the chances of avoiding divorce. The average marriage today lasts only about 7.2 years. Before World War II, only 9 out of every 1,000 marriages ended in divorce; from 1950 to 1994 the divorce rate nearly doubled; and today about one-half of all marriages are estimated to end in divorce.[56]

Divorce is one reason why more women work and why the number of households headed by women has risen. Attitudes about the role of women in marriage and the family have also changed. In 1972, one-third of Americans thought a woman's place is in the home, but in 1994, only one-sixth of all Americans felt this way.[57]

Religion

James Dobson, president of Focus on the Family, holds up a Bible as he speaks to several thousand people attending the 1998 Southern Baptist Convention.

In some parts of the world, religious differences are a source of violent conflict. In Iraq and Turkey the Kurdish people have been subjected to expulsion and even to genocide. The war in Bosnia-Herzegovina was a religious and ethnic battle among Muslims, Serbs, and Catholics, as were the recent killings between Serbs and Muslims in Kosovo. Countries like Afghanistan, Israel, Lebanon, India, and Sri Lanka have also experienced intense religious conflict. Jews have often been the target of religious discrimination and persecution (anti-Semitism), including the Holocaust, during which an estimated 6 million Jews were murdered.[58] The United States has not been immune, despite its principle of religious freedom. In 1838, Governor Lilburn W. Boggs of Missouri issued an extermination order against the Mormons.[59]

RELIGION AND POLITICS

At one time we thought a Catholic could not be elected president. With the election of 1960 that issue was resolved. John F. Kennedy directly confronted the question of whether a Catholic would put aside religious teachings if they conflicted with constitutional obligations. He said, "I am not the Catholic candidate for President. I am the Democratic party's candidate for President who happens also to be Catholic. I do not speak for my church on public matters, and the church does not speak for me." A candidate's religion may still become an issue if religious convictions on sensitive issues such as abortion threaten to conflict with public obligations.

Religion can be an important catalyst for social change, as the Catholic church was in the overthrow of communism in Central Europe and the leadership of the black church was instrumental in the American civil rights movement. As writer Taylor Branch explains, the black church "served not only as a place of worship but also as a bulletin board to a people who owned no organs of communication, a credit union to those without banks, and even a kind of people's court."* African American ministers, like the Reverend Martin Luther King, Jr., became leaders of the civil rights movement; others, like the Reverend Jesse Jackson, have run for national office. Hence religion can be important not only as a source of personal values and attitudes but as a means of political activity and organization.

In recent years there has been an increase in political activity among fundamentalist Christians. Led by ministers like Jerry Falwell and Pat Robertson, they have supported political organizations such as the Moral Majority and Christian Coalition. For the past two decades, they have sought to influence the national agenda, and Robertson ran for president in the Republican party in 1988. They have also focused their attention at the local level—school boards, city councils, mayorships, and local GOP leadership.** Their agenda includes the return of school prayer, the outlawing of abortion, restrictions on homosexuals, and opposition to gun control. They take credit for Republican successes in the 1994 and 1996 congressional elections and are seen as an important political force in some parts of the country.

*Taylor Branch, *Parting the Waters: America in the King Years, 1954–63* (Simon & Schuster, 1988), p. 3.

**Kevin Lange, "An Energized Religious Right? Strategies for the Clinton Era," *Christian Century* 110 (February 17, 1993), pp. 177–79.

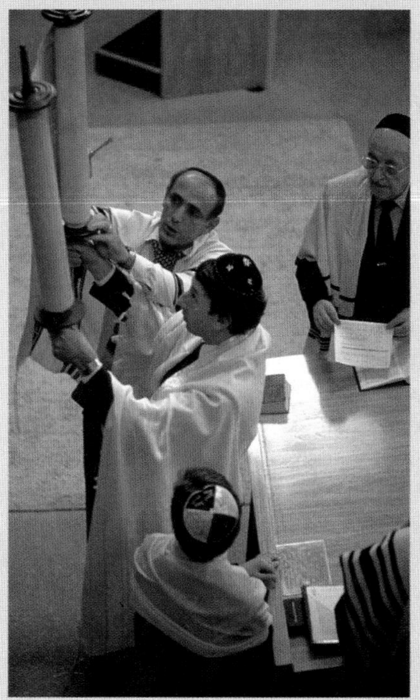

Religious observances in this country are as diverse as the population: Jewish Americans observe the Sabbath, African Americans celebrate Kwanza, and Muslim Americans obey the call to prayer during Ramadan.

You Decide...

How should people be counted?

The Census Bureau, which conducts the once-a-decade count of all persons in the United States, proposed using random sampling rather than attempting to count all households in the 2000 census. Republicans oppose sampling because they consider it unreliable. The Supreme Court ordered actual counting. The Census Bureau countered with a proposal to do both.

The proposed sample approach would contact 90 percent of the households in a census tract consisting of roughly 1,700 individuals. The bureau would then check the accuracy of the sample by surveying 750,000 households throughout the nation and adjusting the final total accordingly.

The sample approach responds to complaints about the flawed 1990 census, which cost $2.6 billion (a 400 percent increase over the cost of the 1980 census) and failed to account for 10 million people and double-counted 6 million others, according to a study by the National Academy of Sciences. Do you think that sampling is a fair and effective solution?

Although the intensity of religious conflict varies, it can become especially strong if there is one predominant or official faith, which is why the framers of our Constitution did not sanction a national church in the United States. In fact, James Madison wrote in *The Federalist*, No. 51, "In a free government the security for civil rights must be the same as that for religious rights. It consists in the one case in the multiplicity of interests, and in the other in the multiplicity of sects" (reprinted in the Appendix).

The absence of an official American church does not mean that religion is unimportant in American politics; indeed, there were established state churches in this country until the 1830s. Politicians frequently refer to God in their speeches or demonstrate their piety in other ways. And many share John Conway's view that "at the root of American political and social values . . . is the distinctive Puritanism of the early New England settlers."[60]

Many Americans take their religious beliefs seriously, more so than people of other industrial democracies.[61] Nearly two-thirds of Americans attend houses of worship several times a year, more than half attend a church or synagogue at least once a month, and more than one-third attend nearly every week.[62] Religion, like ethnicity, is a *shared identity*. People identify themselves as Baptist, Catholic, or Buddhist. Sometimes church attendance or nonattendance is more important than differences between religions in explaining attitudes. "Among both Catholics and Protestants, opposition to abortion increases with frequency of church attendance, but the percentages expressing pro-choice and pro-life sentiments are almost identical for the Catholic and Protestant groups."[63]

One defining characteristic of religion in the United States is the tremendous variety of denominations. About half the people in the United States describe themselves as Protestant (see Figure 8-4). The largest Protestant denomination is Baptist, followed by Methodists, Lutherans, Presbyterians, and Episcopalians. Because there are so many different Protestant churches, Catholics have the largest single membership in the United States, constituting more than one-quarter of the population. Jews constitute less than 2 percent of the population. Protestants came to the United States first; most Catholics and Jews immigrated after the 1840s. It was not until 1960, however, that Americans elected a Catholic president.

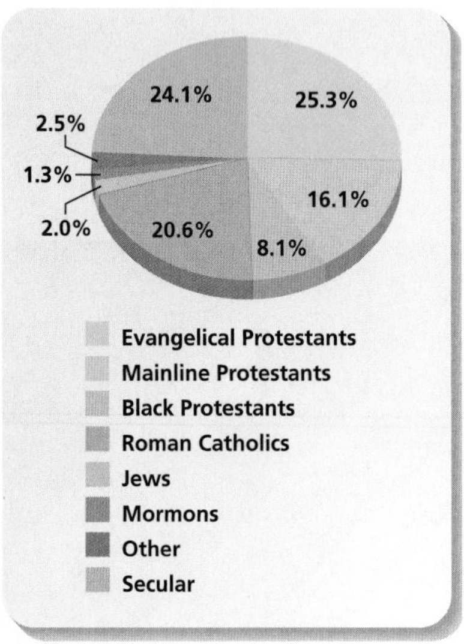

FIGURE 8-4 Religious Groups

SOURCE: "Is There a Culture War: Religion and the 1996 Election." Paper presented at the American Political Association meetings, Washington, D.C., 1997 (http://www.wheaton.edu/polsci/kellstedt).

In recent presidential elections, a majority of Protestants voted Republican, while majorities of Catholics and Jews voted Democratic.[64] The perception among many Catholics and Jews that the Democratic party is more open to them helps explain the strength of their Democratic identification. The Democrats won the loyalty of many Catholics by their willingness to nominate Al Smith for the presidency in 1928 and John Kennedy in 1960. Southern Protestants are Democrats for different reasons, largely having to do with the sectional issues discussed earlier. Religious groups vary in their rates of participation. Jews have the highest rate of reported voter turnout, 79 percent in 1992, while those who claim no religious affiliation have the lowest, 62 percent. Catholics voted at a slightly higher rate than Protestants.[65]

Religion is especially important in American politics because of the clustering of populations. Hence Catholics make up about one-quarter of the U.S. population, yet they are more than 50 percent of the population of Rhode Island, Massachusetts, and Connecticut. Baptists represent 19 percent of the U.S. population, yet they are more than 50 percent of the population of Mississippi, Alabama, and Georgia. Mormons are only 2 percent of the U.S. population, yet they are more than 70 percent of the population of Utah. The South is the most Protestant—61 percent. The state of New York has the highest percentage of Jews, 7 percent; New York City is 14 percent Jewish.

Religion can be related to other politically important characteristics. For instance, Jews are the most prosperous and best educated of any ethnic or religious group. More than 46 percent of Jewish adults graduated from college, compared to

22 percent of Protestants and 20 percent of Catholics.[66] In this example, as in others, religion is a cross-cutting cleavage in American politics; the differences do not reinforce one another. On the basis of income and education, Jews predictably would be Republicans, but 66 percent of American Jews are Democrats.[67] Similarly, southern Protestants would predictably be heavily Republican, but many of them are Democrats.

Wealth and Income

The United States is a wealthy nation in a world of scarcity and intense economic conflict over the distribution of wealth. Indeed, to some knowledgeable observers, "the most striking thing about the United States has been its phenomenal wealth."[68] A large proportion of the people in the United States lead comfortable lives in terms of housing, nutrition, and medical care, and they enjoy a standard of living beyond the reach of many in other countries. But even in affluent societies, the distribution of wealth and income can result in important political divisions and conflicts.

Wealth (total value of possessions) is more concentrated than income (annual earnings). The wealthiest families hold most of the property and other forms of wealth like stocks and savings. Traditionally, one of the problems with concentrated wealth has been that it fosters an aristocracy. Jefferson sought to break up the "aristocracy of wealth" by changing from laws based on *primogeniture* (the eldest son's exclusive right to inherit his father's estate) to laws that encouraged people to divide their estates equally among all their children, the result being smaller landholding. Jefferson sought to foster an "aristocracy of virtue and talent" through a public school system open to all for primary grades and for the best students through the university level.[69] Education has been one of the most important means for Americans to achieve economic and social mobility. Those with an education are wealthier, and those with wealth are more inclined to get an education. Most college students come from the top quarter of American families in income—those earning $50,000 a year or more. In fact, students from these families graduate from college at nearly twice the rate as those from the bottom 75 percent of the socioeconomic ladder.[70]

"The most common and durable source of factions has been the various and unequal distribution of property," wrote James Madison in *The Federalist*, No. 10 (reprinted in the Appendix). He continued, "Those who hold, and those who are without property, have ever formed distinct interests in society." Madison was right. Economic differences often lead to conflict, and Americans remain divided politically along economic lines. Aside from race, income may be the single most important factor in explaining views on issues, partisanship, and ideology. Most rich people are Republicans, and most poor people are Democrats, and this has been true since at least the Great Depression of the 1930s.

Income has been rising in the United States. Even after adjusting for inflation, income doubled in the period between the early 1950s and early 1970s. Since the early 1970s, inflation-adjusted income has gone up and down, but the steady rise seen earlier has not occurred (see Figure 8-5).[71] Economists debate the causes for this change; some cite higher energy costs, low levels of personal savings, and the worldwide slowdown in productivity growth.[72] In terms of income, the Northeast is the most prosperous region and the South the least prosperous. Compared to other nations, our purchasing power is higher than that of any other advanced democracy, including Japan.[73]

Despite the general rise in income, in the last quarter-century, roughly one in every ten Americans has come from a family whose income is below the poverty line. In 1997 the official poverty level for a family of four was an income below $16,404.[74] Most persons classified as below the poverty line are in families in which adults of working age either do not have jobs or work in jobs with low pay. Families headed

Thinking it Through...

The battle over the 2000 census is not so much about *how* to count as *whom* to count. The proposed sampling would enable a more accurate count of inner-city Hispanics and African Americans—the most difficult to count. This approach would likely have resulted in a greater representation for Hispanics and African Americans in state legislatures and the U.S. House of Representatives. A more complete count of minorities could also mean that the Republican party could loose a few seats in the House to Democrats, which is why Republicans generally oppose the sampling approach while Democrats favor it.

The constitutionality of sampling is also disputed, as the Constitution calls for an "actual enumeration" of the people. Democrats are quick to point out that under three presidents—Carter, Bush, and Clinton—the Justice Department concluded that sampling is legal. In order to get a ruling on the constitutionality of sampling, Speaker Newt Gingrich filed suit on behalf of the House of Representatives, and the Supreme Court ordered an actual count.* Whatever the resolution of this dispute, you should monitor the 2000 census and assess the extent to which it corrects the problems of the 1990 census.

SOURCES: Steven A. Holmes, "Political Interests Arouse Raging Debate on Census," *The New York Times*, April 12, 1998, p. 1; and Steven A. Holmes, "Gingrich Files Suit to Prevent Use of Sampling in 2000 Census," *The New York Times*, February 22, 1998, p. 21.

**Department of Commerce et al v United States House of Representatives et al.*

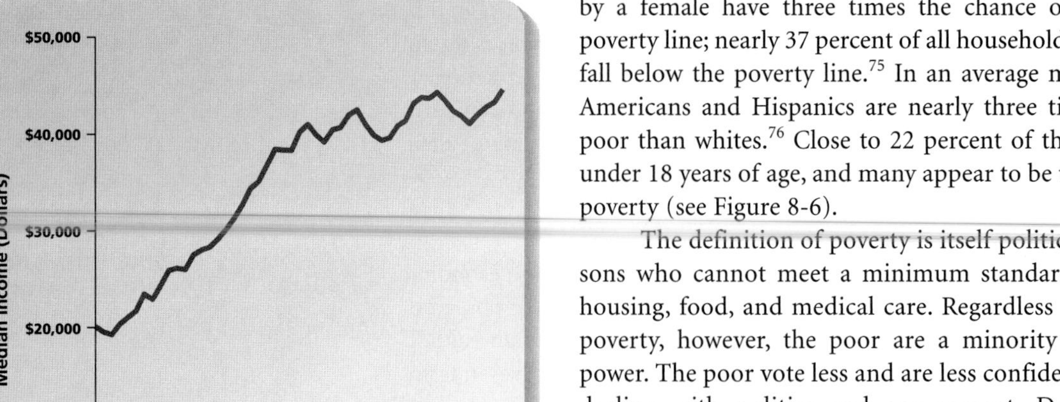

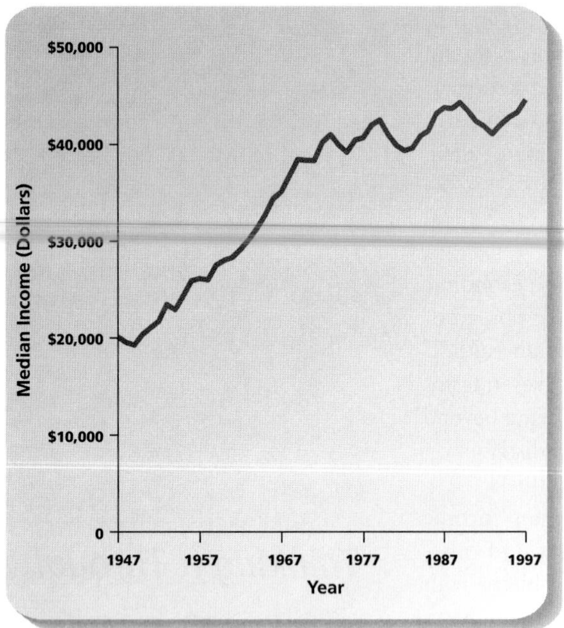

FIGURE 8-5 Median Family Income, 1947–1997

SOURCE: U.S. Bureau of the Census, *The Official Statistics*, July 27, 1998, p. 620.

by a female have three times the chance of falling below the poverty line; nearly 37 percent of all households headed by females fall below the poverty line.[75] In an average month, both African Americans and Hispanics are nearly three times as likely to be poor than whites.[76] Close to 22 percent of the poor are children under 18 years of age, and many appear to be trapped in a cycle of poverty (see Figure 8-6).

The definition of poverty is itself political. It identifies persons who cannot meet a minimum standard in such basics as housing, food, and medical care. Regardless of how one defines poverty, however, the poor are a minority who lack political power. The poor vote less and are less confident and organized in dealing with politics and government. During the last two decades, there has been increasing inequality between rich and poor, a trend quite different from the 1960s, when the gap between rich and poor narrowed. Although the gap did begin to decrease under the Bush administration, since 1992 the inequality between rich and poor has again been on the rise.[77]

The distribution of income within a society can have important consequences for democratic stability. If there is a perception that only the few at the top of the economic ladder can hope to earn enough for an adequate standard of living, then domestic unrest and revolution may follow. Income is related to participation in politics. Poor people who need the most help from government are the least likely to participate. They are also the most likely to favor social welfare programs.

Occupation

Americans at the time of Thomas Jefferson and for several generations after worked primarily in agriculture, but by the end of World War I, the United States had become the world's leading industrial nation. This dramatic transformation also resulted in the expansion of American cities, as workers moved to find jobs. Labor conditions, including child-labor practices, became important political issues. The invention and application of technology, combined with abundant natural and human resources, meant that the U.S. gross domestic product (GDP) rose by more than 565 percent in real terms over the period from 1929 to 1997.[78]

The United States has now entered what Daniel Bell, a noted sociologist, has labeled the "post-industrial phase of our development." "A post-industrial society, being primarily a technical society, awards less on the basis of inheritance or property . . . than on education and skill."[79] *Knowledge* is the organizing device of the post-industrial era. Post-industrial societies have greater affluence and a class structure less defined along traditional labor versus management lines.

The changing dynamics of the American labor force can be seen in Figure 8-7, which shows the percentage of the U.S. labor force in various occupations since 1900. As the figure demonstrates, there has been tremendous growth in the white-collar sector of our economy, rising from under 20 percent of the work force at the turn of the century to more than half by 1980. The white-collar sector includes managers, accountants, and lawyers as well as professionals and technicians in such rapid growth areas as computers, communications, finance, insurance, and research. This shift has been accompanied by a dramatic decline in the number of people engaged in agriculture and a more modest decline in the number of people in manufacturing (blue collar). Today less than one in three working Americans produces goods, and only 3 percent work on farms. Governments are among the biggest employers in this country. Slightly more than one-sixth of our gross domestic product is produced by federal, state, and local governments.[80]

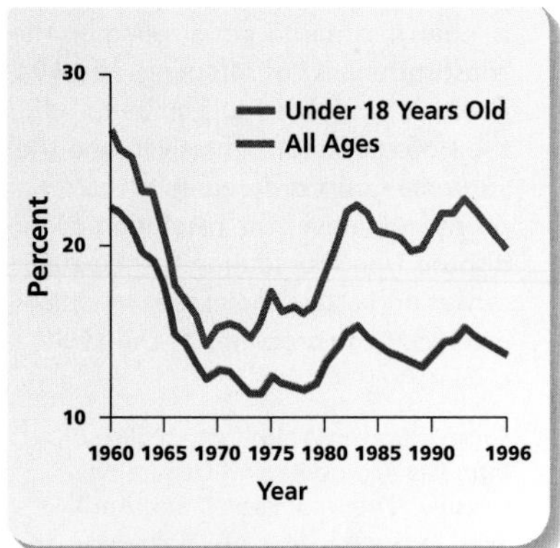

FIGURE 8-6 Percentage of Americans Living in Poverty, by Age, 1960–1996

SOURCE: U.S. Bureau of the Census (http://www.census.gov/prod/3/97pubs/p60-198.pdf).

Women and racial minorities have distinct occupational patterns. Women are much less likely than men to work in blue-collar jobs and more likely to work as professionals and technicians in white-collar jobs. More than one in four working women are employed as clerical workers, and another 18 percent are in service occupations. As noted earlier, women generally earn less than men of the same age and education. Occupations in which women predominate, like teaching and clerical work, are generally lower paying than industrial or management jobs. And as women advance in their careers, especially in management, they encounter the "glass ceiling" as a barrier to advancement.

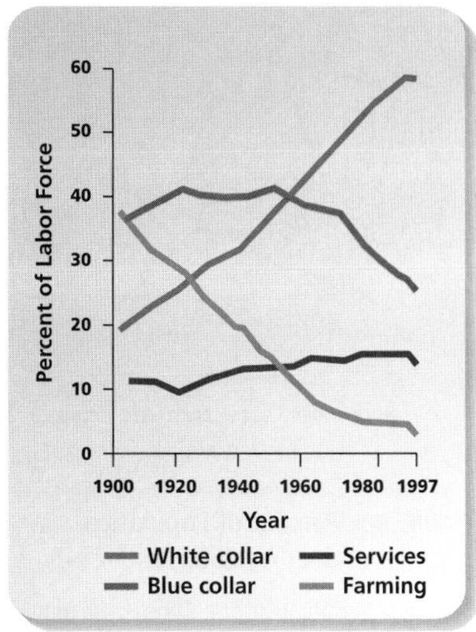

FIGURE 8-7 Occupational Groups, 1990–1997

SOURCE: U.S. Department of Labor, *Employment and Earnings*, vol. 43, no. 1 (Government Printing Office, 1996), p. 30.

Social Class

Many observers have questioned why Americans do not divide themselves into social classes as Europeans do. American workers have not formed their own political parties, nor does class seem to dominate our political life. Marxist categories of *proletariat* (those who sell their labor) and *bourgeoisie* (those who own or control the means of production) are not as important here as they are in Europe. But we do have social classes and what social scientists call **socioeconomic status (SES)**—a division of the population based on occupation, income, and education.

Most Americans, when asked what class they belong to, say "middle class" (see Figure 8-8). Very few see themselves as lower class or upper class. But what constitutes "middle class" is highly subjective. For instance, some individuals perform working-class tasks (such as plumbing), but their income is middle class or even upper middle class. A schoolteacher's income is below that of many working-class jobs, but in terms of status, the job ranks at least with middle-class fields. In many other industrial democracies, large proportions of the population think of themselves as working class instead of middle class.[81] In England, nearly three out of five

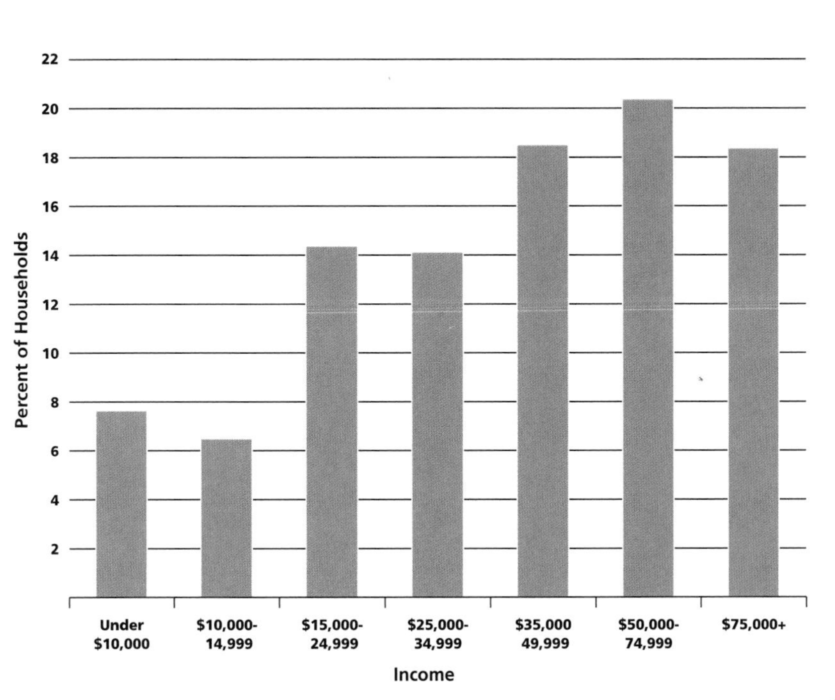

FIGURE 8-8 Total Money Income of Households, 1995

SOURCE: U.S. Bureau of the Census, *Statistical Abstract of the United States, 1997* (Government Printing Office, 1997), p. 469.

"It's like this. If the rich have money, they invest. If the poor have money, they eat."

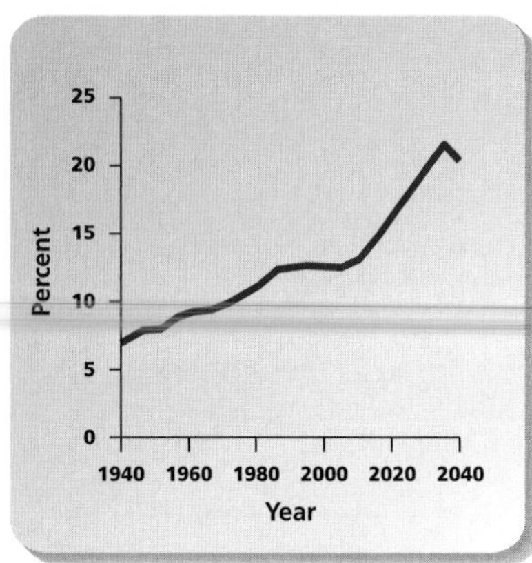

FIGURE 8-9 Percent of Population over Age 65, 1940–2040

SOURCE: U.S. Bureau of the Census, *Current Population Reports* (Government Printing Office, 1995).

persons see themselves as working class.[82] But to many Americans there is something undesirable about the label "working class."

One explanation for Americans' responses may be the elements of the American Dream that involve upward mobility. Or their responses may reflect the hostility many feel toward organized labor. In any case, compared to many countries, class divisions in the United States are less defined and less important to politics. As political scientist Seymour Martin Lipset has written, "The American social structure and values foster an emphasis on competitive individualism, an orientation that is not congruent with class consciousness, support for socialist or social democratic parties, or a strong union movement."[83]

Age

Americans are living longer, a phenomenon that has been called the "graying of America" (Figure 8-9). Not only are we living longer, but fewer babies are being born proportionate to the population. This demographic change is already having important consequences; it has increased the demand for medical care, retirement benefits, and a host of other age-related services. Persons over the age of 65 constitute less than 13 percent of the population yet account for 49 percent of the total medical expenditures.[84] The growing population of older persons was most pronounced in the West during the 1980s, but Florida remains the state with the largest proportion of persons over age 65.

Older Americans have a political agenda, and they vote. In recent presidential elections, less than one-third of all 18–20 year-olds voted; in contrast, 70 percent of those 65 and older turned out to vote.[85] As a group, they fight to ensure that Social Security is protected; they value Medicare and favor catastrophic health insurance. Despite their desire for services that benefit themselves, they also favor tax cuts. Past legislative victories have changed the lives of older citizens. For instance, the poverty rate among this age group dropped from 35 percent in 1959 to 10 percent in 1995, a change partly due to improved medical benefits passed during the 1960s.[86]

The "gray lobby" not only votes in large numbers but also has four other political assets that make it politically powerful—disposable income, discretionary time, a clear focus on issues, and effective organization—factors not found in any other age group. When older Americans compete for their share of the budget pie, the young, minorities, and the poor often lose out. During the prolonged budget fight between

Vigorous, healthy older adults require fewer benefits for medical care than do the frail elderly.

Congress and the president in 1995 and 1996, President Clinton twice vetoed Republican budget proposals, in part, he said, because they cut too deeply into Medicare, the health care program for the elderly. The popularity of this program and the political importance of this group bolstered Clinton's standing in the polls and forced the Republicans to back down, helping reelect Clinton in 1996.

Age is important to politics in two additional ways: life cycle and generation. *Life-cycle effects* have shown that as people become middle-aged, they become more politically conservative, less mobile, and more likely to participate in politics. As they age further and rely more on the government for services, they tend to grow more liberal.[87]

There are also *generational effects* in politics that arise when a particular generation has had experiences that make it politically distinct. An example is the experience of the Great Depression, which, for those who lived through it, shaped lifelong views of parties, issues, and political leaders. Some members of this generation saw Franklin Roosevelt as the leader who saved the country by pulling it out of the Depression; others felt he sold the country down the river by launching too many government programs. A more recent generation that shared a common and distinctive political experience is the baby-boom generation. These Americans came of age politically in the 1960s and 1970s during the Vietnam War and the civil rights movement. As with the Great Depression, not everybody saw the Vietnam War and civil rights battles in the same way. Such differences do not diminish the importance of the experience in shaping a generation's perspective on politics and government.

WE THE PEOPLE

Distribution of Education in the United States

	Population (1,000)	Not a high school graduate	High school graduate	Bachelor's degree	Advanced degree
Age					
25 to 34 years old	40,919	13.1%	32.0%	20.5%	6.0%
35 to 44 years old	43,077	12.1	33.9	17.7	8.5
45 to 54 years old	31,584	13.5	32.7	16.4	11.5
55 to 64 years old	21,084	22.5	37.0	11.8	8.4
65 to 74 years old	18,270	30.7	36.3	9.3	5.6
75 years old or over	13,388	41.2	30.8	8.3	4.3
Sex					
Male	80,339	18.1	31.9	16.4	9.5
Female	87,984	18.4	35.1	15.1	6.2
Race					
White	142,733	17.2	33.9	16.1	8.1
Black	18,715	25.7	35.1	10.0	3.6
Hispanic	14,541	46.9	26.0	6.6	2.6
Other	6,875	18.9	23.7	23.7	12.7

SOURCE: U.S. Bureau of the Census, *Current Population Reports,* P20-493; *Statistical Abstract 1997* (Government Printing Office, 1997), p. 160.

Education

Education has long been linked to citizenship and civic virtue. Differences in education affect not only economic well-being but political participation and involvement. Thomas Jefferson wrote of education, "Enlighten the people generally, and tyranny and oppressions of body and mind will vanish like evil spirits at the dawn of day."[88] The vast majority of people in the United States are educated in public schools. Nine out of every ten students in kindergarten through high school attend public schools, and nearly four out of five students in college are in public institutions.[89]

The number of years of school completed varies greatly in the United States. Only recently did the number of college graduates in America surpass the number of persons who had not graduated from high school.[90] Just over half of all Americans have not gone to college, though many college students assume that the college experience is widely shared. High school dropout rates have declined in the last decade, yet African Americans, Hispanics, and individuals from low-income families still have higher dropout rates than do whites and Asian Americans.

Compared to persons in other industrial democracies, Americans and Canadians are more likely to go to college.[91] Yet the experience of higher education has not been uniformly shared. The proportion of whites who are college graduates is nearly double that for African Americans and more than double that for Hispanics; roughly 26 percent of African Americans and nearly half of all Hispanics stopped their schooling before completing high school.[92]

Education is one of the most important variables in predicting political participation, confidence in dealing with government, and awareness of issues. Education is also related to the acquisition of democratic values. Those who have failed to learn the prevailing norms of American society are far more likely to express opposition to democratic and capitalist ideals than those who are well educated and politically knowledgeable.[93]

Unity in a Land of Diversity

As remarkable as American diversity is, the existence of a strong and widely shared sense of national unity and identity may be even more remarkable. Writing about the United States some years ago, a famous reporter, John Gunther, summarized his insights from extensive travels:

> Whoever invented the motto E Pluribus Unum [one out of many] has given the best three-word description of the United States ever written. The triumph of America is the triumph of a coalescing federal system. Complex as the nation is almost to the point of insufferability, it interlocks. Homogeneity and diversity—these are the stupendous rival magnets. . . . Think of the United States as an immense blanket or patchwork quilt solid with different designs and highlights. But, no matter what colors burn and flash in what corners, the warp and woof, the basic texture and fabric is the same from corner to corner, from end to end.[94]

Americans have always been united by their commitment to liberty. Equally important has been the belief that government should exist to serve the people, rather than the reverse. What shapes our political culture is the persistent commitment to the individual. One author recently concluded that "equality, individualism and openness are the crucial values of American politics in the 1990s."[95]

Part of the explanation for our unity is the unifying effect of the American Dream—the belief that this is the land of opportunity for enterprising individuals. Unity in the midst of diversity has also been enhanced by a sense of a common fate, often highlighted by a crisis. Social and economic differences become less important, for example, when we fight wars. World War II enabled many Americans to experience life in different parts of the country and confirmed the patriotism of diverse groups. One question for the new century will be: Can we maintain the same degree of unity in a world with fewer foreign enemies and only one military superpower? Finally, the United States has achieved a measure of unity through residential mobility, intermarriage, the mass media, and a common culture.

Social scientists sometimes speak of the *melting pot*, meaning that as minorities, especially ethnic groups, associate with other groups, they are assimilated into the rest of American society and come to share democratic values like majority rule, individualism, and the notion that America is the land of opportunity. Recently the melting pot idea has been criticized as assuming that differences between groups are to be discouraged. In its place, critics propose the notion of the *salad bowl*, in which "though the salad is an entity, the lettuce can still be distinguished from the chicory, the tomatoes from the cabbage."[96]

As we have seen, important differences persist among groups, and in that sense the salad bowl analogy is accurate. Divisive issues like immigration, affirmative action, and programs for the poor have reinforced our differences. But in another way, our society has achieved a unity of commitment to democratic values and processes—a political culture—that is, at least in part, a consequence of such elements of the melting pot theory as public schools, a common language, and hope for a better life for one's children. Ethnic divisions in the United States pose challenges to the institutions and processes of government, yet the public has generally accepted diversity in political appointments, government jobs and contracts, and other aspects of policy. This is in sharp contrast to the violent ethnic conflicts in other parts of the world. But what is the appropriate balance among recognition, preservation, and representation of ethnic groups and the needs for assimilation, common commitments, and a shared identity?

online POLITICS

Surfing the Political Landscape

If you assume that opinions expressed on your favorite chat box on the Internet are representative of people generally, or even of young people, you are mistaken. A study by the Pew Research Center for the People and the Press found that online users tend to be young, affluent suburbanites who are better educated than the general public. Fifty-eight percent of online users are men, but there is little difference between Internet users and the public in terms of political ideology.

The Web is an excellent place to learn about different racial, ethnic, economic, religious, and other groups in the United States. Our social and economic diversity is evident in the wide range of home pages devoted to these differences. Latinos, for instance, have a Web page at:

http://www.catalog.com/favision/latnoweb.htm

If you want to learn about the Catholic or Mormon Churches, you can go to:

http://www.catholic.net or **http://www.lds.org**.

The Christian Coalition can be found at:

http://cc.org.

Voices United for Israel is at:

http://knowledge1.knowledge-tree.com/israel/voices.

Labor unions, trade associations, and small business groups also use the Internet and provide a sense of our economic diversity. The largest union organization can be found at:

http://www.aflcio.org/front.htm

The most useful place to go for information on demography is the U.S. Census Bureau at:

http://www.census.gov.

There you can find data on the population, current economic indicators, income, poverty, labor force, households, GDP, wages, prices, and jobs.

For more Internet resources on the American Political Landscape, see our home page at:

http://www.prenhall.com/burns

SUMMARY

1. The character of a political society, its social and economic divisions, its traditions, and its sectional and local identifications are important to understanding public opinion, participation, voting, interest groups, political parties, and the communications process. It is often a mistake to generalize solely from one's own experience, background, beliefs, and values.
2. As a nation of immigrants, Americans are more diverse than the citizens of most other nations, with the potential for a great many demographic characteristics affecting participation in American political and economic life.
3. Geography, room to grow, abundant natural resources, wealth, and relative isolation from "foreign entanglements" help to explain American politics and traditions, including the notions of manifest destiny, ethnocentrism, and isolationism.
4. Until recently, the South was a very distinct region in the United States, in large part because of the issue of slavery and race relations. With in-migration, it is no longer solidly Democratic. Recently the most significant migration has been from cities to suburbs. Today large cities are increasingly poor, African American, and Democratic, surrounded by suburbs that are primarily middle class, white, and Republican.
5. The United States is a land of tremendous diversity in race, ethnicity, family structure, religion, wealth and income, occupation, social class, age, and education. Divisions by gender and sexual orientation have recently become more important. This diversity is often significant in our politics.
6. Race has been among the most important of the differences in our political landscape. Although we fought a civil war over freedom for African Americans, racial equality was largely postponed until the latter half of this century. Race remains an important issue in our politics and government. Ethnicity, including the rising numbers of Hispanics, continues to be a factor in politics, as demonstrated by the controversy over English as the official language.
7. Gender is important in American politics. Women have gradually acquired political rights. They now play important roles in our government, and they differ from men in their attitudes on some issues. Sexual orientation is also becoming increasingly important to politics and policy.
8. Since World War II attitudes towards sexuality, marriage, and family have changed in important ways. The use of birth control and contraception has risen, as has abortion and the number of illegitimate births. People cohabit at much higher rates, and those who marry are older. Divorce has also become much more commonplace. Changing family structures and attitudes affect our tax policies, child care, parental leave, and gender equality. They are also important political issues.
9. Religion is a difference that helps explain political behavior both in terms of persons from different religions behaving differently and in terms of differences between those who are religious and those who are not.
10. While the United States is a land of wealth and is known for its large middle class, not everyone has an adequate share in the American economic success. Poverty has grown over the past two decades, and it is most concentrated among African Americans, Native Americans, Hispanics, and single-parent households. Women as a group continue to earn less than men, even in the same occupations. Differences in income and wealth remain important.
11. America has shifted from an agricultural to an industrial to a post-industrial society, with consequences for occupations and politics. Governments are a major source of employment. Social class is less important in America than in other industrialized democracies.
12. Age and education are important to understanding American politics. Our aging population poses important challenges to public policy. Because they participate so much more than young voters, older Americans are a potent political force. Education not only opens up economic opportunities in America but also explains many important aspects of political participation.
13. Despite our diversity, Americans share an important unity. We are united by our shared commitment to democratic values, economic opportunity, the work ethic, and the American Dream. National experiences like wars and global economic competition have also unified us.

KEY TERMS

ethnocentrism 178
political socialization 178
demographics 179
political predisposition 179
reinforcing cleavages 179
cross-cutting cleavages 179
manifest destiny 180
race 184
ethnicity 184
gender gap 188

FURTHER READING

Douglas L. Anderson, Richard Barnett, and Donald Bogue, *The Population of the United States*, 3d ed. (Free Press, 1996).

David H. Bennett, *The Party of Fear* (University of North Carolina Press, 1990).

Earl Black and Merle Black, *The Vital South: How Presidents Are Elected* (Harvard University Press, 1992).

Urie Brontenbrenner et al., *The State of Americans: The Disturbing Facts and Figures on Changing Values, Crime, the Economy, Poverty, Family, Education, the Aging Population, and What They Mean for Our Future* (Free Press, 1996).

Rodolfo O. de la Garza, Louis DeSipio, F. Chris Garcia, John Garcia, and Angelo Falcon, *Latino Voices: Mexican, Puerto Rican, and Cuban Perspectives on American Politics* (Westview Press, 1992).

Lois Lovelace Duke, ed., *Women in Politics: Outsiders or Insiders?* 2d ed. (Prentice Hall, 1995).

Sarah H. Evans, *Born for Liberty: A History of Women in America* (Free Press, 1989).

Geoffrey Fox, *Hispanic Nation: Culture, Politics and the Constructing of Identity* (Birch Lane Press, 1996).

Donald R. Kinder and Lynn M. Sanders, *Divided by Color: Racial Politics and Democratic Ideals* (University of Chicago Press, 1996).

Seymour Martin Lipset, *Continental Divide: The Values and Institutions of the United States and Canada* (Routledge, 1990).

Nancy E. McGlen and Karen O'Connor, *Women, Politics, and American Society* 2d ed. (Prentice Hall, 1998).

Peter Nabokov, ed., *Native American Testimony: A Chronicle of Indian-White Relations from Prophecy to the Present, 1492–1992* (Viking, 1991).

Kevin Phillips, *The Politics of Rich and Poor: Wealth and the American Electorate in the Reagan Aftermath* (Random House, 1990).

Steven J. Rose, *Social Stratification in the United States: The American Profile Poster Revised and Expanded* (New Press, 1992).

Arthur M. Schlesinger, Jr., *The Disuniting of America* (W. W. Norton, 1992).

Studs Terkel, *Race: How Blacks and Whites Think and Feel About the American Obsession* (W. W. Norton, 1992).

Alexis de Tocqueville, *Democracy in America*, ed. J. P. Mayer, trans. George Lawrence (Doubleday and Company, 1969).

Kenneth D. Wald, *Religion and Politics in the United States*, 3d ed. (CQ Press, 1996).

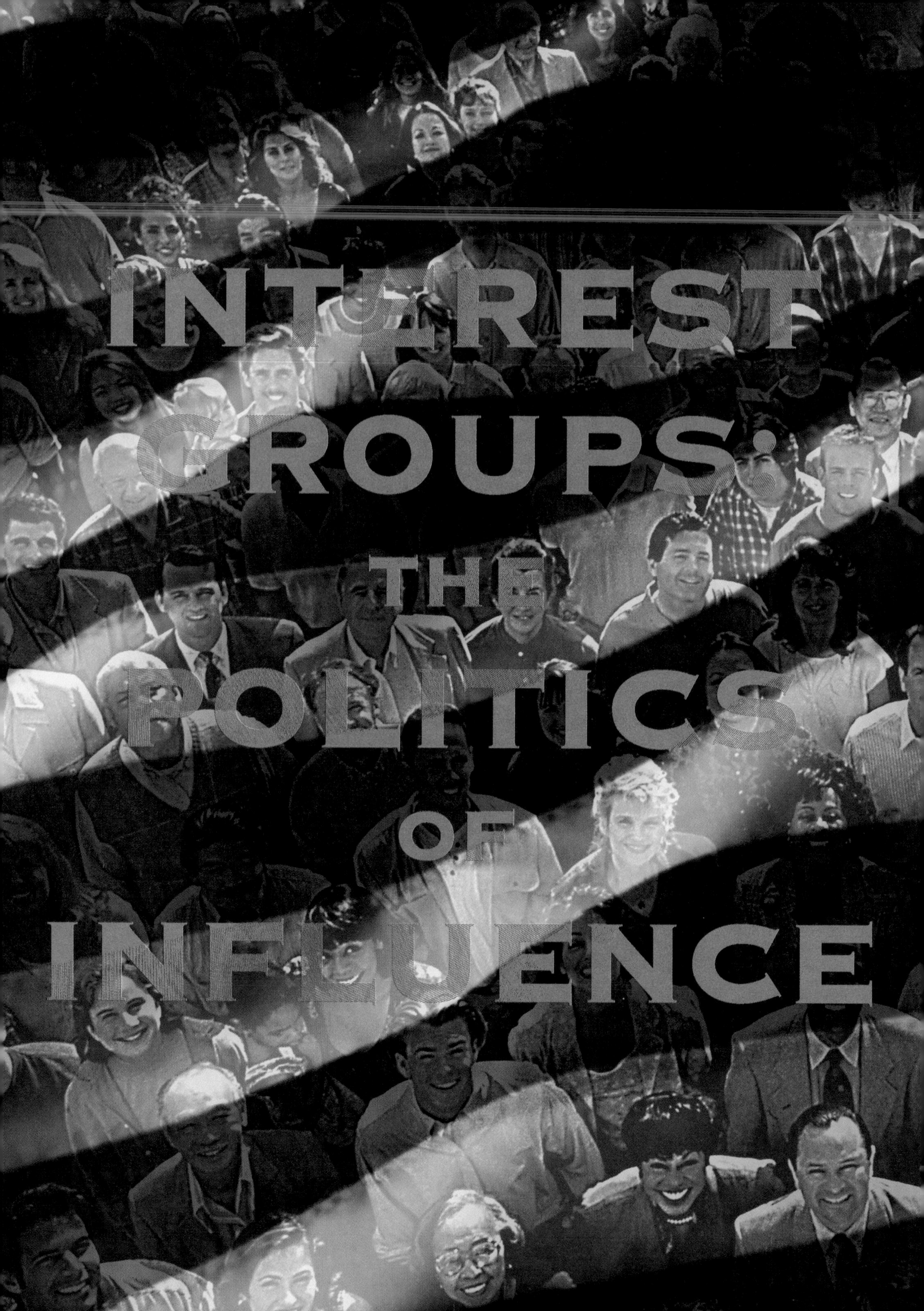
INTEREST GROUPS:
THE
POLITICS
OF
INFLUENCE

9

CHAPTER OUTLINE

- Interest Groups Past and Present—The Mischiefs of Faction
- Types of Interest Groups
- Characteristics and Power of Interest Groups
- The Influence of Lobbyists
- Money and Politics
- Curing the Mischiefs of Faction—Two Hundred Years Later
- Is Reform Possible?

IF YOU BELONG TO A UNION, YOU MAY NOT BE AWARE THAT PART OF YOUR PAYCHECK GOES TO UNION DUES THAT FUND THE UNION'S POLITICAL ACTIVITIES. Similarly, if you are a stockholder, you may not know that part of the corporation profits are spent on political contributions without your input. The use of union dues and corporate funds to elect or defeat candidates has recently come under attack. Ballot initiatives in California and Oregon in 1998 called for "paycheck protection" measures that would require annual written authorization from union members before allowing their dues to be used for any political purpose.

Labor unions understandably saw these initiatives as an effort to reduce their political power, and they launched aggressive campaigns to defeat them. They argued that paycheck protection measures would "silence the voice of working families in the political process." Their ads charged that sponsors of paycheck protection wanted to "privatize Social Security, expand corporate control of our nation's health care system and hold down living standards."[1]

The anti-union initiatives were in part a reaction to a flood of labor advertisements in recent elections financed by union dues. These ads targeted first-term Republican House members by criticizing their voting records. AFL-CIO President John Sweeney explained labor's goal: "We expect that the people who will be elected to Congress will want to address the issues we have raised in this campaign."[2] In response to labor's new tactic, business entered the political advertising game, often defending candidates attacked by labor. Some incumbents who were targets of the ads were defeated, but the overall impact of the effort did not change House party control.

Paycheck protection initiatives would have the short-term effect of forcing labor to spend millions defending their use of labor dues—millions that cannot be spent in advertisements for or against candidates. Although union involvement in politics is effective, the role of corporations is much greater. One credible source estimates that in 1996 corporations outspent labor in this regard by a ratio of 11 to 1.[3]

Businesses and labor unions are only two types of interest groups active in our country. How interest groups compete for influence, the role they play in elections, and how to limit their "mischiefs" are the subjects of this chapter. We begin by discussing the types of interest groups in our political system and the roles they play. Then we turn to one of their most important activities—lobbying. Finally, we examine the problems interest groups pose and ways to regulate them.

Interest Groups Past and Present—The Mischiefs of Faction

What we call interest groups today, James Madison called **factions**. (Madison also thought of political parties as factions.) For Madison and the other framers of the Constitution, the daunting problem was how to establish a stable and orderly constitutional system that at the same time would respect the liberty of free citizens. As a good practical politician and a brilliant theorist, Madison offered both a diagnosis and a solution in *The Federalist*, No. 10 (reprinted in the Appendix).

The genius of *The Federalist*, No. 10, lies in the manner in which Madison describes the factions of the day. He begins with a basic proposition: "The latent causes of faction are thus sown in the nature of man." Madison demonstrated that Americans live in a maze of group interests. He went on to argue that the "most common and durable source of factions has been the various and unequal distribution of property."

A Nation of Interests

As we noted in Chapter 8, Americans form groups according to their race, gender, ethnic background, age, occupation, sexual orientation, and so forth. When such associations share some common outlook or attitude and they seek to influence government in some way, they are **interest groups**.

Interest groups are sometimes called "special interests." Presidents and political candidates often use this term to describe those interest groups that do not support their programs. But what makes an ordinary interest group a "special" one? The answer is highly subjective. One person's special interest is another's national interest. Special interests sometimes claim to be "public interests." Even so-called public interest groups like Common Cause or the Center for Responsive Politics, which presume to speak for the entire public, are called special interests.

When social scientists call something an "interest group" or a "special interest," they are not calling it names. These are analytic terms to describe a group that speaks for some but not all of us. Much of our politics focuses on what is in the national interest. The democratic process exists to decide among those national interests. In a democracy there are many interests and many organized interest groups. Part of the politics of interest groups is to persuade the public that your group's interest is better, broader, more beneficial, and more general and at the same time label groups that oppose yours as "special interests." For this reason we use the neutral term "interest groups."

Social Movements

Interest groups sometimes have their beginnings as movements. A **movement** is a large body of people who are interested in a common issue, idea, or concern that is of continuing significance and who are willing to take action on that issue. Examples of movements include abolitionist, temperance, civil rights, environmental, antitax, animal rights, and women's rights. Each movement represents groups who have felt "left out" of government. Such groups often arise at the grass-roots level and evolve into national groups. Movements tend to see their causes as morally right and the positions of the opposition as morally wrong.

To a marked degree, our Constitution protects the liberties and independence of movements. The Bill of Rights guarantees movements—whether popular or unpopular—free assembly, free speech, and due process. Hence militants do not have to engage in terrorism or other extreme activities in the United States, as they do in some countries, and they need not fear persecution for demonstrating peacefully. In a democratic system that restricts the power of those in authority, movements have considerable room to operate *inside* the constitutional system.

faction
A term used by James Madison and other founders of this country to refer to political parties as well as what we now call special interests or interest groups.

interest group
A collection of people who share some common interest or attitude and seek to influence government for specific ends. Interest groups usually work within the framework of government and employ tactics such as lobbying to achieve their goals.

movement
A large body of people interested in a common issue, idea, or concern that is of continuing significance and who are willing to take action on that issue. Movements seek to change attitudes or institutions, not only policies.

THE MILITIA MOVEMENT

The bombing of the Murrah Federal Office Building in Oklahoma City, Oklahoma, in which 168 people lost their lives was a stark reminder that terrorism could be carried out by American extremists. The arrest and conviction of Timothy McVeigh for the bombing drew attention to the extent of anti-government militia growth in the 1990s. Other instances of militia activity in the United States included the Montana Freemen and the FBI standoff with Randy Weaver in 1992 at Ruby Ridge, Idaho. The Ruby Ridge incident had been a rallying call for the militia movement because Weaver's wife and son were killed by an FBI sniper. The same incident also resulted in the death of an FBI agent. Recently some militia groups have aligned themselves with hate groups and white supremacists like the Aryan Nation and Ku Klux Klan.

Militias have existed in this country since the first Minutemen skirmished against the British on Lexington Green, and militia supporters often point to their Revolutionary War roots. But the militias of the late 1990s are very different from those of 1778, as they exploit the fear of government intrusion into people's lives. Furthering their anti-government hostility are laws like the Brady Bill that limit the right to bear arms. But despite their acts of violence, militia leaders like Montana's John Trochman claim their groups are composed of "regular people" who simply "gather intelligence, dissect it and put it into a picture to show people what's wrong with America. We're solution oriented and non-violent."*

But what should the government do about individuals like McVeigh who clearly are a threat to others? It would be unconstitutional to prohibit such movements, yet most people believe the government cannot wait to take action only after they have committed serious crimes. Some feel the only solution is for government to closely monitor militia groups. Avoiding confrontations like the one that occurred with the Branch Davidian sect in Waco, Texas, would require this kind of careful monitoring. Sometimes violent confrontations can be avoided with patience and forbearance, as was the case in the stand-off with the Montana Freeman in the summer of 1996.

Despite the publicity given these militia groups, they remain relatively few in number and isolated from one another. They continue to attract followers and to engage in military training, but severe government repression would be more likely to strengthen them than to eliminate them.

*Patrick May, "Militia's Retrench with Hard-Core Followers: Extremist's Views Deepen, Overlap," *The Times-Picayune*, August 9, 1998, p. A-19.

Members of the Michigan Militia gather to practice military tactics and rally support for their cause.

TYPES OF INTEREST GROUPS

Interest groups vary widely. Some are formal associations or organizations; others have no formal organization. Some are organized primarily to lobby for goals such as securing wage increases, conducting research, or broadly influencing public opinion by publishing reports and mass mailings.

Interest groups can be categorized into several broad types: (1) economic, including both business and labor, (2) ideological or single-issue, (3) public interest, (4) foreign policy, and (5) government itself. Obviously these categories are not mutually exclusive. The varied and overlapping nature of interest groups in the United States has been described as *interest group pluralism*, meaning that competition among open, responsive, and diverse groups helps preserve democratic values and limits the concentration of power in any single group.

Most Americans' interests are represented by a number of interest groups, some of which they are aware of and others of which they may not be. For instance, older citizens may not be aware that their interests are represented by the American Association of Retired Persons (AARP). Others may not know that when they join the American Automobile Association (AAA), they not only purchase travel assistance and automobile towing when needed, but also join a group that lobbies Congress and the Federal Highway Administration on behalf of motorists.

As Alexis de Tocqueville observed long ago, Americans form associations for every conceivable purpose and function. And as the federal government has become more involved in people's lives, these groups have turned their attention to Washington, where interest groups rival the federal bureaucracy in number and complexity.

Economic Interest Groups

Madison pointed out that some of the most common and durable factions derive from property interests, or how we make our living and manage what we own. There are thousands of economic interests: agriculture, consumers, plumbers, northern businesses, southern businesses, labor unions, the airplane industry, landlords, truckers, bond holders, property owners, and so on.

BUSINESS The most familiar business institution is probably the large corporation. Corporations range from small one-person enterprises to large multinational entities. Large corporations—General Motors, AT&T, and other large companies—exercise considerable political influence, as do hundreds of smaller corporations. Corporate power and the implications of a changing domestic and global economy make business practices important political issues.

TRADE AND OTHER ASSOCIATIONS Businesses with similar interests in government regulations and other issues join together as trade associations. They are as diverse as the products and services they provide. In addition, businesses of all types are organized into large, nationwide associations such as the Conference Board, the National Association for the Self-Employed, the Business Higher-Education Forum, and the Chamber of Commerce.

Local Chambers of Commerce provide a way for business owners to participate in community policy making.

The broadest business trade association is the Chamber of Commerce of the United States. Organized in 1912, the Chamber is a federation of several thousand local Chambers of Commerce representing tens of thousands of business firms. Loosely allied with the Chamber on most issues is the National Association of Manufacturers, which, since its founding in the wake of the depression of 1893, has tended to speak for the more conservative elements of American business.

Business associations often take up issues that may involve many individual businesses throughout the country, for example banks. Three associations that represent banks in Washington, D.C.,[4] have been involved in an ongoing turf dispute with credit unions. Two major credit union associations[5] aggressively lobbied

Congress and eventually were able to obtain more open membership rules and the right to serve small businesses. The banks prevailed upon Congress to impose stringent supervisory and commercial lending requirements on credit unions.[6] While these compromises seem technical to most Americans, they amount to billions of dollars of business that could be open to credit unions, which is why the two groups battled each other.

LABOR Workers' associations have a range of interests, from professional standards to wages and working conditions. Labor unions are one of the most important groups representing workers. The American work force is the least unionized of almost any industrial democracy (Figure 9-1).

Probably the oldest unions in the United States were farm organizations. The largest farm group now is the American Farm Bureau Federation, which is especially strong in the corn belt. Originally organized around government agents who helped farmers in rural counties, the federation today is almost a semi-governmental agency, but it retains full freedom to fight for such goals as price supports and expanded credit. Other farm organizations are based on the interests of producers of specific commodities, such as the American Soybean Association.

Throughout the nineteenth century, workers organized political parties and local unions. Their most ambitious effort at national organization, the Knights of Labor, claimed 700,000 members. By the beginning of this century, the American Federation of Labor (AFL), a confederation of strong and independent-minded national unions mainly representing craft workers, was the dominant organization. During the ferment of the 1930s, unions more responsive to industrial workers broke away from the AFL and formed a rival national organization for workers organized by industry, the Congress of Industrial Organizations (CIO). In 1955 the AFL and CIO reunited in the organization that exists today.

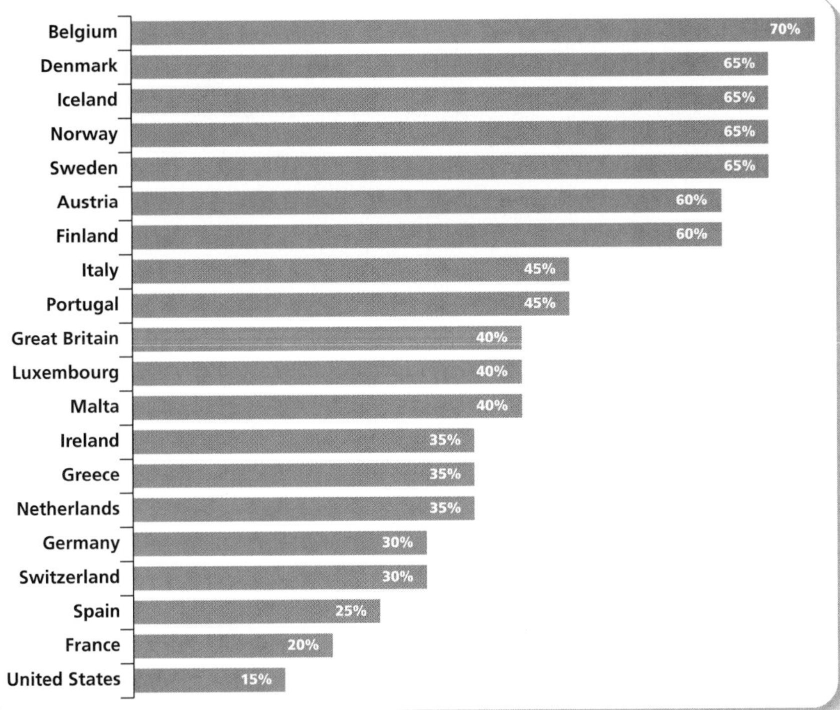

FIGURE 9-1 Union Membership in the United States Compared to Other Countries (Estimated Percentage of the Work Force)

SOURCE: Based on data from Dr. Henri J. Warmenhoven, *Western Europe*, 5th ed. (Dushkin/McGraw-Hill, 1997), p. 46, and *World Almanac Book of Facts, 1998* (K-III Communications Company, 1998), p. 152.

The 1997 strike at United Parcel Service was a protest against the company's extensive use of part-time workers.

For some years the Committee on Political Education (COPE) of the AFL-CIO was one of the most respected—and most feared—political organizations in the country. In the Kennedy-Johnson years it won a reputation for political effectiveness. It encouraged and supervised grass-roots political activity, and at the national level it prepared and adopted a detailed platform that spelled out labor's position on issues. Labor contributed money to candidates, ran registration and get-out-the-vote campaigns, and otherwise supported its favorites. In recent elections COPE has had a fair, but not spectacular, record of wins for its endorsed House and Senate candidates.[7] Labor unions invested heavily in the 1992 fight against the North American Free Trade Agreement (NAFTA), claiming it would cost jobs. Labor's defeat in this battle was compounded by the 1994 and 1996 elections, which put Republicans in charge of Congress.

In 1996 the AFL-CIO mounted a vigorous campaign to elect a Democratic majority in Congress, spending roughly $20 million in issue advertising targeting Republican incumbents.[8] The effort may have helped a few Democrats, but the Republicans retained their majority, and the tactic drew the Chamber of Commerce and other groups into issue advertising, where labor was unlikely to match business spending. The political intervention by labor angered some foes of labor who, as noted, pushed payroll protection in Congress and several state ballot initiatives.

Union membership is optional in states whose laws permit the **open shop**, in which union membership cannot be required as a condition of employment. In states with the **closed shop**, union membership may be required as a condition of employment. In both cases, the unions conduct negotiations with management, and the benefits the unions gain will be shared with all workers. It is understandable in open shop states that many workers choose not to affiliate with the union, as they can secure the same pay without incurring the costs associated with union membership, a condition referred to as the **free rider**.

open shop
A company with a labor agreement whereby union membership cannot be required as a condition of employment.

closed shop
A company with a labor agreement whereby union membership is a condition of employment.

free rider
An individual who does not join an interest group representing his or her interests, yet receives the benefit of the influence the group achieves.

Because the AFL-CIO is a federation of powerful and independent national unions, state and local groups have sometimes been politically divided. Leadership of the AFL-CIO had been in the hands of only a few men who, once elected, held office for a long time. The AFL-CIO speaks for about 80 percent of unionized labor, but unions represent only about 13 percent of the nation's work force (see Figure 9-2).[9] Organized labor's dwindling membership limits its political and lobbying muscle, and its prospects for increasing influence in the future are dim. The decline in the proportion of the work force belonging to unions is explained in part by the shift from an industrial to a service economy; however, there has been growth in public sector unions.

In a much publicized showdown between the United Parcel Service (UPS) and the Teamsters Union in 1997 over such issues as the use of part-time employees, the union's more than 180,000 workers went on strike. UPS management denied that part-time workers were replacing full-time union jobs, but after two weeks UPS settled with the union.[10] The impact of the strike was felt in every state and fostered a debate on the costs and benefits of full-time employees generally.

Traditionally identified with the Democratic party, unions have not enjoyed a close relationship with Republican administrations. Given labor's limited resources, one option for unions is to form temporary coalitions with consumer, public interest, liberal, and sometimes even with industry groups—especially when faced with the issue of foreign imports. But labor pays a price for such collaboration. It must water down or give up some of its own goals. Few of labor's recent legislative initiatives have been successful, and with Reagan and Bush appointees still serving, labor faces a much less sympathetic Supreme Court.

PROFESSIONAL ASSOCIATIONS Professional people have organized some of the strongest unions in the nation. Some are well known, such as the American

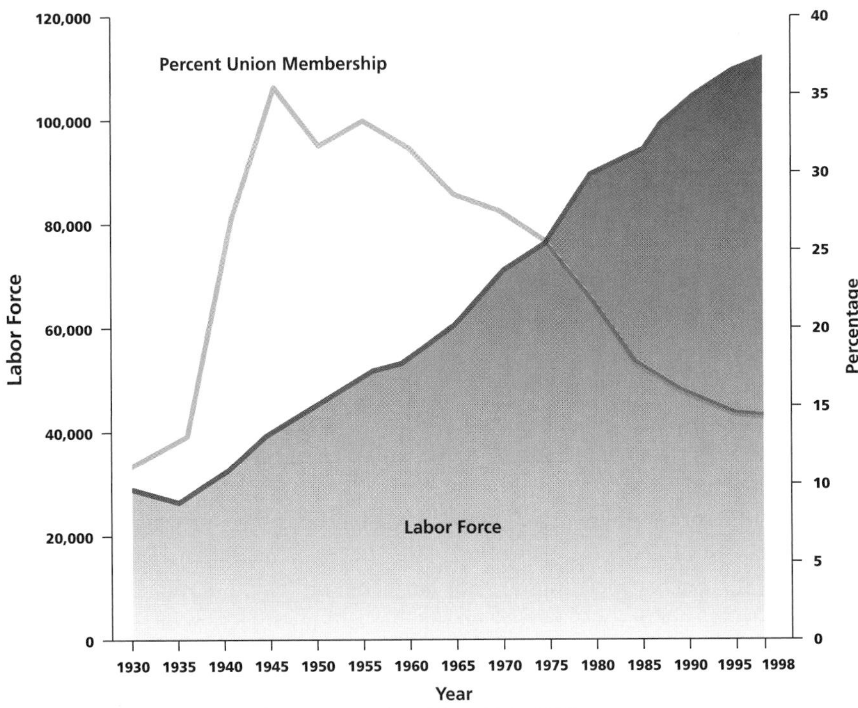

FIGURE 9-2 Labor Force and Union Membership, 1930–1998

SOURCE: *The World Almanac and Book of Facts, 1998.*

Medical Association and the American Bar Association. Others are divided into many subgroups. Teachers, for example, are organized into large groups such as the National Education Association, the American Federation of Teachers, the American Association of University Professors, and also into subgroups based on specialties, such as the Modern Language Association and the American Political Science Association.

Many professions are regulated by government, especially on the state level. Lawyers, for example, are licensed by states, which, often as a result of pressure from lawyers themselves, have set up certain standards of admission to the state bar.

Members of the American Teachers Federation celebrate passage of a motion to merge with the National Education Association at a meeting in New Orleans in July 1998.

Professional associations also use the courts to pursue their agenda. In the area of medical malpractice, for example, doctors lobby hard for limited liability laws, while the trial lawyers association resists such efforts. Teachers, hair stylists, and marriage therapists work for legislation or regulations of concern to them. It is not surprising, then, that among the largest donors to political campaigns through political action committees are those representing professional associations such as the American Medical Association and the American Realtors Association (see Table 9-1).

Ideological or Single-Issue Interest Groups

Ideological groups behave very much like economic interest groups, although they may not be motivated by a desire to make money. Some of these groups are single-issue groups, often highly motivated and seeing politics primarily as a means to pursue their one issue. Such groups are often adamant about their position and unwilling to negotiate compromises. Right-to-life and pro-choice groups on abortion fit this description.

Countless groups have organized around other specific issues, such as civil liberties, birth control, abortion, environmental protection, nuclear energy, and nuclear disarmament.[11] Such associations are not new. The Anti-Saloon League of the 1890s was single-mindedly devoted to barring the sale and manufacture of alcoholic beverages, and it did not care whether legislators were drunk or sober, as long as they voted dry. One of the best-known ideological groups today is the American Civil Liberties Union (ACLU), with roughly one-quarter million members committed to the protection of civil liberties.[12] Some highly ideological religious groups are thriving in the otherwise pragmatic, pluralistic politics of today.[13] Examples include the Christian Coalition, which distributes "Voter Guides" the Sunday before the election.

Public Interest Groups

Out of the political ferment of the 1960s came groups that make a specific claim to promote "the public interest." For example, Common Cause, founded in 1970 by independent Republican John W. Gardner and later led by noted Watergate prosecutor Archibald Cox, campaigns for electoral reform and for making the political process more open. Its Washington staff raises money through direct mail campaigns, oversees state chapters, issues a flood of research reports and press releases on current issues, and lobbies on Capitol Hill and in major government departments.

TABLE 9-1 PACs That Gave the Most to Federal Candidates in 1996–1998 (contributions in millions)

	1996	1998
Democratic Republican Independent Voter Education Committee	$2.61	$2.19
American Federation of State, County, and Municipal Employees	2.51	2.38
United Auto Workers Voluntary Community Action Program	2.47	1.93
Association of Trial Lawyers of America Political Action Committee	2.36	2.43
Dealers Election Action Committee of the National Automobile Dealers Association	2.35	2.10
National Education Association Political Action Committee	2.33	1.86
American Medical Association Political Action Committee	2.32	2.34
Realtors Political Action Committee	2.10	2.47
International Brotherhood of Electrical Workers Committee on Political Education	2.08	1.89
Active Ballot Club, A Department of United Food & Commercial Workers International Union	2.03	1.52

SOURCE: Federal Election Commission, "PAC Activity Increases in 1995–96 Election Cycle," Press Release, April 22, 1997, p. 19; and FEC/Info: Political Action Committee and Party Committee Page (http://www.fecinfo/_pac.htm).

Ralph Nader started a conglomerate of consumer organizations that investigates and reports on governmental and corporate action—or inaction—relating to consumer interests. Public Interest Research Groups (PIRGs) founded by Nader today number among the largest interest groups in the country. PIRGs have become important players on Capitol Hill and in several state legislatures, promoting environmental issues, safe energy, consumer protection, and good government.

A specific type of public interest group is the *tax-exempt public charity*, organized under section 501(c)(3) of the Internal Revenue Code. Examples include the American Heart Association, the Girl Scouts, and the American Cancer Society. Organizations must meet certain conditions, such as educational or philanthropic objectives, to qualify for this preferred status. Not only are public charities tax exempt, but donations to these organizations are tax deductible, and the organizations are not required to disclose information about their donors publicly. These organizations cannot participate in elections or support candidates, nor can they benefit an individual or small group. Despite these limitations, tax-exempt charitable organizations have been very active in voter registration efforts and in advertising campaigns designed to influence public opinion.

Foreign Policy Interest Groups

Issues of domestic policy are not the only matters of concern to interest groups. More and more groups are organizing to promote or oppose certain foreign policies. Among the most prestigious (although not uncontroversial) foreign affairs group is the Council on Foreign Relations in New York City. Other groups, devoted to narrower areas of American foreign policy, exert pressure on legislators or the executive to enact specific policies. Among these are interest groups concerned with the Arab-Israeli conflict and the contending factions in Bosnia. Interest group pressure also influenced U.S. policy toward South Africa and played a role in South Africa's decision to abandon apartheid. Groups ranging from student organizations to national lobbies like the American Committee on Africa urged divestment, sanctions, or other policy measures that ultimately promoted change in South Africa from the outside.

The American-Israel Political Action Committee (AIPAC) has more than 50,000 members and is listed by *Fortune Magazine* as the second most influential lobby.[14] Because AIPAC's primary focus is lobbying and not distributing campaign funds, it is not required to disclose where its money comes from or goes. Included in the long list of AIPAC lobbying successes are enactment of aid packages to Israel, passage of the 1985 United States-Israel Free Trade Agreement, and emergency assistance to Israel in the wake of the 1992 Gulf War. Its counterpart, the National Association of Arab Americans, lobbies for action in support of Arab causes.

Government Interest Groups

Government itself is the source of important interest groups. You may think that odd, but as the size of government has grown and the scope of its activity has expanded, so has governmental lobbying. Many cities and most states retain Washington lobbyists, and cities also hire lobbyists to represent them at the state legislature. Governors are organized through the National Governors Association, cities through the National League of Cities, and counties through the National Association of Counties.

Government is an important source of interest groups in other ways as well. Public employees form a large and well-organized group. The National Education Association (NEA), for example, claims more than 2.3 million members.[15] Public employees are also important to organized labor, and they are the fastest growing unions.

Other Interest Groups

Americans are often emotionally and financially involved in a variety of groups: veterans groups such as American Legion or Veterans of Foreign Wars; nationality groups such as the multitude of German, Irish, Hispanic, and Korean organizations; or religious organizations such as the Knights of Columbus or B'nai B'rith. More than 150 nationwide organizations are based on national origin alone.

In recent years there has been a virtual explosion in the number and variety of interests and associations.[16] This is especially true for single-issue interest groups, and sometimes a variety of environmental groups press for their slightly different perspectives at all levels of government (see Table 9-2).

CHARACTERISTICS AND POWER OF INTEREST GROUPS

Groups vary in their goals, methods, and power. Among the most important group characteristics are size, resources, cohesiveness, leadership, and techniques.

Size and Resources

Obviously size is important to political power; an organization representing five million voters has more influence than one speaking for five thousand. Perhaps even more important than size is the extent to which members are actively involved and focus on the attainment of policy objectives. Often people join an organization for reasons that have little to do with its political objectives. They may want to secure group insurance, take advantage of travel benefits, participate in professional meetings, or get a job. If organizational leaders can depend on the political backing of their followers, the organization is able to put its full strength into pursuing its aims and will have an enormous advantage in the political arena. If the leaders cannot motivate the members, the organization will not be effective.

How do associations motivate potential members to join them? Individuals will not always join an organization for the benefits of collective action. Organizations must provide incentives, material or otherwise, that are compelling enough to attract the potential free rider.[17] Unions are organized not just for lobbying but also to perform other important services for their members. They derive much of their strength from their negotiating position with corporations, which they use to obtain wage increases or improved safety standards. Similarly, the AARP, in

TABLE 9-2 Some Environmental Groups and How They Do Business

Group	Membership	Issues	Activities
Greenpeace USA	Fewer than 400,000	Whales, oceans, and toxins	Media events; mass mailings; (worldwide) door-to-door canvassing; does not lobby government
Natural Resources Defense Council	350,000	Energy, air and water pollution, nuclear waste	Lobbying; litigation; a watchdog; its scientists compete with experts from agencies and industry
Sierra Club	580,000 (nearly one-third in California)	Wildlands, pollution, endangered species	Grass-roots action; liberal, Democratic politics; hierarchy of 382 local groups making up 55 U.S. and 3 Canadian chapters; fierce internal debates
Wilderness Society	370,000	Strictly public lands	No local chapters; once a backpacker advocacy group, now has a more general Washington-insider focus

SOURCE: *Governing*, April 1992, p. 35. Updated from Charles Lawrence, "Struggling Greenpeace Slashes U.S. Operation," *The Daily Telegraph*, September 17, 1997, p. 12.

addition to lobbying against Social Security cuts and speaking out on other issues of concern to older citizens, offers incentives such as a free subscription to its magazine, *Modern Maturity*, and member discounts at certain hotels. This combination of size and strength sets these groups apart from other large organizations in their effectiveness, as members derive numerous benefits from joining.

While the size of an interest group is often important, so, too, is its *spread*—the extent to which membership is concentrated or dispersed. Automobile manufacturing is concentrated in Michigan and a few other states, and as a result its influence does not have the same spread as that of the American Medical Association, which has an active chapter in virtually every congressional district. An association consisting of three million supporters concentrated in a few states will usually have less influence than another group consisting of three million supporters spread out in a large number of states. A group whose goals are contrary to widely accepted values will have a more difficult time than a group that can present its demands as advancing the public interest. Most interest groups cultivate specific and recognizable identities.[18]

Interest groups also differ in the extent to which they preempt a policy area or share it with other groups. Doctors and the AMA have effectively preempted the health care policy area because they play such an important role in the delivery of health care. In the transportation policy area, railroads must compete with interstate trucking and even air-freight companies.

Groups also differ in their *resources*, which include money, volunteers, expertise, and reputation. Some groups can influence many centers of power—both houses of Congress, the White House, federal agencies, the courts, and state and local governments—while others cannot.

Cohesiveness

Usually a mass-membership organization is made up of three types of members.[19] The first type comprises a relatively small number of formal leaders who may hold full-time, paid positions or at least devote much of their extra time, effort, and money to the group's activities. The second includes people intensely involved in the group, organizationally and psychologically. They identify with the group's aims, attend meetings, faithfully pay dues, and do a lot of the legwork. The third type consists of people who are members in name only. They do not participate actively, they do not look on themselves as Teamsters or Rotarians or Legionnaires, and they cannot be depended on to vote in elections or otherwise act as the leadership wants. In a typical large organization, for every top leader there might be a few hundred hard-core activists and thousands of essentially inactive members.

Another factor in group cohesiveness is its organizational structure. Some associations have no formal organization; others are local organizations that have joined together in some sort of loose state or national federation in which they retain a measure of separate power and independence, just as the states did when they entered the Union. Separation of powers may be found as well: the national assembly of an organization establishes, or at least ratifies, policy; an executive committee meets more frequently; a president or director is elected to head and speak for the group; and permanent paid officials form the organization's bureaucracy. Power may be further divided between the organization's main headquarters and its Washington office. An organization of this sort tends to be far less cohesive than a centralized, disciplined group such as the army or some trade unions.

Leadership

Closely related to cohesion is the nature of the leadership. In a group that embraces many attitudes and interests, leaders may either weld the various elements together or sharpen their disunity. The leader of a national business association, for example, must tread cautiously between big business and small business, between exporters and importers, between chain stores and corner grocery stores, and between the producers and the sellers of competing products. Yet leaders must not be at the mercy of different interests, for above all they must lead. The group leader is in the same position as a president or a member of Congress; he or she must know when to lead followers and when to follow them.

Techniques

Interest groups seeking to wield influence choose from a variety of political weapons and targets. They present their case to both houses of Congress, the White House staff, state and local governments, and to federal agencies and departments. They also become involved in litigation. Other techniques include election activities, establishing political parties, and lobbying.

PUBLICITY AND MASS MEDIA APPEALS Interest groups exploit the communications media—television, radio, newspapers, leaflets, signs, direct mail, and word of mouth—to influence voters during elections and to motivate constituents to contact their representatives between elections. Business enjoys a special advantage in this arena, and businesspeople have the money to use propaganda machinery. As large-scale advertisers, they know how to deliver their message effectively or can find an advertising agency to do it for them.

MASS MAILING New technologies have increased the reach and effectiveness of interest groups. One of these new technologies is computerized and targeted mass mailing.[20] For many decades, interest groups have been sending out huge mailings to people whose names are on lists culled from telephone directories and other sources. Most of these mailings are sent out indiscriminately. Mass mailing is used by all kinds of interest groups, but it has been especially refined by public interest groups, which are sometimes accused of being a small headquarters with a good mailing list. Today's technology can produce personalized letters targeted to specific groups. Speaking of the National Rifle Association, former Congressman William J. Hughes (D.-N.J.) said, "It's a lobby that can put 15,000 letters in your district overnight and have people in your town hall meeting interrupting you."[21] Such targeted direct mail can also appeal to people who share a common concern, such as environmental groups.

INFLUENCE ON RULE MAKING Organized groups have ready access to the executive and regulatory agencies that write the rules implementing laws passed by Congress. Government agencies publish proposed regulations in the ***Federal Register*** and invite responses and reactions from all interested persons before the rules are finalized. (The *Federal Register* is published every weekday. You can find it in your school or public library.) Well-staffed associations and corporations peruse the *Register*, ever alert for actions that will affect their interests. Lobbyists, who are often lawyers, prepare written responses to the proposed rules, draft alternative rules, and appear at the hearings to make their case. These lobbyists seek to be on good terms with the staff of the agencies so that they can learn what rules are being considered long before they are released publicly and thus have input in the early stages. Administrative rules are defined over time through legal cases and agency modifications, so even if an interest group fails to get what it wants, it can fight the rules in court or press for a reinterpretation when the agency leadership changes hands.

Finally, an interest group can seek to modify rules it does not like by pressuring Congress to change the legal mandate for the agency or have the agency's budget reduced, making enforcement of existing rules difficult. In short, interest groups and lobbyists never really quit fighting for their point of view.

Federal Register
This official document, published every weekday, lists new and proposed regulations of executive departments and regulatory agencies.

LITIGATION When groups find the usual political channels closed to them, they may turn to the courts.[22] The Legal Defense and Education Fund of the National Association for the Advancement of Colored People (NAACP), for example, initiated and won numerous court cases in its efforts to improve legal protection for African Americans. In recent decades, urban interests and environmental groups, feeling underrepresented in state and national legislatures, have turned to the courts to influence the political agenda.[23] Women's groups—such as the National Organization for Women and the American Civil Liberties Union's Women's Rights Project—have also used the courts to pursue their objectives.[24] Conservative religious groups, often known as the Religious Right or New Christian Right, have also actively used litigation as a strategy to pursue their objectives.[25]

Despite the general impression that association litigants achieve great success in the courts, groups are no more likely than individuals to win their cases at the district court level.[26] In addition to initiating lawsuits, associations can gain a forum for their views in the courts by filing ***amicus curiae* briefs** (literally "friend of the court") in cases in which they are not direct parties.

ELECTION ACTIVITIES Although nearly all large organizations say they are nonpolitical, almost all are politically involved in some way. What they usually mean when they say they are nonpolitical is that they are *nonpartisan*. A distinguishing feature of organized interest groups is that they often try to work through *both* parties.

Labor usually favors Democrats. Although the AFL-CIO has supported every Democratic candidate for president since the New Deal, there are exceptions. The Teamsters Union has often endorsed Republicans. Labor endorsements can become controversial, as happened with the National Education Association (NEA) endorsement of Bill Clinton in 1996, which led Republican presidential candidate Bob Dole to attack teachers in his acceptance speech.

Business groups generally endorse the incumbent but favor Republicans when no incumbent is running. Some organizations are prevented from taking a firm position by the diversity of their members. A local retailers' group, for example, might be composed equally of Republicans and Democrats, and many of its members might refuse to openly support a candidate for fear of losing business.

Ideological groups target certain candidates, seeking to change the candidate's positions or, failing that, to influence voters to vote against that candidate. Americans for Democratic Action and the American Conservative Union publish ratings of incumbents' voting record on liberal and conservative issues, as do the U.S. Chamber of Commerce and the AFL-CIO, among others.

How effective is electioneering by interest groups? In general, the mass-membership organizations' power to mobilize their full strength in elections has been exaggerated in the press. Too many cross-pressures are operating in the pluralistic politics of the United States for any one group to assume a commanding role. Some groups reach their maximum influence only by allying themselves closely with one of the two major parties. They may place their members on local, state, and national party committees and help send them to party conventions as delegates, but such alliances mean losing some independence and singleness of purpose.

FORMING A POLITICAL PARTY Another interest group strategy is to form a political party. These parties are organized less with the intent to *win elections* than to *publicize a cause*. The Free Soil party was formed in the mid-1840s to propagandize against the spread of slavery, and the Prohibition party was organized two decades later to ban the sale of liquor. Farmers have formed a variety of such parties. More often, however, interest groups prefer to work through existing parties.

COOPERATIVE LOBBYING Interest groups often form alliances. An example is the Food Group, a 30-year-old informal conference group in Washington that has

***amicus curiae* brief**
Literally, "friend of the court" brief, this document is filed by an individual or organization to present arguments in addition to those presented by the immediate parties to the case.

lobbying
Activities aimed at influencing public officials, especially legislators, and the policies they enact.

lobbyist
A person who is employed by and acts for an organized interest group or corporation to try to influence policy decisions and positions in the executive and legislative branches.

represented more than 60 business and trade associations. In addition, it spawned an Information Committee on Federal Food Regulations to fight "truth-in-packaging" legislation. Although the Food Group has been fairly effective, it does run into the predictable problem of differences among its constituents over goals and priorities and has found it difficult to put strong and unified pressure on Congress and government agencies.

Other like-minded groups have also joined together as cooperative groups. In 1987 the Leadership Conference on Civil Rights brought together many groups in the battle to defeat the nomination of outspoken federal judge Robert Bork to the U.S. Supreme Court.[27] Different types of environmentalists work together, as do consumer and ideological groups on the right and on the left. Women continue to be represented by a large variety of groups that reflect diverse interests, but the larger the coalition, the greater the chance that members may divide over such issues as abortion.

The Influence of Lobbyists

The terms "lobbying" and "lobbyist" were not generally used until around the middle of the nineteenth century in the United States. The root in these words refers to the lobby or hallway outside House and Senate chambers in the U.S. Capitol. It was also used to refer to hotel lobbies in Washington where petitioners and agents of influence congregated. Thus a senator coming out of the Senate chamber might be accosted politely by several lobbyists seeking to influence his vote on some measure. Or a president might be dining at the Willard Hotel, a few blocks from the White House, and make reference to the number of "lobbyists" hanging around in the hotel lobby. The noun "lobby" has been turned into a verb in this political context. Thus "to lobby" is to seek to influence legislators and government officials, and we call this **lobbying** even if there is no lobby in sight.

Despite their negative public image, lobbyists perform useful functions for government. They provide information for the decision makers of all three branches of government, they help educate and mobilize public opinion, they help prepare legislation and testify before legislative hearings, and they contribute a large share of the costs of campaigns. Yet many people are concerned that lobbyists have too much influence on government and add to legislative gridlock by being able to stop action on pressing problems.

Lobbyists during the administration of President Grant operated in much the same way as today's lobbyists do.

Who Are the Lobbyists?

The typical image of interest groups in action is that of powerful, hard-nosed lobbyists who skillfully employ a combination of knowledge, persuasiveness, personal influence, charm, and money to influence legislators and bureaucrats. **Lobbyists** are the employees of associations who try to influence policy decisions and positions in the executive and especially in the legislative branches of our government. They are experienced in the ways of government, often having been public servants before going to work for an organized interest group or association or corporation. They might start as staff in Congress, perhaps on a congressional committee. Later, when their party wins the White House, they gain an administration post, often in the same policy area as their congressional committee work. After a few years in the administration, they are ready to make the move to lobbying, either by going to work for one of the interests they dealt with while in the government or by obtaining a position with a lobbying firm.

Moving from a government job to one with an interest group is quite common. The practice is sometimes called the **revolving door**. Despite the fact that it is illegal to directly lobby the agency from which they came, contacts made during government service are often helpful to interest groups. Many former members of Congress make use of their congressional experience as full-time lobbyists.

The revolving-door tendency between government and interest groups produces networks of people who care about certain issues. These networks have been called **iron triangles**—meaning mutually supporting relationships among interest groups, congressional committees and subcommittees, and the government agencies that share a common policy concern. Sometimes these relationships become so strong and mutually beneficial that the issue network becomes very powerful. Retired military officers, for example, can go to work for defense contractors after leaving the military, although they are banned for life from selling Department of Defense contracts. This restriction does not preclude them from providing advice to corporations on how best to compete for defense projects.

Legal and political skills, along with specialized knowledge, have become so crucial in executive and legislative policy making as to become a form of power in themselves. Elected representatives increasingly depend on their staffs for guidance, and these staffs in turn are linked to the staffs of executive departments and of lobbyists. Issue specialists know more about Section 504 or Title IX or the amendment of 1972—and who wrote that amendment and why—than most political and administrative leaders, who are usually generalists. It is in this gray area of policy making that many interest groups and lobbyists play a vital role, as people move

WE THE PEOPLE

Tom Korologos, Lobbyist

Tom Korologos is an experienced Washington lobbyist. He first became involved in politics in the 1962 U.S. Senate race for Senator Wallace Bennet (R.-UT) and moved from there to the Nixon and Ford administrations, where he was deputy assistant to the president for Senate relations. He has helped shepherd more than 300 presidential nominees through the Senate confirming process.

Presidents Reagan and Bush drafted Korologos to aid the White House in confirmation efforts for Robert Bork and Justices Rehnquist and Scalia to the Supreme Court, as well as several cabinet appointees. His work for the White House on confirmation lobbying helped reinforce his reputation as an insider with his regular clients.

In 1975 he was a founder of Timmons and Company, a premiere Washington lobbying firm, where he is now president. Korologos has represented, among others, Major League Baseball, Union Pacific, Anheuser-Busch, and the National Rifle Association.

Korologos is from Salt Lake City, Utah. His undergraduate degree at the University of Utah was in journalism, as was his master's degree from Columbia University.

revolving door
The employment cycle in which individuals work, in turn, for governmental agencies regulating interests and then for the interest groups or businesses with the same policy concern.

iron triangle
A mutually supporting relationship among interest groups, congressional committees and subcommittees, and government agencies that share a common policy concern.

freely from congressional or agency staff to association staff and perhaps back again. Even if campaigns and elections were funded entirely by taxpayers instead of our current system, interest groups would remain important because of their ability to provide knowledge and information.

What Do Lobbyists Do?

Thousands of lobbyists are active in Washington, but few of them are as glamorous or as unscrupulous as the media suggest, nor are they necessarily influential. One limit on their power is the competition among interest groups. Rarely does any one group have a policy area all to itself. For example, transportation policy involves airplanes, trucks, cars, railroads, consumers, suppliers, state and local governments—the list goes on and on.

To members of Congress, the single most important thing lobbyists provide is money for their next reelection campaign. "Reelection underlies everything else," writes political scientist David Mayhew.[28] Money from interest groups has become instrumental in this driving need of incumbents. Interest groups also provide volunteers for campaign activity. Also their failure to support the opposition can enhance an incumbent's chances of being reelected.

Some people defend lobbyists as a kind of "third house" of Congress. Whereas the Senate and House are set up on a geographical basis, lobbyists represent people on the basis of interests. Small but important groups can sometimes get representation in the "third house" when they cannot get it in the other two. In a nation of vast and important interests, this kind of functional representation, if it is not abused, can be a useful supplement to geographical representation.

Beyond their central role in campaigns and elections, interest groups provide another essential commodity to legislators: information of two important types, political and substantive. The *political information* provided by lobbyists includes such matters as who supports or opposes legislation and how strongly they feel.[29] *Substantive information* such as the impact of proposed laws might not be available from any other source. Lobbyists often provide technical assistance on the drafting of bills and amendments, identify persons to testify at legislative hearings, and formulate questions to ask of administration officials at oversight hearings.

Money and Politics

A **political action committee** (PAC) is the political arm of an interest group that is legally entitled to raise funds on a voluntary basis from members, stockholders, or employees in order to contribute funds to favored candidates or political parties.[30] PACs link two vital techniques of influence—giving money and other political aid to politicians, and persuading officeholders to act or vote "the right way" on issues. Thus PACs are the means by which interest groups seek to influence which legislators are elected and what they do once they take office.[31] PACs can be categorized according to the type of interest they represent: corporations, trade and health organizations, labor unions, ideological organizations, and others.

political action committee (PAC)
The political arm of an interest group that is legally entitled to raise funds on a voluntary basis from members, stockholders, or employees in order to contribute funds to favored candidates or political parties.

The Growth of PACs

Ironically, considering that the explosion of PACs has occurred mainly in the business world, it was organized labor that invented this device. In the 1930s, John L. Lewis, president of the United Mine Workers, set up the Non-Partisan Political League as the political arm of the newly formed Congress of Industrial Organizations. When the CIO merged with the American Federation of Labor, the new labor group established the Committee on Political Education (COPE), whose activities we have already described. This unit came to be the model for most political action committees: "From the outset, national, state, and local units of COPE have not only raised and distributed funds, but have also served as the mechanism for organized and widespread union activity in the electoral process, for example, in voter registration, political education, and get-out-the-vote drives."[32]

Some years later, manufacturers formed the Business-Industry Political Action Committee, but this committee played a limited role in the 1960s. The 1970s brought a near-revolution in the role and influence of PACs, ironically as the result of post-Watergate reforms. The number of PACs increased dramatically, from about 150 to nearly 4,000 today. Corporations and trade associations contributed most to this growth; today their PACs constitute the majority of all PACs. Labor PACs, on the other hand, increased only slightly in number, representing less than 10 percent of all PACs. But the increase in the number of PACs is less important than the intensity of recent PAC participation in elections and in lobbying.

Campaign fund raisers such as this often charge donors $1,000 a plate for the privilege of meeting the candidates and other influential policy makers.

How PACs Invest Their Money

In response to reporters' questions concerning the influence of money in politics, controversial banker Charles Keating once said, "One question, among the many raised in recent weeks, [has] to do with whether my financial support in any way influenced several political figures to take up my cause. I want to say in the most forceful way I can: I certainly hope so."[33] Another businessman was equally candid before the Senate committee investigating the campaign finance scandals of the Clinton/Gore 1996 campaign. Roger Tamraz had long wanted government support for his idea of building an oil pipeline under the Caspian Sea. When asked if his $300,000 donation to the Democratic party gave him access to the president, he replied, "Of course. The only reason to give money is to get access."[34] Tamraz also said that his "only regret now is that he didn't give $600,000."[35]

PACs take part in the entire election process, but their main influence lies in their capacity to contribute money to candidates. Candidates today need a lot of money to wage their campaigns. It is no longer uncommon for House candidates to spend more than a million dollars, and for many senators or would-be senators to spend ten times that amount.[36]

As PACs contribute more, their influence grows. What counts is not only the amounts they give but to whom they give. PACs give to the most influential incumbents, to committee chairs, party leaders and whips, and to the Speaker. PACs not only give to the majority party but to key incumbents in the minority party as well, because they understand that today's minority could be tomorrow's majority.

PACs, like individuals, are limited by law in the amount of money they can contribute to any single candidate in an election cycle. The Federal Election Campaign Act of 1971 limits PACs to $5,000 per election or $10,000 per election cycle (primary and general elections). Individuals have a limit of $2,000 per candidate per election cycle. PACs have found some creative ways around this limit. They can host fund-raisers attended by other PACs to boost their reputation with the candidate, or they can collect money from several persons and give them to the candidate as a bundle. Through **bundling**, PACs and interested individuals can increase their clout with elected officials.

The Effectiveness of PACs

How much does PAC money influence election outcomes, legislation, and representation? One critic has written, "When politicians start to see a dollar sign behind every vote, every phone call, every solicitation, those other factors sometimes weighed during governance, like the public good and equal access to government, become less and less important."[37] An organization called Citizens Against PACs publishes attacks on members of Congress who, in their opinion, accept too many out-of-state PAC contributions. In this area, as in others, money obviously talks. But it is easy to exaggerate that influence. While a candidate may receive a great amount

bundling
A tactic of political action committees whereby they collect contributions from like-minded individuals (each limited to $2,000) and present them to a candidate or political party as a "bundle," thus increasing their influence.

You Decide . . .

Should PACs be abolished?

As a new member of Congress who almost lost to a candidate supported by PACs in the last election, you are urged by your local newspaper and some constituents to take a bold step and introduce legislation to abolish all PACs. If such legislation were introduced, how would you defend it?

of PAC money, only a fraction of that total comes from any single interest. In addition, it is debatable how much campaign contributions affect election outcomes and uncertain that winning candidates will be willing and able to "remember" their financial angels or that the money in the end produces a real payoff in legislation.

Much depends, however, on the context in which money is given and received. Many campaigns—especially congressional and state and local campaigns—are small-scale undertakings in which a big contribution makes a difference. Amid all the murk of campaigning, a candidate may feel grateful for so tangible and convertible a contribution as money. Studies demonstrate a significant relationship between PACs giving money and receiving favorable treatment in congressional committees.[38]

Curing the Mischiefs of Faction—Two Hundred Years Later

If James Madison were to return today, he would not be surprised by the existence of interest groups. Nor would he be surprised by the variety of interest groups. He might be surprised, however, by the intense expression of *factionalism*—the varied weapons of group influence, the deep involvement of interest groups in the electoral process, and the vast number of lobbyists in Washington and the state capitals. And doubtless Madison, were he alive today, would be concerned about the power of faction, especially its tendency toward instability and injustice.

Concern about the evils of interest groups has been a recurrent theme throughout U.S. history. President Ronald Reagan in his Farewell Address warned of the power of "special interests."[39] President Reagan was not alone in warning about the problems of cozy relationships between special interests and policy makers. President Dwight Eisenhower used his Farewell Address to warn against the military-industrial complex.

Single-interest groups organized for or against particular policies—abortion, handgun control, tobacco subsidies, animal rights—have aroused much concern in recent years. "It is said that citizen groups organizing in ever greater numbers to push single issues ruin the careers of otherwise fine politicians who disagree with them on one emotional issue, paralyze the traditional process of governmental compromise, and ignore the common good in their selfish insistence on getting their own way."[40] But which single issues reflect narrow interests? Women's rights—even a specific issue such as sexual harassment—are hardly "narrow," women's rights leaders contend, because they would help over half the population. Peace groups, too, claim that they represent

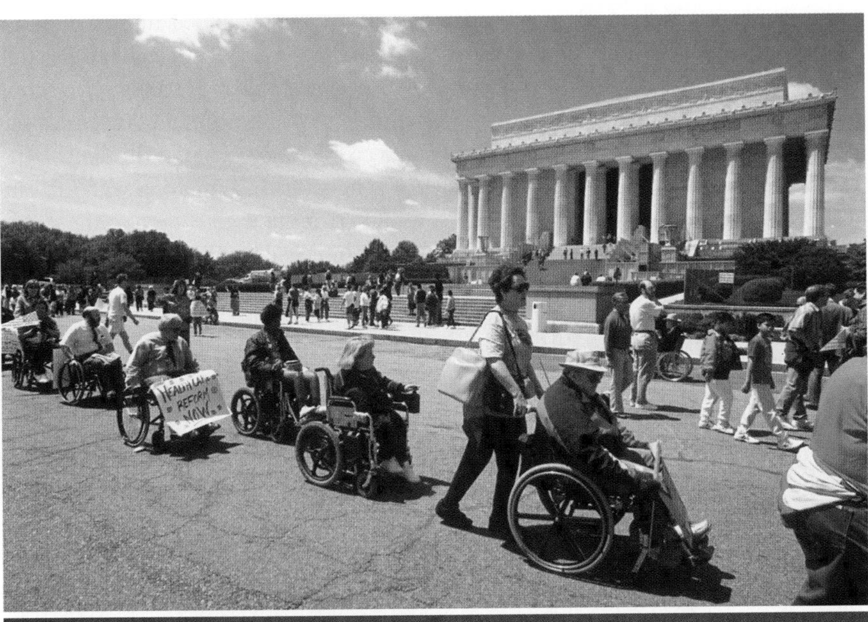

One effective special interest group has been disabled individuals, whose demonstrations in Washington ultimately led to the Americans with Disabilities Act.

the whole population, as do those who support prayer in schools. These issues may seem quite different from those related to subsidies to dairy farmers, for example.

Some of the issues raised by factionalism are:

1. The struggle among factions is not a fair fight because highly organized and better-financed single-issue groups hold a decided advantage over more general groups.
2. The interest-group battle leads to great inequities, because lower-income people are grossly underrepresented among interest groups, as compared to richer, more highly organized people, many of whom are represented by well-financed organizations and lobbyists.
3. Even though the organization of hundreds of single-issue groups has diffused power in government, as the Constitution's framers desired, it has led to incoherent policies, waste and inefficiency, endless delays, and the inability to plan ahead and anticipate crises.
4. The role of interest groups in elections has made incumbents more secure and enhanced the power of interest groups in relation to Congress and state and local governments.

What should be done, if anything? For decades Americans have tried to find ways to keep interest groups in check. They have agreed with James Madison that the "remedy" of outlawing factions would be worse than the disease. It would be absurd to abolish liberty simply because it nourished faction. And the existence and activity of interest groups and lobbies are solidly protected by the Constitution. But by safeguarding the value of *liberty*, have Americans allowed interest groups to threaten *equality*, the second great value in our national heritage? The question remains: How can interest groups be regulated in a way that does not threaten their constitutional liberties?

Federal and State Regulation

Americans have generally responded to this question by seeking to regulate lobbying in general and political money in particular. Concern over the use of money—especially corporate funds—to influence politicians goes back well over a century, to the Crédit Mobilier scandals during the administration of Ulysses S. Grant. During the "progressive" first two decades of this century, Congress legislated against corporate contributions in federal elections and required disclosure of the use of the money.

In 1925, responding to the Teapot Dome scandal during Warren G. Harding's administration, Congress passed the Federal Corrupt Practices Act. It required disclosure reports, both before and after elections, of receipts and expenditures by Senate and House candidates and by political committees that sought to influence federal elections in more than one state. Note that these were *federal* laws applying to *federal* elections; regulation of state lobbying and elections was left to the states.

Federal legislation, including the 1925 Federal Corrupt Practices Act and the 1946 Federal Regulation of Lobbying Act, was not very effective. It was, in fact, largely unenforced. Many candidates filed incomplete reports or none at all. The reform mood of the 1960s brought basic changes, "nurtured by the ever-increasing costs of campaigning, the incidence of millionaire candidates, the large disparities in campaign spending between various candidates and political parties, some clear cases of unique influence on the decision-making process by large contributors and special interests, and the apparent advantages of incumbency in an age of mass communications with a constant focus on the lives and activities of officeholders."[41] The upshot was the Federal Election Campaign Act (FECA) of 1971, which supplanted the earlier legislation.

FECA, which has been amended three times, establishes reporting or disclosure requirements for all candidates for the U.S. House of Representatives, the Senate, and the presidency, as well as their political parties and campaign committees. It also

Thinking it Through . . .

As an incumbent, your self-interest would dictate that you oppose a ban on PACs because you stand to benefit from them and your challengers do not. PAC contributions provide a major advantage to you and a huge obstacle to most challengers. This is why many incumbents who ran against PACs in their first race suddenly discover, once elected, that PACs are not all bad. Defenders of PACs label PAC contributions an important form of participation. They argue that such contributions are constitutionally protected. Or they point to a PAC from their district that has supported them and claim that PACs are merely groups of constituents.

If you want to stand by your original opposition to PACs and win others to your point of view, you will need to find a way to substitute "untainted" money like public financing of elections for what you see as "tainted" PAC money. You will have to overcome an intense lobbying effort by PACs to defend what they have been doing. Your best arguments against them are that they give so heavily to incumbents (especially incumbents on committees that deal with their concerns) that the constitutionality of banning corporate or labor PACs will be tested.

requires disclosure of the amounts spent to influence federal elections by others, including individuals and political action committees. The act established partial public financing for presidential candidates, financed by a voluntary check-off on federal income tax forms. *Spending by candidates* for Congress is not limited, but *contributions to these candidates* and to presidential candidates is limited.

There have been notable problems with the act, including an ineffective Federal Election Commission. The act has had its critics, and Congress has frequently debated reforming campaign financing. (We discuss these reform proposals in greater detail in Chapter 12.) There have also been significant attempts to regulate interest-group activity in elections at the state level. Some states, like Maine, Wisconsin, Minnesota, and Hawaii, provide for public financing of state offices and state legislative races; others, like Michigan, New Jersey, and Massachusetts, provide partial public financing of gubernatorial elections; a dozen more help underwrite parties with public funds.[42]

Recently, there has been renewed interest in regulating not only lobbyists but those who may someday become lobbyists. Bill Clinton required top appointees to his administration to agree "not to lobby their former agencies for five years after leaving the government . . . [and] never to become lobbyists for foreign governments or foreign political parties." The White House staff "pledge[d] not to lobby any agency for which they have had 'substantial personal responsibility' for five years after leaving office."[43]

In his 1995 State of the Union Address, President Clinton challenged the new Republican majority in Congress to send him bills on campaign finance and lobby reform—two elements Republicans had been criticized for leaving out of their Contract with America. Congress has not passed campaign finance reform, but it did produce the first major overhaul of lobbying laws since 1946. Under the Lobbying Disclosure Act of 1995, the definition of lobbyist was significantly expanded to include part-time lobbyists, those who deal with congressional staff or executive branch agencies, and those who represent foreign-owned companies and foreign entities. This act is expected to increase the number of registered lobbyists anywhere from three to ten times its current level.[44] The act also includes specific disclosure requirements and information requirements.

The Effects of Regulation

What have been the effects of these reforms on interest groups? Ironically, one has been to increase the number and importance of such groups. The strategy of the 1971 law was to authorize direct and open participation by both labor and corporate organizations in elections and lobbying in the hopes that a visible role for interest-group activity, backed by effective enforcement, would be constitutional under the First Amendment. The 1971 act allowed unions and corporations to communicate on political matters to members or stockholders, to conduct registration and get-out-the-vote drives, and to spend union and company funds to set up "separate segregated funds" (PACs) to use for political purposes.

The 1971 act opened the door to corporations and trade associations to form PACs, and they made the most of it. The growth in numbers and contributions from corporate and trade association PACs was great.[45] But what changed the rules of the game even more for corporate interests was passage in 1974 of limits on individual contributions, something not part of the 1971 act. An explosion of corporate PACs followed this 1974 amendment.[46] In 1978 there was little difference in the level of campaign activity of PACs representing corporations, labor unions, or trade associations.[47] But that has changed, with corporate PACs spending more than the others, and ideological PACs at roughly half the level of spending of trade and labor PACs. In the 1995–96 election cycle, corporate PACs spent $130 million dollars, nearly $30 million more than labor PACs and $25 million more than trade PACs.[48]

Large corporations are able to contribute to political parties or candidates through their PACs.

With each successive election cycle, PACs spend more money. Most of this money goes to incumbents, especially committee chairs and party leaders. The result, labor leaders contend, has been a greater imbalance than ever between the political action and power of a relatively small number of corporation executives and stockholders, on the one hand, and the labor unions on the other.

A centerpiece of past efforts to regulate interest-group activity was disclosure of how politicians fund their campaigns. Until the 1996 election cycle, and with the important exception of soft money, we had a much better idea of how much money candidates raised and how they spent it. Without disclosure, much of what we have written here about PACs, for instance, would not be public knowledge. Disclosure permits the press and public to assess the implications of how candidates finance their campaigns. The growth of soft money and the advent of issue advocacy now means that we know less and less about how campaigns are financed. Groups and individuals can avoid disclosure, and the public remains uninformed about who is trying to influence their vote.

Candidates and some appointed officials must also disclose their personal finances, permitting voters and the press to see what investments and resources candidates have that may affect their ability to be impartial. Such public disclosure of personal worth, the value of property owned, and outstanding debts no doubt discourages some persons from entering public life, but it also makes officeholders accountable for certain obligations and actions once they enter office.

Is Reform Possible?

Will Congress reform the PACs and campaign finance in general? Not only is reform itself complex and difficult, but it is doubtful that most members of Congress really *want* reform. Many members of Congress thrive on the present arrangements, and the leaders and members of both parties actually compete for PAC dollars (see Table 9-3). When the National Association of Home Builders, a richly funded lobby, began to give more money to Republican candidates, Democratic leaders of the House warned the lobby that it had better help Democrats too, or its "good relationship" with the Democrats might be "damaged." One reason members of Congress become entrenched in their seats is that they become increasingly funded by PACs. Some of them are reluctant to give up such a cozy relationship. Thus the real question may be not whether Congress can reform the interest-group lobbies, but whether Congress can reform itself.[49]

TABLE 9-3 The Big Givers, 1995–96

Donor	Republicans	Democrats	Total
Philip Morris Co. (tobacco)	$2,517,518	$ 481,518	$2,999,036
Joseph E. Seagram & Sons/MCA (liquor, music)	$ 685,145	$1,180,700	$1,865,845
RJR Nabisco (tobacco)	$1,188,175	$ 253,403	$1,441,578
Walt Disney Co. (entertainment)	$ 296,450	$ 997,050	$1,293,500
Atlantic Richfield Co.* (oil, gas)	$ 766,506	$ 486,372	$1,252,878
Communications Workers of America* (labor union)	$ 0	$1,128,425	$1,128,425

SOURCE: Common Cause home page (http://www.commoncause.org/cgi-bin/ccause/soft_money.pl).

*Includes contributions from subsidiaries and/or executives.

Some observers favor tougher regulation of political money and publicly financed congressional elections. Others call for removal of regulation of the political arms of interest groups, hoping that the groups will find a natural and proper balance. Still others believe the balance must be righted between the present wide and intense activity of corporate PACs and the far less influential role of PACs for consumer groups, women's groups, environmental groups, and civil rights groups.[50]

A different school of thought holds that none of these "solutions" will work. The problem lies outside interest groups and PACs rather than within them. This school cites James Madison, who concluded that while the *causes* of faction could not be removed, the *effects* could be controlled only by fundamental changes in the whole political system. His solutions were to extend the sphere of government to take in "a greater variety of parties and interests," create federal-state-local tiers of government, and fragment the power of government so no majority or minority could control it.

Strengthening the political parties might be one way to reduce the power of special interests. If campaign contributions were directed more to parties than to candidates, then candidates would be more accountable to the parties and less tied to any particular interest. Parties are also more likely to invest in challengers than are PACs. Finally, because parties must seek to broaden their appeal, they cannot risk becoming captive of a particular narrow interest. Yet politicians and the interest groups that finance their campaigns strongly favor the current system. This mutually beneficial system is likely to continue until public pressure for change increases.

Finally, some believe the main problem lies not in interest groups but in the way public opinion is formed, managed, and manipulated—above all, by the barons of the electronic media in a new "age of communications" politics. These observers urge Congress to limit what commercial television stations can charge for political advertising and to discourage issue advertising.

POLITICS online

The Christian Coalition

One interest group that has effectively used the new media of computers, fax machines, and talk radio is the Christian Coalition. Ralph Reed, the young and energetic former leader of the group, makes no secret of the importance of these media. In his book, *Politically Incorrect*, Reed makes clear that "people of faith are enthusiastically embracing the emerging technologies of computers and interactive television that will make up the information superhighway of the future." The Christian Coalition has a well-developed home page at:

http://www.cc.org.

The coalition's home page also includes its Congressional Scorecard on how members of Congress voted on matters important to the coalition, announcements of upcoming events, and statements about the goals and purposes of the organization.

Other interest groups also make extensive use of the Web. Labor unions like the AFL-CIO (**http://www.aflcio.org**), animal rights advocates (**http://www.peta-online.org**), and proponents of term limits (**http://www.termlimits.org/homepage.html**) all use this technology. Pick your favorite issue or interest group, and check out what it has to say on the Internet.

For more Internet resources on Interest Groups, see our home page at:

http://www.prenhall.com/burns

SUMMARY

1. Interest groups exist to make demands on government. The dominant interest groups in the United States are economic or occupational, but a variety of other groups—ideological, public interest, foreign policy, government itself, and ethnic, religious, and racial—have memberships that cut across the big economic groupings; thus their influence is both reduced and stabilized.
2. Movements of large numbers of people who are frustrated with government policies have always been with us in the United States. Blacks, women, Native Americans, and the economic underdogs have at various times organized themselves into movements.
3. Elements in interest-group power include size, resources, cohesiveness, leadership, and techniques, especially the ability to contribute to candidates and political parties as well as the ability to fund lobbyists. But the actual power of an interest group stems from the manner in which these elements relate to the political and governmental environment in which the interest group operates.
4. For many decades, interest groups have engaged in lobbying, but these efforts have become far more significant as groups become more deeply involved in the electoral process, especially through the expanded use of political action committees (PACs). Interest groups also take their messages directly to the public through mass mailings, advertising campaigns, and cooperative lobbying.
5. Concern for PACs centers on their ability to raise money and spend it on elections on behalf of endorsed candidates, typically incumbents. This concern has led to proposals to ban PACs or to more strictly limit their authority. Yet their existence and rights are protected by our First Amendment.
6. Reforms of interest-group excess often include strengthened political parties or regulations that seek fairness, disclosure, and balance between interest groups. All reform efforts must operate in such a way as not to take away basic constitutional rights of individuals. The key issue today in "controlling factions" is whether to allow groups to proliferate and so balance each other, to try to regulate groups, or to seek reforms outside the groups by fostering balanced power in political parties or elsewhere.

KEY TERMS

faction 204
interest group 204
movement 204
open shop 208
closed shop 208
free rider 208
***Federal Register* 214**
***amicus curiae* brief 215**
lobbying 216
lobbyist 216
revolving door 217
iron triangle 217
political action committee (PAC) 218
bundling 219

FURTHER READING

JEFFREY M. BERRY, *The Interest Group Society*, 3d ed. (Longman, 1997).

JEFFERY H. BIRNBAUM, *The Lobbyists: How Influence Peddlers Get Their Way in Washington* (Times Books, 1992).

WILLIAM P. BROWNE, *Groups, Interests, and Public Policy* (Georgetown University Press, 1998).

ALLAN J. CIGLER AND BURDETT A. LOOMIS, EDS., *Interest Group Politics*, 5th ed. (Congressional Quarterly Press, 1998).

ALLEN D. HERTZKE, *Representing God in Washington: The Role of Religious Lobbies in the American Polity* (University of Tennessee Press, 1988).

RONALD J. HREBENAR, *Interest Group Politics in America* (M. E. Sharpe, 1997).

MANCUR OLSON, *The Logic of Collective Action* (Harvard University Press, 1965).

MARK P. PETRACCA, ED., *The Politics of Interests: Interest Groups Transformed* (Westview Press, 1992).

DAVID VOGEL, *Kindred Strangers: The Uneasy Relationship Between Politics and Business in America* (Princeton University Press, 1996).

JACK L. WALKER, JR., *Mobilizing Interest Groups in America: Patrons, Professions, and Social Movements* (University of Michigan Press, 1991).

CLYDE WILCOX, *Risky Business? PAC Decision Making in Congressional Elections* (M. E. Sharpe, 1994).

JOHN R. WRIGHT, *Interest Groups and Congress: Lobbying Contributions and Influence* (Allyn and Bacon, 1996).

POLITICAL
PARTIES:
ESSENTIAL
TO
DEMOCRACY

10

Chapter Outline

SOME YEARS AGO A COMMUNITY COLLEGE DISTRICT IN LOS ANGELES HELD A NONPARTISAN ELECTION IN WHICH ANY REGISTERED VOTER COULD RUN IF HE OR SHE paid the $50 filing fee and gathered 500 valid signatures on a petition. One hundred and thirty-three candidates ran, and each voter could cast up to seven votes in the election. Political parties were not allowed to nominate candidates, and party labels did not appear on the ballot to help orient voters to the candidates.[1]

How did people vote in an election without parties? Candidates were listed alphabetically, and those whose names began with the letters A to F did better than those later in the alphabet. Being well known helped. Endorsements by *The Los Angeles Times* also influenced the outcome, as did campaigning by a conservative group. A Mexican-American surname also helped. In this election an important voting cue was absent: incumbency. Because the board of trustees was newly created, none of the candidates were incumbents.

Rarely are American voters faced with such unorganized and unlimited choices, because parties give structure to elections. E. E. Schattschneider, a noted political scientist, once said, "The political parties created democracy, and modern democracy is unthinkable save in terms of the parties."[2] This provocative statement is true, but such a favorable evaluation of political parties runs counter to a long-standing and deep-seated American fear and distrust of them. Experience has taught us that free people create political parties to promote their own goals. Parties are a consequence of freedom, as we learned again with the fall of communism in Eastern Europe. Even though our founders hoped to discourage parties, parties quickly became an integral part of our political system.

Elections have important consequences. They determine who will hold office and have political power. Parties are an integral part of making elections work, and elections serve the vital task of deciding who can legitimately exercise political power. We take for granted the peaceful transfer of power from one elected official to another, from one party to another, yet in new democracies the transfer of power following an election is often problematic.

This chapter begins by examining the purposes parties serve that make them so vital to the functioning of democracy. We then examine the evolution of American political parties. Although American political parties have changed over time, they remain important in three different settings: as institutions, in government, and in the electorate. It is important to understand how parties facilitate democracy in all three settings. Finally, we turn to a discussion of the strength of parties today and the prospects for party reform and renewal.

What Parties Do for Democracy

Parties serve many functions, including an important one of narrowing the choices for voters. But *factions*, as James Madison pointed out in *The Federalist*, No. 10 (reprinted in the Appendix), develop wherever there is freedom. They are both a consequence of democracy and an instrument of it. Parties need not be strong and cohesive like those in Western Europe and Britain, but without some kind of party system, democracies are not likely to survive.[3]

Party Functions

American political parties serve a variety of political and social functions, some obvious and some not so obvious. They perform some functions well and others not so well, and how they perform them differs from place to place and time to time.

ORGANIZE THE COMPETITION One of the most important functions of parties is to organize the competition by choosing candidates to run under their label—an important task we often take for granted. To organize the competition, parties do many things: they recruit and nominate candidates for office; they register and activate voters; they help candidates by training them, raising money for them, providing them with research and voter lists, and enlisting volunteers to work for them.[4] Recently parties have been replaced in some of these functions by campaign consultants and professionals; we explore this topic at some length in Chapter 11.

The ability of parties to influence the selection of candidates varies by the type of nominating system used in the state. A few states use a *caucus or convention system*, which permits party leaders to play a greater role in the selection of nominees. Other states utilize *primary elections*. A party's ability to organize the competition is also influenced by how states organize their ballots. In many states, candidates are listed in party columns—the **party column ballot**—which makes it easier for voters to vote a *straight ticket* for all the party candidates. Straight-ticket voting is also easier in voting machines that permit flipping one switch to vote for all candidates from one party. Other states organize the ballot by office—the **office block ballot**—which makes straight ticket voting harder. Even though many voters cast votes for candidates in more than one party, the party label of a candidate means something to most voters and is important in their voting decision.

Local and judicial elections in most state elections are **nonpartisan**, which means no party affiliation is indicated. Such systems make it more difficult for political parties to operate—which is why many jurisdictions have adopted this reform. Proponents of nonpartisan local and judicial elections contend that party affiliation is not important to being a good judge or operating schools and local governments. One problem with nonpartisan elections, however, is that no one is organizing the competition, which means voters have to search for other ways to make decisions.

UNIFY THE ELECTORATE Parties are often accused of creating conflict, but the fact is that they actually help unify the electorate and moderate conflict. Because our system places such a premium on winning the election, there is a strong incentive in both parties to fight out their differences in the party but then come together to take on the opposition. In presidential elections, for instance, promises made to party leaders about cabinet positions or policies important to states or regions can help unify the party. Moreover, in order to win elections, parties need to reach out to voters outside their party and gain their support. This action also helps unify the electorate, at least into the two large national political parties in our system.

party column ballot
Method of voting in which all candidates are listed under their party designations, making it easy for voters to cast votes for all the candidates of one party.

office block ballot
Method of voting in which all candidates are listed under the office for which they are running.

nonpartisan
A local or judicial election in which candidates are not selected or endorsed by political parties.

When single-issue politics becomes important on controversial issues like abortion or gun control, parties have more difficulty building coalitions. Not surprisingly, candidates and parties generally try to avoid defining themselves or the election in single-issue terms. Rather, they hope that if voters disagree with them on one issue, they will still support them because they agree with them on other issues.

HELP ORGANIZE GOVERNMENT Although American political parties are not as cohesive as those in England and most continental democracies, parties are important to organizing our state and national governments. Congress is organized along party lines. The political party with the most votes in each chamber elects the officers of that chamber, selects the chair of each committee, and has a majority on all the committees. The president operates as the national party leader. State governments, with the notable exception of Nebraska, are also organized along party lines.

Another way in which parties organize government is that the winning party gets the **patronage**, which means they can select members of their party as public officials or judges. Such appointments are limited only by civil service regulations that restrict patronage typically to the top posts, but these posts number in the thousands in the federal government. They are also numerous at the state and local levels.

TRANSLATE PREFERENCE INTO POLICY One of the great strengths of our democracy is that even the party that wins usually has to moderate what it does in order to win reelection. For that reason, public policy does not dramatically change with each election. Nonetheless, the party that wins the election has a chance to enact its policies and implement its campaign promises.

American parties have had only limited success in setting the course of national policy, especially when compared with traditionally strong European parties.[5] The European model of party government, which has been called a *responsible party system*, assumes that parties discipline their members through their control over nominations and campaigns. Officeholders in such party-centered systems are expected to act according to party wishes or they will not be allowed to run again under the party label. Moreover, candidates run on fairly specific party platforms and are expected to implement those policies if they win control in the election.

Because American parties do not tightly control nominations, they are unable to discipline members who express views contrary to those of the party. The American system is *candidate centered*; politicians are nominated largely on the basis of their qualifications and personal appeal, not party loyalty. In fact, it is more correct to say that we have candidate politics rather than party politics. As a consequence, party leaders cannot guarantee passage of their program, even if they are in the majority.

On most important issues in our Congress, most, but not all, Democrats vote together, as do most, but not all, Republicans. And then there are times, rather unusual but not unprecedented, when a president of one party receives more votes from the opposing party than from his own, as President Bill Clinton did on the 1993 North American Free Trade Agreement (NAFTA) vote in the House.

PROVIDE LOYAL OPPOSITION Parties provide a loyal opposition. This role was first played by the Jeffersonians during the Washington administration. After a polite interval following an election—the **honeymoon**—the opposition party begins to criticize the party that controls the White House, especially when the opposition party controls one or both houses of Congress.[6] In his first term, Bill Clinton's honeymoon with the Republicans and even some Democrats was unusually brief as he faced early opposition on permitting gays in the military and had to abandon most of his economic stimulus package. In his second term, Clinton and the Republican-controlled Congress worked together to enact sweeping welfare reform

patronage
Dispensing government jobs to persons who belong to the winning political party.

honeymoon
A period at the beginning of a new president's term in which the president enjoys generally positive relations with the press and Congress, usually lasting about six months.

and move the federal budget from deficit to surplus. His relations with Republicans again soured as the issues of perjury and abuse of office in the Monica Lewinsky matter came to dominate the agenda.

Volunteers crowd around a table in West Des Moines, Iowa, to count ballots for presidential candidates in the 1996 Iowa caucuses.

The Nomination of Candidates

From the beginning, parties have been the mechanism by which candidates for public office are chosen. Massachusetts used the earliest method of nominating candidates—the **caucus**, a closed meeting of local leaders. The caucus played an important part in pre-Revolutionary politics. Elected officials organized themselves into groups or parties and together selected candidates to run for higher office, including the presidency. This method of nomination operated for several decades after the United States was established.

As early as the 1820s, however, charges of "secret deals" and "smoke-filled rooms" were made against this method. Moreover, it was not representative of people from areas where a party was in a minority or nonexistent, as only officeholders took part in the caucus. Efforts were made to make the caucus more representative. The *mixed caucus* brought in delegates from districts in which the party had no elected legislators.

Then, during the 1830s and 1840s, a system of **party conventions** was instituted. Delegates, usually chosen directly by party members in towns and cities, selected the party standard-bearers, debated and adopted a platform, and built party spirit by celebrating noisily. But the convention method soon came under criticism that it was subject to control by the party bosses and their machines.

To involve more voters and reduce the power of the bosses to pick party nominees, states adopted the **direct primary**, in which people could vote for the party's nominees for office. Primaries spread rapidly after Wisconsin adopted them in 1905—in the North as a Progressive era reform and in the South as a way to bring democracy to a region that had seen no meaningful general elections due to one-party rule by the Democrats since the end of Reconstruction. By the end of Woodrow Wilson's second administration in 1920, direct primaries were used for some offices in almost all states.

Today the direct primary is the typical method of picking party candidates. Primaries vary significantly from state to state. They differ in terms of: (1) who may run in a primary and how one qualifies for the ballot; (2) whether the party organization can or does endorse candidates before the primary; (3) who may vote in a party's primary—that is, whether a voter must register with a party in order to vote; and (4) how many votes are needed for nomination—a plurality, a majority, or some other number determined by party rule or state law. The differences among primaries are not trivial; they have an important impact on the role played by party organization and on the strategy used by candidates.

In states with **open primaries**, any voter, regardless of party, can participate in whichever primary he or she may choose. This kind of primary permits **crossover voting**—Republicans and Independents helping to determine who the Democratic nominee will be, and vice versa. Other states use **closed primaries**, in which only persons already registered in a party may participate.

In 1996 California voters approved an initiative (Proposition 198) establishing a *blanket primary* system patterned after those in Washington and Alaska. Under the new system, all candidates from all parties are randomly listed by office, and voters have one vote per office. Proponents of the change contend it will benefit moderates in both parties. It will also give Independents a say in who the nominees will be in the general election. Opponents fear that some voters will vote for the weakest candidate in the other party as a way of helping their own party in the general election. In its first primary, California voters of both parties cast ballots for candi-

caucus
A meeting of local party members to choose party officials and/or candidates for public office and to decide the platform.

party convention
A meeting of party delegates to pass on matters of policy and in some cases to select party candidates for public office.

direct primary
Election open to all members of the party in which voters choose the persons who will be the party's nominees in the general election.

open primary
A primary in which any voter, regardless of party, may vote.

crossover voting
A member of one party voting for a candidate of another party.

closed primary
A primary in which only persons registered in the party holding the primary may vote.

dates from the other party, with exit polls showing the more moderate candidate the beneficiary.[7]

Direct primaries were introduced to reduce the influence of party leaders, which they have done, but many critics believe that this change has had more undesirable than desirable consequences. Leaders now have less influence over who gets to be the party's candidate, and candidates are less accountable to the party for what they do, both during the election and after it. Along with modern communications and fundraising techniques, direct primaries have diminished the influence of leaders of political parties.

The rise of direct primaries has not meant the death of caucuses or conventions. In fact, caucuses have reappeared in a number of states as a step in nominating presidential and other candidates. But they have returned in a much more participatory form, open to all party members. Local party caucuses choose delegates to attend regional meetings, which in turn select delegates to state and national conventions, where they nominate party candidates for offices. The Iowa caucuses, in which hundreds of thousands of Iowans participate, are highly publicized as the first important test of potential presidential nominees.[8]

In a few states, conventions still play a role in the nominating process. In Connecticut, for example, convention choices become the party nominees unless they are challenged. Candidates who attain at least 15 percent of the vote in the convention have an automatic right to challenge, but they do not always exercise this right.[9] In other states, convention nominees are designated as such on the primary ballot; they may or may not receive help from the party organization. Conventions are also used to invigorate the party faithful by enabling them to meet with their leaders.

In all but a few states people can get their names on the ballot for most offices without a party. This seldom-used way of running for office simply requires that the candidate secure the required number of signatures on a nomination petition. This is hard to do, but it can be done, as Ross Perot demonstrated in 1992. He spent his own money to build an organization of volunteers who put his name on the ballot in all 50 states.

Two-Party versus Multiparty Systems

In contrast to the two-party system found in the United States, Canada has a multiparty system. Following the general elections of 1997, the Liberal party led by Jean Chrétien formed Canada's government. In addition, seats were allocated in the House of Commons, Canada's preeminent legislative chamber, to the Progressive Conservative party, the New Democratic party, the Reform party, and the Bloc Québécois. Either the Liberals or the Progressive Conservatives have dominated the national political landscape since Canada became a sovereign nation in 1867, and both are basically centrist parties.

The New Democrats, which have formed several provincial governments in recent years, believe in social democracy and support a strong government role in the economy, an extensive social welfare system, and Canada's withdrawal from both the North Atlantic Treaty Organization (NATO) and the North American Free Trade Agreement (NAFTA). They are outspoken about too much American influence over Canada.

The Reform party receives most of its support from voters in Canada's western provinces and believes in a limited government role in the economic sector and cordial relations with the United States. The Bloc Québécois's primary mission is to promote Quebec's independence from Canada through democratic means. All of Canada's major parties are to the left of the Democratic and Republican parties in the United States, and Canadians in general are much more supportive than Americans of a major government role in the economic and social welfare sectors.

Because of the multiplicity of parties, Canadian voters have more options in linking their own policy preferences to specific party platforms. On the other hand, the multiparty system may occasionally result in a minority government, meaning that no party controls a majority of the seats in parliament. This can make governing a much more precarious process. In addition, Canada's multiparty system has accentuated regional biases and preferences within this vast northern nation, complicating efforts to promote national unity and a national vision of Canada's future.

Party Systems

Ours is a two-party system; most other democracies have a multiparty system. Multiparty systems are almost always found in countries that have a parliamentary government, in contrast to our presidential system. This is, however, not always true. For example, England has a parliamentary system but also a strong two-party system.

Parliamentary systems usually have a *head of the nation*, often called the president, but they also have a *head of the government*, often called the prime minister or chancellor, who is the leader of one of the larger parties in the legislature. In democracies with multiparty systems, such as Israel and Italy, because no one party has a majority of the votes, *coalition* governments are necessary. Minor parties can gain concessions—positions in a cabinet or support of policies they want implemented—in return for their participation in a coalition. Major parties need the minor parties and are therefore willing to bargain. Thus the multiparty system favors the existence of minor parties by giving them incentives to persevere.

In some multiparty parliamentary systems, parties run slates of candidates for legislative positions, and winners are determined by **proportional representation** in which the parties receive a proportion of the legislators corresponding to their proportion of the vote. In our **winner-take-all** system, only the candidate with the most

proportional representation
An election system in which each party running receives the proportion of legislative seats corresponding to its proportion of the vote.

winner-take-all
An election system in which the candidate with the most votes wins.

Minor Parties Past and Present

- **The Natural Law party** was started at the Mahirishi International University in Fairfield, Iowa, with the stated purpose to "bring the light of science into politics." The party's platform includes preventive health care and sustainable agriculture without pesticides; it favors using renewable energy to reduce pollution and create national energy self-sufficiency and advocates transcendental meditation as a solution to major health and crime problems, as well as a foreign policy tool. The Natural Law party also wants a 10 percent flat tax by 2002. The party had more than 700 candidates running for office in 1996.
- **The Libertarian party** places heavy emphasis on individual liberties, personal responsibility, and freedom from government. Its agenda calls for an end to the federal government's role in education and crime control. Libertarians believe the income tax is the "biggest intrusion into the lives of the American people," and they perceive Social Security as a "fraudulent scheme." They think the United States should wash its hands of foreign involvement—bring all U.S. troops home and only maintain sufficient military for our own defense. About 1,000 Libertarians ran for office in 1996.
- **The Green party** takes its name from other pro-environment parties throughout Europe. In the United States, the Greens not only embrace pro-environment positions but are committed to social justice, decentralization, respect for diversity, community-based economics, nonviolence, feminism, ecological wisdom, grass-roots democracy, and personal and global responsibility. Their 1996 presidential candidate, Ralph Nader, calls for public campaign financing, a "none of the above" ballot option, and abandonment of NAFTA.

votes in a district or state takes office. Because a party does not gain anything by finishing second, minor parties in a two-party system can rarely overcome the assumption that a vote for them is a wasted vote.[10] Even if a third-party candidate can keep either major party candidate from receiving more than 50 percent (a *majority*) of the vote, the candidate with the most votes (a *plurality*) wins.

In multiparty systems, parties at the extremes are apt to have more influence than in our two-party system, and their legislatures more accurately reflect the full range of the views of the electorate. Political parties in multiparty systems can be more doctrinaire than ours because they do not have to appeal to masses of people. Even though parties that do not become part of the governing coalition may have little to say in setting government policy, they survive because they appeal to some voters. Under such a system, an incentive exists for third, fourth, or additional parties to run because they may win some seats. In contrast, our two-party system tends to create *centrist* parties that appeal to moderate elements and suppress the views of extremists in the electorate. Moreover, once elected, our parties do not form as cohesive a voting block, as do ideological parties in multiparty systems.

Multiparty parliamentary systems make governments unstable, as coalitions form and collapse. In addition, swings in policy when party control changes can be quite dramatic. In contrast, two-party systems produce governments that tend to be stable and centrist, and as a result, policy changes occur incrementally.

Minor Parties: Persistence and Frustration

In the United States we have a two-party system, but we always have **minor parties**, sometimes called *third parties.* Those that arise around a *candidate* usually disappear when the charismatic personality does. Examples of such parties are Theodore Roosevelt's Bull Moose party and George Wallace's American Independent party. Wallace's party polled more than 13 million votes and won 46 electoral votes in 1968. Ross Perot won 19 million votes, for 19 percent of the total vote in 1992. He did only about half as well in 1996, despite the fact that he had organized a political party. Minor parties that are organized around an *ideology* usually persist over time. Communist, Prohibition, or Libertarian parties are of the ideological type. Minor parties of both types come and go, and there are usually several minor parties running in any given election.[11] Some parties arise around a single issue, like the States' Rights party that split with the Democratic party in 1948 over President Harry Truman's civil rights policies.

Minor parties have had an indirect influence in our country by drawing attention to controversial issues and by organizing such groups as the antislavery and the civil rights movements. However, they have never won the presidency or more than a handful of congressional seats (see Table 10-1).[12] They have never shaped national policy from *inside* the government, and their influence on national policy in general, and on the platforms of the two major parties, has been limited.[13]

minor party
A small political party that rises and falls with a charismatic candidate or, if composed of ideologues on the right or left, usually persists over time.

realigning election
An election that proves to be a turning point, redefining the agenda of politics and the alignment of voters within parties during periods of historic change in the economy and society.

A Brief History of American Political Parties

Our First Parties

To the leaders of the young Republic, parties usually meant bigger, better organized, and more fierce factions, and they did not want that. Benjamin Franklin worried about the "infinite mutual abuse of parties, tearing to pieces the best of characters." In his Farewell Address, George Washington warned against the "baneful effects of the Spirit of Party." And Thomas Jefferson said, "If I could not go to heaven but with a party, I would not go there at all."[14]

How, then, did parties get started? Largely out of practical necessity. The same early leaders who so frequently stated their opposition to political parties also recognized the need to organize officeholders who shared their views so that government could act. To get its measures passed by Congress, the Washington administration had to fashion a coalition among factions. This job fell to Treasury Secretary Alexander Hamilton, who built an informal Federalist party, while Washington stayed "above politics."

Secretary of State Jefferson and other officials, many of whom despised Hamilton and his aristocratic ways as much as they opposed the policies he favored, were uncertain about how to deal with these political differences. The overriding concern was the success of the new government; personal loyalty to Washington was a close second. Thus Jefferson stayed in the cabinet, despite his opposition to administration policies, during most of Washington's first term. When he left the cabinet at the end of 1793, many who joined him in opposition to the administration's economic policies remained in Congress, forming a group of legislators opposed to Federalist fiscal policies and eventually to Federalist foreign policy, which appeared "soft on Britain." This party was later known as Republicans, then as Democratic-Republicans, then as Democrats.[15]

Theodore Roosevelt's Bull Moose party polled 27 percent of the vote for president in 1912, the highest of any minor party candidate.

Realigning Elections

American political parties have evolved and changed over time, but some underlying characteristics have been constant. Historically, we have had a two-party system with minor parties. Our parties are moderate and accommodative, meaning that they are open to people with diverse outlooks. Political scientist V. O. Key and others argue that our party system has been shaped in large part by **realigning elections**, turning points that define the agenda of politics and the alignment of voters within parties during periods of historic change in the economy and society.[16] Realigning elections are characterized by intense electoral involvement by the voters, disruptions of traditional voting patterns, changes in the relations of power within the community, and the formation of new and durable electoral groupings. They have occurred cyclically, not randomly.[17] These elections tend to coincide with expansions of the

Running on a state's rights platform with his American Independent party, George Wallace received 14 percent of the vote for president in 1968.

TABLE 10-1 Minor Parties in the United States

Year	Party	Candidate	Percent of Vote	Electoral Vote
1832	Anti-Masonic	William Wirt	8	7
1856	American (Know-Nothing)	Millard Fillmore	22	8
1860	Democratic (Secessionist)	J.C. Breckinridge	18	72
1860	Constitutional Union	John Bell	13	39
1892	People's (Populist)	James B. Weaver	9	22
1912	Bull Moose	Theodore Roosevelt	27	88
1912	Socialist	Eugene V. Debs	6	0
1924	Progressive	Robert M. La Follette	17	13
1948	States' Rights	Strom Thurmond	2	39
1948	Progressive	Henry A. Wallace	2	0
1968	American Independent	George C. Wallace	14	46
1980	National Unity	John Anderson	7	0
1992	United We Stand, America	Ross Perot	19	0
1996	Reform	Ross Perot	9	0

President Andrew Jackson, organizer of a people's coalition of voters, celebrated his arrival at the White House with an inaugural party open to all that nearly tore the place down.

suffrage or changes in the rate of voting.[18] We focus here on four realigning elections: 1824, 1860, 1896, and 1932.

1824: ANDREW JACKSON AND THE DEMOCRATS Party politics was invigorated following the election of 1824, in which the leader in the popular vote—the hero of the battle of New Orleans, Democrat Andrew Jackson—failed to achieve the necessary majority of the Electoral College and was defeated by John Quincy Adams in the runoff election in the House of Representatives. Jackson, brilliantly aided by Martin Van Buren, a veteran party builder in New York State, later knit together a winning combination of regions, interest groups, and political doctrines to win the presidency in 1828. The Whigs succeeded the Federalists as the opposition party. By the time Van Buren followed Jackson in the White House in 1837, the Democrats had become a large, nationwide movement with national and state leadership, a clear party doctrine, and grass-roots organization. The Whigs were almost as strong; in 1840 they put their own man, General William Henry Harrison ("Old Tippecanoe") into the White House. A two-party system had been born, and we have had that two-party system ever since—one of few such systems worldwide.

1860: THE CIVIL WAR AND THE RISE OF THE REPUBLICANS Out of the crisis over slavery evolved a new party: the second Republican party—ultimately the "Grand Old Party" (GOP).[19] Abraham Lincoln was elected in 1860 with the support not only of financiers, industrialists, and merchants, but also of large numbers of workers and farmers. For 50 years after 1860, the Republican coalition won every presidential race except for Grover Cleveland's victories in 1884 and 1892. The Democratic party survived with its durable white male base in the South.

1896: A PARTY IN TRANSITION The Republican party's response to industrialization and hard times for farmers transformed it in the late 1800s. A combination of western and southern farmers and western mining interests sought an alliance with workers in the East and Midwest to "recapture America from the foreign moneyed interests responsible for industrialization. The crisis of industrialization squarely placed an agrarian-fundamentalist view of life against an industrial-progress view."[20] This realignment of 1896 differs from the others, however, in that the party in power did not change hands. In that sense it was a *converting realignment* because it reinforced the Republican majority status that had been in place since 1860.[21]

The Progressive era, the first two decades of the twentieth century, was a period of political reform led by the Progressive wing of the Republican party. Much of the agenda of the Progressives focused on the corrupt political parties. Civil service reforms shifted some of the patronage out of the hands of party officials. The direct primary election took control of nominations from party leaders and gave it to the rank-and-file. And in a number of cities, nonpartisan governments were instituted, totally eliminating the role of a party. With the ratification of the Seventeenth Amendment to the Constitution in 1913, United States senators came to be popularly elected. Women obtained the right to vote when the Nineteenth Amendment was ratified in 1920. Thus within a short time, the electorate changed, the rules changed, and even the stakes of the game changed. Democrats were unable to build a durable winning coalition during this time. In fact, they remained the minority party until the early 1930s, when the Hoover administration was overwhelmed by the Great Depression.

1932: FRANKLIN ROOSEVELT AND THE NEW DEAL ALIGNMENT The 1932 election was a turning point in American politics. In the 1930s the United States faced a devastating economic collapse. Between 1929 and 1932, the gross national product fell over 10 percent per year, and unemployment rose from 1.5 million to more than 15 million, with millions more working only part-time. Herbert Hoover and the Republican majority in Congress had responded to the

Depression by arguing that the problems with the economy were largely self-correcting and that their long-standing policy of ***laissez-faire***, a hands-off approach to the economy, was appropriate.

Voters wanted more. Franklin D. Roosevelt and the Democrats were swept into office in 1932 by a tide of anti-Hoover and anti-Republican sentiment. Roosevelt rode this wave and labeled his response to the Depression as the New Deal. He rejected *laissez-faire* economics and instead relied on **Keynesian economics**, which asserted that government could influence the direction of the economy through fiscal and monetary policy. After a century of sporadic government action, the New Dealers stepped in and fundamentally altered the relationship between government and society.

The central issue on which the Republicans and Democrats disagreed in this New Deal period was the role of government regarding the economy. Roosevelt Democrats argued that the government had to do something to pull the country out of the Depression. Republicans disagreed with enlarging the scope of government activity and its intrusion into the economy. This basic disagreement about whether the national government should play an active role in regulating and promoting our economy remains one of the most important divisions between the Democratic and Republican parties today, although, with time, the country and both parties accepted many of the New Deal programs. For the two decades following the 1932 election, the Republican party was relegated to watching the majority Democrats—a new coalition of union households, immigrant workers, and people hurt by the Great Depression—implement their domestic policies. During World War II, both parties cooperated in embracing a bipartisan foreign policy.

Some Realities about American Parties

- Parties began in this country as soon as people started taking sides in the debate over ratifying the U.S. Constitution, although it took a few years for them to organize into formal bodies.
- Political parties, and especially our two-party system, have persisted over the course of our history.
- Ours has almost always been a two-party system, differentiating us from most nations, which have a one-party or multiparty system.
- Since 1830 we have witnessed reasonably effective competition in our national party system.
- Our parties have historically been decentralized and fragmented. Parties are organized around states, congressional districts, counties, and cities, with state parties the most important units.
- Winning office and power have been more important to party leaders than specific issues or platforms; political parties in the United States are primarily organized to win and hold political power.
- Our parties can be characterized as moderate, centrist, and pragmatic, with only modest ideological cohesion and voting discipline, especially when compared to European political parties.

Divided Government

Major shifts in the demographics of the parties have occurred in recent decades. The once "Solid South" that Democrats could count on to bolster their legislative majorities and help win the White House has now become the "Solid Republican South" in presidential and increasingly in congressional elections as well. Republican congressional leaders in the 105th Congress—House Speaker Newt Gingrich of Georgia and Senate Majority Leader Trent Lott of Mississippi—both came from states that once rarely elected Republicans. This shift in the South is explained by the movement of whites out of the Democratic party, largely as a result of the party's position on civil rights. The rise of the Republican South reinforced the shift to conservatism in the Grand Old Party. And as the South became more Republican, the Northeast became more Democratic and is increasingly the home of the Democratic party. This shift, combined with the diminished ranks of conservative southern Democrats, made the Democratic party more unified and more liberal.

In recent years both parties have had to reconcile internal differences. For the Republicans it has been between liberal northeastern Republicans like Governors Christine Todd Whitman of New Jersey and William Weld of Massachusetts, and the dominant conservative wing. Bill Clinton was once a leader of the Democratic Leadership Council, a group preaching moderation in the Democratic party against the more liberal core of the party.

Not surprisingly, with the parties shifting their positions and appealing to new blocks of voters, there have also been shifts in election outcomes and a tendency toward a president of one party and a Congress controlled by the other. Since 1953, we have had this type of **divided government** twice as often as we have had one party in control of both legislative and executive branches. Until the 1994 election, the strength of the Republicans had been in presidential elections, where they often

laissez-faire
Doctrine opposing governmental interference in economic affairs beyond what is necessary to protect life and property.

Keynesian economics
Economic principles based on the principles advocated by John Maynard Keynes: increasing government spending during business slumps and curbing spending during booms.

divided government
Governance divided between the parties, especially when one controls the White House and the other controls Congress.

You Decide...

Would government work better without parties?

American government may be intensely partisan—some think much too partisan. In Congress the two parties have been locked in battle over legislation, investigations, and budget priorities. When legislators become intensely partisan, they become more concerned with advancing their own party's fortunes in the next election than with finding an acceptable compromise that would serve the public. And when there is divided government, with a governor or president from a party different from the legislative majority, that difference often leads to gridlock. Finally, partisanship in judicial or executive branch appointments means that qualified people may be excluded from consideration on the basis of party affiliation.

Would we be better off if we did not have political parties? Is intense partisanship destroying our political system?

won with landslide margins. Part of the explanation was their ability to attract popular candidates like Dwight Eisenhower and Ronald Reagan. Republicans also reaped the rewards of Democratic party divisiveness and generally weaker Democratic presidential candidates.

Republican victories in presidential elections between 1952 and 1992 had been achieved with the support of elements of Roosevelt's New Deal coalition. New Deal programs that benefited these voters had expanded the middle class and made possible the conservative "hold onto what we've got" thinking of voters in the 1980s and 1990s. Further evidence that voters are inclined to favor divided government came in the 1990s, when voters elected a Republican majority in 1994 and then retained it in 1996 and 1998.

American Parties Today

What is the state of political parties in the United States today? American parties are weak as organizations. Party leaders no longer make the most crucial decision in national party politics—the choice of the presidential nominee. This choice is made by voters in primary elections and precinct caucuses. Parties have also been weakened by the loss of patronage. Since the founding of the Republic, parties have operated within our system of separation of powers and checks and balances, which limits their ability to dominate our government.[22]

Americans are largely indifferent about political parties. If anything, most people are critical or even fearful of the major parties. Parties are, in a word, distrusted. Some see parties as corrupt institutions, interested only in the spoils of politics. Critics charge that the parties evade the issues; they fail to deliver on their promises; they have no new ideas; they follow public opinion rather than lead it; or they are just one more special interest.

Still, many Americans understand that parties are necessary. They want party labels kept on the ballot, think of themselves as Democrats or Republicans, and typically vote for candidates from their party. They even contribute millions of dollars to the two major parties. Far more individual contributions go to the Republicans than to the Democrats.[23] Thus Americans appreciate, at least vaguely, that you cannot run a big democracy without parties, or something like them.

Both the Democratic and Republican parties are moderate in their policies and leadership.[24] Each party usually takes its extremist supporters more or less for granted and seeks out the voters in the middle. Successful party leaders must be diplomatic; to win presidential elections and congressional majorities, they must find a middle ground among more or less hostile groups so that they can reach agreement on general principles.

Parties as Institutions

Political parties are organizations that seek political power by electing people to office so that their positions and philosophy become public policy. Like other institutions of American government—Congress, the presidency, the courts—parties have rules, procedures, and organizational structure, and they make policy. What are the institutional characteristics of political parties?

NATIONAL PARTY LEADERSHIP The supreme authority in both major parties is the **national party convention**, which meets every four years to nominate candidates for president and vice-president, to ratify the party platform, and to adopt rules. The delegates have only four days in which to accomplish their business, but many key decisions have been made ahead of time.

More directly in charge of the national party is the *national committee*. In recent years both parties have strengthened the role of the national committee and

political party
An organization that seeks political power by electing people to office so that its positions and philosophy become public policy.

national party convention
The national meeting of delegates elected in primaries, caucuses, or state conventions who assemble once every four years to nominate candidates for president and vice-president, ratify the party platform, elect officers, and adopt rules.

soft money
Money contributed for party-building purposes that does not have to be disclosed under federal law.

enhanced the influence of individual committee members. The committees are now more representative of the party rank-and-file. But in neither party is the national committee the center of party leadership.

Each major party has a *national chair* as its top official. The chair is formally elected by the national committee but in reality is the choice of the presidential nominee. Although chairs are the heads of their national party apparatus, they remain largely unknown to the voters. The chair may play a major role in running the national campaign; after the election, the power of the national chair of the victorious party tends to dwindle. Even though he or she serves as a liaison between the party and the White House, the chair actually serves at the pleasure of the president and does the president's bidding. The chair of the party without an incumbent president has considerable independence, yet works closely with the party's congressional leadership. The national committee usually elects a new head after electoral defeats.

In addition to the national party committees, there are also congressional and senatorial *campaign committees*. Senatorial campaign committees are composed of senators chosen for two-year terms by their fellow party members in the Senate; congressional campaign committees are chosen in the same manner by the House. The chairs of these committees, appointed by their party leadership, have much more to say about which candidates get campaign funds. In recent years congressional campaign committees have become very active, recruiting candidates, training them, and assisting with campaign finance.[25] In the 1998 elections the congressional campaign committees, following the lead of the national party committees in previous presidential elections, raised unprecedented amounts of **soft money**, contributions that are unlimited and which can be targeted to states with the most competitive races. Soft money is spent in the most competitive races where it makes the biggest difference. The party committee leaders who make these allocations have grown in power as the amounts of soft money raised have grown. Party committee leaders effectively used the close party balance, especially in the House of Representatives, to justify their soft money spending decisions.

National party organizations are often agents of an incumbent president in securing his renomination. When there is not an incumbent president seeking reelection, the national party committee is generally neutral until the nominee is selected. Although heated primary contests often preclude having a united party in the general election, national parties are helpless to prevent them.[26]

PARTIES AT THE GRASS ROOTS The two major parties are decentralized, organized around elections in states, cities, or congressional districts. Like the government itself, they have national, state, and local organizations. Party organization at the state and local levels is structured much like the national level. Each state has a *state committee* headed by a *state chair*. State law determines the composition of the state committees and sets rules regulating them. Members of state committees are usually elected from local areas. Party auxiliaries such as the Young Democrats or the Federation of Republican Women are sometimes represented as well. In many states these committees are dominated by governors, senators, or coalitions of local elected business and ethnic leaders. State chairs are normally elected by the state committees, although approximately one-quarter are chosen at state conventions. When the party controls the governorship, chairs are often agents of the governor, but some can remain independent.[27]

Some powerful state parties have developed in recent years. Despite much state-to-state variation, the trend is toward stronger state organizations, with Republicans typically much better funded.[28] In some states, third and fourth parties play a role in local elections. New York, for instance, has both a Liberal party and a Conservative party in addition to Democratic and Republican parties. The role minor parties play in statewide elections can be important, even though they rarely win office themselves.

Former Colorado Governor Roy Romer was the Democratic National Committee Chair from 1996 to 1998.

Jim Nicholson is the Republican National Committee Chair.

Thinking it Through...

It is naive to believe that the removal of parties will negate conflict, self-interest, or ambition. A political system without parties would be a society without the means to deal with disagreements over policies, economics, or social values. Americans expect legislators to be partisan, to be contentious, and to make the most of partisan opportunities. Divided government may be inefficient, but that clearly has not bothered voters, who routinely elect legislators from one party and governors or presidents from another. Finally, people with judicial or administrative ambitions understand the role that parties play in appointments, giving them an incentive to get involved in a party. This is not all bad because, as we have seen, it is possible for idealistic individuals to redefine and reshape a party.

Below the state committees are *county committees*, which vary widely in function and power. The key role of these committees is recruiting candidates for such offices as county commissioner, sheriff, and treasurer. The recruiting job often involves finding a candidate for the office, not deciding among competing contenders. For a party that rarely wins an election, the county committee has to struggle to find someone willing to run. When the job is valued by those seeking it, however, primaries, not the party leaders, usually decide the winner.[29] Many county organizations maintain a significant level of activity, distributing campaign literature, organizing telephone campaigns, putting up posters and lawn signs, and canvassing door-to-door. Other county committees do not function at all, and many party leaders are just figureheads.

In recent elections the efforts of state and county organizations have been aided by financial assistance from the party's national committee, which has distributed millions of dollars in soft money. This money must be spent for the benefit of the party rather than for a particular congressional, senatorial, or presidential candidate.

Both parties made soft money a major priority in the 1996 presidential election. Bill Clinton and Bob Dole effectively used soft money to set the stage for the fall campaign and to supplement their hard dollar allocation for the general election campaign. Soon after the Democratic victory, questionable fund-raising practices became the subject of considerable press attention. After months of investigations in both houses of Congress, nothing was done to change the soft money loophole exploited by parties.

As the parties entered the 1998 midterm election, both made raising soft money for congressional elections a high priority. In the past, soft money had been more important in presidential elections than congressional elections. The Republicans wanted soft money in the hands of the party committees to permit the party to respond to advertising by organized labor and other Democratic allies. The Democrats, building on Clinton's proven success as a soft money fund raiser, saw soft money as a key to winning back a congressional majority. In 1998, as in 1996, the Republicans raised substantially more soft money than the Democrats, but the Democrats appeared to put the money to better use.

What are the implications of this surge in soft money in both parties? First, because soft money contributions are unlimited, the priority given to raising soft money has elevated the importance of the large contributor. The post-Watergate reforms had lessened the power of wealthy individuals because they could give only $50,000 in total political contributions to candidates or parties in a two-year period. With the soft money loophole, such individuals could give unlimited amounts. Parties now rely heavily on these large donors.

A second implication is that those who allocate soft money are now very powerful because they can move more money into a race than a candidate could have raised in months of fund raising. Decisions about which races will be targets for soft money spending are critical in an election outcome. Looking ahead to future elections, both parties see targeting soft money resources to competitive races as an essential electoral strategy.

It is not clear that soft money transfers to state parties build stronger parties at the state and local level. Some soft money spending may enhance such party activities as building a list of active partisans in the state or district, improving the computer technology of the party offices, or secondary benefits when party supporters are mobilized for a U.S. Senate or U.S. House race. But for most soft money spending, the state parties simply become local bank accounts for candidate endorsements.

One possible benefit of soft money would be strengthening parties at the grass-roots level. At the base of the party pyramid—at the city, town, ward, and precinct level—we find the grass roots of the party, if we find any party activity at all.

THE ROLE OF CONVENTIONS

Every four years since 1856 both major parties have held conventions to nominate candidates for president and vice-president. Conventions bring together delegates from the state parties to represent the wishes of their voters. Successful conventions build party unity, mobilize support for the party nominees, and capture the interest and attention of the nation. Conventions also decide on rules and regulations governing the party, deciding controversies surrounding delegate selection (credentials) and party platforms.

The 1968 Democratic National Convention in Chicago will long be remembered for the more than ten thousand protesters who came to Chicago to oppose the war in Vietnam. Televised images of Chicago police using tear gas and night sticks to disperse the crowd not only hurt the Democrats in 1968 but meant neither party held a convention in Chicago for the following twenty-eight years. Security concerns were high because earlier in 1968 Martin Luther King and Robert Kennedy had been assassinated.

The intense battle in the streets of Chicago carried over onto the convention floor as delegates debated the Vietnam plank of the party platform into the early hours of the morning. Civil rights issues nearly tore the Democratic party apart as some Southern states still had all-white delegations to the convention. African American delegates sought recognition, and the convention voted to seat some of them over the protest of the white delegates. The party remained badly divided after the Chicago convention and later changed its rules to encourage greater diversity in delegations and more extensive use of direct primaries.

Who attends conventions? Delegates come from all walks of life, yet many are former party leaders or public officials. Republican delegates are more likely to be male than their Democrat counterparts. Democratic delegates at the 1996 convention were roughly 30 percent from minority backgrounds, compared to 6.7 percent for Republican delegates.

Aside from the candidates and delegates, the most important people at the conventions are journalists and TV reporters. Thousands from all over the world view these festivities. The parties have an interest in getting a positive "spin" out of the convention, so they work hard to manage the news coverage. Reporters, on the other hand, have an interest in stirring up controversy.

Because the choice of the party nominees has been decided well before the convention, there has been relatively little controversy on the floor of the conventions in recent years. The parties have turned to theatrics and celebrities in an effort to boost the audience watching the televised conventions. They have also shortened the proceedings on network television coverage to only a few hours in the evening. Even with these changes, audience share continued to drop in 1996.

Why continue to hold conventions? One reason is that some day we may again have an election in which there is no clear winner in the preconvention process. If that happens, the party needs to select its nominee, and the convention would accomplish that purpose. But if the public and media continue to lose interest in conventions, they may well be replaced with some other means of deciding essential party business.

A young protester is confronted by national guard troops that had been called in to quell the street demonstrations during the 1968 Democratic convention.

Delegates on the Republican Party Platform Committee rise to vote against an amendment that would have moderated the party's strong opposition to abortion rights.

Strong local party organization is rare. Most local committees are poorly financed and inactive except during the few weeks before election day.[30] In a few places, local ward and precinct leaders still do favors for constituents, from fixing parking tickets, to organizing clambakes, to obtaining horse-racing passes in a state like Arkansas.

Party Platforms

The typical **party platform**—the official statement of party policy—is often a vague and ponderous document that hardly anyone reads. Platforms are ambiguous by design, giving voters few obvious reasons to vote against the party. This generalization about party platforms does not mean that political parties do not stand for anything. Thus most business and professional people believe the Republican party best serves their interests, while working people tend to look to the Democrats to speak for them. The proportion of voters discerning important differences between the parties increased sharply in recent years, as the parties became more polarized.[31]

Many politicians contend platforms rarely help elect anybody, but platform positions can hurt a presidential candidate. Because the platform-writing process is not always controlled by the nominee, it is possible for presidential candidates to disagree with their own party platform. Jimmy Carter ended up with a platform in 1980 that was more liberal than his administration had been.[32] But the platform-drafting process gives partisans, especially those motivated by particular issues, an opportunity to express their views, and it serves to identify the most important values and principles upon which the two parties are based.

Once elected, politicians are rarely reminded of what their platform position was on a given issue. One major exception to this was President George Bush's promise not to raise taxes if elected in 1988 with his memorable "Read my lips—no new taxes." Bush was forced to eat those words when taxes were raised. Clinton had to backpedal on his 1992 promise that if elected he would lower taxes on the middle class; his budget and tax recommendations raised taxes on wealthy Americans but did not lower taxes on the middle class. The Republican Contract with America in 1994 was an explicit set of promises that became the focus of legislative activity in 1995 and 1996, when Republicans took control of both houses of Congress for the first time in 40 years, but only a limited number of the legislative provisions of the Contract were actually enacted.[33]

Party platforms in 1996 were carefully controlled by the Dole and Clinton campaigns and were largely designed to minimize problems for the candidates in their general election campaigns. The Democratic platform, for example, stressed opportunity, responsibility, security, freedom, peace, and community. Like apple pie and motherhood, these were not issues delegates or voters were likely to oppose. The platform spelled out the Democrats' commitment to improving education, guaranteeing economic security for families, fighting crime, and strengthening national security. In part because Bill Clinton so thoroughly dominated his party's nomination process, the document provided no targets for Republican attacks. Differences between 1996 Democratic and Republican platforms are highlighted in Table 10-2.

Many parts of the Republican platform were also intended to reinforce broad areas of political consensus, but the Republican platform of 1996 was more explicit in its discussion of social issues. The GOP platform opposed same-sex marriages, supported California's Proposition 209 to eliminate affirmative action programs in the public sector, and called for the abolition of the Department of Education. The most contentious issue in the 1996 Republican platform deliberations was abortion.

party platform
The official statement of party policy.

TABLE 10-2 Key Party Differences: Excerpts from Republican and Democratic Party Platforms, 1996

Issue	Democratic	Republican
Taxes	America cannot afford to return to the era of "something-for-nothing tax cuts." Supports a "$500 tax cut for children" and additional reductions for college tuition payments, small businesses, and the self-employed. Allows money in individual retirement accounts to be used to buy a first home and to pay education and medical expenses.	Supports a 15 percent reduction in tax rates, a $500-per-child tax credit, a 50 percent cut in the capital gains rate, expansion of Individual Retirement Accounts (IRAs), and lower taxes on Social Security benefits. These are "interim steps toward comprehensive tax reform." The Internal Revenue Service "must be dramatically downsized."
Balanced budget	Promises to balance the budget by 2002.	Supports a constitutional amendment requiring a balanced budget.
Economy	"Today, America is moving forward. The economy is stronger, the deficit is lower, and the government is smaller."	"We cannot go on like this. For millions of families, the American dream is fading."
Education	Supports strengthening public schools.	Favors using federal money to help parents pay private-school tuition.
Environment	Emphasizes government regulation to protect the environment.	Emphasizes consideration of private property rights and economic development in conjunction with environmental protection.
Foreign affairs	Opposes revival of the land-based missile defense system known as Star Wars (Strategic Defense Initiative). In the area of trade, insists that international trade agreements include standards to protect children, workers, and the environment.	Favors development of the Strategic Defense Initiative missile defense system. In the area of trade, opposes using trade policy to pursue "social agenda items."
Gun control	Supports a waiting period for buying handguns and a ban on the sale of certain assault weapons.	Defends "the constitutional right to keep and bear arms" and favors mandatory penalties for crimes committed with guns.
Homosexuality	Supports attempts "to end discrimination against gay men and lesbians, and further their full inclusion in the life of the nation."	Rejects the "distortion" of civil rights laws that would "cover sexual preference."
Immigration	Would permit the children of illegal immigrants to attend public schools, allow legal immigrants to receive welfare and other benefits, and make it easier for eligible immigrants to become United States citizens.	Would prohibit the children of illegal immigrants from attending public schools and restrict welfare to legal immigrants. Supports a constitutional amendment denying automatic citizenship to children born in the United States to illegal immigrants and legal immigrants who are in this country for a short time.
Abortion	Supports a woman's right to choose to have an abortion in all circumstances currently legal. "Respect the individual conscience of each American on this difficult issue."	Supports a constitutional amendment that would outlaw abortion in all circumstances. Only mention of tolerance for other views on abortion is in an appendix at the end of the platform.
Affirmative action	"We should mend it, not end it."	"We will attain our nation's goal of equal rights without quotas or other forms of preferential treatment."

SOURCE: Based on "Party Platforms: How They Compare," *The New York Times*, August 27, 1996, p. A11.

Republican platforms between 1976 and 1992 had endorsed a human-life constitutional amendment making abortion illegal. Prominent Republican governors like William Weld of Massachusetts, Pete Wilson of California, and Christine Todd Whitman of New Jersey pushed the party to moderate this language in 1996. Nominee Bob Dole wanted to come part way to meet the concerns of these influential Republican moderates. Rather than modify the language of the platform, the

Republicans added a clause in the appendix to the platform that expressed "tolerance" for differing views on abortion.

Both parties have considerable ideological diversity. The Democratic umbrella encompasses the conservative Coalition for a Democratic Majority, the moderate Democratic Leadership Council (dominated by an array of southern governors and senators), and the liberal Americans for Democratic Action. The Democratic coalition embraces activists in the civil rights and other liberal-left movements. Republicans, while more homogeneous, have their contentious factions as well. On the more conservative side are the Religious Right, staunch supporters of the right to bear arms, and antitax activists. More moderate Republican conservatives include governors in northeastern and midwestern states who may be pro-choice on abortion and favor some limits on gun ownership.

Parties in Government

Despite the organizational weakness of political parties, they remain central to the operation of government in the United States. Party organizations play a more important role after the election in the operation of government than they play in the elections.

IN THE LEGISLATIVE BRANCH Members of Congress take their partisanship seriously, at least while they are in Washington. Their power and influence are determined by whether their party is in control of the House or Senate; they also have a stake in which party controls the White House. The chairs of all standing committees in Congress come from the majority party, as do the presiding officials of both chambers. Members of both houses sit together with fellow partisans on the floor and in committee, leading to the expression often heard in floor debate, "the other side of the aisle."

Members of congressional staffs are also partisan. From the volunteer intern to the senior staffer, members of Congress expect their staff to be loyal first to them and then to their party. Should you decide to go to work for a representative or senator, you would be expected to identify yourself with that person's party, and you would have some difficulty working for the other party later. Employees of the House and Senate—from elevator operators to the Capitol Hill police and even including the chaplain—hold patronage jobs. With few exceptions, such jobs go to persons from the party that has a majority in the House or the Senate.

IN THE EXECUTIVE BRANCH Presidents select almost all senior White House staff and cabinet members from their own party. However, it is not unusual for them to chose one or two advisers or cabinet members from the opposition party, as Clinton did when he picked a former Republican senator from Maine, William Cohen, to be his secretary of defense. Presidents, however, typically surround themselves with advisers who have campaigned with them and proven their loyalty.

Partisanship is also important in presidential appointments to the highest levels of the federal bureaucracy. The party that wins the White House has more than 4,000 noncareer positions to fill.[34] Included in these positions are cabinet-level appointments and ambassadorships around the world. Party commitment, including making campaign contributions, is expected of those who seek these positions.

IN THE JUDICIAL BRANCH The judicial branch of the national government, with its lifetime tenure and political independence, is designed to operate in an expressly nonpartisan manner. Judges, unlike Congress, do not sit together by political party. But the appointment process for judges has been partisan from the beginning. The landmark case establishing the principle of judicial review, *Marbury v Madison* (1803), concerned the efforts of one party to stack the judiciary with fellow partisans before leaving office. Today party remains an important consideration in the naming of federal judges. While the party of a judicial nominee is not called for on any form,

party registration
The act of declaring party affiliation; in some states required when one registers to vote.

those responsible for the screening and evaluating of candidates certainly take party and ideology into account. Appointees must be acceptable to certain power centers in the party. For example, Republicans in the Reagan and Bush administrations insisted on conservative judges; Clinton gave more emphasis to gender and race than to ideology in selecting judges.

STATE AND LOCAL LEVELS The importance of party in the operation of local government varies among states and localities. In some states, such as New York and Illinois, local parties play an even stronger role than they do at the national level. In others, such as Nebraska, parties play almost no role. In Nebraska, the state legislature is expressly nonpartisan, though factions perform like parties and still play a role. Parties are likewise unimportant in the government of most city councils. But in most states and many cities, parties are important to the operation of the legislature, governor, or mayor. Judicial selection in most states is also a partisan matter.

Parties in the Electorate

Political parties would be of little significance if they did not have meaning to the electorate. Adherents of the two parties are drawn to them by a combination of factors: stand on issues; personal or party history; religious, racial, or social peer grouping; attractiveness of candidates. The emphases among these factors change over time, but they are remarkably consistent with those identified by political scientists more than 40 years ago.[35]

PARTY REGISTRATION For citizens in most states, "party" has a particular legal meaning—**party registration**. At the time voters register to vote in these states, they are asked to state their party preference. They then become registered Democrats, Republicans, Libertarians, or whatever. Voters can subsequently change their party registration. The purpose of party registration is to limit the participants in primary elections to members of that party and to make it easier for parties to contact people who might vote for their party.

PARTY ACTIVISTS This group tends to fall into three broad categories: party regulars, candidate activists, and issue

WE THE PEOPLE

Portrait of the Electorate

	Republican	Democrat	Independent
Sex			
Male	**41**	**49**	**10**
Female	35	54	11
Race			
White	42	47	11
Black	7	86	7
Hispanic	32	60	8
Age			
18–34	40	49	11
35–45	42	46	12
46–55	37	52	11
56–64	32	61	6
65+	31	58	10
Income			
Less than $10,000	34	54	12
$10,000–$19,999	29	62	9
$20,000–$29,999	35	53	12
$30,000–$39,999	32	54	14
$40,000–$59,999	37	53	10
$60,000+	48	42	10
Religion			
Protestant	41	51	8
Catholic	38	52	10
Jewish	18	82	0
Ideology			
Liberal	14	81	5
Moderate/DK	30	56	15
Conservative	67	28	5
Region			
Northeast	36	48	16
Northcentral	38	53	9
South	39	51	10
West	35	56	9
Total	**37**	**52**	**11**

Source: *1998 American National Election Study*, Center for Political Studies, University of Michigan.

How to Tell 'em Apart

- Republicans usually wear hats. Democrats usually don't.
- Democrats buy banned books. Republicans form censorship committees and read them.
- Democrats eat the fish they catch. Republicans hang them on the wall.
- Republicans study the financial pages of the newspaper. Democrats put them on the bottom of the bird cage.
- On Saturday, Republicans head for the golf course, the yacht club, or the hunting lodge. Democrats get a haircut, wash the car, or go bowling.
- Republicans have guest rooms. Democrats have spare rooms filled with old baby furniture.
- Republicans hire exterminators. Democrats step on the bugs.
- Republicans sleep in twin beds—some even in separate rooms. That is why there are more Democrats.

SOURCE: The National Republican Congressional Committee Newsletter.

activists. *Party regulars* place the party first. They value winning elections and understand that compromise and moderation may be necessary to reach that objective. They also realize that it is important to keep the party together as much as possible, because a fractured party only helps the opposition.

Candidate activists are followers of a particular candidate who see the party as the means to place their candidate in power. Candidate activists are often not concerned with the other operations of the party—with nominees for other offices or with raising money for the party. For example, people who supported David Duke in his Louisiana contest for governor and his unsuccessful run for the presidency in 1992 would be classified as candidate activists. Duke, a former Ku Klux Klan leader with an antiblack and anti-Semitic record, disavowed his past in hopes of becoming governor of Louisiana. While ultimately losing the gubernatorial election, he generated national attention. Candidate activists like those who supported Duke fade in interest and involvement when their candidate loses and leaves the political scene.

Issue activists wish to push the parties in a particular direction on a single issue or narrow range of issues: abortion, taxes, school prayer, the environment, or civil rights. To issue activists, the party platform is an important battleground because they seek the party endorsement for their position. Issue activists are also often candidate activists if they can find a candidate willing to embrace their position.

Both issue activists and candidate activists insist on making their "statement" regardless of the electoral consequences. They prefer to lose the election rather than compromise. Party activists thus include a diverse group of people who come to the political party with different objectives. It is not surprising, then, that some of the most interesting politics you will observe are over candidate selection and issue positions within the political parties. Fights over strategy and party position are conducted in open meetings and under democratic procedures. Political parties foster democracy not only by competition *between* the parties but *within* the parties as well.

Party Identification

The vast majority of Americans are mere spectators of party activity. They lack the partisan commitment and interest needed for this level of involvement. This is not to say that parties are irrelevant or unimportant to them. For them, partisanship is what political scientists call **party identification**—an informal and subjective affiliation with a political party that most people acquire in childhood, a standing preference for one party over another.[36] This type of voter may sometimes vote for a candidate from the other party, yet in the absence of a compelling reason to do otherwise, most will vote according to their party identification. Party identification, generally acquired from parents, is reinforced by peers and early political experiences. It is part of the political socialization process described in Chapter 7.

Party identification is measured by the answers to the following questions:

> Generally speaking, in politics do you usually think of yourself as a Republican, a Democrat, an Independent, or what?

Persons who answer Republican or Democrat to this question are then asked:

> Would you call yourself a strong or a not very strong Republican/Democrat?

Persons who answered Independent to the first question are asked this follow-up question:

> Do you think of yourself as closer to the Republican or the Democratic party?

party identification
An informal and subjective affiliation with a political party that most people acquire in childhood.

Persons who did not indicate Democrat, Republican, or Independent to the first question rarely exceed 2 percent of the electorate and include persons who are apolit-

TABLE 10-3 **Party Identification, 1950s to 1990s**

Decade	Strong Democrat	Weak Democrat	Independent-Leaning Democrat	Independent	Independent-Leaning Republican	Weak Republican	Strong Republican	Apolitical
1950s*	23.3%	23.3%	7.6%	7.3%	6.7%	15%	13.3%	3.7%
1960s	21.6	25.2	8.2	9.8	7	14.8	11.8	2
1970s	16.6	24	12	14	9.6	14	8.8	1.6
1980s	18.2	26.2	11	11.6	10.8	14.4	11.2	2.2
1990s	17.6	18.8	13	10.2	12	15.2	12.8	1.4

SOURCE: American National Election Studies, Center for Political Studies, University of Michigan.

Note: data may not sum to 100% due to averaged data.

*1950s percentages based on years 1952, 1956, 1958.

ical or who identify with one of the minor political parties. Because of their consistently small numbers, they are typically not very important to election outcomes.

Party identification questionnaires produce seven categories of persons: Strong Democrats, Weak Democrats, Independent-leaning Democrats, Pure Independents, Independent-leaning Republicans, Weak Republicans, and Strong Republicans. Over the 40-year period during which political scientists have been conducting such surveys, the partisan preferences of the American public have been remarkably stable. Table 10-3 presents the party identification breakdown for the period from the 1950s to the 1990s.

Party identification is the single best predictor of how people will vote. Unlike candidates and issues, which come and go, party identification is a long-term element in voting choice. The strength of party identification is also important in predicting participation and political interest. Strong Republicans and Strong Democrats participate more actively in politics than any other groups and are generally more knowledgeable and informed. Pure Independents are just the opposite; they vote at the lowest rates and have the lowest levels of interest and awareness of any of the categories of party identification. This evidence runs counter to the notion that persons who are strong partisans are unthinking party adherents.[37]

Partisan Realignment and Dealignment

The current system of party identification is built upon a foundation of the New Deal and the critical election of 1932, events that took place nearly 70 years ago. How can events so removed from the present still be important in shaping our party system? When will there be another realignment—an election that dramatically changes the voters' partisan identification? Whether a realignment has occurred is frequently debated in the literature of political science, but most researchers believe we have not experienced any major realignment since 1932.[38] Partisan identification for the past four decades has been stable, and while new voters have been added to the electorate—minorities and 18-to-21-year-olds—the basic character of the party system has not changed dramatically.

In presidential voting, Republicans have done well, winning five of the last eight presidential elections. Bill Clinton's victories in 1992 and 1996 demonstrated, however, that Democrats could assemble a winning coalition. Many so-called Reagan Democrats returned to the Democratic party to vote for Bill Clinton, especially in heavily populated states. Although people may not be changing their underlying party preference, they seem willing to vote for candidates from the other party: Democrats have supported Republicans, and people defected from both parties to vote for Ross Perot in 1992. Perot's support waned in 1996, and many voters returned to their underlying partisan preferences in presidential voting.

"Very Republican. I love it."

dealignment
Change in the composition of the electorate or its partisan preferences that points to a rejection of both major parties and a rise in the number of Independents.

Possible evidence of a voting realignment came in the early 1980s, when Republicans won several close Senate elections and gained a majority in that body. Democrats, however, won back the Senate in 1986, and until 1994 they appeared to have a permanent majority in the House. All that changed with the 1994 election, as Republicans were swept into office on a tidal wave of victories. Republicans made major inroads in the South and strengthened their share of the vote among white males.

The 1998 election gave the Democrats renewed hope that they could regain control of Congress, or at least the House of Representatives, in the 2000 elections. Overcoming their worst fears that the Clinton/Lewinsky scandal would enlarge the Republican majorities in the Senate and House, the Democrats effectively mobilized their core voters and actually picked up five seats in the House of Representatives. Allies of the Democratic party like organized labor were also encouraged by gains they saw in 1998. Republicans were disheartened by the congressional election outcome but pointed to their strength in several key governorships as cause for optimism about regaining control of the White House in 2000. Moreover, if they could retain their majorities in the House and Senate in 2000, they would achieve Republican control of both houses and the presidency for the first time in 43 years.

The 1990s can thus be characterized as a decade in which voters did not demonstrate a consistent preference for one party over the other. In a time of such electoral volatility and low turnout, the winners and losers are determined by basics of politics: who turns out their vote, who strikes a theme that motivates voters to participate, or who does a better job in communicating with the voters. Party identification remains important for those voters who come out to vote, and strength of partisanship remains positively correlated with turnout. There are few signs of a realignment but there are signs of disengagement.

Some think that, instead of a realignment, we are experiencing the rejection of partisanship in favor of becoming Independents, and there has indeed been an increase in the number of persons who characterize themselves as Independents. Journalist Hedrick Smith expresses a widespread view: "The most important phenomenon of American politics in the past quarter century has been the rise of independent voters who have at times outnumbered Republicans."[39]

The **dealignment** argument—that people have abandoned both parties to become Independents—would be more persuasive were it not that two-thirds of all Independents are really partisans in their voting behavior and attitudes. One third of those who claim to be Independents lean toward the Democratic party and vote Democratic election after election. Another third of Independents lean toward Republicans and just as predictably vote Republican. The remaining third, who

TABLE 10-4 Voting Behavior of Partisans and Independents, 1992–1998

	Percent Democratic Vote				
	President		U.S. House		
	1992	1996	1994	1996	1998
Strong Democrats	93%	96%	88%	87%	77%
Weak Democrats	68	82	73	70	57
Independent-leaning Democrats	70	76	68	69	63
Pure Independents	41	35	55	41	41
Independent-leaning Republicans	11	20	25	21	24
Weak Republicans	14	20	21	21	25
Strong Republicans	3	5	7	3	7

SOURCE: 1998 *American National Election Study*, Center for Political Studies, University of Michigan.

appear to be genuine Independents and who do not vote predictably for one party, turn out to be people with little interest in politics. Despite the reported growth in Independents, there were proportionately about the same number of Pure Independents in 1992 as there were in 1956.[40] There are, in short, at least three types of Independents, and most of them are predictably partisan. Table 10-4 summarizes voting behavior in contests for president in 1992 and 1996 and for U.S. House of Representatives in 1994, 1996, and 1998.

Because most Independents are really closet partisans in their voting behavior and have been so for a long time, much of the case for the dealignment theory fails. Something about the parties inhibits most Independents from labeling themselves as partisans. However, it is a mistake to assume that all Independents see the political world in similar terms and constitute a monolithic force. There are instead at least three groups, and most of them are predictably partisan.

Why has realignment moved so slowly? Why aren't all conservatives now happily ensconced in the Republican party and all liberals gladly lodged in the Democratic party? Americans do not casually cross party lines. If you grew up in a conservative New Hampshire family whose forebears voted Republican for a century, you are pretty much conditioned to stay with the GOP. Even if that party took a direction you disliked, you might continue to register as a Republican but quietly vote Democratic to avoid friction in the family. Or if you come from a "yellow dog" Democratic family in Texas (meaning your family would vote for a "yellow dog" before it would vote for a Republican), you might continue to vote for Democrats locally even though you disliked various Democratic candidates for president or senator. Evidence indicates that this pattern is common throughout the South.

The other reason for slow realignment is the local nature of the parties. For decades, conservative Democrats in the South have been voting for Republican candidates for president—not only Dole and Reagan but Nixon and even Eisenhower—without changing their identification from the Democratic party to the Republican. Why? Partly because they still see themselves as Democrats, but also because the Democratic party remains much stronger at the state and local level in the South. So if candidates and voters want to have an impact on local politics, in which the only meaningful elections may be in the Democratic primaries, they retain their Democratic affiliation.

Are the Political Parties Dying?

Critics of the American party system make three allegations against it: (1) parties do not take meaningful and contrasting positions on issues, especially the issues of the 1990s; (2) party membership is essentially meaningless; and (3) parties are so concerned with accommodating those on the middle of the ideological spectrum that they are incapable of serving as an avenue for social progress. Are these statements true, and if true, are they important?

Some experts fear parties are so weak they may be mortally ill, or at least in a severe decline. They point first to the long-run impact of the Progressive reforms early in this century, reforms that robbed party organizations of their control of the nomination process by allowing masses of independent and "uninformed" voters to enter the primaries and vote for candidates who might not be acceptable to party leaders. They also point to nonpartisan elections in cities and towns and the staggering of national, state, and local elections that made it harder for parties to influence the election process.

Legislation limiting the viability and functions of parties was bad enough, say the party pessimists, but parties suffer from further ills today. The rise of television and electronic technology and the parallel rise in campaign, media, and direct-mail consultants may have made parties irrelevant in educating, mobilizing, and organizing the electorate. These new media have strengthened the role of candidates and lessened the role of parties. (See Chapter 13 for more on the media in this role.)

Advocates of strong parties concede parts of this diagnosis may be correct: the demise of political machines at the local level, the decline in strong partisan affiliations, the weakness of grass-roots party membership. Yet they also see signs of party revival. The national party organizations—the national committees and the congressional and senatorial campaign committees—are significantly better funded than they were in earlier days; they even own permanent, modern headquarters in Washington, D.C. Moreover, the parties are more capable of providing assistance to candidates and to state and local party organizations because of their strong financial base from political contributions and because they have defined their role as providing expertise to those who need it but cannot otherwise obtain it. Optimists hope these services will give the national parties some leverage over the positions that candidates and officeholders take on party issues.[41]

During the first years of the Reagan administration, the Republican party demonstrated a remarkable cohesiveness in Congress on issues of importance to the president's program. This trend can be measured by the *party unity score*, defined as the percentage of members of a party who vote together on roll call votes in Congress on which a majority of the members of one party vote against a majority of the members of the other party. Clinton had higher party unity scores from his party in 1993 than any party gave its president in the past 40 years; 88 percent of the Democrats voted together, while 87 percent of the Republicans voted together.[42] Clinton needed the strong support of his party in key votes on the budget and tax proposals, but he also benefited from strong Republican support on the NAFTA vote. During the Republican-controlled 105th Congress, House and Senate Republicans voted together 89 percent of the time—a new all-time high. Democrats in both houses were less unified than they had been in Clinton's first two years in office, dropping to 80 percent in the House and 83 percent in the Senate.[43] Thus, while rank-and-file voters do not seem to be returning to strong partisan ties, party organizations and the party in government do show significant signs of strength.[44]

Reform Among the Democrats

A wave of party reform occurred after the 1968 election, when the Democrats, responding to the disarray during their Chicago convention and disputes about the fairness of delegate selection procedures, agreed to a process that led to greater use of direct primaries and greater representation of younger voters, women, and minorities as elected delegates. Another reform was the abolition of the rule that a winner of a state's convention or primaries got all the state's delegates (the *unit rule*). This rule was replaced by a system of *proportionality* in which candidates won delegates in rough proportion to the votes they received in the primary election.

Chicago's mayor Richard Daley, father of the current mayor of Chicago, and many other party stalwarts argued that these reforms would make the party reflective of the views of college professors and intellectuals, and not working-class people, unionists, the elderly, and elected officials. Responding to this criticism, the party created "superdelegate" positions for elected officials and party leaders.

Reform Among the Republicans

Republicans were not immune to criticism that their party conventions and party procedures were keeping out the rank-and-file. They did not make changes as drastic as those made by the Democrats, but they did give the national committee more control over presidential campaigns, and state parties were urged to encourage broader participation by all groups, including women, minorities, youth, and the poor. While making these concessions to reformers within their own party, Republicans put more emphasis on improving the party structure and finances.

The Republican party entered the 1980s with a party organization far superior to that of the Democrats. The GOP emphasized grass-roots organization and membership recruitment. Seminars were held to teach Republican candidates how to make speeches and hold press conferences, and weekend conferences were organized for training young professionals. Both parties now conduct training sessions for candidates on campaign planning, advertising, fund raising, using phone banks, recruiting volunteers, and campaign scheduling.[45]

Soft Money and Stronger Parties

The outcry over President Clinton and Vice-President Gore's campaign fund raising in 1995 and 1996 and the ensuing congressional investigations reinforced public cynicism over the role of money in politics, but because the system so clearly benefits incumbents of both parties, Congress had little incentive to change. Over the objections of the House leadership, the House enacted modest campaign finance reform, but the legislation was killed by filibusters in the Senate in 1998.

Our election system now lacks candidate accountability for the content and tone of the campaign. The parties can spend unlimited and largely undisclosed amounts of soft money, and the candidate that benefits can deny any role in the message. Accountability is also diminished by the large amounts of money spent by interest groups supporting one candidate or opposing another. Some groups are prepared to spend large amounts of money on advertisements, a factor that requires candidates to raise even more money so they have the resources to respond to them.

One political consequence of this outside money in elections may be to encourage incumbents to enact reform because these outside ads make them more vulnerable to attack. If the system is not changed, we will almost certainly see more expensive campaigns and an increasingly negative tone to campaigning.

online POLITICS

Parties Online

Our major and minor parties now have websites where you can learn about the party, its platform, and its issue positions. The sites are interactive in the sense that you can volunteer for a host of party activities. A constant of party home pages is fund raising—both directly through contributions and indirectly by purchasing party paraphernalia.

Democratic party activists use the Internet as a means of mobilizing people to party causes. Calling themselves "Digital Democrats," they provide an online newsletter and make available a software package called Precinct Walker, which helps manage a precinct, ward, or neighborhood and provides information on recruiting volunteers, raising funds, identifying voters, processing absentee ballot requests, and managing get-out-the-vote efforts. You can also register to vote through their site:

http://www.digitals.org/digitals/

Republicans ask visitors to their Website to sign the official Petition for Balancing the Budget and Real Tax Cuts. Republicans provide a frequently updated survey to get feedback from the party faithful on policy issues.

If you would like to volunteer for a party, you can do so through party home pages:

http://www.rnc.org/ or www.republicanweb.com

http://www.democrats.org/

http://www.reformparty.org

http://www.libertarian.org

For more Internet resources on Political Parties, see our home page:

http://www.prenhall.com/burns

SUMMARY

1. Political parties are essential to democracy—simplifying voting choices, organizing the competition, unifying the electorate, helping to organize government by bridging the separation of powers and fostering cooperation among branches of government, translating public preferences into policy, and providing loyal opposition.
2. Political parties help structure voting choice by nominating candidates to run for office. Before the advent of direct primaries, in which voters determine the party nominees, the parties had more control of who ran under their label. States determine the nomination rules. While most states employ the direct primary, some use a caucus or mixed caucus system where more committed partisans have a larger role in the decision of who gets nominated.
3. American parties are moderate. Bringing factions and interests together, they are broad enough to win the presidency and other elections. Third parties have been notably less successful. One reason for this is our single-member district, winner-take-all election rules. In systems with proportional representation or multimember districts, there is a greater tendency for more parties and the need to assemble governing coalitions across parties.
4. American parties have experienced critical elections and realignments. Most political scientists agree the last realignment occurred in 1932. In recent years, there has been divided government and an increase in the number of persons who call themselves Independents. This trend is sometimes called dealignment, but most Independents are closet partisans who vote for the party toward which they lean.
5. Parties are governed by their national and state committees, and the focal point of party organization is the national and state party chairs. When the party controls the executive branch of government, the executive (governor or president) usually has a determining say in selecting the party chair. With the rise of soft money in recent elections, parties now have more resources to spend on politics.
6. Party platforms are vague and generalized by design, giving the other party and voters little to oppose.
7. Parties are vital in the operation of government. They are organized around elected offices at the state and local levels. Congress is also organized around parties, and judicial and many executive branch appointments are based in large part on partisanship.
8. Parties are also active in the electorate, seeking to organize elections, simplify voting choices, provide a line between the people and government, broker diverse positions, and strengthen party identification.
9. Frequent efforts have been made to reform our parties. The Progressive movement saw parties, as then organized, as an impediment to democracy and pushed direct primaries as a means to reform them. Following the 1968 election, the Democratic party took the lead in pushing primaries and stressing greater diversity in those elected as delegates. Republicans have also encouraged broader participation, and they have improved party structure and finances.
10. Compared to some European parties, ours remain organizationally weak. There has been some party renewal in recent years as party competition has grown in the South and the parties themselves have initiated reforms.

KEY TERMS

party column ballot 228
office block ballot 228
nonpartisan 228
patronage 229
honeymoon 229
caucus 230
party convention 230
direct primary 230
open primary 230
crossover voting 230
closed primary 230
proportional representation 230
winner-take-all 230
minor party 231
realigning election 231
***laissez-faire* 235**
Keynesian economics 235
divided government 235
political party 236
national party convention 236
soft money 237
party platform 238
party registration 242
party identification 244
dealignment 246

FURTHER READING

JOHN H. ALDRICH, *Why Parties? The Origin and Transformation of Party Politics in America* (University of Chicago Press, 1995).

PAUL ALLEN BECK, *Party Politics in America*, 8th ed. (Longman, 1997).

JOHN F. BIBBY, *Politics, Parties, and Elections in America*, 3d ed. (Nelson-Hall, 1996).

DAVID BOAZ, *Libertarianism: A Primer* (Free Press, 1998).

MARY C. BRENNAN, *Turning Right in the Sixties: The Conservative Capture of the GOP* (University of North Carolina Press, 1995).

STEPHEN C. CRAIG, ED., *Broken Contract: Changing Relationships Between Americans and Their Government* (Westview Press, 1996).

LEON EPSTEIN, *Political Parties in the American Mold* (University of Wisconsin Press, 1986).

JEFF FAUX, *The Party's Not Over: A New Vision for Democrats* (Basic Books, 1996).

J. DAVID GILLESPIE, *Politics at the Periphery: Third Parties in Two-Party America* (University of South Carolina Press, 1993).

JOHN C. GREEN AND DANIEL M. SHEA, EDS., *The State of the Parties: The Changing Role of Contemporary American Parties*, 2d ed. (Rowman and Littlefield, 1996).

PAUL S. HERRNSON, *Party Campaigning in the 1980s: Have the National Parties Made a Comeback as Key Players in Congressional Elections?* (Harvard University Press, 1988).

PAUL S. HERRNSON AND JOHN C. GREEN, EDS., *Multiparty Politics in America* (Rowman and Littlefield, 1997).

WILLIAM J. KEEFE, *Parties, Politics, and Public Policy in America*, 8th ed. (Congressional Quarterly Press, 1998).

BRUCE E. KEITH, DAVID B. MAGLEBY, CANDICE J. NELSON, ELIZABETH ORR, MARK C. WESTLYE, AND RAYMOND E. WOLFINGER, *The Myth of the Independent Voter* (University of California Press, 1992).

G. CALVIN MACKENZIE, *The Irony of Reform: Roots of American Political Disenchantment* (Westview Press, 1996).

L. SANDY MAISEL, ED., *The Parties Respond: Changes in American Parties and Campaigns*, 3d ed. (Westview, 1998).

WILLIAM G. MAYER, *The Divided Democrats: Ideological Unity, Party Reform, and Presidential Elections* (Westview, 1996).

SIDNEY M. MILKIS, *The President and the Parties: The Transformation of the American Party System Since the New Deal* (Oxford University Press, 1993).

WARREN E. MILLER AND J. MERRILL SHANKS, *The New American Voter* (Harvard University Press, 1996).

KELLY D. PATTERSON, *Political Parties and the Maintenance of Liberal Democracy* (Columbia University Press, 1996).

STEVEN J. ROSENSTONE, ROY L. BEHR, AND EDWARD H. LAZARUS, *Third Parties in America: Citizen Response to Major Party Failure*, 2d ed. (Princeton University Press, 1996).

JAMES SUNDQUIST, *Dynamics of the Party System: Alignment and Realignment of Political Parties in the United States*, rev. ed. (Brookings, 1983).

MARTIN P. WATTENBERG, *The Decline of American Political Parties, 1952–1992* (Harvard University Press, 1994).

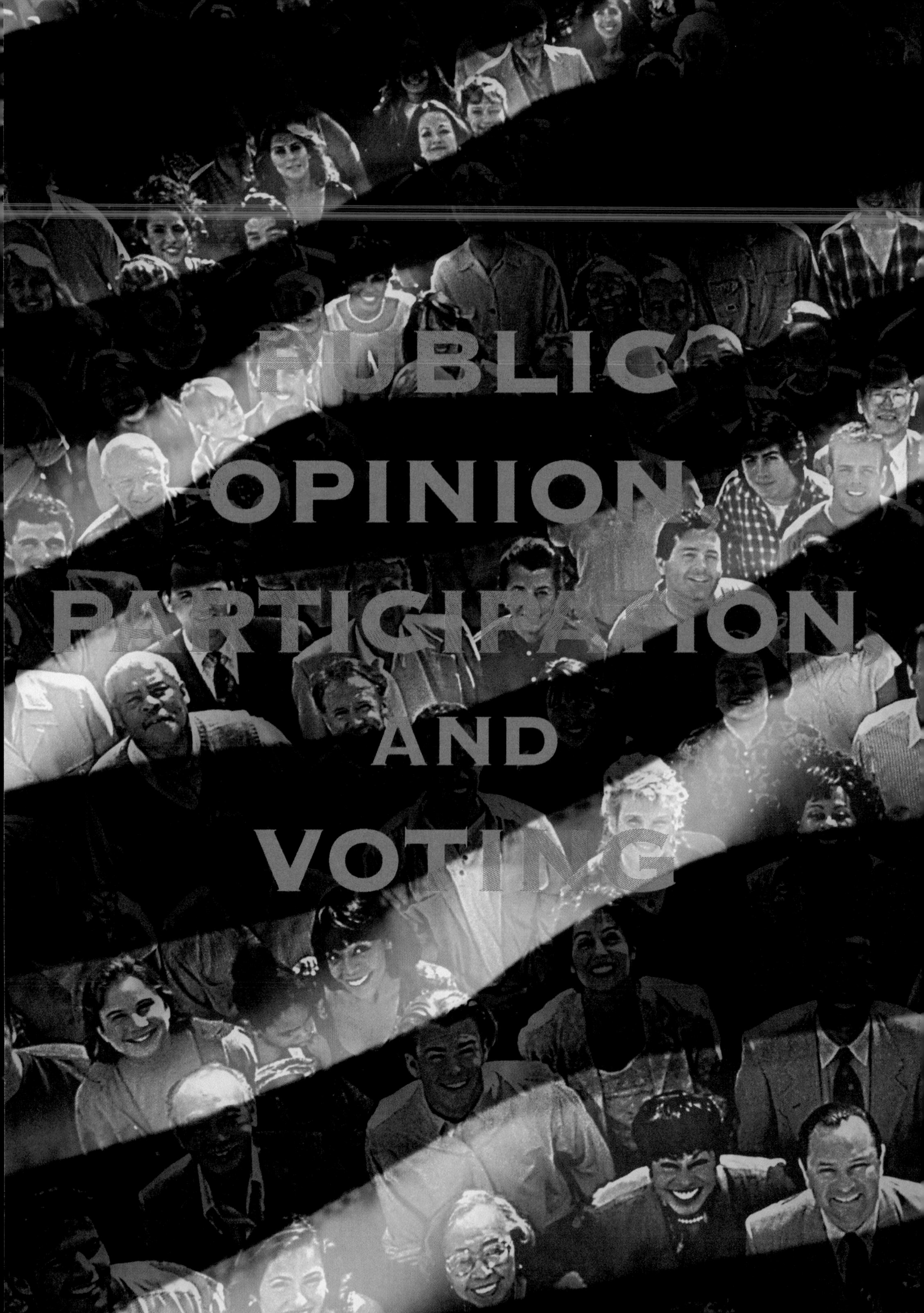
PUBLIC
OPINION
PARTICIPATION
AND
VOTING

11

CHAPTER OUTLINE

- Public Opinion
- Participation: Translating Opinions into Action
- Voting Choices

THROUGHOUT THE DEBATE OVER IMPEACHMENT OF PRESIDENT BILL CLINTON, OPPONENTS OF THE IMPEACHMENT FREQUENTLY CITED POLLS THAT SHOWED THE public did not favor such drastic action. As an organizer of a pro-Clinton rally in Boston put it, "We want this process over. We're driven by one phrase: listen to the people."[1] But others thought too much was being made of the polls. As one journalist put it, "President Clinton's popularity appears to be speaking louder than the evidence."[2] The public reacted negatively to the impeachment vote in the House of Representatives. A poll conducted on the same day as the House impeachment vote showed an *increase* in Clinton's approval rating to 71 percent, an approval rating higher than any ever achieved by President Ronald Reagan.[3]

Those who favored impeachment insisted that elected officials should do what is right rather than what is popular. William F. Buckley, Jr., host of *Firing Line*, said, "Still, though it is tiresome to repeat it, those of us terminally committed to the correctness of impeachment have to say it: a president was the principal enforcer of the laws, and this president flouted those laws."[4] Supporters of impeachment also countered that Clinton's job approval rating was high because of the robust economy, but that the public held him in low regard on honesty, integrity, and moral leadership. Indeed, "seven in ten Americans—including a majority of Baby Boomers—said in a survey that Clinton does not have high personal moral or ethical standards."[5]

The reality was that the public was very much divided about what, if any, action should be taken against the president. Soon after the House voted for two articles of impeachment, about a third of those surveyed felt Congress should proceed with the trial, slightly more favored a vote to censure, and another third favored not holding a trial or censuring the president.[6] When the public is so divided on a controversial matter, it is not surprising that elected officials are also divided. There was, in short, no clear consensus on what should be done.

But polling data on impeachment assumed the public knew and understood what the process meant. However, studies demonstrated that most people thought the House impeachment vote meant removing Clinton from office, when in fact it meant only that the Senate would hold a trial *to decide whether to remove him from office.* When asked what vote was needed in the House for impeachment, only 18 percent correctly said a majority. When asked what vote was needed in the Senate for removal, slightly more than half the voters knew it was a two-thirds vote. Finally, when asked who would succeed Bill Clinton if he were removed from office, 83 percent correctly identified Al Gore as his successor.[7]

How You Ask It Shapes How You Answer It

How you ask a polling question makes a lot of difference in the responses people give, as demonstrated by the way three different polls asked about special interests and campaign finance. The first question was written by Ross Perot's organization, not by a survey researcher. It was published in *TV Guide* and asked individuals to send in their answers. Perot's survey was criticized widely by survey organizations for its skewed sample and biased questions. The second and third questions were part of national surveys conducted by professional polling firms using random samples.

1. Should laws be passed to eliminate all possibilities of special interests giving huge sums of money to candidates?

   Yes 99%

2. Should laws be passed to prohibit interest groups from contributing to campaigns, or do groups have a right to contribute to the candidate they support?

Prohibit contribution	40%
Groups have right	55%

3. Please tell me whether you favor or oppose this proposal: The passage of new laws that would eliminate all possibility of special interests giving large sums of money to candidates.

Favor	70%
Oppose	28%

SOURCE: Daniel Goleman, "Pollsters Enlist Psychologists in Quest for Unbiased Results," *The New York Times*, September 7, 1993, pp. C1, C11.

These data clearly demonstrate that it was a mistake to assume the public knew what was meant by a constitutional process like impeachment, so interpreting polling data about such a topic is fraught with possible misunderstanding.

One reason polls were relevant to the debate about impeachment and removal from office for Bill Clinton is that these processes undo the vote of the people. The framers assigned the removal of a president from office to Congress—the political branch presumed to be most in tune with the will of the voters. This context made it appropriate for Congress to assess public opinion. The number and consistency of public opinion supporting Clinton saved him, because without polls Congress would have been left to speculate about "what the people think."

In this chapter we look at the nature of public opinion, how to measure it, the factors that affect the formation of opinions, the nature and level of political participation in the United States, and why people vote as they do.

PUBLIC OPINION

All governments in all nations must be concerned with public opinion, for unrest and protest can topple them. But in a constitutional democracy like ours, public opinion plays an even larger role. Citizens have opinions and express them in a variety of ways, including protest demonstrations, letters to newspaper editors, and voting in free and regularly scheduled elections. Elected officials refer often to public opinion as a basis for their actions. In short, democracy and public opinion go hand in hand.

What Is Public Opinion?

We define **public opinion** as the distribution of individual preferences or evaluations of a given issue, candidate, or institution within a population. *Distribution* means the proportion of the population that holds a particular opinion, as compared to people with opposing opinions or those with no opinion at all. For instance, final pre-election polls in 1996 by the Gallup Organization predicted Bill Clinton would get 52 percent of the popular vote, Robert Dole 41 percent, and Ross Perot 7 percent. This would be the distribution. Clinton actually got 49 percent of the popular vote, Dole 41 percent, and Perot 8 percent.

TAKING THE PULSE OF THE PEOPLE *Proper sampling* is based on random choices of the appropriate set of people to survey. *Random choice* means that every individual has an equal chance of being selected. The sample of randomly selected respondents should be appropriate for the questions being asked. For instance, a survey of 18-to-24-year-olds should not be done solely among college students, since roughly three-quarters of this age group do not attend college.

The art of asking questions is also important to scientific polling. The wording of questions can influence the answers given. Good questions have been pretested and are delivered by trained and professional interviewers, who read the questions exactly as written and without any intonation in their voices. Questions are worded in different ways to measure factual knowledge, opinions, the intensity of opinion, or views on hypothetical situations. Sometimes *open-ended questions* are asked that permit the respondents to answer in their own words. The order of questions can also alter the responses.

Thorough analysis and reporting of the results are expected of scientific polls. Scientific polls inform the public of the sample size, the margin of expected statistical error for a standard question, and when the poll was conducted.

It is important to remember that public opinion can change and that most polls are really snapshots of opinion at a point in time rather than moving pictures of opinions over time.

public opinion
The distribution of individual preferences or evaluations of a given issue, candidate, or institution within a population.

TABLE 11-1 How Opinions Differ on Abortion

	Percent Saying Abortion Should Be			
	Legal Under Any Circumstances	Legal Under Certain Circumstances	Illegal in All Circumstances	Don't Know
Total Adults	23%	59%	17%	1%
Age				
18–29	25	58	17	—
30–49	27	55	17	1
50–64	22	63	14	1
65+	13	64	21	2
Sex				
Men	21	62	16	1
Women	24	56	18	2
Education				
High school graduate or less	18	61	19	2
Some college	22	61	15	2
College graduate	35	47	18	—
Postgraduate	33	55	11	1
Race				
White	22	60	17	1
Nonwhite	25	55	18	2
Black	21	55	23	1
Religion				
Protestant	21	61	17	1
Catholic	23	57	19	1
Political Philosophy				
Liberal	35	55	9	1
Moderate	27	59	13	1
Conservative	11	63	26	—
Party Identification				
Republican	18	62	19	1
Democrat	27	57	15	1
Independent	25	55	19	1
Income				
Less than $20,000	17	57	25	1
$20,000–$29,999	21	59	19	1
$30,000–$49,999	24	59	15	2
More than $50,000	29	60	10	1

SOURCE: Data for Total Adults and for sex are from a national survey by the Gallup Organization, January 1998; other data are from the Gallup Organization, January 1992.

Figures may not add up to 100 percent due to rounding.

"It should be 'yes' or 'no' or 'undecided'—we don't accept a 'don't give a damn' answer!"

The Wall Street Journal.

Individual preference means that when we measure public opinion, we are asking *individuals*—not groups, elected officials, or journalists—about their opinions. The *universe* or *population* is the relevant group of people for the question. When a substantial percentage of a sample agree on an issue—for example, that we should honor the American flag—there is a *consensus.* But on most issues, opinions are divided in various proportions. When a large portion of opposing sides feels intensely about an issue, voters are said to be *polarized.* Vietnam in the 1960s and abortion in the 1990s were polarizing issues (see Table 11-1).

Newspapers and television stations conduct polls to measure the popularity of candidates and to discover public attitudes on current issues.

INTENSITY This factor produces the brightest and deepest hues in the fabric of public opinion. The fervor of people's beliefs varies greatly. For example, some individuals mildly favor gun control legislation and others mildly oppose it; but some people are emphatically for or against it, and some have no interest in the matter at all; still others may not even have heard of it. Intensity is typically measured by asking people how strongly they feel on an issue or about a politician. Such a question is often called a *scale.*

LATENCY Latency refers to political opinions that exist merely as a potential; they may not have crystallized, yet they are still important, for they can be aroused by leaders and converted into action. Latent opinions set rough boundaries for leaders who know that if they take certain actions they will trigger either opposition or support from millions of people. If leaders have some understanding of latent opinions—people's real wants, needs, and hopes—they will know how to mobilize them and draw them to the polls on election day. Many who lived in communist Poland, East Germany, Czechoslovakia, or Yugoslavia must have had latent opinions favorable to democracy—opinions supporting majority rule, freedom, meaningful elections. The speed with which these countries embraced democratic reforms was possible when leaders encouraged widespread expression of such ideas.

SALIENCE By *salience* we mean the extent to which people feel that issues are relevant to them. Most people are more concerned about personal issues like paying their bills and keeping their jobs than about national issues, but if national issues somehow threaten their security or safety, salience rises sharply.

Salience may change over time. During the Great Depression of the 1930s, Americans were concerned mainly about jobs, wages, and economic security. By the 1940s, foreign affairs came to the fore. In the 1960s, problems of race and poverty aroused intense feeling. In the 1970s, Vietnam and then Watergate riveted people's attention. By the early 2000s, concern about drugs, crime, health care, and the state of the environment had become salient issues.

How Do We Get Our Political Opinions and Values?

No one is born with political views. We learn them from many teachers. The process by which we develop our political attitudes, values, and beliefs is called **political socialization**. This process starts in childhood, and the family and the schools are probably the two most important political teachers. Children learn the content of our culture in childhood and adolescence but reshape it as they live their lives.[8] Socialization lays the foundation for political beliefs, values, ideology, and partisanship.

A common element of political socialization in all cultures is *nationalism*, a consciousness of the nation-state and of belonging to that entity. Robert Coles describes it this way:

> As soon as we are born, in most places on this earth, we acquire a nationality, a membership in a community. . . . A royal doll, a flag to wave in a parade, coins with their engraved messages—these are sources of instruction and connect a young person to a country. The attachment can be strong, indeed even among children yet to attend school, wherever the flag is saluted, the national anthem sung. The attachment is as parental as the words imply—homeland, motherland, fatherland. . . . Nationalism works its way into just about every corner of the mind's life.[9]

political socialization
The process by which we develop our political attitudes, values, and beliefs.

The sources of our views are immensely varied in the pluralistic political culture of the United States. Political attitudes may stem from religious, racial, gender, ethnic, or economic beliefs and values. But we can make at least one generalization safely: We form our attitudes in *groups*, and not only in groups such as schools and social organizations, but especially in close-knit groups like the family. When we identify closely with the attitudes and interests of a particular group, we tend to see politics through the "eyes" of that group.[10]

Group affiliation does not necessarily mean that individual members of the group do not think for themselves. Each member brings his or her own emotions, feelings, memories, and resistances to groups. The extent to which people are captive to groups is indeed a running argument among scholars from different disciplines. Sociologists tend to emphasize the pervasive influence of groups over their members. Psychologists focus more on the developmental stages within individuals that prompt them to be joiners or loners. Political scientists have traditionally tended to agree more with the sociological approach.[11] Political psychologists seek to combine both approaches.

The considerable variation in the factors that influence our political beliefs produces a wide array of attitudes in society. However, children in the United States at an early age adopt common values that provide continuity with the past and legitimize the American political system. Young children know what country they live in, and their loyalty to the nation develops early. Although the details of our political system may still elude them, most young Americans acquire a respect for the Constitution and for the concept of participatory democracy, as well as an initially positive view of the most visible figure in our democracy—the president.

FAMILY American children typically show political interest by the age of ten or even earlier, and by the early teens their interest may be fairly high. Consider your own political learning process. You probably formed your picture of the world by listening to a parent at dinner or by absorbing the tales your older brothers and sisters brought home from school. Perhaps you heard about politics from grandparents, aunts, and uncles. You, in turn, influenced your family, if only by bringing some of your own hopes and problems home from school. What we first learn in the family is not so much specific political opinions as basic *attitudes* that shape our opinions—attitudes toward our neighbors, political parties, other classes or types of people, particular leaders (especially presidents), and society in general.

Studies of high school students indicate a high correlation between the political party of the parents and the partisan choice of the child. This relatively high degree of correspondence continues throughout life. Such a finding raises some interesting questions: Does the direct influence of parents create the correspondence? Or are parents and children equally influenced by living in the same social environment—neighborhood, church, socioeconomic group? The answer is *both*, and one influence often strengthens the other. A daughter of Democratic parents growing up in a small southern town with strong Democratic leanings will be affected by friends, by other adults, and perhaps by youngsters in a church group, all of whom may reinforce the attitudes of her parents.[12]

SCHOOLS Schools also mold young citizens' values and attitudes. American schools see part of their purpose as preparing students to be citizens and active participants in governing their communities and nation. At an early age, schoolchildren begin to pick up specific political values and acquire basic attitudes toward our system of government. Education, like the family, prepares Americans to live in society.

From kindergarten through college, children generally develop political values that will enhance their citizenship and legitimize the American political system. In their study of American history, they are introduced to our nation's heroes and heroines, the important events in our history, and the ideals of our society. Other aspects of the student's experience, such as the daily Pledge of Allegiance, usually reinforce respect of country. Children also gain practical experience in the workings of democracy through elections for class or school officers and student government. In some colleges, the state legislature or college trustees have made courses in U.S. history or American government a graduation requirement.

Do school influences give young people greater faith in political institutions? Yes and no. A classic study examined civics texts and students' attitudes in three Boston communities—one upper-middle class, one lower-middle class, and one working class. The textbooks in all three communities stressed the right of citizens to try to influence government, but only the texts used in the upper-middle-class community stressed politics as conflict and as a process for resolving differing group demands. Edgar Litt, a political scientist, concluded that the lower-middle-class students were learning that government was a process carried out by institutions on their behalf, while the upper-middle-class students were learning that the political process was something they could influence.[13]

How does college influence political opinions? One study suggests that students planning to attend college are more likely to be knowledgeable about politics, more in favor of free speech, and more likely to talk and read about politics.[14] Conservatism and Republican party preference on college campuses increased in the 1980s, but there are indications from the same study that college students in the 1990s are again more liberal.[15] Is this the influence of the professors, the curriculum, or the students? It is difficult to generalize. Parents sometimes fear professors have too much influence on their college-age children; however, most professors doubt they have significant influence over students. The debate about whether there is peer pressure on college campuses to conform to certain acceptable ideas—*political correctness* (PC)—highlights the role higher education can play in shaping attitudes and values.

The Chicago Herald Tribune was so sure of its polling data in the 1948 election predicting a win for Thomas Dewey, they printed this headline before the results were final. A victorious Harry Truman displays the mistaken headline.

MASS MEDIA Family and school are not the only influences on children and adolescents. Like everybody else, students are exposed to a wide range of media—school newspapers, national newspapers, the Internet, movies, television—all of which influence what they think. They pick and choose the media with which they agree, so their exposure is *selective.* The mass media also serve as agents of socialization by providing a link between individuals and the values and behavior of others. When people watch, listen, and read, they discover which values and role models are considered important. News broadcasts present information about our society; events that get intensive media coverage often focus our attention on certain issues. For example, the televised Clinton impeachment hearings directed widespread attention to constitutional procedures and requirements for the removal of a president.

By Margulies for *The Record,* Hackensack, NJ.

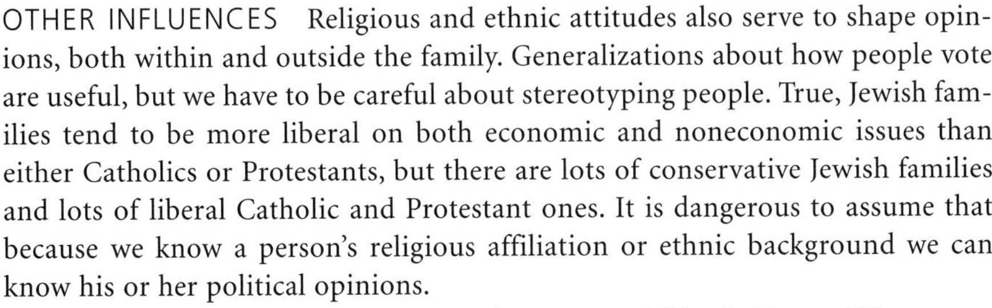

OTHER INFLUENCES Religious and ethnic attitudes also serve to shape opinions, both within and outside the family. Generalizations about how people vote are useful, but we have to be careful about stereotyping people. True, Jewish families tend to be more liberal on both economic and noneconomic issues than either Catholics or Protestants, but there are lots of conservative Jewish families and lots of liberal Catholic and Protestant ones. It is dangerous to assume that because we know a person's religious affiliation or ethnic background we can know his or her political opinions.

What happens when a young person's parents and friends disagree? Young people tend to go along with parents rather than friends on party affiliation, with friends rather than parents on issues like the death penalty or gun control, and somewhere in between in their actual votes in presidential elections.[16]

Stability and Change in Public Opinion

Most of us do not change our opinions very often. Even if the world changes rapidly around us, we are slow to shift our loyalties or to change our minds about things that matter to us. In general, people who remain in the same place, in the same occupation, and in the same income group throughout their lives tend to have stable opinions. But people carry their attitudes with them, and families who move from cities to suburbs often retain their big-city attitudes long after they have moved.

Adults are not simply the sum of all their early experiences, however. Political analysts are becoming more interested in the ways in which adults modify their views. A major factor may be a harsh experience—a war, economic depression, or loss of a job—that shocks people out of their existing attitudes.

Some of our opinions change very little because they are part of our basic values. Thus our views on abortion, the death penalty, and doctor-assisted suicide remain basically stable over time. On issues that are less central to our values, such as our view of how a president is performing his job, opinions can show substantial change over time. On many issues, public opinion can change once the public learns more about the issue or perceives there is another side to the question. It is on these issues that politicians can help shape attitudes.

Public Opinion and Public Policy

For much of human history it has been difficult to measure public opinion. "What I want," Abraham Lincoln once said, "is to get done what the people desire to be done, and the question for me is how to find that out exactly." Another president, Woodrow Wilson, once complained to the newspapers that they had no business saying what people thought: "You do not know, and the worst of it, since the responsibility is mine, I do not know, what they are thinking about. I have the most

What If They Held an Election and No One Voted?

Such an election actually happened in Centreville, Mississippi, in 1993. Candidate Danny Jones appeared to be a sure winner for a seat on the board of aldermen (city council), in part because he was the only candidate. But no one actually voted, including Jones, who had to work late on election day. State law requires winners to get at least one vote, so a special election had to be held, at which Jones received 45 votes.

SOURCE: *Parade Magazine*, January 2, 1994, p. 4.

imperfect means of finding out, and yet I have got to act as if I knew." Politicians in our day do not face the uncertainty about public opinion faced by Lincoln and Wilson. They do know what public opinion is on all major policy issues.

A clear example of how public opinion can shape policy occurred during the Vietnam War. Antiwar demonstrations on college campuses soon spread to cities all over the country. "Public opinion had a substantial impact on the rate of troop withdrawals."[17] In the Persian Gulf War, opposition to the use of U.S. forces was greatly reduced after a few days of success in the air and ground war. When American forces were dispatched to Somalia in Operation Restore Hope in January 1993, 79 percent approved of the use of troops to ensure the delivery of humanitarian aid, food, and medical provisions. But when U.S. soldiers were killed and dragged through the streets of Mogadishu, support fell to only 17 percent in October of the same year.[18]

Typically, elected officials seek to follow public opinion. Winning reelection is a strong motive for members of Congress.[19] "Legislators show greater attention to public opinion as election day looms," and the closeness of fit between constituent opinion and roll call voting reflects that connection.[20] Candidates use polls to determine where to campaign, how to campaign, and even whether to campaign. In the years and months preceding a national convention, politicians watch the polls to determine who among the hopefuls has political appeal. Have polls become more important than voters in influencing who can mount a viable campaign?

More than 80 percent of newspapers and half of television stations conduct or commission their own polls.[21] These media polls are often not conducted as carefully as the academic polls conducted at major universities, but they play a major role in shaping public opinion.[22]

Surely polls are no substitute for elections. Faced with a ballot, voters must translate their opinions into concrete decisions. They must decide what is important and what is not. Democracy is more than the expression of views, more than a simple mirror of opinion. It also involves choosing among leaders, taking sides on certain issues, and selecting the governmental actions that may follow. Democracy is the thoughtful participation of people in the political process. It means using heads as well as counting them. Elections, with all their failings, still establish the link between the many voices of "We the People" and the decisions of their leaders.

Awareness and Interest

For most people, politics is of secondary importance to earning a living, raising a family, and having a good time; some Americans are more concerned about which team wins the Super Bowl than they are about who wins the school board elections, who gets to be mayor, or even who gets to be president of the United States. Most people find politics complicated and difficult to understand. And they should, for democracy *is* complicated and difficult to understand. But it helps to understand the mechanics and structures of our government: how the government operates, how the Electoral College works, how many chambers there are in Congress, the length of terms for the president and for members of the Senate and House of Representatives, for example.

Details about how the government works are typically best known by younger persons, who remember learning them in school. The general adult public, however, fares poorly when quizzed about their elected officials. Just over a quarter of Americans are able to recall the name of their member of Congress, and only 60 percent can name even one of their U.S. senators.[23] With so many voters not knowing who represents them in Congress, it is not surprising that "on even hotly debated congressional issues, few people know where their Congress member stands."[24]

Although the public's knowledge of institutional and candidate issues is poor, its knowledge of important public policy issues is worse. In 1982, after years of debate over ratification of the Equal Rights Amendment, nearly one-third of the adults in the United States indicated they had never heard of it. In late August 1993, several weeks before the vote in Congress on the North American Free Trade Agreement (NAFTA), six out of ten Americans reported they were not following the NAFTA story at all.[25]

Fortunately, not all Americans are uninformed or uninterested. About 25 percent of the public are interested in politics most of the time. They are the **attentive public**, people who know and understand how the government works. They vote in most elections, read a daily newspaper, and "talk politics" with their families and friends. They tend to be better educated and more committed to democratic values than are other Americans.

At the opposite end of the spectrum are *nonvoters*, people who are rarely interested in politics or public affairs and who rarely vote. About 35 percent of Americans have indicated that they have little interest in politics or are only occasionally interested.[26] A subset of this group might be called *political know-nothings*. These individuals not only avoid political activity but have little interest in government and limited knowledge about it.

Between the attentive public and the nonvoters are the *part-time citizens*, roughly 40 percent of the American public. These individuals participate selectively in elections, voting in presidential elections but usually not in others. Politics and government do not greatly interest them; they pay only minimal attention to the news, and they rarely discuss candidates or elections with others.

Democracy can survive even when a large number of citizens are passive and uninformed, as long as a substantial number of people serve as opinion leaders and are interested and informed about public affairs. Obviously, these activists will have much greater influence than their less active fellow citizens.

Participation: Translating Opinions into Action

Americans influence their government's actions in several different ways, many of which are protected by the Constitution. They vote in elections, join interest groups, go to political party meetings, ring doorbells, call friends urging them to vote for issues or candidates, sign petitions, write letters to the editors of newspapers, and make calls to radio talk shows.

Protest is also a form of political participation. Our political system is remarkably tolerant of protest that is not destructive or violent; boycotts, picketing, sit-ins, and marches are all legally protected. Rosa Parks and Martin Luther King, Jr., used the peaceful breaking of the law to protest what they saw as unfair laws. The number of Americans who participate in protests is small, but the impact of their actions in shaping public opinion can be substantial.

A distinguishing characteristic of a democracy is that citizens can influence government decisions by participating in politics. In totalitarian societies, participation is very limited, forcing people who want to influence government to resort to violence or revolution. When the citizens of Belgrade turned out night after night to protest the nullification of their local elections, they forced Slobodan Milosevic to recognize the opposition victories. But protests and responses are not always peaceful or successful. The protest of Chinese students in Tiananmen Square failed to stop the onslaught of tanks and the repression that followed. Americans sometimes forget that our democracy was born of

attentive public
Those who follow public affairs carefully.

Street demonstrations in Belgrade, Yugoslavia, forced President Milosovic to recognize his party's defeat in local elections in 1997.

revolution, but that maintaining a constitutional democracy is also difficult and demands public participation. The people of Belgrade experienced these difficulties firsthand during 1999.

Even in an established democracy, people may feel so strongly about an issue that they would rather fight than accept the verdict of an election. The classic example is the American Civil War. Following the election of 1860, in which the presidency was won by an antislavery candidate who did not receive a single electoral vote from a slave state, the South took up arms. War marked the breakdown of democracy. Examples in our own time include antiabortion groups that use violence to press their political agenda and militia groups that arm themselves for battle against government restrictions.

Large numbers of Americans routinely participate in such rituals of democracy as singing the National Anthem or reciting the Pledge of Allegiance. They communicate their views about government and politics to their representatives in Washington and the state capital. They serve as jurors in courtrooms and enlist in the military. They express concern about the involvement of American military forces in foreign hostilities. They complain about taxes and government regulations. And each year millions of Americans visit Washington, D.C., and other historic sights.

TABLE 11-2 Political Participation and Awareness in the United States

Vote in presidential elections	49%
Vote in congressional elections	34
Know name of U.S. representative	28
Sign a petition	48
Write congressman or state representative	30
Vote in local elections	10–30
Try to persuade vote of others	19
Display campaign button, sticker, or sign	7
Attend dinner, meeting, or rally for candidate	5
Contribute to candidate	4
Contribute to party	4

SOURCE: U.S. Bureau of the Census, *Statistical Abstract of the United States, 1998* (Government Printing Office, 1998), p. 297; *1998 American National Election Study*, Center for Political Studies, University of Michigan.

For most people, politics is a private activity. Some books on manners still consider it impolite to discuss politics at dinner parties. To say that politics is private does not mean people do not have opinions or will not discuss them when asked by others, including pollsters. But often politics is avoided in discussions with neighbors, work associates, even friends and family, as too divisive or upsetting. Typically, less than one person in four attempts to influence how another person votes in an election. An even smaller number actually work for a candidate or party. Only one in twenty people make a contribution to a candidate, and only one in four designate one dollar of their taxes to the fund that pays for presidential general elections (see Table 11-2).

Few individuals attempt to influence others by writing letters to elected officials or to editors of newspapers for publication. Even smaller numbers participate in protest groups or activities. Despite the small number of persons who engage in these activities, it would be a mistake to assume that small numbers of individuals cannot make a difference to politics and government. Often an individual or small group can generate media interest in an issue and expand the impact. Peaceful protests for civil rights, environmental issues, and abortion have generated public attention and perhaps even changed opinions.

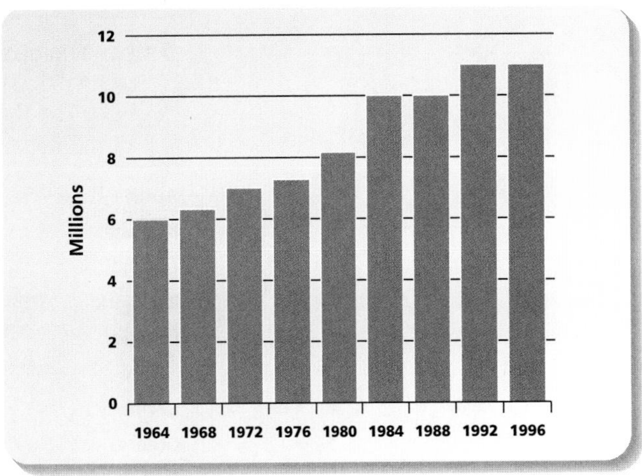

Figure 11-1 African American Registered Voters, 1964–1996

SOURCE: U.S. Bureau of the Census, *Statistical Abstract of the United States, 1998* (Government Printing Office, 1998), p. 297.

Voting

Americans' most typical political activity is voting. The United States is a constitutional democracy with many decades of free and frequent elections and a tradition of the peaceful transfer of power between competing groups and parties.

Originally the Constitution left it to the individual states to determine the crucial question of who could vote, and the qualifications for voting differed considerably from state to state. All states except New Jersey barred women from voting, many did not permit African Americans to vote, and property ownership was often a requirement. By the time of the Civil War, the franchise had been extended to all white male citizens in every state. Since that time, eligibility standards for voting have been expanded by legislation and constitutional amendments:

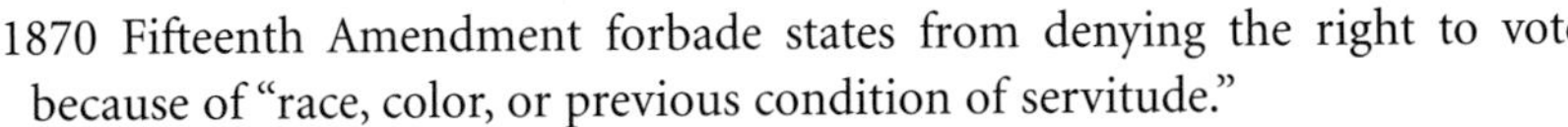

1870 Fifteenth Amendment forbade states from denying the right to vote because of "race, color, or previous condition of servitude."

1920 Nineteenth Amendment gave women the right to vote.

1924 Congress granted Native Americans citizenship and voting rights.

1961 Twenty-third Amendment permitted District of Columbia residents to vote in federal elections.

1964 Twenty-fourth Amendment prohibited the use of poll taxes.

1965 Voting Rights Act removed restrictions that kept blacks from voting.

1971 Twenty-sixth Amendment extended the vote to citizens age 18 and older.

The civil rights movement in the 1960s, which made voting rights a central issue, secured adoption of the Twenty-fourth Amendment and passage of the 1965 Voting Rights Act. The Voting Rights Act banned literacy tests, eased registration requirements, and provided for the replacement of local election officials with federal registrars in areas where the denial of the right to vote had been most blatant. Its passage resulted in a dramatic expansion of African American registration and voting. Once African Americans were permitted to register to vote, "the focus of voting discrimination shifted . . . to preventing them from winning elections."[27] In southern legislative districts where African Americans are in the majority, however, there has been a "dramatic increase in the proportion of African American legislators elected"[28] (see Figure 11-1).

Registration

One peculiarly American legal requirement—**voter registration**—discourages voting. Most other democracies have automatic voter registration. Average turnout in the United States is more than 30 percentage points lower than in countries like Australia, Austria, Belgium, Denmark, Germany, and Italy; only

voter registration
System designed to reduce voter fraud by limiting voting to those who have established eligibility by submitting the proper form.

TABLE 11-3 Registration and Voting in the World's Democracies

	Turnout as Percent of Eligible Vote	Compulsion Penalties*	Automatic Registration**
Australia	94%	Yes	No
Austria	91	No	Yes
Belgium	93	Yes	Yes
Canada	76	No	Yes
Denmark	86	No	Yes
Finland	78	No	Yes
France	66	No	No
Germany	84	No	Yes
Greece	85	Yes	Yes
Ireland	69	No	Yes
Israel	80	No	Yes
Italy	91	Yes	Yes
Japan	71	No	Yes
Netherlands	86	No	Yes
New Zealand	87	No	No
Norway	84	No	Yes
Spain	71	No	Yes
Sweden	86	No	Yes
Switzerland	46	No	Yes
United Kingdom	75	No	Yes
United States	53	No	No

SOURCE: Thomas T. Mackie and Richard Rose, *The International Almanac of Electoral History*, 3d ed. (Congressional Quarterly Press, 1991); G. Bingham Powell, Jr., "American Voter Turnout in Comparative Perspective," *American Political Science Review* 80 (March 1986), p. 38. Iceland, Luxembourg, Malta, and Portugal were not included in the Powell study and were therefore omitted from this table.

*Compulsion penalties are fines or other possible state actions against nonvoters.

**Automatic registration utilizes other forms of citizen identification like a driver's license.

Switzerland has lower average turnout[29] (see Table 11-3). This was not always the case. In fact, in the 1800s, turnout in the United States was much like that of Europe today. Turnout began to drop significantly around the turn of the century, in part as a result of election reform (see Figure 11-2).

American elections in the 1800s were different from those of today. Ballots were prepared by the parties, often using different colors of paper that allowed them to monitor how people had voted. In some areas charges of multiple voting generated a reform movement that substituted the **Australian ballot**, a secret ballot printed by the state, and initiated voter registration to reduce multiple voting and limit voting to those who had previously established their eligibility.

Australian ballot
A secret ballot printed by the state.

Registration laws vary by state, but in every state except North Dakota registration is required in order to vote. Three states permit election-day voter registration. The most important provision regarding voter registration may be the closing date. A few years ago it was not uncommon for closing dates to be six months before the election; now, by federal law, no state can stop registration more than 30 days before an election.[30] Voter registration places a responsibility on voters to take an extra step—usually filling out a form at the county courthouse, when renewing a driver's license, or with a roving registrar—some days or weeks before the election. Other important provisions include places and hours of registration, and the closing date for registration.[31]

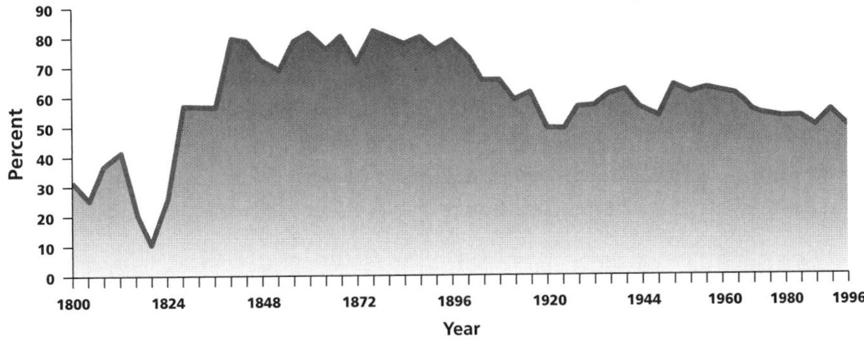

Figure 11-2 Voter Turnout in Presidential Elections, 1800–1996

SOURCE: Walter Dean Burnham, "The Turnout Problem," in *Elections American Style*, ed. A. James Reichley (Brookings Institution, 1987), pp. 113–14; Committee for the Study of the American Electorate.

Motor-Voter

Voter registration was eased a bit when, on May 20, 1993, President Clinton signed the National Voter Registration Act—called the "Motor-Voter" bill because it allows people to register to vote while applying for or renewing a driver's license. Offices that provide welfare and disabled assistance can also facilitate voter registration. States have the option to include public schools, libraries, and city and county clerks' offices as registration sites. The law also requires states to allow registration by mail using a standardized form. Motor-Voter requires a questionnaire be mailed to registered voters every four years to purge for death and change of residence, but forbids purging for any other reasons, such as nonvoting.

Proponents of the law say it will reach the 49 million Americans of voting age with driver's licenses who have not registered to vote. Opponents claim the new law is another federal mandate that does not provide money to pay for the costs involved. They also assert it will increase election fraud because of the difficulty in removing names from voting rolls.

It appears that the law has been successful, at least in terms of numbers of new voters registered. One source estimates that Motor-Voter meant that "for the

In an effort to make voter registration easier, states have made registration forms available at motor vehicle stations, schools, public buildings, and even at highway toll booths.

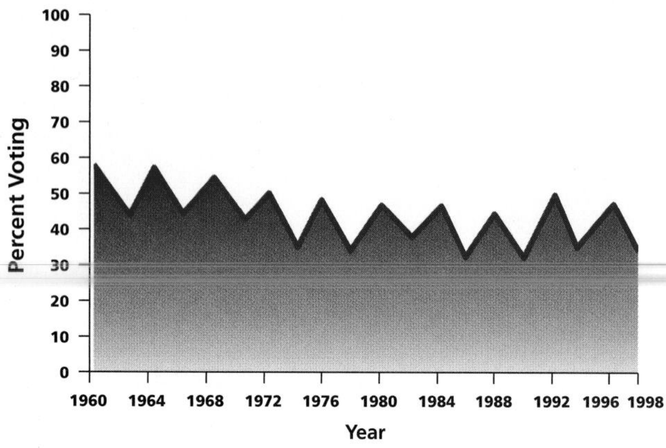

Figure 11-3 Voter Turnout in Presidential and Midterm Elections, 1990–1996

SOURCE: U.S. Bureau of the Census, *Statistical Abstract of the United States, 1998* (Government Printing Office, 1998), p. 97. Louis V. Gerstner, "Next Time Let Us Boldly Vote as No Democracy Has Before," *USA Today*, November, 16, 1998. p. A15.

1996 election there were 12 million new registered voters and an estimated 3 million more by the start of 1997."[32] Early data on the impact of Motor-Voter suggest that neither Democrats nor Republicans are the primary beneficiaries because most who have registered claim to be Independent. Motor-Voter does not appear to have increased turnout.[33]

Turnout

Americans hold more elections for more offices than do citizens of any other democracy. In part because there are so many elections, American voters tend to pick and choose which elections to vote in. Americans elect officeholders in *general elections*, determine party nominees in *primary elections*, and replace senators who have died or left office in *special elections*. For example, in a two-year period, voters in Pasadena, California, had the option of voting in as many as five elections.

Elections held in years when the president is on the ballot are called *presidential elections*, elections held midway between presidential elections are called *midterm elections*, and elections held in odd-numbered calendar years are called *off-year elections*. Midterm elections (like the one in 1998) elect about one-third of the U.S. Senate, all members of the House of Representatives, and most governors and other statewide officeholders as well as large numbers of state legislators. Many local elections are held in the spring of odd-numbered years to elect city councils and mayors.

Turnout—the proportion of the voting-age public that votes—is highest in presidential general elections (see Figure 11-3). Turnout is higher in general elections than in primary elections and higher in primary elections than in special elections. Turnout is higher in presidential general elections than in midterm general elections, and higher in presidential primary elections than in midterm primary elections.[34] Turnout is higher in elections in which candidates for federal office are on the ballot (U.S. senator, member of the House of Representatives, president) than in state elections in years when there are no federal contests. Some states elect their governor and other state officials in odd-numbered years to separate state from national politics. The result is generally lower turnout. Finally, local or municipal elections have lower turnout than state elections, and municipal primaries have even lower rates of participation.

Turnout peaked in 1960 at almost 63 percent of persons over 21 years of age, but it has since declined to 34 percent in 1998.[35] Turnout should have gone up since 1960 because the Voting Rights Act of 1965 added large numbers of African Americans to the pool of registered voters. Women, another historically underrepresented group, have also increased their voting levels.[36] Finally, our electorate has grown richer and more educated since the 1960s, and since wealth and education are related to voting, we should have seen an increase instead of a decrease in voting. However, 85 million Americans failed to vote in recent presidential elections; the nonvoting figures are even higher for congressional, state, county, and local elections.[37]

Who Votes?

turnout
The proportion of the voting-age public that votes.

The extent of voting varies widely among different groups. The level of education especially helps predict whether people will vote; as education increases, so does the propensity to vote. "Education increases one's capacity for understanding complex and intangible subjects such as politics," according to one study, "as well as encouraging the ethic of civil responsibility. Moreover, schools provide experience dealing with a variety of bureaucratic problems, such as coping with requirements, filling out forms, and meeting deadlines."[38] Race and ethnic background are linked with different levels of voting, in large part because they correlate with education. Blacks in general turn out at lower rates than whites. However, women, another historically underrepresented group, increased their voting levels to the point where, in 1988, 1992, and again in 1996, turnout among women actually exceeded that of men.[39]

Income and age are also important factors. Those with higher family incomes are more likely to vote than those with lower incomes. Income, of course, corresponds to occupation, and those with higher-status careers are more likely to vote than those with lower-status jobs. Poor people are less likely to feel politically involved and confident, and their social norms tend to de-emphasize politics.[40] Older people, unless they are very old and infirm, are more likely to vote than younger people. Women's recent higher turnout is generally attributed to increasing levels of education and employment; black women in particular are influenced by their party identification and by attitudes on gender issues.[41]

WE THE PEOPLE

Voter Turnout by Demographic Factors

	1992	1994	1996	1998
Sex				
Men	60.2%	44.4%	52.8%	49%
Women	62.3	44.9	55.5	51
Race				
White	63.6	46.9	56.0	82
Black	54.0	37.0	50.6	10
Hispanic	28.9	19.1	26.7	5
Education				
Some high school	41.2	27.0	33.8	5
High school graduate	57.5	40.5	49.1	22
Some college	68.7	49.1	60.5	27
College graduate	81.0	63.1	73.0	27

SOURCE: U.S. Bureau of the Census, *Statistical Abstract of the United States, 1998* (Government Printing Office, 1998), p. 296; Marjorie Connelly, "A Look at Voting Patterns of 115 Demographic Groups in the House Race," *The New York Times*, November 9, 1998, p. A20.

How Serious Is Nonvoting?

Some political scientists argue that nonvoting is not a critical problem. "Nonvoting is not a social disease," contends Austin Ranney, a noted scholar of politics. He points out that legal and extralegal denial of the vote to African Americans, women, Hispanics, persons over 18, and other groups has now been outlawed, so nonvoting is voluntary. He quotes the late Senator Sam Ervin: "I don't believe in making it easy for apathetic, lazy people to vote."[42]

Those who argue that nonvoting is a critical problem cite the "class bias" of those who do vote. The social makeup and attitudes of nonvoters are significantly different from those of voters and hence greatly distort the representative system. "The very poor . . . have about two-thirds the representation among voters than their numbers would suggest." Thus the people who need help the most from the government lack their fair share of electoral power to obtain it. And, it is argued, this situation is growing worse.[43]

Those who contend that there is a class bias in voting restrictions defend their observations. Low voting, they say, reflects "the underdevelopment of political attitudes resulting from the historic exclusion of low-income groups from active electoral participation." In short, part of the problem of low-income, less-educated people is their failure to be conscious of their real interests. Dynamic leadership or strong party organization, or both, would not only attract the poor to the polls but make clear their "class grievances and aspirations."[44]

Others reject this class-bias argument. They admit nonvoters are demographically different, yet they cite polls showing that nonvoters' attitudes are not much different from voters' attitudes. One study, comparing the party

A Closer Look

WHY IS TURNOUT SO LOW?

Although Americans can hardly avoid reading or hearing about political campaigns, roughly 85 million Americans fail to vote in presidential elections. Who are they? Why don't they vote? Is the fact that so many Americans choose not to vote a cause for alarm? If so, what can we do about it?

The simplest explanation for low turnout is that people are lazy, but there is more to it than that. Of course, some people are apathetic, but the vast majority of Americans are not. Paradoxically, we compare favorably with other nations in political interest and awareness, but for a variety of institutional and political reasons, we fail to convert these qualities into votes.

The difficulty of voting in the United States, the cost in time and effort, is higher than in other democracies. In our system, individuals are required to register to vote, and they must make sense of a range of political alternatives that do not necessarily meet their interests.

Another factor in the decline of voter turnout since the 1960s is the Twenty-sixth Amendment, which lowered the voting age to 18. It increased the number of eligible voters, but that group is the least likely to vote. With ratification of the amendment in 1971, turnout fell from 61 percent in 1968 to 55 percent in 1972.* The effect of adding this low turnout group to the electorate has been to lower the overall turnout rate. Efforts to activate younger voters through programs like "Rock the Vote" fostered increases in voter registration in 1996, but turnout in 1998 declined to 49 percent.

In other large industrialized democracies, political parties shoulder much of the burden of persuading people to vote, but American parties are too weak to take on this task. In particular, the Democratic party, which has an enormous stake in a heavy voter turnout from lower-income Americans, seldom achieves the voting participation it wants.

Critics say the reason people do not vote is that our political leaders do not appeal to the voters, and they do not offer real choices. They are not exciting, or they avoid taking positions on important issues. Yet in 1998 in Minnesota, Jesse "The Body" Ventura attracted a large enough following among young and new voters to be elected governor.

*David E. Rosenbaum, "Democrats Keep Solid Hold in Congress," *The New York Times*, November 9, 1988, p. A24.

MTV's "Choose or Lose" bus toured college campuses to register young people to vote.

Why People Don't Vote

Not registered to vote	35%
Didn't have time to go	6
No campaign or organization contacted them	6
Was not convenient	24
Not interested in the candidates	22
Election just didn't seem important	10
Too young at the time	1
Other	2
Not sure	8

Note: Results add up to more than 100 percent due to multiple responses.

SOURCE: Roper Center at University of Connecticut, February 1997, Public Opinion Online, Question ID (Ushare.97govn, rf03b).

identification of voters with that of all Americans, found the proportion of Democrats was nearly identical (51.4 percent of all citizens and 51.3 percent of voters), while Republicans as voters were slightly overrepresented (36 percent of citizens and 39.7 percent of voters). All other political differences are considered to be much smaller than this 3.7 percent gap. Further, voters are not "disproportionately hostile" to social welfare policies.[45]

What effect might increased voter turnout have in national elections? It might make a difference, since there are partisan differences between different demographic groups, and candidates would have to adjust to the demands of an expanded electorate. A noted political scientist, while acknowledging that no political system could achieve 100 percent participation, pointed out that the entire balance of power in the political system could be overturned if the large nonvoter population decided to vote.[46] However, others argue that the difference may not be as pronounced. Nonvoters are not more in favor of government ownership or control of industry, and they are not more egalitarian. Nonvoters are, however, more inclined to favor additional spending on welfare programs.[47]

Another way to think of low voter turnout is to see it as a sign of approval with things as they are, whereas high voter turnout would signify disapproval and widespread desire for change. Even on the subject of how to interpret low turnout there is disagreement.

VOTING CHOICES

Why do people vote as they do? Political scientists have identified three main elements of the voting choice: party identification, candidate appeal, and issues. These elements often overlap.

Voting on the Basis of Party

Party identification is the subjective sense of identification or affiliation that a person has with a political party, a long-standing preference for one party over the other (see Chapter 10). Party identification often predicts a person's stand on issues. It is part of our national mythology that Americans vote for the person and not the party, but, as you will see, the person we vote for is most often from the party we prefer.

Partisanship is typically acquired in childhood or adolescence as a result of the socialization process in the family, then reinforced by peer groups in adolescence. In the absence of reasons to vote otherwise, people depend on party identification to simplify their voting choices. Party identification is not party registration; it is not party membership in the sense of being a dues-paying, card-carrying member, as in some European parties. Rather, it is a psychological sense of attachment to one party or another.

There has been a dramatic increase in the number of Independents beginning in the mid-1970s. Nominally there are more Independents in the electorate today than Republicans. But two-thirds of all Independents are, in fact, partisans in their voting behavior. Independent Democrats are predictably Democratic in their voting behavior, and Independent Republicans vote heavily Republican. Independent-leaners are thus very different from each other and from the Pure Independents. Pure Independents have the lowest rate of turnout but generally do side with the eventual winner in presidential elections. These data on Independents only reinforce the importance of partisanship as an explanation of voting choice, because when we consider Independent Democrats and Independent Republicans as Democrats and Republicans respectively, there were only 8 percent Pure Independents or others without a party in 1996, and the average for the period 1952–96 was only 11 percent.[48]

Although party identification has fluctuated somewhat in the past 40 years, it remains more stable than attitudes about issues or political ideology. Fluctuations in party identification appear to come in response to economic conditions and political performance, especially of the president. The election in 2000 may produce some changes in party preference as a result of the Clinton impeachment and its highly partisan treatment in Congress.[49] The more information voters have about their choices, the more likely they are to defect from their party and vote for a candidate from the other party.

Voting on the Basis of Candidates

While long-term party identification is important, it is clearly not the only factor in voting choices; otherwise the Democrats would have won every presidential election since the last realignment in 1932. In fact, since 1952, Republicans have been more successful in winning the White House than Democrats. The answer to this puzzle is largely found in a second major explanation of voting choice—candidate appeal.

party identification
An informal and subjective affiliation with a political party that most people acquire in childhood.

You Decide . . .

Should we allow voting by mail and on the Internet?

During the past two centuries of constitutional government, this nation has gradually adopted a more expansive view of popular participation. Not only has the right to vote been extended to more people, but what decisions will be made in the voting booth have been expanded as well, to include primary elections to nominate party candidates and ballot referenda in which state constitutional amendments and state laws are adopted.

It seems logical that the next step in our democratic progress is permitting voters to cast ballots through the mail or through the Internet. Not only would such a reform make voting easier, but it would permit us to have more elections. For example, when a city council wants voters to decide whether to build a new football stadium, or when there is need for a special election to fill the term of a member of Congress who has died or resigned, election officials could mail out the ballots, and then in two or three weeks count up those that have been returned. The state of Oregon has already conducted several general elections by mail, and other states are considering adopting the Oregon system.

What do you think? Should we move toward a system in which we replace the ballot box with the mailbox or the computer? What arguments would you make for and against such an idea?

The elections of the 1980s marked a critical threshold in the emergence of the candidate-centered era in American electoral politics. This change in focus from parties to candidates is an important historical trend that has been gradually taking place over the last several decades.[50] Clinton's election victories in 1992 and 1996 reinforce the importance of candidates. He was especially popular among younger voters, women, and African Americans, but he also persuaded many "Reagan Democrats"—those who had defected to the Republicans in the 1980s—to return to their party. Evidence that his 1996 victory was largely candidate-centered is the Democrats' inability to regain a majority in the House or Senate. The 1998 elections may have marked a change to more party-centered and interest group-centered voting, at least in the competitive elections. But these elections were relatively rare, with most incumbents effectively unchallenged.

Candidate appeal or the lack of it—in terms of leadership, experience, good judgment, integrity, competence, strength, and energy—is often more important than party or issues. Dwight Eisenhower had great candidate appeal. He was a legendary five-star hero of the Allied effort in World War II. His unmilitary manner, his moderation, his personal charm, and his lack of a strong party position made him appealing across the ideological spectrum. Ronald Reagan generated positive candidate appeal, in part by asserting mainstream values the public found lacking in Jimmy Carter—leadership and strength.

Candidate appeal often involves an assessment of a candidate's character. Is the candidate honest? Is the candidate consistent? Is the candidate dedicated to "family values"? Does the candidate have religious or spiritual commitments? The American press in recent elections has sometimes played the role of "character cop," often asking, as Robert Livingston and Bill Clinton learned, questions about private lives and lifestyles. The press asks these questions because voters are interested in a political leader's background—perhaps even more interested in his character than in his position on hard-to-understand health care or regulatory policy issues.

Ronald Reagan's effort to generate positive candidate appeal was successful. Carter had hoped that Reagan would behave more like Barry Goldwater, who in his acceptance speech in 1964 had said, "Extremism in the defense of liberty is no vice. . . . Moderation in the pursuit of justice is no virtue."[51] Lyndon Johnson, Goldwater's opponent, benefited from public perception that Goldwater and those who nominated him were out of the mainstream of American politics.

Like Barry Goldwater in 1964, George McGovern was a candidate with negative appeal. Many of his supporters, by their dress and manner, appeared out of the mainstream of American politics. McGovern raised doubts about his judgment and leadership by how he handled his choice of a vice-president. McGovern named Missouri Senator Tom Eagleton as his running mate, only to discover that Eagleton had once been hospitalized for treatment of emotional exhaustion and depression. McGovern initially stood behind Eagleton, but as press coverage and criticism of McGovern's lack of investigation into Eagleton's past grew, McGovern dropped Eagleton and named a new running mate. In the end, "only about one-third of the public thought McGovern could be trusted as president."[52]

Increasingly, campaigns today focus on the negative elements of candidates. Opponents and the media are quick to point out the limitations or problems of any given candidate. In the 1992 election, George Bush did his best to attack Bill Clinton's unwillingness to serve in the Vietnam War, and Ross Perot and Clinton attacked Bush's economic record. Both Bush and Clinton, however, were gentle toward Perot, as they both hoped to get his endorsement or his supporters' votes.

The 1996 primary campaigns in the Republican party were often negative in tone, with candidates claiming that Bob Dole had been in Washington too long and was too old, that Pat Buchanan had never held public office and was an extremist, or that Steve Forbes lacked experience and was attempting to buy the election.

What did Americans make of the character issue in 1996? On dimensions of candidate character like "has high personal and moral standards" and "honest and trustworthy," people found Dole more appealing. On other elements of candidate character like "has new ideas" or "understands the problems of people like me," pollsters found that voters preferred Clinton to Dole. Polls taken soon after Clinton's reelection show that more than half the voters did not see him as honest and forthcoming regarding Whitewater.[53] But to most voters in 1996, issues like the economy and jobs mattered more than a candidate's character.

Voting on the Basis of Issues

Most political scientists agree that issues, while important, are not as central to the decision process as partisanship and candidate appeal.[54] Part of the reason is that candidates often intentionally obscure their positions on issues—an understandable strategy.[55] Richard Nixon said he had a plan to end the Vietnam War in 1968, clearly the most important issue in that year, but he would not reveal the specifics of that plan. By not detailing his plan, he stood to gain votes from those who wanted a more aggressive war effort as well as those who wanted a cease-fire.

For issue voting to occur, the issue must be important to voters, opposing candidates must take opposing stands on the issues, and voters must know these positions and vote accordingly. Rarely do candidates focus on only one issue. Voters often will agree with one candidate on one issue and with the opposing candidate on another. In such an instance, issues will likely not be the determining factor. But lack of interest by voters in issues does not mean candidates can take any issue position they wish.[56]

More likely than *prospective issue voting* (voting based on what a candidate pledges to do about an issue if elected) is *retrospective issue voting* (holding incumbents, usually the president's party, responsible for performance on issues such as the economy or foreign policy).[57] In times of peace and prosperity, voters will reward the incumbent; if the nation falls short on either, voters will elect the opposition.

Scholars have found that voter approval or disapproval of the performance of an outgoing president like Ronald Reagan in 1988 can have an impact on the vote for a presidentially endorsed successor. For example, 92 percent of those who strongly approved of Reagan's handling of the economy voted for George Bush in 1988.[58] But by 1992, Bush's handling of the economy came to be the most important issue in his defeat by Bill Clinton. More than two-thirds of Americans responding to exit polls described the economy in negative terms.

The state of the economy is often the central issue in midterm elections as well as presidential ones. Several studies have found a positive relationship between the state of the economy and "out" party gains and "in" party losses in congressional seats.[59] Political scientists have been able to locate the sources of this effect in individual voter's decision making. Voters tend to vote against the party in power if they perceive a decline or standstill in their personal financial situations.[60] Voters see responsibility for the economy resting with the president and Congress more than with governors or local officials.[61]

Despite generally good economic news and success in lowering the federal budget deficit, Democrats suffered a substantial defeat in 1994. Why? Part of the explanation lies in Bill Clinton's low approval ratings. In spite of his efforts to improve his popularity by trips to the Middle East shortly before the election, the public continued to have doubts about his leadership. Clinton, who had won election in 1992 on the theme of change, found that he and Democrats in Congress were targets of the same voter frustrations they had directed at George Bush. Republicans in Congress had used the filibuster and other tactics to defeat much of the Clinton agenda and then succeeded in arguing that Congress was in need of wholesale change. Republicans captured the "change" theme in 1994 by presenting their Contract with America, which included a commitment to a Balanced Budget Amendment, term limits for members

Thinking it Through . . .

One of the problems with making elections more frequent is that voters will get fed up. Americans already vote more frequently and for more offices than citizens of any other democracy do. Asking them to make voting choices even more frequently could result in lower turnout and less rational consideration. Many voters may be unaware an election is going on. Yet the advantage of the vote-by-mail system employed by Oregon and some cities and counties is that it increases turnout, at least initially. What political scientists dispute is whether such increases in participation will continue when the novelty wears off.

Some critics of voting by mail or electronic democracy worry about fraud. Even when voters are required to sign their mailed-in ballots, the possibility for forgery still exists. Also voting by mail or computer has the possibility of allowing people to pressure or harass voters.

Another criticism is that mail and electronic voting could be skewed toward participation by better-educated and higher-income voters, who routinely pay their bills by mail, make purchases on their computer, and own a personal computer with Internet access. Advocates of these new voting procedures contend that voters who do not own computers can drop off their ballots in some public building, and that eventually computers will be available widely enough that access will not be a problem.

However, if voting can be made easier and more convenient, why not do it? If the integrity of the vote can be protected and the new ways of voting become widely accessible, then such changes are probably inevitable.

SOURCE: David B. Magleby, "Participation in Mail Ballot Elections," *Western Political Quarterly* 40 (March 1987), pp. 79–91; Michael W. Traugott, "An Evaluation of Voting by Mail in Oregon," paper prepared for workshop cosponsored by the University of Michigan and the League of Women Voters, Washington, D.C., August 27, 1997.

of Congress, and other reforms. This strategy kept Democrats off balance and enabled Republicans to take advantage of voter anger.

The Clinton campaign won the battle of issues in 1996. Clinton made the economy and job creation a centerpiece of his reelection bid, and voters rewarded him with a second term in office. Exit polls indicated that voters, by a margin of three to two, saw the condition of the nation's economy as excellent or good, compared to those who saw it as poor or not so good. The Dole campaign countered that the economy was not growing fast enough and there was uncertainty about the stability of employment. Dole, Clinton, and Perot all stressed deficit reduction. Voters, however, by a margin greater than two to one, rejected Dole's supply-side argument that he could lower taxes by 15 percent and still reduce the federal budget deficit.

In varying degrees the Democrats focused the 1998 midterm election on four issues: Social Security, education, health care, and the environment. In contrast, the Republicans had a less clear and concrete agenda. The party wanted to emphasize the accomplishments of the 105th Congress and the reasons to return that Congress to power. The Republican party also decided to raise the impeachment issue late in the campaign, in part to activate their core supporters. Exit polls demonstrated that this strategy did not resonate well with voters, who wanted to move beyond the impeachment debate. The Democrats' emphasis on concrete issues, when combined with strong candidates in the relative few competitive races, helped them surprise even themselves by picking up a net gain of five House seats. This reinforced the sense that both parties have a lot to gain or lose in the 2000 elections.

POLITICS online

Internet Polling

As more and more people gain access to the Internet, scholars are interested in learning who uses this technology and why. Graphics Visualization Center at the Georgia Institute of Technology is a pioneer in Internet user surveys. Every six months, this group conducts a survey with some questions of political significance. For instance, they ask respondents if they are registered to vote, and they report these data for different demographic groups. You will find this survey at:

http://www.cc.gatech.edu/gvu

There are places on the Web where any user can log on and express an opinion on current events. The reliability of these results has the same problem with self-selection we discussed in the chapter; Internet polls are essentially like a newspaper call-in poll. One example is:

http://nt.excite.com/poll

A more reliable poll, run by the Harris firm, draws a representative sample from users who have registered online. The polling firm then e-mails them questionnaires periodically. A self-selection problem remains with this poll, but the researcher can at least control for demographics. This poll covers a wide range of topics, but the focus becomes explicitly political around election time. You will find this report at:

http://www.harrispollonline.com

As people become accessible via Internet polling, this communications medium may eventually replace telephone polling.

For more Internet resources on Public Opinion, Participation, and Voting, see our home page at:

http://www.prenhall.com/burns

SUMMARY

1. Public opinion is a complex combination of views and attitudes individuals acquire through various influences from childhood on. Public opinion takes on qualities of stability, fluidity, intensity, latency, consensus, or polarization—each of which is affected by people's feelings about the salience of issues.
2. The American public has a generally low level of interest in politics, and most people do not follow politics and government closely. The public's knowledge of political issues is poor.
3. Those Americans who are interested in public affairs can participate by voting, joining interest groups and political parties, working on campaigns, writing letters to newspaper editors or elected officials, or attempting to influence how another person will vote, or even protesting.
4. Better educated, older, and party- and group-involved people tend to vote more; the young tend to vote the least. Voter turnout tends to be higher in national than in state and local elections, and higher in presidential than in midterm elections.
5. Party identification remains an important element in the voting choice of most Americans. It represents a long-term attachment and is a "lens" through which voters view candidates and issues as they make their voting choices. Candidate appeal, including character and record, are another key factor in voter choice. Voters decide their vote less frequently on the basis of issues.

KEY TERMS

public opinion 254
political socialization 256
attentive public 261
voter registration 263
Australian ballot 264
turnout 266
party identification 269

FURTHER READING

JOSEPH A. AISTRIP, *The Southern Strategy Revisited: Republican Top-Down Advancement in the South* (University of Kentucky Press, 1996).

HERBERT ASHER, *Polling and the Public: What Every Citizen Should Know*, 3d ed. (Congressional Quarterly Press, 1995).

EARL BLACK AND MERLE BLACK, *The Vital South: How Presidents Are Elected* (Harvard University Press, 1992).

M. MARGARET CONWAY, *Political Participation in the United States*, 2d ed. (Congressional Quarterly Press, 1991).

ROBERT S. ERIKSON AND KENT L. TEDIN, *American Public Opinion: Its Origins, Content and Impact*, 5th ed. (Allyn and Bacon, 1995).

WILLIAM H. FLANIGAN AND NANCY H. ZINGALE, *Political Behavior of the American Electorate*, 8th ed. (Congressional Quarterly Press, 1994).

JOHN G. GEER, *From Tea Leaves to Opinion Polls: A Theory of Democratic Leadership* (Columbia University Press, 1996).

ROBERT HUCKFELDT AND JOHN SPRAGUE, *Citizens, Politics, and Social Communication: Information and Influence in an Election Campaign* (Cambridge University Press, 1995).

BRYAN D. JONES, *Reconceiving Decision-Making in Democratic Politics: Attention, Choice and Public Policy* (University of Chicago Press, 1994).

BRUCE E. KEITH, DAVID B. MAGLEBY, CANDICE J. NELSON, ELIZABETH ORR, MARK C. WESTLYE, AND RAYMOND E. WOLFINGER, *The Myth of the Independent Voter* (University of California Press, 1992).

V. O. KEY, JR., *Public Opinion and American Democracy* (Alfred A. Knopf, 1961).

ANTHONY KING, *Running Scared: Why America's Politicians Campaign Too Much and Govern Too Little* (Free Press, 1997).

PHILIP A. KLINKNER, ED., *Midterm: The Elections of 1994 in Context* (Westview Press, 1996).

WARREN E. MILLER AND J. MERRILL SHANKS, *The New American Voter* (Harvard University Press, 1996).

MICHAEL NELSON, ED., *The Elections of 1996* (Congressional Quarterly Press, 1997).

RICHARD G. NIEMI AND HERBERT F. WEISBERG, *Classics in Voting Behavior* (Congressional Quarterly Press, 1993).

RICHARD G. NIEMI AND HERBERT F. WEISBERG, *Controversies in Voting Behavior*, 3d ed. (Congressional Quarterly Press, 1993).

BENJAMIN I. PAGE AND ROBERT Y. SHAPIRO, *The Rational Public: Fifty Years of Trends in Americans' Policy Preferences* (University of Chicago Press, 1992).

FRANK R. PARKER, *Black Votes Count: Political Empowerment in Mississippi After 1965* (University of North Carolina Press, 1990).

GERALD M. POMPER, ED., *The Election of 1996: Reports and Interpretations* (Chatham House, 1997).

SAMUEL L. POPKIN, *The Reasoning Voter: Communication and Persuasion in Presidential Campaigns* (University of Chicago Press, 1991).

SUSAN J. TOLCHIN, *The Angry Citizen: How Voter Rage Is Changing the Nation* (Westview Press, 1996).

JOHN ZALLER, *The Origins and Nature of Mass Opinion* (Cambridge University Press, 1992).

See also *Public Opinion Quarterly, American Journal of Political Science*, and *American Political Science Review*.

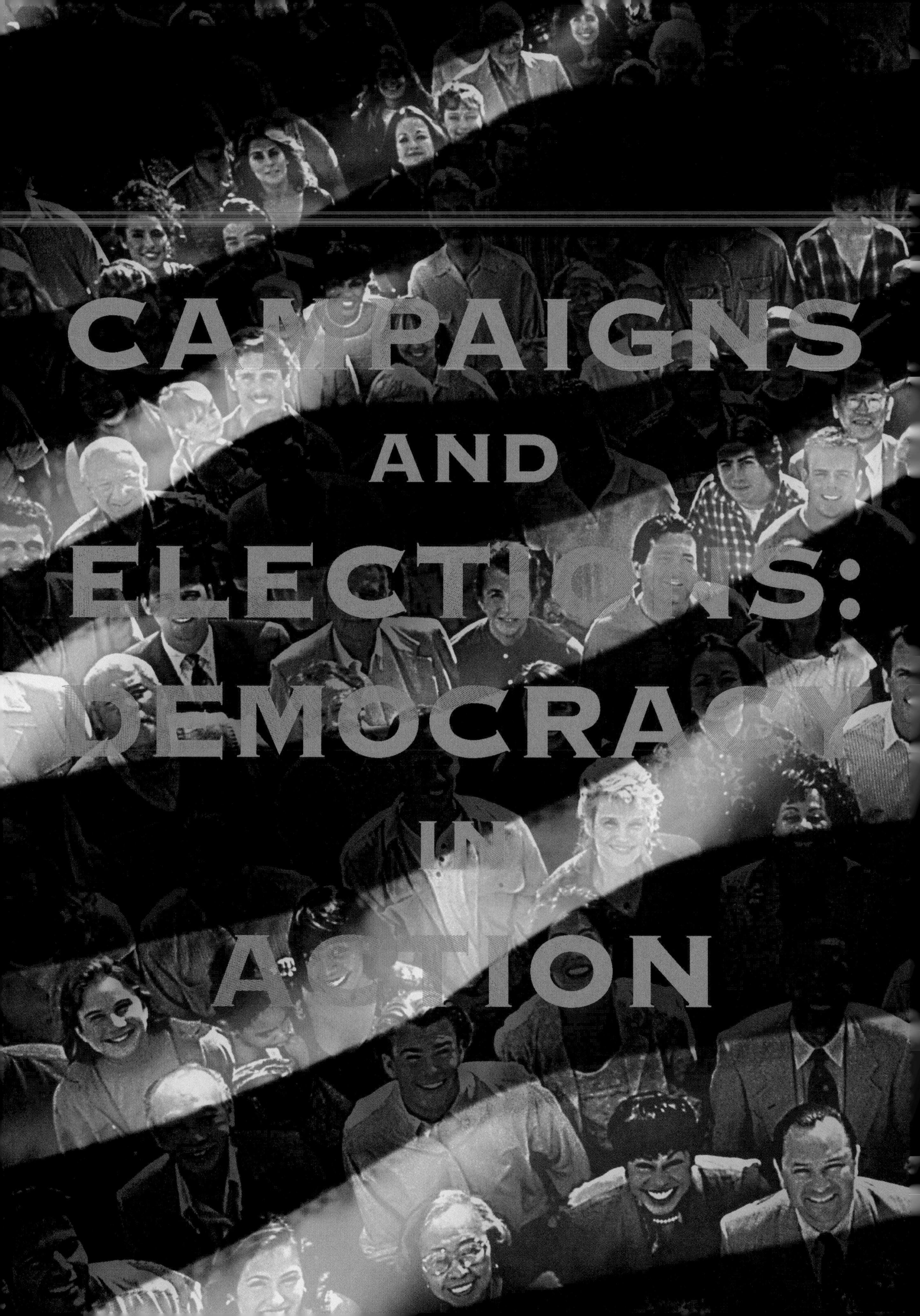

CAMPAIGNS AND ELECTIONS: DEMOCRACY IN ACTION

12

CHAPTER OUTLINE

- Elections: The Rules of the Game
- Running for Congress
- Running for President
- Money in American Elections
- Improving Elections

SOME CYNICS CONTEND THAT ELECTIONS DO NOT MATTER, AND THERE IS LITTLE POINT IN VOTING. STRONG EVIDENCE TO THE CONTRARY COMES FROM THE 1998 midterm election, in which the Democrats bucked the historic tradition of the president's party losing seats in a midterm election. They not only did not lose seats but actually picked up five seats in the House of Representatives, while holding the Republicans to no gains in the Senate. The fallout from this election toppled House Speaker Newt Gingrich, who was quoted some weeks before the election as expecting that Republicans would pick up as many as 40 seats.[1] The outcome of the election was frequently cited by Democrats as a "referendum on the president's future," in part because some Republicans had run commercials late in the campaign on the Monica Lewinsky scandal. Exit polls found President Bill Clinton's relationship with the young White House intern was not very important to voters.[2]

Competitive contests in the 1998 House elections took place in a little more than 1 in 10 of the 435 elections.[3] The small number of competitive elections compared to previous years was the result of few incumbents retiring in 1998 and the reality that most districts are now dominated either by Republicans or Democrats as a result of how district boundaries were drawn by state legislatures following the 1990 census. The relatively small number of competitive contests meant that political parties and interest groups focused their money and attention on the few battlegrounds for control of the House of Representatives.

Even in these days of campaigning primarily on television and radio, the outcome of elections is still determined by who can best mobilize voters and get them to the polls. This is especially the case in lower turnout primary and midterm elections. The Democrats clearly won the voter mobilization battle in 1998. Part of their success can be attributed to their consistent message, while Republican campaigns were less focused. Another part of the explanation was the activity of political parties and interest groups, who spent millions of dollars on the election, in addition to campaigns run by the candidates. Labor unions mounted person-to-person drives in competitive states to identify voters supportive of candidates endorsed by labor. Then on election day, they reminded those voters to get out and vote, and in some cases even drove them to the polls. Other interest groups sent letters and postcards to likely voters suggesting which candidate was better on issues of interest to the group's agenda—the environment, abortion, trade, or health care. Hiding behind names masking their identity like

"Foundation for Responsible Government" or the "Eagle Forum," some interest groups attacked one candidate or supported another. These campaign activities, so long as they do not explicitly call for the election or defeat of a candidate, are not subject to the disclosure requirement of campaign contributions, nor are they limited in amount spent.

Parties are permitted to raise unlimited contributions from individuals and interest groups for party-building purposes. Party building has been expanded to include advertising on behalf of candidates. The political parties, recognizing the growth in interest group campaigning, responded in 1998 by doubling the amount of soft money they raised and spent, as compared to the midterm election in 1994. The parties not only placed ads on radio and television but used extensive mailings and phone banks. Democrats, for instance, often ran phone banks with recorded messages from President Clinton and First Lady Hillary Rodham Clinton. Republicans roughly doubled Democrats' soft money activity in 1998, focusing on the battle for the House. House Republicans titled their effort "Operation Breakout" and did not hide their goal of raising and spending $35 million in soft money.[4] Increased activity by candidates, parties, and interest groups is likely to continue, especially given the close party balance in both houses of Congress and an open seat for president in 2000.

The American electoral system permits citizens to vote more often and for more offices than citizens of any other democracy. In 2000 we are electing not only a president and vice-president but 11 governors, 33 U.S. senators, and all 435 members of the U.S. House of Representatives. At the state level, we are electing treasurers, secretaries of state, and, in most states, judges.

Americans hold thousands of elections for everything from community college directors to county sheriffs. About half a million persons hold elected state and local offices.[5] In addition to electing people, voters can place laws or constitutional amendments on the ballot by petition in 27 states. In all states except Delaware, voters must approve all changes in the state constitution. Voters decide directly on issues such as limiting automobile insurance rates, lowering taxes, and setting term limits for elected officials.

In this chapter we begin by explaining the implications of our election rules. We note four important problems that deserve attention: lack of competition for some offices, problems associated with nominating presidential candidates, complexities and distortions of the Electoral College, and the influence of money in our elections. We also discuss proposed reforms in each of these areas.

Elections: The Rules of the Game

The rules of the game—the electoral game—make a difference. Although the Constitution sets certain conditions and requirements, most electoral rules remain matters of state law.

Regularly Scheduled Elections

In our system, elections are set in advance and at fixed intervals that cannot be changed by the party in power. It does not make any difference if the nation is at war, as we were during the Civil War, or in the midst of a crisis; when the calendar calls for an election, the election is held. Elections for members of Congress occur the first Tuesday after the first Monday in November of even-numbered years. Although there are some exceptions (special elections or peculiar state provisions), participants know *in advance* just when the next election will be. In many parliamentary democracies, such as Great Britain and Canada, elections are called by the government at a time of its choosing.

Fixed, Staggered, and Sometimes Limited Terms

Our electoral system is based on *fixed terms*, meaning that the length of a term in office is specified, not indefinite. The Constitution has set the term of office for the U.S. House of Representatives at two years, the Senate at six years, and the presidency at four years. Fixed terms of office mean that politicians can anticipate the next election for a given office and plan for it.

Our system also has *staggered terms* for some offices, meaning that not all offices are up for election at the same time. All House members are up for election every two years, but only one-third of the senators are up for election at the same time. Because House members must be campaigning perpetually, many have expressed support for lengthening their terms to four years. Also, House members must now give up their seats to run for the Senate; with a four-year term, they could run for the Senate at the middle of their term and, if they lost, still retain their House seat. Senators strongly oppose this change, even though the same concern affects senators when they run for the presidency. If the presidential election occurs two or four years into their six-year term, senators can run for the presidency without fear of losing their seat. But if their Senate term expires the same year as the presidential election, the laws of all states except Texas require them to give up their Senate seat to run for president or vice-president or any other position. (Texas is an exception because Lyndon Johnson had state law changed to permit him to run for both vice-president and the Senate in 1960. This same rule permitted Lloyd Bentsen to run for both offices in 1988.)

Term Limits

Limits on the number of terms a person can hold a particular office are another feature of our electoral system with important consequences. The Twenty-second Amendment to the Constitution, adopted in 1951, limits presidents to two terms. Knowing that a president cannot run again changes the way Congress, the opposing party, and the press regard the president. A politician who cannot, or has announced he or she will not, run again is called a **lame duck**. Efforts to limit the terms of other politicians have become a major issue in several American states. The most frequent targets have been state legislators. One consequence of term limits is more lame ducks.

Term limits are popular. Proposals to impose constitutional limits on terms have been defeated in only three states (Washington, Utah, and Mississippi); 22 states have enacted them on their own.[6] Three-fourths of all voters favor term limits, as do 9 out of 10 Strong Republicans and 7 out of 10 Strong Democrats.[7] Still, despite their popularity, proposals for term limits have repeatedly lost when they have come to a vote in recent sessions of Congress.

The Supreme Court, by a vote of 5 to 4, declared that a state does not have the constitutional power to impose limits on the number of terms for which its members of the U.S. Congress are eligible, either by amending its own constitution or state law.[8] If term limits were to be imposed on members of Congress, it would have to be either by an amendment to the U.S. Constitution or by reversal of the Supreme Court decision.

Winner-Takes-All

One of the most important features of our electoral system is the **winner-takes-all** rule.[9] In most American electoral settings, the candidate with the most votes wins. The winner does not necessarily need to have a *majority* (more than half the votes cast); in a multicandidate race the winner may have only a *plurality* (the largest number of votes), as did Harry Truman in 1948, John Kennedy in 1960, Richard Nixon in 1968, and Bill Clinton in 1992 and 1996.

lame duck
A politician who cannot, or has announced that he or she will not, run again.

winner-takes-all
An election system in which the candidate with the most votes wins.

Most American electoral districts are **single-member districts**, meaning that in any district for any given election—senator, governor, U.S. House, state legislative seat—the voters choose *one* representative or official.[10] When a single-member district system is combined with the winner-takes-all rule, minor parties find it hard to win. For example, even if a third party gets 25 percent of the vote in several districts, it still gets no seats. Under our electoral rules, the best way for a party to win an election is to assemble a large coalition that produces a majority or at least a plurality.

The single-member district and winner-takes-all system is different from **proportional representation** systems, in which political parties secure legislative seats and power in proportion to the number of votes they receive in the election. Let's assume a hypothetical state has three representatives up for election. In each of the three contests, the Republican defeats the Democrat, but in one district by only a narrow margin. If you add up the statewide vote, the Republicans get 67 percent and the Democrats 33 percent. Under our winner-takes-all and single-member district system, the Republicans get all three seats. But under a system of proportional representation, in which the three seats represent the whole state, the Democrats would receive one seat because they got roughly one-third of the vote in the entire state. Proportional representation thus rewards minor parties and permits them to participate in government. Countries that practice some form of proportional representation include Germany, Israel, and Japan.

The Electoral College

We elect our president and vice-president by an indirect device known as the **Electoral College**. The framers of the U.S. Constitution devised this system to remove the choice of president from a direct vote of the people. Under this system each state has as many electors as it has representatives and senators. Thus California, for instance, has 54 electoral votes, and Vermont has 3. Following the 2000 census, California's electoral votes will increase because of population growth, while the least populated states will retain only one electoral vote each. Each state is free to determine how its electors are selected. Electors are often longtime party workers who are appointed by the state parties. They are expected to cast their electoral votes for the party's candidates for president and vice-president.

The Twelfth Amendment requires electors to vote separately for president and vice-president. To demonstrate how this works, if you vote for the Republican candidate for president in 2000, you actually vote for electors pledged to vote for that candidate and his or her vice-presidential running mate. If you voted for the Democratic candidate in 1996, you actually voted for the electors pledged to support Bill Clinton for president and Al Gore for vice-president.

Candidates who win a plurality of the popular vote in a state secure all that state's electoral votes, except in Nebraska and Maine, which allocate electoral votes to the winner in each congressional district plus two electoral votes for whoever carries the state as a whole. The winning electors go to their state capital on the first Monday after the second Wednesday in December to cast their ballots. These ballots are then sent to Congress, and early in January, Congress formally counts the ballots and declares to the world what everybody already knows—who won the election for president and vice-president.

It takes a majority of the electoral votes to win. If no candidate gets a majority of the electoral votes for president, the House chooses among the top three candidates, with each state delegation having one vote. If no candidate gets a majority of the electoral votes for vice-president, the Senate chooses among the top two candidates, with each senator casting one vote.

Concern about the Electoral College is renewed every time there is a serious third-party candidate for the presidency, as was the case in 1992 and 1996 when Ross Perot ran for president. People began to ask questions like: Which Congress casts the

single-member district
An electoral district in which voters choose one representative or official.

proportional representation
An election system in which each party receives the proportion of legislative seats corresponding to its proportion of the vote.

Electoral College
The electoral system used in electing the president and vice-president, in which voters vote for electors pledged to cast their ballots for a particular party's candidates.

vote, the one now serving or the new one just elected? The answer is the new one, the one elected in November and taking office the first week in January. But what happens if a state's delegation cannot agree on a candidate? Then its vote does not count. Would it be possible to have a president of one party and a vice-president of another? Yes, if the election were thrown into the House and Senate.

When there are only two major candidates for the presidency, the chances of an election being thrown into the House are remote. But twice in our history the House has had to act: in 1800, before the Twelfth Amendment was written, the House had to choose in a tie vote between Thomas Jefferson and Aaron Burr; in 1824 the House picked John Quincy Adams over Andrew Jackson and William Crawford. Henry Clay, who was forced out of the race when he came in fourth in the Electoral College, threw his support behind Adams. When Adams was elected, he made Clay his secretary of state. The 1824 vote in the House was especially contentious. Jackson, winner of the popular vote, was passed over when the vote went to the House. This outcome infuriated Jackson, who won the Electoral College vote by a wide margin four years later.

The rules of the Electoral College sharply influence presidential politics. To win a presidential election, a candidate must appeal successfully to the big states of California, Texas, Ohio, and Illinois.[11] California's electoral vote of 54 currently exceeds the combined electoral votes of the 14 least populated states plus the District of Columbia. The map inside the front cover of this book provides a visual comparison of state size based on electoral votes.

Presidential candidates do not ordinarily waste time campaigning in a state unless they have at least a fighting chance of carrying that state; nor do they waste time in a state in which their party is a sure winner. Richard Nixon in 1960 was the last candidate to promise to campaign in all 50 states. He did so, but lost valuable time traveling to and from Alaska, while John Kennedy focused on the more populous states. The contest usually narrows down to the medium-sized and big states, where the balance between the parties tends to be fairly even.

Our Electoral College system makes it possible for a person to receive the most popular votes and not get enough electoral votes. This happened in 1824, when Andrew Jackson won 12 percent more of the vote than John Quincy Adams; in 1876, when Samuel Tilden received more popular votes than Rutherford B. Hayes; and again in 1888, when Benjamin Harrison won in the Electoral College although Grover Cleveland received more popular votes. It almost happened in close elections in 1960 and 1976, when the shift of a few votes in a few key states could have resulted in the election of a president without a popular majority. In a year with a serious minor party candidate, the result could be the election of a president without a plurality of the vote.

In two of the three elections in which popular vote winners did not become president, the Electoral College did not decide the winner. The 1824 election was decided by the U.S. House of Representatives. In 1876 the electoral vote in three southern states was disputed, resulting in the Hayes-Tilden Commission deciding how those votes should be counted. Only in 1888 did the Electoral College award the presidency to the candidate with fewer popular votes.[12]

Running for Congress

How candidates run for Congress depends on the nature of their district or state, on whether candidates are incumbents or challengers, on the strength of their personal organization, on how well known they are, and on how much money they have to spend on their campaign. We can, however, note several similarities in House and Senate elections.

First, most congressional elections are not close. In districts where most people belong to one party or where incumbents are popular and enjoy fund-raising and other campaign advantages, there is often little competition.[13] Those who believe competition is essential to constitutional democracy are concerned that so many officeholders have **safe seats.** When officeholders do not have to fight to retain their seat, elections are not performing their proper role.[14]

Congressional elections tend to be more competitive than state legislature elections; mayoral elections are often hotly contested also. Competition is also more likely when funding is adequate for both candidates, which is not often the case in U.S. House elections. Elections for governor and for the U.S. Senate are more seriously contested and adequately financed than those for the U.S. House of Representatives.

Presidential popularity affects both House and Senate elections during presidential election years as well as midterm elections. The impact of presidential popularity in a presidential election is the **coattail effect**, the boost candidates from the president's party get from a popular presidential candidate running in the same election. Winning presidential candidates do not always provide such a boost. The Republicans suffered a net loss of six seats when George Bush won the presidency in 1988, and the Democrats suffered a net loss of ten seats when Bill Clinton won the 1992 presidential election. Democrats fared better in 1996, picking up a net gain of nine seats in the House, but this was not enough to permit them to regain control of the chamber. Overall, "measurable coattail effects continue to appear," according to congressional elections scholar Gary Jacobson, but they are "erratic and usually modest" in their impact.[15]

In midterm elections, presidential popularity and economic conditions have long been associated with the number of House seats a president's party loses.[16] These same factors are associated with how well the president's party does in Senate races, but the association is not as strong.[17] Figure 12-1 shows the number of seats in the House of Representatives and U.S. Senate gained or lost by the party controlling the White House in midterm elections since 1938. In each of these elections until 1998, the party controlling the White House lost seats in the House. The range of losses, however, is quite wide, from a low of 4 seats for the Democrats in 1962 to a high of 71 seats for the Democrats in 1938. The robust economy and President Clinton's high job approval ratings contributed to the success of the Democrats in the 1998 elections.

Republicans did better in 1994 than in any midterm election since 1946, picking up 53 seats. The Republican tide was not limited to the House but included a net gain of nine seats in the Senate.[18] When presidential landslides occur, as they did with Lyndon Johnson in 1964, the victorious party is especially vulnerable to lose seats in the next midterm election, as the Democrats did in 1966.

The House of Representatives

Every two years, as many as 1,000 candidates—including approximately 400 incumbents—campaign for Congress. After deciding to take the plunge, candidates must first plan a primary race, unless they face no opponents. Incumbents are rarely challenged for renomination from within their own party, and when they are, the challenges are seldom serious. In the 1990s, for example, on average only two House incumbents were denied renomination each election cycle. Challengers running against entrenched incumbents rarely encounter opposition in their own party.[19]

safe seat
An elected office that is predictably won by one party or the other.

coattail effect
The boost candidates of the president's party receive in an election because of the president's popularity.

MOUNTING A PRIMARY CAMPAIGN The first step for would-be challengers in contested primaries or for those seeking open seats is to raise hundreds of thousands of dollars to mount a serious campaign. This requires asking friends and acquaintances as well as interest groups for money. Parties can sometimes help, but they shy away from giving money before a candidate's nomination.

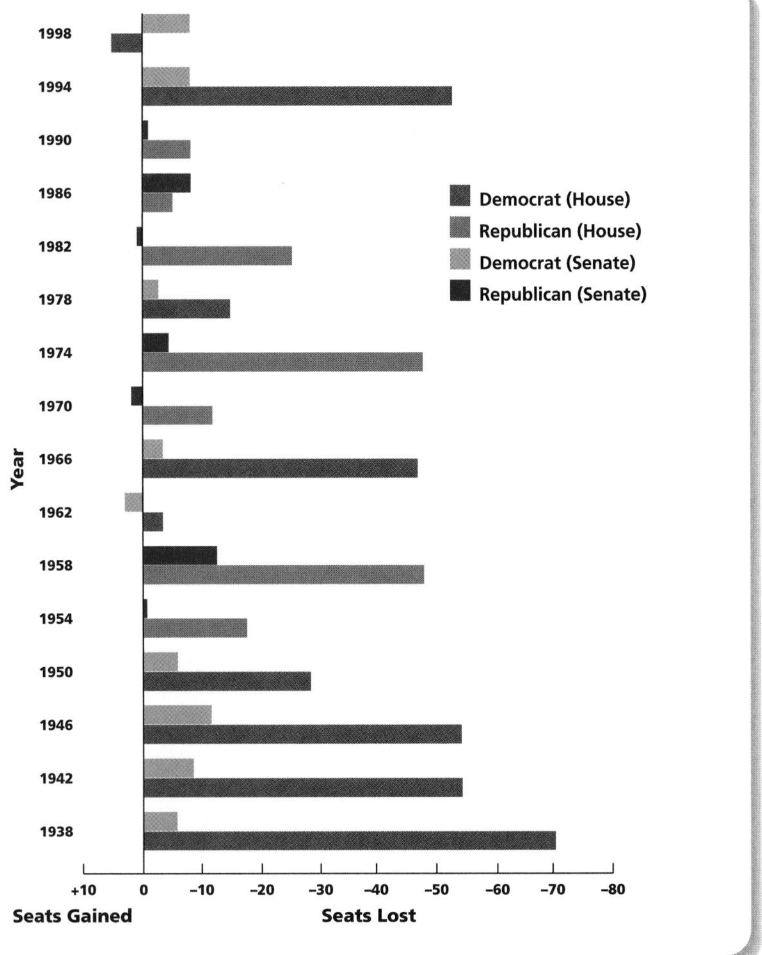

FIGURE 12-1 Seats Lost by the President's Party in Midterm Elections for the House of Representatives and the Senate (1938–1998)

The second step is to build a *personal organization.* The party organization usually stays neutral until the nomination is decided. A candidate can build an organization while holding another office, such as a seat in the state legislature, or by serving in civic causes, helping other candidates, and being conspicuous without being controversial.

The next steps are to hire campaign managers and technicians, buy television and other advertising, conduct polls, and pay for a variety of activities. All these things depend on raising funds, which most candidates find difficult before they have secured the nomination.

A candidate's main hurdle is gaining visibility. Candidates work hard to be mentioned by the media. As the old cliché goes, "It doesn't matter what they say about you as long as they spell your name right." In large cities with many simultaneous campaigns, congressional candidates are frequently lost in media "noise," and in rural areas the press often plays down political news. Candidates rely on personal contacts, on hand shaking and door-to-door campaigning, and on identifying likely supporters and courting their favor—the same techniques used in campaigns for lesser offices. The turnout in primaries tends to be low, except in campaigns in which large sums of money are expended on advertising.

CAMPAIGNING FOR THE GENERAL ELECTION As we have mentioned, most members of Congress win reelection.[20] Since 1970, over 95 percent of incumbent House members seeking reelection have won, and in 1998 over 98

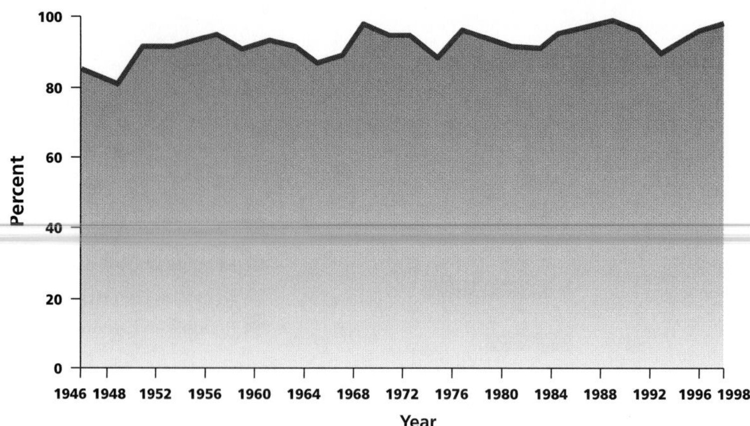

FIGURE 12-2 Congressional Incumbents Reelected

SOURCE: Federal Election Commission, press release, April 14, 1997, pp. 32–51; "House Membership in the 106th Congress," *Congressional Quarterly Weekly*, November 7, 1998, p. 3010.

percent of incumbent House members running for reelection were successful (see Figure 12-2).[21] Knowing the advantage of incumbency, potential challengers often choose not to run, thereby helping the incumbent further.[22] In recent House elections, incumbents outspent their challengers roughly 3 to 1; in the Senate the difference was closer to 2 to 1.[23] Most challengers spend little money, run campaigns that are not significantly more visible than primary campaigns, contact few voters, and lose badly.

A few challengers in each election mount serious challenges because of the incumbent's perceived vulnerability, the challenger's own wealth, party, or political action committee efforts, or a combination of factors. Serious challengers in House races are hard to find. Many are scared away by the prospect of having to raise close to a million dollars in campaign funds; others realize the district has been drawn with fewer persons from their party than the incumbent's; and some do not want to face the media scrutiny that comes with a serious race for Congress.

Why is keeping a House seat so much easier than gaining it? Incumbents have a host of advantages that help them gain reelection. These "perks" include free mailings to constituents (the *franking* privilege), the free use of broadcast studios to record radio and television tapes to be sent to local media outlets, and perhaps most important of all, a large staff to perform countless favors for constituents and send a stream of press reports and mail back to the district.[24] Representatives also try to win committee posts, even on minor committees, that relate to the needs of their districts and build connections with constituents.[25]

If incumbents win so often, how do we get any significant turnover in the House of Representatives? Turnover comes when incumbents die, decide to retire, or seek some other office. *Redistricting*, which happens once each decade, often promotes some turnover, as it will in 2002 when incumbents are forced to run in new districts. More than one-third of the U.S. House retired between 1992 and 1996. This was an unusual amount of turnover and included some members who were disillusioned by partisan bickering.

Retirements and redistricting create open seats, which often result in more competitive elections. Potential candidates, as well as political action committees and political party committees, all watch open seat races closely. But as noted, most races have incumbents and most incumbents win, lending credibility to the charge that we have a "permanent Congress." One solution to the problem of the permanent Congress is to limit the number of terms a person can serve.

The Senate

Running for the Senate is big-time politics. The six-year term and the national exposure make a Senate seat a glittering prize, so competition is usually intense. Senate campaigns generally feature state-of-the-art campaign technology; a race normally costs millions of dollars (see Figure 12-3).[26] Still, Senate races tend to be much like those for the House. The essential tactics are to raise lots of money, get good people involved, make as many personal contacts as possible (especially in the states with smaller populations), avoid giving the opposition any positive publicity, and have a simple campaign theme.

Incumbency is an advantage for senators, although not as much as for representatives.[27] Incumbent senators are more widely known through the media, but so are many of their opponents. Because Senate candidates are far more visible than House candidates, they cannot easily duck tough issues. Further, senators normally face tougher competition—challengers who frequently are already well known or who raise and spend significant amounts of money.[28]

When one party controls the Senate by only a few seats, as has been the case in recent years, more good candidates run, and the number of competitive elections increases. But the cost of Senate campaigns can vary greatly. California has 69 times the number of potential voters as Wyoming, so a seat from Wyoming is much cheaper than a seat from California. As a result, disproportionately large amounts of money are spent in small states when the stakes for control of the Senate are high.[29]

Running for President

Presidential elections are major media events, with candidates seeking as much positive television coverage as possible, and trying at the same time to avoid negative coverage. The formal campaign has three stages: winning the nomination, campaigning at the convention, and mobilizing support in the general election.

Stage 1: The Nomination

Presidential hopefuls must make a series of critical tactical decisions. The first is when to start campaigning. Some candidates, like Steve Forbes and Lamarr Alexander, begin almost as soon as the last presidential election is over. Early decisions are increasingly necessary for candidates to raise the money and assemble an organization. The problem with having to decide on a race for the presidency years

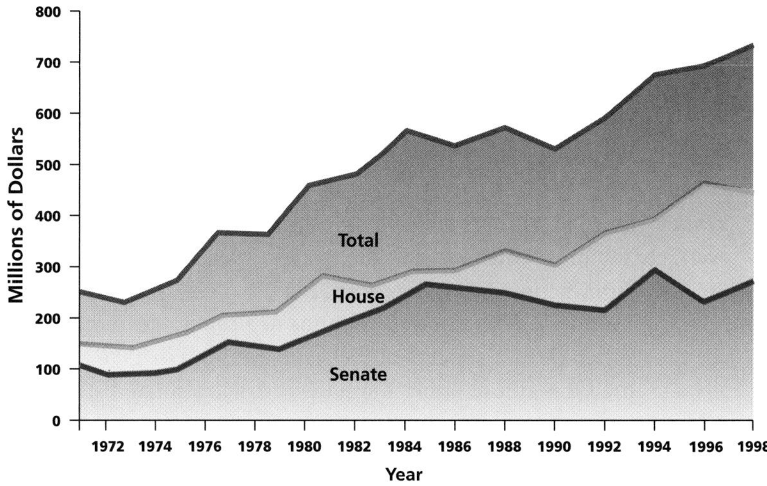

FIGURE 12-3 Rising Campaign Costs (General Elections)

SOURCE: Federal Election Commission, press release, April 14, 1997, pp. 12–13; and press release, December 29, 1998, p. 1.

"My former opponent is supporting me in the general election. Please disregard all the things I said about him in the primary."

Dunagin's People by Ralph Dunagin. Reprinted with special permission of NAS, Inc.

before the next election is that circumstances change. A president who is popular can suffer a dramatic loss of popularity, and a front runner who appears invincible may stumble. Campaigning begins well before any actual declaration of candidacy, as candidates try to line up supporters to win caucuses or primaries in key states and to raise money for their nomination effort.

One of the hardest jobs for candidates and their strategists is calculating how to deal with the complex maze of presidential primaries and caucuses that constitutes the delegate selection system. The system varies from state to state and often from one party to the other in the same state. Although the process is influenced somewhat by federal regulation of campaign financing and national party rules, within broad limits states can set up the systems they prefer.

PRESIDENTIAL PRIMARIES State presidential primaries, unknown before this century, have become the main method of choosing delegates. Today more than three-fourths of the states use presidential primaries. In 1996 primaries selected 78 percent of the Democratic delegates and 88 percent of the Republican delegates.[30] The rest of the states use caucuses or conventions.

Voters in states like Iowa and New Hampshire bask in media attention for weeks and even months before they cast the first ballots in the presidential sweepstakes. Because these early contests have had the effect of limiting the choices of voters in states that come later in the process, there has been a tendency for states to move their primaries up. California, which traditionally held its primary in June, moved it to March in 1996 so that its voters would play a more important role in selecting the nominee. Other states did the same thing. As a result, the 1996 primary season was compressed into several weeks of intense activity. The trend of compressing the primaries continues in 2000 as several states are considering holding a primary between the regional primary in the South and the California primary.

Presidential primaries have two main features: a *beauty contest*, or popularity vote in which voters indicate which candidate they prefer but do not actually elect delegates to the convention, and *actual voting* for delegates pledged to a candidate. Candidates may win the beauty contest and find their opponents doing better in actual delegates elected because they failed to put a full slate of delegates on the ballot or because local notables were running for a delegate pledged to another candidate. Different combinations of these two features have produced the following systems:

1. *Proportional representation*: Delegates to the national convention are allocated on the basis of the votes candidates win in the beauty contest. This system has been used in most of the states, including several of the largest ones. The Democrats now mandate a proportional representation rule for all their primaries.[31] In some states Republicans use this same system, but Republicans are much more varied in their delegate selection processes.[32]
2. *Winner-takes-all*: In some states there is a winner-takes-all rule that whoever gets the most votes wins all that state's delegates, as Bob Dole did in the California Republican primary in 1996. To win all the delegates of a state like California is an enormous bonus to a candidate. Republicans still use the winner-takes-all system at the state level, and in 1996 about half of all states used this rule at either the state or congressional district levels.
3. *Delegate selection*: In several states, large and small, voters choose delegates who may or may not have pledged how they will vote in the national party convention. The names of the presidential hopefuls do not appear separately on the ballot, and there is no declared presidential preference. Under this arrangement, delegates are free to exercise their independent judgment

at the convention. This system is used only by the Republicans; in 1996 it was used most prominently in New York and Illinois.

4. *Delegate selection and separate presidential poll*: In several states voters decide twice: once to indicate their choice for president, and again to choose delegates pledged, or at least favorable, to a presidential candidate. This system is one of the oldest kinds of presidential primary.[33]

CAUCUSES AND CONVENTIONS A **caucus** is a meeting of party members and supporters of various candidates. About a dozen states use a caucus and/or convention system for choosing delegates.[34] There are many variations of the caucus and convention system because they are regulated by each state's parties and legislature. The caucus or convention is the oldest method of choosing delegates and is fundamentally different from the primary system because it centers on the party organization. In principle, the caucus and convention system is far simpler than the primary method.

Delegates who will attend the national party conventions are chosen by delegates to state or district conventions, who themselves are chosen earlier in county, precinct, or town caucuses. The process starts at local meetings open to all party members, who discuss and take positions on candidates and issues and elect delegates to represent their views at the next level. This process is repeated until national nominating convention delegates are chosen by conventions of delegates throughout a district or state.

Whether caucus or primary, nominations require candidates to mobilize voters in generally low turnout settings. This situation pushes candidates to appeal to more committed and ideological voters. However, the policies that motivate these voters to support a candidate at the caucus or in a primary may brand the candidate as "extreme" for the general election, when more moderate voters participate.

The best-known example of a caucus is in Iowa, because Iowa has held the earliest caucuses in most recent presidential nominating contests. Every February in a presidential election year, Iowans have the opportunity to attend Republican and Democratic precinct meetings. Large numbers of voters attend these small town meetings and have a chance to meet and exchange views on issues and candidates, rather than merely pulling a lever in a voting booth or placing an *X* on a ballot. A special feature of the Iowa meetings is that college students can attend local caucuses in their college towns or hometowns with a minimum of hassle.

STRATEGIES Strategies for gaining delegates to the national convention have changed over the years. Some candidates think it wise to skip some of the earlier contests and enter first in states where their strength lies. Most candidates choose to run hard in Iowa and New Hampshire, hoping that early showings in these states, which receive a great deal of media attention, will move them into the spotlight for later efforts.

During this early phase, candidates win or lose by their ability to adapt their own strengths to changing circumstances: the number of candidates running, the ideological splits among the candidates, the calendar of events, the amount of money available for the campaign, the ways in which the media cover a particular state, and the events that disrupt planning. Especially important is the ability of candidates to manage the media's expectations of their performance. Lyndon Johnson actually won the New Hampshire primary in 1968, but because Eugene McCarthy did better than the press had predicted, McCarthy was interpreted as the "winner."

Winning in the primaries thus becomes a game of expectations, and candidates may intentionally downplay their expectations so that "doing better than expected" might generate momentum for their campaign. Pat Buchanan made the most of his early victories in Alaska, Louisiana, and New Hampshire in 1996 and generated a lot

caucus
A meeting of local party members to choose party officials and/or candidates for public office and to decide the platform.

national party convention
The national meeting of delegates elected in primaries, caucuses, or state conventions who assemble once every four years to nominate candidates for president and vice-president, ratify the party platform, elect officers, and adopt rules.

of free publicity. As the field of candidates narrowed, however, Bob Dole picked up supporters and handily defeated Buchanan. Steve Forbes spent approximately $37 million of his own money in a few selected states early in the process, and as a result he won in Arizona and Delaware. Forbes, however, was unable to sustain his strong showing and dropped out of the race soon after the New York primary.

Stage 2: The Convention

National party conventions are the national meeting of the delegates elected in primaries, caucuses, or state conventions who assemble in the summer before the election to pick the party's presidential and vice-presidential candidates. Historically, delegates arrived at national nominating conventions with differing degrees of commitment to presidential candidates; some delegates were pledged to no candidate at all, others to a specific candidate for one or two ballots, and others firmly to one candidate only. Recent conventions have merely ratified decisions already made in the primaries and caucuses, in part because delegates were required to pledge themselves to a specific presidential hopeful (in the Democratic party) or because one candidate was able to amass the necessary number of delegates in advance. And because of reforms encouraging delegates to stick with the person to whom they are pledged, there has been less room to maneuver at conventions. National party conventions used to be events of high excitement because they determined who would be the party nominees, but in every election since the Republican convention of 1948 and the Democratic convention of 1952, the nominee has been chosen on the first ballot.

As recently as 1988, Democratic and Republican national conventions were given gavel-to-gavel coverage by the major networks, meaning that from the beginning of the first night to the end of the fourth night, millions of people watched. Now the major networks leave comprehensive coverage to C-SPAN and CNN. National nominating conventions have ceased to dominate the national news, for the very good reason that they are no longer the place where candidates are selected.[35] The long-term trend of declining viewership and reduced hours of coverage has altered the parties' strategies for evening prime time. In 1996, even more than in previous years, the parties featured their most important speakers and highlighted their most important messages in the limited time given them by the networks.

Conventions follow standard rules, routines, and rituals. Usually the first day is devoted to a keynote address and other speeches touting the party and denouncing the opposition; the second day to committee reports, including party and convention

The hoopla and excitement of the national convention reaches a nationwide audience on TV.

rules and the party platform; the third day to presidential balloting; and the fourth to choosing the vice-presidential nominee and winding up with the presidential candidate's acceptance speech.[36]

Balloting for president used to be the highlight of the proceedings, but now dramatic struggles occur over the adoption of the rules and the platform. Not long ago sharp encounters occurred over credentials—that is, over which delegates should be seated. The matter was most often in dispute when southern states sent all-white delegations to the Democratic convention. Credential fights have decreased since standard procedures for choosing delegates have been enforced and African Americans have secured the right to vote.

Important Factors in Winning an Election

Uncontrollable Factors

- Incumbent running
- Strength of party organization
- National tides or landslide possibility
- Socioeconomic makeup of district

Organizational Factors

- Registration drives
- Fund-raising machinery
- Campaign organization
- Volunteers
- Media campaign
- Direct-mail campaign efforts
- Get-out-the-vote efforts

Candidate's Personal Leadership Factors

- Personal appeal
- Knowledge of issues
- Speaking and debating ability
- Commitment and determination
- Ability to earn free, positive media coverage

THE PARTY PLATFORM Delegates to the national party conventions decide upon the platform, which sometimes involves a divisive fight. Why? Critics have long pointed out that the party platform is binding on no one and is more likely to hurt than help a candidate. But presidential candidates as well as delegates take the platform seriously because it defines the direction a party wants to take. Also, despite the charge that the platform is ignored, most presidents make an effort to implement it.[37] In recent years the parties have been successful in working out their platform before the convention so that delegates seldom debate and vote on more than a couple of controversial issues.

THE VICE-PRESIDENTIAL NOMINEE The choice of the vice-presidential nominee generates widespread attention. The presidential nominee generally selects a running mate, although this could be left to the convention. Rarely does a person actually "run" for the vice-presidential nomination because only the presidential nominee's "vote" counts, but there is a good deal of maneuvering to capture that one vote. Sometimes the choice of a running mate is made at the convention—not a time conducive to careful and deliberate thought. More often the choice is made before the convention, and the announcement is timed to enhance media coverage and momentum going into the convention.

Traditionally the presidential nominee chooses a running mate who will "balance the ticket." Democratic presidential nominee Walter Mondale raised this tradition to a dramatic new height in 1984 by selecting a woman, Representative Geraldine A. Ferraro, to run with him. Mondale's bold decision was an effort to strengthen his appeal to women voters. Presidential candidates sometimes ignore the idea of a balanced ticket, as Bill Clinton did when he chose another southern white male, Al Gore, to be his running mate.

THE VALUE OF CONVENTIONS Why do the parties continue to have conventions if the nominee is known in advance and the vice-presidential nominee is the choice of one person? What role do conventions play in our system? For the parties, they are a time of "coming together" to endorse a party program and to build unity and enthusiasm for the fall campaign. For future candidates, they are a chance to capture the national spotlight and further their political ambitions. For nominees, they are an opportunity to define themselves in positive ways. The potential is there to heal wounds festering from the primary campaign and move into the general election united, but the potential is not always achieved. Conventions can be potentially dangerous, as Bill Clinton discovered when his keynote speech at the 1988 Democratic convention ran so long that the audience began to walk out.

NOMINATION BY PETITION There is a way to run for president of the United States that avoids the grueling process of primary elections and conventions—if you are rich enough or well known enough. John Anderson in 1980 and H. Ross Perot in

President Perot?

In 1992 H. Ross Perot and his running mate, James Stockdale, got nearly one-fifth of the popular vote. Perot was not nominated by any political party, did not run in any primaries, and had not sought any office before. How did he do it? He spent about $65 million of his own money to promote himself as a candidate.

Perot's candidacy was unusual because it generated so much media attention. He skillfully used free media, like the television program *Larry King Live* on which he opened his campaign and appeared many times during its course. Perot's anti-politician, anti-Washington, and anti-deficit message struck a responsive chord in the American public. His folksy and often humorous manner of communicating reinforced his appeal.

Despite some early mistakes and difficulties with his staff, Perot ran a respectable campaign in 1992 and played an important role in defining the issues. In fact, there was the possibility that he might come in second in the race or win enough electoral votes to throw the election into the House of Representatives. Perot did come in second in two states—Utah and Maine—and he garnered almost 20 million votes. However, he did not carry any states in the Electoral College.

Following the election, Perot continued to be courted by both Republicans and Democrats, who hoped to win back his supporters. His influence fell after the televised debate over the North American Free Trade Agreement (NAFTA) with Vice-President Al Gore, in which Perot was widely seen as testy, whiney, and a "bossy, old billionaire bully."*

Perot's 1996 campaign, run under the banner of his Reform party, never generated the kind of media attention or popular support that his 1992 campaign did. Perot's 1996 popular vote dropped substantially, and again he won no electoral votes, but Perot's Reform party surprised many when its candidate for governor of Minnesota, Jesse Ventura, won election in 1998.

*William Safire, "Gore Flattens Perot," *The New York Times*, November 11, 1993, p. A27.

1992 met the various state petition requirements or paid the $500 filing fee in Louisiana and made it onto the ballot in all 50 states. In 1996, the petition process was as simple as submitting the signatures of 200 registered voters in Washington State, or as difficult as getting the signatures of 3 percent of registered voters (72,784 signatures) in Maryland. Perot and Anderson demonstrated that you do not need a political party to run for president.

Stage 3: The General Election

The national party convention adjourns immediately after the presidential and vice-presidential candidates deliver their acceptance speeches to the delegates and the national television audience. The time between the conventions and Labor Day was traditionally a time for resting, binding up convention wounds, gearing up for action, and planning campaign strategy. In recent elections, however, the campaigns have hardly paused after the convention.[38]

Strategy differs from one election to another, but politicians, pollsters, and political scientists have collected enough information to agree broadly on a number of basic factors that affect election outcomes. Whether the nation is prosperous probably has the most to do with who wins a presidential election, but, as we have noted, most voters vote on the basis of party and candidate appeal.[39] Much depends on voter turnout as well. The Democrats' advantage in number of people who identify themselves as Democrats is mitigated by the higher voter turnout among Republicans. Republicans also usually have better access to money.

PRESIDENTIAL DEBATES Televised presidential debates are now a major feature of presidential elections. The 1960 debate between John Kennedy and Richard Nixon boosted Kennedy's campaign and elevated the role of television in national politics.[40] In 1976, President Gerald Ford debated Jimmy Carter and mistakenly said that each country in Eastern Europe "is independent, autonomous, it has its own territorial integrity, and none was under Soviet domination." That mistake damaged his credibility. Ronald Reagan's performance in the 1980 and 1984 debates confirmed the public view of him as decent, warm, and dignified. Bill Clinton's skirmishes with George Bush in 1992 and Bob Dole in 1996 showed him to be a skilled performer.

In 1980 the question arose whether to include third-party candidate John Anderson in the televised debates, as it did again with Ross Perot. Perot and his running mate, James Stockdale, were included in the 1992 presidential and vice-presidential debates, which generated large viewing audiences, averaging more than 80 million for each debate. Each debate used a different format, one of which had undecided voters asking George Bush, Bill Clinton, and Ross Perot questions. The debates did not result in large numbers of voters changing their minds about the candidates; rather, they reinforced voters' prior choices and brought additional attention to Ross Perot. In 1996 Perot was excluded because he failed to meet one of the criteria, a plausible chance of winning any electoral votes.

Although some critics are quick to express their dissatisfaction with presidential candidates for being so concerned with makeup and rehearsed answers, and although the debates have not significantly affected the election outcomes, they have provided important opportunities for candidates to distinguish themselves and for the public to weigh their qualifications. Candidates who do well in these

In the 1996 presidential debates, candidate Bob Dole appeared rather tense and serious, compared to the relaxed and polished president.

debates are at a great advantage. They have to be quick on their feet, well rehearsed, and project a positive image. But these are not necessarily the qualities that make for a successful presidency.

Money in American Elections

Election campaigns cost money, and the methods of obtaining the money have long been controversial. Campaign money can come from a variety of sources: a candidate's own wealth, political parties, interested individuals, or interest groups. Money is contributed to candidates for a variety of reasons, ranging from altruism to self-interest. **Interested money** is given by individuals or groups in hopes of influencing the outcome of an election and subsequently influencing policy. Concern about campaign finance stems from the possibility that candidates, in their pursuit of campaign funds, will decide it is more important to represent their contributors than their conscience or the voters. The potential corruption that results from politicians' dependence on interested money concerns many observers of American politics.

Scandals about money influencing policy are not new. In 1925, responding to the Teapot Dome scandal in which a cabinet member was convicted of accepting bribes, Congress passed the Corrupt Practices Act, which required disclosure of campaign funds but was "written in such a way as to exempt virtually all of them [members of Congress] from its provisions."[41]

The 1972 Watergate scandal—an illegal break-in of Democratic party headquarters by persons associated with the Nixon campaign to steal campaign documents and plant listening devices—led to discoveries by news reporters and congressional investigators that large amounts of money from corporations and individuals were "laundered" in secret bank accounts outside the country for political and campaign purposes. Nixon's 1972 campaign spent more than $60 million, more than twice what it had expended in 1968. Investigators discovered that wealthy individuals made large contributions to influence the outcome of the election or secure ambassadorships and administrative appointments.

interested money
Contributions by individuals or groups in hopes of influencing the outcome of an election and subsequently influencing policy.

In the early 1990s, Charles Keating and his failed Lincoln Savings and Loan spotlighted the possibility that undue influence comes with large contributions. Keating asked five U.S. senators, all of whom had received substantial campaign contributions or other "perks" from him, to intervene on his behalf with federal bank

SOFT MONEY IS BAD BUSINESS

Jerome Kohlberg

The system has become an industry unto itself.

Jerome Kohlberg, founding partner in a large investment company, explains that political contributions are a small price for big corporations to pay to gain political influence. They can easily justify these expenditures because they get an outstanding return on their investment.

"It's no wonder that business is seen as part of the campaign finance problem. Critics point to the tens of millions contributed by corporate donors in the last election cycle and to the geometric growth of soft-money contributions, and label business an 'enemy.' But such surface analysis begs the more important issue: Do all business and business leaders embrace the current system? The answer is no."

Kohlberg points out that the overwhelming majority of companies don't participate in the giving game at all. He found that contributors resent the implied quid pro quo nature of the system and object to being pressured by officeholders to make contributions. Moreover, officeholders also dislike having to go begging for money and feel uncomfortable when contributors ask for favors.

"In short, both business leaders and many of the politicians we talk to are increasingly frustrated with and disgusted by a cash race gone out of control. Even as they participate, they feel the system has become an industry unto itself, caught in a perpetual cycle that increasingly undermines both democracy and genuine business interests."

He warns that the price for access is rising rapidly. "The result will be an increasingly loud voice for big-moneyed interests, an increasingly alienated electorate, and an increasingly fragile democracy." He urges Congress to restore some dignity to democracy and pass real campaign finance reform. ★

SOURCE: Jerome Kohlberg, "Soft Money Is Bad Business," *The New York Times*, July 5, 1998, section 4, p. 11.

THE PRICE OF POLITICS

Robert J. Samuelson

Robert J. Samuelson maintains that campaign contributions haven't corrupted Congress. In this era of casual cynicism, "it is somehow comforting to think that Congress submits to those who make the biggest contributions."

"The crusade for campaign reform captures a defining delusion of our time. It is that our democracy is beseiged by some sinister cabal whose destruction would restore confidence in government. The nature of the cabal is constantly shifting. Sometimes it's 'big interests' and 'big money.' At other times its 'career politicians' or arrogant 'elites.' But someone is messing with the system and must be obliterated."

However, Samuelson argues, the real problem is not the corrupting influence of money, but rather that Americans are deeply divided on how to solve the serious issues on which Congress must legislate: budget deficits, affirmative action, abortion, regulation, for example. Assigning the blame for these decisions to some outside force exempts people from responsibility for dealing with them.

He concludes that "campaign contributions matter a lot less than most people assume. The more important an issue, the less campaign money matters. Social Security, Medicare, and other programs for the elderly constitute more than a third of all federal spending. They have regularly expanded, not because their supporters make big campaign gifts but because these programs have huge constituencies and are highly popular."

Samuelson charges that the idea that campaign money corrupts politics persists "because it is endlessly repeated by groups like Common Cause, echoed by journalists, and proclaimed by politicians themselves. This last act is highly cynical. Politicians pander to the public's antipolitical mood by bewailing the corruption of politics and then innocently wonder why the public thinks ill of them. But the true damage of our cabal theory of politics is self-deception. Exaggerating the evil of campaign money diverts us from wrestling with the important issues that divide the nation."★

SOURCE: Robert J. Samuelson, "The Price of Politics," *Newsweek*, August 28, 1995, p. 65.

Exaggerating the evil of campaign money diverts us from wrestling with the important issues that divide the nation.

For more information about this debate, go to **http://www.prenhall.com/burns** *and click on the Debate Icon in Chapter 12.*

The Federal Election Campaign Act (1971) and Amendments (1974)

- Establishes a Federal Election Commission appointed by the president with the advice and consent of the Senate to regulate the campaign financing of candidates for president, senator, and representative.
- Provides for public financing of presidential general election campaigns with funds from the income tax checkoff.
- Provides for partial public financing on a matching basis of presidential nominating campaigns.
- Provides for subsidies to the two national parties for their convention expenses and to any minor party that polled 5 percent of the total vote in the previous presidential election.
- Limits spending by candidates for presidential nominations (on a state-by-state basis and in total) and in the presidential general elections for those candidates who accept public funding.
- Limits the amounts that national parties may spend on presidential campaigns and on individual congressional and senatorial campaigns.
- Sets a limit of $1,000 on the amount that any individual can give to a candidate for the U.S. Senate or for the U.S. House of Representatives in the primary election; a limit of $1,000 per candidate in the general election; and a limit of $5,000 per candidate per election ($5,000 in primary and $5,000 in general election) for political action committees.
- Sets an overall limitation of $25,000 on the amount that any individual can donate to all candidates for federal office in an election cycle; no similar limitation applicable to political action committees.
- Sets no limit on the amount of their own money candidates can spend on their campaign.
- Sets no limit on the amount that individuals or groups can spend independently.

regulators looking into his savings and loan business. These senators came to be called the Keating Five. The reelection campaign of California Senator Alan Cranston, in particular, had clearly benefited from the more than $1 million Keating had contributed to a voter registration and get-out-the-vote effort run by the senator's son.

The high costs of television advertising diminish the ability of challengers to mount visible campaigns. Declining competition is explained in part by the difficulty challengers have in raising money. Incumbents have a substantial advantage in raising interested money from wealthy individuals and political action committees (PACs). Hence it is not only the source of campaign money that is a problem but the pattern of unequal distribution as well.

Efforts to Reform

In the past, reformers have tried three basic strategies to prevent abuse in political contributions: (1) imposing limitations on giving, receiving, and spending political money; (2) requiring public disclosure of the sources and uses of political money; and (3) giving governmental subsidies to presidential candidates, campaigns, and parties, including incentive arrangements. Recent campaign finance laws have tended to use all three strategies for dealing with a problem that sometimes seems unsolvable.

THE FEDERAL ELECTION CAMPAIGN ACT In 1971 Congress passed two significant laws dealing with campaign funding. The Federal Election Campaign Act (FECA) limits amounts that candidates for federal office can spend on media advertising, requires the disclosure of the sources of campaign funds as well as how they were spent, and requires political action committees active in federal campaigns to register with the government and report all major contributions and expenditures. This 1971 law also provided a tax checkoff that allows taxpayers to direct $1 to a fund to subsidize presidential campaigns by checking a box on their income tax form.

The public subsidy of candidates worked rather well. All presidential candidates except wealthy self-financed candidates have accepted the voluntary limitations that come with partial public financing of presidential campaigns. Three exceptions are John Connally, who sought the Republican nomination in 1980, Ross Perot in 1992, and Steven Forbes in 1996. Even Ronald Reagan, who opposed public financing, accepted public subsidies in all three of his major presidential campaigns. But the system is not without problems. The number of taxpayers checking off on their income tax forms that they want $1 of their taxes to be directed to the presidential campaign fund has been declining, although enough did so to cover all the costs of the 1996 elections.[42]

POST-WATERGATE REFORMS Further campaign funding reform was prompted by Watergate and widespread public concern about money in elections. In 1974 Congress passed and President Gerald Ford signed the most sweeping campaign reform measure in U.S. history. These amendments to the Federal Election Campaign Act established realistic limits on contributions and spending, tightened disclosure, and provided for public financing of presidential campaigns.

The 1974 law had to be extensively amended after the 1976 *Buckley v Valeo* decision, which overturned several of its provisions on grounds that they violated the First Amendment.[43] The Supreme Court made a distinction between campaign spending and campaign contributions, holding that the First Amendment protects spending, and legislatures may not limit how much people spend of their own

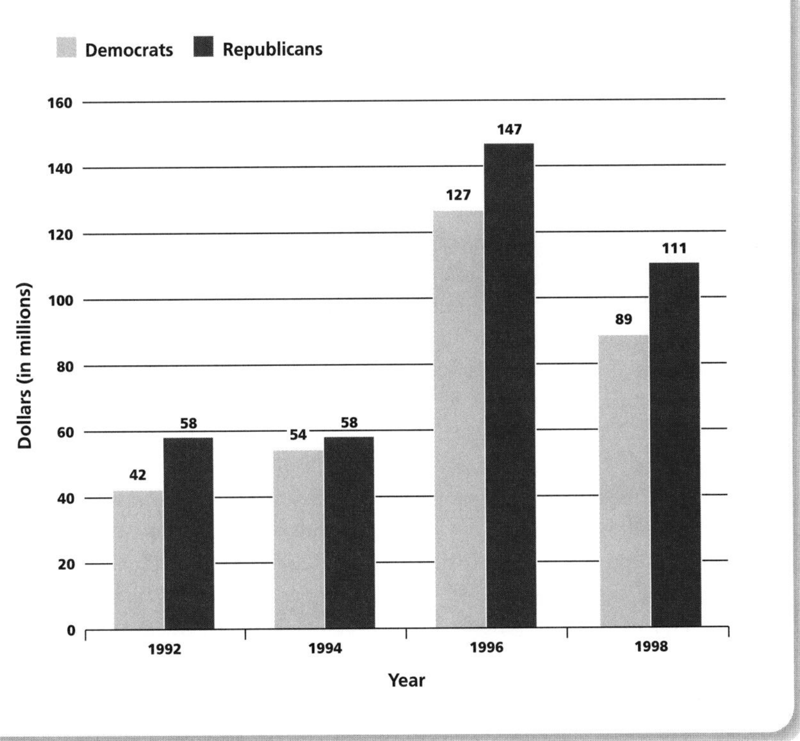

FIGURE 12-4 National Soft Money Contributions, 1992–1998 (in 1998 Dollars)

SOURCE: Federal Election Commission.

money on elections, but may limit how much they contribute to somebody else's campaign. The *Buckley* decision emphasized limitations on contributions and full and open disclosure of all fund-raising activities by candidates for federal office, as well as the system of public financing for presidential elections.[44] Later amendments sought to encourage volunteer activities and party building by permitting national political parties, corporations, labor unions, and individuals to give unlimited amounts to state parties.

THE UNSOLVED PROBLEM OF SOFT MONEY The most serious problem with the presidential campaign finance system is **soft money**—funds given to state and local parties by political parties, individuals, or political action committees for voter registration drives, party mailings, and advertising. No limits are set on the amount of such contributions. The money is called "soft" because federal law does not require disclosure of its source or use. Although soft money is supposed to benefit only state and local parties, it influences federal elections. Presidential candidates in both parties have made raising soft money a high priority. Soft money has risen in presidential campaigns from roughly $19 million in 1980 to $250 million in 1996 (see Figure 12-4).[45]

Soft money contributions circumvent the more limited and disclosed "hard money" sources in federal campaigns. Soft money has brought back the large donors as major players in our system of campaign finance. It also strengthened the power of the national party committees, which allocate the money to state parties and indirectly to candidates.

Soft money had been more important in presidential elections than in congressional contests, but that changed in a dramatic way with the 1998 congressional elections, in which both parties poured soft money into states with competitive House and Senate races. In some cases in 1998, well over $3 million in soft money was transferred to a state.[46]

soft money
Money contributed to a state or local party for party-building purposes that does not have to be disclosed under federal law.

A Closer Look

CAMPAIGN FINANCE REFORM

In his first few months in office, President Bill Clinton proposed comprehensive campaign finance reform—partial public financing of congressional elections, limitations on the amount of money congressional candidates could accept from PACs, and virtual elimination of soft money in presidential elections. Not surprisingly, Democrats and Republicans in Congress objected and quickly embarked on their own campaign finance reform agendas. House Democrats were less eager for change than Clinton was, and the president was forced to downplay his campaign promise for change.

Public disgust with the excesses of the 1996 elections, including foreign money, letting wealthy contributors spend a night in the Lincoln Bedroom of the White House, unlimited and unchecked use of issue advertising, and the willingness of both parties to raise and spend large amounts of soft money, failed to provide enough pressure for Congress to pass campaign finance legislation in 1997–98.

Congress considered legislation narrowing the definition of who may donate soft money to exclude labor unions and corporations. Proponents of the law argued that because it was Congress that created the soft money exemption, Congress could take it away. Proposals also required any issue advertising that mentions candidates by name or shows their image to disclose who is paying for the ad. Opponents of these reforms countered that limiting who may contribute soft money or the content of issue ads infringes upon First Amendment rights. Should such a law be passed, it would immediately be challenged in court.

The same disincentives that stopped legislative action in the past remain. For the 535 members of Congress, the current system works well. They won under the rules now in place, and they know they have tremendous advantages under the present campaign finance system. Winning reelection is one of the most central motives of incumbents, so it will take a major public outcry for them to change a campaign finance system that benefits them.

Senators John McCain and Russ Feingold proposed legislation to outlaw soft money contributions to political campaigns, but it failed to gain Senate approval in 1997 and 1998.

"Sorry, Socks . . . only fat cats are allowed in here."

Marshall Ramsey. Courtesy Jackson Clarion-Ledger.

One reason for the dramatic rise in soft money spending was a Supreme Court decision in a case involving the Republican party in Colorado. The decision was interpreted to mean that parties could spend unlimited amounts of soft money when combined with a smaller amount of hard money on advertisements, as long as the advertisements *did not explicitly call for a vote for or against a specific candidate.*[47] Both parties responded immediately to this opening. The Republican senatorial committee opened an office one mile from national party headquarters and funneled $10 million into soft money ads in the 1996 election.[48] In 1998 the use of this form of party spending grew even more.

Soft money has also been linked to foreign contributions, at least in Bill Clinton's 1996 campaign. A possible connection to the Chinese government raised the issue of foreign governments using campaign contributions to influence U.S. policy. John Huang, who helped raise money from an Indonesian family with close connections to the Chinese government, became controversial because he was granted access to sensitive documents in the Commerce Department.[49] Foreign nationals living in America have long been allowed to contribute to political parties. Restrictions on foreign corporations may be made more restrictive as a result of the fund-raising scandals of the 1990s.

ISSUE ADVERTISING The 1996 election saw a surge in a new form of campaign activity called **issue advertising**, which is also unlimited because it presumably deals with issues, not candidates. Issue ad campaigns in some U.S. House races have exceeded $1 million in recent elections. In the 1998 elections businesses, labor unions, HMOs, the Sierra Club, the League of Conservation Voters, the Business Roundtable, and Americans for Limited Terms ran issue ads (see Table 12-1). For interest groups, these ads not only help the candidate they prefer or punish the candidate they oppose; they also force candidates to support the group's agenda. The use of issue ads and the growth in soft money mean that in competitive congressional elections we are shifting from candidate-centered elections to party-centered and interest group-centered campaigns.[50]

One of the problems with issue ads is accountability. Because these groups are not required to disclose how much they spend or how they raise their money, voters have a hard time knowing who they are. Often candidates get blamed for the attacks made by these groups because voters assume the campaign is being run by the candidates. Finally, because they are willing to spend so much money and the tone of their communications is often negative, these groups have reinforced cynicism and alienation among voters.

Recent reforms before Congress have placed limitations on issue advertising in the 30 or 60 days before an election. Groups are also prohibited from using the image or likeness of the candidates in issue ads. Here the argument is that using such photos makes the commercials look like candidate-sponsored ads.

Do Issue Ads Work?

A recent report evaluated 107 television and radio advertisements produced by 29 different political organizations. The report polled over 1,000 voters to see the impact of these ads. It found that 57.2 percent of the people remembered at least one issue ad during the 1996 campaign. The report also noted that although ostensibly these issue ads were to support a position and not a person, 86.9 percent of respondents mentioned a candidate for office by name, and 59.2 percent pictured a candidate. The report also recorded that 41.1 percent of all issue ads were solely attacks.

Business Roundtable, a political organization whose members are CEOs of the largest corporations in America, tripled its membership dues to raise more than $27 million for issue ads in 1998. Organized labor planned on spending at least $15 million, and the Sierra Club planned to spend at least $7 million.

One example of an issue ad comes from a congressional race between Democrat Bill Yellowtail and Republican Rick Hill. The add said, "Who is Bill Yellowtail? He preaches family values, but he took a swing at his wife. And Yellowtail's explanation? He only slapped her. But her nose was broken." The ad was considered an issue ad because it didn't say vote for Hill or vote against Yellowtail but was supporting family values.

SOURCES: Jack W. Germond and Jules Witcover, "Turning Issue Ads into a Big Issue," *National Journal* 38, September 9, 1997, p. 1848; Jim Drinkard, "'Issue-Advocacy' Groups: The New Electoral Power," *USA Today*, March 9, 1998, p. 13A.

TABLE 12-1 Top Ten Issue Advertisers, 1998

National Republican Congressional Committee	$37 million
American Federation of Labor-Congress of Industrial Organizations	$28 million ($5 million on TV and radio ads alone)
National Republican Senatorial Committee	$9 million
U.S. Term Limits	$8 million
Democratic Senatorial Campaign Committee	$8 million
Democratic Congressional Campaign Committee	$7 million
Sierra Club	$6 million
Christian Coalition	$3 million
Citizens Flag Alliance	$2 million
Business Roundtable	$2 million

SOURCE: Annenberg Public Policy website (www.appcpenn.org/issueads/gindex).

All amounts are estimates mentioned in press releases or reported in the media.

issue advertising
Commercial advertising on radio and television advocating a particular position on an issue, paid for by interest groups and designed to influence voters' choices on election day.

The Soft Money Loophole in Japan

The Japanese strategy to combat corruption and money politics has been to create some of the most stringent campaign regulations in the world:

- Door-to-door campaigning is banned.
- Candidates may not run campaign advertisements in the media although parties may.
- Each campaign may produce only two versions of its campaign brochure, and only a limited number may be distributed; the number varies according to the number of registered voters in a district.
- Campaign posters are allowed only on government-provided poster boards that are set up in several locations across a district during the campaign.
- Direct mailing of campaign literature is not allowed except for a specified number of government-provided campaign postcards.
- The number of campaign offices, employees, and vehicles is restricted by law.

These regulations should make it impossible for candidates to raise and spend large sums of money in a campaign, but Japanese candidates have found a giant loophole in these restrictions by avoiding "official" campaign activities. A candidate will go door-to-door or mail out literature to voters or put up posters *before* the official campaign period. In these precampaign activities, the candidates will be very careful never to mention the upcoming election, so their efforts are not covered by law.

Attempts to limit these activities have run into constitutional concerns. If a campaign has not begun and a person has not declared his or her candidacy, how can the Japanese government restrict the right of a citizen to hold meetings, discuss issues with people, mail information to people, or put up posters? In a similar manner, concern for free speech led to the soft money loophole in U.S. campaign restrictions.

Defenders of issue ads point to recent ad campaigns that focused on legislation, like those mounted by tobacco companies in 1998 to defeat a tobacco tax in the Senate or ads run by insurance companies attacking the Clinton health care plan in 1994.

CANDIDATES' PERSONAL WEALTH Campaign finance legislation cannot constitutionally restrict rich candidates—the Rockefellers, the Kennedys, the Perots—from giving heavily to their own campaigns. Big money makes a big difference, and wealthy candidates can afford to spend big money. In presidential politics, this advantage can be most meaningful in the period before the primaries begin. There may be no constitutional way to limit how much money people can spend on their own campaigns.

INDEPENDENT EXPENDITURES Similarly, current finance laws do not constrain **independent expenditures** by groups or individuals who are separate from political candidates. This loophole has been permitted by the Supreme Court on free speech grounds. Groups sympathetic to, but independent of, candidates are allowed to raise and spend funds to help elect them or to defeat their opponents. For example, in 1984 Michael Goland, a Californian, spent $1,100,740 as an independent expenditure to defeat Illinois Senator Charles Percy.[51] As long as there is no collusion between the independent spender and the candidate, an individual or PAC can spend an unlimited amount of money for or against a candidate.

Independent expenditures are not soft money; they are fully disclosed. Soft money is given to state parties for "party building." It is not limited, and if state law does not require disclosure, it is not disclosed. Issue ads have largely replaced independent expenditures in recent election cycles because interest groups can spend the same amount of money without having to disclose the activity. Some groups like the National Rifle Association continue to use independent expenditures, however, perhaps because they want to urge voters to "vote for" or "vote against" specific candidates, words you cannot include in an issue ad.

Consequences of Current Campaign Financing

The problems with federal election campaigns are easy to identify: dramatically escalating costs, a growing dependence on PAC money, decreasing visibility and competitiveness of challengers (especially in the House), the ability of wealthy individuals to fund their own campaigns, and the danger of large contributions altering election outcomes.

RISING COSTS OF CAMPAIGNS Since the Federal Election Campaign Act became law in 1972, total expenditures by candidates for the House of Representatives have more than doubled after controlling for inflation, and they have risen even more in Senate elections (see Table 12-2). Television advertising is expensive, limiting the field of challengers to those who can spend more than a year raising money. The American ideal that anyone—a person from humble beginnings or of modest wealth—can seek and hold high public office is no longer true. And rising costs mean incumbents spend more time raising funds and therefore less time legislating and representing their districts.

independent expenditures
Money spent by individuals or groups not associated with candidates to elect or defeat candidates for office.

Candidates for federal office spent an estimated $2.7 billion in 1996, of which $765 million was spent on congressional campaigns. These are big sums, but they must be put into perspective. The $2.7 billion spent on national elections is but a

TABLE 12-2 Average Campaign Expenditures of Candidates for the House of Representatives, 1988–1998 General Election (1998 Dollars in Thousands)

	Incumbent	Challenger	Open Seat
Republican			
1988	$563.8	$138.4	$1123.5
1990	496.5	138.2	1036.8
1992	617.7	219.3	727.5
1994	506.4	263.1	1111.8
1996	766.9	219.6	653.5
1998	668.9	245.1	709.2
Democrat			
1988	$493.6	$198.1	$616.0
1990	501.3	137.8	667.8
1992	702.6	186.8	560.2
1994	665.0	174.2	639.6
1996	593.7	307.9	652.5
1998	539.5	232.9	709.8

SOURCES: Federal Election Commission, "Congressional Fundraising and Spending Up Again in 1996," press release, April 14, 1997, p. 13; Federal Election Commission, "1998 Congressional Financial Activity Declines," press release, December 29, 1998, p. 5.

fraction of a percent of the total cost of government. One Trident submarine, for example, costs hundreds of millions of dollars. In the 1988 presidential campaign, the candidates collectively spent around $500 million.

DECLINING COMPETITION Unless something is done to help finance challengers, incumbents will continue to have the advantage in seeking reelection. Challengers in both parties are typically underfunded. House Democratic challengers averaged $240,700 in spending in 1998.[52] In today's expensive campaigns, candidates are invisible if they can spend only $200,000 to $250,000.

The high cost of campaigns dampens competition by discouraging individuals from running for office. Potential challengers look at the fund-raising advantages enjoyed by incumbents—at incumbents' campaign chests, which sometimes have $1 million before the campaign even starts, and at the time it will take for them to raise enough money to launch a minimal campaign—and they decide to direct their energies elsewhere. Moreover, unlike incumbents, who are being paid while campaigning and fund raising, most challengers have to support themselves and their families for the duration of the campaign, which for the House and Senate now is roughly two years.

INCREASING DEPENDENCE ON PACS AND WEALTHY DONORS Where does the money come from to finance these expensive election campaigns? For most House incumbents the answer is political action committees (PACs). In 1996, for instance, 174 of the 387 incumbents seeking reelection raised more money from PACs than from individuals (see Figure 12-5).[53] Senators are somewhat less dependent on PACs, but because they spend so much more, they need to raise even more money from PACs than House incumbents do. Challengers for seats in either chamber receive little from PACs because PACs do not want to offend politicians in power, and politicians in power want to stay in office. This marriage of interests has

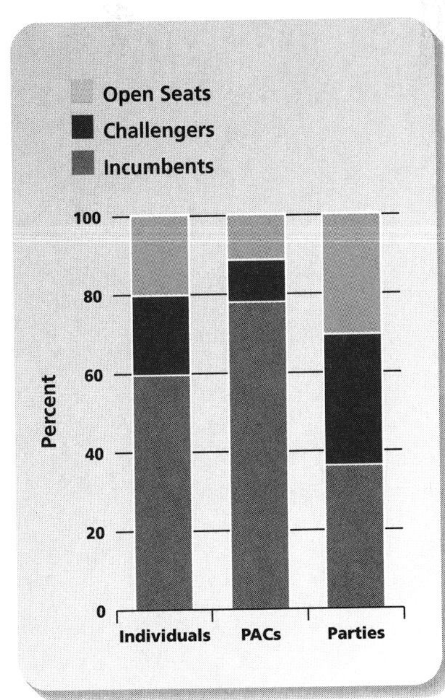

FIGURE 12-5 Incumbents' Dependence on PAC Money

SOURCE: Federal Election Commission.

You Decide...

Should people who are not American citizens be allowed to influence American elections through campaign contributions?

The role of foreign money in our election process was placed on the agenda of campaign finance reform following the 1996 election. Under current law, foreign-owned corporations can engage in election activities as long as the individuals making the contribution are U.S. citizens, and foreign corporations or foreign citizens do not provide funds for the PAC.

Since American corporations and trade associations can contribute to campaigns, should their foreign counterparts be permitted to do the same? While there is an abiding concern about foreign money influencing our democracy, the law says foreign citizens living in the United States can contribute to our campaigns. The issue of corporations and trade associations is murkier because many corporations have multinational subsidiaries, and virtually all foreign corporations doing business in the United States can influence our electoral process through their American partners. An example might be the Toyota Dealers of America, who are affiliated with Toyota, a Japanese corporation, but are generally American citizens competing with other auto dealers selling domestic and foreign automobiles.

meant that congressional incumbents court PAC contributions, and PACs are happy to oblige.

Politicians also turn to donors who can contribute $500 or $1,000 to their campaigns. People who make such contributions expect that the legislators they have helped will respond to their concerns. Given congressional incumbents' preoccupation with reelection, contributions from PACs or large individual contributions are likely to be remembered.

To be sure, PACs and individuals give political money for many reasons. But the hundreds of interest groups that contribute to campaigns share something in common: they want certain laws to be passed or repealed, certain funds appropriated, or certain administrative decisions rendered. At a minimum, they want access to officeholders, a chance to talk with members before key votes.

Defenders of PACs point out that there is no demonstrable relationship between contributions and roll call votes. But influence in the legislative process depends on *access* to staff and members of Congress, and most agree that campaign contributions give donors unusual access. PACs influence the legislative process in other ways as well. Their access helps them structure the legislative agenda with friendly legislators and influence the drafting of legislation or amendments to existing bills. These are all advantages that others do not have.

IMPROVING ELECTIONS

Concern over how we choose presidents now centers on two issues: (1) the number, timing, and representativeness of presidential primaries, and (2) the role of the Electoral College, including the possibility that a presidential election might be thrown into the House of Representatives, with possibly controversial results.[54] Electoral reform also focuses on encouraging greater turnout and changing the way we finance elections.

Reforming Presidential Primaries

The main argument in favor of presidential primaries is that they open the nominating process to more voters than do caucus or convention methods. Today the media play up the primary in every important state, and voters follow the races in other states as well as their own. In so doing, they can judge the candidates' political qualities: their abilities to organize campaigns, communicate through the media, stand up under pressure, avoid making mistakes (or recover if they do make them), adjust their appeals to shifting events and to different regions of the country, control their staffs as well as utilize them, and be decisive, articulate, resilient, humorous, informed, and ultimately successful in winning votes. In short, supporters claim, primaries test candidates on the very qualities they must exhibit in the presidency.[55]

Critics of primaries grant that more voters take part in primaries than in the caucus and convention methods of choosing delegates, but they question the quality of the participation. For one thing, supporters of the different candidates have no opportunity to deliberate together in public. Voters in primaries must depend largely on the news media and advertising for their information and basis for judgment. Voters in presidential primaries tend to be more influenced by candidates' personalities and media skills than their positions on vital issues.[56] Participation has been low in recent years (see Figure 12-6). In the 1996 primaries, turnout was generally under 20 percent of the voting age population, and it declined as the primary season progressed and the field of candidates narrowed.[57]

Low levels of turnout in primaries open the possibility that extreme groups will have a disproportionate say; the "selectorate" replaces the electorate. In addition, candidates are forced to appeal to highly motivated voters, usually from the

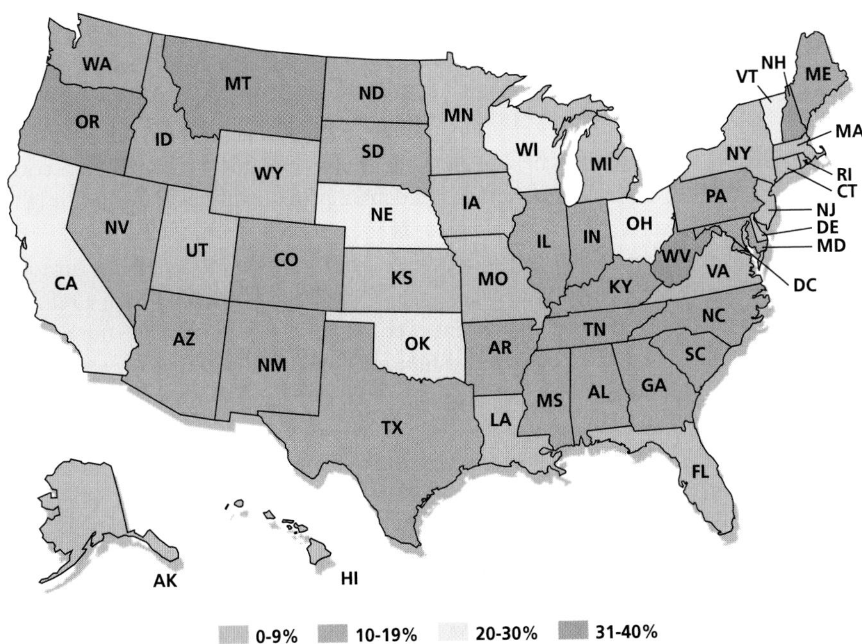

FIGURE 12-6 Voter Turnout in the 1996 Presidential Primaries

conservative wing of the Republican party and the liberal wing of the Democratic party. As a result, candidates often take ideologically extreme positions during the primaries.

The primary voting mechanism—each citizen casting one vote for one candidate, often in a multicandidate field—does not allow voters to express relative preferences. In 1976, for instance, a number of liberal Democratic candidates ran in the New Hampshire primary. Jimmy Carter was the only one seen as moderate or conservative. Liberal candidates split the liberal vote; Carter received the moderate and conservative vote. Thus, liberal voters had no opportunity to say they preferred any of the liberal candidates over Carter. Such an electoral system does not allow for rank ordering that may reflect voter preferences.[58]

For many years the primary season was criticized for being too long.[59] Some states, by virtue of coming early in the process, had a disproportionate say in determining the nominee and therefore were more influential with presidents. This is one reason why most southern states bound together to hold their primaries the same day—Super Tuesday—in March. The intention of this schedule was to enhance the position of the South in the nominating process, helping moderate candidates or candidates from the region.[60] States that came later in the process often found the nominee had already been selected. This is why California and several other states are moving their dates earlier in the process. Rather than being criticized as too long, the process for 2000 is now challenged as too short, with the nominee selected five months before the fall campaign begins, and giving the advantage to the candidate who can raise the most money early in the process.

Finally, some critics question whether primaries test the qualities needed to be president. To win "the media game," candidates must be witty, resourceful, attractive, and articulate—not the most important qualities to be a good president. Thomas Jefferson, Abraham Lincoln, and Harry Truman were able presidents, but they did not have great "media appeal." Critics are disturbed by the gap between the qualities required to carry primary contests and the qualities needed to govern: to organize an administration, get support on issues, make hard decisions, and deal with congressional leaders, governors, and mayors.

Thinking it Through...

Current law permits contributions from subsidiaries of foreign corporations as long as they are directed by American employees and the money does not come from the foreign corporate parent. In recent campaigns, American subsidiaries of foreign concerns gave millions of dollars to both political parties. Republicans received the most, but Democrats were not far behind. Charges about the role of foreign contributions led to congressional hearings in 1997.

SOURCE: Robert Hershey, Jr., "Panel Chairman Says Inquiry into Fund Raising Is Expanding," *The New York Times*, February 17, 1997, p. A12.

Campaign Financing in Britain and Canada

U.S. election campaigns go on for months or even years and are very expensive. In contrast, Canadian general election campaigns are limited by law to about five weeks. Public opinion polls cannot be published during the last three days of a campaign, and the media are prohibited by law from reporting results from earlier time zones on the evening of the election in any district where voting is still taking place.

Expenditures are strictly limited for Canadian political parties and individual candidates. During the 1997 general election campaign to fill the 301 seats in the House of Commons, political parties that fielded candidates in all districts were limited by law to spending no more than approximately $8 million each for the entire election, and individual candidates could spend from about $35,000 to $45,000, depending on the number of voters per district. In return, media outlets were required to sell a certain amount of airtime to the parties, and national and regional television and radio networks had to donate some free airtime to these parties. If individual candidates received more than 15 percent of the vote in their districts, the government reimbursed 50 percent of their election-related expenses. Political parties receiving at least 2 percent of the national vote or at least 5 percent of the votes cast in electoral districts where they ran candidates were reimbursed 22.5 percent of their expenses.

In the June 1997 Canadian elections, 1,672 candidates ran for office, and 10 political parties received registered status. Total spending by the parliamentary candidates and political parties was approximately $70 million—much less than the $29 million spent by candidates in the United States seeking seats in the House of Representatives and the $128 million spent by candidates seeking seats in the Senate during the 1996 election campaign.

British general elections also offer an interesting contrast to elections in the United States. The election campaign lasts only three weeks. Candidates for the House of Commons, the most critical election in Britain, are allowed to raise and spend only $15,000. If they spend more, they are disqualified. Each candidate gets the same amount of free airtime, and each candidate is allowed one free election leaflet mailed to each voter in the constituency. About 75 percent of voters turn out, and about 95 percent of eligible voters are registered to vote. At the voting booth, the voter is handed a slip of paper with the names of three or four candidates for the House of Commons. No other offices or ballot questions are presented at the same time.

SOURCE: Adapted from Dudley Fishburn (a candidate for Parliament in 1992), "British Campaigning—How Civilized!" *The New York Times*, April 14, 1992, p. 25.

Reforming the Nominating Process

What would the critics substitute for state presidential primaries? Some argue in favor of a *national presidential primary* that would take the form of a single nationwide election, probably held in May or September, or separate state primaries held in all the states on the same day. Supporters contend that a one-shot national presidential primary (though a runoff might be necessary) would be simple, direct, and representative. It would cut down the wear and tear on candidates, and it would attract a large turnout because of intensive media coverage. Opponents argue that such a reform would make the present system even worse. It would enhance the role of showmanship and gamesmanship; and, being enormously expensive, it would hurt the chances of candidates who lack strong financial backing.[61]

A more modest proposal is to hold *regional primaries*, possibly at two- or three-week intervals across the country—in other words, expand on the South's Super Tuesday idea. Regional primaries might bring more coherence to the process, encourage more emphasis on issues of regional concern, and also cut down on wear and tear. But such primaries would retain most of the disadvantages of the present system—especially the emphasis on money and media. Clearly, they would give an advantage to candidates from whatever region held the first primary, and this advantage would encourage regional candidates and might increase polarization among sections of the country.

A different proposal is to drastically reduce the number of presidential primaries and make more use of the caucus system. The turnout of voters in the Iowa caucuses in recent elections shows that participation can be high, and the time participants spent discussing candidates and issues shows that such participation can be thoughtful and informed. In caucus states, candidates are less dependent on the media and more dependent on convincing political activists. By centering delegate selection in party meetings, the caucus system would also, some say, enhance the role of the party.[62]

Still another idea—used by Colorado for nominations to state offices and by Utah for nominations to federal and state office—would turn the process around. Beginning in May, local caucuses and then state conventions would be held in every state. They would then send delegates—a certain percentage of whom would be unpledged to any presidential candidate—to the national party conventions, which would be held in the summer. The national conventions would select two or three candidates to compete in a national primary to be held in September. In this plan, voters registered by party would be allowed to vote for their party nominee in the September primaries.[63]

How we choose nominees for president is determined by a combination of party rules and state laws. Reformers agree that the current process is flawed but disagree over which aspects require change. Democrats have been most unhappy with the current system because, until 1992, it had produced nominees who did not fare well in the general election. Some blamed the rules for these defeats, but others expressed doubt that a change of rules would produce more successful Democratic candidates. The debate now will probably shift to the Republican party, where the race for the 2000 election may include a fight over nominating rules and procedures because of their defeats in 1992 and 1996.

Reforming the Electoral College

The possibility of three viable presidential candidates in the 1990s once again put reform of the Electoral College on the national agenda. Defenders claimed that the system has not broken down, and "if it ain't broke, don't fix it." "The Electoral College avoids uncertainty when the popular vote is extremely close (as in 1960, 1968, and 1976) and prevents candidates with narrow appeal from making it to the White House."[64]

The most frequently proposed reform of the Electoral College system is *direct popular election* of the president. Presidents would be elected directly by the voters, just as governors are, and the Electoral College and individual electors would be abolished. Such proposals usually provide that, if no candidate receives at least 40 percent of the total popular vote, a *runoff election* would be held between the two contenders with the most votes. Supporters argue that direct election would give every voter the same weight in the presidential balloting in accordance with the one-person, one-vote doctrine. Winners would take on more legitimacy because their victories would reflect the will of the voters.

Opponents contend that the plan would further undermine federalism, that it would encourage unrestrained majority rule and hence political extremism, and that it would hurt the smaller states, which would lose some of their present influence. Others fear that the plan would make presidential campaigns more remote from the voters; candidates might stress television and give up their forays into shopping centers and city malls.[65] Some also fear that the plan would increase the reliance of presidential campaigns on television.

From time to time, Congress considers proposals for a constitutional amendment to elect presidents directly. Such proposals, however, seldom get far because of the strong opposition of various interests that believe they may be disadvantaged by such a change. Groups such as African Americans and farmers, for example, fear they might lose their swing vote power—their ability to make a difference in key states that may tip the Electoral College balance.

The failure of attempts to change the system of elections points to an important conclusion about procedural reform: Americans normally do not focus on procedures. Only after a major Electoral College crisis is any significant change likely. Then citizens will focus on actual problems with the electoral system, not on hypothetical problems discussed by political scientists and democratic theorists.

online POLITICS

Rock the Vote

In 1990 people from the recording industry organized Rock the Vote to fight "a wave of political attacks on freedom of speech and artistic expression":

http://www.rockthevote.org/INSIDERTV/155/15_5.html

Millions watched their commercials that encouraged young people to vote. What is less known is that Rock the Vote has become involved in legislation on issues like health care reform and in support of Americorps, the national service program for young adults. Rock the Vote uses its home page not only to provide information on public issues but to register voters as well. Perhaps some of the readers of this book registered to vote through the Rock the Vote home page:

http://www.rockthevote.org

The Internet is a wonderful resource for current information on campaigns and elections, polling information, and even political jokes:

http://www.abc.com/pi

More good places to go are:

http://www.newpolitics.com

http://www.agora.stm.it/politic

For more Internet resources on Campaigns and Elections, see our home page at:

http://www.prenhall.com/burns

SUMMARY

1. Our electoral system is based on winner-takes-all rules, with typically single-member district or single-officeholder arrangements. These rules encourage a moderate, two-party system. That we have fixed and staggered terms of office adds predictability to our electoral system.
2. The Electoral College is the means by which presidents are actually elected. To win a state's electoral votes, a candidate must have a plurality of votes in that state. Except in two states, the winner takes all. Thus candidates cannot afford to lose the popular vote in the most populous states. The Electoral College also gives disproportionate power to the largest states and has the potential for defeat of the popular vote winner. Reform efforts have been unsuccessful because the system has worked in the past.
3. Many congressional, state, and local races are not seriously contested. The extent to which a campaign is likely to be hotly contested varies with the importance of the office and the chance a challenger has of winning. Senate races are more likely to be contested, though most incumbents win.
4. The race for the presidency actually takes place in three stages: winning enough delegate support in presidential primaries and caucuses to secure the nomination, campaigning at the national party convention, and mobilizing voters for a win in the Electoral College.
5. Even though presidential nominations today are usually decided weeks or months before the national party conventions, these conventions still have an important role in setting the parties' direction, unifying their ranks, and firing up enthusiasm. Speakers who are highlighted are positioned to pursue nominations in future years.
6. Because large campaign contributors are suspected of improperly influencing public officials, Congress has long sought to regulate political contributions. The main approaches to reform have been: (1) imposing limitations on giving, receiving, and spending political money; (2) requiring public disclosure of the sources and uses of political money; and (3) giving governmental subsidies to presidential candidates, campaigns, and parties, including incentive arrangements. Present regulation includes all three approaches.
7. Loopholes in federal law and rising costs of campaigns have led to declining competition for Congressional seats and increasing dependence on PACs and wealthy donors.
8. The present presidential selection system is under criticism because of its length and expense and because it seems to test candidates for media skills less needed in the White House than the ability to govern, including the capacity to form coalitions and make hard decisions.
9. Reform efforts center on presidential primaries and the Electoral College as well as on voter turnout and campaign finances.

KEY TERMS

lame duck 277
winner-takes-all 277
single-member district 278
proportional representation 278
Electoral College 278
safe seat 280
coattail effect 280
caucus 285
national party convention 286
interested money 289
soft money 293
issue advertising 295
independent expenditures 296

FURTHER READING

LARRY M. BARTELS, *Presidential Primaries and the Dynamics of Public Choice* (Princeton University Press, 1988).

JUDITH A. BEST, *The Choice of the People? Debating the Electoral College* (Rowman and Littlefield, 1996).

EARL BLACK AND MERLE BLACK, *The Vital South: How Presidents Are Elected* (Harvard University Press, 1992).

ALAN EHRENHALT, *The United States of Ambition: Politicians, Power, and the Pursuit of Office* (Times Books, 1991).

THOMAS FERGUSON, *Golden Rule: The Investment Theory of Party Competition and the Logic of Money-Driven Political Systems* (University of Chicago Press, 1995).

LINDA L. FOWLER AND ROBERT D. MCCLURE, *Political Ambition: Who Decides to Run for Congress* (Yale University Press, 1989).

THOMAS GAIS, *Improper Influence: Campaign Finance Law, Political Interest Groups, and the Problem of Equality* (University of Michigan Press, 1996).

PAUL S. HERRNSON, *Congressional Elections: Campaigning at Home and in Washington* (Congressional Quarterly Press, 1995).

GARY C. JACOBSON, *The Politics of Congressional Elections*, 4th ed. (Longman, 1997).

MARION R. JUST, ANN N. CRIGLER, DEAN E. ALGER, TIMOTHY E. COOK, MONTAGUE KERN, AND DARREL M. WEST, *Crosstalk: Citizens, Candidates and the Media in a Presidential Campaign* (University of Chicago Press, 1996).

JOHN KESSEL, *Presidential Campaign Politics*, 4th ed. (Brooks Cole, 1992).

JONATHAN S. KRASNO, *Challengers, Competition, and Reelection: Comparing Senate and House Elections* (Yale University Press, 1994).

ROBERT D. LOEVY, *The Flawed Path to the Presidency, 1992: Unfairness and Inequality in the Presidential Selection Process* (State University of New York Press, 1994).

DAVID B. MAGLEBY AND CANDICE J. NELSON, *The Money Chase: Congressional Campaign Finance Reform* (Brookings Institution, 1990).

NELSON W. POLSBY AND AARON B. WILDAVSKY, *Presidential Elections: Contemporary Strategies of American Politics*, 9th ed. (Chatham House, 1995).

GERALD M. POMPER ET AL., *The Election of 1992* (Chatham House, 1993).

SAMUEL L. POPKIN, *The Reasoning Voter: Communication and Persuasion in Presidential Campaigns* (University of Chicago Press, 1991).

FRANK J. SORAUF, *Inside Campaign Finance: Myths and Realities* (Yale University Press, 1992).

JAMES A. THURBER AND CANDICE J. NELSON, EDS., *Campaigns and Elections American Style* (Westview Press, 1995).

STEPHEN J. WAYNE, *The Road to the White House, 1996: The Politics of Presidential Elections* (St. Martin's Press, 1996).

See also *Public Opinion Quarterly, American Journal of Politics,* and *American Political Science Review.*

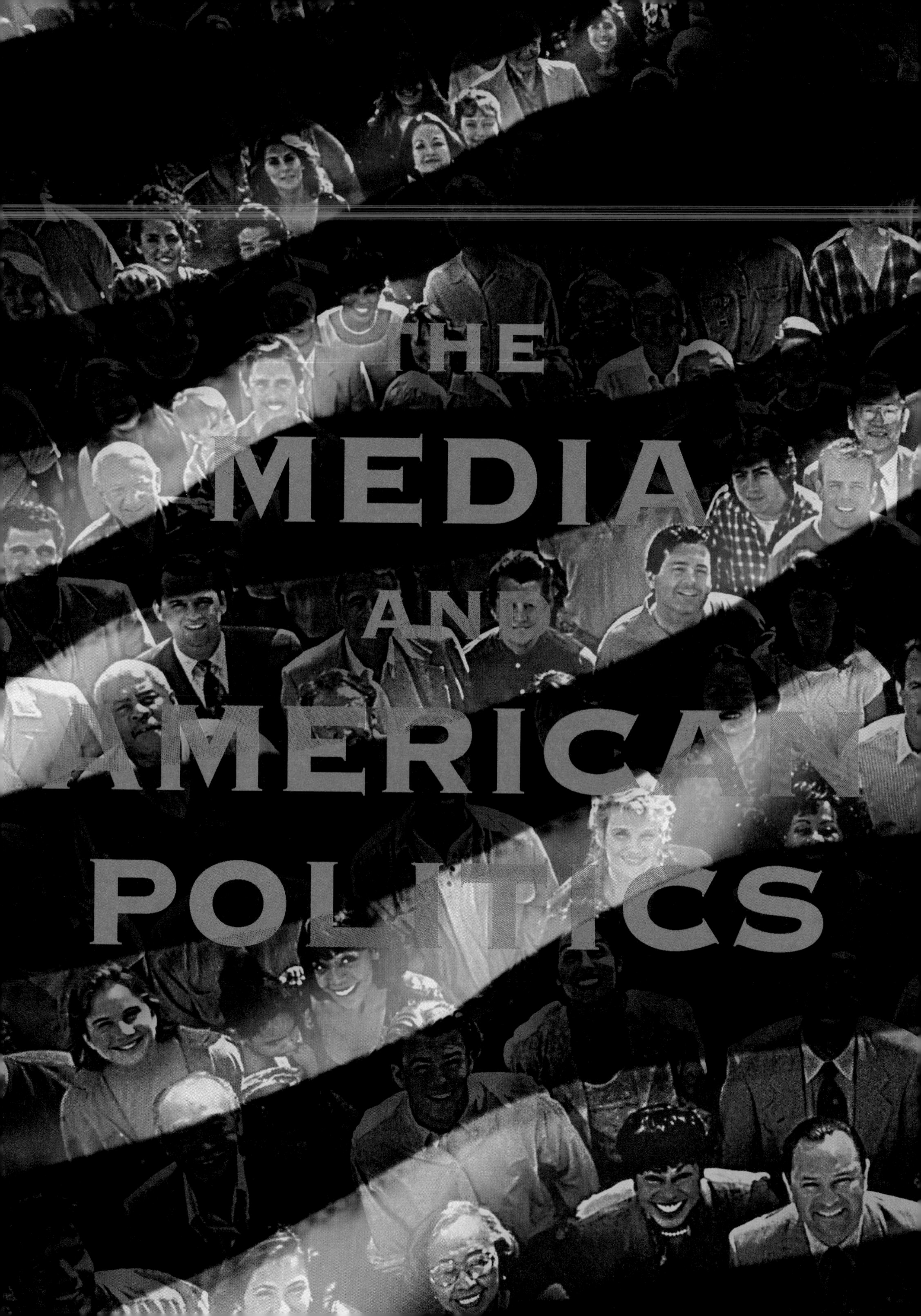

THE MEDIA AND AMERICAN POLITICS

13

CHAPTER OUTLINE

AMERICANS HAVE MORE WAYS TO FIND OUT WHAT IS GOING ON IN THE WORLD THAN DO CITIZENS OF ANY OTHER DEMOCRACY. WE HAVE WIDESPREAD ACCESS TO television, on which we get around-the-clock news and opinion. The Internet provides millions with a wide range of news options and even permits individuals to interact with journalists and newsmakers. Our magazines reflect all kinds of perspectives and promote every conceivable cause. We have some of the world's greatest newspapers. Although we have experienced some censorship of the news during wartime, with very few exceptions people in this country are free to say or write whatever they wish.

Americans make use of their access to the news and spend, on average, an hour a day consuming it. As people grow older, they devote even more time attending to the news.[1] Despite the ready access to our media and its wide variety, Americans are quick to criticize the media. James Fallows, a journalist himself, begins his book on the media by saying: "Americans have never been truly fond of their press. Through the last decade, however, their disdain for the media establishment has reached new levels. Americans believe that the news media have become too arrogant, cynical, scandal-minded, and destructive."[2]

How often have you or your friends blamed the media for insufficient information on issues during elections, criticized the frenzy that surrounded the Monica Lewinsky story, or denounced the "if it bleeds it leads" mentality of nightly television news? Polling data reveal that people criticize the press for being biased, negative, and prone to sensationalism and for focusing too much on private matters. Some Americans would even go so far as to limit the freedom of speech and of the press in order to curb what they consider the excesses of some television shows or other media outlets, but when it comes to election coverage, most people think the press is "fair," although they only give press coverage a grade of C.[3] Although a free press is an important guarantee that our government is not only democratic but honest, this is not to say that press coverage of politics and government in the United States is without problems. Our Constitution guarantees a free press, not a responsible one.

People often blame the media for many of our ills—for increasing tension between the races, biased attacks upon public officials, sleaze and sensationalism—and for being more interested in making money than in conveying information. Media bashing has become something of a national pastime, and there is considerable merit to all of these charges. Many in the media even agree with them.[4] But complaints about the media may simply be a case of criticizing the messenger in order to avoid dealing with

"Hey, do you want to be on the news tonight or not? This is a sound bite, not the Gettysburg Address. Just say what you have to say, Senator, and get the hell off."

the message. Comments like, "It is the media's fault that we have lost our social values," or "The media's preoccupation with the private lives of politicians turns Americans off to politics," are overly broad assertions. Americans tend to blame far more problems on the media than they deserve.

No discussion of politics today is complete without assessing the role of the media. The media are the major source of information, even for policy makers. This chapter examines the media's role in American politics, beginning with the factors that promoted their rise as an independent force, continuing with a discussion of the media's influence on us as citizens and on election campaigns, and culminating in an appraisal of the media's role in the governance of our nation.

The Influence of the Media on Politics

Is the influence of the media on politics real or a myth? The media, in particular the print media, have been called "the other government," "the fourth estate," and "the fourth branch of government."[5] Evidence that the media influence our culture and politics is plentiful. Before we can examine that influence, however, we must define some terms. The **mass media**—that is, newspapers and magazines, radio, television (broadcast, cable, and satellite), films, recordings, books, and electronic communication—are the means of communication that reach the mass public.[6] The **news media** are that part of the mass media that emphasizes the news, although the distinctions between entertainment and news are sometimes blurred. News programs often have entertainment value, and entertainment programs often convey the news. Programs in this latter category include newsmagazines such as *60 Minutes*, *Primetime*, *20/20*, and talk shows with hosts like Rush Limbaugh, Larry King, and Oprah Winfrey.

By definition, the mass media disseminate messages to a large and often heterogeneous audience. Because they must have broad appeal, their messages are often simplified, stereotyped, and formulaic. The mass media are big business and make money by appealing to large numbers of people. But do large audiences equal political clout? Two factors are important in answering this question: the media's pervasiveness and their role as a linking mechanism.

Where do Americans get their news? As late as 1959 most people got their news from newspapers. Today they primarily rely on television, although many people use several sources. Whenever there is a crisis, say the release of Kenneth Starr's "referral" on the investigation of President Bill Clinton, or a major news event such as the funeral of Princess Diana, people stay glued to the TV set. Another new and rapidly growing source of news is the Internet. In 1998 about 20 percent of Americans visited online for news.[7]

The Pervasiveness of Television

Perhaps more than any single other invention, television has changed the character of American politics. Almost all Americans see television every day, and most homes have at least two sets, turned on for an average of seven hours per day. While television is primarily an entertainment medium, most Americans use it for news as well. Four out of ten Americans start their day with some kind of television news; even more tune in to the news in the afternoon and evening.[8] Television provides instant news from around the country and the globe, permitting citizens and leaders alike to observe, firsthand, a refugee crisis in Kosovo or the bombing of a U.S. embassy in Nairobi. This instant coverage increases the pressure on world leaders to respond quickly to crises, permits terrorists to gain widespread coverage of their actions, and elevates the role played by the president in both domestic and international politics.

Perhaps the single biggest change in American electoral politics in the last half century is that most voters now rely on television commercials for information about candidates and issues. As a result, electoral campaigns now focus on image and slogans

mass media
Means of communication that reach the mass public. The mass media include newspapers and magazines, radio, television (broadcast, cable, and satellite), films, recordings, books, and electronic communication.

news media
That part of the mass media that emphasizes the news.

rather than on substance. Successful candidates must be able to communicate with voters through this medium. To get their message across to TV audiences, politicians increasingly communicate with citizens through "sound bites"—15-to-45-second statements for the television or radio news—and 30-second political commercials. Interest groups advocating one position or another—health care reform, trade agreements, affirmative action—also use paid advertising on television and radio to influence voters' choices on election day. These so-called **issue ads** permit groups to spend unlimited and undisclosed amounts of money so long as they do not explicitly call for the election or defeat of a candidate. Interest groups have mounted expensive advertising campaigns on health care reform and tobacco taxes in an effort to sway votes in Congress.

issue ad
Commercial advertising on radio and television advocating a particular position on an issue, paid for by interest groups and designed to influence voters' choices on election day.

For several decades the network evening news programs on CBS, NBC, and ABC captured more than 90 percent of the audience for television news at set times in the morning and early evening hours. Today, Americans can get around-the-clock news information from alternative sources. Two in five Americans are regular viewers of CNN, CNBC, or MSNBC; and nearly three in five regularly watch network prime-time news shows.[9]

The Persistence of Radio

Television has not displaced radio. On the contrary, radio continues to reach more American households than does television. Only one household in a hundred does not have a radio, compared with four in a hundred without a TV. Nine out of ten Americans listen to the radio every day.[10] Cars and radios seem to go together.

Americans get more than "the facts" from radio. They also get analysis and opinion from their favorite commentators and talk show hosts like Rush Limbaugh, Alan Colmes, Michael Reagan, Tom Leykis, and G. Gordon Liddy. These hosts have their own home pages on the World Wide Web and provide around-the-clock opinion on politics. Talk radio has been closely identified with conservatives and Republicans. Newt Gingrich and other leaders in the Republican resurgence in the U.S. House of Representatives made widespread use of it. The popularity of the format has been applied as well to television. Ross Perot announced his candidacy for the presidency on *Larry King Live*, which was also the forum for a major debate between Vice-President Al Gore and Perot over the North American Free Trade Agreement (NAFTA). Talk radio had been a major growth medium, but listeners seem to have dropped off in recent years.[11]

The Continuing Importance of Newspapers

Despite vigorous competition from the broadcast media, Americans still read newspapers. Newspaper circulation has held steady at about 63 million nationwide—or about one copy for every four people—for the past 20 years. Another indication of the print media's pervasiveness is the rise of nationwide newspapers. *The Wall Street Journal*, with a circulation of 1.7 million, has long acted as a national newspaper specializing in business and finance. Other national newspapers with more general interests have also emerged. *USA Today*, created in 1982 by the Gannett Corporation, now has a circulation of over 1.6 million. In addition, *The New York Times* has a national edition that is read by more than 1 million people (see Table 13-1).

TABLE 13-1 Top Ten Newspapers in Circulation, 1997

Newspaper	Circulation
The Wall Street Journal	1,740,000
USA Today	1,650,000
The New York Times	1,070,000
The Los Angeles Times	1,070,000
The Washington Post	759,000
The Daily News (New York)	723,000
The Chicago Tribune	652,000
Newsday	572,000
The Houston Chronicle	551,000
Chicago Sun-Times	486,000

SOURCE: Delwyn Swingewood, "Still Spreading the News," *Media International*, February 1999, p. 30.

The Electronic Media

Recent technological advances have created intense competition for advertising revenues and contributed to sweeping changes in the manner in which news is transmitted and received. Satellites, cable television, computers, and videocassette recorders (VCRs) make vast amounts of political information available 24 hours a day. These technologies eliminate the obstacles of time and distance and increase the volume of information that can be stored, retrieved, and viewed.

An example of the multiplicity of media available to many Americans is the Internet or World Wide Web. From its humble beginnings as a Pentagon research project in the 1970s, the Internet/www has blossomed in the 1990s into an international phenomenon. There are now more than 30 million home pages, including one for this book, which you can find at **http://www.prenhall.com/burns**.

Evidence of the widespread use of the Web is that in recent elections hundreds of candidates for Congress established home pages. Use of the Web has increased dramatically. One study found "a quarter of the public (25%) went online from home or work yesterday, a sharp increase from the 4% who did so three years ago. To put this in perspective, almost as many people use the Internet on a typical weekday as spend time reading a magazine (29%)."[12] Americans use the Internet for more than recreation; they are turning to it in greater numbers for news. Use of the Internet, one study found, is a supplement to rather than a substitute for other news sources.[13] Users of the Internet can read news from a variety of sources and obtain direct links to politicians and candidates. They can also interact with other people or politicians about politics through electronic mail and chat rooms.

THE CHANGING ROLE OF AMERICAN NEWS MEDIA

Political Mouthpiece

At the time of the ratification of the Constitution, newspapers consisted of a single sheet, often printed irregularly by store owners to hawk their services or goods. Newspapers rarely lasted more than a year, due to delinquent subscribers and high costs.[14] But the framers understood the important role the press should play as a watchdog of politicians and government, and they included freedom of the press in the Bill of Rights.

The new nation's political leaders, such as Alexander Hamilton and Thomas Jefferson, recognized the need to keep voters informed. Political party organizations as we know them did not exist, but the active role of the press in supporting the Revolution had fostered a growing awareness of the political potential of newspapers. Hamilton recruited staunch Federalist John Fenno to edit and publish a newspaper in the new national capital of Philadelphia. Jefferson responded by attracting Philip Freneau, a talented writer and editor and a loyal Republican, to do the same for the Republicans. (Jefferson's Republicans later became the Democratic party.) The two papers became the nucleus of competing partisan newspaper networks throughout the nation.

Although the two newspapers competed in Philadelphia only several years, their lasting significance was as a model for future partisan newspapers. Federalist and Republican editors relied on each other for government news and editorials. The free mailing of newspapers granted by the U.S. Post Office allowed broader coverage.

The early American press served as a political mouthpiece for political leaders. Its close connection with politicians and political parties offered the opportunity for financial stability, but at the cost of journalistic independence.

Financial Independence

The Jacksonian era of the 1820s and 1830s was characterized by increased participation in American politics through the elimination of property qualifications for voting. As the vehicle for communication with the public, the press began to shift its appeal away from elite readers and toward large masses of less educated and less politically interested readers. This movement was reinforced by rising literacy rates that supported greater circulation for newspapers. These two forces—increased political participation by the common people and the rise of literacy among Americans—began to alter the relationship between politicians and the press.

Some newspaper publishers began to experiment with a new financing structure called the "penny press." They charged a penny a paper, paid on delivery, instead of the traditional annual subscription fee of $8 to $10, which was beyond the ability of most readers to pay. Through expanded circulation and more emphasis on advertising, newspapers could become financially independent of the political parties.

The changing finances of newspapers also affected the definition of news. Before the penny press, all news was political—speeches, documents, editorials—directed at politically interested readers. The penny press reshaped the definition of news as it sought to appeal to less politically aware readers with human interest stories, sports, crime and public trials, and social activities.

"Objective Journalism"

The death knell of the partisan press sounded with the rise of "objective journalism." By the early decades of the twentieth century many journalists began to argue that the press should be independent of the political parties. *New York Tribune* editor Whitelaw Reid eloquently expressed this sentiment: "Independent journalism! That is the watchword of the future in the profession. An end of concealments because it would hurt the party; an end of one-sided expositions . . . an end of assaults that are not believed fully just but must be made because the exigency of party warfare demands them."[15]

Journalists began to view their work as a profession and established professional associations with codes of ethics and the publication of journals. This professionalization of journalism reinforced the notion that journalists should be independent of partisan politics—a notion that still holds true today. The rise of the wire services as the primary source for national news (they were politically neutral in order to attract more customers) further strengthened the trend toward objectivity.

The Impact of Broadcasting

Radio and television changed the media's role in politics by nationalizing and personalizing the news. Radio did it first, beginning with the creation of networks in the 1920s. Political speeches, campaign advertising, and coverage of political events such as national party conventions were carried on radio.[16] Radio provided a means to bypass the editorial screening of the press, since politicians could speak directly to listeners. It also contributed to increased interest in national and international news, since activities outside a listener's local area could be heard as if one were actually there.

President Franklin Roosevelt used radio with a new effectiveness. Before 1933 most radio addresses were formal orations, but Roosevelt spoke to his audience on a personal level that showed how radio could be used as a one-to-one conversation. Roosevelt's "fireside chats" established a standard for presidential use of the broadcast media still followed today. When Roosevelt began speaking over the microphone, he would visualize the average citizen in front of him. "His face would smile and light up as though he were actually sitting on the front porch or in the parlor with them."[17]

President Franklin Roosevelt was the first president to recognize the effectiveness of radio to reach the public. HIs fireside chats were the model for today's Saturday morning talks on radio by Bill Clinton.

Television added a visual dimension, which contributed to rising audience interest in national events. By 1963 the then two largest networks expanded their evening news programs from 15 to 30 minutes. Today news broadcasting has expanded to the point where many local stations provide 90 minutes of local news every evening as well as a half-hour in the morning and at noon. Programs such

Media in Japan and the United States: Watch Dog or Lap Dog?

A comparison of the media in Japan and the United States illustrates the strengths and weaknesses of both. In Japan the media are independently owned but work closely with one another in alliances, whereas in the United States media conglomerates include diverse businesses like General Electric or Westinghouse. Compare this list of the six largest media outlets in Japan and the United States; for U.S. firms we also provide the business that owns the media outlet.

Japan*	United States
Asahi (newspaper)	General Electric (owns NBC and CNBC and, in partnership with Microsoft, MSNBC)
Yomiuri (newspaper)	
Tokyo Broadcasting	
Shueisha (publishing house)	Dun and Bradstreet (owns *The Wall Street Journal*)
Nihon Television Broadcasting	Westinghouse (owns CBS)
Nihon Keizai Newspaper	Gannett (*USA Today*)
	Walt Disney (ABC)
	Time Warner (TBS, CNN)

While media firms are owned separately in Japan, this does not foster greater media independence, nor are the media in Japan more challenging and investigative than U.S. media. Rather, Japanese reporters are organized into reporter clubs that are affiliated with a specific government news source, and they gain all their information through that source. Japanese reporters know more about the inner workings of politics in their country than most investigative reporters in the United States know about the inner workings of our government. Yet Japanese reporters rarely print what they know, often reporting only the official government line. As a result, whatever stories are printed are the same in each of Japan's newspapers.

For these reasons, the Japanese media has earned a reputation for being a lap dog of its government rather than a watch dog. Despite the trend toward large corporations owning the major news providers in the United States, there remains strong support for journalistic independence, and news reporting is more driven by competition between news media to get the story.

*D. Eleanor Westney, "Mass Media as Business Organizations: A U.S.-Japanese Comparison," in *Media and Politics in Japan*, ed. Susan J. Pharr and Ellis S. Krauss (University of Hawaii Press, 1996), pp. 47–88.

as *60 Minutes*, *20/20*, and other newsmagazine shows are among the most popular in the prime-time evening hours. The rise of cable television brought 24-hour news coverage. During the Persian Gulf War and the Clinton impeachment hearings, American cable news was watched at home and around the world for its instantaneous coverage. Other stations now provide coverage of Congress, the courts, and state and local government.

Investigatory Journalism

Today news reporters do more than convey the news. They investigate it, and their investigations often have political consequences. Notable examples of influential investigatory reporters include Seymour Hersh of *The New York Times*, who exposed *The Pentagon Papers* on how the United States became involved in the Vietnam War; Robert Woodward and Carl Bernstein of *The Washington Post*, who played an important role in uncovering the Watergate conspiracy; Nina Totenberg of National Public Radio, whose reporting on sexual harassment charges against Clarence Thomas helped force the Senate Judiciary Committee to extend the hearings on his confirmation to the U.S. Supreme Court; and Michael Isikoff of *Newsweek*, who broke the story of Bill Clinton's alleged perjury involving sexual relations with Monica Lewinsky.

Media Conglomerates

Newspapers and television are big business. What happens if a few people corner the market on newspapers and television stations? Is the free flow of information to the public endangered? Is too much power to influence public opinion in the hands of too few people?

As in other sectors of the economy, media companies have merged with others and created large conglomerates. Radio networks and newspapers were among the first to purchase television stations when television was in its infancy. These mergers established cross-ownership patterns that persist in media ownership today. The Gannett Corporation, for example, owns 87 daily newspapers and 21 television stations and cable television systems—assets that provide news coverage to nearly 17 percent of the United States.[18] The Federal Communications Commission (FCC) has reinforced the trend toward media conglomeration by permitting one owner to control up to 30 AM and 30 FM radio stations. Previously, ownership was less concentrated, in part because the government was granting licenses to a finite number of stations.

Media conglomerates with large financial resources now dominate the media business and have contributed to the control of news. Are a few media conglomerates likely to provide sufficient competition of ideas to support a democratic system?[19] And without them, can local populations scattered around the country, depending only on local media, find out what is happening in the nation's capital? Why not have government-owned media carry out educational and information functions as well as entertainment functions, as they do in Great Britain and France?[20] The answer is that Americans continue to put great stock in an independent press and news media and find centralized, government-owned media unacceptable.

Another concern has been the gobbling up of American communication assets by large corporations and foreign interests. Local newspapers, radio, and television stations used to be owned primarily by local firms; today large firms, many of them foreign, have acquired ownership of many newspapers and broadcasting stations. The merger of the Disney organization with ABC/Capital Cities, approved early in 1996, cost Disney $19 billion but gave it control not only of the ABC television network but also ESPN, the cable sports station. Months later, the Westinghouse Company bought the CBS television network for $7.5 billion.[21] Time Warner purchased Turner Broadcasting System in late 1996 for reportedly just under $7 billion.[22] The foremost example of foreign interest in our news media is Australian Rupert Murdoch, founder of the Fox network, who owns 22 television stations in the United States and the Family Channel. Murdoch also owns HarperCollins and *TV Guide* magazine, which has the largest magazine circulation in America.

Local outlets depend heavily on news that is gathered, edited, and distributed by national organizations like United Press International and Associated Press. As a result, some people contend that information these days is more diluted, homogenized, and moderated than it would be if the newspapers and broadcast stations were locally owned and the news was gathered and edited locally.[23]

"Ever since we installed a V-chip, I haven't been able to watch the news."

Parade Magazine, October 11, 1998, p. 21.

Regulation of the Media

Regulation of the broadcast media has existed in some form since its inception. Because of the limited number of television and radio frequencies, government has overseen matters like licensing, financing, and even content. One such regulation required "fairness" in news programming.[24] As written into law and interpreted by the Federal Communications Commission, the **fairness doctrine** imposed an obligation on radio and television license holders to ensure that differing viewpoints are presented about controversial issues or persons. With the advent of cable television and the Reagan administration's antiregulatory campaign, the fairness doctrine was repealed in 1987.

The New Mediator in American Politics

The pervasiveness of the media alone does not prove their political influence. But it does place the media in a position to be influential because they can reach so much of the American public so quickly. With a large population scattered over a continent, both the reach and speed of the modern media elevate their importance.

The extensive use of computers by young children opens questions of whether government should protect them from sexual predators. Parental supervision remains the best protection.

fairness doctrine
Doctrine interpreted by the Federal Communication Commission that imposed on radio and television licensees an obligation to ensure that different viewpoints were presented about controversial issues or persons; repealed in 1987.

You Decide . . .

Should the government protect children from excessive violence and sex on TV?

The media are a powerful socializing agent. Many agree that there is too much violence and sex on television. Hillary Rodham Clinton told a national media literacy conference that television "shapes young people's beliefs and aspirations, their sense of self and understanding of the world around them . . . We all have a responsibility to create an environment in which our children can grow and learn to the best of their God-given ability."* Mrs. Clinton then went on to discuss her husband's support of the V-chip and a ratings system for television programs other than news and sports.

The V-chip is a computer chip that can be installed in a television set to permit parents to restrict access to certain television programs. Some favor this type of system as a means of informing parents of the content of programs and permitting them to limit access to inappropriate programs. Others oppose such ratings systems and say the V-chip is a form of censorship. Shouldn't parents enforce their own standards by monitoring what their children watch? Will the V-chip exert any pressure on the television industry to clean up its act?

*Hillary Rodham Clinton, remarks to the 1996 National Media Literacy Conference, October 4, 1996.

Political parties and interest groups have long been political mediators between private individuals and the government—mediators that help organize the world of politics for the average citizen. This role is less important today because the media now serve that function, and political parties have largely lost control over the nominating process (see Chapters 10 and 12). Moreover, there is much greater attention given today to judging candidates not so much in terms of party affiliation and platform but in terms of character and competence. The press, not the parties, is performing this evaluative function.

News media have also taken over the role of "speaking for the people." Journalists tell politicians what "the people" want and think, and then they tell the people what politicians and policy makers are doing about it. Politicians understand this and realize how dependent they are on the media for getting their message out to voters. They also know a hostile press can hurt them. Clearly, today's politicians have to spend much of their time cultivating the press.

The Media and Public Opinion

Scholars, journalists, politicians, and political pundits have long debated the power of the media over public opinion. Do journalists and editors really shape opinions? Do they alter people's behavior? Can they even affect our core values? For a long time, analysts tended to play down the influence wielded by the media in American politics as compared with the influence wielded by political leaders. The impact of Franklin D. Roosevelt's fireside chats came to symbolize the power of the politician against that of the news editor. Roosevelt spoke directly to his listeners over the radio in a way and at a time of his own choosing, and no network official was able to block or influence that direct connection. President John Kennedy's use of the televised press conference represented a similar direct contact with the public. President Ronald Reagan was nicknamed the "Great Communicator" because of his ability to talk persuasively and often passionately about public policy issues with the people through television. Ross Perot emerged on the national scene because of his skill in using television talk shows and his use of his personal wealth to buy time for television "infomercials."

Broadcasters and journalists are now so important to the political process that elected officials and politicians spend considerable time trying to learn how to use them. Presidential events and "photo opportunities" are planned with the evening news and its format in mind.[25] Members of Congress use Capitol Hill recording studios to tape messages for local television and radio stations. White House press briefings are frequently included in the evening news. How government officials use the press, how the press uses government officials, and to what extent the press and television can and should be regulated are critical questions for study.

Factors that Limit Media Influence on Public Opinion

People are not just empty vessels into which politicians and media pour information and ideas. How people interpret political messages depends on a variety of factors: political socialization, selectivity, needs, and the individual's ability to recall and comprehend the message.

political socialization
The process by which we develop our political attitudes, values, and beliefs.

selective exposure
The process by which individuals screen out those messages that do not conform to their own biases.

selective perception
The process by which individuals perceive what they want to in media messages and disregard the rest.

POLITICAL SOCIALIZATION Although we would like to believe we consume the news with an open mind, the reality is that we employ a set of *filters*, or screens that help us interpret and integrate information. When we watch television or read newspapers, magazines, and books, we bring with us values and attitudes that have been shaped by family, peers, school, and the groups to which we belong.[26] We develop our political attitudes, values, and beliefs through an education process that social scientists call **political socialization**. (See Chapters 7 and 11 for more detail on this process.) The media, particularly television, may influence our values and attitudes, but they are not as important as family in the formation of our political attitudes.[27] Face-to-face contacts often have far more impact than the impersonal television or newspaper. Strong identification with a party also acts as a powerful filter.[28] A conservative Republican from Arizona might watch the "liberal Eastern networks" night after night and year after year and complain about their biased news coverage while sticking to his or her own opinions.

SELECTIVITY People practice **selective exposure**—screening out those messages that do not conform to their own biases. They subscribe to newspapers or magazines that already support their views. People also practice **selective perception**—perceiving what they want to in media messages and disregarding the rest.[29] One dramatic example was the differing views of whites and blacks on the guilt or innocence of O. J. Simpson in his widely followed criminal and civil trials. Another example is the differing reactions of Democrats and Republicans to reports of President Clinton's sexual relationship with Monica Lewinsky, a former White House intern, and the possibility he encouraged her to lie under oath. In the first weeks after the story broke, Republicans were four times more likely than Democrats to believe that Clinton had been sexually involved with Lewinsky.[30] Following the release of the Starr report, more than two-thirds of Republicans and Democrats agreed that Clinton committed perjury before Starr's grand jury, but they had dramatically different opinions on whether Clinton should remain in office. Just over one-third of Republicans wanted Clinton to remain in office, while 63 percent of Independents and 87 percent of Democrats felt that Clinton should continue as president.[31]

NEEDS People read newspapers, listen to the radio, or watch television for very different reasons—sometimes because they are bored, tired, or have nothing better to do, sometimes because they want information.[32] People who seek information and cultivate an interest in politics are affected by what they read and see in a way that differs from the effects experienced by those who use media primarily for entertainment.[33] For those who are seeking entertainment, gossip about President Clinton's alleged affairs or Senator Phil Gramm's financing of an X-rated movie is more important than Clinton's or Gramm's political opinions or deeds. Members of the broader audience are also more likely to follow news that directly affects their lives, such as interest rate changes and stock market fluctuations.[34]

RECALL AND COMPREHENSION Still another limitation of media influence on public opinion is the extent to which the audience can recall the stories or comprehend their importance. Candidates and officials send out vast amounts of information designed to influence what people think and do, especially how they vote, but people forget or fail to comprehend much of it.[35] The fragmentary and rapid mode of presentation of television news contributes to the problem.

Given all the information available about politics and government, it is not surprising that most people pick and choose which media source—television, radio, newspapers—they pay attention to and which news stories they consider important. One scholar who studied the process of selecting which news people pay attention to and remember found that comprehension varied widely, "depending on the nature of stories, the use of visuals, and the concerns and lifestyles of the audience."[36] The best predictor of retention of news stories is political interest. People tend to fit today's news stories into their general assumptions or beliefs about government, politicians, or the media itself.

Are the Media Biased?

Americans tend to blame the media for lots of things. Conservatives complain "the media are too liberal." Liberals claim "the media are controlled by the establishment." Politicians complain that their messages do not come across. Although people blame

Thinking it Through...

The movement to have a ratings system for television programs gained enough support that all major television networks except NBC proposed their own rating system similar to that used for movies, in part to avoid one legislated by Congress. The ratings indicate if the program contains violence, sex, or language that might be objectionable.

Jack Valenti, president of the Motion Picture Association of America, argues that these ratings help parents make decisions. Valenti and others in the television industry say that to go further than their proposal would violate First Amendment rights.

The opposition, led by Representative Ed Markey (D-Mass.), says these ratings are insufficient because they do not give enough information about the programs, such as the degree of violence or the type of sexual material. Markey and most parent and family groups want a more detailed system of ratings and description of program content.

Those who oppose such ratings systems contend that, once started, they can become a type of censorship. Moreover, they assert there is a lot of subjectivity in evaluating programs. What some may see as too violent or sexually explicit, others may not find objectionable. Then there is the added cost to equip televisions with V-chips and to employ people to rate the programs. Ultimately it will be advertisers who pay the costs of the ratings and consumers who pay for the V-chip.

The counterargument is that children learn what is acceptable behavior from the media, especially television. Critics point to an increasing incidence of violent and sexually explicit actions and language on TV. They contend the industry will not regulate itself. The V-chip, when combined with content disclosure and a detailed ratings system, would give parents control over this powerful socializing force.

You Decide . . .

How should the media report sex scandals?

During the 1992 presidential campaign, Bill Clinton saw his press coverage turn negative as reports circulated in the *Star*, a supermarket tabloid, that he and Gennifer Flowers, a former Arkansas state employee, had had a twelve-year-long extramarital affair. Clinton, with Mrs. Clinton by his side, denied the Flowers account in an interview on *60 Minutes*, a CBS-TV news program, on Superbowl Sunday. Because Flowers had been paid for her story by the *Star*, some people discounted the story. Others were doubtful that tabloid papers like the *Star* ever print anything close to the truth. Despite the existence of tapes that appeared to confirm the Flowers account, the press essentially dropped the story.

After winning the presidency, Clinton was dogged by a series of accusations of unwanted sexual advances toward Paula Jones and Kathleen Willey and of a consensual affair with Monica Lewinsky. In a transcript of his deposition in the Jones sexual harassment suit, Clinton admitted having an affair with Gennifer Flowers. This raised anew questions of how the media had reported the original accusations. Did the press handle those stories properly?

many things on the media, they do not always give the media a failing grade. Most felt press treatment of the candidates during the 1996 election was fair. In contrast, voters were more critical of campaign advertising, believing that political advertisements "rarely" or "almost never" could be trusted.[37]

Are the news media biased? True, television networks are business corporations concerned about profits. This means they work to boost ratings and must please advertisers, sponsors, and stockholders. Do the preferences of advertisers or corporate owners show up in news reporting? Reporters and editors pride themselves on impartial reporting of the facts.[38] Yet one group of media critics holds that the media reflect a conservative bias not only in what they report but in what they choose to ignore. Political scientist Michael Parenti states that journalists "rarely doubt their own objectivity even as they faithfully echo the established political vocabularies and the prevailing politico-economic orthodoxy."[39]

Another source of possible bias is that reporters and editors become too friendly with those they write about. David Broder of *The Washington Post* voices his concern about the confusion of roles by journalists who have served in government. According to Broder, a line should divide objective journalism from partisan politics, but many in the print and television media have crossed this line. Broder opposes the idea of journalists becoming government officials and vice versa.[40] Others argue that journalists with previous government service have close working relationships with politicians and can give us a valuable perspective on government without losing their professional neutrality.

Equally disturbing to some observers is the media's alleged political bias, whether liberal or conservative (see Table 13-2). But to whom are these critics referring? To reporters, writers, editors, producers, or owners of TV and newspapers? Do they assume a journalist's personal politics will be translated into biased reporting? And does the public think so?

Conservatives say the press is too liberal. They criticize the press for advocating liberal social causes and ignoring the conservative viewpoint.[41] Influential conservative radio talk show host Rush Limbaugh, speaking of the media, argues, "They all just happen to believe the same way. . . . They are part of the same culture as Bill Clinton."[42]

The far left also accuses the media of bias. Leftist critics contend the mainstream press is purely a propaganda device of the ruling class, creating the boundaries of acceptable thinking and thereby shutting out left-wing viewpoints. Leftist

Gennifer Flowers and her attorney are questioned by reporters after she revealed her affair with Bill Clinton in the supermarket tabloid Star.

TABLE 13-2 The Politics of Journalists and the Public

	Washington-Based Reporters	Newspaper Editors (National)	Public
Party Identification			
Democrat	50%	31%	34%
Republican	4	14	28
Independent	37	39	25
Other	9	7	8
Self-Described Ideology			
Liberal	61	32	20
Moderate	30	35	34
Conservative	9	25	27

Source: The Roper Center, *The Public Perspective*, October/November 1996, p. 8. Based on a Media Studies Center/Roper Center survey of 1,200 persons conducted in September 1995.

critics see the mass media as capitalist enterprises that dislike airing anticapitalist sentiments. As well as being a tool of the business class, according to these critics, the media are also a tool of government propaganda that seeks to distort the facts.[43] Others see this "conspiracy theory" as merely a rationalization by leftists who are disgruntled over the failure of their views to take hold with the American people.[44]

Conservatives and the far left are not the only ones who perceive bias. Liberals point to newspaper endorsements of Republican presidential candidates to support their claim that newspapers are biased toward conservative policies and candidates. Daily newspapers tend to endorse Republicans over Democrats for president by a ratio of roughly 2 to 1.[45]

Another charge of bias has to do with the possible cultural bias of journalists. Journalists usually are more liberal than the population as a whole; editors tend to be a bit more conservative than their reporters; and media owners are more conservative still. Polling data demonstrate that slightly more than half the journalists classify themselves as liberals, compared with only about one-fourth of the general public.[46] Elite journalists—those who work for national news media organizations—tend to share a similar culture: cosmopolitan, urban, upper class. Their approach to the events and issues they cover is governed by their common worldview, which may be derived from their professional training.[47] The result is an almost unconscious bias, because elite journalists give greater weight to the side of issues that corresponds to their own version of reality.[48] Newspapers and television news often set a tone of dissatisfaction with the performance of the national government and cynicism about politics and politicians.

A critical tone may be an inevitable element in the mindset of the press. But to whose benefit does that critical tone work? The question is not whether the press is biased, but whether a press bias—whatever the direction—seeps into the content of the news. The answer to that question is still not settled. Empirical studies of news content have failed to find the expected liberal bias.[49] But the media are accused of more than a liberal bias. Others think they have an anti-incumbent bias, a generational bias, and a bias fostering continuing crises.[50] And still others, as noted above, contend that they have a bias in favor of their ownership and top management.

Public Opinion

The media can make a big difference in what Americans believe. Television is especially important in shaping opinion; with all its concreteness and drama, it has an emotional impact that print cannot hope to match.[51] And television news exposure

Thinking it Through...

Some dismiss reporting on sex scandals as prudish and unrelated to governing. Others, like Larry Sabato, a political scientist who has written on the media, disagree. Sabato says the press "didn't reveal what most of them knew then about Clinton and all the other women. They said, 'Oh we've already been through all that.' No we hadn't. In fact, they left it with most Americans believing Gennifer Flowers had been lying. If the press had done its job in '92, the country would not be facing this horrible dilemma in '98."*

The question of how to report accusations against political candidates is unresolved. It is debatable whether such matters ought to be reported at all. Reporters appear to be looking for ways to avoid such stories.** The public wants to know whether candidates meet high standards of personal conduct but react negatively to coverage that is too aggressive. Public reaction to the explicit details of the Starr report is instructive: 84 percent of the public wanted to know the conclusions of the investigation, but 70 percent felt that Congress should have omitted the details of the sexual encounters.†

*Larry J. Sabato, quoted in William Power, "News at Warp Speed," *National Journal*, January 31, 1998, p. 220.

**See Larry J. Sabato and S. Robert Lichter, *When Should the Watchdogs Bark? Media Coverage of the Clinton Scandals* (Center for Media and Public Affairs, 1994), pp. 41–52.

†Frank Newport, "Initial Reaction Mixed on Delivery of Starr Report to Congress," Gallup Organization, September 12, 1998. See also www.gallup.com/poll_archives/980912.htm.

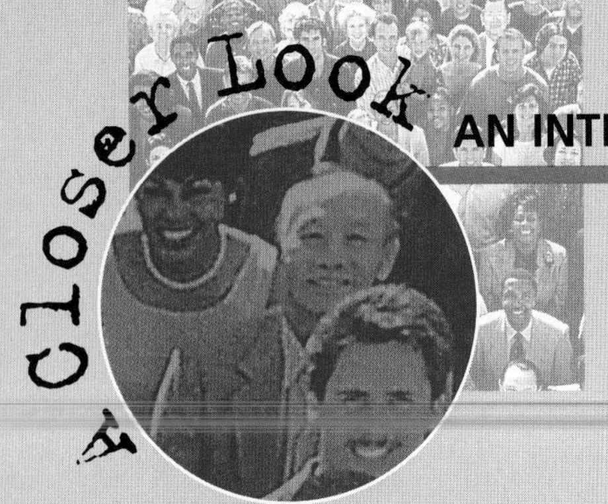

AN INTERNET TOWN MEETING

With the Internet, citizens now have the opportunity to interact with each other on a wide range of political topics. In this sense, the Internet is something like a town meeting, but without people leaving their homes or offices. In chat rooms, on the World Wide Web, people express ideas and respond to each other's opinions. Examples of such chat rooms include Abortion Chat, Democrat Chat, Environment Chat, Republican Chat, and Congress Chat. Most chat rooms offer group discussions in which anyone in the group can read and send messages, but some chat rooms also permit private messages to be sent.

As with town meetings, politicians can learn about public sentiment via the Web. They can participate in the chat room or read postings on the Internet in what is called Usenet. Reading messages posted on Usenet permits politicians to gauge public opinion and tap into particular segments of the population. But because those who use the Internet are not a representative sample of the general public, politicians should be wary not to generalize from the opinions expressed through this medium.

Reporters also use the messages posted on the Web as leads for stories. Elements of the Clinton-Lewinsky scandal were posted on the Internet long before they made it into newspapers or on television. Because rumors on the Web are not substantiated, reporters and others should beware of the possibility of inaccuracy.

Matt Drudge was the first to break the story of the Lewinsky/Clinton scandal on the Internet. Mainstream press and TV quickly jumped in to spread the news.

cuts across age groups, educational levels, social classes, and races. Newspapers, on the other hand, provide more detail about the news and often contain contrasting points of view, at least on the editorial pages, that help inform the public more substantially. Both print and broadcast media are a potent influence in agenda setting and issue framing.

AGENDA SETTING The power to set the public agenda is a significant one. By calling public attention to certain issues, the media help to determine what topics will become the subject of public debate and legislation.[52] However, the agenda-setting function of the media is not uniformly pervasive. It is limited by the audience and the nature of the issue.[53]

Ronald Reagan, more than any president before him, effectively used the media to set the nation's agenda. Reagan and his advisers carefully crafted the images and scenes of his presidency to fit television. Thus television became an "electronic throne." According to former Vice-President Walter Mondale, "If I had to give up . . . the opportunity to get on the evening news or the veto power, . . . I'd throw the veto power away. [Television news] is the President's most indispensable power."[54]

ISSUE FRAMING How politicians and journalists frame issues affects how they will be perceived. Politicians, like everybody else, try to frame issues to win arguments, and they try to influence the "spin" the media will give to their actions or issues. Examples abound. Those who opposed U.S. intervention in Bosnia tried to portray such action as another Vietnam. When George Bush sought support for U.S. intervention in the Persian Gulf War, he compared Saddam Hussein to Adolf Hitler. When Bill Clinton wanted to forestall a Republican tax cut, he framed the use of the budget surplus to rescue Social Security. Those who favor abortion define the issue as one of freedom of choice; those who oppose it define it as murder. In referendum campaigns the side that wins the battle of interpreting what the referendum is about wins the election.[55]

The Media and Elections

Do news stories determine who wins or loses elections, who gets nominated for office, or which referenda get passed? News stories arguably have more influence today because of the shift to greater direct democracy in our political system. Primaries now nominate candidates, with little role left for political parties, and voters decide many important issues directly through initiatives and referenda. Although the influence of the media may be greater due to these changes, there is little evidence such influence controls elections. Generally, the more attention given the campaign, the less likely voters are to be swayed by any one source. Hence, news coverage is likely to be more important in a city referendum than in an election for president or the Senate.

Diversification of the news media also lessens the ability of any one medium to dominate politics. Newspaper publishers who were once seen as very important in state and local politics know that today politicians and their media advisers can communicate their message through television, radio, direct mail, videocassettes, the Internet, and cable television. Hence, there is now more competition among the various media, and politicians and candidates can get their message out regardless of what the editor of the state's largest newspaper may think.

The Role of the Media in Elections

A generation ago campaigns were waged as much to impress party leaders and power brokers as to win votes. Today candidates bypass the party and use the media to go directly to the voters. This extensive use of television has made being "good on television" much more important, fostered a growth industry in political consulting, and made visibility the watchword in nomination politics.

CHOICE OF CANDIDATES The role of the media begins with the decision of who will run. Television greatly affects the public's idea of what traits are important in a candidate. A hundred years ago, successful candidates needed a strong pair of lungs; today it is a telegenic appearance, a pleasing voice, and no obvious physical impairments. Back in the 1930s, the press chose not to show Franklin Roosevelt in his wheelchair or using braces, whereas today the country knows every intimate detail of the president's health. The importance of the public's perception of these traits is evident in the ridicule often directed at candidates. In 1996, Bob Dole was criticized for his boring speaking style and Ross Perot was teased about his haircut.

If the news media pay no attention to a candidate, he or she is not likely to win any elections. Although the media insist they pay attention to all who have a chance to win, they also influence who has such a chance. So candidates have to come up with creative ways to attract media attention. Lawton Chiles, running for the U.S. Senate from Florida, captured media attention by walking across the state. The novelty of the idea meant that reporters gave Chiles lots of free media coverage. Paul Wellstone used creative advertisements in his first Minnesota Senate campaign in which he said that he did not have much money to pay for ads, so he would have to talk fast to cram what he had to say into fewer commercials. The witty way he did this became a news event itself—and got Wellstone additional coverage. Both Chiles and Wellstone won.

CAMPAIGN EVENTS Candidates schedule events—press conferences, interviews, "photo ops"—in settings that reinforce their verbal messages. Even the national convention has become less a place to choose the nominee and more of an elaborate photo opportunity. Since party primaries are now where the presidential candidates are selected, fewer people watch the convention proceedings. Political parties have sought, in vain, to regain audience interest by relying on "movie stars, entertainment routines, and professionally produced documentaries to spice up their conventions."[56] In 1952 the average television set was tuned to the political conventions for 26 hours,[57] or an average of more than three hours a night for the eight nights of convention coverage. In 1996, in contrast, the major networks provided only one hour of prime-time coverage each night, and only C-SPAN provided gavel-to-gavel coverage.[58]

MEDIA TECHNOLOGY Thanks to new media technology, candidates finally can be in more than one place at a time. Satellites allow candidates to conduct local television interviews without actually traveling to the area and to communicate with party workers across the country. Specific voter groups can be targeted through cable television or low-power television stations that reach homogeneous neighborhoods and small towns. Videocassettes sent to voters with messages from the candidates further extend the campaign's reach.[59] Many candidates for Congress and governor in 1998 made themselves and their positions available through a home page on the World Wide Web. The expense associated with media technology has contributed to the skyrocketing costs of campaigning.

Image Making

Public interest in the image of candidates is not new. Presidential campaign sloganeering such as "Tippecanoe and Tyler Too" in 1840 and "Abe the Rail Splitter" in 1860 were used to convey the candidate's image. Radio, television, and the Web have expanded this image-making role, which in turn has affected candidates' vote-getting strategies and their manner of communicating messages. Television is especially important because of the power of the visual image.

Candidates recognize that their messages about issues are often ignored. The press tends to emphasize goofs and gossip or tensions among party leaders. In the 1996 election, for instance, the press reported on a $1,000 campaign contribution given to Bob Dole by the Log Cabin Republicans, a gay and lesbian group. It was initially returned by the Dole campaign, but Dole later reversed the decision of his campaign staff and said the staff had not consulted him.[60]

Media Consultants

James Carville, a key adviser to Bill Clinton in 1992 and 1996 and a staunch defender during the Clinton/Lewinsky scandal.

Image making has contributed to the rise of new players in campaign politics—media consultants, campaign professionals who provide candidates with advice and services on media relations, advertising strategy, and opinion polling.[61] For instance, when Bill Clinton was running for president in 1992, his consultants countered the impression that Hillary Clinton was too assertive by having her discuss her cookie-making skills, drop her maiden name in campaign references, and play the role of the supportive spouse.[62]

Some media consultants have been credited with propelling candidates to success. Dick Morris was seen as important to Clinton's resurgence after the 1994 election defeats, until he had to resign from the campaign following a personal scandal. Republican consultants Roger Ailes and Don Sipple and Democratic consultants James Carville and Robert Squire have acquired powerful reputations. But media consultants have also been blamed for the negativity of recent presidential campaigns. The classic example was a 1988 ad sponsored by George Bush's campaign, linking Democratic nominee Michael Dukakis to Willie Horton, a convicted murderer who committed violent crimes while on a prison furlough program.

Media consultants have taken over the role formerly played by party politicians. Before World War II, candidates for office at all levels from president to dog catcher were advised by party professionals. Such leaders made their judgments about possible candidates on the basis of long observation of the candidates' performances under fire, decisiveness, conviction, political skill, and other "presidential" qualities (in addition to their chances of victory). Party professionals told candidates which party and interest group leaders to placate, which issues to stress, and which topics to avoid.

Today candidates are more dependent upon a media consultant. Consultants advise them on television technique, flexibility, "salability," and the like. Consultants report the results of *focus groups* (small sample groups of people who are asked questions about candidates and issues in a discussion setting) and *public opinion polls*, which in turn determine what the candidate says and does. Some critics allege that political consultants have become a new "political elite" who can virtually choose candidates by determining in advance which men and women have the right images, or at least images that can be restyled for the widest popularity.[63] But political consultants who specialize in media advertising and image making realize their own limitations in packaging candidates. As one media consultant put it, "It is a very hard job to turn a turkey into a movie star; you try instead to make people like the turkey."[64]

WE THE PEOPLE

Profile of a Media Consultant

Martin Hamburger is a partner in the political consulting firm of Seder, Laguens & Hamburger. He first became involved with politics while in college where he majored in political science and organized a nuclear freeze campaign. Upon graduation, he began working for the public interest group, Council for a Livable World, where he later directed its Peace PAC. He has also worked for the National Wildlife Federation. Frustration with the lobbying process caused Hamburger to try his hand at campaigning. His first campaign was for Michigan Democratic Senator Carl Levin in his 1990 reelection campaign. After spending time as a congressional staffer, Hamburger was hired by the Democratic Congressional Campaign Committee (DCCC) to manage a special election for the U.S. House in Massachusetts. By 1992 he had become the DCCC's deputy political director. Soon after the 1992 elections, he joined Joe Slade White and Co., a media consulting firm, and then worked for a year at Campaign Performance Group, a direct-mail firm. This revolving door from campaign staff to legislative staff, to party committee staff, to consulting firms is not unusual.

In 1997 he joined his current firm. Hamburger sees his relationship to campaigns as a consultant as different from his relationship as a committee staffer, primarily because he works on fewer campaigns and therefore has the opportunity to become more involved with a candidate. He also feels that as a consultant he is responsible to his clients rather than to the party as a whole. These responsibilities include telling the absolute truth to his client and being honorable; yet while remaining within these parameters, doing whatever it takes to win. He feels, as a consultant, his responsibility is to the candidate, not to the electorate.

Source: Interview with Martin Hamburger and Candice J. Nelson, "Inside the Beltway: Profiles of Two Political Consultants," *PS: Political Science and Politics* 31 (June 1998), pp. 162–66.

The Media and Voter Choice

As television has become increasingly important to politics and as the political parties have been weakened with such reforms as primary elections, news coverage of candidates has taken on added significance. Although some critics think reporters pay too much attention to candidates' personality and background, others say character and personality are among the most important characteristics for readers and viewers to know about. What is not in dispute is the central role the news media play in our democratic process.

INFORMATION ABOUT CANDIDATES What voters know about candidates is based largely on media coverage. If the media do not cover a candidate, voters generally know little about him or her. Journalists are more likely to comment on a

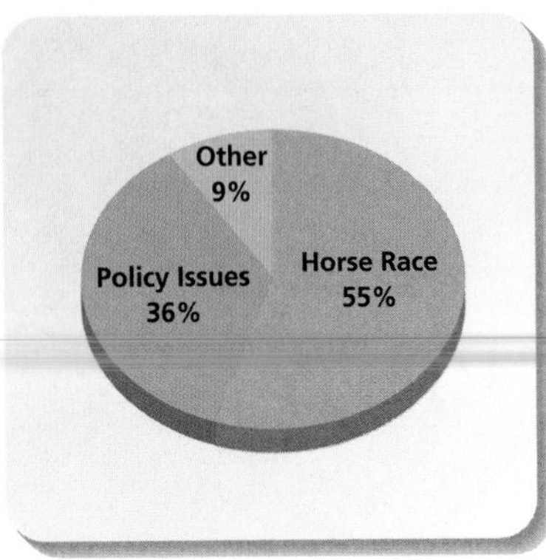

Figure 13-1 Focus of Coverage, 1988–1996 Presidential Elections*

SOURCE: *Media Monitor,* November/December 1996.

*Average percentage of stories based on evaluation of election stories on ABC, CBS, and NBC evening newscasts, by nonpartisan sources.

candidate's standing in the polls compared to other candidates—what is sometimes called the "horse race"[65] (see Figure 13-1). "Many stories focus on who is ahead, who is behind, who is going to win, and who is going to lose, rather than examining how and why the race is as it is."[66] Reporters focus on the tactics and strategy of campaigns because they perceive that the public is interested and influenced by such coverage.[67]

INFORMATION ABOUT ISSUES It is often difficult for voters to learn much about the candidates' stands on issues. The media's propensity to focus on the "game" of campaigns displaces coverage of issues. When there is a scarcity of issue information on television news, voters may learn more about issue positions from issue ads on television and in newspapers.[68] But advertising is becoming increasingly negative in tone. A rule of thumb in the old politics was to ignore the charges of the opposition, thus according one's rival no importance or standing. That practice has changed as candidates trade charges and countercharges.

Voters say they are turned off by the attack style of politics, but the widespread perception among consultants is that negative campaigning works. This seeming inconsistency may be explained by recent evidence suggesting that campaigns fostering negative impressions of the candidates contribute to lower turnout.[69] Negative advertising thus may discourage some voters who would be inclined to support your opponent, while reinforcing the inclination of your supporters to come out to vote. In referendum elections, advertising is the most important source of information in voter decision making.[70]

In recent elections the media have attempted to bring back a more issues-centered focus through what has been called *civic journalism.* With funding from charitable foundations, some newspapers have emphasized talking to ordinary voters and writing campaign stories from the point of view of ordinary voters. The news media interviewed people in 1998 and used these interviews to structure their campaign coverage.[71]

MAKING A DECISION Newspapers and television seem to have more influence in determining the outcome of primaries than of general elections.[72] This is probably because voters are less likely to know about the candidates and have fewer clues

Projecting the outcome of the 1996 presidential election early in the evening may have discouraged voters on the West Coast, who felt the results were a foregone conclusion.

about how they stand in a primary. By the time of the November general election, however, party affiliation, incumbency, and other factors moderate the impact of media messages. The mass media are more likely to influence undecided voters who, in a close election, can determine who wins and who loses.

ELECTION NIGHT REPORTING Does TV coverage on election night affect the outcome of elections? Election returns from the East come in three hours before the polls close on the West Coast. Because major networks often project the presidential winner well ahead of poll closings in western states, some western voters have been discouraged from voting. As a result, voter turnout in congressional and local elections has been affected. In a close presidential election, however, such early reporting may well stimulate turnout because voters will know their vote could determine the outcome. In short, it is only in elections in which one candidate appears to be winning by a large margin that television reporting makes voters believe their vote is meaningless.[73]

THE MEDIA AND GOVERNANCE

The press serves as both observer and participant.[74] As observer, it records and transmits information to and from actors in policy making. As participant, it acts as watchdog or critic, helps set the agenda of policy issues, and serves as a check on the abuse of power.

But the press's role as participant rarely follows the policy process to its conclusion. Rather, it leaves the issue at the doorstep of public officials. By the time an issue reaches the stages of policy formulation and implementation, the press has moved on to another issue. When policies are being formulated and implemented, decision makers are at their most impressionable, yet the press has little impact at this stage.[75]

Lack of press attention to how policies are implemented explains in part why we know less about how bureaucrats go about their business than we do about heated legislative debates or presidential scandals. Only in the case of a policy scandal, such as the savings and loan debacle in the early 1990s, does the press take notice. Ignoring the policy process is fine with many agency heads, who prefer bureaucratic anonymity. "Most executives would be satisfied with a press strategy of no surprises. All their press officers need do to be doing their job is provide a rudimentary early warning system [for crises] and issue routine announcements."[76] But the assumption of most policy makers, even those handling classified national security information, is that their actions will leak out to the media sooner or later.

Some media critics contend a negative consequence of the media's approach to policy coverage is pressure on policy makers to resolve a problem immediately once it receives media focus. Foreign policy may be in particular danger from such quick responses. Presidential adviser Lloyd Cutler asserts the press's pressure on a president can be difficult to resist:

> If an ominous foreign event is featured on TV news, the president and his advisers feel bound to make a response in time for the next evening news broadcast. . . . If he does not have a response ready by the late afternoon deadline, the evening news may report that the president's advisers are divided, that the president cannot make up his mind, or that while the president hesitates, his political opponents know exactly what to do.[77]

Political Institutions and the News Media

Presidents have become stars of media coverage, particularly television, and have made the media their forum for setting the public agenda and achieving their legislative aims. Presidential news conferences command attention (see Table

TABLE 13-3 Presidential News Conferences with White House Correspondents

President	Average per Month	Total Number
Herbert Hoover (1929–33)	5.6	268
Franklin D. Roosevelt (1933–45)	6.9	998
Harry Truman (1945–53)	3.4	334
Dwight Eisenhower (1953–61)	2.0	193
John Kennedy (1961–63)	1.9	64
Lyndon Johnson (1963–69)	2.2	135
Richard Nixon (1969–74)	0.5	37
Gerald Ford (1974–77)	1.3	39
Jimmy Carter (1977–81)	0.8	59
Ronald Reagan (1981–89)	0.5	44
George Bush (1989–93)	3.0	142
Bill Clinton (1993–97)	2.3	167

Source: *Weekly Compilation of Presidential Documents*, vol. 31, *Annual Index*, p. C12.

13-3). Every public activity, both professional and personal, is potentially newsworthy; a presidential cold or sickness can become front page news, as can presidential vacations and family pets.

A president attempts to manipulate news coverage to his benefit. Speeches are used to set the national agenda or spur congressional action. Travel to foreign countries usually boosts popular support at home, thanks to the largely favorable news coverage. Better yet for the president, most coverage of the president—either at home or abroad—is favorable or at worst neutral.[78] President Clinton's trip to Israel and Gaza during the height of the impeachment furor may have helped distract attention.

Congress, on the other hand, often gets negative coverage. Congress's problems are that it is a fragmented body unable to act quickly on much of anything.[79] Unlike the presidency, it lacks an ultimate spokesperson—a single individual who can speak for the whole institution.[80] Congress does not make it easy for the press to cover it. While the White House engages in the "care and feeding" of the press corps, Congress does not arrange its schedule to suit the media; floor debates, for example, often compete with committee hearings and press conferences.[81] Singularly dramatic

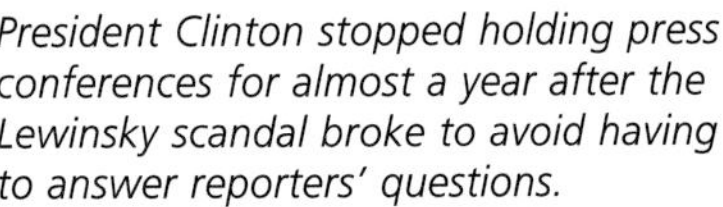
President Clinton stopped holding press conferences for almost a year after the Lewinsky scandal broke to avoid having to answer reporters' questions.

actions rarely occur in Congress, but such actions constitute news for the press. The press, therefore, turns to the president to describe federal government activity on a day-to-day basis and treats Congress largely as a foil to the president. Most coverage of Congress is of its reaction to the initiatives of the president.[82]

The federal institution least dependent on the press is the Supreme Court, which relies little on public communication for political support. Rather, it relies indirectly on public opinion for continued deference to and compliance with its decisions.[83] The Court has strong incentives to avoid the perception of direct manipulation of the press, so it retains an image of aloofness from politics and public opinion. The justices' manipulation of press coverage of the Court is far more subtle and complex than that of the other two institutions.[84]

The news media's greatest role as a participant in the governing process may be at the local level. Most of us have multiple sources for finding out what is happening in Washington that act as a check on the biases and limitations of reporters who cover national government and policy. But when it comes to finding out about the city council, the school board, or the local water district, most of us are dependent on the work of a single reporter. Consequently the media's influence is much greater when there are fewer news sources.

Not all who think the media are powerful agree that their power is harmful. After all, they argue, the media perform a vital educative function. Further, they continue, almost 70 percent of the public think the press is a watchdog that keeps government leaders from doing bad things.[85] At the very least, the media have the power to mold the agenda of the day; at most, in the words of the late Theodore White, they have the power to "determine what people will talk and think about—an authority that in other nations is reserved for tyrants, priests, parties, and mandarins."[86]

online POLITICS

Computer Users Watching TV Less?

During the last few years, there has been a general decline in viewing television news programs. This decline may be related to the use of personal computers, which has increased markedly among young people. National television networks and major newspapers all have extensive websites with the day's news as well as archived past editions, and many local newspapers are also available on the Internet.

Watched TV News Yesterday

	June 1995	April 1996	Difference
Computer User	63%	56%	-7
Online User	63	56	-9
Nonuser	66	63	-3

SOURCE: The Pew Research Center for The People and The Press, "TV News Viewership Declines," May 13, 1996.

News consumption over the Internet allows flexibility. Instead of sitting through an entire news program waiting for your topic of interest, you can use a search engine to find a specific news item immediately. Are you among those who still consume their news the old-fashioned way, through the newspaper or nightly news? If so, check out these websites:

http://www.nbc.com

http://www.abc.com

http://www.nytimes.com

http://www.cbs.com

http://www.cnn.com

For more Internet resources on The Media in Politics, see our home page at:

http://www.prenhall.com/burns

SUMMARY

1. The news media include newspapers, magazines, radio, television, films, recordings, books, and electronic communications, in all their forms. These means of communication have been called "the other government" and "the fourth branch of government."
2. The news media are a pervasive feature of American politics and generally help to define our culture. The rise of new communications technologies has made the media more influential throughout American society. The news media provide a "linking" function between politicians and government officials and the public.
3. Our modern news media emerged from a more partisan and less professionalized past. The autonomy of the media from political parties is one of the important changes. Now journalists strive for objectivity and see themselves as important to the political process. They also engage in investigative journalism. Broadcasting on radio and television has changed the news media, and most Americans use television and radio as primary news sources. The role of corporate ownership of media outlets, especially media conglomerates, has emerged in the past few years and raises questions about media competition and orientation.
4. The influence of the mass media over public opinion is significant yet not overwhelming. People may not pay much attention to the media or believe all they read or see or hear. They may be critical or suspicious of the media and hence resistant to it. People tend to "filter" the news in part through their political socialization, selectivity, needs, and ability to recall or comprehend the content of the news.
5. The media are criticized as biased both by conservatives (who charge that the media are too liberal) and by liberals (who claim that the media are captive of corporate interests and major advertisers). Little evidence exists of actual, deliberate bias in news reporting.
6. A major effect of mass media news is agenda setting—that is, determining what problems will become salient issues for people to form opinions about and to discuss. The media are also influential in defining issues for the general public.
7. The media are under attack for sensationalism, superficial reporting, biased coverage, and overemphasis on the "theatrical." Efforts to significantly change the media will be frustrated by at least two factors: reformers do not agree on what course to follow, and virtually all Americans fear taking any action that might threaten the freedom of the press.
8. Presidential campaigns are dominated by media coverage during both the pre- and postconvention stages. One effect of media influence is that most people seem more interested in the contest as a "game" or "horse race" than as an occasion for serious discussion of issues and candidates. Another effect has been the rise of image making and the media consultant.
9. The press serves as observer of and participant in politics, as watch dog, agenda setter, and check on the abuse of power, but it rarely follows the policy process to its conclusion. Political institutions depend on the media.

KEY TERMS

mass media 306
news media 306
issue ad 307
fairness doctrine 311
political socialization 312
selective exposure 312
selective perception 312

FURTHER READING

STEPHEN ANSOLABEHERE AND SHANTO IYENGAR, *Going Negative: How Attack Ads Shrink and Polarize the Electorate* (Free Press, 1996).

LANCE W. BENNETT, *Governing Crisis: Media, Money, and Marketing in American Elections* (St. Martin's Press, 1992).

JOSEPH N. CAPPELLA AND KATHLEEN HALL JAMIESON, *Spiral of Cynicism* (Oxford University Press, 1997).

TIMOTHY COOK, *Governing with the News: The News Media as a Political Institution* (University of Chicago Press, 1998).

TIMOTHY COOK, *Making Laws and Making News: Press Strategies in the U.S. House of Representatives* (Brookings Institution, 1990).

RICHARD DAVIS, *The Press and American Politics: The New Mediator*, 2d ed. (Prentice Hall, 1996).

RICHARD DAVIS, ED., *Politics and the Media* (Prentice Hall, 1994).

JAMES FALLOWS, *Breaking the News: How the Media Undermine American Democracy* (Pantheon Books, 1996).

SUZANNE GARMENT, *Scandal: The Culture of Mistrust in American Politics* (Times Books, 1991).

DORIS A. GRABER, *Mass Media and American Politics*, 5th ed. (Congressional Quarterly Press, 1997).

LAWRENCE K. GROSSMAN, *The Electronic Republic: Reshaping Democracy in the Information Age* (Viking, 1995).

ROD HART, *Seducing America: How Television Charms the Modern Voter* (Oxford University Press, 1994).

STEPHEN HESS, *Live from Capitol Hill: Studies of Congress and the Media* (Brookings Institution, 1991).

KATHLEEN HALL JAMIESON, *Dirty Politics: Deception, Distraction, and Democracy* (Oxford University Press, 1992).

PHYLISS KANISS, *Making Local News* (University of Chicago Press, 1991).

HOWARD KURTZ, *Spin Cycle: Inside the Clinton Propaganda Machine* (Free Press, 1998).

S. ROBERT LICHTER AND RICHARD E. NOYES, *Good Intentions Make Bad News: Why Americans Hate Campaign Journalism* (Rowman and Littlefield, 1995).

S. ROBERT LICHTER, STANLEY ROTHMAN, AND LINDA S. LICHTER, *The Media Elite* (Adler and Adler, 1986).

JOHN ANTHONY MALTESE, *Spin Control: The White House Office of Communications and the Management of Presidential News* (University of North Carolina Press, 1992).

RUSSELL W. NEWMAN, *Common Knowledge: News and the Construction of Political Meaning* (University of Chicago Press, 1991).

THOMAS E. PATTERSON, *Out of Order* (Knopf, 1993).

TOM ROSENSTEIL, *Strange Bedfellows: How Television and the Presidential Candidates Changed American Politics, 1992* (Hyperion, 1993).

LARRY J. SABATO AND S. ROBERT LICHTER, *When Should the Watchdogs Bark? Media Coverage of the Clinton Scandals* (Center for Media and Public Affairs, 1994), pp. 41–52.

SIMON SEFATY, *The Media and Foreign Policy* (St. Martin's Press, 1990).

KENNETH T. WALSH, *Feeding the Beast: The White House versus the Press* (Random House, 1996).

DARRELL M. WEST, *Air Wars: Television Advertising in Election Campaigns, 1952–1992* (Congressional Quarterly Press, 1993).

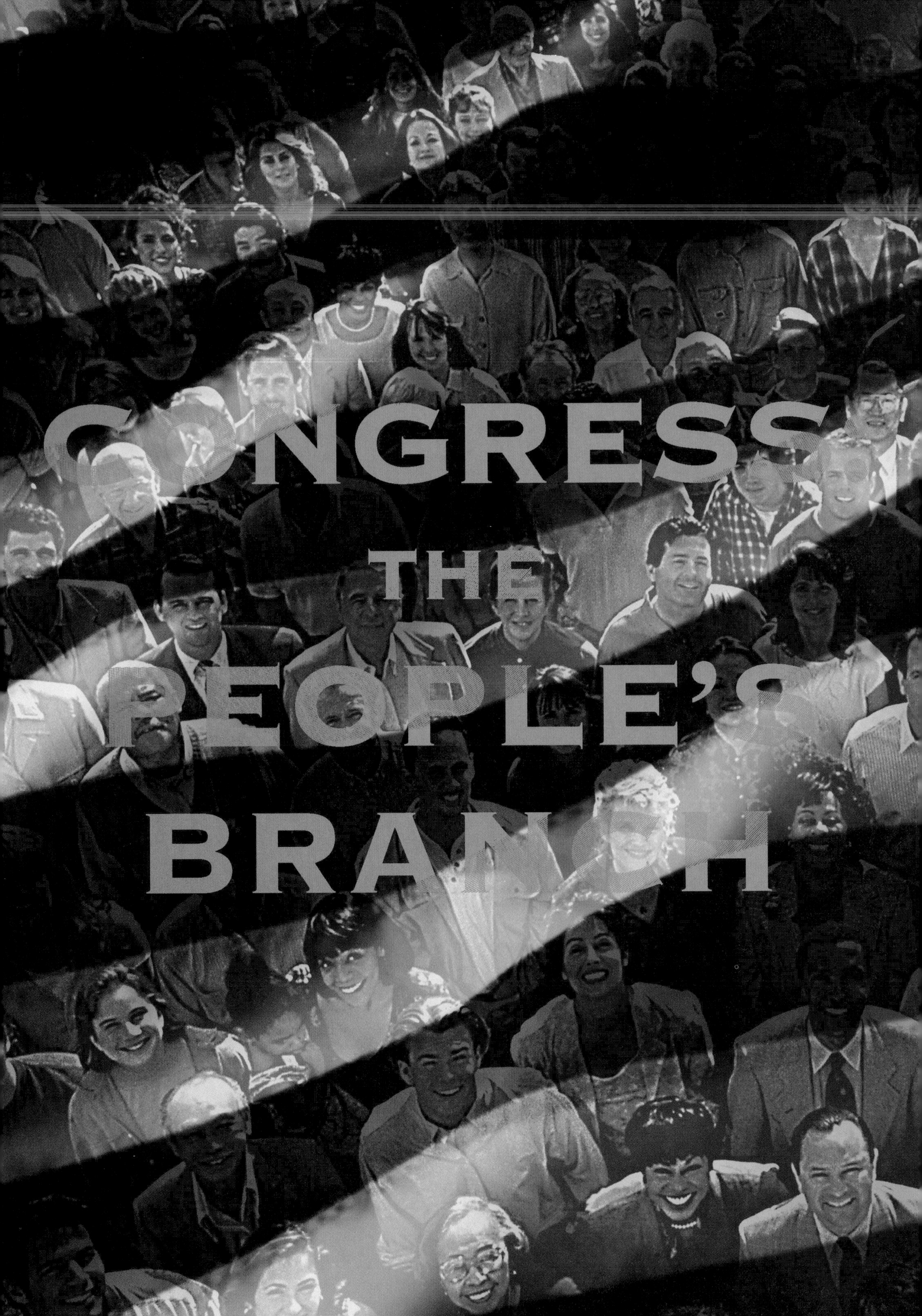
CONGRESS
THE
PEOPLE'S
BRANCH

14

THE UNITED STATES CONGRESS IS ONE OF THE MOST PRAISED YET MOST CRITICIZED POLITICAL INSTITUTIONS IN THE WORLD. IT IS PRAISED BECAUSE IT IS A REPRESENTATIVE and democratic institution. It is praised, too, because it is deliberative and open. And it is revered because it has nurtured many outstanding legislators who have contributed greatly to the success of the American political experiment.

Yet Americans relentlessly criticize both Congress and its members: citizens not only think members of Congress don't understand their needs but also think members of Congress put the concerns of special interests ahead of those of the average person. Sixty-two percent of participants in one national survey in 1997 agreed that "Congress creates more problems than it solves."[1] Congress is also criticized for being irrelevant, slow, and overly partisan.

Complicating matters, however, is the fact that although most Americans profess a devotion to democracy, many have little or no appreciation of what a practicing democracy requires. Political scientists John Hibbing and Elizabeth Theiss-Morse note, "People do not wish to see uncertainty, conflicting options, long debate, competing interests, confusion, bargaining, and compromised, imperfect solutions." Instead, they would like their government to perform its job quietly, efficiently, and without public bickering and gridlock. "In short," Hibbing and Theiss-Morse conclude, the American people "often seek a patently unrealistic form of democracy."[2]

Congress may be widely criticized, but it plays an absolutely crucial role in the American political system. Presidents cannot lead if they do not have a working relationship with both chambers of Congress. Congress controls key decisions on budgets, taxes, trade policy, the shape of the federal bureaucracy, and appointments to the cabinet, the embassies, and the courts. A president has a certain amount of freedom in foreign policy, yet even here a president's policies will rarely be successful or properly implemented without support from Congress. For this reason President George Bush sought congressional support before the Persian Gulf War, and President Bill Clinton tried to gain approval of congressional leaders for the 1998 bombing of Iraq.

Because ours is a system of shared powers, Congress and the president are inevitably engaged in a collaborative process. Part of the reason why it is difficult to appreciate or understand Congress is that much of what it does depends on its relationships with the other branches of government as well as with state and local governments.

In this chapter we examine the politics of representation and how Congress organizes itself to do its work of making laws and representing the people. We also

CHAPTER OUTLINE

Why Do Incumbent Members of Congress Usually Win?

- They enjoy better name recognition, and to be known at all is generally to be known favorably. Challengers are almost always less well known.
- They enjoy free mailings (called the franking privilege) to every household in the state or district. These mailings—which often resemble campaign brochures—portray members as hardworking and influential.
- They have greater access to the media.
- They raise campaign money more easily than challengers, because lobbyists and political action committees (PACs) seek their ears and their favors. Also, many campaign contributors know that incumbents are more likely than challengers to get reelected, so they give to those they know will win. (PACs in recent elections have given as much as $8 out of every $10 to incumbents.)
- They usually have had more campaign experience, and they can claim to have had more experience in Congress and in Washington.
- They have staffs to help with casework and constituency services for the folks back home.
- They take credit for federal money that gets allocated to their region.
- They are in a better position than challengers to take advantage of government research staffs, new government studies, and even classified information.

No one of these factors can guarantee a member's reelection, yet skillful use of them makes it difficult to unseat a healthy incumbent.

look at how this highly public, open, and genuinely political institution cannot avoid provoking conflicts that lead to sometimes bitter clashes with the White House and other rivals for influence in the shaping of American public policies.

Congressional Elections

The entire membership of the House of Representatives (435) is elected to two-year terms in even-numbered years. Elections for the six-year Senate terms are staggered, so that one-third of the Senate's 100 members are chosen every two years. Members of the House of Representatives must be 25 years old and have been citizens for seven years. Senators must be at least 30 years old and have been citizens for nine years.

Members of Congress are politicians, and they get their jobs by winning an election. Ironically, it is often good politics for them to deny they are politicians and to lead the charge against the institution they serve in. The willingness of "House members to stand and defend their own votes or voting record contrasts sharply with their disposition to run and hide when a defense of Congress might be called for," writes political scientist Richard F. Fenno, Jr. "Members of Congress run *for* Congress by running *against* Congress. The strategy is ubiquitous, addictive, cost-free, and foolproof. . . . In the short run, everybody plays and nearly everybody wins. Yet the institution bleeds from 435 separate cuts."[3]

The outcome of any congressional election depends on many factors. By far the most important is the nature of the state or district in which the candidate runs. Is it a **safe seat**—one that is predictably won by one party or the other—or is it a competitive one? Other factors affecting winning elections are personal appeal of the candidate, whether the opponent is an incumbent or a newcomer, local issues, campaign strategies, the fund-raising abilities of the candidate, and, occasionally, national political tides, such as in the 1964, 1974, and 1994 elections.

Incumbents have traditionally enjoyed a great advantage over challengers, but incumbency isn't always an advantage. "Outsiders" like Ross Perot, Ralph Nader, Steve Forbes, and Rush Limbaugh have targeted the "Washington insiders" and helped create a climate of antagonism toward Congress as an institution. Because of this climate, there have been repeated yet unsuccessful efforts in Congress to pass constitutional limits on congressional terms. But more than 90 percent of incumbents who run for reelection to Congress continue to beat their challengers; 94 percent did so in 1996, and 97 percent of incumbent members running for reelection won in 1998. In the House, 395 out of 401 incumbents won; in the Senate 26 of 29 incumbents won.

safe seat
An elected office that is predictably won by one party or the other, so reelection is almost taken for granted.

gerrymandering
The drawing of election district boundaries to benefit a party, group, or incumbent.

redistricting
The redrawing of congressional and other legislative district lines following the census, to accommodate population shifts and keep districts as equal as possible in population. Also called *reapportionment*.

bicameralism
The principle of a two-house legislature.

Districting and Apportionment

The Constitution gives Congress the right to apportion representatives among the states according to population, and Congress, in turn, has given state legislatures control over drawing congressional districts. Senators, of course, represent entire states, but House seats are distributed among the states according to population; each state receives at least one seat. Subject to a gubernatorial veto, state legislatures draw the district lines for the House of Representatives. The party in control of the state legislature traditionally draws the lines to enhance its own political fortunes.[4] This process is known as **gerrymandering**, after Governor Elbridge Gerry of Massachusetts, who, in 1811, reluctantly signed a redistricting bill that created a distinctly partisan district shaped like a salamander.

To accommodate population shifts, **redistricting** occurs once a decade, after each national census. Because population shifts also occur between states, it is necessary after each census to reapportion seats for the U.S. House of Representatives. Thus, after the census in 1990, 13 states lost representatives and 8 gained new seats in the House. After the census in 2000, Congress will again reapportion representatives among the states, and due to population shifts, some eastern and northern states such as New York and Pennsylvania will lose House seats, and a few sun belt and western states such as Arizona, California, and Texas will gain seats.

State legislatures draw up congressional districts subject to constitutional limitations and requirements of national laws. Federal courts are playing an increasing role in ensuring that the legislatures comply with these national requirements. Thus a state legislature can, and almost all do, provide for districts with equal population.[5] But they often do so in a manner that favors one major political party over the other. This party gerrymandering explains why so many districts are "safe" for one party. However, if the partisanship is so biased that it makes it impossible for the other party to win, it might run into judicial objections. The Supreme Court has held that under certain circumstances, which it has never specified, excessive partisan gerrymandering might be unconstitutional.[6]

Finally, although a state legislature can design congressional districts to virtually guarantee the election of a member of a particular minority, it must be careful not to do so in a fashion that focuses *only* on racial considerations and ignores such matters as county lines and city boundaries.[7] Indeed, the Supreme Court has ruled that making race "the predominant factor," while ignoring traditional redistricting principles such as compactness, is unconstitutional.[8]

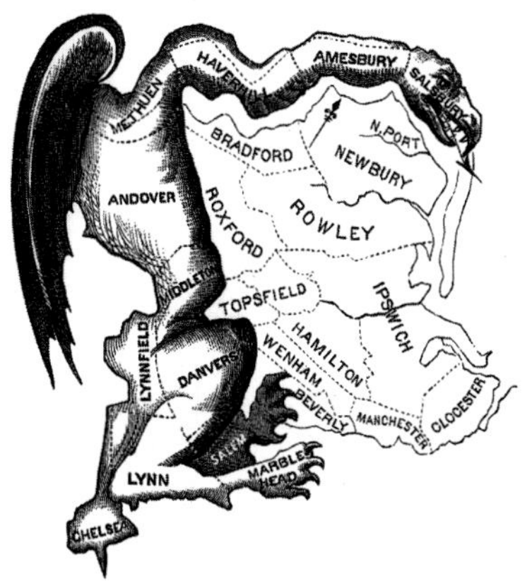

The word "gerrymander" comes from the name of a governor of Massachusetts, Elbridge Gerry, and the salamander-shaped district that was created to favor his party in 1811.

The Structure and Powers of Congress

The most important feature of Congress is its **bicameralism**—that is, it is made up of two houses. Few other national legislatures are genuinely bicameral. Many have two houses, but one is usually largely ceremonial. In the United States, the Senate and the House each have an absolute veto over the other's law making. Each chamber runs its own affairs, sets its own rules, and conducts its own investigations. The law-making role, however, is shared. Each must be seen as a separate institution, even though both houses reflect similar political forces and share common organizational patterns.

In other countries the "upper" house often has significantly fewer powers than the supposed people's house. For example, the British House of Lords (composed of hereditary and appointed nobility) is unable to do more than delay for a few weeks legislation passed by the more powerful and popularly elected House of Commons. And Prime Minister Tony Blair recently proposed legislation to strip the hereditary lords of any voting rights. The French Senate (indirectly elected by local and regional officeholders) has full powers of debate and amendment, but the government can push through legislation blocked or amended in the Senate by obtaining a favorable vote in the lower house (the National Assembly).

In Germany, the upper house (Bundesrat) is composed of delegates named by the state governments. The size of the delegation is based on population, but each state's delegation casts its votes as a bloc in Bundesrat votes. The Bundesrat lacks the legislative powers of the lower house (Bundestag), but it does allow for the involvement of the states in legislation that affects them and their relationship to the federal government. The Bundesrat often plays a key political role, especially when its majority differs from the majority in the Bundestag.

The Consequences of Bicameralism

As James Madison explained in *The Federalist*, No. 51, the protection against giving too much power to the legislature "is to divide the legislature into different branches; and to render them, by different modes of election and different principles of action, as little connected with each other as the nature of their common functions, and their common dependence on the society will admit." (*The Federalist*, No. 51, is reprinted in the Appendix.)

The House of Representatives was expected to reflect the popular will of the average citizen, whereas the Senate was to provide for stability, continuity, and in-depth deliberation. Many of the framers hoped the Senate would stem any rash populist impulses of the other chamber. Although the Seventeenth Amendment to the Constitution (1913), which provides for direct election of U.S. senators, altered the character of the Senate's membership, the two chambers still have many differences (see Table 14-1). However, the two houses are more similar today in their membership and operations than they were two hundred or even one hundred years ago.

Defenders of bicameralism say it serves as a moderating influence on the partisanship or possible errors of either of the chambers. This constitutionally mandated structure also guarantees that many votes will be taken before a policy is finally approved. It provides more opportunities, too, for bargaining and allows legislators with different policy goals a role in the shaping of national laws.

James Madison and the framers of the Constitution hailed this feature of our system as desirable protection of our liberties. The Senate is the only legislature in the United States where the principle of equal representation does not apply. That is, the number of senators from each state is not based on population. Because each state has two senators regardless of population, the Senate represents constituencies that are more rural, white, and conservative than would be the case if the one-person, one-vote norm applied to Senate elections.

WE THE PEOPLE

Profile of the 106th Congress, 1999–2001

	U.S. Senate (100)	U.S. House (435)
Republicans	55	223
Democrats	45	211
Independents	0	1
Sex		
Men	91	377
Women	9	58
Religion		
Catholic	25	126
Jewish	11	23
Protestant	53	251
Other	11	35
Average Age	58	53
Racial/Ethnic Minorities	3	63
Lawyers	57	172
Business	24	159
Agriculture	6	22
Engineering	0	9
Real Estate	4	20

SOURCES: *Congressional Quarterly Weekly*, January 9, 1999, pp. 62–63.

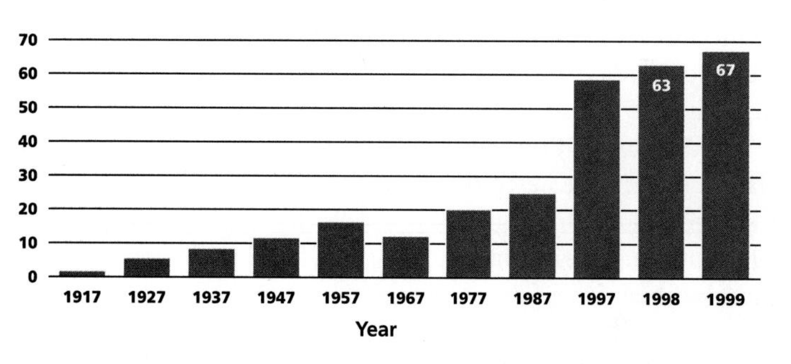

Figure 14-1 Number of Women in U.S. Congress

SOURCE: Rutgers University Center for the American Woman and Politics. Reprinted from *The Washington Post*, October 12, 1998, p.10. Updated by the authors.

TABLE 14-1 Differences Between the House of Representatives and the Senate

House of Representatives	Senate
Two-year term	Six-year term
435 members	100 members
Smaller constituencies	Larger constituencies
Fewer personal staff	More personal staff
Equal populations represented	States represented
Less flexible rules	More flexible rules
Limited debate	Extended debate
More policy specialists	Policy generalists
Less media coverage	More media coverage
Less prestige	More prestige
Less reliance on staff	More reliance on staff
More powerful committee leaders	More equal distribution of power
Very important committees	Less important committees
20 major committees	20 major committees
Nongermane amendments (riders) not allowed	Nongermane amendments (riders) allowed
Important Rules Committee	Special treaty ratification power
Some bills permit no floor amendments (closed rule)	Special "advise and consent" confirmation power
	Filibuster is allowed

The Constitutional Separation of Powers

In Article I, the Constitution outlined the structure, powers, and responsibilities of Congress, giving it "All legislative Powers herein granted": the power to spend and tax in order to "provide for the common Defense and general Welfare of the United States"; the power to borrow money; the power to regulate commerce with foreign nations and among the states; the power to declare war, raise and support armies, and provide and

Incoming members of the 106th Congress pose on the steps of the Capitol in November 1998.

maintain a navy; the power to establish post offices; and the power to set up the federal courts under the Supreme Court. As a final catchall, the Constitution gave Congress the right "to make all Laws which shall be necessary and proper for carrying into Execution" the powers set out. Several nonlegislative functions were also granted, such as participating in the process of constitutional amendment and impeachment (given to the House) and trying an impeached federal officer (given to the Senate).

The framers empowered Congress to remove presidents, vice-presidents and federal judges who have committed "High Crimes and Misdemeanors." The House sits to determine whether or not their actions reach the level of impeachable offenses, and they can impeach by a majority vote. The Senate sits as a court to decide if the impeached official should be convicted, and whether the nature of the offense warrants removal from office. A two-thirds vote is needed to convict; thus a minority of just 34 senators can reject a conviction or removal of an impeached official.

The Constitution confers additional responsibilities on the Senate. The Senate has the power to confirm many presidential nominations—sometimes as many as 500 key executive and judicial nominees a year. In a two-year session of Congress there may be more than 5,000 civilian nominations and 90,000 military nominations needing senatorial approval. The Senate must also give its consent, by a two-thirds vote of the senators present, for presidential ratification of treaties.

The House has some distinctive responsibilities, but they are not as important as those given to the Senate. For example, although all revenue bills must originate in the House, this practice does not give the House much advantage, because the Senate can freely amend spending bills, sometimes changing everything except the title.

The framers did not intend Congress to be all-powerful. They reserved certain authority for the states and for the people and gave other powers to the executive and judicial branches of the national government. As time passed, Congress gained power in some respects and lost it in others. The power of Congress also changed with the president and the times. For example, Bill Clinton was more effective in getting legislation passed in his first two years in office (1993–95) than he was after the Republican takeover of both houses in 1995.

As the role and authority of the national government have expanded, so have the policy-making and oversight responsibilities of Congress. Still, Congress has difficulty keeping pace with its great rival, the president. The president's national security responsibilities, preparation of the budget, media visibility, and agenda-setting influence have all enhanced the position of the presidency. The growth of executive authority may be part of a worldwide trend. Legislative bodies almost everywhere have become subordinate to the executive at all levels of government.

Congress performs seven important functions:

1. *Representation*: expressing the diversity and conflicting views of the regional, economic, social, racial, religious, and other interests in the United States.
2. *Law making*: enacting measures to help solve substantive problems.
3. *Consensus building*: the bargaining process by which these interests are reconciled.
4. *Overseeing the bureaucracy*: ensuring that laws and policies approved by Congress are faithfully carried out by the executive branch and accomplish what was intended.
5. *Policy clarification*: the identification and publicizing of issues.
6. For the Senate, *confirming by a majority vote presidential appointees* and ratifying treaties by a two-thirds vote.
7. *Investigating the operation of government agencies*, including the White House; this responsibility includes impeachment processes.

The House of Representatives

The organization and procedures in the House are different from those in the Senate, if only because the House is more than four times as large as the Senate. *How* things are done affects *what* is done. The House assigns different types of bills to different calendars. For instance, finance measures—tax or appropriations bills—are put on a special calendar for quicker action.

The House has other ways to speed up law making, including electronic voting. Ordinary rules may be suspended by a two-thirds vote, or immediate action may be taken by *unanimous consent* of the members on the floor. By sitting as the *committee of the whole,* the House is able to operate more informally and more quickly than under its regular rules. A quorum in the committee of the whole is composed of only 100 members, rather than a majority of the whole chamber, and voting is quicker and simpler. Members are limited in how long they can speak, and debate may be cut off simply by majority vote.

Well-wishers greeted Newt Gingrich after he announced he was stepping down as Speaker of the House.

THE SPEAKER The **Speaker** is the presiding officer in the House of Representatives.[9] The Constitution mandates that the House of Representatives shall choose its Speaker, yet it does not say anything about the duties or powers of the office. This officer is formally elected by the entire House yet is actually selected by the majority party. As the highest-ranking officer in Congress, the Speaker represents it on ceremonial occasions. Third in line of succession to the presidency (in case of death, resignation, or impeachment), the Speaker must keep the White House informed about his whereabouts.

The routine powers of the Speaker include recognizing members who wish to speak, ruling on questions of parliamentary procedure, and appointing members to temporary committees, not the major regular committees. Revolts in 1910 by rank-and-file Progressives stripped Speakers of much of their power, including control over who served on which congressional committees. In general, the Speaker directs business on the floor of the House. More significant, of course, is a Speaker's political and behind-the-scenes influence.

When the Republicans won control of the House in 1994, they elected Newt Gingrich as Speaker. As the first Republican Speaker in 40 years, he was a novelty in Washington. "I had set out to do a very unusual job," said Gingrich, "which was part revolutionary, part national political figure, part Speaker, part intellectual."[10]

Gingrich established his authority—naming committee chairs, bypassing the seniority rule, reorganizing House committees, and reducing perks and committee staffs. He delegated considerable power to fellow Republican leaders, yet claimed for himself the main role as spokesperson for major policy initiatives. He published books detailing his ideas about government and his party, and he cheerfully took on the White House and the national press.[11]

Gingrich eventually found it impossible to control many of his highly conservative colleagues, especially the 73 Republican first-term members elected in 1994. He sometimes lost his temper with the press, and after a while, he became a lightning rod for the public's discontent with Congress.[12]

Following a spate of charges and a two-year investigation, the House Ethics Committee found Gingrich had disregarded standards of conduct that applied to the use of tax-exempt funds. For at least three years he had insisted there was little overlap between his partisan political activities and his supposedly nonpartisan educational endeavors. But the committee recommended, and the House of Representatives quickly passed, a reprimand of Gingrich and imposed a fine of $300,000 for misusing charitable deductions for political purposes and for misleading the House Ethics Committee. This was an unprecedented rebuke for a Speaker; indeed, it was the only such reprimand of a Speaker in the history of the House.[13]

Speaker
The presiding officer in the House of Representatives, formally elected by the House but actually selected by the majority party.

majority leader
The legislative leader selected by the majority party, who helps plan party strategy, confers with other party leaders, and tries to keep members of the party in line.

minority leader
The legislative leader selected by the minority party as spokesperson for the opposition.

whip
Party leader who is the liaison between the leadership and the rank-and-file in the legislature.

party caucus
Meeting of party members in a chamber of the legislature to select the party leadership in that chamber and to develop party policy. Called a *conference* by Republicans.

closed rule
A procedural rule in the House of Representatives that prohibits any amendments to bills or provides that only members of the committee reporting the bill may offer amendments.

open rule
A procedural rule in the House of Representatives that permits floor amendments within the overall time allocated to the bill.

hold
A practice in the Senate whereby a senator temporarily blocks the consideration of a bill or nomination.

president pro tempore
Officer of the Senate selected by the majority party to act as chair in the absence of the vice-president.

filibuster
A practice in the Senate whereby a senator holds the floor and thereby delays proceedings and prevents a vote on a controversial issue.

Gingrich retired both as Speaker and as a member of Congress following his party's poor showing in the midterm election of 1998. He was replaced by Illinois Congressman Dennis Hastert. Hastert, a former high school teacher and wrestling coach, had served for six years in the Illinois state legislature and twelve in the U.S. House of Representatives before becoming Speaker of the House. "It's a calling that I have not sought," said Hastert. "However, it is a duty that I cannot ignore."[14] His colleagues viewed him as soft-spoken, genial, and hard-working, and they plainly expected him to be less of a lightning rod than his predecessor. "I've always tried to be an honest broker," said Hastert.[15]

OTHER HOUSE OFFICERS The Speaker is assisted by a **majority leader**, who helps plan party strategy, confers with other party leaders, and tries to keep members of the party in line. The minority party elects a **minority leader**, who usually steps into the Speakership when his or her party gains a majority in the House. (These positions are also sometimes called majority and minority floor leaders.) Assisting each floor leader are the party **whips**. The term comes from the "whipper-in," who in fox hunts keeps the hounds bunched in a pack. The whips serve as liaisons between the House leadership of each party and the rank-and-file. They inform members when important bills will come up for a vote, prepare summaries of the bills, do nose counts for the leadership, exert pressure (sometimes mild and sometimes heavy) on members to support the leadership, and try to ensure maximum attendance on the floor for critical votes. Current Speaker Hastert was the deputy majority whip before becoming Speaker; he and Majority Whip Tom DeLay (R.-Tex.) were known for their effective efforts to "encourage" House Republicans to vote the party line on key votes.

At the beginning of the session and occasionally afterward, each party holds a **party caucus** of all its members (called a *conference* by Republicans) to elect party officers, approve committee assignments, elect committee leaders, discuss important legislation, and perhaps try to agree on party policy.

THE HOUSE RULES COMMITTEE The House, unlike the Senate, has a Rules Committee that regulates the time of floor debate for each bill and sets limitations on floor amendments. By refusing to grant a rule, the committee can delay consideration of a bill. A **closed rule** prohibits amendments altogether or provides that only members of the committee reporting the bill may offer amendments; closed rules are usually reserved for tax and spending bills. An **open rule** permits debate within the overall time allocated to the bill.

From the New Deal era in the mid-1930s until the mid-1960s, the Rules Committee was dominated by a coalition of Republicans and conservative Democrats. Liberals denounced it as unrepresentative, unfair, and dictatorial. More recently, the Rules Committee membership has come to reflect the views of the total membership of the majority party. The Rules Committee today is an arm of the leadership, and rather than block legislation, it offers a "dress rehearsal" on procedural issues like time allotted for debate to those trying to press for new measures.

The Senate

The Senate has the same basic committee structure, elected party leadership, and decentralized power as the House, but because the Senate is a smaller body, its procedures are more informal, and it permits more time for debate.

The contemporary Senate is individualistic. The Senate is a more open, fluid, and decentralized body now than it was a generation or two ago. Indeed, it is often said that the Senate has one hundred separate power centers and is so splintered that the party leaders have difficulty arranging the day-to-day schedule.[16]

The Senate has always operated under rules that vest great power in the individual senator. Extended debate allows senators to hold the floor as long as they wish unless a supermajority of 60 colleagues votes to end debate. "The Senate's permissive amending rules enable any senator to offer any and as many amendments as she pleases to almost any bill and those amendments need not even be germane [related to the measure]."[17]

In recent years, senators have used a practice called the **hold**. A hold is a procedure allowing any senator to block temporarily the consideration of either a legislative bill or a presidential nomination. Nowhere found in the Constitution or in Senate rules, the hold has "evolved as a courtesy for senators who could not be present when a vote was scheduled or who needed time to bone up on a subject before the floor debate began."[18] But in the 1990s the hold was expanded beyond its past purposes and is now often a tactic to kill a bill or nomination.

Senator Trent Lott, Republican majority leader.

The president of the Senate (the vice-president of the United States) has little influence over Senate proceedings. A vice-president can vote only in case of a tie. The Senate elects from among the majority party a **president pro tempore**, usually the most senior member, who acts as chair in the absence of the vice-president. Presiding over the Senate on most occasions is a thankless chore, so the president pro tempore regularly delegates this responsibility to junior members of the chamber's majority party.

The *Senate majority leader*—the elected leader of the majority party in the Senate—is an influential person within the Senate and sometimes nationally. The current majority leader, Senator Trent Lott (R.-Miss.), for example, has become a spokesperson for the Republican party. As the Senate's power broker, the majority leader has the right to be the first senator heard on the floor. In consultation with the *Senate minority leader*, the majority leader determines the Senate's agenda and has much to say about committee assignments for members of the majority party. The position confers somewhat less authority than the Speakership in the House, and its influence depends on the person's political and parliamentary skills and on the national political situation.[19]

Party machinery in the Senate is somewhat similar to that of the House. There are party caucuses (conferences), majority and minority floor leaders, and party whips. Each party has a *policy committee*, composed of the leaders of the party, which is theoretically responsible for the party's overall legislative program. In the Senate the party policy committees handle only committee assignments. Unlike the House party committees, the Senate's party policy committees are formally provided for by law, and each has a regular staff and a budget. Although the Senate party policy committees have some influence on legislation, they have not asserted strong legislative leadership or managed to coordinate policy.

THE FILIBUSTER A major difference between the Senate and the House is that debate is less limited in the Senate. A senator who gains the floor may go on talking until he or she relinquishes the right to talk voluntarily or through exhaustion. This right to unlimited debate may be used by a small group of senators to **filibuster**—that is, delay Senate proceedings by talking continually in order to delay or prevent a vote.

Tom Daschle, minority leader of the Senate, is the official spokesperson for the Democrats in the Senate.

At one time the filibuster was a favorite weapon of southern senators intent on blocking civil rights legislation. More recently the filibuster has been used for a wider range of issues. The Senate in 1987 had, for instance, a week-long filibuster opposing a congressional campaign finance reform bill. And in 1993, Republicans used a filibuster to kill President Clinton's economic stimulus package. Former Senator Alfonse D'Amato (R.-N.Y.) used the threat of a filibuster to get his policy preferences incorporated into legislation. Thus he once threatened to shut down the Senate unless a breast cancer measure he sponsored was

Representative J.C. Watts of Oklahoma is chairman of the Republican Party Conference in the U.S. House of Representatives.

brought to the floor for a vote. The Finance Committee soon agreed to attach his legislation to a tobacco regulation bill they were processing. On another occasion he vowed a filibuster to block a major transportation bill unless more money was provided for mass transit. Again, D'Amato won a deal from Senate colleagues to increase funds for mass transit.[20]

A filibuster, or the threat of a filibuster, is typically most potent at the end of a congressional session, when there is a fixed date for adjournment, because it could mean that many bills that have made it to the end of the legislation process will die for lack of a floor vote. The knowledge that a bill might be subject to a filibuster is often enough to force a compromise satisfactory to its opponents. Sometimes the leaders, knowing that a filibuster will tie up the Senate and keep it from enacting other needed legislation, do not bring a controversial bill to the floor.

A filibuster can be defeated. Until 1917 the Senate could terminate a filibuster only if every member agreed. That year, however, the Senate adopted its first debate-ending rule or **cloture**. Now, as long as the senators who are doing the talking stay on their feet, debate can be stopped only by a cloture vote. The rule of cloture specifies that two days after 16 members sign a petition, the question of curtailing debate must be put to a vote. If three-fifths of the total number of senators (60 of the 100 members) vote for cloture, no senator may speak for more than one hour. A final vote must be taken after no more than 30 hours of debate, including all delaying tactics, such as quorum calls and roll call votes on procedure. After the 30 hours of debate, the motion before the Senate must be brought to a vote.

There has been a noticeable increase in the use of filibusters in the 1990s, and they have been used for partisan and parochial purposes. Indeed, senators usually anticipate a filibuster on contested controversial measures.[21] The tactic is available to Senate minorities to force the majority to compromise and modify its position, and both parties have learned to use it well when they are in the minority.

THE POWER TO CONFIRM The Senate has the constitutional power to confirm presidential appointments to the cabinet, the U.S. Supreme Court and other federal courts, all ambassadorial positions, and many executive branch positions. As with other legislative business, the confirmation process starts in committees, with the relevant standing committee having jurisdiction. For example, the Judiciary Committee considers judges and Supreme Court nominees; the Foreign Relations Committee considers ambassadorial appointments. Nominees appear before the committee to answer questions, and they typically meet individually with key senators before the hearing.

The framers of the Constitution regarded the confirmation process and its advice and consent by the Senate as an important check on executive power. Alexander Hamilton viewed it as a way for Congress to prevent the appointment of "unfit characters." The Constitution leaves the precise practices of the confirmation process somewhat ambiguous: "The President . . . shall nominate, and by and with the Advice and Consent of the Senate, shall appoint Ambassadors, other public Ministers and Consuls, Judges of the Supreme Court, all other officers of the United States."

Presidents, however, have never enjoyed exclusive control over hiring and firing in the executive branch. The Senate jealously guards its right to confirm or reject or even delay major appointments; during the period of strong Congresses after the Civil War, presidents had to struggle to keep their power to appoint and dismiss. But for most of the twentieth century, presidents gained a reasonable amount of control over top appointments, in part because a growing number of people in and out of Congress believe that chief executives without compatible cabinet-level appointees of their choice cannot be held accountable. The Senate's advise and consent powers sometimes force presidents to make compromises,

cloture
Procedure for terminating debate, especially filibusters, in the Senate.

plainly constraining their ability to use the presidential appointment power to direct the federal bureaucracy to embrace the administration's goals.

The Senate's role in the confirmation process was never intended to eliminate politics but rather to use politics as a safeguard against weak or ill-advised nominees. When the Senate was Democratic and the White House Republican, conservatives complained that the Senate was interfering with the executive power of the president by rejecting nominees because of their political beliefs. Yet when the Republicans controlled the Senate and the Democrats the White House, it was the liberals who made the same complaint. Political conflict induced by **divided government** (one branch controlled by one party, the other by another) and increased partisanship have led to a more drawn out confirmation process than in the past. "The ease in which these dilatory tactics can be employed is likely to give partisan and ideological minorities much more leverage over the process than they would have in a more majoritarian body."[22]

In recent years the Senate has taken a tough stand on some presidential appointments and spent more time evaluating and screening presidential nominations. The Senate rejected several nominees of Presidents Ronald Reagan and George Bush, and President Clinton had to withdraw nominees for attorney general and several other posts because of Senate opposition. In 1997, for example, Anthony Lake, Clinton's nominee for director of the Central Intelligence Agency, withdrew his name after a particularly grueling week of confirmation hearings indicated he might not win confirmation in a Senate vote. Governor William Weld (R.-Mass.), a Clinton nominee for ambassador to Mexico, also withdrew his name for consideration after his confirmation was effectively blocked by Senator Jesse Helms (R.-N.C.), who refused to hold hearings on his nomination.[23]

By a tradition called **senatorial courtesy**, a president confers with the senator or senators from the state where an appointee is to work. A nomination is less likely to secure Senate approval against the objection of these senators, especially if these senators are members of the president's party. Thus, for nearly all district court judgeships and a variety of other positions, senators can exercise what is, in fact, a veto that can be overridden only with difficulty. Further, it is usually exercised in secret and subject to little accountability. But this form of patronage or influence is sufficiently important to senators that senatorial courtesy is likely to continue.

As noted earlier, a controversial practice has emerged in recent years that allows an individual senator to request of the Senate leadership that a hold be placed on a nomination. The hold is requested to permit that senator to meet with the nominee, to gain more information about the nominee, or similar purposes. Such holds have become more frequent and are used to delay an appointment, to extract concessions from the president or other senators, or sometimes even to kill a nomination. Presidents have protested this recent practice.[24]

It is useful to note a distinction between *judicial* appointments, especially those to the Supreme Court, and *administration* appointments. The Senate plays a greater role in judicial appointments because judges serve for life and constitute an independent and vital branch of the government.[25] When it comes to cabinet-level positions in the executive branch, it is assumed that a president ought to be able to choose those who will carry out the general views of the White House; in contrast, a president is not expected to enjoy partisan loyalty from those nominated to the bench.

The confirmation provisions in the Constitution have fulfilled most of the intentions of the framers. The Senate has been able to use its power to reject unqualified nominees, and it has also been able to prevent those with serious conflicts of interest from taking office. In addition, senators have been able to use the confirmation process to make their views known to prospective executive officials. Indeed, the very existence of the confirmation process generally deters presidents from appointing weak, questionable, or "unfit characters."

divided government
Governance divided between the parties, as when one holds the presidency and the other controls Congress.

senatorial courtesy
Presidential custom of submitting the names of prospective appointees for approval to senators from the states in which the appointees are to work.

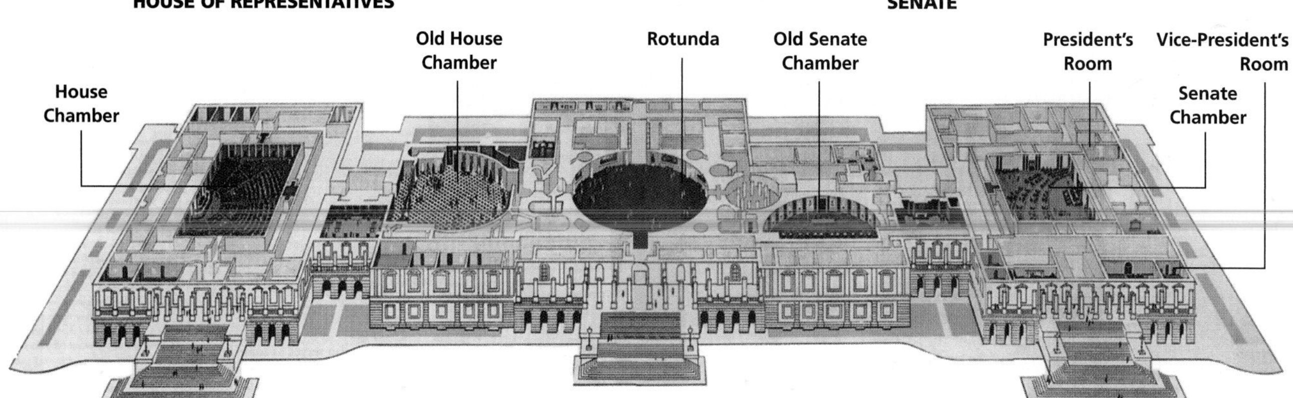

FIGURE 14-1 The Capitol Building

The Job of the Legislator

The elegant U.S. Capitol building is the working center of our nation's legislative process. It is flanked by half a dozen House and Senate office buildings, the sprawling Library of Congress, and a number of other office buildings that help Congress do its work (Figure 14-1). Although staff size has been cut in recent years, members of Congress still employ about 16,000 staff aides who work in Washington, D.C., or in local district offices. Another 5,000 work for the General Accounting Office, the Congressional Research Office, the Congressional Budget Office, the Architect of the Capitol, and other agencies under the direct control of Congress. (We exclude for this count the Library of Congress and the U.S. Government Printing Office, which technically report to Congress, yet in fact serve the entire government as well as the general public.)

Congressional staffs grew enormously in the 1960s and 1970s. But in more recent years, critics as well as elected officials have called for major reductions in the number of both staffs and committees.[26] These staffs are now nearly 10 percent smaller than they were a decade ago.

Legislators as Representatives

Congress has a split personality. On the one hand, it is a *law-making institution* that writes laws and makes policy for the entire nation. In this capacity, all the members are expected to set aside their personal ambitions and perhaps even the concerns of their own constituencies. Yet Congress is also a *representative assembly*, made up of 535 elected officials who serve as links between their constituents and the national government. The dual roles of making laws and responding to constituents' demands force members to balance national concerns against the specific interests of their states or districts.

Members of Congress perceive their roles differently. Some believe they should serve as **delegates** from their districts. These legislators believe it is their duty to find out what "the folks back home" want and act accordingly.

Other members see their role as that of **trustee**. Their constituents, they contend, did not send them to Congress to serve as mere robots or "errand-runners." They act and vote according to their own view of what is best for their district or state as well as the nation. As one member explained, "I have a responsibility not only to follow [my constituents], but to inform them and lead them. I'm not going to betray my responsibility to my constituents. I owe them not only my industry but my judgment. That's why they sent me here."[27] In this view a legislature is a place for deliberation and learning, not a mere gathering of ambassadors from localities.

delegate
A view of the role of legislators that holds that they should represent the views of their constituents even when personally holding different views.

trustee
A view of the role of legislators that holds that they should vote independently based on their judgment of the facts.

Representation is one of the most challenging concepts in political science, yet one of the most important. These definitions may be helpful.

- *Formal representation* is the authority to act in another's behalf, gained through an institutional process or arrangement such as free and open elections.

- *Descriptive or demographic representation* is the extent to which a representative mirrors the characteristics of the people he or she formally represents. According to this usage of the term, a representative legislature should be an exact portrait, in miniature, of the people.

- *Symbolic representation* is the extent to which a legislator is accepted as believable and as "one of their own" by the folks back home. This usage has a lot to do with a legislator's style and nonverbal signals.

- *Substantive representation* is a legislator's responsiveness to constituents. Do the policy and voting views of a legislator match those of constituents, or does the legislator rely primarily on his or her own judgment?

Most legislators shift back and forth between the delegate and trustee role, depending on their perception of the public interest, their standing in the last and next elections, and the pressures of the moment. Most also view themselves more as free agents than as instructed delegates for their districts. Still, nearly everyone in Congress spends a lot of time building constituency connections, mending political fences, and worrying about how a vote on a controversial issue will "play" back home.[28]

Legislators as Lawmakers

Members of Congress cast more than a thousand votes each year.[29] When they vote, members of Congress are influenced by their own philosophy and values, their perceptions of their constituents' interests, and the views of their trusted colleagues, staff, party leaders, lobbyists, and the president.

POLICY AND PHILOSOPHICAL CONVICTIONS Members vote their ideological beliefs most of the time because, especially in the case of the House, people who got elected share the beliefs of most of the voters back home. But constituents also grant most members of Congress considerable leeway. A liberal on social issues is also likely to be a liberal on tax and national security issues. Thus, on controversial issues such as social security reform, tax cuts, or defense spending, knowing the general philosophical leanings of individual members provides a helpful guide both to how they make up their minds and how they will vote.

VOTERS Rarely does a legislator consistently and deliberately vote against the wishes of the people back home, but a paradox is evident here. Members of Congress sometimes think what they do and how they vote makes a lot of difference to voters back home. Yet the fact is most voters don't have the slightest idea of how their members of Congress vote. In practice, most voters don't care about most issues that come before Congress. Most citizens don't even know the names of their senators and representatives.[30] Aside from periodic polls, members hear most often from the **attentive public**—those who follow public affairs carefully—rather than the general public. Still, members of Congress are generally concerned about how they will explain their votes, especially around election day. Even if only a few voters are aware of their stand on a given issue, this group might make the difference between victory and defeat.

COLLEAGUES Legislators are often influenced by the advice of their close friends in Congress. Their busy schedules and the great number of votes force them to depend on the advice of like-minded colleagues. In particular, they look to respected members of the committee who worked on a bill.[31] Legislators find out how their friends stand

attentive public
Those who follow public affairs carefully.

Bill Bradley on What Influences a Senator's Decisions and Votes

"Every day, an effective Senator calculates the interaction of substance, procedure, and personality in his dealings with his fellow Senators. To have command of only one of these and not the other two dooms one to failure. The skillful Senators know what they're talking about and have mastered the substance of at least two or three subject areas. . . . The skillful Senators use procedures to further their goals. They don't let Senate leadership arrange their procedural lives. The skillful Senators are at home with their colleagues. . . .

Finally, the behavior of every Senator, be that Senator collegial or not, is affected by the quest for reelection. Senators running for reelection do not act normally. They justify an egregious legislative position or their sudden support of the other party's amendment or their participation in outrageous pandering to special interests as being absolutely necessary for reelection."

SOURCE: Bill Bradley, *Time Past, Time Present: A Memoir* (Knopf, 1996), pp. 88–89.

on an issue, listen to the party leadership's advice, and take into account the various committee reports. Sometimes, members are influenced to vote one way merely because they know a colleague is on the other side of the issue. For some legislators, the **state delegation** (senators and representatives from their home state) reinforces a common identity. Texas Democrats have long been a strong and cohesive delegation; other states, like California, have less cohesive state delegations.

A member may also vote with a colleague in the expectation that the colleague will later vote for a measure about which the member is concerned—called **log rolling**. Some vote trading takes place to build coalitions so that members can "bring home the bacon" to their constituents. Other vote trading reflects reciprocity in congressional relations or deference to colleagues' superior information or expertise.

CONGRESSIONAL STAFF Representatives and senators used to be at a distinct disadvantage in dealing with the executive branch because they were overly dependent on information supplied by the White House or lobbyists. Complexity of the issues and increasingly demanding schedules created pressures for additional staff. Congress responded and gradually expanded their staffs, and this expansion has strengthened the role of Congress in the public policy process.

All members of Congress have personal staff members working for them both in their Washington and home-district offices. About one-third of the House of Representatives staff and one-fourth of the Senate staff are based back home. Local staff members help members of Congress communicate with the voters and provide constituency services and casework. Much of the work done in district offices is akin to a continuous campaign effort: generating favorable publicity, arranging for local appearances and newspaper interviews, scheduling, and contacting important civic and business leaders in the region.

Congressional staffers become knowledgeable about special policy areas and deal on a day-to-day basis with their counterparts in the executive departments and interest groups. Indeed, some observers say that congressional staffers are some of the most powerful people in Washington. Staffers draft bills, conduct research, and often do much of the legislative negotiating and coalition building. Professional staffers have the opportunity to influence legislative decisions. And certainly there is some truth to the notion that the more staffers there are, the more they look for things to do, such as preparing more legislation, suggesting more investigations, and in general making more work for themselves.

But we should not exaggerate the independent power base of staffers. They can be summarily fired at the whim of those they serve. Although they cannot be dismissed because of their race, sex, or national origin, they know that if they wander too far from the views of the one person who can fire them, they will quickly be called back into line.

PARTY Members generally vote with their party. Whether as a result of party pressure or natural affinity, on major bills there is a tendency for most Democrats to be arrayed against most Republicans.

Partisan voting has been increasing in the House since the early 1970s and has intensified since the 1994 elections. Indeed, party-line voting has been greater in recent years than at any time in recent decades. Party differences are stronger over domestic, regulatory, and welfare reform measures than over foreign policy or civil liberty issues. Ninety-eight percent of House Republicans, for example, voted to impeach Bill Clinton in a historic vote in late 1998; 98 percent of House Democrats voted against impeachment.

Party leaders in both chambers do their best to get their members to vote together. Republican leaders claim cohesive voting is the only way Republicans can

state delegation
The senators and representatives from the same state.

log rolling
Mutual aid and vote trading among legislators.

implement their party platform and satisfy the majorities who elected them in recent years. Senators are usually more independent, so party leaders in the Senate have a harder time encouraging party discipline than do leaders in the House.

The regional realignment in the American South has had the effect of diminishing the number of Democratic conservatives and strengthening Republican conservatives. There has been a similar decline of Republican moderates and a rise in more uniformly liberal Democratic districts.

A key factor in increasing partisanship in congressional voting has been the science of congressional redistricting. "Advances in computer-driven mapping capabilities have made an art form of the old-fashioned gerrymandering that occurs where congressional districts are redrawn after each decennial census."[32] Party operatives in the states can with great precision draw district lines to create relatively safe Democratic or Republican districts, "increasing the number of secure members answerable to only their own party's primary votes."[33]

In 1998, for example, on important party-unity legislation, that is, where the party leadership tried to rally its forces to vote with it, Republicans succeeded in holding an average of 86 percent of their conference in line in the House and 86 percent in the Senate. "Democrats kept an average of 87 percent of caucus members unified on these votes in the Senate, and 82 percent in the House."[34] Republican moderates from the Northwest were most likely to split from their party ranks, while the few remaining conservative Democrats from the South "were generally the most willing to cross over to the GOP side when the parties locked horns."[35]

Many forces—regional, local, ties of friendship—can override party influence. Members are sometimes influenced by informal groups (ideological groups, ethnic caucuses, regional groupings, and even the class of colleagues with whom they were elected—for example, "the class of 1994"). Ideological groups in Congress ranging from the Congressional Progressive Caucus to the more conservative Family Concerns or New Federalists groups can also provide voting cues.

INTEREST GROUPS Interest groups, acting through their lobbyists and political action committees (PACs), make substantial contributions to congressional elections, giving largely to incumbents. In addition to their role as financiers of elections, interest groups are important participants in the legislative process because they provide information.

Interest groups can also be effective when they mobilize grass-roots activists and rally various constituencies to lobby their home state members of Congress. For example, higher education lobbying groups have effectively mobilized students and educators to write and call members of Congress on behalf of student aid and related provisions in various measures before the Congress.[36] And tobacco companies spent huge sums to fight taxes on cigarettes.

THE PRESIDENT Through effective use of their constitutional and political powers, presidents are usually partners with Congress in the legislative process. Members of Congress are invariably reluctant to admit that they are influenced by pressure from the White House. On key domestic issues, legislators generally say they are more likely to be influenced by their own convictions or by their constituents than by what the White House wants. But presidents and their aides work hard to influence public opinion and to win members over to the president's point of view.

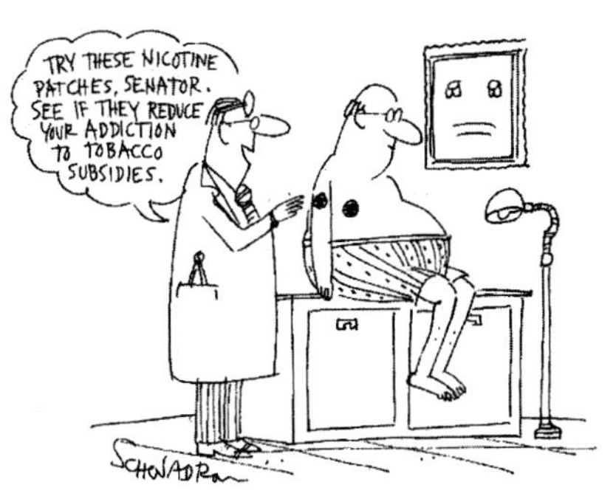

The Wall Street Journal

On key votes, presidents usually win needed majority support more than half the time. In his first term, Bill Clinton won an impressive 64 percent support from Congress on roll call votes on which he had taken a clear position.[37] He fared less well in his controversy-packed second term yet still better than what most people would expect.[38]

Presidents exert greater influence on how members of Congress vote on foreign policy or national security issues than on domestic policy.[39] President Bush benefited from a bipartisan coalition that passed the resolution authorizing the use of military force in the Persian Gulf. President Clinton benefited from strong Republican support in Congress to help win approval for the North American Free Trade Agreement, even when large numbers in his own party opposed this measure.

During the last two decades Congress has become better staffed and more capable of vying with the president for policy leadership, but mainly as a check on presidents.[40] President Clinton was, however, able to co-opt several Republican issues and thereby claim credit for legislative successes as much as, and sometimes more than, the Republicans who controlled the Congress in the late 1990s.[41]

THE LEGISLATIVE OBSTACLE COURSE

Congress operates under a system of multiple vetoes. The framers intentionally dispersed powers so they could not be accumulated by any would-be tyrant. Follow a bill through the legislative process, and you clearly see this dispersion of power (see Figure 14-2). The procedures and rules of the Senate differ somewhat from those of the House, but in each chamber power is fragmented and influence is decentralized.

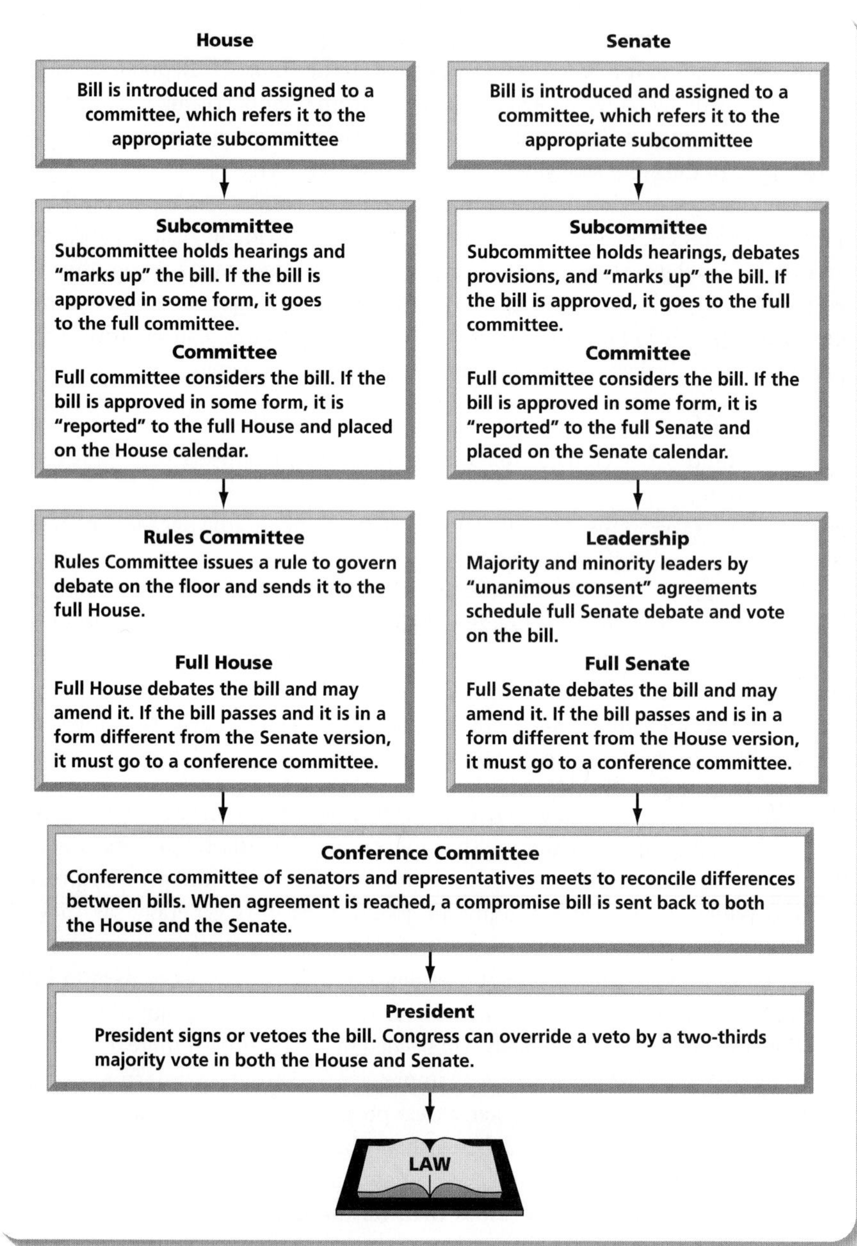

FIGURE 14-2 **How a Bill Becomes a Law**

Every bill, including those drawn up in the executive branch, must be *introduced* in the House and the Senate by a member of that body. Bills are then *referred* by the leadership to the appropriate **standing committee.** A standing committee is one of the permanent working units established in the rules of the House and the Senate. Standing committees continue from one session to the next and are generally organized along policy lines (foreign policy, agriculture, and so forth). Their importance arises from the fact that most legislative measures are first considered in the appropriate standing committee or one of its relevant subcommittees (see Table 14-2).

Roughly 90 percent of the bills introduced in every two-year session of Congress die in a subcommittee for lack of support. When bills have significant backing, a committee or subcommittee holds *hearings* to receive opinions. It then meets to *mark up* (discuss and amend) and vote on the bill. If the subcommittee and then the parent committee vote in favor of the bill, it is *reported*—that is, sent to the full chamber—where it is *debated* and *voted* on. In the House the bill must go first to the Rules Committee for a *rule.*

In the Senate, it is not uncommon for legislators to attach **riders**—provisions that may have little relationship to the bill they are riding on. For example, riders that have little to do with spending money can be attached to appropriations bills. The House of Representatives has stricter rules that require amendments to be relevant to the bill, but no such rule is enforced in the Senate. Senators use riders to force the president to accept legislation attached to a bill that was otherwise popular, because the president has either to accept the entire bill or to veto it.

There has been an increase in the number of riders to appropriation bills in recent years. Republicans in both the House and Senate skirmished with President Clinton by adding riders concerning restrictions on abortion, on enforcement of environmental laws, and the right of nonprofit groups that receive federal grants to lobby.[42]

standing committee
A permanent committee established in a legislature, usually focusing on a policy area.

rider
A provision that may have little relationship to the bill it is attached to in order to secure its passage.

TABLE 14-2 Congressional Standing Committees

House	Senate
Agriculture	Agriculture, Nutrition, and Forestry
Appropriations	Appropriations
Banking and Financial Services	Armed Services
Budget	Banking, Housing, and Urban Affairs
Commerce	Budget
Education and the Workforce	Commerce, Science, and Transportation
Government Reform and Oversight	Energy and Natural Resources
House Oversight	Environment and Public Works
International Relations	Finance
Judiciary	Foreign Relations
National Security	Governmental Affairs
Resources	Indian Affairs
Rules	Judiciary
Science	Labor and Human Resources
Select Intelligence	Rules
Small Business	Select Ethics
Standards of Official Conduct (Ethics)	Select Intelligence
Transportation and Infrastructure	Small Business
Veterans' Affairs	Special Aging
Ways and Means	Veterans' Affairs

How to Kill a Bill

The complexity of the congressional system provides a tremendous built-in advantage for opponents of any measure. Multiple opportunities to kill a bill exist because of the dispersion of influence. At a dozen or more points a bill may be stopped or allowed to die (inaction is the same as killing a bill). Those who sponsor a bill must win at every step; opponents need to win only once. Whether good or bad, a proposal can be delayed or rejected by any one of the following:

1. The House subcommittee and its chair
2. The chair of the House standing committee
3. The House standing committee and its leaders
4. The House Rules Committee
5. The majority of the House
6. The Senate subcommittee and its chair
7. The Senate standing committee
8. The majority of the Senate
9. The floor leaders in both chambers
10. A few senators, in the case of a filibuster
11. The House-Senate conference committee, if the chambers disagree
12. The president (by veto)

Except for tax bills, the House and Senate discuss bills simultaneously rather than waiting for one to act first. If only one chamber passes a bill, it dies. If both houses pass bills on the same subject but there are differences between the bills—and there often are—the two versions must go to a *conference committee* for reconciliation. If a bill does not make it through both chambers in identical form in the same Congress (two-year term), it must begin the entire process again in the next Congress.

When a bill has passed both houses in identical form, it then goes to the president, who may *sign* it into law or *veto* it. If Congress is in session and the president waits ten days (excluding Sundays), then the bill becomes law *without* his signature. If Congress has adjourned and the president waits ten days without signing the bill, it is then defeated by a **pocket veto**. Except for the pocket veto, when a bill is vetoed it is returned to the chamber of its origin by the president with a message explaining the reasons for the veto. Congress can vote to **override** the veto with a two-thirds vote in each chamber, but assembling such an extraordinary majority is often difficult.

Authorization and Appropriation

Congress legislates by a two-step process; it *authorizes* and it *appropriates.* After Congress and the president authorize a program by passing a law, Congress, with the president's concurrence, has to appropriate the funds to implement it. Appropriations are processed by the House and Senate Appropriations Committees and their subcommittees. For example, the 1997 Education Act and its several titles reauthorized a variety of programs for a five-year period, including those for federal loans and grants for college students. The authorization act set the limits on the amount that students may borrow and the conditions under which they must pay back the loan. But the authorization is useless until Congress appropriates funds and the president signs the appropriations bill into law each year. Congress is often likely to appropriate less money for student loans and grants than it has authorized.

The Importance of Compromise

Clearly, a bill does not become law unless its sponsors are willing to compromise to get the votes necessary for its passage. One tactical decision at the start is whether to push for action in the Senate first, in the House first, or in both simultaneously. For example, if it appears that a bill could not be passed in the Senate, its sponsors may seek passage in the House and hope that a sizable victory there will spur the Senate into action. Another decision concerns the committee to which the bill is assigned. Normally, referral to a committee is automatic. Sometimes, however, a bill involves more than one jurisdiction and can be written in such a way that it may go to a committee that will look more kindly on it.

Getting a bill through Congress requires that majorities and sometimes supermajorities be mobilized over and over again—in subcommittee, in committee, in chamber, and possibly again in chamber to override a presidential veto. These majorities shift and change, and they involve different legislators in different situations at different points in time. Thus coalitions must be built again and again.[43]

pocket veto
A veto exercised by the president after Congress has adjourned; if the president takes no action for ten days, the bill does not become law and is not returned to Congress for a possible override.

override
An action taken by Congress to reverse a presidential veto that requires a two-thirds majority in each chamber.

Committees: The Little Legislatures

It is sometimes said that Congress is a collection of committees that come together in a chamber every once in a while to approve one another's actions. There is much truth in this. Congress has long relied on committees to get its work done. Woodrow Wilson, a teacher of political science before he became president, expressed a similar thought: "Congress in session is Congress on display. Congress in committee is Congress at work."[44] More precisely, Congress in subcommittee is Congress at work, because the initial struggle over legislation takes place in subcommittees.[45]

Congress utilizes **joint committees** whose members are selected from both houses to oversee such institutions as the Library of Congress or to investigate issues like campaign finance reform. Committees organized to conduct investigations are called **select or special committees.**

The House of Representatives divides standing committees into three categories:

1. *Exclusive committees* include Appropriations, Ways and Means, and Rules; members who serve on one of these committees may not serve on any other standing committee.
2. *Major committees* include committees like National Security; members can serve on only one of these committees, but can add assignments to two nonmajor committees.
3. *Nonmajor committees*, such as Small Business, permit membership in two or three of these. House members rarely serve on more than three standing committees.

Bills can be pigeonholed for weeks, amended beyond recognition, or kept in committee forever. Or a bill can fly through a committee in a hurry. A committee reports out favorably only a small fraction of all the bills that come to it. Although a bill can be forced to the floor of the House through a **discharge petition** signed by a majority of the membership, legislators are reluctant to bypass committees. They regard committee members as experts in their fields. Sometimes, too, they are reluctant to risk the anger of committee leaders. And there is a strong sense of *reciprocity*: "You respect my committee's jurisdiction, and I will respect yours." Not surprisingly, few discharge petitions gain the necessary number of signatures.

While members of the House hold relatively few committee assignments, each senator normally serves on three standing committees and at least seven subcommittees. Among the most important Senate committees are Appropriations, Budget, Finance, and Foreign Relations.

Committees are not all alike. Some are powerful; others are less important. Because of the Senate's special role in foreign policy, for example, the Senate Foreign Relations Committee is usually more influential than the House Committee on National Security. For the two Appropriations Committees, however, the reverse is true; the House Appropriations Committee plays a more significant role than the Senate Appropriations Committee, although these differences are less than they used to be.

Choosing Committee Members

Control and staffing of standing committees are partisan matters. The chair and a majority of each standing committee come from the majority party. The minority party is represented on each committee roughly in proportion to its membership in the entire chamber, except on some powerful committees on which the majority may want to enhance its position. Getting on a politically advantageous committee is important to members of Congress. A representative from Kansas, for example, would much rather serve on the Agriculture Committee than on the Banking and Financial Services Committee. Members usually stay on the same committees from one Congress to the next, although less senior members who have had less desirable assignments often seek better committees when places become available.

How are committee members chosen? In the House of Representatives, a Committee on Committees of the Republican membership allots places to Republican members. This committee is composed of one member from each state

joint committee
Committee composed of members of both the House of Representatives and the Senate; such committees oversee the Library of Congress and conduct investigations.

select or special committee
A congressional committee created for a specific purpose, sometimes to conduct an investigation.

discharge petition
Petition that, if signed by a majority of the members of the House of Representatives, will pry a bill from committee and bring it to the floor for consideration.

The House Judiciary Committee investigated the charges against President Clinton to determine if they warranted impeachment. Although Chairman Henry Hyde (center) announced his intention to make the proceedings bipartisan, they became highly partisan.

having Republican representation in the House; the member is generally the senior member of the state's delegation. Because each member has as many votes in the committee as there are Republicans in the delegation, the group is dominated by senior members from the large state delegations. On the Democratic side, assignment to committees is handled by the Steering and Policy Committee of the Democratic caucus in negotiation with senior Democrats from the state delegations.

In the Senate, veteran members also dominate the assignment process. Each party has a small Steering Committee that makes committee assignments. In making assignments, leaders are guided by various considerations: how talented and cooperative a member is, whether his or her region is already well represented on a committee, and whether the assignment will aid in reelecting the member. There sometimes are fierce battles within these committees, battles about liberal/conservative, rural/urban, environment/industry, and other differences.

One reason Congress copes with its huge workload is that its committees and subcommittees are organized around subject matter specialties. This specialization allows members to develop technical expertise in specific areas and to recruit skilled staffs. Thus Congress is often able to challenge experts from the bureaucracy. Interest groups and lobbyists realize the great power a specific committee has in certain areas and focus their attention on its members. Similarly, members of executive departments are careful to cultivate the committee and subcommittee chairs and members of "their" committees.

How Congress uses committees is critical in its role as a partner in policy making. In recent years progress has been made in opening hearings to the public and improving the quality of committee staffs, but it is difficult to restructure committee jurisdictions so they do not overlap. Thus, a dozen different committees deal with energy, education, and the war on drugs. Efforts to make the committee system more efficient are often considered threats to the delicate balance of power within the chamber.

THE IMPEACHMENT OF BILL CLINTON

A Closer Look

In all of our history only two presidents have been impeached—Andrew Johnson in 1868 and Bill Clinton in 1998. Richard Nixon was about to be impeached in 1974 when he abruptly resigned from office.

The Clinton impeachment hearings dramatized the House Judiciary Committee and its role in establishing whether an impeachment is called for. Nationally televised debates by the full House of Representatives were heated and highly partisan. Opinion polls showed the public solidly opposed to impeachment and conviction, yet House Republicans remained unified in the effort to impeach. Two articles of impeachment were passed by the House: for perjury before a federal grand jury (228 to 206) and for obstruction of justice (221 to 212). Most Republicans voted for impeachment, and most Democrats voted against impeachment.

The proceedings in the Senate were in marked contrast to the House deliberations. They were more formal, less heated, and in the end less partisan. Representatives from the House Judiciary Committee acted as the prosecutors, while lawyers for the president defended Bill Clinton. It would have taken a two-thirds majority, or 67 votes in the Senate, to convict Clinton, but only 45 senators voted to convict him on perjury charges; ten Republicans defected to join 45 Democrats in voting "not guilty." Fifty senators (all Republicans) voted to convict Clinton on the obstruction of justice charges, while 5 Republicans joined all 45 Democrats in voting "not guilty."

In the end it was the office of the presidency that saved the president. Republicans argued that when Clinton chose not to tell the truth, he put himself above the law and his oath of office. Democrats agreed that the president's conduct was wrong, boorish, indefensible, and even reprehensible, but they did not believe what Clinton did threatened the Republic. The president's legal team argued convincingly that Clinton's wrongdoings in the Monica Lewinsky affair were simply not fit subjects for impeachment. To remove a president on this basis, they contended, would lower the impeachment bar too far and create an unhealthy precedent.

Some scholars believe this whole process was very damaging for the presidency and perhaps, too, for Congress. But most observers think our national institutions will bounce back and carry on with their assigned responsibilities. Most people also believe that the Constitution prevailed.

One lesson of the Clinton impeachment process is that an impeachment conducted primarily along partisan lines is unlikely to succeed under our constitutional system of checks and balances. A second lesson is that impeachment was designed primarily for crimes against the state, against the system of government itself.

The first article of impeachment against Bill Clinton, which concerned his testimony in the Paula Jones case, was defeated in the House of Representatives.

Members of the House Judiciary Committee present the two articles of impeachment to the clerk of the Senate.

Congressional committee hearings perform the investigative and oversight functions of Congress.

Seniority Rule

Forty years ago committee chairs determined the workload of committees, hired and fired staff, formed subcommittees, and assigned them jurisdictions, members, and aides. Chairs also managed the most important bills assigned to their committees. Since the mid-1970s, however, junior members have insisted they be given more authority. Subcommittee chairs have also become more independent. In recent years there have also been moves to strengthen the powers of the party leaders and caucuses at the expense of the committee chairs.

Until recently, most chairs were selected on the basis of the **seniority rule**; the member of the majority party with the longest continuous service on the committee became chair upon the retirement of the current chair or a change in the party in control of Congress. The seniority rule gives power to representatives who come from safe districts where one party is dominant and a member can build up years of continuous service. Conversely, the seniority rule lessens the influence of states or districts where the two parties are more evenly matched and where there is more turnover.

Both Democrats and Republicans have occasionally passed over the most senior committee member in order to place someone with more energy or with a more compatible policy perspective in a committee chair position. In 1975 Democrats removed a few aging committee chairs and generally appointed the next ranking members to chair several committees. It is not uncommon these days for a member of Congress to become chair of an important subcommittee after only one or two terms, and indeed such placement is the tradition in the Senate.

Still, the practice of elevating the senior member of a committee to serve as committee chair remains a general rule. It has long been respected in Congress for several reasons: It encourages members to stay on a committee; it encourages specialization and expertise; it also reduces the interpersonal politics that would arise if several members of a committee "ran" for election to become chair. However, one legacy from the Gingrich era that remains, although it may be changed later, is a Republican House rule that limits committee chairs to just three terms.

Investigations and Oversight

The power to *investigate* is one of Congress's most important functions. Congress conducts investigations to determine if legislation is needed, to gather facts relevant to legislation, to assess the efficiency of executive agencies, to build public support, to expose corruption, and to enhance the image or reputation of its members.[46] Hearings by standing committees, their subcommittees, or special select committees are an important source of information and opinion. They provide an arena in which experts can submit their views.

Another important function of congressional hearings is the *oversight* function—the responsibility to question executive branch officials to see whether their agencies are complying with the wishes of the Congress and conducting their programs efficiently. Authorization committees regularly hold oversight hearings, and appropriations committees, exercising "the congressional power of the purse," often use appropriations hearings to communicate committee members' views about how agency officials should carry out their business. Cabinet members and agency heads have been known to dread the loaded questions of hostile members of Congress and to hate having to watch themselves on the evening news trying to explain why their agency made some mistakes.

seniority rule
A legislative practice that assigns the chair of a committee or subcommittee to the member of the majority party with the longest continuous service on the committee.

Conference Committees

When the framers created a two-house national legislature, they anticipated the two chambers would represent sharply different interests. The Senate was to be a small chamber of persons elected indirectly by the state legislatures to hold long, overlapping terms. It was to be a chamber of scrutiny, a gathering of wise leaders who would counsel and sanction a president. The House of Representatives, elected anew every two years, was to be a more direct reflection of the people.

The Senate did serve as a conservative check on the House, especially in the late nineteenth and early twentieth centuries, when it was extremely conservative and something of a rich man's club. But today the House tends to be more conservative than the Senate. Executive departments and agencies, for instance, occasionally consider the Senate to be a court of appeals for appropriations that have been shot down by the House.

Given the differences between the House and the Senate, it is not surprising that the version of a bill passed by one chamber may differ substantially from the version passed by the other. Only if both houses pass an absolutely identical measure can it become law. Most of the time one house accepts the language of the other, but at least 15 percent of all bills passed (usually major ones) must be referred to a **conference committee**—a special committee of members from each chamber—that settles the differences between versions. Both parties are represented, but the majority party has more members.

The proceedings of a conference committee are usually an elaborate bargaining process. When the proposed bill is brought back to the two chambers, the conference report can be accepted or rejected (often with further negotiations ordered), but it cannot be amended. Conference members of each chamber must convince their colleagues that any concessions made to the other chamber were on unimportant points and that nothing basic to the original version of the bill was surrendered.

How much leeway does a conference committee have? Ordinarily members are expected to stay somewhere between the different versions. On matters for which there is no clear middle ground, members are sometimes accused of exceeding their instructions and producing an entirely new bill. The conference committee has even been called a "third house" of Congress, one that arbitrarily revises policy.

Which chamber, House or Senate, wins more often in conference committees? On the surface it appears that the Senate's version wins more often, but this is partly because the Senate more often than not acts on its legislation after the House. Political scientist David J. Vogler concludes that "by creating the original bill and setting the agenda for debate on the issue, the House is judged to have the more real impact on the final shape of legislation as it passes through conference than does the Senate."[47] In effect, the House plays a dominant law-making role, while the Senate plays a key representational role through amendments.

Congress: An Assessment and a View on Reform

More than two hundred years after its creation, Congress is a larger, more vital, and very different kind of institution from the one envisioned by the framers. Yet most of its major functions remain the same, and their effective exercise is crucial to the health of our constitutional democracy. Even as we enter the twenty-first century, we still look to Congress to make laws, raise revenues, represent citizens, investigate abuses of power, and oversee the executive branch.

Today most members must engage in continual electioneering to stay in office. Members appear driven by their desire to win reelection, so that much of what takes place in Congress seems mainly designed to promote reelection. These efforts usually pay off for members of Congress: most who want to get reelected do. But at the same time, these efforts also pay off for our democracy. The concern of members with reelection fosters *accountability* and the desire to please the voters.

conference committee
Committee appointed by the presiding officers of each chamber to adjust differences on a particular bill passed by each but in different forms.

You Decide . . .

How would you "reform" Congress?

Which of these proposed reforms do you think should be adopted to improve Congress?

- Move to a European-style parliamentary system
- Extend House terms to four years
- Limit House and Senate tenure to 12 years
- Provide for public financing of campaigns and ban campaign contributions
- Permit only people who live in a district or state to contribute to candidates for Congress
- Radically reduce the number of committees and subcommittees
- Strengthen the power and resources of the party leaders
- Reduce the size of congressional staffs
- Abide by an agenda agreed to at the beginning of each session
- Have shorter sessions for Congress so members can spend more time in their districts

William Cohen, a popular Republican senator from Maine (later secretary of defense in the Clinton cabinet), observed as he was retiring from the Senate that he admired Congress's deliberative process, yet he worried that too many checks and too much partisanship made it hard for Congress to get needed results:

> Our republic, we know, was designed to be slow-moving and deliberative. Our founding fathers were convinced that power had to be entrusted to someone, but that no one could be entirely trusted with power. They devised a brilliant system of checks and balances to prevent the tyranny of the many by the few. They constructed a perfect triangle of allocated and checked power. . . . There could be no rash action, no rush to judgment, no legislative mob rule, no unrestrained chief executive.
>
> The difficulty with this diffusion of power in today's cyberspace age is that everyone is in check, but no one is in charge. . . .
>
> But more than the constitutional separation of powers is leading to the unprecedented stalemate that exists today. There has been a breakdown in civil debates and discourse. Enmity at times has become so intense that members of Congress have resorted to shoving matches outside the legislative chambers.[48]

How does such a Congress make any progress? In an institution where most members act as individual entrepreneurs and consider themselves leaders, the task of providing institutional leadership is increasingly difficult. With limited resources, and only sometimes aided by the president, congressional leaders are asked to bring together a diverse, fragmented, and independent institution. The congressional system acts only when majorities can be achieved. That the framers accomplished their original objective—creating a Congress that would not move with imprudent haste—has been generally well realized.

Americans often characterize Congress as a bickering, timid, ignorant, selfish, or narrow-minded body. Yet they also admire the stamina and civic responsibility of their own member of Congress. Individual members of Congress are invariably more popular than the institution, perhaps because people judge individual members primarily on how well they serve the interests of their states and districts and on their personal appeal (see Figure 14-3).

Some of the criticism of Congress is justified. Yet critics usually forget that our national legislature is particularly exposed, and some of our expectations of it are unrealistic. First, Congress does nearly all its work directly in the public eye, even more public now that it is televised live on C-SPAN. Unfortunate incidents—quarrels, name calling, evasive actions, inaccurate statements, and ethical lapses—that might be hushed up in the executive or judicial branches are observed and duly reported by the ever-present media, most especially by CNN, Fox, MSNBC, *Roll Call*, *The Hill*, *National Journal*, *Congressional Quarterly*, or *The Washington Post.*

Second, Congress by its nature is controversial and argumentative. Its 535 members are found on both sides, sometimes on half a dozen sides, of every important question. Moreover, during the 1990s Congress has both raised taxes and cut services, closed military bases, reduced spending for welfare, the arts, and many research programs, shut down the government, and impeached a highly approved president—not a recipe for popularity!

Criticisms of Congress

CONGRESS IS INEFFICIENT House and Senate procedures are, some charge, simply not suited to the needs of a modern information-age nation. Some of this criticism is exaggerated. Evaluating procedure and structure is difficult to separate from evaluating policy, about which everyone has an individual preference. Congress deals with an enormous number of complex measures. Many procedures expedite

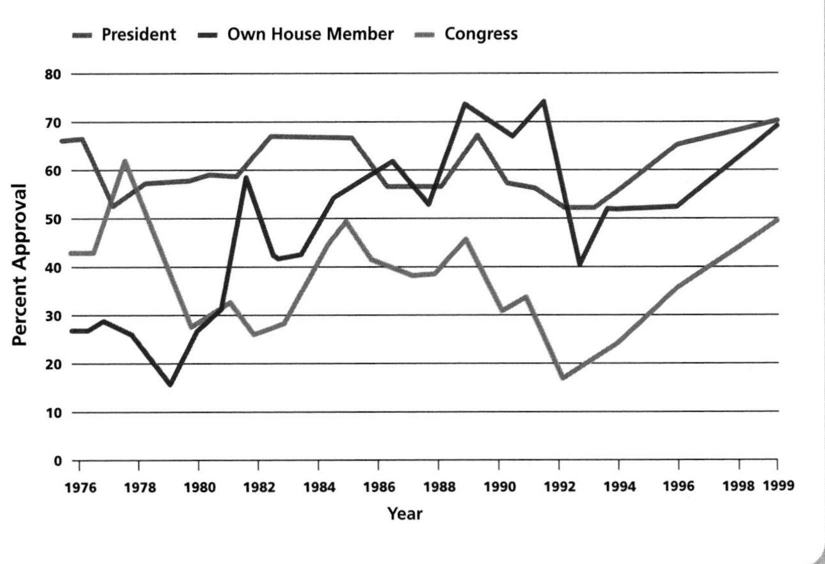

Figure 14-3 Presidential, Congressional, and Own House Member Approval Ratings, 1976–1999

SOURCES: The Gallup Poll, CBS News/New York Times Poll, NBC News/Wall Street Journal Poll.

handling of bills, and the committee and subcommittee system is a reasonable device for hearing arguments and compiling information.

Still, the question of efficiency remains. Study groups inside and outside Congress have urged the chambers to reduce the number of committee assignments, establish better information systems, centralize more power in their leadership positions, and strengthen majority rule. Congress has done many of these things recently, yet the pace of legislation has not improved.

CONGRESS IS UNREPRESENTATIVE The complaint is often made that Congress represents constituents' interests over the national interest. Defenders of Congress respond that representing their districts is precisely what Congress was designed to do. Legislators are described as being obsessed with staying in office—indeed, as concentrating solely on winning reelection—often at the expense of critical national issues such as Social Security, drug abuse, foreign policy, and trade.

Congress is supposed to reflect geographical and narrow interests, to register the diversity of the United States. In *The Federalist*, No. 57, James Madison wrote: "Who are to be the electors of the Federal Representatives? Not the rich more than the poor; not the learned more than the ignorant; not the haughty heirs of distinguished names more than the humble sons of obscure and unpropitious fortune."[49] Yet as the costs of campaigning increase, and as the majority of elected officials continue to come from the upper and upper-middle classes, we do have to ask whether ours is the open, representative, responsive, and responsible legislative system we can point to with pride as a model for those in other parts of the world who yearn for constitutional democracy. Can a Congress that has only 12 percent women and 7 percent African American membership truly represent our 51 percent female and 13 percent black populations?[50] That most members are the products of middle- and upper-middle-class families does not necessarily mean they are interested only in improving the position of that portion of the population. Senators like Edward Kennedy

Thinking it Through . . .

No reform is neutral in terms of effects. Some groups will benefit more than others from the passage of each reform proposal. Most reforms also have unanticipated consequences that may create more problems than they solve. Some would require amendments to our Constitution. Still, the search goes on for practical ways to improve Congress's ability to do the people's work.

Congress spent a lot of time in the 1990s trying to come up with procedural and fund-raising reforms, but despite great public pressure to reform, Congress did little to alter its traditional ways.

(D.-Mass.) and Jay Rockefeller (D.-W.Va.), for instance, are affluent white males, yet they are strong advocates of legislation to protect women, minorities, and poor people.

CONGRESS IS UNETHICAL Some critics claim we have "the best Congress money can buy."[51] Many people allege that special interests and single-issue groups are stronger than ever, and that they are able to delay or block proceedings in Congress. The current system of financing congressional elections has been called a scandal because it forces members of Congress to beg for money from wealthy individuals and political action committees representing interest groups whose primary purpose is to seek support for pet legislation.

In response to occasional scandals, both houses have passed ethics codes and created ethics subcommittees. These codes require public disclosure of income and property holdings by legislators, key aides, and spouses. They also ban most gifts of over $100 to a legislator, a staff member, or a legislator's family from a registered lobbyist, an organization with a political action committee, a foreign government, or a business with an interest in legislation before Congress. But valuable as these changes have been, they have apparently failed to improve the image of Congress.[52]

Defenders of Congress insist these charges are overstated. They say money would hardly influence the three dozen or more millionaires who are members of the Senate and the one hundred or so members of the House who are well-off financially. Defenders of Congress also point out that some members of Congress regularly turn down certain types of campaign contributions.

CONGRESS LACKS COLLECTIVE RESPONSIBILITY Some critics see the main problem in Congress as the dispersion of power among committee and subcommittee leaders, elected party officials, factional leaders, informal caucus leaders, and other legislators. It is a "nobody's-in-charge" system. This dispersion of power means that to get things done, congressional leaders must bargain and negotiate. The result of this "brokering" system is that laws may be watered down, defeated, delayed, or written in vague language. According to some critics, too much leeway is given to unelected bureaucrats to develop the regulations that will enforce the legislation. Accountability is confused, responsibility is eroded, and well-organized special interests that know how to work the system have an unfair advantage.

A Defense of Congress

Attacking or poking fun at Congress has been a national pastime for generations. Will Rogers told some of his best jokes at the expense of Congress, as Jay Leno and David Letterman do today. Cartoonists love Congress for its unfailing ability to put its worst foot forward. Even members of Congress, as noted earlier, often run against Congress when they are at home in their districts.

The challenge that confronted the framers—how to reconcile the need for executive energy with republican liberty—is still with us. The history of constitutional democracy has always been the search for limitations on absolute power and for techniques of sharing power. Our American style of constitutionalism and separation of powers, especially in the absence of a major crisis, often means a slow-moving and sometimes inefficient decision-making system. It means a system that often hinders rather than facilitates leadership. It is a system that invites contention, division, debate, delay, and political conflict. Critics often call this gridlock or deadlock or even paralysis. Defenders of the Congress prefer to call it the world's greatest deliberative body. They point out, too, that the framers of the U.S. Constitution took great efforts to insulate policymaking processes from the momentary fancies of the people.

Newly elected presidents and members of Congress always arrive enthusiastically ready to enact the people's wishes. But governing is invariably tougher and slower than they or most voters appreciate. This is so because governments deal with complex issues about which there often is little consensus. Building policy majorities will always be hard because complex problems generate complex solutions, and the structure of Congress requires supermajorities to agree to serious changes. Thus the president's veto, the filibuster practice, the use of holds and legislative riders all make it harder to build a consensus for change.

Finally, not only is there often a lack of consensus in Congress, "there is a lack of consensus [on most major issues] among the public about what should be done."[53] And this makes it hard for legislators who are, after all, eager to please voters and remain in office.

Criticism of Congress—its alleged incompetence, its overresponsiveness to organized interests, its inefficiencies—are difficult to separate from the context of policy preferences and democratic procedures. Sometimes criticism tells us more about the critic than it does about the effectiveness of Congress. Constitutional democracy is not the most efficient form of government. Congress was never intended to act swiftly; it was not created to be a rubber stamp or even a cooperative partner for presidents. Its greatest strengths—its diversity and deliberative character—also weaken its position in dealing with the more centralized executive branch. Its members will rarely be fast on their feet. The 535 members, divided into two houses, two parties, dozens of committees, and nearly two hundred subcommittees, will often have a difficult time arriving at a common strategy to collaborate with or to resist whoever is president.

online POLITICS

Thomas

For political science students, the legislative process and consideration of actual bills hold great interest. What hot bills are coming up this week? Is the House about to vote on a matter of concern to you? How many times has the Senate voted to save the Social Security system?

The Legislative Reference Service of the Library of Congress provides just this kind of information on its website named Thomas, after Thomas Jefferson. Some of the options it offers are bill tracking, congressional records, committee information, historical documents, and what's going on in Congress this week. Just for fun, you might click on Congressional Record Text, where you will find summaries and even complete texts of what Congress has passed into law during this session. You can also use Thomas to search for bills on specific issues like welfare reform:

http://thomas.loc.gov

Most members of Congress also maintain their own home page. Why not check out your representative or senator, either from your home district or your college's district? What kinds of resources does your member of Congress make available to constituents? What kind of image is portrayed? How are votes explained? You might contrast your member with one from another state or party and see what differences emerge. Political scientists have long believed that members use different home styles to relate to constituents. To what extent does their home style permeate their electronic style?

For more Internet resources on Congress, see our home page at:

http://www.prenhall.com/burns

SUMMARY

1. Congress plays a crucial role in our system of shared powers, controlling key decisions and constraining presidents. Yet, over time, Congress has lost some influence as the presidency has gained influence. In the last two decades, however, Congress has become more capable as a policy-making competitor for presidents.
2. Senators and representatives come primarily from middle- and upper-middle-class backgrounds. They are better educated than Americans as a whole. The typical member of Congress is still a middle-aged, white, male lawyer. Redistricting and reapportionment have shaped a Congress that somewhat more accurately reflects the population.
3. The most distinctive feature of Congress is its bicameralism, which the framers intended as a moderating influence on partisanship and possible error. Each chamber has a few distinctive functions. Their organizations and procedures also differ slightly, as do their political environments.
4. Congress performs these functions: representation, law making, consensus building, overseeing the bureaucracy, policy clarification, and investigating. The Senate also confirms or denies presidential appointments and participates in the ratification of treaties.
5. As a collective body, Congress must attempt to accomplish its tasks even as most of its members serve as delegates or trustees for their constituents. When they vote, members are influenced by their philosophy and values, their perceptions of constituents' interests, and the views of trusted colleagues, staff, party leaders, lobbyists, and the president.
6. Most of the work in Congress is done in committees and subcommittees. Congress has attempted in recent years to streamline its committee system and modify its methods of selecting committee chairs. Seniority practices are still generally followed, yet the threat of removal forces committee chairs to consult with younger members of the majority party. Subcommittees are important. They can prevent or delay legislation from being enacted. But there are numerous other stages where bills can be killed, making it easier to stop legislation than to enact it.
7. Members of Congress are motivated by the desire to win reelection, and much of what Congress does is in response to this motive. Members work hard to get favors for their districts, to serve the needs of constituents, and to maintain a high visibility in their districts or states. Incumbents have advantages that help explain their success at reelection: they have greater name recognition; they have large staffs; they are much better able to raise campaign money; and they have greater access to the media.
8. Individual members of Congress are more popular than the institution. Congress is criticized for being inefficient, unrepresentative, unethical, and lacking in collective responsibility. Yet criticisms of Congress are difficult to separate from the context of policy preference and democratic procedures. Congress's greatest strengths—its diversity and deliberative character—also contribute to its weaknesses.

KEY TERMS

safe seat 328
gerrymandering 328
redistricting 328
bicameralism 328
Speaker 333
majority leader 334
minority leader 334
whip 334
party caucus 334
closed rule 334
open rule 334
hold 334
president pro tempore 334
filibuster 335
cloture 336
divided government 337
senatorial courtesy 337
delegate 338
trustee 338
attentive public 339
state delegation 340
log rolling 340
standing committee 343
rider 343
pocket veto 344
override 344
joint committee 345
select or special committee 345
discharge petition 345
seniority rule 348
conference committee 349

FURTHER READING

Joel D. Aberbach, *Keeping a Watchful Eye: The Politics of Congressional Oversight* (Brookings Institution, 1990).

Sarah A. Binder and Steven S. Smith, *Politics or Principles? Filibustering in the United States Senate* (Brookings Institution, 1997).

Barbara Boxer, *Strangers in the Senate* (National Press, 1993).

Bill Bradley, *Time Present, Time Past: A Memoir* (Knopf, 1996).

David W. Brady and Craig Volden, *Revolving Gridlock: Politics and Policy from Carter to Clinton* (Westview Press, 1998).

Stephen L. Carter, *The Confirmation Mess: Cleaning Up the Federal Appointments Process* (Basic Books, 1994).

Kenneth E. Collier, *Between the Branches: The White House Office of Legislative Affairs* (University of Pittsburgh Press, 1997).

Constance Ewing Cook, *Lobbying for Higher Education: How Colleges and Universities Influence Federal Policy* (Vanderbilt University Press, 1998).

Roger H. Davidson and Walter J. Oleszek, *Congress and Its Members*, 5th ed. (Congressional Quarterly Press, 1996).

Christopher J. Deering and Steven S. Smith, *Committees in Congress*, 3d ed. (Congressional Quarterly Press, 1997).

Lawrence C. Dodd and Bruce J. Oppenheimer, eds., *Congress Reconsidered*, 5th ed. (Congressional Quarterly Books, 1993).

Richard F. Fenno, Jr., *Home Style: House Members in Their Districts* (Little, Brown, 1978).

RICHARD F. FENNO, JR., *Learning to Govern: An Institutional View of the 104th Congress* (Brookings Institution, 1997).

RICHARD F. FENNO, JR., *Senators on the Campaign Trail: The Politics of Representation* (University of Oklahoma Press, 1996).

MORRIS FIORINA, *Congress: Keystone of the Washington Establishment*, 2d ed. (Yale University Press, 1989).

PAUL HERRNSON, *Congressional Elections* (Congressional Quarterly Press, 1998).

JOHN R. HIBBING AND ELIZABETH THEISS-MORSE, *Congress as Public Enemy: Public Attitudes Toward American Political Institutions* (Cambridge University Press, 1995).

GARY C. JACOBSON, *The Electoral Origins of Divided Government: Competition in U.S. House Elections, 1946–1988* (Westview Press, 1990).

GARY C. JACOBSON, *The Politics of Congressional Elections*, 3d ed. (HarperCollins, 1992).

VICTOR KAMBER, *Giving Up on Democracy: Why Term Limits Are Bad for America* (Regnery, 1995).

MARCY KAPTUR, *Women in Congress* (Congressional Quarterly Press, 1996).

LINDA KILLIAN, *The Freshmen: What Happened to the Republican Revolution?* (Westview Press, 1998).

BURDETTE A. LOOMIS, *The Contemporary Congress* (St. Martin's Press, 1996).

THOMAS MANN AND NORMAN ORNSTEIN, EDS., *Renewing Congress: A Second Report* (American Enterprise Institute and Brookings Institution, 1993).

JANET M. MARTIN, *Lessons from the Hill: The Legislative Journey of an Education Program* (St. Martin's Press, 1993).

DAVID R. MAYHEW, *Congress: The Electoral Connection* (Yale University Press, 1974).

WALTER J. OLESZEK, *Congressional Procedures and the Policy Process*, 4th ed. (Congressional Quarterly Press, 1995).

TIMOTHY PENNY AND MAJOR GARRETT, *Common Cents* (Little, Brown, 1995).

RONALD M. PETERS, JR., ED., *The Speaker: Leadership in the U.S. House of Representatives* (Congressional Quarterly Press, 1995).

DAVID E. PRICE, *The Congressional Experience: A View from the Hill* (Westview Press, 1993).

WARREN B. RUDMAN, *Combat: Twelve Years in the U.S. Senate* (Random House, 1996).

DAVID SCHOENBROD, *Power Without Responsibility: How Congress Abuses the People Through Delegation* (Yale University Press, 1994).

PAUL SIMON, *Advice and Consent: Clarence Thomas, Robert Bork and the Intriguing History of the Supreme Court's Nominating Battles* (National Press Books, 1992).

BARBARA SINCLAIR, *The Transformation of the U.S. Senate* (Johns Hopkins University Press, 1989).

BARBARA SINCLAIR, *Unorthodox Lawmaking: New Legislative Processes in the U.S. Congress* (Congressional Quarterly Press, 1997).

CAROL M. SWAIN, *Black Faces, Black Interests: The Representation of African-Americans in Congress* (Harvard University Press, 1993).

DENNIS F. THOMPSON, *Ethics in Congress* (Brookings Institution, 1995).

STEVEN WALDMAN, *The Bill—How Legislation Really Becomes Law: A Case Study of the National Service Bill* (Penguin, 1996).

Students of Congress also should consult *Congressional Quarterly Weekly*, *National Journal*, *Roll Call*, and *The Hill*.

THE
PRESIDENCY:
THE
LEADERSHIP
BRANCH

15

As he traveled slowly up the East coast from Mount Vernon to New York (the temporary seat of government) in 1789, newly elected President George Washington was showered with parades and fireworks. His whole trip was one long ovation, a celebration of the people's yearning for a strong individual who could provide continuity and leadership for the nation.

Yet Washington and his compatriots were of two minds about the power of the presidency. The framers both admired and feared leadership. They realized the country needed a more effective, centralized government, yet they were suspicious of the potential abuses of power, especially power vested in a single individual. Given what they had lived through in the preceding decades, they had every right to these fears. Moreover, they hardly wanted to jeopardize the rights and liberties they had fought so hard to win in the recent Revolution.

Today, as we begin the twenty-first century, we still have not resolved our ambivalence toward the presidency. Should a president be "above politics" and wait for a consensus to emerge from the people and Congress? Or should presidents be clearly political, leading the people and leading Congress? Should presidential powers be narrowly defined? Or should the presidency be granted broad authority to respond to national and international emergencies? Does the enlarged role of the presidency under today's circumstances undermine some of the fundamental checks and balances in our constitutional democracy? Should we be willing to overlook a president's personal failings if his performance of official duties meets with public approval? We try to answer these questions as we look at the jobs we ask presidents to perform.

The Politics of Shared Powers

Original Intent

The framers of the Constitution created a presidency of limited powers. They wanted a presidential office that would steer clear of parties and factions, enforce the laws passed by Congress, handle relations with foreign governments, and help states put down disorders. They wanted a presidency strong enough to match Congress, yet not so strong it would overpower Congress.

They combined the ceremonial head of government with the actual head of government. The term of office would be four years, and presidents would be indefinitely

Presidentialism in Other Democracies

The United States is among a very few democracies in which a strong presidential system has coincided with democratic rule. Elsewhere, democratic presidential regimes have often given way to authoritarian presidential rule.

Most democracies are based on the parliamentary system of government (as in Australia, Britain, and Israel) that confers full powers on a parliament, which then delegates executive powers to a handful of its members. These officials, the head of government (a prime minister or premier or chancellor), and cabinet ministers make up what is known as "the Government." The Government serves only so long as it *maintains the confidence of a majority* in the lower house of parliament. If the parliament indicates its loss of support for the Government by a vote of censure, or a vote of no confidence, or even by defeating a major piece of Government-sponsored legislation, the Government resigns, either to allow a new Government to be formed or to call for new parliamentary elections. In parliamentary systems, the head of state (usually a president elected by parliament but sometimes, as in Britain, a hereditary monarch) has only ceremonial responsibilities.

In the recent wave of democratizations, a number of countries have experimented with a mixed presidential-parliamentary system. Based on the French Fifth Republic (1958–present), the mixed system includes a popularly elected presidency that has extensive powers of its own, notably in foreign and defense matters, *and* a prime minister and cabinet accountable to the parliament. This mixed presidential-parliamentary system has been adopted in Russia, Poland, the Czech Republic, and several other new democracies.

There is a lively debate on which pattern of government—presidential, parliamentary, or the mixed presidential-parliamentary system—is most conducive to democracy. Some fear that powerful presidents are a source of authoritarianism. Others claim that a strong president is needed to give leadership and coherence to the often fragmented parliaments in newer democracies. Still others see the solution in some kind of hybrid.

It is true that historically most presidential regimes have given way to dictatorships. But in most of these cases, the causes for the failure of democracy were less with the specific institutions than with the attitudes and commitments of the people and their leaders. It is unlikely that any single set of institutions can create or perpetuate democratic government. The presence of democratic values is more important in building and maintaining democracy than the existence of a particular institutional arrangement.

eligible to succeed themselves. (The two-term limit was added as the Twenty-second Amendment to the Constitution in 1951.)

Although independent from the legislature, presidents would still share considerable power with Congress. To enact government business, the separate branches would have to cooperate and consult with one another. A president's major appointments would have to be approved by the Senate; Congress could override the chief executive's veto by a two-thirds vote of each chamber, and the president could make treaties only with the advice and consent of two-thirds of the senators. All appropriations would be legislated by Congress, not the president.

But even a president whose power was limited by the system of checks and balances worried many Americans in 1787. The framers deliberately outlined the powers of the president broadly. The president, they thought, should have discretionary power to act when other governmental branches failed to meet their responsibilities or to respond to the urgencies of the day. But Congress retained the right to impeach and remove a president if members of Congress believed a president had failed to abide by the Constitution.

Divided Powers

Our constitutional democracy was designed to be one of both shared powers and divided powers. The framers wanted disagreement as well as cooperation because they assumed that the checks and balances within the government would prevent the president and Congress from "ganging up" against the people's liberties. The framers actually made disagreement inevitable by providing that the president, Senate, and House of Representatives would be elected by different constituencies and for different lengths of service.

The United States is rare among major world powers because it is neither a parliamentary democracy nor a wholly executive-dominated government. Our Constitution plainly invites both Congress and the president to set policy and govern the nation. Leadership and policy change are encouraged only when two, and sometimes all three, branches of government concur on the desirability of new directions.

A president and members of Congress are legitimate participants in a whole range of policy activities. Triumphs for a president acting alone in a system of separated powers are rare. "Whenever powers are shared, attention must be devoted to the other decision makers," writes political scientist Charles O. Jones. "How do they view the problem? What are their present commitments? On what basis will they compromise? The test in a separated system is not simply one of presidential success. It is rather one of achievement by the system, with presidents and members of Congress inextricably bonded and similarly judged."[1]

The politics of shared power has often been stormy, as the Clinton impeachment, health reform battles, and Social Security policy fights illustrate. Making systems of shared powers—that is, a separation of powers system—work is never easy. Sometimes presidents are helped when majorities of their party are in control of Congress, which can join together what the framers separated. In recent decades, however, **divided government**, in which one party controls the executive branch and the other the legislative branch, has been the norm.

divided government
Governance divided between the parties, especially when one holds the presidency and the other controls Congress.

The Evolution of Presidential Influence

The executive powers of the president as vested by our constitutional system has not changed over the last two centuries. But the actual powers or influences of a given president are partly the consequence of the incumbent's character and energy, combined with the needs of the time, the party balance in Congress, the values of the citizenry, and the challenges to our nation's survival. By and large, the history of presidential power is one of steady, if uneven, growth. Of the individuals who have filled the office, about one-third have enlarged its powers. Andrew Jackson, Abraham Lincoln, and both Roosevelts, for example, redefined both the institution and many of its powers by the way they set priorities and responded to crises.

In the evolution of executive power, Congress and the courts have sometimes been willing partners. In emergencies Congress often delegates discretion to the executive branch. In resolving complex problems, the legislature sometimes seems incapable of dealing with matters that are highly technical or that require immediate response and constant management. The weakness of Congress is not unique among legislative bodies. During the last two centuries in all democracies, and at all levels, power has drifted from legislators to executives. The English prime minister, the French president, governors of our states, and mayors of our cities all play more dominant roles than they did, generally speaking, one hundred years ago. This has been so in large part because people turn to executives to make government responsive to democratic needs, encourage a growing economy, and press national interest in the international system.

Two centuries of national expansion and recurrent crises have increased the influence of the president beyond that specified by the Constitution. The complexity of Congress's decision-making procedures, its unwieldy numbers, and its constitutional role make Congress a more public, deliberative, and divided organization than the presidency. When crises occur, Congress traditionally holds debates and, almost as predictably, delegates authority to the president, charging the executive branch to take whatever actions are deemed necessary. This is essentially what Congress has done in the 1990s in response to presidential calls for U.S. involvement in Kuwait, Somalia, Iraq, and Yugoslavia.

In the history of presidential–Supreme Court relations, the nation's highest court has generally favored an expansive interpretation of presidential power. The Court has on occasion halted a presidential action or ruled a presidential decision unconstitutional, but it has more frequently given legitimacy to the growth of presidential power.

Several factors strengthened the presidency in the twentieth century. The danger of war and the destructive potential of new weaponry plainly increased a president's influence. The cold war—with its enormous standing armies, nuclear weapons, and widespread intelligence and alliance operations—invited presidential leadership in national security matters. Television also contributed to the growth of presidential influence. With access to prime time, presidents can take their case directly to the people, and this invitation to bypass and sometimes ignore Congress, the Washington press, and even party leaders weakens the checks once imposed on the presidency.

Growth of the federal role in domestic and economic matters increases presidential responsibility and contributes to an enlarged presidential establishment. Problems not easily delegated to any one department often get pulled into the White House. When new programs involve several federal agencies, someone near the president is often asked to set a consistent policy and reconcile conflicts. White House aides, with some justification, claim the presidency is the only place in government where it is possible to establish and coordinate national priorities.

Who Were the Best and Worst Presidents?

Two extensive surveys of noted presidential historians and political scientists concluded the following:

The Ten Best	The Ten Worst
1. Abraham Lincoln	1. Warren Harding
2. George Washington	2. James Buchanan
3. Franklin Roosevelt	3. Franklin Pierce
4. Thomas Jefferson	4. Ulysses Grant
5. Theodore Roosevelt	5. Andrew Johnson
6. Woodrow Wilson	6. Millard Fillmore
7. Harry Truman	7. Richard Nixon
8. Andrew Jackson	8. John Tyler
9. James Polk	9. Calvin Coolidge
10. Dwight Eisenhower	10. Herbert Hoover

The Neal survey put Eisenhower about one notch higher than the Schlesinger poll. The Schlesinger tabulations added Zachary Taylor as also among the worst presidents. Yet overall these two attempts to evaluate the performance of presidents yielded strikingly similar findings.

SOURCE: Steve Neal, "Putting Presidents in Their Place," *Chicago Sun-Times*, November 19, 1995, pp. 30–31; Arthur M. Schlesinger, Jr., "The Ultimate Approval Rating," *The New York Times Magazine*, December 15, 1996, pp. 46–51.

Presidents set up central review and coordination units that help formulate new policies, settle jurisdictional disputes among departments, and provide access for the well-organized interest groups that want their views to be given weight in decision making.

The growth of the presidency is encouraged by public expectations. Although we may dislike or condemn individual presidents, the public's attitude toward the institution of the presidency remains positive. We want very much to believe in our presidents, perhaps because we have no royal family, no established religion, and no common ceremonial leadership.

George Washington was inaugurated as first president of the United States at Federal Hall in New York City on April 30, 1789.

What We Yearn for in Presidents (and Sometimes Don't Get)

The framers conceived their president in the image of George Washington, the man they expected would first occupy the office. Like Washington, the American executive was to be a wise, moderate, dignified, nonpartisan leader of all the people. No one commanded the trust and respect that Washington did, and he was unanimously elected as the first president of the new republic in 1789. George Washington knew the people needed to have confidence in their fledgling government, a sense of continuity with the past, and a time of calmness and stability free of emergencies and crises. He knew, too, that the new nation faced foreign dangers.

Today we are still not clear about how much authority and influence we want to vest in the president. When presidents take charge and try to run the country, they are accused of being dictatorial and trying to impose their will on the nation. If they are not activist leaders, however, they are criticized because they do nothing, and, even more likely, they are blamed for whatever happens to be wrong with the country. People who like what a president is doing are champions of presidential leadership, but people who disapprove of what a president is doing point to the dangers of dictatorship.

Article II of the Constitution outlined the nature and scope of presidential power (see page 47 of this text). It responded to George Washington's calls for executive leadership. He was sensitive to the fine line between providing strong leadership and infringing on individual rights and liberties. He knew then—as every president after him has either known or learned—that Americans have a strong streak of antigovernment and even anti-authority sentiment.[2]

What kind of person does it take to perform this delicate balancing act? Our Constitution establishes only three qualifications for the office: a president must be at least 35 years of age, have lived in the United States for 14 years, and be a natural-born citizen. Our "unwritten presidential job description"—the one we carry around in our heads—says a president has to be many things to many people.

Voters sometimes place as much emphasis on a presidential candidate's character and integrity as they do on a candidate's political philosophy and past experiences. Such emphasis is not misguided. Presidents have enormous influence, especially in times of crisis. They select the people who run the executive departments and serve on our courts, and thus they have much to do with governmental performance and ethics. Hence it is important to weigh their character and their allegiance to democratic values and to the spirit of the Constitution.[3]

President Grover Cleveland was mocked in cartoons for fathering an illegitimate child.

Concerns about presidential character are as old as the presidency itself. In 1800, for example, religious leaders denounced Thomas Jefferson from their pulpits as "godless," and Andrew Jackson was pilloried as a barbarian and adulterer.

The election of 1884 provides a fascinating case study of character in politics. In that election, Democratic candidate Grover Cleveland was charged with fathering a child out of wedlock. Cleveland took responsibility and agreed to pay for the child's upbringing. Not surprisingly, this became a hot issue for his opponent, James G. Blaine. The dilemma was that while Cleveland's private life did indeed raise doubts, he was highly responsible in his political and professional life. Blaine, on the other hand, had an "upright" private life yet was far less well regarded for his political integrity. Voters elected Cleveland.

It is said that Bill Clinton was "character challenged." His supporters in 1992 and 1996 were willing to overlook his past indiscretions in the hope that he would avoid reckless behavior and concentrate on domestic and foreign policy initiatives that they favored. "But he broke the bargain," noted *New York Times* columnist Thomas Friedman. "I knew he was a charming rogue with an appealing agenda, but I didn't think he was a reckless idiot with an appealing agenda."[4]

What was somewhat confusing after the Monica Lewinsky affair was exposed is that 60 to 70 percent of the American public continued to approve Clinton's handling of the presidency while decidedly disapproving Clinton's ethics and flawed character. At least in this case, most people judged the president on how well the economy was doing and on traditional "peace and prosperity" measures rather than on his character flaws.[5]

The One Quality Voters Say They Want Most in a President

Quality	Percent
Honesty/integrity	43%
Leadership/ability to make decisions	11
Sense of responsibility to people	6
Believes United States rates first	5
Understanding of the poor	4
Sound economic program	4
Intelligence	2
Good judgment	2
Self-confidence	2
Experience	2
High moral standards	2
Accessibility	1
Other	3
No answer/don't know	12

SOURCE: CBS News/New York Times Poll, April, 1996.

We pick presidential candidates in terms of their personalities. Can they get along with members of Congress, the press, fellow party leaders, and leaders of other nations? Will they display vision, judgment, moral character, a grasp of history, a sense of proportion, and a sense of humor? To be sure, people prefer candidates whose views on issues accord with their own; if they like a person's personality, they trust that individual's policy proposals. A candidate's character and policy preferences sometimes get blurred—if not reversed—in the voter's mind.

The Many Jobs of the President

The traditional responsibilities assigned to presidents are mostly well known:

- To serve as chief executive of the federal bureaucracy
- To nominate and appoint key officials
- To propose the yearly budget
- To implement and enforce laws
- To veto unwise laws
- To negotiate treaties
- To recognize foreign nations
- To serve as commander in chief
- To serve as chief of state
- To pardon or grant clemency
- To develop policies that promote peace and prosperity

This famous photo of Bill Clinton embracing Monica Lewinsky was played repeatedly on TV during the months that the scandal occupied the attention of the nation and the world.

Most of these responsibilities are spelled out in the Constitution, while a few are designated by laws enacted by Congress. But today a president is asked to perform additional roles that were not spelled out in the Constitution. We want the chief executive to be an international peacemaker as well as a national morale builder, a politician in chief as well as a commander in chief. We want the president to be the architect of "a new world order," or at least a peaceful world, who negotiates favorable trade pacts with major trading partners. In addition to the obvious leadership responsibilities a president has in foreign policy, economics, and domestic policy, six broad functional kinds of leadership are expected of a

TABLE 15-1 A Presidential Job Description

	Examples of Policy Responsibilities		
	Foreign Policy	**Economic Policy**	**Domestic Policy**
Crisis management	Clinton's authorizing bombing of Iraq	FDR's handling of the Depression, 1930s	Federal disaster relief
Symbolic and morale-building leadership	Clinton's trip to Ireland to support peace plan	Granting most favored status to China	Visiting flood and disaster victims
Recruitment of top officials	Selecting Joint Chiefs of Staff chair	Reappointing Alan Greenspan to head Fed	Nominating Supreme Court justices
Priority setting and problem clarification	Working with United Nations on peacekeeping priorities	Outlining tax-cut or revenue-producing programs	Setting priorities in environmental protection and health care
Legislative and political coalition building	Negotiating with Congress on new members of NATO	Balanced budget agreement with Congress	Clinton's efforts to pass health care reform
Program implementation, administration, and oversight	Hosting Middle East peace accords	Monitoring Internal Revenue Service performance	Appraising the impact of federal social programs

president. These policy areas and functions permit us to develop a presidential job profile (see Table 15-1).

Presidents as Crisis Managers

"The President shall be Commander in Chief of the Army and Navy of the United States," reads Section 2 of Article II of the Constitution. Even though this is the first of the president's powers listed in the Constitution, the framers intended the military role to be a limited one—far less than a king's. Congress would declare war, call up the army and navy, and control the funding of wars. Yet it was important, the framers insisted, that the people's elected representative—the president—be in charge of the military. This principle of *civilian control over the military* is a central element in our constitutional democracy.[6]

When crises and national emergencies occur, Americans instinctively turn to the chief executive, who is expected to provide the appearance of a confident, "take-charge" executive who has a steady hand at the helm. Public necessity forces presidents to do what Lincoln and Franklin Roosevelt did during the national emergencies of their day: provide the stability and continuity needed to protect the union and safeguard vital American interests.

The primary factor underlying this transformation in the president's function as commander in chief has been the changed role of the United States in the world, especially since World War II. In the postwar years, every president from Harry Truman to Bill Clinton has argued for and won support for the use of U.S. troops overseas as part of the North Atlantic Treaty Organization (NATO) or the various United Nations peacekeeping forces. Nations grew dependent on our assistance, which often was spelled out in treaties, pacts, and diplomatic agreements. These commitments, plus the fear of nuclear war and the importance of deterrence, prompted Congress to give presidents flexibility in the foreign policy area.

President Bill Clinton was warmly received by the people of Limerick, Ireland, on a 1998 visit to support peace in Northern Ireland.

Presidents are expected to be crisis managers in the domestic sphere as well. Whenever things go wrong, we demand presidential-level planning and problem solving. When terrorists attack U.S. citizens, people assume their president will retaliate. When a disastrous oil spill occurs, or a hurricane, or a flood, or a drought, people expect the head of state to step in and assist. When riots occur in our cities, we ask what the president is going to do about it. In many crises, however, presidents are little more than victims of fast-breaking events and forces outside of their control. They are sometimes surprised, overtaken by developments, and placed on the defensive.

THE PRESIDENTIAL WAR POWER The Constitution delegates to Congress the authority to declare the legal state of war (with the consent of the president), but in practice the president often starts the fighting or initiates actions that lead to war. This power has often been used by our presidents. From George Washington's time until Clinton's, the president, by ordering troops into battle, has often decided when Americans will fight and when they will not. When the cause has had political support, the president's use of this authority has been approved.

Abraham Lincoln called up troops, spent money, set up a blockade, and fought the first few months of the Civil War, without even calling Congress into session. William McKinley's dispatch of a battleship to Havana harbor, where it blew up, helped precipitate war with Spain in 1898. The United States was not formally at war with Germany until late 1941, but prior to the Japanese attack on Pearl Harbor, Franklin Roosevelt ordered the navy to guard convoys to Great Britain and to open fire on submarines threatening the convoys. Since World War II, presidents have sent forces without specific congressional authorization to Korea, Berlin, Vietnam, Lebanon, Grenada, Cuba, Libya, Panama, Kuwait, Somalia, Rwanda, Bosnia, and Iraq—in short, around the world.

President Franklin D. Roosevelt signed the declaration of war against Japan on December 8, 1941, as leaders of Congress looked on. It was the last time a president of the United States signed a formal declaration of war.

In 1973, Congress overrode Richard Nixon's presidential veto and enacted the War Powers Resolution, which declared that henceforth the president can commit the armed forces of the United States only: (1) after a declaration of war by Congress; (2) by specific statutory authorization; or (3) in a national emergency created by an attack on the United States or its armed forces. After committing the armed forces under the third circumstance, the president is required to report to Congress within 48 hours. Unless Congress has declared war, the troop commitment must be ended within 60 days. The president is allowed another 30 days if the chief executive claims the safety of the United States forces requires their continued use. A president is also obligated by this resolution to consult Congress "in every possible instance" before committing troops to battle. Moreover, at any time, by concurrent resolution not subject to presidential veto, Congress may direct the president to disengage such troops.

Not everyone was pleased by the passage of the War Powers Resolution. President Nixon vetoed it because he said it encroached on presidential powers. Others said it gave away a constitutional power plainly belonging to Congress—namely, the war-making power. Still other observers, however much they may have thought this resolution was defective, believed nonetheless that war powers legislation was of symbolic and institutional significance because it reflected a new determination in Congress at the time.

Presidents from Nixon to Clinton have not changed their behavior much, yet they have been put on notice that the commitment of American troops is subject to congressional approval. According to the resolution, presidents have to persuade Congress and the nation that their actions are justified by the gravest of national emergencies. Presidents in the future may, at least occasionally, hold back from conflict until they get a congressional declaration of war.

Presidents as Morale Builders

Presidents are the nation's number-one celebrities; almost anything they do is news. Presidents command attention merely by jogging, fishing, golfing, or going to church. By their actions they can arouse a sense of hope or despair, honor or dishonor.

What Is the Pardon Power?

Article II, Section 2, of the U.S. Constitution provides that the president shall have the power to grant "Reprieves" and "Pardons" for offenses against the United States, except in cases of impeachment. This authority, the roots of which can be traced directly to the royal authority of the king of England, is probably the most imperial and often the most delicate power a president exercises. The pardon power is generally a tool of mercy, an instrument to correct miscarriages of justice and to restore full civil rights to those who have served their sentences and are expected to be law abiding.

The pardon power permits a president to be merciful, but it can also be used strategically when a pardon can restore peace and stability. George Washington used this power to help end the Whiskey Rebellion. Presidents Abraham Lincoln and Andrew Johnson used it to provide amnesty to Confederate leaders and soldiers. Presidents Gerald Ford and Jimmy Carter used it for Vietnam War draft evaders. President Ford also used it to pardon Richard Nixon, probably the most controversial exercise of the pardon power.

The framers of the Constitution did not fully anticipate the symbolic and morale-building functions a president must perform. Certain magisterial functions, such as receiving ambassadors and granting pardons, were conferred. But over time the presidency has acquired enormous symbolic significance.

The morale-building job of the president involves much more than just ceremonial cheerleading or quasi-chaplain duties. Presidential leadership, at its finest, radiates national self-confidence and helps unlock the possibility for good that exists in the nation. Our best leaders have been able to provide this special and often intangible element.

Presidents as Recruiters

Presidents make more than 4,000 appointments, including hundreds of federal judgeships and top positions in the military and diplomatic service. Recall, however, that many appointments require the approval of the Senate. Effective presidents shrewdly use their appointment powers not only to reward campaign supporters and enhance ties to Congress, but also to communicate priorities and policy directions. Moreover, the White House in recent decades has often placed campaign aides in key deputy positions to ensure loyalty to the White House.[7]

Besides identifying and recruiting them, the president must also try to keep the most talented of these officials in government as long as possible. The turnover problem is acute. Many able people come to top positions in the cabinet or subcabinet and stay for just two years; less than one-third stay for more than three years. These top federal posts do not pay as much as similar positions in the private sector, and living in Washington is expensive.

Presidents have a lasting impact beyond their terms of office by their power to nominate federal judges. For example, President Dwight Eisenhower's nomination of Earl Warren to be chief justice of the United States was one of his most significant decisions in the area of domestic policy. Warren served for more than 15 years and presided over vast changes in civil rights and civil liberties. President Clinton nominated about three hundred federal judges, including Supreme Court justices Ruth Bader Ginsburg and Stephen Breyer, who are likely to have long-term effects. In a similar way, the selection of a secretary of state, a top economic adviser, a secretary of the treasury, or top White House aides can have an enormous impact on long-term national policy.

Various financial disclosure and conflict-of-interest requirements, imposed on presidential appointees as a result of the Ethics in Government Act of 1978, discourage some potential appointees from accepting government jobs. They must fill out many forms, and they must testify at sometimes complicated, time-consuming, confusing, and embarrassing congressional hearings. Media scrutiny of citizen-leaders called to government service has also become more intensive. Recruiters for recent presidents report they often have to go to their second or third choice before they find someone willing to accept an appointment.[8] A president must strengthen the hand of the ablest people working in the bureaucracy and promote them to higher positions at the senior reaches of the executive branch.[9]

Presidents as Priority Setters

A president can set national goals and propose legislation. Close inspection indicates, however, that in many if not most instances, "new initiatives" in domestic policy are measures that have been under consideration for a long time. Just as the celebrated New Deal legislation had a fairly well-defined history extending back several years before its embrace by Franklin Roosevelt, many of Bill Clinton's initiatives—health care and "the end of welfare as we know it"—are the fruits of long campaigns by congressional activists and certain interest groups. Many policy ideas percolate up from citizen groups and popular movements.

Presidents, by custom, have become responsible for proposing initiatives in foreign policy, economic growth and stability, and the quality of life. This was not always the case. But beginning with Woodrow Wilson, and especially since the New Deal, a president is expected to propose reforms to ensure domestic progress. New ideas are seized upon by a presidential candidate searching for campaign issues, and they are later refined and implemented by the executive office staff, by special presidential task forces, and by Congress.

NATIONAL SECURITY POLICY The framers foresaw a special need for speed and unity in dealing with other nations. As a result, presidents generally have more leeway in foreign policy and military affairs than they have in domestic matters. The Constitution vests in a president command of the two major instruments of foreign policy—the diplomatic corps and the armed services. It also gives the chief executive responsibility for negotiating treaties and commitments with other nations, although Congress usually gets to vote on these matters.

Congress has granted presidents discretion in initiating foreign policies, for diplomacy frequently requires quick action. The Supreme Court has upheld strong presidential authority in this area. In *United States v Curtiss-Wright* (1936), the Court referred to the "exclusive power of the president as the sole organ of the federal government in the field of international relations—a power which does not require as a basis for its exercise an act of Congress, but which, of course, like every other governmental power, must be exercised in subordination to the applicable provisions of the Constitution."[10] These are sweeping words.[11] Yet a determined Congress that knows what it wants and can agree on action does not lack power in foreign relations. Congress must authorize and appropriate the funds that back up the president's policies abroad.

ECONOMIC POLICY Ever since the New Deal, presidents have been expected to keep unemployment low, fight inflation, keep taxes down, and promote economic growth and prosperity. The Constitution did not specify these duties for the executive, yet presidents know that when the nation is not prosperous and jobs are scarce, they may suffer the fate of Herbert Hoover, who was denounced for his alleged inaction at the beginning of the Great Depression. The growth and complexity of economic problems since the Depression of the 1930s have placed more economic responsibility in the president's hands. The delicate balancing required to keep a modern economy operating means that presidents must make key fiscal and budgetary policy decisions.[12] The presidential elections in 1980, 1992, and 1996 turned largely on economics.

Although presidents sometimes get their economic advice elsewhere, their chief advisers on economic policy are the secretary of the treasury, the three members of the Council of Economic Advisers, and the director of the Office of Management and Budget. The chair of the Federal Reserve Board of Governors is also an influential, if independent, adviser on the economy.

An effective president must be an effective politician who both leads and follows his supporters. Here President Lyndon Johnson celebrates with Martin Luther King, Jr., the passage of the Civil Rights Act of 1964.

DOMESTIC POLICY A leader is one who knows where the followers are. Abraham Lincoln did not invent the antislavery movement. John Kennedy and Lyndon Johnson did not begin the civil rights movement. Clinton was hardly the first leader to notice the

Steve Kelley, *San Diego Union-Tribune*. Copley News Service.

unfairness of health care and welfare policies. But they all, in their respective times, became embroiled in these controversies, for a president cannot long ignore what divides or inspires a nation.

Presidents as Molders of Public Opinion

The press conference is an example of how a president can employ the machinery of communication to build legislative and political coalitions. Years ago press conferences were rather casual affairs. Franklin Roosevelt ran his get-togethers informally and was a master at withholding information as well as giving it. Under Harry Truman the conference became an institutionalized part of the presidential communications apparatus. John Kennedy authorized live telecasts of press conferences and used them frequently for direct communication with the people. Ronald Reagan effectively used five-minute Saturday afternoon radio chats to communicate his views, ask for support, and win Sunday morning media coverage. Bill Clinton occasionally uses the press conference, and also speaks directly to the public on his Saturday morning radio broadcasts.[13]

Presidents regularly commission polls to find out how they are doing. They want to learn about the public's views, estimate the strength and direction of its thinking, and respond to it. Public opinion can be unstable and unpredictable. Richard Nixon's dramatic drop of nearly 40 percentage points in public opinion polls as a result of the Watergate scandal helped force his resignation. George Bush won solid public approval during and after the successful military efforts in the Persian Gulf in early 1991, but his popular approval diminished sharply during the economic downturn that followed (see Figure 15-1). Most presidents lose support the longer they are in office. Dissatisfaction sets in; interest groups grow impatient; unkept promises must be accounted for; and the president gets blamed for things that go wrong.

Bill Clinton surprisingly retained and even gained popularity the longer he was in office. Indeed, the more personal trouble Clinton got into, the more his public approval ratings went up—even after he was impeached by the U.S. House of Representatives. The Clinton years of "peace, prosperity, and moderation" kept his approval ratings high.[14] He also reinvented himself as a warrior against the Newt Gingrich–led Congress, yet he prudently collaborated, when necessary, on a number of Republican initiatives, such as welfare reform, balancing the budget, and crime pre-

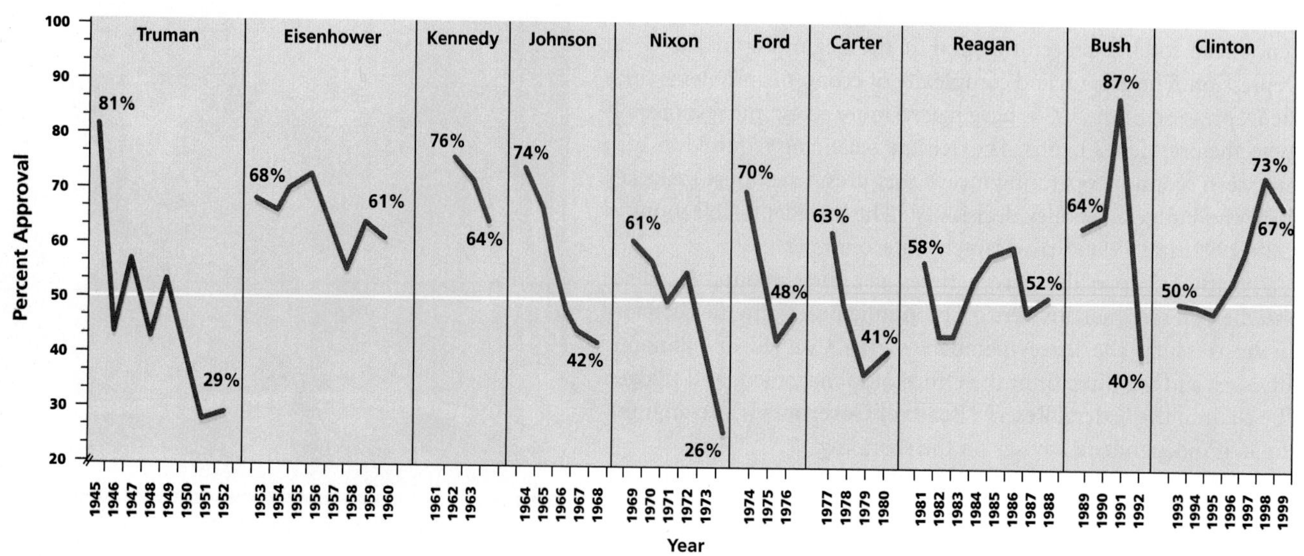

FIGURE 15-1 Presidential Approval Ratings, 1945–1999

SOURCE: The Gallup Organization.

Members of the Democratic party rallied strongly behind their president after the House of Representatives passed two articles of impeachment against him.

vention. Clinton and his supporters were often able to challenge his opponents, including Independent Counsel Kenneth Starr, Speaker Newt Gingrich, the House Republican Judiciary Committee, and Linda Tripp—the wired woman who helped make the case against Clinton. Finally, Clinton benefited from the fact that people believed being an effective president was far more important than being a role model.[15]

Bill Clinton had especially testy relations with the press and complained a lot about the media.[16] He used every available means to get his message out to the American public.[17] He was the first president to appear on MTV, and at least in his early years, he turned up at town meetings and talk shows with regularity. He had to deal with the press in an era of "in your face journalism," where many of the old rules and courtesies about the separation of public and private life had disappeared, especially those having to do with marital and extramarital relations. We have to remember, however, that Thomas Jefferson, Abraham Lincoln, and Franklin Roosevelt were all vilified by the press and rarely shown much reverence in their lifetimes. Presidents, along with members of Congress, are always fair game for media critics.[18]

Presidents as Party Leaders

Another potential source of influence for the president is the political party. Most presidents since Thomas Jefferson have been party leaders, and generally the more effective the president, the more use he has made of party support. Woodrow Wilson, the two Roosevelts, and Ronald Reagan fortified their executive and legislative influence by mobilizing support within their party.

Someone or something is needed to grease the wheels of government, which, if left to their own devices, grind slowly if at all. A president who can use help from his party and galvinize a relatively cohesive party sometimes supplies the needed push to overcome gridlock. Yet presidents are often led by their party, or at least constrained by it, as much as they lead it; no president has ever wholly dominated his party.[19]

Presidents as Administrators

The Constitution charges the president to "take Care that the Laws be faithfully executed." Presidents, however, must delegate much of their administrative authority. Because their other responsibilities demand most of their attention,

First Lady: A Search for the Appropriate Role

A president cannot by law appoint a spouse to a federal job. Yet Hillary Rodham Clinton became an influential and important adviser to President Bill Clinton. In his first term she headed the planning for national health care; however, her proposals failed to win majority support in Congress. She also took an active role in the selection of various nominees for cabinet and judicial posts.

Political spouses have often influenced their husbands or wives. Earlier presidential spouses—including Eleanor Roosevelt, Edith Wilson, and Dolley Madison—counseled and lobbied their presidential husbands. Every "first spouse" defines her responsibilities differently. Bess Truman and Pat Nixon chose to remain in the background. Lady Bird Johnson, Betty Ford, and Roslyn Carter undertook projects of special interest to them.

Hillary Clinton was as controversial as she was influential. Her role as an advocate of health care initiatives and women's rights attracted criticism as well as praise. Her role in the Whitewater real estate development and her alleged failure to answer specific questions about it caused additional concerns. She became the first First Lady to be subpoenaed to testify before a grand jury, and she, along with her husband, was questioned by a federal independent counsel.

Hillary Clinton has been hailed as a first lady for our times and a model for contemporary women who choose to have both a career and a family. She was criticized in the press, satirized in the novel *Primary Colors,* and ridiculed by opposition politicians and pundits—especially William Safire, Alfonse D'Amato, Rush Limbaugh, and Pat Buchanan. She resolutely stood by her husband throughout the Lewinsky scandal and energized Democratic opposition.

Future presidential partners doubtless will carefully weigh the Hillary Clinton experience. The question also arises of whether the husband of our first woman president will continue with his career, be active in policy planning, or play a passive, ceremonial role.

presidents are dependent on their subordinates. Theoretically, at least, orders flow down an administrative line: from president, to cabinet members, to bureau chiefs, to smaller offices. Like all top executives, a president is assisted by a staff who advise the chief executive. This *line and staff organization* is typical of every large administrative entity, whether it be the army, General Motors, or the United Nations.

THE WHITE HOUSE STAFF Presidents have come to rely heavily on their personal staffs. Nowhere else—not in Congress, not in the cabinet, not in the party—can presidents find the loyalty and single-mindedness that often develops among their closest White House aides. Cabinet heads, on the other hand, are often perceived as staunch advocates of their departments and the constituencies their departments serve. Presidents assume, however, that their aides will provide them with neutral and objective advice, but there are substantial costs to listening only to one's closest aides. The White House can usually be thought of as a palace court in which strong presidents create an environment that weeds out any assistant who persists in presenting irritating or opposing views.

The number of employees in the presidential entourage grew steadily from the early 1900s through the early 1990s. Today a White House staff of about 400 operates at a slight reduction from previous years. This staff makes up just one part of the Executive Office of the President.[20]

The staff of the White House office can be categorized by their primary functions: (1) domestic policy; (2) economic policy; (3) national security or foreign policy; (4) administration and personnel matters (as well as personal paperwork and scheduling for the president); (5) congressional relations; and (6) public relations.

Presidential aides sometimes insist they are simply the eyes and ears of the president, that they make few important decisions, and that they never intrude between the chief executive and the heads of departments. But the White House staff and the inevitable emergence of a few strong White House advisers made this traditional picture inaccurate. Some White House aides, impatient with bureaucratic and congressional bottlenecks or even political sabotage, come to view the presidency as if it alone were the whole government.

Executive Office of the President
The cluster of presidential staff agencies that help the president carry out his responsibilities. Currently the office includes the Office of Management and Budget, the Council of Economic Advisers, and several other units.

Office of Management and Budget
Presidential staff agency that serves as a clearinghouse for budgetary requests and management improvements.

cabinet
Advisory council for a president, consisting of the heads of the executive departments, the vice-president, and a few others the president considers cabinet-level officials.

THE INSTITUTIONALIZED EXECUTIVE OFFICE Approved by Congress in 1939, the **Executive Office of the President** was the recommendation of Franklin Roosevelt's Committee on Administrative Management. The intention was to provide presidents with the help they obviously needed to carry out the growing responsibilities imposed by the Great Depression and by the enlarged role of government. The Executive Office of the President consists of the Office of Management and Budget, the Council of Economic Advisers, and several other staff units (see Figure 15-2).

The **Office of Management and Budget (OMB)** is the central presidential staff agency. Its director advises the president in detail about the hundreds of government agencies—how much money they should be allotted in the budget and what kind of job they are doing. OMB seeks to improve the planning, management, and statistical work of the agencies. It makes a special effort to see that each agency conforms to presidential policies in its dealings with Congress; each agency has to clear its policy recommendations to Congress through OMB first.[21]

Through the long budget preparation process, presidents use OMB as a way of conserving and centralizing their own influence. A budget is more than just a financial plan, because it reflects power struggles and indicates national priorities (and wishful thinking). To the president, the budget is a means of control over administrators who may be trying to join ranks with politicians or interest groups to thwart presidential priorities.

THE CABINET It is hard to find a more unusual institution than the president's **cabinet**. The cabinet is not specifically mentioned by name in the Constitution, yet since George Washington's administration, every president has had one. Washington's consisted of his secretaries of state, treasury, and war, plus his attorney general.

Today the selection of cabinet members is the first major job for the president-elect. The cabinet consists of the president, the vice-president, the heads of the 14 executive departments, and a few others a president considers cabinet-level officials. The cabinet has always been a loosely designated body, and it is not always clear who belongs in it. In recent years, certain executive branch administrators and White House counselors have been accorded cabinet rank. Presidents need a strong cabinet and allies in Congress to provide alternative views to help ensure that they do not become isolated by an overly protective entourage.[22]

Cabinet government as practiced in parliamentary systems—where the voice and the vote of the cabinet members count for a lot—simply does not exist in the United States. In fact, an American president is not required by the Constitution to form a cabinet or to hold regular meetings. Presidents John Kennedy, Lyndon Johnson, and Richard Nixon all preferred small conferences with individuals specifically involved in a problem. Kennedy saw no reason to discuss defense department matters with his secretaries of agriculture and labor, and he thought cabinet meetings wasted valuable time. Both Jimmy Carter and Ronald Reagan tried to revive the cabinet, and both met often with their cabinets during their first two years. But the longer they remained in office, the less frequently they met with their cabinets as a whole. Bill Clinton, like those he followed, seldom called for full Cabinet

The Cabinet

- Vice-President
- Secretary of State
- Secretary of Treasury
- Secretary of Defense
- Attorney General
- Secretary of Interior
- Secretary of Agriculture
- Secretary of Commerce
- Secretary of Labor
- Secretary of Health and Human Services
- Secretary of Housing and Urban Development
- Secretary of Transportation
- Secretary of Energy
- Secretary of Education
- Secretary of Veterans Affairs
- Chief of Staff at the White House
- Director of the Office of Management and Budget
- U.S. Trade Representative
- U.S. Representative to the United Nations
- Chair, Council of Economic Advisers
- Administrator, Environmental Protection Agency
- Director, Drug Control Office

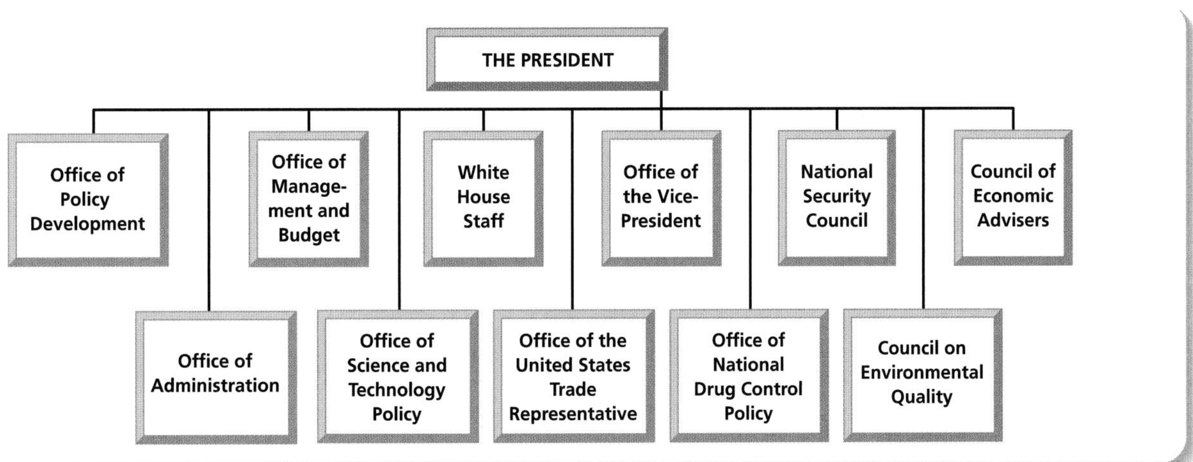

FIGURE 15-2 Executive Office of the President

SOURCE: *United States Government Manual, 1989/1999* (Government Printing Office, 1998), pp. 90–108.

You Decide . . .

Should presidents be limited to two terms in office?

Before he left office, former President Ronald Reagan called for the repeal of the Twenty-second Amendment to the Constitution, the one that limits a president to two terms. Why do you think he opposed the amendment? What additional reasons could be put forth to persuade people to repeal this relatively new (1951) provision in the Constitution? What are the best reasons for retaining the Twenty-second Amendment?

meetings, holding just 18 full cabinet meetings in his first term and even fewer during his second.[23]

Presidential advisers and the heads of various White House–based cabinet-level councils, such as the National Security Council and the Office of Management and Budget, have gained equal or even superior status to many cabinet secretaries. This shift occurred in part because these advisers are physically located in or next door to the White House (see Figure 15-3). Further, presidents are aware that some cabinet members adopt narrow "advocate" views: the agriculture cabinet secretary as a strident advocate for the farmers; the Housing and Urban Development cabinet secretary as an ambassador for the housing industry and, to some extent, also for big city mayors; and so on through much of the cabinet, especially those preoccupied with domestic policy matters.

Working with Congress

The Constitution provides that the president "shall from time to time give to the Congress information on the State of the Union, and recommend to their Consideration such Measures as he shall judge necessary and expedient." From the start, strong presidents have exploited this power. George Washington and John Adams went in person to Congress to deliver information and recommendations. Thomas Jefferson and many presidents after him sent written messages, but Woodrow Wilson restored the practice of delivering a personal, and often dramatic, message.

Less public, yet equally important, are the frequent written policy messages dispatched from the White House to the members of Congress on a range of public problems. These messages are important in defining the administration's position and in giving assistance to friendly legislators. Moreover, these messages are often accompanied by detailed drafts of legislation, which members of Congress sponsor with little or no change. These White House proposals, the products of bill-drafting experts on the president's staff or in the executive departments and agencies, may be strengthened or diluted by Congress, but many of the original provisions survive.

Presidents cannot escape political coalition building. As candidates, they made promises to the people. To get things done and to get reelected, they must work with

President Clinton with several members of his cabinet at the start of his second term: (left to right) Deputy Treasury Secretary Larry Summers, Budget Director Franklin Raines, Treasury Secretary Robert Rubin, Vice-president Al Gore, Commerce Secretary Bill Daley, United Nations Ambassador Bill Richardson, Economic Council Chair Larry Sperling, and Assistant to the President for International Economic Affairs Dan Tarullo.

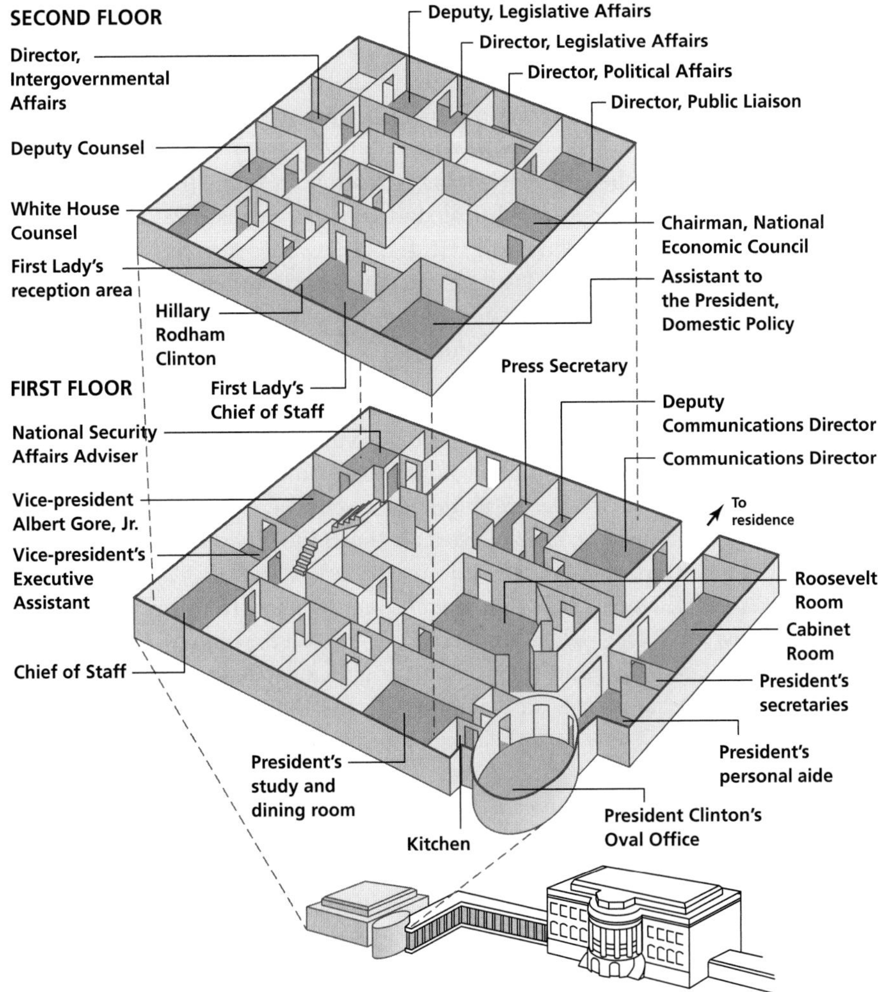

FIGURE 15-3 The White House

SOURCE: Adapted from *The Washington Post*, February 5, 1993, p. A23.

interest groups and people who have differing loyalties and responsibilities.[24] Inevitably, presidents become embroiled in legislative, bureaucratic, and lobbying politics, and their approval ratings usually suffer as a consequence.

Despite their formal powers, presidents can rarely command; they spend most of their time *persuading* people. The power to persuade is the president's chief resource, and that power comes through bargaining. Bargaining, in turn, comes primarily through getting others to believe it is in their self-interest to cooperate. Presidents and their aides spend a lot of time dispensing favors to various members of Congress from whom they are seeking votes and political support.[25] Hence the skill of a president in communicating and winning others over is the necessary energizing factor in moving the institutions of the national government to action.

From a president's vantage point, it is seldom helpful to punish legislators from one's own party who, for whatever reason, decide not to support part of the president's legislative program. With power dispersed and decentralized in Congress, it is just too risky for a president to single out a few party "disloyalists" for retribution. White House congressional relations aides abide by the motto "No permanent allies, no permanent enemies." Someone whose vote is lost today may cast the crucial supportive vote on some other measure next week.

Thinking it Through . . .

Reagan said the people should be able to reelect a president as many times as they want, just as they now reelect House and Senate members. He also hinted that the Twenty-second Amendment might weaken a president late in his second term by making him a lame duck, less powerful because everyone knows he will not be around in a year or so. Advocates of repeal also say we may sometimes need to keep a veteran president in office during a crisis period, much as we retained Franklin Roosevelt in 1940. Others say eight years may not be enough time to resolve certain major problems.

The Twenty-second Amendment is not only a limit on the incumbent but also on the electorate, the first since the ratification of the Constitution to restrict the power of the electorate rather than expand it. It is based, advocates of repeal suggest, on the assumption that the voters cannot be trusted.

Those who favor keeping the Twenty-second Amendment cite these reasons: First, the presidency is so powerful today that we need the Twenty-second Amendment as an additional check and balance against abuse of this power. Second, the amendment encourages both parties to seek out effective candidates to succeed to office and discourages dependence on a single ruler. Third, few leaders are likely to have the health, the intellectual energy, and the new ideas needed to perform the demanding responsibilities of the presidency beyond eight years in office. Finally, Americans have always believed in citizen-leaders rather than career politicians, and this amendment encourages this ideal.

Executive Orders

A presidential *executive order* is nowhere defined in the Constitution, yet is generally accepted as a directive presidents can send to government agencies that has the force of law. Its legal authority comes from existing laws or from the president's other constitutional assignments of authority.

Executive orders are used to set up agencies, modify rules, or give emphasis to certain laws. Executive orders are essential because Congress very often has not spelled out in detail how laws it has passed are to be implemented. Congress, in effect, expects presidents to perform a quasi-legislative role in adapting vague laws to complex and sometimes changing circumstances. Franklin D. Roosevelt issued more than 3,500 executive orders; Ronald Reagan issued more than 400.

Sometimes a presidential executive order will be challenged in federal court, but the courts generally side with the president, especially if Congress has failed to be precise in prescribing how a law will be applied.

Presidents and their aides sometimes stretch this authority more broadly than Congress might have intended. When this happens, Congress responds by passing more detailed or restrictive legislation with more precise specifications. But too many restrictions or too narrow a leeway can lead to inefficiencies or chaos or both, which in turn can lead to demands for broader discretion.

Presidents are often in a good position to bargain and trade for votes with members of Congress. In addition to receiving presidential help in their reelection campaigns, members of Congress also want federal projects for their districts, patronage for their supporters, help with their own pet legislative measures, and defense contracts and benefits for major industries in their districts or states. "The White House political staff controls a great deal of patronage and becomes expert at wielding it," writes former U.S. Senator Warren Rudman. "Typically, senators traded their votes on foreign policy issues . . . for a new highway for their state or a new science center for their state university."[26]

THE PRESIDENTIAL VETO A president can veto a bill by returning it, together with specific objections, to the house in which it originated. Congress, by a two-thirds vote in each chamber, may override the president's veto. Another variation of the veto is known as the pocket veto. In the ordinary course of events, if the president does not sign or veto a bill within ten weekdays after receiving it, it becomes law without the chief executive's signature. But if Congress adjourns within the ten days, the president—by taking no action—can kill the bill.

The veto's strength lies in the difficulty Congress has in getting a two-thirds majority of both houses. From 1789 through mid 1999, presidents have exercised their regular veto power 1,437 times; only 105 of these vetoes have been overridden by Congress (see Table 15-2). However, when scholars separate out the vetoes of private bills (bills dealing with individual claims against the government, or land titles, or matters such as immigration and naturalization) from public bills, they find that about 19 percent of the public bill vetoes have been overridden by Congress. Still, writes political scientist Robert Spitzer, "a presidential success rate of more than 80 percent for important legislation poses a daunting challenge to anyone seeking to overturn a veto."[27]

Presidents can also use the veto power in a positive way. Even the threat of the veto can sometimes strengthen their hand in negotiating and persuading. They can announce that bills under consideration by Congress will be turned back unless certain changes are made. They can use the threat of a veto against a bill Congress wants badly in exchange for other bills that they want. A presidential veto can also protect a national minority from hasty, unfair legislation passed in the heat of the moment. But the veto is essentially a negative weapon of limited use to a president who is pressing for action.

TABLE 15-2 Presidential Vetoes, 1933–mid-1999

President	Vetoes*
Franklin D. Roosevelt	635
Harry S. Truman	250
Dwight D. Eisenhower	181
John F. Kennedy	21
Lyndon B. Johnson	30
Richard M. Nixon	43
Gerald R. Ford	66
Jimmy Carter	31
Ronald Reagan	78
George Bush	46
Bill Clinton	25

SOURCE: Office of the Secretary, U.S. Senate Library, 1999.

*Regular and pocket vetoes combined.

THE RISE AND FALL OF THE ITEM VETO President Clinton in 1996 signed into law a bill passed by Congress authorizing the **item veto**, which he said would allow future presidents to fight "special interest boondoggles, tax loopholes, and pure pork."[28] ("Pork," or **pork-barrel legislation**, refers to government benefits or programs that may help the economy of a member's district—as in "bring home the bacon.") Clinton was only the most recent in a long list of presidents to call for the right to veto subsections within major appropriation bills passed by Congress.[29] To fight deficit spending and to cut expenditures whose main purpose was to help members of Congress win reelection, presidents sought the authority to remove "pork" and **riders**—unrelated items added to appropriations bills, often at the last minute, because their proponents knew there was little chance a president would veto an entire bill, especially an appropriations bill, because of them.

The item veto applied to discretionary spending, new direct spending, and items of limited tax benefit. The president had five calendar days following Congress's passing of a bill to notify Congress of his decision to "rescind" (propose for elimination) an item. Congress had 30 days to respond by passing the item again by a majority vote, not a two-thirds vote, of each house. Or Congress could choose not to act.

What was remarkable about the enactment of the item veto legislation in 1996 was that a Congress controlled by Republicans noted for their intent to reassert congressional powers, particularly with Clinton in the White House, "nevertheless voted to give that president, and the office, an important new power that could be used only against the priorities of the institution that granted the power—that is Congress."[30]

President Clinton cautiously exercised this item veto authority on ten occasions in 1997, striking out 82 spending provisions. One cut of $287 million in a military construction bill was overridden by Congress. Members of Congress whose districts suffered because of the item veto protested loudly, even though most had voted to give this authority to the president.

The item veto was challenged in the federal courts. Then in June 1998, the Supreme Court ruled, in a 6 to 3 decision, that Congress had improperly ceded to the president the power to rewrite legislation when it approved the Line Item Veto Act of 1996.[31] "The decision is a defeat for all Americans," Clinton lamented. "It deprives the president of a valuable tool for eliminating waste in the federal budget and for enlivening the public debate over how to make the best use of public funds."[32]

Opponents, on the other hand, were jubilant. Some said the Court saved Congress from itself. Senator Robert C. Byrd (D.-W.V.) declared, "This is a great day for the Constitution of the United States of America. . . . The liberties of the American people have been assured. God save this honorable court!"[33] Supreme Court Justice Anthony Kennedy, in his concurring

Line of Succession to the Presidency

The Constitution leaves succession after the vice-president up to Congress. Thus this is the line of succession according to law passed by Congress. However, the constitutional qualifications still apply. For example, if the secretary of state was born in a foreign country of parents who were not U.S. citizens, he or she would be bypassed in this line.

1. Vice-President
2. Speaker of the House of Representatives
3. Senate President Pro Tempore
4. Secretary of State
5. Secretary of the Treasury
6. Secretary of Defense
7. Attorney General
8. Secretary of the Interior
9. Secretary of Agriculture
10. Secretary of Commerce
11. Secretary of Labor
12. Secretary of Health and Human Services
13. Secretary of Housing and Urban Development
14. Secretary of Transportation
15. Secretary of Energy
16. Secretary of Education
17. Secretary of Veterans Affairs

President Clinton's State of the Union address on January 19, 1999 was delivered in the same chamber where he had been impeached a few weeks earlier.

item veto
A measure passed by Congress in 1996 and ruled unconstitutional by the Supreme Court in 1998 whereby the president was given the authority to strike specific spending programs from the budget passed by Congress. Also permits governors in some states to veto individual items in an appropriations bill while signing the remainder of the bill into law.

pork-barrel legislation
Government benefits or programs that may help the economy of a member of Congress's district.

rider
A provision that may have little relationship to the bill it is attached to in order to secure its passage.

Presidential versus Prime Ministerial Authority

The president of the United States is widely considered one of the most powerful persons on earth. This is undoubtedly true when one takes into account the economic, political, and military capabilities of the United States. On the other hand, it may be inaccurate in terms of the president's personal ability to control the making of policy.

The president can propose policies to Congress, but only members of the legislative branch can pass laws. Because of separation of powers and relatively loose party discipline, presidents often see their pet projects (such as Jimmy Carter's energy program and Bill Clinton's health care reforms) either drastically modified or totally rejected by Congress, even when the president's own party controls a majority of seats in the House of Representatives and the Senate.

In contrast, if the Canadian prime minister's party controls a majority of seats in the House of Commons, his legislative proposals are almost always enacted. This occurs because executive and legislative powers overlap much more extensively in Canada than in the United States. Further, there is strict party discipline within the House of Commons, meaning that party members must vote in accordance with the prime minister's instructions on important issues or risk being expelled from the party caucus. Party discipline is much more important in Canada than the United States, because if the prime minister is defeated on a major issue in Parliament, custom requires that he submit his resignation, often leading to a new general election.

Consequently, with majority support in the House of Commons and with a weak Canadian Senate usually rubber stamping whatever is passed by the House, the prime minister can enact the lion's share of his policy agenda, unlike the U.S. president. Indeed, the major check on the prime minister's policy preferences will usually not occur until the next election, when the voters will decide how well the prime minister and his or her party have served the interests of Canada.

opinion, aptly summarized why the Court brought an end to the brief experiment. "By increasing the power of the President beyond what the framers envisioned," Justice Kennedy wrote, "the statute compromises the political liberty of our citizens, liberty which the separation of powers seeks to secure."[34]

Congress Often Sees Things Differently

For presidents to get much done, they need the cooperation of Congress. But congressional cooperation can never be taken for granted. We can point to several causes of the inevitable balancing and checking Congress performs in its dealing with presidents: constitutional ambiguities, different constituencies, varying terms of office, divided party control of the branches (most of the time in recent years), weak political parties, and fluctuating public support.

CONSTITUTIONAL AMBIGUITIES Article I of the Constitution grants to Congress "all legislative Powers" but limits them to those "herein granted." It then sets forth in some detail the powers vested in Congress. In contrast, Article II vests in the president "the executive Power" without limiting it to such powers as are "herein granted" and then proceeds to describe those powers in very general terms. Is this difference in language between Articles I and II significant? Some scholars and most presidents have argued that a president is granted by Article II a general and undefined power to act to promote the well-being of the United States, subject only to precise constitutional limits. Therefore, they contend, a president is *not* limited to the specific powers spelled out in the Constitution, as is Congress, but has all the executive powers of the United States.[35] Other scholars and many members of Congress say the president either has no such inherent power or has it only in extraordinary circumstances.[36]

Whatever the language of the Constitution, the president has often exercised powers not expressly defined in it. These powers have been given a variety of names: *implied, inherent,* or *emergency powers.* For example, Bill Clinton ordered retaliatory bombings in Sudan and Afghanistan after U.S. embassies in Africa were bombed, and he did so without asking for a declaration of war and without consulting Congress. Clinton was criticized by Congress for acting without congressional approval, and some suggested the action was intended to distract attention from the Lewinsky affair. Yet even the most faithful defenders of congressional prerogatives recognize that in extraordinary emergencies a president "may have to act promptly without clear constitutional or statutory support."[37] Bill Clinton also figured out a way to lend Mexico billions of dollars to overcome a financial crisis even though Congress essentially refused to do so.

DIFFERENT CONSTITUENCIES Members of Congress represent state and local districts, and hence reflect specific geographic, ethnic, and economic interests. James Madison and other framers of the Constitution anticipated legislators would often be pressured by local and state interests to adopt a narrow or parochial view, as opposed to a national view on certain policy issues, and presidents and their aides often think Madison was right. Members of Congress, of course, see sensitivity to state and local concerns as essential to their job as representatives and to their prospects for reelection. As a result, members of Congress—even those from a president's own party and own region—may look at problems and solutions somewhat differently from the way a president does, as a president represents a national perspective.

There is an old saying in Washington that "where you stand depends on where you sit." President Lyndon Johnson, for example, viewed the importance of civil rights legislation when he was in the White House differently from the way he viewed it when he represented Texas in the U.S. House and Senate.

VARYING TERMS OF OFFICE Presidents serve for four years with a chance of reelection to a second term; senators have the luxury of six-year terms; members of the House of Representatives are elected for two-year terms. Different constituencies and lengths of service make these national offices responsive to different moods and points of view. Different electoral forces are at work in different election years. A majority of the voters can win control over only part of the national government at a time, and this arrangement, too, was by design.

Presidents often act quickly to shape national priorities in their first year following the flush of their electoral victories. They act to win support for their agendas before a possible decline in public approval. Congress, on the other hand, usually moves more slowly. Congress moves at a slower pace in part "because it represents a vast array of local interests. Congress passes new laws slowly and reviews old ones carefully."[38] The decision-making pace of Congress and of the president is not the same because of their different terms of office. The result is often conflict and deadlock.

Why Presidential Approval (in Polls) Usually Declines the Longer Presidents Are in Office

- Expectations that are raised in campaigns are dashed as time forecloses resources and options.
- Things that go wrong get blamed, rightly or wrongly, on presidents, whether or not presidents have the power to deal with these matters.
- Rising disapproval of incumbent presidents is often influenced by inflation and unemployment.
- Major negative events, such as the Vietnam War, Watergate scandal, or Iranian hostage crisis, influence how people evaluate presidents.
- Press and media criticism accumulates over time and sharpens the public's dissatisfaction with a president. Perhaps, too, time in office simply wears out our welcome for a president.

Political scientists are not exactly sure of the precise relationships among the above factors; different studies produce different findings. These factors are, however, plainly some of the more important ones, and some of them are doubtless interrelated.

DIVIDED GOVERNMENT Since 1952 there has been a split in partisan control of the presidency and Congress for most of the time. Republican Presidents Dwight Eisenhower, Ronald Reagan, George Bush, Gerald Ford, and Richard Nixon had to deal with Congresses that were most of the time under the control of Democrats. Only John Kennedy, Lyndon Johnson, and Jimmy Carter enjoyed majority control by their own party in Congress, and even then they had considerable trouble getting support for their legislative programs.

In the days, weeks, and sometimes months following their inauguration, presidents usually enjoy what has been called the **honeymoon**, a period of generally positive relations with the press and Congress. Franklin Roosevelt, Lyndon Johnson, and Ronald Reagan all enjoyed legislative success in their first year in office.

The opposition party in Congress regularly mounts its own programs. It will, when possible, defeat a president's policy initiatives and substitute its own. This effort becomes all the more troublesome for a president when Congress is controlled by the opposition party—as Bill Clinton clearly learned when the Republicans swept into power in Congress following the 1994 elections.

WEAK POLITICAL PARTIES Most members of Congress finance their elections with only minimal assistance from their national party. They customarily respond to local conditions and run their campaigns independently of their party's presidential candidate or national platform. Thus they feel few obligations to go along with the president of their own party, unless a measure converges with their own political philosophy and is in the interest of their home district or state. And although parties have recently become somewhat stronger inside Congress, especially in the House of Representatives, there are always a few independent thinkers who will at times—sometimes crucial times for the White House—go their own way rather than cooperate with the White House even when the president is a member of the same party.[39]

FLUCTUATING PUBLIC SUPPORT In recent years Americans have generally held presidents in higher esteem than Congress as an institution—this was even the case after Clinton had been impeached—and this fluctuating prestige has had consequences. Greater prestige for the presidency can give the incumbent in the White House a slight edge in battles with Congress.

honeymoon
A period at the beginning of a new president's term in which the president enjoys generally positive relations with the press and Congress.

Congress may be viewed by many people as slow or inefficient, in part because it has to represent local interests and respond (some think too much) to narrow-minded constituencies.[40] Yet when presidents decline in popularity, such as after the Watergate scandal, or when a president loses his moral authority, Americans turn to Congress to hold the president and the presidency accountable.

Congress Also Cooperates

Although separation of powers and divided government are checks on any president, they are not insurmountable barriers to good policy making. Presidents and Congress can legislate when the leaders of both institutions bargain and compromise in ways that overcome the roots of division discussed here. In fact, although the Constitution disperses power and invites a continual struggle between these two branches, it also requires the two branches to integrate the fragmented parts of the system into a workable government. And usually these two branches of government do work together. Even when the relationship is regarded as hostile, "bills get passed and signed into law. Presidential appointments are approved by the Senate. Budgets are enacted and the government is kept afloat. This necessary cooperation goes on even when control of the White House and the Capitol is divided between the two major parties."[41]

The presidential record of dealing with Congress in recent decades is mixed (see Figure 15-4). Presidents enjoy considerable success in getting most of their nominations confirmed by the Senate, and relatively few presidential vetoes are overturned by Congress. Also, most presidential budget requests eventually win approval, although Congress jealously guards its right to modify them, especially in certain areas such as defense and agriculture. On the other hand, Congress approves only about 50 percent of the president's major policy recommendations.[42] Congress itself is, in fact, the source of many laws offered as part of the president's program.

CONSTRAINTS ON PRESIDENTS

Presidential power may be greater today than ever before; it is misleading, however, to infer from a president's capacity to begin a nuclear war that the chief executive has similar power in most policy-making areas. Seldom are presidents free agents in bringing about significant social change. Presidents who

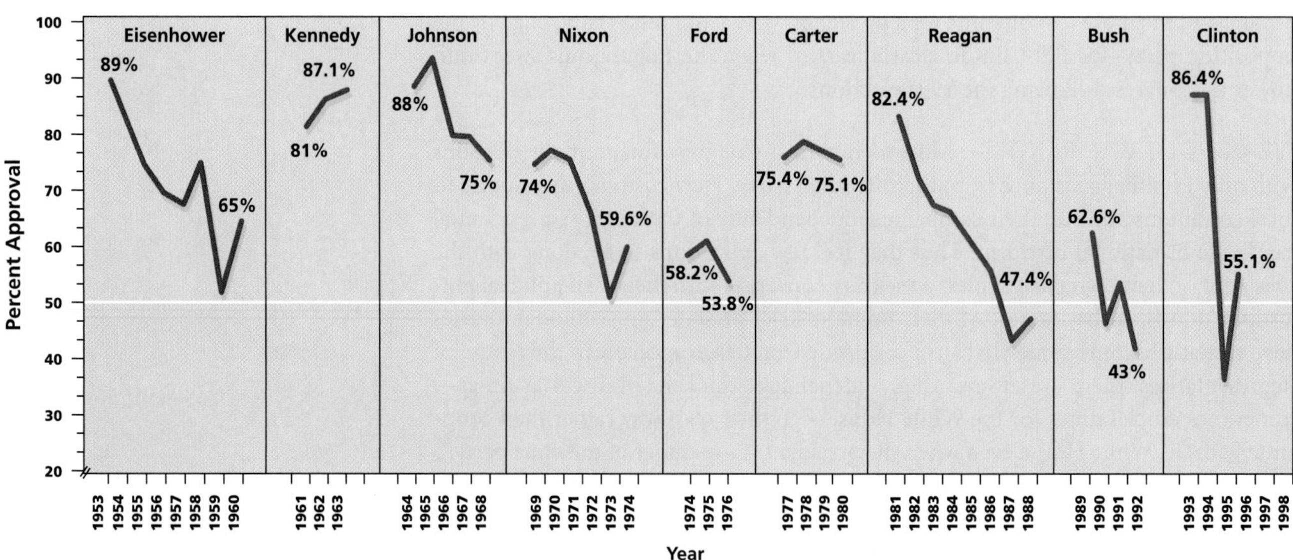

FIGURE 15-4 Presidential Support from Congress, 1953–1998

SOURCE: *Congressional Quarterly*, January 9, 1999, p. 86.

Note: Percentages represent average scores for both chambers of Congress.

INDEPENDENT COUNSEL INVESTIGATIONS

The Watergate scandal in the early 1970s demonstrated that the executive branch could not investigate itself lest there be an appearance, if not the reality, of a conflict of interest. As a result, Congress passed the Special Prosecutor Act of 1978. The law was reauthorized in 1982, 1987, and again in 1994, each time for a five-year term.

Here is how it worked: If an attorney general decided there was sufficient evidence to appoint an independent counsel, a panel of three federal judges actually made the appointment. An independent counsel had unusually wide discretion to expand an inquiry, even to charges not related to the initial inquiry. At least 20 independent counsels were appointed in the 1978–98 period, with Kenneth Starr being the best known.

When Independent Counsel Lawrence Walsh spent seven years investigating Reagan administration officials involved in the Iran-contra affair, it was Republicans who loudly howled about the abuse, expense, waste, and injustice of this new check on presidents. Later, of course, Democrats complained just as bitterly of what they felt were Kenneth Starr's overly partisan and entrapment methods of investigating Clinton's private life. It is in part a question of which party's ox is being gored.

Independent Counsel Kenneth Starr holds up a copy of his report while testifying before the House Judiciary Committee impeachment hearing.

Critics repeatedly urged the repeal of the Independent Counsel Act because of overzealous prosecution. "The independent counsel statute is too flawed, and its out-of-control investigative process has become too politicized." It is a legally sanctioned witch hunt, and it has cost both the government and public servants a lot of money with little good to show for it.*

Many Republicans and Democrats agree the independent counsel provisions should be limited to presidents and cabinet-level officials, and also limited to crimes committed in national office. The whole process should have some reasonable time limit, such as a one-year duration. Former Watergate special prosecutor Archibald Cox concludes: "Independent counsels must see their function not as pursuit of a target to be wounded or destroyed, but as an impartial inquiry with as much concern for public exoneration of the innocent as for indictment of the guilty."**

Source: CBS News-*New York Times* Poll, April 1996.

*Walter Shapiro, "Special Council Is No Answer for What's Wrong with Politics," *U.S.A. Today*, December 3, 1997, p. 10A. See also Kathleen M. Sullivan, "Have Independent Counsels Gone Too Far?" *Public Affairs Report*, July 1998, pp. 10–11.

**Archibald Cox, "Curbing Special Counsels," *The New York Times*, December 12, 1996, p. A21.

want to be effective in implementing policy changes know they face a number of constraints. Besides the formal system of checks and balances, which includes impeachment, effective presidents learn to deal with a media that today plays a feisty watchdog role, with judicial investigations, and with various international pressures. Presidents are, of course, also shaped by their times, by the ideological leanings of the people, and by the successes and failures of their immediate predecessors.[43]

A Watchdog Media as a Constraint

Ronald Reagan once walked away from one of his news conferences and, turning to an aide, blasted the reporters, not realizing a microphone was picking up every word. John F. Kennedy canceled more than 50 White House subscriptions to the *New York Herald Tribune* because he was furious about the way the paper treated

You Decide . . .

Should a president be sued?

In May 1994, Paula Jones brought sexual harassment charges against President Bill Clinton and a former Arkansas state trooper for a 1991 incident she alleges occurred in an Arkansas hotel room when Clinton was governor of Arkansas and she was a state employee. No one had ever before filed a civil suit against a sitting president involving his private behavior.

Clinton denied the charges and hired a lawyer, who asked a federal judge in Arkansas to postpone the suit until the end of Clinton's presidency. He especially asked the court to rule on whether presidents are immune from having to answer civil suits during their tenure. This case was heard by the Supreme Court in 1997. The Supreme Court, in a unanimous 9 to 0 vote, ruled that a sitting president can indeed be sued for actions that fall outside the scope of presidential duties. The Court rejected Clinton's and his lawyer's request to delay proceeding in the sexual harassment civil suit. The Court ruled that neither the U.S. Constitution nor public policy justified delaying pretrial proceedings and a trial until after Clinton left office, but made no reference to the validity of the charges.

Do you think the public interest was served by permitting the president to be sued?

SOURCE: *The New York Times*, January 12, 1997, p. 11.

his administration. Bill Clinton complained about "gotcha journalism." All recent presidents complain that the modern media misrepresent them and disproportionately report bad news.

Enjoying enormous First Amendment rights in this country, reporters usually go about their business of analyzing and criticizing presidents with gusto. Scores of media representatives are stationed at the White House, and they travel everywhere the president goes, reporting on every move.

Presidents, of course, want all their initiatives publicized and praised as much as possible. But media people believe they should provide a context in which presidential statements can be understood; hence they not only tell people what a president says, but often try to explain what the statement means. This type of interpretation is offered primarily by columnists, editorial writers, cable television commentators, and talk radio hosts. Those who manage newspapers and radio and television stations try to balance their coverage of what presidents say—especially in presidential speeches—with an equal amount of time for spokespersons of the opposition party or persons who hold different points of view. In recent years this kind of *adversarial* media coverage has often left the impression that a president's influence is more divisive than unifying.

What have presidents done about this? Typically, they have been patient and respected the criticism as essential in a democracy. However, presidents and their aides engage in extensive public relations efforts aimed at winning admiration and support for the president and White House policies.[44] Out-of-town editors are invited in for special briefings, and extra effort is made to get the president out of Washington for meetings with local and regional media representatives, who are generally viewed as less critical than Washington-based media. White House media experts devise ways to get the president's point of view out to the public, to get the president on prime-time television, or to arrange for flattering photo opportunities.

The modern media are indeed a formidable adversary of the modern presidency. But the presidency is not being brutally wounded, and its capacity for leadership is seldom sapped because of aggressive media coverage. Defenders of the press like to quote Thomas Jefferson, who, although angered by the press when he was president, said: "Were it left to me to decide whether we should have a government without newspapers or newspapers without a government, I should not hesitate to prefer the latter."

No matter who is in the White House, presidents and the media will be in conflict. This ongoing struggle is inherent in a constitutional democracy. Exposés of the campaign-contribution scandals and the Monica Lewinsky affair fortified the media through their important role in bringing these events to public attention. Further, because the media—especially television—are viewed as more trustworthy and believable than some other national institutions, most Americans, most of the time, believe what they hear and see on television. But the resources of the White House and the amount of free media coverage given presidents—especially communicators like Franklin Roosevelt, John Kennedy, and Ronald Reagan—provide an effective counterpoint to the media.

Impeachment and Removal: The Ultimate Constraint

The ultimate constraint on presidents is removal from office through the impeachment process provided in the U.S. Constitution. Article II, Section 4, gives Congress power to remove from office the president, vice-president, federal judges, and other top officials upon impeachment for and conviction of "Treason, bribery, or other high crimes and misdemeanors." The House functions as a grand jury and is governed by a majority vote principle. The Senate acts like a trial jury in a criminal case, with conviction and removal from office determined by a two-thirds vote of senators present.

Including Presidents Andrew Johnson in 1868 and Bill Clinton in 1998, only 14 national officials have been impeached by the House of Representatives. Of these, 12 were tried in the Senate. Only four were convicted. President Richard Nixon resigned in 1974 before he would most likely have been impeached.

Some observers have argued that an official can be impeached and removed only on criminal charges or on offenses that would be indictable in a criminal court. Most scholars contend, however, that the construction of "High Crimes and Misdemeanors" is not limited to offenses under ordinary criminal law.

The framers of the Constitution placed the power of impeachment, not in the hands of some unaccountable persons, but in the most politically responsive body of government—the House of Representatives. Because electing a president to office is a political act, so too is removing a president from office a political act. The checks and balances built into the Constitution made it very difficult to overthrow the results of an election.

Impeachment of a president is fraught with emotion and often strident partisanship. It can be time consuming and highly traumatic. But its very existence and its use against three presidents, in one form or another, make it a constant reminder for presidents that their power must be exercised in an accountable manner—and that Congress is the final judge of what is acceptable behavior.

International Checks and Realities

The task facing American leaders as the nation enters the twenty-first century is to recognize that broad trends are under way on a global scale, and that there is a need for presidents and leaders to cooperate with and persuade allies, and they must have the ability to win the support of leaders elsewhere as well.[45]

Increasingly, our problems are international in scope and rarely can be solved by one nation acting alone. Environmental matters, terrorism, drugs, trade—all demand multilateral agreement and collaboration. In this post–cold war era, presidents are challenged by these realities. It is increasingly clear that the international system, especially the international economy, is stronger than any president or prime minister.

Presidents today are forced to deal with a much stronger European Union and with a world in which nuclear proliferation is inevitable. Multilateral action usually makes far more sense than unilateral action. Presidents have to secure not only the support of Congress and the American people; they must also win the cooperation of foreign nations. Bill Clinton had to overcome resistance among the NATO members to continue weapons inspections and the embargo against Iraq.

Most other nations long ago learned that to succeed in an international system requires understanding other nations as well as one's own. Current and future presidents will have to be even better prepared than in the past to take global needs, aspirations, and politics into account.

The Vice-Presidency

Although the vice-presidency is now a part of the presidential establishment, it has not been so for long. Most vice-presidents served mainly as president of the Senate. Up to the 1950s, the vice-president was at best a "fifth wheel" and at worst a political rival who sometimes connived against the president. The office was often dismissed as a joke. One reason for the vice-president's posture as an outsider was that presidential nominees prior to Bill Clinton usually chose running mates who were geographically, ideologically, demographically, and in

Thinking it Through . . .

Defenders of the presidency, not necessarily supporters of Clinton, said the presidency must be immune from civil lawsuits such as this—at least while they are serving as president. Otherwise, presidents cannot properly perform their decidedly full-time job.

Defenders of Paula Jones obviously saw it differently. One of her attorneys asked, "Do we have a nation of kings or a nation where there are truly public servants? Or do we have a nation where people are accountable for their own personal, private conduct, or where some, because of their positions of power, aren't accountable?"

People who believe a president should be immune from civil suits contend a president's responsibilities are unique, and therefore a president should be protected from distractions such as civil lawsuits until he or she leaves the White House. If a president were subject to such suits, it could lead to a flood of frivolous lawsuits that would distract the president from effectively conducting the nation's business.

Clinton, of course, was sued, and his deposition in the Paula Jones case later led to his impeachment. Some scholars believe it was unwise to let this type of suit be conducted during a president's term in office, and after the year-long turmoil of the Lewinsky affair, many people agreed. But it is still a highly debatable matter.

Vice-president Al Gore worked closely with President Clinton and was groomed to step into the presidency in 2000.

other ways likely to "balance the ticket." Clinton ignored that tradition and picked another white, male, progressive southerner who has been not only a like-minded partner to Clinton but has assumed increased responsibility for presidential policy.

Today the vice-presidency brings both advantages and liabilities to a person who aspires to the presidency. The job surely provides exposure to the issues and to the office, but it is sometimes hard to appear "presidential" while at the same time avoiding the appearance of being disloyal to or upstaging the president.

Ideally, a vice-president performs several tasks in addition to the ceremonial function of acting as president of the Senate. A vice-president gets to cast the tie-breaking vote if the Senate has a tie vote, but this situation usually occurs less than once a year. The vice-president is also a member of the National Security Council.

The real test of the role of vice-president is whether he or she is fully integrated into the decision-making process in the White House. All vice-presidents are "back-up equipment" in case something happens to the president. They can head up any number of councils, visit any number of countries, and still not be much involved in the day-to-day operations of the presidency. President Jimmy Carter included Walter Mondale in the daily processes of decision making in the White House; President Reagan sometimes included George Bush in a similar way; President Clinton used Al Gore as an important adviser and confidant on domestic as well as foreign policy matters and key appointments. Al Gore headed a national review of the federal bureaucracy for President Clinton, a temporary yet highly visible presidential assignment.[46] He also spearheaded various "information superhighway" initiatives for Clinton.

The vice-presidency has been significantly affected by two constitutional amendments. The Twenty-second Amendment, ratified in 1951, imposes a two-term limit on presidents; consequently, vice-presidents have a better chance of moving up to the Oval Office. The Twenty-fifth Amendment, ratified in 1967, confirms the practice of making the vice-president not an acting president, but president, in the event of the death of a president. Also of significance, this amendment outlines a procedure to determine whether an incumbent president is unable to discharge the powers and duties of the office and establishes procedures to fill a vacancy in the vice-presidency.[47] For a few hours in 1985, George Bush became the first "acting president" when President Reagan underwent a minor cancer operation.

The amendment also provides that in the event of a vacancy in the office of vice-president, the president nominates a vice-president, who takes office upon confirmation by a majority vote of both houses of Congress. This procedure generally ensures the appointment of a vice-president in whom the president has confidence. Thus vice-presidents who have to take over the presidency can be expected to reflect most of their predecessor's policies.

Although the sort of tensions between president and vice-president that existed in the past did not plague Clinton and Gore, common tension between a president and a vice-president is natural. After all, except for the vice-president, everybody who works closely with a president can be fired. It is almost certain that vice-presidents will continue to have an undefined ad hoc set of assignments, subject more to the good will and mood of the president than to any fixed description.[48]

Presidential Leadership in a Constitutional Democracy

James Madison warned that our country could never trust "parchment barriers" to halt the encroaching abuse of power. In the end, constitutions survive only if they embody the spirit, values, and deeply held civic beliefs of the people. As the poet Walt Whitman reminded us, tyranny is always a possibility—if the people lose their supreme confidence in themselves and their spirit of defiance. Tyranny may always enter; there is no bar or charm against it. The only bar against it is a large, resolute breed of citizens.

The most compelling restraint on presidential power is the opinion of the American people. Citizens have more power than they realize. Presidents listen when citizens are "sending a message." Citizens can also "vote" between elections in innumerable ways—by changing parties, by organizing protests, by voting for the opposition party in off-year elections, by voting in state referenda, and by protests.

Ultimately, there is, of course, no foolproof way to guarantee our presidents will possess the leadership skills and moral character the job requires. America has had several great presidents, yet we have also had several flawed and ineffective presidents. The presidency is a unique, necessary yet always potentially dangerous institution. Thus James Madison's advice remains useful: "A dependence on the people is, no doubt, the primary control of the government; but experience has taught mankind the necessity of auxiliary precautions" (see *The Federalist*, No. 51, in the Appendix). Americans must maintain the effectiveness of these "auxiliary precautions"—Congress, political parties, the courts, the press, the Bill of Rights, and concerned citizens' groups—to ensure a properly balanced and constitutional presidency.

online POLITICS

Protesting Via the Internet

On February 8, 1996, President Clinton signed the Telecommunications Reform Bill, which was seen by many as imposing too many constraints on the Internet. Online protests were organized by the Center for Democracy and Technology (**http://www.cdt.org**), along with the Voters Telecommunications Watch (**http://www.vtw.org**), and the Citizens Internet Empowerment Coalition (**http://www.ciec.org**). To highlight their opposition, they organized an Internet blackout. The protest was supported by thousands of Web pages, including major sites like Yahoo, Netscape, Infoseek, Webcrawler, Surfwatch Software, and the home pages of Senator Patrick Leahy (D.-Vt.) and Congressman Jerrold Nadler (D.-N.Y.). Surfing the net today, you will find a campaign program to support free speech online, as promoted by the Libertarians' Blue Ribbon Campaign:

http://www.eff.org/blueribbon.html

Using the Internet to protest an action by President Clinton is somewhat ironic, because he has been an outspoken advocate of connecting schools to the Internet and has made use of the Web for White House communications. If you want to send a message to the White House, visit its home page at:

http://www.whitehouse.gov

This website also provides the text of presidential speeches, copies of news releases, current events at the White House, information regarding the federal government, and White House tours.

The vice-president and various departments of the executive branch also maintain home pages; if you need information relating to the State Department, Treasury Department, or the Bureau of Land Management, just search out their home pages.

For more Internet resources on The Presidency, see our home page at:

http://www.prenhall.com/burns

SUMMARY

1. The framers created a presidency with limited powers. To enact government business, the president must cooperate with Congress, but powers are divided among the branches, and the politics of shared power has often been stormy. In general, however, the role and influence of presidents have increased in the course of the nation's history.
2. The expansion of presidential influence has been a continual development during the past several decades. Crises, both foreign and economic, have enlarged these powers. When there is a need for decisive action, presidents are asked to supply it. Congress, of course, is traditionally expected to share in the formulation of national policy. Yet Congress is often so fragmented that it has been a willing partner in the growth of the presidency. At the same time, Congress is constantly setting boundaries on how far presidents can extend their influence. Every president must learn anew the need to work closely with the members of Congress.
3. Presidents must act as crisis-managing, morale-building, personnel-recruiting, priority-setting, coalition-building, and managerial leaders. No president can divide the job into tidy compartments. Ultimately, these responsibilities overlap.
4. Presidents use their persuasive power in dealing with Congress. They generally exercise more leadership in foreign and national security policy than does Congress, and generally, though not always, Congress is more supportive of presidential requests in these areas.
5. Several factors can cause conflict in our system of divided government. Among them are constitutional ambiguities, different constituencies, varying terms of office, divided party control of the different branches, weak political parties, and fluctuating public support for Congress or the president. The separation of powers and necessity of shared decision making, especially in foreign affairs, produce a creative tension between the White House and Congress. Both presidents and Congress have occasionally overstepped their roles in recent years; the process is never neat and tidy; complete accord is only sometimes achieved. Yet the two branches do cooperate, and somehow the business of government does get done.
6. Constraints on presidential power have included the media, with its watchdog role, independent counsel investigations, impeachment, and various international pressures.
7. The vice-presidency is now a part of the presidential establishment, and most vice-presidents have been increasingly integrated into the White House decision-making process.

KEY TERMS

divided government 358
Executive Office of the President 368
Office of Management and Budget 368
cabinet 368
item veto 373
pork-barrel legislation 373
rider 373
honeymoon 375

FURTHER READING

David Gray Adler and Larry N. George, eds., *The Constitution and the Conduct of American Foreign Policy: Essays on Law and History* (University Press of Kansas, 1996).

James David Barber, *The Presidential Character*, 4th ed. (Prentice Hall, 1992).

Jon R. Bond and Richard Fleisher, *The Presidents in the Legislative Arena* (University of Chicago Press, 1990).

Paul Brace and Barbara Hinckley, *Follow the Leader: Opinion Polls and the Modern Presidents* (Basic Books, 1992).

Thomas E. Cronin, ed., *Inventing the American Presidency* (University Press of Kansas, 1989).

Thomas E. Cronin and Michael Genovese, *The Paradoxes of the American Presidency* (Oxford University Press, 1998).

Terry Eastland, *Energy in the Executive* (Free Press, 1992).

Louis Fisher, *The Politics of Shared Power: Congress and the Executive*, 4th ed. (Texas A & M Press, 1998).

Louis Fisher, *Presidential War Power* (University Press of Kansas, 1995).

Alexander L. George and Juliette L. George, *Presidential Personality and Performance* (Westview Press, 1998).

Erwin C. Hargrove, *The President as Leader: Appealing to the Better Angels of Our Nature* (University Press of Kansas, 1998).

Charles O. Jones, *Passages to the Presidency, From Campaigning to Governing* (Brookings Institution, 1998).

Charles O. Jones, *The Presidency in a Separated System* (Brookings Institution, 1994).

LEONARD W. LEVY AND LOUIS FISHER, EDS., *Encyclopedia of the American Presidency* (Simon & Schuster, 1994).

JOHN A. MALTESE, *Spin Control: The White House Office of Communications and the Management of the Presidential News* (University of North Carolina Press, 1992).

SIDNEY M. MILKIS, *The President and the Parties: The Transformation of the American Party System Since the New Deal* (Oxford University Press, 1993).

SIDNEY M. MILKIS AND MICHAEL NELSON, *The American Presidency: Origins and Development, 1976–1998,* 3rd ed. (Congressional Quarterly Books, 1999).

MICHAEL NELSON, ED., *The Presidency and the Political System* (Congressional Quarterly Press, 1998).

RICHARD E. NEUSTADT, *Presidential Power and the Modern Presidents* (Free Press, 1991).

HUBERT S. PARMET, *George Bush: The Life of a Lone Star Yankee* (Scribner's, 1998).

MARK A. PETERSON, *Legislating Together: The White House and Capitol Hill from Eisenhower to Reagan* (Harvard University Press, 1990).

JAMES P. PFIFFNER, *The Strategic Presidency: Hitting the Ground Running,* 2d ed. (University Press of Kansas, 1996).

GLENN A. PHELPS, *George Washington and American Constitutionalism* (University Press of Kansas, 1993).

LYN RAGSDALE, *Vital Statistics on the Presidency,* rev. ed. (Congressional Quarterly Press, 1998).

STANLEY A. RENSHON, *The Psychological Assessment of Presidential Candidates* (New York University Press, 1996).

ALLEN SCHICK, *The Federal Budget: Politics, Policy, Process* (Brookings Institution, 1995).

ARTHUR M. SCHLESINGER, JR., *The Imperial Presidency* (Houghton Mifflin, 1973).

ROBERT J. SPITZER, *The President and Congress: Executive Hegemony at the Crossroads of American Government* (McGraw-Hill, 1993).

SHELLEY LYNNE TOMKINS, *Inside OMB: Politics and Process in the President's Budget Office* (M. E. Sharpe, 1998).

KENNETH T. WALSH, *Feeding the Beast: The White House Versus the Press* (Random House, 1996).

SHIRLEY ANNE WARSHAW, *Powersharing: White House-Cabinet Relations in the Modern Presidency* (State University of New York Press, 1996).

THE
JUDICIA
THE
BALANC
BRANCH

16

FOREIGN VISITORS ARE OFTEN AMAZED AT THE POWER AMERICANS GIVE THEIR JUDGES. IN 1834, AFTER HIS VISIT TO THE UNITED STATES, FRENCH ARISTOCRAT ALEXIS de Tocqueville wrote: "If I were asked where I place the American aristocracy, I should reply without hesitation . . . that it occupies the judicial bench and bar. . . . Scarcely any political question arises in the United States that is not resolved, sooner or later, into a judicial question."[1] A century later the British political scientist Harold J. Laski observed, "The respect in which federal courts and, above all, the Supreme Court are held is hardly surpassed by the influence they exert on the life of the United States."[2]

Why do judges play such a central role in our political life? In 1803 Chief Justice John Marshall successfully claimed for judges the power of judicial review, that is, the power to interpret the Constitution authoritatively. Only a constitutional amendment or a later Supreme Court can modify the Court's doctrine. Justice Felix Frankfurter put it tersely: "The Supreme Court is the Constitution."

Judges—and not just those on the Supreme Court—resolve disputes involving millions of dollars, decide conflicts among interests, supervise the criminal justice system, and make rules that affect the lives of millions of people. They are not only resolvers of legal conflicts, but they have, in effect, become managers of schools, prisons, mental hospitals, and complex businesses.[3] Sometimes, in fact, they decide the details of how these institutions should be run. Still, the scope and nature of judicial power limit the role of our judges.

CHAPTER OUTLINE

- The Scope of Judicial Power
- Federal Justice
- Prosecution and Defense
- The Politics of Judicial Selection
- How the Supreme Court Operates
- Judicial Power in a Constitutional Democracy

THE SCOPE OF JUDICIAL POWER

The American judicial process rests on an **adversary system**. A court of law is a neutral arena in which two parties argue their differences and present their points of view before an impartial arbiter. The adversary system, or *fight theory*, may or may not be adequate to arrive at the truth, but it is the basis of our judicial system. The logic of the adversary system imposes formal restraints on the scope of judicial power, and its rhetoric leads us to conceive the role of the judge in a special way.

Judicial power is essentially *passive*. Judges cannot reach out and instigate a case. Furthermore, not all disputes are within the scope of judicial power. Judges decide only **justiciable disputes**—those that grow out of actual cases and are capable of settlement by legal methods. Judges are not supposed to use their power unless there is a real case or controversy. "It was never thought that . . . a party beaten in the legislature could transfer to the courts an inquiry as to the constitutionality of a legislative act."[4] In addition, litigants must have *standing to sue*; that is, they must have sustained or be in immediate danger of sustaining a direct and substantial injury. It is not enough merely to have a general interest in a subject or to believe that a law is unconstitutional.[5]

Of increasing importance in recent years are **class action suits** in which a small number of persons are allowed to represent all other persons similarly situated—a suit on behalf of all students in a university, for example, or all patients in a hospital, or all persons who bought a particular model of an automobile. "Would-be class action litigants must show that they are proper representatives for the class of persons they seek to champion, that the types of issues they wish to raise are common to the class, and they must be able to demonstrate how a remedy can be formed that will meet the needs of the class."[6]

Not all constitutional disputes can be resolved by the courts. Some raise **political questions**, which require knowledge of a nonlegal character, or the use of techniques not suitable for a court, or are explicitly assigned by the Constitution to Congress or the president. Which of two competing state governments is the proper one? What does the Constitution mean when it provides that the national government should guarantee to each state a republican form of state government? Which group of officials of a foreign nation should the United States recognize as the government of that nation?[7] These are all political questions.

adversary system
A judicial system in which a court of law is a neutral arena where two parties argue their differences.

justiciable dispute
A dispute that grows out of an actual case and is capable of settlement by legal methods.

class action suit
Lawsuit brought by an individual or a group of people on behalf of all those similarly situated.

political question
A dispute that requires knowledge of a nonlegal character, or the use of techniques not suitable for a court, or explicitly assigned by the Constitution to Congress or the president; judges refuse to answer constitutional questions that they declare are political.

stare decisis
The rule of precedent, whereby a rule or law contained in a judicial decision is commonly viewed as binding on judges whenever the same question is presented.

appellate jurisdiction
The authority of a court to review a decision of a lower court.

Do Judges Make Law?

"Do judges make law? Course they do. Made some myself," remarked Jeremiah Smith, judge of the New Hampshire Supreme Court.[8] Most judges are less candid. Judges obviously make law, but to admit it is somehow disturbing. Such statements do not conform to our notions of what a judge should do.

Why do we think judges should not make law? Many people equate a judge's role with that of a referee in a prizefight. We expect referees to be impartial and disinterested, to treat both parties as equals. We expect them to apply rules, not make them.

Laws are not made, however, in the same way as the rules of a sport, and herein lies the answer to our question. Not only do judges make law, but also they *must*. Legislatures make law by enacting statutes, but judges apply the statutes to concrete situations. Statutes are drawn in broad terms: drivers shall act with "reasonable care"; no one may make "excessive noise" in the vicinity of a hospital; employers must maintain "safe working conditions." Such broad terms must be used because legislators cannot know exactly what will happen in the future.

These problems are intensified when judges are asked—as American judges are—to apply the Constitution, which was written more than 200 years ago. The Constitution is full of generalizations: "due process of law," "equal protection of the laws," "unreasonable searches and seizures," "Commerce . . . among the several States." Recourse to the intent of the framers or to the words of the Constitution is not likely to help judges faced with cases involving electronic wiretaps, multinational corporations, or birth control pills.

Adherence to Precedent

Just because judges make policy, however, does not mean they are free to make it as they wish. They are subject to a variety of limits on what they decide—some imposed by the political system of which they are a part, some by their own professional obligations as lawyers. Among these constraints is the rule of ***stare decisis***, the rule of precedent.

Stare decisis pervades our judicial system. Judges are expected to abide by all previous decisions of their own courts and all rulings of superior courts. Although adherence to precedent is normal, the doctrine of *stare decisis* is not nearly as restrictive as some people think.[9] The judge can distinguish precedents because of differences in context. In addition, many areas of law have conflicting precedents, one of which can be chosen to support a decision for either party.

The doctrine of *stare decisis* is even less controlling in the field of constitutional law. Because the Constitution itself, rather than any one interpretation of it, is binding, the Court can *reverse* a previous decision it no longer wishes to follow, as it has done dozens of times. Supreme Court justices are, therefore, not seriously restricted by *stare decisis.* As the first Justice John Marshall Harlan told a group of law students, "I want to say to you young gentlemen that if we don't like an act of Congress, we don't have too much trouble to find grounds for declaring it unconstitutional."[10] Since 1789 the Supreme Court has reversed more than 204 of its own decisions as well as overturned more than 1088 acts of Congress, more than 925 pieces of state legislation and state constitutional provisions, and more than 124 city ordinances.

FEDERAL JUSTICE

"The judicial Power of the United States," says Article III of the Constitution, "shall be vested in one supreme Court, and in such inferior Courts as the Congress may from time to time ordain and establish." Courts created to carry out this judicial power are called *Article III* or *constitutional courts.* Congress may also establish *Article I* or *legislative courts* to carry out the legislative powers the Constitution has granted to it. The main difference between a legislative and a constitutional court is that the judges of a legislative court need not be appointed to "hold their Offices during good Behavior" and may be assigned other than purely judicial duties, such as supervising tax collections and arbitrating disputes.

The Constitution requires a Supreme Court. It is a necessity if the national government is to have the power to frame and enforce laws that take precedence over those of the states. The lack of such an agency to maintain national supremacy, to ensure uniform interpretation of national legislation, and to resolve conflicts among the states was one of the glaring deficiencies of the central government under the Articles of Confederation.

Congress decides whether there will be other courts in addition to the Supreme Court ordained by the Constitution. The Constitution also allows Congress to determine the size of the Supreme Court. The First Congress divided the nation into districts and created lower courts for each district. That decision, though often supplemented, has never been seriously questioned.

Federal Courts of General Jurisdiction

Today the hierarchy of national courts of general jurisdiction consists of district courts, courts of appeals, and one Supreme Court (see Figure 16-1).

In all cases affecting ambassadors, other public ministers, and consuls, and in cases in which a state is a party, the Supreme Court has original jurisdiction. In all other cases arising under the judicial power of the United States, the Supreme Court has **appellate jurisdiction**—power to review decisions of other courts—except when Congress determines otherwise.

Types of Courts

Examples of Special Article III (Constitutional) Courts

In addition to courts of general jurisdiction, Congress has created constitutional courts with special jurisdiction:

United States Court of International Trade (formerly U.S. Customs Court)

Consists of nine judges who review rulings of customs collectors and conflicts arising under various tariff and trade laws.

United States Court of Appeals for the Federal Circuit

Consists of 12 judges who sit in panels of three to hear appeals of cases from all federal courts relating to patents and review decisions of the Patent Office and of the Court of International Trade.

Foreign Intelligence Surveillance Court

Composed of seven district court judges appointed by the chief justice. They serve on a regular rotation and meet in secret to hear requests from the Department of Justice acting on behalf of the National Security Agency, the Federal Bureau of Investigation, and other intelligence agencies that engage in electronic surveillance and physical searches of the homes and offices of foreign agents.

Examples of Article I (Legislative) Courts

United States Court of Claims

Consists of 16 judges appointed for 15-year terms who have jurisdiction over all property and contract damage suits against the United States.

United States Court of Appeals for the Armed Forces

Consists of five civilian judges appointed for 15 years each by the president with the consent of the Senate. This court, created by Congress under its grant of authority to make the rules and regulations for "land and naval forces," applies military law, which is separate from the body of law that governs the rest of the federal court system.

Bankruptcy Judges

Almost 300 judges appointed by the courts of appeals to serve as adjuncts to the federal district courts for terms of 14 years each. These judges handle bankruptcy matters subject to review by federal district judges.

United States Court of Veteran Appeals

Consists of two to six judges who hear appeals from certain administrative decisions of the Veterans Administration.

SOURCE: Lawrence Baum, "Specializing the Federal Courts: Neutral Reforms or Efforts to Shape Judicial Policy?" *Judicature*, December 1990/January 1991, pp. 217–24.

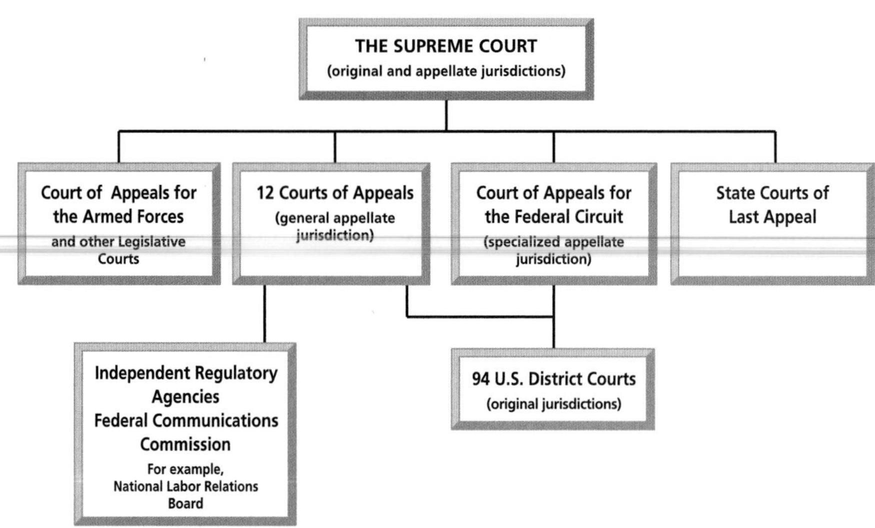

FIGURE 16-1 **The Structure of the Federal Courts**

Although the Supreme Court and its justices receive most of the attention, the workhorses of the federal judiciary are the district courts within the states, in the District of Columbia, and in the territories. Each state has at least one district court. Larger states have as many as the demands of judicial business and the pressure of politics require, although no state has more than four. There are 94 district courts in the 50 states, the District of Columbia, and the Commonwealth of Puerto Rico. Each has at least 2 judges but may have as many as 28. District judges normally sit separately and hold court by themselves, and most hold office for life.

District courts are the trial courts of **original jurisdiction**. They are the only federal courts that regularly employ **grand juries** (indicting) and **petit juries** (trial). Many cases tried before district judges involve citizens of different states, and the

original jurisdiction
The authority of a court to hear a case "in the first instance."

grand jury
A jury of 12 to 23 persons who, in private, hear evidence presented by the government to determine whether persons shall be required to stand trial. If the jury believes there is sufficient evidence that a crime was committed, it issues an indictment.

petit jury
A jury of 6 to 12 persons that determines guilt or innocence in a civil or criminal action.

magistrate judge
An official who performs a variety of limited judicial duties.

court of appeals
A court with appellate jurisdiction, which hears appeals from the decisions of lower courts.

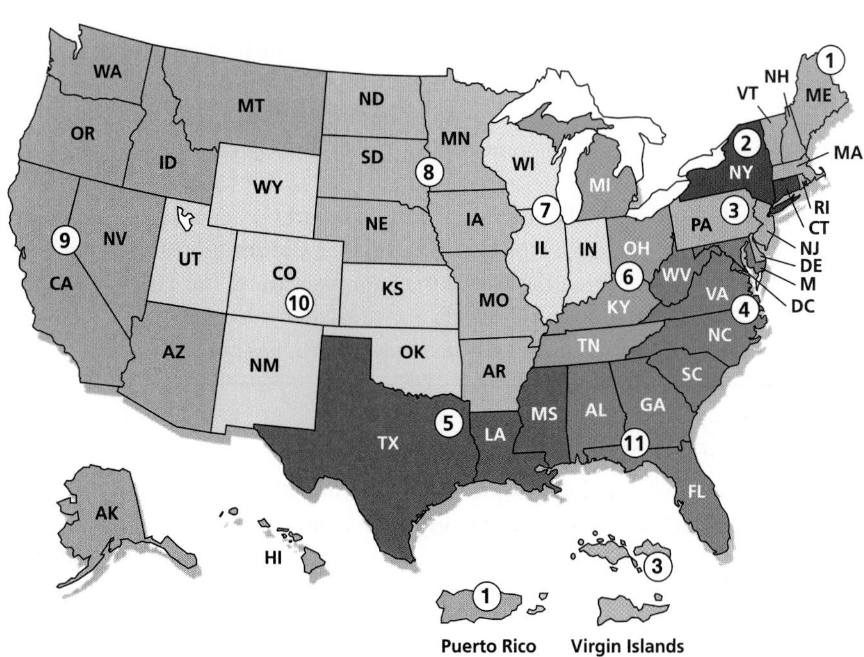

FIGURE 16-2 **The U.S. Court of Appeals**

Source: *The Federal Register.*

judges apply the appropriate state laws. Otherwise, district judges are concerned with federal laws. For example, they hear and decide cases involving crimes against the United States—suits under the national revenue, postal, patent, copyright, trademark, bankruptcy, and civil rights laws.[11]

District judges are assisted by clerks, bailiffs, stenographers, law clerks, court reporters, probation officers, and magistrate judges. All these officials are appointed by the judges. The 429 full-time and 76 part-time federal **magistrate judges** are becoming increasingly important.[12] After being screened by panels composed of residents of the judicial districts, full-time magistrates are appointed by the judges of the district court for eight-year renewable terms, part-time magistrates for four-year renewable terms.

Magistrates "look like a judge, act like a judge, and speak like a judge."[13] Magistrates, most of whom wear robes and since 1990 are called "Judge," issue warrants for arrest, hold hearings to determine whether arrested persons should be held for action by the grand jury, and, if so, set bail. They hear motions subject to varying kinds of review by their district judges. They preside over civil trials—jury and nonjury—with the consent of both parties, and over nonjury trials for petty offenses with the consent of the defendants.[14] Under the supervision of the district judge, and with the consent of the accused, they may preside over the selection of a jury for a felony trial.[15]

District judges are bound by the precedents of the appellate courts that review their decisions, but these judges have considerable discretion in applying these precedents. Except for the few cases that may be taken directly to the Supreme Court, a final decision of a district court is reviewable by a **court of appeals**. The United States is divided into 12 *judicial circuits*, one of which is the District of Columbia (see Figure 16-2). Each circuit has a court of appeals consisting of 6 to 28 permanent judgeships (179 in all). The Court of Appeals for the Federal Circuit has national jurisdiction. Each court of appeals normally hears cases in panels of three, but for especially important and controversial cases, all judges may be present; that is, they may sit *en banc*.

Courts of appeals have only appellate jurisdiction. These courts are powerful policy makers.[16] Less than 1 percent of the cases from these courts are looked at carefully by the Supreme Court. As the policy role of federal courts has become a prominent political issue, more attention is being focused on these courts and the judges who serve on them.[17]

The Ninth Circuit, the largest, consists of a Court of Appeals of 28 circuit judges and 99 district judges who serve in California, Arizona, Nevada, Oregon, Washington, Idaho, Montana, Alaska, and Hawaii. The Ninth's liberalism often brings it into conflict with the more conservative United States and California Supreme Courts. Republicans have been trying to split the Ninth, isolating California and possibly Nevada in one circuit and putting the other states in a new one, ostensibly because it is too large. But the battle is essentially over politics and public policy. Proponents of the change hoped it would "isolate and diminish the power of progressive judges" from California left in the Ninth.[18] Mining and oil interests from the Northwest hoped to remove judges from California, who tend to be rigorous on environmental issues.

Types of Law

Statutory Law

Law that comes from authoritative and specific lawmaking sources, primarily legislatures but also including treaties and executive orders.

Common Law

Judge-made law that originated in England in the twelfth century, when royal judges traveled around the country settling disputes in each locality according to prevailing custom. The common law continues to develop according to the rule of *stare decisis*, which means "let the decision stand." This is the rule of precedent, which implies that a rule established by a court is to be followed in all similar cases.

Equity Law

Law used whenever common law remedies are inadequate. For example, if an injury done to property may do irreparable harm for which money damages cannot provide compensation, under equity a person may ask the judge to issue an injunction ordering the offending person not to take the threatened action. If the wrongdoer persists, he or she may be punished for contempt of court.

Constitutional Law

Statements interpreting the United States Constitution that have been given Supreme Court approval.

Admiralty and Maritime Law

Law applicable to cases concerning shipping and waterway commerce on the high seas and on the navigable waters of the United States.

Administrative Law

Law relating to the authority and procedures of administrative agencies as well as to the rules and regulations issued by those agencies.

Criminal Law

Law that defines crimes against the public order and provides for punishment. Government is responsible for enforcing criminal law, the great body of which is enacted by states and enforced by state officials in state courts. The criminal caseload of federal judges is growing.

Civil Law

Law that governs the relations between individuals and defines their legal rights. However, the government can also be a party to a civil action. Under the Sherman Antitrust Act, for example, the federal government may initiate civil as well as criminal action to prevent violations of the law.

SURE JUSTICES LEGISLATE. THEY HAVE TO.

Linda Greenhouse

Judicial law making is not only routine, but necessary and beneficial as well.

Linda Greenhouse, a writer for *The New York Times*, argues that the Supreme Court constantly makes law. "By substantial majorities that cut across the ideological spectrum, the justices in the term that just ended essentially rewrote the law of sexual harassment in the workplace . . ." Interpreting a law that forbade sexual harassment, the Court went beyond what was specified in the law and held that "Employers could be held liable even for conduct they were not aware of, and for conduct that did not cause any tangible job-related harm to the victimized employee . . ." Greenhouse claims that the Court went even further beyond the specified dictates of the law by formulating regulations for compliance with the law. This judicial regulation was accomplished by the Court's assertion that "If there was no harm, an employer could establish an 'affirmative defense' against liability by having an effective anti-harassment policy in place, and by showing that the complaining employee unreasonably failed to invoke it."

Greenhouse maintains that this sort of judicial law making is not only routine, but necessary and beneficial as well. It "fills in all-important statutory gaps attributable to congressional neglect or, often, to deliberate omission in the face of political gridlock." In other words, when Congress writes a law in general terms, many questions arise about how it is to be implemented. The courts provide the service of filling in the information that Congress, due to politics or neglect, leaves out. Greenhouse agrees with University of Pennsylvania law professor Geoffrey C. Hazard, Jr., who maintains that "no institution other than the Supreme Court has both the credibility and the responsibility to fill in the blanks . . . What service would they really be performing for anyone if they talked at an equal level of generality?"★

Source: Linda Greenhouse, "Sure Justices Legislate. They Have To," *The New York Times*, July 5, 1998.

INJUDICIOUS JUDICIARY

Steve Forbes

In an article entitled "Injudicious Judiciary" Steve Forbes, publisher and presidential candidate, declares that "The Supreme Court in its last session continued a disturbing 30-year trend in American governance: usurping powers that properly belong to Congress." Forbes is even more disturbed by the tendency of Congress to accede to judicial initiative and contends that, even though the "founding fathers never intended unelected lifetime judges to act as legislators," the Supreme Court has become an unofficial permanent legislature.

Forbes rejects the idea that Congress needs the Court to fill in gaps in legislation. In some cases Congress intentionally writes broad, nonspecific laws to allow states and localities latitude in implementing them. In other situations, Congress is capable of filling the gaps in legislation itself, if it chooses to do so.

If judicial usurpation of congressional power is such a problem, Forbes asks, why doesn't Congress do something about it? The answer is that both state and national legislators are neglecting their duty. "Obsessed with staying in office for a lifetime, many of them are content to let the judiciary, not to mention independent regulatory agencies, take the heat for making difficult decisions. National, state and local legislators sat by, while judges administered schools and prisons, right down to the brand of toilet paper used."

For Forbes, it is time for Congress to accept its constitutional responsibility. "If they create a mess, they clean it up; that's their job." He is not optimistic, however, that Congress will rise to the challenge: "Alas, such restraint, in the face of an open invitation to seize more power, is asking too much of human nature." ★

SOURCE: Steve Forbes, "Injudicious Judiciary," *Forbes* 162, October 5, 1998, pp. 29–30.

The founding fathers never intended unelected lifetime judges to act as legislators.

For more information about this debate, go to **http://www.prenhall.com/burns** *and click on the Debate Icon in Chapter 16.*

Jurisdiction of the Federal Courts

Federal courts can hear and decide cases or controversies in law and equity if:

1. They arise under the Constitution, a federal law, or a treaty.
2. They arise under admiralty and maritime laws.
3. They arise because of a dispute involving land claimed under titles granted by two or more states.
4. The United States is a party to the case.
5. A state is a party to the case (but not if a suit was begun or prosecuted against a state by an individual or a foreign nation).
6. They are between citizens of different states. Congress has chosen to limit this *diversity jurisdiction* of federal courts, as it is called, to cases in which the amount in controversy exceeds $50,000.
7. They affect the accredited representatives of a foreign nation.

In 1997, after the Senate approved splitting the Ninth but the House of Representatives did not, it was agreed that the chief justice of the Supreme Court would select five commissioners to conduct a study of the federal courts of appeals with special attention to the Ninth Circuit.[19] The commission, headed by retired Justice Byron White, recommended that the circuit be kept intact but be divided into three geographical divisions, with northern and southern California in separate divisions. Another division would be formed to resolve any conflicts that might arise between the two California divisions. The White Commission also recommended that any circuit that exceeded 15 judges should be given the choice of creating divisions.[20] The commission also suggested that courts of appeals might be allowed to use two-judge panels to dispose of some cases instead of the traditional three-judge ones.[21]

Chief Justice William H. Rehnquist has endorsed the commission's report, and four Supreme Court justices have expressed the view that some kind of change is needed, including Justice Antonin Scalia, who noted that the Ninth circuit is the most frequently reversed circuit.[22] The matter is again before Congress, where there is still no consensus on what needs to be done, with some endorsing the commission's recommendation, some calling for a complete split and the creation of a new circuit, and some favoring the status quo.

The last circuit to be divided was the old Fifth Circuit in 1981. Texas, Louisiana, and Mississippi remained in the Fifth; Georgia, Florida, and Alabama became the Eleventh Circuit. This split was opposed by some of the more liberal judges who had presided over the abolition of public school segregation.

Some members of Congress have called for a term limit for members of the federal judiciary, perhaps for a nonrenewable term of 18 years. If adopted, this legislation would allow presidents to appoint one member every two years but would prevent any president, including one who served for two terms, to appoint a majority of the Supreme Court.[23]

State and Federal Courts

In addition to federal courts, each state maintains a judicial system of its own, and many large municipalities have judicial systems as complex as those of the states. State courts have sole jurisdiction to try all cases not within the judicial power the Constitution grants to the United States.

The federal and state court systems are related, but they do not exist in a superior-inferior relationship. Except for the limited **habeas corpus** jurisdiction of the district courts (the power to release persons from custody if the judge is not satisfied that the person is being constitutionally detained), the Supreme Court is the only federal court that may review state court decisions. And it may do so only under special conditions.

habeas corpus
Court order requiring explanation to a judge why a prisoner is held in custody.

Other than the original jurisdiction the Constitution vests directly in the Supreme Court, no federal court has any jurisdiction except that granted to it by an act of Congress. Congress also determines whether this judicial power of the United States will be exercised exclusively by federal courts or concurrently by both federal and state courts.

Prosecution and Defense

Federal Lawyers

Judges decide cases; they do not prosecute persons. On the federal level, the job of prosecution falls to the Department of Justice: the attorney general, the solicitor general, the 94 United States attorneys, and some 1,200 assistant attorneys. The president, with the consent of the Senate, appoints a United States attorney for each district court.

United States attorneys serve a four-year term but may be dismissed by the president at any time. These appointments are of great interest to senators, who exercise significant influence over the selection process. Because U.S. attorneys are almost always members of the president's political party, it is customary for them to resign if the opposition party wins the White House.

The attorney general, in consultation with the U.S. attorney in each district, appoints assistant attorneys. Some districts have only one; the largest, the Southern District of New York, has more than 65. These attorneys, working with the U.S. attorney and assisted by the Federal Bureau of Investigation and other federal law-enforcement agencies, begin proceedings against those alleged to have broken federal laws. They also represent the United States in civil suits.

Factors Constraining Federal Judges

- The Constitution
- Precedent (*stare decisis*)
- Statutory law
- Legal thought as found in books and law reviews
- Opinions of other courts
- Interest groups
- Public opinion
- Media opinion
- Views of colleagues
- Views of law clerks
- Contemporary events and general social environment
- Traditions of the law
- Actions of the legislature, past and future
- Actions of executives, past and future
- Limitations of time and staffing

Prosecutors and the Solicitor General

Prosecutors decide whether to charge an offense and which offense to charge. They have largely unreviewable discretion. "So long as the prosecutor has probable cause to believe that the accused committed an offense defined by statute, the decision whether or not to prosecute, and what charge to file or bring before a grand jury, generally rests entirely in his [or her] discretion."[24]

Prosecutors negotiate with the lawyers for **defendants** (those accused of an offense) and often work out a **plea bargain**, whereby defendants agree to plead guilty to a lesser offense to avoid having to stand trial for a more serious offense. Prosecutors make recommendations to judges about what sentences to impose.

Attorneys from the Department of Justice and from other federal agencies participate in well over half the cases on the Supreme Court's docket. Of special importance is the *solicitor general* (SG), who represents the government before the Supreme Court. (When the SG appears before the Supreme Court, he wears a formal dark vest, tails, and striped pants.) When the solicitor general petitions the Supreme Court and asks it to review an opinion of a lower court, the Court is likely to do so. "Overall, the government is involved in about two-thirds of all cases heard during a term, and the solicitor general's record of wins has been fairly consistent in the past decade. About 75 percent of all rulings go his way."[25] Moreover, no appeal may be taken in behalf of the United States to any appellate court without the approval of the solicitor general.[26]

The solicitor general (sometimes called the "Tenth Justice") has traditionally been given some measure of independence from the White House. In recent decades that independence has been reduced. The Reagan and Bush administrations used the SG to try to persuade the justices to limit affirmative action and to restrict the right of women to have abortions.[27] The Clinton administration continued in the activist manner, although on the opposite side on many issues.

A Department of Justice office that is becoming increasingly important is the *assistant attorney general*, who heads up the Office of Legal Counsel. The OLC is "the principal legal guardian in the executive branch of the constitutional prerogatives and powers of the presidency"[28] and works closely with the Office of the Counsel to the President on official matters.

Federal Defense Lawyers

The federal government provides lawyers for poor defendants in criminal trials. District courts have some discretion in how they provide this assistance. Most districts use the traditional system of assigning a private attorney. About half of the judicial districts, however, have opted to use the **public defender system**. Salaried public defenders operate under the general supervision of the Administrative Office of the United States Courts. The Judicial Conference of the United States has said the most important problem confronting the federal defender program is lack of money.[29] Congress is now reviewing the effectiveness of this system.

defendant
In a criminal action, the person or party accused of an offense.

plea bargain
Negotiations between a prosecutor and defendant aimed at getting the defendant to plead guilty for a lesser offense to avoid having to stand trial for a more serious offense.

public defender system
Arrangement whereby public officials are hired to provide legal assistance to those persons accused of crimes who are unable to hire their own attorneys.

The Tort Law Explosion

In recent decades, there has been a huge increase in *tort law*, that part of civil law covering the liability of those whose conduct injures others and the compensation they must pay.

"Throughout most of American history, liability law has been an obscure legal byway . . . with little discernible effect on the wider society or economy."* Today liability has dramatically expanded, and the targets are mainly manufacturers, physicians, hospitals, towns and counties, and their insurance carriers.

Judges have played a leading role in this liability revolution, to the praise of some who believe judges have provided protection for the weak against the powerful, to the criticism of others who believe judges have usurped legislative responsibilities and impaired the effectiveness of our economy.

*Walter Olson, "The Liability Revolution: New Directions in Liability Law," *Proceedings of the Academy of Political Science* 37, no. 1 (1988), p. 1.

The Legal Services Corporation (LSC) provides financial assistance to 323 organizations that furnish legal help to the poor in noncriminal legal matters.[30] The corporation is the center of controversy. There are those, primarily Republicans, who would like to abolish it. They have barred it from filing class action suits; from representing prisoners, illegal aliens, and people being evicted from public housing for alleged drug activity; from litigating abortion or redistricting issues; and from challenging the legality of state or federal welfare laws. These restrictions extended not just to the use of federal funds but also to the use by legal services organizations of nonfederal money raised from private or state sources. The Legal Services Corporation is thus restricted to suing landlords, employers, husbands, or wives in traditional legal battles.

On the other side are those, primarily Democrats, who would fund the Legal Services Corporation more fully and would allow it to use class action suits to challenge the status quo. Some legal aid lawyers and organizations have challenged the restrictions against class action as being unconstitutional.[31]

The LSC is governed by an 11-member board of directors appointed by the president with the advice and consent of the Senate. Hillary Rodham Clinton was chair of the Legal Services Corporation when her husband was governor of Arkansas.

The Politics of Judicial Selection

The selection of federal judges has always been part of the political process. It makes a difference who serves on the federal courts. It has always been so, but as the courts have come to play an even more important role in the political process, and as more and more interests—African Americans and women, for example—participate in that process, judicial selection politics has come front and center on the political stage.

The president selects federal judges with the advice and consent of the Senate. Political reality imposes constraints on the president's discretion, and the selection of a federal judge is actually a complex bargaining process. The principal figures involved are the candidates, the president, and the "subpresidency for judicial selection"[32] consisting of key members of the Department of Justice, United States senators, the American Bar Association, party leaders, and, increasingly, interest groups.

Recent presidents have inserted the White House much more directly into the process than did their predecessors. Department of Justice officials and key White House staff meet often to review proposed names.[33] Before the White House submits names of nominees for the federal district courts to the Senate, the president observes the practice of **senatorial courtesy**—the presidential custom of submitting the names of prospective appointees for approval to senators from the states in which the appointees are to work. Even a senator from the opposition party is usually consulted. If negotiations are deadlocked between the senators or between the senators and the Department of Justice, a seat may stay vacant for years.[34]

The custom of senatorial courtesy no longer applies to Supreme Court appointments and is not often applied to the selection of judges for the courts of appeals because these judges do not serve in any one senator's domain. This difference in selection politics means that district court judges often reflect values different from those of persons appointed to the courts of appeal or the Supreme Court.[35]

senatorial courtesy
Presidential custom of submitting the names of prospective appointees for approval to senators from the states in which the appointees are to work.

Liberal interest groups, such as People for the American Way and Alliance for Justice, as well as conservative groups, such as the Heritage Foundation and a coalition of 260 conservative organizations and 35 talk show hosts called the Judicial Selection Monitoring Project offer their views about candidates. These organizations used to wait until after the president had sent the name of a nominee to the Senate, but they are now active in the preliminaries, making known their views even before the names of nominees are released to the public or sent to the Senate Judiciary Committee.

The American Bar Association's Standing Committee on the Federal Judiciary plays a special role in evaluating candidates. Presidents are hesitant to submit for Senate confirmation a candidate rated "not qualified" by the ABA. In recent years, conservative groups have mounted an attack on the ABA's role, contending it reflects a liberal bias and gives low ratings to "sandbag conservative nominees." In response to this criticism, Senator Orrin Hatch, current chair of the Judiciary Committee, announced that the ABA committee no longer has any special status and no longer is part of the official process. However, since the ABA sends a letter to each senator on the Judiciary Committee indicating its rating of the candidates, this new policy creates a subtle difference, "but as a practical matter the effect is about the same."[36]

WE THE PEOPLE

Female and Minority Appointments to Federal Judgeships

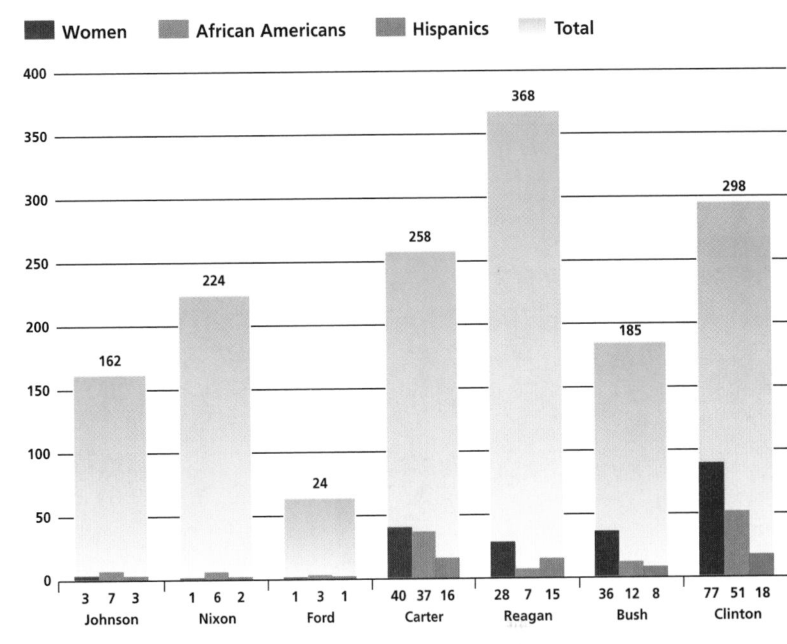

SOURCE: Sheldon Goldman and Elliott Slotnick, "Clinton's Second Term Judiciary: Selection under Fire," *Judicature*, May/June 1999.

Senate: Advice and Consent

The normal presumption is that the president should be allowed considerable discretion in the selection of federal judges. Despite this presumption, the Senate takes seriously its responsibility to confirm presidential nominations, especially when the party controlling the Senate is different from that of the president, as has often been the case in recent years.

Until recently, most judicial appointments, especially those for the lower federal courts, were processed without much controversy. However, "now that lower court judges are more commonly viewed as political actors, there is increasing Senate scrutiny of these nominees."[37]

The battle over judicial confirmations ordinarily takes place before the Senate Judiciary Committee. The Senate usually goes along with the recommendations of its Judiciary Committee without much debate, yet floor debates are not all that rare. Overall, the Senate has refused to confirm 29 of the 138 presidential nominations for Supreme Court justices.[38]

Prior to 1955, the common practice was for the Senate to look into candidates' qualifications and background but not examine them in person. More recently, the committee has felt free to ask judicial candidates a full range of questions in the glare of television cameras, since a candidate's political orientation is a major factor in determining how he or she will vote on the cases that come before the Court.

Except for Robert Bork, nominated by President Ronald Reagan in 1987, judicial nominees have steadfastly refused to answer questions when the answer might reveal how they would decide a case likely to come up to the Supreme Court. Judge Bork had written so many articles, made so many speeches, and decided so many cases that he thought he had to clarify his constitutional views. His candor may well

CONFIRMATION POLITICS

Examination of recent nomination battles highlights the interplay of party, race, gender, ideology, and judicial philosophy in the process of selecting and confirming a Supreme Court justice.

Robert Bork.

The Bork Battle

When Justice Lewis F. Powell, Jr., who had had the swing vote on such critical issues as affirmative action and abortion, announced his retirement as he neared 80 years of age at the end of the term in July 1987, President Reagan quickly nominated Judge Robert Bork, a member of the Court of Appeals for the District of Columbia and a noted jurist and legal scholar. Despite Bork's controversial writings on many current constitutional issues, his scholarly and legal qualifications made it appear initially that he would be confirmed. However, his nomination so offended women's and black organizations that they organized a campaign to block the Bork nomination. After almost four months of national debate, 12 days of acrimonious questioning by the members of the Senate Judiciary Committee, and 23 hours of debate on the Senate floor, the Senate voted 58 to 42 against Bork's confirmation.

David Souter.

The Souter Solution

The political bruises resulting from the Bork confirmation proceedings were traumatic. Political pundits speculated that in the future, presidents would seek noncontroversial candidates for the Supreme Court. This prediction came true in 1990 with George Bush's nominee to replace William J. Brennan, Jr., leader of the liberal bloc on the Supreme Court. President Bush chose David Souter, a member of the New Hampshire Supreme Court. Educated at Harvard and Oxford, he had written no law articles, made practically no speeches, and lived the secluded life of a sitting judge. When he appeared before the Judiciary Committee, Souter steadfastly refused to answer any questions that might reveal his orientation on abortion and privacy issues, to the frustration of the Senate Democrats. He was confirmed by an overwhelming vote. He became one of the more liberal judges.

Clarence Thomas.

The Thomas Tangle

When Justice Thurgood Marshall retired in 1991, President Bush sent to the Senate the name of a controversial jurist, Judge Clarence Thomas, then sitting on

have contributed to the Senate's rejection of him and is likely to scare off future nominees from responding to similar questions.

The Role of Party, Race, and Gender

Presidents so seldom nominate judges from the opposing party (around 90 percent of judicial appointments since the time of Franklin Roosevelt have gone to candidates from the president's party) that partisan considerations are taken for granted, and partisan affiliation is rarely mentioned (see Table 16-1). Today journalists pay more attention to other characteristics, such as race and gender.[39]

the Court of Appeals for the District of Columbia. Thomas was a conservative African American. Prior to his brief service on the Court of Appeals, he had served as chair of the Equal Employment Opportunity Commission (EEOC) and in the Office of Civil Rights. During five days of grueling questions about his constitutional views, Judge Thomas, as had his predecessor, refused to respond. The Senate Judiciary Committee narrowly recommended his confirmation.

Two days before the Senate was due to vote on his confirmation, documents leaked to the press revealed that a former associate of Judge Thomas, Anita Hill, had accused him of sexually harassing her when she worked for him in the Department of Education and the EEOC. Women's and liberal groups exploded in outrage. There followed three days of dramatic and emotion-charged hearings telecast to the nation in which Judge Thomas categorically denied the charges presented persuasively by his accuser. Panels of witnesses pro and con came forward to testify. Thomas was confirmed by the Senate 52 to 48, the closest Supreme Court confirmation vote in modern times.

Ruth Bader Ginsburg.

The Clinton Choices

Almost as soon as President Clinton took office, Justice Byron White announced he would leave the Court at the end of its 1992–93 term. It was clear that with this appointment, Clinton could arrest the Court's conservative drift and fulfill his campaign pledge to appoint justices committed to protect the right of privacy—that is, to preserve a woman's freedom to choose an abortion.

After several months of deliberation, including the embarrassingly public consideration of other candidates, President Clinton nominated Ruth Bader Ginsburg. Judge Ginsburg was a 13-year veteran of the Court of Appeals for the District of Columbia, to which she had been appointed by President Carter. On the Court of Appeals she had earned a reputation for fairness and moderation. She was readily confirmed by the Senate and took her seat for the opening of the 1993–94 term.

Clinton had a second opportunity when Harry A. Blackmun, at age 85, announced his intention to leave the Court during the spring of 1994. Blackmun, best known for writing the opinion in *Roe v Wade*, was thought at first to be a judicial conservative, but by the time of his retirement, he had become the most liberal member of the Court. President Clinton nominated Stephen G. Breyer, chief judge of the First Circuit, a noncontroversial judicial moderate. Justice Breyer, a graduate of Stanford University, Oxford, and Harvard Law School, served as Supreme Court law clerk for Justice Arthur Goldberg and was a member of the faculty at Harvard Law School before being appointed by President Carter as a Federal Appeals Court judge. After a cordial hearing before the Senate Judiciary Committee in July 1994, Breyer was easily confirmed by the Senate.

Stephen G. Breyer.

President Jimmy Carter, who had no opportunity to appoint anyone to the Supreme Court, selected more African Americans, Hispanics, and women for the lower federal courts than all other prior presidents combined—40 women, 37 African Americans, and 16 Hispanics. President Ronald Reagan, although the first to appoint a woman to the Supreme Court, appointed fewer minority members or women than did Carter, perhaps in part because fewer minorities and women could pass the Reagan administration's ideological screening.[40] Twenty percent of George Bush's appointees were women, 7 percent African Americans, and 4 percent Hispanics.[41]

TABLE 16-1 Party Affiliation of District and Appeals Judges Appointed by Presidents

President	Party	Appointees from Same Party
Roosevelt	Democrat	97%
Truman	Democrat	92
Eisenhower	Republican	95
Kennedy	Democrat	92
Johnson	Democrat	96
Nixon	Republican	93
Ford	Republican	81
Carter	Democrat	90
Reagan	Republican	94
Bush	Republican	89
Clinton	Democrat	88*

SOURCE: Sheldon Goldman, "Judicial Selection Under Clinton: A Midterm Examination," *Judicature*, May/June 1995, p. 280; Sheldon Goldman and Elliot Slotnick, "Clinton's Second Term Judiciary: Selection under Fire," *Judicature*, May/June 1999.

*Figures for President Clinton are for nominations to April 1999. Figures for other presidents are for confirmed appointments.

Bill Clinton promised to appoint federal judges who would be more representative of the ethnic makeup of the United States. "There will not be an ideological blood test, like there was during the Reagan and Bush years, to see if the candidate is a moderate or liberal," said a prominent Democratic member of the Senate Judiciary Committee, "but there will be an insistence upon diversity."[42] Clinton lived up to his pledge; almost one third of his appointees have been women or minorities.[43]

The Role of Ideology

Finding a party member is not enough; presidents want to pick the "right" kind of Republican or "our" kind of Democrat to serve as judge. By and large they have been able to achieve this goal. Republican judges picked by Republican presidents tend to be judicial conservatives (with the notable exception of President Dwight Eisenhower's nomination of Chief Justice Earl Warren); Democratic judges picked by Democratic presidents are more likely to be liberals. Both of these orientations have had to be tempered by the fact that judges had to go through a senatorial confirmation screen that, during the administrations of Reagan and Bush, and during most of Clinton's term in office, has been of the opposite persuasion from that of the White House.[44]

President Ronald Reagan's two terms made it possible for him to join Presidents Franklin D. Roosevelt and Dwight D. Eisenhower as the only presidents in modern times to appoint a majority of the federal bench. All told, Reagan appointed 368 lifetime judges. His administration acted carefully to nominate only those whose views about the role of the courts and constitutional issues were consistent with Reagan's own.[45] Not only were a large number of judicial conservatives appointed, but many of them—because they were comparatively young—will continue to have an effect on judicial policy well into the twenty-first century. But despite the care given to their selection, there is some evidence that the Reagan judges may not be that much more conservative than judges appointed by other presidents.[46]

As President Bush's commitment to conservatism was somewhat less well established than Reagan's, conservative organizations—the Heritage Foundation, the Pacific Legal Foundation, and the Federalist Society—focused their attention on Bush's judicial appointments. Bush appointed 148 district judges, 37 appellate judges, and 2 Supreme Court justices—David Souter and Clarence Thomas. His appointees were among the most conservative in recent history.[47] Their conservative constitutional views helped consolidate the Court's "turn to the right."[48]

President Clinton gave Democratic senators "clear guidelines about the kind of judges he wants."[49] But after the Republicans took control of the Senate in 1994, President Clinton instructed his "judge-pickers" to consult closely with Republican Senator Orrin Hatch, chair of the Senate Judiciary Committee, and Clinton dropped from consideration any candidates that were likely to "engender serious opposition."[50]

By the end of his first term, Clinton had nominated and the Senate had confirmed 198 judges and 2 justices of the Supreme Court.[51] At the start of his second term, Clinton was faced with nearly 100 judicial vacancies because the Republican-controlled Senate, hoping that a Republican would be in the White House after the 1996 election, confirmed only 17 district judges and, for the first time in 40 years, failed to confirm any judges for the courts of appeals.[52]

Even after President Clinton was reelected for his second term, the Senate continued to slow down confirmations to such an extent that Chief Justice Rehnquist, in his annual report on the federal judiciary, scolded the Senate for jeopardizing the ability of the federal judiciary to do its work. His message, plus criticism from newspaper editorials, seemed to have an effect. In the next year 65 judges were confirmed by the Senate. Despite the slowdown in Senate confirmations, by the time Clinton leaves office he will have picked more than 300 of the approximate total of 800 federal judges.[53]

The Role of Judicial Philosophy

What about a candidate's judicial philosophy? Does a candidate believe that judges should interpret the Constitution to reflect what the framers intended and what its words literally say; that is, Does the candidate believe in **judicial restraint**? Or does the candidate believe the Constitution should be adapted to reflect current conditions and philosophies; that is, Does the candidate believe in **judicial activism**?

Throughout most of our history, federal courts have been more conservative than Congress, the White House, or state legislatures. Prior to 1937, judicial self-restraint was the battle cry of liberals who objected to judges interpreting the due process clauses of the Fifth and Fourteenth Amendments to strike down many laws passed to protect labor and women and to keep the national and state governments from regulating the economy. These judges broadly construed the words of the Constitution to prevent what they thought to be unreasonable regulations of property.

By the time of Richard Nixon, Ronald Reagan, and George Bush, however, the judicial shoe was on the other foot, and it was conservatives who were advocates of judicial self-restraint. What is needed, they argued, are judges who will let Congress, the president, and the state legislatures regulate or forbid abortions, adopt prayers for public schools, impose capital punishment, or authorize police to engage in wiretapping.

It would be wrong to assume that judicial philosophy is nothing more than another way to argue about political ideology. Some conservatives, for example, favor judicial activism because they want current judges to reverse the last half-century of precedents and to protect property rights from government regulation. Some liberals favor judicial restraint because they believe democracy will flourish when judges stay out of policy debates. The debate over the Supreme Court's role today is less about activism and restraint than it is about competing conceptions of the proper balance between government authority and individual rights.

Judicial Longevity and Presidential Tenure

Ideology and judicial philosophy affect not only presidents' nominations for the federal courts but also when sitting judges choose to retire. Because federal judges serve for life, they may be able to schedule their retirement to allow a president whose views they approve to nominate their successors. Chief Justice Roger B. Taney stayed on the bench long after his health began to fail to prevent President Abraham Lincoln from nominating a Republican. In 1929 Chief Justice William Howard Taft wrote: "I am older and slower and less acute and more confused. However, as long as things continue as they are, and I am able to answer in my place, I must stay on the court in order to prevent the Bolsheviki [Herbert Hoover, a conservative Republican, was in the White House] from getting control."[54]

Although former Chief Justice Warren Burger denied that he retired in 1986 in order to permit President Ronald Reagan to replace him with a constitutional conservative, his retirement did give Reagan an opportunity to rejuvenate the conservative wing of the Court by promoting 61-year-old William H. Rehnquist. Reagan then picked another constitutional conservative, 50-year-old Antonin Scalia, to take the seat vacated by Rehnquist.[55] Liberal Supreme Court justices William J. Brennan, Jr., and Thurgood Marshall held onto their seats well into their 80s, and many assumed that they were doing so in the hope that they might be able to stay on the Court until

judicial restraint
Judicial philosophy proposing that judges should interpret the Constitution to reflect what the framers intended and what its words literally say.

judicial activism
Judicial philosophy proposing that judges should interpret the Constitution to reflect current conditions and values.

a president more congenial to their views might be in the White House. They did not make it, and their successors were appointed by Republican President Bush rather than by a Democrat.

Reforming the Selection Process?

The televised Bork and Thomas confirmation hearings aroused considerable criticism from both liberals and conservatives and created widespread complaints that "something is wrong with the process." Subsequently a group of experts recommended that an attempt be made to constrain the partisan politics surrounding the confirmation process for Supreme Court justices. They proposed that "Supreme Court nominees should no longer be expected to appear as witnesses during the Senate Judiciary Committee's hearings on their confirmation" and that the Senate should return to the practice of judging nominees on their written record and on the testimony of legal experts.[56] A bipartisan commission on judicial selection from the Miller Center of Public Affairs at the University of Virginia recommended that the increasingly prolonged time between nominations and confirmation be reduced.[57]

The politics of judicial selection may shock those who like to think judges are picked strictly on the basis of legal merit and without regard for party, race, gender, or ideology. But as a former Justice Department official has said, "When courts cease being an instrument for political change, then maybe the judges will stop being politically selected."[58] Moreover, as another scholar put it, "Supreme Court Justices have always been appointed for political reasons by politicians, and their confirmation process has always been dictated by politicians for political purposes." He concludes, "In fact, however, not despite the politicization of the appointment and confirmation process, but because of it, the Supreme Court has endured as a flexible, viable force in the American democracy for over 200 years."[59]

CHANGING THE NUMBERS One of the first actions of a political party after gaining control of the White House and Congress is to increase the number of federal judgeships. With divided government, however, when one party controls Congress and the other holds the White House, a stalemate is likely to occur, and relatively few new judicial positions will be created. During Andrew Johnson's administration, Congress went so far as to reduce the size of the Supreme Court to prevent the president from filling two vacancies. After Johnson left the White House, Congress returned the Court to its former size to permit Ulysses S. Grant to fill the vacancies.

In 1937, President Franklin Roosevelt proposed an increase in the size of the Supreme Court by one additional justice for every member of the Court over the age of 70, up to a total of 15 members. Ostensibly, the proposal was aimed at making the Court more efficient. In fact, Roosevelt and his advisers were frustrated because the Court had declared much New Deal legislation unconstitutional. Despite Roosevelt's popularity, his "court-packing scheme" aroused intense opposition. Roosevelt's proposals to change the Court's size failed. He lost the battle but won the war, as the Court began to sustain some important New Deal legislation.

CHANGING THE JURISDICTION Congressional control over the structure and jurisdiction of federal courts has been used to influence the course of judicial policy making. Although unable to get rid of Federalist judges by impeachment, the Jeffersonians abolished the circuit courts created by the Federalist Congress just prior to their losing control. In 1869 radical Republicans in Congress altered the Supreme Court's appellate jurisdiction in order to snatch from the Court a case it was about to review involving the constitutionality of some Reconstruction legislation.[60]

Each year a number of bills are introduced in Congress to eliminate the jurisdiction of federal courts over cases relating to abortion, school prayer, and school busing, or to eliminate the appellate jurisdiction of the Supreme Court over such matters. In the Clinton second term, some Republicans returned to an attack on federal judges to limit their power to review state constitutional initiatives, especially after federal judges slowed down the implementation of several constitutional initiatives passed by California voters, including Proposition 209 limiting the state's power to adopt affirmative action programs.

These attacks on federal court jurisdiction spark debate about whether the Constitution gives Congress authority to take such actions. Congress has not yet decided to make what could amount to a fundamental shift in the nature of the relationship between Congress and the Supreme Court. As one scholar concluded: "History suggests the public has seen such attempts for precisely what they are, as attacks on judicial independence, and such attacks have been resisted."[61]

How the Supreme Court Operates

Supreme Court justices are in session from the first Monday in October through the end of June. They listen to oral arguments for two weeks and then adjourn for two weeks to consider the cases and write their opinions. By agreement, six justices must participate in each decision. Cases are decided by a majority. In the event of a tie vote, the decision of the lower court is sustained, although, on rare occasions, the case may be reargued.

At 10:00 a.m. on the days when the Supreme Court sits, the eight associate justices and the chief justice, dressed in their robes (Chief Justice Rehnquist has four gold stripes on each sleeve of his robe)[62] file into the court (see Figure 16-3). As they take their seats—arranged according to seniority, with the chief justice in the center—the clerk of the Court introduces them as the "Honorable Chief Justice and Associate Justices of the Supreme Court of the United States." Those present in the courtroom, asked to stand when the justices enter, are seated, and counsel take their

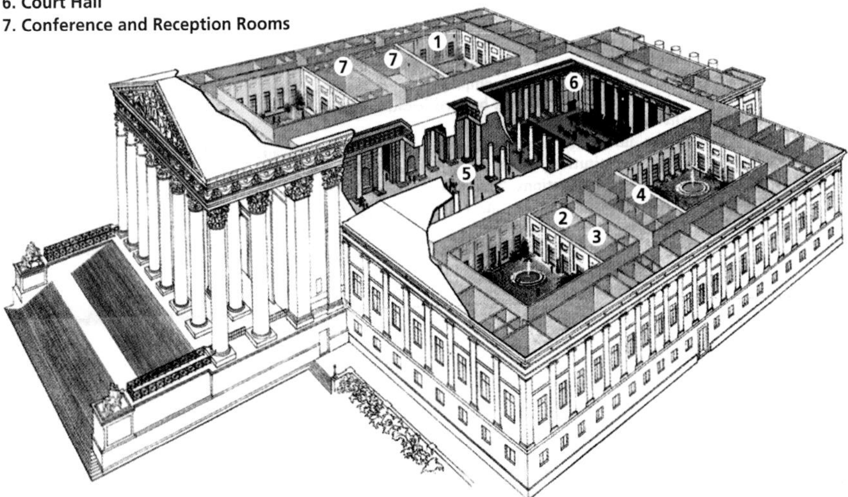

FIGURE 16-3 The Supreme Court Building

Don't Call Me Judge

A member of the United States Supreme Court is called "Justice," not "Judge," and the chief justice is the "Chief Justice of the United States," not the "Chief Justice of the Supreme Court." Members of the Court call him "The Chief," but nobody else should. In the years before Justice Sandra Day O'Connor was appointed to the Court, justices were often called "Mr. Justice" and were collectively known as "The Brethren." Nowadays "Justice" will do, and so will "Your Honor."

A member of the lower federal court is "Judge," not "Justice." The practice among the states varies, but members of state supreme courts are coming to be called "Justices."

SOURCE: David Margolick, "Here Comes the Chief Justice (Please Don't Call Him Judge)," *The New York Times*, April 26, 1991, p. B1.

places along tables in front of the bench. The attorneys for the Department of Justice, dressed in formal morning clothes, are at the right. The other attorneys are dressed conservatively; sport coats are not considered proper. Dress and ceremony are all part of the high ritual of the Court:

> The majesty of its courtroom; the black robes of the justices; the ritual of its proceedings at oral argument and on decision day; the secrecy and isolation of its decision-making conferences; the formal opinions invoking the symbols of Constitution, precedent, and framers' intent; and all the other elements of setting and conduct distinguish the Supreme Court, a body of constitutional guardians, from all other government officials.[63]

Which Cases Reach the Supreme Court?

When citizens vow they will take their cases to the highest court of the land even if it costs their last penny, they underestimate the difficulty of securing Supreme Court review, overestimate the cost (although it costs plenty), and reveal a basic misunderstanding of the Court's role. The rules for appealing a case to the Supreme Court are established by act of Congress. Until 1988 there were a few types of cases the Supreme Court was obliged by law to review. Today, however, almost all appellate cases come before the Court by means of a discretionary **writ of *certiorari***, a formal writ used to bring a case before the Court.

The Constitution stipulates the Supreme Court has original jurisdiction in a few specified situations. But the fact is the Supreme Court has control of its agenda and decides which cases it wants to consider. In recent years the justices have closely reviewed and issued signed opinions in less than 100 of the thousands of cases presented to them.[64] This is half the number of cases decided by written opinions a decade ago.[65]

The crucial factor in determining whether the Supreme Court will hear a case is its importance to the operation of the governmental system as a whole. The Supreme Court will review a case only if the claim has broad public significance. For instance, the rulings among the courts of appeals may conflict; by deciding the case, the Supreme Court can establish which ruling is to be followed. Or a case may raise a constitutional issue on which a state supreme court has presented an interpretation with which the Court disagrees.

The Court accepts cases under the *rule of four*. If four justices are sufficiently interested in a petition for a writ of *certiorari*, the petition will be granted and the case brought forward for review. Law clerks (called the "cert pool") read the petitions and write a memorandum on each for circulation to all the justices in the pool. Only Justice John Paul Stevens stays out of the pool, and even he, it is rumored, divides up the cert petitions among his own clerks and reads only a few of them himself.[66]

Denial of a writ of *certiorari* does not mean that the justices agree with the decision of the lower court, nor does it establish precedent. Refusal to grant such a writ may indicate all kinds of possibilities. The justices may not wish to become involved in a political "hot potato," or the Court may be so divided on an issue that it is not yet prepared to take a stand.[67]

The Role of the Law Clerks

writ of *certiorari*
A formal writ used to bring a case before the Supreme Court.

Beginning in the 1930s, federal judges began the practice of hiring the best recent graduates of law schools to serve as clerks for a year or two. As the judicial work load increased, more law clerks have been appointed. Today each Supreme Court justice is entitled to four clerks. Clerks draft opinions and screen writs of *certiorari.* Justices often talk through their cases with their law clerks.

Law clerks are young and energetic, and they know how to use computers to do research and prepare drafts of opinions. As the number of law clerks and computers has increased, so has the number of concurring and dissenting opinions. As a result, today's opinions are longer and have more substantive footnotes and elaborate citations of cases and law review articles.

Briefs and Oral Arguments

Before a case is heard in open court, the justices receive printed *briefs* in which each side presents legal arguments, historical materials, and relevant precedents. In addition, the Supreme Court may receive briefs from ***amici curiae*** (literally, "friends of the court"), who may be individuals, organizations, or government agencies that have an interest in the case and claim they have information of value to the Court. This procedure guarantees that the Department of Justice is represented if a suit between two private parties calls the constitutionality of an act of Congress into question. The *amicus curiae* brief is also used by presidents to see that the views of the current administration are brought to the Court's attention.[68]

Often organizations file *amicus curiae* briefs before the Supreme Court grants a writ of *certiorari* in order to lobby the Supreme Court to review the case. Their doing so enhances the probability that the court will take the case for review but has almost no influence on how the case is decided.[69] An *amicus* brief may help the justices by presenting an argument or point of law that the parties to the case have not raised. Often the briefs are filed as a means of pressuring the Court to reach a particular decision.

In *Webster v Reproductive Health Services,* dealing with a Missouri law regulating abortions and a request for the Court to reverse *Roe v Wade,* 78 *amicus* briefs were filed.[70] In *United States v Lopez,* which challenged congressional authority to ban guns in and around schools, more than 40 parties filed a dozen *amicus* briefs. Ohio, New York, and the District of Columbia argued in favor of federal power, as did associations of police and school officials. On the other side were some conservative public interest firms, the National Governors' Association, and the National League of Cities.[71]

Formal oratory before the Supreme Court, perhaps lasting for several days, is a thing of the past. As a rule, counsel for each side is limited to 30 minutes. Lawyers use a lectern to which two lights are attached. A white light flashes five minutes before time is up; when the red light goes on, the lawyer must stop, even in the middle of an "if."

WE THE PEOPLE

Needed: Minority Clerks at the Court

A Congressional hearing on the Supreme Court's annual budget took a valuable detour as Justices Clarence Thomas and David Souter engaged in a lengthy colloquy with lawmakers about the Court's dismal record in recruiting and hiring minority law clerks.

Each of the nine justices personally selects up to four law clerks each term to help with screening appeals and drafting opinions.

The current term's crop of 34 clerks includes only one minority member—a Hispanic woman—and for the second year running, the Court hired no African-American clerks. Of the 428 clerks hired over the years by the current justices, only 7 have been black, according to figures compiled by *USA Today.* Chief Justice William Rehnquist has not hired even one African-American clerk in 27 years on the Court.

"There is not a person at the Court who would not want to change this," said Justice Thomas, the second African-American to sit on the Court, responding to questioning by Democratic lawmakers. Justice Souter also expressed displeasure with the lopsided numbers and the perception they create. But other comments by the two Justices suggested a reluctance to alter the clubby "feeder system" from top-tier law schools and judges that produces a nearly all-white coterie of high-caliber clerks.

SOURCE: Editorial, *The New York Times,* March 18, 1999, p. A24.

amicus curiae
Literally, "friend of the court" brief, filed by an individual or organization to present arguments in addition to those presented by the immediate party to the case.

You Decide . . .

Can states refuse to provide free education for undocumented aliens?

A few years ago the Texas state legislature decided Texas taxpayers should no longer provide a free public education for the children of undocumented aliens. Then, in 1994, Californians adopted Proposition 187, which forbids schools and colleges to admit undocumented aliens and public hospitals to provide any treatment other than emergency care to them.

Setting aside for a moment whether you think such a policy is desirable, in your judgment, is there anything in the United States Constitution, especially in the equal protection clause, that should prevent the Texas legislature or the California electorate from making such a choice? What dilemmas of democracy does this case illustrate?

The entire procedure is formally informal. Sometimes, to the annoyance of attorneys, justices talk among themselves or consult briefs or legal volumes during the oral presentation. Sometimes, if justices find a presentation particularly bad, they ostentatiously consult their watches. Justices freely interrupt the lawyers to ask questions and request additional information. In recent years, "the justices seem barely able to contain themselves, often interrupting the answer to one question with another query."[72] The 30-minute limit is becoming a problem, especially when the solicitor general participates, since his ten minutes comes out of the time of the two parties before the Court.

If a lawyer seems to be having a difficult time, the justices may try to help him or her present a better case. Occasionally, justices bounce arguments off a hapless attorney and at one another. Justice Antonin Scalia is a harsh questioner. "When Scalia prepares to ask a question, he doesn't just adjust himself in his chair to get closer to the microphone like the others; he looks like a vulture, zooming in for the kill. He strains way forward, pinches his eyebrows, and poses the question, like '. . . do you want us to believe?'"[73] Justice Sandra Day O'Connor commented about him, "Some of our members are former law professors and haven't lost their technique of asking questions."[74] Justice Ruth Bader Ginsburg is a particularly persistent questioner, frequently rivaling Justice Scalia in asking the most questions.[75] Justice Clarence Thomas almost never asks a question. Justice David Souter has a thick New England accent. He once asked an attorney during oral arguments in an affirmative action case, "What's the floor?" The attorney hemmed and hawed until, with a smile, Souter explained he meant, "What's the flaw?"[76]

Behind the Curtains: The Conference

Wednesday afternoons and all day Friday the justices meet in conference. They have heard the oral arguments, read and studied the briefs, and examined the petitions. Before every conference, each justice receives a list of the cases to be discussed. Each brings to the meeting a red leather book in which the cases and the votes of the justices are recorded. These conferences are secret affairs, although in recent years the secrecy has been penetrated. They are marked by informality and by vigorous give-and-take; they are both "collegial and substantive."[77]

The chief justice presides, usually opening the discussion by stating the facts, summarizing the questions of law, and making suggestions for disposing of the case. Each member of the Court is then asked, in order of seniority, to give his or her views and conclusions. Chief Justice Rehnquist tries to see to it during the course of discussion that "everybody [speaks] once before the vote is taken."[78] Recently the justices have not bothered with formal votes because they make it clear how they will vote when they discuss the case.[79]

Opinions

opinion of the court
An opinion and explanation of the decision of the Supreme Court or any other appelate court.

dissenting opinion
An opinion that conflicts with the decision of the Court.

concurring opinion
An opinion that agrees with the decision of the Court but differs on the reasoning.

As a general rule, Supreme Court opinions state the facts, present the issues, announce the decision, and, most important, explain the reasoning of the Court. These opinions are the Court's principal method of expressing its views to the world. Perhaps the primary function of opinions is to instruct the judges of all other state and federal courts in the United States on how to decide similar cases in the future.

Judicial opinions may be directed at Congress or at the president. If the Court regrets that "in the absence of action by Congress, we have no choice but to . . ." or insists that "relief of the sort that petitioner demands can only come from the political branches of government," it is clearly asking Congress to act.[80] Justices also use opinions to communicate with the public. A well-handled opinion may increase support for a policy the Court favors.

ASSIGNING OPINIONS The justice to whom writing an opinion is assigned knows that he or she must influence the outcome, for no vote in conference is final. Justices are free to change their minds if persuaded by the draft opinion. When voting with the majority, the chief justice decides who drafts the **opinion of the court**. When the chief justice is in the minority, the senior justice among the majority makes the assignment, often to himself or herself.

Justices are free to write a **dissenting opinion** if they wish. Dissenting opinions are, in Chief Justice Charles Evans Hughes's words, "an appeal to the brooding spirit of the law, to the intelligence of a later day."[81] Dissenting opinions are quite common, as justices hope that someday these dissenting opinions will command a majority of the court. If a justice agrees with the majority on how the case should be decided but differs on the reasoning, that justice may write a **concurring opinion**.

CIRCULATING DRAFTS Writing an opinion for the Court is an exacting task. The document must win the support of at least four—even more, if possible—intelligent, strong-willed persons. Assisted by the law clerks, the assigned justice writes a draft and sends it to colleagues for comments. If the justice is lucky, the majority will accept the draft, perhaps with only minor changes. If the draft is not satisfactory to the other justices, it must be redrafted and recirculated until a majority can reach agreement.

The two weapons justices can use against their colleagues are their votes and their willingness to write dissenting opinions attacking a doctrine the majority wishes to see adopted. Especially if the Court is closely divided, one justice may be in a position to demand that a given argument be included in, or removed from, the opinion as the price of his or her vote. Sometimes this bargaining occurs even though the Court is not closely divided. An opinion writer who anticipates that a decision will bring critical public reaction may wish to have it presented as the view of a unanimous Court and may be prepared to compromise to achieve unanimity. For this reason, the Court delayed declaring school segregation unconstitutional until unanimity could be secured. The justices understood that any sign of dissension on the bench on this major social issue would be an invitation to evade the Court's ruling.

The Powers of the Chief Justice

The chief justice of the United States is appointed by the president and confirmed by the Senate and holds tenure for life. This method of selecting the chief justice gives him (in our entire history they have all been men) greater visibility than if selected by rotation of fellow justices, as is the practice in the state supreme courts, or by seniority, as is the practice in the federal courts of appeals. But as Chief Justice Rehnquist said when he was still an associate justice, the chief deals not with "eight subordinates whom he may direct or instruct, but eight associates who, like him, have tenure during good behavior, and who are as independent as hogs on ice."[82]

The ability of the chief justice to influence the Court has varied considerably.[83] Chief Justice Charles Evans Hughes ran the conferences like a stern schoolmaster, keeping the justices on the point, moving the discussion along, and doing his best to work out compromises. He tried to achieve unanimous votes in order to give decisions greater weight. Chief Justice Harlan F. Stone, on the other hand, encouraged justices to state their own points of view and let the discussions wander. Chief Justice Warren Burger devoted much of his time to judicial reform, speaking to bar and lay groups and trying to build political support for modernizing the judicial process.

Thinking it Through...

Proposition 187 is currently being challenged in the courts, but in *Plyler v Doe* (1982), five members of the United States Supreme Court ruled that the Texas law violated the equal protection clause because Texas had failed to show its action would, as alleged, protect the state from an influx of illegal immigrants, improve the overall quality of education, or save substantial sums of money. "If the state," wrote Justice William J. Brennan, Jr., "is to deny a discrete group of innocent children the free public education it offers to other children residing within its borders, that denial must be justified by a showing that it furthers some substantial state interests. No such showing was made here."*

Chief Justice Warren Burger, dissenting along with Justices Byron R. White, William H. Rehnquist, and Sandra Day O'Connor, wrote: "I agree without hesitation that it is senseless for an enlightened society to deprive any children—including illegal aliens—of an elementary education. However, the Constitution does not vest in this Court the authority to strike down laws because they do not meet our standards of desirable social policy, 'wisdom,' or 'common sense.' . . . Today's cases, I regret to say, present yet another example of unwarranted judicial action which in the long run tends to contribute to the weakening of our political process."

**Plyler v Doe*, 465 US 202 (1982).

Who Were the Great Justices?

Although this question is asked often, the answers tell you as much about the values of the evaluators as they do about the merits of the justices. Nonetheless, two law professors surveyed about 65 law school deans and professors of law and political science. Respondents were asked to evaluate the performance of 96 justices who had served from 1789 to 1970. The 12 rated "best" or "great" were:

John Marshall* (1801–35)

Joseph Story (1812–45)

Roger B. Taney* (1836–64)

John Marshall Harlan (1877–1911)

Oliver W. Holmes, Jr. (1902–32)

Charles Evans Hughes* (1910–16, 1930–41)

Louis D. Brandeis (1916–39)

Harlan F. Stone* (1925–46)

Benjamin Cardozo (1932–38)

Hugo Black (1937–71)

Felix Frankfurter (1939–62)

Earl Warren* (1953–69)

*Chief justices

SOURCE: Henry J. Abraham, *Justices and Presidents: A Political History of Appointments to the Supreme Court*, 3d ed. (Oxford University Press, 1992), p. 412. Copyright © 1992 by Henry J. Abraham. Reprinted by permission of Oxford University Press.

Chief Justice William H. Rehnquist had 15 years of Court experience prior to his elevation to the post of chief justice. He "has not utilized his position as Chief Justice to shape the decisions of the Court."[84] But as the Reagan-Bush justices are still a majority, his constitutional views, formerly expressed only in his dissenting opinions, are now the opinions of the Court.[85]

"The Chief Justiceship does not guarantee leadership. It only offers its incumbent an opportunity to lead."[86] Yet the chief justice "sets the tone, controls the conference, assigns the most opinions, and usually, takes the most important, nation-changing decisions for himself. . . . The Chief Justice remains first among equals." Periods in Court history are named after the chief justice, who is responsible for the institution's character."[87]

After the Lawsuit Is Over

Victory in the Supreme Court does not necessarily mean that winning parties get what they want. As a rule, the Court does not implement its own decision but *remands*, that is, sends the case back to the lower court with instructions to act in accordance with the Supreme Court's opinion. The lower court often has considerable leeway in interpreting the Court's mandate as it disposes of the case.

Decisions whose enforcement requires only the action of a central governmental agency usually become effective immediately. Thus, when the Supreme Court held that President Harry Truman lacked constitutional authority to seize steel companies temporarily to avoid a shutdown during the Korean War,[88] the president promptly complied.

The impact of a particular Supreme Court ruling on the behavior of those who are not immediate parties to a lawsuit is even more uncertain. Most important decisions contain constitutional rulings that require a change in the behavior of thousands of administrative and elected officials. Sometimes Supreme Court pronouncements are simply ignored. For example, despite the Court's holding that it is unconstitutional for school boards to require students to pray within school, some schools continue this practice.[89] And for years after the Supreme Court held public school segregation unconstitutional, many school districts remained segregated.[90]

The most difficult Supreme Court decisions to implement are those that require the cooperation of large numbers of officials. For example, a Supreme Court decision announcing a new standard for warrantless searches is not likely to have an impact on the way police make arrests for some time, since not many police officers subscribe to the *United States Supreme Court Reports.* The process is more complex. Local prosecutors, state attorneys general, chiefs of police, and state and federal trial court judges must all participate to give meaning to Supreme Court decisions. The Constitution may be what the Supreme Court says it is, but a Supreme Court opinion, for the moment at least, is what a trial judge or police officer or a prosecutor or a school board or a city council says it is.

Judicial Power in a Constitutional Democracy

An independent judiciary is one of the hallmarks of a free society. As impartial dispensers of equal justice under the law, judges should not be dependent on the executive, the legislature, the parties to the case, the electorate, or a mob outside the courtroom. But this very independence, essential to protect judges in their roles as legal umpires, raises basic problems when a democratic society decides—as ours has—also to allow these same judges to make policy. Perhaps in no other society do the people resort to litigation as a means of making public policy as much as they do in the United States.

The involvement of our courts in politics exposes the judiciary to political criticism. Throughout our history, the Supreme Court has been attacked for engaging in "judicial legislation." This is nothing new. Yet the active role of the federal courts on behalf of liberal causes since 1937 and the Republican attacks on that role have returned these issues to the forefront of public debate.

Whereas in earlier times judges occasionally told public officials what they could not do, today they often tell them what they *must* do. For example, federal judges, responding to class action complaints, have told Congress, state legislatures, and local officials that they must provide attorneys for the poor, ensure adequate care for mental patients, modernize prisons, and even break up the telephone system. (In this last case, the Department of Justice initiated the action.) Often judges retain jurisdiction for years as they preside over the implementation of the decrees they have issued.[91] Judges have always been policy makers; that role is not a matter of choice but flows from the roles they play in deciding cases. But today they also govern.[92]

Chief Justice William Hubbs Rehnquist was formerly an assistant attorney general and then an associate justice of the Supreme Court from 1971 to 1986.

The Great Debate over the Proper Role of the Courts

Some people contend that the courts have a duty to protect the long-range interests of the public as defined in the Constitution, even against the short-range wishes of the voters (but then what is and is not defined by the Constitution is the issue). Defenders of this *activist* judicial role argue that if Congress, the White House, and the state legislatures are unable to resolve pressing problems when people are being denied justice and their constitutional rights, then the courts should resolve those problems. The Supreme Court, they say, should be "a leader in a vital national seminar that leads to the formulation of values for the American people."[93]

Critics of judicial activism contend that for the last half century the federal courts, in their zeal to protect people, became unhinged from their political moorings in the political and constitutional system. Even if courts make the "right" decisions, these critics argue, it is not right for courts to take over the legislative function of elected representatives.

Others claim the debate between those who favor judicial restraint and those who favor judicial activism oversimplifies the choices. Judges, they argue, should take a leadership role in some areas but a restrained role in others. They stand with Chief Justice Harlan F. Stone, who argued that courts have a special duty to intervene: (1) whenever legislation restricts the political process by which decisions are made, or (2) whenever legislation restricts the rights of "discrete and insular minorities." In all other areas, the political process should be allowed to work, and judges should not set aside legislation or interfere with administrative agencies merely because judges would prefer some other policy or even some other interpretation of the Constitution.[94]

The People and the Court

Whether judges are liberal or conservative, defer to legislatures or not, try to apply the Constitution as they think the framers intended, or interpret it to conform to current values, there are linkages between what the judges do and what the people want done. The linkages are not direct, and the people never speak with one mind, but these linkages are the heart of the matter.[95] In the first place, the president and the Senate are likely to appoint justices whose decisions reflect their values. When the people elected George Bush, they got judges who reflected his perspectives; when they elected Bill Clinton, they got judges who reflected his values and preferences.

"Do you ever have one of those days when *nothing* seems constitutional?"

The Wall Street Journal, August 3, 1998.

At the end of the 1991–92 term, the Supreme Court, by a 5 to 4 vote in *Planned Parenthood v Casey*, refused to overturn *Roe v Wade* and upheld its core holding—that the Constitution protects the right of a woman to an abortion—although subjecting that right to state regulations that do not "unduly burden" it.[96] This close vote on abortion made it clear that the 1992 presidential election would determine whether that right would continue to be protected by the Constitution. At stake was whether it would be George Bush or Bill Clinton who would nominate new members of the Supreme Court. Clinton pledged to nominate only persons committed to the view that the Constitution protects a woman's right to choose. Bush made it clear that he would continue to appoint conservative jurists who could be expected to vote to reverse *Roe v Wade.*

During most of his time in office, President Clinton had to filter his judicial appointments through a conservative, Republican-controlled Senate and Judiciary Committee. His appointees tended to be moderates. Some liberal critics accused him of working so closely with the Republicans that he was unable to reverse the conservative legacy of the Reagan-Bush years, but Clinton was able to increase substantially the number of African Americans and women on the federal bench.

By the 1996 elections, the conservative hold on the Supreme Court was clear yet tenuous. After decades of effort, the Nixon-Reagan-Bush attempts to alter the course of constitutional direction were having results. Chief Justice Rehnquist and Justices Thomas and Scalia were joined by Justices Kennedy and O'Connor to provide a five-person majority.

When the voters returned Clinton for a second term but left Republicans in control of the Senate, they increased the probability that centrists would be selected as federal judges, since only candidates who would please both President Clinton and the conservative Republicans who dominate the Senate Judiciary Committee would be likely to be nominated and confirmed. But they also enhanced the likelihood that constitutional conservatives would not be able to consolidate further their control over the Supreme Court.

Scholars debate how public opinion influences what judges decide, whether it is direct or indirect through presidential appointments and Senate confirmations, but there is little question that there is a correlation between public opinion and judicial decisions.[97] Judicial opinions that reflect what the people want have the greatest survival value. When a new political coalition takes over the White House or Congress, the old regime stays on in the federal courts, or as one unknown wit put it: "The good a president does is oft interred with his bones, but his choice of Supreme Court Justices lives after him."[98] New electoral coalitions eventually take over the federal courts, and before long, new interpretations of the Constitution reflect the dominant political ideology.

Judges have neither armies nor police to execute their rulings. Although Congress cannot reverse Supreme Court decisions that relate to constitutional interpretations, and only three Supreme Court decisions have been reversed by formal constitutional amendment, the political system alters judicial policy in more subtle ways. Decisions are binding on the parties to a particular case, but the policies involved in judicial decisions are effective and durable only if they are supported by the electorate. To win a favorable Supreme Court decision is to win something of considerable political value, but the policies reflected by that decision may or may not alter the way people behave.

"American courts are not all-powerful institutions."[99] If the Court's policies are too far out of step with the values of the country, the Court is likely to be reversed. As Chief Justice William H. Rehnquist has written, "No judge worthy of his salt would ever cast his vote in a particular case simply because he thought the majority of the public wanted him to vote that way, but that is quite a different thing from saying that no judge is ever influenced by the great tides of public opinion that run a country such as ours."[100]

"The people" speak in many ways and with many voices. The Supreme Court—and the other courts—represent and reflect the values of some of these people. Although the Court is not the defenseless institution portrayed by some commentators, and its decisions are as much shapers of public opinion as reflections of it, ultimately the power of the Court in a constitutional democracy rests on retaining the support of most of the people most of the time. No better standard for determining the legitimacy of a governmental institution has been discovered.

online POLITICS

Lexis/Nexis, Westlaw, and the Practice of Law

The Public Affairs Video Archives at Purdue University can supply videotapes and videoguides for the Senate Judiciary Committee hearings on recent Supreme Court nominations. For information, see your local librarian or write to Public Affairs Video Archives, Stewart Center, Purdue University, West Lafayette, Indiana 47907. Also available at

http://www.pava.purdue.edu

The legal profession was one of the first professions to go online, and the early pioneers in providing interactive computer service were Westlaw and Lexis/Nexis. Beginning in 1973, Lexis provided access to full texts of federal and state cases, statutes, regulations, and public records from several states. In 1979, the Nexis news and information service became a companion to Lexis, offering online information from newspapers, news wires, magazines, trade journals, and business publications. Nexis also provides stock and brokerage house information, information on corporations, and political analysis and information. Each week more than 9.5 million documents are added to the more than 1 billion documents online at Lexis/Nexis.

Lexis/Nexis and other online services like Westlaw are now part of most law school curricula, and students are instructed in their use in their first year of law school. The service is given to law schools at a discounted rate, but students must use it only for academic purposes. Lawyers, judges, clerks, and legal academics use these tools extensively. Lawyers can search for similar cases and make sure there are no more recent cases with conflicting rulings.

Many college libraries make these services available. Talk to your librarian or check out home pages at:

http://www.westlaw.com

http://www.lexis-nexis.com

For a description of the federal courts and documents relating to them, go to:

http://www.uscourts.gov/

Supreme Court decisions can be found at:

http://www.findlaw.com

http://www.usscplus.com/

For more Internet resources on the Judiciary, see our home page at:

http://www.prenhall.com/burns

SUMMARY

1. The American judicial process rests on an adversary system. Judges in the United States play a more active role in the political process than they do in other democracies. Federal courts are established by and receive their jurisdiction directly from Congress, which must decide the constitutional division of responsibilities among federal and state courts.
2. Federal judges apply statutory law, common law, equity law, constitutional law, admiralty and maritime law, and administrative law. They apply federal, criminal, and civil law. Although bound by procedural requirements, including *stare decisis*, they can exercise discretion.
3. Partisanship and ideology are important factors in the selection of federal judges, and these factors ensure a linkage between the courts and the rest of the political system, so that the views of the people are reflected, even if indirectly, in the work of the courts.
4. The Supreme Court, which has almost complete control over the cases it chooses to review as they come up from the state courts, the courts of appeals, and district courts, is a revered but somewhat mysterious branch of our government. Annually its nine justices dispose of thousands of cases, but most of their time is concentrated on the 75 to 100 cases per year that establish guidelines for lower courts and the country.
5. A continuing concern of major importance is the reconciliation of the role of judges—especially those on the Supreme Court—as independent and fair dispensers of justice with their vital role as interpreters of the Constitution. This is an especially complex problem in our democracy because of the power of judicial review and the significant role courts play in making public policy.
6. The debate about how judges should interpret the Constitution is almost as old as the Republic. More than two hundred years after the Constitution was adopted, the argument between those who contend judges should interpret the document literally and those who believe they cannot, and should not, has returned to the headlines.

KEY TERMS

FURTHER READING

HENRY J. ABRAHAM, *The Judiciary: The Supreme Court in the Governmental Process*, 10th ed. (New York University Press, 1996).

HENRY J. ABRAHAM, *Justices and Presidents: A Political History of Appointments to the Supreme Court*, 3d ed. (Oxford University Press, 1992).

STEPHEN L. CARTER, *The Confirmation Mess: Cleaning Up the Federal Appointments Process* (Basic Books, 1994).

PHILLIP J. COOPER, *Battles on the Bench: Conflict Inside the Supreme Court* (University Press of Kansas, 1995).

PHILLIP COOPER AND HOWARD BALL, *The United States Supreme Court: From the Inside Out* (Prentice Hall, 1996).

CLARE CUSHMAN, *The Supreme Court Justices: Illustrated Biographies, 1789–1995*, 2d ed. (Congressional Quarterly Press, 1996).

LEE EPSTEIN AND JOSEPH F. KOBYLKA, *The Supreme Court and Legal Change: Abortion and the Death Penalty* (University of North Carolina Press, 1993).

SHELDON GOLDMAN, *Picking Federal Judges: Lower Court Selection from Roosevelt Through Reagan* (Yale University Press, 1997).

STEPHEN GRIFFIN, *American Constitutionals* (Princeton University Press, 1997).

KERMIT L. HALL, ED., *The Oxford Companion to the Supreme Court of the United States* (Oxford University Press, 1992).

PETER IRONS AND STEPHANIE GUITTON, EDS., *May It Please the Court: Transcripts of 23 Recordings of Landmark Cases as Argued Before the Supreme Court* (New Press, 1993).

ROBERT A. KATZMAN, *Courts & Congress* (Brookings Institution Press, 1997).

EDWARD LAZARUS, *Closed Chambers: The First Eyewitness Account of the Epic Struggles Inside the Supreme Court* (Free Press, 1998).

DAVID W. NEUBAUER, *Judicial Process, Law, Courts, and Politics in the United States*, 2d ed. (Harcourt Brace, 1997).

DAVID M. O'BRIEN, *Storm Center: The Supreme Court in American Politics*, 5th ed. (W. W. Norton, 2000).

DAVID M. O'BRIEN, ED., *Judges on Judging: View from the Bench* (Chatham House, 1997).

J. W. PELTASON, *Federal Courts in the Political Process* (Doubleday, 1955).

BARBARA A. PERRY, *A "Representative" Supreme Court? The Impact of Race, Religion, and Gender on Appointments* (Greenwood Press, 1991).

GERALD N. ROSENBERG, *The Hollow Hope: Can Courts Bring About Social Change?* (University of Chicago Press, 1991).

C. K. ROWLAND AND ROBERT A. CARP, *Politics and Judgment in Federal District Courts* (University Press of Kansas, 1996).

ANTONIN SCALIA, *A Matter of Interpretation: Federal Courts and the Law* (Princeton University Press, 1997)

BERNARD SCHWARTZ, *A History of the Supreme Court* (Oxford University Press, 1993).

JAMES F. SIMON, *The Center Holds: The Power Struggle Inside the Rehnquist Court* (Simon & Schuster, 1995).

PAUL SIMON, *Advice and Consent: Clarence Thomas, Robert Bork, and the Intriguing History of the Supreme Court Battles* (National Press Books, 1992).

ELLIOT E. SLOTNICK, *Judicial Politics: Readings from "Judicature"* (Nelson-Hall, 1992).

HARRY P. STUMPF, *American Judicial Politics*, 2d ed. (Prentice Hall, 1998).

STEPHEN L. WASBY, *The Supreme Court in the Federal Judicial System*, 4th ed. (Nelson-Hall, 1993).

THE
BUREAUCRACY:
THE
REAL POWER?

17

CHAPTER OUTLINE

- Reinventing Government in the 1990s
- The Federal Bureaucracy
- The Bureaucracy in Action
- Bureaucratic Responsiveness
- Bureaucratic Accountability
- What the Public Thinks of Bureaucrats and the Bureaucracy

THE CLINTON-GORE ADMINISTRATION HAS DEVOTED MORE SUSTAINED, PRESIDENTIAL-LEVEL ATTENTION TO REFORMING THE FEDERAL BUREAUCRACY THAN HAS ANY administration in history.[1] With help and some prodding from Congress, the administration eliminated about 400,000 federal jobs and made significant improvements in customer service and government procurement processes. Some agencies have been eliminated, and many programs have been consolidated.

Yet the government is still very big, and nobody now believes, as Bill Clinton once proclaimed, that "the era of big government is over." Bureaucracy is a fact of modern life. We still have a lot of "red tape" and overlap in our federal government and its processes. To see the true picture, writes political scientist Paul Light, "one must count all the heads, including full-time federal civil servants, uniformed military personnel, postal workers, and people who deliver goods and services on behalf of the federal government under contracts, grants and mandates to state and local governments."[2] When this is done, the size of federal government and its extended employment runs to nearly 17 million (see Figure 17-1). When Thomas Jefferson was president, the federal government employed 2,120 persons: Indian commissioners, postmasters, collectors of customs, tax collectors, marshals, lighthouse keepers, and clerks.

Bashing the always unpopular Internal Revenue Service and other government bureaucracies is a great American pastime. There is hardly a citizen who has not been offended, irritated, or at least frustrated at one time or another in dealing with the Internal Revenue Service (IRS), the Federal Bureau of Investigation (FBI), the U.S. Customs agents, the Environmental Protection Agency (EPA), the Food and Drug Administration (FDA), or similar federal agents. No matter that these same agencies can also be a big help to us or serve the country well; we mainly remember the hassles and mistakes.

As many as 2 million people, for example, are audited each year by some of the 100,000 employees of the IRS. And despite the fact that most IRS agents do their job well and are fair-minded as they go after tax evaders or tax cheaters, there are well-documented instances of IRS intimidation and abuse.[3]

For most people, everything in life now seems to be regulated. The rules are numerous and inflexible. One critic writes that government "acts like some extraterrestrial power, not an institution that exists to serve us. Its actions have an arbitrary quality. It almost never deals with real-life problems in a way that reflects understanding of the situation."[4]

Red Tape

The term "red tape" comes from the ribbon English civil servants once used to tie up and bind legal documents. Today, along with taxes and death, we think of red tape as inevitable. We are annoyed when we have to wait in lines while officials check files or consult with their supervisors. We are furious when officials lose important documents. Red tape often takes the form of an official's punctilious adherence to rigid procedures. We may view it as a hopeless tangle of rules and regulations that keep public servants from doing anything but stamping and shuffling papers.

But these same rules and regulations help ensure that public servants act impartially. In other words, red tape stems from our desire not to give public servants too much discretion and to hold them accountable. After all, they are spending our money. Remember, too, that one person's red tape is another person's prudent system or proper cautiousness.

In this chapter we explain who the bureaucrats are, examine the origins, functions, and realities of our national public bureaucracy, and explore how elected officials in both Congress and the executive branch are trying to make the bureaucracy leaner, more responsive, and more accountable to the American people. It is important to ask, at the beginning of the twenty-first century, whether our bureaucracy and its methods are stifling innovation, productivity, and common sense.

REINVENTING GOVERNMENT IN THE 1990S

Early in his presidency Clinton appointed Vice-President Al Gore to conduct a major review of the bureaucracy's performance. Both Clinton and Gore took this effort seriously. They clearly wanted to change the way the government did business: how it bought goods and services, how it dealt with vendors, how it served citizens, how it listened to its citizen customers, and how it could do a better job with fewer employees and less red tape. That was a tall order.

Al Gore's National Performance Review team made exhaustive studies, held numerous conferences, and issued hundreds of recommendations for encouraging efficiency, productivity, and responsiveness in government operations. Early recommendations included closing or consolidating 1,200 field offices of the Department of Agriculture, reducing the number of Department of Education programs from 230 to 189, encouraging market-based approaches to reducing pollution, reducing the time required to fire incompetent federal employees, and insisting that all agencies survey customers, measure customer satisfaction, and establish service standards equal to the best in business.[5]

Clinton and Gore, with the enthusiastic backing of most members of Congress, worked hard throughout the 1990s to cut the size of the federal government's civilian and military work force. The end of the cold war obviously made it somewhat easier to close military bases and to downsize the post–cold war military ranks.

After about three years, the executive branch claimed considerable progress in "putting customers first, empowering employees to get results, cutting red tape, and cutting back to basics." The departments and agencies "established customer service standards and streamlined their operations," said Clinton. "They also are working with my Office of Management and Budget to focus more on 'performance'—what federal programs actually accomplish."[6] In his Second Inaugural Address, Clinton boasted that the federal bureaucracy was the smallest since the administration of John Kennedy.

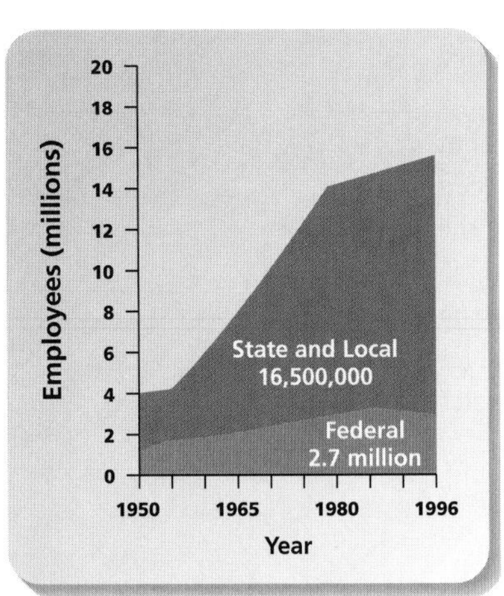

FIGURE 17-1 Civilian Government Employees, 1950–1996

SOURCE: Bureau of Labor Statistics, U.S. Department of Labor.

Clinton and Gore were responding to the widespread popular perception that there was too much waste and inadequate responsiveness by federal bureaucrats. They borrowed ideas about privatization, competition, choices, and reliance on a market orientation.[7] And they usually, though not always, went along with Republican calls to shift responsibility to the states when possible. (This last "solution" hardly solves the problem of bureaucracy; it merely shifts the problem from national to state bureaucracies.)

Many federal departments and agencies have improved their procedures to encourage common sense and accountability. There is growing recognition, both in and out of government circles, that "a reinvented civil service will have to invest more in people than in process. People will have to be more mobile and faster to learn; agencies will have to acquire more flexibility to attract the people they need."[8]

Public attitudes toward the federal government and its institutions, we should note, have become more favorable in recent years. Public attitudes toward federal agencies such as the Postal Service, Park Service, Defense Department, National Aeronautics and Space Administration (NASA), and the Federal Aviation

Administration, among others, have become noticeably more favorable in the late 1990s than a decade earlier.[9] To be sure, this increased favorability may be due to good economic times, yet it may also be due to the Clinton-Gore bureaucratic reform initiatives.

Executive Branch Departments

- Department of State (1789)
- Department of the Treasury (1789)
- Department of Defense (1947, originally War, 1789)
- Department of Justice (1789)
- Department of the Interior (1849)
- Department of Agriculture (1862)
- Department of Commerce (1913, originally Commerce and Labor, 1903)
- Department of Labor (1913, originally Commerce and Labor, 1903)
- Department of Health and Human Services (1979, originally Health, Education and Welfare, 1953)
- Department of Housing and Urban Development (1965)
- Department of Transportation (1966)
- Department of Energy (1977)
- Department of Education (1979)
- Department of Veterans Affairs (1989)

Dates indicate when the department was established.

The Federal Bureaucracy

Bureaucrats, or career government employees, work in the executive branch, in the 14 cabinet-level departments, and in the more than 50 independent agencies embracing about 2,000 bureaus, divisions, branches, offices, services, and other subunits of government. Five big agencies—the Departments of the Army, the Navy, and the Air Force (all three in the Department of Defense), the Department of Veterans Affairs, and the U.S. Postal Service—tower over the others in size. Most agencies are directly responsible to the president, yet some, like the Postal Service, are partly independent. Agencies exist by act of Congress; legislators can abolish them either by passing a new law or by withholding funds.[10]

The terms "bureaucrat" and "bureaucracy" are of recent origin. Initially referring to a cloth covering the desks of French government officials in the eighteenth century, the term "bureau" came to be linked with the suffix "ocracy" signifying rule of government (as in "democracy" or "aristocracy"). **Bureaucracy**, as the term came to be used a century ago, referred to a rational, efficient method of organization. "Bureaucracy" today can refer to a professional corps of officials organized in a pyramidal hierarchy and functioning under impersonal, uniform rules and procedures. The term "bureaucracy" typically refers to the whole body of nonelected and non–presidentially appointed government officials in the executive branch who work for presidents and their political appointees. In this chapter we use the terms "bureaucracy" and "bureaucrat" in their neutral sense, although popular usage of these terms is typically negative.

Bureaucracies are public or private organizations that are large and hierarchical in structure, with each employee accountable to a superior through a chain of command. They provide each employee with a defined role or responsibility, base their decisions on impersonal rules, and hire and promote employees according to skills related to their jobs.[11] Bureaucracies in the modern sense came into being in government to provide predictability and efficiency and to minimize the arbitrary practices that so often characterized rule under dictatorial monarchs.

Some critics believe the federal bureaucracy is an overzealous guardian of the status quo and is too lazy or unimaginative to innovate or experiment. Others fear that a powerful national bureaucracy encourages a wasteful welfare state. Many people also think the federal bureaucracy is too large, too powerful, too unaccountable; 64 percent of respondents in a national survey complained that the federal government controls too much of our daily lives.[12] And nearly everyone surveyed was suspicious that there was waste and "fat" in government, especially those who had heard about Defense Department procurement cost overruns, welfare fraud, Central Intelligence Agency (CIA) tragedies, and general inefficiencies. Such stereotypes are widespread, for bureaucracies have never been popular.

Bureaucracy in a large, complex society is virtually inevitable. Most of us will work in some public or private bureaucracy for part, if not most, of our careers. Public bureaucracies pose special challenges because they report to competing political institutions and must function within our constitutional democracy of shared powers and multiple checks and balances.

bureaucrat
Career government employee.

bureaucracy
A professional corps of officials organized in a pyramidal hierarchy and functioning under impersonal, uniform rules and procedures.

This cartoon by Thomas Nast shows Andrew Jackson riding the hog of political patronage.

How Did the Bureaucracy Evolve?

From 1789 until about 1829, the federal service in this country was drawn from an upper-class, white male elite. In 1829 President Andrew Jackson called for greater participation by the middle and lower classes. He introduced what was labeled a **spoils system**, which his successors in office followed until well into the 1890s. This system, epitomized by the phrase "to the victor belong the spoils," operated on the theory that party loyalists should be rewarded, and that government would be effective and responsive only if supporters of the president held most key federal posts. Besides, it was thought that government should not be complicated; anybody should be able to do the job. With each new president came a full turnover in the federal service.

Later in the nineteenth century, however, a sharp reaction set in against the spoils system. In response to the various abuses and most immediately to the assassination of President James Garfield in 1881 by a disappointed office seeker, Congress passed the Pendleton Act. It set up a limited **merit system** based on a testing program for evaluating candidates. Federal employees were to be selected and retained according to their "merit," not their party connections or loyalty. Federal service was placed under the control of a three-person bipartisan board called the Civil Service Commission, which functioned from 1883 to 1978.[13]

By the 1950s coverage under the merit system had grown from 10 percent of all federal employees when it was first established to about 90 percent. In 1978 the Civil Service Reform Act abolished the Civil Service Commission and split its functions between two new agencies. This split was made to avoid a conflict of interest inherent in the agency that recruits, hires, and promotes employees also being the same agency that passes judgment on employee grievances about fairness and discrimination.

Today the **Office of Personnel Management (OPM)** administers civil service laws, rules, and regulations. An independent Merit Systems Protection Board is charged with protecting the integrity of the federal merit system and the rights of federal employees. The board conducts studies of the merit system, hears and decides charges of wrongdoing, considers employee appeals against adverse agency actions, and orders corrective and disciplinary actions against an agency executive or employee when appropriate.

Who Are the Bureaucrats?

We are mainly interested here in the approximately 4 million people (2.7 million civilians, including postal workers, and about 1.4 million in the military services) who make up the executive branch of the federal government. Certain facts about these people need to be emphasized:

1. Only about 10 percent of the career civilian employees work in the Washington area. The vast majority are scattered throughout the country and around the world. California alone has more federal employees than does the District of Columbia.
2. Nearly 30 percent of the civilian employees work for the army, the navy, the air force, or some other defense agency.
3. The welfare state may consume a sizable portion of the U.S. budget, yet the size of the federal bureaucracy that administers it is relatively small. Less than 15 percent of the bureaucrats work for welfare agencies such as the Social Security Administration or the Rural Electrification Administration. Almost half of those who do work for the Department of Veterans Affairs.
4. In terms of social origin, education, religion, and other background factors, bureaucrats are more broadly representative of the nation than are legislators or politically appointed executives.

spoils system
System of public employment based on rewarding party loyalists and friends.

merit system
A system in which selection and employment depend on demonstrated performance rather than political patronage.

Office of Personnel Management (OPM)
Agency that administers civil service laws, rules, and regulations.

5. More than 15,000 different personnel skills are represented in the federal government. Unlike Americans as a whole, however, most federal employees are white-collar workers: secretaries, clerks, lawyers, inspectors, engineers.

Most bureaucrats are honest professionals and experts at their business. Presidents, Congress, and other elected officials ignore the bureaucracy's advice at their peril. A compelling example is provided by the CIA's perceptive memoranda (many of them later published in the celebrated *Pentagon Papers*) warning that the Vietnam War as President Lyndon Johnson wanted to conduct it would be a failure. This was good advice from an expert bureaucracy, but Johnson paid little attention.

What Do Bureaucrats Do?

After the president has signed a bill into law, it must be implemented. Implementation of policy is the function of the executive branch, its bureaucracy, and in some instances, state, county, and local governments as well.

More is involved in policy implementation than the mechanical translation of goals into practice. Indeed, it is during this stage that many key decisions are made. Legislation is often deliberately vague to conceal serious policy differences among supporters of a bill. Frequently legislators are more concerned with the symbolic potency of legislation than with its content. Thus Congress often sets general goals and passes the responsibility for interpretation on to the bureaucrats, who then have considerable latitude to translate general guidelines into specific directives. Bureaucrats are sometimes blamed for the confusion, yet they are merely trying to carry out ambiguous policies in a political atmosphere characterized by conflict and competition.

Consider civil rights legislation. Often differences among women's groups, African American groups, Latino groups, employer groups, and trade unions are momentarily resolved and a bill becomes law. But after the bill has been enacted, the coalition that supported the bill falls apart, and conflicting pressures are felt by the agencies trying to implement the policies. Employers claim that the regulations are unrealistic and interfere with their rights; women's groups contend agencies are failing to enforce the law vigorously enough; African American groups claim agencies favor the women's groups but ignore African Americans. The more controversial the issue, the greater the chance of delay, as powerful interest groups clash over a program and force bureaucrats to move cautiously.

The implementation process involves a long chain of decision points. At each point a public official or community leader can advance or delay the program. The more decision points a program needs to clear, the greater the chance of failure or delay. Special problems result if the successful implementation of a national program depends on the cooperation of state and local officials. One state or community may be eager to help; another may be opposed to a program and try to stop it.

A number of federal programs have failed to accomplish their desired goals because of problems in implementation. Sometimes these difficulties lead to the outright failure of a program, but more often they mean excessive delay, watered-down goals, or cost overruns. John Kennedy's economic reform programs in Latin America, Lyndon Johnson's Model Cities program, Richard Nixon's and Gerald Ford's crime control programs, the Reagan-Bush antidrug crusade, and Bill Clinton's national service program all faced problems of implementation.[14] When such failures occur, it is easier to blame the legislation than the implementation.

Like so much of politics, successful policy implementation cannot be guaranteed. It depends on the creation of effective routines, the ability to adjust to changing circumstances, the quality of the working relationship between implementers at various levels, the degree of conflict invoked by the policy, and its general level of public support.

How Is the Bureaucracy Organized?

FORMAL ORGANIZATION The executive branch departments are headed by cabinet members called *secretaries* (except Justice, which is headed by the attorney general). Cabinet secretaries are directly responsible to the president. Although departments vary greatly in size, they have certain features in common. A *deputy* or an *undersecretary* takes part of the administrative load off the secretary's shoulders, and several assistant secretaries direct major programs. The secretaries have assistants who help them in planning, budget, personnel, legal services, public relations, and other staff functions.

Departments are subdivided into smaller units. The basis for their division may differ. The most common basis is function. For example, the Commerce Department is divided into the Bureau of the Census, the Patent and Trademark Office, and so on. The basis may also be clientele (for example, the Bureau of Indian Affairs of the Interior Department), or work processes (for example, the Economic Research Service of the Agriculture Department), or geography (for example, the Alaskan Air Command of the Department of the Air Force).

The standard name for the largest subunit is the **bureau**, although it is sometimes called an office, administration, or service. Bureaus are the working units of the federal government. In contrast to the big departments, which often consist of a variety of agencies, bureaus usually have fairly definite and clear-cut duties, as their names show: the Bureau of the Census in the Commerce Department, the Forest Service in the Agriculture Department, the Social Security Administration in the Department of Health and Human Services, the Bureau of the Mint in the Treasury Department, the Bureau of Indian Affairs and the National Park Service in the Interior Department, and the Bureau of Prisons, Federal Bureau of Investigation, and Drug Enforcement Administration in the Justice Department.

Government corporations, such as the Corporation for Public Broadcasting and the Federal Deposit Insurance Corporation, are a cross between business corporations and regular government agencies. Government corporations were designed to make possible a freedom of action and flexibility not always found in the regular agencies. These corporations have been freed from certain regulations of the Office of Management and Budget and the comptroller general. They also have more leeway in using their own earnings. Still, because these corporations are a part of the government, the government retains control over their activities.

Government entities that are not corporations and do not fall within cabinet departments are called **independent agencies**. They consist of many types of organizations with differing degrees of independence. Many, however, are no more independent of the president and Congress than the cabinet departments. The huge General Services Administration (GSA), for example, the function of which is to operate and maintain federal properties, is not represented in the cabinet, but its director is responsible to the White House and its actions are closely watched by Congress.

Another type of agency is the **independent regulatory board** or **commission**. Examples are the Securities and Exchange Commission, the National Labor Relations Board, and the Federal Reserve Board. Congress deliberately set up these boards to keep them somewhat free from White House influence; the president nominates their members and Congress confirms them, but the president cannot fire them. Congress has protected their independence in several ways: the boards are headed by three or more commissioners with overlapping terms; they often have to be bipartisan in membership (that is, they must have some Democrats as well as some Republicans); and members are appointed for fixed terms in office, some for only 3 years but others for up to 14 years.

government corporation
Cross between a business corporation and a government agency, created to secure greater freedom of action and flexibility for a particular program.

bureau
The largest subunit of a government department or agency.

independent agency
A government entity that is independent of the legislative, executive, and judicial branch.

independent regulatory board
An independent agency with regulatory power whose independence is protected by Congress.

By assigning specific functions to each unit, placing an official at the head, and holding that official responsible for performance, formal bureaucracy allows for both specialization and coordination, permits ready communication, and in general makes a large and complex organization more manageable.

ASSISTANT SECRETARIES: A WEAK LINK Although presidents can usually recruit people of prominence and influence as cabinet secretaries, they find it harder to hire outstanding people at the assistant secretary level. Assistant secretaries are supposed to infuse the views and values of the White House into the federal bureaucracy. These citizen policy makers serve as links between the people who elect the presidents and the civil servants.

Many people, however, are not willing to interrupt their professional or business careers to become assistant secretaries. Over the last three decades the position has become one of relatively low pay, little prestige in Washington, short tenure (people stay, on average, about two years in these posts), and high cost to one's family. As a result, presidents often fill these slots with relatively young people who, from the day they arrive in Washington, are looking for their next job. These assistant secretaries are forced to wear "kid gloves" with those they are supposed to regulate because it is from them that their next job is often likely to come. Others have strong ideological convictions but little experience in administration and congressional politics. Still others use the position as a transition to retirement.

Most civil servants have virtually secure jobs, and sometimes all they have to do to ignore assistant secretaries is to wait them out for a year or two. Moreover, in and around Washington, government workers constitute a powerful political group. Assistant secretaries who try to significantly alter the policy directions of those who are supposedly under their supervision may do so at considerable political and legal peril.

THE SENIOR EXECUTIVE SERVICE The Civil Service Reform Act of 1978 created a Senior Executive Service. This pool of about 8,000 career officials (which can include up to 10 percent political appointees by an administration) can be filled without senatorial confirmation. The service was created to make senior career bureaucrats more responsive to the goals and policy preferences of the White House. This new service gave presidents greater flexibility in selecting, promoting, and rewarding with financial bonuses those in the top career service who are productive and responsive.

The Senior Executive Service has not lived up to expectations. It has had little impact on the federal workers it was supposed to help. Because of federal budgetary problems, their bonuses and related incentives have been less than was expected. Morale in the senior ranks of the federal bureaucracy has not improved. Presidents and their top aides, however, have enjoyed an increase in the flexibility of assignments, and recent presidents have shrewdly used this flexibility to their advantage to discipline the upper reaches of the executive branch.

THE OFFICE OF MANAGEMENT AND BUDGET Ever since Franklin Roosevelt strengthened the presidential staffs, the budget bureau (currently called the **Office of Management and Budget**) has been a key resource. OMB's primary task is to prepare the president's annual budget. The budget is a major vehicle for shaping a president's policy priorities. It is the place and the process that determines which programs will get more funds, which will be cut, and which will remain the same. Departments and agencies fight to win larger chunks of the president's budget projections. OMB supervises the preparation of the budget and hence assists very directly in the formulation of policy. It weighs and evaluates the merits of the countless proposals and pleas that constantly pour in upon the White House.

Ninety-six percent of OMB's staff are career officials trained to evaluate ongoing projects and new spending requests. OMB's top officials are presidential

Office of Management and Budget
Presidential staff agency that serves as a clearinghouse for budgetary requests and management improvements.

You Decide...

Should civil servants be given unannounced drug tests?

Some 50 million Americans have tried marijuana, and 20 million are reputed to use it regularly. About 6 million use cocaine, and about 500,000 are heroin addicts. The rise of "crack" is rapidly destroying lives and neighborhoods. Drug use and abuse cost the economy tens of billions in health and criminal justice expenses and lost productivity. The trade puts everyone at risk, not just those who use drugs. Drug use by federal employees can be particularly hazardous, especially by air traffic controllers and top governmental policy makers.

Do the consequences of drug use justify across-the-board, random, unannounced drug and urinalysis tests for policy makers, senior civil servants, and other civil servants as a condition of employment?

appointees, and they are often among a president's most important advisers. They help a president make critical decisions not only about the budget but also about management practices, collaboration among government agencies, and legislative planning. OMB makes sure that both the departments and Congress are informed of the president's legislative preferences, and it plays an important role in expanding the policy and administrative options open to a president.

INFORMAL ORGANIZATION To study a formal organization is only to begin to understand how bureaucracy works, for we also need to understand the informal organization (see Figure 17-2). Bureaucrats differ in attitudes, motives, abilities, experiences, and political clout, and these differences matter. Leadership in an organization is exercised in a variety of places; some officials may have considerably more influence than others with the same formal status. Further, loyalties of officials cut across the formal aims of the agency.

Informal organization can have a significant effect on administration. A subordinate official in an agency may be especially close to the chief because they went to the same college, or because they play racquetball together, or because the subordinate knows how to ingratiate himself with the chief. A staff official may have tremendous influence not because of formal authority but because of experience, fairness, common sense, and personality. If an agency is headed by a chief who is

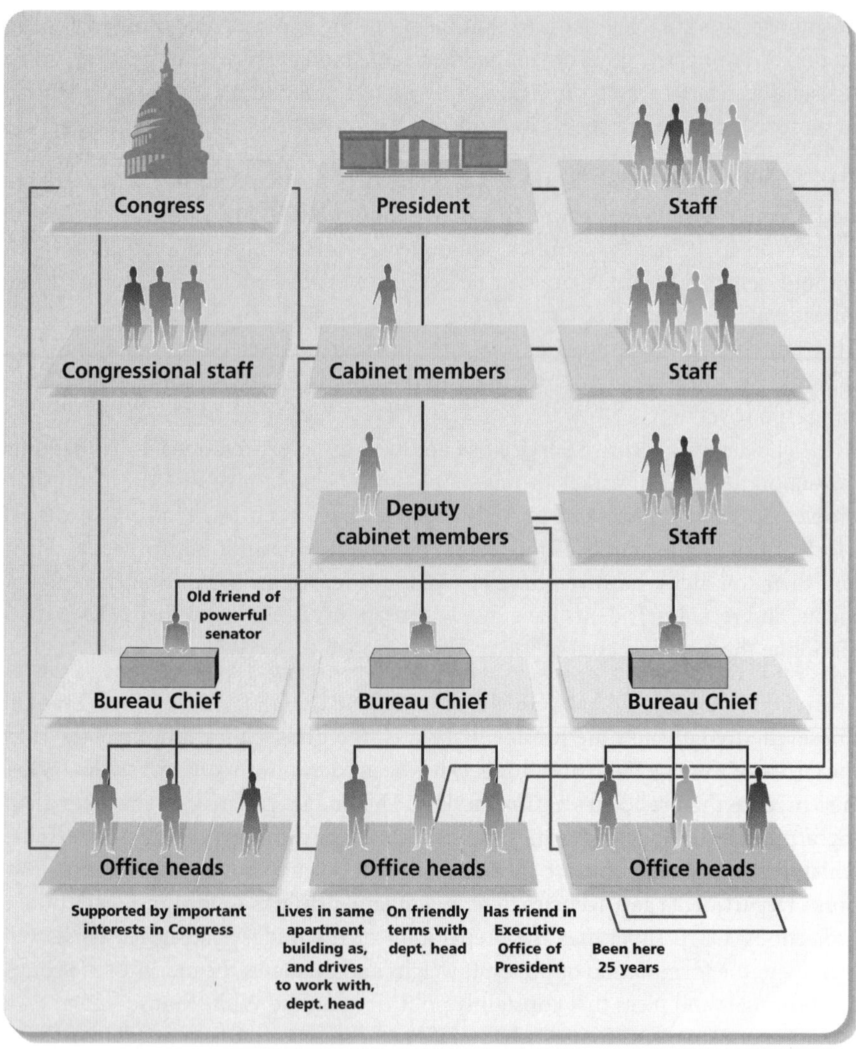

FIGURE 17-2 **Hypothetical Relationships within the Executive Branch**

weak or unimaginative, a vacuum may develop that encourages others to take over. Such informal organization and communication, cutting across regular channels, is inevitable in any organization—public or private, civilian or military.

Hatch Act
Federal statute barring federal employees from active participation in certain kinds of politics and protecting them from being fired on partisan grounds.

THE BUREAUCRACY IN ACTION

Hiring Practices and Employee Regulations

Senior government administrators work with the Office of Personnel Management in staffing their agencies. OPM acts as a policy maker for recruiting, examining, and appointing government workers. It advertises for new employees, prepares and administers oral and written examinations throughout the country, and compiles a roster of names of those who pass the tests. OPM delegates to the individual agencies the responsibility for hiring new personnel, subject to its standards. Individual agencies may promote people from within or transfer a civil servant already in the government. If, however, they wish to consider an "outsider," they request OPM to certify possible candidates from its roster of applicants. OPM typically certifies the top three applicants who have applied for the departmental or agency opening, and the agency normally selects one of these. However, the agency can decide to make no appointment or to request other applicants if it thinks none of the three is qualified.

These procedures are intended to protect the merit principle and to meet agencies' needs for qualified personnel. In practice, the two objectives sometimes come into conflict. Trade-offs have to be made, particularly between central control by OPM and delegation of discretionary authority to the agencies. Further, the pursuit of both objectives is enfeebled by the introduction of additional and often incompatible objectives—the veteran preference system, for example.

THE HATCH ACT, OLD AND NEW In 1939 Congress passed an Act to Prevent Pernicious Political Activities, usually called the **Hatch Act** after its chief sponsor, Senator Carl Hatch of New Mexico. The act was designed to neutralize the danger of a federal civil service being able to shape, if not dictate, the election of presidents and members of Congress. In essence, the Hatch Act permitted federal employees to vote in government elections, but not to take an active part in partisan politics. The Hatch Act also made it illegal to dismiss federal officials below cabinet and subcabinet rank for partisan reasons.[15]

In 1993 Congress, with the encouragement of the Clinton administration, overhauled the Hatch Act and made many forms of participation in partisan politics permissible. The revised Hatch Act still bars federal officials from running as candidates in partisan elections, but it does permit most federal civil servants to hold party positions and involve themselves in party fund raising and campaigning. This new law was welcomed by those who believed the old Hatch Act discouraged political participation by more than 2 million individuals who might otherwise be vigorous political activists.[16]

The new Hatch Act spells out many restrictions on federal bureaucrats; they cannot raise campaign funds in their agencies, and those who work in such highly sensitive federal agencies as the CIA, FBI, Secret Service, and certain divisions of the Internal Revenue Service are specifically barred from nearly all partisan activity. Those who work in the U.S. military have stricter rules regulating their political involvement. The rules for federal civilian employees specify that they:

May register and vote as they choose

May assist in voter registration

May express opinions about candidates and issues

May participate in campaigns as off-duty activities

Thinking it Through...

Unannounced drug testing raises serious Fourth Amendment questions. The idea that a group of people should be subjected to random searches without reasonable individual cause has been resisted since the outset of our life as a nation. When Congress, or the president, or the head of a federal agency requires testing as a condition of employment, even if evidence of drug use would not be used to dismiss employees, skeptical judges must be persuaded that the testing is not an "unreasonable" search and seizure.

The Supreme Court ruled in two 1989 decisions involving railway workers and U.S. Customs Service employees that mandatory blood and urine tests may be required for certain workers without a showing of "individualized suspicion." Writing for the Court in the railway workers' case, Justice Anthony Kennedy said the government's interest in testing even without a showing of individual suspicion is compelling. Employees subject to the tests discharge duties fraught with such risks of injury to others that even a momentary lapse of attention can have disastrous results.

The two cases dealt with post-accident testing of railway personnel on duty at the time of a major accident and with customs officials who carry firearms, handle classified information, or intercept drugs.

Drug testing of all federal employees, or even only those in policy-making positions, presents difficult constitutional issues. Supporters of privacy rights and civil liberties are uncomfortable with carrying this policy too far. Drug testing, some concede, may be necessary for certain individuals where public safety is genuinely involved, but it is not needed and would be an unconstitutional deprivation of privacy rights under the Fourth Amendment as a general policy.

May contribute money to political organizations or attend political fund-raising functions

May wear or display political badges, buttons, or stickers

May attend political rallies and meetings

May join political clubs or parties

May seek and hold positions in political parties

May campaign for or against referendum questions, constitutional amendments, and municipal ordinances

May not be candidates for public office in partisan elections

May not use official authority to interfere with or affect the results of an election

May not collect contributions or sell tickets to political fund-raising functions from subordinate employees

May not solicit funds or discourage the political activity of any person who has business before the employees office

May not solicit funds or discourage political activity by any person who is the subject of an ongoing audit, investigation, or enforcement action[17]

EMPLOYEE UNIONS Since 1962, federal civilian employees have had the right to form unions or associations that represent them in seeking to improve government personnel policies, and about one-third of them have joined such unions. Some of the more important unions representing federal employees today are the American Federation of Government Employees, the National Treasury Employees Union, the National Association of Government Employees, and the National Federation of Federal Employees.

Unlike unions in the private sector, these groups lack the right to strike and are not able to bargain over pay and benefits. What can they do? They can attempt to negotiate better personnel policies and practices for federal workers; they can represent federal bureaucrats at grievance and disciplinary proceedings; and they can also lobby Congress on measures affecting personnel changes.

Principles of Bureaucratic Management

Followers of the noted German sociologist Max Weber contended that a properly run bureaucracy could be a model of efficiency based on rational and impartial management.[18] President Woodrow Wilson, while still a Princeton University professor, adopted many of these views in his writings. Politics and public administration, he said, should be carefully separated. Leave politics to Congress and management to administrators who adhere to the laws passed by Congress.

According to the textbook model, bureaucrats should be closely controlled by established rules and regulations. Although this is not always true in practice, it is generally the case. Administrators are not free to make any rules they wish or to decide disputes any way they please. Several kinds of limitations exist:

1. The legislative power of Congress compels agencies to interpret and apply laws as Congress would wish. Congress can amend a law to make its intent clearer, conduct oversight hearings and investigations, or restrict appropriations.
2. Congress has closely regulated the procedures to be followed by regulatory agencies. Under the Administrative Procedures Act of 1946, agencies must publicize their procedures and organization, give advance informa-

tion of proposed rules to interested persons, allow such persons to present written information and arguments, and allow parties appearing before the agency to be accompanied by counsel and to cross-examine witnesses.

3. Under certain conditions, final actions of agencies may be appealed to the courts.
4. Some federal agencies are created for the specific purpose of overseeing and limiting their fellow agencies. Examples are the Office of Management and Budget (OMB), which is supervised by the White House, and the General Accounting Office (GAO), which is supervised by Congress.
5. Administrators must keep in mind the demands of professional ethics, the advice and criticism of experts, and the attitudes of Congress, the president, interest groups, political parties, and citizens. In the long run, these informal safeguards may be the most important of all.

This textbook model remains influential because it reflects reality. Laws of Congress, although not the whole story, are an important part of the story. Federal agencies and career servants are creatures of the enabling laws under which they work.

Reformers in the 1990s junked all but a few sections of the 10,000-page *Federal Personnel Manual* that had specified everything down to the color of personnel folders. "We actually hauled it out to a dumpster in a wheelbarrow. The death of the manual gave agencies more freedom to tailor things to fit their own operations."[19]

Many federal agencies are changing how they hire people and go about their work. Innovation and customer service became government priorities in the 1990s. Hierarchical pyramids have become somewhat flatter. Applicants can now use regular résumés instead of federal forms in applying for government jobs. A World Wide Web site lets people find out what jobs are available, and applicants can apply by phone or fax for many jobs. And workers are being evaluated and rewarded in terms of how well their teams achieve measurable results.

The government is also trying to make the federal bureaucracy a more family-friendly workplace. The Clinton-Gore administration supported the Family Leave Act (1993) and encouraged job sharing, part-time work, alternative work schedules, telecommuting from home, and child and elder services.

The Japanese Bureaucracy

In Japan the most prestigious job a college student can aspire to is not a doctor, lawyer, corporate executive, or even a politician. It is to become a top-level member of the national bureaucracy. One recent college graduate who passed the entrance exam for Japan's Ministry of Foreign Affairs (the equivalent of the U.S. State Department) was featured in his local newspaper and received congratulatory messages from his governor and national politicians from his home province.

A comparison of television news programs in Japan and the United States found that 26 percent of the news stories in Japan were about the bureaucracy, whereas only 2 percent in the United States were about the bureaucracy. The most news stories in the United States were about the president (25 percent); in Japan the prime minister was the subject of only 7 percent of news stories.

The popularity of a top-level bureaucratic job is also shown by the recruitment patterns of bureaucrats. More than 50 percent of all of Japan's top bureaucrats graduated from Japan's best university, Tokyo University, with the most difficult major, an undergraduate degree in law. When Japan's second-best university, Kyoto University, is included, fully three-fourths of all of Japan's high-level bureaucrats came from these two universities. In Japan, only the best and brightest students go on to elite careers in the national bureaucracy.

SOURCE: Ellis S. Krauss, "Portraying the State: NHK Television News and Politics," in *Media and Politics in Japan*, ed. Susan J. Pharr and Ellis S. Krauss (University of Hawai'i Press, 1996).

Bureaucratic Realities

Career administrators are in a good position to know when a program is not operating properly and what action is needed. But one of the major complaints about bureaucrats is that they do not go out of their way to make things better. The problem is that many bureaucrats often learn by hard experience that they are more likely to get into trouble by attempting to improve or change programs than if they just do nothing. Hardening of administrative arteries is more likely, some critics say, than administrative aggressiveness.

Often the fiercest battles in Washington are not over principles or programs but over jurisdictional boundaries, personnel cuts, and fringe benefits. Career employees come to believe the expansion of their organization is vital to the public interest. They sometimes become more skillful at building political alliances to protect their own organization than at building political alliances to ensure their programs' effectiveness.

Organizations, both public and private, tend to resent "outside" direction, whether by a president or by other external supervisors or boards. A department head in the government, a large corporation, or a university is often likely to consider the president of the organization to be an outsider whose judgment in matters affecting his or her bureau is always suspect.

Career administrators often become involved in politics. Some of them have more bargaining and alliance-building skills than the elected and appointed officials to whom they report. In one sense, agency leaders are at the center of action in Washington. Over time, administrative agencies may come to resemble entrenched pressure groups in that they operate to advance their own interests. The FBI is a good example; it is always seeking more funds, new projects, and as much independence as possible from the Justice Department in which it is located.

Career bureaucrats develop a keen sensitivity to the political environment and get caught up in a network of issue experts and politicians who specialize in certain policy areas. The growth of federal programs from the 1930s through the 1970s brought an increase in the number of policy aides on Capitol Hill, of Washington law firms that specialize in assisting clients who are interested in policy development, and of lobbyists (some say at least 40,000) who work with Congress and the federal bureaucracy to advance various economic and professional interests.

Groups that perceive real or potential harm to their interests cultivate the bureau chiefs and agency staffs who have jurisdiction over their programs. They also work closely with the committees and subcommittees of Congress that authorize, appropriate, and oversee programs run by these key bureaucracies. Some bureaucrats become entangled with these external coalitions. Bureau chiefs are logical targets for the efforts of concerned interest groups. On the other hand, recognizing the power of interest groups, bureau chiefs frequently recruit them as allies in pursuing common goals. What these bureau officials have in common with interest groups and their allies in Congress is a shared view that more money should be spent on federal programs run by the bureau in question. These alliances among bureaucrats, interest groups, and subcommittee members and their staffs on Capitol Hill are sometimes described as **iron triangles**.

The executive branch is not the smooth operating hierarchy it is made to appear on an organization chart. The president, cabinet members, and their politically appointed undersecretaries and assistant secretaries have their work cut out for them as they try to impose their will on the permanent civil service. Bureaucrats, with their strong allies in Congress and the interest groups, often resist change and direction from their appointed or elected political "superiors." Some view these external relations as "administrative guerrilla warfare" and a serious roadblock to holding elected leaders accountable. Others view the clash over values as inevitable in a system that provides ample opportunities for such clashes. After all, the bureaucracy is merely one more forum for registering the many demands that people make upon government.

The Case of Bureau Chief George Brown

The following case is fictional, yet based on actual experiences of typical bureaucrats. (Note that not only is our main character, George Brown, fictitious, but so are the Bureau of Erosion and the Department of Conservation. Other agencies mentioned do exist.) This case illustrates some of the painful choices bureaucrats have to make.

George Brown, age 47, is chief of the Bureau of Erosion in the Department of Conservation. A graduate of North Dakota State University, Brown is a career official in the federal service and a member of the Senior Executive Service. His appointment to the post was a result of both ability and luck. When his old bureau chief retired, the president wanted to bring in an erosion expert from Illinois, but influential members of Congress pressed for the selection of a recently "retired" (actually he was

iron triangle

A mutually supporting relationship among interest groups, congressional committees and subcommittees, and government agencies that share a common policy concern.

defeated in the last election!) member of the House of Representatives from a farm state. After deadlock and delay, Brown, then a division head in the Bureau of Erosion, was promoted to bureau chief as a compromise.

Early in March of Brown's second year in his new post, his boss, the secretary of conservation, summoned him and the other bureau heads to an important conference and informed them that he had just attended a cabinet meeting in which the president had called on each department to make at least a 10 percent cut in spending in the coming fiscal year. The president, the secretary reported, was responding to popular demands for federal fiscal restraint.

Brown quickly calculated what this cutback would mean for his agency. For several years the Bureau of Erosion had been spending about $1.7 billion a year to help farmers protect their farmland. Could it get along on about $1.4 billion, and where could savings be made? Returning to his office, Brown called a meeting of his personnel, budget, and management officials. After hours of discussion, it was agreed that savings could be effected only by decreasing the scope of the program, a step that would involve terminating about 1,500 of the bureau's employees. Brown asked his subordinates to prepare a list of employees who were the least useful to the bureau. He would decide which to drop after checking with the affected members of Congress.

A few weeks later Brown presented a $1.5 billion budget to Conservation Secretary Jones, who approved it and passed it along to the White House. The president then went over the figures with the director of the Office of Management and Budget, and a few weeks later the White House submitted the budget for the whole executive department to Congress.

Meanwhile Brown was running into trouble. News of the proposed budget cut had leaked immediately to the bureau's personnel in the field. Nobody knew who would be dropped, and some employees were already looking around for other positions. Morale fell. Hearing of the cut, farmers' representatives in Washington notified local farm organizations throughout the country. Soon Brown began to receive letters demanding certain services be maintained. Members of the farm bloc in Congress were also becoming restless.

Shortly after the president's budget went to Congress, Representative Jim Smith of Kansas asked Brown to meet with him. Smith was chair of the Subcommittee on Agriculture of the influential House Appropriations Committee. Smith said his fellow subcommittee members, both Democratic and Republican, all agreed the Erosion Bureau's budget must not be cut. The farmers needed even more than the usual $1.7 billion because of severe flood conditions in some sections of the country. He warned they would vote against the party if the program were reduced. Members of Congress from agricultural states, Smith went on, were under tremendous pressure. Leaders of farm groups in Washington were mobilizing farmers everywhere. Besides, Smith said, the president was unfair in cutting down on the farm program; he did not understand agricultural problems, and he failed to recognize that programs designed to increase agricultural output were the best way to reduce the trade imbalance. Let the cuts in federal programs be made elsewhere.

Smith then came to the point. Brown, he said, must vigorously oppose the budget cut. Hearings on appropriations would begin in a few days, and Brown as bureau chief would, of course, testify. At that time he must insist that the cuts would hurt the bureau and undermine its whole program. Brown would not have to volunteer this statement, Smith said. He could just respond to leading questions put by committee members. Brown's testimony, Smith thought, would help clinch the argument against the cut because the committee would respect the judgment of the administrator closest to the problem. Other bureaucrats were fighting to save their appropriations. Obviously, said Smith, they are counting on public reaction to get them exemptions from the 10 percent cutback, and Brown would be foolish not to do the same.

Brown was in an embarrassing position. He had submitted his estimates to the secretary of conservation and to the president, and it was his duty to back them up. The rules of the game demanded, moreover, that agency heads defend budget estimates submitted to Congress, whatever their personal feelings might be. The president had appointed Brown to his position and had a right to expect loyalty. On the other hand, Brown was on the spot with his own agency. His employees all expected their chief to look out for them. Brown had developed cordial relations with his staff, and he squirmed at the thought of having to let more than a thousand employees go. What would they think when they heard him defend the cut? More important, he needed to maintain friendly relations with the farmers, the farm organizations, and the farm bloc in Congress. Finally, Brown was committed to the work of his department. He grasped its true importance, whereas the president's budget advisers did not. And he knew that his pet project—aid to poverty-stricken areas in Appalachia—would probably be sacrificed because it was not supported by a powerful constituency.

Brown turned for advice to an old friend in the Office of Management and Budget. This friend urged him to defend the president's budget. He appealed to Brown's professional pride as an administrator and career public servant. He reminded him that the chief executive must have control of the budget and that agency heads must subordinate their interests to the executive program. He said the only way to balance the budget would be for all agencies to make program cuts. As for the employees to be dropped—well, that was part of the game. Some of them might be able to get jobs in other government agencies; civil service would protect their status. Anyway, they would understand Brown's position. In a parting shot he mentioned that the president had Brown in mind for bigger things.

The next day Brown had lunch with a North Dakota senator, wise and experienced in Washington ways, who had helped him get his start in government. The senator was sympathetic. But there was no doubt about what Brown should do, the senator said. He should follow Representative Smith's plan, of course, being as diplomatic as possible about it. That way he would protect his position with those who would be most important in the long run.

"After all," the senator said, "presidents come and go, parties rise and fall, but Smith and the other members of Congress will be here a long time, and so will the farm organizations. They can do a lot for you in future years. And remember one other thing," the senator concluded. "These people are the elected representatives of the people. Constitutionally, Congress has the power to spend money as it sees fit. Why should you object if they want to spend an extra \$90 or \$100 million?"

Brown realized his dilemma was worse than ever. The arguments on both sides were persuasive. He felt hopelessly divided in his loyalties and responsibilities. The president expected one thing of him; Congress expected another. As a professional administrator, he felt obliged to side with the president. As head of a bureau, however, he wanted to protect his team and his programs. His future? Whatever decision he made, he was bound to antagonize important people and interests.

After much soul searching, Brown decided the issue involved more than loyalties, ambitions, and programs. Ultimately it boiled down to two questions: First, to whom was he, Brown, legally and administratively responsible? Formally, of course, he was responsible to the chief executive who appointed him, who was accountable to the people. Brown knew, too, that he was accountable to Congress, which after all has the power over all fiscal matters. Second, which course of action did he think was better for the welfare of all the people? Looking at the question this way, he believed the president was right in asking for fiscal restraint. As a taxpayer and consumer himself, Brown recognized the need to reduce the federal budget deficit. To be sure, Congress must make the final decision. Yet to make the decision, Congress had to act on the advice of the administration, and the administration should speak with one voice for the majority of the people, or it should not be speaking out at all.

With mixed feelings, Brown decided to support the president. Being a seasoned alliance builder, however, he hedged his bets. He came out strongly for the president's budget, yet at the same time he sent friendly members of Congress some questions to be asked of him in future congressional hearings so he could explain the impact of the cutbacks. He also circulated to some of these same members of Congress an analysis of the impact of personnel and funding cuts in their states and districts.

BUREAUCRATIC RESPONSIVENESS

One of the most complex questions concerning public bureaucracies is whether they are responsive enough to the citizens and the elected officials who employ them. Determining how responsive an agency is depends on the perceptions of the person involved. A person who has had to stand for hours in a long line, whether at the post office or at a welfare agency, will complain about unresponsive bureaucrats. Someone who feels that a federal bureaucrat treats him or her "by the book" rather than by common sense also develops a critical view.

Standard Operating Procedures

Bureaucracies develop routines and standard operating procedures to ensure efficiency and productivity. Unfortunately, reliance on routine reduces flexibility. Just about everyone has at one time or another been turned away from the local post office because a package to be mailed was too large, or too small, or in the wrong kind of container. It is hard on such occasions to hold back our anger: Why can't they be flexible? Why can't they be reasonable? Why can't they deal with me in a personal way?

Procedures that allow the post office, the army, or the Internal Revenue Service to perform efficiently sometimes also diminish their ability to respond to the personalized needs of individuals. Routines help to prevent chaos and allow government behavior to be consistent, uniform, and impartial. The inevitable and necessary result of big bureaucracy is often a trade-off; quick, personalized, and sympathetic service is sacrificed for order.

Privatization

Can certain problems be better handled by agencies other than government bureaucracies? For example, should the government run railways, prisons, and a public television channel, or should we encourage the private sector and free market mechanisms to handle these responsibilities?

Privatization is the process of contracting public services to private organizations. Examples of privatization include the contracting out by the Air Force of the building of fighter planes, and the contracting out by several state governments of the construction and operation of prisons. The National Aeronautics and Space Administration contracts out most of the manufacturing of its space vehicles.

Private or nonprofit firms handle a vast array of services, from repairing ships to delivering meals-on-wheels to the home-bound elderly. Some people contend that our public schools might be more effectively operated by private firms. Advocates of privatization claim it would reduce costs and provide better service than reliance on the federal and state bureaucracies.[20]

Critics of privatization point to the cost overruns and waste in the procurement of weapons systems as failures of privatization. According to David Osborne and Ted Gaebler, privatization is one answer, but not *the* answer:

> Services can be contracted out or turned over to the private sector. But governance cannot. We can privatize discrete [governmental programs], but not the overall process of governance. If we did, we would have no mechanism by which

privatization
The contracting out to the private sector of services that are usually provided by government.

You Decide...

To whom should bureaucrats be accountable?

One of the important challenges in American government is how to keep nonelected government workers (bureaucrats) accountable to the taxpayers. After all, whose bureaucracy is this, anyway? Part of the challenge is figuring out how accountability can be guaranteed. How should the day-to-day operations and behavior of the typical U.S. public bureaucrat be controlled?

Most bureaucrats, most of the time, follow guidelines provided either in the law or by their administrative superiors, but at times many factors come into play as bureaucrats have to exercise judgment and discretion. Many of the considerations listed in the box on the facing page shape bureaucratic behavior implicitly rather than explicitly. Much of this chapter has analyzed the question of bureaucratic accountability. Perhaps it will revise your thinking.

> to make collective decisions, no way to set the rules of the marketplace, no means to enforce rules of behavior. We would lose all sense of equity and altruism: services that could not generate a profit, whether housing for the homeless or health care for the poor, would barely exist. . . .
>
> Business does some things better than government, but government does some things better than business. The public sector tends to be better, for instance, at policy management, regulation, ensuring equity, preventing discrimination or exploitation, ensuring continuity and stability of services, and ensuring social cohesion. . . . Business tends to do better at performing economic tasks, innovating, replicating successful experiments, adapting to rapid change, abandoning unsuccessful or obsolete activities, and performing complex or technical tasks.[21]

Would we be better off if the U.S. Postal Service were turned over to private firms? A business executive who served as postmaster general, Anthony Frank, says no. He praises the Postal Service for its high on-time delivery and points out that all Americans, no matter where they live, get essentially the same service at the same price. "If you privatize it," Frank pointed out, "the cost would go up for a lot of Americans. [Thirty-three] cents compared to anywhere else in the world is an incredible bargain," says Frank. "It's 67 cents in Germany, 47 cents in Japan, and 42 cents in Canada. And they don't have any overnight service."[22]

Bureaucratic Accountability

The question of bureaucratic *responsiveness* is extremely difficult to disentangle from the question of bureaucratic *accountability*. In determining the responsiveness of the U.S. Navy or the FBI or the Department of Transportation, we must also ask who should oversee and control them.

Should bureaucrats be accountable to the president, the cabinet, the majority in Congress, or the people who elected the president? Plainly, most Americans would like the bureaucracy to be responsive to them as taxpaying customers. In general terms, they would say the bureaucracy should be responsive to the public interest. But defining the public interest is the crucial problem. The president and the House and the Senate and the committees of Congress all claim to speak on behalf of the public interest. Moreover, to whom bureaucrats should be accountable is an inherently political question. Accountability to the White House, for example, depends in large measure on the supporters' partisanship toward the president. Republicans, not surprisingly, favor strong presidential control over the bureaucracy when Republicans occupy the White House, as do Democrats when their party wins the White House.

Attorney General Janet Reno was pressured by congressional Republicans to name an independent counsel to investigate fund-raising irregularities by President Clinton and the Democrats, but she refused to do so. She had earlier, however, approved investigations of several Clinton cabinet members.

To the President

Modern presidents invariably contend the president should be in charge, for the chief executive is responsive to the broadest constituency. A president, it is argued, must see that popular needs and expectations are converted into administrative action. When the nation elects a conservative president who favors cutbacks in federal programs and less governmental intervention in the economy, his policies must be carried out by the bureaucracy. The voters' wishes can be translated into action only if the bureaucrats support presidential policies.

Yet, as we have seen, under the American system of checks and balances the party winning a presidential election does not acquire total control of the national government. Under our Constitution, the president is not even the undisputed master of the executive structure. Congress sets up the agencies, broadly determines their organization, provides the money, and establishes the ground rules under which they operate. Congress constantly reviews the activities of the bureaucrats in appropriation hearings, special investigations, or informal inquiries. And, as we have also seen, the Senate confirms important cabinet-level leaders.

Presidents come into an ongoing system over which they have little control and within which they have little leeway to make the bureaucracy responsive. Still, some presidential control over the bureaucracy may be exercised through the president's powers of appointment, reorganization, and budgeting. More specifically, a president can attempt to control the bureaucracy by appointing or promoting sympathetic personnel, mobilizing public opinion and congressional pressure, changing the administrative apparatus, influencing budget decisions, using extensive personal persuasion, and if all else fails, shifting a bureaucracy's assignment to another department or agency (although this shift requires tacit if not explicit congressional approval).

Presidents appoint about 4,000 people to top positions within the executive branch; however, many of these are confidential assistants or special aides to cabinet officers, and many require Senate confirmation and are not exclusively a president's choice. Some suggest that a president's hand could be strengthened if the chief executive were able to make two or three times as many political appointments.

"Think of it. Presidents come and go, but WE go on forever!"

Berry's World. Reproduced by permission of Newspaper Enterprise Association, Inc.

To Congress

Congress has a number of ways to exercise control over the bureaucracy: by establishing agencies, formulating budgets, appropriating funds, confirming personnel, authorizing new programs or new shifts in direction, conducting investigations and hearings, reorganizing authority, and rebuking officials.

The foundation of this bureaucratic power is legal authority. A bureaucrat's information and expertise augment this legal authority. Ordinarily, bureaucrats know more than anyone else about their programs and the consequences of what they are doing. Recognizing this, Congress may request agency heads to make initial proposals and provide cost and price estimates. To reduce bureaucratic deception, Congress has imposed stiff penalties for providing misleading information.

Most constituents, especially businesspeople, turn to their members of Congress for help as they battle federal red tape. Hence, as the federal bureaucracy and its funds grow, so does the influence of members of Congress. Members of Congress regularly earn political credit by interceding in federal agencies on behalf of their constituents. Still, Congress is under fire, at least in some quarters, for encouraging the growth of federal spending and allowing the bureaucracy to remain too independent. Members of Congress, so this reasoning goes, profit from the growth and complexity of the federal government.

> The brutal fact is that only a small minority of our 535 members of Congress would trade the present bureaucratic structure for one which was an efficient, effective agent of the general interest—the political payoffs of the latter are lower than those of the former. Congressional talk of inefficient, irresponsible, out-of-control bureaucracy is typically just that—talk—and when it is not, it usually refers to agencies under the jurisdiction of other legislators' committees. Why do reformers continually ignore the fact that Congress has all the power necessary to enforce the "people's will" on the bureaucracy? Congress can abolish or reorganize an agency. Congress can limit or expand an agency's jurisdiction, or allow its authority to lapse entirely. Congress can slash an agency's appropriations. Congress can investigate. Congress can do all these things, but individual congressmen generally find reasons not to do so.[23]

Congress, it is charged, anxious whenever possible to avoid conflict, adopts such sweeping legislation and delegates so much authority to the bureaucracy that bureaucrats, in effect, have become the nation's lawmakers. Congress could pass laws with precise wording, but it would get too bogged down in details to complete its work.

It is not Congress as a whole that shares direction over the bureaucracy with the president. More accurately, individual members and committees specialize in

Thinking it Through...

From this list of possibilities, select one or more as your preferences:

- The Constitution
- Laws and statutes
- Congress
- The president
- Their administrative superiors, including bureau chiefs and cabinet officers
- Their own view of "the public interest"
- Court rulings
- Public opinion
- Interest groups
- The media
- Their profession
- Public-employee unions
- Political parties and their platforms
- Intellectual opinion
- Their co-workers and colleagues
- Taxpayers

Why Presidents Like to Reorganize the Bureaucracy

- Shake up an organization to increase managerial control
- Simplify or streamline the bureaucracy or a specific agency
- Reduce costs by lessening overlap, duplication, inefficiencies
- Symbolize priorities by signaling new responsibilities in new agencies
- Improve program effectiveness by bringing separate but logically related programs to the same agency
- Improve policy integration by placing competitive or conflicting interests within a single organization
- Downgrade the importance of a program to weaken it
- Increase power over an unresponsive agency by installing their own people.

the appropriations and oversight processes. They oversee policies of a particular cluster of agencies—often the agencies serving constituents in their own districts. Some legislators stake out a claim over more general policies. Members of Congress, who see presidents come and go, come to think they know more about particular agencies than the president does (and often they do). Some congressional leaders prefer to seal off "their" agencies from presidential direction and maintain their influence over public policy. Sometimes their power is institutionalized; the Army Corps of Engineers, for example, is given authority by law to plan public works and report to Congress without going through the president.

Whose Bureaucracy Is This Anyway?

Presidents and members of Congress both strive to exercise control over the bureaucracy, each in their own way. Interest groups and court rulings also influence the way the bureaucracy operates. For their part, career bureaucrats say they are responsive to the laws and statutes they work under and to their own standards of professionalism and responsibility. The search for improved means of ensuring bureaucratic accountability is never ending. Experiments with countless reforms—reorganization, deregulating the public service, sunset practices, selective privatization, budgetary planning, and oversight hearings—also continue.

It is increasingly clear, moreover, that virtually all national bureaucracies are more responsive today than once was the case. Even organizations such as the FBI or the Corps of Engineers are now more accountable to Congress and the White House, and ultimately to the American people. "Thanks to Freedom of Information statutes and other 'sunshine' legislation, [the bureaucracy] has become less selective, and the weakening of iron triangles has made it much more responsive to broad constituencies and much less the creature of its own clients."[24] Also, new restrictions in the Clinton era prohibit those who leave government from working for the agency they recently left on any contractual basis.

What the Public Thinks of Bureaucrats and the Bureaucracy

Big bureaucracy in the abstract is unpopular. It engages in many activities that most people find offensive, like taxing them, inspecting them, or regulating them. Big bureaucracy is sometimes defined as that part of the government people dislike.

As individuals, civil servants are appreciated, but as a class they are not. Citizens who have dealings with federal employees on a face-to-face basis say they are pleased by employees' performance. In contrast to scorn for bureaucrats and bureaucracy in general, Americans seem to approve the conduct of individual federal employees—Postal Service delivery persons, forest rangers, Veterans Affairs Department officials, or county field agents who help with the local 4-H programs. They also admire astronauts, marines, FBI agents, and Coast Guard officers, all of whom are also federal employees.

An irreverent journal in the nation's capital, *The Washington Monthly*, rails against clumsy bureaucracy in every issue. Most newspapers and magazines feature stories and cartoons critical of the federal bureaucracy. Some members of Congress like to joke that there is a parlor game played in the nation's capital: "It's called Bureaucracy," they say. "And there is only one rule. The first one to move loses."

Red Tape and Waste

Americans are skeptical of, if not cynical about, big government. They equate bigness with remoteness, incompetence, and unresponsiveness. They also assume that the bigger government gets, the less efficient it is, and the more it wastes. Perhaps the most criticized aspect of the federal bureaucracy is that career public employees seem to enjoy the closest thing to job security; they are almost as secure in their jobs as if they were confirmed for life on the Supreme Court.

A central problem with the bureaucracy, critics say, is that we have failed to subject it to the control and discipline alleged to operate in the private sector. Despite the talk about numerous federal programs facing the guillotine, most federal agencies survive. The tests of efficiency and cost effectiveness that are the basic standards of business are much less important in decisions about which federal programs will survive. Outdated and ineffective programs endure because both Republicans and Democrats have forged coalitions of convenience based on a desire to deliver favors and protect programs located in their particular districts.

Defining what is truly in the national interest is hard. And deciding what is no longer in the national interest is also equally hard for presidents and members of Congress. Take, for example, the subsidies for public radio and public television. Many Republicans in Congress wanted to end support for public broadcasting, saying that *Sesame Street*, *Car Talk*, and *Wall Street Week* would all be picked up by the networks, and that today's abundance of cable television channels makes publicly subsidized broadcasting no longer necessary.[25]

Congress throughout the 1990s took steps to downsize federal agencies. It abolished the Interstate Commerce Commission; it called for the gradual privatization of Amtrak; and it scaled back the Environmental Protection Agency, the Bureau of Mines, the Bureau of Indian Affairs, and several scientific advisory boards and projects. Still, many Americans believe Congress has spared too many programs and agencies that no longer serve us well.

In the mid-1990s there was a Republican crusade to dismantle the Departments of Energy, Commerce, Housing and Urban Development, and Education. "But even as they claimed a mandate to end 'big government,' these Republicans discovered that voter sentiment about closing down agencies typically ranged from apathy to uneasiness to outright opposition."[26]

Republicans showed less eagerness to cut cabinet departments in Clinton's second term, due in part to the downsizing of some of these departments, in part to many programs being made into block grants to states and localities, and in part because they knew President Clinton would wield his veto power to retain these departments. Moreover, various interest groups came to the defense of these departments. For example, a coalition of major corporations—including AT&T, IBM, Boeing, General Electric, and Motorola—came together to support the Commerce Department and its trade promotion and industrial research operations.[27]

Still another charge leveled against bureaucrats is that once a program is established, the people assigned to it become committed to "the cause." In the Office of Civil Rights in the Department of Education, for example, appointments generally go to those concerned about protecting the rights of women and minorities. The protection of rights is their assigned task, and in their zeal they demand more authority and more spending. Groups outside the government who want their programs carried forward pressure the agencies; women's groups and minority advocacy groups carefully watch the Office of Civil Rights.

Two Cheers for Bureaucracy

Recent efforts at some state and local government levels have made their bureaucracies more entrepreneurial. The cities of St. Paul, Minnesota, and Indianapolis, Indiana, and the states of Florida and Massachusetts have introduced various market incentives, rewards, and public-private partnerships that encourage efficiency and responsiveness.[28] Competition and incentives can prudently be built into various government monopolies so that bureaucracies become more responsive to their customers.

In the private sector, if you are displeased with the service provided by a company such as AT&T, you can switch to MCI or Sprint, and this is now happening to some government services. It used to be that you could use only the U.S. Postal Service to deliver your messages, whether you liked the service or not. Now numerous delivery services compete with the postal service; fax and e-mail have become popular means of communication. (It should be noted that the postal service is getting better—credit this to the competition.)

Compared to most other nations, U.S. government employment has declined. Government employment grew by more than 20 percent in Sweden in the past generation and by over 11 percent in Italy and Germany during the same period. There has been a steady decline in U.S. government employment during the last 12 years.

A comparison of the performance of the U.S. bureaucracy with most bureaucracies in the world suggests we should be grateful for the service we get from our public employees. The U.S. Postal Service provides a good example. Although it is sometimes criticized as being a dinosaur, it is more efficient and less costly than comparable services around the world. And, as noted, it is getting better. Another example is the United States tax system; although it is constantly cursed and has been properly chided for its abuses of power, it is the most effective and efficient such system in the world.

POLITICS online

Government Business on the Web

In forming the National Information Infrastructure Advisory Council, Bill Clinton and Al Gore have made information technology a priority. Its goal was to centralize Internet policy at the highest level, advocating a market-driven approach to Internet regulation. They encouraged all governmental units to make use of the Internet and have done so themselves through their home page:

http://www.whitehouse.gov

One application of information technology is found in the Federal Acquisition Streamlining Act, which created a Federal Acquisition Network (FACNET). Under this act, all federal agencies were to use electronic means for routine purchasing. Previously, procurement of things government uses—from paper clips to paint—required purchase orders and supporting memos. Implementing such a change ran into problems involving computer hardware and software. FACNET, which was to have been fully implemented by early 1997, fell behind schedule. Still, no one doubts that new technologies are becoming an integral part of the federal bureaucracy.

SUMMARY

1. We often condemn bureaucracy and bureaucrats, yet we continue to turn to them to solve our toughest problems and to render more and better services. Our bureaucratic agencies reflect how our political system has tried to identify our most important national goals and how policies are implemented.
2. The 1990s witnessed major efforts to overhaul and improve the workings of the federal bureaucracy. Vice-President Al Gore recommended numerous initiatives to streamline the government, eliminate waste, and make government more like an effective business.

3. Most of the 2.7 million civilian employees of the federal government serve under a merit system that protects their independence of politics. They work in one of the 14 cabinet departments as well as government corporations, independent agencies, and independent regulatory boards or commissions. A major responsibility is policy implementation.
4. The American bureaucracy does not fully adhere to the textbook model of management organization, as it is not fully subordinate to any branch of government. It has at least two immediate bosses: Congress and the president. It must pay considerable attention as well to the courts and their rulings and, of course, to well-organized interest groups and public opinion. In many ways the bureaucracy is a semi-independent force—a fourth branch of government—in American politics.
5. Debates and controversy over big government and big bureaucracy, and over how to reorganize and eliminate waste in them, continue. Compared with many other nations and their centralized bureaucracies, the hand of bureaucracy rests more gently and less oppressively on Americans than on citizens elsewhere. Efforts to make the bureaucracy more responsive are enduring struggles in a constitutional democracy.

KEY TERMS

bureaucrat 415
bureaucracy 415
spoils system 416
merit system 416
Office of Personnel Management (OPM) 416
government corporation 418
bureau 418
independent agency 418
independent regulatory board 418
Office of Management and Budget 419
Hatch Act 421
iron triangle 424
privatization 427

FURTHER READING

Joel D. Aberbach, *Keeping a Watchful Eye: The Politics of Congressional Oversight* (Brookings Institution, 1990).

Dan Baum, *Smoke and Mirrors: The War on Drugs and the Politics of Failure* (Little, Brown, 1996).

Shelley L. Davis, *Unbridled Power: Inside the Secret Culture of the IRS* (Harper Business, 1997).

John J. DiIulio, Jr., ed., *Deregulating the Public Service: Can Government Be Improved?* (Brookings Institution, 1994).

John J. DiIulio Jr., Gerald Garvey, and Donald F. Kettl, *Improving Government Performance: An Owner's Manual* (Brookings Institution, 1993).

Anthony Downs, *Inside Bureaucracy* (Little, Brown, 1967).

James W. Fesler and Donald F. Kettl, *The Politics of the Administrative Process* (Chatham House, 1991).

Charles T. Goodsell, *The Case for Bureaucracy*, 3d ed. (Chatham House, 1994).

Al Gore, *The Best Kept Secrets in Government: How the Clinton Administration Is Reinventing the Way Washington Works* (Random House, 1996).

Al Gore, *Creating a Government That Works Better and Costs Less: The Report of the National Performance Review* (Plume-Penguin, 1993).

Larry Hill, ed., *The State of Public Bureaucracy* (M. E. Sharpe, 1992).

Philip K. Howard, *The Death of Common Sense: How Law Is Suffocating America* (Random House, 1994).

Patricia Ingraham and David Rosenbloom, eds., *The Promise and Paradox of Civil Service Reform* (University of Pittsburgh Press, 1992).

Ronald N. Johnson and Gary D. Libecap, *The Federal Civil Service System and the Problem of Bureaucracy* (University of Chicago Press, 1994).

Herbert Kaufman, *The Administrative Behavior of Federal Bureau Chiefs* (Brookings Institution, 1981).

Donald F. Kettl, *Reinventing Government: A Fifth Year Report Card* (Brookings Institution, 1998).

Donald F. Kettl and John J. DiIulio, Jr., eds., *Inside the Reinvention Machine: Appraising Governmental Reform* (Brookings Institution, 1995).

Andrew Kohut, ed., *Deconstructing Distrust: How Americans View Government* (Pew Research Center for the People and the Press, 1998).

Everett C. Ladd and Karlyn H. Bowman, *What's Wrong: A Survey of American Satisfaction and Complaint* (AEI Press, 1998).

Paul C. Light, *Monitoring Government: Inspectors General and the Search for Accountability* (Brookings Institution, 1993).

Paul C. Light, *Thickening Government: Federal Hierarchy and the Diffusion of Accountability* (Brookings Institution, 1995).

Paul C. Light, *The Tides of Reform: Making Government Work, 1945–1995* (Yale University Press, 1997).

David Osborne and Ted Gaebler, *Reinventing Government: How the Entrepreneurial Spirit Is Transforming the Public Sector* (Addison-Wesley, 1992).

David Osborne and Peter Plastrik, *Banishing Bureaucracy: The Five Strategies for Reinventing Government* (Addison-Wesley, 1997).

Elliot Richardson, *Reflections of a Radical Moderate* (Pantheon Books, 1996).

James Q. Wilson, *Bureaucracy: What Government Agencies Do and Why They Do It* (Basic Books, 1989).

B. Don Wood and Richard W. Waterman, *Bureaucratic Dynamics: The Role of Bureaucracy in a Democracy* (Westview Press, 1994).

Four useful journals are *Journal of Policy Analysis and Management*, *National Journal*, *Public Administration Review*, and *Government Executive*.

MAKING
ECONOMIC
AND
REGULATORY
POLICY

18

CHAPTER OUTLINE

- Public Policy
- Economic Policy
- Monetary Policy
- Trade Policy
- Regulatory Policy
- Regulating Business
- Regulating Labor and Management
- Environmental Protection
- The Deregulation Debate

GOVERNMENT BY THE PEOPLE IS ENCOURAGED BY AN ECONOMY IN WHICH ECONOMIC ENTERPRISES ARE MAINLY OWNED PRIVATELY, NOT BY THE STATE. YET THE close and favorable association between democracy and market capitalism conceals a paradox. "A market-capitalist economy inevitably generates inequalities in the political resources to which different citizens have access," writes political scientist Robert Dahl. "Thus a market-capitalist economy seriously impairs political equality."[1]

No matter how much a society may strive to be democratic, if its citizens are economically unequal, they are unlikely to be politically equal. Consequently, there is always a tension between democracy and a capitalist economy. Plainly, economics matters. And so does the way in which a nation makes its economic, social, and foreign policies.

In the preceding chapters we have concentrated on the structure of our federal system and how government institutions are organized and operate. In this chapter and the two chapters that follow, we focus on what the national government *does*, how voters, interest groups, and institutions (Congress, the White House, the executive branch, the courts) all interact to promote the general welfare and to provide for the common defense. We will be talking about making and implementing public policy.

Public Policy

Thousands of individuals work in Washington in the policy-making process. One of the most fascinating aspects of Washington politics is the way these policy activists in government and nongovernmental organizations (research institutes, foundations, the media) join forces. These policy subsystems grow up around interrelated issues. Formal titles are less important for participation in the group than information, imagination, energy, and persistence. Important players include White House staff and executive branch officials, senior congressional committee staff, lobbyists, professional political consultants, and unelected policy specialists. Also influential are journalists and TV pundits and nongovernmental research organizations—"think tanks" such as the Brookings Institution, American Enterprise Institute, or Heritage Foundation. Policy activists help clarify issues, resolve conflicts, and facilitate cooperation across institutions.

There are numerous approaches to the study of public policy making. The choice of which approach is most appropriate depends on what policies are being considered, the particular stage of the process selected for analysis, and the analyst's assumptions and political values. Nevertheless, the following distinct stages in the policy-making process can be identified.

- *Problem Identification*: What is the problem? How and by whom is the problem defined? How does the problem fit with existing policy categories and priorities? Does the government need to help out, intervene, regulate, or make some kind of decision? Should the issue or problem even be placed on the government's agenda? What forces determine whether the problem will reach the attention of government officials? A variety of factors and people are involved in problem identification: events, crises, changes in expert opinion, changes in mass opinion, interest-group agitation, and involvement by elected officials and their staffs.
- *Policy Formulation*: What should be done? What alternatives should analysts consider? How should the alternatives be assessed? Who should be involved in the planning and design of the policy?
- *Policy Adoption*: Who needs to act? What branch of government should get involved? What constitutional, legal, or political requirements must be met? How specific or how general must the decision be? Should Congress or some regulatory body be asked to hold hearings on the matter and come up with recommendations? Or should the matter be turned over to the president, who can issue executive orders and deliver major addresses urging the public to comply?
- *Policy Implementation*: Once adopted, how should the policy be carried out? At what level of government—federal, state, local, or all three—will the policy be most effectively implemented? How much money should be spent, where, and how? How can the policy be administered effectively? How and by whom will the implementation of the policy be defined? During this stage policy is translated into practice.
- *Policy Evaluation*: Is the policy working? How is the effectiveness of the policy measured? Who evaluates the policy? What are the consequences of policy evaluation and congressional oversight? Program supporters and administrators tend to exaggerate the success of their favorite programs to justify the funds allocated to them. On the other hand, an agency may build in delays and deficiencies during evaluation to hide the real cost of its operations. Evaluation is never entirely nonpolitical; it is sometimes used by one party, branch of government, department, or agency against another.

But some matters of great importance never get on the public agenda. Matters like the inadequacies of our educational system and the unresolved problems of our cities fail to get the attention that some people think they deserve.[2] Indeed, there are many ways in which issues fail to reach the national political agenda, and one of the advantages of our federal system is that some issues are dealt with at the state and local level. However, "nondecisions" can occur at any level of government. The absence of government activity does not necessarily mean government is without a policy in that area, for *inaction is itself a policy*. Inattention to an issue can be as important as decisive action.

fiscal policy
Government policy that attempts to manage the economy by controlling taxing and spending.

monetary policy
Government policy that attempts to manage the economy by controlling the money supply and interest rates.

Economic Policy

Our national government has tremendous economic power. Through two types of policy—**fiscal policy** (taxing and spending) and **monetary policy** (control of the money supply and interest rates)—the government attempts to manage the economy's ups and downs, moderating both while encouraging steady economic growth. The goal is to smooth out the booms and busts of the business cycle so that unemployment and inflation are kept at a minimum and to allow real income to rise. This management power emerged earlier this century through such developments as the Federal Reserve System, the income tax, deficit spending, and the growth of government spending.

Does the government have the same direct control over the national economy that it has, say, over the military or national parks? No. Only if we had a socialized economy administered from Washington would we have a *managed* economy in that sense. In our capitalist economy, a great deal of power is left to private individuals and enterprises. Yet the government keeps a firm hand on many of the gears and levers that guide not only the economy's general direction but the rate at which it moves. These controls are taxes, spending, and borrowing.

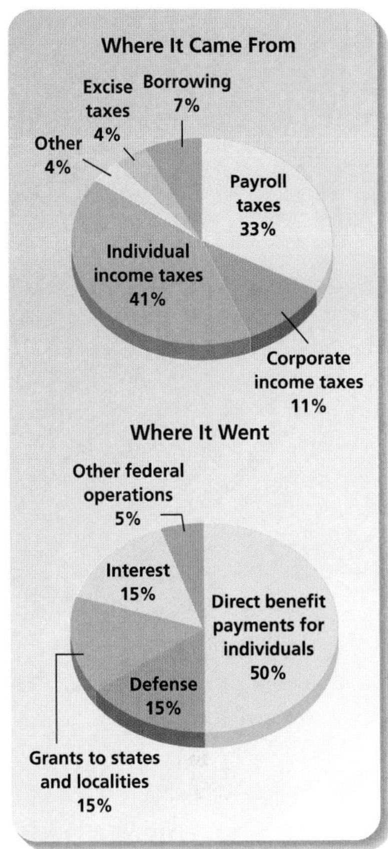

FIGURE 18-1 The Federal Government Dollar

SOURCE: *Budget of the United States Government, Fiscal Year 2000* (Government Printing Office, 1999).

Fiscal Policy

Of the two great instruments used to manage the economy we begin with *fiscal policy*—federal taxing and spending. Nothing reflects the growth of federal programs and the rise of big government more clearly than the increased spending by the national government. In 1933 the national government spent only $4 billion, about $30 per capita. In 2001 the respective figures are estimated to be 1.8 trillion, about $6,500 per capita.

Today federal, state, and local governments spend sums of money equal to about one-third of the income of all Americans. The national government is the biggest spender of all—more than all state and local governments combined. Our national government annually spends about 23 percent of the gross domestic product (GDP), or nearly one dollar out of every four. The national debt is $5.8 trillion, and we pay $205 billion each year in interest payments on that debt[3] (see Table 18-1).

Where the Money Comes From

"In this world," Benjamin Franklin once said, "nothing is certain but death and taxes." Tax collecting is one of the oldest activities of government. Today the federal government gets most of its funds from personal and corporate income taxes (see Figure 18-1). Other moneys come from borrowing, special fees and fines, grants and gifts, and administrative and commercial revenues.

TABLE 18-1 Trends in the Gross Federal Debt

Year	Amount, in Billions	Amount as a Percentage of Gross Domestic Product
1950	$256.8	94.2%
1955	274.3	69.4
1960	290.5	56.1
1965	322.3	46.9
1970	380.9	37.7
1975	541.9	34.9
1980	909.0	44.3
1985	1,817.5	33.4
1990	3,206.5	56.4
1995	4,921.0	68.5
2001*	5,781	61.0

*Figures are estimates.

SOURCE: *Budget of the U.S. Government (Historical Tables), Fiscal Year 2000.*

Putting power over taxation into the hands of the people was a major achievement in the development of self-government. "No taxation without representation" has been a battle cry the world over. The Constitution clearly provided that Congress "shall have Power To lay and collect Taxes, Duties, Imposts, and Excises." **Tariffs** (import duties) and **excise taxes** (consumer taxes on a specific kind of merchandise) have to be levied uniformly throughout the United States, while direct taxes other than income taxes have to be apportioned among the states according to population.

Raising money is only one objective of taxation. Regulation and, more recently, promoting economic growth are others. In a broad sense all taxation regulates human behavior. For example, a **progressive tax**—by which people with high incomes pay larger fractions of their incomes than people with lower incomes—has a leveling tendency on people's wealth.

In the federal budget for Fiscal Year 2000, federal receipts include the following:

1. *Individual income taxes.* Taxes on individuals' incomes account for about 48 percent of the federal government's tax revenue. Over the years, the income tax has grown increasingly complex as Congress responded to claims for differing kinds of exemptions and rates. Some members of Congress have advocated simplification or even elimination of the income tax in favor of a national sales tax.
2. *Corporate income taxes.* These account for just over 10 percent of the national government's tax revenues. As late as 1942, revenue from corporate income taxes exceeded that from individual income taxes.
3. *Social insurance receipts.* These payroll taxes are the second largest and most rapidly rising source of federal revenue, accounting for 34 percent of all federal revenue, not including borrowing. Most people pay more in Social Security taxes than in federal income taxes. These are highly **regressive taxes**, meaning that low-income people generally pay larger fractions of their income than do high-income people.
4. *Excise taxes.* These taxes on liquor, tobacco, gasoline, telephones, air travel, and other so-called "luxury items" account for roughly 4 percent of federal revenue.
5. *Customs duties and tariffs.* Although no longer the main source of federal income, in recent years these taxes provided an annual yield of almost $20 billion.
6. *Borrowing.* Since World War II, the government has regularly resorted to borrowing money to finance itself. Between 1969 and 1998, the government never had a surplus.[4]

The **deficit** is the difference between the annual revenues raised and the expenditures of government, including the interest on past borrowing. The deficit is not to be confused with the **debt**, which is the total of our deficits, minus our surpluses, over the years. Today the total debt reaches nearly $6 trillion.

When ordinary people are faced with emergency expenses, they borrow money. The same is true of governments. During past military and economic crises, our federal government went heavily into debt; it engaged in *deficit spending.* But recently, we have also incurred great debts during a period of peace with a relatively healthy economy. The federal government borrowed $23 billion during World War I, about $13 billion during the Great Depression of the 1930s, and $200 billion during World War II. As of 2000, the total federal debt was about $5.9 trillion. Each individual's share of the national debt now is about $21,000.

Borrowing costs money. Although the federal government can borrow at a relatively low rate, the interest on the federal debt is more than $240 billion a year. The federal government borrows from investors who buy treasury notes, treasury bills,

tariff
Tax levied on imports to help protect a nation's industries, labor, or farmers from foreign competition. It can also be used to raise additional revenue.

excise tax
Consumer tax on a specific kind of merchandise, such as tobacco.

progressive tax
A tax graduated so that people with higher incomes pay a larger fraction of their income than people with lower incomes.

regressive tax
A tax whereby people with lower incomes pay a higher fraction of their income than people with higher incomes.

deficit
The difference between the revenues raised annually from sources of income other than borrowing and the expenditures of government, including paying the interest on past borrowing.

debt
The accumulated total of federal deficits, minus surpluses, over the years.

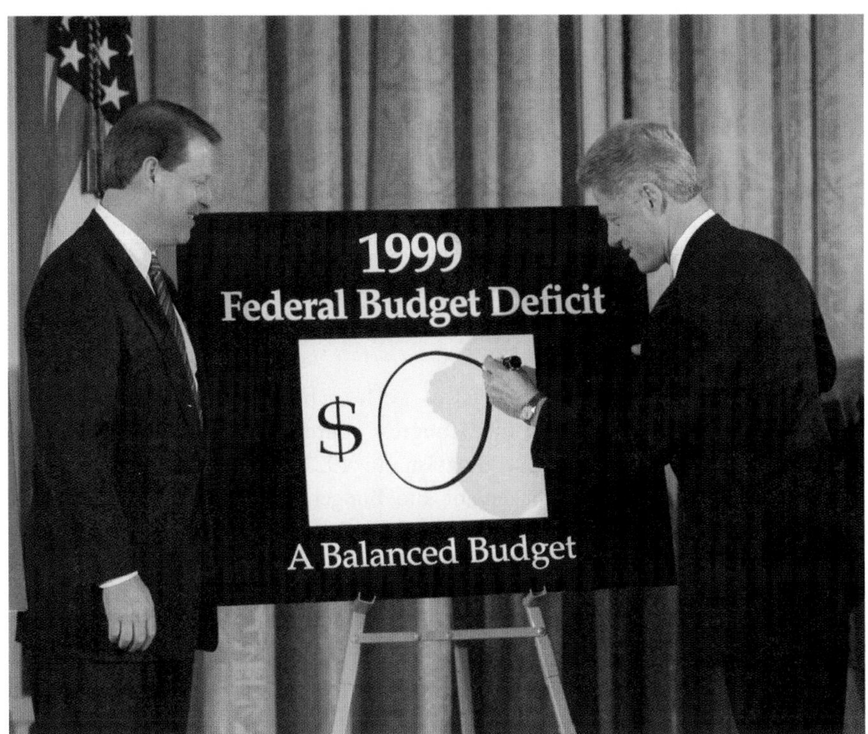

Vice-President Gore and President Clinton took great pride in announcing that the 1999 budget would have a zero deficit—the first in three decades.

and U.S. savings bonds. These investors include individuals (foreign and domestic), U.S. government accounts, banks, and other investors.

The size of the debt and the interest payments alarm many Americans. How did we allow the debt to grow to such an extent? When dealing with this question, keep two considerations in mind. First, the government owes roughly 90 percent of the money to its own citizens rather than to foreign governments or investors, although the amount owed to foreigners is growing. Second, the economic strength and resources of the country are more significant than the size of the debt. Still, interest payments on the debt are a cause for concern.

Where the Money Goes

Where does the money go? Much of it, of course, goes for benefit payments and national defense. As we enter a new century, 15 percent goes to national defense; 15 percent to interest on the national debt; 15 percent to grants for states and localities; 50 percent to direct benefit payments for individuals (such as Social Security, Medicare, Medicaid, and other major social programs), and 5 percent for all other federal operations (see Figure 18-1).

Another way of understanding how the money is spent is to consider federal outlays as a percentage of the nation's **gross domestic product (GDP)**, an estimate of the total output of all U.S. economic activity. In fiscal year 2000, our GDP is estimated to be close to $8 trillion. Spending on domestic **entitlement programs**—programs such as Social Security, Medicare, and unemployment insurance to which qualified citizens are "entitled" by national legislation—runs at about 11 percent of the GDP. Spending for defense is a little more than 3 percent of GDP; payments on the deficit make up another 3 percent of GDP; and nondefense discretionary spending is around 3.3 percent.

Years ago, federal revenues and outlays were so small that national taxing and spending had little impact on the overall economy. Today the federal government extracts billions of dollars from certain areas of the economy and pumps them back into others, with profound effects on the United States and world economies.

gross domestic product (GDP)
An estimate of the total output of all economic activity in the nation, including goods and services.

entitlement program
Government programs such as Social Security, Medicare, and unemployment insurance to which qualified citizens are "entitled" by national legislation.

Office of Management and Budget (OMB)
Presidential staff agency that serves as a clearinghouse for budgetary requests and management improvements.

Much of the federal budget is "uncontrollable" in the sense that "mandatory growth" (cost of living increases) in many programs is built into the law. These programs do not come up for annual review or decision by either the Congress or the president; they just keep on growing automatically. The most uncontrollable parts of the budget are Social Security, Medicare, unemployment benefits, outstanding contracts, and other fiscal obligations. The most controllable part of the budget is defense spending. Since the collapse of the Soviet Union, real cuts in defense spending have been achieved, dozens of bases closed, and significant reductions made in the size of our military services.

The Budget Process

Before the Budget and Accounting Act of 1921, each executive agency dealt with Congress on its own, requesting that Congress appropriate funds for its activities with little or no presidential coordination. In 1921 the Bureau of the Budget (changed to the Office of Management and Budget in 1970) was created in the Treasury Department, and for the first time, the executive branch presented one budget to Congress.

THE EXECUTIVE BRANCH The federal government's fiscal year begins on October 1. The budget process begins nearly two years in advance, when the various departments and agencies estimate their needs and propose their budgets to the president.[5] While Congress is debating the budget for the coming fiscal year, the agencies are making estimates for the year after that (see Table 18-2). Agency officials take into account not only their needs as they see them, but also the overall presidential program and the probable reactions of Congress. Departmental budgets are detailed; they include estimates on expected needs for personnel, supplies, office space, and the like.

The **Office of Management and Budget (OMB)**, a staff agency of the president, handles the next phase. Budget examiners in the OMB review each agency budget and bring it into line with the president's overall plans. Executive branch hearings are then held to give agency people a chance to clarify and defend their estimates. The OMB director and staff often prune the agencies' requests severely.

Finally, the OMB director goes to the president with a single, consolidated set of estimates of both revenue and expenditures—the product of perhaps a year's work. The president takes several days to review these figures and make adjustments. The budget director also helps the president prepare a budget message that will stress key aspects of the budget and tie it to broad national goals. The president must submit the budget recommendations and accompanying message to Congress between the first Monday in January and the first Monday in February. The president's budget recommendations cover thousands of pages.

TABLE 18-2 Steps in the Budget Process

February–December 2000	Executive branch agencies develop requests for funds and submit them to the Office of Management and Budget. The president reviews the requests and makes the fiscal decisions on what goes in his budget.
December 2000	The budget documents are prepared.
January–February 2001	Budget is transmitted to Congress.
March–September 2001	Congress reviews the president's proposed budget, develops its own budget, and approves spending and revenue bills.
October 1, 2001	The fiscal year begins.
October 1, 2001–September 30, 2002	Program managers execute the budget provided in law.
October–November 2002	Data on actual spending and receipts for the completed fiscal year become available.

THE LEGISLATIVE BRANCH Presidential submission of a budget proposal is only the beginning. Under our Constitution, Congress must appropriate the funds and raise the taxes. But the president also plays a role, since all appropriation and tax proposals are subject to a presidential veto. Thus the White House is an active participant in the congressional budget battles. When Congress acts on the budget, it does so by first approving the overall budget resolution. Then the actual appropriation of funds is detailed in 13 different bills, each of which is presented to the president for approval.

In 1974 Congress adopted the Budget Reform Act to give Congress a more effective role in the budget process. This act specifies that the president must include proposed changes in tax laws, estimates of amounts of revenue lost through existing preferential tax treatments, and five-year estimates of the costs of new and continuing federal programs. The act also calls on the president to seek authorizing legislation for a program a year before asking Congress to fund it.

The 1974 Budget Reform Act also created the **Congressional Budget Office (CBO)**, which gave Congress its own independent agency to prepare budget data and analyze budgetary issues. By February 15 of each year, the CBO furnishes its analysis of the presidential recommendations to the House and Senate Budget Committees. The CBO also provides Congress with biannual forecasts of the economy, analyzes alternative fiscal policies, prepares five-year cost estimates for bills proposed by congressional committees, and undertakes studies requested by committees. The CBO also monitors the results of congressional action on individual appropriations and revenues against the targets or ceilings specified by legislation.

The Gramm-Rudman-Hollings Act (1985), as modified by the 1990 Budget Enforcement Act, called for Congress to adopt a **concurrent resolution** for the next fiscal year by April 15. This resolution set levels of new budget authority and spending, which became the ceiling for the Appropriations Committees. Congress could later adopt a budget resolution that revised or reaffirmed the earlier resolution. In recent years Congress has been resorting to **reconciliation**, in which Congress, by a budget resolution, sets ceilings on what the various Appropriations Subcommittees can appropriate, and then leaves the decision of how to achieve the required limits to the committees.

In the Gramm-Rudman-Hollings Act, Congress also established a procedure designed to gradually reduce the federal deficit to zero. Under this procedure, if it appears that there will be a deficit beyond a stipulated level, then across-the-board cuts in discretionary spending are put into effect automatically and become the ceiling limits for the Appropriations Committees. It is important to note that the fastest growing part of the budget—entitlement spending—is exempt from the Gramm-Rudman caps. Hence no automatic cuts are permitted in Social Security, Medicare, interest on the national debt, veterans' compensation, veterans' pensions, unemployment assistance, and student loans.

These various budget reform efforts did not by themselves balance the budget, yet they did set in place a discipline and a mind-set that helped move toward balancing the budget. Equally, if not more important, was the economic boom of the 1980s and 1990s that generated huge tax revenues that, together with budget reforms, helped achieve balanced budgets in the late 1990s.

Indeed, by the close of the century the U.S. economy was robust enough that the federal budget enjoyed a surplus. This unfamiliar event triggered extensive debates about what should be done with the surplus. Republicans proposed tax cuts. President Clinton said he would favor tax cuts only after Social Security was properly funded, and he also fought to ensure that tax cuts would not come at the expense of various social programs, such as financial aid and loan programs for needy college students. Still others thought it would be wise to build up the surplus.

Congressional Budget Office (CBO)
An agency of Congress that analyzes presidential budget recommendations and estimates the costs of proposed legislation.

concurrent resolution
A resolution passed in the same form by both houses of Congress that expresses the "sense" of Congress on some question. It is not sent to the president and does not have the force of law.

reconciliation
Process by which Congress sets ceilings on what Appropriations Subcommittees can appropriate.

THE GENERAL ACCOUNTING OFFICE After Congress appropriates money, it checks on the way that money is being spent by two methods: (1) congressional committees hold *oversight hearings* in which they call on agency heads to explain how they have spent the money; (2) the **General Accounting Office (GAO)** uses spot sampling to check vouchers and make audits in the field. The GAO is headed by the **comptroller general**, who is appointed by the president with the approval of the Senate for a 15-year term. Although the comptroller general has the authority to disallow expenditures, approval is no longer needed for the disbursement of funds. In the past 20 years, the GAO has taken on broader responsibilities in investigating and evaluating programs by checking on the adequacy and effectiveness, as well as the honesty, of a program's performance.

The Politics of Taxing and Spending

In addition to raising funds to run the government, taxes also promote economic growth and reward certain types of behavior, such as owning a home, contributing to charities, and investing in high-risk but desirable (from a national standpoint) energy or housing ventures. Cynics suggest, too, that from a member of Congress's point of view, tax legislation has the additional and important function of raising campaign funds. As long as tax legislation is under consideration in Congress, swarms of lobbyists are eager to contribute generously to campaign coffers.[6]

THE TAX BURDEN No one likes taxes. Most of us complain our tax load is too heavy and that other people are not paying their fair share. People with high incomes who pay a high percentage of their income for federal taxes naturally grumble. People with low incomes complain that even a low tax deprives them of the necessities of life. People with middle incomes consider their situation the worst of all; their incomes are not high, but their taxes are.

What is the best type of tax? Some say a *progressive income tax* (also called a *graduated income tax*) is best because it is relatively easy to collect, hits hardest those who are most able to pay, and hardly touches those at the bottom of the income ladder. Others argue that *excise taxes* are the fairest because they are paid by people who spend money for luxury goods and thus obviously have money to spare. In addition, by discouraging people from buying expensive goods, excise taxes occasionally have a deflationary effect when prices are on the rise. On the other hand, excise taxes are more expensive to collect than income taxes. In some cases, such as the tax on tobacco, they may hit the poor the hardest. Excise taxes also face strong resistance from affected industries: tobacco, liquor, and airlines, for example. An excise tax on yachts passed by Congress in 1990 but repealed in 1993 had the unintended consequence of putting several thousand yacht builders out of business.

The most controversial tax is a general **sales tax**, which is levied by almost all states on the sale of most goods, sometimes exempting food and drugs. Labor and liberal organizations see sales taxes as *regressive*, meaning that because a sales tax is the same for all persons, these taxes are not related to a taxpayer's ability to pay. Poor persons pay a higher percentage of their income in sales taxes for the goods and services they buy than do rich ones. Proponents of a national sales tax stress its potential anti-inflationary effect and point to its successful use in a number of states.

The sales tax is exclusively a state and local tax in the United States, but in Europe a similar tax, a **value-added tax (VAT)**, is used to raise revenues for national governments. The VAT differs from a sales tax in that it collects a tax on the increased value of a product *at each stage of production and distribution* rather than just at the point of sale, as with a sales tax. A loaf of bread would thus have value added at each stage of production: the farmer would pay a value-added tax on the grain before selling to the miller, who would be taxed before selling to the baker, and so forth. The value-added tax is seen by some as a way to infuse a large amount of new revenue

General Accounting Office (GAO)
An independent investigative arm of Congress established in 1921 to check on receipt and disbursement of public funds and review the performance of government agencies.

comptroller general
Head of the General Accounting Office, appointed by the president with the approval of the Senate for a 15-year term.

sales tax
General tax on sales transactions, sometimes exempting food and drugs.

value-added tax (VAT)
A tax on increased value of a product at each stage of production and distribution rather than just at the point of sale.

into the federal government. Opponents of the tax see it as regressive and increasing the tax burden. States see a federal VAT as invading their turf. Since it taxes consumption and not savings, a VAT could encourage savings and investment, both of which are vital to economic growth.

Antitax protests erupted all over the country after Californians in 1978 passed Proposition 13, which placed strict limits on state government spending.

THE ANTITAX MOVEMENT California voters set the tax agenda for the entire nation when they passed a tax limitation in June 1978—Proposition 13, a citizen initiative to lower and permanently cap property taxes. Tax limitation measures like Proposition 13 were later approved in scores of states and localities, and the success of the issue at the local level gave antitax activists at the national level renewed energy.

Ronald Reagan in his 1980 presidential campaign promised a 30 percent reduction in income taxes, phased in over a three-year period. Once elected, he made cutting taxes his highest priority. In a stunning victory over the House Democratic leadership, he got most of what he wanted. He had promised that by cutting taxes and government spending in nondefense areas, he could stimulate the economy and fund his other priority—national defense. This policy, dubbed "Reaganomics," was based on *supply-side economics*, which holds that economic growth will result from people having more money to spend because of lower taxes, permitting these additional expenditures also to be taxed.

Whether Reaganomics worked is still a partisan issue, because after the tax cuts budget deficits grew by leaps and bounds. It certainly did not work as promised, yet few question that it worked politically. Since the 1981 tax cut, the agenda of American politics has largely been to reduce spending in hopes of reducing the high federal budget deficits. Hence the Democrats, who typically would want to propose new or expanded government programs, were put on the defensive. By the late 1990s, a strong economy and restraint on government spending meant that for the first time in decades there is a budget surplus. Whether these surpluses should be used to help fund Social Security, buy down the debt, or lower taxes is, as noted above, a subject of intense debate. But it is an enduring legacy of Reaganomics that few are proposing using the surplus for new government programs.

Tax Expenditures

Tax expenditures are government revenue losses due to federal tax laws that provide special tax incentives or benefits to individuals and businesses. These benefits, more than $400 billion of them, come from special exclusions, exemptions, or reductions from gross income or from special credits, preferential tax rates, or deferrals of tax liability.

Tax expenditures are one means by which the national government carries out public policy objectives. For example, the government encourages investment in research and development by allowing such costs to be deducted from a company's taxes. Federal grants could also achieve this objective. One of the largest tax expenditures permits persons buying a home to deduct the mortgage interest from their taxes. In 2000 this deduction amounts to over $56 billion.[7]

Critics assert that the rich get their "welfare" through such loopholes and tax expenditures. This form of "welfare" does not require a visible appropriation of money—one plainly identified in the budget. However meritorious the objectives of tax expenditures are—encouraging home ownership, research and development, retirement savings—these tax benefits are a cost to government that does not benefit all levels of society. In many instances, they cause investors to waste their resources on low-yield investments in order to obtain large tax benefits.

tax expenditure
Loss of tax revenue due to federal tax laws that provide special tax incentives or benefits to individuals or businesses.

How the Fed Controls Inflation

1. The board sets the *discount rate*, the rate the Fed charges to lend money to banks. Raising rates is deflationary by increasing costs for money and credit; lowering rates is inflationary by decreasing the cost for money and credit.
2. The Fed's *open market operations* are its most flexible and important monetary policy tool. The Fed buys or sells federal bonds. Selling is deflationary by taking money and credit out of circulation; buying is inflationary by increasing money and credit in circulation. For example, if the Fed purchases $1 billion of government securities, the Fed pays for it by adding $1 billion to the reserve account that the security dealer keeps at the Fed, and the bank in turn credits the security dealer's account for that amount. As these funds are spent and respent, the stock of money and credit will increase by much more than the original $1 billion. If the Fed sells $1 billion, the amount is deducted from the security dealer's account, with less money flowing through the economy.
3. The Fed sets *reserve requirements* for nationally charted banks. Raising reserves is deflationary by reducing the funds banks have available to lend; decreasing reserves is inflationary by increasing funds banks have available to lend. The Fed seldom changes reserve requirements because such changes can have a dramatic effect on institutions and the economy.

SOURCE: "The Fed: Our Central Bank," the Federal Reserve System on the Internet (http://www.frbkc.or/infofrs/ifrsmain.htm).

The Rise and Demise of the Item Veto

In 1996, after years of debate, Congress passed and President Clinton signed into law the **item veto**. This measure gave the president the authority to strike specific spending programs from the budget passed by Congress. Governors in nearly all of the states have long had this power, and most presidents, going back as far as Ulysses Grant, had advocated giving it to a president in order to eliminate wasteful spending projects that are quietly added to congressional appropriations measures at the last moment before they pass.

Clinton was delighted to have this new power and exercised it on dozens of occasions. But in June 1998, the Supreme Court ruled in a 6 to 3 decision that Congress acted unconstitutionally in granting this authority to the White House. The Court said that this was too sweeping a power to grant to the president by statutory (lawmaking) means, a violation of the doctrine of separation of powers, and contrary to the powers granted Congress by Article I of the Constitution. "Separation of powers was designed to implement a fundamental insight," wrote Justice Anthony Kennedy. "Concentration of power in the hands of a single branch is a threat to liberty."[8] The only way, according to the Court, that a president could be granted the item veto authority, would be if the Constitution were amended.

MONETARY POLICY

Monetary policy is the second way the national government affects the economy. The core element of **monetarism** is the idea that prices, income, and economic stability are primarily a function of growth in the money supply. Monetarists contend the money supply is the key factor affecting the economy's performance, and restrained yet steady growth in the money supply would encourage solid economic growth but not inflation.

The Federal Reserve System

Monetary policy is not made by either Congress or the president but by the **Federal Reserve System**, most especially its Federal Open Market Committee. The members of that committee, some of the most powerful people in the United States, have a lot to say about how much interest you pay on the car you are buying and whether you refinance your home because of lower interest rates. They can stimulate the economy so that it could be easier for you to find a job, or slow it down so that it could be harder. Who are these people with so much power, and how do they influence economic policy?

The Board of Governors of the Federal Reserve System, or "The Fed," as it is called, consists of a chair and six other members who are appointed by the president with the consent of the Senate for 14-year terms, with one member's term expiring every two years. These long, staggered terms for members of the board are intended to insulate its members from politics as much as possible. There are 12 Regional Federal Reserve Banks, each headed by a president, with a nine-member board of directors chosen from the private banking business in that district.

The 12 members of the Federal Open Market Committee are all professional economists or bankers, most of whose names are unfamiliar to most people. Yet this group, which meets about every six to eight weeks, decides how much money will be allowed to enter the economy, manages foreign currency operations, and regulates banks. It does this by buying and selling government securities, which can encourage

item veto
A measure passed by Congress in 1996 and ruled unconstitutional by the Supreme Court in 1998 whereby the president was given the authority to strike specific spending programs from the budget passed by Congress.

monetarism
A theory that government should control the money supply to encourage economic growth and restrain inflation.

Federal Reserve System
The system created by Congress in 1913 to establish banking practices and regulate currency in circulation and the amount of credit available. It is comprised of 12 regional banks, and its major responsibilities are supervised by the Federal Reserve Board of Governors.

either lower or higher interest rates. Other lenders closely watch the decisions of the Fed and typically make their interest rates consistent with Fed decisions. Because lenders make it either more or less expensive to borrow money, they influence a wide range of economic activity.

The chair of the Board of Governors, by tradition an economist, is appointed by the president to a four-year term. The current chair, Alan Greenspan, is one of the most influential national public policy officials. Greenspan was first appointed by President Ronald Reagan in 1987, reappointed by President George Bush, and reappointed in 1996 by President Clinton. Greenspan's leadership had helped foster economic growth and was widely respected by financial leaders, factors that influenced Clinton's decision to reappoint him. The staff of the Federal Reserve System reports directly to the chair, not to the board, and the chair is the one who appears before Congress and the country to explain the policies of the Federal Reserve System. The chair heads the Federal Open Market Committee and is credited or blamed for the decisions made by the Fed.

Comments about the state of the economy by Federal Reserve Chairman Alan Greenspan often influence stock market fluctuations.

At the time the Federal Reserve System was established in 1913, regional banks were located according to the population, economy, and politics of that time. As John R. Wilke has written, "Today, these locations make little sense. Missouri, once an economic and political power because of its riverboat economy, has two Fed Banks; booming Florida has none. California and its vast economy have only one Fed Bank—which also serves eight other states and covers 20 percent of the population."[9]

The 12 Fed Banks process one-third of the checks written in the United States, and the electronic network dollar volume of transfers is approaching $200 trillion annually. As its check-clearing business begins to be altered by competition from private clearinghouses, and as new technologies proliferate in the years ahead, Fed operations may come under closer scrutiny. But as one insider commented, "The market has changed, and the technology has changed. . . . [But] do we really want to fool around with the Fed's independence just to save a few hundred million dollars a year?"[10]

Government and Economic Policy

Depression is a hard teacher, and the 1930s had a tremendous impact on American thinking about the role of government in the economy. The Great Depression that began in 1929 brought mass misery. "One vivid, gruesome moment of those dark days we shall never forget," wrote one observer. "We saw a crowd of some fifty men fighting over a barrel of garbage which had been set outside the back door of a restaurant. American citizens fighting for scraps of food like animals!"[11]

Despite the efforts of the Franklin Roosevelt administration to cope with the Depression, it hung on. Faint signs of recovery could be seen in the mid-1930s, but the recession of 1937–38 indicated that the country was by no means out of the woods. Between 8 and 9 million people were jobless in 1939. Then came World War II, and unemployment seemed cured. Millions of people had more income, more security, and higher standards of living. Lord Beveridge in England posed a question that bothered many thoughtful Americans: "Unemployment has been practically abolished twice in the lives of most of us—in the last war and in this war. Why does war solve the problem of unemployment which is so insoluble in peace?"[12]

What can government do to foster jobs and economic growth? Some economists urged the government to reduce spending, lower taxes, curb the power of labor, and generally leave business and the economy alone. This is called **laissez- faire economics**. Another group said that the trouble with the New Deal was not that it had done too much, but that it had done too little. This group's thinking was deeply influenced by the work of English economist John Maynard Keynes.[13] Keynes recommended that when consumer spending and investment decline, government

laissez-faire economics
Economic theory that opposes governmental interference in the economy beyond what is necessary to protect life and property.

spending and investing should increase. In a recession, government must do the spending and investing if private enterprise will not or can not. Laissez-faire economics is identified with President Herbert Hoover, while Keynesian economics is identified with President Franklin Roosevelt, at least in his first term.

Keynesian economics influences government management of the economy. Yet politically, Keynesian economics presents a problem. It is much easier to increase spending and government programs than it is to curb them. As a result, deficit spending became a habit in this country for 50 years. To stimulate demand, the government spent more money than it took in. For many years, this policy was thought to be beneficial to the economy. It was also convenient politically. However, when the national debt soared, both Congress and the president searched for ways to balance the budget.

Economists also found that Keynesian policies, when accompanied by a loose-money policy by the Federal Reserve, resulted in a hidden cost: **inflation**. Because government programs introduced extra money into the economy without a corresponding increase in goods, each dollar became worth less, and prices rose to compensate. Although government spending was not responsible for all inflation, it was viewed as a major contributor; as a result, new economic remedies have been sought.

A Balancing Act

Republicans and Democrats alike have been concentrating on getting the federal budget into balance by the year 2002. In May 1997, President Clinton and congressional leaders agreed to a plan to achieve that goal and procure a surplus by fiscal 1998, which would remain in surplus until 2002. But the question remains: What about 2003 and beyond? The real problem comes when members of the baby-boom generation start to reach retirement age around 2008, and the costs of Medicare, Medicaid, and Social Security begin to explode.

Robert D. Reischauer, a Brookings Institution budget expert who headed the Congressional Budget Office from 1989 to 1995, warned that unless lawmakers made sweeping changes, the deficit would come back after 2002 with a vengeance. Barring a major restructuring, the deficit would mushroom from zero in 2002 to 4.5 percent of the gross domestic product by 2010 and 9.5 percent by 2025.

Promoting Business and Agriculture

The national government promotes a prosperous economy through its monetary and fiscal policies. It also provides various services to business and industry. The Department of Commerce is sometimes known as the nation's "service center for business." Its cabinet secretary, usually a person with an extensive business background, is a spokesperson for business interests. Historically, the department has been at the center of the government's efforts to promote economic growth and encourage business research and development. Its National Institute of Standards and Technology (NIST) provides highly valued technical assistance to corporations like General Electric, DuPont, and IBM. The NIST has helped companies study the structures of enzymes, look at submicroscopic flaws in jet-engine turbine blades, and probe the structure and properties of various materials used in biotechnology, electronics, fiber optics, and other fields. The Department of Commerce also undertakes basic research in ocean science and engineering, meteorology, and weather forecasting. Its National Oceanic and Atmospheric Administration is currently performing research on hurricane predictions, acid rain, marine fisheries, and a wide assortment of undersea research activities.

Also part of the Department of Commerce, the Patent and Trademark Office (PTO) administers the patent system that Congress established "to promote the Progress of Science and useful Arts" under Article I of the Constitution. Each year the United

Keynesian economics
Economic theory based on the principles of John Maynard Keynes stating that government spending should increase during business slumps and be curbed during booms.

inflation
A rise in the general price level (and decrease in dollar value) owing to an increase in the volume of money and credit in relation to available goods.

States Patent and Trademark Office issues more than 100,000 patents to cover new and useful inventions that provide their owners certain exclusive rights for 17 years.[14]

The impressive success and competitiveness of American agriculture owe much to the federal government and its subsidies—almost as much as to fertile soil, hard work, and the technology revolution. Agriculture and food-related businesses are our largest industry, bigger than computers, or automobiles, or the movie and recording industries. Agribusiness generates nearly one out of every five jobs in the private sector and accounts for almost 20 percent of the GDP and 15 percent of our exports. It is also an industry with a high rate of productivity. Thanks in part to federal support for research, agricultural productivity has increased at a rate of about 3 percent a year in the past decades. Farmers in the United States produce about ten times as much per work hour today as they did 50 years ago.

Ed Gamble. © 1997 The Florida Times Union

Our great agricultural production reflects one of the most successful partnerships between government and private enterprise. The federal government has invested large sums in basic and applied agricultural research. Much of this work is done at land-grant state universities and colleges. What is learned in the laboratories is tested on experimental farms, and new techniques and products are then made available to farmers through the Agricultural Extension Services of these schools. Local county agents, part of the Agricultural Extension Service, are supported by a combination of national, state, and local funds.

The Great Depression of the 1930s ravaged virtually every farmer. The New Deal helped to get farmers back on their feet by means of credit support, loans, and crop price supports. Federal initiatives in irrigation and rural electrification fostered significant strides in productivity. Loans and credit programs were established to help farmers purchase needed equipment. Some of these programs were eventually self-financing, even though they began with public money. Other federal initiatives stabilized income and output with price supports and acreage controls.

Plainly, the array of subsidies, loans, credits, and related programs of research and investment helped American farmers be successful in the past, but economists point out that not only do the biggest farmers gain the most from federal programs, but farm subsidies hurt poor people by driving up the price of food. Thus, although helping farmers encourages productivity, it also increases poverty. Why do we do this? Farmers are well organized, and like senior citizens, unions, and the banking industry, they know how to present their case to Congress. Nonetheless, as the century comes to a close and the nation faces the need to cut federal expenditures, political support is eroding for the continuation of farm programs costing billions of dollars to subsidize farmers not to grow things.

The 1996 Federal Agriculture Improvement and Reform Act (FAIR) is a massive and complex piece of legislation. It calls for an end of subsidies to wheat, corn, feed grain, cotton, and rice farmers over seven years, to be replaced by fixed but declining Freedom to Farm payments. The act continues subsidies at a reduced rate for peanut, sugar, and dairy programs, continues conservation programs that pay farmers to leave idle 36.4 million acres of cropland, provides for crop insurance, and maintains food stamps and other nutrition programs for two years. The assumption behind this act is that the farmers who receive these Freedom to Farm payments, while still being allowed to plant anything they want in any amount they want, will use these cash payments to cushion the loss of subsidies. At the end of the seven years, it is hoped that the marketplace will work, and farmers will be able to make a living by producing what the nation needs at lower prices for consumers. However, if farm incomes substantially decline or food prices go way up, it is very likely that the Freedom to Farm plan will come under attack and be modified by Congress. And it should be noted that the 1996 act only *authorized* this program, which means that each year Congress must *appropriate* the funds to implement it. These yearly battles provide ample opportunities for the many interests involved in farming to alter how the law is funded.

You Decide...

What does it mean to "Buy American"?

The answer may surprise you. One of these cars is made only in the United States. Can you name it? For extra points, match all the cars to their countries of origin.

1. Pontiac LeMans	A. Canada
2. Chevrolet Lumina	B. Korea
3. Mercury Capri	C. Mexico
4. Honda Accord Coupe	D. United States
5. Dodge Stealth	E. Japan
6. Mercury Tracer	F. Australia

Answer: 1-B, 2-A, 3-F, 4-D, 5-E, 6-C

Trade Policy

In 1971 the United States experienced its first **trade deficit**—the value of imports exceeded the value of exports—in more than a century. Since then we have had trade deficits in billions of dollars every year.[15] Congress and the president are under continuing pressure from industry, unions, and regional political leaders to save American jobs, companies, and communities from foreign competition. These pressures come not only from the textile and auto industries but from glass, steel, shoe, lumber, electronics, book publishing, aluminum, farming, and domestic wine and spirit coalitions, to name just a few. They claim that the trade deficit justifies the imposition of trade sanctions.

The problem is not that we are importing too much but that we are exporting too little. German cars, Japanese radios, and Indonesian textiles are fine products; if other countries produce better cars or shoes at a lower price, then free traders argue we should deploy our labor and capital in areas in which we can do better.

The question is also whether our products are given fair treatment by other nations. American agricultural products are denied entry into some countries and are subject to high tariffs in others. American automobile manufacturers complain of unfair restrictions imposed by the Japanese on our cars. Finally, some countries exploit the U.S. advantage in technology by slavishly copying our products and then selling them back to us or to other countries at a profit.

Another unfair trade practice is *dumping*—selling products in a country below the cost of manufacturing or below their domestic price with the intention of driving other producers out of the market and then raising prices to profitable levels. Another practice is *subsidizing* certain industries. Some countries, for example, subsidize steel for export; others require lengthy inspection procedures for imported goods. Japan has protected several of its industries—producers of automobiles and baseball bats, for example—by specifying standards that are virtually impossible for us to meet. The United States, of course, often retaliates. In recent years, we have imposed "voluntary" limits on Japanese automobiles and European steel imports. Japan opened its markets to U.S. cellular phone companies in 1994 because of stiff trade sanction threats against Japanese electronics industries.

In 1947 a group of countries formed a trade organization to negotiate free trade by lowering tariffs (taxes on imports that raises their price) and **quotas** (limits on the quantity of a particular product that may be imported) and other disadvantages countries face when trading. Today a world trade organization has grown out of the **General Agreement on Tariffs and Trade (GATT)**. It includes 125 countries, and its membership accounts for four-fifths of the world's trade. GATT has negotiated agreements through eight rounds of trade negotiations (the most recent was called the *Uruguay Round*, named after the site of the initial conference). The United States has tried to focus GATT negotiations on trade in agricultural items, foreign investment, and protection of technological innovations and intellectual property. Although many trade restrictions still face U.S. imports and those of other countries, GATT has greatly helped to lower tariffs and quotas as well as to increase "fair" trade throughout the world. GATT has also devised several methods of retaliating against countries that practice unfair trade. Many maintain that GATT is one of the most successful innovations in the history of international relations and one of the contributing factors to the post–cold war economic success of the United States.[16]

trade deficit
An imbalance in international trade in which the value of imports exceeds the value of exports.

quota
In a trade context, a limit on the quantity of a particular product that may be imported.

General Agreement on Tariffs and Trade (GATT)
An international trade organization with 125 members, including the United States, that seeks to encourage free trade by lowering tariffs and other trade restrictions.

North American Free Trade Agreement (NAFTA)
Agreement signed by the United States, Canada, and Mexico in 1992 to form the largest free-trade zone in the world.

The North American Free Trade Agreement

On December 17, 1992, leaders of the United States, Canada, and Mexico signed the **North American Free Trade Agreement (NAFTA)**, which formed the largest free-trade zone in the world, even surpassing the European Community's 13-country conglomerate. Although President Bush signed NAFTA near the end of his presidency, the agreement could not become law until ratified by Congress. President Clinton promoted NAFTA, even though many members of his own party were its most vigorous opponents. Congress passed NAFTA by a thin margin in a bipartisan vote in which the Democrats were the minority.

Though trade among the United States, Canada, and Mexico will not be absolutely "free" or unimpeded, the agreement will have a tremendous impact on the economies of all three countries. Today Mexico is the United States' third most important trading partner, and the United States is Mexico's most important trading partner. Critics of NAFTA remain concerned because Mexican antipollution laws are significantly less stringent than those in the United States, and Mexican workers work for considerably lower wages. Both of these factors could make relocation to Mexico attractive to many U.S. companies seeking to lower labor and pollution-control costs.

Early estimates had indicated that 112,000 U.S. jobs would be eliminated as U.S. firms expanded in Mexico, but as many as 130,000 new U.S. jobs would be created, many of them high-tech, high-wage jobs. Not all studies came to the same conclusion, however. Some studies estimated that 1.5 million U.S. jobs would be created by the end of the decade due to NAFTA, while others concluded the United States would lose up to 900,000 jobs.[17]

Advocates of NAFTA—including Gerald Ford, Jimmy Carter, George Bush, and Bill Clinton—claim a free-trade zone will create jobs for Americans in the long run and increase profits for U.S.-owned companies. These proponents predict exports to Mexico will increase when tariff barriers are eliminated. In addition, Mexico has a responsibility to enforce health and environmental laws according to NAFTA's side agreements—a matter that remains in contention.

Three years after NAFTA went into effect, a study by researchers at the University of California at Los Angeles concluded that the claims of both those who argued that it would dramatically increase jobs as well as those who predicted there would be great job losses were exaggerated. Despite the collapse of the Mexican economy during that period, NAFTA's impact on jobs had been slight. The increase in imports eliminated an estimated 28,000 jobs; the increase in exports created 31,000 jobs.[18] It is still too early to come to any firm conclusions about how NAFTA will work, but the recovery of the Mexican economy is having a positive effect on job creation.

Barriers to Trade

Protectionism—erecting barriers to protect domestic industry—sounds easy and workable as a solution to trade deficits, but trade deficits are only symptomatic of more profound economic problems. Most economists favor free trade and strongly dislike protectionism because it prevents efficient use of resources and because consumers pay much more for protected products than they would otherwise. Tariffs merely divert attention away from real solutions like increased productivity and capital investments and inevitably invite retaliation from foreign countries.

In the 1930s many nations experienced high unemployment, low production, and general economic misery. The United States was no exception. In an effort to aid ailing American industries, Congress passed the Smoot-Hawley tariff, the highest general tariff the United States had ever had. Supporters hoped high tariffs on imported goods would increase the demand for goods produced in the United States and thus help get the country out of the Great Depression. The exact opposite occurred. Other nations retaliated with high tariffs on American goods. Demand fell, intensifying the Depression.

In 1934, Congress gave the president power to negotiate mutual tariff reductions with other nations, subject to certain restrictions, and by the early 1970s, tariffs on industrial products had been substantially reduced. As we enter the twenty-first century, trade barriers are less severe than they were back in the 1930s. But

protectionism
Policy of erecting trade barriers to protect domestic industry.

Thinking it Through...

What constitutes an "American" car? After finishing this short quiz, you know (if you did not know already) that company name has little relevance. Many foreign companies have plants in the United States that employ American workers and use a high percentage of American parts. General Motors, Ford, and Chrysler all have joint ventures with foreign-owned companies that place some of their models in the "import" category. Is a Toyota Camry an American car if it is built in Mexico in a plant partially owned by Ford? What defines an American product? Ownership of company? Nationality of employees? Location of physical plant? Domestic content of components?

The "Buy American" movement reached its apex in 1992. In January of that year, the president of Monsanto (an American chemicals manufacturer) offered each of its 12,000 employees $1,000 to buy or lease a new American car. Other countries charged discrimination, arguing that our government should have no role in promoting homegrown products over imports. Citizens, they maintained, should choose the best product available, not the one that says "Made in the U.S.A."

SOURCE: Jacqueline Mitchell, "Growing Movement to 'Buy American' Debates the Term," *The Wall Street Journal*, January 24, 1992, p. A1.

American automobile manufacturers encourage consumers to "buy American," but these same manufacturers often sell cars made abroad.

restrictions still exist. Certain tariffs, quotas on imported goods, and import regulations limit American consumption of foreign products. Most exist to protect American farmers, or businesses, or U.S. workers in certain industries. Thus we have certain restrictions on clothing and textile imports. Invariably these restrictions cost U.S. consumers a lot more than they benefit workers' wages.

America has generally backed increased trade and fewer trade barriers. Yet many Americans fear "globalization." Free trade and globalization policies do not confer equal benefits on everyone. Some workers inevitably are worse off as a result of freer international flow of goods and capital. All told, trade barriers cost American consumers $80 billion a year—equal to more than $1,200 per family.[19]

U.S. economic policy in the future will probably be some combination of free trade and selective protectionism. Though protectionism shields highly visible industries from competition at home or abroad, such measures are often another kind of subsidy that protects one industry at the expense of another—and always at high cost to American consumers. Instead, the United States must continue, through negotiations with trading partners, to remove unfair trade practices, encourage greater investments in what we have traditionally done well (science, technology, and medical and agricultural research), educate workers with better skills, and encourage labor-management experiments that can maximize productivity with an eye toward higher-quality products that will be highly prized abroad. We will also have to continue our trade adjustment assistance to aid displaced workers and help retrain those who lose their jobs as a direct result of freer trade arrangements.

Regulatory Policy

What do lawn mowers, cellular phones, roller blades, Viagra pills, fat substitutes, nicotine patches, pornography, banks, breast implants, cable TV, animal cloning, baby food, and workers' wages have in common? They are all *regulated* in some way by government. Because virtually every activity in the United States is supervised by government in one form or another, regulation is a vast enterprise. Not surprisingly, any activity as pervasive as this generates controversy. From small business owners who have to spend several days each year filling out dozens of forms and complying with federal regulations, to Microsoft's Bill Gates, there is constant criticism of government's regulatory intrusiveness.

The Constitution explicitly authorized Congress to regulate commerce among the states and with foreign nations. In our earliest years, Congress used this regulatory power to impose or suspend tariffs on imports from other nations. In the nineteenth century, the federal government created a number of agencies to regulate the conduct of citizens and commercial enterprises with an eye toward promoting economic development. Among these were the Army Corps of Engineers (1824), the Patent and Trademark Office (1836), the Steamboat Inspecting Service (1837), and the Copyright Office of the Library of Congress (1870). In 1887, Congress created the Interstate Commerce Commission to deal with the widespread dissatisfaction over the practices of railroads.

regulation
The attempt by government to control the behavior of corporations, other governments, or citizens through altering the natural workings of the open market to achieve some desired goal.

Additional regulations came into existence to break up monopolies, to clean up meat-packing conditions such as those exposed in Upton Sinclair's *Jungle* (1906), to prevent the kind of pesticide contamination described in Rachel Carson's *Silent Spring* (1962), to correct the lack of auto safety documented in Ralph Nader's *Unsafe at Any Speed* (1965), and to respond to discrimination in employment on the basis of race, color, national origin, religion, sex, and age. More recently, regulations have been enacted to protect us from raw sewage in rivers, lead in paint and gasoline, toxins in the air, radon gas in our homes, and asbestos, cotton dust, and hazardous products and environments. Current expenditures mandated by federal regulations cost about $200 billion annually for environmental, health, and safety rules alone.[20]

Presidents and members of Congress are frequently embroiled in the politics of making regulatory policy. There were partisan battles in the 1990s over legislation to enable cable TV, local phone companies, and long-distance carriers to join together. The Brady Bill antagonized many politicians by mandating a waiting period before handguns could be purchased, and battles have been waged over air bags and their protection or harm of children. Meat inspections have been overhauled by new government rules. The Food and Drug Administration and the Federal Aviation Administration are continually issuing new guidelines about the foods we eat and the planes we fly. Some members of Congress question whether the health benefits from cleaning up auto emissions are compelling enough to justify the enormous expense of stricter pollution control.[21]

In 1935 there were 4,000 pages of regulations in the *Federal Register* (a daily publication of proposed and existing federal regulations). Today there are about 70,000 pages of regulations.[22] Both political parties say regulatory overkill threatens to overwhelm entrepreneurs and divert them from building vital, innovative companies. "Regulations add as much as 33 percent to the cost of building an airplane engine and as much as 95 percent to the price of a new vaccine. Federal regulation also adds about $3,000 to the cost of a new car."[23]

Regulation in the News

The politics of regulation and new regulatory rules seldom make front page news. Yet every week you read about new regulations or debates about regulatory policy, such as:

- "EPA to Require New Pollution Emissions Controls"
- "Nutrition Labeling on Products for Kids Proposed"
- "FAA Finds Minor Shortcomings at Boeing"
- "FAA to Tighten Rule on Takeoffs in Snow and Ice"
- "FCC Considers Rules to Spur Economic Growth"
- "Meat Inspections Facing Overhaul"
- "Bid to Save Fish Puts West on Notice"
- "FDA to Set Limits on Breast Implants"
- "FDA Approves Laser System for Angioplasty"
- "Panel Urges FDA to Approve Female Condom"
- "FDA Revises Labeling on Antacids"
- "Bank Mergers Pose Challenge to Regulators"
- "FAA Plans Close Look at Plane Braking Mechanism"
- "FCC Adopts Limits on TV Ads Aimed at Children"
- "EPA to Shame Industries into Reducing Pollution"
- "FTC Sues Intel"
- "President Bans Federal Research on Cloning"

Regulation Defined

In a broad sense, **regulation** is any attempt by the government to control the behavior of corporations, other governments, or citizens. Regulation, as we use the term, occurs when the government steps in and alters the natural workings of the open market to achieve some desired goal. Regulation by government interjects political goals and values into the economy in the form of rules that direct behavior in the marketplace. These rules have the force of law and are backed by the government's police power.

All economies follow sets of rules and regulations; there simply are no unregulated economies. The United States operates in a competitive market economy in which wages, prices, the allocation of goods and services, and the employment of resources are generally regulated by the laws of supply and demand. We rely on private enterprise and market incentives to carry out most of our production and distribution.

The presumption in the United States is against government regulation. Most people feel that businesses should be allowed to buy and sell products and produce goods without government regulation. Our government and our courts have to justify regulations, and they do so only because people, through the representative process, have come to demand certain protections. Regulation is assumed to be necessary to protect people from undesirable side effects of the market, such as pollution or discrimination or false advertising.

In 1997 federal inspectors at the Hudson Foods plant in Columbus, Nebraska, recalled 1.2 million pounds of hamburger suspected of contamination with E. coli bacteria.

Types of Regulations

It is customary to talk of two general categories of regulation: economic and social regulation. *Economic regulation* generally refers to government controls on the behavior of business in the marketplace: the entry of individual firms into particular lines of business, the prices

independent regulatory agency
A government agency that exists outside the three branches of government and is responsible for enforcing particular statutes.

monopoly
Domination of an industry by a single company; also the company that dominates.

antitrust regulation
Federal laws and regulations that try to prevent businesses from dominating a particular market through monopoly or restraint of trade.

that firms may charge, the standards of service they must offer. Public utilities, transportation, and television are examples of regulated industries. As already noted, economic regulation began almost as early as the founding of the republic and expanded in earnest in 1887, when the Interstate Commerce Commission (ICC) was established; it continued in the twentieth century with the Federal Communications Commission (FCC), Commodity Futures Trading Commission (CFTC), and a host of regulatory agencies, boards, or commissions responsible for enforcing statutes in particular industries (see Table 18-3). In the twentieth century, regulatory bodies grew from five to about 80 regulatory organizations and employed at least 100,000 people to enforce thousands of federal regulations.

The second type of regulation, *social regulation*, refers to government correction of a wide variety of side effects, usually unintended, brought about by economic activity. Concern for worker health and safety and for environmental hazards has led to social regulation. Social regulation also includes the efforts by government to ensure equal rights in employment, education, and housing. Whereas economic regulation is usually organized along industry lines, social regulation cuts across these lines.

The Environmental Protection Agency (EPA), the Consumer Product Safety Commission (CPSC), and the Occupational Safety and Health Administration (OSHA) are regulatory agencies engaged in social regulation. In economic terms, producers regulated by social regulation must now pay for external costs that once were free, such as using rivers, landfills, or the atmosphere for waste disposal. These costs, however, are then passed along to the consumer, so the true cost of the product is more accurately reflected in its price. Some goods subsequently become too costly, and demand drops. Others become more popular (for instance, safe toys), and demand increases. The final goal of social regulation is the socially beneficial allocation of resources.

Congress has created two types of regulatory agencies: those within the executive branch and those that deal with policy areas in which independence from Congress and

TABLE 18-3 Some Regulatory Agencies and Their Missions

	Year Established	Primary Functions
Federal Trade Commission (FTC)	1914	Administers certain antitrust laws concerning advertising, labeling, and packaging to protect consumers from unfair business practices
Food and Drug Administration (FDA)	1931	Establishes regulations concerning purity, safety, and labeling accuracy of certain foods and drugs; issues licenses for manufacturing and distribution.
Federal Communications Commission (FCC)	1934	Licenses civilian radio and television communication; licenses and sets rates for interstate and international communication
Animal and Plant Health Inspection Service	1953	Sets standards; inspects and enforces laws relating to meat, poultry, and plant safety
Environmental Protection Agency (EPA)	1970	Develops environmental quality standards; approves state environmental plans
Occupational Safety and Health Administration (OSHA)	1970	Develops and enforces worker safety and health regulations
Bureau of Alcohol, Tobacco and Firearms	1972	Enforces laws and regulates legal flow of these materials
Consumer Product Safety Commission (CPSC)	1972	Establishes mandatory product safety standards and bans sales of products that do not comply
Nuclear Regulatory Commission (NRC)	1974	Licenses the construction and operation of nuclear reactors and similar facilities and regulates nuclear materials; also licenses the export of nuclear reactors and the export and import of uranium and plutonium

the president is desired. Members of executive branch agencies serve at the pleasure of the president. Executive branch regulatory agencies include the Food and Drug Administration (FDA), the Office of Surface Mining, and the National Highway Traffic Safety Administration. Members of **independent regulatory agencies** are appointed by the president, confirmed by the Senate, and cannot be removed by a president. Independent agencies, usually headed by a board composed of seven members, include the Federal Communications Commission, the Equal Employment Opportunities Commission, and the Nuclear Regulatory Commission.

The Regulation Debate

Perhaps the number one responsibility of government regulation in our free market system is to maintain competition. Where one company gains a **monopoly**, the market system operates ineffectively. The aim of **antitrust regulations** is to prevent monopolies, break up those that exist, and to restore competition.

In the past there were what were called "natural monopolies" such as electric utilities and telephone companies, which were protected by the government because it was assumed that in these fields more than one company would be grossly inefficient.

Regulation also compensates for market imperfections. Even those who oppose regulation recognize that the market does not always solve every problem. Consider pollution. For a long time no price was imposed on a business for using air and water to discharge toxic wastes. Therefore, market forces did not consider what it cost society to have its air and water polluted. When the market fails to set appropriate costs and benefits, pressures develop for the government to step in. The government can, for example, pass regulations that impose penalties for air pollution. Market forces also do not encourage taking a bus instead of a car to work. If government enacted higher taxes on gasoline, our fuel costs would be brought more in line with Europe's. Such a policy would also reduce our dependency on Middle East oil and promote domestic energy production.

The debate about regulation is usually about less versus more, rather than all or nothing. Few Americans call for unlimited government intervention in economic and social activity. And few advocate absolute removal of government participation from the marketplace. Indeed, most people call for more regulation in some areas and less in others. Sometimes those who call for more regulation are surprised by the results, as mandatory air bags in automobiles illustrated.

WE THE PEOPLE

Farewell Reflections of a Former FDA Commissioner

David Kessler was appointed Food and Drug Administration commissioner by President George Bush in 1990 and stayed on until 1997, when he became dean of Yale Medical School. Many of his initiatives began during the Bush administration, but his role became even more controversial under President Bill Clinton. His efforts to change food labeling laws and tighten vitamin supplement regulations generated applause and criticism. Under his leadership, the FDA first studied and then concluded that nicotine should be a "controlled substance." Kessler looked back on his years at the Food and Drug Administration as "a good fight":

> My six years at the agency . . . have been a challenge. I have had to deal with the issues that the FDA faces as a public-health agency and learn to cope with the relentless pressures that are always part of the job. Both the agency and I have been vilified. I feel very strongly, however, that if you believe in what you're doing, all the name calling in the world won't stop you. . . .
>
> For a public-health agency to make a difference, there is no better strategy than prevention. The two chief causes of preventable death in the United States are poor diet and smoking. The new food labels that FDA developed are helping millions of Americans make healthier choices. . . .
>
> Then there's smoking. In August [1996], President Clinton took a historic and unprecedented action when he announced that the FDA was asserting its jurisdiction over cigarettes and smokeless tobacco. We issued a regulation that will make it more difficult for children and adolescents to obtain tobacco products and tougher for the industry to aim its advertising at young people. . . . Our goal over the next seven years is to cut in half the number of children who start to smoke. . . .
>
> Maybe the world in which our children live will be a little bit safer. . . . The things we have done at FDA can and will affect the public's health—and that means we've fought the good fight.

SOURCES: Jeffrey Goldberg, "Next Target: Nicotine," *The New York Times Magazine*, August 4, 1996, pp. 22–27, 36–44; also David Kessler, "We've Fought the Good Fight," *Newsweek*, December 9, 1996, p. 28.

Regulations that Have Improved the Quality of Our Lives

- Bans on "quack medicines"
- Inspections for livestock diseases
- Recalls of defective automobiles
- Regulations on industrial pollution
- Regulations on lead poisoning
- Regulations to encourage clean water
- Regulations on asbestos
- Regulations on vinyl chloride
- Regulations on unsafe toys
- Regulations on breast implants
- Regulations on fraudulent labeling of children's foods

Automobile air bags have saved thousands of lives since they were made mandatory in the 1980s, but they have also killed dozens of people, including as many as 40 children who were riding in the front passenger seat. Thus a piece of equipment designed as a safety measure turns out to have serious risks to the people it should protect. The federal government issued warnings in 1997 that small children should never sit in the front seat, and car manufacturers rushed to redesign their air bags to prevent injury or death to children or small adults, as the government created new regulations for their installation and use.[24]

The deregulation of cable television offers yet another example of unintended results. Soon after the deregulation of television in the mid-1990s, the number of cable subscribers increased. The dramatic growth in access to cable was accompanied by an increase in fees, something the Department of Justice attributed in part to the monopoly held by local cable companies. The Federal Communications Commission and Congress were pressured to address the rapid increases in the cost of cable television, so Congress passed legislation regulating fees. Ironically, rates went up for about half of the country following regulation. Defenders of Congress's law see the fee increases as part of an effort to establish a "benchmark" from which prices will not grow as rapidly in the future. Opponents point not only to the higher costs associated with regulation, but to the fear Congress may seek to regulate subscriber fees as well as the rates the companies pay for programs.

Congress often legislates broad objectives for the regulatory agencies, which then set specific rules for meeting these goals. Agency regulations have been largely in the form of specific rules that a firm may not violate without being punished. Under pressure from businesses and their allies in Congress, recent administrations have cut back some of these regulations. For example, the Occupational Safety and Health Administration trimmed more than a thousand "nitpicking" regulations that governed such things as the shape of toilet seats. Congress also began to acquire better information on the benefits and costs of regulation and increased its oversight of federal regulatory efforts.[25]

REGULATING BUSINESS

During most of the nineteenth century our national policy was to leave business pretty much alone. However, four major waves of regulatory legislation have occurred: at the turn of the century, in the 1910s, in the 1930s, and in the late 1960s through 1980. In each case, changing circumstances gave rise to the legislation.

Antitrust Policy

In the late nineteenth century, social critics and populist reformers believed consumers were being cheated, especially in the oil, sugar, whiskey, and steel industries, where large monopolies, called **trusts**, worked to reduce competition. People began to have mixed feelings about big business. Americans, who have often been impressed by bigness—the tallest skyscraper, the largest football stadium, the biggest steel mill—and the efficiency that often goes with bigness, became skeptical about giant enterprises.

In 1890, Congress responded by passing the Sherman Antitrust Act, which was designed "to protect trade and commerce against unlawful restraints and monopolies." Henceforth, persons making contracts, combinations, or conspiracies in restraint of trade in interstate and foreign commerce could be sued for damages, required to stop their illegal practices, and subjected to criminal penalties. However, the Sherman Antitrust Act had little immediate impact; presidents made little attempt to enforce it, and the Supreme Court's early interpretation of the act limited its scope.

trust
A monopoly that controls goods and services, often in combinations that reduce competition.

In 1914, during the administration of Woodrow Wilson, Congress added the Clayton Act to the antitrust arsenal. This act outlawed such specific abuses as charging different prices to different buyers in order to destroy a weaker competitor, granting rebates, making false statements about competitors and their products, buying up supplies to stifle competition, and bribing competitors' employees. In addition, **interlocking directorates** (by which an officer or director in one corporation serves on the board of a competitor) were banned, and corporations were prohibited from acquiring stock in competing concerns if such acquisitions substantially lessened interstate competition. That same year Congress established the Federal Trade Commission (FTC), run by a five-person board, to enforce the Clayton Act and prevent unfair competitive practices. The FTC was to be the "traffic cop" for competition.[26]

Merger Mania

During recent years thousands of mergers have taken place, many of them among competing companies: General Motors bought Hughes Aircraft; R.J. Reynolds absorbed Nabisco; GE and RCA merged with General Foods; Warner Communications merged with Time; and McDonnell Douglas became part of Boeing. Airlines have merged. Many banks and financial services companies merged.

With a staff of 350 lawyers, the Antitrust Division of the Department of Justice investigates mergers and acquisitions to determine whether they violate the antitrust laws by unreasonably restraining interstate trade and commerce. If it so determines, it may seek to prevent the merger. The Antitrust Division also has authority to prosecute violators of the laws against price fixing, and it investigates and prepares cases to prevent anticompetitive bid rigging."[27]

The Reagan and Bush administrations generally adopted a permissive policy toward mergers, and few were prevented. These Republican administrations assumed that most mergers were inherently good for the consumer and the economy, not—as the common wisdom had it in the 1960s—that such mergers were suspect. The Clinton administration has been more vigorous in enforcing antitrust laws, yet the Justice Department's Antitrust Division and the Federal Trade Commission have generally looked favorably on most mergers.

REGULATING LABOR AND MANAGEMENT

Government regulation of business is essentially restrictive. Most laws and rules curb business practices and steer private enterprise into socially useful channels. But regulation cuts two ways. In the case of American workers, most laws in recent decades have tended not to restrict labor but to confer rights and opportunities on it. Actually, many labor laws do not touch labor directly; instead they regulate its relations with employers.

Among the more important federal regulations designed to protect workers are:

1. *Public contract.* The Walsh-Healy Act of 1936, as amended, requires that no worker employed under contracts with the national government in excess of $10,000 be paid less than the prevailing wage, and that he or she be paid overtime for all work in excess of 8 hours per day or 40 hours per week.
2. *Wages and hours.* The Fair Labor Standards Act of 1938 set a maximum work week of 40 hours for all employees engaged in interstate commerce or in the production of goods for interstate commerce (with certain exemptions). Work beyond that amount must be paid for at one-and-one-half times the regular rate. Minimum wages, originally set as 25 cents an hour, were progressively increased; the minimum wage was increased to $5.15 an hour as a result of the Minimum Wage Increase Act of 1996.

The Case of OSHA

The Occupational Safety and Health Administration, a unit in the Department of Labor, has been one of the most criticized federal regulatory agencies, although that criticism has decreased in recent years. You have no doubt come across reports of its endless rules or its allegedly patronizing warnings to business operators. OSHA has thousands of rules in the *Code of Federal Regulations.* Despite vigorous efforts by antiregulation groups to slash its budget and cut its staff, OSHA still employs over 2,000 persons, about half of whom are safety and health inspectors.

OSHA was created because interest groups effectively publicized that many people were becoming disabled or were dying from work-related accidents. By 1970, for example, more than 14,000 people were dying each year in industrial accidents, and an estimated 100,000 a year were being permanently disabled in workplace injuries.

The mandate of OSHA is to protect the health and safety of more than 60 million workers in about 5 million workplaces. It is also asked to issue compulsory safety and health standards and to monitor compliance. To achieve these objectives, OSHA is empowered to inspect businesses and to issue notices of violation and fines.

OSHA will celebrate its thirtieth anniversary in 2000. It has not been as bad as its critics maintain, but neither has it been as effective as its proponents hoped would be the case. OSHA deserves credit for the decrease in work-related injuries and illnesses and for its action against polyvinyl chloride and other serious threats to workers' health. OSHA has tried to concentrate its limited energies on severe health hazards and make more use of its emergency power to restrict dangerous substances. It has dropped many trivial safety rules and focuses on four major industries—construction, heavy manufacturing, transportation, and petrochemicals—that are considered hazardous. It also keeps pressure on a few industries it considers potentially dangerous, such as auto repair, dry cleaning, and building materials.

interlocking directorate
A corporation in which an officer or director sits on the board of a competitor, with the effect of restraining trade.

3. *Child labor.* The Fair Labor Standards Act of 1938 prohibits child labor (under 16 years of age, or under 18 in hazardous occupations) in industries that engage in, or that produce goods for, interstate commerce.
4. *Industrial safety and occupational health.* The Occupational Safety and Health Act of 1970 created the first comprehensive federal industrial safety program. It gave the secretary of labor broad authority to set safety and health standards for companies engaged in interstate commerce.

During the first half of this century, labor's basic struggle was for the right to organize into unions. For many decades trade unions had been held lawful by state legislatures, but the courts had chipped away at their status by legalizing anti-union devices. The most notorious was the **yellow-dog contract**, by which employers made new workers, as a condition of employment, promise not to join labor organizations. If labor organizers later tried to unionize the workers, the employers could apply for court orders to stop the organizers. In 1932, the Norris–La Guardia Act made yellow-dog contracts unenforceable and granted labor the right to organize. Under President Franklin D. Roosevelt, Congress enacted a series of laws to protect workers and their right to form trade unions.

Do unions need federal laws to protect their right to organize? The history of union efforts before 1933 suggests that organizing without federal protection was extremely difficult. Indeed, union membership and strength were waning fast until New Deal measures granted workers the right to organize and bargain collectively. The 1935 National Labor Relations Act (usually called the Wagner Act) made these guarantees permanent and gave them federal backing. The act makes five types of employer action unfair: (1) interfering with workers in their attempt to organize unions or bargain collectively; (2) supporting company unions (unions set up and dominated by the employer); (3) discriminating against members of unions; (4) firing or otherwise victimizing an employee for having taken action under the act; (5) refusing to bargain with union representatives. The act prevents employers from using violence, espionage, propaganda, and community pressure to resist unionization.

yellow-dog contract
Contract by an anti-union employer that forces new workers to promise they will not join a union as a condition of employment.

closed shop
A company with a labor agreement whereby union membership is a condition of employment.

union shop
A company in which new employees must join a union within a stated time period.

labor injunction
A court order forbidding specific individuals or groups from performing certain acts (such as striking) that the court considers harmful to the rights and property of an employer or community.

collective bargaining
Method whereby representatives of the union and employer determine wages, hours, and other conditions of employment through direct negotiation.

A regulatory commission was established to administer the act. The National Labor Relations Board (NLRB), consisting of five members holding overlapping terms of five years each, operates largely through regional officers, who investigate charges of unfair labor practices and issue formal complaints, and through trial examiners, who hold hearings and submit reports to the board in Washington.

Congress passed a major modification of the labor laws in 1947, the Labor-Management Relations Act, commonly called the Taft-Hartley Act. It remains the most important legislation regulating union activity in the United States.

- It outlaws the **closed shop** (a company that requires an employer to hire and retain only union members in good standing) and permits the **union shop** (a company in which new employees must join the union within a stated period of time).
- It makes it an unfair labor practice for unions to refuse to bargain with employers.
- It allows limited use of the **labor injunction** (a court order forbidding specific individuals or groups to perform acts the court considers harmful to the rights or property of an employer or community).
- It permits states to outlaw union shops. Right-to-work laws, which states could now adopt, typically make it illegal for **collective bargaining** agreements (terms and conditions of employment negotiated by representatives of the union and the employer) to contain closed shop, union shop, preferential hiring, or any other clauses calling for compulsory union membership.

THE MICROSOFT DEBATE

A Closer Look

For years Microsoft has been adding functions to its operating systems, such as Windows 95 and Windows 98. Critics charge that these functions give a distinct advantage to compatible software produced by Microsoft, enabling it to win a greater share of the market. This tactic can be illegal if it can be demonstrated that it stifles competition.

The Justice Department's Antitrust Division investigated whether Microsoft was actually stifling competition, and Senate hearings were also held.

The Justice Department took Microsoft to court for allegedly violating past agreements in which it agreed that it would not engage in anticompetitive practices. Microsoft co-founder and chief executive officer, Bill Gates, fumed at the Justice Department's efforts, saying incorporating fewer functions in operating systems would be a major setback not only for Microsoft but for consumers, innovation, and the high-tech industry:

> The government wants to force us to ship a browser made by a leading competitor, Netscape, with every copy of Windows—a demand that would benefit only Netscape, not consumers. Such a demand is both unprecedented and unreasonable. It's like ordering Ford to sell autos fitted with Chrysler engines. Not only would these proposals undermine our ability to compete, they run counter to the way every industry has evolved over the years—and, more importantly, to what consumers expect when they buy products.*

Is Bill Gates right? Or is Microsoft creating an unfair monopoly? Microsoft's critics argue that if the Justice Department does not restrain Microsoft's expansion into new markets, its monopoly will mow down rivals with market muscle and not necessarily with superior products.** Others contend that because of Microsoft's dominance in important computer markets, it deserves close government scrutiny. Yet they point out that "the purpose of antitrust law is to protect consumers, not to help rivals."†

Federal Reserve Chair Alan Greenspan, though not commenting directly on the Microsoft case, cautioned that what appear to be monopolies very often tend to fade over time with changes in markets and technology. He cited IBM, U. S. Steel, and General Motors as examples. "I would feel uncomfortable if we inhibited various different types of mergers or acquisitions on the basis of some presumed projection as to how the markets would evolve," Greenspan told a congressional panel. "History is strewn with people making projections that have turned out to be grossly inaccurate."††

Bill Gates and Microsoft have previously fought off federal regulations and court challenges, yet they have also had to compromise on a number of important issues. This debate could establish the rules and limits for the vast computer industry and other hi-tech fields.

Microsoft President Bill Gates (left), along with Sun Microsystems President Scott McNealy and Netscape President Jim Barksdale, testifying before the Senate Judiciary Committee.

*Bill Gates, "We're Defending Our Right to Innovate," *The Wall Street Journal*, May 20, 1998, p. A14.

**See Robert Bork, "The Most Misunderstood Antitrust Case," *The Wall Street Journal*, May 22, 1998, p. A16. See also Steve Lohr, "Gates on Capital Hill, Presents Case for Microsoft," *The New York Times*, March 4, 1998, pp. A1, C4.

†Robert E. Hale, "Antitrust Excess?" *The New York Times*, May 20, 1998, p. A23.

††Quoted in Jon R. Wilke, "Greenspan Questions Antitrust Efforts," *The Wall Street Journal*, June 17, 1998, p. A2.

The Taft-Hartley Act set up machinery for handling disputes if a work stoppage threatens national health or safety. It has been invoked against strikes in vital sectors of the economy such as atomic energy, coal, shipping, steel, and telephone service. The president or the secretary of labor can attempt to mediate strikes without resorting to the act.

Environmental Protection

The issue of pollution vividly illustrates the regulatory dilemma. Critics of strict controls on air, water, and noise pollution say the pursuit of a clean environment hampers our economy and causes unemployment. They call attention, for example, to the disastrous economic consequences of the shutdown of companies for pollution violations. Until relatively recently, governments at all levels did little to protect the environment, and what little was done was by state and local governments. In recent years the national government has taken on new responsibilities, primarily because local governments have failed to act.

The primary federal agencies concerned with the environment are the Council on Environmental Quality in the Executive Office of the President, which develops and recommends policy options to the president and Congress, and the Environmental Protection Agency (EPA), which is responsible for enforcing federal environmental laws and regulations. Other federal agencies that regulate the environment include the Interior Department, the Food and Drug Administration, and the Departments of Energy and Transportation.

The National Environmental Policy Act of 1969 set up the controversial requirement of **environmental impact statements** to assess the potential effects of new construction or development on the environment. Most projects utilizing federal funds must file such statements. Since 1970 thousands of statements have been filed. Supporters contend that such statements point out major flaws in projects and can lead to cost saving along with greater environmental awareness. Critics claim environmental impact reviews simply represent more government interference, paperwork, and delays in the private sector.

A 1970 amendment to the Air Quality Act of 1967 established national standards for states, pollution guidelines for automobiles, and regulations concerning stationary sources of pollution. Yet enforcement of the act greatly disappointed environmentalists, who noted that EPA had brought only about seven of some nearly 300 industrial air toxins under federal regulation. Amendments to the act passed in 1977 extended but did not greatly strengthen the original legislation. Throughout the 1980s the fear of lost jobs and costs for industry and consumers stalled more rigorous enforcement and tighter restrictions.

But in 1989 George Bush introduced a bold clean air bill. The 1990 Clean Air Act was designed to remedy the failings and lax enforcement of the 1970 and 1977 acts. It tightened controls on automobiles and the fuel they use. It required automakers to install pollution controls to reduce emissions of hydrocarbons and nitrogen oxides and set stiff standards for the kinds of gas that can be sold. The 1990 act stipulated that plants that emit any of 189 toxic substances have to cut those emissions to the average level of the 12 cleanest similar facilities. Plants posing a 1 in 10,000 risk of cancer to nearby residents by the year 2003 may be shut down. The act also promoted the phasing out of chlorofluorocarbons and other chemicals that harm the earth's protective ozone layer and may contribute to global warming.

The 1990 Clean Air Act has been called the most expensive piece of environmental legislation ever passed, with some estimates saying compliance will cost as much as $25 billion per year. But most people, including leaders in our nation's basic industries, acknowledge we have made a mess of the environment, and the sooner we clean it up the better.

environmental impact statement
A statement required by federal law from all agencies for any project using federal funds to assess the potential effect of the new construction or development on the environment.

Some economists suggest that the profit motive may be harnessed in the pursuit of pollution control. With this in mind, EPA has pressed for new regulatory strategies that encourage market solutions for ecological problems: "Government sets broad limits on the amount of pollution allowed for a region or industry and allots permits to firms for their share of that total. Polluters can buy or sell these allowances, so that firms that can reduce a pollutant inexpensively will benefit by selling their allowances to dirtier neighbors."[28] Initial efforts along these lines have been successful, saving billions.

Bill Clinton won election in 1992 on a platform that promised aggressive leadership on environmental matters. His vice-president, Al Gore, had long been associated with environmental reform. Gore was the author of a best-selling book, *Earth in the Balance*, and vigorously championed more research and action on global warming.[29] Clinton's appointments to key environmental policy positions were praised, but he generally tried to strike a middle ground between business interests on the one hand and vigorous environmentalists on the other. In both his first and second term, Clinton promised more leadership in environmental matters than he was able to exercise. His efforts to cut regulations, reduce staff, and balance the federal budget made it difficult to strengthen EPA and similar agencies to do their job effectively. Clinton raised expectations yet achieved only modest success in this policy area.

THE DEREGULATION DEBATE

One solution to criticism about government regulation has been **deregulation**—cutbacks in the amount of regulation attempted by the federal government, not the dismantling of all regulatory procedures. Deregulation has been tried in the transportation industries, the banking industry, and telecommunications, to name a few. No industry has undergone more extensive deregulation than the transportation industry. Over the past generation, airlines, trucking, and railroads have been granted considerable freedom in conducting their operations.

Airline Deregulation

The Civil Aeronautics Board (CAB) was established by the federal government in 1938 to protect airlines from unreasonable competition by controlling rates and fares. Critics charged that airlines competed only in the frequency of flights and in the services they offered. Because there was no competition over price, consumers were forced to pay high rates for services they may not have desired. Others claimed CAB regulation of fares kept them higher than they would have been under competitive conditions. It was also charged that airlines were too slow to open new routes under CAB supervision.

In light of these and other considerations, Congress in 1978 passed the Airline Deregulation Act. The Civil Aeronautics Board was legislated out of existence in 1985, and airlines were free to set whatever fares their markets would bear. Free entry and free exit were allowed in all markets.

One of the first results of deregulation was that some medium-sized cities lost service because carriers found it more profitable to use their aircraft in busier markets. Airlines were raising fares on routes over which they had monopolies in order to subsidize lower fares on more competitive routes. Critics charged that safety precautions and maintenance suffered as a result of cutthroat competition and the ease with which new airlines could enter the market.

Although problems have been associated with airline deregulation, it has resulted in generally lower fares, greater choice of routes and fares in most markets, and more efficient use of assets by the industry.[30] Some airlines have been driven into bankruptcy and others have merged, but deregulation of the airlines has been judged a success by the surviving airlines and most observers of the industry. If an airline is overcharging passengers, a competitor will eventually steal those travelers away. Southwest Airlines is an example of a discount airline that took advantage of

deregulation
A policy promoting cutbacks in the amount of federal regulation in specific areas of economic activity.

Assigning Blame for the Valujet Crash

In May of 1996, Valujet Flight 592 crashed in the Florida Everglades, killing 110 people. Critics charged that the Federal Aviation Agency (FAA) should have inspected Valujet's planes more closely and warned about possible violations. Valujet had grown rapidly over a two and a half year period from two planes to a fleet of more than fifty planes, many of them refurbished older planes.

FAA Director David Hinsen told Congress in a 1996 hearing into the crash, "It is apparent now that the extraordinarily rapid growth [of Valujet] created problems that should have been more clearly recognized and dealt with sooner and more aggressively."*

Valujet Flight 592 crashed because it was carrying hazardous materials that were incorrectly labelled. But the crash highlighted lax inspection procedures and focused attention on the operations of a regulatory agency that had had its funds and personnel cut back as a result of federal downsizing.

The FAA has the unreachable goal of zero airplane accidents. Its officials are constantly searching for inspection systems and training programs that will make a zero accident record possible. Flying is still the safest way to travel, but it can never be accident-free.

*Quoted in Douglas B. Feaver, "A New Route to Safety," *The Washington Post Weekly Edition*, August 12–18, 1996, p. 22. See also Mary Schiavo with Sabra Chartrand, *Flying Blind, Flying Safe* (Avon, 1997).

deregulation to take on larger airlines in the West.[31] In the long run, deregulation is strengthening the industry by forcing companies to streamline their operations in order to survive in a competitive market.

Telecommunications Reform

After years of debate, President Clinton signed into law the Telecommunications Act of 1996, the most sweeping regulatory reform of telecommunications since the Communications Act of 1934. The act opened up large areas of telecommunications to companies that once were regulated both in the services they could provide and the prices they could charge. The main objective of the new law was to increase competition among phone, cable, and other communications companies. Telephone companies that were once divided into seven local "mini-Bell companies" were allowed to offer services outside their defined regions. Local telephone companies won the freedom to provide long distance service, manufacture communications equipment, and offer video service in competition with cable television. At the same time, local telephone companies opened their networks to competition for local telephone service from cable television and long distance companies. In short, restrictions were removed so that cable television and local and long distance telephone companies could effectively compete with one another.

Two controversial aspects of the Telecommunications Act of 1996 were regulation of Internet content and the advent of the V-chip to allow parents to block out television shows with objectionable content. The act prohibits any person or company knowingly to make indecent material accessible to minors by a computer; selling or obtaining drugs are similarly prohibited. But the rating system based on age level that was proposed by industry has been criticized by parent groups. They prefer ratings for excessive violence, offensive language, or nudity. The constitutionality of these restrictions is being challenged and will be settled by the courts, but the debate continues on who will decide what is deemed violent or offensive.[32]

Regulatory Outcomes and Issues

While the need for regulation, especially in areas affecting health and safety, is widely accepted, there are concerns about the negative consequences of regulation. A marked decrease in lead paint poisonings, the use of childproof bottle tops, and the banning of many cancer-producing pesticides are all positive outcomes of federal regulatory activity. On the negative side, regulations have increased the cost of some products and may have hampered some industries.

- *Regulation distorts and disrupts the operation of the market.* Some governmental intervention upsets the normal adjustment processes of the market and thus encourages higher prices, misallocation of resources, and inefficiency.
- *Regulation may discourage competition.* Some forms of regulation (often the kind desired by industry) actually have the reverse of their desired effect. This is especially true when the government grants operating licenses and charters to maintain a certain level of quality or stability in the market. Regulatory red tape has also been charged with discouraging entry into industries and driving small businesses out.
- *Regulation may discourage technological development.* If the reward for innovation is a new set of rules and a struggle for permission to use a new product, business may not find it worth the effort to innovate.

- *Regulatory agencies are often "captured" by the industries they regulate.* It is suggested that some regulatory bodies are controlled by the businesses they are supposed to be regulating. There is evidence, too, that some bureaucrats consider jobs in regulatory agencies as stepping-stones to lucrative careers in private industry, and the industries encourage this connection.
- *Regulation increases costs to industry and to the consumer.* Some critics estimate that government regulations cost $8,000 to $10,000 annually to every household in the United States. Such figures are disputed by many labor and consumer advocates, who say health and safety standards are the best investment we can make. Every life and every limb we save, and every disease we prevent, represents not only a valuable achievement but also a reduction in the nation's enormous hospital and medical bills.
- *Regulation has often been introduced without cost-benefit analysis.* Critics say too little attention is given to whether the benefits of a particular piece of regulation are great enough to justify its cost. Is it worth it to delay approval of new drugs while some who would benefit may die? Is it worth it to clean up 95 percent of automobile emissions if the cost is many times that of an 85 percent cleanup? Is it worth spending $2 million per cancer case arising from exposure to hazardous waste?
- *Regulatory agencies lack qualified personnel.* Critics of regulation, and some heads of regulatory agencies themselves, say regulators lack the expertise to do their jobs properly. Regulatory agencies complain they need larger budgets to do their job properly and attract more qualified staff. Critics argue, too, that government should not meddle in technological industries about which it knows little.

Deregulation of the airlines may have reduced fares in some areas, but it also led to reductions in service and long lines at the counters in other areas.

Evaluating Regulation

Deregulation appears to be working better in some areas than in others. In the area of drug deregulation, the results are mixed. The Food and Drug Administration, especially since the early 1980s, relaxed the requirements for introducing new medicines. People in the drug industry applaud these efforts. They argue that as a result of deregulation, the public gets better medicines faster and cheaper. Opponents contend, and with some evidence, that the accelerated approval process is endangering public health by prematurely allowing potentially hazardous drugs on the market.

In our federal system the mere fact that the national government stops regulating an industry does not mean the particular industry will be unregulated. On the contrary, sometimes 50 different state regulators take over, making it even more difficult for an industry to operate on a large scale. California, for example, has much tougher automobile emission rules than does the national government. Variations in state regulations are the reason businesspeople themselves sometimes call for more, not less, national regulation; they would prefer one set of national guidelines to 50 different state ones.

In sum, the federal government is heavily involved in making economic and regulatory policies. It collects taxes, regulates the money supply, tries to prevent monopolies that would hurt the consumer, and seeks to promote free trade. It does all this while trying to let the market, not government bureaucrats, shape the demand and price of products and services. Most Americans want their government to play only a limited role in the economy, but competing values such as fairness, equality, protecting the environment, and encouraging healthy competition inevitably encourage elected officials to perform certain balancing or referee responsibilities in order to promote the common good.

FEDS, GET OFF OF MY CLOUD

James K. Glassman

It's not a perfect system, but it's a lot better than the alternative.

Professor James K. Glassman argues that deregulation has had numerous benefits. In the case of airline regulation, fares have declined as anticipated. One study indicated that air travelers paid 28 percent less in 1996 than they would have if regulation were still in place. In addition, more Americans are flying more safely now than before deregulation. Flight mileage increased three times as fast as automobile mileage between 1980 and 1995, while air fatalities per mile were cut in half in the same period.

The overall savings to consumers resulting from airline deregulation was estimated at $18.4 billion in 1993, but the South and West have benefited at the expense of the East and Midwest, because airlines have shifted some operations to warmer climates. Glassman admits that deregulation "has been messy and confusing." He cites a *New York Times* study indicating that on a single flight from Chicago to Los Angeles in 1997, 33 coach passengers paid 27 different fares in amounts varying from $87 to $728.

Another problem is that airlines have reduced fares by offering poorer quality food, reducing space between seats, and flying aging planes longer. The greatest complaint about deregulation is the tendency of airlines to try to monopolize traffic in their hub cities. When smaller competitors try to enter a major hub, the large airlines drop their fares in an attempt to run the competitors out of the hub city business.

Glassman insists, however, that on the whole, deregulation is better than the alternative. Even if airlines cut fares suspiciously, "the government is on shaky ground in trying to determine whether price-cutting—which, after all, helps passengers in the here and now—is 'predatory' or robust." Government regulation can hardly increase or guarantee competition. Good intentions do not guarantee the best results. Glassman concludes that "Federal officials also have to understand their own limits. A certain amount of chaos in pricing and service—as well as unfairness to stagnant communities and even to smaller airlines—is inevitable and largely unfixable with deregulation. It's not a perfect system, but, when you judge from the past 20 years' experience, it's a lot better than the alternative."★

SOURCE: James K. Glassman, "Feds, Get Off of My Cloud," *US News & World Report* 124, April 27, 1998, p. 61.

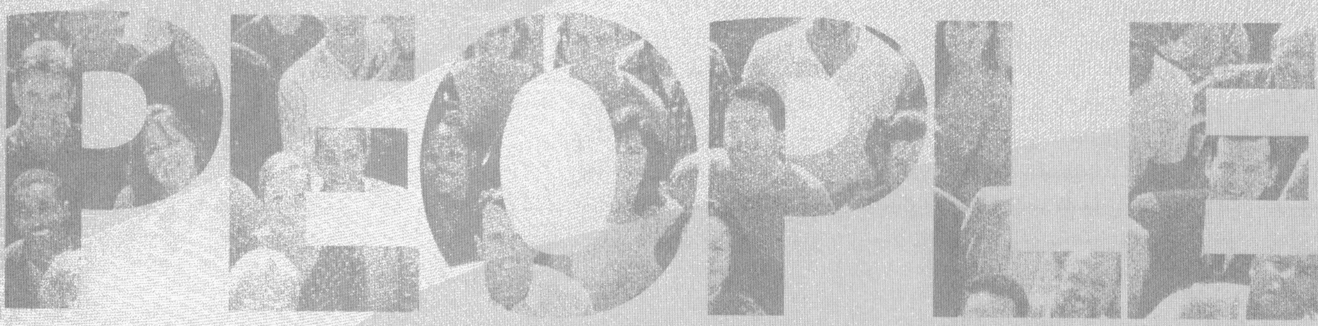

WHY DEREGULATION HAS GONE TOO FAR

Robert Worth

Robert Worth, an editor at *Washington Monthly*, argues that government has a legitimate role in regulating business in the public interest, and the effects of deregulation to date give us reason to pause before proceeding further.

First, claims Worth, the large airlines have effectively kept small competitors out of the market. Second, although air travel fatalities have decreased since deregulation, the number of new flights has outpaced the number of air traffic controllers available to handle them, leading to an increasing number of near misses.

If we turn to other industries where deregulation has occurred, notes Worth, we find combinations of large companies monopolizing the telephone industry and cable television. Of particular significance is the fact that "more than half of big-city [radio] stations are in the hands of just five companies." The large firms play only the old favorites, limiting the selection available to the general public. Worth complains that the Justice Department is often too weak to break up monopolies. Deregulation of the banking business led to practices that allowed Charles Keating and his friends to cheat Americans out of $130 billion. As electric companies are deregulated, they tend to charge their residential customers higher rates than business customers as they compete for factories and other high-volume clients.

Worth insists that proponents of deregulation miss the point when they claim that the cash benefits outweigh the costs. "Left to its own devices, the economy—no matter how large or small—always inflicts some unfairness on those who don't own a lot of stock. The purpose of regulation in areas like telecom, electricity, and banking was to defray the cost of service for ordinary people at the expense of the high-volume users—businesses, mostly—who could better afford it."

Worth admits that some unwise regulations appear from time to time. "The Equal Employment Opportunity Commission has been after the Hooters restaurant chain for years because Hooters doesn't employ male waiters (if you don't know why, God bless you)." But occasional problems like this should not deter us from securing public health and safety. Although the FDA is called a "job killer," it has provided consumers much needed protection. Worth concludes that "When you look at the human damage weak regulation can do, the question becomes not whether to regulate at all but how to do it better." ★

SOURCE: Robert Worth, "Why Deregulation Has Gone Too Far: Toxic Drugs, Tainted Meat, Exploding Airplanes, and Other Dangers of Unfettered Capitalism," *Washington Monthly* 30 (July/August 1998), pp. 10–14.

Government has a legitimate role in regulating business in the public interest, and the effects of deregulation to date give us reason to pause before proceeding further.

For further discussion of this debate, go to **http://www.prenhall.com/burns.** *Click on the Debate Icon under Chapter 17.*

POLITICS online

Regulation and Economic Policy on the Internet

One group promoting the use of electronic communications in policy matters is the Consumer Project on Technology, a site created by Ralph Nader to disseminate information on telecommunications, intellectual property, privacy, and antitrust legislation:

http://www.cptech.org

For a sampling of home pages of agencies and interest groups involved in regulatory policy, go to:

http://www.public-domain.org

or

http://www.essential.org/antitrust

One of the most important and least understood institutions in economic policy is the Federal Reserve Board. To learn more about it, go to:

http://www.bog.frb.fed.us

Information on the federal budget can be found at:

http://www/acces.gpo.gov

For more Internet resources on Economic and Regulatory Policy, see our home page:

http://www.prenhall.com/burns

SUMMARY

1. There are five stages in the policy-making process: problem identification, policy formulation, policy adoption, policy implementation, and policy evaluation. When the process turns to implementation and evaluation, new problems are identified, and the process begins again. Inaction is also a policy. Every policy has political consequences.
2. The national government influences how wealth is produced and distributed primarily via fiscal policy (taxing and spending), monetary policy (control of the money supply), and regulatory policy.
3. Fiscal policy is implemented by the federal budget, which is annually negotiated between the president and Congress. Monetary policy is primarily under the control of the Federal Reserve System, which has considerable independence from both Congress and the president as it works to supply sufficient amounts of money and credit so that the economy will grow, but not so much that it will lead to inflation.
4. The role of government as promoter of economic growth and jobs is not new. It is as old as the Republic itself. The federal government has long been involved in promoting agriculture and concerned about the health of producers and consumers of these commodities. Working through the Department of Commerce, it also promotes business. The national government is also involved in promoting trade and commerce with other nations. Our ability to buy from other nations and sell them our goods and services has much to do with the health of our economy.
5. Regulation, now a major activity of government, involves altering the natural workings of the open market to achieve some desired goal. Economic regulation aims to control the behavior of business in the marketplace. Social regulation aims to correct the unintended side effects of economic activity and to ensure equal rights in employment, education, and housing.
6. Even though the members of regulatory bodies are nominated by the president, their powers derive from legislative delegation, and their decisions are subject to review by the courts. Independent regulatory agencies have a scope of responsibility in the American economy that sometimes exceeds that of the three regular branches of government.
7. Regulation is a means of eliminating some of the abuses and problems generated by the private economy, while avoiding government ownership and the risks of too much centralization. Regulation is an inevitable by-product of a complex, industrialized, high-technology society.
8. A deregulation movement designed to get the government out of the regulation of certain businesses has taken place during the last 30 years. Liberals sometimes favor deregulation if they believe it will foster more competition. Conservatives generally favor deregulation that will get federal regulators off their backs in areas such as safety, health, and environmental and consumer-protection standards.

KEY WORDS

fiscal policy 436
monetary policy 436
tariff 438
excise tax 438
progressive tax 438
regressive tax 438
deficit 438
debt 438
gross domestic product (GDP) 439
entitlement program 439
Office of Management and Budget (OMB) 440
Congressional Budget Office (CBO) 441
concurrent resolution 441
reconciliation 441
General Accounting Office (GAO) 442
comptroller general 442
sales tax 442
value-added tax (VAT) 442
tax expenditure 443
item veto 444
monetarism 444
Federal Reserve System 444
laissez-faire economics 445
Keynesian economics 446
inflation 446
trade deficit 448
quota 448
General Agreement on Tariffs and Trade (GATT) 448
North American Free Trade Agreement (NAFTA) 448
protectionism 449
regulation 450
independent regulatory agency 452
monopoly 452
antitrust regulation 452
trust 454
interlocking directorate 455
yellow-dog contract 456
closed shop 456
union shop 456
labor injunction 456
collective bargaining 456
environmental impact statement 458
deregulation 459

FURTHER READING

JAGDISH BHAGWATI, *The World Trading System at Risk* (Princeton University Press, 1991).

JEFFREY H. BIRNBAUM AND ALAN S. MURRAY, *Showdown at Gucci Gulch: Lawmakers, Lobbyists, and the Unlikely Triumph of Tax Reform* (Vintage, 1988).

STEPHEN G. BREYER, *Breaking the Vicious Circle: Toward Effective Risk Regulating* (Harvard University Press, 1993).

GARY BRYNER, *Blue Skies, Green Politics: The Clean Air Act of 1990 and Its Interpretation*, 2d ed. (Congressional Quarterly Press, 1995).

GARY BURTLESS, ROBERT Z. LAWRENCE, ROBERT E. LITAN, AND ROBERT J. SHAPIRO, *Globaphobia: Confronting Fears About Open Trade* (Brookings Institution, 1998).

THOMAS W. CHURCH AND ROBERT T. NAKAMURA, *Cleaning Up the Mess: Implementation Strategies in Superfund* (Brookings Institution, 1993).

ROBERT W. CRANDALL ET AL., *An Agenda for Federal Regulatory Reform* (American Enterprise Institute and the Brookings Institution, 1997).

ROBERT W. CRANDALL AND HAROLD FURCHTGOTT-ROTH, *Cable TV: Regulation or Competition?* (Brookings Institution, 1996).

ROBERT M. ENTMAN, *Competition, Innovation and Investment in Telecommunications* (Aspen Institute, 1998).

AL GORE, *Earth in the Balance: Ecology and the Human Spirit* (Houghton Mifflin, 1992).

WILLIAM GREIDER, *Secrets of the Temple: How the Federal Reserve Runs the Country* (Simon & Schuster, 1987).

PHILIP K. HOWARD, *The Death of Common Sense: How Law Is Suffocating America* (Random House, 1994).

RICHARD KLINGLER, *The New Information Industry: Regulatory Challenges and the First Amendment* (Brookings Institution, 1996).

ROBERT KUTTNER, *Everything for Sale: The Virtues and Limits of Markets* (Knopf, 1997).

CALVIN MACKENZIE AND SARANNA THORTON, *Bucking the Deficit: Economic Policy-making in America* (Westview Press, 1996).

PAUL MCCLURE, ED., *Congressional Quarterly's Federal Regulatory Directory*, 8th ed. (Congressional Quarterly Press, 1997).

STEVEN A. MORRISON AND CLIFFORD WINSTON, *The Evolution of the Airline Industry* (Brookings Institution, 1995).

PETER G. PETERSON, *Facing Up: Paying Our Nation's Debt and Saving Our Children's Future* (Simon & Schuster, 1994).

ALLEN SCHICK, *The Federal Budget: Politics, Policy, Process* (Brookings Institution, 1995).

JOHN WARGO, *Our Children's Toxic Legacy: How Science and Law Fail to Protect Us from Pesticides* (Yale University Press, 1997).

JEFFREY WORSHAW, *Other People's Money: Policy Changes, Congress and Bank Regulation* (Westview Press, 1997).

DANIEL YERGIN AND JOSEPH STANISLAW, *The Commanding Heights: The Battle Between Government and the Marketplace That Is Remaking the Modern World* (Simon & Schuster, 1998).

MAKING
SOCIAL
POLICY

19

One of the most important policy changes of the past decade occurred in 1996 when Bill Clinton and the Republican-controlled Congress abandoned the large welfare program called Aid to Families with Dependent Children (AFDC) and replaced it with Temporary Assistance for Needy Families (TANF). Dating back to the days of the New Deal, the AFDC program was largely federally funded but locally administered. Politicians in both parties had long criticized AFDC as creating a permanent underclass and providing incentives for husbands to abandon their families and for mothers to have illegitimate children. The debate at the state and national levels was not about abandoning welfare entirely, but about replacing it with a different kind of public assistance, the Personal Responsibility and Work Opportunity Reconciliation Act of 1996, a name that captures two themes of the new approach—individuals taking more responsibility for themselves and replacing welfare with work.

The administrative burden for the new program was shifted entirely to the states. The federal government now gives *block grants* of money to states and generally requires states to match those funds. Public assistance is limited to five years over a person's lifetime; recipients must engage in work activities within two months of receiving benefits; and states can exempt up to 20 percent of cases from the work requirements and lifetime limits—an exemption intended for blind and disabled persons. The law excluded legal immigrants from 19 welfare programs and illegal immigrants from 23, but at the strong urging of the governors, several welfare benefits were later restored to legal immigrants. To discourage persons on welfare from moving to states with more generous assistance payments, the law gives states the option of limiting welfare to newcomers from another state.

Reforming welfare illustrates the complexity of making social policy. What is the responsibility of government in assisting people who, for whatever reason, cannot provide for themselves? Where should the line be drawn in excluding certain groups from assistance or in limiting their benefits? The purpose of this chapter is to introduce the basic elements of social policy as an illustration of some broader themes and issues discussed earlier in this book. The making of social policy teaches us a lot about how the separation of powers, the overlapping roles of Congress and the presidency, the implications of federalism, and the role of ideology and public opinion in the making of domestic policy actually work in practice.

CHAPTER OUTLINE

The extremes of wealth and poverty in our country are epitomized by this homeless man bedded down in front of a billboard on the streets of New York.

The Role of Government in Social Policy

What is the proper role of government in welfare, education, health care, housing, job security, care for the elderly, and public safety? These responsibilities encompass a large part of the agenda of our national government today, yet such functions were once thought to be mostly private matters or were left to local government. Debates over private versus public responsibilities in social policy and the role of different levels of government have shaped the partisan and ideological differences of this century, and they continue to be important as the nation initiates major changes in social policy.

Public versus Private

Those who favor private approaches to social policy do so for a host of reasons, including a belief that individuals need to take responsibility for their own lives rather than relying on the government to care for them. They doubt the efficiency and effectiveness of public solutions to social problems and are confident the free market will provide opportunities for those with ambition and a willingness to work hard. Opponents of government solutions say public assistance robs people of ambition and defeats the work ethic.

A preference for private solutions to social problems is closely linked with conservatism in American politics and has long been a central precept of the Republican party. Some conservatives today advocate a purely private form of health insurance, with no government requirement or participation. Allowing parents to choose where to send their children to school by giving them vouchers that can be redeemed at any private or public school is another example of a conservative approach to a social policy issue.

Conservatives often point to the long-standing tradition in the United States that private charities, churches, and foundations should raise contributions from individuals and businesses to build hospitals and nursing homes, fund medical research, provide scholarships for students, feed and house the homeless, care for abandoned children, and perform many similar services. The private approach to social policy points to such activities as evidence that people can and will seek to remedy social problems on their own, without the higher taxes, bigger government, and wasteful bureaucracy of public remedies.

Advocates of public solutions to social problems believe it is the responsibility of government to provide some minimum standard of living—a job, an education, health care, housing, and basic nutrition—for all citizens. They argue that human dignity not only requires some minimum standard of living, but that such a policy is also pragmatic. Without it, our cities would have far more homeless and hungry people, desperate for survival. Advocates of government solutions also say that private solutions to social problems do not work because there is simply not enough charitable giving to address the social needs of poor people, the elderly, and those without health insurance. Moreover, the United States is far behind other countries in social service programs and funding. Government support for public housing, welfare, health care, and education is a necessity in the modern nation-state, they contend.

National versus State and Local

The ideological debate about social policy also involves debate about which level of government should address social problems—the national government or the state and local governments. Conservatives advocate leaving most social policy matters to states and localities, where programs can be adapted to local needs. Liberals counter that history has taught that state and local governments are often unable or unwilling to address problems like health care, homelessness, and crime on their own, so the national government has had to play a major role in funding programs and setting policy standards.

Governors have been increasingly vocal about the tendency of the national government to mandate programs that the states must then administer with little or no federal funding for implementation. Such *unfunded mandates* force state governments to raise taxes or reduce funding for various other state programs. The governors make the point that whatever new national programs are enacted, they need to be fully funded by the national government.

public goods
Services or commodities that individuals benefit from but that cannot be separately sold or given to individuals. Examples are clean air, national defense, roads, harbors, and public order.

A Brief History of Social Policy in the United States

Promoting "the general welfare" is listed in the Preamble to the Constitution as one of the tasks of government. In today's terms, the general welfare could include welfare, health care, public education, and crime control. This more expansive view of the role of government is relatively new.

Long after other Western democracies had expanded their social services, welfare in the United States was left to private charities and to local governments. Why? Part of the answer is that this nation was seen as the land of opportunity. Our millions of acres of free land, our enormous natural resources, and our technical advances all helped absorb people who otherwise might not have made a go of it. Closely linked with this growth and opportunity was the widely held philosophy of *rugged individualism*: If people did not get ahead, it was their own fault. The idea of equality of opportunity meant that government played only a limited role in people's lives. Government's primary function was to secure traditional individual rights and provide **public goods**, such as roads, harbors, postal services, and public order. Rather grudgingly, state governments in the early twentieth century extended relief to needy groups, especially the old, the blind, and the orphaned. But government aid was limited, and much reliance was placed on private charity.[1]

Most Americans today expect government to play a greater role in the delivery of social services than did their predecessors. These expectations have changed as a result of wave after wave of reformers who pushed their agenda of social services. Two social policy reform efforts deserve special attention: the New Deal and the Great Society.

The New Deal

The Great Depression of the 1930s drastically expanded the involvement of the national government in social programs. As the value of stocks and real estate fell after the 1929 stock market crash, and unemployment, homelessness, and poverty

The WPA program, part of President Roosevelt's New Deal, created jobs for thousands of workers during the Great Depression of the 1930s.

rose to unprecedented heights, the inadequacy of state and local government programs and private charities became apparent. In 1933 the federal government began making loans to states and localities for public relief. When state and local funds dried up, the federal government assumed more responsibility.

Franklin D. Roosevelt's administration established relief programs designed to stimulate the economy and put people back to work:

- *The Works Progress Administration* (WPA) spent billions of dollars on local projects such as public housing, courthouses, and parks.
- *The Public Works Administration* (PWA) built larger permanent projects, like dams and roads.
- *The Agricultural Adjustment Act* (AAA) raised farm prices.
- *The Civilian Conservation Corps* (CCC) put people to work protecting natural resources on federal land.
- *The Tennessee Valley Authority* (TVA) supervised the construction of dams and power plants on the Tennessee River to electrify and modernize the rural South.

As the economy recovered, people grew critical of so-called "make-work projects" and the cost and waste of relief programs. They wanted to go back to simple handouts of food or cash by the government. But there was growing support for a well-planned, long-term program that would foster both the security and self-respect of the people needing assistance. However, the first federal attempt at an extensive security program—the Railroad Retirement Act of 1934—was declared unconstitutional by the Supreme Court.[2] The act permitted the establishment of a fund that all railroad workers would pay into, and then at their retirement or disability, they would receive payments from this fund. The Court declared the act unconstitutional because Congress had established the fund under the Constitution's commerce clause. When Congress passed the same act the next year under the general welfare clause, the act was upheld.

Social Security

As a part of the New Deal, the United States inaugurated **Social Security** in 1935, perhaps the most significant social legislation in our history. At the time it was controversial; today it is politically untouchable. Social Security is actually many programs, the most important being a retirement program supported by a combination of employee and employer taxes, now covering more than 90 percent of the American work force. Social Security was expanded in 1939 to include financial support for survivors of workers covered by Social Security when the retired worker died, and in 1954 the program was again expanded to include support for disabled workers and for children of deceased or disabled workers.

Social Security issues checks to more than 44 million Americans every month, and three times as many working people contribute to the fund. The average retired person receives about $768 per month.[3] Full benefits are paid to those between the ages of 65 and 70 who are not currently earning more than a certain amount; after age 70, people are entitled to retirement benefits regardless of wage earnings. The universal nature of Social Security is one reason it is politically so popular: everyone benefits, regardless of need.

Social Security is based on the assumption that society must take care of the elderly and the unemployed. Before Social Security, when large families were common, much of the cost of caring for the elderly was borne by children and grandchildren. Families usually had the resources to provide the necessities of life for Grandma, Aunt Suzie, and Uncle George. But during the 1930s, "taking care of one's own" was no longer a practical solution, given the extensive economic dislocation and fractured families caused by the Depression.

Social Security
A combination of entitlement programs, paid for by employer and employee taxes, that includes retirement benefits, health insurance, and support for disabled workers and the children of deceased or disabled workers.

Until the 1970s, growth in Social Security benefits was relatively noncontroversial, largely because "the costs were initially deceptively low," while the benefits increased steadily, making the system politically painless.[4] Since Social Security began, the program has experienced steady growth and is now the world's largest insurance program for retirees, survivors, and people with disabilities. Combined with the cost of Medicare, its expenditures totaled over $580 billion by 1998.[5]

Social Security, unlike many other welfare programs, is financed not from general taxes but from a *trust fund* into which taxes on employees and employers are placed—the Federal Insurance Contribution Act, commonly known as FICA. In some ways, this fund is like a private pension plan in which an investor puts money into a pension account. Over the years, Congress has added benefits to the Social Security system without adding enough money to the trust fund to cover the added expense. In 1983, Congress was forced to put Social Security on a more sound financial foundation by passing reforms that raised the retirement age at which one qualifies for Social Security benefits, increasing Social Security taxes, and taxing 50 percent of the Social Security payments of upper-income individuals—a percentage that was raised to 85 percent in 1993.

Social Security taxes are now the largest tax paid by roughly two-thirds of all Americans, and for three-quarters of Americans their Social Security tax now exceeds their income tax. Both employers and employees are required to pay 7.65 percent, up to more than $5,000 per year, of their earnings into the Social Security fund. A single person with no dependents would have to earn $30,000 before paying more federal income tax than Social Security tax; families with two children would have to earn over $40,000 before their income tax would exceed their Social Security tax. Some experts believe that if Social Security expenditures are not controlled, more than half of every paycheck will be used to finance the program by 2040.[6]

Because people are living longer and demanding more benefits, the future financial stability of Social Security has become a major political issue. When the baby boomers retire, the number of people receiving benefits will increase in proportion to those contributing to the system. This increase would not be a problem if the money being contributed to Social Security by today's workers was put away for their eventual retirement. But much of the money taken from today's workers goes to pay for today's retirees. Social Security is thus a transfer program in which today's young workers finance the retirement of today's elderly. At some point, this reality is likely to foster intergenerational tension between workers and retirees.

The Social Security system is presently running a surplus, meaning that the amount that is brought in through Social Security taxes is greater than the amount of money going out in benefits. The surpluses are invested in Treasury bonds, with the promise that they will be repaid with interest later. Experts predict that the Social Security system will feel its next financial strain in about 2010, when baby boomers start to retire and the system has to start spending the interest on today's investments.[7]

In his State of the Union address in 1998, President Clinton announced that the budget surplus should "Save Social Security First!" Republicans would have preferred to use it for tax cuts, but the pressure to support Social Security was so strong that they had to yield to the president.

President Lyndon Johnson's vision of a Great Society relied upon the principle of government action to solve economic and social problems.

The Great Society

Another significant expansion of social services came in the 1960s. At a commencement speech at the University of Michigan in May 1964, President Lyndon Johnson described a vision of a Great Society:

> The Great Society rests on abundance and liberty for all. It demands an end to poverty and racial injustice. . . . But that is just the beginning. The Great Society is a place where every child can find knowledge to enrich his mind and to enlarge his talents. . . . It is a challenge constantly renewed, beckoning us toward a destiny where the meaning of our lives matches the marvelous products of our labors.[8]

Major Legislation of the Great Society

1964

- *Civil Rights Act*—the most comprehensive civil rights legislation since Reconstruction
- *Food Stamp Act*—expansion of the New Deal program to improve the nutrition of the poor
- *Economic Opportunity Act*—job training, adult education, and loans to small businesses to attack the roots of unemployment and poverty
- *Nurses Training Act*—grants for training nurses and construction of nursing schools
- *Omnibus Housing Act*—addition of four federal housing programs to existing programs
- *Community Mental Health Centers Act*—federal grants for staffing mental health centers

1965

- *Medicare*—health care benefits for the elderly, linked to Social Security
- *Medicaid*—health care benefits for the poor, linked to Aid to Families with Dependent Children (AFDC)
- *Elementary and Secondary Education Act*—federal funding and programs in public education for disadvantaged children
- *Higher Education Act*—federal funding for colleges and college students
- *Department of Housing and Urban Development*—new department with responsibility for low-rent housing and urban renewal programs
- *Older Americans Act*—Administration on Aging and grants to the states
- *Voting Rights Act*—federal enforcement of right to vote in federal elections within the state voting process

1968

- *Housing and Urban Development Act*—expansion of federal housing and urban development programs
- *Omnibus Crime Control and Safe Streets Act*—federal aid for local law enforcement, crime prevention, and corrections programs

Sources: *Congress and the Nation, 1945–1964: A Review of Government and Politics* (Congressional Quarterly Press, 1965); *Congress and the Nation, 1965–1968: A Review of Government and Politics During the Johnson Years* (Congressional Quarterly Press, 1969).

Johnson's agenda was as broad as his rhetoric, and as with the New Deal, Congress enacted much of it in a fairly short period of time. Great Society programs dramatically increased the role of the federal government in education, extended voting and civil rights, expanded Social Security to include medical benefits for retired Americans, provided health care to poor Americans, financed housing programs to provide decent housing to the poor, offered job training through the Job Corps, and offered preschool education to poor children in a program called Head Start.[9]

Changes in social policy are typically led by presidents who have made social policy a key part of their agenda. Many of the ideas of the Great Society, for instance, had been discussed during the Roosevelt and Truman administrations but had not been acted on. The leadership and political skill of President Lyndon Johnson were critical. His motivation stemmed from his own values but also reflected a response to pressures within his party and the country and, some might argue, a desire to deflect attention away from the Vietnam War.

Johnson combined a passion for the agenda with great skill in working with Congress. During Johnson's five years as president, 1,902 proposals were submitted to Congress. Only 57 percent of them were approved, yet of Johnson's 115 Great Society proposals submitted to Congress, 78 percent were passed.[10] Johnson's effectiveness was enhanced by his party's large majority in Congress following his landslide victory in 1964, his ability to mobilize public opinion for his programs, and his skill in dealing with individual legislators, which came from his years of experience in Congress, including several years as Senate majority leader.

The central article of faith in the Great Society agenda was that social and economic problems could be solved, or at least reduced, by government action. In the period since 1968, there has been considerable debate over whether the Great Society was a success or failure.[11] Some Great Society programs were later disbanded during the Reagan and Bush administrations, while spending on other programs was reduced. The 1994 Republican Contract with America proposed drastic cuts in domestic social programs. Republicans, controlling the House of Representatives for the first time in 40 years, passed legislation to cut welfare spending and Medicare. President Bill Clinton's declaration that "the era of big government is over"[12] and his willingness to "end welfare as we know it"[13] reflected a sense that government should do less and that government services should be decentralized as much as possible.

The Burden of Entitlements and Budget Constraints on Social Policy

The end of New Deal and Great Society approaches to social policy can trace its roots to Ronald Reagan's two terms as president. Reagan's policy of a 25 percent reduction in marginal tax rates and a 20 percent increase in defense spending resulted in large budget deficits, with no money left for new social programs. Since the Reagan years, the policy debate has shifted from funding new programs to cutting taxes and devoting resources to save Social Security and Medicare.

entitlement programs
Programs such as Social Security, Medicare, and unemployment insurance that provide a specified set of benefits as a matter of right to all who meet the criteria established by law.

Programs like Social Security are called **entitlement programs** because they provide a specified set of benefits as a matter of right to all who meet the criteria established by law. Entitlements act as a constraint on social policy change precisely because people believe these programs are *guaranteed.* Entitlements constrain any new social policy initiatives because they take up such a large part of the budget.

When added up, the portion of the federal budget earmarked for defense spending, entitlements, and interest on the national debt equals 82 percent, with roughly half going to entitlements alone.

The Clinton years have not resulted in a return to a pre-Reagan agenda for social policy. As a "New Democrat," Clinton emphasized economic growth, policy reform, business and government partnerships, and improved efficiency. His program reflected the goals of the social policy liberals, especially his unsuccessful efforts to reform health care, but his willingness to compromise with Republicans on welfare reform alienated many liberals.

WELFARE

Welfare programs in the United States incorporate job training, transportation subsidies, housing subsidies, free school lunches, food stamps, food for pregnant mothers and babies, and tax credits for low-income people (see Table 19-1). The government also provides financial assistance to farmers and certain industries and underwrites the cost of such "middle-class welfare" as national parks (supported by taxpayers but rarely used by poor people) and loans to college students. But when we hear the term "welfare," we tend to think only of public assistance for poor, handicapped, or disadvantaged people.

Public assistance can take many forms:

- Direct payments to single parents with young children, the unemployed, and the disabled
- Vouchers that can be exchanged for food
- Subsidies that reduce the cost of housing or the provision of public housing
- Reduced cost or free access to public transportation, higher education, or job training
- Subsidized medical care.

These programs are targeted to the more than 35 million people living under the official poverty line of just under $16,400 for a family of four in 1998, or roughly 13 percent of the population.[14]

The poor tend to be disproportionately African American, Hispanic, young, and female. Because most poor people tend to be women and children, scholars refer to the *feminization of poverty.*[15] Women usually get paid less than men for doing the same work and tend to be employed in low-paying jobs. Divorce adversely affects the living standards of women more than men, and women provide most of the child care.

TABLE 19-1 Growth in Social Insurance and Benefit Program Payments, 1980–2000 (in billions of 1996 dollars)

Program	1980	1985	1990	1995	2000 (estimated)
Social Security	$227.7	$275.3	$298.5	$345.6	$381.6
Medicaid	60.4	94.8	116.0	163.1	207.8
Medicare	27.2	33.43	49.8	92.4	107.9
Family support (AFDC and TANF)	14.2	13.5	14.8	17.8	20.4
Food stamps	17.3	18.2	19.1	26.4	28.4

SOURCE: Office of Management and Budget, *Budget of the United States Government, Fiscal Year 1998* (Government Printing Office, 1997), pp. 118–22, 193; and *Budget of the United States Government* (http://www.access.gpo.gov).

WILL THE BABY BOOM BE READY FOR RETIREMENT?

William G. Gale

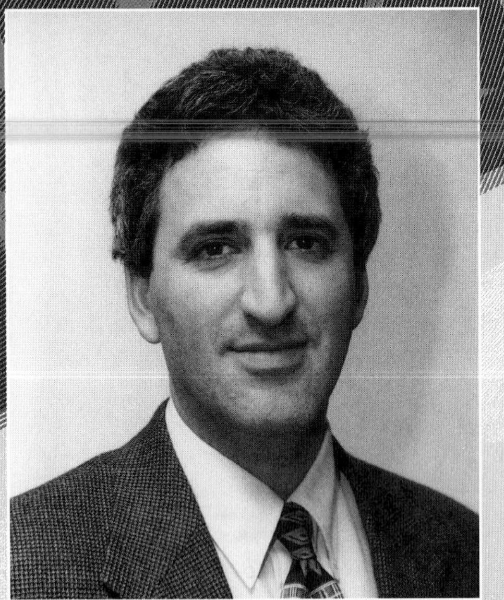

No general agreement exists about what an adequate retirement income is.

William G. Gale, a fellow in the Brookings Economic Studies program, argues that we should revise and retain Social Security while promoting private saving. Gale begins by considering the extent to which baby boomers will be prepared for retirement.

One problem is that no general agreement exists about what an adequate retirement income is. Financial planners suggest a goal of 60 percent to 80 percent of pre-retirement income, which will maintain a pre-retirement standard of living for most people. Retired people normally have more free time and fewer expenses, and most retirees have paid off their mortgages, pay less income tax, and have no children living with them. They do, however, pay high medical costs.

The prospects for most Americans for attaining this suggested level of retirement income are bleak. A 1991 study indicated that, apart from pensions, Social Security, and houses, the median retiree had only $14,000 in savings—hardly enough to extend a pre-retirement lifestyle into retirement. In 1995, 18 percent of retirees were living below the minimum standard of a decent living, which is 125 percent above the poverty line. The problem is that baby boomers are not saving enough money to maintain their lifestyles beyond retirement. This does not mean that everyone is doing poorly, for some are doing much better than others. A recent study, however, leads Gale to this conclusion about baby boomers' readiness for retirement: "Roughly speaking, a third of the sample is doing well by any measure, a third is doing poorly by any measure, and the middle third is (or may be) just hanging in there."

Gale does not argue that Social Security should be called upon to maintain retirement incomes at their pre-retirement levels. He does, however, see it as a foundational element in the retirement system as a whole, because people at the poorer end of the spectrum, the ones who need it most, are able to save little if anything on their own.

What is the best public policy to secure America's retirement plans? Gale suggests that government (1) reduce the budget deficit without cutting into private savings, (2) promote financial education, (3) encourage savings incentives, and (4) continue "judicious Social Security and pension reform."★

SOURCE: William G. Gale, "Will the Baby Boom Be Ready for Retirement?" *The Brookings Review* (Summer 1997), pp. 5–9.

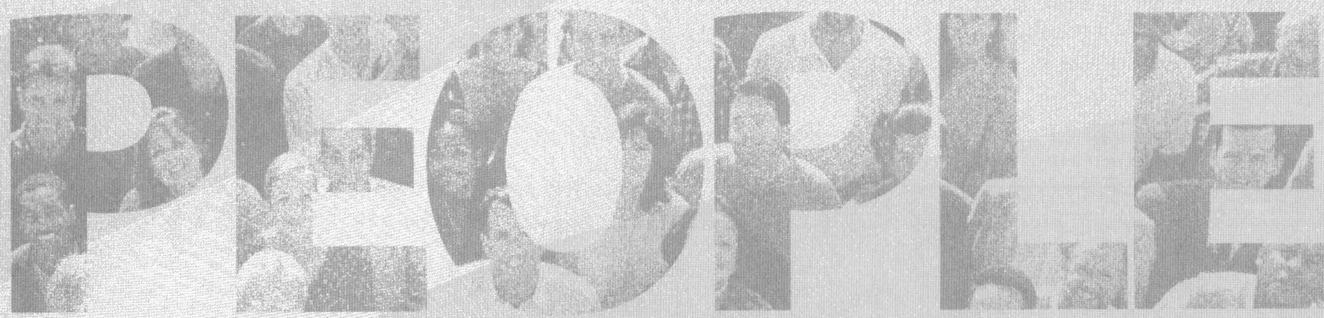

THE CASE FOR PRIVATIZATION

Martin Feldstein

Martin Feldstein is professor of economics at Harvard University and president of the National Bureau of Economic Research. He argues that we should replace Social Security with a system of mandatory contributions to private retirement funds. Feldstein agrees with Gale that the baby boom generation is placing increasing stress on the Social Security system, but his focus, unlike Gale's, is upon the effectiveness of the system itself. Feldstein maintains that the Social Security system is simply wasteful and inefficient, and that mandatory private retirement investment plans could accomplish the goals of Social Security at less cost and with greater benefits for the population.

"The obvious solution is to shift to a privatized system of pre-funding those benefits through mandatory contributions to individual accounts." If people had to pay into investment accounts, more capital would be available for investment, spurring economic growth. For the first time, lower-income people could acquire substantial savings. This system is working successfully in Australia and Latin America; Sweden has a partially privatized plan; and Britain is moving in the same direction.

Feldstein proposes mandatory payments to 401K plans that would pay annuity benefits upon retirement. Since the average investment return for the last 40 years has been 9 percent per year, workers would have far more resources for retirement than they now enjoy under Social Security's return of only 1.5 percent. Feldstein then asks: "What about the baby boomers, who are counting on the future contributions of others to finance their retirements? Who will pay for them?" His answer is that the new system would be phased in gradually; higher costs in the short run would be more than compensated for in the long run. Even the first baby boomers, born in 1946, are still eleven years from retirement, and they could contribute to the new system as well.

How will the poor, who have little to invest, be protected? The best way, according to Feldstein, is for the government simply to provide an income supplement at age 65 so that everyone receives at least 50 percent of an average benefit. "The cost of bringing them up to half of the median value could be financed by a one-time tax of 4.7 percent on all mandatory accounts at age 65. Each individual could save enough to finance that one-time tax by raising his lifetime mandatory savings by 4.7 percent." In the end, Feldstein maintains that Social Security is "a very risky asset for anyone who expects to depend on Social Security benefits as the primary source of retirement income." ★

Mandatory private retirement investment plans could accomplish the goals of Social Security at less cost and with greater benefits for the population.

SOURCE: Martin Feldstein, "The Case for Privatization," *Foreign Affairs* 76 (July/August 1997), pp. 24–39.

For more information on this debate, go to **http://www.prenhall.com/burns** *and click on the Debate Icon under Chapter 18.*

The CPI: A Technical or a Social Problem?

In December of 1996, a commission led by Michael J. Boskin of Stanford University reported that the Consumer Price Index (CPI) overstates inflation by 1.1 percent. The commission went on to recommend that Congress revise the CPI, and that the Bureau of Labor Statistics redesign its methods of calculating it. If the CPI were simply one of the many obscure government statistics that is reported almost daily, there would be little to talk about. The CPI, however, is the government's measure of inflation, which is used to adjust government spending on programs such as Social Security, Medicare, and pensions for retired government workers.

While economists may view the CPI as a mere statistic to be examined technically, politicians are surrounded by recipients of entitlements arguing for more relief and by others demanding a balanced budget. The CPI is the political equivalent of a "silver bullet" because much of the entitlement spending in the budget could be reduced if the CPI were adjusted. Politicians in both parties have been reluctant to make this change in the CPI, fearing the wrath of those who benefit from the current CPI formula. But the widespread consensus among economists, that the CPI is an overestimate of true inflation persists, as does the temptation not to lower entitlement spending.

SOURCE: Louis Uchitelle, "Measuring Inflation: Can't Do It, Can't Stop Trying," *The New York Times*, March 16, 1997, p. D4.

1996 Welfare Legislation

The landmark welfare reform legislation of 1996 reflected a growing sentiment that welfare recipients are not victims; they just need help to break the cycle of unemployment and low skills. The "safety net" provided by government should be only temporary, and more should be required of recipients. The Republican-controlled Congress in 1995 and 1996 proposed block grants to the states for welfare instead of the dozens of programs then in place. In addition, Congress proposed reducing welfare eligibility, placing a cap on federal funding of welfare, and making the states responsible to run the revamped welfare programs. These changes were part of the 1996 budget proposal, which President Clinton vetoed, saying Republican budget cuts were too deep, although he continued to support time limits for welfare, work requirements, tougher child support enforcement, and requiring teen-age mothers to live at home as a condition of assistance.

The National Governor's Association (NGA) then came forward with compromise welfare reform proposals. The NGA plan was based on the defeated budget in that it embraced the block-grant approach and state discretion and responsibility. With bipartisan support, the governors agreed that more money for child care was needed than Congress offered, that states must spend funds to match federal block grants, and that school lunch programs should stay intact and not become a block grant. The states would be relatively free of interference from Washington, but they would have access to a federal "rainy-day fund" during times of recession or when demand for welfare services exceeded state capacity.

The governors' proposals served as a basis for compromise in August 1996 on a welfare reform bill. House proposals for a lifetime limit on benefits and decreasing aid to legal immigrants were included, as were Clinton's proposals that welfare be linked to work and that welfare benefits have a time limit. The federal government would continue to fund about three-quarters of welfare costs, but that figure could change as the reforms are instituted. The compromise bill gave Clinton and the Republicans in Congress an important legislative accomplishment as they entered the presidential election of 1996.

Evaluating Welfare Reform

Besides reflecting a fundamental American belief in self-help and individualism, the new welfare bill has significant ramifications for our federal system. This *devolution* of power to the states in the area of welfare is seen as a testing ground for the future. Based upon how well states perform their new responsibilities, there may be a resurgence in the role played by the states in setting and implementing policy. If states are creative and successful in enacting welfare reform, other federal programs and powers may also be handed down to the states. Giving more discretion over welfare to the states may not end the decentralization of this program. Some advocate further decentralization to counties, and others even call for privatization.[16]

What difference has the massive overhaul of welfare had? Since passage of welfare reform in 1996, the number of people on welfare has declined in every state except Hawaii. In fact, from 1996 to 1998 the number of families receiving welfare nationally decreased by 1.6 million families, or 39 percent of the total number of families receiving welfare.[17] Governors and reformers are quick to claim credit for this good news, but others point out that the decline in welfare case loads is due at least in part to the robust economy and low unemployment. The real test for welfare reform will come, they say, when the economy hits a downturn.

Health Care

The federal government is involved with health care in three ways: research, access, and cost control. First, the government has adopted a wide range of programs to promote research, target particular diseases, regulate drugs, monitor health care providers, gather and disseminate information, and in general deal with health issues with a public dimension. States receive federal money to construct hospital and research facilities and maintain medical programs, including maternal and child welfare services. State and federal governments underwrite part of the costs of training doctors, dentists, nurses, and pharmacists. The government gathers data on infant mortality, life spans, and diseases in an effort to monitor the success of its programs.

The surgeon general of the United States heads the Public Health Service (PHS), the national government's health agency. The service carries out its research through the National Institutes of Health. Researchers in these institutes, working closely with experts in private laboratories, study causes and seek cures for serious diseases. Fellowships for health research are granted to able scientists and physicians. The Public Health Service also administers grants to states and local communities to help them improve public health. Another agency promoting health is the Food and Drug Administration (FDA).

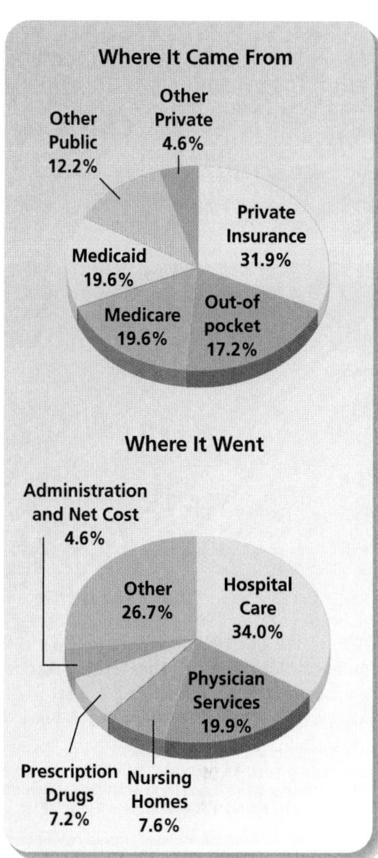

FIGURE 19-1 The Nation's Health Dollar

SOURCE: Health Care Financing Administration, Office of the Actuary, National Health Statistics Group (http://www.hcfa.gov/stats/nhe-oact/tables/chart.htm).

Most Americans have private insurance, usually through their employers, which pays for health care and hospitalization. Private health insurance began in 1910 when the Montgomery Ward Company started the first health insurance plan for its employees. Limited access to health care and hospitals for those who could not afford private insurance resurfaced during the Great Depression, when large numbers of Americans were unemployed. President Franklin Roosevelt organized a Committee on Economic Security, which recommended compulsory national health insurance, but those recommendations did not go far. However, the committee's recommendations that Social Security provide money for maternal and child health care as well as aid for the disabled were adopted as part of the original Social Security legislation. Harry Truman was reelected in 1948 with universal health care as one of his stated policy goals, but the idea was labeled as socialism and was not seriously pursued.

In 1965, as part of Lyndon Johnson's Great Society legislation, Congress passed Medicare and Medicaid. **Medicare** is the national health insurance program for the elderly and disabled; it provides hospital and medical insurance for people 65 years of age and older. The Medicare program covers most charges for most illnesses, but some catastrophic and long-term conditions result in major costs to patients for which there is no Medicare coverage. **Medicaid** provides medical benefits for low-income persons; it is funded largely by the federal government but also requires state funding and administration. Eligibility for Medicaid is limited to persons who receive welfare cash payments—the visually impaired, the elderly, the disabled, and families with dependent children where one parent is absent, incapacitated, or unemployed. Both programs took effect in 1966.[18] Disabled people are entitled to both Medicare and Medicaid.

Another approach to health care policy is cost control. Government pays for over 40 percent of the health care costs through veterans' hospitals and programs for the poor, elderly, and disabled (see Figure 19-1). Developments in health care thus have a profound impact on government. Take the 1996 budget, in which we allocated nearly $351 billion on health care.[19] This total is more than state and federal governments combined spend on education. If that amount were reduced by 1.8 percent, it would fund the entire Pell Grant program for college students.[20]

Medicare
National health insurance program for the elderly and disabled.

Medicaid
Federal program that provides medical benefits for low-income persons.

fee for service
System of health care payment in which patients can choose their own physician, whose bills are then covered by insurance companies.

A Mostly Private Health Care System

Health care for most Americans has traditionally been provided by physicians of their choice whose bills were largely covered by insurance companies. This arrangement is known as **fee for service**. When these patients go to a hospital,

TABLE 19-2 National Health Expenditures, 1970–1996 (in millions of 1996 dollars)

Year	Total Amount Spent	
	Nominal*	Real
1970	$73.2	$296.1
1975	130.7	381.3
1980	247.2	470.9
1985	428.2	624.6
1990	697.5	837.7
1991	61.3	877.5
1992	833.6	932.7
1993	892.3	969.3
1994	949.4	978.1
1995	988.5	1018.2
1996	1035.1	1035.1

SOURCE: U.S. Bureau of the Census, *Statistical Abstract of the United States, 1997* (Government Printing Office, 1997), p. 112; for 1996, Health Care Financing Administration, Office of the Actuary, *National Health Care Expenditures*, September 28, 1998 (http://www.hcfa.gov/stats/NHE-Proh/tables/t01.htm).

**Nominal* dollars are the actual dollars spent per year. To compare spending over time, we need to take inflation into account. The *Real* column accounts for inflation by converting nominal dollars into inflation-adjusted dollars against the base year, which in this case is 1995.

their costs are covered by insurance—the third-party payer—meaning neither the doctor nor hospitals that provide the service nor the patient who gets the service covers the costs. Generally, big companies provide better benefits than do small businesses with fewer than 100 workers. For instance, large companies are much more likely to provide extras like dental and eyeglass benefits to their employees.

The traditional ways of paying for health care are rapidly being challenged by other forms of coverage—especially **health maintenance organizations (HMOs)** in which people or their employers are charged a set amount and the HMO provides health care and covers hospital costs. However, approximately 40 million Americans are uninsured and are not covered by Medicaid.[21] They often rely on government or charity to pay for their medical care. More than 27 percent of all households in the United States donate an average of $214 a year to volunteer health organizations to help those in need, an amount second only to religious donations.[22]

Under current law, employers have a tax incentive to provide health insurance to employees. The government treats employers' costs of insurance as a deductible business expense, reducing their corporate tax obligations. These benefits are not counted as taxable income for employees either. In addition, employees may deduct any medical expenses that exceed 7.5 percent of their gross adjusted income when they pay their income taxes.

Problems with Health Care

The problems with health care in the United States include rising costs, an increasing number of uninsured Americans, unnecessary procedures, endless paperwork, high costs of litigation, and avoidable illnesses. Generally speaking, the quality of health care in the United States is not a problem. We have the best health care money can buy. But that is precisely the problem. Those who have insurance and money also have greater access to new and expensive procedures like organ transplants or new treatments. Those without insurance or money either forgo needed services or simply make do with minimum care.

RISING COST OF HEALTH CARE Health care costs in the United States have risen nearly 400 percent since 1970[23] (see Table 19-2). Another measure of the rising cost of health care is the percentage of the gross domestic product (GDP) devoted to health care. Even as our economy has grown, the share of it devoted to health care has grown even faster. In specific areas, pharmaceutical costs have soared, and the costs of children's vaccines have risen 1,000 percent in one decade.[24]

Who pays for the rapid rise in costs? Employers pay a large share of the costs of health insurance. The cost of employer-sponsored health plans is about 7 percent of employee compensation.[25] Individual consumers also pay more for health care, and the health care costs paid by government have risen 12-fold over the last 20 years; the government now pays for nearly half of all health expenditures in the United States.[26]

health maintenance organization (HMO)
Alternative means of health care in which people or their employers are charged a set amount and the HMO provides health care and covers hospital costs.

One reason costs have risen is that advances in medicine mean people live longer. Life expectancy has increased by more than five years between 1970 and 1995, and most experts believe it will continue to rise.[27] As people live longer, they place greater demands on the health care system. New and advanced medical technology—life-support systems, ultrasound, sophisticated x-ray equipment, and genetic counseling—have all increased the costs of health care.

Americans also seek elective health care in comparatively high numbers. Examples of elective health care include cosmetic surgery that is not medically necessary like liposuction, and some dermatology and orthopedic surgery. Advances in medications, such as the AIDS "cocktail" of drugs, are also expensive and have significantly added to the rising costs of health care. Rising health care costs are likely to continue to grow in importance and increase the demand for medical care.

THE UNINSURED As noted, roughly 40 million people in the U.S. are not covered by any private health insurance or state or federal Medicaid benefits. The proportion of people without insurance has been rising. Between 1996 and 1997, the number without coverage increased by an estimated 1.7 million.[28] A large proportion of this number are full-time employees, but because their incomes fall just above the poverty line, they do not qualify for Medicaid. And because they work in jobs that are part-time, seasonal, or full-time but menial, their employer does not provide health insurance. Uninsured individuals usually seek care in hospital emergency rooms only when their illness has reached a critical stage. Delay drives up costs because critical care is much more expensive than preventive medicine or early treatment.

But it is not just the poor who may end up uninsured. Persons who change jobs may often go without coverage for several months before their new insurance takes effect. And people with serious medical conditions may find the insurance company unwilling to cover their expenses, claiming that the illness is a "preexisting condition." Some insurance companies set limits on their coverage, meaning that families faced with very expensive illnesses end up essentially uninsured.

UNNECESSARY PROCEDURES Doctors and insurance companies claim that they have to perform and pay for procedures that may be unnecessary medically but are needed to reduce the risk of being sued by patients. These procedures add up to billions in unnecessary costs, but they do not improve the quality of care provided to patients.[29] To avoid malpractice suits, obstetricians may perform as many as 500,000 unnecessary caesarean sections each year.[30] Critics also accuse hospitals of charging high prices for items that are not used or not needed. Since few patients are knowledgeable enough to audit their hospital bills, insurance companies must monitor these expenses.

There are understandable reasons for the penchant for expensive new tests and procedures. People want to do everything possible to prolong life, and if a test or procedure has a chance, however limited, of doing so, they want it. But the question of who pays the costs of these expensive new tests is disputed.

ENDLESS PAPERWORK In medicine as in other activities, paperwork is necessary to document what services were provided and to prevent fraud. But virtually all health care reformers criticize the inefficient and uncoordinated system of paperwork and administration in the present system. The large number of insurance forms combined with abundant government forms cost health consumers more than $60 billion in 1996, accounting for roughly 6 percent of total health costs.[31] A standardized insurance form that could be submitted electronically could save billions of dollars.[32] Computerized patient records, electronically transmitted prescriptions, and hand-held computers that send doctors' orders and comments to a computer could also cut down on paperwork. Some estimate that computerization of the medical industry could save almost 15 percent on overall medical expenditures in the United States.[33]

LITIGATION EXPENSES Physicians frequently complain about the high cost of malpractice insurance. Malpractice premiums in the United States are nine times higher than in Canada. Malpractice insurance costs for all physicians have more

A Closer Look

TOBACCO LEGISLATION GOES UP IN SMOKE IN THE 105TH CONGRESS

As the 105th Congress (1997–98) was meeting, tobacco companies were already on the defensive because of the aggressive litigation by some state attorneys general, the willingness of judges to hold them liable in some cases where people died of lung cancer, growing evidence that they had misled the public about the harmful effects of smoking, and evidence they deliberately lured young people into smoking cigarettes. In 1996, President Clinton had ordered the Food and Drug Administration to treat tobacco as a drug, essentially expanding government power to regulate tobacco.

Republican Senator John McCain led the Senate effort to respond to the growing public pressure to force tobacco manufacturers to reduce their appeals to teen smokers, to pay a larger share of the public health care costs for treating smokers, and generally to discourage the use of the life-threatening substance. The bill he proposed enjoyed widespread support in committee, where it passed by a margin of 19 to 1.

As is often the case, as the bill moved through the legislative process, amendments were added. Some had no relationship to the tobacco issue, like a tax break for married couples making less than $50,000 a year. Before the bill was defeated on the Senate floor, it had been expanded to include costs to tobacco companies in excess of $516 billion over the next 25 years, which was estimated to increase the cost of a pack of cigarettes by $1.10 per pack.

How did tobacco companies who lost resoundingly in committee win on the Senate floor? They launched a $40 million advertising campaign, particularly in the tobacco states and in states with senators facing tough election campaigns. Their message was that the Senate was going to increase the cost of smoking dramatically and was raising taxes, especially on working people. They also contributed heavily to the campaign funds of key senators.

The power of the advertising blitz was real. A bill that seemed certain to pass failed by three votes on the Senate floor. The bill then went back to committee, where it died in the 105th Congress. After Congress was unable to enact the tobacco tax, many states working together settled with the tobacco companies in an agreement costing tobacco companies $206 billion over 25 years, but permitting tobacco companies to avoid the possibility of even more costly litigation.

SOURCES: Allan Freedman, "Big Tobacco, Big Government and the Senate's Nicotine Plan," *Congressional Quarterly Weekly Report*, April 18, 1998, p. 99; Janine Yagielski, "Analysis: Tobacco Battle Ends But Battle for the Issue Continues," CNN, *All Politics*, June 19, 1998, pp. 1–4; John King and Gene Randall, "Senate Kills Tobacco Bill," CNN, *All Politics*, June 17, 1998, pp. 1–4; "Feinstein and Hatch Announce Bipartisan Tobacco Bill," CNN, *All Politics*, June 23, 1998, pp. 1–3.

Heads of the major cigarette companies, testifying before the Senate Commerce Committee, denied that they intensified nicotine levels.

Attorneys General unveiled the details of a $206 billion agreement to settle their lawsuits against tobacco companies at a November 1998 news conference.

than doubled in a decade. Insurance coverage can cost as much as $40,000 a year for specialists.[34]

Huge malpractice awards are defended by trial lawyers who represent people whose health was damaged or families of those whose lives were lost due to medical malpractice. They argue that physicians, like all professionals, have a responsibility to exercise sound professional judgment in their jobs, and when they do not, they should provide restitution to victims.

PREVENTION: LIFESTYLE AND ENVIRONMENTAL CAUSES OF ILLNESS Part of the health care "crisis" in the United States is avoidable. Medicare alone spends billions of dollars each year treating smoking-related diseases, and over the next 20 years the costs will continue to rise.[35] The relationship between cancer and smoking has been clearly established. Other illnesses at least partly related to lifestyle include heart disease, liver disease, and Acquired Immune Deficiency Syndrome (AIDS). Some states have recently sued tobacco companies to recover Medicaid expenses, and others use educational programs to discourage teenagers from beginning to smoke.

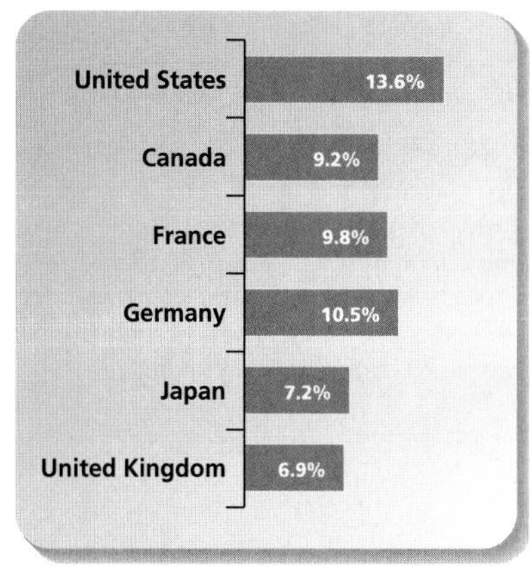

FIGURE 19-2 Total Health Care Expenditures as a Share of Gross Domestic Product, 1996

SOURCE: Frequently Asked Data—OECD Health Data 98—National Expenditure on Health (http://cs9-hq.oecd.org/health/fad_l.htm).

Health Care in Advanced Industrial Democracies

Advanced industrial democracies like Canada, Germany, Japan, the Netherlands, and the United Kingdom provide health care for their entire population either through national health insurance or a national health service. Although one-seventh of all U.S. citizens do not have health insurance and do not regularly receive health care, the United States outspends all these countries in terms of health expenditures as a percent of the gross domestic product (see Figure 19-2).

Our high spending on health care does not mean we are a more healthy population. Our infant mortality rates, for instance, are among the worst in all industrialized countries, and we rank below average in male and female life expectancy at birth (see Table 19-3). However, the United States does rank first in the quality and access to first-rate medical technology, and for those Americans who can afford the best health care, our system is excellent.

TABLE 19-3 Infant Mortality and Life Expectancy Rates in Ten Industrialized Nations, 1998

Country	Infant Mortality*	Life Expectancy
United States	6.4	76.1
Japan	4.1	80.0
Sweden	3.9	79.2
Netherlands	5.2	78.0
Germany	5.2	77.0
France	5.7	78.5
Canada	5.6	79.2
Australia	5.3	79.9
United Kingdom	5.9	77.2
Italy	6.4	78.4

SOURCE: U.S. Bureau of the Census, *Statistical Abstract of the United States, 1998* (Government Printing Office, 1997), pp. 831–32.

*Infant mortality rate is the number of deaths of children under one year of age per 1,000 live births in a calendar year.

You Decide...

What health care reform option do you prefer?

Of the many different health care reform options, which one do you think is best? Would you be willing to accept restrictions on your choice of doctors and hospitals? Do you think that the nation spends too much or too little on health care?

The United States also differs from other countries in the extent to which health care costs are paid by public funds. Approximately three-quarters of the cost of health care in most advanced industrial democracies is funded by central or local governments. In 1992, for instance, the government paid 72 percent of the costs of health care in Japan and Germany, 84 percent in the United Kingdom, and 86 percent in Sweden. In 1992, the U.S. government paid 46 percent of the costs.[36]

In neighboring Canada, about 10 percent of the nation's GDP is devoted to health care spending, and all Canadians are covered by provincial health insurance. Canada's administration of health care is based on a publicly funded system, whereas the program in the United States is divided among public and private insurers. Canada's administrative costs per patient are at least three times less than ours, and companies in the United States often pay three to five times more than Canadian companies to fund employee health and social benefits, including taxes collected by governments to pay for some of these benefits.[37]

The Canadian health care system is not without its faults. Canadians are taxed at a much higher rate than Americans, in part to pay for the publicly funded system. In addition, patients may face delays in receiving services, especially for routine health problems and elective surgery. Doctors and nurses are also paid less in Canada, and thousands have moved to the United States, where salaries are much higher. Costs for health care are also increasing well above the rate of inflation, and the Canadian federal and provincial governments have begun to cut back on funding certain services. Nevertheless, most Canadians express satisfaction with their health care system, and Canada manages to insure all of its people, while spending far less per capita than the United States spends.

Health Care Reform

Bill Clinton made health care reform a major priority in his first administration, appointing Hillary Rodham Clinton to head the National Task Force on Health Care Reform, but its proposals, which were complicated and bureaucratic, were defeated by Congress in 1993.

While there are many different proposals for health care reform, the essential approaches include single-payer, managed competition, employer-mandated coverage, spending caps, individual responsibility, and medical savings accounts.

SINGLE-PAYER Under a single-payer system the government, using broad-based taxes, covers the costs of health care and hospitalization and sets the rates. Like the system used in Canada, such a plan would provide universal coverage and benefits to all Americans. No longer would people need to worry about the costs of catastrophic illnesses or a change in jobs that would exclude them from coverage. Proponents claim that the single-payer system would save billions of dollars in administrative expenses by reducing the number of insurers from about 1,200 to 1. Opponents of the single-payer system claim it would lead to a bureaucratic mess, with little incentive for innovation, cost control, or diversity of coverage. They further claim that the government would be put in the position of deciding which procedures to pay for and how to ration access to these procedures. As a result, they contend, Americans would lose not only quality in their health care but their freedom of choice.

Business leaders generally oppose single-payer coverage out of concern for costs and what the program would do to taxes and the federal budget deficit. The American Medical Association, U.S. Chamber of Commerce, Health Insurance Association of America, and other interest groups representing health care providers oppose the single-payer system. Labor unions, some senior citizens groups, and most consumer groups advocate this type of plan.

MANAGED COMPETITION Cost containment has been a frequent refrain of large corporations and consumer groups. In the 1970s and 1980s, business owners reduced benefits, increased payments, and encouraged employees to join managed care plans, especially health maintenance organizations. During the 1980s and 1990s, HMO enrollment increased fourfold, from just under 10 million in 1980 to almost 67 million patients in 1997.[38]

In the 1990s the quality of HMO care and limitations on patient choice became issues. Because there are no national standards of heath care quality, consumer groups are pressing HMOs to improve treatment of specific conditions and are urging Congress to enter the battle.[39] HMOs counter that they provide adequate care at reasonable costs and that national standards would drive up costs. Consumers want the reduced costs associated with HMOs but do not like the limitations on choice of physicians and the lack of coverage for some procedures.[40]

The politics of HMOs was an issue in the 1998 elections. President Clinton presented a "patient's bill of rights" in 1998. Legislation stalled in both houses, due in part to an aggressive advertising campaign against the reforms funded by insurance companies and HMOs. A patient's bill of rights would include permitting women to see a gynecologist as her primary care physician; allowing for review of the need for medical procedures; leaving it to the doctor to determine the length of stay in the hospital; requiring coverage of emergency care a "prudent layperson" would deem necessary; and removing rules that deny doctors permission to talk to patients. In addition, one of the bills proposed in Congress would lift restrictions on medical savings accounts, and another would allow small businesses to pool their resources to bid for reasonable rates with HMOs.[41]

EMPLOYER-MANDATED COVERAGE Currently, more than 160 million Americans get some form of medical insurance as a benefit that goes with their job.[42] President Richard Nixon proposed in 1971 that employers be required to provide and pay all employees' health insurance.[43] The Clinton administration also recommended in 1993–94 that all employers be required to provide employees with health insurance. But many small businesses contended that they could not afford to provide this benefit and stay in business. Some have estimated that costs of health care to small businesses may be 10 to 40 percent higher than for large businesses. In businesses with fewer than 25 employees, only about one-third of the workers receive coverage directly from their employer.[44] Mandating coverage does not solve this economic problem, nor does it take care of those who do not have jobs.

Proponents counter that these negative consequences can be mitigated through tax credits and higher levels of productivity. They also point out that if all small businesses provide health insurance, none of them will be put at a disadvantage compared to other small businesses. As noted, the federal government allows businesses to deduct what they pay in health benefits to employees as a business expense and gives tax credits to low-income families to purchase coverage for their children. The cost of these tax deductions and credits under the current system has been estimated to be as high as $50 billion.[45]

SPENDING CAPS Because the cost of providing health care each year consumes a larger and larger share of our gross domestic product, some have proposed an overall expenditure cap on health care that applies not only to public expenditures but to private ones as well. Supporters of a cap include the business-dominated National Leadership Coalition for Health Care Reform, some economists, and some prominent Democrats. The American Hospital Association, American Medical Association, and Pharmaceutical Manufacturers Association vigorously oppose the idea. They argue that spending caps would limit research and development in medicine and reduce the quality of people entering the medical profession.

Thinking it Through . . .

Although we all have our own ideas about health care reform, the American people are split over what approach is best. More than half do not want restrictions on their choice of doctors and hospitals, and half do not think that the country spends enough on health care. A 1998 Roper poll found these results:

Question: The United States government spends close to one trillion dollars on health care annually. As it stands today, there are roughly 40 million people lacking basic health coverage. In your estimation, do you think the role of government in shouldering health care costs should increase, remain the same, or decrease?

Increase	50%
Remain the same	26
Decrease	22

Question: Thinking about health care, do you think the country's health care system needs a great deal of reform, only some reform, or no reform at all?

Great deal	52%
Only some	40
No reform at all	4
Not sure	4

SOURCE: Public Opinion Online: Roper Center at University of Connecticut, June 30, 1998.

INDIVIDUAL RESPONSIBILITY FOR COVERAGE Another reform seeks to apply a free-market approach to health care by abolishing *all* employer-provided benefits and encouraging individuals to buy health insurance on their own in much the same way that individuals are now responsible for purchasing their own automobile insurance. Those with low incomes, including people not now covered, would have tax credits or vouchers to assist in the purchase of insurance.

Those who advocate such a proposal say that if individuals purchased their own insurance, they might pay more attention to costs and more closely monitor doctor and hospital fees. When higher wages are combined with tax credits, some individuals could end up with improved benefits tailored to their individual needs. Such a plan would also eliminate the need to impose price controls or pay for a large health care bureaucracy. It is unlikely, however, that employees would recover all they now spend on health care from their employers, so costs to individual consumers might increase. It is also unlikely that all uninsured persons who need government assistance could be taken care of without a tax increase to pay for it. Perhaps most important, such a proposal would run into so much political opposition that it presents an unlikely alternative.

MEDICAL SAVINGS ACCOUNTS A new item on the health care agenda is **medical savings accounts**, which Congress enacted as a viable alternative in 1996. Medical savings accounts allow individuals to make tax deductible contributions to a special medical savings account, which can be saved from year to year and can be used to pay for any medical expenses. Withdrawals for other purposes are taxable and subject to an early withdrawal penalty.

Supporters of medical savings accounts say that they will lower health care costs by giving people the incentive to spend their own money more carefully. They will also allow people to go to a doctor of their own choosing without needing approval from their insurance company. Opponents of medical savings accounts say that they amount to nothing more than a tax break for the wealthy and the healthy. Because of high deductibles, people will be discouraged from getting needed services and preventive care. Opponents also argue that because healthier people are more likely to sign up for medical savings accounts, sicker people will pay higher premiums.

Prospects for Reform

Most proposals for health care reform would not reorganize the industry but would address problems within the existing system. Proposals include greater government regulation of insurance companies; group purchasing agreements among small companies; expanded Medicare and Medicaid coverage to include more of the presently uninsured; standardized insurance forms that would reduce paperwork and lower the cost of administration for doctors and hospitals; medical malpractice reform; and regulation of the rates doctors and hospitals can charge for certain procedures.

Bill Clinton's health care proposals lost momentum and ultimately did not pass for several reasons. A major problem with the complex health care program Clinton envisioned was the expense. Although many Americans were in favor of reform, they were not willing to pay the costs associated with such large-scale changes. In addition, the various measures fell under the jurisdiction of different committees and subcommittees in Congress, thus greatly complicating and lengthening the process of creating coherent legislation. Because of these difficulties, Congress ultimately ran out of time before the 1994 congressional elections.

Perhaps the most troubling problems with Clinton's health care plan were ideological. With its goal of universal health care, the plan was labeled as social-

medical savings account
Alternative means of health care in which individuals make tax deductible contributions to a special account that can be saved from year to year and used to pay for medical expenses.

ism by its opponents. They maintained that America was built on foundations of individual hard work and achievement that are embodied in the American Dream, and these values seemed to conflict with the goals set forth in Clinton's plan. Clinton has had to be satisfied with limited incremental reforms, such as portability of coverage.

EDUCATION

Americans have always given a high priority to educating their children. To our nation's founders, education was closely connected with the survival of democracy because it provided the citizenry with a moral sense, an ability to reason, and a general knowledge about history and government.[46] The founders believed education should not be limited to the rich, but rather should be widely shared. Public education, like much of social policy generally, was left to state and local governments, and a strong tradition of private education existed as well. Today education is one of the areas still solidly under the control of state and local governments.

Education, especially in a competitive global economy, is essential for the economic well-being of society. For nations in a world of high technology and rapid change, a work force that has the necessary skills is crucial. For individuals, education is the route to a job and an adequate standard of living. Education can also have the effect of bridging the gaps between the races and between rich and poor, although it has not always done so.[47]

The United States is committed to a system of public education with local control. Most children go to public schools run by local school boards and funded, at least partly, by property taxes. Since local districts vary from areas with large homes to very poor neighborhoods, the funds for local schools vary. The effect is that children from poor districts are more likely to have lower quality public schools than those from rich districts. Other enduring problems in public schools are the uneven quality of teacher preparation and performance, high dropout rates, and inequality in the educational opportunities provided people of color.

The Federal Role in Education

The federal government's first involvement in education policy came with the Northwest Ordinance of 1785, in which Congress set aside one section in each township for support of public schools. In 1862, the Morrill Land Grant Act provided grants of land to state colleges if they specialized in mechanical or agricultural arts. As early as 1867, a U.S. Office of Education was established to oversee these programs, but the scope of federal involvement was modest by today's standards.

In 1944 Congress passed the G.I. Bill, which paid tuition at any college or university for veterans. The G.I. Bill helped provide college education to approximately 20 million veterans. During the cold war, the view that education, especially in the sciences, was closely linked to national defense became popular. When the Soviet Union launched *Sputnik*—the first satellite to orbit the earth—in 1957, efforts to expand the federal role in funding education grew. In 1958 Congress passed the National Defense Education Act to upgrade science, language, and mathematics courses.

The next expansion of federal government activity in education came with President Johnson's Great Society. In 1964 Congress created the Head Start program and college-level work-study programs. Then in 1965 Congress passed the Elementary and Secondary Education Act (ESEA), which focused on poverty-stricken schools, supplied educational materials for underprivileged public school students, and provided funding for educational research on how to assist children from underprivileged backgrounds. Even with this expanded role, the federal government today funds only 10.4 percent of the estimated $595 billion spent on public education in the United States.[48]

The new federal programs left intact local control over school construction, curriculum, teacher salaries, teacher standards, and governance. The federal government took a keen interest, however, in school desegregation. The Supreme Court's landmark 1954 decision in *Brown v Board of Education of Topeka* held that the previous education policy of "separate but equal" was inherently unconstitutional. This decision gave the federal government an added incentive to improve schools for poor and underprivileged students of all races and put added pressure on local school officials and district courts to end segregation. School desegregation efforts also led to forced busing programs mandated by state and federal courts.

College and university students also benefited from federal funding. Many college students today receive Pell Grants or Stafford Loans, present-day versions of federally insured student loans. Over half of all college students receive some federal financial aid. Pell Grants for low-income students and low-interest Guaranteed Student Loans continue to be the most available and most used payment for college expenses.

Goals 2000: Education for the Next Century

As governor of Arkansas, Bill Clinton led an effort to reform public education in his state, so it is not surprising that when he became president he proposed legislation that built on his earlier experience. The Goals 2000: Educate America Act had as its centerpiece a set of national standards for education by the year 2000. The project was actually started by President George Bush and the nation's governors at a meeting in 1990 during which they agreed on such goals as higher graduation rates, lower drug and crime rates, higher literacy, and improved curricula. The Clinton administration translated these goals into more precise objectives and standards that stressed the need for cooperation among local schools, school districts, states, and the federal government. The program is voluntary, and states may choose not to participate.

To overcome concerns about excessive federal regulation with Goals 2000, the program identifies goals that virtually everyone can agree on, and the federal role is minimal. There are no regulations, and no goals have been implemented for Goals 2000. All a state must do to apply for Goals 2000 funding is fill out a simple four-page document. The application process has been so streamlined that "review, approval and the obligation of funds generally take less than three weeks" after the application is approved.[49] All states are receiving or have applied for Goals 2000 monies. One of the last states, Virginia, finally accepted use of the funds "for the sole purpose of purchasing classroom computers and related technology."[50]

The Goals 2000 legislation has renewed the debate over how best to improve the quality of education in the United States. Proponents assert that real educational change requires the infusion of new resources from the federal government that are conditioned on real improvement at the state and especially local levels. The program is a way to help states and local school districts help themselves. Proponents also point to greater accountability based on measurable student achievement. They argue that local control will be maintained because the legislation does not contain any new federal mandates.

Critics of the program counter that Goals 2000 is a first step toward a centralized administration of education and the loss of local autonomy. Few states or localities have the political will to turn down federal dollars; consequently, they will forsake local control. They also argue that this program will remove incentives for local experimentation. As one opponent put it, "This debate is about one issue: Who can best determine what is right for the child? Is it the parent or is it the government?"[51]

Educational Choice

The issue of parental control has surfaced in recent years in two other ways. One proposal would provide parents with a *voucher* or check toward their child's education. The voucher could be redeemed at a public or private school of the parents' choosing. Vouchers, proponents argue, introduce the element of competition into the educational system. Voucher plans have been tried in a few states and cities with some success. In Milwaukee one of the largest programs has been specifically targeted to help low-income students, covering the full cost of tuition and allowing them to go to private schools.[52] Republicans proposed vouchers in the 1996 presidential campaign, but they have been rejected by voters when they have been on the ballot in states, as they were, for example, in Oregon.

A second type of reform proposal calls for charter schools. A *charter school* receives public funds but has a contract or charter giving it greater autonomy and flexibility than public schools. Proponents of charter schools argue that this autonomy leads to greater accountability. Charter schools have only been in existence since the early 1990s. The states with the greatest activity in this area are Arizona, California, and Michigan.[53]

Educational Reform

The role of schools in our society has gone through a dramatic transformation. We ask a lot more of our schools than just to educate students. Schools are now a major means by which basic nutrition is provided to millions of poor children; schools screen at-risk children and attempt to get them psychological assistance; schools provide sex education and sometimes condoms; schools seek to socialize students into socially acceptable behaviors, often in the face of increasing violence in the surrounding neighborhoods. The presence of police officers in most American high schools is relatively new and speaks to the problems of maintaining some minimal control over violence, drugs, and gangs.

The importance of an educated work force, concerns over equality of educational opportunity, civil liberties, and individual freedoms, and the increasing mobility of Americans all create pressures for national policies and programs. But national intervention collides with strongly held views that schools are primarily a local matter. Satisfying demands for more effective programs and more accountability to parents may be beyond the reach of the federal government without the option of dramatic increases in federal funds. As a result, more attention has been directed to innovative efforts by states and local communities to improve their schools.

Gun Control: U.S. and Canada

In recent years the average annual homicide rate in the United States has been four times that of Canada. Between 1984 and 1995 the average annual homicide rate in the United States was 8.8 per 100,000 people, versus only 2.3 in Canada. The homicide rate involving firearms was even greater, with the U.S. rate 15 times higher in homicides involving the use of handguns.

There are 30 times more firearms in the United States than in Canada, even though the U.S. population is only 9 times larger than Canada's. The handgun differential is far greater, with 76 million weapons in the United States compared with 1 million in Canada.*

Possessing weapons in Canada, especially handguns, has traditionally been much more difficult than in the United States, and a law passed by the Canadian parliament in 1995 imposed even more stringent regulations. All weapons, including rifles and shotguns, have to be registered with the police, extensive background searches are required before new weapons can be purchased, and many owners of handguns are required to turn over their weapons to government authorities for safekeeping or disposal.

Some Canadians oppose these tough standards, claiming they lead to growing government interference in the lives of the citizens. They also complain about the high costs of administering the program and the strict limits placed on those who like to hunt. They also argue that criminals will always be able to procure illegal weapons, placing law-abiding citizens at an unfair disadvantage. However, surveys indicate that most Canadians support these gun control measures and perceive that such restrictions help make Canadian society much less violent than its neighbor south of Canada's border.

*Canada, Department of Justice, 1997.

CRIME

In recent years crime control, once a state and local issue, has been forced onto the national political agenda. The issue of getting tough on crime surfaced in recent presidential campaigns and has been a primary concern in many public opinion polls. President Clinton discovered that some of his most popular lines in speeches

You Decide...

Should all semiautomatic weapons be banned?

Semiautomatic weapons permit those who use them to fire multiple rounds rapidly, and thus may result in numerous deaths before someone can subdue the assailant. In recent years these weapons have been used not only by terrorists, as in the case of a man who opened fire from the observation deck of the Empire State Building, wounding six tourists and killing two men, including himself. In three other incidents, public school students brought semiautomatic guns to school, opened fire, and killed or wounded classmates.

Should semiautomatic weapons with little or no hunting purpose be banned in the United States? Does the government have the right to tell citizens what guns they can and cannot use?

had to do with getting tough on crime, so his administration joined the ongoing efforts in Congress to fight crime.

The fact remains that crime control is primarily a state and local matter. The national government usually acts as a banker, providing grants to states and local governments to hire more police officers, improve the enforcement of drug laws, or deal with organized crime. An exception to this decentralized criminal justice system is the Federal Bureau of Investigation (FBI), created in 1908 and charged with gathering and reporting evidence in matters relating to federal laws or to crimes that cross state boundaries. In addition, the FBI provides investigative services on a cooperative basis to local law enforcement in fingerprint identification and laboratory services. Other agencies of the federal government that take on law enforcement activities include the Drug Enforcement Agency (DEA), which is responsible for controlling the flow of illegal narcotics into the United States, patrols U.S. borders, and conducts joint operations with countries where drugs are produced, and the Bureau of Alcohol, Tobacco and Firearms (ATF), which monitors the sale of destructive weapons and guns inside the United States.

Legislation to Control Crime

Congress has made more and more crimes federal ones and increased the severity of punishments. As more people are put in prisons, the costs for building and running them has increased dramatically.

After years of debate, in 1993 Congress passed and President Clinton signed into law the Brady Bill, which provides for a five-day waiting period and requires a background check when purchasing a handgun. Although the Supreme Court struck down the responsibility of local sheriffs for conducting this background check, under an expanded version of the Brady Bill the background checks are done by the FBI rather than by local law enforcement. Congress has also banned the sale of some semiautomatic assault weapons.[54] The National Rifle Association (NRA) has been powerful enough to stop most antigun legislation, even though such legislation has had the support of police chiefs and victims of crime. The debate over gun control at the local, state, and national levels remains intense.

In 1994, after an initial defeat in the House and an intense lobbying effort by President Clinton, Congress passed an omnibus anticrime bill that authorized $30.2 billion in spending on federal crime initiatives. The money funded a long list of programs, including hiring up to 100,000 new police officers and constructing new prisons and "boot camps" for juvenile offenders. The bill added new

President Clinton signs the Brady Bill, which limited access to certain types of guns, as James Brady (seated) and (left to right) Vice-President Al Gore, Attorney General Janet Reno, Sarah Brady, and the Brady children look on. Brady was wounded during an assassination attempt on President Reagan's life, after which he and his wife campaigned for gun control legislation.

assault rifle restrictions, a long list of federal offenses punishable by the death penalty, federal penalties and programs aimed at curbing domestic violence, and the "three-strikes-and-you're-out" provision mandating life imprisonment upon conviction for a third violent felony.

In recent years, the number of serious violent crimes has declined while the number of drug abuse violations has increased.[55] There is good evidence that there is a systematic underreporting of some crimes, but that is not a new phenomenon. The widespread perception, however, is that crime and violence are increasing and the federal government needs to step in.

Domestic terrorism, long a worry, became a reality with the bombing of the Federal Building in Oklahoma City in 1995 and with the Olympic Park bombing during the 1996 Atlanta Olympic Games. Concerns about armed militia movements also became part of the domestic terrorism debate. Finally, the serial bomber known as the "Unabomber" had an explicit political agenda. As with terrorist groups everywhere, domestic terrorism seeks to use fear and violence to achieve political goals. In 1996 President Clinton signed the Terrorism Act, which limits federal appeals by inmates sentenced to death, makes it easier to deport foreign terrorists, bans fund raising by Americans for foreign terrorist groups, and authorizes spending $1 billion to fight terrorism.

Fighting crime may be a major social policy challenge of the next century, but the goal of reducing crime must compete with other expectations we have for our government. Can we combat crime in ways that protect traditional civil liberties? Random drug tests, searches of private automobiles, curfews in urban areas, electronic eavesdropping, sting operations to catch criminals, and other steps law enforcement officials believe are necessary often conflict with the individual liberty and freedom from government restraint that Americans cherish. Must we give up some of those individual freedoms in order to fight crime? Should we build more prisons and impose harsher sentences on convicted criminals? Or should we focus on remedying the poverty and lack of opportunity that lead to criminal behavior? Like other social policies, policies aimed at fighting crime must ultimately balance competing values, one of the most complex and difficult tasks we delegate to government.

The Politics of Social Policy

Social policy issues along with the economy now dominate the agenda of American politics. Welfare, health care, education, and crime, and their costs are the political battleground between the parties and between contending interest groups. Both Republicans and Democrats are attempting to address key domestic issues that win broad support. Recent elections demonstrate how unsettled public opinion is on these issues.

The nation long ago answered questions about whether the government is responsible to provide decent housing, adequate health care, and a solid education to all of its citizens. The answer—to use Ronald Reagan's phrase—is that government provides a "safety net" for those who cannot provide for themselves. But how to provide that net and what programs or approaches to try are very much debated. And what we can afford and are willing to pay for expanded social services is the main issue. The social policy battles of recent years have demonstrated that expensive national social policy programs are unlikely to pass. As Bill Clinton put it, "the era of big government is over." But a party or president who ignores the social policy area is in political peril, as George Bush learned in 1992. Voters expect candidates to create programs to improve education, reduce crime, save Social Security, and expand health care. These issues remain central to American politics as we enter the twenty-first century.

Thinking it Through . . .

Opponents of any limitations on gun ownership point to the Second Amendment, which protects the right to keep and bear arms—a right valued by more people than just gun owners. But as technology has created more powerful guns, we have had to define what types of arms are protected. Few would assert that individuals have the right to use their own missiles. During Prohibition, Congress banned machine guns; and now we have added semiautomatic weapons to the list.

The number of guns in the United States has increased dramatically since 1950, up from 54 million to more than 200 million today. Today, one of every three households in this country has a gun. Guns, particularly handguns, are used in violent crimes. Nearly 11,000 murders are committed each year with guns; and 450,000 crimes are committed with guns annually.*

In 1994, Congress voted to ban 19 semiautomatic rifles. This ban left 670 guns other than semiautomatic rifles legal for use in hunting and target practice. Though supporters of this measure say these guns have made killing humans much easier, opponents point out that less than 1 percent of all violent crime is committed by criminals using assault rifles. Though banning only 19 out of nearly 700 assault rifles seems trivial, it could be regarded as a first step toward tight gun control. For two centuries, gun rights advocates have had the power and influence to stop any gun regulation in Congress; today, however, public demands for safe streets and a reduction in crime are pushing Congress to adopt controls.

*Mike Adams, "Gun Fight: Sometimes 911 Just Isn't Quick Enough," *The Arizona Republic*, January 10, 1999. See also U.S. Bureau of the Census, *Statistical Abstract of the United States, 1998* (Government Printing Office, 1998), p. 210.

POLITICS online

Tracking Social Policy

One of the great resources of the Web is its ability to research current policy issues using primary sources. In many instances, you can get more current information than you will find in newspapers or journal articles. Take, for example, the Goals 2000 legislation discussed in this chapter. To find out about the program generally, go to the U.S. Department of Education website. As with many websites, it opens up a set of additional resources:

http://www.ed.bov/G2K/

What if you want to compare how states are implementing this legislation? One way to research this question is through any of the standard search engines using key words like Goals 2000, or Educate America Act, or National Education Standards.

To track other social policy questions like health care reform, smoking regulation, or crime policy, begin with the home page of the relevant agency or department of national government. Also check congressional resources like Thomas:

http://thomas.loc.gov

or groups interested in the issue, like the American Medical Association for health policy:

http://www.ama-assn.org

or the American Cancer Society for tobacco policy:

http://forces.org/pages/p07-95-1.htm

For more Internet resources on Social Policy, see our home page at:

http://www.prenhall.com/burns.

SUMMARY

1. Conservatives advocate private solutions to most social problems, while liberals argue that it is the responsibility of government to provide a minimum standard of living—including a job, education, health care, housing, and nutrition—for all citizens. Since the New Deal, some government involvement in social programs has been widely accepted, although the extent of involvement has waxed (under Lyndon Johnson) and waned (under Ronald Reagan and George Bush).
2. Social Security, inaugurated in 1935 as part of the New Deal, is perhaps the most significant social legislation in U.S. history. Through a system of employee and employer taxes, retired workers and disabled individuals receive monthly payments and health benefits. With the country's changing demographic profile, tensions in the system are likely to increase.
3. Welfare takes many forms, including direct payments to the poor, the unemployed, and the disabled; food stamps; job training; housing subsidies; free school lunches; tax credits; subsidized medical care; and others. Public assistance programs began with the New Deal and have grown ever since; the federal government pays about three-fourths of their costs.
4. Welfare has long been criticized as creating disincentives to work, and many proposals have been put forward to make programs more effective and efficient. The most recent welfare reform, which became law in August 1996, transferred the administrative burden to the states, including giving them more discretion over recipients and their benefits, while helping to fund welfare programs through block grants of federal money.
5. The federal government supports medical research and has increased its role in health care cost control and access as the country's mostly private health care system is beset by rising costs, increasing numbers of uninsured Americans, unnecessary procedures, endless paperwork, high litigation costs, avoidable illnesses, and limited access. A variety of proposals for reform are under consideration, including a single-payer system, managed competition, employer-mandated coverage, spending caps, individual responsibility for coverage, and medical savings accounts.
6. Education continues to be primarily a state and local government function in the United States. The federal government plays an important role in helping fund public schools and by pushing national goals for better education.
7. Crime control has been forced onto the national agenda by public perceptions of increases in crime and violence and by politicians eager to accuse opponents of being "soft on crime." Although crime rates since 1991 have actually declined, during the Clinton administration pressures for federal action resulted in passage of the Brady Bill, which imposes a five-day waiting period on the sale of handguns, a ban on some semiautomatic assault weapons, and other proposals that would add to the number of police officers and further restrict gun sales.

KEY TERMS

public goods 469
Social Security 470
entitlement programs 472
Medicare 477
Medicaid 477
fee for service 477
health maintenance organization (HMO) 478
medical savings account 484

FURTHER READING

MARY JO BANE AND DAVID T. ELLWOOD, *Welfare Realities: From Rhetoric to Reform* (Harvard University Press, 1994).

ANNE MARIE CAMMISA, *From Rhetoric to Reform? Welfare Policy in American Politics* (Westview, 1998).

FRANK FISCHER, *Evaluating Public Policy* (Nelson-Hall, 1995).

LAURENE A. GRAIG, *Health of Nations: An International Perspective on U.S. Health Care Reform* (Congressional Quarterly Press, 1993).

CHRISTOPHER JENCKS, *The Homeless* (Harvard University Press, 1994).

THOMAS E. MANN AND NORMAN J. ORNSTEIN, EDS., *Intensive Care: How Congress Shapes Health Policy* (Brookings Institution, 1995).

THEODORE R. MARMOR, JERRY L. MASHAW, AND PHILIP L. HARVEY, *America's Misunderstood Welfare State: Persistent Myths, Enduring Realities* (Basic Books, 1990).

DANIEL PATRICK MOYNIHAN, *Miles to Go: A Personal History of Social Policy* (Harvard University Press, 1996).

CHARLES MURRAY, *Losing Ground: American Social Policy, 1950–80* (Basic Books, 1984).

DAVID OSBOURNE AND TED GAEBLER, *Reinventing Government: How the Entrepreneurial Spirit Is Transforming the Public Sector* (Addison-Wesley, 1993).

B. GUY PETERS, *American Public Policy: Promise and Performance*, 4th ed. (Chatham House, 1996).

THEDA SKOCPOL, *Social Policy in the United States: Future Possibilities in Historical Perspective* (Princeton University Press, 1995).

BOB WOODWARD, *Agenda: Inside the Clinton White House* (Simon & Schuster, 1994).

MAKING
FOREIGN
AND
DEFENSE
POLICY

20

THE UNITED STATES FINDS ITSELF TODAY IN A NEW ERA OF WORLD AFFAIRS. "IT IS AN AGE WHICH, FOR ALL ITS CONFUSIONS AND DANGERS," OBSERVED DISTINGUISHED diplomat George F. Kennan, "is marked by one major blessing: for the first time in centuries, there are no great-power rivalries that threaten immediately the peace of the world."[1] Yet Kennan and most U.S. citizens understand that even if the cold war is behind us, and even if the United States is the world's dominant military power, the world remains full of conflicts between and within nations. In addition, the population explosion, drugs, poverty, terrorism, environmental problems, and the spread of weapons of mass destruction create a highly unsettled world.

Both American public opinion and congressional actions have swung, sometimes unpredictably, between support and opposition to the deployment of U.S. troops in places such as Somalia, Haiti, Bosnia, Kosovo, and Iraq. Our hopes and aspirations are often contradictory. That we want to promote democratic values abroad yet also secure our sources of energy sometimes forces us to support nondemocratic governments such as Saudi Arabia. We want to protect the environment yet also support American business overseas; we want to encourage human rights in China yet want China to buy our airplanes; we want to reprimand India and Pakistan for testing nuclear bombs, but rigorous enforcement of economic sanctions against them would devastate our midwestern and northwestern wheat growers who ship much of their wheat to Asia. We favor progressive free-trade and immigration policies yet worry about job losses that sometimes result from such policies.

Congress and the American people want the United States to remain the premier global power, yet we balk at the costs. We question the need for foreign aid. We wonder whether the Central Intelligence Agency is as necessary now as it was during the cold war. We fret about the bloated and inefficient United Nations and question whether it is worth supporting. We want to scale down defense spending but want to maintain instant readiness and superior military strength.

How should we restructure our foreign and defense policies to meet twenty-first century conditions? And is it possible—or desirable—to fashion a single grand strategy of foreign policy to replace our longtime goal of containing and defeating the Soviet Union? As the once-clear lines between foreign and domestic policy become blurred, how will the increased participation by Congress and the increased influence of public opinion affect the traditional primacy of the American president in the politics of foreign policy decision making? In short, what should our foreign

CHAPTER OUTLINE

policy be, and who should make it? In this chapter we explore possible answers to these difficult questions.

President Bill Clinton and Chinese President Jiang Zemin at welcoming ceremonies in Tiananmen Square in June 1998. Critics felt it was inappropriate for Clinton to appear at the scene of a brutal repression of democracy.

VITAL INTERESTS IN THE POST–COLD WAR WORLD

Our foreign policy goal remains, as it has been, to maintain our sovereignty and freedom. Over the past several generations, the United States has become involved in world affairs to a degree unprecedented in our history. Much of this activity was due to the cold war, 1945 to 1990. Yet there are other reasons as well. U.S. security and economic interests are closely tied to what happens in the rest of the world. Whether we like it or not, events far from home affect our life, liberty, and pursuit of happiness.

Defining Our Vital Interests

Our political values are a critical factor in defining our vital interests. We want peace. We favor human rights. We generally support United Nations peacekeeping missions. We have a commitment to protect weaker nations against aggression. We want to encourage democracy and market-oriented economies. We want, where possible, to improve the standard of living in less-developed nations. We are also committed to improving the global environment. As a global trader, the United States needs markets for its products, imports of raw materials, and adequate supplies of energy. Plainly, the task of defining our interests requires extensive balancing of sometimes competing goals.

Making foreign and defense policy involves not simply defining our interests, but making tough choices about what to do, especially when resources are limited, risks are high, and our objectives are sometimes in conflict. Policy making invariably involves deciding among options. "Foreign policy, unlike baseball, has no world championships; there are no permanent victories and no 70th home runs," writes Secretary of State Madeleine Albright. "In our era, moreover, neither the adversaries, nor the rules, nor even the location of the playing field are fully fixed."[2]

New Foreign Policy Challenges

The end of the cold war surely has not meant that the United States no longer faces challenges to its security or economic well-being. The removal of communism as a constraint has led to the reemergence of old national hatreds throughout Eastern Europe. Some nations, such as Yugoslavia and Czechoslovakia, have broken apart. The Middle East remains unsettled. In Latin America, democracies have emerged, yet there have also been setbacks. China, Burma, North Korea, and Indonesia remain under military rule.

The United States may be militarily strong, yet we face stiff competition for influence in the world as the power base shifts from military might to economic strength. Our foreign policy has to address vital issues that have been simmering for many years, plus some recent concerns. Table 20-1 lists issues of major concern both to leaders and to the general public. Notice here again how what people think is important is often contradictory.

POPULATION GROWTH AND POVERTY Americans are alarmed at the world's population explosion and the resulting widespread poverty. Still, our support for population control programs abroad is embroiled in controversy in Congress between anti-abortion and pro-choice interest groups. Many of the world's nearly 6 billion people are virtually excluded from economic opportunity. In China alone, more than 300 million live below the international poverty level. Moreover, there continues to be a significant transfer of wealth from poor countries to rich, and the information technology revolution accelerates this disparity.

TABLE 20-1 Foreign Policy Goals: What Is Important?

	Percent Answering "Very Important"	
	Leaders	The Public
Stopping flow of illegal drugs into the United States	57%	81%
Protecting jobs of American workers	45	80
Preventing the spread of nuclear weapons	85	82
Controlling and reducing illegal immigration	21	55
Securing adequate supplies of energy	55	64
Reducing our trade deficit with foreign countries	34	56
Improving global environment	46	53
Combating world hunger	56	62
Protecting the jobs of American workers	45	80
Strengthening the United Nations	32	45
Maintaining superior military power worldwide	58	59
Defending our allies' security	58	44
Promoting and defending human rights in other countries	41	39
Helping to bring a democratic form of government to other nations	27	29
Protecting weaker nations against foreign aggression	29	32
Helping to improve standards of living in less-developed nations	36	29

SOURCE: John E. Rielly, ed., *American Public Opinion and U.S. Foreign Policy, 1999* (The Chicago Council on Foreign Relations, 1999), p. 16.

Leaders sample included elected officials, business leaders, educators, editors, and union officers.

TRADE WITH JAPAN AND CHINA A serious trade imbalance exists between the United States and Japan and China. We have tried to force Japan to open its markets to imports of our products and have imposed restrictions on the importing of Japanese products, even though such restrictions made those products cost more. And with the downturn in the Japanese economy, we have tried to be a supportive trade partner.

Trade with China poses other concerns. China has one of the fastest growing economies in the world. Our exports to China have tripled in the last several years, and imports from China have grown rapidly. But human rights advocates believe we should link trade and tariff agreements to China's human rights record. It is well known that China does not regard human rights in the same way that constitutional democracies do. President Bill Clinton, from time to time, threatened to withhold most-favored-nation status from China unless there was a marked improvement in China's treatment of dissidents. **Most-favored-nation status**, now called by many people simply "normal trade" status, is an international trade policy whereby we grant to a country the same favorable trade concessions and tariffs that our best trading partners receive.

Loss of trade with China would deal a serious blow to the American economy, especially on the West Coast and especially to huge companies such as Boeing. In 1998 President Clinton "separated" the two issues and extended China's most-favored-nation status. His visit to China and the reception in Tiananmen Square angered some Americans, who felt it was an affront to the memory of the Chinese democracy movement that had been brutally assaulted by government troops there.

most-favored-nation status
Trade status granted as part of an international trade policy that gives a nation the same favorable trade concessions and tariffs that our best trading partners receive.

NUCLEAR AND BIOLOGICAL ARMS CONTROL Probably the single greatest threat to the security of the United States and the rest of the world is the proliferation of weapons of mass destruction. At present, only a handful of nations have usable

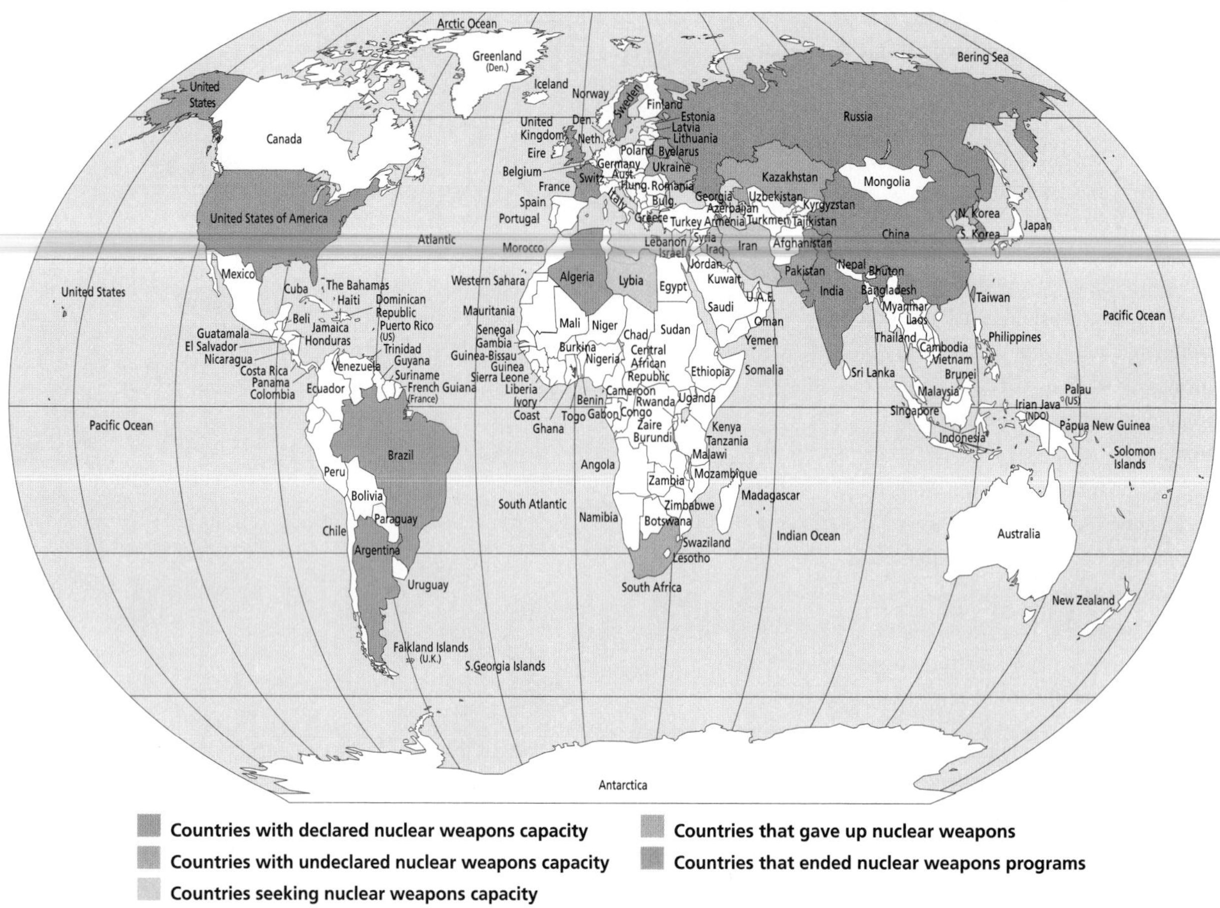

FIGURE 20-1 The Spread of Nuclear Weapons

SOURCE: Natural Resources Defense Council, Arms Control Association, Institute for Science and International Security; *Congressional Quarterly Weekly*, May 23, 1998, p. 1366.

nuclear weapons (see Figure 20-1). What happens if such weapons fall into the hands of so-called "rogue nations" like Libya, Iraq, and North Korea, which have no democratic controls on their governments and whose leaders may have dreams of world conquest, or at least retaliation against the United States?

A few dozen nations, including the United States and Russia, have agreed to curb the sale of materials that could be used in the manufacture of nuclear weapons. This agreement was a direct result of a close call in early 1990, when Iraq was detected trying to build nuclear weapons. Although the agreement established limits on the sale of materials or machinery that can be used either for peaceful purposes or for building nuclear bombs, experts still caution that "good intentions on export controls are often undermined by ignorance and greed."[3]

Some foreign policy experts suggest that the United States may some day have to resort to "preemptive intervention" in nations like North Korea, Iran, Iraq, Syria, Libya, or Algeria to prevent a rogue nation from acquiring menacing nuclear weapons.[4] This is hardly a strategy most Americans would like, and no government official has espoused it. Still, modern warfare writers note that "modern missiles and bombs are so powerful that each side will have a strong incentive to strike first and thus stop the enemy doing anything."[5]

THE CHEMICAL WEAPONS CONVENTION The United States has entered into a variety of agreements to restrict the use of biological or chemical materials. President Clinton and his supporters waged a major legislative battle in 1997 against Senator Jesse Helms and many conservatives over whether the United States should ratify the Chemical Weapons Convention. Treaty supporters, such as Bill Clinton, George Bush, and Senator John McCain (R.-Ariz.), said the security of our soldiers and citizens was at stake. They noted we were already destroying our chemical weapons stockpile and argued that other nations must do the same. Routine inspections would take place in all member nations, and this convention (or treaty) would punish nonmembers by restricting their ability to import or export restricted chemicals.

Critics called the Chemical Weapons Convention a dangerous treaty because cheaters could easily evade detection. They also opposed it because Libya, Iraq, Syria, and North Korea were not going to join: "How can a treaty that professes to address the problem of chemical weapons be credible unless it addresses the threat from the very countries, such as Syria and Iraq, that have actually deployed these weapons?"[6] After heated and prolonged debate, the Senate voted in 1997 to ratify our participation in the Chemical Weapons Convention.

THE FORMER SOVIET UNION AND EASTERN EUROPE Russia and other countries that emerged from the former Soviet Union and its satellites are now torn by economic chaos and shortages. Americans want to be of assistance yet are weary of giving direct aid that will raise U.S. taxes and enlarge the national debt. Still, foreign policy experts contend such investment is essential to help with the transition to a market economy and to encourage the gradual development of healthy constitutional democracies in that region.

THE EUROPEAN ECONOMIC UNION AND THE FUTURE OF NATO The European Economic Union has adopted measures that bind European nations together for the purpose of economic growth. They now have a common currency and have eliminated many tariffs and trade restrictions. An economically powerful Europe poses challenges for U.S. companies and trade. With the end of the cold war, the mission, goals, and even membership of the North Atlantic Treaty Organization (NATO) have been redefined. In Bosnia, NATO forces conducted the alliance's first "out of the area" military operation, and in 1997 NATO was expanded to include former Warsaw Pact nations—Poland, The Czech Republic, and Hungary.

DRUG TRAFFIC U.S. relations with Mexico, Colombia, and other Latin American nations are greatly affected by the drug traffic. Extensive domestic demand in the United States is fed by drugs smuggled into this country from Western Hemisphere nations. Are drugs a domestic problem that needs to be solved at home, or should American addictions be perceived as a combined domestic, economic, and foreign policy problem? A cooperative program of destroying drug crops and interdicting drug imports has been carried out by the United States and some of its neighbors.

THE GLOBAL ENVIRONMENT The United States is at the same time one of the world's leading promoters of environmental concerns and one of its major polluters. A 1992 U.N. conference in Rio de Janeiro on conserving and improving the world's natural resources pointed the way toward many new policies, but most nations, including the United States, have moved slowly on implementing policies to achieve these goals, despite grim warnings about global warming.

BUDGETING FOR AN EFFECTIVE FOREIGN POLICY An effective foreign policy is impossible to sustain by rhetoric or repeated statements of noble intentions. "Talk is cheap; leadership is not," said former Secretary of State Warren Christopher. "Leadership in foreign policy requires resources: enough to keep our embassies open and our people trained; enough to maintain constructive relations with the world's great powers; enough to multiply our leverage through

Secretaries of State and the Presidents They Served

George Marshall (Truman)

John Foster Dulles (Eisenhower)

Dean Rusk (Kennedy and Johnson)

Henry Kissinger (Nixon and Ford)

international institutions; enough to provide targeted aid to struggling democracies that can one day emerge as allies and export markets; enough to meet threats like terrorism and international crime."[7]

We have closed at least 25 consulates and several embassies in recent years. Many embassies operate with obsolete technology and in decaying buildings. We rank last among industrialized nations in our foreign aid investments abroad. We are the number one debtor both to the United Nations and multilateral development banks. "We lack the funds to provide full security for our people overseas," says Secretary of State Madeleine Albright. "And under the current budget agreement, we face a further reduction in buying power of at least 12 percent over the next 5 years."[8] Critics of Clinton's foreign policy say it is not a question of money but a question of imagination or good policy that we are lacking. And they especially question subsidizing the United Nations.

In this post–cold war era, the success or failure of U.S. foreign policy may not seem a matter of life and death to many people. Thus we invest fewer resources in foreign policy and in national defense than in the recent past. But all this deserves to be questioned and debated. How much is an effective foreign policy worth? What are the obligations of a foreign policy that seeks to prevent conflicts, promote prosperity, strengthen freedom, block the transfers of destructive arms and technologies, and advocate democratic institutions and practices?

Key Players in Foreign Policy

Although presidents share with Congress the responsibility for making overall foreign policy decisions, the operations of foreign policy are directly under the president. In practice, a president has the primary responsibility to shape foreign policy. Presidents can bargain, negotiate, persuade, apply economic pressures, threaten, or even use armed force.

The Constitution put control of foreign policy in the hands of those who run the national government: the president, the Senate, and, in some cases, the Congress as a whole. In eighteenth-century England, the king controlled foreign policy. The framers of our Constitution thus tried to redress the balance of power, and many of the powers given to Congress by the Constitution reflect the decision to limit the powers of the executive branch. Congress has the power to declare war, to appropriate funds, and to make rules for the armed forces. But the president is commander in chief of the armed forces and is expected to negotiate treaties and receive and send ambassadors—that is, to recognize or refuse to recognize other governments. The Senate confirms ambassadors and gives consent to treaty ratification. The courts have the power to interpret treaties, but by and large they have ruled that relations with other nations are matters for the executive to negotiate. The primacy of the executive in foreign policy is a fact of political life of all nations, including constitutional democracies.

The President's Foreign Policy Advisers

Officially, the president's principal foreign policy adviser is the secretary of state, though today competing advisers are sometimes more influential. The secretary of state administers the State Department, receives visits from foreign diplomats, attends international conferences, and usually heads our delegation in the General Assembly of the United Nations. The secretary also serves as the administration's chief coordinator of all governmental actions that affect our relations with other nations. In practice, a secretary of state delegates the day-to-day responsibilities for running the State Department and spends most of his or her time negotiating with the leaders of other countries.[9]

Today, because of the interdependence of foreign, economic, and domestic policies, the president calls on an increasing number of civilian and economic advisers in addition to the secretary of state. The conduct of foreign affairs is now the business of several major departments and agencies: State, Defense, Treasury, Agriculture, Commerce, Labor, Energy, the Central Intelligence Agency (CIA), and others. The need for immediate reaction and preparedness has transferred more responsibilities directly to the president, and, to a great extent, to the senior White House aides who assist in coordinating information and advice. Yet no matter what the system for advice and coordination, there are always overlap, redundancy, and competition.

Secretaries, agency chiefs, and their senior subordinates are chosen by the president and are expected to support and carry out White House decisions. At the same time, they retain a measure of independence; they naturally tend to reflect and defend the views of the departments and agencies they head. As a result, presidents have found a need to appoint White House advisers whose loyalties lie solely with the chief executive.

The National Security Council

The key coordinating agency for the president is the National Security Council (NSC). Created by Congress in 1947, it is intended to help presidents integrate foreign, military, and economic policies that affect national security. The National Security Council serves directly under the president. By law, it consists of the president, vice-president, secretary of state, and secretary of defense. Recent presidents have sometimes included the director of the CIA, the White House chief of staff, and the national security adviser as *ex officio* members of the NSC.

The national security adviser, appointed by the president, has gradually emerged as one of the most influential foreign policy makers, sometimes rivaling in influence the secretary of state. Presidents come to rely on these White House aides both because of their proximity (down the hall in the west wing of the White House) and because they owe their primary loyalties to the president, not to any department or program. Each president has shaped the NSC structure and adapted its staff procedures to suit his personal preferences, but over the years the NSC, as both a committee and a staff, has taken on a major role in making and implementing foreign policy.[10]

The State Department

The primary duty of the State Department has always been the security of the nation. Although our armed forces remain our ultimate line of defense, the State Department is our first line. It is dedicated to an around-the-clock, worldwide effort to promote diplomacy and secure negotiated settlements of international disputes—to see to it that troops and weapons are not used except in genuine emergencies. It is also the central agency in the day-to-day management of foreign affairs. Among the State Department's main priorities are the following:

1. To promote peace and human rights
2. To negotiate with other nations and international organizations
3. To protect American citizens and interests abroad

Secretaries of State and the Presidents They Served

Cyrus Vance (Carter)

George Shultz (Reagan)

James Baker (Bush)

Warren Christopher (Clinton)

The Peace Corps

The Peace Corps, established by the Peace Corps Act of 1961 in the Kennedy administration, has a mission to encourage world peace and friendship, help other countries in meeting their social and development needs, and promote greater understanding between Americans and other peoples. Peace Corps volunteers are expected to serve in another nation for two years and become part of the community they are serving. Volunteers work on a variety of projects, such as teaching math and science, doing community development work, and improving water and sanitation systems.

What qualifications does one need to apply? Generally a college degree, experience, or a combination of both. There is no age limit. In fact, about 10 percent of the 6,500 current volunteers are over 50 years old. The Peace Corps picks up the expenses and typically trains each volunteer in language and job skills for about three months prior to service abroad.

The Peace Corps operates in about 95 nations and has had funding of about $230 million a year. More than 150,000 Americans have been Peace Corps volunteers. Eight Peace Corps alumni have served in Congress. The Peace Corps is wholly separate from the State and Defense Departments and the intelligence agencies.

The Peace Corps motto to would-be volunteers says, "The Peace Corps—the toughest job you'll ever love."

For more information, write Peace Corps, Volunteer Service Office, 1990 K Street, NW, Washington, D.C. 20526, or call 1-800-424-8580. For a useful study of the Peace Corps, see Elizabeth Cobbs Hoffman, *All You Need Is Love: The Peace Corps and the Spirit of the 1960s* (Harvard University Press, 1998).

4. To promote American commercial interests and enterprises
5. To collect and interpret intelligence
6. To represent an American "presence" abroad.

The State Department's budget of about $5.5 billion (not counting foreign aid) is the lowest of all the cabinet departments—less than 2 percent of the Department of Defense's over $270 billion budget. Considering the State Department's role and prestige, its staff of 24,000 worldwide is small, especially compared with the 2.2 million civilian and military personnel in the Department of Defense. Like most other federal agencies, State had to eliminate more than 10 percent of its staff in the 1990s. If Republican Senator Jesse Helms, who has chaired the Senate Foreign Relations Committee, had his way, it would have cut twice that amount.

The Foreign Service

The American Foreign Service is the eyes and ears of the United States in other countries. Although part of the State Department, the service represents the entire government and performs jobs for many other agencies. Its main duties are to carry out foreign policy as expressed in the directives of the secretary of state; gather political, economic, and intelligence data for American policy makers; protect Americans and American interests in foreign countries; and cultivate friendly relations with host governments and foreign peoples.

The Foreign Service is composed of officers, reserve officers, and staff officers. At its core are the foreign service officers, comparable to army officers in the military. They are a select, specially trained group expected to take assignments any place in the world on short notice. There are approximately 4,000 such officers; in recent years fewer than 250 junior officers won appointment each year. Approximately two-thirds of our U.S. ambassadors to about 160 nations come from the ranks of the Foreign Service. The others are usually political appointees, such as former Tennessee Senator James Sasser, the current ambassador to China, or large donors or friends of the president.

The Foreign Service is one of the most prestigious yet most criticized career services of the national government. Criticism sometimes comes as much from within as from outside. Critics claim the organizational culture of the Foreign Service stifles creativity; attracts officers who are, or at least become, more concerned about their status than their responsibilities; and requires new recruits to wait 15 years or more before being considered for positions of responsibility. These problems are recognized in Washington, and the task of improving the service continues. Outside critics point to a social homogeneity among the Foreign Service, but that is probably overstated. More women and minorities have been recruited in recent years.

Madeleine Albright is the first woman secretary of state. She has had to deal with sensitive negotiations backed by threats of military intervention in Iraq and Kosovo.

Perhaps the greatest challenge for foreign service diplomats is how to function effectively in a high-tech world. Some have even suggested that diplomats be replaced altogether and most of their work be conducted by e-mail, fax, and videoconferencing from Washington.[11] Yet having a diplomat on the scene in Iran or Saudi Arabia who speaks Farsi and Arabic and who knows a country's major leaders personally is often a better method than relying on even the most advanced new technologies—especially when making subtle judgments about a nation's political, economic, and military policies.[12]

Intelligence and the CIA

What is the nuclear capability of the North Korean military? How strong are the rebel forces in Kosovo? What are the internal political struggles in Indonesia? How stable is the political situation in North Korea? Before our foreign policy makers can act on important issues, they have to know as much as possible about other countries: their possible reactions to a particular policy, their strengths and weaknesses, the character of their leaders, and if possible, their strategic plans and intentions. Thus those who gather and analyze intelligence data are among the most important advisers to policy makers.[13]

The Central Intelligence Agency, an outgrowth of the World War II Office of Strategic Services, was created in 1947 to coordinate the gathering and analysis of information that flows into various parts of the U.S. government from all over the world. In recent years, the CIA has had nearly 20,000 employees and has helped direct and integrate the intelligence products of the State Department's Bureau of Intelligence and Research, the Defense Intelligence Agency (which combines the intelligence operations of the Army, Navy, Air Force, and Marine Corps), the National Security Agency (which specializes in electronic reconnaissance and code breaking), the supersecret National Reconnaissance Office (which runs the U.S. satellite surveillance programs), the Federal Bureau of Investigation (FBI), and a small intelligence operation run by the Departments of Energy and Treasury. These agencies spend nearly $30 billion a year on intelligence work.[14]

Although most of the information the CIA gathers comes from open sources, the term "intelligence" conjures up visions of spies and undercover agents. Secret intelligence occasionally does supply crucial data. But it is not all glamour; much is routine. Intelligence work involves three basic operations: reporting, research, and dissemination. *Reporting* is based on the close and rigorous observation of developments around the world; *research* is the attempt to detect meaningful patterns out of what was observed in the past and to understand what appears to be going on now; and *dissemination* means getting the right information to the right people at the right time.

CIA analysts detected the military buildup by Iraq's Saddam Hussein in 1990, but their warnings about an invasion of Kuwait were too cautious and too late, according to later analyses. Indeed, President George Bush, himself a former CIA director, is reported to have been misinformed that Iraq really was not adequately recovered from its war with Iran to mount another military invasion.[15]

For 40 years the CIA and other intelligence agencies used their best personnel to understand and help undermine our primary enemy—the Soviet Union. Now that the Soviet Union is gone, the CIA has had to redefine its role, address new challenges, and reverse its long-term growth pattern. Among its new challenges are gathering intelligence on terrorism, drug trafficking, and the growing number of nations that have ballistic missiles with chemical, biological, and nuclear warheads. Our intelligence agencies are also asked to prevent industrial espionage by other nations.

What about the need for *covert operations*—operations that deliberately try to destabilize governments or insurgent groups in other nations? The CIA has been credited with both successful and failed covert operations abroad. The ill-fated Bay of Pigs invasion of Cuba in 1961 was directed by the CIA. Later the CIA supported the anti-Allende forces in Chile. Because of its past record and because it must act when our government cannot intervene officially, there is a tendency to credit (or blame) the CIA for many coups, purges, and revolts, whether the agency was involved or not.

The CIA's influence, its information, its secrecy, its speed in communication, its ability to act, and its enormous budget make the CIA controversial. Congress has tried to see that this power is used only by publicly accountable decision makers. Committees have been set up in both the Senate and the House of Representatives to hold the CIA accountable to Congress, although earlier efforts by similar committees sometimes failed to do an adequate job.[16]

Congress became especially outraged at the CIA's leadership in 1994, when it was discovered that a senior CIA agent, Aldrich Ames, had spied for the Soviets and

Former CIA officer Aldrich Ames leaves court after being sentenced to life in prison for revealing secrets to Russia.

The American public concerns itself with foreign affairs mainly when it involves the use of our troops abroad.

the KGB for much of the 1980s. Ames confessed to what is considered the worst betrayal of U.S. intelligence in the history of the CIA; it is estimated that at least 12 overseas agents or friendly sources were killed because of his deeds.

Senator Daniel Patrick Moynihan has called for dismantling the CIA. He argues it has grown fat and lazy over the years and there is no justification for intelligence agencies to have a budget five times as large as the State Department's. Moynihan agrees that the U.S. cannot put a complete end to secrecy. "It is at times legitimate and necessary." But a widely established culture of secrecy need not remain the tradition in diplomacy and national security operations. "A case can be made . . . that secrecy is for losers. For people who don't know how important information really is. The Soviet Union realized this too late," writes Moynihan. "Openness is now a singular, and singularly American, advantage. . . . It is time to dismantle government secrecy, this most pervasive of Cold War–era regulations. It is time to begin building the supports for the era of openness that is already upon us."[17]

While the U.S. intelligence agencies have made mistakes over the years, many experts still believe these agencies are needed. Political scientist Loch Johnson writes that "the likelihood that they contributed significantly to warding off a third world war has been enough to earn their keep."[18] Their analysis of complicated political and military developments in the Middle East has also proved strategically important.

An extensive review of the CIA by a bipartisan commission in 1996 recommended strengthening the hand of the director of central intelligence, reducing the work force of these agencies, and "refocusing its efforts on global crime such as terrorism, narcotics trafficking, proliferation of weapons of mass destruction and international organized crime syndicates."[19] The commission recommended that the intelligence agencies strengthen their accountability to the executive and legislative branches, yet concluded their missions of information gathering and analysis remain vital to the security of the United States.[20]

The Politics of Making Foreign and Defense Policy

Foreign policy flows through the same institutional and constitutional structures as domestic policy. Public opinion, interest groups, foreign countries, political parties, and Congress, all affect the politics of making foreign policy. Yet these structures operate somewhat differently from the way they do in domestic affairs. Of course, international organizations and foreign governments and their embassies also play an important role.

Public Opinion

Different foreign and defense issues evoke different degrees of public interest and involvement. In crisis situations—such as the bombing of Iraq in 1998—decisions are made by the president and his military advisers. Yet even in these situations, presidents and their advisers know their decisions will ultimately require support from the public and from Congress.

In noncrisis situations, the public appears to consist of three subcategories. The largest, constituting perhaps as much as 75 percent of the adult population, is the *mass public.* This group knows little about the details of foreign affairs, despite the subject's importance. The mass public concerns itself with foreign affairs mainly in conflict situations, especially those involving the use of American troops abroad. The second group is the *attentive public,* constituting perhaps 15 to 20 percent of the population. It maintains an active interest in foreign policy. The *opinion makers* are the third and smallest public; as editors, teachers, writers, political and business leaders, they transmit information and judgments on foreign affairs and mobilize the support of the other two publics.

Still, many people in this country are indifferent or uninformed about foreign and defense policy. Foreign affairs issues are more remote than domestic issues. People have more firsthand information about unemployment, inflation, crime, and health care costs than about Japanese economic reform or Indonesian political problems. Most Americans have a poor sense of world geography and an even weaker grasp of geopolitics. Sometimes it seems that only when American soldiers or civilians overseas are killed does the mass public become directly concerned with foreign affairs.

Most Americans do recognize that their lives, jobs, and security inevitably reflect international developments. "Contrary to a widely held assumption, their concern does not stop at the water's edge," writes Steven Kull.[21] And a survey of American views on foreign and defense policy concludes that most Americans accept that the United States has serious obligations:

> Relief from the long competition with the Soviet Union and the lack of a clear external threat have made Americans more reluctant to use force abroad and become involved in the affairs of other countries. But they want to maintain current levels of defense in an uncertain world and are committed to diplomatic engagement through alliances and multilateral organizations.[22]

The State and Defense Departments make an effort to keep people informed about those areas of policy they think should be discussed publicly and to keep themselves informed about public opinion. Yet despite occasional talk about open and democratic policy making, most foreign policy negotiations are conducted in secret. Even Congress is sometimes kept at a distance, as was the case when the Iranians were encouraged to send arms to Bosnia while President Clinton was assuring Congress that the United States supported the arms embargo.

Special Interests

The mass media can be powerful in shaping public opinion. Certain reporters and newspapers have helped rally public opinion on behalf of human rights, and press coverage of government treatment of dissidents in China and South Africa put pressure on the White House and Congress to reconsider our policies toward those countries.

It is difficult to generalize about the impact of interest groups on American foreign policies. At moments of international crisis, such as after President Clinton ordered the retaliatory bombings in Sudan and Afghanistan in 1998, a president is usually able to mobilize so much public support that interest groups find it difficult to exert much influence. As a general rule, special interest groups other than major economic interests rarely have a decisive role in the formulation of foreign policy.

Ethnic interest groups, however, sometimes play an important role in foreign policy decisions. As a nation of immigrants and the children and grandchildren of immigrants, our citizens often retain a special bond with their country of origin. Thus Irish Americans, Jewish Americans, African Americans, Asian Americans, Polish Americans, Greek Americans, and Mexican Americans take a keen interest in decisions affecting Ireland, Israel, South Africa, China, Indonesia, Poland, Greece, and Mexico. These interest groups sometimes exert powerful pressures on policy makers to support the country to which they are emotionally linked. Congress is attuned to these pressures.

Governmental entities can also be a special interest. Thus the Air Force may be as influential in determining the size and shape of the U.S. strategic bomber force as any contractor, or party, or interest group. And members of Congress can influence where to purchase military equipment or whether to shut down a military installation.

Foreign Countries

Most countries have embassies that lobby for their interests in Washington. In addition, some countries like Japan have built up a powerful network of lawyers, lobbyists, and Washington-based publicists who are retained by Japanese companies and trade associations, as well as by the Japanese government, to defend their extensive economic interests in the United States.[23] Lobbyists representing newly industrialized countries like South Korea, Taiwan, Singapore, Brazil, and Mexico have also expanded their Washington lobbying efforts to fight U.S. protectionism and import quotas on textiles, shoes, and other exports.

Whether foreign governments and business interests influence our foreign policy became an issue after large Chinese and Indonesian contributions to Bill Clinton's 1996 reelection campaign came to light. The president vigorously denied that contributions bought influence, and the money was returned by the Democratic National Committee.

Political Parties

Political parties do not usually play a major role in shaping foreign and defense policy for two reasons: (1) many Americans still prefer to keep partisan politics out of foreign policy; (2) parties usually take less clear and candid stands on foreign policy than they do on domestic policy. Party platforms often obscure the issues instead of highlighting them, and many members of Congress fail to follow a general party line.

Should parties be concerned with foreign policy? At the end of World War II, sentiment grew stronger for a bipartisan approach to foreign policy. An ambiguous term, **bipartisanship** generally means: (1) collaboration between the executive and the congressional foreign policy leaders of both parties; (2) support of presidential foreign policies by both parties in Congress; and (3) downplaying foreign policy issues in national elections and especially in presidential debates. Overall, bipartisanship is an attempt to remove the issues of foreign policy from partisan politics.

The Role of Congress

Despite the importance of foreign and defense policy, and even though Congress can block the president's policy and undermine the chief executive's decisions, Congress as an institution seldom makes foreign policy directly. Individual members of Congress, however, are sometimes included within the circle of those who make foreign and defense policy decisions. The power of Congress is mainly consultative, although the legislature has taken the initiative in some trade and foreign economic and military assistance questions. In addition, Congress regularly tries to define the limits of presidential war-making powers.[24] And, of course, Congress, through its budget-making powers, can encourage or discourage foreign policy initiatives.

Congress is a crucial link between policy makers and the public. Congress wants a voice—especially "meaningful consultation" with the president in matters of foreign relations. Some members of Congress, for example, asked for a full-scale debate before President Clinton made any commitment of U.S. troops to bombing Iraq in 1998, but were not given that opportunity. Congress is often divided on issues of foreign and defense policy—as it has been, for example, on the Chemical Weapons Convention, foreign aid, and funding for the United Nations.

For the most part, presidents and their advisers initiate foreign policy, yet members of Congress stimulate, prod, amend, modify, and sometimes block what the White House proposes.

bipartisanship
A policy that emphasizes a united front and cooperation between the major political parties, especially on sensitive foreign policy issues.

The Potential for a Democratic Foreign Policy

A democratic foreign policy is presumably one in which policy makers are known and are held accountable to the people. That is a tough test for any policy, but it is especially tough for foreign policy because of the frequent need to act with speed and sometimes with secrecy, the generally low level of information among the general public, the anonymity of most foreign policy leaders, and, of course, the complexity of most international issues and strategic policy options. Still, the American public wants to be consulted and informed, and it wants its leaders accountable.[25]

In Vietnam, American policy makers miscalculated the character of the war as well as the commitment of the Vietnamese who opposed the Saigon government. And because these policy makers knew to some extent that they had made mistakes and believed the American people and Congress might not support them in what they thought necessary, they sometimes concealed these difficulties.[26]

A constitutional democracy may not be able to keep leaders from making mistakes, but in a policy area in which big mistakes can be made, the mistakes eventually become public. It is then that the safeguarding agencies of democracy—the opposition party, the press, and public opinion—go to work. Changes are demanded, and policies are changed. In the case of Vietnam, public resistance to the war eventually forced the United States to get out. The way in which these agencies of democracy worked in the United States doubtless encouraged the United States to exit from both the Vietnam and Somalia conflicts faster than the Soviets got out of their ill-fated engagement in Afghanistan.

U.S. Formal Military Alliances

- The North Atlantic Treaty Organization (NATO)
- The Australian-New Zealand-United States (ANZUS) Alliance (although U.S. obligations to New Zealand are suspended)
- The Treaty of Mutual Cooperation and Security between the United States and Japan
- The Mutual Defense Treaty between the United States and the Republic of Korea
- The Mutual Defense Treaty between the United States and the Republic of the Philippines
- The Southeast Asia Collective Defense Treaty (which remains in effect on a bilateral basis with Thailand)
- The InterAmerican Treaty of Reciprocal Assistance between the United States and most Latin and Central American countries (Rio Treaty)

Foreign and Defense Policy Options

How are foreign and defense policies actually implemented? As a major power, the United States can choose a variety of options or tools, but it usually employs the following six, or some combination of them. Whether these tools will work, either alone or in combination with others, usually depends on whether they fit the particular strategic situation in which policy makers find themselves and also whether the domestic conditions for pursuing such a strategy are favorable.

Conventional Diplomacy

Much of U.S. foreign policy is conducted by the foreign service and ambassadors in face-to-face discussions in Washington and other capitals, at the United Nations, in Geneva (at arms talks), and elsewhere around the world in regional or international organizations and world conferences. International summit meetings, with their high-profile pomp and drama, are another form of conventional diplomacy. Even though traditional diplomacy appears more subdued and somewhat less vital in this era of personal leader-to-leader communication by telephone, fax, and teleconferencing, it is still an important, if slow, process by which nations can gain information, talk about mutual interests, and try to resolve bilateral and multilateral disputes.

Much of the conventional diplomacy carried out by the State Department may not produce important breakthroughs, yet it is difficult to measure the value of diplomatic representation. No price tag can be placed on close personal relations with foreign officials or on information gathered and arguments made to promote American interests around the world. Surely the closing of one embassy or the withdrawal from international organizations is unlikely to cause the United States major setbacks, yet a less active diplomatic corps could mean a less effective foreign policy.

President Bill Clinton and Jordan's King Hussein were instrumental in the 1998 accords signed by Palestinian President Yasser Arafat and Israeli Prime Minister Benjamin Netanyahu.

Foreign Aid

The United States regularly grants economic and military assistance to foreign countries, in part for humanitarian reasons and in part to further good relations with other nations. The United States offers aid to more

You Decide . . .

Should the United States stay in or get out of the United Nations?

The United Nations has had major financial and bureaucratic problems, and some writers and politicians have called for the United States to get out of the United Nations. We are currently asked to pay about 25 percent of the U.N.'s bills. Republican Jesse Helms, while not calling for getting out of the United Nations, insists that we stop placing the agenda of the United Nations before the interests of the United States. Democrat Bill Clinton strongly favors staying in the United Nations, yet insists the organization needs to be restructured and revitalized and should do more with less. What do you think most Americans believe, and where do you stand?

than 100 countries directly and to a number of other nations through contributions to various United Nations development funds. Since 1945 we have provided about $400 billion in economic assistance to foreign countries—a figure that sounds impressive. From 1948 to 1951, the Marshall Plan gave $13 billion worth of money, goods, and services to help rebuild war-devastated Western Europe. That amount is equivalent to about $90 billion in today's current dollars. "For more than three years, Americans, who wanted nothing more than to throw away their ration cards, buy consumables and enjoy the peace, instead turned over as much as 3 percent of what they produced to Europe."[27] In recent years, however, foreign aid spending has declined to around $13 billion, or less than .18 percent of our gross domestic product, five times lower than it was back in the 1950s.[28]

Most foreign aid goes to a few countries the United States deems to be of strategic importance—Israel, Egypt, Bosnia, Ukraine, Jordan, India, Russia, South Africa, and Haiti. But much of what constitutes foreign aid is actually spent in the United States, where it pays for the purchase of American services and products being sent to those countries. It thus amounts to a hefty subsidy for American companies and their employees.

Ever since the United States began giving serious amounts of foreign aid after World War II, many Americans and members of Congress have opposed it. Few powerful interest groups or constituencies back foreign aid initiatives. State department officials are invariably the biggest advocates of foreign aid. Presidents also recognize the vital role foreign aid plays in advancing U.S. interests, so presidents keep asking Congress for funds for foreign aid. Successive presidents have all wanted to maintain the leverage with key countries that economic and military assistance aid provides. One of the major debates today is how much economic aid the United States should provide to Russia and the republics that once constituted the Soviet Union.

Despite the assertion by presidents and their secretaries of state that foreign aid is an investment to secure our vital national interests and a peaceful future, Congress invariably trims these requests by 15 to 20 percent, saying there is too much waste. Congress doubtless is responding to polls that indicate at least three-quarters of the general public feels the United States spends too much on foreign aid. The average citizen mistakenly believes we spend five times or more on foreign aid than we do.[29]

Economic Sanctions

The United States has frequently practiced the art of economic pressure in response to a nation's unwillingness to abide by what we perceive to be international law or proper relations. **Economic sanctions** entail a denial of export, import, or financial relations with a target country in an effort to change that nation's policies. Economic sanctions imposed on South Africa helped in encouraging democracy in that nation. But sanctions imposed on Iraq and Cuba have not had much effect on dislodging Saddam Hussein or Fidel Castro. The United States imposed some economic sanctions on India and Pakistan in 1998 when both nations began a round of nuclear testing, but because of economic distress both in Pakistan and among U.S. wheat growers, Congress and President Clinton lifted many of these economic sanctions within months of imposing them.

The United States has imposed stringent economic sanctions on Burma because of a repressive military regime that refuses to hold meaningful talks with the democratic opposition led by Nobel Peace Prize winner Aung San Suu Kyi. Burma, with its government's connivance or neglect, has become the world's leading source of heroin and that region's worst area for AIDS.

economic sanctions
A denial of export, import, or financial relations with a target country in an effort to change that nation's policies.

"Political change is essential if Burma is to transform itself into a source of stability in Southeast Asia. Sanctions may well work," says Secretary of State Madeleine Albright. "Having driven the economy into the ground, the regime desperately needs foreign investment, loans, and aid. By denying these benefits—and encouraging others to do the same—we may eventually persuade Burmese leaders to rethink where their own best interests lie."[30]

The popularity of economic sanctions has waxed and waned over the years, yet it can be a potentially important weapon in the arsenal of diplomatic and foreign policy strategies. "Economic sanctions often emerge as the centerpiece when a balance is needed between actions that seem too soft or too strident. In these situations, sanctions are seldom regarded as the 'ideal' weapon; rather they are seen as the 'least bad' alternative."[31]

Sanctions are unpopular among farmers or corporations that have to sacrifice part of their overseas markets to comply with government controls. Indeed, business and farm lobbyists try to convince Congress and the White House that unilateral embargoes hurt our economy and produce unwanted results more often than desired ones.

No nation has employed sanctions as often as the United States has—more than 100 times in the twentieth century. Sanctions rarely work as effectively as intended. Brookings Institution scholar Richard Haass claims, "sanctions have caused humanitarian suffering (Haiti), weakened friendly governments (Bosnia), bolstered tyrants (Cuba), and left countries with little choice but to develop nuclear weapons (Pakistan)."[32] They can also be costly to U.S. businesses and U.S. workers.

Senator Richard Lugar (R.-Ind.) believes sanctions seldom work unless they are multilateral, as opposed to being imposed by the United States alone.[33] Scholars suggest when dealing with authoritarian regimes, the United States should direct sanctions at rulers, not the populace at large. "Iraqis are not our enemies. Nor are the Cubans," writes Gary Hufbauer. "Where the president imposes comprehensive sanctions on an authoritarian regime, he should view those sanctions as a prelude to the exercise of military force, not as a substitute for force. Unless we are prepared to remove bad governments with military force, we have no business heaping prolonged punishment on innocent people."[34]

Political Coercion

When relations between nations become especially strained, diplomatic relations are sometimes broken as a means of political coercion. When the United States breaks diplomatic ties, it greatly restricts tourist and business travel to a country and, in effect, curbs political as well as certain economic relations with a nation. The consequences are thus more than merely symbolic.

Breaking off diplomatic relations, however, is a next-to-last resort (force is the last resort), for such action undermines the ability to reason with a nation's leaders or to use other diplomatic strategies to resolve conflicts. The act also undermines our ability to get valuable information about what is going on in a nation and to have a presence in that nation.

Covert Operations

Covert activities are planned and executed to conceal the identity of the sponsor. U.S. support for the shah of Iran and the overthrow of the government in Guatemala in the 1950s are examples. During the cold war years, several presidents authorized covert operations in Vietnam and Central America. But covert activities in Cuba, Chile, and elsewhere have backfired, and support for this strategy has cooled in the post–cold war era.[35]

Military Intervention

War, it is said, is not merely an extension of diplomacy; it is also a total breakdown of diplomacy. The United States has intervened militarily in other nations on the average of almost once a year since 1789, although usually in relatively minor or short-term episodes, such as Ronald Reagan's use of troops in Grenada, George

Thinking it Through...

There have always been Americans who wanted to "go it alone." And there are quite a number, perhaps a majority in the U.S. Congress, who want to emasculate U.N. peacekeeping missions and end U.N.-sponsored conferences on major social and scientific issues.

Critics point out that the United Nations is neither more wise nor more farsighted than the governments that constitute it, and thus is subject to the same kind of waste, inefficiency, and abuse.

Former Secretary of State Warren Christopher believes the U.N. is indispensable as an ally in most aspects of our foreign policy. But he warns that because of the U.S. dues delinquencies, "the U.N. is hobbled in doing tasks of great importance to our interests—in peacekeeping, in refugee operations, in human rights, in world health, to take only a few examples."* Christopher says we face stark choices: We can meet global challenges through the U.N., where we can share the burden with 185 nations, or we can attempt to go it alone, forcing U.S. soldiers to take all the risks and U.S. taxpayers to foot all the bills. The latter will strike most people as not much of a choice.

Defenders of the United Nations claim that the United States has a complete veto over anything the organization does, so it is nonsense to say this country puts the U.N.'s interests ahead of our own.

*Warren Christopher, *In the Stream of History: Shaping Foreign Policy for a New Era* (Stanford University Press, 1998), p. 535.

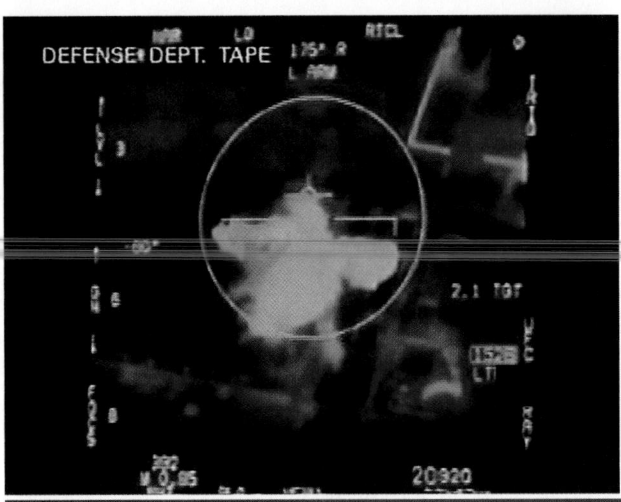

Secretary of Defense William Cohen and General Henry Hugh Shelton describe the bombing of Iraq in December 1998 to force Saddam Hussein to cooperate in eliminating his weapons of mass destruction.

Bush's invasion of Panama in 1989, Bill Clinton's peaceful invasion of Haiti in 1994, and NATO's military activities in Bosnia and Serbia. Of course, these may not be considered minor events by the target nations or by the American families who lost sons in these forays.

Intervention with force is plainly the ultimate strategy—the last resort—in trying to resolve a conflict. Military action by the United States is most successful when it involves small and even medium-sized countries (Grenada, Panama, and Kuwait). But military intervention "often proves ineffective in the context of national civil wars (the United States in Vietnam; Israel in Lebanon)."[36] Lessons from past interventions are one reason Americans were reluctant, if not opposed, to U.S. military intervention in Haiti, Bosnia, and Kosovo.

The United Nations

The United States belongs to the 185-nation United Nations and is a member of at least 200 other international organizations. The United Nations was set up in 1945 by the victors of World War II. Its main goal was to promote peace. But when the two superpowers—the United States and the former Soviet Union—became major military rivals, the United Nations was less able to achieve its central objectives.

Kofi Annan, secretary general of the United Nations.

For most of its first 45 years, the United Nations earned a reputation for ineffectiveness. Critics contend it either ducked or was politically unable to tackle crucial global issues. During much of that time, the U.N. General Assembly, dominated by a combination of Third World and communist nations, was hostile to many U.S. interests. The General Assembly often became a talk shop, passing vague resolutions. But when the cold war ended, the five permanent members of the U.N. Security Council—the United States, China, Russia (which replaced the Soviet Union), Britain, and France—usually worked in harmony. Moreover, the U.N.'s assumption of responsibilities in the Persian Gulf War and its extensive peacekeeping missions in Cyprus and Lebanon won it respect. U.N. efforts in Cambodia and Somalia were less successful.

Blue-helmeted U.N. peacekeeping forces are now monitoring cease-fires, elections, and human rights in several areas. These efforts are costly, and the United Nations constantly finds itself pleading with leading nations such as the United States to underwrite the costs of these peace initiatives. Some of the U.N.'s peacekeeping missions are popular, yet as these efforts increase in number and in cost, the negotiations to raise funds for this new international peace army get harder.

Some conservatives have long been skeptical of U.S. involvement in the United Nations, fearing that the United States risks being trapped or outvoted. Critics across the ideological spectrum question whether it makes sense to give every U.N. member an equal vote in the General Assembly, regardless of its size, population, and contribution to the U.N. budget. Critics also worry about creating a standing U.N. army with a large contingent of U.S. troops under foreign command. Some U.S. officials call this current system "taxation without representation." Critics also continue to question the efficiency of the organization's bureaucracy. Table 20-2 compares public attitudes toward the United Nations in 1996 and 1998.

TABLE 20-2 Assessing the United Nations

In general, do you think the United Nations is doing a good job or a poor job in trying to solve the problems it has had to face?

	1996	1998
Good job	49%	60%
Poor job	38	37
Don't know/Refused to answer	13	3

SOURCE: The Roper Center, University of Connecticut, August 1998.

Conservatives insist Congress needs to have a greater say in how the United Nations uses taxpayers' dollars and puts our soldiers' lives at risk. "When the U.N. Security Council votes," said former senator and Republican presidential candidate Bob Dole, "American taxpayers should grab their wallets. Once the council approves a peacekeeping operation, the United States is obligated to pay nearly one-third of the cost."[37] Several members of Congress have introduced legislation that would bar U.S. forces from any standing U.N. army and prohibit U.S. troops from serving under foreign command in U.N. operations. Some critics on both the left and right suggest that the United Nations should be allowed to wither away into irrelevance.[38]

The United Nations has certainly disappointed many of the grander hopes of its ardent founders, who dreamed it would help end all international conflicts. The United States, which is assessed 25 percent of the organization's annual budget, is almost always delinquent in its payment. "The U.N.," said President Clinton, "must be able to show that the money it receives supports saving and enriching people's lives, not unneeded overhead."[39] With mixed success, Clinton worked with Congress to get the United States to pay most of its back dues assessments. And the United Nations under Kofi Annan significantly reduced its budgets, staff, and peacekeeping operations.

When Secretary of State Madeleine Albright was U.S. ambassador to the United Nations, she defended our U.N. dues and peacekeeping expenses: "When the United States intervenes alone, we pay all of the costs and run all of the risks. When the U.N. acts, we pay one-fourth of the costs, and others provide the vast majority of troops." Our annual U.N. bills, she pointed out, are about equal to the annualized cost of a single aircraft carrier battle group.[40]

National Security and Defense

The United States has a long history of involvement in world affairs, often by means of military intervention. We have formally declared war by an act of Congress on only five occasions. Although the 1991 Persian Gulf War was not declared formally, Congress, in effect, declared war when it authorized the use of troops to repel Iraq. But we have intervened with military forces on about 190 occasions. "Since 1945 more than 100,000 U.S. military personnel have died in undeclared wars; more than 400,000 have suffered battle injuries."[41] Military intervention is likely to continue. In this new post–cold war era, "We are the ones who can deter," says General Colin Powell, former chair of the Joint Chiefs of Staff. "We have the overwhelming power, and we have demonstrated the willingness to use it."[42]

Some Americans are concerned the United States will use its military clout unwisely or irresponsibly. Some believe we should resist the temptation to send our military into regional conflicts around the world when other means are available to

The Pentagon, headquarters for the Defense Department, is the world's largest building. It has 20 miles of corridors and houses nearly 25,000 workers, who tell time by 4,200 clocks, drink water from 685 fountains, consume 30,000 cups of coffee daily, and place 200,000 calls a day on 87,000 phones connected by 100,000 miles of cable.

achieve our objectives.[43] And there is probably widespread agreement that we should not intervene in conflicts unless the action is backed by a broad public consensus at home and an alliance of nations abroad. Still, virtually all Americans say it would be a grave mistake to forsake our leadership position and abandon our friends and allies at this time of global change.

Civilian Control over the Military

One of the bedrock principles of our constitutional democracy is that a civilian, the president of the United States, is the commander in chief. Members of the military have freedom of speech, yet to ensure civilian supremacy, commissioned officers who use "contemptuous words" against a president are subject to punishment. When a popular World War II hero, General Douglas MacArthur, challenged President Harry Truman's decisions, MacArthur was removed from his command in Korea. When a two-star general made rude and critical remarks about President Bill Clinton in a speech, he was fined $7,000 and retired from the service. And military leaders, in the aftermath of the Clinton–Monica Lewinsky affair, took the unusual step of warning military personnel that they could face punishment for speaking "contemptuous words" against the president.[44]

Defense Organization

The president, Congress, the National Security Council, the State Department, and the Defense Department make overall defense policy and attempt to integrate U.S. national security programs. But the day-to-day work of organizing for defense is the job of the Defense Department. Its headquarters, the Pentagon, houses within its miles of corridors 25,000 top military and civilian personnel. The offices of several hundred generals and admirals are there, as is the office of the secretary of defense, who provides civilian control of the armed services.

A major issue in recent decades has been how to organize the Department of Defense to ensure that it can provide both strategic vision and practical coordination among the military services. Prior to 1947 there were two separate military departments, War and Navy. The difficulty of coordinating them during World War II led to demands for unification. In 1947 the Air Force, already an autonomous unit within the War Department, was made an independent department, and all three military departments—Army, Navy, and Air Force—were placed under the general supervision of the secretary of defense. The Unification Act of 1947 was a bundle of compromises between the Army, which favored a tightly integrated department, and the Navy, which wanted a loosely federated structure, but the act at least brought the military services under a common organizational chart.

The Joint Chiefs of Staff (JCS) serves as the principal military adviser to the president, the National Security Council, and the secretary of defense. It includes the heads of the three armed services, plus the commandant of the Marine Corps, the chair, and the vice-chair. All the service chiefs are appointed by the president with the consent of the Senate for four-year, nonrenewable terms. The chair of the JCS, a top-ranking military officer from one of the three services or the Marine Corps, is appointed by the president with the consent of the Senate for a two-year term that may be renewed once. Note that their short two-year term is part of the process of ensuring civilian control over the military.

Before 1986 the members of the Joint Chiefs of Staff were, collectively, very powerful. They advised the president and the secretary of defense. Because they functioned as a committee and could not act until unanimous agreement was reached, however, they often produced overly broad decisions. Critics, therefore, viewed much of the work of the Joint Chiefs as wasteful and even dangerous.

The Department of Defense Reorganization Act of 1986 shifted considerable power to the chair. Reporting through the secretary of defense, the chair now advises the president on military matters, exercises authority over the forces in the field, and is responsible for overall military planning. In theory, the chair of the Joint Chiefs can even make a military decision that the chiefs of the other services oppose. On paper at least, these other chiefs now serve the chair merely as advisers, and even the chair's deputy, the vice-chair, outranks the other service chiefs. The chair has a mandate to encourage "jointness" in military education and in other spheres to integrate the services for maximum effectiveness. Disputes still continue, but the chair is now much stronger than was previously the case. The chair of the Joint Chiefs in the 1990s is the most powerful peacetime military officer in U.S. history. The Reorganization Act also

WE THE PEOPLE

Kelly Flinn, Bomber Pilot

Kelly Flinn, a graduate of the Air Force Academy, made history twice in her life. In 1995 she became the nation's first female B-52 bomber pilot. The following year, Flinn began a relationship with a man who told her he was legally separated from his wife. She fell in love with him. She was accused of fraternization, adultery, lying about the affair to investigators, disobeying an order to end the affair, and conduct unbecoming an officer.

Air Force Secretary Sheila Widnall agreed to grant Flinn a general discharge, allowing her to leave the service without facing a court martial. "Although it is the adultery charge that has received the greatest public focus, it is the allegations of lack of integrity and disobedience to order that have been of principal concern to the Air Force," Widnall said. "It is primarily those allegations that made an honorable discharge unacceptable."

Flinn plans to appeal her discharge and hopes to rejoin the military. "I'd love to put on a uniform and serve my country again," Flinn said in an interview on "Larry King Live." She did not rule out becoming a pilot for a commercial airline if she were unable to resume her military career.

SOURCE: "Air Force Gives Pilot a General Discharge" (cnn.com/9705/flinn/index/htm).

strengthened the powers of the theater commanders who actually command forces in various parts of the world.

It is critical to appreciate, however, that the chair of the Joint Chiefs is not the head of the military. The chair and the JCS are *advisers* to the secretary of defense and the president, but the president can, and has on occasion, disregarded their advice. A president must weigh military action or inaction against the larger foreign and security interests of the nation.

The Confederational Nature of the Defense Bureaucracy

It is common to hear criticisms of the "Pentagon machine" or the "national military establishment." The defense bureaucracy is, however, best understood—as is any bureaucracy—as something less than a monolith. Insiders often stress that this policy-making structure is best thought of as a *confederation*, or bargaining arena, as opposed to a tight chain-of-command hierarchy. In fact, in recent years strong sentiment has emerged for more centralized control and direction of the nation's defense bureaucracy.

Disputes among military services involve more than professional jealousies. The technological revolution in warfare has rendered obsolete many concepts about military missions, thereby threatening the traditional roles of some of the services. In the past it made sense to divide command among land, sea, and air forces. Today defense research and development are constantly altering formerly established roles and missions, yet the individual services are reluctant to give up their traditional functions or to serve each other's crucial needs. The Navy, for example, is interested in waging sea warfare, not in running a freight service for the Army. Interservice rivalries erupt when the Army and Air Force quarrel over who should provide air support for ground troops. Each branch also supports weapons that bring it prestige. The Air Force and Navy dispute, for example, the effectiveness of land-based versus sea-based missiles.

Whether strategic policies are worked out within the Defense Department, the White House, or Congress, the decisions result from a political process in which some measure of consensus is essential. The Joint Chiefs engage in the same type of vote trading used in Congress. On budget issues the chiefs often endorse all the programs desired by each service. When forced to choose on an issue of policy, the chiefs have traditionally compromised among the different service positions rather than attempt to develop a position based on a unified military point of view.

The Draft

Military conscription (the draft) was first instituted by the Confederacy in 1862 and by the Union in 1863 during the Civil War. It was used during World War I, when Congress passed the Selective Service Act. This act called for a draft of males between the ages of 21 and 30, with exemptions for certain public officials and for clergy. In both instances, conscription ended when the conflicts ended. The first peacetime draft began in 1940, with the Selective Service Training Act. By the time of Pearl Harbor in late 1941, men between the ages of 18 and 35 were eligible for the draft. When World War II ended, the draft continued in various forms for almost three decades. Soon after the Vietnam War, the all-volunteer force (AVF) was established by Congress. This force was charged with providing for our peacetime military personnel needs; in time of war, a draft could be reinstituted.

Women in the Military and in Combat

Women constitute 14 percent of the total enlistment in the armed forces; 6 percent of our forces in the Persian Gulf War were female, and 10 percent of the U.S. troops serving in the NATO mission to implement the Dayton peace accord in Bosnia were also women.[45] The women in Operation Desert Storm piloted troop transport and supply aircraft, helped to operate Patriot antimissile sys-

Women now make up 14 percent of the total enlistment in the armed forces.

tems, and worked as tank mechanics and military police guarding Iraqi prisoners of war.

Congress has lifted any legal restrictions on Air Force and Navy women becoming combat pilots, and the Pentagon, after prodding by the Clinton administration, has now opened thousands of combat-related positions in the military services for women. The military is redesigning its assignments to ensure that equal opportunity exists within its ranks.

A majority of Americans think women should be assigned to ground combat units, but others are still concerned about women in combat situations. According to reports from the Persian Gulf War, few women who served in combat support units recommended the experience. Similarly, many women in the military have said that while they would like to have the right to serve in combat positions, most of them would not opt for these roles.

The difficulty in deciding whether women should participate in combat often comes in defining what is combat. Women working in support units in the Panama conflict of 1989 engaged in fighting. "I find it very difficult to separate this from other jobs where women are at risk, on police and fire departments, as truck drivers," says retired Air Force General Wilma Vaught.[46]

Despite their accomplishments, women in the armed forces have faced countless problems, including sexual harassment and rape, and women officers have complained of men refusing to take orders from them and giving them inappropriate assignments. Female Navy combat pilots complain about "the silent treatment" and gender prejudice.[47] Still, women are generally winning acceptance in the military at all levels and will continue to play increasingly significant roles in virtually all aspects of the armed forces. And just as we have had women ambassadors to the United Nations and a woman secretary of state, some day there will probably be a woman chair of the Joint Chiefs of Staff or a woman secretary of defense.

The Politics of Defense Spending

The U.S. defense budget is over $270 billion a year. Over half the people employed by the national government work in the Defense Department. About three-quarters of federal purchases of goods and services originate in the defense budget; several thousand defense installations are scattered across the country. Contracts in excess of $100 billion result in defense-related civilian employment of nearly 2 million workers. More than 1.5 million retired Defense

Pentagon-Style Pork

A new beneficiary of federal defense spending is a small Illinois company that produces neither weapons nor widgets. It makes chewing gum. "Stay Alert" is a caffeinated gum so potent each stick supposedly packs the power of a hearty cup of coffee. Why is the military interested? Well, it seems the gum could be an aid in energizing sleep-deprived troops.

So goes the reasoning from the office of Republican Representative J. Dennis Hastert (elected Speaker of the House of Representatives in 1999), who at the last minute quietly slipped in $250,000 in research funds to study the potential uses of Stay Alert. It is one of at least 30 items that appear in the fine print of the defense spending bill Congress sent to President Clinton in 1998.

It turns out that Stay Alert is produced by Amurol Confections Company of Yorkville, Illinois—Hastert's hometown. Hastert spokesman Pete Jeffries says the allocation was added late because Amurol officials didn't approach the congressman until the House defense appropriation had already passed. He says the Army enthusiastically backed the addition. For the company's part, "We were thrilled," said Amurol official Janet Sweeney. "We didn't have the money in our budget for this kind of research."

SOURCE: Charles R. Babcock, "Some Last Minute Pork to Chew On," *The Washington Post Weekly Edition*, October 19, 1998, p. 32.

Department personnel draw pensions and other fringe benefits. The defense budget also includes about $12 billion dedicated to nuclear weapons research and maintenance and environmental cleanup that actually is run by the Department of Energy.

Reflecting the end of the cold war, the demise of the Soviet Union, and the lack of support for maintaining defense spending at the 1980s level, defense spending has decreased over the past decade. Weapons systems have been canceled or postponed, bases closed, ships retired, and large numbers of troops brought home from Germany, the Philippines, and elsewhere. A number of major weapons systems whose primary justification was to fight the former Soviet Union have been canceled or their production greatly curtailed in the past few years. All the services have lost personnel. The Army was cut over 30 percent, and the National Guard and the military reserve have been cut back about 25 percent.

By the year 2000, defense spending will represent about 15.5 percent of the federal budget, where 20 years earlier it averaged about 25 percent of federal spending. Most analysts believe downsizing has been achieved without weakening the nation's national security interests. Defense spending "remains sufficient to leave the United States the world's only global military power and permit it to deter conflict and instability in several key overseas theaters at once."[48] The United States spends more on defense than all of our NATO allies, Japan, Israel, and South Korea combined. Further, the United States spends more on defense than all of its declared or potential adversaries combined.

President Clinton defended his defense spending cuts and insisted we have maintained the necessary strength. But he also added: "We can't be the world's policeman. We can't be everywhere. We can't do everything. But we can make a difference, and when it is consistent with our values and our interests, we have to try."[49] Public opinion on defense spending is divided (see Table 20-3).

It is no secret in Washington, however, that the Pentagon's top military brass would like to see Congress appropriate significantly more funds for new

TABLE 20-3 Public Opinion and Defense Spending

Question: Is the U.S. spending too much, about right, or too little on defense?

Year	Too Much	About Right	Too Little	No Opinion
1998	22%	45%	26%	7%
1995	42	40	15	3
1993	42	38	17	3
1991	50	36	10	4
1989	49	37	11	3
1987	44	36	14	6
1986	47	36	13	4
1980	14	24	49	13
1976	36	32	22	10
1974	44	32	12	12
1971	49	31	11	9
1969	52	31	8	9

SOURCE: The Gallup Organization, November 1998.

THE "DON'T ASK, DON'T TELL" CONTROVERSY

Controversy persists over whether the military has the right to expel homosexuals because of their sexual orientation. In the mid-1990s, the U.S. military expelled about 1,000 men and women every year because of sexual preference. The Pentagon defended the ban by saying that homosexuals in a military setting create difficulty because there is no privacy, no choice of association or living quarters, and no provision for those who prefer gay and lesbian lifestyles.

Many leaders in Congress and elsewhere criticized the ban, calling it the final bastion of discrimination in the military and saying it reminded them of the army's former official opposition to African Americans in uniform. Bill Clinton called for a complete end to the ban when he campaigned for his first term as president. Once in office, however, he had to settle for a compromise that merely modified the ban. Under a "don't ask, don't tell" policy, military officials are now not permitted to question recruits about their sexual orientation, and gays and lesbians are required to refrain from sexual practices while on duty or assignments. Those who commit homosexual acts are still subject to discharge.

Even after the Clinton compromise was implemented, harassment of gays was common. Some commanders continue to ask, and under duress, some soldiers continue to tell. In fact, the "military is discharging 67 percent more gay and lesbian troops today than when the Clinton administration adopted its 'don't ask, don't tell' policy," according to a Defense Department study. Critics claim this policy may well be as bad, or even worse, than the previous policy. It has created a world of fear and deceit among gays and their friends.[*]

Gay and homosexual groups have turned to the courts to try to get the new Clinton-era regulations overruled as unconstitutional. Some U.S. district courts have ruled that the military may not discharge a person simply because of declared sexual orientation. Various federal court rulings have upheld the regulations set by the Clinton White House, saying they were properly based on a law enacted by Congress and that courts are traditionally obligated to defer to the other branches of government, especially when the matter involves military policy.[**]

The U.S. Supreme Court has never ruled definitely on the "don't ask, don't tell" policy. But several federal appeals courts have upheld the policy, and the Supreme Court has on several occasions rejected a challenge to the policy.[†]

Americans are divided over this issue. Many conservatives would like an unambiguous rejection of gays in the military. However, as former Republican presidential candidate Barry Goldwater said, "You don't need to be 'straight' to fight and die for your country. You just need to shoot straight."[††]

[*] Tim Weiner, "Military Discharges of Homosexuals Soar," *The New York Times*, April 7, 1998, p. A21; Andrew Sullivan, "Undone by 'Don't Ask, Don't Tell,'" *The New York Times*, April 9, 1998, p. A22.

[**] See Neil A. Lewis, "Court Upholds Clinton Policy on Gay Troops," *New York Times*, April 6, 1996, pp. 1, 7.

[†] Richard Carelli, "'Don't Ask, Don't Tell' Survives First Test in Supreme Court," *U.S.A. Today*, October 20, 1998, p. 4A.

[††] Barry M. Goldwater, "The Gay Ban: Just Plain Un-American," *The Washington Post National Weekly Edition*, June 21–27, 1993, p. 28.

Keith Meinhold, who was discharged after he announced he was gay, reenlists in the Navy. The officer administering the oath, Zoe Dunning, is a lesbian who, like Meinhold, is fighting efforts to discharge her.

Some Key Foreign Policy Strategies

- *Internationalism*: A foreign policy that recognizes that concern for trade, human rights, and international peace requires not only a strong military but also the willingness to intervene where U.S. vital interests are at stake. The goal is to create an international order consistent with American values.
- *Isolationism*: A foreign policy that curtails U.S. military aid and intervention abroad as much as possible. It was the dominant policy in this country during the nineteenth century and to some degree in the 1920s and 1930s. It was put forward again by Pat Buchanan during the 1996 presidential primaries.
- *Realpolitik*: A foreign policy based on practical and self-interest factors rather than on moral, idealistic, or theoretical considerations. Realists say the United States should intervene in world affairs only if its vital interests are in jeopardy or if a dispute involves overt outside aggression, not simply internal rebellion.
- *Containment*: A foreign policy aimed at halting the spread of communism, especially the influence of the former Soviet Union. This was the underlying foreign and national security policy of the United States between 1947 and 1990.
- *New World Order*: A vague and often confusing label pinned on the post-cold war period—one in which the United States presumably plays a vital role as the only remaining superpower in preserving peace and encouraging economic and human rights throughout the world.

weapons systems, new ships, and new technologies. The 1990s saw constant U.S. involvement in international peacekeeping and humanitarian relief operations that military officials believe strained the military's resources. Some in the military view such tasks as "peripheral" or diversionary from the Pentagon's main mission, yet in today's world, these peacekeeping activities are viewed by many other people as a primary mission.

The Army always wants more tanks, the Air Force wants more planes, and the Navy always likes more carriers and submarines. And Republicans continue to lobby for an extensive missile defense system. But the one area where the Pentagon needs more money is for pay raises. Military pay is 13 percent lower than comparable private-sector wages, and recruiting and retaining qualified troops has become a vital necessity.[50]

Resistance to Making Cuts

One of the problems with cutting defense spending is that it immediately costs jobs in congressional districts. Weapons systems continue to be protected by members of Congress more concerned with jobs and reelection hopes than with strategic needs.[51] The B-52 Stealth bomber is a notable case in point. After 15 years of design and manufacturing, it has difficulty distinguishing a rainstorm from a mountain. The Pentagon has not asked for more of these billion-dollar planes, yet Congress often approves funds for them because cuts in weapons systems and plant closings mean not only that people in the Defense Department and on bases lose their jobs but also that local shopkeepers, bankers, lawyers, doctors, contractors, housekeepers, baby sitters—the list goes on and on—are put out of work.

Weapons are, in fact, a major American industry, and the industry and members of Congress work hard to promote its products. The agreement that operates in other pork-barrel areas works here as well: "You help me in my district, and I'll help you in yours." Even the most ardent, balance-the-budget conservatives change their tune when a contract termination hits close to their district. Similarly, vigorous antiwar doves in Congress often shout the loudest when a base closing is proposed for their home region.

This is not to say that members of Congress cast their votes on military spending solely on whether their district would profit from the decisions. An analysis of the relationships between campaign contributors and votes on weapons systems concludes that issues of defense strategy, cost, and a legislator's political philosophy are equally important.[52]

Still, the Defense Department was repeatedly frustrated in its efforts to close unneeded military bases in the United States. Influential members of Congress sometimes went to great lengths lobbying their colleagues that bases in their districts were too important to shut down. Military officials and members of Congress eventually agreed that new procedures were needed to handle congressional approval of base closings.

To thwart efforts by legislators to block closings of individual bases, Congress in 1988 set up a blue-ribbon commission to identify military bases that should be closed for budgetary reasons. At least three additional commissions have been appointed in subsequent years. These commissions are appointed by Congress and the president, but they work independently of both branches. They review the base-closing suggestions made by the Pentagon and make recommendations, which have to be accepted in toto or else be rejected by the president. If the president accepts the closings, the package then goes to Congress, where each chamber is allowed 45 days to consider the entire package. Congress also has to accept the entire package or else no closings take place.[53]

This procedure has generally succeeded. Dozens of bases have been closed or are in the process of being shut down—and the savings will run into billions of dollars. While there have been predictable grumblings from the big losers and some lawsuits, the federal courts have upheld these procedures, and more bases are being closed as we begin the twenty-first century. Many members of Congress in the late 1990s tried to delay base closings. This led Secretary of Defense William Cohen to say at least another $20 billion could have been saved in recent years if more obsolete bases could have been closed down.

deterrence
Defense policy of maintaining the ability to threaten massive retaliation on any attacking nation.

Military Strategy

After World War II, the nation's primary defense against nuclear attack was a strategy of **deterrence**, or maintaining the ability to threaten massive retaliation on any nation that attacked us. Effective deterrence is commonly measured by the strength of survivable second-strike force. Thus, the United States has maintained a large, diversified, and well-protected defense system so that a first strike by another nation would not cripple our ability to retaliate decisively. This strategy of "mutual assured destruction" (MAD) is still the core of American defense policy. Pentagon officials claim it has worked, even if it is costly. At least, they point out, it has succeeded in winning for the United States and our allies more than five decades of peace—a period twice as long as the period between World Wars I and II.

Foreign and defense policy making converge on a common list of priorities that include protecting jobs, protecting borders and energy supplies, and reducing the risk of nuclear and biochemical war. The stakes will always be high in the twenty-first century as we learn to live with the inevitable spread of nuclear weapons, as well as persistant ethnic and religious conflicts between, and sadly, within many nations.

online

Foreign Countries on the Internet

The State Department issues useful travel information, including warnings and information regarding tourist locations, passports, and visa requirements; tips for travelers to all areas of the world, such as how to contact U.S. consuls for help abroad; tips for Americans residing abroad; and business and medical information for travelers. The next time you are planning a trip overseas, be sure to check out the State Department website so you can be fully informed on current conditions and special requirements in foreign countries:

http://www.whitehouse.gov/WH/Services/Agency/dos.html

Many different interests can use this new communications tool to press their claims or deliver their demands. Governments can also use the Internet to distribute information about foreign and defense policy:

http://www.dtic.mil/defenselink

For more Internet resources on Foreign and Defense Policy, see our home page at:

http://www.prenhall.com/burns

SUMMARY

1. American foreign policy from 1945 through 1990 was shaped and at times completely dominated by relations with the superpower rival, the Soviet Union. The competition between these two military giants also dominated world politics. With the passing of the cold war have come new debates over foreign policy goals. The rise of Japan and Europe as economic powers and the increasing importance of economic and trading interests have transformed foreign policy debates as America prepares for the twenty-first century.
2. New foreign policy challenges include population growth in the face of poverty; a serious trade imbalance with Japan; the relationship of trade status to human rights violations, especially in relations with China; nuclear and biological arms control; the Chemical Weapons Convention; aid to former Soviet-bloc nations; the European Economic Union and the future of NATO; drug traffic; the degradation of the global environment; and budget issues.
3. The president has the primary responsibility to shape foreign policy. The principal foreign policy advisor is the secretary of state, although other cabinet secretaries are also influential. The National Security Council and the intelligence agencies also play key roles.
4. Presidents, Congress, and the American people all become involved in defining our vital national security interests, but they often have contradictory views. Presidents must sometimes act swiftly and decisively. Plainly, the role of the president in foreign affairs was strengthened during the cold war years as the United States developed an enormous standing military capability and an extensive intelligence network. Presidents are often in a good position to see the nation's long-term interests above the tugging of bureaucratic and special interests. But in our constitutional democracy, presidents and their advisers must consult with Congress and inform the American people. The media and special interests also play a role.
5. U.S. foreign policy interests are advanced by one or a combination of the following strategies: diplomacy, foreign aid, economic sanctions, political coercion (including the breaking off of diplomatic relations), covert action, and military intervention.
6. The United States is an active participant in numerous international organizations, especially the United Nations. The United Nations is likely to play an even greater role in the post–cold war world, even if many Americans, especially conservatives, are highly critical of the way the U.N. works. The primacy of the nation-state is not in question, yet more and more of our global policy problems will be solved through international organizations of one type or another.
7. Our system is designed to provide civilian control over the military. Although the military in any society has enormous potential for direct political involvement, this has not occurred in the United States. The president, Congress, the secretary of defense, the Joint Chiefs of Staff, and cabinet officers continually weigh national security against competing claims.
8. Although the 1990s witnessed major reductions in the size of the military and major cuts in military spending, some critics say the defense budget can be cut much further. Critics on the right, however, claim we have weakened our defense preparedness. The nature of warfare and the preventing of wars may be considerably different in the twenty-first century.

KEY TERMS

most-favored-nation status 445 **bipartisanship 504** **economic sanctions 506** **deterrence 507**

FURTHER READING

CHRISTOPHER ANDREW, *For the President's Eyes Only: Secret Intelligence and the American Presidency from Washington to Bush* (HarperCollins, 1995).

GEORGE BUSH AND BRENT SCOWCRAFT, *A World Transformed* (Knopf, 1998).

WARREN CHRISTOPHER, *In the Stream of History: Shaping Foreign Policy for a New Era* (Stanford University Press, 1998).

STEPHEN J. CIMBALA, *The Politics of Warfare: The Great Powers in the Twentieth Century* (Penn State Press, 1997).

ANGELO CODEVILLA, *Informing Statecraft: Intelligence for a New Century* (Free Press, 1992).

JOSEPH G. DAWSON III, ED., *Commanders-in-Chief: Presidential Leadership in Modern Wars* (University Press of Kansas, 1993).

LOUIS FISHER, *Presidential War Power* (University Press of Kansas, 1995).

JOHN LEWIS GADDIS, *The United States and the End of the Cold War* (Oxford University Press, 1992).

MARK D. GEARAN, ED., *At Home in the World: The Peace Corps Story* (Peace Corps, 1996).

ALLEN E. GOODMAN ET AL., *In from the Cold: Task Force on the Future of U.S. Intelligence* (Twentieth Century Fund, 1996).

RICHARD N. HAASS, *The Reluctant Sheriff: The United States After the Cold War* (Council on Foreign Relations, 1997).

OLE HOLSTI, *Public Opinion and American Foreign Policy* (University of Michigan Press, 1996).

SAMUEL HUNTINGTON, *The Clash of Civilization and the Remaking of World Order* (Simon & Schuster, 1996).

RHODRI JEFFREYS-JONES, *The CIA and American Democracy*, 2d ed. (Yale University Press, 1998).

LOCH K. JOHNSON, *Secret Agencies: U.S. Intelligence in a Hostile World* (Yale University Press, 1996).

HENRY KISSINGER, *Diplomacy* (Simon & Schuster, 1994).

HAROLD HONGJU KOH, *The National Security Constitution: Sharing Power After the Iran-Contra Affair* (Yale University Press, 1990).

MARY LOCKE AND CASIMIR A. YOST, EDS., *Who Needs Embassies? How U.S. Missions Abroad Help Shape Our World* (Georgetown University School of Foreign Policy, 1997).

KENNETH R. MAYER, *The Political Economy of Defense Contracting* (Yale University Press, 1991).

ROBERT S. MCNAMARA, *In Retrospect: The Tragedy and Lessons of Vietnam* (Times Books, 1995).

CHARLES C. MOSKOS AND JOHN SIBLEY BUTLER, *All That We Can Be: Black Leadership and Racial Integration the Army Way* (Twentieth Century Fund, 1996).

DANIEL PATRICK MOYNIHAN, *Secrecy: The American Experience* (Yale University Press, 1998).

JOHN PRADOS, *Keepers of the Keys: A History of the National Security Council from Truman to Bush* (William Morrow, 1991).

ROSEMARY RIGHTER, *Utopia Lost: The United Nations and World Order* (Twentieth Century Fund, 1995).

CRAIG A. RIMMERMAN, *Gay Rights, Military Wrongs: Political Perspectives on Lesbians and Gays in the Military* (Garland Publishing, 1996).

JOSEPH ROMM, *Defining National Security: The Nonmilitary Aspect* (Council on Foreign Relations, 1993).

JAMES N. ROSENAU, *The United Nations in a Turbulent World* (Lynne Rienner, 1992).

HENRY SHUE, *Basic Rights: Subsistence, Affluence and U.S. Foreign Policy*, 2d ed. (Princeton University Press, 1996).

GEORGE SHULTZ, *Turmoil and Triumph: My Years as Secretary of State* (Scribner's, 1993).

RONALD STEEL, *Temptations of a Superpower* (Harvard University Press, 1995).

ROBERT W. TUCKER AND DAVID C. HENDRICKSON, *The Imperial Temptation: The New World Order and America's Purpose* (Council on Foreign Relations, 1992).

STEPHEN R. WEISSMAN, *A Culture of Deference: Congress's Failure of Leadership in Foreign Affairs* (Basic Books, 1995).

BOB WOODWARD, *The Commanders* (Simon & Schuster, 1991).

THE
DEMOCRATIC
FAITH

21

CHAPTER OUTLINE

- The Case for Government by the People
- Participation and Representation
- The Role of the Politician
- Leadership for a Constitutional Democracy
- Reconciling Democracy and Leadership
- The Democratic Faith

AMERICA'S FOUNDING GENERATION FOUGHT A REVOLUTION TO SECURE THEIR RIGHTS AND LIBERTY. THEN THEY FACED THE CHALLENGE OF CREATING A GOVERNMENT, writing a Constitution, and drafting a Bill of Rights that would protect the rights to life, liberty, and self-government for themselves and for those who would come later. But they knew, as we also know, that passive allegiance to ideas and rights is never enough. Every generation must see itself as having a duty to nurture these ideals by actively renewing the community and government of which it is a part.

The framers knew about the rise and decline of ancient Athens. Athens had flourished as a shining beacon of what a civilized city might be, but it foundered when greed, self-centeredness, and smugness set in. As time went on, the Athenians wanted security more than they wanted liberty; they wanted comfort more than they wanted freedom. In the end they lost it all—security, comfort, and freedom. "Responsibility was the price every man must pay for freedom. It was to be had on no other terms."[1]

If we are to be citizens of the United States in the truest meaning of the term, our dreams must transcend personal ambition and the accumulation of material goods. Our country needs citizens who understand that our well-being is tied to the well-being of neighbors, community, country, and world.

As democracy movements around the world gain strength and formerly totalitarian governments topple, we Americans are reminded of our democratic roots. Over the past generation, black South Africans, Chinese students, Polish Solidarity members, Bosnian Muslims, Russian communists, and Kosovo Albanians have been willing to protest, fight, and even die for the democratic values Thomas Jefferson emphasized in the Declaration of Independence. We have been delighted by the success of most of these movements, but we have also been saddened by the setbacks many of them have encountered. Translating democratic values into a working democratic government is difficult. We in the United States gain renewed appreciation for our system of constitutional democracy as we watch these new republics struggle with social and economic divisions, federalism, the lack of an effective party system, and a poorly developed free press.

Our theme in this last chapter is simple: elected leadership and constitutional structures and protections are important, but an active, committed citizenry is equally important. Freedom and obligation go together. Liberty and duty go together. The answer to a nation's problems lies not in producing a perfect

Willing to Die

During my lifetime I have dedicated myself to this struggle of the African people. I have fought against white domination, and I have fought against black domination. I have cherished the ideal of a democratic and free society in which all persons live together in harmony and with equal opportunities. It is an ideal I hope to live for and to achieve. But if needs be, it is an ideal for which I am prepared to die.

Nelson Mandela,
Statement at the Rivonia Trial, 1964

constitution or a few larger-than-life leaders. The answer lies in educating a nation of citizen-leaders who will, regardless of their professional and private ambitions, care about the concerns of the Republic and strive to make democracy work.

The Case for Government by the People

More than any other form of government, the kind of democracy that has emerged under our Constitution requires a certain kind of faith—and a certain kind of skepticism. It requires faith concerning our common human enterprise, a belief that if the people are informed and caring, they can be trusted with their own self-government, and an optimism that when things begin to go wrong, the people can be relied upon to set them right. But a healthy skepticism is needed as well. Democracy requires us to question our leaders and leadership institutions and never trust any group with too much power. Although we prize majority rule, we must always be skeptical enough to ask whether the majority is right.

Constitutional democracy requires us to be constantly concerned about whether we really tolerate and protect the rights and opinions of others and whether democratic processes are in fact serving the principles of liberty, equality, and justice. In short, the democratic faith rests upon a peculiar blend of faith in the people and skepticism of them.

Thomas Jefferson, one of our best-known champions of the democratic faith, believed in the common sense of the people and in the flowering of the human spirit. Jefferson believed deeply that every government degenerates when it is trusted to its rulers alone. The people themselves, he wrote, are the only safe repositories of government. His was a robust commitment to popular control, to representative processes, and to accountable leadership. But he was no believer in the simple participatory democracy of ancient Greece or revolutionary France. The people, too, must have their power checked and balanced.

Our founders set up a government based on the consent of the governed. Our Bill of Rights specifically denies government authorities the right to coerce that consent. Indeed, as Justice Robert H. Jackson wrote in a 1943 Supreme Court decision, "Authority here is to be controlled by public opinion, not public opinion by authority." Jackson added, "If there is any fixed star in our constitutional constellation, it is that no official, high or petty, can prescribe what shall be orthodox in politics, nationalism, religion, or other matters of opinion or force citizens to confess by word or act their faith therein."[2]

The essence of our Constitution is that it both grants power to and withholds power from the national government. Fearing national weakness and popular disorder, the framers wanted to grant the government only enough power to do its basic jobs, such as maintaining national defense and providing financial stability. Valuing above all the principle of individual liberty, the framers wanted to protect the people from too much government. They wanted a limited government—yet one that would work. The solution was to make government responsive to the people, but at the same time insulate the government from momentary and passionate majorities.

We want a government that is efficient and effective but also caring. We want to maintain our commitment to liberty and freedom. We want a government that acts for the majority yet also protects minorities. We want to safeguard our nation and our streets in a world full of change and violence. We want to protect the rights of the poor, the elderly, and minorities. Do we expect too much from government? Of course we do.

Participation and Representation

In essence, the challenge to the future of democracy is whether we can make our representative process work better. For one thing, representation is impossible in the literal sense. Every man and woman has a host of conflicting desires, fears, hopes, and expectations, and no government can represent them all. But even if millions of voters could be represented in their many interests, the question of how they would be represented would remain. Through direct representation, such as a New England town meeting or ballot initiatives and referenda? Through economic or professional associations, such as labor unions or political action committees? Through a coalition of minority groups? All these and other alternatives can be defended as proper forms of representation in a constitutional democracy.

This participant in a Black Voter Awareness Rally in Austin, Texas, urges citizens to accept responsibility for perpetuating democracy.

If we must have representatives, who shall represent whom? Although this question can be answered in countless ways, in practice there are two basic ways to organize representation. By electing representatives in a multitude of districts, it is possible to build into representative institutions—the U.S. Congress, for example—most minority interests and attitudes. The other way is through an election system that emphasizes majority representation. This system can be achieved by creating a nationwide electorate that elects one representative (the American president, for example) or by developing a strong two-party system that knits all the local constituencies into coalitions that can elect and sustain national majorities. A nation does not have to choose between these alternatives. It can have both, as we do in the United States.

Which is better: a government that represents coalitions of minorities or a government that represents a relatively clear-cut majority and has little or no obligation to the minority? The answer depends on what you expect from government. A system that represents coalitions of minorities usually reflects the trading, competition, and compromising that must take place in order to reach agreement among the various groups. Such a government has been called *broker rule*; the government acts essentially as a go-between, as a mediator among organized groups that have definite policy goals. Under broker rule, leaders cannot get too far ahead of their followers; they must tack back and forth, shifting in response to changing group pressures. Instead of acting for a united popular majority with a fairly definite program, either liberal or conservative, the government tries to satisfy all major interests by giving them a voice in decisions and sometimes a veto over actions. In the pushing and hauling of political groups, the government is continually involved in delicate balancing acts.

Some critics believe in broker rule but point out that fair representation has not been achieved in the American system. They point to the extent of nonvoting and other forms of nonparticipation in politics; the fact that low-income persons are less well organized than upper-income persons; the bias of strong organized groups toward the status quo; the domination of television and the press by a few corporations; and the virtual monopoly of party politics by the two major parties, which do not always offer the voters meaningful alternatives.

In the government itself, critics note devices in Congress like the filibuster and committee control that block majority will and overrepresent certain minorities; the distortion of representation embodied in the U.S. Senate and Electoral College; and the power of the Supreme Court to invalidate laws demanded by popular majorities acting through the legislative and executive branches.

Such charges may be exaggerated, yet they cannot be denied. Those who believe in fairer representation, however, can point to steady improvement in recent years. There have been changes in election laws to simplify voter registration and extend voting and to enforce one-person, one-vote standards. Pressure has been building to regulate campaign finance. And some progress has been made in Congress to strengthen majority rule.

Poking Fun at Politicians

"Don't vote, it only encourages them!"
"Thank God only one of them can win!"
"Old politicians never die, they just evade away."
"A politician is a person who approaches every question with an open mouth."
"Politicians are there when they need you."
"Politicians divide their time between running for office and running for cover."
"Political promises go in one year and out the other."

Some propose to bypass the thorny problem of representation by vastly increasing participation in decision making. Direct participation in decision making, its advocates contend, will serve two major purposes. It will enhance the dignity, self-respect, and understanding of individuals by giving them responsibility for the decisions that shape their lives. And it will act as a safeguard against undemocratic and antidemocratic forms of government and prevent the replacement of democracy by dictatorship. This idea rests on a theory of self-protection that says interests can be represented, furthered, and defended best by those whom they concern directly.

Experience with many forms of participatory democracy, however, suggests that it has limitations as a form of decision making. In an age of rapidly growing population, increasingly complex economic and social systems, and multiple decision-making units of government, direct participation can work only in smaller communities or at the neighborhood level. As a practical matter, people simply cannot put in endless hours taking part in every political decision that affects their lives. Participatory democracy still can play an important role in smaller units—in neighborhood associations, local party committees, and the like. And perhaps the idea of participation could be greatly extended, for example, to greater influence of workers in running certain factories and corporations.

The Role of the Politician

Americans have decidedly mixed views about elected officials. They realize that at their best politicians are skillful at compromising, mediating, negotiating, brokering—and that governing often requires these qualities. But Americans also suspect politicians of being ambitious, conniving, unprincipled, opportunistic, and corrupt. Compared to people in other professions, Americans hold most politicians in low esteem.

Still, we often find that individual officeholders are responsive, bright, hardworking, and friendly (even though we may suspect they are simply trying to get our vote). And our liking sometimes turns into reverence after these same politicians die. George Washington, Abraham Lincoln, Dwight D. Eisenhower, and John F. Kennedy are acclaimed today. Harry Truman liked to joke that a statesman is merely a politician who has been dead for about ten years.

Of course, we must put the problem in perspective. In all democracies the public probably expects too much from politicians. Moreover, people naturally dislike those who wield power. Public officeholders, after all, tax us, regulate us, and conscript us. We dislike political compromisers and ambitious opportunists—even though we may need such people to get things done.

Why the gap between expectations about the typical and the ideal politician? This gap exists, as we noted back in Chapter 1, because we have high expectations. We want politicians to be like us but better than us. We want politicians to have all the right answers and all the right values. When things go wrong in our government or election system, as is often the case, we seldom blame the U.S. Constitution; we revere it too much. "Our belief in popular sovereignty makes us reluctant to blame ourselves. And so we blame the only people left—the politicians. And they, wanting to please us, confirm us in our belief that politicians are at fault by pointing fingers at each other."[3]

Leadership for a Constitutional Democracy

Americans are fond of saying, "It is all politics, you know." This greatly oversimplified insight is offered as profound. More important, it is intended as a negative judgment, as if things somehow would be improved if we did not have politics and politicians.

But politics is the lifeblood of democracy, and without politics there is no freedom. To conclude that politicians are interested in winning elections is about as profound as to conclude that business-people are interested in profits. Of course they are! We do not expect our economy to operate because manufacturers want to make people happy. Rather, we harness their desire to make a profit as a way to see to it that the largest number of people get the products they need at the lowest possible price. So also we harness the elected officials' desire for reelection as the way to ensure that they do what most of the voters want them to do. It is the politician's need to please the voters that is the indispensable link in making democracy work.

Leadership can be understood only in the context of both leaders and followers. A leader without followers is a contradiction in terms. Leadership is also situational and contextual. Leadership is not necessarily transferable; a person is often effective in only one kind of situation. James Madison, for example, was a brilliant political and constitutional theorist; he was also a superb politician. Still, he was not a brilliant president. The leadership required to lead a marine platoon up a hill in battle is different from the leadership needed to change racist or sexist attitudes in city governments. The leadership required of a campaign manager differs from that required of a candidate. Leaders of thought are not always effective as leaders of action.

Although leaders are often skilled managers, they need more than just managerial skills. Managers are concerned with efficiency and process, especially routines and standard operating procedures. Leaders, on the other hand, concentrate on goals and purposes. Managers are concerned with doing things the right way; leaders are concerned with doing the right thing.

Proud to Be a Politician

Must a politician gain public office by denouncing the profession? From the tone of many recent congressional races, it would appear that this is a growing trend. Journalist Charles McDowell of the Richmond Times-Dispatch noted this trend on the PBS series "The Lawmakers" and suggested that such a tactic "demeans an honorable and essential profession—that of the politician." McDowell proposed that every member of Congress be required to take the following oath:

> I affirm that I am a politician. That I am willing to associate with other known politicians. That I have no moral reservations about committing acts of politics. Under the Constitution, I insist that politicians have as much right to indulge in politics as preachers, single-issue zealots, generals, bird-watchers, labor leaders, big business lobbyists, and all other truth-givers.
>
> I confess that, as a politician, I participate in negotiation, compromise, and tradeoffs in order to achieve something that seems reasonable to a majority. And, although I try to be guided by principle, I confess that I often find people of principle on the other side, too.
>
> So help me God.

Some leaders have indispensable qualities of contagious self-confidence, relentless optimism, and dogged perseverance that attract and mobilize others to undertake tasks they never dreamed they could accomplish. In short, they empower others and enable many of their followers to become leaders in their own right. Most of the significant breakthroughs in our nation as well as in our communities have been made or shaped by people who, while seeing all the complexities and obstacles ahead of them, believed in themselves and in their goals so much that they refused to be overwhelmed and paralyzed by self-doubts. They were willing to gamble, to take risks, to look at things in a fresh way, and often to invent new rules.[4]

Leaders recognize the fundamental—unexpressed as well as expressed—wants and needs of potential followers. By bringing followers to a fuller consciousness of their needs, they help convert people's dreams and aspirations into practical demands on other leaders, especially leaders in government.

Reconciling Democracy and Leadership

As we begin the twenty-first century, one of our major political challenges is to reconcile democracy and leadership. Too often in the past we have held a view of leaders as dictatorial. Yet a nation of subservient followers can never be a democratic one. A democratic nation requires educated, skeptical, caring, engaged, and conscientious citizen-leaders. It also requires citizen-leaders who recognize when change is needed and have the courage to bring about necessary reforms and progress.[5]

Such democratic citizen-leaders appreciate that power wielded justly today may be wielded corruptly tomorrow. They are moved to protest when they know a policy is wrong or when the rights of other citizens are diminished. Such leaders appreciate that criticism of official error is not rejection of their country. Citizen-leaders recognize as well that democracy rests solidly upon a realistic view of human nature. Our capacity for justice, as Reinhold Niebuhr observed, makes democracy possible. But our "inclination to injustice makes democracy necessary."[6]

Leadership thought of as an engagement among equals can empower people and enlarge their opinions, choices, and freedoms. The answer for our democracy lies not in producing a handful of great, charismatic, Mount Rushmore leaders, but in educating a citizenry who can boast that we are no longer in need of great leaders or superheroes because we have become a nation of citizens who believe that each of us can make a difference.

Leaders will always be needed. However, our system of government is designed to prevent unrestrained leaders, lest too much political power be placed in the hands of too few people. Thus, while we have emphasized the role of leadership in constitutional democracies in these last few pages, the potential for abuse is checked not only by an involved citizenry but also by the very structure of our constitutional system—separation of powers, checks and balances, federalism, bicameral legislatures, and the rule of law so constantly emphasized throughout this book.

Thomas Jefferson, main author of the Declaration of Independence, first secretary of state, and third president of the United States.

The Democratic Faith

The ultimate test of a democratic system is the legal existence of an officially recognized opposition. A cardinal characteristic of a constitutional democracy is that it not only recognizes the need for the free organization of opposing views but positively encourages such organization. Freedom for dissent is basic—even freedom for nonsense to be spoken so that good sense not yet recognized gets a chance to be heard.[7]

Crucial to the democratic faith is the belief that a constitutional democracy cherishes the free play of ideas. Only where the safety valve of public discussion is available and where almost any policy is subject to perpetual questioning and challenge can there be the assurance that both minority and majority rights will be served. To be afraid of public debate is to be afraid of self-government.

> But why be so considerate of dissent and criticism? To answer this question is to state one of the strongest tenets of our political philosophy. We do not expect organizations or societies to be above criticism, nor do we trust the men who run them to be adequately self-critical. We believe that even those aspects of society that are healthy today may deteriorate tomorrow. We believe that power wielded justly today may be wielded corruptly tomorrow. We know that from the ranks of the critics come cranks and troublemakers, but from the same ranks come the saviors and innovators. And since the spirit that welcomes nonconformity is a fragile thing, we have not depended on that spirit alone. We have devised explicit legal and constitutional arrangements to protect the dissenter.[8]

Your authors hold with Thomas Jefferson that there is nothing in the country so radically wrong that it cannot be cured by good newspapers, sound schoolmasters, and a critical reading of history. Inform and educate the citizenry, and a major hurdle is overcome. Jefferson had boundless faith in education. He believed people are rationally endowed by nature with an innate sense of justice; the average person has only to be informed to act wisely. In the long run, said Jefferson, only an educated and enlightened democracy can hope to endure.

Education is one of the best predictors of voting, participation in politics, and knowledge of public affairs. People may not be equally involved or equally willing to invest in democracy, but an attentive public—frequently those like yourself who have gone to college—has the idealism and self-confidence to see government and politics as necessary and important. An educated public has an understanding of how government works, how individuals can influence decision makers, and how to elect like-minded people.

Recent years have sadly witnessed an increase in racial and ethnic tensions in the United States. When carried to the extreme, these tensions promote groups that exaggerate differences, intensify resentments, and drive deep wedges between nationalities and races. "The genius of America" writes historian Arthur M. Schlesinger, Jr., "lies in its capacity to forge a single nation from peoples of remarkably diverse racial, religious, and ethnic origins." Schlesinger acknowledges that our government and society have been more open to some groups than to others, "but it is more open to all today than it was yesterday and it is likely to be even more open tomorrow than today."[9]

We are a restless, dissatisfied, and searching people. We are our own toughest critics. Our political system is far from perfect, but it still is an open system. People *can* fight city hall. People who disagree with policies in the nation *can* band together and be heard. We know only too well that the American Dream is never fully attained, and it is certainly not inherited. It must always be achieved.

The future of this democracy will be shaped by those citizens (and we trust you will be among them) who care about extending and preserving our political rights and freedoms. Our individual liberties will never be assured unless there are people willing to take responsibility for the progress of the whole community, people willing to exercise their determination and democratic faith. Carved in granite on one of the long corridors in a building on the Harvard University campus are these words of American poet Archibald MacLeish:

> How shall freedom be defended? By arms when it is attacked by arms; by truth when it is attacked by lies, by democratic faith when it is attacked by authoritarian dogma. Always, in the final act, by determination and faith.

APPENDIX

THE DECLARATION OF INDEPENDENCE

Drafted mainly by Thomas Jefferson, this document adopted by the Second Continental Congress, and signed by John Hancock and fifty-five others, outlined the rights of man and the rights to rebellion and self-government. It declared the independence of the colonies from Great Britain, justified rebellion, and listed the grievances against George the III and his government. What is memorable about this famous document is not only that it declared the birth of a new nation, but that it set forth, with eloquence, our basic philosophy of liberty and representative democracy.

IN CONGRESS, JULY 4, 1776
(The unanimous Declaration of the Thirteen United States of America)

Preamble
When, in the course of human events, it becomes necessary for one people to dissolve the political bands which have connected them with another, and to assume, among the powers of the earth, the separate and equal station to which the laws of nature and of nature's God entitle them, a decent respect to the opinions of mankind requires that they should declare the causes which impel them to the separation.

New Principles of Government

We hold these truths to be self-evident; that all men are created equal, that they are endowed by their Creator with certain unalienable rights, that among these are life, liberty, and the pursuit of happiness.

That, to secure these rights, governments are instituted among men, deriving their just powers from the consent of the governed.

That whenever any form of government becomes destructive of these ends, it is the right of the people to alter or to abolish it, and to institute new government, laying its foundation on such principles, and organizing its powers in such form, as to them shall seem most likely to effect their safety and happiness. Prudence, indeed will dictate that governments long established should not be changed for light and transient causes; and accordingly all experience hath shown that mankind are more disposed to suffer while evils are sufferable, than to right themselves by abolishing the forms to which they are accustomed. But when a long train of abuses and usurpations, pursuing invariably the same object, evinces a design to reduce them under absolute despotism, it is their right, it is their duty, to throw off such government, and to provide new guards for their future security.

Reasons for Separation

Such has been the patient sufferance of these colonies; and such is now the necessity which constrains them to alter their former systems of government. The history of the present king of Great Britain is a history of repeated injuries and usurpations, all having in direct object the establishment of an absolute tyranny over these states. To prove this, let facts be submitted to a candid world.

He has refused his assent to laws, the most wholesome and necessary for the public good.

He has forbidden his governors to pass laws of immediate and pressing importance unless suspended in their operation till his assent should be obtained; and when so suspended, he has utterly neglected to attend to them.

He has refused to pass other laws for the accommodation of large districts of people, unless those people would relinquish the right of representation in the legislature, a right inestimable to them, and formidable to tyrants only.

He has called together legislative bodies at places unusual, uncomfortable, and distant for the depository of their public records, for the sole purpose of fatiguing them into compliance with his measures.

He has dissolved representative houses repeatedly, for opposing, with manly firmness, his invasions on the rights of people.

He has refused, for a long time after such dissolutions, to cause others to be elected; whereby the legislative powers incapable of annihilation, have returned to the people at large for their exercise; the state remaining, in the meantime, exposed to all the dangers of invasion from without and convulsions within.

He has endeavored to prevent the population of these states; for that purpose obstructing the laws of naturalization of foreigners, refusing to pass others to encourage their migration hither, and raising the conditions of new appropriations of lands.

He has obstructed the administration of justice, by refusing his assent to laws for establishing judiciary powers.

He has made judges dependent on his will alone for the tenure of their offices, and the amount and payment of their salaries.

He has erected a multitude of new offices, and sent hither swarms of officers to harass our people and eat out their substance.

He has kept among us, in times of peace, standing armies, without the consent of our legislature.

He has affected to render the military independent of, and superior to, the civil power.

He has combined with others to subject us to jurisdiction foreign to our constitution and unacknowledged by our laws, giving his assent to their acts of pretended legislation:

For quartering large bodies of armed troops among us;

For protecting them, by a mock trial, from punishment for any murders which they should commit on the inhabitants of these states;

For cutting off our trade with all parts of the world;

For imposing taxes on us without our consent;

For depriving us, in many cases, of the benefits of trial by jury;

For transporting us beyond seas, to be tried for pretended offenses;

For abolishing the free system of English laws in a neighboring province, establishing therein an arbitrary government, and enlarging its boundaries, so as to render it at once an example and fit instrument for introducing the same absolute rule into these colonies;

For taking away our charters, abolishing our most valuable laws, and altering, fundamentally, the forms of our governments;

For suspending our own legislatures, and declaring themselves invented with power to legislate for us in all cases whatsoever.

He has abdicated government here, by declaring us out of his protection and waging war against us.

He has plundered our seas, ravaged our coasts, burned our towns, and destroyed the lives of our people.

He is at this time transporting large armies of foreign mercenaries to complete the works of death, desolation, and tyranny already begun with circumstances of cruelty and perfidy scarcely paralleled in the most barbarous ages and totally unworthy of the head of a civilized nation.

He has constrained our fellow-citizens, taken captive on the high seas, to bear arms against their country, to become the executioners of their friends and brethren, or to fall themselves by their hands.

He has excited domestic insurrections among us, and has endeavored to bring on the inhabitants of our frontiers the merciless Indian savages, whose known rule of warfare is an undistinguished destruction of all ages, sexes, and conditions.

In every stage of these oppressions we have petitioned for redress in the most humble terms; our repeated petitions have been answered only by repeated injury. A prince whose character is thus marked by every act which may define a tyrant is unfit to be the ruler of a free people.

Nor have we been wanting in attention to our British brethren. We have warned them, from time to time, of attempts by their legislature to extend an unwarrantable jurisdiction over us. We have reminded them of the circumstances of our emigration and settlement here. We have appealed to their native justice and magnanimity; and we have conjured them, by the ties of our common kindred, to disavow these usurpations, which would inevitably interrupt our connections and correspondence. They, too, have been deaf to the voice of justice and of consanguinity. We must, therefore, acquiesce in the necessity which denounces our separation, and hold them, as we hold the rest of mankind, enemies in war, in peace, friends.

We, therefore, the representatives of the United States of America, in General Congress assembled, appealing to the Supreme Judge of the world for the rectitude of our intentions, do, in the name and by authority of the good people of these colonies, solemnly publish and declare, that these united colonies are, and of right ought to be, free and independent states; that they are absolved from all allegiance to the British crown, and that all political connection between them and the state of Great Britain is, and ought to be, totally dissolved; and that, as free and independent states, they have full power to levy war, conclude peace, contract alliances, establish commerce, and do all other acts and things which independent states may of a right do. And, for the support of this declaration, with a firm reliance on the protection of Divine Providence, we mutually pledge to each other our lives, our fortunes, and our sacred honor.

THE FEDERALIST, NO. 10, JAMES MADISON

The Federalist, *No. 10, written by James Madison soon after the Constitutional Convention, was prepared as one of several dozen newspaper essays aimed at persuading New Yorkers to ratify the proposed constitution. One of the most important basic documents in American political history, it outlines the need for and the general principles of a democratic republic. It also provides a political and economic analysis of the realities of interest group or faction politics.*

To the People of the State of New York: Among the numerous advantages promised by a well-constructed union, none deserves to be more accurately developed than its tendency to break and control the violence of faction. The friend of popular governments, never finds himself so much alarmed for their character and fate, as when he contemplates their propensity of this dangerous vice. He will not fail, therefore, to set a due value on any plan which, without violating the principles to which he is attached, provides a proper cure for it. The instability, injustice, and confusion introduced into the public councils, have, in truth, been the mortal diseases under which popular governments have everywhere perished; as they continue to be the favorite and fruitful topics from which the adversaries to liberty derive their most specious declamations. The valuable improvements made by the American constitutions on the popular models, both ancient and modern, cannot certainly be too much admired; but it would be an unwarrantable partiality, to contend that they have as effectually obviated the danger on this side, as was wished and expected. Complaints are everywhere heard from our most considerate and virtuous citizens, equally the friends of public and private faith, and of public and personal liberty, that our governments are too unstable; that the public good is disregarded in the conflicts of rival parties; and that measures are too often decided, not according to the rules of justice, and the rights of the minor party, but by the superior force of an interested and overbearing majority. However anxiously we may wish that these complaints had no foundation, the evidence of known facts will not permit us to deny that they are in some degree true. It will be found, indeed, on a candid review of our situation, that some of the distresses under which we labor have been erroneously charged on the operations of our governments; but it will be found, at the same time, that other causes will not alone account for many of our heaviest misfortunes; and, particularly, for that prevailing and increasing distrust of public engagements, and alarm for private rights, which are echoed from one end of the continent to the other. These must be chiefly, if not wholly, effects of the unsteadiness and injustice, with which a factious spirit has tainted our public administrations.

By a faction, I understand a number of citizens, whether amounting to a majority of the whole, who are united and actuated by some common impulse of passion, or of interest, adverse to the rights of other citizens, or to the permanent and aggregate interests of the community.

There are two methods of curing the mischiefs of faction: the one, by removing its causes; the other, by controlling its effects.

There are again two methods of removing the causes of faction: the one, by destroying the liberty which is essential to its existence; the other, by giving to every citizen the same opinions, the same passions, and the same interests.

It could never be more truly said, than of the first remedy, that it was worse than the disease. Liberty is to faction what air is to fire, an aliment without which it instantly expires. But it could not be a less folly to abolish liberty, which is essential to political life, because it nourishes faction, than it would be to wish the annihilation of air, which is essential to animal life, because it imparts to fire its destructive agency.

The second expedient is as impracticable, as the first would be unwise. As long as the reason of man continues fallible, and he is at liberty to exercise it, different opinions will be formed. As long as the connection subsists between his reason and his self-love, his opinions and his passions will have a reciprocal influence on each other; and the former will be objects to which the latter will attach themselves. The diversity in the faculties of men, from which the rights of property originate, is not less an insuperable obstacle to an uniformity of interests. The protection of these faculties is the first object of government. From the protection of different and unequal faculties of acquiring property, the possession of different degrees and kinds of property immediately results; and from the influence of these on the sentiments and views of the respective proprietors, ensues a division of the society into different interests and parties.

The latent causes of faction are thus sown in the nature of man; and we see them everywhere brought into different degrees of activity, according to the different circumstances of civil society. A zeal for different opinions concerning religion, concerning government, and many other points, as well of speculation as of practice; an attachment to different leaders ambitiously contending for preeminence and power; or to persons of other descriptions whose fortunes have been interesting to the human passions, have, in turn, divided mankind into parties, inflamed them with mutual animosity, and rendered them much more disposed to vex and oppress each other, than to cooperate for their common good. So strong is this propensity of mankind, to fall into mutual animosities, that where no substantial occasion presents itself, the most frivolous and fanciful distinctions have been sufficient to kindle their unfriendly passions and excite their most violent conflicts. But the most common and durable source of factions, has been the various and unequal distribution of property. Those who hold, and those who are without property, have ever formed distinct interests in society. Those who are creditors, and those who are debtors, fall under a like discrimination. A landed interest, a manufacturing interest, a mercantile interest, a moneyed interest, with many lesser interests, grow up of necessity in civilized nations, and divide them into different classes, actuated by different sentiments and views. The regulation of these various and interfering interests forms the principal task of modern legislation, and involves the spirit of the party and faction in the necessary and ordinary operations of the government.

No man is allowed to be a judge in his own cause; because his interest will certainly bias his judgment, and, not improbably, corrupt his integrity. With equal, nay, with greater reason, a body of men are unfit to be both judges and parties at the same time; yet what are many of the most important acts of legislation, but so many judicial determinations, not indeed concerning the right of single persons, but concerning the rights of large bodies of citizens? And what are the different classes of legislators, but advocates and parties to the causes which they determine? Is a law proposed concerning private debts? It is a questions to which the creditors are parties on one side, and the debtors on the other. Justice ought to hold the balance between them. Yet the parties are, and must be, themselves the judges; and the most numerous party, or, in other words, the most powerful faction, must be expected to prevail. Shall domestic manufacturers be encouraged, and in what degree, by restrictions on foreign manufacturers? Are questions which would be differently decided by the landed and the manufacturing classes; and probably by neither with a sole regard to justice and the public good. The apportionment of taxes, on the various descriptions of property, is an act which seems to require the most exact impartiality; yet there is, perhaps, no legislative act, in which greater opportunity and temptation are given to a predominant party to trample on the rules of justice. Every shilling, with which they overburden the inferior number, is a shilling saved to their own pockets.

It is in vain to say, that enlightened statesmen will be able to adjust these clashing interests, and render them all subservient to the public good. Enlightened statesmen will not always be at the helm, nor, in many cases, can such an adjustment be made at all, without taking into view indirect and remote considerations, which will rarely prevail over the immediate interest which one party may find in disregarding the rights of another, or the good of the whole.

The inference to which we are brought is, that the causes of faction cannot be removed; and that relief is only to be sought in the means of controlling its *effects.*

If a faction consists of less than a majority, relief is supplied by the republican principle, which enables the majority to defeat its sinister views, by regular vote. It may clog the administration, it may convulse the society; but it will be unable to execute and mask its violence under the forms of the Constitution. When a majority is included in a faction, the form of popular government, on the other hand, enables it to sacrifice to its ruling passion or interest, both the public good and the rights of other citizens. To secure the public good, and private rights, against the danger of such a faction, and at the same time to preserve the spirit and the form of popular government, is then the great object to which our inquiries are directed. Let me add, that it is the great desideratum, by which alone this form of government can be rescued from the opprobrium under which it has so long laboured, and be recommended to the esteem and adoption of mankind.

By what means is this object attainable? Evidently by one of two only. Either the existence of the same passion or interest in a majority, at the same time, must be prevented; or the majority, having such coexistent passion or interest, must be rendered, by their number and local situation, unable to concert and carry into effect schemes of oppression. If the impulse and the opportunity be suffered to coincide, we well know that neither moral nor religious motives can be relied on as an adequate control. They are not found to be such on the injustice and violence of individuals, and lose their efficacy in proportion to the number combined together; that is, in proportion as their efficacy becomes needful.

From this view of the subject, it may be concluded, that a pure democracy, by which I mean a society consisting of a small number of citizens, who assemble and administer the government in person, can admit of no cure for the mischiefs of faction. A common passion or interest will, in almost every case, be felt by a majority of the whole; a communication and concert, results from the form of government itself; and there is nothing to check the inducements to sacrifice the weaker party, or an obnoxious individual. Hence, it is, that such democracies have ever been spectacles of turbulence and contention; have ever been found incompatible with personal security, or the rights of property; and have in general been as short in their lives, as they have been violent in their deaths. Theoretic politicians, who have patronized this species of government, have erroneously supposed, that by reducing mankind to a perfect equality in their political rights, they would, at the same time be perfectly equalized and assimilated in their possessions, their opinions, and their passions.

A republic, by which I mean a government in which the scheme of representation takes place, opens a different prospect, and promises the cure for which we are seeking. Let us examine the points in which it varies from pure democracy, and we shall comprehend both the nature of the cure and the efficacy which it must derive from the union.

The two great points of difference, between a democracy and a republic, are, first, the delegation of the government, in the latter, to a small number of citizens, elected by the rest; secondly, the greater number of citizens, and greater sphere of country, over which the latter may be extended.

The effect of the first difference is, on the one hand, to refine and enlarge the public views, by passing them through the medium of a chosen body of citizens, whose wisdom may best discern the true interest of their country, and whose patriotism and love of justice, will be least likely to sacrifice it to temporary or partial considerations. Under such a regulation, it may well happen, that the public voice, pronounced by the representatives of the people, will be more consonant to the public good, than if pronounced by the people themselves, convened for the purpose. On the other hand the effect may be inverted. Men of factious tempers, of local prejudices, or of sinister designs, may by intrigue, by corruption, or by other means, first obtain the suffrages, and then betray the interest of the people. The question resulting is, whether small or extensive republics are most favourable to the election of proper guardians of the public weal; and it is clearly decided in favour of the latter by two obvious considerations.

In the first place, it is to be remarked that, however small the republic may be, the representatives must be raised to a certain number, in order to guard against the cabals of a few; and that however large it may be, they must be limited to a certain number, in order to guard against the confusion of a multitude. Hence, the number of representatives in the two cases not being in proportion to that of the constituents, and being proportionally greatest in the small republic, it follows, that if the proportion of fit characters be not less in the large than in the small republic, the former will present a greater option, and consequently a greater probability of a fit choice.

In the next place, as each representative will be chosen by a greater number of citizens in the large than in the small republic, it will be more difficult for unworthy candidates to practice with success the vicious arts, by which elections are too often carried; and the suffrages of the people being more free, will be more likely to centre in men who possess the most attractive merit, and the most diffusive and established characters.

It must be confessed, that in this, as in most other cases, there is a mean, on both sides of which inconveniences will be found to lie. By enlarging too much the number of electors, you render the representatives too little acquainted with all their local circumstances and lesser interests; as by reducing it too much, you render him unduly attached to these, and too little fit to comprehend and pursue great and national objects. The federal constitution forms a happy combination in this respect; the great and aggregate interests being referred to the national, the local and particular to the state legislatures.

The other point of difference is, the greater number of citizens, and extent of territory, which may be brought within the compass of republican, than of democratic government; and it is this circumstance principally which renders factious combinations less to be dreaded in the former, than in the latter. The smaller the society, the fewer probably will be the distinct parties and interests composing it; the fewer the distinct parties and interests, the more frequently will a majority be found of the same party; and the smaller the number of individuals composing a majority, and the smaller the compass within which they are placed, the more easily will they concert and execute their plans of oppression. Extend the sphere, and you take in a greater variety of parties and interests; you make it less probable that a majority of the whole will have a common motive to invade the rights of other citizens; or if such a common motive exists, it will be more difficult for all who feel it to discover their own strength, and to act in unison with each other. Besides other impediments, it may be remarked, that where there is a consciousness of unjust or dishonourable purposes, communication is always checked by distrust, in proportion to the number whose concurrence is necessary.

Hence, it clearly appears, that the same advantage, which a republic has over a democracy, in controlling the effects of faction, is enjoyed by a large over a small republic—is enjoyed by the union over the states composing it. Does this advantage consist in the substitution of representatives, whose enlightened views and virtuous sentiments render them superior to local prejudices, and to schemes of injustice? It will not be denied that the representation of the union will be most likely to possess these requisite endowments. Does it consist in the greater security afforded by a greater variety of parties, against the event of any one party being able to outnumber and oppress the rest? In an equal degree does the increased variety of parties, comprised within the union, increase the security? Does it, in fine, consist in the greater obstacles opposed to the concert and accomplishment of the secret wishes of an unjust and interested majority? Here, again, the extent of the union gives it the most palpable advantage.

The influence of factious leaders may kindle a flame within their particular states, but will be unable to spread a general conflagration through the other states; a religious sect may degenerate into a political faction in a part of the confederacy; but the variety of sects dispersed over the entire face of it, must secure the national councils against any danger from that source: a rage for paper money, for an abolition of debts, for an equal division of property, or for any other improper or wicked project, will be less apt to pervade the whole body of the union than a particular member of it; in the same proportion as such a malady is more likely to taint a particular county or district, than an entire state.

In the extent and proper structure of the union, therefore, we behold a republican remedy for the diseases most incident to republican government. And according to the degree of pleasure and pride we feel in being republicans, ought to be our zeal in cherishing the spirit, and supporting the character of federalists.

THE FEDERALIST, NO. 51, JAMES MADISON

The Federalist, *No. 51, also written by Madison, is a classic statement in defense of separation of powers and republican processes. Its fourth paragraph is especially famous and is frequently quoted by students of government.*

To what expedient, then, shall we finally resort, for maintaining in practice the necessary partition of power among the several departments as laid down in the Constitution? The only answer that can be given is that as all these exterior provisions are found to be inadequate the defect must be supplied, by so contriving the interior structure of the government as that its several constituent parts may, by their mutual relations, be the means of keeping each other in their proper places. Without presuming to undertake a full development of this important idea I will hazard a few general observations which may perhaps place it in a clearer light, and enable us to form a more correct judgment of the principles and structure of the government planned by the convention.

In order to lay a due foundation for that separate and distinct exercise of the different powers of government, which to a certain extent is admitted on all hands to be essential to the preservation of liberty, it is evident that each department should have a will of its own; and consequently should be so constituted that the members of each should have as little agency as possible in the appointment of the members of the others. Were this principle rigorously adhered to, it would require that all the appointments for the supreme executive, legislative, and judiciary magistracies should be drawn from the same fountain of authority, the people, through channels having no communication whatever with one another. Perhaps such a plan of constructing the several departments would be less difficult in practice than it may in contemplation appear. Some difficulties, however, and some additional expense would attend the execution of it. Some deviations, therefore, from the principle must be admitted. In the constitution of the judiciary department in particular, it might be inexpedient to insist rigorously on the principle: first, because peculiar qualifications being essential in the members, the primary consideration ought to be to select that mode of choice which best secures these qualifications; second, because the permanent tenure by which the appointments are held in that department must soon destroy all sense of dependence on the authority conferring them.

It is equally evident that the members of each department should be as little dependent as possible on those of the others for the emoluments annexed to their offices. Were the executive magistrate, or the judges, not independent of the legislature in this particular, their independence in every other would be merely nominal.

But the great security against a gradual concentration of the several powers in the same department consists in giving to those who administer each department the necessary constitutional means and personal motives to resist encroachments of the others. The provision for defense must in this, as in all other cases, be made commensurate to the danger of attack. Ambition must be made to counteract ambition. The interest of the man must be connected with the constitutional rights of the place. It may be a reflection on human nature that such devices should be necessary to control the abuses of government. But what is government itself but the greatest of all reflections on human nature? If men were angels, no government would be necessary. If angels were to govern men, neither external nor internal controls on government would be necessary. In framing a government which is to be administered by men over men, the great difficulty lies in this: you must first enable the government to control the governed; and in the next place oblige it to control itself. A dependence on the people is, no doubt, the primary control on the government; but experience has taught mankind the necessity of auxiliary precautions.

This policy of supplying, by opposite and rival interests, the defect of better motives, might be traced through the whole system of human affairs, private as well as public. We see it particularly displayed in all the subordinate distributions of power, where the constant aim is to divide and arrange the several offices in such a manner as that each may be a check on the other—that the private interest of every individual may be a sentinel over the public rights. These inventions of prudence cannot be less requisite in the distribution of the supreme powers of the State.

But it is not possible to give to each department an equal power of self-defense. In republican government, the legislative authority necessarily predominates. The remedy for this inconveniency is to divide the legislature into different branches; and to render them, by modes of election and different principles of action, as little connected with each other as the nature of their common functions and their common dependence on the society will admit. It may even be necessary to guard against dangerous encroachments by still further precautions. As the weight of the legislative authority requires that it should be thus divided, the weakness of the executive may require, on the other hand, that it should be fortified. An absolute negative on the legislature appears, at first view, to be the natural defense with which the executive magistrate should be armed. But perhaps it would be neither altogether safe nor alone sufficient. On ordinary occasions it might not be exerted with the requisite firmness, and on extraordinary occasions it might be perfidiously abused. May not this defect of an absolute negative be supplied by some qualified connection between this weaker department and the weaker branch of the stronger department, by which the latter may be led to support the constitutional rights of the former, without being too much detached from the rights of its own department?

If the principles on which these observations are founded be just, as I persuade myself they are, and they be applied as a criterion to the several State constitutions, and to the federal Constitution, it will be found that if the latter does not perfectly correspond with them, the former are infinitely less able to bear such a test.

There are, moreover, two considerations particularly applicable to the federal system of America, which place that system in a very interesting point of view.

First. In a single republic, all the power surrendered by the people is submitted to the administration of a single government; and the usurpations are guarded against by a division of the government into distinct and separate departments. In the compound republic of America, the power surrendered by the people is first divided between two distinct governments, and then the portion allotted to each subdivided among distinct and separate departments. Hence a double security arises to the rights of the people. The different governments will control each other, at the same time that each will be controlled by itself.

Second. It is of great importance in a republic not only to guard the society against the oppression of its rulers, but to guard one part of the society against the injustice of the other part. Different interests necessarily exist in different classes of citizens. If a majority be united by a common interest, the rights of the minority will be insecure. There are but two methods of providing against this evil: the one by creating a will in the community independent of the majority—that is, of the society itself; the other, by comprehending in the society so many separate descriptions of citizens as will render an unjust combination of a majority of the whole very improbable, if not impracticable. The first method prevails in all governments possessing an hereditary or self-appointed authority. This, at best, is but a precarious security; because a power independent of the society may as well espouse the unjust views of the major as the rightful interests of the minor party, and may possibly be turned against both parties. The second method will be exemplified in the federal republic of the United States. Whilst all authority in it will be derived from and dependent on the society, the society itself will be broken into so many parts, interests and classes of citizens, that the rights of individuals, or of the minority, will be in little danger from interested combinations of the majority. In a free government the security for civil rights must be the same as that for religious rights. It consists in the one case in the multiplicity of interests, and in the other in the multiplicity of sects. The degree of security in both cases will depend on the number of interests and sects; and this may be presumed to depend on the extent of country and number of people comprehended under the same government. This view of the subject must particularly recommend a proper federal system to all the sincere and considerate friends of republican government, since it shows that in exact proportion as the territory of the Union may be formed into more circumscribed Confederacies, or States, oppressive combinations of a majority will be facilitated; the best security, under the republican forms, for the rights of every class of citizen, will be diminished; and consequently the stability and independence of some member of the government, the only other security, must be proportionally increased. Justice is the end of government. It is the end of civil society. It ever has been and ever will be pursued until it be obtained, or until liberty be lost in the pursuit. In a society under the forms of which the stronger faction can readily unite and oppress the weaker, anarchy may as truly be said to reign as in a state of nature, where the weaker individual is not secured against the violence of the stronger; and as, in the latter state, even the stronger individuals are prompted, by the uncertainty of their condition, to submit to a government which may protect the weak as well as themselves; so, in the former state, will the more powerful factions or parties be gradually induced, by a like motive, to wish for a government which will protect all parties, the weaker as well as the more powerful. It can be little doubted that if the State of Rhode Island was separated from the Confederacy and left to itself, the insecurity of rights under the popular form of government within such narrow limits would be displayed by such reiterated oppressions of factious majorities that some power altogether independent of the people would soon be called for by the voice of the very factions whose misrule had proved the necessity to it. In the extended republic of the United States, and among the great variety of interests, parties, and sects which it embraces, a coalition of a majority of the whole society could seldom take place on any other principles than those of justice and the general good; whilst there being thus less danger to a minor from the will of a major party, there must be less pretext, also, to provide for the security of the former, by introducing into the government a will not dependent on the latter, or, in other words, a will independent of the society itself. It is no less certain that it is important, notwithstanding the contrary opinions which have been entertained that the larger the society, provided it lie within a practicable sphere, the more duly capable it will be of self-government. And happily for the *republican cause*, the practicable sphere may be carried to a very great extent by a judicious modification and mixture of the *federal principle.*

THE FEDERALIST, NO. 78, ALEXANDER HAMILTON

The Federalist, *No. 78, written by Alexander Hamilton, explains and praises the provisions for the judiciary in the newly drafted Constitution. Notice especially how Hamilton asserts that the courts have a key responsibility in determining the meaning of the Constitution as fundamental law. Hamilton is outlining here the doctrine of* judicial review *as we now know it.*

We proceed now to an examination of the judiciary department of the proposed government.

In unfolding the defects of the existing Confederation, the utility and necessity of a federal judicature have been clearly pointed out. It is the less necessary to recapitulate the considerations there urged as the propriety of the institution in the abstract is not disputed; the only questions which have been raised being relative to the manner of constituting it, and to its extent. To these points, therefore, our observations shall be confined.

The manner of constituting it seems to embrace these several objects: 1st. The mode of appointing the judges. 2nd. The tenure by which they are to hold their places. 3rd. The partition of the judiciary authority between different courts and their relations to each other.

First. As to the mode of appointing the judges: this is the same with that of appointing the officers of the Union in general and has been so fully discussed in the two last numbers that nothing can be said here which would not be useless repetition.

Second. As to the tenure by which the judges are to hold their places: this chiefly concerns their duration in office, the provisions for their support, the precautions for their responsibility.

According to the plan of the convention, all judges who may be appointed by the United States are to hold their offices *during good behavior*, which is conformable to the most approved of the State constitutions, and among the rest, to that of this State. Its propriety having been drawn into question by the adversaries of that plan is no light symptom of the rage for objection which disorders their imaginations and judgments. The standard of good behavior for the continuance in office of the judicial magistracy is certainly one of the most valuable of the modern improvements in the practice of government. In a monarchy it is an excellent barrier to the despotism of the prince; in a republic it is a no less excellent barrier to the encroachments and oppressions of the representative body. And it is the best expedient which can be devised in any government to secure a steady, upright, and impartial administration of the laws.

Whoever attentively considers the different departments of power must perceive that, in a government in which they are separated from each other, the judiciary, from the nature of its functions, will always be the least dangerous to the political rights of the Constitution; because it will be least in a capacity to annoy or injure them. The executive not only dispenses the honors but holds the sword of the community. The legislature not only commands the purse but prescribes the rules by which the duties and rights of every citizen are to be regulated. The judiciary, on the contrary, has no influence over either the sword or the purse; no direction either of the strength or of the wealth of the society, and can take no active resolution whatever. It may truly be said to have neither FORCE NOR WILL but merely judgment; and must ultimately depend upon the aid of the executive arm even for the efficacy of its judgments.

This simple view of the matter suggests several important consequences. It proves incontestably that the judiciary is beyond comparison the weakest of the three departments of power; that it can never attack with success either of the other two; and that all possible care is requisite to enable it to defend itself against their attacks. It equally proves that though individual oppression may now and then proceed from the courts of justice, the general liberty of the people can never be endangered from that quarter; I mean so long as the judiciary remains truly distinct from both the legislature and the executive. For I agree that "there is no liberty if the power of judging be not separated from the legislative and executive powers." And it proves, in the last place, that as liberty can have nothing to fear from the judiciary alone, but would have everything to fear from its union with either of the other departments, that as all the effects of such a union must ensue from a dependence of the former on the latter, notwithstanding a nominal and apparent separation; that as, from the natural feebleness of the judiciary, it is in continual jeopardy of being overpowered, awed, or influenced by its co-ordinate branches; and that as nothing can contribute so much to its firmness and independence as permanency in office, this quality may therefore be justly regarded as an indispensable ingredient in its constitution, and, in a great measure, as the citadel for the public justice and the public security.

The complete independence of the courts of justice is peculiarly essential in a limited Constitution. By a limited Constitution, I understand one which contains certain specified exceptions to the legislative authority; such, for instance, as that it shall pass no bills of attainder, no *ex post facto laws*, and the like. Limitations of this kind can be preserved in practice no other way than through the medium of courts of justice, whose duty it must be to declare all acts contrary to the manifest tenor of the Constitution void. Without this, all the reservations of particular rights or privileges would amount to nothing.

Some perplexity respecting the rights of the courts to pronounce legislative acts void, because contrary to the Constitution, has arisen from an imagination that the doctrine would imply a superiority to the judiciary to the legislative power. It is urged that the authority which can declare the acts of another void must necessarily be superior to the one whose acts may be declared void. As this doctrine is of great importance in all the American constitutions, a brief discussion of the grounds on which it rests cannot be unacceptable.

There is no position which depends on clearer principles than that every act of a delegated authority, contrary to the tenor of the commission under which it is exercised, is void. No legislative act, therefore, contrary to the Constitution, can be valid. To deny this would be to affirm that the deputy is greater than his principal; that the servant is above his master; that the representatives of the people are superior to the people themselves; that men acting by virtue of powers do not authorize, but what they forbid.

If it be said that the legislative body are themselves the constitutional judges of their own powers and that the construction they put upon them is conclusive upon the other departments it may be answered that this cannot be the natural presumption where it is not to be collected from any particular provisions in the Constitution. It is not otherwise to be supposed that the Constitution could intend to enable the representatives of the people to substitute their *will* to that of their constituents. It is far more rational to suppose that the courts were designed to be an intermediate body between the people and the legislature in order, among other things, to keep the latter within the limits assigned to their authority. The interpretation of the laws is the proper and peculiar province of the courts. A constitution is, in fact, and must be regarded by the judges as, a fundamental law. It therefore belongs to them to ascertain its meaning as well as the meaning of any particular act proceeding from the legislative body. If there should happen to be an irreconcilable variance between the two, that which has the superior obligation and validity ought, of course, to be preferred; or, in other words, the Constitution ought to be preferred to the statute, the intention of the people to the intention of their agents.

Nor does this conclusion by any means suppose a superiority of the judicial to the legislative power. It only supposes that the power of the people is superior to both, and that where the will of the legislature, declared in its statutes, stands in opposition to that of the people, declared in the Constitution, the judges ought to be governed by the latter rather than the former. They ought to regulate their decisions by the fundamental laws rather than by those which are not fundamental.

This exercise of judicial discretion in determining between two contradictory laws is exemplified in a familiar instance. It not uncommonly happens that there are two statutes existing at one time, clashing in whole or in part with each other and neither of them containing any repealing clause or expression. In such a case, it is the province of the courts to liquidate and fix their meaning and operation. So far as they can, by any fair construction, be reconciled to each other, reason and law conspire to dictate that this should be done; where this is impracticable, it becomes a matter of necessity to give effect to one in exclusion of the other. The rule which has obtained in the courts for determining their relative validity is that the last in order of time shall be preferred to the first. But this is a mere rule of construction, not derived from any positive law but from the nature and reason of the thing. It is a rule not enjoined upon the courts by legislative provision but adopted by themselves, as consonant to truth and propriety, for the direction of their conduct as interpreters of the law. They thought it reasonable that between the interfering acts of an *equal* authority that which was the last indication of its will should have the preference.

But in regard to the interfering acts of a superior and subordinate authority of an original and derivative power, the nature and reason of the thing indicates the converse of that rule as proper to be followed. They teach us that the prior act of a superior ought to be preferred to the subsequent act of an inferior and subordinate authority; and that accordingly, whenever a particular statute contravenes the Constitution, it will be the duty of the judicial tribunals to adhere to the latter and disregard the former.

It can be of no weight to say that the courts, on the pretense of a repugnancy, may substitute their own pleasure to the constitutional intentions of the legislature. This might as well happen in the case of two contradictory statutes; or it might as well happen in every adjudication upon any single statute. The courts must declare the sense of the law; and if they should be disposed to exercise WILL instead of JUDGMENT, the consequence would equally be the substitution of their pleasure to that of the legislative body. The observation, if it prove anything, would prove that there ought to be no judges distinct from that body.

If, then, the courts of justice are to be considered as the bulwarks of a limited Constitution against legislative encroachments, this consideration will afford a strong argument for the permanent tenure of judicial offices, since nothing will contribute so much as this to that independent spirit in the judges which must be essential to the faithful performance of so arduous a duty.

This independence of the judges is equally requisite to guard the Constitution and the rights of individuals from the effects of those ill humors which the arts of designing men, or the influence of particular conjunctures, sometimes disseminate among the people themselves, and which, though they speedily give place to better information, and more deliberate reflection, have a tendency, in the meantime, to occasion dangerous innovations in the government, and serious oppressions of the minor party in the community. Though I trust the friends of the proposed Constitution will never concur with its enemies in questioning that fundamental principal of Republican government which admits the right of the people to alter or abolish the established Constitution whenever they find it inconsistent with their happiness; yet it is not to be inferred from this principle that the representatives of the people, whenever a momentary inclination happens to lay hold of a majority of their constituents incompatible with the provisions in the existing Constitution would, on that account, be justifiable in a violation of those provisions; or that the courts would be under a greater obligation to connive at infractions in this shape than when they had proceeded wholly from the cabals of the representative body. Until the people have, by some solemn and authoritative act, annulled or changed the established form, it is binding upon themselves collectively, as well as individually; and no presumption, or even knowledge of their sentiments, can warrant their representatives in a departure from it prior to such an act. But it is easy to see that it would require an uncommon portion of fortitude in the judges to do their duty as faithful guardians of the Constitution, where legislative invasions of it had been instigated by the major voice of the community.

But it is not with a view to infractions of the Constitution only that the independence of the judges may be an essential safeguard against the effects of occasional ill humors in the society. These sometimes extend no farther than to the injury of the private rights of particular classes of citizens, by unjust and partial laws. Here also the firmness of the judicial magistracy is of vast importance in mitigating the severity and confining the operation of such laws. It not only serves to moderate the immediate mischiefs of those which may have been passed but it operates as a check upon the legislative body in passing them; who, perceiving that obstacles to the success of iniquitous intention are to be expected from the scruples of the courts, are in a manner compelled, by the very motives of the injustice they mediate, to qualify their attempts. This is a circumstance calculated to have more influence upon the character of our governments than but a few may be aware of. The benefits of the integrity and moderation of the judiciary have already been felt in more States than one; and though they may have displeased those whose sinister expectations they may have disappointed, they must have commanded the esteem and applause of all the virtuous and disinterested. Considerate men of every description ought to prize whatever will tend to beget or fortify that temper in the courts; as no man can be sure that he may not be tomorrow the victim of a spirit of injustice, by which he may be a gainer today. And every man must now feel that the inevitable tendency of such a spirit is to sap the foundations of public and private confidence and to introduce in its stead universal distrust and distress.

That inflexible and uniform adherence to the rights of the Constitution, and of individuals, which we perceive to be indispensable in the courts of justice, can certainly not be expected from judges who hold their offices by a temporary commission. Periodical appointments, however regulated, or by whomsoever made, would, in some way or other, be fatal to their necessary independence. If the power of making them was committed either to the executive or legislature there would be danger of an improper complaisance to the branch which possessed it; if to both, there would be an unwillingness to hazard the displeasure of either; if to the people, or to persons chosen by them for the special purpose, there would be too great a disposition to consult popularity to justify a reliance that nothing would be consulted by the Constitution and the laws.

There is yet a further and a weighty reason for the permanency of the judicial offices which is deducible from the nature of the qualifications they require. It has been frequently remarked with great propriety that a voluminous code of laws is one of the inconveniences necessarily connected with the advantages of a free government. To avoid an arbitrary discretion in the courts, it is indispensable that they should be bound down by strict rules and precedents which serve to define and point out their duty in every particular case that comes before them; and it will readily be conceived from the variety of controversies which grow out of the folly and wickedness of mankind that the records of those precedents must unavoidably swell to a very considerable bulk and must demand long and laborious study to acquire a competent knowledge of them. Hence it is that there can be but few men in the society who will have sufficient skill in the laws to qualify them for the stations of judges. And making the proper deductions for the ordinary depravity of human nature, the number must be still smaller of those who unite the requisite integrity with the requisite knowledge. These considerations apprise us that the government can have no great option between fit characters; and that a temporary duration in office which would naturally discourage such characters from quitting a lucrative line of practice to accept a seat on the bench would have a tendency to throw the administration of justice into hands less able and less well qualified to conduct it with utility and dignity. In the present circumstances of this country and in those in which it is likely to be for a long time to come, the disadvantages on this score would be greater than they may at first sight appear; but it must be confessed that they are far inferior to those which present themselves under the other aspects of the subject.

Upon the whole, there can be no room to doubt that the convention acted wisely in copying from the models of those constitutions which have established *good behavior* as the tenure of their judicial offices in point of duration, and that so far from being blamable on this account, their plan would have been inexcusably defective if it had wanted this important feature of good government. The experience of Great Britain affords an illustrious comment on the excellence of the institution.

Presidential Election Results 1789–1996

Year	Candidates	Party	Popular Vote	Electoral Vote
1789	George Washington			69
	John Adams			34
	Others			35
1793	George Washington			132
	John Adams			77
	George Clinton			50
	Others			5
1796	John Adams	Federalist		71
	Thomas Jefferson	Democratic-Republican		68
	Thomas Pinckney	Federalist		59
	Aaron Burr	Democratic-Republican		30
	Others			48
1800	Thomas Jefferson	Democratic-Republican		73
	Aaron Burr	Democratic-Republican		73
	John Adams	Federalist		65
	Charles C. Pinckney	Federalist		64
1804	Thomas Jefferson	Democratic-Republican		162
	Charles C. Pinckney	Federalist		14
1808	James Madison	Democratic-Republican		122
	Charles C. Pinckney	Federalist		47
	George Clinton	Independent-Republican		6
1812	James Madison	Democratic-Republican		128
	DeWitt Clinton	Federalist		89
1816	James Monroe	Democratic-Republican		183
	Rufus King	Federalist		34
1820	James Monroe	Democratic-Republican		231
	John Quincy Adams	Independent-Republican		1
1824	John Quincy Adams	Democratic-Republican	108,740(30.5%)	84
	Andrew Jackson	Democratic-Republican	153,544(43.1%)	99
	Henry Clay	Democratic-Republican	47,136(13.2%)	37
	William H. Crawford	Democratic-Republican	46,618(13.1%)	41
1828	Andrew Jackson	Democratic	647,231(56.0%)	178
	John Quincy Adams	National Republican	509,097(44.0%)	83
1832	Andrew Jackson	Democratic	687,502(55.0%)	219
	Henry Clay	National Republican	530,189(42.4%)	49
	William Wirt	Anti-Masonic		7
	John Floyd	National Republican	33,108(2.6%)	11
1836	Martin Van Buren	Democratic	761,549(50.9%)	170
	William H. Harrison	Whig	549,567(36.7%)	73
	Hugh L. White	Whig	145,396(9.7%)	26
	Daniel Webster	Whig	41,287(2.7%)	14
1840	William H. Harrison	Whig	1,275,017(53.1%)	234
	Martin Van Buren	Democratic	1,128,702(46.9%)	60
1844	James K. Polk	Democratic	1,337,243(49.6%)	170
	Henry Clay	Whig	1,299,068(48.1%)	105
	James G. Birney	Liberty	63,300(2.3%)	
1848	Zachary Taylor	Whig	1,360,101(47.4%)	163
	Lewis Cass	Democratic	1,220,544(42.5%)	127
	Martin Van Buren	Free Soil	291,163(10.1%)	
1852	Franklin Pierce	Democratic	1,601,474(50.9%)	254
	Winfield Scott	Whig	1,386,578(44.1%)	42
1856	James Buchanan	Democratic	1,838,169(45.4%)	174
	John C. Fremont	Republican	1,335,264(33.0%)	114
	Millard Fillmore	American	874,534(21.6%)	8
1860	Abraham Lincoln	Republican	1,865,593(39.8%)	180
	Stephen A. Douglas	Democratic	1,381,713(29.5%)	12
	John C. Breckinridge	Democratic	848,356(18.1%)	72
	John Bell	Constitutional Union	592,906(12.6%)	79
1864	Abraham Lincoln	Republican	2,206,938(55.0%)	212
	George B. McClellan	Democratic	1,803,787(45.0%)	21
1868	Ulysses S. Grant	Republican	3,013,421(52.7%)	214
	Horatio Seymour	Democratic	2,706,829(47.3%)	80
1872	Ulysses S. Grant	Republican	3,596,745(55.6%)	286
	Horace Greeley	Democratic	2,843,446(43.9%)	66
1876	Rutherford B. Hayes	Republican	4,036,571(48.0%)	185
	Samuel J. Tilden	Democratic	4,284,020(51.0%)	184
1880	James A. Garfield	Republican	4,449,053(48.3%)	214
	Winfield S. Hancock	Democratic	4,442,035(48.2%)	155
	James B. Weaver	Greenback-Labor	308,578(3.4%)	
1884	Grover Cleveland	Democratic	4,874,986(48.5%)	219
	James G. Blaine	Republican	4,851,931(48.2%)	182
	Benjamin F. Butler	Greenback-Labor	175,370(1.8%)	

Presidential Election Results 1789–1996

Year	Candidates	Party	Popular Vote	Electoral Vote
1888	Benjamin Harrison	Republican	5,444,337(47.8%)	233
	Grover Cleveland	Democratic	5,540,050(48.6%)	168
1892	Grover Cleveland	Democratic	5,554,414(46.0%)	277
	Benjamin Harrison	Republican	5,190,802(43.0%)	145
	James B. Weaver	Peoples	1,027,329(8.5%)	22
1896	William McKinley	Republican	7,035,638(50.8%)	271
	William J. Bryan	Democratic; Populist	6,467,946(46.7%)	176
1900	William McKinley	Republican	7,219,530(51.7%)	292
	William J. Bryan	Democratic; Populist	6,356,734(45.5%)	155
1904	Theodore Roosevelt	Republican	7,628,834(56.4%)	336
	Alton B. Parker	Democrat	5,084,401(37.6%)	140
	Eugene V. Debs	Socialist	402,460(3.0%)	0
1908	William H. Taft	Republican	7,679,006(51.6%)	321
	William J. Bryan	Democratic	6,409,106(43.1%)	162
	Eugene V. Debs	Socialist	420,820(2.8%)	0
1912	Woodrow Wilson	Democratic	6,286,820(41.8%)	435
	Theodore Roosevelt	Progressive	4,126,020(27.4%)	88
	William H. Taft	Republican	3,483,922(23.2%)	8
	Eugene V. Debs	Socialist	897,011(6.0%)	0
1916	Woodrow Wilson	Democratic	9,129,606(49.3%)	277
	Charles E. Hughes	Republican	8,538,211(46.1%)	254
1920	Warren G. Harding	Republican	16,152,200(61.0%)	404
	James M. Cox	Democratic	9,147,353(34.6%)	127
	Eugene V. Debs	Socialist	919,799(3.5%)	0
1924	Calvin Coolidge	Republican	15,725,016(54.1%)	382
	John W. Davis	Democratic	8,385,586(28.8%)	136
	Robert M. La Follette	Progressive	4,822,856(16.6%)	13
1928	Herbert C. Hoover	Republican	21,392,190(58.2%)	444
	Alfred E. Smith	Democratic	15,016,443(40.8%)	87
1932	Franklin D. Roosevelt	Democratic	22,809,638(57.3%)	472
	Herbert C. Hoover	Republican	15,758,901(39.6%)	59
	Norman Thomas	Socialist	881,951(2.2%)	0
1936	Franklin D. Roosevelt	Democratic	27,751,612(60.7%)	523
	Alfred M. Landon	Republican	16,681,913(36.4%)	8
	William Lemke	Union	891,858(1.9%)	0
1940	Franklin D. Roosevelt	Democratic	27,243,466(54.7%)	449
	Wendell L. Wilkie	Republican	22,304,755(44.8%)	82
1944	Franklin D. Roosevelt	Democratic	25,602,505(52.8%)	432
	Thomas E. Dewey	Republican	22,006,278(44.5%)	99
1948	Harry S. Truman	Democratic	24,105,812(49.5%)	303
	Thomas E. Dewey	Republican	21,970,065(45.1%)	189
	J. Strom Thurmond	States' Rights	1,169,063(2.4%)	39
	Henry A. Wallace	Progressive	1,157,172(2.4%)	0
1952	Dwight D. Eisenhower	Republican	33,936,234(55.2%)	442
	Adlai E. Stevenson	Democratic	27,314,992(44.5%)	89
1956	Dwight D. Eisenhower	Republican	35,590,472(57.4%)	457
	Adlai E. Stevenson	Democratic	26,022,752(42.0%)	73
1960	John F. Kennedy	Democratic	34,227,096(49.9%)	303
	Richard M. Nixon	Republican	34,108,546(49.6%)	219
1964	Lyndon B Johnson	Democratic	43,126,233(61.1%)	486
	Barry Goldwater	Republican	27,174,989(38.5%)	52
1968	Richard M. Nixon	Republican	31,783,783(43.4%)	301
	Hubert H. Humphrey	Democratic	31,271,839(42.7%)	191
	George C. Wallace	American Independent	9,899,557(13.5%)	46
1972	Richard M. Nixon	Republican	46,632,189(61.3%)	520
	George McGovern	Democratic	28,422,015(37.3%)	17
1976	Jimmy Carter	Democratic	40,828,587(50.1%)	297
	Gerald R. Ford	Republican	39,147,613(48.0%)	240
1980	Ronald Reagan	Republican	42,941,145(51.0%)	489
	Jimmy Carter	Democratic	34,663,037(41.0%)	49
	John B. Anderson	Independent	5,551,551(6.6%)	0
1984	Ronald Reagan	Republican	53,428,357(59%)	525
	Walter F. Mondale	Democratic	36,930,923(41%)	13
1988	George Bush	Republican	48,881,011(53%)	426
	Michael Dukakis	Democratic	41,828,350(46%)	111
1992	Bill Clinton	Democratic	38,394,210(43%)	370
	George Bush	Republican	33,974,386(38%)	168
	H. Ross Perot	Independent	16,573,465(19%)	0
1996	Bill Clinton	Democratic	45,628,667(49%)	379
	Bob Dole	Republican	37,869,435(41%)	159
	H. Ross Perot	Reform	7,874,283(8%)	0

GLOSSARY

adversary system A judicial system in which the court of law is a neutral arena where two parties argue their differences.

advisory opinion An opinion unrelated to a particular case that gives a court's view about a constitutional or legal issue.

affirmative action Remedial action designed to overcome the effects of past discrimination against minorities and women.

amendatory veto The power of governors in a few states to return a bill to the legislature with suggested language changes, conditions, or amendments. Legislators then decide either to accept the governor's recommendations or to pass the bill in its original form over the veto.

American Dream The widespread belief that individual initiative and hard work can bring economic success, and that the United States is a land of opportunity.

***amicus curiae* brief** Literally, "friend of the court" brief, this document is filed by an individual or organization to present arguments in addition to those presented by the immediate parties to the case.

Annapolis Convention A convention held in September 1786 to consider problems of trade and navigation, attended by five states and important because it issued the call to Congress and the states for what became the Constitutional Convention.

Antifederalists Opponents of ratification of the Constitution and of a strong central government generally.

antitrust regulation Federal laws and regulations that try to prevent businesses from dominating a particular market through monopoly or restraint of trade.

appellate jurisdiction The authority of a court to review a decision of a lower court.

Articles of Confederation The first constitution of the American states, drafted in 1777, ratified in 1781, and replaced by the present Constitution in 1789.

assessment The valuation a government places on property for the purposes of taxation.

assigned council system Arrangement whereby attorneys are provided for persons accused of crime who are unable to hire their own attorneys. The judge assigns a member of the bar to provide counsel to a particular defendant.

attentive public Those who follow public affairs carefully.

Australian ballot A secret ballot printed by the state.

bad tendency doctrine Interpretation of the First Amendment that would permit legislatures to forbid speech that has a tendency to cause people to engage in illegal action.

bicameral legislature A two-house legislature.

bicameralism The principle of a two-house legislature.

bill of attainder Legislative act inflicting punishment, including deprivation of property, without trial on named individuals or members of a specified group.

binding arbitration A collective bargaining situation in which both parties agrees to adhere to the decision of an arbitrator.

bipartisanship A policy that emphasizes a united front and cooperation between the major political parties, especially on sensitive foreign policy issues.

blanket primary A primary open to all voters, who may vote for candidates from any party for each office.

bundling A tactic of political action committees whereby they collect contributions from like-minded individuals (each limited to $2,000) and present them to a candidate or political party as a "bundle," thus increasing their influence.

bureau The largest subunit of a government department or agency.

bureaucracy A professional corps of officials organized in a pyramidal hierarchy and functioning under impersonal, uniform rules and procedures.

bureaucrat Career government employee.

cabinet Advisory council for a president, consisting of the heads of the executive departments, the vice-president, and a few others the president considers cabinet-level officials.

capitalism An economic system characterized by private property, competitive markets, economic incentives, and limited government involvement in the production and pricing of goods and services.

caucus A meeting of local party members to choose party officials and/or candidates for public office and to decide the platform.

centralists Those who favor national action over action at the state and local levels.

charter A city "constitution" that outlines the structure of city government, defines the authority of the various officials, and provides for their selection.

charter school A publicly funded alternative to standard public schools in some states, initiated when individuals or groups receive charters; charter schools must meet state standards

checks and balances Constitutional grant of powers that enables each of the three branches of government to stop some acts of the others and therefore ensure than no branch can dominate.

civil disobedience When people refuse to obey the law or comply with the orders of public officials as a means of expressing their opposition to the government or some of its laws.

civil law Law that evolved from Roman law; in contrast to *common law*, which has evolved from English tradition; also in contrast to *criminal law*, which refers to law that applies to disputes between individuals or between individuals and the government.

civil liberties Rights of all people that cannot be denied by governmental power: freedom of conscience, religion, or expression; generally the freedoms secured by the First Amendment.

civil rights Rights of all persons to equal protection of the laws: the constitutional right not to be discriminated against by government because of race, religion, gender, or ethnic origin; guaranteed by the Fifth and Fourteenth Amendments.

class action suit Lawsuit brought by an individual or a group of people on behalf of all those similarly situated.

clear and present danger doctrine Interpretation of the First Amendment that holds government cannot punish a person for speech unless the speech presents a clear and present danger that it will lead to illegal acts. To shout "Fire!" falsely in a crowded theater is Justice Oliver Wendell Holmes's famous example.

closed primary A primary in which only persons registered in the party holding the primary may vote.

closed rule A procedural rule in the House of Representatives that prohibits any amendments to bills or provides that only members of the committee reporting the bill may offer amendments.

closed shop A company with a labor agreement whereby union membership is a condition of employment.

cloture Procedure for terminating debate, especially filibusters, in the Senate.

coattail effect The boost candidates of the president's party receive in a presidential election from the president's popularity.

collective bargaining Method whereby representatives of the union and employer determine wages, hours, and other conditions of employment through direct negotiation.

commerce clause The clause (Article I) of the Constitution that gives Congress the power to regulate commerce among the states, with other nations, and with the Indian tribes. This clause provides the constitutional basis for most national regulations of our economy, as well as for much civil rights legislation.

community policing Recent programs to move police from patrol cars into neighborhoods, where they walk the beat and work with churches and other community groups to reduce crime and improve relations with minorities.

comptroller general Head of the General Accounting Office, appointed by the president with the approval of the Senate for a 15-year term.

concurrent powers Powers the Constitution gives to both the national and state governments, such as the power to levy taxes.

concurrent resolution A resolution passed in the same form by both houses of Congress that expresses the "sense" of Congress on some question. It is not sent to the president and does not have the force of law.

concurring opinion An opinion that agrees with the decision of the court but differs on the reasoning.

confederation A constitutional arrangement in which sovereign nations or states, by compact, create a central government but carefully limit its power and do not give it direct authority over individuals.

conference committee Committee appointed by the presiding officers of each chamber to adjust differences on a particular bill passed by each but in different forms.

Congressional Budget Office (CBO) An agency of Congress that analyzes presidential budget recommendations and estimates the costs of proposed legislation.

Connecticut Compromise Compromise agreement by states at the Constitutional Convention for a bicameral legislature with a lower house in which representation would be based on population, and upper house in which each state would have two senators.

conservatism A belief that limited government ensures order, competitive markets, and personal opportunity.

Constitutional Convention The convention in Philadelphia, May 25–September 17, 1787, that framed the Constitution of the United States.

constitutional democracy A government in which those who exercise governmental powers do so as a result of winning free and relatively frequent elections and are subject to recognized, enforced limits on the power of all government officials. It is the elections that make the government democratic; it is the recognized and enforced limits on power that make it constitutional.

constitutional home rule State constitutional authorization for local governments to conduct their own affairs.

constitutionalism The set of arrangements such as checks and balances, federalism, separation of powers, rule of law, due process, and a bill of rights that requires our leaders to listen, think, bargain, and explain before they make laws. We then hold them politically and legally accountable for how they exercise their powers.

contract clause Clause of the Constitution that was originally intended to forbid state governments to modify contracts made between individuals; for a while interpreted to forbid state governments from adversely affecting property rights; no longer interpreted so broadly and no longer constrains states from exercising their police powers.

council-manager plan Form of local government in which the city council hires a professional administrator to manage city affairs; also known as the *city-manager plan.*

court of appeals A court with appellate jurisdiction, which hears appeals from the decisions of lower courts.

cross-cutting cleavages Divisions within society that make groups more heterogeneous or different.

crossover voting A member of one party voting for a candidate of another party.

***de facto* segregation** Segregation that comes about because of economic or social conditions or results from individual choices.

***de jure* segregation** Laws that made it a crime for black or white people to go to school together, or to be served together in public places, or to sit together in public transportation.

dealignment Dramatic change in the composition of the electorate or its partisan preferences that points to a rejection of both major parties and a rise in the number of Independents.

debt The accumulated total of federal deficits, minus surpluses, over the years.

decentralists Those who favor state or local action rather than national action.

defendant In a criminal action, the person or party accused of an offense.

deficit The difference between the revenues raised annually from sources of income other than borrowing and the expenditure of government, including paying the interest on past borrowing.

delegate A view of the role of legislators that holds that they should represent the views of their constituents even when personally holding different views.

democracy Government by the people, either directly or indirectly, with free and frequent elections.

demographics The study of the characteristics of populations.

deregulation A policy promoting cutbacks in the amount of federal regulation in specific areas of economic activity.

deterrence Defense policy of maintaining the ability to threaten massive retaliation on any attacking nation.

devolution revolution Movement beginning with the 1984 congressional elections to transfer functions and responsibilities from the national government to the states; for example, for providing welfare.

direct democracy Government in which citizens come together to discuss and pass laws and select rulers.

direct primary Election open to all members of the party in which voters choose the persons who will be the party's nominees in the general election.

discharge petition Petition that, if signed by a majority of the members of the House of Representatives, will pry a bill from committee and bring it to the floor for consideration.

disclosure A requirement that candidates specify where the money came from to finance their campaign.

dissenting opinion An opinion that conflicts with the decision of the court.

divided government Governance divided between the parties, especially when one holds the presidency and the other controls Congress.

double jeopardy Trial or punishment for the same crime by the same government; forbidden by the Constitution.

dual citizenship Citizenship in two or more nations.

due process Established rules and regulations that restrain those in government who exercise power.

due process clause Clause in the Fifth Amendment limiting the power of the national government; similar to clause in the Fifteenth Amendment prohibiting state governments from depriving any person of life, liberty, or property without due process of law.

economic sanction A denial of export, import, or financial relations with a target country in an effort to change that nation's policies.

Electoral College The electoral system used in electing the president and vice-president, in which voters vote for electors pledged to cast their ballots for a particular party's candidates.

eminent domain Power of a government to take private property for public use; the U.S. Constitution gives national and state governments this power and requires them to provide just compensation for property so taken.

enterprise zone Inner-city areas designated as offering tax incentives to companies that invest in plants there and provide job training for the unemployed.

entitlement program Government programs such as Social Security, Medicare, and unemployment insurance that provide a specified set of benefits as a matter of right to all who meet the criteria established by law.

environmental impact statement A statement required by federal law from all agencies for any project using federal funds to assess the potential effect of the new construction or development on the environment.

equal protection clause Clause in the Constitution that forbids any state to deny to any person within its jurisdiction the equal protection of the laws. By interpretation, the Fifth Amendment imposes the same limitation on the national government. This clause is the major constitutional restraint on the power of governments to discriminate against persons because of race, national origin, or sex.

establishment clause Clause in the First Amendment that states that Congress shall make no law respecting an establishment of religion. It has been interpreted by the Supreme Court to forbid governmental support of any or all religions.

ethnicity A social division based on national origin, religion, language, and often race.

ethnocentrism Selective perception based on individual background, attitudes, and biases that leads one to believe in the superiority of one's nation or ethnic group.

ex post facto law Retroactive criminal law that works to the disadvantage of an individual; forbidden in the Constitution.

excise tax Consumer tax on a specific kind of merchandise, such as tobacco.

exclusionary rule Requirement that evidence unconstitutionally or illegally obtained be excluded from a criminal trial.

Executive Office of the President The cluster of presidential staff agencies that help the president carry out his responsibilities. Currently the office includes the Office of Management and Budget, the Council of Economic Advisers, and several other units.

executive order An order issued by a president or governor that has the force of law.

executive privilege The right to confidentiality of executive communications, especially those that relate to national security.

express powers Powers specifically granted to one of the branches of the national government by the Constitution.

extradition Legal process whereby an alleged criminal offender is surrendered by the officials of one state to officials of the state in which the crime is alleged to have been committed.

faction A term used by James Madison and other founders of this country to refer to political parties as well as what we now call special interests or interest groups.

fairness doctrine Doctrine interpreted by the Federal Communications Commission that imposed on radio and television licensees an obligation to ensure that different viewpoints were presented about controversial issues or persons; repealed in 1987.

federal mandate A requirement imposed by the federal government as a condition of receipt of federal funds.

Federal Register This official document, published every weekday, lists new and proposed regulations of executive departments and regulatory agencies.

Federal Reserve System The system created by Congress in 1913 to establish banking practices and regulate currency in circulation and the amount of credit available. It is comprised of 12 regional banks, and its major responsibilities are supervised by the Federal Reserve Board of Governors.

federalism Constitutional arrangement whereby power is distributed between a central government and subdivisional governments, called states in the United States. The national and the subdivisional governments both exercise direct authority over individuals.

Federalists Supporters of ratification of the Constitution whose position promoting a strong central government was later voiced in the Federalist party.

fee for service System of health care payment in which patients can choose their own physician, whose bills are then covered by insurance companies.

felony A serious crime, the penalty for which can range from death to imprisonment for over a year in a penitentiary.

fighting words Words that by their very nature inflict injury upon those to whom they are addressed or cause acts of violence by them.

filibuster A practice in the Senate whereby a senator holds the floor and thereby delays proceedings and prevents a vote on a controversial issue.

fiscal policy Government policy that attempts to manage the economy by controlling taxing and spending.

free exercise clause Clause in the First Amendment that states that Congress shall make no law prohibiting the free exercise of religion.

free rider An individual who does not join an interest group representing his or her interests, yet receives the benefit of the influence the group achieves.

full faith and credit clause Clause in the Constitution requiring each state to recognize the civil judgments rendered by the courts of the other states and to accept their public records and acts as valid documents.

gender gap The difference between the political opinions or political behavior of men and women.

General Accounting Office (GAO) An independent investigative arm of Congress established in 1921 to check on receipt and disbursement of public funds and review the performance of government agencies.

General Agreement on Tariffs and Trade (GATT) An international trade organization with 125 members, including the United States, that seeks to encourage free trade by lowering tariffs and other trade restrictions.

general property tax Tax levied by local and some state governments on real property or personal, tangible property, the major portion of which is on the estimated value of one's home and land.

gerrymandering The drawing of election district boundaries to benefit a party, group, or incumbent.

government corporation Cross between a business corporation and a government agency, created to secure greater freedom of action and flexibility for a particular program.

grand jury A jury of 12 to 23 persons who, in private, hear evidence presented by the government to determine whether persons shall be required to stand trial. If the jury believes there is sufficient evidence that a crime was committed, it issues an indictment.

gross domestic product (GDP) An estimate of the total output of all economic activity in the nation, including goods and services.

habeas corpus Court order requiring explanation to a judge why a prisoner is held in custody.

Hatch Act Federal statute barring federal employees from active participation in certain kinds of politics and protecting them from being fired on partisan grounds.

health maintenance organization (HMO) Alternative means of health care in which people or their employers are charged a set amount, and the HMO provides health care and covers hospital costs.

hold A practice in the Senate whereby a senator temporarily blocks the consideration of a bill or nomination.

honeymoon A period at the beginning of a new president's term in which the president enjoys generally positive relations with the press and Congress.

ideology One's basic beliefs about power, political values, and the role of government—beliefs that arise out of educational, economic, and social conditions and experiences.

immunity Protection granted by prosecutors to witnesses in exchange for giving up their constitutional right not to testify against themselves. There are various kinds of immunity; the most extensive is *transactional,*which means witnesses cannot be prosecuted for any offenses uncovered by their testimony; *use immunity* only protects witnesses from having their testimony used in subsequent criminal trials.

impeachment Formal accusation against a public official and the first step in removal from office.

implied powers Powers inferred from express powers that allow Congress to carry out its functions.

impoundment Presidential refusal to allow an agency to spend funds authorized and appropriated by Congress.

independent agency A government entity that is independent of the legislative, executive, and judicial branch.

independent expenditures Money spent by individuals or groups not associated with candidates to elect or defeat candidates for office.

independent regulatory agency A government agency that exists outside the three branches of government and is responsible for enforcing particular statutes.

independent regulatory board An independent agency with regulatory power whose independence is protected by Congress.

indexing Automatic adjustment of income tax rates to rise with inflation so that, in effect, income tax rates remain constant.

indictment A formal charge issued by a grand jury against an individual for a specified crime; also called a *true bill.*

inflation A rise in the general price level (and decrease in dollar value) owing to an increase in the volume of money and credit in relation to available goods.

information affidavit Certification by a public prosecutor that there is evidence to justify bringing named individuals to trial.

inherent powers Those powers of the national government in the field of foreign affairs that the Supreme Court has declared do not depend upon constitutional grants but rather grow out of the very existence of the national government.

initiative Procedure whereby a certain number of voters may, by petition, propose a law or constitutional amendment and have it submitted to the voters.

initiative petition A device that permits voters to place specific amendments to a state constitution on the ballot by petition.

interest group A collection of people who share some common interest or attitude and seek to influence government for specific ends. Interest groups usually work within the framework of government and employ tactics such as lobbying to achieve their goals.

interested money Contributions by individuals or groups in hopes of influencing the outcome of an election and subsequently influencing policy.

interlocking directorate A corporation in which an officer or director sits on the board of a competitor, with the effect of restraining trade.

interstate compact An agreement among two or more states. The Constitution requires that most such agreements be approved by Congress.

iron triangle A mutually supporting relationship among interest groups, congressional committees and subcommittees, and government agencies that share a common policy concern.

issue advertising Commercial advertising on radio and television advocating a particular position on an issue, paid for by interest groups and designed to influence voters' choices on election day.

issue advocacy Promoting a particular position on an issue, often funded by interest groups and designed to influence voters' choices on election day. The money is unlimited and undisclosed.

item veto A measure passed by Congress in 1996 and ruled unconstitutional by the Supreme Court in 1998 whereby the president was given the authority to strike specific spending programs from the budget passed by Congress. Also permits governors in some states to veto individual items in an appropriations bill while signing the remainder of the bill into law.

Jim Crow laws State laws formerly pervasive throughout the South requiring public facilities and accommodations to be segregated by race; ruled unconstitutional.

joint committee Committee composed of members of both the House of Representatives and the Senate; such committees oversee the Library of Congress and conduct investigations.

judiciable dispute A dispute that grows out of an actual case and is capable of settlement by legal methods.

judicial activism Judicial philosophy proposing that judges should interpret the Constitution to reflect current conditions and values.

judicial interpretation A method whereby judges can modify a constitutional provision's restrictive force by a narrow interpretation of its meaning.

judicial restraint Judicial philosophy proposing that judges should interpret the Constitution to reflect what the framers intended and what its words literally say.

judicial review The power of a court to refuse to enforce a law or a government regulation that in the opinion of the judges conflicts with the Constitution, or, in a state court, that conflicts with the state constitution.

Keynesian economics Economic theory based on the principles of John Maynard Keynes stating that government spending should increase during business slumps and be curbed during booms.

labor injunction A court order forbidding specific individuals or groups from performing certain acts (such as striking) that the court considers harmful to the rights and property of an employer or community.

laissez-faire economics Economic theory that opposes governmental interference in the economy beyond what is necessary to protect life and property.

lame duck A politician who cannot, or has announced that he or she will not, run again.

legal privileges Privileges granted by the government to which we have no constitutional or legal right; once granted they cannot be denied except by appropriate procedures.

legislative caucus Party members in a legislative chamber who meet to select party leadership, decide policy positions, and distribute campaign funds.

libel Written defamation of another person. Especially in the case of public officials and public figures, the constitutional tests designed to restrict libel actions are very rigid.

liberalism A belief in the positive uses of government to bring about justice and equality of opportunity.

libertarianism An ideology that cherishes individual liberty and insists on a sharply limited government, promoting a free-market economy, a noninterventionist foreign policy, and an absence of regulation in the moral and social spheres.

literacy test Literacy requirement imposed by some states as a condition of voting, generally used to disqualify blacks from voting in the South; now illegal.

lobby To attempt to influence public officials, especially legislators, and the policies they enact.

lobbying Activities aimed at influencing public officials, especially legislators, and the policies they enact.

lobbyist A person who is employed by and acts for an organized interest group or corporation to try to influence policy decisions and positions in the executive and legislative branches.

log rolling Mutual aid and vote trading among legislators.

magistrate judge An official appointed for renewable terms who performs a variety of limited judicial duties.

majority A candidate or party wins more than half the votes cast to win an election.

majority leader The legislative leader selected by the majority party who helps plan party strategy, confers with other party leaders, and tries to keep members of the party in line.

majority-minority district A congressional district created to include a majority of minority voters; ruled constitutional so long as race is not the only factor.

majority rule Governance according to the expressed preferences of the majority.

manifest destiny A notion held by nineteenth-century Americans that the United States was destined to rule the continent, from the Atlantic to the Pacific Oceans.

mass media Means of communication that reach the mass public. The mass media include newspapers and magazines, radio, television (broadcast, cable, and satellite), films, recordings, books, and electronic communication.

mayor-council charter The oldest and most common form of city government, consisting of either a weak mayor and a city council or a strong mayor and council.

Medicaid Federal program that provides medical benefits for low-income persons.

medical savings account Alternative means of health care in which individuals make tax deductible contributions to a special account that can be saved from year to year and used to pay for medical expenses.

Medicare National health insurance program for the elderly and disabled.

merit system A system of public employment in which selection and promotion depend on demonstrated performance rather than political patronage.

minor party A small political party that rises and falls with a charismatic candidate or, if composed of ideologues on the right or left, usually persists over time.

minority leader The legislative leader selected by the minority party as spokesperson for the opposition.

misdemeanor A minor crime; the penalty is a fine or imprisonment for a short time, usually less than a year in a local jail.

Missouri Plan A system for selecting judges that combines features of the appointive and elective methods. The governor selects judges from lists presented by panels of lawyers and laypersons, and at the end of their term the judges may run against their own record in retention elections.

monetarism A theory that government should control the money supply to encourage economic growth and restrain inflation.

monetary policy Government policy that attempts to manage the economy by controlling the money supply and interest rates.

monopoly Domination of an industry by a single company; also the company that dominates.

most-favored-nation status Trade status granted as part of an international trade policy that gives a nation the same favorable trade concessions and tariffs that our best trading partners receive.

movement A large body of people interested in a common issue, idea, or concern that is of continuing significance and who are willing to take action on that issue. Movements seek to change attitudes or institutions, not only policies.

national party convention The national meeting of delegates elected in primaries, caucuses, or state conventions who assemble once every four years to nominate candidates for president and vice-president, ratify the party platform, elect officers, and adopt rules.

national supremacy Constitutional doctrine that whenever conflict occurs between the constitutionally authorized actions of the national government and those of a state or local government, the actions of the national government take priority.

natural law God's or nature's law that defines right from wrong and is higher than human law.

natural rights Rights of all people to dignity and worth.

naturalization A legal action conferring citizenship upon an alien.

necessary and proper clause Clause of the Constitution setting forth the implied powers of Congress. It states that Congress, in addition to its express powers, has the power to make all laws necessary and proper for carrying out all powers vested by the Constitution in the national government.

New Jersey Plan Proposal at the Constitutional Convention made by William Paterson of New Jersey for a central government with a single-house legislature in which each state would be represented equally.

new judicial federalism The practice whereby state courts use the bill of rights in their state constitution to provide more protection for some rights than is provided by the Supreme Court's interpretation of the Bill of Rights in the U.S. Constitution.

news media That part of the mass media that emphasizes the news.

nonpartisan A local or judicial election in which candidates are not selected or endorsed by political parties.

North American Free Trade Agreement (NAFTA) Agreement signed by the United States, Canada, and Mexico in 1992 to form the largest free-trade zone in the world.

obscenity Quality or state of a work that taken as a whole appeals to a prurient interest in sex by depicting sexual conduct in a patently offensive way and that lacks serious literary, artistic, political, or scientific value.

office block ballot Method of voting in which all candidates are listed under the office for which they are running.

Office of Management and Budget (OMB) Presidential staff agency that serves as a clearinghouse for budgetary requests and management improvements.

Office of Personnel Management (OPM) Agency that administers civil service laws, rules, and regulations.

opinion of the court An opinion and explanation of a decision by the Supreme Court or any other appelate court.

one-party state A state in which one party wins all or nearly all the offices, and the other party receives only a small proportion of the popular vote.

open primary A primary in which any voter, regardless of party, may vote.

open rule A procedural rule in the House of Representatives that permits floor amendments within the overall time allocated to the bill.

open shop A company with a labor agreement whereby union membership cannot be required as a condition of employment.

original jurisdiction The authority of a court to hear a case "in the first instance."

override An action taken by Congress to reverse a presidential veto that requires a two-thirds majority in each chamber.

party caucus Meeting of party members in a chamber of the legislature to select the party leadership in that chamber and develop party policy. Called a *conference* by Republicans.

party column ballot Method of voting in which all candidates are listed under their party designations, making it easy for voters to cast votes for all the candidates of one party.

party convention A meeting of party delegates to pass on matters of policy and in some cases to select party candidates for public office.

party identification An informal and subjective affiliation with a political party that most people acquire in childhood.

party platform The official statement of party policy.

party registration The act of declaring party affiliation; in some states required when one registers to vote.

patronage Dispensing government jobs to persons who belong to the winning political party.

petit jury A jury of 6 to 12 persons that determines guilt or innocence in a civil or criminal action.

plea bargain Negotiations between a prosecutor and defendant aimed at getting the defendant to plead guilty in return for the prosecutor's agreeing to reduce the seriousness of the crime for which the defendant will be convicted.

plurality A candidate or party wins the most votes cast, not necessarily more than half.

pocket veto A veto exercised by the president after Congress has adjourned; if the president takes no action for ten days, the bill does not become law and is not returned to Congress for a possible override.

police powers Inherent powers of state governments to pass laws to protect the public health, safety, and welfare; the national government has no directly granted police powers, but through other delegated powers accomplishes the same goals.

political action committee (PAC) The political arm of an interest group that is legally entitled to raise funds on a voluntary basis from members, stockholders, or employees in order to contribute funds to favored candidates or political parties.

political culture The widely shared beliefs, values, and norms concerning the relationship of citizens to government and to one another.

political predisposition A characteristic of individuals that is predictive of political behavior.

political party An organization that seeks political power by electing people to office so that its positions and philosophy become public policy.

political question A dispute that requires knowledge of a nonlegal character, or the use of techniques not suitable for a court, or explicitly assigned by the Constitution to Congress or the president; judges refuse to answer constitutional questions that they declare are political.

political rights Rights of citizens to participate in the process of governance flowing from the right to vote; secured by the Fifteenth, Nineteenth, and Twenty-Third Amendments

political socialization The process by which we develop our political attitudes, values, and beliefs.

poll tax Payment required as a condition for voting; prohibited for national elections by the Twenty-fourth Amendment (1964) and ruled unconstitutional for all elections in *Harper v Virginia Board of Elections* (1966).

popular consent The idea that a just government must derive its powers from the consent of the people it governs.

popular sovereignty A belief that ultimate power resides in the people.

pork-barrel legislation Government benefits or programs that may help the economy of a member of Congress's district.

preemption The right of a federal law or regulation to preclude enforcement of a state or local law or regulation.

preferred position doctrine Interpretation of the First Amendment that holds that freedom of expression is so essential to the operation of a democracy that judges should give it special protection and should almost never allow governments to punish persons for what they say, only for what they do.

president pro tempore Officer of the Senate selected by the majority party to act as chair in the absence of the vice-president.

prior restraint Restraint or censorship imposed before a speech is made or a newspaper published, usually presumed to be unconstitutional.

privatization The contracting out to the private sector of services that are usually provided by government.

pro bono Term used to describe the work lawyers (or other professionals) do to serve the public good and for which they either receive no fees or decline to receive fees.

procedural due process Constitutional requirement that governments proceed by proper methods; places limits on how governmental power may be exercised.

progressive tax A tax graduated so that people with higher incomes pay a larger fraction of their income than people with lower incomes.

property rights The rights of an individual to own, use, rent, invest in, buy, and sell property.

proportional representation An election system in which each party receives the proportion of legislative seats corresponding to its proportion of the vote.

protectionism Policy of erecting trade barriers to protect domestic industry.

public defender system Arrangement whereby public officials are hired to provide legal assistance to those persons accused of crimes who are unable to hire their own attorneys.

public goods Services or commodities that individuals benefit from but that cannot be sold separately or given to individuals. Examples are clean air, national defense, roads, harbors, and public order.

public opinion The distribution of individual preferences or evaluations of a given issue, candidate, or institution within a population.

quota In a trade context, a limit on the quantity of a particular product that may be imported.

race A grouping of human beings with common characteristics presumed to be transmitted genetically.

racial gerrymandering The drawing of election districts so as to ensure that members of a certain race are always a minority in the district; ruled unconstitutional in *Gomillion v Lightfoot* (1960).

racial or religious restrictive covenants A provision in a deed to real property excluding its sale to persons of a particular race or religion. Judicial enforcement of such deeds is unconstitutional.

realigning election An election that proves to be a turning point, redefining the agenda of politics and the alignment of voters within parties during periods of historic change in the economy and society.

recall Procedure for submitting to popular vote the removal of public officials from office before the end of their term.

recidivist A repeat offender.

reconciliation Process by which Congress sets ceilings on what Appropriations Subcommittees can appropriate.

redistributive policies Governmental tax and social programs that shift wealth or benefits from one segment of the population to another, often from the rich to the poor.

redistricting The redrawing of congressional and other legislative district lines following the census to accommodate population shifts and keep districts as equal as possible in population. Also called *reapportionment.*

reduction veto The power of governors in a few states to reduce a particular appropriation.

referendum Procedure for submitting to popular vote measures passed by the legislature or proposed amendments to a state's constitution.

regressive tax A tax whereby people with lower incomes pay a higher fraction of their income than people with lower incomes.

regulation The attempt by government to control the behavior of corporations, other governments, or citizens through altering the natural workings of the open market to achieve some desired goal.

regulatory taking Government regulation of property so extensive that government is deemed to have taken the property by the power of eminent domain, for which it must compensate the property owners.

reinforcing cleavages Divisions within society that reinforce one another, making groups more homogeneous or similar.

representative democracy Government that derives its powers indirectly from the people, who elect those who will govern; also called a *republic.*

responsibility contract A welfare strategy adopted by some states in which recipients sign a written agreement specifying their responsibilities and outlining a plan for obtaining work and achieving self-sufficiency.

revenue sharing Program from 1972 to 1987 whereby federal funds were provided to state and local governments to be spent largely at the discretion of the receiving governments, subject to very general conditions.

revision commission A state commission that recommends changes in the state constitution for action by the legislature and vote by the voters.

revolving door The employment cycle in which individuals work, in turn, for governmental agencies regulating interests and then for the interest groups or businesses with the same policy concern.

rider A provision that may have little relationship to the bill it is attached to in order to secure its passage.

right of expatriation Right of individuals to renounce their citizenship.

rights of persons accused of crimes Rights that protect all persons from abusive use by the government of the power to prosecute and punish persons who violate the criminal laws; secured by the Fourth, Fifth, Sixth, Eighth, and Fourteenth Amendments.

safe seat An elected office that is predictably won by one party or the other.

sales tax General tax on sales transactions, sometimes exempting food and drugs.

search warrant A warrant issued by a magistrate that authorizes the police to search a particular place or person, specifying the place to be searched and the objects to be seized.

sedition Attempting to overthrow the government by force or to interrupt its activities by violence.

select or special committee A congressional committee created for a specific purpose, sometimes to conduct an investigation.

selective exposure The process by which individuals screen out those messages that do not conform to their own biases.

selective perception The process by which individuals perceive what they want to in media messages and disregard the rest.

selectively incorporated Process by which the provisions of the Bill of Rights are brought within the scope of the Fourteenth Amendment and so applied to state and local governments.

senatorial courtesy Presidential custom of submitting the names of prospective appointees for approval to senators from the states in which the appointees are to work.

seniority rule A legislative practice that assigns the chair of a committee or subcommittee to the member of the majority party with the longest continuous service on the committee.

separation of powers Constitutional division of powers among the legislative, executive, and judicial branches, with the legislative branch making law, the executive branch applying and enforcing the law, and the judiciary interpreting the law.

severance tax A tax on the privilege of "severing" such natural resources as coal, oil, timber, and gas from the land.

Shays' Rebellion Rebellion by farmers in western Massachusetts in 1786–87, protesting mortgage foreclosures; led by Daniel Shays, and important because it highlighted the need for a strong national government just as the call for a Constitutional Convention went out.

single-member district An electoral district in which voters choose one representative or official.

social capital Participation in associations that reinforce democratic habits of discussion, compromise, and respect for differences.

Social Security A combination of entitlement programs, paid for by employer and employee taxes, that includes retirement benefits, health insurance, and support for disabled workers and the children of deceased or disabled workers.

social stratification Divisions in a community among socioeconomic groups or classes.

socialism An economic and governmental system based on public ownership of the means of production and exchange.

soft money Money contributed to a state or local political party for party-building purposes that does not have to be disclosed under federal law.

Speaker The presiding officer in the House of Representatives, formally elected by the House but actually selected by the majority party.

split ticket Voting for some of one party's candidates and some from another party.

spoils system System of public employment based on rewarding party loyalists and friends.

standing committee A permanent committee established in a legislature, usually focusing on a policy area.

stare decisis The rule of precedent, whereby a rule or law contained in a judicial decision is commonly viewed as binding on judges whenever the same question is presented.

state delegation The senators and representatives from the same state.

statism The idea that the rights of the state (meaning nation) are supreme over the rights of the individual.

straight ticket Voting for all of one party's candidates.

strong mayor-council Form of local government in which the voters directly elect the city council and the mayor, who enjoys almost total administrative authority and appoints the department heads.

substantive due process Constitutional requirement that governments act reasonably and that the substance of the laws themselves be fair and reasonable; places limits on what a government may do.

tariff Tax levied on imports to help protect a nation's industries, labor, or farmers from foreign competition. It can also be used to raise additional revenue.

tax expenditure Loss of tax revenue due to federal tax laws that provide special tax incentives or benefits to individuals or businesses.

The Federalist Series of essays promoting ratification of the Constitution, written by Alexander Hamilton, John Jay, and James Madison in 1787 and 1788.

theocracy Government by religious leaders, who claim divine guidance.

three-fifths compromise Compromise agreement between northern and southern states at the Constitutional Convention in which the slave population would be counted at three-fifths for determining direct taxation and representation in the House of Representatives.

tort law Law relating to noncontractual injuries to person, reputation, or property.

trade deficit An imbalance in international trade in which the value of imports exceeds the value of exports.

trust A monopoly that controls goods and services, often in combinations that reduce competition.

trustee A view of the role of legislators that holds that they should think and vote independently based on their judgment of the facts.

turnout The proportion of the voting-age public that votes.

two-party state A state in which the two major parties alternate in winning majorities.

unicameral legislature A one-house legislature.

union shop A company in which new employees must join a union within a stated time period.

unitary system A constitutional arrangement in which power is concentrated in a central government.

user fees Fees charged directly to individuals who use certain public services on the basis of service consumed; also called a *user charge.*

value-added tax (VAT) A tax on increased value of a product at each stage of production and distribution rather than just at the point of sale.

veto Rejection by a president or governor of legislation passed by a legislature.

Virginia Plan Proposal at the Constitutional Convention made by the Virginia delegation for a strong central government with a bicameral legislature, the lower house to be elected by the voters and the upper chosen by the lower.

voter registration System designed to reduce voter fraud by limiting voting to those who have established eligibility by submitting the proper form.

voucher A school reform program whereby a set amount of money is provided by government to parents for their use in paying for their child's education, in a public or private school of their choice.

weak mayor-council Form of local government in which the members of the city council select the mayor, who then shares power with other elected or appointed boards and commissions.

whip Party leader who is the liaison between the leadership and the rank-and-file in the legislature.

white primary Primary operated by the Democratic party in southern states that, before Republicans gained strength in the "one-party South," essentially constituted an election; ruled unconstitutional in *Smith v Allwright* (1944).

winner-takes-all An election system in which the candidate with the most votes wins.

women's suffrage The right of women to vote.

workfare A welfare strategy adopted by some states that gives able-bodied adults who do not have preschool-aged children the opportunity to learn job skills that can lead to employment.

writ of *certiorari* A formal writ used to bring a case before the Supreme Court.

writ of *habeas corpus* Court order directing any official having a person in custody to produce the prisoner in court and explain to the judge why the prisoner is being held.

writ of *mandamus* Court order directing an official to perform an official duty.

yellow-dog contract Contract by an anti-union employer that forces new workers to promise they will not join a union as a condition of employment.

NOTES

CHAPTER 1

1. "White House Scandal Has Families Talking: Teens Losing Respect for Politicians," Pew Research Center for People & The Press, press release, September 30, 1998.
2. For a major theoretical work on the principle of majority rule, see Robert A. Dahl, *Democracy and Its Critics* (Yale University Press, 1989).
3. Seymor Martin Lipset, "The Social Requisites of Democracy Revisited," *American Sociological Review* 59 (1994), pp. 1–22.
4. For a discussion of the importance for democracy of such overlapping group memberships, see David Truman's seminal work, *The Governmental Process*, 2d ed. (Knopf, 1971).
5. Harry Eckstein, *Lessons for the "Third Wave" from the First* (Center for the Study of Democracy, University of California, Irvine, 1996), p. 20.
6. Joyce Appleby, "The American Heritage: The Heirs and the Disinherited," *Journal of American History* (December 1987), p. 808.
7. Maryland and Massachusetts documents quoted in Bernard Schwartz, *Roots of the Bill of Rights* (Chelsea House, 1980), 1:68–73.
8. Richard L. Hillard, "Liberalism, Civic Humanism and the American Revolutionary Bills of Rights, 1775–1790," paper presented at the annual meeting of the Organization of American Historians, Reno, Nevada, 1988.
9. Lance Banning, *The Sacred Fire of Liberty: James Madison and the Founding of the Federal Republic* (Cornell University Press, 1995).
10. See the essays in Thomas E. Cronin, ed., *Inventing the American Presidency* (University Press of Kansas, 1989).
11. Charles A. Beard and Mary R. Beard, *A Basic History of the United States* (New Home Library, 1944), p. 136.
12. See Herbert J. Storing, ed., abridgment by Murray Dry, *The Anti-Federalist: Writings by the Opponents of the Constitution* (University of Chicago Press, 1985).
13. On the role of the promised bill of rights amendments in the ratification of the Constitution, see Leonard W. Levy, *Constitutional Opinions* (Oxford University Press, 1986), chap. 6.

CHAPTER 2

1. Max Lerner, *Ideas for the Ice Age* (Viking, 1941), pp. 241–42. See also *The American Public's Knowledge of the U.S. Constitution: A National Survey of Public Awareness and Personal Opinion* (Hearst Corporation, 1987).
2. Sanford Levinson, *Constitutional Faith* (Princeton University Press, 1988), pp. 9–52.
3. Richard Morin, "We Love It—What We Know of It," *The Washington Post National Weekly Edition*, September 22, 1997, p. 35.
4. Thomas Jefferson, quoted in Alpheus T. Mason, *The Supreme Court: Palladium of Freedom* (University of Michigan Press, 1962), p. 10.
5. James L. Sundquist, "Needed: A Political Theory for the New Era of Coalition Government in the United States," *Political Science Quarterly* (Winter 1988–89), pp. 613–35; Robert A. Godwin and Art Kaufman, eds., *Separation of Powers: Does It Still Work?* (AEI Press, 1986).
6. Charles O. Jones, "The Separate Presidency," in *The New American Political System*, ed. Anthony King, 2d ed. (AEI Press, 1990), p. 3.
7. Morris P. Fiorina, "An Era of Divided Government," *Political Science Quarterly* 107, no. 3 (1992), p. 407.
8. David R. Mayhew, *Divided We Govern: Party Control, Lawmaking, and Investigations, 1946–1990* (Yale University Press, 1991), p. 4. See also James A. Thurber, ed., *Divided Democracy: Presidents and Congress in Cooperation and Conflict* (Congressional Quarterly, 1991).
9. Charles O. Jones, *Separate But Equal Branches: Congress and the Presidency* (Chatham House, 1995).
10. Robert C. Vipond, *Liberty and Community: Canadian Federalism and the Failure of the Constitution* (State University of New York Press, 1991), p. 192.
11. Alec Stone, "Governing with Judges: The New Constitutionalism," in Jack Hayward and Edward C. Page, *Governing the New Europe* (Polity Press, 1995), pp. 286–313; Donald P. Kommers, "The Federal Constitutional Court in the German Political System," *Comparative Political Studies* 26 (January 1994), pp. 470–91; Martin J. Shapiro, "The European Court of Justice," in *Euro-Politics*, ed. Alberta M. Sbrdagia (Brookings Institution, 1992); Martin J. Shapiro and Alec Stone, "The New Constitutional Politics," *Comparative Political Studies* 26 (January 1994), pp. 397–420; Alec Stone, *The Birth of Judicial Politics in France* (Oxford University Press, 1993).
12. Edward S. Corwin, "The Constitution as Instrument and as Symbol," *American Political Science Review* (December 1936), p. 1078. J. M. Sosin argues that these earlier precedents do not support the opinion that judicial review was "in the air," in *The Aristocracy of the Long Robe: The Origins of Judicial Review in America* (Greenwood Press, 1989).
13. *Marbury v Madison*, 1 Cranch 137 (1803).
14. Dumas Malone, *Jefferson the President: First Term, 1801–1805* (Little, Brown, 1970), p. 145.
15. *Dred Scott v Sandford*, 19 Howard 393 (1857).
16. Robert Lowry Clinton, *Marbury v. Madison and Judicial Review* (University Press of Kansas, 1989), pp. 4–42.
17. J. W. Peltason, *Federal Courts in the Political Process* (Random House, 1955).
18. See Eleanore Bushnell, *Crimes, Follies, and Misfortunes: The Federal Impeachment Trials* (University of Illinois Press, 1992); Michael J. Gerhardt, *The Federal Impeachment Process: A Constitutional and Historical Analysis* (Princeton University Press, 1996).
19. *Nixon v United States*, 506 US 224 (1993).
20. Ibid. Stephen Gettinger, "When Congress Decides a President's 'High Crimes and Misdemeanors,'" *Congressional Quarterly*, March 7, 1998, pp. 565–68.
21. John R. Labovitz, *Presidential Impeachment* (Yale University Press, 1978); Alison Mitchell, "Clinton Acquitted Decisively: No Majority for Either Charge," *The New York Times*, February 13, 1999, p. 1.
22. Richard E. Neustadt, *Presidential Power* (Free Press, 1990), pp. 180–81.
23. John Vile, review of *Explicit and Authentic Acts*, by David Kyvig, *Constitutional Commentary* (University of Minnesota Law School) 14, no. 2 (Summer 1997), p. 423.
24. Ronald L. Goldfarb, "The 11,000th Amendment: There's a Rush to Amend the Constitution, and It Shows No Signs of Letting Up," *The Washington Post National Weekly Edition*, November 25–December 1, 1996, p. 22.
25. See Committee on the Constitutional System, *A Bicentennial Analysis of the American Political Structure: Report and Recommendations of the Committee on the Constitutional System* (1987), for recommendations of a committee co-chaired by Senator Nancy L. Kassebaum, C. Douglas Dillon, and Lloyd Cutler. For critical comments, see Mark P. Petracca, "To Right What the Constitution Has Wrought or To Wrong What Is Right," presented at annual meeting of the American Political Science Association, Washington, D.C., 1988.
26. Ann Stuart Diamond, "A Convention for Proposing Amendments: The Constitution's Other Method," *Publius* (Summer 1981), pp. 113–46; Wilbur Edel, "Amending the Constitution by Convention: Myths and Realities," *State Government* 55 (1982), pp. 51–56.

27. Russell L. Caplan, *Constitutional Brinksmanship: Amending the Constitution by National Convention* (Oxford University Press, 1988), p. x. See also David E. Kyvig, *Explicit and Authentic Acts: Amending the U.S. Constitution, 1776–1995* (University Press of Kansas, 1996), p. 440.
28. Samuel S. Freedman and Pamela J. Naughton, *ERA: May a State Change Its Vote?* (Wayne State University Press, 1979).
29. Kyvig, *Explicit and Authentic Acts*, p. 286.
30. Ibid., p. 286; *Dillon v Gloss*, 256 US 368 (1921).
31. William Van Alstyne, "What Do You Think About the Twenty-seventh Amendment," *Constitutional Commentary* 10, no. 1 (University of Minnesota Law School, 1993), p. 15.
32. Gregory A. Caldeira, "Constitutional Change in America: Dynamics of Ratification Under Article V," *Publius* (Fall 1985), p. 29.
33. Mark R. Daniels, Robert Darcy, and Joseph W. Westphal, "The ERA Won—At Least in the Opinion Polls," *PS: Political Science and Politics* (Fall 1982), p. 583.
34. Ibid.
35. Janet K. Boles, *The Politics of the Equal Rights Amendment: Conflict and Decision-Making Powers* (Longman, 1979), p. 4.
36. Gilbert Y. Steiner, *Constitutional Inequality: The Political Fortunes of the Equal Rights Amendment* (Brookings Institution, 1985), p. 64. See also Mary Frances Berry, *Why the ERA Failed: Politics, Women's Rights, and the Amending Process of the Constitution* (Indiana University Press, 1986).

CHAPTER 3

1. For background, see Samuel H. Beer, *To Make a Nation: The Rediscovery of American Federalism* (Harvard University Press, 1993).
2. Ronald L. Watts, "Canadian Federalism in the 1990's: Once More in Question," *Publius* 21 (Summer 1991), pp. 169–90; Robert C. Vipond, "The Canadian Constitutional Crisis: Who's Right on Rights?" *Intergovernmental Perspective* (Fall 1991), pp. 49–52; Vipond, *Liberty and Community: Canadian Federalism and the Failure of the Constitution* (State University of New York Press, 1991).
3. "Wales Gives Narrow Approval to Home Rule," CNN World News (http://www.cnn.com/WORLD/9709/18/britain.wales/index.html). Michael Keating, "Reforging the Union: Devolution and Constitutional Change in the United Kingdom," *Publius 28* (Winter 1998) pp. 217–234.
4. The term "devolution revolution" was coined by Richard P. Nathan in testimony before the Senate Finance Committee, as quoted by Daniel Patrick Moynihan, "The Devolution Revolution," *The New York Times*, August 6, 1995, p. B15.
5. *U.S. Term Limits, Inc. v Thornton*, 514 US 779 (1995).
6. *United States v Lopez*, 514 US 549 (1995).
7. William H. Stewart, *Concepts of Federalism* (Center for the Study of Federalism and University Press of America, 1984). See also Edward L. Rubin and Malcolm Feeley, "Federalism: Some Notes on a National Neurosis," *UCLA Law Review* 41 (April 1994), pp. 903–52.
8. Morton Grodzins, "The Federal System," in *Goals for Americans: The Report of the President's Commission on National Goals* (Columbia University Press, 1960).
9. Thomas R. Dye, *American Federalism: Competition Among Governments* (Lexington Books, 1990), pp. 13–17.
10. Michael D. Reagan and John G. Sanzone, *The New Federalism* (Oxford University Press, 1981), p. 175.
11. Daniel J. Elazar, *Exploring Federalism* (University of Alabama Press, 1987), p. 6.
12. Frederick K. Lister, *The European Union, the United Nations and the Revival of Confederal Governance* (Greenwood Press, 1996).
13. See Beer, *To Make a Nation.*
14. William H. Riker, *The Development of American Federalism* (Academic Publishers, 1987), pp. 14–15. Riker contends that not only does federalism not guarantee freedom but that the framers of our federal system, as well as those of other nations, were not animated by considerations of safeguarding freedom but by practical considerations of preserving unity.
15. *Gibbons v Ogden*, 9 Wheaton 1 (1824).
16. *Heart of Atlanta Motel v United States*, 379 US 241 (1964).
17. *Luther v Borden*, 7 Howard 1 (1849).
18. *California v Superior Courts of California*, 482 US 400 (1987).
19. David C. Nice, "State Participation in Interstate Compacts," *Publius* 17 (Spring 1987), p. 70. See also Council of State Governments, *Interstate Compacts & Agencies* (1995) for list of compacts by subject and by state with brief description.
20. *McCulloch v Maryland*, 4 Wheaton 316 (1819).
21. *Missouri v Jenkins*, 495 US 33 (1990); *Missouri v Jenkins*, 515 US 70 (1995).
22. *Oklahoma City v Tuttle*, 471 US 808 (1985); *Maine v Thiboutot*, 488 US1 (1980); *Monell v New York City Dept. of Social Welfare*, 436 US 658 (1978).
23. David Rapp, "The FEDS: Washington and the States: The Politics of Distrust," *Governing*, September 1, 1992, p. 67; *Florence County School District Four v Carter*, 510 US 7 (1993).
24. Joseph F. Zimmerman, "Federal Preemption Under Reagan's New Federalism," *Publius* 21 (Winter 1991), pp. 7–28.
25. *Webster v Reproductive Health Services*, 492 US 490 (1989); *Planned Parenthood of Southeastern Pennsylvania v Casey*, 505 US 833 (1992).
26. Oliver Wendell Holmes, Jr., *Collected Legal Papers* (Harcourt, 1920), pp. 295–96.
27. *U.S. Term Limits, Inc. v Thornton*, 514 US 779 (1995).
28. *Garcia v San Antonio Metro*, 469 US 528 (1985).
29. *United States v Lopez*, 514 US 549 (1995). Richard A. Brisbin, Jr., "The Reconstitution of American Federalism? The Rehnquist Court and Federal-State Relations, 1991-1997," *Publius* (Winter 1998), pp. 189–217.
30. *U.S. Term Limits v Thornton*, 514 US 779 (1995).
31. *Seminole Tribe of Florida v Florida*, 517 US 44 (1996).
32. *City of Boerne v Flores*, 138 L Ed 2d 624 (1997).
33. *Printz v United States*, 138 L Ed 2d 914 (1997).
34. John E. Chubb, "The Political Economy of Federalism," *American Political Science Review* 79 (December 1985), p. 1005.
35. Paul E. Peterson, *The Price of Federalism* (Brookings Institution, 1995), p. 127.
36. William Weld, "The States Won't Be Cruel," *The New York Times*, February 9, 1996, p. A15; *Congressional Quarterly Weekly Report*, August 3, 1996, pp. 2190–96.
37. Donald F. Kettl, *The Regulation of American Federalism* (Johns Hopkins University Press, 1987), pp. 154–55.
38. *Congressional Quarterly Weekly Report*, April 15, 1995, p. 1087.
39. Advisory Commission on Intergovernmental Relations, *Restoring Confidence and Competence* (ACIR, 1981), p. 30.
40. Cynthia Cates Colella, "The Creation, Care and Feeding of the Leviathan: Who and What Makes Government Grow," *Intergovernmental Perspective* (Fall 1979), p. 9.
41. Aaron Wildavsky, "Bare Bones: Putting Flesh on the Skeleton of American Federalism," in Advisory Commission on Intergovernmental Relations, *The Future of Federalism in the 1980s* (ACIR, 1981), p. 79.
42. Peterson, *Price of Federalism*, p. 182.
43. "GOP Confounds Expectations, Expands Federal Authority," *Congressional Quarterly Weekly Report*, November 2, 1996, p. 3117.
44. Eliza Newlin Carney, "Power Grab," *National Journal*, April 11, 1998, p. 798. See also Joshua Wolf Shenk, "Washington's Counter-Devolutionaries," *U.S. News & World Report*, November 24, 1997, p. 34.
45. Luther Gulick, "Reorganization of the States," *Civil Engineering* (August 1933), pp. 420–21.
46. David E. Osborne, *Laboratories of Democracy* (Harvard Business School Press, 1988), p. 363.
47. Thomas R. Dye, *American Federalism: Competition Among Governments* (Lexington Books, 1990), p. 199.
48. Daniel J. Elazar, *American Federalism: A View from the States*, 3d ed. (Harper and Row, 1984), p. 241.
49. Martha M. Hamilton, "If You Want Something Done Right, Do It Yourself," *Washington Post National Weekly Edition*, September 5–11, 1988, p. 31.
50. Edward Felsenthal, "Firms Ask Congress to Pass Uniform Rules," *The Wall Street Journal*, May 10, 1993, p. B4.
51. John J. DiIulio, Jr., and Donald F. Kettl, *Fine Print: The Contract with America, Devolution, and the Administrative Realities of American Federalism* (Brookings Institution, 1995), p. 60.

CHAPTER 4

1. Craig Smith, *To Form a More Perfect Union: The Ratification of the Constitution and the Bill of Rights, 1788–1791* (University Press of America, 1993).
2. Charles R. Epp, "Do Bills of Rights Matter? The Canadian Charter of Rights and Freedoms," *American Political Science Review* 90, no. 4 (December 1996), p. 765.
3. *Barron v Baltimore*, 7 Peters 243 (1833).
4. *Gitlow v New York*, 268 US 652 (1925).
5. "Project Report: Toward an Activist Role for State Bills of Rights," *Harvard Civil Rights–Civil Liberties Law Review* 8 (March 1973), p. 274.
6. Stanley H. Friedelbaum, ed., *Human Rights in the States: New Directions in Constitutional Policy Making* (Greenwood, 1988); Dorothy Toth Beasley, "Federalism and the Protection of Individual Rights: The American State Constitutional Perspective," in Ellis Katz and G. Alan Tarr, eds., *Federalism and Rights* (Rowman & Littlefield, 1996).
7. Peter J. Galie, "State Supreme Courts, Judicial Federalism and the Other Constitutions," *Judicature* (August/September 1987), pp. 100–110. See also Jeff Rosen, "Altered States: Liberals and Forgotten Constitutions," *The New Republican*, July 1, 1991, p. 19; Steven Pressman, "Protecting Rights in State Courts," Editorial Research Reports, *Congressional Quarterly* 1, no. 20 (1988), p. 277; Dorothy Beasley, "State Bills of Rights: Dead or Alive?" *Intergovernmental Perspective* (June 1989), pp. 13–17.
8. Rosen, "Altered States," p. 20.
9. Barry Latzer, "The Hidden Conservatism of the State Court 'Revolution,'" *Judicature* (December 1990/January 1991), p. 193.
10. *Walz v Tax Commission*, 397 US 644 (1970).
11. *Lemon v Kurtzman*, 403 US 602 (1971).
12. *Everson v Board of Education*, 333 U.S. 203 (1947). See also Leonard W. Levy, *The Establishment Clause: Religion and the First Amendment* (Macmillan, 1986).
13. *Lemon v Kurtzman*, 403 US 602 (1971).
14. *Capital Square Review Board v Pinette*, 132 L Ed 2d 650 (1995).
15. *Lynch v Donnelly*, 465 U.S. 669 (1984).
16. *Allegheny County v. Greater Pittsburgh ACLU*, 492 US 573 (1989).
17. *Bowen v Kendrick*, 487 US 589 (1988); *Texas Monthly, Inc. v Bullock*, 489 U.S. 1 (1989); *Lee v Weisman*, 505 US 577 (1992); *Board of Education of Kiryas Joel Village School District v Grumet*, 512 US 687 (1994).
18. *Lee v Weisman*, 505 US 577 (1992).
19. *Engel v Vitale*, 370 US 421 (1962).
20. *Edwards v Aguillard*, 482 US 578 (1987).
21. *Marsh v Chambers*, 463 US 783 (1983).
22. *Writters v. Washington Department of Service for Blind*, 474 US 481 (1986).
23. Donald L. Brakeman, *Church-State Constitutional Issues: Making Sense of the Establishment Clause* (Greenwood, 1991), p. 125.
24. *Mueller v Allen*, 463 US 388 (1983).
25. *Agostini v Felton*, 521 US 74 (1997).
26. *Aguilar v Felton*, 473 US 402 (1985) and *School Dist. of Grand Rapids v Ball*, 473 US 373 (1985), overruled by *Agostini v Felton*, 521 US 74 (1997).
27. *Zobrest v Catalina Foothills School District*, 509 US 1 (1993).
28. *Rosenberger v University of Virginia*, 515 US 819 (1995).
29. *Wisconsin v Yoder*, 406 US 205 (1972).
30. *Employment Division, Department of Human Resources of Oregon v Smith*, 494 US 872 (1990).
31. Jesse H. Choper, *Securing Religious Liberty: Principles for Judicial Interpretation of the Religion Clauses* (University of Chicago Press, 1995), p. 55.
32. *Weekly Compendium of Presidential Documents* 2377 (November 16, 1993).
33. *City of Boerne v Flores*, 138 L Ed 2d 624 (1997).
34. Jeremy Learning, "Senators Told New Religious-Protection Act is Needed and Constitutional," *The Freedom Forum OnLine*, June 25, 1998, http://www.freedomforum.org/religion.
35. John Stuart Mill, *Essay on Liberty* (1859), in *The English Philosophers from Bacon to Mill*, ed. Arthur Burtt (Random House, 1939), p. 961.
36. *Abrams v United States*, 250 US 616 (1919).
37. *Hustler Magazine v Falwell*, 485 US 46 (1988).
38. *West Virginia State Board of Education v Barnette*, 319 US 624 (1943).
39. *Brown v Hartlage*, 456 US 45 (1982), in which the Supreme Court reversed a decision of the Kentucky Court of Appeals based on the bad tendency doctrine.
40. *Schenck v United States*, 249 US 47 (1919).
41. *Whitney v California*, 274 US 357 (1927).
42. *Nebraska Press Association v Stuart*, 427 US 539 (1976). See also Fred W. Friendly, *Minnesota Rag: The Dramatic Story of the Landmark Supreme Court Case That Gave New Meaning to Freedom of the Press* (Random House, 1981).
43. *Hazelwood School District v Kuhlmeier*, 484 US 260 (1988).
44. *Winters v New York*, 333 US 507 (1948). See also *Burstyn v Wilson*, 343 US 495 (1952).
45. *Regan v Time, Inc.*, 468 US 641 (1984).
46. *R.A.V. v St. Paul*, 505 US 377 (1992). See also Edward J. Cleary, *Beyond the Burning Cross: The First Amendment and the Landmark R.A.V. Case* (Random House, 1995) by the attorney for the cross burner.
47. *Branzburg v Hayes*, 408 US 665 (1972).
48. *Richmond Newspapers, Inc. v Virginia*, 448 US 555 (1980). See also David M. O'Brien, *The Public's Right to Know: The Supreme Court and the First Amendment* (Praeger, 1981).
49. See Frank Reuven, "Don't Hide the News from Hidden Cameras: The Ethics of Undercover Reporting in Light of Food Lion-ABC News," *Los Angeles Times*, February 17, 1997, p. B5; and Terry Tange, "Revisiting the Food Lion Case: Can Deception Serve a Useful Purpose?" *The New York Times*, February 17, 1997, p. 22.
50. Page Putnam Miller, "Status Report on the Freedom of Information Act," *PS: Political Science and Politics* (Winter 1988), pp. 87–90. See also Michael Moss, "Federal Service Gets Wider Use by Sleuths, Snoops—and Senators: Freedom of Information Act Offers Surprise Benefits for Business, Investors," *Wall Street Journal*, January 3, 1996, p. A1; Cheryl Arvidson, "Government Agencies Slow to Make Info Available Online," http://www.freedomforum.org/press/1998; Steven Aftergood, "Press Aids Argentine Democracy, openness-with help from U.S. FOIA," Freedom Forum.
51. Susanna Barber, *News Cameras in the Courtroom: A Free Press–Fair Trial Debate* (Ablex, 1987), p. 9.
52. *Milwaukee Pub. Co. v Burleson*, 255 US 407 (1921).
53. *Lamont v Postmaster General*, 381 US 301 (1965).
54. *Rowan v Post Office Department*, 397 US 728 (1970).
55. *Southeastern Promotions, Ltd. v Conrad*, 420 US 546 (1975).
56. *McIntyre v Ohio Election Commission*, 514 US 334 (1995).
57. *Burson v Freeman*, 504 US 191 (1992).
58. Phillip Taylor, "Court Orders FCC to Rule on 'Personal Attack' Petition," May 12, 1998, *The Freedom Forum onLine*, http://www.freedomforum.org/press/1998; see also Taylor, "Broadcasters to Ask Court to Force FCC Action on 'Personal Attack' Rules," June 24, 1998, ibid.
59. Lucas A. Powe, Jr., *American Broadcasting and the First Amendment* (University of California Press, 1987).
60. *Arkansas Educational Television Commission v Forbes*, 140 L Ed 2d 875 (1998).
61. *Turner Broadcasting System v FCC*, 518 US 180 (1997).
62. *Denver Area Educational Television v FCC*, 518 US 727 (1996).
63. Lizette Alvarez, "Internet Is New Pet Issue in Congress," *The New York Times*, national ed., June 28, 1998, p. 14; Juliana Gruenwald, "Who's Minding Whose Business on the Internet?" *Congressional Quarterly Weekly Report*, July 25, 1998, p. 1986.
64. *Sable Communications v Federal Communications Commission*, 492 US 115 (1989).
65. Barnaby J. Feder, "Toward Defining Free Speech in the Computer Age," *The New York Times*, November 3, 1991, p. E5; Don Oldenburg, "Computers: Rights on the Line," and "The Law: Lost in Cyberspace," *The Washington Post*, October 1, 1991, p. E5; Dan Carney, "TeleCommunications: Conferees Favor 'Indency' Standard," *Congressional Quarterly Weekly Report*, December 9, 1995, p. 3734.
66. *The New York Times v Sullivan*, 376 US 254 (1964). See also Anthony Lewis, *Make No Law: The Sullivan Case and the First Amendment* (Random House, 1991), p. 140.
67. *Harte-Hanks, Inc. v Connaughton*, 491 US 657 (1989).

68. *Hustler Magazine v Falwell*, 485 US 46 (1988).
69. *Masson v New Yorker Magazine, Inc.*, 501 US 496 (1991).
70. *Brockett v Spokane Arcades, Inc.*, 472 US 491 (1985).
71. *Miller v California*, 413 US 15 (1973).
72. *Young v American Mini Theatres*, 427 US 51 (1976). See also *Renton v Playtime Theatres, Inc.*, 475 US 41 (1986).
73. *Ginsberg v New York*, 390 US 629 (1968).
74. *Reno v ACLU*, 138 L Ed 2d 874 (1997).
75. *General Media Communications v Cohen*, 141 L Ed 2d 736 (1998).
76. "From Preamble to Indianapolis City-County Ordinance," cited by Joel B. Grossman, "The First Amendment and the New Anti-Pornography Statutes," *News for Teachers of Political Science* (American Political Science Association, 1985), p. 18. See also Catharine A. MacKinnon, *Only Words* (Harvard University Press, 1993). For a rebuttal to MacKinnon by another feminist, see Nadine Strossen, *Defending Pornography: Free Speech, Sex, and the Fight for Women's Rights* (Scribner's, 1995).
77. Cass R. Sunstein, *The Partial Constitution* (Harvard University Press, 1993), p. 268.
78. "Anti-Pornography Laws and First Amendment Values," *Harvard Law Review* 98 (1984), p. 460. See also Donald Alexander Downs, *The New Politics of Pornography* (University of Chicago Press, 1990).
79. *Butler v Her Majesty the Queen*, 1 S.C.R. 452 (1992). See also "Pornography, Equality, and a Discrimination-Free Workplace: A Comparative Perspective," *Harvard Law Review* 106 (March 1993), pp. 1075–92; Kent Greenawalt, *Fighting Words* (Princeton University Press, 1995), pp. 113–23.
80. *Hudnut v American Booksellers*, 475 US 1001 (1986); *Sable Communications v Federal Communications Commission*, 492 US 115 (1989).
81. *Chaplinsky v New Hampshire*, 315 US 568 (1942).
82. *Cohen v California*, 403 US 115 (1971). See also *NAACP v Claiborne Hardware Co.*, 458 US 886 (1982); *R.A.V. v St. Paul*, 505 US 377 (1992).
83. *Cohen v California*, 403 US 115 (1971).
84. *West Virginia State Board of Education v Barnette*, 319 US 624 (1943).
85. See two works by Leonard W. Levy: *Legacy of Suppression* (Harvard University Press, 1960) and *Freedom of the Press from Zenger to Jefferson* (Bobbs-Merrill, 1966).
86. *Dennis v United States*, 341 US 494 (1950).
87. *Yates v United States*, 354 US 298 (1957).
88. *Brandenburg v Ohio*, 395 US 444 (1969).
89. David M. Hamlin, "Swastikas and Survivors: Inside the Skokie-Nazi Free Speech Case," *Civil Liberties Review* (March/April 1978).
90. Lee C. Bollinger, *The Tolerant Society: Freedom of Speech and Extremist Speech in America* (Oxford University Press, 1986), pp. 24–32. See also Donald A. Downs, *Nazis in Skokie: Freedom, Community, and the First Amendment* (University of Notre Dame Press, 1985).
91. Freedom Forum Online (http://www.freedomforum.org/assembly/1998/9/2/ march.asp).
92. Lee C. Bollinger, *Images of a Free Press* (University of Chicago Press, 1991).
93. *Walker v. Birmingham*, 388 US 307 (1967).
94. *Madsen v. Women's Health Center*, 512 US 753 (1994); *Schenck v Pro-Choice Network*, 519 US 357 (1997).
95. *Pruneyard Shopping Center v Robins*, 447 US 74 (1980).

CHAPTER 5

1. Michael R. Belknap, *Federal Law and Southern Order: Racial Violence and Constitutional Conflict in the Post-Brown South* (University of Georgia, 1987), pp. 128–204.
2. Taylor Branch, *Parting the Waters: America in the King Years, 1954–1963* (Simon & Schuster, 1988). See also Harris Wofford, *Of Kennedys and Kings: Making Sense of the Sixties* (Farrar, Strauss and Giroux, 1980).
3. See Robert D. Loevy, *To End All Segregation: The Politics and Passage of the Civil Rights Act of 1964* (University Press of America, 1990).
4. Aldon D. Morris, *The Origins of the Civil Rights Movement: Black Communities Organizing for Change* (Free Press/Macmillan, 1985); James Farmer, *Lay Bare the Heart: An Autobiography of the Civil Rights Movement* (Arbor House, 1985).
5. National Advisory Commission on Civil Disorders, *The Kerner Report* (Washington, D.C.: Government Printing Office, 1968), p. 1.
6. Ellen Carol DuBois, *Feminism and Suffrage: The Emergence of an Independent Women's Movement in America, 1848–1869* (Cornell University Press, 1978); Joan Hoff-Wilson, "Women and the Constitution," *News for Teachers of Political Science* (American Political Science Association), Summer 1985, pp. 10–15.
7. Susan M. Hartmann, *From Margin to Mainstream: American Women and Politics since 1960* (Temple University Press, 1989); Susan Gluck Mezey, *In Pursuit of Equality: Women, Public Policy, and the Federal Courts* (St. Martin's Press, 1992).
8. U.S. Bureau of the Census, *Population Profile of the United States, 1998* (Government Printing Office, 1998), p. 44.
9. Celia W. Dugger, "U.S. Study Says Asian-Americans Face Widespread Discrimination," *The New York Times*, February 29, 1992, p. 1, reporting on U.S. Civil Rights Commission, *Civil Rights Issues Facing Asian Americans in the 1990s.*
10. Won Moo Hurh, *Korean Immigrants in America* (Fairleigh Dickinson University Press, 1984).
11. Antonio J. A. Pido, *The Filipinos in America: Macro/Micro Dimensions of Immigration and Integration* (Center for Migration Studies of New York, 1986).
12. Harold L. Hodgkinson, *The Demographics of American Indians: One Percent of the People, Fifty Percent of the Diversity* (Institute for Educational Leadership/Center for Demographic Policy, 1990), pp. 1–5. See also *1998 Almanac* (Houghton Mifflin, 1998) p. 680.
13. Charles F. Wilkinson, *American Indians, Times, and the Law* (Yale University Press, 1987), p. 62; Vine Deloria, Jr., and Clifford M. Lytle, *The Nations Within: The Past and Future of American Indian Sovereignty* (Pantheon Books, 1984).
14. *County of Yakima v Yakima Indian Nation*, 502 US 251 (1992).
15. Theodora Lurie, "Shattering the Myth of the Vanishing American," *The Ford Foundation Letter* 22 (Winter 1991), p. 5.
16. Office of Technology Assessment, quoted by Spencer Rich in "Native Americans, They Can Still Get Free Health Care If They're Indian Enough," *The Washington Post National Weekly Edition*, July 14, 1986, p. 34.
17. *Idaho Employment v Smith*, 434 US 1 (1974).
18. *San Antonio School District v Rodriguez*, 411 US 1 (1973).
19. *Frontiero v Richardson*, 411 US 677 (1973).
20. *Califano v Webster*, 430 US 313 (1977).
21. *Mississippi University for Women v Hogan*, 458 US 718 (1982).
22. *Rostker v Goldberg*, 453 US 57 (1981).
23. *San Antonio School District v Rodriguez*, 411 US 1 (1973).
24. *Washington v Davis*, 426 US 229 (1976). See also *Hunter v Underwood*, 471 US 522 (1985).
25. Justice Sandra Day O'Connor, concurring in *Hernandez v New York*, 500 US 352 (1991).
26. *Personnel Administrator of Massachusetts v Feeney*, 442 US 256 (1979).
27. *Smith v Allwright*, 321 US 649 (1944).
28. *Gomillion v Lightfoot*, 364 US 339 (1960).
29. *Harper v Virginia Board of Elections*, 383 US 663 (1966).
30. Harold W. Stanley, *Voter Mobilization and the Politics of Race: The South and Universal Suffrage, 1952–1984* (Praeger, 1987).
31. Abigail M. Thernstrom, *Whose Votes Count? Affirmative Action and Minority Voting Rights* (Harvard University Press, 1987), p. 15.
32. *Report of the United States Commission on Civil Rights* (Government Printing Office, 1959), pp. 103–4.
33. Thernstrom, *Whose Votes Count?* For a contrary view, see Bernard Grofman, Lisa Handley, and Richard G. Niemi, *Minority Representation and the Quest for Voting Equality* (Cambridge University Press, 1992).
34. *Morse v Republican Party of Virginia*, 134 L Ed 2d 347 (1996).
35. Ellen Perlman, "Feds on Remaps: No Go," *City and State*, July 29–August 11, 1991.

36. *Shaw v Reno*, 509 US 630 (1993). See also *Shaw v Reno*, 509 US 874; *Johnson v De Grandy*, 512 US 997 (1994).
37. *Abrams v Johnson*, 518 US 74 (1997); *Miller v. Johnson*, 515 US 900 (1995).
38. Orlando Patterson, *The Ordeal of Integration: Progress and Resentment in America's "Racial" Crisis* (Civitas/Counterpoint, 1997), p. 67.
39. *Plessy v Ferguson*, 163 US 537 (1896).
40. *Brown v Board of Education of Topeka*, 347 US 483 (1954). See also J. W. Peltason, *Fifty-eight Lonely Men: Southern Federal Judges and School Desegregation* (University of Illinois Press, 1971), p. 248.
41. *Brown v Board of Education*, 349 US 294 (1955).
42. *Alexander v Board of Education*, 396 US 802 (1969).
43. William Celis III, "Study Finds Rising Concentration of Black and Hispanic Students," *The New York Times*, December 14, 1993, p. A1.
44. *Missouri v Jenkins*, 495 US 33 (1990).
45. See Gary Orfield, Susan E. Eaton, and the Harvard Project on School Desegregation, *Dismantling Desegregation: The Quiet Reversal of Brown v Board of Education* (New Press, 1996). See also Peter Appelbome, "Schools See Reemergence of 'Separate But Equal'," *The New York Times*, April 8, 1997, p. A8.
46. Raymond Hernandez, "NAACP Suspends Yonkers Leader After Criticism of Usefulness of School Busing," *The New York Times*, November 1, 1995, p. A13.
47. Quoted by Peter Applebome, "Opponents' Moves Refueling Debate on School Busing," *The New York Times*, September 26, 1995, p. A1.
48. Justice William O. Douglas, dissenting in *Moose Lodge No. 107 v Irvis*, 407 US 163 (1972).
49. *New York State Club Association v New York City*, 487 US 1 (1988).
50. *Civil Rights Cases*, 109 US 3 (1883).
51. *Heart of Atlanta Motel v United States*, 379 US 421 (1964).
52. Darryl Van Duch, "Plagued by Politics, EEOC Backlog Grows," *The Recorder*, August 18, 1998, p. 1; David Rovella, "EEOC Chairman Casellas, 'We Are Being Selective'," *The National Law Journal*, November 20, 1995, p. 1.
53. Charles M. Lamb, "Housing Discrimination and Segregation," *Catholic University Law Review* (Spring 1981), p. 370.
54. *Shelley v Kraemer*, 334 US 1 (1948).
55. Timothy Noah, "Housing Report Says Racial Bias Remains Prevalent," *The Wall Street Journal*, August 30, 1991, reporting on findings of report prepared by the Urban Institute commissioned by the Department of Housing and Urban Development.
56. Daniel Mitchell, quoted in CQ Researcher, *Housing Discrimination* 5 (February 24, 1995), p. 174.
57. Justice John Marshall Harlan, dissenting in *Plessy v Ferguson*, 163 US 537 (1896).
58. *University of California Regents v Bakke*, 438 US 265 (1978).
59. Justice Byron White, concurring in *Wygant v Jackson Board of Education*, 476 US 267 (1986).
60. Justice Sandra Day O'Connor, majority opinion, and Justice Thurgood Marshall, dissenting in *Richmond v Croson*, 488 US 469 (1989).
61. Justice William J. Brennan, majority opinion, and Justice Sandra Day O'Connor, dissenting in *Metro Broadcasting v Federal Communications Commission*, 497 US 547 (1990).
62. *Shaw v Reno*, 509 US 630 (1993); *Miller v Johnson*, 515 US 900 (1995).
63. *Hopwood v Texas*, 518 US 1016 (1996).
64. Ibid.
65. Kathleen M. Sullivan, "Getting Around the Supreme Court," *The Washington Post National Edition*, December 15, 1997, p. 21.
66. Romel Hernandez, "Universities Will End Offers of Scholarships Based on Race," *The Oregonian*, March 21, 1998; http://www.oregonlive.com/todaynews.
67. Carol M. Swain et al., "When Whites and Blacks Agree: Fairness in Educational Opportunities," Institute of Governmental Studies, University of California at Berkeley, Working Paper 98-11, 1998, p. 6. See also Lee Sigelman and Susan Welch, *Black Americans' Views of Racial Inequality: The Dream Deferred* (Cambridge University Press, 1994); Peter Skerry, "The Affirmative Action Paradox," *Society* 35, no. 6 (September/October 1998), p. 11.
68. Sam Howe Verhovek, *The New York Times*, November 6, 1997, A1.
69. John Leo, "Hold the 'Wrong' Story," *U.S. News & World Report*, August 10, 1998, p. 12.
70. Steven A. Holmes, "Victorious Preference Foes Look for New Battles," *The New York Times*, November 10, 1998, p. A25.
71. James Farmer, quoted in Rochelle L. Stanfield, "Black Complaints Haven't Translated into Political Organization and Power," *National Journal*, June 14, 1980, p. 465.
72. National Academy of Science, *A Common Destiny: Blacks and American Society* (National Academy Press, 1989).
73. Gary Orfield, "Separate Societies: Have the Kerner Warnings Come True?" in *Quiet Riots: Race and Poverty in the United States—The Kerner Report Twenty Years Later*, ed. Fred R. Harris and Roger W. Wilkins (Pantheon, 1988), p. 103. See also Madeline Landau, "Race, Poverty and the Cities: Hyperinnovation in Complex Policy Systems," *Public Affairs Report* (Bulletin of the Institute of Governmental Studies, University of California, Berkeley) 30 (January 1989), p. 1; Margaret C. Simms, ed., *Black Economic Progress: An Agenda for the 1990's* (Joint Center for Political Studies, 1988); Nicholas Lehmann, *The Promised Land* (Knopf, 1991).
74. Gary Orfield and Carole Ashkinaze, *The Closing Door: Conservative Policy and Black Opportunity* (University of Chicago Press, 1991), p. 26.
75. William J. Wilson, *The Truly Disadvantaged: The Inner City, the Underclass, and Public Policy* (University of Chicago Press, 1987), esp. chap. 5.
76. Orfield and Ashkinaze, *Closing Door*, pp. 221–34.
77. Patterson, p. 54.
78. Gleen C. Loury and Christopher Edley, Jr., "Will All This Talk About Race Lead to Any Action?" *The Washington Post National Weekly Edition*, December 18, 1997, p. 19.
79. Advisory Board of the President's Initiative on Race, *One America in the 21st Century: Forging a New Future* (Government Printing Office, 1998).
80. Council of Economic Advisers, *Changing America: Indicators of Social and Economic Well-Being by Race and Hispanic Origin* (Government Printing Office, 1998).

CHAPTER 6

1. *Presser v Rodriguez*, 411 US 475 (1973).
2. *Stone v Powell*, 428 US 465 (1976); *McCleskey v Zant*, 499 US 467 (1991); *Winthow v Williams*, 507 US 680 (1993). For a review of these decisions, see Jordan Steiker, "Innocence and Federal Habeas," *UCLA Law Review* 41 (December 1993), pp. 303–89.
3. *Felker v Turpin*, 518 US 651 (1996).
4. Martin Edelman, *Democratic Theories and the Constitution* (State University of New York Press, 1984), p. 304; Judith N. Shklar, *American Citizenship: The Quest for Inclusion* (Harvard University Press, 1991), p. 3.
5. *Vance v Terrazas*, 444 US 252 (1980).
6. G. Pascal Zachary, "Dual Citizenship Is Double-Edged Sword," *The Wall Street Journal*, March 25, 1998, p. B1, B15, quoting T. Alexander Aleinikoff of the Carnegie Endowment for International Peace. See also Mark Fritz,"Dual Citizenships Create Dueling Family Allegiances," *Los Angeles Times*, April 6, 1998, p. A1; William Branigin, "Pledging Allegiance to Two Flags," *The Washington Post National Weekly Edition*, June 8, 1998, p. 14.
7. *Slaughter-House Cases*, 16 Wallace 36 (1873).
8. Plyler v Doe, 457 US 202 (1982).
9. Arnold H. Leibowitz, "The Refugee Act of 1980: Problems and Congressional Concerns," *Annals of the American Academy of Political and Social Sciences* (May 1983), pp. 163–71. See also Gil Loescher and John Scanlan, *Calculated Kindness: Refugees and America's Half-Open Door, 1945 to Present* (Free Press, 1986).

10. *Sale v Haitian Centers Council, Inc.*, 509 US 155 (1993).
11. *Plyler v Doe*, 457 US 202 (1982). See also Paul Yoshihashi, "Employer Sanctions and Illegal Workers," *The Wall Street Journal*, May 26, 1989, p. B1.
12. Dan Carney, "Law Restricts Illegal Immigration," *Congressional Quarterly Weekly Report*, November 16, 1996, pp. 3287–88.
13. Sam Dillon, "U.S.-Mexico Study Sees Exaggeration of Migration Data," *The New York Times National Edition*, August 31, 1997, p. 6. See also Bilateral Commission on the Future of United States–Mexican Relations, *The Challenge of Interdependence: Mexico and the United States* (University Press of America, 1989), p. 185.
14. Belinda Reyes, "Why Return Migration Matters: The Case of Immigration from Western Mexico," Public Policy Institute of California, p. 4, and Belinda Reyes, "Dynamics of Immigration: Return Migration to Western Mexico," Public Policy Institute of California, 1997.
15. *Kleindienst v Mandel*, 408 US 753 (1972).
16. Senator Alan Simpson, quoted by Justice John Paul Stevens in *McNary v Haitian Refugee Center*, 498 US 479 (1991).
17. Bilateral Commission, *Challenge of Interdependence*, p. 77.
18. *Chicago Home Building & Loan Assn. v Blaisdell*, 290 US 398 (1934).
19. *Chicago, Burlington & Quincy Railway Co. v Chicago*, 166 US 226 (1897).
20. Richard A. Epstein, *Taking: Private Property and the Power of Eminent Domain* (Harvard University Press, 1985).
21. *First English Evangelical v Los Angeles County*, 482 US 304 (1987).
22. *United States v 564.54 Acres of Land*, 441 US 506 (1979).
23. Ibid.
24. *Nollan v California Coastal Commission*, 483 US 825 (1987); *Dolan v City of Tigard*, 512 US 374 (1994).
25. *Mathews v Eldridge*, 424 US 319 (1976), restated in *Connecticut v Doeher*, 501 US 1 (1991).
26. *Leary v United States*, 395 US 6 (1969); *Turner v United States*, 369 US 398 (1970).
27. *Meyer v Nebraska*, 262 US 390 (1923).
28. *Morrissey v Brewer*, 408 US 471 (1972).
29. Philip B. Kurland, *Some Reflections on Privacy and the Constitution* (University of Chicago Center for Policy Study, 1976), p. 9. A classic and influential article about privacy is S. D. Warren and L. D. Brandeis, "The Right to Privacy," *Harvard Law Review*, December 15, 1890, pp. 193–220.
30. *Roe v Wade*, 410 US 113 (1973).
31. *Planned Parenthood of Southeastern Pennsylvania v Casey*, 505 US 833 (1992).
32. *Ohio v Akron Center for Reproductive Health*, 497 US 502 (1990); *Hodgson v Minnesota*, 497 US 417 (1990); *Planned Parenthood of Southeastern Pennsylvania v Casey*, 505 US 833 (1992).
33. Trisha Renaud, "Georgia Overturns Sodomy Law," *The Recorder*, November 24, 1998, p. 1.
34. *Roemer v Evans*, 517 US 620 (1996).
35. The most comprehensive analysis of these complicated issues is Wayne R. LaFave, *Search and Seizure: A Treatise on the Fourth Amendment*, 2d ed. (West Publishing Co., 1987).
36. *County of Riverside v McLaughlin*, 500 US 44 (1991).
37. *California v Hodari D.*, 499 US 621 (1991).
38. *Chandler v Miller*, 520 US 305 (1997).
39. *Treasury Employees v Von Raab*, 489 US 656 (1989); *Skinner v Railway Labor Executives' Assn.*, 489 US 602 (1989); *Vernonia School Dist. 47J v Action*, 515 US 646 (1995); *Chandler v Miller*, 520 US 305 (1997).
40. *United States v Ross*, 456 US 798 (1982).
41. *Pennsylvania v Mimms*, 434 US 110 (1977), reaffirmed in *Ohio v Robinette*, 519 US 33 (1997).
42. *Terry v Ohio*, 392 US 1 (1968); *United States v Sharpe*, 470 US 675 (1985); *Hayes v Florida*, 470 US 811 (1985).
43. *Minnesota v Dickerson*, 508 US 366 (1993).
44. *Chimel v California*, 395 US 752 (1969); *United States v Edward*, 415 US 800 (1974); *Illinois v Lafayette*, 462 US 640 (1983).
45. *Cupp v Murphy*, 412 US 291 (1973).
46. *Schneckloth v Bustamonte*, 412 US 218 (1973); *Ohio v Robinette*, 519 US 33 (1997); *United States v Matlock*, 415 US 164 (1974).
47. *Almeida-Sanchez v United States*, 413 US 266 (1973); *United States v Ortiz*, 422 US 891 (1975).
48. *United States v Ramsey*, 431 US 606 (1977).
49. *Coolidge v New Hampshire*, 403 US 443 (1971); *Texas v Brown*, 460 US 730 (1983); *Arizona v Hicks*, 480 US 321 (1987).
50. *Michigan v Tyler*, 436 US 499 (1978); *Mincey v Arizona*, 437 US 385 (1978).
51. Benjamin Wittes, "Ames Case Leads to More Powerful Spy Court," *The Recorder*, November 8, 1994, p. 16.
52. *Tennessee v Garner*, 471 US 1 (1985).
53. *Mapp v Ohio*, 367 US 643 (1961).
54. Senate Committee on the Judiciary, *The Jury and the Search for Truth: The Case Against Excluding Relevant Evidence at Trial: Hearing before the Committee*, 104th Cong., 1st sess., 1997.
55. *United States v Leon*, 468 US 897 (1984).
56. *Blau v United States*, 340 US 332 (1951).
57. David Stout, "Lewinsky Gets Total Immunity As Long as She Speaks the Truth," *The New York Times National Edition*, July 29, 1998, p. A14.
58. *Mincey v Arizona*, 437 US 385 (1978).
59. *Miranda v Arizona*, 384 US 436 (1966). Liva Baker, *Miranda: Crime, Law and Politics* (Atheneum, 1983), explores every aspect of the decision, including subsequent controversy about its effects.
60. *Rhodes v Chapman*, 452 US 337 (1981); *Wilson v Seither*, 501 US 294 (1991).
61. Hutto v Davis, 454 US 370 (1982); *Solem v Helm*, 463 US 277 (1983).
62. *Graham v Collins*, 506 US 461 (1993).
63. Fox Butterfield, "Behind the Death Row Bottleneck," *The New York Times*, January 25, 1998, sec. 4, p. 5. See also WWW//Smu.edu/~deathpen/summary.html, and the U.S. Department of Justice, *Bureau of Justice Statistics, Capital Punishment, 1997* (December 1998).
64. Henry Weinstein, "Execution Halt Sought by American Bar Assn.," *Los Angeles Times*, February 4, 1997, p. A13.
65. Felix Frankfurter, dissenting in *United States v Rabinowitz*, 339 US 56 (1950).
66. *United States v Salerno*, 481 US 739 (1987).
67. *United States v Enterprises, Inc.*, 498 US 292 (1991).
68. *Blanton et al. v North Las Vegas*, 489 US 538 (1989).
69. *J.E.B. v Alabama ex rel T. B.*, 511 US 127 (1994); *Batson v Kentucky*, 476 US 79 (1986); *Powers v Ohio*, 499 US 400 (1991); *Hernandez v New York*, 500 US 352 (1991); *Georgia v McCollum*, 505 US 42 (1990).
70. *Benton v Maryland*, 395 US 784 (1969).
71. See also *Kansas v Hendricks*, 138 L Ed 2d 501 (1997).
72. Jerome Frank, *Courts on Trial* (Princeton University Press, 1949), p. 122. See also Rita James Simon, ed., *The Jury System in America: A Critical Overview* (Sage Publications, 1975); John Guinther, *The Jury in America* (Facts-on-File Publications, 1988); Steven Brill, *Trial by Jury* (American Lawyer Books/Touchstone, 1989).
73. Laura Mansnerus, "Rewriting the Rules of the Jury System," *The New York Times*, November 4, 1995, p. Y7.
74. See comments of Jeffrey Abramson in *The New York Times*, November 4, 1995, p. Y7.
75. Harry Kalven, Jr., and Hans Zeisel, *The American Jury* (University of Chicago Press, 1971), p. 57. See also Jeffrey Abramson, *We, The Jury: The Jury System and the Ideal of Democracy* (Basic Books, 1994).
76. William O. Douglas, dissenting in *United States v Mara*, 410 US 19 (1973).
77. *M.L.B. v M.L.J.*, 519 US 102 (1997) and cases cited therein.
78. Jonathan Kaufman, Wade Lambert, and Benjamin A. Holden, "Fuhrman's Comments Bolster Black Concerns About Police Conduct," *The Wall Street Journal*, August 31, 1995, p. A1.
79. George Edwards, *The Police on the Urban Frontier* (Institute of Human Relations Press and the American Jewish Committee, 1968), p. 28.
80. Sandra Bass, "Blacks, Browns, and the Blues: Police and Minorities in California," *Public Affairs Report* (IGS, University of California, Berkeley) 38 (November 1997), p. 10.
81. Associated Press, "Civilian Police-Review Agencies on Rise Nationwide," *The Recorder*, September 9, 1996, p. 8. See also *Understanding Community Policing* (Bureau of Justice Administrations, August 1994); www.community policy.org
82. *West Virginia State Board of Education v Barnette*, 319 US 624 (1943).
83. Robert H. Jackson, *The Supreme Court in the American System of Government* (Harvard University Press, 1955), pp. 81–82.
84. Richard Behar, "Who's Reading Your E-mail?" *Fortune*, February 3, 1997, pp. 56–70.

CHAPTER 7

1. Robert D. Putnam, "Bowling Alone: America's Declining Social Capital," *Journal of Democracy* 6, no. 1 (January 1995), pp. 65–78. See also Robert D. Putnam, *Bowling Alone: Civic Disengagement in America and What to Do About It* (Simon & Schuster, 2000).
2. Ibid., p. 4.
3. Margaret Levi, "Social and Unsocial Capital: A Review Essay of Robert Putnam's *Making Democracy Work*," *Politics and Society* 24, no. 1 (March 1996), pp. 45–55.
4. Michael W. Folley and Bob Edwards, "Escape from Politics? Social Theory and the Social Capital Debate," *American Behavioral Science* 40, no. 5 (1997), pp. 55–56.
5. Katha Pollitt, "For Whom the Ball Rolls," *The Nation* 262, no. 15 (April 15, 1996), p. 9.
6. Jean Bethke Elshtain, "Not a Cure-All," *The Brookings Review* 15, no. 4 (Fall 1997), pp.13–15.
7. Clinton Rossiter, *Conservatism in America* (Vintage, 1962), p. 72.
8. See Ronald Dworkin, *Taking Rights Seriously* (Harvard University Press, 1977).
9. *Marbury v Madison*, 1 Cranch 137 (1803).
10. For an analysis of one aspect of the underclass, see Paul M. Sniderman and Michael Hagen, *Race and Inequality: A Study in American Values* (Chatham House, 1985).
11. When adjusted using the consumer price index (CPI), the percent of people earning over $75,000 a year has risen from 6.4 percent in 1970 to 12.5 percent in 1993. U.S. Bureau of the Census, *Statistical Abstract of the United States, 1995* (Government Printing Office, 1995), table 723.
12. See, generally, Bernard Bailyn, *The Ideological Origins of the American Revolution* (Harvard University Press, 1967).
13. Robert A. Dahl, "Liberal Democracy in the United States," in *A Prospect of Liberal Democracy*, ed. William Livingston (University of Texas Press, 1979), p. 64.
14. Ibid., pp. 59–60.
15. Franklin D. Roosevelt, State of the Union Address, January 11, 1944, *The Public Papers of the President of the United States, 1944* (Government Printing Office, 1962), pp. 371–94.
16. Bill Clinton, Address to Congress on Health Care, *The New York Times*, September 23, 1993, pp. A24–25.
17. Harry S Truman, State of the Union Address, 1949, *The Public Papers of the President of the United States, 1949* (Government Printing Office, 1964), pp. 1–7.
18. See Charles Peters and Philip Keisling, eds., *A New Road for America: The Neoliberal Movement* (University Press of America, 1984); Randall Rothenberg, *The Neoliberals: Creating the New American Politics* (Simon & Schuster, 1984).
19. E. J. Dionne, Jr., *They Only Look Dead: Why Progressives Will Dominate the Next Political Era* (Simon & Schuster, 1996), p. 13.
20. Ibid.
21. Newt Gingrich, *To Renew America* (HarperCollins, 1995), p. 102.
22. Barry Goldwater with Jack Casserly, *Goldwater* (Doubleday, 1988), p. 387.
23. Ronald Reagan, Inaugural Address, 1981, *The Public Papers of the President of the United States, 1981* (Government Printing Office, 1982), p. 1.
24. Kathleen Day, *S & L Hell: The People and the Politics Behind the $1 Trillion Savings and Loan Scandal* (W.W. Norton & Co., 1993).
25. Sylvia Nasar, "Even Among the Well-Off, the Rich Get Richer," *The New York Times*, March 5, 1992, p. A1.
26. Karl Marx, "Critique of the Gotha Program," in *Marx Selections*, ed. Allen W. Wood (Macmillan Publishing, 1988), p. 190.
27. Irving Howe, *Socialism and America* (Harcourt, 1985); Michael Harrington, *Socialism: Past and Future* (Arcade, 1989).
28. Daniel Yergin and Joseph Stainslaw, *The Commanding Heights: The Battle Between Government and the Marketplace That is Remaking the Modern World* (Simon & Schuster, 1998).
29. Charles Murray, *What It Means to Be a Libertarian* (Broadway Books, 1997).
30. Center for Political Studies, University of Michigan, *American National Election Study, 1990: Post Election Survey* (April 1991).
31. Nat Hentoff, "Liberal Trimmers of the First Amendment," *The Washington Post*, January 17, 1998, p. A25.
32. Dinesh D'Sousa, *Illiberal Education: The Politics of Race and Sex on Campus* (Free Press, 1991), p. 313.

CHAPTER 8

1. Glenn Garvin, "Loco, Completamente Loco," *Reason 29*, January 1998.
2. "Bilingual Education: A Squandered Opportunity; for the Sake of Youngsters, A 3 Year Limit Should be Sought," *Los Angeles Times*, October 26, 1997, p. M4.
3. National Clearinghouse for Bilingual Education, "Which School Districts in the U.S. Have the Highest LEP Enrollments?" and "How Has the LEP Student Population Changed in Recent Years?" at http://www.ncbe.gwu.edu/askncbe/faqs, February, 1998.
4. Quoted in William Booth, "A Plan to Write Off Bilingual Education: Californians to Vote on English-Immersion Proposal," *The Washington Post*, February 28, 1998, p. A9.
5. Quoted in ibid.
6. Albert Einstein, quoted in Laurence J. Peter, *Peter's Quotations* (William Morrow, 1977), p. 358.
7. Alexis de Tocqueville, *Democracy in America*, ed. J. P. Mayer, trans. George Lawrence (Doubleday and Company, 1969), p. 278.
8. Ibid., p. 280.
9. U.S. Bureau of the Census, *Statistical Abstract of the United States, 1997* (Government Printing Office, 1997), p. 289.
10. V. O. Key, Jr., *Politics, Parties, and Pressure Groups*, 5th ed. (Thomas Y. Crowell, 1964), p. 232.
11. Earl Black and Merle Black, *The Vital South: How Presidents Are Elected* (Harvard University Press, 1992), p. 4.
12. Joseph A. Pika and Richard A. Watson, *The Presidential Contest*, 5th ed. (Congressional Quarterly Press, 1996), pp. 80–81.
13. Tim Currant and John Mercurio, "A Seat at the Table," *Roll Call*, March 19, 1998.
14. Robert S. Erikson, Gerald C. Wright, and John P. McIver, *Statehouse Democracy: Public Opinion and Policy in the American States* (Cambridge University Press, 1993).
15. *Statistical Abstract, 1997*, p. 28.
16. Holly Idelson, "Count Adds Seats in Eight States," *Congressional Quarterly Weekly Report* 48 (December 29, 1990), p. 4240.
17. U.S. Bureau of the Census, *Statistical Abstract of the United States, 1993* (Government Printing Office, 1993), p. 8.
18. Douglas S. Massey, "The Age of Extremes: Concentrated Affluence and Poverty in the Twenty-First Century," *Demography* 33, no. 4 (November 1996), p. 404.
19. U.S. Bureau of the Census, *Population Profile of the United States, 1993*, U.S. Population Reports P-23, no. 185 (Government Printing Office, 1993), p. 34.
20. *Statistical Abstract, 1997*, pp. 45–47.
21. Ibid., p. 14.
22. Dale Rogers Marshall, "The Continuing Significance of Race: The Transformation of American Politics," *American Political Science Review* 84 (June 1990), pp. 611–16.
23. Robert D. Ballard, "Introduction: Lure of the New South," in *Search of the New South: The Black Urban Experience in the 1970s and 1980s*, ed. Robert D. Ballard (University of Alabama Press, 1989), p. 5.
24. *Statistical Abstract, 1997*, p. 36.
25. Ibid., p. 49.
26. U.S. Bureau of the Census, *Household Wealth and Asset Ownership, 1991*, Current Population Reports P-70, no. 34 (Government Printing Office, 1991), table H.

27. *Statistical Abstract, 1997,* p. 465.
28. Ibid., p. 149.
29. Ibid., p. 176.
30. Ibid., p. 23.
31. Mark R. Levy and Michael S. Karmer, *The Ethnic Factor: How America's Minorities Decide Elections* (Simon & Schuster, 1973); also Mark Stern, "Democratic Presidency and Voting Rights," in *Blacks in Southern Politics,* ed. Lawrence W. Mooreland, Robert P. Steed, and Todd A. Baker (Praeger, 1987), pp. 50–51.
32. David Bositis, *Blacks and the 1992 Republican National Convention* (Joint Center for Political and Economic Studies, 1992), p. 5; "Portrait of the Electorate," *The New York Times,* November 10, 1996, p. 16.
33. *Statistical Abstract, 1997,* pp. 35–37 (based on projections for 2000).
34. See Frank R. Parker, *Black Votes Count: Political Empowerment in Mississippi After 1965* (University of North Carolina Press, 1990).
35. Black Caucus of State Legislators, Washington, D.C.
36. Rodolfo O. de la Garza, Louis DeSipio, F. Chris Garcia, John Garcia, and Angelo Falcon, *Latino Voices: Mexican, Puerto Rican, and Cuban Perspectives on American Politics* (Westview Press, 1992), p. 14.
37. U.S. Bureau of the Census home page: http://www.census.gov/population/socdemo/hispanic/cps96/sumtab-1.txt, May 1998.
38. De la Garza et al., *Latino Voices,* p. 14.
39. *Statistical Abstract, 1997,* p. 38 (estimates for the year 2000).
40. U.S. Bureau of the Census home page: http://www.census.gov/ftp/pub/population/socdem/race/api/tab-01.txt, May 1998 and *Statistical Abstract,* 1997, p. 49.
41. *Statistical Abstract, 1997,* p. 34.
42. Ibid., p. 10.
43. U.S. Census Bureau, May 1998 (www.census.gov/prod/3/98pubs/p20-507.pdf).
44. James West Davidson, William E. Gienapp, Christine Leigh Heyrman, Mark H. Lytle, and Michael B. Stoff, *Nation of Nations* (McGraw-Hill, 1990), pp. 833–34.
45. G. Thomas Edwards, *Sowing Good Seeds: The Northwest Suffrage Campaigns of Susan B. Anthony* (Oregon Historical Society Press, 1990), p. 136.
46. Paul Kleppner, *Continuity and Change in Electoral Politics, 1893–1928* (Greenwood Press, 1987), p. 172.
47. Carol Mueller, "The Gender Gap and Women's Political Influence," *Annals of the American Academy of Political and Social Sciences* 515 (May 1991), p. 25.
48. Barbara C. Burrell, *A Woman's Place Is in the House: Campaigning for Congress in the Feminist Era* (University of Michigan Press, 1994).
49. Diane L. Fowlkes, "Feminist Theory: Reconstructing Research and Teaching About American Politics and Government," *News for Teachers of Political Science* (Winter 1987), pp. 6–9. See also Sally Helgesen, *Everyday Revolutionaries: Working Women and the Transformation of American Life* (Doubleday, 1998); Karen Lehrman, *The Lipstick Proviso: Women, Sex and Power in the Real World* (Anchor Books and Doubleday, 1997); Tanya Melich, *The Republican War Against Women: An Insider's Report from Behind the Lines: Updated Edition* (Ingram Publisher, 1998); and Virginia Valian, *Why So Slow? The Advancement of Women* (MIT Press, 1998).
50. E. J. Dionne, Jr., "Struggle for Work and Family Fueling Women's Movement," *The New York Times,* August 22, 1989, p. A1.
51. Jeffrey Schmalz, "Clinton Carves a Wide Path Deep into Reagan Country," *The New York Times,* November 4, 1992, p. B1.
52. *Statistical Abstract, 1997,* p. 429.
53. U.S. Bureau of the Census, *Statistical Abstract of the United States, 1996* (Government Printing Office, 1996), p. 470.
54. U.S. Bureau of the Census, Table p. 33 (http://www.census.gov/hhes/income/histinc/p33.html).
55. *Statistical Abstract, 1997,* p. 474.
56. *Statistical Abstract, 1997,* p. 74.
57. Reynolds Farley, *The American Reality: Who We Are, How We Got Here, Where We Are Going* (Russell Sage Foundation, 1996), p. 44.
58. For a discussion of the Holocaust, see Leni Yahil, *The Holocaust: The Fate of European Jewry* (Oxford University Press, 1990).
59. Stephen C. LeSuer, *The 1838 Mormon War in Missouri* (University of Missouri Press, 1987), pp. 151–53.
60. John Conway, "An Adapted Organic Tradition," *Daedalus* 117 (Fall 1988), p. 382. For an extended comparison of the impact of religion on politics in the United States and Canada, see Seymour Martin Lipset, *Continental Divide: The Values and Institutions of the United States and Canada* (Routledge, 1990), pp. 74–89.
61. Robert N. Bellah, *Beyond Belief: Essays on Religion in a Post-Traditional World* (University of California Press, 1991), pp. 168–90.
62. National Opinion Research Center, General Social Survey, 1972–94.
63. William H. Flanigan and Nancy H. Zingale, *Political Behavior of the American Electorate,* 9th ed. (CQ Press, 1998), p. 118.
64. Center for Political Studies, Inter-University Consortium for Political and Social Research, University of Michigan, *American National Election Study, 1992.*
65. Ibid.
66. Lyman A. Kellstedt and John C. Green, "Is There a Culture War: Religion and the 1996 Election." Paper presented at the American Political Science Association Annual Meeting, Washington, D.C., 1997 (www.wheaton.edu\polsci\kellstedt).
67. Telephone survey of 113,000 households in the 48 contiguous states, April 1989–April 1990, Graduate School of the City University of New York.
68. Raymond E. Wolfinger, Fred I. Greenstein, and Martin Shapiro, *Dynamics of American Politics,* 2d ed. (Prentice Hall, 1980), p. 19.
69. Thomas Jefferson, "Autobiography," in *The Life and Selected Writings of Thomas Jefferson,* ed. Adrienne Koch and William Peden (Modern Library, 1944), p. 38.
70. U.S. Department of Education, *Digest of Education Statistics, 1991* (Government Printing Office, 1991), p. 294.
71. U.S. Bureau of the Census, *Historical Statistics of the United States, Colonial Times to 1970* (Government Printing Office, 1976), p. 297; *Statistical Abstract, 1993,* p. 457.
72. Stanley Fischer, "Symposium on the Slowdown in Productivity Growth," *Journal of Economic Perspectives* 2 (Fall 1988), pp. 3–7.
73. Organization for Economic Cooperation and Development (OECD), *National Accounts,* vol. 1, *Main Aggregates, 1960–89* (OECD, 1991), p. 145.
74. U.S. Bureau of the Census, *Preliminary Estimates of Poverty Threshold, 1997* (U.S. Census Bureau website: www.census.gov/hhes/poverty/prelim97.html.
75. *Statistical Abstract, 1997,* p. 478.
76. Ibid., p. 476.
77. U.S. Census Bureau website: http://www.census.gov/hhes/income/incineq/p60tb3.html.
78. *Statistical Abstract, 1997,* p. 447. "Real" means that inflation has already been taken into account.
79. Daniel Bell, *The Coming of Post-Industrial Society: A Venture in Social Forecasting* (Basic Books, 1973), p. xviii.
80. *Statistical Abstract, 1997,* p. 447; U.S. Department of Labor, *Employment and Earnings,* vol. 44, no. 9, p. 24 (Government Printing Office, 1997).
81. Mattei Dogan and Dominique Pelassy, *How to Compare Nations: Strategies in Comparative Politics,* 2d ed. (Chatham House, 1990), p. 47.
82. Responses for subjective social class vary somewhat with wording of the question. The data on Great Britain are from the *Index to International Public Opinion, 1991–92* (Greenwood Press, 1992), p. 462.
83. Lipset, *Continental Divide,* p. 170.
84. *Statistical Abstract, 1997,* pp. 15, 119.
85. U.S. Bureau of the Census home page: www.census.gov/population/socdemo/voting/history/vot23/txt, May 1998.
86. *Statistical Abstract, 1997,* p. 476.
87. Seymour Martin Lipset, *Political Man* (Doubleday, 1963), pp. 283–86.
88. Thomas Jefferson to P. S. du Pont de Nemours, April 24, 1816, *The Writings of Thomas Jefferson,* ed. Paul L. Ford (G. P. Putnam's Sons, 1899), 10:25.
89. *Statistical Abstract, 1997,* p. 153; *Population Profile, 1993,* p. 113.
90. *Statistical Abstract, 1997,* p. 161.
91. World Development Report, *The Challenge of Development* (Oxford University Press, 1991), p. 261.
92. *Statistical Abstract, 1997,* p. 159.
93. Herbert McClosky and John Zaller, *The American Ethos: Public Attitudes Toward Capitalism and Democracy* (Harvard University Press, 1984), p. 261.
94. John Gunther, *Inside U.S.A.* (Harper & Brothers, 1947), p. 911.
95. Alan Ehrenhalt, *The United States of Ambition: Politicians, Power, and the Pursuit of Office* (Times Books, 1991), p. 275.
96. Carl N. Degler, *Out of Our Past: The Forces That Shaped Modern America,* 3d ed. (Harper & Row, 1984), p. 322.

CHAPTER 9

1. Jack Germond and Jules Witcover, "California Labor Launches TV Blitz at Paycheck Protection," *The Salt Lake Tribune*, May 16, 1998, p. A11.
2. Jonathan Weisman, "Union Leaders Predict Victory Even Before Votes Tallied," *Congressional Quarterly Weekly Report*, November 2, 1996, p. 3164.
3. Robert A. Jordan, "David vs. Goliath, Without a Slingshot," *The Boston Globe*, March 3, 1998, p. D4.
4. The American Bankers Association (ABA), which represents large and small banks; the Independent Bankers Association of America (IBAA), which exclusively represents small community banks; the Bankers Roundtable, which represents the 125 largest banks; and the Consumer Bankers Association, which represents banks involved in retail business. Interview with Dean Anason, writer for *American Banker*, May 18, 1998.
5. Credit Union National Association (CUNA) and National Association of Federal Credit Unions (NAFCU).
6. Personal communication with Dean Anason, writer for *American Banker*, May 18, 1998.
7. James Parks, "COPE Endorsements, 1968–1992," AFL-CIO, Department of Information, personal communication, January 6, 1994.
8. Estimate provided by Robert Biersack of the Federal Election Commission, January 16, 1997.
9. U.S. Bureau of the Census, *Statistical Abstract of the United States, 1997* (Government Printing Office, 1997), pp. 398, 400.
10. James P. Kelly, "Chairman and CEO of UPS Responds to Strike Allegations," *Workforce*, November 1997.
11. James MacGregor Burns and Stewart Burns, *A People's Charter: The Pursuit of Rights in America* (Knopf, 1991).
12. William R. Donohue, *The Politics of the American Civil Liberties Union* (Transaction, 1985).
13. Michael Lienesch, "Right-Wing Religion: Christian Conservatism as a Political Movement," *Political Science Quarterly* 97 (Fall 1982), pp. 403–25.
14. John W. Huey, Jr., "Power Lobbying," *Fortune* 136, no. 11 (December 8, 1997), p. 16.
15. See NEA home page (http://www.nea.org/index.html).
16. There is a debate in the literature about whether group membership has grown. For the view that it has, see Frank R. Baumgartner and Jack L. Walker, "Survey Research and Membership in Voluntary Associations," *American Journal of Political Science* 32 (November 1988), pp. 908–27. For a different perspective, see Tom W. Smith, "Trends in Voluntary Group Membership: Comments on Baumgartner and Walker," *American Journal of Political Science* 34 (August 1990), pp. 646–61, which in turn led to Frank R. Baumgartner and Jack L. Walker, "Measurement Validity and the Continuity of Results in Survey Research," *American Journal of Political Science* 34 (August 1990), pp. 662–70.
17. Robert Salisbury, "Interest Representation: The Dominance of Institutions," *American Political Science Review* 78 (March 1984), p. 66.
18. William P. Browne, "Organized Interests and Their Issue Niches: A Search for Pluralism in a Policy Domain," *Journal of Politics* 52 (May 1990), pp. 477–509.
19. V. O. Key, Jr., *Public Opinion and American Democracy* (Knopf, 1961), pp. 504–507.
20. R. Kenneth Godwin, *One Billion Dollars of Influence: The Direct Marketing of Politics* (Chatham House, 1988).
21. Quoted in Joan Biskupic, "NRA, Gun-Control Supporters Take Aim at Swing Votes," *Congressional Quarterly Weekly Report*, March 9, 1991, p. 604.
22. Lucius J. Barker, "Third Parties in Litigation: A Systemic View of the Judicial Function," *Journal of Politics* 29 (February 1967), pp. 41–69; Jethro K. Lieberman, *Litigious Society*, rev. ed. (Basic Books, 1983).
23. Gregory A. Calderia and John R. Wright, "Organized Interests and Agenda Setting in the U.S. Supreme Court," *American Political Science Review* 82 (December 1988), pp. 1109–27. See also Gregory A. Calderia and John R. Wright, "Amici Curiae before the Supreme Court: Who Participates, When, and How Much?" *Journal of Politics* 52 (August 1990), pp. 782–806.
24. Karen O'Connor, *Women's Organizations' Use of the Courts* (Lexington Books, 1980).
25. Steven Preston Brown, "Restoring Faith: The New Christian Right, Religious Liberty and the Courts" (Ph.D. diss. University of Virginia, May 1998).
26. Lee Epstein and C. K. Rowland, "Debunking the Myth of Interest Group Invincibility in the Courts," *American Political Science Review* 85 (March 1991), pp. 205–17.
27. Ethan Bronner, *Battle for Justice: How the Bork Nomination Shook America* (Norton, 1989), pp. 50–55.
28. David Mayhew, *Congress: The Electoral Connection* (Yale University Press, 1974), p. 45.
29. One indication of the importance of transmitting information may be the frequency of contact by lobbyists. See John R. Wright, "Contributions, Lobbying, and Committee Voting in the U.S. House of Representatives," *American Political Science Review* 84 (June 1990), pp. 417–38.
30. Herbert E. Alexander, *PACs: What They Are, How They Are Changing Political Campaign Financing Patterns* (Grass Roots Guides, 1979), p. 3.
31. For evidence of the impact of PAC expenditures on legislative committee behavior and legislative involvement generally, see Richard L. Hall and Frank W. Wayman, "Buying Time: Moneyed Interests and the Mobilization of Bias in Congressional Committees," *American Political Science Review* 84 (September 1990), pp. 797–820.
32. Edwin M. Epstein, "Business and Labor Under the Federal Election Campaign Act of 1971," in *Parties, Interest Groups, and Campaign Finance Laws*, ed. Michael J. Malbin (American Enterprise Institute for Public Policy Research, 1980), p. 112. See also Gary Jacobson, *Money in Congressional Elections* (Yale University Press, 1980).
33. Charles Keating, quoted in David J. Jefferson, "Keating of American Continental Corporation Comes Out Fighting," *The Wall Street Journal*, April 18, 1989, p. B2.
34. Phil Sudo, "Show Me the Soft Money! Campaign Contributions as a Corrupting Influence," *Scholastic Update*, December 8, 1997.
35. "Janet Reno's Last Chance to Order Independent Counsel Investigation into Campaign Finance Abuses," *National Review* 49, no. 19, October 13, 1997, p.18.
36. Senator Charles C. Mathias, statement in *The New York Times*, February 27, 1986, p. A31.
37. Amy Dockster, "Nice PAC You've Got Here ... A Pity If Anything Should Happen to It: How Politicians Shake Down the Special Interests," *Washington Monthly*, January 27, 1987, p. 24, quoted in Margaret Cates Nugent and John R. Johannes, eds., *Money, Elections, and Democracy: Reforming Congressional Campaign Finance* (Westview Press, 1990), p. 1.
38. Hall and Wayman, "Buying Time," pp. 797–820. A different study of the House Ways and Means Committee found campaign contributions to be part of the representatives' policy decisions, but even more important was the number of lobbying contacts. See Wright, "Contributions, Lobbying, and Committee Voting," pp. 417–38.
39. Ronald Reagan, "Remarks to Administration Officials on Domestic Policy," December 13, 1988, *Weekly Compilation of Presidential Documents* 24 (December 1988), pp. 1615–20.
40. Sylvia Tesh, "In Support of Single-Interest Politics," *Political Science Quarterly* 99 (Spring 1984), pp. 27–44.
41. Herbert E. Alexander, *PACs: What They Are, How They Are Changing Political Campaign Financing Patterns* (Grass Roots Guides, 1979), p. 5.
42. Report and Recommendations of the California Commission on Campaign Financing, *The New Gold Rush: Financing California's Legislative Campaigns* (Center for Responsive Government, 1985), pp. 177–97. For a study of state lobby regulation, see Cynthia Opheim, "Explaining the Differences in State Lobby Regulation," *Western Political Quarterly* 44 (June 1991), pp. 405–21.
43. Douglas Jehl and Sara Fritz, "Clinton Team Issues Ethics Rules for Top Appointees," *Los Angeles Times*, December 10, 1992, p. A26.
44. Adam Clymer, "Congress Sends Lobbying Overhaul to Clinton," *The New York Times*, December 16, 1995, sec. 1, p. 36.
45. David B. Magleby and Candice J. Nelson, *The Money Chase: Congressional Campaign Finance Reform* (Brookings Institution, 1990), p. 20. See also Brooks Jackson, *Honest Graft: Big Money and the American Political Process* (Knopf, 1988).
46. Magleby and Nelson, *Money Chase*, pp. 72–97.
47. Factors that predict the formation of PACs include company size and the degree of regulation for corporations. See Craig Humphries,

"Corporations, PACs and the Strategic Link Between Contributions and Lobbying Activities," *Western Political Quarterly* 44 (June 1991), pp. 353–72.

48. Federal Election Commission, "PAC Activity Increases in 1995–96 Election Cycle," Press Release, April 22, 1997, p. 5 (http://www.fec.gov/finance/pacgrpol.htm).
49. See Jackson, *Honest Graft*; Robert Kuttner, "Protection Racket," review of *Honest Graft*, by Brooks Jackson, *The New Republic*, March 16, 1989, pp. 40–42.
50. See David Jessup, "Can Political Influence Be Democratized? A Labor Perspective," in *Parties, Interest Groups, and Campaign Finance Laws*, ed. Malbin, pp. 26–55.

CHAPTER 10

1. John E. Mueller, "Choosing Among 133 Candidates," *Public Opinion Quarterly* 34 (Fall 1970), pp. 395–402.
2. E. E. Schattschneider, *Party Government* (Holt, Rinehart and Winston, 1942), p. 1.
3. See Scott Mainwaring, "Party Systems in the Third Wave," *Journal of Democracy* (July 1998), pp. 67–81.
4. Joseph A. Schlesinger, *Political Parties and the Winning of Office* (University of Michigan Press, 1994).
5. See, for example, David W. Brady and Charles S. Bullock IV, "Party and Faction Within Legislatures," in *Handbook of Legislative Research*, ed. Gerhard Loewenberg, Samuel C. Patterson, and Malcolm E. Jewell (Harvard University Press, 1985), chap. 4; see also David W. Brady and Kara Z. Buckley, "Coalitions and Policy in the U.S. Congress: Lessons from the 103rd and 104th Congresses," in *The Parties Respond: Changes in American Parties and Campaigns*, ed. L. Sandy Maisel, 3d ed. (Westview Press, 1998), pp. 286–315.
6. David W. Brady and Craig Volden, *Revolving Gridlock: Politics and Policy from Carter to Clinton* (Westview Press, 1998); James A. Thurber, ed., *Divided Democracy: Cooperation and Conflict Between the President and Congress* (CQ Press, 1991); James A. Thurber, ed., *Rivals for Power: Presidential-Congressional Relations* (CQ Press, 1996); Charles O. Jones, *Separate But Equal Branches: Congress and the Presidency* (Chatham House, 1995), chaps. 5, 6; Jon R. Bond and Richard Fleisher, *The President in the Legislative Arena* (University of Chicago Press, 1990).
7. Mark Paul, "Primary Gave Political Theorists a Reason to Smile," *The Sacramento Bee*, June 8, 1998, p. B5.
8. David Dodenhoff and Kenneth Goldstein, "Resources, Racehorses, and Rules: Nominations in the 1990s," in *Parties Respond*, ed. Maisel, pp. 180–81; Peverill Squire, ed., *The Iowa Caucuses and the Presidential Nominating Process* (Westview Press, 1989).
9. *The Book of the States, 1998–1999* (Council of State Governments, 1998), pp. 159–60.
10. William H. Riker, "The Two-Party System and Duverger's Law: An Essay on the History of Political Science," *American Political Science Review* 76 (December 1982), pp. 753–66. For a classic analysis, see Schattschneider, *Party Government*.
11. See Paul S. Herrnson and John C. Green, eds., *Multiparty Politics in America* (Rowman and Littlefield, 1997); J. David Gillespie, *Politics at the Periphery: Third Parties in Two-Party America* (University of South Carolina Press, 1993).
12. Steven J. Rosenstone, Roy L. Behr, and Edward H. Lazarus, *Third Parties in America: Citizen Response to Major Party Failure*, 2d ed. (Princeton University Press, 1996). See also Xandra Kayden and Eddie Mahe, Jr., *The Party Goes On: The Persistence of the Two Party System in the United States* (Basic Books, 1985), pp. 143–44.
13. On the impact of third parties, see Howard R. Penniman, "Presidential Third Parties and the Modern American Two-Party System," in *The Party Symbol*, ed. William J. Crotty (W. H. Freeman, 1980), pp. 101–17. See also Frank Smallwood, *The Other Candidates: Third Parties in Presidential Elections* (University Press of New England, 1983).
14. Benjamin Franklin, George Washington, and Thomas Jefferson, quoted in Richard Hofstadter, *The Idea of a Party System* (University of California Press, 1969), pp. 2, 123.
15. For concise histories of the two parties, see two studies by Robert A. Rutland, *The Democrats: From Jefferson to Clinton* (University of Missouri Press, 1996), and *The Republicans: From Lincoln to Bush* (University of Missouri Press, 1996).
16. V. O. Key, "A Theory of Critical Elections," *Journal of Politics* 17 (February 1955), pp. 3–18.
17. Walter Dean Burnham, *Critical Elections and the Mainsprings of American Politics* (Norton, 1970), pp. 1–10.
18. E. E. Schattschneider, *The Semisovereign People: A Realist's View of Democracy in America* (Holt, Rinehart and Winston, 1975), pp. 78–80.
19. William E. Gienapp, *The Origins of the Republican Party, 1852–1856* (Oxford University Press, 1987).
20. David W. Brady, "Elections, Congress and Public Policy Changes: 1886–1960," in *Realignment in American Politics: Toward a Theory*, ed. Bruce A. Campbell and Richard Trilling (Texas University Press, 1980), p. 188.
21. Gerald Pomper, "Classification of Presidential Elections," *Journal of Politics* 29 (1967), p. 538.
22. For an examination of American attitudes toward parties over the breadth of American history, see Austin Ranney, *Curing the Mischiefs of Faction: Party Reform in America* (University of California Press, 1975).
23. Federal Election Commission, "15-Month Summary on Political Party Finances," June 8, 1998.
24. Paul Allen Beck, *Party Politics in America*, 8th ed. (Longman, 1997), chap. 2.
25. The early Republican efforts and advantages over the Democrats are well documented in Thomas B. Edsall, *The New Politics of Inequality* (Norton, 1984); Gary C. Jacobson, "The Republican Advantage in Campaign Finances," in *New Direction in American Politics*, ed. John E. Chubb and Paul E. Peterson, p. 6.
26. See L. Sandy Maisel, *From Obscurity to Oblivion: Running in the Congressional Primary*, rev. ed. (University of Tennessee Press, 1986).
27. John F. Bibby, *Politics, Parties, and Elections in America* (Nelson-Hall, 1992). For further data on these roles, see Cornelius P. Cotter, James L. Gibson, John F. Bibby, and Robert J. Huckshorn, *Party Organizations in American Politics* (Praeger, 1984).
28. See James L. Gibson, Cornelius P. Cotter, John F. Bibby, and Robert J. Huckshorn, "Assessing Party Organizational Strength," *American Journal of Political Science* 27 (May 1983), pp. 193–222; Cotter et al., *Party Organizations in American Politics*.
29. Paul S. Herrnson, *Party Campaigning in the 1980s: Have the National Parties Made a Comeback as Key Players in Congressional Elections?* (Harvard University Press, 1988), p. 122.
30. On the influence of local parties, see Kayden and Mahe, *Party Goes On*. See also John C. Green and Daniel M. Shea, ed., *The State of the Parties: The Changing Role of Contemporary Parties*, 2d ed. (Rowman and Littlefield, 1996), which presents their recent case studies of parties at the local level.
31. See Bruce E. Keith, David B. Magleby, Candice J. Nelson, Elizabeth Orr, Mark C. Westlye, and Raymond E. Wolfinger, *The Myth of the Independent Voter* (University of California Press, 1992), p. 148.
32. Michael J. Malbin, "The Conventions, Platforms, and Issue Activists," in *The American Elections of 1980*, ed. Austin Ranney (American Enterprise Institute, 1982), pp. 116–41; L. Sandy Maisel, "The Platform Writing Process: Candidate Centered Platforms in 1992," in *State of Parties*, 2nd ed. Green and Shea, pp. 289–313.
33. Robin Koldny, "The Contract with America in the 104th Congress," in *State of Parties*, ed. Green and Shea, pp. 314–27.
34. Bob Nash, director, White House Office of Personnel, interview with David Magleby, October 26, 1998. A listing of many of these positions is presented in *Policy and Supporting Positions* (Government Printing Office, November 9, 1988). For a general

discussion of this topic, see G. Calvin Mackenzie, "Partisan Presidential Leadership: The President's Appointees," in *Parties Respond*, 3rd ed., Maisel, pp. 316–37.

35. See Angus Campbell, Philip E. Converse, Warren E. Miller, and Donald E. Stokes, *The American Voter* (Wiley, 1960); Norman A. Nie, Sidney Verba, and John R. Petrocik, *The Changing American Voter*, enlarged ed. (Harvard University Press, 1979); Warren E. Miller and J. Merrill Shanks, *The New American Voter* (Harvard University Press, 1996).
36. Campbell et al., *American Voter*, pp. 121–28.
37. Keith et al., *Myth of the Independent Voter.*
38. See Byron E. Shafer, *The End of Realignment: Interpreting American Electoral Eras* (University of Wisconsin Press, 1991).
39. Hedrick Smith, *The Power Game: How Washington Works* (Random House, 1988), p. 671.
40. Nine percent of all voters were Pure Independents in 1956 and 1960. Keith et al., *Myth of the Independent Voter*, p. 51. In 1992 the same percent were Pure Independents. *1992 American National Election Study*, Center for Political Studies, University of Michigan.
41. For the "optimistic view," see Ralph M. Goldman, *Search for Consensus: The Story of the Democratic Party* (Temple University Press, 1979), pp. 366–73; Kayden and Mahe, *Party Goes On;* Larry Sabato, *The Party's Just Begun: Shaping Political Parties in America's Future* (Scott, Foresman, 1988); Joseph A. Schlesinger, "The New American Political Party," *American Political Science Review* 79 (December 1985), pp. 1152–69; David E. Price, *Bringing Back the Parties* (Congressional Quarterly Press, 1984).
42. "With Democrats in the White House, Partisanship Hits New High," *Congressional Quarterly Weekly Report*, December 18, 1993, pp. 3432–34.
43. "Vote Studies," *Congressional Quarterly Weekly Report*, December 21, 1996, p. 3461.
44. Barbara Sinclair, "Evolution or Revolution?" in *Parties Respond*, ed. Maisel, pp. 263–85.
45. Herrnson, *Party Campaigning in the 1980s*, pp. 80–81.

CHAPTER 11

1. Brian MacQuarrie, "The Impeachment Case on to the Full House—The Local View," *The Boston Globe*, December 16, 1998.
2. William Neikerk, "For GOP Leaders, President's Popularity Speaks Louder Than Evidence," *The Milwaukee Journal Sentinel*, January 3, 1999 (Lexis-Nexis).
3. Pew Research Center, "People and the Press Impeachment Vote Re-Interview Survey," December 22, 1998.
4. Robert L. Bartley, "Clinton, the Country, and the Political Culture," Vol. 107, *American Jewish Committee Commentary*, January 1999, p. 20.
5. David S. Broder and Richard Morin, "Struggle over New Standards; Impeachment Reveals Nation's Changing Standards," *The Washington Post*, December 27, 1998, p. A1.
6. Roper Center, University of Connecticut, Gallup Poll, December 20, 1998.
7. Data are from the KBYU-Utah Colleges Exit Poll, 1998.
8. Robert Coles, *The Moral Life of Children* (Atlantic Monthly Press, 1986); Robert Coles, *The Political Life of Children* (Atlantic Monthly Press, 1986).
9. Coles, *Political Life of Children*, pp. 59–60.
10. Pamela Johnston Conover, "The Influence of Group Identifications on Political Perception and Evaluation," *Journal of Politics* 46 (August 1984), pp. 760–85; Henry E. Brady and Paul M. Sniderman, "Attitude Attribution: A Group Basis for Political Reasoning," *American Political Science Review* 79 (December 1985), pp. 1061–78.
11. Shawn W. Rosenberg, "Sociology, Psychology, and the Study of Political Behavior: The Case of the Research on Political Socialization," *Journal of Politics* 47 (May 1985), pp. 715–31.
12. Russell J. Dalton, "Reassessing Parental Socialization: Indicator Unreliability versus Generational Transfer," *American Political Science Review* 74 (June 1980), pp. 421–31.
13. Edgar Litt, "Civic Education Norms and Political Indoctrination," *American Sociological Review* 28 (February 1963), pp. 69–75. See also Elizabeth Leonie Simpson, *Democracy's Stepchildren* (Jossey-Bass, 1971); M. Kent Jennings and Richard G. Niemi, *The Political Character of Adolescence* (Princeton University Press, 1974); Stanley Allen Renshon, "Personality and Family Dynamics in the Political Socialization Process," *American Journal of Political Science* 19 (February 1975), pp. 63–80; Frances Fitzgerald, *America Revised* (Atlantic-Little, Brown, 1979).
14. Kenneth Feldman and Theodore M. Newcomb, *The Impact of College on Students*, vol. 2 (Jossey-Bass, 1969), pp. 16–24, 49–56.
15. Alexander N. Astin et al., *The American Freshmen: National Norms for 1990* (UCLA Graduate School of Education, 1991).
16. Suzanne Koprince Sebert, M. Kent Jennings, and Richard G. Niemi, "The Political Texture of Peer Groups," in Jennings and Niemi, *Political Character of Adolescence*, p. 246.
17. Benjamin I. Page and Robert Y. Shapiro, *The Rational Public: Fifty Years of Trends in Americans' Policy Preferences* (University of Chicago Press, 1992), p. 237.
18. George J. Church, "What in the World Are We Doing?" *Time*, October 18, 1993, p. 42.
19. David Mayhew, *Congress: The Electoral Connection* (Yale University Press, 1974); Richard F. Fenno, Jr., *Home Style: House Members in Their Districts* (Little, Brown, 1978).
20. Warren E. Miller and Donald E. Stokes, "Constituency Influence in Congress," *American Political Science Review* 57 (March 1963), pp. 45–46; Robert S. Erikson and Kent L. Tedin, *American Public Opinion: Its Origins, Content and Impact*, 5th ed. (Allyn and Bacon, 1995), p. 279.
21. Everett C. Ladd and John Benson, "The Growth of News Polls in American Politics," in *Media Polls in American Politics*, ed. Thomas Mann and Gary Orren (Washington, D.C.: Brookings Institution, 1992), pp. 19–31.
22. Scott L. Althaus, "Opinion Polls, Information Effects and Political Equality: Exploring Ideological Biases in Collective Opinion," *Political Communication*, January–March, 1996, pp. 5–7.
23. Thomas E. Mann and Raymond E. Wolfinger, "Candidates and Parties in Congressional Elections," *American Political Science Review* 74 (September 1980), pp. 617–40.
24. Erikson and Tedin, *American Public Opinion*, p. 304.
25. Neil S. Newhouse and Christine L. Matthews, "NAFTA Revisited: Most Americans Just Weren't Deeply Engaged," *Public Perspective* 5 (January/February 1994), pp. 31–32.
26. Center for Political Studies, *American National Election Studies, 1960–90* (Ann Arbor, Michigan, 1990).
27. Frank R. Parker, *Black Votes Count: Political Empowerment in Mississippi After 1965* (University of North Carolina Press, 1990), p. 3.
28. Bernard Grofman and Lisa Handley, "The Impact of the Voting Rights Act on Black Representation in Southern State Legislatures," *Legislative Studies Quarterly* 16 (February 1991), pp. 111–28.
29. G. Bingham Powell, Jr., "American Voter Turnout in Comparative Perspective," *American Political Science Review* 80 (March 1986), p. 38.
30. Raymond E. Wolfinger and Steven J. Rosenstone, "The Effect of Registration Laws on Voter Turnout," *American Political Science Review* 72 (March 1978), p. 24.
31. Raymond E. Wolfinger and Steven J. Rosenstone, *Who Votes?* (Yale University Press, 1980), pp. 78, 88.
32. Human SERVE, "The Impact of the National Voter Registration Act (NVRA), January 1995–June 1996: The First Eighteen Months" (October 1996). See also http://www.esential.org/human_serve.html
33. "Voter Turnout Drops in 1998 Primaries," *The New York Times*, June 30, 1998, p. A18.
34. For a discussion of the differences in the turnout between presidential and midterm elections, see James E. Campbell, "The Presidential Surge and Its Midterm Decline in Congressional Elections, 1868–1988," *Journal of Politics* 53 (May 1991), pp. 477–87.

35. David E. Rosenbaum, "Democrats Keep Solid Hold on Congress," *The New York Times*, November 9, 1988, p. A24; Louis V. Gerstner, "Next Time, Let Us Boldly Vote as No Democracy Has Before," *USA Today*, November 16, 1998, p. A15.
36. Paula Ries and Anne J. Stone, eds., *The American Women 1992–93: A Status Report* (Women's Research and Education Institute, 1992), p. 415.
37. Congressional Research Service, "Voter Turnout in the Presidential Election of 1992: The States," January 26, 1993, pp. 4–5. See also Powell, "American Voter Turnout," pp. 17–43.
38. Wolfinger and Rosenstone, *Who Votes?* p. 102.
39. Sandra Baxter and Marjorie Lansing, *Women and Politics: The Invisible Majority* (University of Michigan Press, 1980), pp. 106–7.
40. See Angus Campbell, Philip E. Converse, Warren E. Miller, and Donald E. Stokes, *The American Voter* (Wiley, 1960). This volume is a foundation of modern voting analysis despite much new evidence and reinterpretation. See also Norman H. Nie, Sidney Verba, and John R. Petrocik, *The Changing American Voter* (Harvard University Press, 1976); Ruy A. Teixeira, *Why Americans Don't Vote: Turnout Decline in the United States, 1960–1984* (Greenwood, 1987).
41. Wolfinger and Rosenstone, *Who Votes?*
42. Austin Ranney, "Nonvoting Is Not a Social Disease," *Public Opinion*, October/November 1983, pp. 16–19.
43. Thomas Byrne Edsall, *The New Politics of Inequality* (W. W. Norton, 1984), p. 181.
44. Frances Fox Piven and Richard A. Cloward, "Prospects for Voter Registration Reform: A Report on the Experiences of the Human SERVE Campaign," *PS: Political Science and Politics* 18 (Summer 1985), pp. 582–92.
45. Wolfinger and Rosenstone, *Who Votes?* p. 109.
46. E. E. Schattschneider, *The Semisovereign People* (Dryden Press, 1975), p. 96.
47. Stephen Earl Bennett and David Resnick, "The Implications of Nonvoting for Democracy in the United States," *American Journal of Political Science* 84 (August 1990), pp. 771–802.
48. Bruce E. Keith, David B. Magleby, Candice J. Nelson, Elizabeth Orr, Mark C. Westlye, and Raymond E. Wolfinger, *The Myth of the Independent Voter* (University of California Press, 1992), pp. 60–75; 1992 American National Election Study, Center for Political Studies, University of Michigan, Ann Arbor.
49. Michael B. MacKuen, Robert S. Erikson, and James A. Stimson, "Macropartisanship," *American Political Science Review* 83 (December 1989), pp. 1125–42.
50. Martin P. Wattenberg, *The Rise of Candidate Centered Politics: Presidential Elections of the 1980s* (Harvard University Press, 1991), p. 1.
51. Barry Goldwater, quoted in Theodore H. White, *The Making of the President, 1964* (Athenaeum Publishers, 1965), p. 217.
52. William H. Flanigan and Nancy H. Zingale, *Political Behavior of the American Electorate*, 8th ed. (Congressional Quarterly Press, 1994), p. 173.
53. Roper Center, University of Connecticut, "Public Opinion Online," CBS News/New York Times Poll, January 19, 1997.
54. J. Merril Shanks and Warren E. Miller, "Policy Direction and Performance Evaluation: Complementary Explanations of the Reagan Elections," *British Journal of Political Science* 20 (1990), pp. 143–235; Warren E. Miller and J. Merril Shanks, "Policy Direction and Performance Evaluation: Comparing George Bush's Victory With Those of Ronald Reagan in 1980 and 1984," paper presented at the American Political Science Association Annual Meeting, Atlanta, August 31–September 2, 1989.
55. Amihai Glazer, "The Strategy of Candidate Ambiguity," *American Political Science Review* 84 (March 1990), pp. 237–41.
56. Robert S. Erikson and David W. Romero, "Candidate Equilibrium and the Behavioral Model of the Vote," *American Political Science Review* 84 (December 1990), p. 1122.
57. Morris P. Fiorina, *Retrospective Voting in American National Elections* (Yale University Press, 1981).
58. Miller and Shanks, "Alternative Interpretations of the 1988 Election." See also Warren E. Miller and J. Merrill Shanks, *The New American Voter* (Harvard University Press, 1966).
59. Gerald H. Kramer, "Short-Term Fluctuations in U.S. Voting Behavior, 1896–1964," *American Political Science Review* 65 (March 1971), pp. 131–43. See also Edward R. Tufte, "Determinants of the Outcomes of Midterm Congressional Elections," *American Political Science Review* 69 (September 1975), pp. 812–26.
60. John R. Hibbing and John R. Alford, "The Educational Impact of Economic Conditions: Who Is Held Responsible?" *American Journal of Political Science* 25 (August 1981), pp. 423–39; Morris P. Fiorina, "Who Is Held Responsible? Further Evidence on the Hibbing-Alford Thesis," *American Journal of Political Science* (February 1983), pp. 158–64.
61. Robert M. Stein, "Economic Voting for Governor and U.S. Senator: The Electoral Consequences of Federalism," *Journal of Politics* 52 (February 1990), pp. 29–53.

CHAPTER 12

1. Jim VandeHei, "Speaker Predicts Republicans Could Gain Up to 40 Seats in Fall," *Roll Call*, July 16, 1998.
2. William Schneider, "To the 'New Rich,' Bill's OK," *National Journal*, November 14, 1998, p. 2746.
3. Charlie Cook, "How Big Will Republican Gains Be?" *National Journal*, September 26, 1998, p. 2251.
4. House Republicans raised just under $28 million, while all Republican committees combined exceeded $111 million in receipts in 1998. See David B. Magleby and Marianne Holt, eds., "Outside Money: Soft Money and Issue Ads in Competitive 1998 Congressional Elections," report of a grant funded by the Pew Charitable Trusts, National Press Club, February 1, 1999, p. 15.
5. *1994 Census of Governments* (Government Printing Office, 1995), vol. 1, no. 2, p. 1.
6. Washington voters enacted term limits in 1992 after defeating them in 1991.
7. In the 1992 and 1994 National Election Studies, 77–78 percent of Americans favored term limits. Center for Political Studies, University of Michigan.
8. *U.S. Term Limits Inc. v Thornton*, 114 S.Ct. 2703.
9. For an insightful examination of electoral rules, see Bernard Grofman and Arend Lijphart, eds., *Electoral Laws and Their Political Consequences* (Agathon Press, 1986).
10. Arend Lijphart, "The Political Consequences of Electoral Laws, 1945–85," *American Political Science Review* 84 (June 1990), pp. 481–95.
11. George Rabinowitz and Stuart Elaine MacDonald, "The Power of the States in U.S. Presidential Elections," *American Political Science Review* 80 (March 1986), pp. 65–87.
12. Dany M. Adkison and Christopher Elliott, "The Electoral College: A Misunderstood Institution," *PS: Political Science and Politics* 30 (March 1997), pp. 77–80.
13. See, as examples, David Mayhew, *Congress: The Electoral Connection* (Yale University Press, 1974); Richard F. Fenno, Jr., *Home Style: House Members in Their Districts* (Little, Brown, 1978); James E. Campbell, "The Return of Incumbents: The Nature of Incumbency Advantage," *Western Political Quarterly* 36 (September 1983), pp. 434–44.
14. Gary King and Andrew Gelman, "Systemic Consequences of Incumbency Advantage in U.S. House Elections," *American Journal of Political Science* 35 (February 1991), pp. 110–37.
15. See Gary C. Jacobson, *The Politics of Congressional Elections*, 4th ed. (Longman, 1997), chap. 6; Alan I. Abramowitz, "Economic Conditions, Presidential Popularity, and Voting Behavior in Midterm Congressional Elections," *Journal of Politics* (February 1985), p. 130.
16. See Edward R. Tufte, *Political Control of the Economy* (Princeton University Press, 1978); see also his "Determinants of the Outcomes of Midterm Congressional Elections," *American Political Science Review* 69

(1975), pp. 812–26. For a more recent discussion of the same subject, see Jacobson, *Politics of Congressional Elections*, pp. 123–78.

17. Alan I. Abramowitz and Jeffrey A. Segal, "Determinants of the Outcomes of U.S. Senate Elections," *Journal of Politics* 48 (1986), pp. 433–39.
18. This includes the postelection switch of Alabama Senator Richard Shelby to the Republican party.
19. Linda L. Fowler and Robert D. McClure, *Political Ambition: Who Decides to Run for Congress* (Yale University Press, 1989); David T. Canon, "Political Conditions and Experienced Challengers in Congressional Elections, 1972–1984," paper presented at the American Political Science Association Annual Meeting, New Orleans, August 29–September 1, 1985.
20. Keith Krehbiel and John R. Wright, "The Incumbency Effect in Congressional Elections: A Test of Two Explanations," *American Journal of Political Science* 27 (February 1983), p. 140.
21. Roll Call, "Roll Call Casualty List," *Roll Call Politics*, November 5, 1998, p. 15.
22. Gary C. Jacobson and Samuel Kernell, *Strategy and Choice in Congressional Elections* (Yale University Press, 1981).
23. "Financial Activity of Senate and House General Election Campaigns," www.fec.gov/en30981.htm
24. Albert D. Cover, "One Good Term Deserves Another: The Advantages of Incumbency in Congressional Elections," *American Journal of Political Science* 21 (August 1977), pp. 523–42; Morris P. Fiorina, *Congress: Keystone of the Washington Establishment* (Yale University Press, 1978); Mayhew, *Congress*, pp. 52–53.
25. Mayhew, *Congress*, p. 61; Richard F. Fenno, Jr., *Congressmen in Committees* (Little, Brown, 1973); Steven S. Smith and Christopher J. Deering, *Committees in Congress*, 3d ed. (Congressional Quarterly Press, 1997).
26. Candice J. Nelson, "Campaign Finance in Presidential and Congressional Elections," *Political Science Teacher* (Summer 1988), p. 6.
27. Jonathan S. Krasno, *Challengers, Competition, and Reelection: Comparing Senate and House Elections* (Yale University Press, 1994).
28. Alan I. Abramowitz, "Explaining Senate Election Outcomes," *American Political Science Review* 82 (June 1988), pp. 385–403.
29. David B. Magleby, "More Bang for the Buck: Campaign Spending in Small State U.S. Senate Elections," paper presented at the Western Political Science Association Annual Meeting, Salt Lake City, March 30–April 1, 1989.
30. Rhodes Cook, "GOP Shows Dramatic Growth, Especially in the South," *Congressional Quarterly Weekly Report*, January 13, 1996, pp. 97–100.
31. Paul T. David and James W. Caesar, *Proportional Representation in Presidential Nominating Politics* (University Press of Virginia, 1980).
32. For a discussion of the 1996 primary rules, see Rhodes Cook, "GOP's Rules Favor Dole, If He Doesn't Stumble," *Congressional Quarterly Weekly Report*, January 27, 1996, pp. 228–31.
33. The descriptions of these types of primaries are drawn from James W. Davis, *Presidential Primaries*, rev. ed. (Greenwood Press, 1984), chap. 3. See pp. 56–63 for specifics on each state (and Puerto Rico). This material is used with the permission of the publisher.
34. *The Book of the States, 1996–1997* (Council of State Governments, 1996), pp. 157–58.
35. The viewership of conventions has declined as the amount of time devoted to conventions dropped. In 1988, Democrats averaged 27.1 million viewers and Republicans 24.5 million. By 1996 viewership for the Democrats was 18 million viewers on average and Republicans averaged 16.6 million viewers. See John Carmody, "The TV Column," *The Washington Post*, September 2, 1996, p. D4.
36. Stephen J. Wayne, *The Road to the White House, 1996: The Politics of Presidential Elections* (St. Martin's Press, 1996), chap. 5.
37. Jeff Fishel, *Presidents and Promises* (Congressional Quarterly Press, 1984).
38. Jules Witcover uses the image of a marathon to describe the 1976 presidential campaign in *Marathon: The Pursuit of the Presidency, 1972–1976* (Viking, 1977).
39. Robert S. Erikson, "Economic Conditions and the Presidential Vote," *American Political Science Review* 83 (June 1989), pp. 567–75. Class-based voting has also become more important. See Robert S. Erikson, Thomas O. Lancaster, and David W. Romers, "Group Components of the Presidential Vote, 1952–1984," *Journal of Politics* 51 (May 1989), pp. 337–46.
40. Sidney Kraus, *The Great Debates: Kennedy vs Nixon, 1960* (Indiana University Press, 1962). See also Myles Martel, *Political Campaign Debates* (Longman, 1983).
41. David B. Magleby and Candice J. Nelson, *The Money Chase: Congressional Campaign Finance Reform* (Brookings Institution, 1990), pp. 13–14.
42. The Federal Election Commission was late in some payments to 1996 primary candidates because of the heavy early expenditures by several candidates. Eventually, all candidates received their entitlement of FEC money.
43. *Buckley v Valeo*, 424 US 1 (1976).
44. For a discussion of recent legislation, see Herbert E. Alexander and Monica Bauer, *Financing the 1988 Election* (Westview, 1991); Frank J. Sorauf, *Money in American Elections* (Scott, Foresman, 1988).
45. Beth Donovan, "Parties Turned Soft Money Law into Hard and Fast Spending," *Congressional Quarterly Weekly Report*, May 15, 1993, pp. 1196–97; David E. Rosenbaum, "In Political Money Game, the Year of Big Loopholes," *The New York Times*, December 26, 1996, p. A1.
46. Magleby and Holt, eds., "Outside Money."
47. See *Colorado Republican Federal Campaign Committee v FEC*, 518 U.S. 604 (1996).
48. Ruth Marcus and Chuck Babcock, "The System Cracks Under the Weight of Cash: Candidates, Parties and Outside Interests Dropped a Record 2.7 Billion," *Washington Post*, February 9, 1997, p. A1.
49. Edward Timperlake and William C. Triplett II, *The Year of the Rat: How Bill Clinton Compromised U.S. Security for Chinese Cash* (Regnery, 1998).
50. Ibid.
51. Sorauf, *Money in American Elections*, pp. 64–65.
52. Federal Election Commission, "Congressional Financial Activity Declines," press release, December 29, 1998.
53. Federal Election Commission, "Congressional Fundraising and Spending Up Again in 1996," press release, April 14, 1997, pp. 32–51.
54. See Robert Hunter, ed., *Electing the President: A Program for Reform, Final Report of the Commission on National Election* (Center for Strategic and International Studies, 1986); James L. Sundquist, *Constitutional Reform* (Brookings Institution, 1986); Edward N. Kearny, "Presidential Nominations and Representative Democracy: Proposals for Change," *Presidential Studies Quarterly* 14 (Summer 1984), pp. 348–56.
55. Barbara Norrander and Greg W. Smith, "Type of Contest, Candidate Strategy, and Turnout in Presidential Primaries," *American Politics Quarterly* 13 (January 1985), p. 28.
56. John G. Geer, "Voting in Presidential Primaries," paper presented at the American Political Science Association Annual Meeting, Washington, D.C., September 1984. See also Albert R. Hunt, "The Media and Presidential Campaigns," in *Elections American Style*, ed. A. James Reichley (Brookings Institution, 1987), pp. 52–74.
57. On the Internet: http://www.fec.gov/pages/96to.htm; also http://www.fec.gov/pages/intro.htm
58. Steven J. Brams and Peter Fishburn, *Approval Voting* (Birkhauser, 1983).
59. George S. McGovern, "Considerations on Our Political Processes," *Presidential Studies Quarterly* 14 (Summer 1984), pp. 341–47.
60. Gary R. Orren and Nelson W. Polsby, eds., *Media and Momentum: The New Hampshire Primary and Nomination Politics* (Chatham House, 1987).
61. *A National Agenda for the Eighties*, Report of the President's Commission for a National Agenda for the Eighties (Government Printing Office, 1980), p. 97, proposes holding only four presidential primaries, scheduled about one month apart.
62. Nelson Polsby, *Consequences of Party Reform* (Oxford University Press, 1983), p. 118.
63. Thomas E. Cronin and Robert Loevy, "The Case for a National Primary Convention Plan," *Public Opinion*, December 1982/January 1983, pp. 50–53.
64. See Judith A. Best, *The Choice of the People? Debating the Electoral College* (Rowman and Littlefield, 1996); Malcolm S. Forbes, Jr., "Helpful, Useful Antique," *Forbes*, February 6, 1989, p. 27.
65. Neal R. Peirce and Lawrence Longley, *The People's President: The Electoral College in American History and the Direct-Vote Alternative*, 2d ed. (Yale University Press, 1981), describes and advocates the direct-vote alternative. Nelson W. Polsby and Aaron B. Wildavsky, *Presidential Elections: Contemporary Strategies of American Politics*, 9th ed. (Chatham House, 1995), favors the present system.

CHAPTER 13

1. Pew Research Center for the People and the Press, "Internet News Takes Off," press release, June 8, 1998, p. 1.
2. James Fallows, *Breaking the News: How the Media Undermine American Democracy* (Pantheon Books, 1996), p. 3.
3. Pew Research Center for the People and the Press, "Fewer Happy with Clinton Victory than with GOP Congressional Win," press release, December 6, 1996. http://www.people.press.org/postmor.htm
4. Paul Starobin, "Heeding the Call," *National Journal*, November 30, 1996, pp. 2584–89.
5. William Rivers, *The Other Government* (Universe Books, 1982); Douglas Cater, *The Fourth Branch of Government* (Houghton Mifflin, 1959); Dom Bonafede, "The Washington Press: An Interpreter or a Participant in Policy Making?" *National Journal*, April 24, 1982, pp. 716–21; Michael Ledeen, "Learning to Say 'No' to the Press," *Public Interest* 73 (Fall 1983), p. 113.
6. Leslie G. Moeller, "The Big Four: Mass Media Actualities and Expectations," in *Beyond Media: New Approaches to Mass Communication*, ed. Richard W. Budd and Brent D. Ruben (Transaction Books, 1988), p. 15.
7. Pew Center, "Internet News Takes Off," p. 2.
8. Ibid.
9. Ibid.
10. See Ray Hiebert, Donald Ungarait, and Thomas Bohn, *Mass Media VI* (Longman, 1991), chap. 11.
11. Pew Center, "Internet News Takes Off," p. 5.
12. Ibid. p. 1.
13. Ibid.
14. See Robert A. Rutland, *Newsmongers: Journalism in the Life of the Nation, 1690–1972* (Dial Press, 1973).
15. Quoted in Frank Luther Mott, *American Journalism*, 3d ed. (Macmillan, 1962), p. 412.
16. During the 1930s, more than one thousand speeches were made by members of Congress on one network alone. See Edward W. Chester, *Radio, Television and American Politics* (Sheed and Ward, 1969), p. 62.
17. Frances Perkins, quoted in James MacGregor Burns, *Roosevelt: The Lion and the Fox* (Harcourt Brace, 1956), p. 205.
18. www.gannett.com/map/gan/007.htm
19. Ben H. Bagdikian, *The Media Monopoly* (Beacon Press, 1983).
20. See Doris A. Graber, *Mass Media and American Politics*, 5th ed. (Congressional Quarterly Press, 1997); Gina M. Garramone and Charles K. Atkin, "Mass Communication and Political Socialization: Specifying the Effects," *Public Opinion Quarterly* 50 (Spring 1986), pp. 76–86.
21. Stephanie Storm, "Mergers for Year Approach Record," *The New York Times*, October 31, 1996, p. A1.
22. Geraldine Fabrikant, "The Media Business," *The New York Times*, October 11, 1996.
23. Shanto Iyengar and Donald R. Kinder, *News That Matters* (University of Chicago Press, 1987).
24. Steven J. Simmons, *The Fairness Doctrine and the Media* (University of California Press, 1978).
25. Harvey G. Zeidenstein, "News Media Perception of White House News Management," *Presidential Studies Quarterly* 24 (Summer 1984), pp. 391–98.
26. See, for example, Jack Dennis, "Preadult Learning of Political Independence: Media and Family Communications Effects," *Communication Research* 13 (July 1987), pp. 401–33; Olive Stevens, *Children Talking Politics* (Martin Robertson, 1982).
27. Elihu Katz and Paul Lazarsfeld, *Personal Influence: The Part Played by People in the Flow of Mass Communications* (Free Press, 1955).
28. See the classic, Angus Campbell, Philip E. Converse, Warren E. Miller, and Donald E. Stokes, *The American Voter* (Wiley, 1960).
29. See other classic works, Paul Lazarsfeld, Bernard Berelson, and Hazel Gaudet, *The People's Choice: How the Voter Makes Up His Mind in a Presidential Campaign*, 3d ed. (Columbia University Press, 1968); Bernard Berelson, Paul Lazarsfeld, and William McPhee, *Voting: A Study of Opinion Formation in a Presidential Campaign* (University of Chicago Press, 1954).
30. Pew Research Center for the People and the Press, "Scandal Reporting Faulted for Bias and Inaccuracy: Popular Policies and Unpopular Press Lift Clinton Ratings," press release, February 6, 1998, p. 6.
31. http://www.gallup.com/poll-archives/980926.htm
32. Stuart Oskamp, ed., *Television as a Social Issue* (Sage Publications, 1988); James W. Carey, ed., *Media, Myths, and Narratives: Television and the Press* (Sage Publications, 1988).
33. Doris A. Graber, *Processing the News: How People Tame the Information Tide*, 2d ed. (Longman, 1988), pp. 107–13.
34. Times Mirror Center for the People and the Press, "Times Mirror News Interest Index," press releases, January 16 and February 28, 1992.
35. John K. Robinson and Mark R. Levy, eds., *The Main Source: Learning from Television News* (Sage Publications, 1986).
36. Graber, *Processing the News*, p. 115.
37. Media Studies Center, "Media Get High Marks for Campaign Coverage," press release, November 19, 1996.
38. See Nelson Polsby, *Consequences of Party Reform* (Oxford University Press, 1983), pp. 142–46. See also Stanley Rothman and S. Robert Lichter, "Media and Business Elites: Two Classes in Conflict!" *Public Interest* 69 (Fall 1982), pp. 119–25.
39. Michael Parenti, *Inventing Reality: The Politics of the Mass Media* (St. Martin's Press, 1986), p. 35.
40. David Broder, "Beware of the 'Insider' Syndrome: Why Newsmakers and News Reporters Shouldn't Get Too Cozy," *The Washington Post*, December 4, 1988, Outlook sec.; see also Broder, "Thin-Skinned Journalists," *The Washington Post*, January 11, 1989, p. A21.
41. See, for example, William A. Rusher, *The Coming Battle for the Media* (William Morrow, 1988).
42. Rush Limbaugh, *See, I Told You So* (Pocket Books, 1993), p. 326.
43. See, for example, Parenti, *Inventing Reality*.
44. Todd Gitlin, *The Whole World Is Watching: Mass Media in the Making and Unmaking of the New Left* (University of California Press, 1980).
45. Dorothy Giobbe, "Dole Wins . . . In Endorsements," *Editor and Publisher Magazine*, November 9, 1996, p. 7.
46. Robert Lichter, "Consistently Liberal: But Does It Matter?" *Forbes Media Critic* 4 (Fall 1996), pp. 26–39. These data are essentially the same as data reported a decade earlier. See David Shaw, "The Times Poll: Public and Press—Two Viewpoints," *Los Angeles Times*, August 11, 1985, part 1, p. 1.
47. Daniel P. Moynihan, "The Presidency and the Press," *Commentary* 51 (March 1971), p. 43.
48. S. Robert Lichter, Stanley Rothman, and Linda S. Lichter, *The Media Elite* (Adler and Adler, 1986).
49. See, for example, Michael J. Robinson and Margaret A. Sheehan, *Over the Wire and on TV: CBS and UPI in Campaign '80* (Russell Sage Foundation, 1983); Lichter, Rothman, and Lichter, *Media Elite*.
50. See Thomas Patterson, *Out of Order* (Knopf, 1996); Paul Weaver, *News and the Culture of Lying* (Free Press, 1993); Anthony Munro, "Yet Another Conspiracy Theory," *Columbia Journalism Review* 33 (November 1994), p. 71.
51. Among others researching this topic, see Doris A. Graber, "Say It with Pictures: The Impact of Audio-Visual News on Public Opinion Formation," paper presented at the Midwest Political Science Association Annual Meeting, Chicago, April 1987; Benjamin I. Page, Robert Y. Shapiro, and Glenn R. Dempsey, "What Moves Public Opinion?" *American Political Science Review* 76 (March 1987), pp. 23–43.
52. Shanto Iyengar, Mark D. Peters, and Donald R. Kinder, "Experimental Demonstrations of the 'Not-So-Minimal' Consequences of Television News Programs," *American Political Science Review* 76 (December 1982), pp. 848–58.
53. Maxwell E. McCombs and Donald L. Shaw, "The Agenda-Setting Function of the Mass Media," *Public Opinion Quarterly* 36 (1972), pp. 176–87; Iyengar, Peters, and Kinder, "Experimental Demonstrations," pp. 848–58; Maxwell E. McCombs and Sheldon Gilbert, "News Influence on Our Pictures of the World," in *Perspectives on Media Effects*, ed. Jennings Bryant and Dolf Gillman (Lawrence Erlbaum, 1986), pp. 1–15. Iyengar and Kinder, *News That Matters*.
54. Quoted in Robinson and Sheehan, *Over the Wire and on TV*, p. xiii.
55. David B. Magleby, *Direct Legislation: Voting on Ballot Propositions in the United States* (Johns Hopkins University Press, 1984).
56. Richard Davis, *The Press and American Politics: The New Mediator*, 2d ed. (Prentice Hall, 1996), p. 279.

57. Paul T. David, Ralph M. Goldman, Richard C. Bain, *The Politics of the National Party Conventions* (Brookings Institution, 1960), pp. 300–301.
58. Martin Schram, "Eye on the Media/Next Conventions: Networks Pull a Fade," *Newsday*, September 4, 1996, p. A36.
59. Frank I. Lutz, *Candidates, Consultants, and Campaigns* (Basil Blackwell, 1988), chap. 7.
60. Frank Rich, "Journal: The Log Cabin Lesson," *The New York Times*, October 21, 1995, p. A21.
61. Larry J. Sabato, *The Rise of Political Consultants* (Basic Books, 1981).
62. Mimi Hall and Judy Keen, "Hillary Clinton's Image Undergoes a Change," *USA Today*, July 16, 1986, p. 16.
63. See, in general, Sabato, *Rise of Political Consultants*; James David Barber, *The Pulse of Politics: Electing Presidents in the Media Age* (Norton, 1980). See also Fred Barnes, "The Myth of Political Consultants," *New Republic*, June 16, 1986, p. 16.
64. Quoted in Sabato, *Rise of Political Consultants*, p. 144.
65. Thomas E. Patterson, *The Mass Media Election: How Americans Choose Their President* (Praeger, 1980), chap. 12.
66. John H. Aldrich, *Before the Convention* (University of Chicago Press, 1980), p. 65. This book is a study of candidates' choices and strategies. See also Patterson, *Mass Media Election*.
67. John Foley et al., *Nominating a President: The Process and the Press* (Praeger, 1980), p. 39. For the press's treatment of incumbents, see James Glen Stovall, "Incumbency and News Coverage of the 1980 Presidential Election Campaign," *Western Political Quarterly* 37 (December 1984), p. 621.
68. Thomas E. Patterson and Robert McClure, *The Myth of Television Power in National Elections* (Putnam, 1976); Patterson, *Mass Media Election*, chap. 13.
69. Priscilla Southwell, "Voter Turnout in the 1986 Congressional Elections: The Media as Demobilizer?" *American Politics Quarterly* 19 (January 1991), pp. 96–108.
70. David B. Magleby, "Direct Legislation in the American States," in *Referendums Around the World: The Growing Use of Direct Democracy*, ed. David Butler and Austin Ranney (AEI Press, 1994), pp. 218–57.
71. Pew Center for Civic Journalism, press release, newswire, July 9, 1998.
72. Patterson, *Mass Media Election*, pp. 115–17.
73. Raymond Wolfinger and Peter Linguiti, "Tuning In and Tuning Out," *Public Opinion* 4 (February/March 1981), pp. 56–60.
74. Bernard Cohen, *The Press and Foreign Policy* (Princeton University Press, 1963); Gary Orren, "Thinking About the Press and Government," in *Impact: How the Press Affects Federal Policymaking*, ed. Martin Linsky (Norton, 1986), pp. 1–20.
75. Lewis Wolfson, *The Untapped Power of the Press* (Praeger, 1985), p. 79.
76. Stephen Hess, *The Government/Press Connection* (Brookings Institution, 1984), p. 106.
77. Lloyd Cutler, "Foreign Policy on Deadline," *Foreign Policy* 56 (Fall 1984), p. 114.
78. Michael B. Grossman and Martha Joynt Kumar, *Portraying the President* (Johns Hopkins University Press, 1981), pp. 255–63; Fredric T. Smoller, *The Six O'Clock Presidency: A Theory of Presidential Press Relations in the Age of Television* (Praeger, 1990), pp. 31–49.
79. Michael J. Robinson and Kevin R. Appel, "Network News Coverage of Congress," *Political Science Quarterly* 94 (Fall 1979), pp. 407–18; Charles Tidmarch and John C. Pitney, Jr., "Covering Congress," *Polity* 17 (Spring 1984), pp. 463–83.
80. Susan Heilmann Miller, "News Coverage of Congress: The Search for the Ultimate Spokesperson," *Journalism Quarterly* 54 (Autumn 1977), pp. 459–65.
81. See Stephen Hess, *Live From Capitol Hill: Studies of Congress and the Media* (Brookings Institution, 1991), pp. 102–10.
82. Richard Davis, "Whither the Congress and the Supreme Court? The Television News Portrayal of American National Government," *Television Quarterly* 22 (1987), pp. 55–63.
83. For a discussion of the Supreme Court and public opinion, see Thomas R. Marshall, *Public Opinion and the Supreme Court* (Unwin Hyman, 1989); Gregory Caldiera, "Neither the Purse nor the Sword: Dynamics of Public Confidence in the Supreme Court," *American Political Science Review* 80 (December 1986), pp. 1209–28.
84. For a discussion of the relationship between the Supreme Court and the press, see Richard Davis, "Lifting the Shroud: News Media Portrayal of the U.S. Supreme Court," *Communications and the Law* 9 (October 1987), pp. 43–58; Elliot E. Slotnick, "Media Coverage of Supreme Court Decision Making: Problems and Prospects," *Judicature*, October/November 1991, pp. 128–42.
85. Times Mirror Center, "Campaign '92," January 16, 1992.
86. Quoted in Herbert Schmertz, "The Making of the Presidency," *Presidential Studies Quarterly* 16 (Winter 1986), p. 25.

CHAPTER 14

1. From a poll by Opinion Dynamics, Inc., for Fox News Channel, cited in *National Journal*, September 20, 1998, p. 1856.
2. John R. Hibbing and Elizabeth Theiss-Morse, *Congress as Public Enemy: Public Attitudes Toward American Political Institutions* (Cambridge University Press, 1995), p. 147.
3. Richard F. Fenno, Jr., *Home Style: House Members in Their Districts* (Little, Brown, 1978), p. 168.
4. For an examination of this practice, see Michael Lyons and Peter F. Galderisi, "Incumbency, Reapportionment, and U.S. House Redistricting," *Political Research Quarterly* (December 1995), pp. 857–71.
5. See *Wesberry v Sanders*, 376 US 1 (1964).
6. *Davis v Bandemer*, 478 US 109 (1986).
7. *Shaw v Reno*, 509 US 630 (1993).
8. *Miller v Johnson*, 132 L Ed 2d 762 (1995); *Bush v Vera*, 135 L Ed 2d 248 (1996).
9. For a brief discussion of the speakership in the 1990s, see Barbara Sinclair, "House Majority Party Leadership in an Era of Legislative Constraint," in *The Postreform Congress*, ed. Roger H. Davison (St. Martin's Press, 1992), pp. 91–111. See also Ronald M. Peters, Jr., ed., *The Speaker: Leadership in the U.S. House of Representatives* (Congressional Quarterly Press, 1995).
10. Quoted in Adam Clymer, "Firebrand Who Got Singed Says Being Speaker Suffices," *The New York Times*, January 22, 1996, p. 1.
11. Newt Gingrich, *To Renew America* (HarperCollins, 1995) and *Lessons Learned the Hard Way* (HarperCollins, 1998).
12. Gingrich shares his shortcomings and difficulties in his candid *Lessons Learned the Hard Way*.
13. See Charles R. Babcock and Ruth Marcus, "The Speaker's About-Face on the Ethics Question," *The Washington Post National Weekly Edition*, January 6, 1997, pp. 13–14; "The Gingrich Case: The Findings of the Special Counsel," *The New York Times*, January 18, 1997, p. 11.
14. Quoted in Greg Hitt, "Hastert Is Tapped as House Speaker to Fill Vacuum Created by Livingston," *The Wall Street Journal*, December 21, 1998, p. A20.
15. Quoted in a profile by Jeffrey L. Katz in *Congressional Quarterly Weekly Report*, November 21, 1998, p. 3150.
16. For insightful memoirs by three recently retired U.S. Senators, see Bill Bradley, *Time Present, Time Past: A Memoir* (Knopf, 1996); Warren B. Rudman, *Combat: Twelve Years in the U.S. Senate* (Random House, 1996); and Alan K. Simpson, *Right in the Old Kazoo: A Lifetime of Scrapping with the Press* (Morrow, 1997).
17. Barbara Sinclair, "Unorthodox Lawmaking in the Individualist Senate," *Extensions: A Journal of the Carl Albert Congressional Research and Studies Center* (Fall 1997), p. 11. See also Sinclair, *Unorthodox Lawmaking: New Legislative Processes in the U.S. Congress* (Congressional Quarterly Press, 1997), chap. 3.
18. Norman J. Ornstein, "Prima Donna Senate," *The New York Times*, September 4, 1997, p. A17. See also Carroll J. Doherty, "Senate Caught in the Grip of Its Own 'Holds' System," *Congressional Quarterly Weekly Report*, August 15, 1998, pp. 2241–43.
19. For an insightful set of essays on Senate leadership, see Richard A. Baker and Roger H. Davidson, eds., *First Among Equals: Outstanding Senate Leaders of the Twentieth Century* (Congressional Quarterly Press, 1991).
20. See Karen Foerstel, "D'Amato: A Streetfighter Prepares for Battle," *Congressional Quarterly Weekly*, June 6, 1998, p. 1510.

21. Sarah A. Binder and Steven S. Smith, *Politics or Principles? Filibustering in the United States Senate* (Brookings Institution, 1997).
22. Nolan McCarty and Rose Razaghian, "Advice and Consent: Senate Responses to Executive Branch Nominations, 1885–1996," paper presented at the American Political Science Association Annual Meeting, Boston, September 3–6, 1998, p. 22.
23. Katherine Q. Seelye, "Weld Ends Fight over Nomination by Withdrawing," *The New York Times*, September 16, 1997, pp. 1, 14.
24. Sheldon Goldman, "The Judicial Confirmation Crisis and the Clinton Presidency," *Presidential Studies Quarterly* (Fall 1998), pp. 838–44.
25. For a criticism of recent confirmation hearings and various reform proposals, see Stephen L. Carter, *The Confirmation Mess: Cleaning Up the Federal Appointments Process* (Basic Books, 1994). See also G. Calvin Mackenzie and Robert Shogan, eds., *Obstacle Course: The Report of the Twentieth Century Fund Task Force on the Presidential Appointment Process* (Twentieth Century Fund Press, 1996).
26. See Gingrich, *To Renew America*, p. 121. See also Timothy Penny and Major Garrett, *Common Cents* (Little, Brown, 1995), p. 209.
27. Robert C. Byrd (D.-W.Va.), quoted in David J. Vogler, *The Politics of Congress* (Allyn and Bacon, 1983), p. 77.
28. See the case studies in Richard F. Fenno, Jr., *Senators on the Campaign Trail: The Politics of Representation* (University of Oklahoma Press, 1996), p. 331.
29. Reported in *National Journal*, January 4, 1997, p. 30. Members of Congress cast more than 1,321 votes in one record session of Congress.
30. See Richard Morrin, "Tuned Out, Turned Off: Millions of Americans Know Little About How Their Government Works," *The Washington Post National Weekly Edition*, February 5–11, 1996, pp. 6–7.
31. Bill Bradley, *Time Present, Time Past: A Memoir* (Knopf, 1996), chap. 4.
32. Jackie Clames, "House Divided: Why Congress Hews to the Party Line on Impeachment," *The Wall Street Journal*, December 16, 1998, p. 1.
33. Ibid., p. 9.
34. Alan K. Ota, "Partisan Voting on the Rise," *Congressional Quarterly Weekly Report*, January 9, 1999, p. 80.
35. Ibid., p. 80.
36. Constance Ewing Cook, *Lobbying for Higher Education* (Vanderbilt University Press, 1998). See, too, Ken Kolman, *Outside Lobbying* (Princeton University Press, 1998).
37. Carroll J. Doherty, "Clinton's Big Comeback Shown in Vote Score," *Congressional Quarterly Weekly Report*, December 21, 1996, pp. 3427–30.
38. 54 percent in 1997 and 51 percent in 1998. Carroll J. Doherty, "Clinton Finds Support on Hill. . . . ," *Congressional Quarterly Weekly Report*, January 3, 1998, p. 14. And David Hosansky, "Clinton's Biggest Prize Was a Frustrated GOP," *Congressional Quarterly Weekly*, January 9, 1999, p. 76.
39. See Jeffrey S. Peake, "Presidential Agenda Setting in Foreign Policy . . .," paper presented at the American Political Science Association Annual Meeting, Boston, September 3–6, 1998.
40. Lance T. Leloup and Steven A. Shull, *The President and Congress: Collaboration and Combat in National Policymaking* (Allyn and Bacon, 1999), p. 264.
41. See Kenneth E. Collier, *Between the Branches: The White House Office of Legislative Affairs* (University of Pittsburgh Press, 1997).
42. Sinclair, *Unorthodox Lawmaking*, p. 58. For a defense of riders as a means to cut wasteful spending, see Slade Gorton and Larry E. Craig, "Congressional Riders Rein in Excesses," *Walla Walla Union-Bulletin*, July 31, 1998, p. 4.
43. See David W. Brady and Craig Volden, *Revolving Gridlock: Politics and Policy from Carter to Clinton* (Westview Press, 1998). For two case studies on the way bills get treated in Congress, see Janet M. Martin, *Lessons from the Hill: The Legislative Journey of an Education Program* (St. Martin's Press, 1993); Steven Waldman, *The Bill—How Legislation Really Becomes Law: A Case Study of the National Service Bill* (Penguin, 1996).
44. Woodrow Wilson, *Congressional Government* (Houghton, Mifflin, 1885; reprint, Johns Hopkins University Press, 1981), p. 69.
45. Christopher J. Deering and Steven S. Smith, *Committees in Congress*, 3d ed. (Congressional Quarterly Press, 1997).
46. Joel D. Aberbach, *Keeping a Watchful Eye: The Politics of Congressional Oversight* (Brookings Institution, 1990).
47. David J. Vogler, *The Politics of Congress*, 5th ed. (Allyn and Bacon, 1988), p. 213.
48. William S. Cohen, "Why I Am Leaving," *The Washington Post National Weekly Edition*, January 28–February 4, 1996, p. 29.
49. James Madison, *The Federalist*, No. 57, in *The Federalist*, ed. Jacob E. Cooke (Meridan Books, 1961), p. 385.
50. See Kenny J. Whitby, *The Color of Representation: Congressional Behavior and Black Interests* (University of Michigan Press, 1998).
51. See Charles Lewis and the Center for Public Integrity, *The Buying of the Congress: How Special Interests Have Stolen Your Right to Life, Liberty and the Pursuit of Happiness* (Avon, 1998).
52. For an excellent treatment of ethical problems faced by members of Congress and what has been and might be done about them, see Dennis F. Thompson, *Ethics in Congress* (Brookings Institution, 1995).
53. Brady and Volden, *Revolving Gridlock*, p. 178.

CHAPTER 15

1. Charles O. Jones, *The Presidency in a Separated System* (Brookings Institution, 1994), p. 295. See also Jean Reith Schroedl, *Congress, the President, and Policymaking* (M.E. Sharpe, 1994).
2. Glenn A. Phelps, *George Washington and American Constitutionalism* (University Press of Kansas, 1993).
3. It is difficult for the average citizen to assess systematically the psychological health and character of presidential candidates, but voters still try to do so. For a specialist's efforts, see Stanley A. Renshon, *The Psychological Assessment of Presidential Candidates* (New York University Press, 1996); see also Alexander L. George and Juliette L. George, *Presidential Personality and Performance* (Westview Press, 1998).
4. Thomas Friedman, "Character Suicide," *The New York Times*, January 27, 1998, p. A23.
5. For a longer discussion of these points, see Thomas E. Cronin and Michael A. Genovese, "President Clinton and Character Questions," *Presidential Studies Quarterly* (Fall 1998), pp. 892–97. See also Robert Shogan, *The Double-Edged Sword: How Character Makes and Ruins Presidents, from Washington to Clinton* (Westview Press, 1998).
6. See, in general, Joseph G. Dawson III, ed., *Commanders in Chief: Presidential Leadership in Modern Wars* (University Press of Kansas, 1993).
7. See Thomas J. Weko, *The Politicizing Presidency: The White House Personnel Office, 1948–1994* (University Press of Kansas, 1995).
8. See G. Calvin MacKenzie and Robert Shogan, eds., *Obstacle Course: The Report of the Twentieth Century Fund Task Force on the Presidential Appointment Process* (Twentieth Century Fund Press, 1996).
9. See James P. Pfiffner, *The Strategic Presidency: Hitting the Ground Running*, 2nd ed. (University Press of Kansas, 1996).
10. *United States v Curtiss-Wright Export Corp.*, 299 US 304 (1936).
11. For those who believe the Curtiss-Wright ruling was too sweeping, see Harold H. Koh, *The National Security Constitution* (Yale University Press, 1990); Louis Fisher, *Presidential War Power* (University Press of Kansas, 1995); David Gray Adler and Larry N. George, eds., *The Constitution and the Conduct of American Foreign Policy: Essays on Law and History* (University Press of Kansas, 1996).
12. On the president's major involvement in the budget process, see Allen Schick, *The Federal Budget: Politics, Policy, Process* (Brookings Institution, 1995).
13. On presidential press conferences, see Carolyn Smith, *Presidential Press Conferences: A Critical Approach* (Praeger, 1990).
14. See the essay by John Zaller, "Monica Lewinsky's Contribution to Political Science," *PS: Political Science and Politics* (July 1998), pp. 182–89.
15. See table "Public View of the President," *The New York Times*, September 25, 1998, p. A18.

16. See Kenneth T. Walsh, *Feeding the Beast: The White House Versus the Press* (Random House, 1996). See also Richard Morris, *Behind the Oval Office* (Random House, 1997).
17. See Howard Kurtz, *Spin Cycle: Inside the Clinton Propaganda Machine* (Free Press, 1998).
18. See also the vigorous criticism of the Washington media and their biases by former U.S. Senator Alan K. Simpson, *Right in the Old Kazoo* (Morrow, 1997).
19. See Sidney M. Milkis, *The President and the Parties: The Transformation of the American Party System Since the New Deal* (Oxford University Press, 1993); James W. Davis, *The President as Party Leader* (Praeger, 1992).
20. See Charles E. Walcott and Karen M. Holt, *Governing the White House* (University Press of Kansas, 1995).
21. See Shelley Lynne Tomkins, *Inside OMB: Politics and Process in the President's Budget Office* (M. E. Sharpe, 1998).
22. See Thomas E. Cronin and Michael A. Genovese, *The Paradoxes of the American Presidency* (Oxford University Press, 1998), chap. 9.
23. Information provided to Thomas E. Cronin in a letter, February 1997, from Ms. Kathryn Hughes, secretary of the cabinet in the Clinton White House. See also Robert B. Reich, *Locked in the Cabinet* (Knopf, 1997).
24. See Robert J. Spitzer, *The President and Congress: Executive Hegemony at the Crossroads of American Government* (McGraw-Hill, 1993); Lester G. Seligman and Cary R. Covington, *The Coalition Presidency* (Dorsey Press, 1989).
25. See Cary R. Covington and Kedron Bardwell, "Helping Friends or Wooing Enemies? How Presidents Use Favors to Build Support in Congress," paper presented at the Annual Meeting of the American Political Science Association, Boston, September 3–6, 1998.
26. Warren B. Rudman, *Combat: Twelve Years in the U.S. Senate* (Random House, 1996), p. 251.
27. Robert J. Spitzer, "Regular Veto," in *Encyclopedia of the American Presidency*, vol. 4, eds. Leonard W. Levy and Louis Fisher (Simon & Schuster, 1994), p. 553. Updated through mid 1999 by the Office of the Secretary, U.S. Senate Library.
28. Quoted in Alison Mitchell, "With Ceremony, Clinton Signs a Line-Item Veto Measure," *The New York Times*, April 10, 1996, p. C20.
29. For a detailed review of the arguments for and against the item veto, see Thomas E. Cronin and Jeffrey Weill, "An Item Veto for Presidents?" *Congress and the Presidency* (Autumn 1985), pp. 127–51.
30. Robert J. Spitzer, "The Item Veto Dispute and the Secular Crisis of the Presidency," *Presidential Studies Quarterly* (Fall 1998), p. 804.
31. *Clinton v. City of New York*, 141 L Ed 2d 393 (1998).
32. Quoted in Andrew Taylor, "Few in Congress Grieve as Justices Give Line-Item Veto the Ax," *Congressional Quarterly Weekly Report*, June 27, 1998, p. 1748.
33. Quoted in *ibid.*, p. 1747.
34. *Clinton v. City of New York*, 141 L Ed 2d 393 (1998).
35. See, for example, Terry Eastland, *Energy in the Executive* (Free Press, 1992); Harvey Mansfield, Jr., *Taming the Prince: The Ambivalence of Modern Executive Power* (Free Press, 1989).
36. See Louis Fisher, *Presidential War Power* (University Press of Kansas, 1995); Adler and George, eds., *Constitution and the Conduct of American Foreign Policy.*
37. Louis Fisher, *Constitutional Conflicts Between Congress and the President*, 3d ed. (University Press of Kansas, 1991), p. 285.
38. James A. Thurber, "The Roots of Divided Democracy," in *Divided Democracy*, ed. James A. Thurber (Congressional Quarterly Press, 1991).
39. See, for example, former Republican Senator Warren B. Rudman's memoir, *Combat*, chaps. 2, 3. See also former Democratic Congressman Timothy Penny and Major Garrett, *Common Cents* (Little, Brown, 1995).
40. John R. Hibbing and Elizabeth Theiss-Morse, *Congress as Public Enemy: Public Attitudes Toward American Political Institutions* (Cambridge University Press, 1995).
41. Roger Davidson and Walter J. Oleszek, *Congress and Its Members*, 5th ed. (Congressional Quarterly Press, 1996), p. 289. See also Mark A. Peterson, *Legislating Together: The White House and Capitol Hill from Eisenhower to Reagan* (Harvard University Press, 1990); David R. Mayhew, *Divided We Govern: Party Control and Investigations, 1946–1990* (Yale University Press, 1991); Burdett A. Loomis, *The Contemporary Congress* (St. Martin's Press, 1996).
42. An excellent case study of a presidential program initiative that Congress refused to enact was Clinton's health care reforms. See Jacob S. Hacker, *The Road to Nowhere* (Princeton University Press, 1997).
43. See Stephen Skowronek, *The Politics Presidents Make: Leadership from John Adams to George Bush* (Harvard University Press, 1993), chaps. 1–3.
44. Mark Hertsgaard, *On Bended Knee: The Press and the Reagan Presidency* (Farrar, Straus, Giroux, 1988). See also John A. Maltese, *Spin Control: The White House Office of Communications and the Management of Presidential News* (University of North Carolina Press, 1992).
45. Paul Kennedy, *The Rise and Fall of the Great Powers* (Random House, 1987), p. 534.
46. One of several publications from this assignment was Al Gore, *Creating a Government That Works Better and Costs Less* (Plume, 1993).
47. There has been a certain amount of controversy about the Twenty-fifth Amendment. See Herbert L. Abrams, *The President Has Been Shot: Confusion, Disability and the Twenty-fifth Amendment* (Stanford University Press, 1994); Laura Myers, "Transfer-of-Power-Rules Urged for Impaired Presidents," *Seattle-Post Intelligencer*, December 4, 1996, p. A3.
48. Former Vice-president Dan Quayle's views are of interest: *Standing Firm* (Harper Paperbacks, 1995). Three useful general treatments on the vice-presidency are Jules Witcover, *Crapshoot: Rolling the Dice on the Vice Presidency* (Crown, 1992); Paul Light, *Vice Presidential Power* (Johns Hopkins University Press, 1984); Joel Goldstein, *The Modern Vice Presidency* (Princeton University Press, 1982).

CHAPTER 16

1. Alexis de Tocqueville, *Democracy in America*, ed. Phillips Bradley (Knopf, 1944), 1:278–80.
2. Harold J. Laski, *The American Democracy* (Viking, 1948), p. 110.
3. Joseph F. DiMento and Dean W. Hestermann, "Ordering the Elephants to Dance: Consent Degrees and Organizational Behavior," *Journal of Urban and Contemporary Law* 43 (1993), p. 303.
4. *Chicago Grand Trunk Railway Co. v Wellman*, 143 US 339 (1892).
5. Karen Orren, "Standing to Sue: Interest Group Conflict in the Federal Courts," *American Political Science Review* 70 (September 1976), p. 7.
6. Philip J. Cooper, *Hard Judicial Choices: Federal District Court Judges and State and Local Officials* (Oxford University Press, 1988), p. 15.
7. *Luther v Borden*, 7 Howard 1 (1849).
8. Quoted in Paul E. Freund, *Understanding the Supreme Court* (Little, Brown, 1949), p. 3.
9. For one of the great classics, see Benjamin N. Cardozo, *The Nature of the Judicial Process* (Yale University Press, 1921).
10. Quoted in H.L.A. Hart, *The Concept of Law* (Oxford University Press, 1961), pp. 121–22.
11. C. K. Rowland, "The Federal District Courts," in *The American Courts: A Critical Assessment*, ed. John B. Gates and Charles A. Johnson (Congressional Quarterly Press, 1991), pp. 61–80.
12. Christopher E. Smith, *United States Magistrates in the Federal Courts: Subordinate Judges* (Praeger, 1990); Christopher E. Smith, "From U.S. Magistrates to U.S. Magistrate Judges," *Judicature*, December 1991/January 1992, pp. 210–15.
13. Quoted in Smith, *United States Magistrates in the Federal Courts*, p. 183.
14. Steven Puro and Roger Goldman, "U.S. Magistrates: Changing Dimensions of First-Echelon Federal Judicial Officers," in *The Politics of Judicial Reform*, ed. Philip L. Dubois (Heath, 1982). See also Caroll Seron, "Magistrates and the Work of Federal Courts: A New Division of Labor," *Judicature*, April/May 1986, pp. 353–59; Christopher E. Smith, "Who Are the U.S. Magistrates?" *Judicature*, October/November 1987, pp. 143–50.

15. *Peretz v United States*, 501 US 923 (1991).
16. Donald R. Songer, "The Circuit Courts of Appeals," in *American Courts*, ed. Gates and Johnson, pp. 35–37.
17. Deborah J. Barrow and Thomas G. Walker, *A Court Divided: The Fifth Circuit Court of Appeals and the Politics of Judicial Reform* (Yale University Press, 1988); Arthur D. Hellman, ed., *Reconstructing Justice: The Innovations of the Ninth Circuit and the Future of the Federal Courts* (Cornell University Press, 1991).
18. Editorial, "Short-Circuiting the 9th Circuit," *Los Angeles Times*, November 5, 1995, p. M4. See also Neil A. Lewis, "Partisan Gridlock Blocks Senate Confirmations of Federal Judges," *The New York Times*, November 30, 1995, p. A15.
19. Bill Kisliuk, "9th Circuit Split Postponed for Further Study," *The Recorder*, November 11, 1997, p. 1.
20. Paul Elias, "Final 9th Circuit Study Calls for Three Divisions," *The Recorder*, December 21, 1998, p. 3.
21. Paul Elias, "Splitting Circuit Is Not 1st Choice," *The Recorder*, October 8, 1998, p. 1.
22. Paul Elias, "North-South Split Backed by Seven Ninth Circuit Judges," *The Recorder*, November 9, 1998, p.3.
23. John Gruhl, "The Impact of Term Limits for Supreme Court Justices," *Judicature*, September/October 1997, pp. 67–68.
24. *Bordenkircher v Hayes*, 434 US 357 (1978). See also James Eisenstein, *Counsel for the United States: U.S. Attorneys in the Political and Legal Systems* (Johns Hopkins Press, 1978); *Wayte v United States*, 470 US 598 (1985); *United States v Armstrong*, C.D.O.S., May 13, 1996, p. 3351.
25. Joan Biskupic, "For Court Advocate, a Nominee Who Seeks 'Different Solutions,' " *The Washington Post*, April 19, 1993, p. A21; John G. Roberts, Jr., "The New Solicitor General and the Power of the Amicus," *The Wall Street Journal*, May 5, 1993, p. A21.
26. Karen O'Connor, "The Amicus Curiae Role of the U.S. Solicitor General in Supreme Court Litigation," *Judicature*, December 1982/January 1983, pp. 256–64; Jeffrey A. Segal, "Amicus Curiae Briefs by the Solicitor General During the Warren and Burger Courts," *Western Political Quarterly* 41 (March 1988), pp. 134–44.
27. For a critical analysis, see Lincoln Caplan, *The Tenth Justice: The Solicitor General and the Rule of Law* (Knopf, 1987). For a defense, see former Solicitor General Charles Fried, *Order and Law: Arguing the Reagan Revolution—A Firsthand Account* (Simon & Schuster, 1991). For a more neutral account, see Rebecca Mae Salokar, *The Solicitor General: The Politics of Law* (Temple University Press, 1992).
28. David Leitch, "The Deal for Walter Dellinger," *The Recorder*, June 1993, p. 6.
29. Charley Roberts, "Federal Defender Program to Be Studied," *Los Angeles Daily Journal*, August 19, 1991, p. 7; *United States Law Week*, April 20, 1993, p. 2627.
30. Naftali Bendavid, "D-Day for Advocates of the Poor," *The Recorder*, February 22, 1994, p. 10; editorial, "Legal Services Survives, Barely," *The New York Times*, May 6, 1996, p. A14.
31. David Cole, "Confining Compromise: How the Legal Services Corp. Sold Out the Poor," *The Recorder*, February 12, 1997, p. 5.
32. Neil D. McFeeley, *Appointment of Judges: The Johnson Presidency* (University of Texas Press, 1987), p. 1.
33. Stephen LaBaton, "Shifting List of Prospects to Be Justice," *The New York Times*, May 9, 1993, p. A12; Paul M. Barrett, "More Minorities, Women Named to U.S. Courts," *The Wall Street Journal*, December 23, 1993, p. B1.
34. Harold W. Chase, *Federal Judges: The Appointing Process* (University of Minnesota Press, 1972), pp. 3–47; Paul Simon, "The Senate's Role in Judicial Appointments," *Judicature*, June/July 1986, pp. 55–58; Elliot E. Slotnick, "Federal Judicial Recruitment and Selection Research: A Review Essay," *Judicature*, April/May 1988, pp. 317–24.
35. Lettie McSpadden Wenner and Lee F. Dutter, "Contextual Influences on Court Outcomes," *Western Political Quarterly* 41 (March 1988), pp. 115–34; Ronald Stidham and Robert A. Carp, "Exploring Regionalism in the Federal District Courts," *Los Angeles Daily Journal* 18 (Fall 1988), pp. 113–25.
36. January 9, 1999, e-mail to authors from Sheldon Goldman, professor of political science, University of Massachusetts, Amherst, who is the pre-eminent author on federal judicial selection.
37. Lisa M. Holmes and Roger E. Hartley, "Increasing Senate Scrutiny of Lower Federal Court Nominees," *Judicature*, May/June 1997, p. 275.
38. George Watson and John Stookey, "Supreme Court Confirmation Hearings: A View from the Senate," *Judicature*, December 1987/January 1988, p. 193. See also John Massaro, *Supremely Political: The Role of Ideology and Presidential Management in Unsuccessful Supreme Court Nominations* (State University of New York Press, 1990).
39. Barbara A. Perry and Henry J. Abraham, "A 'Representative' Supreme Court? The Thomas, Ginsburg, and Breyer Appointments," *Judicature*, January/February 1998, pp. 158–65.
40. Sheldon Goldman, *Picking Federal Judges: Lower Court Selection from Roosevelt Through Reagan* (Yale University Press, 1998), pp. 161, 327–36.
41. Sheldon Goldman, "Bush's Judicial Legacy: The Final Imprint," *Judicature*, April/May 1993, p. 291.
42. Quoted in Sheldon Goldman, "Judicial Selection Under Clinton: A Midterm Examination," *Judicature*, May/June 1995, p. 281.
43. Ibid.
44. Robert A. Carp and C. K. Rowland, *Policymaking and Politics in the Federal District Courts* (University of Tennessee Press, 1983), p. 82.
45. Sheldon Goldman, "Reagan's Judicial Legacy: Completing the Puzzle and Summing Up," *Judicature*, April/May 1989, pp. 318–30.
46. Leo V. Hennessy, "Redrawing the Political Map? An Impact Analysis of the Reagan Appointments on the U.S. Courts of Appeals," paper presented at the Southern Political Science Association, Tampa, Florida, November 7–9, 1991.
47. Robert A. Carp, Donald Songer, C. K. Rowland, Ronald Stidham, and Lisa Richey-Tracey, "The Voting Behavior of Judges Appointed by President Bush," *Judicature*, April/May 1993, pp. 298–302.
48. David G. Savage, *Turning Right: The Making of the Rehnquist Supreme Court* (John Wiley & Sons, 1992), pp. 451–58.
49. Naftali Bendavid, "Diversity Marks Clinton Judiciary," *The Recorder*, December 30, 1993, p. 11.
50. Naftali Bendavid, "Seeking Diversity, Not Confrontation," *The Recorder*, December 30, 1995, p. 1.
51. Dan Carney, "Battle Looms Between Clinton, GOP Over Court Nominees," *Congressional Quarterly Weekly Report*, February 8, 1997, p. 369.
52. Editorial, "Too Many Federal Court Vacancies," *The New York Times*, February 14, 1997, p. A22. See also Neil Lewis, "Republicans Seek Greater Influence in Naming Judges," *The New York Times*, April 27, 1997, p. A1.
53. Cited in Stephen Labaton, "Clinton Expected to Change Makeup of Federal Courts," *The New York Times*, March 8, 1993, p. A1; Neil A. Lewis, "Clinton Has a Chance to Shape the Courts," *The New York Times*, February 9, 1997.
54. William Howard Taft to Horace Taft, November 14, 1929; quoted in Henry Pringle, *The Life and Times of William Howard Taft* (Farrar, 1939), 2:967.
55. Sue Davis, "Federalism and Property Rights: An Examination of Justice Rehnquist's Legal Positivism," *Western Reserve Political Quarterly* 39 (June 1986), pp. 250–64.
56. David M. O'Brien, *Judicial Roulette: Report of the Twentieth Century Fund Task Force on Judicial Selection* (Priority Press Publications, 1988), pp. 10–11.
57. White Burkett Miller Center of Public Affairs, *Improving the Process of Appointing Federal Judges* (Miller Center, University of Virginia, 1996).
58. Donald Santarelli, quoted in Jerry Landauer, "Shaping the Bench," *The Wall Street Journal*, December 10, 1970, p. 1. See also J. W. Peltason, *Federal Courts in the Political Process* (Doubleday, 1955), p. 32.
59. Michale A. Kahn, "The Appointment of a Supreme Court Justice: A Political Process from Beginning to End," *Presidential Studies Quarterly* 25 (Winter 1995), pp. 26, 39.
60. Ex parte *McCardle*, *Wallace* 506 (1869).
61. Barry Friedman, "Attacks on Judges: Why They Fail," *Judicature*, January/February 1998, p. 152.
62. Tony Mauro, "Yipes! Stripes!" *The Recorder*, February 8, 1995, p. 8.
63. Richard Johnson, *The Dynamics of Compliance* (Wiley, 1967), pp. 33–41, as summarized in David Adamany, "Legitimacy, Realigning Elections, and the Supreme Court," *Wisconsin Law Review* (1973), p. 792.
64. Tony Mauro, "Supreme Court Calendar Begs for More Arguments," *The Recorder*, February 13, 1996, p. 1.
65. David M. O'Brien, "The Rehnquist Court's Shrinking Plenary Docket," *Judicature*, September/October 1997, p. 58.
66. David M. O'Brien, *Storm Center: The Supreme Court in American Politics*, 2d. ed. (W. W. Norton, 1990), p. 63. See also Tony Mauro, "Jumping into the Pool," *The Recorder*, September 14, 1993, p. 6.

67. Sidney Ulmer, "The Supreme Court's Certiorari Decisions: Conflict as a Predictive Variable," *American Political Science Review* 78 (December 1984), pp. 901–11.
68. Elder Witt, "Reagan Crusade Before Court Unprecedented in Intensity," *Congressional Quarterly Weekly Report*, March 15, 1986, p. 616.
69. Gregory A. Caldeira and John R. Wright, "Organized Interest and Agenda Setting in the U.S. Supreme Court," *American Political Science Review* 82 (December 1988), p. 1110; Donald R. Songer and Reginald S. Sheehan, "Interest Groups' Success in the Courts: Amicus Participation in the Supreme Court," *Political Research Quarterly* 46 (June 1993), pp. 339–54.
70. *Webster v Reproductive Health Services*, 492 US 490 (1989); *Roe v Wade*, 410 US 113 (1973). See also Susan Behuniak-Long, "Friendly Fire: *Amici Curiae* and *Webster v Reproductive Health Services*," *Judicature*, February/March 1991, pp. 261–70.
71. *United States v Lopez*, 514 US 549 (1951).
72. Tony Mauro, "The Supreme Court as Quiz Show," *The Recorder*, December 8, 1993, p. 10.
73. Joyce O'Connor, "Selections from Notes Kept on an Internship at the U.S. Supreme Court, Fall 1988," *Law, Courts, and Judicial Process* (Department of Political Science, Purdue University) 6 (Spring 1989), p. 44.
74. Quoted in Mauro, "Jumping into the Pool," p. 7.
75. Tony Mauro, "No Comfort for Counsel After Court Review," *The Recorder*, November 10, 1997, p. 8.
76. Mauro, "Yipes! Stripes!" p. 8.
77. Anthony M. Kennedy, Jr., address to Pasadena Bar Association, June 1991, quoted in Richard C. Reuben, "Kennedy Remembers William Brennan," *The Los Angeles Daily Journal*, July 2, 1991, p. 7.
78. Joan Biskupke, "Supreme Court Film Offers Glimpse Behind Justices' Closed Doors," *The Washington Post*, June 17, 1997, p. A15.
79. William H. Rehnquist, *The Supreme Court: How It Was, How It Is* (William Morrow, 1987), pp. 289–90.
80. Daniel M. Berman, *It Is So Ordered: The Supreme Court Rules on School Segregation* (Norton, 1986), p. 114; Walter F. Murphy, *Elements of Judicial Strategy* (University of Chicago Press, 1964), p. 66; David M. O'Brien, *Storm Center: The Supreme Court in American Politics*, 2d ed. (W. W. Norton, 1990), pp. 262–72.
81. Charles Evans Hughes, quoted in Donald E. Lively, *Foreshadows of the Law: Supreme Court Dissents and Constitutional Development* (Praeger, 1992), p. xx.
82. Quoted in John R. Vile, "The Selection and Tenure of Chief Justices," *Judicature*, September/October 1994, p. 98.
83. Robert J. Steamer, *Chief Justice: Leadership and the Supreme Court* (University of South Carolina Press, 1986). See also White Burkett Miller Center of Public Affairs, *The Office of Chief Justice* (University Press of Virginia, 1984).
84. Sue Davis, "The Supreme Court: Rehnquist's or Reagan's," *Western Political Quarterly* 44 (March 1991), p. 98.
85. David G. Savage, "The Rehnquist Court," *Los Angeles Times Magazine*, September 29, 1991, p. 13; David W. Rohde and Harold J. Spaeth, "Ideology, Strategy and Supreme Court Decisions: William Rehnquist as Chief Justice," *Judicature*, December 1988/January 1989, pp. 247–50. See also Joseph F. Kobylka, "Leadership on the Supreme Court of the United States: Chief Justice Burger and the Establishment Clause," *Western Political Quarterly* 42 (December 1989), pp. 545–68.
86. David Danelski, "The Influence of the Chief Justice in the Decisional Process of the Supreme Court," in *The Federal Judicial System: Readings in Process and Behavior*, ed. Thomas P. Jahnige and Sheldon Goldman (Holt, Rinehart and Winston, 1968), p. 148.
87. Edward Lazarus, *Closed Chambers: The First Eyewitness Account of the Epic Struggles Inside the Supreme Court* (Times Books, Random House, 1998), p. 423.
88. *Youngstown Sheet and Tube Co. v Sawyer*, 343 US 579 (1952).
89. Stephen L. Wasby, *The Impact of the United States Supreme Court* (Dorsey Press, 1970).
90. J. W. Peltason, *Fifty-Eight Lonely Men: Southern Federal Judges and School Desegregation* (University of Illinois Press, 1971), p. 19.
91. Cooper, *Hard Judicial Choices*, pp. 347–50.
92. Peter W. Huber, *Liability: The Legal Revolution and Its Consequences* (Basic Books, 1988).
93. Arthur S. Miller, "In Defense of Judicial Activism," in *Supreme Court Activism and Restraint*, ed. Stephen C. Halpern and Charles M. Lamb (Heath, 1982), p. 177. See also, by the chief justice of the West Virginia Supreme Court, Richard Neely, *How Courts Govern America* (Yale University Press, 1981).
94. *United States v Carolene Products*, 304 US 144 (1938). Variations on this basic position have been restated in dozens of books. Halpern and Lamb, eds., *Supreme Court Activism and Restraint*, and Mark Tushnet, *Red, White, and Blue: A Critical Analysis of Constitutional Law* (Harvard University Press, 1988), provide balanced analysis from all perspectives. For another analysis of this great debate, see Lief H. Carter, *Contemporary Constitutional Lawmaking* (Pergamon Press, 1985). See also David J. Richards, *Toleration and the Constitution* (Oxford University Press, 1986); Stephen Macedo, *The New Right v the Constitution* (Cato, 1986). Leslie F. Goldstein, "Judicial Review and Democratic Theory: Guardian Democracy vs. Representative Democracy," *Western Political Quarterly* 40 (September 1987), pp. 391–412, also contains a bibliography.
95. J. W. Peltason, "The Supreme Court: Transactional or Transformational Leadership," in *Essays in Honor of James MacGregor Burns*, eds. Michael R. Beschloss and Thomas E. Cronin (Prentice Hall, 1988), pp. 165–80; Mark Silverstein and Benjamin Ginsburg, "The Supreme Court and the New Politics of Judicial Power," *Political Science Quarterly* 102 (Fall 1987), pp. 371–88.
96. *Planned Parenthood v Casey*, 505 US 833 (1992).
97. Thomas R. Marshall, *Public Opinion and the Supreme Court* (Unwin Hyman, 1989), p. 193. See also Thomas R. Marshall, "The Supreme Court and the Grass Roots: Whom Does the Court Represent Best?" *Judicature*, June/July 1992, pp. 22–28; Michael Comiskey, "The Rehnquist Court and American Values," *Judicature*, March/April 1994, pp. 261–67; William Mishler and Reginald S. Sheehan, "The Supreme Court as a Counter-Majoritarian Institution? The Impact of Public Opinion on Supreme Court Decisions," *American Political Science Review* 87 (1993), pp. 87–101; response along with Mishler and Sheehan response, Helmut Norpoth and Jeffrey A. Segal, "Popular Influence on Supreme Court Decisions," *American Political Science Review* 88 (September 1994), pp. 711–24.
98. Quoted in Fred Rodell, *Nine Men: A Political History of the Supreme Court from 1790 to 1995* (Random House, 1995).
99. Gerald N. Rosenberg, *The Hollow Hope: Can Courts Bring About Social Change?* (University of Chicago Press, 1991), p. 343.
100. Rehnquist, *Supreme Court*, p. 98.

CHAPTER 17

1. Donald F. Kettl, *Reinventing Government: A Fifth Year Report Card* (Brookings Institution, 1998), p. ix.
2. Paul C. Light, "Big Government Is Bigger Than You Think," *The Wall Street Journal*, January 13, 1999, p. A22.
3. Shelley L. Davis, *Unbridled Power: Inside the Secret Culture of the IRS* (Harper Business, 1997); Michael Hirsh, "Infernal Revenue Disservice," *Newsweek*, October 13, 1997, pp. 33–35.
4. Philip K. Howard, *The Death of Common Sense: How Law Is Suffocating America* (Random House, 1994), p. 9.
5. Al Gore, *Creating a Government That Works Better and Costs Less: The Report of the National Performance Review* (Plume-Penguin, 1993).
6. President Bill Clinton, *Budget Message: Budget of U.S. Government for Fiscal Year 1996* (Government Printing Office, 1995), p. 5. See also Al Gore, *The Best Kept Secrets in Government: How the Clinton Administration Is Reinventing the Way Washington Works* (Random House, 1996).
7. Influential writings that helped shape the debate about reforming the bureaucracy include James Q. Wilson, *Bureaucracy: What Government Agencies Do and Why They Do It* (Basic Books, 1989); David Osborne and Ted Gaebler, *Reinventing Government: How the Entrepreneurial Spirit Is Transforming the Public Sector* (Addison-Wesley, 1992); John J. DiIulio, Jr., Gerald Garvey, and Donald F. Kettl, *Improving Government*

Performance: An Owner's Manual (Brookings Institution, 1993); Howard, *Death of Common Sense.*
8. Donald F. Kettl, "Building Lasting Reform: Enduring Questions, Missing Answers," in *Inside the Reinvention Machine: Appraising Governmental Reform,* ed. Donald F. Kettl and John J. DiIulio, Jr. (Brookings Institution, 1995), p. 30. See also Kettl, *Reinventing Government: A Fifth Year Report Card.*
9. Data reported in detail in Andrew Kohut, ed., *Deconstructing Distrust: How Americans View Government* (Pew Research Center for the People and the Press, 1998), p. 16.
10. For a study of bureaucracies and their strategies to keep as much autonomy as possible, see Wilson, *Bureaucracy.*
11. Adapted from Dennis Palumbo and Steven Maynard-Moody, *Contemporary Public Administration* (Longman, 1991), p. 26.
12. See data provided in Kohut, ed., *Deconstructing Distrust,* p. 124.
13. For an analysis of the use and abuse of the civil service system in the early twentieth century, see Stephen Skowronek, *Building a New American State* (Cambridge University Press, 1982).
14. See, for example, Dan Baum, *Smoke and Mirrors: The War on Drugs and the Politics of Failure* (Little, Brown, 1996).
15. A history of the old Hatch Act is provided in James Eccles, *The Hatch Act and the American Bureaucracy* (Vantage Press, 1981).
16. For the 1994 revisions of this act, see Jeanne Ponessa, "The Hatch Act Rewrite," *Congressional Quarterly Weekly Report,* November 13, 1993, pp. 3146–47.
17. Adapted from the U.S. Merit Systems Protection Board publications and from *Congressional Quarterly Weekly Report,* November 13, 1993, p. 3146.
18. For an examination of Max Weber's ideas on bureaucracy, see Brian Fry, *Mastering Public Administration: From Max Weber to Dwight Waldo* (Chatham House, 1989).
19. Gore, *Best Kept Secrets in Government,* p. 24.
20. E. S. Savas, *Privatization: The Key to Better Government* (Chatham House, 1987).
21. Osborne and Gaebler, *Reinventing Government,* pp. 45–46.
22. Anthony Frank, quoted in an interview in *USA Today,* January 8, 1992, p. 7A.
23. Morris P. Fiorina, "Flagellating the Federal Bureaucracy," *Society,* March/April 1983, p. 73.
24. Francis E. Rourke, "Whose Bureaucracy Is This, Anyway?" *PS: Political Science and Politics,* December 1993, p. 691.
25. For the general philosophy of the congressional Republican leadership in the 1990s, see Newt Gingrich, *To Renew America* (HarperCollins, 1995); Dick Armey, *The Freedom Revolution* (Regnery, 1995).
26. Jonathan Weisman, "Republicans Showing Less Zeal to Cut Cabinet Departments," *Congressional Quarterly Weekly Report,* January 18, 1997, p. 171.
27. Ibid., p. 172.
28. The strategies used in these places and elsewhere are detailed in Osborne and Gaebler, *Reinventing Government*; and in David Osborne and Peter Plastrik, *Banishing Bureaucracy: The Five Strategies for Reinventing Government* (Addison-Wesley, 1997).

CHAPTER 18

1. Robert A. Dahl, *On Democracy* (Yale University Press, 1998), p. 158.
2. Peter Bachrach and Morton Baratz, *Power and Poverty* (Oxford University Press, 1970); Charles E. Lindblom, "Another State of Mind," *American Political Science Review* 76 (March 1982), pp. 9–21.
3. *Budget of the United States Government, Fiscal Year 2000* (Government Printing Office, 1999).
4. *A Citizen's Guide to the Federal Budget* (http://www.doc. gov/Budget FY 99/guide2.html).
5. For a discussion of the budgetary cycle, see Allen Schick, *The Federal Budget: Politics, Policy, Process* (Brookings Institution, 1995).
6. Efforts at past tax reform are described by Jeffrey H. Birnbaum and Alan S. Murray, *Showdown at Gucci Gulch: Lawmakers, Lobbyists, and the Unlikely Triumph of Tax Reform* (Vintage, 1988). See also Timothy J. Conlan, Margaret T. Wrightson, and David R. Beam, *Taxing Choices: The Politics of Tax Reform* (Congressional Quarterly Press, 1990).
7. Bureau of the Census, *Statistical Abstract of the United States, 1998* (Government Printing Office, 1998), p. 343, Table 544.
8. Anthony Kennedy, quoted in Andrew Taylor, "Few in Congress Grieve as Justices Give Line-Item Veto the Ax," *Congressional Quarterly Weekly,* June 27, 1998, p. 1747. See also *Clinton v City of New York,* 177 L Ed 2d, 1998.
9. John R. Wilke, "Showing Its Age: Fed's Huge Empire, Set Up Years Ago, Is Costly and Inefficient," *The Wall Street Journal,* September 12, 1996, p. 1.
10. Arthur Rolnick, research director at the Minneapolis Fed, quoted in ibid., p. 2.
11. Quoted in Frederick Lewis Allen, *Since Yesterday* (Harper, 1940), p. 64.
12. W. H. Beveridge, *The Pillars of Security* (Macmillan, 1943), p. 51.
13. The debate over Keynes and his economic theories is still alive in the United States. See, for example, the special issue on Keynes in *The Economist* (American Enterprise Institute, June 1983); see also Robert Eisner, *How Real Is the Federal Deficit?* (Free Press, 1986), and Donald E. Moggridge, *Maynard Keynes: An Economist's Biography* (Routledge, 1992).
14. Superintendent of Documents, *Annual Report of the United States Patent Office* (Government Printing Office), or on the World Wide Web (http://www.uspto.gov/web/offices/com/annual/annual html).
15. U.S. Bureau of the Census, *Statistical Abstract of the United States, 1998* (Government Printing Office, 1998), p. 798, table 1284; Patrick G. Marshall, "U.S. Trade Policy," *Congressional Quarterly Weekly Report,* January 29, 1994, pp. 75–88. See also Martin Crutsinger, Associated Press, "U.S. Trade Deficit Improves," February 8, 1996 (http://www.kern.com/tbc/art/BIZ/25688Ahtml).
16. Gary Burtless, Robert J. Lawrence, Robert E. Litan, and Robert J. Shapiro, *Globaphobia: Confronting Fears About Open Trade* (Brookings Institution, 1998), p. 29.
17. Arlene Wilson, "NAFTA: How Many U.S. Jobs Are at Risk?" Congressional Research Service Report for Congress, May 19, 1993, p. 3.
18. Richard W. Stevenson, "NAFTA's Impact on Jobs Has Been Slight, Study Says," *The New York Times,* December 19, 1996, p. C1.
19. Burtless et al., *Globaphobia,* p. 126.
20. Robert W. Crandall et al., *An Agenda for Federal Regulatory Reform* (American Enterprise Institute and the Brookings Institution, 1997), p. 1.
21. John Cushman, Jr., "Surprise Senate Challenge to Pollution Plan," *The New York Times,* December 7, 1996, p. 7. See also Robert Kuttner, *Everything for Sale: The Virtues and Limits of Markets* (Knopf, 1997); Gary Bryner, *Blue Skies, Green Politics: The Clean Air Act of 1990 and Its Interpretation,* 2d ed. (Congressional Quarterly Press, 1995).
22. Harold W. Stanley and Richard G. Niemi, *Vital Statistics in American Politics* (Congressional Quarterly Press, 1999), p. 258.
23. Stephen Moore, ed., *Restoring the Dream: The Bold New Plan by House Republicans* (Times Books, 1995), p. 156.
24. Ben Wildavsky, "Deflating Air Bags," *National Journal,* February 15, 1997, pp. 322–24.
25. But more progress is encouraged by Crandall et al., *An Agenda for Federal Regulatory Reform,* pp. 12–16.
26. On the origins of the Federal Trade Commission and the role of Louis D. Brandeis, see Thomas K. McCraw, *Prophets of Regulation* (Belknap, 1984), chap. 3.
27. Paul McClure, ed., *Congressional Quarterly's Federal Regulatory Directory,* 8th ed. (Congressional Quarterly Press, 1997), p. 507.
28. Don L. Boroughs with Betsy Carpenter, "Cleaning Up the Environment," *U.S. News and World Report,* March 25, 1991, p. 46.
29. Al Gore, *Earth in the Balance: Ecology and the Human Spirit* (Houghton Mifflin, 1992).
30. See John E. Robson, "Airline Deregulation," *Regulation,* Spring 1998, pp. 17–22. For a useful history of airline deregulation, see Steven A.

Morrison and Clifford Winston, *The Evolution of the Airline Industry* (Brookings Institution, 1995).

31. See the book on Southwest Airlines and its longtime chief executive Herb Kelliher by Kevin Freiberg and Jackie Freiberg, *Nuts!* (Bard Press, 1996).
32. For discussion of the telecommunications industry and its regulatory issues, see Robert W. Crandall and Harold Furchtgott-Roth, *Cable TV: Regulation or Competition?* (Brookings Institution, 1996); Richard Klingler, *The New Information Industry: Regulatory Challenges and the First Amendment* (Brookings Institution, 1996).

CHAPTER 19

1. Michael B. Katz, *In the Shadow of the Poorhouse: A Social History of Welfare in America* (Basic Books, 1986).
2. *Railroad Retirement Board v Alton Railroad Company*, 295 US 300 (1934).
3. Social Security Administration, *Highlights of Social Security Data*, August 1998, October 29, 1998, http://www.ssa.gov/statistics/highssd.html
4. Martha Derthick, "No More Easy Votes for Social Security," *Brookings Review* 10 (Fall 1992), pp. 50–53.
5. U.S. Bureau of the Census, *Statistical Abstract of the United States, 1998* (Government Printing Office, 1998), p. 339.
6. Peter Francese, "Social Security Solution," *American Demographics* 15 (February 1993), p. 2. See also Terry Savage, "Can Social Security Find Its Way Back to Stability?" *Chicago Sun Times*, December 8, 1998, p. 6.
7. David S. Cloud, "Social Security Funds Not Immune Forever," *Congressional Quarterly Weekly Report*, March 18, 1995, p. 838.
8. Quoted in *Congress and the Nation, 1965–1968: A Review of Government and Politics During the Johnson Years* (Congressional Quarterly Press, 1969), II: 650.
9. *Congress and the Nation, 1945–1964: A Review of Government and Politics I* (Congressional Quarterly Press, 1965), 1:49.
10. *Congress and the Nation, 1965–1968*, 2:1–13, 625.
11. For examples on both sides of this debate, see John E. Schwartz, *America's Hidden Success: A Reassessment of Twenty Years of Public Policy* (Norton, 1983); Charles Murray, *Losing Ground: American Social Policy, 1950–80* (Basic Books, 1984).
12. William J. Clinton, State of the Union Address, January 23, 1996, *House Document 104-168* (Government Printing Office, 1996).
13. William J. Clinton, acceptance speech at the Democratic National Convention, Chicago, 1992, *Los Angeles Times*, July 7, 1992, p. A10.
14. U.S. Bureau of the Census, "Poverty Rate Down, Household Income Up—Both Return to 1989 Pre-Recession Levels," press release, September 24, 1998, http://www.census.gov/PressRelease/cb98-175.html
15. Gertrude Schaffner Goldberg and Eleanor Kremen, eds., *The Feminization of Poverty: Only in America?* (Greenwood Press, 1990).
16. "The Newest New Federalism for Welfare: Where Are We Now and Where Are We Headed," *Rockefeller Reports*, October 30, 1997.
17. The Web Site for Administration for Children and Families, www.acf.dhhs.gov/news/caseload.htm
18. For a description of issues surrounding Medicaid, see Kathleen N. Lohr and M. Susan Maquis, *Medicare and Medicaid: Past, Present and Future* (Rand Corporation, 1984); Congressional Research Service, *Medicaid Source Book* (Library of Congress, 1993). For a discussion of Medicare generally, see Theodore R. Marmor, Jerry L. Mashaw, and Philip L. Harvey, *America's Misunderstood Welfare State: Persistent Myths, Enduring Realities* (Basic Books, 1990), p. 97.
19. Health Care Financing Administration, Office of the Actuary, *National Health Expenditure Amounts*, September 28, 1998, http://www.hcfa.gov/stats/NHE-Proj/tables/t01.htm
20. *Statistical Abstract, 1998*, pp. 119, 161.
21. Health Care Financing Administration, Bureau of Data Management and Strategy: Data from the Division of Health Care Information Services and the Office of the Actuary: Data from the Office of Medicaid Cost Estimates, *1996 HCFA Statistics*, October 30, 1998, http://www.hcfa.gov/stats/hstats96/blustats.htm
22. *Statistical Abstract, 1997*, p. 391.
23. Health Care Financing Administration, Office of the Acutary, *National Health Expenditures*, September 28, 1998, http://www.hcfa.gov/stats/NHE-Proj/tables/t02.htm
24. John Greenwald, "Ouch!" *Time*, March 8, 1993, p. 53.
25. *Statistical Abstract, 1997*, p. 440.
26. Health Care Financing Administration homepage, October 4, 1998, Table 11, http://www.hcfa.gov/stats/nhe-oact/tables/t11/htm
27. U.S. Bureau of the Census, *Statistical Abstract of the United States, 1996* (Government Printing Office, 1996), p. 88.
28. U.S. Census Bureau, press release, September 28, 1998, http://www.census.gov/PressRelease/cb98-172.html
29. Laurene A. Graig, *Health of Nations: An International Perspective on U.S. Health Care Reform* (Congressional Quarterly Press, 1993), p. 20.
30. "Defensive Deliveries," *Time*, February 1, 1993, p. 23.
31. Health Care Financing Administration, Office of the Actuary, National Health Statistics, December 15, 1997, http://www.hcfa.gov/stats/nhe-oact/tables/t11.htm
32. Christopher Georges, "Bad Forms," *Washington Monthly* 25 (April 1993), pp. 10–33.
33. Mark M. Hagland, "Physicians Using Computers Show Lower Resource Utilization," *Hospitals*, May 5, 1993, p. 17.
34. Peter C. Coyte, Donald N. Dewees, and Michael Trebilock, "Medical Malpractice: The Canadian Experience," *New England Journal of Medicine*, January 10, 1991, pp. 89–93; *Statistical Abstract, 1996*, p. 125; *Statistical Abstract, 1997*, p. 125.
35. Associated Press, "Medicare Funds Going Up in Smoke," *Deseret News*, May 17, 1994, p. A1.
36. Organization for Economic Cooperation and Development, *Health Care Reform: The Will to Change*, Health Policy Studies 8 (1996).
37. David C. Dingwall, minister of health, "Building a Better Health System for Canadians," speech presented to the Board of Trade of Metropolitan Toronto, April 22, 1997.
38. U.S. Bureau of the Census, *Statistical Abstract of the United States, 1998* (Government Printing Office, 1998), p. 128.
39. "Measuring the HMOs," *Los Angeles Times*, October 3, 1998, p. B7.
40. Keith Hammonds, "Listen to Your Patients—Or Else," *Business Week*, October 19, 1998, p. 175.
41. See Mary Agnes Cary, "Lobbyist Intensifying Debate over Health Care Regulation," *Congressional Quarterly Weekly Report*, February 21, 1998, p. 441; Cary, "GOP Tries to Claim Middle Ground with Managed Care Overhaul Plan," *Congressional Quarterly Weekly Report*, June 27, 1998, p. 1753.
42. James A. Klein, "Should Employers Select Health-Insurance Options for Workers?" *The Dallas Morning News*, August 2, 1998, p. 1J.
43. "Health Programs," *Congress and the Nation, 1969–1972: A Review of Government and Politics During Nixon's First Term* (Congressional Quarterly Press, 1973), 3:551.
44. Institute of Medicine, Committee on Employer-Based Health Benefits, *Employment and Health Benefits: A Connection at Risk*, ed. Marilyn J. Field and Harold T. Shapiro (National Academy Press, 1993), p. 5.
45. Beth C. Fuchs and Mark Merlis, "Health Care Reform: Tax System Approaches," *CRS Issue Brief*, October 27, 1993, p. i.
46. Philip B. Kurland and Ralph Lerner, eds., *The Founders' Constitution* (University of Chicago Press, 1987).
47. Mickey Kaus, *The End of Equality* (Basic Books, 1992).
48. U.S. Department of Education, *National Center for Education Statistics, Federal Support for Education: Fiscal Years 1980 to 1998, NCES 98-115 (Washington, D.C., 1998), p. iii.*
49. U.S. Department of Education, *Goals 2000: Increasing Student Achievement Through State and Local Initiatives: Report to Congress* (Government Printing Office, April 30, 1996), p. 23.

50. Governor George Allen, *Announcement on Goals 2000* (Commonwealth of Virginia Office of the Governor, January 10, 1997).
51. Representative John A. Boehner (R.-Ohio), quoted in *Congressional Digest*, January 1994, p. 25.
52. B. Guy Peters, *American Public Policy: Promise and Performance*, 4th ed. (Chatham House, 1996), p. 338.
53. Center for Education Reform, *Charter School Highlights and Statistics*, updated November 18, 1996, http://edreform.com/pugs/chglance.html
54. "House Passes Bill Clarifying Gun-Crimes Law," *Congressional Quarterly Weekly Report*, February 28, 1998, p. 498.
55. Bureau of Justice Statistics, *Key Crime and Justice Facts @ a Glance*, April 1998, http://www.ojp.usdoj.gov/bjs/glance/htm

CHAPTER 20

1. George F. Kennan, "The Failure in Our Success," *The New York Times*, March 14, 1994, p. A13.
2. Madeleine K. Albright, "The Testing of American Foreign Policy," *Foreign Affairs*, November/December 1998, p. 51.
3. William J. Broad, "27 Countries Support New Atom Accord," *The New York Times National Edition*, May 3, 1992, sec. 1, p. 9.
4. Michael Mandelbaum, "Lessons of the Next Nuclear War," *Foreign Affairs*, March/April 1995, pp. 22–37.
5. "The Future of Warfare," *The Economist*, March 8, 1997, p. 15.
6. "A Dangerous Treaty," editorial, *The Wall Street Journal*, February 19, 1997, p. A16. But see Pat Towell, "Clinton Pressures GOP to Act on Chemical Arms Ban," *Congressional Quarterly Weekly Report*, March 11, 1997, pp. 545–50.
7. Warren Christopher, *In the Stream of History: Shaping Foreign Policy for a New Era* (Stanford University Press, 1998), p. 533.
8. Albright, "Testing of American Foreign Policy," p. 62.
9. For the views of two recent secretaries of state, see James Baker with Thomas M. DeFrank, *The Politics of Diplomacy* (Putnam's, 1995), and Warren Christopher, *In the Stream of History*.
10. For different perspectives on the National Security Council under various presidents, see Harold Hongju Koh, *The National Security Constitution: Sharing Power After the Iran-Contra Affair* (Yale University Press, 1990); John Prados, *Keepers of the Keys: A History of the National Security Council from Truman to Bush* (William Morrow, 1991).
11. See Tim Zimmerman, "Twilight of the Diplomats," *U.S. News and World Report*, January 27, 1997, pp. 48–49.
12. The case for continued reliance on vital and well-supported U.S. embassies abroad is well made in Mary Locke and Casimir A. Yost, eds., *Who Needs Embassies? How U.S. Missions Abroad Help Shape Our World* (Georgetown University School of Foreign Policy, 1997).
13. For a fascinating history of U.S. intelligence operations, see Christopher Andrew, *For the President's Eyes Only: Secret Intelligence and the American Presidency from Washington to Bush* (HarperCollins, 1995). See also Rhodri Jeffreys-Jones, *The CIA and American Democracy*, 2d ed. (Yale University Press, 1998).
14. Tim Weiner, "The U.S. Intelligence Chief Steps Up to the Plate," *The New York Times*, October 23, 1998, p. A8.
15. For President Bush's recollections and surprise, see George Bush and Brent Scowcraft, *A World Transformed* (Knopf, 1998), pp. 302–333.
16. See Loch K. Johnson, *Secret Agencies: U.S. Intelligence in a Hostile World* (Yale University Press, 1996).
17. Daniel Patrick Moynihan, *Secrecy: The American Experience* (Yale University Press, 1998), pp. 221, 227.
18. Johnson, *Secret Agencies.*
19. James Kitfield, "What Now for the Spooks?" *National Journal*, March 1, 1996, p. 597.
20. The full report of this commission headed by Les Aspin and Harold Brown is *Preparing for the 21st Century: An Appraisal of U.S. Intelligence*, Report of the Commission on the Roles and Capabilities of the U.S. Intelligence Community (Government Printing Office, March 1, 1996).
21. Steven Kull, "What the Public Knows That Washington Doesn't," *Foreign Policy* (Winter 1995–96), p. 115.
22. John E. Rielly, ed., *American Public Opinion and U.S. Foreign Policy, 1995* (The Chicago Council of Foreign Relations, 1995), p. 40.
23. For an examination of how Japanese companies try to influence foreign policy and trade officials in Washington, see Pat Choate, *Agents of Influence* (Knopf, 1990).
24. For a useful review of how Congress has occasionally challenged and even more often has failed to challenge the White House when it comes to the war power, see Louis Fisher, *Presidential War Power* (University Press of Kansas, 1995).
25. For an analysis that asserts U.S. foreign policy is almost entirely shaped by self-appointed elites, see Eric Alterman, *Who Speaks for America? Why Democracy Matters* (Cornell University Press, 1998). More generally see Ole Holsti, *Public Opinion and American Foreign Policy* (University of Michigan Press, 1996).
26. See Robert S. McNamara, *In Retrospect: The Tragedy and Lessons of Vietnam* (Times Books, 1995).
27. Anne Swardson, "The Marshall Plan's Success," *The Washington Post National Weekly Edition*, June 2, 1997, p. 8.
28. "U.S. Foreign Aid Spending Since World War II," data presentation in *The Public Perspective* 8, no. 5 (August/September 1997), p. 11.
29. Ibid.
30. Albright, "Testing of American Foreign Policy," p. 57.
31. Gary Clyde Hufbauer and Jeffrey J. Schott, "Economic Sanctions and Foreign Policy," *PS: Political Science and Politics* (Fall 1985), p. 727.
32. Richard N. Haass, "Sanctions Almost Never Work," *The Wall Street Journal*, June 19, 1998, p. A14.
33. Cited in Gerald F. Seib, "Capital Journal," *The Wall Street Journal*, June 17, 1998, p. A18.
34. Gary Hufbauer, "Foreign Policy on the Cheap," *The Washington Post National Weekly Edition*, July 20–27, 1998, p. 22.
35. John Prados, *The President's Secret Wars: CIA and Pentagon Covert Operations Since World War II* (Morrow, 1986); Moynihan, *Secrecy.*
36. Hufbauer and Schott, "Economic Sanctions," p. 278.
37. Bob Dole, "Peacekeepers and Politics," *The New York Times*, January 24, 1994, p. A11. Dole reiterated this general theme in Robert Dole, "Shaping America's Global Future," *Foreign Policy* (Spring 1995), pp. 29–43.
38. See, for example, Michael Lind, "Twilight of the U.N.," *The New Republic*, October 30, 1995, pp. 25–33; Rosemary Righter, *Utopia Lost: The United Nations and World Order* (Twentieth Century Fund, 1995).
39. Quoted in "The UN at 50," *The New York Times*, October 23, 1995, p. A6. For similar and even stronger views, see Nancy Landon Kassebaum and Lee Hamilton, "Fix the UN," *The Washington Post National Weekly Edition*, July 3–9, 1995, p. 28.
40. Quoted in Tim Zimmerman, "Why the UN Might Be Worth Saving," *U.S. News and World Report*, December 16, 1996, p. 44. See also James Kitfield, "Not-So-United," *National Journal*, January 1, 1997, pp. 69–72.
41. Norman A. Graebner, "The President as Commander in Chief: A Study in Power," in *Commander In Chief: Presidential Leadership in Modern Wars*, ed. Joseph G. Dawson (University Press of Kansas, 1993), p. 31.
42. Quoted in Don Oberdorfer, "Strategy for Solo Superpower: The U.S. Plans to Keep Its Powder Dry," *The Washington Post National Weekly Edition*, May 27–June 2, 1991, p. 8.
43. See the arguments in Robert W. Tucker and David C. Hendrickson, *The Imperial Temptation: The New World Order and America's Purpose* (Council on Foreign Relations, 1992). See also Ronald

Steel, *Temptations of a Superpower* (Harvard University Press, 1995).

44. Steven Lee Myers, "Military Warns Soldiers of Failure to Hail Chief," *The New York Times*, October 21, 1998, p. A22.
45. Dana Priest, "Peacekeeping Is Putting Women in the Trenches," *The Washington Post National Edition*, January 26, 1998, p. 9; Mark Thompson, "Boys and Girls Apart," *Time*, January 5, 1998, p. 104.
46. Quoted in Genevieve Anton, "Having Women Fight Riddled with Issues," *Colorado Springs Gazette Telegraph*, August 11, 1991, pp. 1, 10.
47. Evan Thomas and Gregory L. Vistica, "Falling Out of the Sky," *Newsweek*, March 17, 1997, p. 26.
48. Michael O'Hanlon, *How to be a Cheap Hawk: The 1999 and 2000 Defense Budget* (Brookings Institution, 1998), p. 46.
49. Bill Clinton, speech at the McDonnell Douglas plant in Long Beach, Calif., February 23, 1996, reprinted in *Vital Speeches of the Day*, March 15, 1996, p. 323.
50. Lawrence J. Korb, "Money to Burn at the Pentagon," *The New York Times*, September 25, 1998, p. A27.
51. See, for example, James Kitfield, "Ships Galore!" *National Journal*, February 10, 1996, pp. 298–302.
52. Kenneth R. Mayer, *The Political Economy of Defense Contracting* (Yale University Press, 1991), p. 223.
53. On the bureacractic and congressional politics of these panels, see Robert Scott Dering, "The Politics of Military Base Closures, 1988–1995," paper presented at the American Political Science Association, Annual Meeting, Boston, September 3–6, 1998.

CHAPTER 21

1. Edith Hamilton, *The Echo of Greece* (W.W. Norton, 1957), p. 47.
2. Robert H. Jackson, *West Virginia State Board of Education v Barnette*, 319 US 624 (1943).
3. Michael Nelson, "Politics as a Vital, and Sometimes Noble, Human Activity," *Chronicle of Higher Education*, August 18, 1995, p. A44.
4. See Thomas E. Cronin, "Thinking and Learning about Leadership," *Presidential Studies Quarterly* (Winter 1984), pp. 22–34. See also Warren Bennis and Patricia Ward Biederman, *Organizing Genius: The Secrets of Creative Collaboration* (Addison Wesley, 1997).
5. See Kareem Abdul-Jabar and Alan Steinberg, *Black Profiles in Courage* (Morrow, 1996).
6. Reinhold Niebuhr, *The Children of Light and the Children of Darkness* (Charles Scribner's Sons, 1944), p. xi.
7. See Nat Hentoff, *Free Speech for Me—But Not for Thee: How the American Left and Right Relentlessly Censor Each Other* (Harper Perrenial, 1993).
8. John W. Gardner, *Self-Renewal*, rev. ed. (Norton, 1981), p. 72.
9. Arthur M. Schlesinger, Jr., *The Disuniting of America* (W.W. Norton, 1993), p. 134.

PHOTO CREDITS

Chapter 1: 1 Library of Congress **10** The Granger Collection **11** The Boston Tea Party, December 1773; colored engraving, 19th century; The Granger Collection **12** The Granger Collection **13** (left) The Granger Collection; (right) Corbis **18** Louise Turner Arnold **19** Firdia Lisnawati/AP/Wide World Photos

Chapter 2: 23 The Boston Massacre, March 1770; colored engraving, Paul Revere; The Granger Collection **29** The Granger Collection **32** The Granger Collection **35** (top) The Granger Collection; (bottom) Fabian Bachrach/FPG International **36** Reuters/Gary Cameron/Archive Photos **41** Arthur Grace/Sygma

Chapter 3: 53 Chuck Nacke/Woodfin Camp & Associates **54** Santiago Lyon/AP/Wide World Photos **59** Corbis **62** Jim Wilson/New York Times Pictures **71** John Duricka/AP/Wide World Photos

Chapter 4: 75 Win McNamee/Reuters/Corbis **77** Patricia Miklik, Montgomery Advertiser/AP/Wide World Photos **79** Robert Fried/Stock Boston **80** L.M. Otero/AP/Wide World Photos **81** Charles Tasnadi/AP/Wide World Photos **83** Najlah Feanny/SABA Press Photos, Inc. **88** Stephen Jaffe/The Image Works **89** James Wilson/Woodfin Camp & Associates **93** (left and right) Adam Nadel/AP/Wide World Photos **94** McGlynn/The Image Works

Chapter 5: 99 Archive Photos **100** (top) Simon & Schuster Corporate Digital Archive; (bottom) Owen Franken/Stock Boston **104** AP/Wide World Phtotos **105** AP/Wide World Photos **107** Corbis **108** Hal Gabrb/SIPA Press **110** Eric Haase/Contact Press Images Inc. **116** UPI/Corbis **120** Ron Edmonds/UPI/Corbis **123** Wilfredo Lee/AP/Wide World Photos

Chapter 6: 127 Brian Bohannon/Booth News Service/Sygma **130** Corbis **133** Jeffrey Boan/AP/Wide World Photos **139** Blair Seitz/Photo Researchers, Inc. **142** James Wilson/Woodfin Camp & Associates **147** (top) Mingasson/Liaison Agency, Inc.; (bottom) Lee Celano/Reuters/Corbis; (right) Stephen Savoia/AP/Wide World Photos **150** Librado Romero/New York Times Pictures

Chapter 7: 155 Spencer Grant/Photo Researchers, Inc. **160** Lewis Hine/Corbis/Bettmann; **161** UPI/Corbis **163** (top) Richard Shock/Liaison Agency, Inc.; (left) Stephen McBrady/PhotoEdit; (right) Michal Heron/Simon & Schuster/PH College **167** Librado Romero/New York Times Pictures **170** Greg Gibson/AP/Wide World Photos **171** Courtesy of the Libertarian National Committee, Inc.

Chapter 8: 177 Ken Fisher/Tony Stone Images **180** Library of Congress **184** Steve Mason/PhotoDisc, Inc. **190** Mark J. Terrill/AP/Wide World Photos **191** (left) Nathan Benn/Woodfin Camp & Associates; (center) Chester Higgins, Jr./Photo Researchers, Inc. (right) D. Greco/The Image Works **196** (left) Tony Neste; (right) Alan Oddie/ PhotoEdit

Chapter 9: 203 Alan S. Weiner/New York Times Pictures **205** Cynthia Howe/Sygma **206** James Shaffer/PhotoEdit **208** Paul Schumann/Courier-Journal **209** Bill Haber/AP/Wide World Photos **216** (left) Corbis; (right) Roswell Angier/Stock Boston **217** Ralph A. Burns **219** Crandall/the Image Works **220** Charles Tasnadi/AP/Wide World Photos **222** Catherine Ursillo/Photo Researchers, Inc.

Chapter 10: 227 Mathew McVay/Stock Boston **230** Reuters/Jim Bourg/Archive Photos **233** (top) Brown Brothers; (bottom) AP/Wide World Photos **234** The Granger Collection **237** (top) Ed Andrieski/AP/Wide World Photos; (bottom) Denis Paquin/AP/Wide World Photos **239** UPI/Corbis **240** Greg Gibson/AP/Wide World Photos

Chapter 11: 253 AP/Wide World Photos **256** Billy E. Barnes/Jeroboam, Inc. **258** UPI/Corbis **261** SIPA Press **265** Julia Malakie/AP/World Wide Photos **268** Dale Atkins/AP/Wide World Photos

Chapter 12: 275 Richard Ellis/Sygma **286** Bucci/Nelson/Andrews/Corbis **288** AP/Wide World Photos **289** Mike Nelson/Agence France Presse/Corbis **294** AP/Wide World Photos

Chapter 13: 305 Richard Ellis/Sygma **309** UPI/Corbis **311** Geostock/PhotoDisk, Inc. **314** Richard Drew/AP/Wide World Photos **316** Brian K. Diggs/AP/Wide World Photos **318** Joe Marquette/AP/Wide World Photos **319** Ralph A. Burns **320** Maria Melin, ABC, Inc. **322** Trippett/SIPA Press

Chapter 14: 327 Bill Fitzpatrick/The White House Photo Office **329** (top and bottom) Corbis **331** Joe Marquette/AP/Wide World Photos **333** Doug Mills/AP/Wide World Photos **335** (top) J. Scott Applewhite/AP/Wide World Photos; (bottom) Trippett/SIPA Press 336 Doug Mills/AP/Wide World Photos **346** Joe Marquette/AP/Wide World Photos **347** (left) Archive Photos; (right) Reuters/Larry Downing/Archive Photos **348** John Duricka/AP/Wide World Photos

Chapter 15: 357 Bruce Chambers/SABA Press Photos, Inc. **360** (top) The Granger Collection; (bottom) Culver Pictures, Inc. **361** APTV/AP/Wide World Photos **362** Alalstair Grant/AP/Wide World Photos **363** AP/Wide World Photos **365** UPI/Corbis **367** David Hume Kennerly/Sygma **370** Denis Paquin/AP/Wide World Photos **373** Doug Mills/AP/Wide World Photos **377** Doug Mills/AP/Wide World Photos **380** Jeffrey Markowitz/Sygma

Chapter 16: 385 Brad Markel/Liaison Agency, Inc. **396** (left) Clary/UPI/Corbis; (center) Carol T. Powers/AP/Wide World Photos; (right) Reuters/Corbis **397** (left) Reuters/Gary Hershorn/Corbis; (right) Reuters/Steve Jaffe/Corbis **407** Reuters/Gary Hershorn/Corbis

Chapter 17: 413 Louie Psihoyos/Matrix International, Inc. **416** Corbis **428** Doug Mills/AP/Wide World Photos

Chapter 18: 435 Brian J. Gill/ImpactVisuals Photo & Graphics, Inc. **439** J. Scott Applewhite/AP/Wide World Photos **443** Stock Boston **445** Mike Theiler/Reuters/Corbis **450** Tony Freeman/PhotoEdit **451** Dennis Grundman/AP/Wide World Photos **457** Joe Marquette/AP/Wide World Photos **461** Alvis Upitis/The Image Bank

Chapter 19: 467 Mark Lennihan/AP/Wide World Photos **468** Mark Lennihan/AP/Wide World Photos **469** Brown Brothers **471** The White House Photo Office **480** (left) Trippett/SIPA Press; (right) Reuters/Mark Wilson/Archive Photos **488** John Ficara/Sygma

Chapter 20: 493 Hasan Jamal/AP/Wide World Photos **494** AP/Wide World Photos **498** (top to bottom) UPI/Corbis; Corbis; UPI/Corbis; UPI/ P. Skingley/Corbis **499** (top to bottom) UPI/Corbis; UPI/Don Rypka/Corbis; Reuters/Mark Cardwell/Corbis; Reuters/Jeff Mitchell/Corbis **500** Joe Marquette/AP/Wide World Photos **501** Archive Photos **502** UPI/Paul Richards/Corbis **505** Sygma **508** (left) Sygma; (right) Sygma; (bottom) UN-DPI, John Isaac/AP/Wide World Photos **510** UPI/Corbis **511** Robert Petry/Liaison Agency, Inc. **512** (top) James Montgomery Flagg/The Granger Collection; (bottom) Howard Chandler Christy/The Granger Collection **513** T. Campion/Sygma **515** Blake Sell/SIPA Press

Chapter 21: 521 Gary Hershorn/Reuters/Archive Photos **523** Bob Daemmrich Photo, Inc. **526** The Granger Collection

INDEX

C

D

E

F

G

H

I

J

K

L

M

N

O

P

T

U

V

W

Y

Z

SINGLE PC LICENSE AGREEMENT AND LIMITED WARRANTY

READ THIS LICENSE CAREFULLY BEFORE OPENING THIS PACKAGE. BY OPENING THIS PACKAGE, YOU ARE AGREEING TO THE TERMS AND CONDITIONS OF THIS LICENSE. IF YOU DO NOT AGREE, DO NOT OPEN THE PACKAGE. PROMPTLY RETURN THE UNOPENED PACKAGE AND ALL ACCOMPANYING ITEMS TO THE PLACE YOU OBTAINED THEM.

1. GRANT OF LICENSE and OWNERSHIP: The enclosed computer programs ("Software") are licensed, not sold, to you by Prentice-Hall, Inc. ("We" or the "Company") and in consideration of your purchase or adoption of the accompanying Company textbooks and/or other materials, and your agreement to these terms. We reserve any rights not granted to you. You own only the disk(s) but we and/or our licensors own the Software itself. This license allows you to use and display your copy of the Software on a single computer (i.e., with a single CPU) at a single location for academic use only, so long as you comply with the terms of this Agreement. You may make one copy for back up, or transfer your copy to another CPU, provided that the Software is usable on only one computer.

2. RESTRICTIONS: You may not transfer or distribute the Software or documentation to anyone else. Except for backup, you may not copy the documentation or the Software. You may not network the Software or otherwise use it on more than one computer or computer terminal at the same time. You may not reverse engineer, disassemble, decompile, modify, adapt, translate, or create derivative works based on the Software or the Documentation. You may be held legally responsible for any copying or copyright infringement which is caused by your failure to abide by the terms of these restrictions.

3. TERMINATION: This license is effective until terminated. This license will terminate automatically without notice from the Company if you fail to comply with any provisions or limitations of this license. Upon termination, you shall destroy the Documentation and all copies of the Software. All provisions of this Agreement as to limitation and disclaimer of warranties, limitation of liability, remedies or damages, and our ownership rights shall survive termination.

4. LIMITED WARRANTY AND DISCLAIMER OF WARRANTY: Company warrants that for a period of 60 days from the date you purchase this SOFTWARE (or purchase or adopt the accompanying textbook), the Software, when properly installed and used in accordance with the Documentation, will operate in substantial conformity with the description of the Software set forth in the Documentation, and that for a period of 30 days the disk(s) on which the Software is delivered shall be free from defects in materials and workmanship under normal use. The Company does not warrant that the Software will meet your requirements or that the operation of the Software will be uninterrupted or error-free. Your only remedy and the Company's only obligation under these limited warranties is, at the Company's option, return of the disk for a refund of any amounts paid for it by you or replacement of the disk. THIS LIMITED WARRANTY IS THE ONLY WARRANTY PROVIDED BY THE COMPANY AND ITS LICENSORS, AND THE COMPANY AND ITS LICENSORS DISCLAIM ALL OTHER WARRANTIES, EXPRESSED OR IMPLIED, INCLUDING WITHOUT LIMITATION, THE IMPLIED WARRANTIES OF MERCHANTABILITY AND FITNESS FOR A PARTICULAR PURPOSE. THE COMPANY DOES NOT WARRANT, GUARANTEE, OR MAKE ANY REPRESENTATION REGARDING THE ACCURACY, RELIABILITY, CURRENTNESS, USE, OR RESULTS OF USE, OF THE SOFTWARE.

5. LIMITATION OF REMEDIES AND DAMAGES: IN NO EVENT, SHALL THE COMPANY OR ITS EMPLOYEES, AGENTS, LICENSORS, OR CONTRACTORS BE LIABLE FOR ANY INCIDENTAL, INDIRECT, SPECIAL, OR CONSEQUENTIAL DAMAGES ARISING OUT OF OR IN CONNECTION WITH THIS LICENSE OR THE SOFTWARE, INCLUDING FOR LOSS OF USE, LOSS OF DATA, LOSS OF INCOME OR PROFIT, OR OTHER LOSSES, SUSTAINED AS A RESULT OF INJURY TO ANY PERSON, OR LOSS OF OR DAMAGE TO PROPERTY, OR CLAIMS OF THIRD PARTIES, EVEN IF THE COMPANY OR AN AUTHORIZED REPRESENTATIVE OF THE COMPANY HAS BEEN ADVISED OF THE POSSIBILITY OF SUCH DAMAGES. IN NO EVENT SHALL THE LIABILITY OF THE COMPANY FOR DAMAGES WITH RESPECT TO THE SOFTWARE EXCEED THE AMOUNTS ACTUALLY PAID BY YOU, IF ANY, FOR THE SOFTWARE OR THE ACCOMPANYING TEXTBOOK. BECAUSE SOME JURISDICTIONS DO NOT ALLOW THE LIMITATION OF LIABILITY IN CERTAIN CIRCUMSTANCES, THE ABOVE LIMITATIONS MAY NOT ALWAYS APPLY TO YOU.

6. GENERAL: THIS AGREEMENT SHALL BE CONSTRUED IN ACCORDANCE WITH THE LAWS OF THE UNITED STATES OF AMERICA AND THE STATE OF NEW YORK, APPLICABLE TO CONTRACTS MADE IN NEW YORK, AND SHALL BENEFIT THE COMPANY, ITS AFFILIATES AND ASSIGNEES. THIS AGREEMENT IS THE COMPLETE AND EXCLUSIVE STATEMENT OF THE AGREEMENT BETWEEN YOU AND THE COMPANY AND SUPERSEDES ALL PROPOSALS OR PRIOR AGREEMENTS, ORAL, OR WRITTEN, AND ANY OTHER COMMUNICATIONS BETWEEN YOU AND THE COMPANY OR ANY REPRESENTATIVE OF THE COMPANY RELATING TO THE SUBJECT MATTER OF THIS AGREEMENT. If you are a U.S. Government user, this Software is licensed with "restricted rights" as set forth in subparagraphs (a)-(d) of the Commercial Computer-Restricted Rights clause at FAR 52.227-19 or in subparagraphs (c)(1)(ii) of the Rights in Technical Data and Computer Software clause at DFARS 252.227-7013, and similar clauses, as applicable.

Should you have any questions concerning this agreement or if you wish to contact the Company for any reason, please contact in writing: Executive Manager, HSS Media Technology, Prentice Hall, One Lake Street, Upper Saddle River, NJ 07458.

SYSTEM REQUIREMENTS

MACINTOSH: minimum 68040/33MHz, System 7.5 or above, 12mb RAM (16mb recommended), 1mb free HD space, 2x CD-ROM, 640X480 screen resolution, color monitor (thousands of colors required). QuickTime 3.0 installed from CD.

PC: minimum 486/DX25, Windows 3.x (minimum 8mb RAM) or Windows 95/98 (minimum 16mb RAM), 1mb free HD space, 2X CD-ROM, SVGA monitor, thousands of colors, sound and video cards required. For Windows 3.x, Video for Windows installed from CD.